ATTENTION-DEFICIT HYPERACTIVITY DISORDER

ATTENTION-DEFICIT HYPERACTIVITY DISORDER:
A Handbook for Diagnosis and Treatment

RUSSELL A. BARKLEY, PhD
University of Massachusetts Medical Center

THE GUILFORD PRESS
New York   London

© 1990 The Guilford Press
A Division of Guilford Publications, Inc.
72 Spring Street, New York, NY 10012

Printed in the United States of America

This book is printed on acid-free paper.

Last digit is print number: 9 8 7 6

Library of Congress Cataloging-in-Publication Data

Barkley, Russell A., 1949–
    Attention deficit hyperactivity disorder : a handbook for
diagnosis and treatment / Russell A. Barkley.
        p.   cm.
    Includes bibliographical references (p.).
    ISBN 0-89862-443-6
    1. Attention deficit disorders.   I. Title.
RJ496.A86B37   1990   90-3186
618.92′8589—dc20   CIP

To my sons, Ken and Steve,
and my wife, Pat

If you would thoroughly know anything,
teach it to others.

—Tryon Edwards (1809–94)

Contributors

Arthur Anastopoulos, Ph.D., Department of Psychiatry, University of Massachusetts Medical Center, Worcester, MA

Sheldon Benjamin, M.D., Department of Psychiatry, University of Massachusetts Medical Center, Worcester, MA

Charles E. Cunningham, Ph.D., Departments of Psychology and Psychiatry, Chedoke–McMaster Hospitals, McMaster University Medical Centre, Hamilton, Ontario, Canada

George J. DuPaul, Ph.D., Department of Psychiatry, University of Massachusetts Medical Center, Worcester, MA

David Guevremont, Ph.D., Department of Psychiatry, University of Massachusetts Medical Center, Worcester, MA

Robert L. Kane, Ph.D., Departments of Psychiatry and Neurology, University of Massachusetts Medical Center, Worcester, MA

Cecilia Mikalac, M.D., Department of Psychiatry, University of Massachusetts Medical Center, Worcester, MA

Linda J. Pfiffner, Ph.D., Department of Pediatrics, Child Development Center, University of California–Irvine, Irvine, CA

Arthur L. Robin, Ph.D., Department of Psychology, Children's Hospital of Michigan, Detroit, MI; Department of Psychiatry, Wayne State University Medical Center, Detroit, MI

Terri Shelton, Ph.D., Department of Psychiatry, University of Massachusetts Medical Center, Worcester, MA

Preface

This book was intended as a revision of my first text on hyperactive children (Barkley, 1981), published almost a decade ago. However, so much research had occurred in the interim, and so sweeping were some of the changes in the diagnosis, conceptualization, assessment, and treatment of the disorder, that an entirely new volume had to be created. Despite this completely new text, the purpose of this volume remains the same as its predecessor—to pro-vide a highly useful handbook for the clinical practitioner on the provision of clinical services to children, adolescents, and adults with Attention-deficit Hyperactivity Disorder (ADHD). Also like the first, this volume is not in-tended as an exhaustive or critical review of the research literature on ADHD, as other books exist that have accomplished that mission nicely (Campbell, 1990; Ross & Ross, 1976, 1982; Taylor, 1986a; Weiss & Hechtman, 1986; Whalen & Henker, 1980). Instead, its purpose remains to wring out as much useful and practical information as possible from the existing empirical re-search and place it together into a single volume that can guide clinical and educational practice with these children. I can only hope that I have come close to again achieving this goal.

It continues to be the cornerstone of this text that ADHD must be viewed as a developmentally disabling disorder of inattention, behavioral disinhibi-tion, and the regulation of activity level to situational demands. The evidence accumulating in the past 10 years has more than proven this initial view to be correct; indeed, it is the only humane perspective on this disorder. My colleagues' and my own recent follow-up study of more than 100 ADHD children, reviewed in Chapter 4, has resoundingly supported this perspective more than any other professional experience of my career. One cannot help being affected by the plight of these children, the struggles of their families in coping with and managing the disorder, and the successes of many in overcoming their limitations when one has personally followed them for a decade of their development. More strongly than before, I now appreciate the striking and reciprocal interplay between environmental demands and the handicapped capacities of these children; between social prejudice and family advocacy; and between the sincere desire to be good and the strong pull of disinhibition within these children in defining where, when, and for how long they will be disabled by their condition. ADHD is a disorder that cries out now, as mental retardation, autism, and learning disabilities did in preceding decades, for broad societal recognition as a neuropsychological impairment of the individual shaped to final form by its environmental context. It is high time it received it.

The wealth of new articles on ADHD, now more than tripled since 1978, required that I take on the expert assistance of some of my friends and colleagues to accomplish this goal, especially in the domain of treatment. I am very grateful to Terri Shelton (Chapter 7) for her insight into the developmental issues inherent in clinical practice with these children, based on her years of dedication to working with a variety of developmentally disabled infants and preschoolers. She has articulated well the biopsychosocial perspective taken in our clinic for ADHD children. Sincere appreciation is also due to her husband, Arthur Anastopoulos—a close friend, golfing companion, and Chief of the ADHD Clinic at the University of Massachusetts Medical Center—for his assistance with a review of our parent training program (Chapter 12). His cognitive-behavioral approach has broadened my own horizons on working with families and added a significant component to the treatment program I originally developed for ADHD and defiant children (Barkley, 1981, 1987). He has also provided invaluable insights into the construction of our family therapy treatments in a recent three-year study of ADHD adolescents.

To my dear friend, Charles Cunningham, who has become like a brother to me, I turned for assistance in providing a description of his creative and highly useful family systems approach to parent training (Chapter 13). No one in my career has so challenged and stimulated my ideas about ADHD children and their families as has he, and often in the most splendid of settings—while tramping the snowy pastures outside his home (a converted 1800s schoolhouse) near Hamilton, Ontario, Canada; while running the sun-soaked beaches of southern California together; or while fishing the coves on Buck Lake, Ontario, in the early morning sun of autumn, to name but a few. His substantial insight into the communication and family systems problems that arise in the care and raising of an ADHD child were first made evident to me, and several hundred other psychologists, when he presented this program at the American Psychological Association meetings in Atlanta in 1988. His wisdom and talent in this area are well represented in his chapter here.

The rise of another highly ingenious approach to working with adolescents with ADHD, developed by my friends Arthur Robin and Sharon Foster (1989), demanded inclusion in this volume. This behavioral–family systems approach to work with ADHD adolescents is virtually the only proven alternative or adjunct to medication treatment currently available, and Arthur has outlined its clinical elegance here quite well. His superlative compassion and sensitivity for these often difficult teenagers cannot go unnoticed in his chapter (Chapter 14).

To update the recommended approach to educational management, there seemed little choice but to turn to the insights of a young yet highly accomplished psychologist whose substantial work in classroom management has been repeatedly noticed lately in many of the most prestigious child psychology journals—Linda Pfiffner. Linda trained with Susan O'Leary, whose own work laid the empirical foundations for classroom management approaches to behavior problem children, and later with James Swanson, founder of the best educational program specifically designed for ADHD children in this country. She demonstrates here (Chapter 15) that she was a quick study under these senior scientist/practitioners, clearly showing that she is wiser than her youth would suggest. Her future in this field seems bright indeed.

The field of social skills training has flourished in the last decade, yet its results with behavior-problem and ADHD children have been most conflicting. This was an area outside my own clinical expertise, and so I turned to my colleague, David Guevremont, for assistance with this portion of the text. Trained by Sharon Foster and others at West Virginia University, and specializing early in a behavioral–social systems approach to the analysis and treatment of children's social skills, David was a prime choice for the topic. He has also ably assisted me with a three-year research study of family training with ADHD adolescents. His chapter here (Chapter 16) reflects his wealth of personal experience in conducting clinical and research programs on social skills training at our ADHD clinic and with the Worcester, Massachusetts, Public Schools.

And I could think of few others to invite than George J. DuPaul to assist me with the revision of the chapter on medication treatments for ADHD (Chapter 17). As noted earlier, this area of research has literally exploded in volume over the past decade, making it difficult for me to stay abreast of all of the literature and the clinical nuances contained therein. Having trained with Mark Rapport at the University of Rhode Island, authored more research articles on medication in his graduate training than almost any psychologist I know, and assisted me with a two-year study of medication effects on subtypes of ADHD, George was clearly the choice to bring renewed sense to this controversial topic. He has done so nicely here, and I am most appreciative of his assistance.

Finally, I asked my colleagues, Robert Kane, Cecilia Mikalac, and Sheldon Benjamin, to use their substantial clinical experience in our clinic for adults with ADHD in assisting me in preparing a chapter on the diagnosis, assessment, and treatment of adults with this disorder (Chapter 18). Now that it is clear that 50 to 80% of ADHD children continue to have some degree of their symptoms in adulthood, clinicians must be prepared to confront the unique challenges these clients will present. We have tried to provide some clinical recommendations for doing so, recognizing that little research exists to guide us in this endeavor.

Behind any extensive endeavor such as this, there stands the support of one's family, and mine is no exception. I am deeply indebted to my wife, Pat, and my sons, Ken and Steve, for their patience with the demands this project made on our family time, for their encouragement to see it to its timely completion, and for the insights they have given me on children and on family life. I am also grateful to the many families of ADHD children, now numbering several thousand, whom I have had the honor and pleasure to serve over the past 15 years of clinical research and practice. As in the first volume, their influence is undoubtedly woven throughout the fabric of this text.

And finally, I must once again express my continued gratitude to Seymour Weingarten and Robert Matloff of The Guilford Press for their support of and patience with this revision, for their friendship and kindnesses over the past decade, and for the yeomen's work of their staff in bringing this text to fruition. In particular, I am grateful to Rowena Howells and Marie Sprayberry for their meticulous editing and polishing of this text and escorting it through the publishing process. Few authors can claim as attentive, enthusiastic, and professional a publishing house as this one.

RUSSELL A. BARKLEY
January 1990

Contents

PART I. NATURE AND DIAGNOSIS

PART III. TREATMENT

Chapter 12. Counseling and Training Parents
Arthur Anastopoulos and Russell A. Barkley

397

Chapter 13. A Family Systems Approach to Parent Training
Charles E. Cunningham

432

Chapter 14. Training Families with ADHD Adolescents
Arthur L. Robin

462

Chapter 15. Educational Placement and Classroom Management
Linda J. Pfiffner and Russell A. Barkley

498

ATTENTION-DEFICIT
HYPERACTIVITY DISORDER

PART I

NATURE AND DIAGNOSIS

It is not so important to know everything as to know the
exact value of everything, to appreciate what we learn,
and to arrange what we know.

—HANNAH MORE (1745–1833)

1

History

Attention-deficit Hyperactivity Disorder (ADHD) is the most recent diagnostic label for children presenting with significant problems with attention, impulse control, and overactivity. Children with ADHD are a heterogeneous population who display considerable variation in the degree of their symptoms, the pervasiveness across situations of these problems, and the extent to which other disorders occur in association with it. The disorder represents one of the most common reasons why children are referred to mental health practitioners in the United States, and it is one of the most prevalent childhood psychiatric disorders. Throughout the rich and varied history of this disorder, it has received multiple labels; this has been due in part to the particular symptoms believed to be of import at the time, in part to the view of etiology in vogue, and in part (no doubt) to the professional identification of various authors. This chapter presents a brief overview of the history of this disorder. In these earlier writings lie the nascent concepts that served as antecedents to the current conceptualizations of the disorder and its treatment. It is therefore important to have some passing familiarity with them, not only for their insight into this important developmental disorder, but also for an appreciation of why our perspective on these children has come to its present status. Readers wishing a more detailed discussion are referred to other sources (Kessler, 1980; Ross & Ross, 1976, 1982; Schachar, 1986).

THE PERIOD 1900 TO 1960: THE AGE OF THE BRAIN-DAMAGED CHILD

The few papers about this disorder that appeared prior to 1900 were clearly medical in nature and often described the residual cognitive and behavioral effects of various central nervous system (CNS) injuries to children, such as trauma and infections. Credit is typically awarded to George Still and Alfred Tredgold, however, as being the first to focus serious medical attention on the behavioral condition in children that most closely approximates what is today known as ADHD.

Still's Description

In Still's series of lectures to the Royal College of Physicians (Still, 1902), he described 20 children in his clinical practice who were often aggressive, defiant, and resistant to discipline; were excessively emotional or "passionate" (p. 1009); and showed little "inhibitory volition" (p. 1008). "Lawlessness" (p. 1009), spitefulness and cruelty, and dishonesty were also associated with this disorder. Most of these children were impaired in attention and were quite overactive. Still believed that these children displayed a major "defect in moral control" (p. 1009) in their behavior, and that this was relatively chronic in most cases. In some cases, it was acquired secondary to an acute brain disease and might remit upon recovery from the disease. In the chronic cases, a higher risk for criminal acts in later development was noted in some instances, though not all. Although this defect could be associated with intellectual retardation, it could also arise in children of near-normal intelligence.

Still was the first to note that the symptoms of the disorder were defined as unnatural relative to the behavior of normal children at a given age, suggesting that age-referenced criteria were important in the diagnosis. A greater proportion of males than females presented with these characteristics (3:1); it appeared to arise in most cases before 8 years of age. Many displayed a higher incidence of minor anomalies in their physical appearance, or "stigmata of degeneration," such as abnormally large head size, malformed palate, or increased epicanthal fold. We must not forget, however, that in this Victorian era, medical scientists were frankly obsessed with head size and physical stigmata as reflecting defective intellect or morals—associations that were sometimes exaggerated or frankly fabricated and have now been disconfirmed (Gould, 1981). A proneness to accidental injuries was reported in these children, as was an increased threat to the safety of other children because of their aggressiveness. Alcoholism, criminality, and affective disorders, such as depression and suicide, were noted to be more common among their biological relatives. Some of the children displayed a history of significant brain damage or convulsions, while others did not. A few had associated tic disorders, or "microkinesia"; this was perhaps the first time that tic disorders and ADHD were noted to be comorbid conditions. We now recognize that as many as 70% of children with tic disorders and Tourette's syndrome have associated ADHD (Barkley, 1988b).

Although a chaotic family life was reported in many children, many others came from households with seemingly adequate upbringing. In fact, Still believed that cases where poor child rearing was clearly involved should be exempt from this category, and that it should be reserved for children who displayed a morbid failure of moral control despite adequate training. He proposed a biological predisposition to this behavioral condition, suggesting that it was probably hereditary in some children and the result of pre- or postnatal injury in others.

Still, following the theorizing of William James (1890), hypothesized that the deficits in inhibitory volition, moral control, and sustained attention were causally related to each other and to the same underlying neurological deficiency. He cautiously speculated on the possibility of either a decreased threshold for inhibition of responding to stimuli, or a cortical disconnection syndrome (that might be due to neuronal cell modification) in which intellect was dissociated from "will" or social conduct. Any biologically compromising event that could cause significant brain damage (cell modification) and retardation could, he conjectured, in its milder forms lead only to this defective moral control. Later Tredgold (1908), and much later Pasamanick, Rogers, and Lilienfeld (1956), would use such a theory of early, mild, and undetected damage to account for these developmentally late-arising behavioral and learning deficiencies. Temporary improvements in conduct might be achieved by alterations in the environment or by medications, both Still and Tredgold found, but they stressed the relative permanence of the defect even in these cases. The need for special educational environments for these children was strongly emphasized. We see here the origins of many later and even current notions about ADHD and oppositional defiant children, although it would take almost 70 years to return to the more heuristic among them. The children whom Still and Tredgold described would probably now be diagnosed as having not only ADHD, but also Oppositional Defiant Disorder or Conduct Disorder and most likely some sort of learning disability as well (see Chapter 6 for diagnostic criteria for these disorders).

Problematic in these early views was their implicit foundation on a social Darwinist perspective of childhood behavioral disorders that was highly pessimistic about prognosis, viewed most or all abnormal behavioral characteristics as biologically determined to a large degree, and discounted the role of environmental disadvantage and deprivation (Schachar, 1986). Schachar vehemently criticizes these early studies as reductionistic, uncritical, and ignorant of the substantial degree to which hyperactivity is more socially than objectively defined. He also points to the social prejudices of the time, which resulted in these findings' being used to justify segregation of the lower classes and of behaviorally disordered individuals, rather than to address the societal problems often associated with them.

Although much of what Schachar concludes about these early papers appears both appropriate and reasonable, his denigration of these works because they were imbedded in the social contexts, values, and prejudices of their time can be leveled against virtually all sciences and against the social and psychological ones in particular, even to this day. In my view, Schachar risks throwing the proverbial baby out with the bath water. No scientific undertakings or hypotheses are completely divorced from the social values of their time and place; this includes Schachar's own critique, occurring as it does within his now more socialistic Canadian society. We should therefore not allow such criticisms to obscure either the dedication these early scientist/practitioners brought to the children within their professional care or the valuable theoretical insights they provided about this disorder, tainted as the latter may have been with the cultural biases of their time.

North American Interest in ADHD

The history of interest in ADHD in North America is frequently traced to the outbreak of an encephalitis epidemic in 1917–1918, when clinicians were presented with a number of children who survived this brain infection yet were left with significant behavioral and cognitive sequelae (Cantwell, 1981; Kessler, 1980; Stewart, 1970). Numerous papers reported these sequelae (Ebaugh, 1923; Hohman, 1922; Strecker & Ebaugh, 1924; Stryker, 1925), and they included many of the characteristics we now incorporate into the concept of ADHD. Such children were described as being impaired in attention, regulation of activity, and impulse control (the "holy trinity" of ADHD symptoms to the present day). They also showed impairments in other cognitive abilities (including memory), and were often noted to be socially disruptive. Symptoms of oppositional and defiant behavior, as well as delinquency and conduct problems, also arose in some cases. The disorder was referred to as "postencephalitic behavior disorder," and was clearly the result of CNS damage. The large number of children affected resulted in significant professional and educational interest. The severity of this behavioral syndrome was such that many children were recommended for care and education outside of the home and normal educational facilities. Despite a rather pessimistic view of the prognosis of these children, some facilities reported significant success in their treatment, using simple behavior modification programs and increased supervision (Bender, 1942; Bond & Appel, 1931).

The Origins of a Brain Damage Syndrome

This association of a brain disease with behavioral pathology apparently led early investigators to study other potential causes of brain injury in children and their behavioral manifestations. Birth trauma (Shirley, 1939), infections such as measles (Meyer & Byers, 1952), lead toxicities (Byers & Lord, 1943), epilepsy (Levin, 1938), and head injury (Blau, 1936; Werner & Strauss, 1941) were studied in children and were found to be associated with numerous cognitive and behavioral impairments, including the triad of ADHD symptoms noted above. Other terms introduced during this era for children displaying these behavioral characteristics were "organic driveness" (Kahn & Cohen, 1934) and "restlessness syndrome" (Childers, 1935; Levin, 1938). Many of the children seen in these samples were also mentally retarded or more seriously behaviorally disordered than are children today who are described as having ADHD. It would be some time before investigators would attempt to parse out the separate contributions of intellectual delay, learning disabilities, or other neuropsychological deficits from those of the behavioral deficits to the maladjustment of these children. Even so, scientists at this time would discover that activity level was often inversely related to intelligence in children, increasing as intelligence declined in a sample—a finding supported in many subsequent studies to this day (Rutter, 1989). It should also be noted that a large number of children in these older studies were, in fact, brain-damaged or had signs of such damage (e.g., epilepsy, hemiplegias, etc.).

Notable during this era was also the recognition of the striking similarity between the symptoms exhibited by hyperactive children and the behavioral sequelae of frontal lobe lesions in primates (Blau, 1936; Levin, 1938). Frontal lobe ablation studies of monkeys had been done since 1876 (Ferrier, 1878) and were known to result in excessive restlessness, poor ability to sustain interest in activities, aimless wandering, and excessive appetite, among other behavioral changes. Several investigators, such as Levin (1938), would use these similarities to postulate that severe restlessness in children was most likely the result of pathological defects in the forebrain structures, although gross evidence of such defects was not always apparent in many of these children. Later investigators (Chelune, Ferguson, Koon, & Dickey, 1986; Lou, Henriksen, & Bruhn, 1984; Lou, Henriksen, Bruhn, Borner, & Nielsen, 1989; Mattes, 1980) would return to this notion, but with greater evidence to substantiate their claims, Milder forms of hyperactivity, in contrast, were attributed in this era to psychological causes, such as poor child-rearing practices or delinquent family environments. This theme would also be resurrected in the 1970s.

Over the next decade, it became fashionable to consider most children hospitalized in psychiatric facilities with this symptom picture to have suffered from some type of brain damage, such as encephalitis or pre-/perinatal trauma, whether or not the clinical history of the case contained evidence of such. It is easy to see how this logical circularity might emerge. Cases of legitimate CNS damage that gave rise to this behavioral pattern were seen in practice, mixed in with those cases having a similar behavioral pattern but with an ambiguous history of damage. This would naturally lead professionals at the time to believe that the behavioral pattern was a reliable indicator of the underlying CNS etiology or damage, even where evidence of such was lacking. This seems to be close to what happened, as the concept of the "brain-injured child" was to be developed in this era (Strauss & Lehtinen, 1947) and applied to children with these behavioral characteristics, many of whom had insufficient or no evidence of brain pathology. In fact, Strauss argued that the psychological disturbances were de facto evidence of brain injury as the etiology. This term would later evolve into the concept of "minimal brain damage" and eventually "minimal brain dysfunction" (MBD; see below) by the 1950s and 1960s. Even so, a few early voices, such as Childers (1935), would raise serious questions about the notion of brain damage in these children where no historical documentation of damage existed. Substantial recommendations for educating these "brain-damaged" children were made in the classic text by Strauss and Lehtinen (1947); these included placing them in smaller, more carefully regulated classrooms and reducing the amount of distracting stimulation in the environment. Strikingly austere classrooms were developed, in which teachers could not wear jewelry or brightly colored clothing and few pictures could adorn the walls.

Although the population served by the Pennsylvania center in which Strauss, Werner, and Lehtinen worked principally consisted of mentally retarded children, their neuropsychological findings were later extended to cerebral-palsied children of near-normal or normal intelligence by Cruickshank and his students (Dolphin & Cruickshank, 1951a, 1951b, 1951c). This resulted in the extension of the educational recommendations of Strauss to nonretarded children who manifested behavioral or perceptual disturbances (Cruickshank & Dolphin, 1951; Strauss & Kephhart, 1955). Echoes of these recommendations are still commonplace today in most educational assessments of ADHD or learning-disabled children, despite the utter lack of scientific support for their efficacy (Kessler, 1980; Routh, 1978; Zentall, 1984). These classrooms are historically significant, as they were the predecessors as well as instigators of the types of educational resources that would be incorporated in the mid-1970s into U.S. Public Law 94-142, mandating the special education of learning-disabled and behaviorally disordered children.

Beginnings of Child Psychopharmacology with ADHD

Another significant series of papers on treatment of these children appeared in 1937–1941; these were to mark the beginnings of medication therapy for behaviorally disordered children specifically, as well as the origins of the field of child psychopharmacology in general (Bradley, 1937; Bradley & Bowen, 1940; Molitch & Eccles, 1937). These papers reported on the efficacy of the amphetamines in reducing the disruptive behavior and improving the academic performance of behaviorally disordered children hospitalized at the Emma Pendleton Bradley Home in Providence, Rhode Island. Later studies would also confirm such a positive drug response in half or more of hyperactive hospitalized children (Laufer, Denhoff, & Solomons, 1957). As a result, by the 1970s, stimulant medications were to become the treatment of choice for the characteristics of ADHD.

The Emergence of a Hyperkinetic Syndrome

In the 1950s, a number of investigations into the neurological mechanisms underlying these behavioral symptoms were undertaken, the most famous of which was probably that by Laufer et al. (1957). These writers referred to ADHD children as having "hyperkinetic impulse disorder" and reasoned that the CNS deficit occurred in the thalamic area. Here poor filtering of stimulation was thought to occur, allowing an excess of stimulation to reach the brain. Their evidence was based upon a study of the effects of the photo-Metrozol method, in which the drug Metrozol was administered while flashes of light were presented to the child. The amount of drug required to induce a muscle jerk of the forearms, along with a spike-wave pattern on the electrocencephalogram, served as the measure of interest. Laufer et al. found that hyperactive inpatient children required less Metrozol than nonhyperactive inpatient children to induce this pattern of response. This suggested that hyperactive children had a lower threshold for stimulation in the thalamic area. The study was never replicated, and it is unlikely that such research would pass the standards of ethical conduct required by today's institutional review boards on research with human subjects. Nevertheless, it remains a milestone in the history of the disorder for its delineation of a more specific mechanism that might give rise to hyperactivity (i.e., cortical overstimulation). Others at the time also conjectured that an imbalance between cortical and subcortical areas existed, such that there was diminished control of subcortical areas responsible for sensory filtering, which permitted excess stimulation to reach the cortex (Knobel, Wolman, & Mason, 1959).

By the end of this era it seemed well accepted that hyperactivity was a brain damage syndrome, even where evidence of damage was lacking. The disorder was thought to be best treated through severely austere minimal stimulation educational classrooms or residential centers. Its prognosis was considered fair to poor. The possibility that a relatively new class of medications, the stimulants, might hold promise for its treatment was only beginning to be appreciated.

THE PERIOD 1960 TO 1969: THE GOLDEN AGE OF HYPERACTIVITY

The Decline of MBD

In the late 1950s and early 1960s, critical reviews began questioning the concept of a unitary syndrome of brain damage in children. They also pointed out the logical fallacy inherent in the assumption that if brain damage resulted in some of these behavioral symptoms, these symptoms could be pathognomonic of brain damage without any other corroborating evidence of CNS lesions. Chief among these critical reviews were those of Birch (1964), Herbert (1964), and Rapin (1964), who all questioned the validity of applying the concept of "minimal brain damage" to children who had only equivocal signs of neurological involvement, not necessarily damage. As an article by Gomez (1965) was entitled at the time, "Minimal Brain Damage Equals Maximal Neurologic Confusion." Apparently as a result of this controversy, a change in terms came about, with MBD (see above) being substituted. A plethora of research followed on MBD children (see Rie & Rie, 1980, for reviews); in addition, a task force of the National Institute of Neurological Diseases and Blindness (Clements, 1966) recognized at least 99 symptoms for this disorder.

The concept of MBD eventually died a slow death as it became recognized as vague, overinclusive, of little or no prescriptive value, and without much neurological evidence (Kirk, 1963). Its value remained in its emphasis on neurological mechanisms over the often excessive, pedantic, and convoluted environmental ones proposed at that time. This was particularly true of those etiological hypotheses stemming from psychoanalytic theory, which blamed parental and family factors entirely for these problems (Hertzig, Bortner, & Birch, 1969; Kessler, 1980; Taylor, 1983). The term MBD was eventually replaced by more specific labels applying to somewhat more circumscribed cognitive, learning, and behavioral disorders, such as "dyslexia," "language disorders," "learning disabilities," and "hyperactivity." These labels were based on the observable and verifiable deficits of the children they described, rather than on some underlying unobservable etiological mechanism in the brain.

The Hyperactive Child Syndrome

As dissatisfaction with the term MBD was occurring, there arose concurrently the concept of a "hyperactive child syndrome," described in the classic papers by Laufer and Denhoff (1957) and Stella Chess (1960), and in other papers of this era (Burks, 1960; Ounsted, 1955; Prechtl & Stemmer, 1962). Chess defined hyperactivity as follows: "The hyperactive child is one who carries out activities at a higher than normal rate of speed than the average child, or who is constantly in motion, or both" (p. 2379). The official catalogue of diagnostic nomenclature at the time, the second edition of the *Diagnostic and Statistical Manual of Mental Disorders* (DSM-II; American Psychiatric Association, 1968), followed suit in creating the Hyperkinetic Reaction of Childhood disorder. However, other than briefly describing the excessive activity level of these children, this diagnostic manual provided few useful details for reliable clinical diagnosis.

Chess's paper was historically significant for several reasons: (1) She strongly emphasized activity as the defining feature of the disorder, as other scientists of the time were beginning to do; (2) she stressed the need to consider objective evidence of the symptom beyond the subjective reports of parents or teachers; (3) her formulation removed the blame for the child's problems from the parents; and (4) she separated the concept of a syndrome of hyperactivity from the concept of a brain damage syndrome. Other scientists of this era emphasized similar points (Werry & Sprague, 1970). It was now recognized that hyperactivity was a behavioral syndrome that could arise from organic pathology but could also occur in its absence. Even so, it continued to be viewed as the result of some biological difficulty rather than as due solely to environmental causes.

Chess described the characteristics of 36 children diagnosed as having "physiologic hyperactivity" from a total of 881 children seen in a private practice. The ratio of males to females was approximately 4:1, and many children had been referred prior to 6 years of age, intimating a relatively earlier age of onset than that for other childhood behavioral disorders. Educational difficulties were common in this group, particularly scholastic underachievement, and many displayed oppositional defiant behavior and poor peer relationships. Impulsive and aggressive behavior and poor attention span were commonly associated characteristics. Chess believed that the hyperactivity could also be associated with mental retardation, organic brain damage, or serious mental illness such as schizophrenia. Similar findings in later research led others to question the specificity and hence utility of hyperactivity as a symptom for the diagnosis of ADHD (Douglas, 1972). Echoing many of today's prescriptions, a multimodal treatment approach incorporating parent counseling, behavior modification, psychotherapy, medication, and special education was recommended. Unlike Still, Chess and others writing in this era stressed the relatively benign nature of these ADHD symptoms and claimed that in most cases the disorder was resolved by puberty (Laufer & Denhoff, 1957; Solomons, 1965).

Europe and North America Part Company

It was perhaps during this period, or even a little earlier, that the perspective on hyperactivity taken in North America began to diverge from that taken in Europe, particularly Great Britain. In North America, hyperactivity came to be seen as a behavioral syndrome characterized chiefly by greater-than-normal levels of activity; was viewed as a relatively common disturbance of childhood; was not necessarily associated with demonstrable brain pathology; and was considered more of an extreme degree in the normal variation of temperament in children. In Great Britain, the narrower view continued into the 1970s that hyperactivity or hyperkinesis was an extreme state of excessive activity of almost driven quality; was highly uncommon; and usually occurred in conjunction with other signs of brain damage (such as epilepsy, hemiplegias, or retardation) or a clearer history of brain insult (such as trauma or infection) (Taylor, 1988). The divergence in views led to large discrepancies between North American and European investigators in their estimations of the prevalence of the disorder, their diagnostic criteria, and their preferred treatment modalities. A rapprochement between these views was not undertaken until well into the 1980s (Rutter, 1988, 1989; Taylor, 1986a, 1988).

The Prevailing View by 1969

As Ross and Ross (1976) noted, the perspective on hyperactivity in this era was that it remained a brain dysfunction syndrome, although of a milder magnitude than was previously believed. The disorder was no longer ascribed to brain damage, but a focus on brain mechanisms prevailed. The disorder was also viewed as having a relatively homogeneous set of symptoms, predominant among which was excessive activity level or hyperactivity. Its prognosis was now felt to be relatively benign, as it was thought to be often outgrown by puberty. The recommended treatments now consisted of stimulant medication and psychotherapy, in addition to the minimum-stimulation type of classrooms recommended in earlier years.

THE PERIOD 1970 to 1979: THE ASCENDANCE OF ATTENTION DEFICITS

Research in the 1970s on the disorder took a quantum leap forward, with over 2,000 published studies existing by the end of the decade (Weiss & Hechtman, 1979). Numerous clinical and scientific textbooks (Cantwell, 1975; Safer & Allen, 1976; Trites, 1979; Wender, 1971) appeared along with the most thorough and scholarly review of the literature yet published—that by Dorothea and Sheila Ross (1976). Special journal issues were devoted to the topic (*Journal of Abnormal Child Psychology, 4,* 1976; *Journal of Pediatric Psychology, 3,* 1978) along with numerous scientific gatherings (Knights & Bakker, 1976, 1980). Clearly, hyperactivity had become a subject of serious professional and scientific, as well as popular, attention.

By the early 1970s, the defining features of the hyperactive or hyperkinetic child syndrome had been broadened to include what were previously felt to be only associated characteristics, including impulsivity, short attention span, low frustration tolerance, distractibility, and aggressiveness (Marwit & Stenner, 1972; Safer & Allen, 1976). Others (Wender, 1971, 1973) nevertheless persisted with the excessively inclusive concept of MBD, in which even more features—such as motor clumsiness, cognitive impairments, and parent-child conflict—were viewed as hallmarks of the syndrome and in which hyperactivity was unnecessary for the diagnosis. As noted earlier, the concept of MBD faded from clinical and scientific usage by the end of this decade, due in no small part to the scholarly tome by Herbert and Ellen Rie (1980) and the critical reviews by Michael Rutter (1977, 1982). These writings emphasized the lack of evidence for a syndrome, in that the symptoms were not well defined, did not correlate significantly among themselves, had no well-specified etiology, and displayed no common course and outcome. The heterogeneity of the disorder was overwhelming, and more than a few took note of the apparent hypocrisy in defining an MBD syndrome with statements that there was often little or no evidence of neurological abnormality (Wender, 1971). Moreover, even in cases of well-established cerebral damage, the behavioral sequelae were not uniform across cases, and hyperactivity was seen in only a minority. Hence, contrary to 25 years of theorizing to this point, hyperactivity was not a common sequela of brain damage; truly brain-damaged children did not display a uniform pattern of behavioral deficits; and children with hyperactivity rarely had substantiated evidence of neurological damage (Rutter, 1989).

The Emergence of Attention Deficits

There also developed at this time a disenchantment with the exclusive focus on hyperactivity as the sine qua non of this disorder (Werry & Sprague, 1970). Significant at this historical juncture was the presidential address of Virginia Douglas to the Canadian Psychological Association (Douglas, 1972), in which it was argued that deficits in sustained attention and impulse control were more likely to account for the difficulties seen in these children than was hyperactivity. These were also seen as the major areas of impact of the stimulant medications used to treat the disorder. Douglas's paper is historically significant in other ways as well. Her extensive and thorough battery of objective measures of various behavioral and cognitive domains allowed her to rule in or out various characteristics felt to be typical for these children in earlier clinical and scientific lore. For instance, she found that hyperactive children were not necessarily more reading- or learning-disabled, did not perseverate on concept learning tasks, did not manifest auditory or right-left discrimination problems, and had no difficulties with short-term memory. Most importantly, she and Susan Campbell demonstrated that hyperactive children were not more distractible than normal children and that the sustained attention problems could emerge in conditions where no significant distractions existed (Douglas, 1972).

The McGill research team repeatedly demonstrated that hyperactive children had their greatest difficulties on tasks assessing vigilance or sustained attention, such as the continuous-performance test. This test later became the most widely used laboratory measure in subsequent studies on attention in hyperactive, or ADHD, children and was eventually standardized and commercially marketed for diagnosis of the disorder (Gordon, 1983). Douglas remarked on the extreme degree of variability demonstrated during task performances by these children—a characteristic that was later advanced as one of the defining features of the disorder. The McGill team (Freibergs, 1965; Freibergs & Douglas, 1969; Parry, 1973) also found that hyperactive children could perform at normal or near-normal levels of sustained attention under conditions of continuous and immediate reinforcement, but that their performance deteriorated dramatically when partial reinforcement was introduced, particularly at schedules below 50% reinforcement. Campbell (Campbell, Douglas, & Morgenstern, 1971) further demonstrated substantial problems with impulse control and field dependence in the cognitive styles of hyperactive children.

Like Still 70 years earlier, Douglas commented on the probable association between deficits in attention/impulse control and deficiencies in moral development that were plaguing her subjects, particularly in their adolescent years. The research of this team on stimulant medication effects showed dramatic improvements in these attention deficiencies during medication treatment, as did the research in other laboratories at the time (Conners & Rothschild, 1968; Sprague, Barnes, & Werry, 1970). Finally, of substantial significance were the observations of Douglas's colleague, Gabrielle Weiss, from her follow-up studies (see Weiss & Hechtman, 1986) that while the hyperactivity of these children often diminished by adolescence, their problems with poor sustained attention and impulsivity persisted. This alarm concerning both the persistence of the disabilities and the risk for greater academic and social maladjustment was sounded by other research teams from their own follow-up investigations (Mendelson, Johnson, & Stewart, 1971), and was better substantiated by more rigorous studies in the next decade (see Brown & Borden, 1986; Gittelman, Mannuzza, Shenker, & Bonagura, 1985; Barkley, Fischer, Edelbrock, & Smallish, in press-a).

Douglas's Model of Attention Deficits

Douglas later elaborated, refined, and further substantiated this theory of hyperactivity (Douglas, 1980a, 1980b, 1983; Douglas & Peters, 1979). Her ultimate view was that four major deficits could account for symptoms of ADHD: (1) deficits in the investment, organization, and maintenance of attention and effort; (2) inability to inhibit impulsive responding; (3) inability to modulate arousal levels to meet situational demands; and (4) an unusually strong inclination to seek immediate reinforcement. This theory initiated or guided a substantial amount of research over the next 15 years, including my own (Barkley & Ullman, 1975, 1977a), constituting a model as close to a scientific paradigm as the field of hyperactivity is likely to have in its history to date. Only in the 1980s did results begin to emerge that were significantly at odds with this theory. Scientists began to seriously question the adequacy of an attentional model in accounting for the behavioral deficits seen in ADHD children, as well as for the effects of stimulant medications on them (Barkley, 1981, 1984; Haenlein & Caul, 1987; Draeger, Prior, & Sanson, 1986; van der Meere & Sergeant, 1988a, 1988b; see Chapter 5).

So influential were Douglas's paper and the subsequent research published by the team of students and colleagues working with her at McGill University, that this research was probably the major reason the disorder was renamed Attention Deficit Disorder (ADD) in 1980 with the publication of the DSM-III (American Psychiatric Association, 1980). In this revised official taxonomy, deficits in sustained attention and impulse control were now formally recognized as of greater significance in the diagnosis than hyperactivity. The shift to attention deficits rather than hyperactivity as the major difficulty of these children was useful, at least for a time, because of the growing evidence that hyperactivity was not specific to this particular condition, but could be noted in other psychiatric disorders (e.g., anxiety, mania, autism, etc.); that there was no clear delineation between normal and abnormal levels of activity; that activity was in fact a multidimensional construct; and that the symptoms of hyperactivity were quite situational in nature in many children (Rutter, 1989). But this approach only corrected the problem of definition for less than a decade before these same concerns began to be raised about the construct of attention as well (e.g., multidimensional, situationally variable, etc.). Yet some research showed that at least deficits in vigilance or sustained attention could be used to discriminate this disorder from other psychiatric disorders (Werry, 1988).

Other Historical Developments

A number of other historical developments during the 1970s are deserving of mention.

The Rise of Medication Therapy

One of these developments was the rapidly increasing use of stimulant medication with school-age hyperactive children. This was no doubt spawned by the significant increase in research on the effects, often dramatic, of stimulants on hyperactive children. A second development was the use of much more rigorous scientific methodology in drug studies, due in large measure to the early studies by C. Keith Conners (then working with Leon Eisenberg at Harvard), and somewhat later to Robert Sprague at the University of Illinois, Virginia Douglas at McGill University, and John Werry in New Zealand. This body of literature became voluminous (Barkley, 1977b; Ross & Ross, 1976), with over 120 studies published through 1976—a trend that continued well into the next decade, making this treatment approach the most well-studied therapy in child psychiatry.

Despite its proven efficacy, public and professional misgivings about its increasingly widespread use with children emerged. In an incident in Omaha, Nebraska (Maynard, 1970), news accounts reported that as many as 5 to 10% of the children in grade schools were receiving behavior-modifying drugs. Although these would later be shown to be grossly exaggerated estimates of drug treatment (by as much as 10-fold), the public interest that arose around the initial reports led to a congressional review of the use of psychotropic medications for school children. At this same time, the claim was being advanced that hyperactivity was a "myth" created by intolerant teachers and parents and an inadequate educational system (Conrad, 1975; Schrag & Divoky, 1975).

Environment as Etiology

Almost simultaneously with this backlash against "drugging" school children for behavior problems, there came another significant development in this decade: a growing belief that hyperactivity was due to environmental causes. It is not just coincidental that this occurred at the same time that Americans were expressing a great interest in natural foods, health consciousness, and life expectancy extension via environmental manipulations. An extremely popular view among these individuals was that an allergic or toxic reaction to food additives, such as dyes, preservatives, and salicylates (Feingold, 1975), caused hyperactive behavior. It was claimed that over half of all hyperactive children had developed their difficulties because of their diet. The most effective treatment was said to be buying or making foods for these children that did not contain the offending substances.

So widespread became this view that Feingold Associations, comprised mainly of parents, developed in almost every state within the United States. Legislation was introduced, although not passed, in California requiring that all school cafeteria foods be prepared in such a way that these substances were absent from the diet. A sizeable number of research investigations were undertaken (see Conners, 1980, for a review), the more rigorous of which found little if any effect of these substances on children's behavior. A National Advisory Committee on Hyperkinesis and Food Additives (1980) was convened to review this literature and concluded more strongly than Conners that the available evidence clearly refuted Feingold's claims. Nevertheless, it was over 10 years before this notion receded in popularity, to be replaced by the equally unproven hypothesis that refined sugar was more to blame for hyperactivity than food additives (see Milich, Wolraich, & Lindgren, 1986, for a review).

The emphasis on environmental causes, however, spread to other possible sources than diet. Block (1977) advanced the notion that technological development and more rapid cultural change were resulting in an increasing societal "tempo," causing increasing excitation or environmental stimulation. This was interacting with a predisposition in some children toward hyperactivity, making it manifest. It was felt that this explained the apparently increasing incidence of hyperactivity in developed cultures. Ross and Ross (1982) provide an excellent critique of this theory and conclude that there is insufficient evidence in support of it and some that would contradict it. There is little evidence that hyperactivity is increasing or that its prevalence varies as a function of societal development.

Instead, Ross and Ross propose that cultural effects on hyperactivity have more to do with whether important institutions of enculturation are consistent or inconsistent in the demands made and standards set for child behavior and development. These cultural views, it is said, will both determine the threshold for deviance that will be tolerated in children and exaggerate a predisposition to hyperactivity in some children. Consistent cultures will have fewer children diagnosed with hyperactivity, because they minimize individual differences among children and provide clear and consistent expectations and consequences for behavior that conforms to the expected norms. Inconsistent cultures, by contrast, will have more children diagnosed as hyperactive, because they maximize or stress individual differences and provide ambiguous expectations and consequences to children regarding appropriate conduct. This intriguing hypothesis remains unstudied at this time. However, on these grounds an equally compelling case could be made for the opposite effects of cultural influences. That is, in highly consistent, high-conformity cultures, hyperactive behavior may be considerably more obvious in children, because they are unable to conform to these societal expectations; inconsistent, low-conformity cultures may tolerate deviant behavior to a greater degree.

A different environmental view was advanced by schools of psychology/psychiatry at diametrically opposite poles, and this was that poor child rearing leads to hyperactivity. Both psychoanalysts (Bettelheim, 1973) and behaviorists (Willis & Lovaas, 1977) promulgated this view; the former claimed that mothers intolerant of negative or hyperactive temperament in their infants react with excessively negative parental responses, giving rise to clinical levels of hyperactivity. The latter, behavioral view stressed poor conditioning of children to stimulus control by commands and instructions that give rise to noncompliant and hyperactive behavior. Both could derive some support from prospective studies that found negative mother-child interactions in the preschool years to be associated with the continuation of hyperactivity into the late childhood (Campbell, 1987) and adolescent (Barkley, Fischer, et al., in press-a) years.

However, such correlational data do not prove that poor child rearing or negative parent-child interactions cause hyperactivity—only that they are associated with its persistence. It could just as easily be that the severity of hyperactivity elicits greater maternal negative reactions, and that this severity is related to persistence of the disorder over time. In support of this interpretation have been the studies of stimulant drug effects on hyperactive children's interactions with their mothers; these show that mothers' negative and directive behavior is greatly reduced when stimulant medication is used to reduce the hyperactivity in their children (Barkley, 1989b; Barkley & Cunningham, 1979a; Barkley, Karlsson, Pollard, & Murphy, 1985). Moreover, follow-up studies have also shown that the degree of hyperactivity in childhood is predictive of its persistence into later childhood and adolescence (Barkley, Fischer, et al., in press-a; Campbell & Ewing, in press). Nevertheless, family context is still important in predicting the outcome of hyperactive children, even though the mechanism of its action has not yet been specified (Weiss & Hechtman, 1986). Furthermore, parent training in child behavior management has been increasingly recommended as an important therapy in its own right (Dubey & Kaufman, 1978; Pelham, 1977), despite a paucity of studies concerning its actual efficacy (Barkley, 1989a).

The Passage of Public Law 94-142

Another significant development was the passing of Public Law 94-142 in 1975, mandating special educational services for handicapping and behavioral disabilities of children in addition to those already available for mental retardation (see Henker & Whalen, 1980, for a review of the legal precedents leading up to this law). Although many of its recommendations were foreshadowed by Section 504 of the Rehabilitation Act (PL 93-112), it was the financial incentives for each state associated with the adoption of PL 94-142 that probably encouraged its immediate and widespread implementation by the states. Programs for learning disabilities, behavioral–emotional disturbance, language disorders, physical handicaps, and motor disabilities, among others, were now required to be provided to all eligible children in all public schools in the United States.

The full impact of these widely available educational treatment programs on hyperactive children cannot yet be completely appreciated for several reasons. First, hyperactivity, by itself, was overlooked in the criteria set forth for behavioral and learning disabilities that make children eligible for these special classes. Such children must typically also have another condition, such as a learning disability, language delay, or emotional disorder, to receive exceptional educational services. The effects of special educational resources on the outcome of hyperactivity will be difficult to assess, given this confounding of multiple disorders. Second, the mandated services have been in existence for little more than a decade, and so long-term outcome studies begun in the late 1970s are only now being reported. Those that have (Barkley, Fischer, et al., in press-a) suggest that over 35% of ADHD children receive some type of special educational placement. Although the availability of these services seems to have reduced the percentage of ADHD children being retained in grade for their academic problems, compared to percentages in earlier follow-up studies, the rates of school suspensions and expulsions have not declined appreciably from pre-1977 rates. A more careful analysis of the effects of PL 94-142, however, is in order before its efficacy for ADHD children can be judged.

The Rise of Behavior Modification

This growing emphasis on educational intervention for behavior- and learning-disordered children was accompanied by a plethora of research on the use of behavior modification techniques in the management of disruptive classroom behavior, particularly as an alternative to stimulant medication (Allyon, Layman, & Kandel, 1975; O'Leary, Pelham, Rosenbaum, & Price, 1976). Although these studies demonstrated considerable efficacy of these techniques in the management of inattentive and hyperactive behavior, they were not found to achieve the same degree of behavioral improvement as the stimulants (Gittelman-Klein, Klein, Abikoff, Katz, Gloisten, & Kates, 1976), and so did not replace them as a treatment of choice. Nevertheless, there was a growing consensus that the stimulant drugs should never be used as a sole intervention, but should be combined with parent training and behavioral intervention in the classroom.

Developments in Assessment

Another hallmark of this era was the widespread adoption of the parent and teacher rating scales developed by C. Keith Conners (1969) for the assessment of symptoms of hyperactivity, particularly during trials on stimulant medication. For at least 20 years, these simply constructed ratings of behavioral items served as the "gold standard" for selecting children as hyperactive, both for research purposes and for treatment with medication. Large-scale normative data were collected, particularly for the teacher scale, and epidemiological studies throughout the world relied upon them for assessing the prevalence of hyperactivity in their populations (see Appendix A for a review). Their use moved the practice of diagnosis and assessment of treatment effects from one of clinical impression alone to one in which at least some more objective measure of behavioral deviance was employed. These scales were later criticized for their confounding of hyperactivity with aggression. This called into question whether the findings of research that relied upon the scales were the results of oppositional, defiant, and hostile (aggressive) features of the population or of their hyperactivity (Ullmann, Sleator, & Sprague, 1985). Nevertheless, the widespread adoption of the Conners rating scales in this era marks a historical turning point toward the use of assessment methods that can be empirically tested and that can assist in determining developmental deviance.

Also significant during this decade was the effort to study the social-ecological impact of hyperactive/inattentive behavior. This line of research set about evaluating the effects produced on family interactions by the hyperactive child. Originally initiated by Campbell (1973, 1975), this line of inquiry came to dominate my own research (Barkley & Cunningham, 1979a; Cunningham & Barkley, 1978, 1979), particularly evaluation of the effects of stimulant medication on these social exchanges. These studies showed that hyperactive children were much less compliant and more oppositional during parent-child exchanges than normal children, and that their mothers were more directive, commanding, and negative than mothers of normal children. These difficulties increased substantially when the situation changed from free play to task-oriented demands. Studies also demonstrated that stimulant medication resulted in significant improvements in child compliance and decreases in maternal control and directiveness. Simultaneously, Humphries, Kinsbourne, and Swanson (1978) reported similar effects of stimulant medication, all of which suggested that much of parental controlling and negative behavior toward hyperactive children was the result rather than the cause of the children's poor self-control and inattention. At this same time, Carol Whalen and Barbara Henker at the University of California–Irvine demonstrated similar interaction conflicts between hyperactive children and their teachers and peers, as well as similar effects of stimulant medication on these social interactions (Whalen & Henker, 1980; Whalen, Henker, & Dotemoto, 1980). This line of research increased substantially in the next decade.

A Focus on Psychophysiology

Finally, the 1970s were noteworthy for an explosion in the number of research studies undertaken on the psychophysiology of hyperactivity in children. Numerous studies were published measuring galvanic skin response,

heart rate acceleration–deceleration, various parameters of the electroencephalogram, electropupillography, averaged evoked responses, and other aspects
of electrophysiology in hyperactive children. Many were investigating the evidence for theories of over- or underarousal of the CNS in hyperactivity, which
grew out of the speculations in the 1950s on cortical overstimulation. Most
studies would be seriously methodologically flawed, difficult to interpret, and
often contradictory in their findings. Two influential reviews at the time
(Hastings & Barkley, 1978; Rosenthal & Allen, 1978) were highly critical of
most investigations, but concluded that if there was any consistency across
findings, it might be that hyperactive children showed a sluggish or under-
reactive electrophysiological response to stimulation. This laid to rest the belief in an overstimulated cerebral cortex as the cause of the symptoms in
hyperactive children, but did little to suggest a specific neurophysiological
mechanism for this underreactivity. Further advances in the contributions of
psychophysiology to understanding hyperactivity had to await further refinements in instrumentation and in definition and diagnosis of the disorder, along
with advances in computer-assisted analysis of electrophysiological measures.

The Prevailing View by 1979

The decade closed with the prevailing view that hyperactivity was not the
only or the most important behavioral deficit seen in hyperactive children;
poor attention span and impulse control were seen as equally if not more
important in explaining their problems. Brain damage had been relegated to
an extremely minor role as a cause of the disorder, although other brain
mechanisms, such as underarousal or underreactivity, brain neurotransmitter
deficiencies (Wender, 1971), or neurological immaturity (Kinsbourne, 1973),
were viewed as promising. A greater appreciation for potential environmental
causes or irritants had emerged, particularly diet and child rearing; as a result, the most frequently recommended therapies for hyperactivity included
not only stimulant medication, but widely available special education programs, classroom behavior modification, dietary management, and parent
training in child management skills. A greater appreciation for the effects of
hyperactive children on their immediate social ecology was beginning to emerge,
as well as for the impact of stimulant medication in altering these social conflicts. There remained a sizeable discrepancy in North American and European views of the disorder: North American professionals continued to recognize the disorder as more common, in need of medication, and more likely
to be an attentional deficit, whereas those in Europe viewed it as uncommon,
defined by severe overactivity, and associated with brain damage. Those children in North America being diagnosed as hyperactive or attention deficit
would most likely have been diagnosed as having a conduct disorder in Europe, where treatment would consist of psychotherapy, family therapy, and
parent training in child management, while medication would be little used.
Nevertheless, the view that attentional deficits were as important in the dis-

order as hyperactivity was beginning to make its way into European taxonomies, such as the ninth edition of the *International Classification of Diseases* (ICD-9; World Health Organization, 1978).

THE PERIOD 1980 TO 1989: THE AGE OF DIAGNOSTIC CRITERIA AND THE WANING OF ATTENTION DEFICITS

The exponential increase in research on hyperactivity characteristic of the 1970s continued unabated into the 1980s, making hyperactivity the most well-studied childhood psychiatric disorder in existence. More books were written, conferences convened, and scientific papers presented during this decade than in any previous historical period. This decade became notable for its emphasis on attempts to develop more specific diagnostic criteria; the differential conceptualization and diagnosis of hyperactivity from other psychiatric disorders; and, later in the decade, critical attacks on the notion that deficits in sustained attention and impulsivity were the core behavioral deficits in ADHD.

The Creation of an ADD Syndrome

Marking the beginning of this decade was the publication of the DSM-III by the American Psychiatric Association (1980), and its radical reconceptualization of the disorder from the DSM-II category Hyperkinetic Reaction of Childhood to ADD (with or without Hyperactivity). These criteria are set forth in Table 1.1. The new diagnostic criteria were noteworthy not only for their greater emphasis on inattention and impulsivity as defining features of the disorder, but also for their creation of much more specific symptom lists, numerical cutoff scores for symptoms, guidelines for age of onset and duration of symptoms, and the exclusion of other childhood psychiatric conditions as essential to defining the disorder. The DSM-III criteria were also a radical departure from the ICD-9 criteria set forth by the World Health Organization (1978) in its own taxonomy of child psychiatric disorders, which continued to emphasize pervasive hyperactivity as a hallmark of this disorder.

Even more controversial was the creation of subtypes of Attention Deficit Disorder (ADD), based on the presence or absence of Hyperactivity (+ H or − H), in the DSM-III criteria. Little, if any, empirical research existed at the time these subtypes were formulated. Their creation in the official nomenclature of psychiatric disorders initiated numerous research studies by the end of this decade into the validity and utility of this subtyping approach, along with a search for other useful ways of subtyping ADD (i.e., pervasiveness across situations, presence of aggression, stimulant drug response, etc.). Although results at times were conflicting, the trend in the findings of these studies was that ADD/−H children differed from those with ADD/+H in important domains of current adjustment. Children with ADD/−H were

TABLE 1.1. DSM-III Diagnostic Criteria for Attention Deficit Disorder with and without Hyperactivity

The child displays, for his or her mental and chronological age, signs of developmentally inappropriate inattention, impulsivity, and hyperactivity. The signs must be reported by adults in the child's environment, such as parents and teachers. Because the symptoms are typically variable, they may not be observed directly by the clinician. When the reports of teachers and parents conflict, primary consideration should be given to the teacher reports because of greater familiarity with age-appropriate norms. Symptoms typically worsen in situations that require self-application, as in the classroom. Signs of the disorder may be absent when the child is in a new or a one-to-one situation.

The number of symptoms specified is for children between the ages of eight and ten, the peak age range for referral. In younger children, more severe forms of the symptoms and a greater number of symptoms are usually present. The opposite is true of older children.

A. *Inattention.* At least three of the following:
  (1) often fails to finish things he or she starts
  (2) often doesn't seem to listen
  (3) easily distracted
  (4) has difficulty concentrating on schoolwork or other tasks requiring sustained attention
  (5) has difficulty sticking to a play activity
B. *Impulsivity.* At least three of the following:
  (1) often acts before thinking
  (2) shifts excessively from one activity to another
  (3) has difficulty organizing work (this not being due to cognitive impairment)
  (4) needs a lot of supervision
  (5) frequently calls out in class
  (6) has difficulty awaiting turn in games or group situations
C. *Hyperactivity.* At least two of the following:
  (1) runs about or climbs on things excessively
  (2) has difficulty sitting still or fidgets excessively
  (3) has difficulty staying seated
  (4) moves about excessively during sleep
  (5) is always "on the go" or acts as if "driven by a motor"
D. Onset before the age of seven.
E. Duration of at least six months.
F. Not due to Schizophrenia, Affective Disorder, or Severe or Profound Mental Retardation.

Note. From the *Diagnostic and Statistical Manual of Mental Disorders* (3rd ed., pp. 43–44) by the American Psychiatric Association, 1980, Washington, DC: Author. Copyright 1980 by the American Psychiatric Association. Reprinted by permission.

characterized as more daydreamy, hypoactive, lethargic, and learning-disabled in academic achievement, but substantially less aggressive and less rejected by their peers (Carlson, 1986).

Unfortunately, this research came too late to be considered in the subsequent revision of the DSM-III (DSM-III-R), published by the American Psychiatric Association in 1987. ADD/−H was no longer officially recognized as a subtype of ADD, but was relegated to a minimally defined category called "Undifferentiated ADD," with a call for more research on its utility as a diagnostic category. Despite the controversy that arose over the demotion of ADD/−H in this fashion, it was actually a prudent gesture on the part of the committee asked to formulate these criteria. At the time, the committee had little available research to guide its deliberations in this matter. There was simply no indication of whether ADD/−H children had a similar or qualitatively different type of attentional deficit; the latter would make ADD/−H a separate childhood psychiatric disorder in its own right (Barkley, Spitzer, & Costello, 1990). Rather than continue merely to conjecture about the nature of the subtype and how it should be diagnosed, the committee essentially placed the concept in abeyance until more research could be available to its successor committee to guide its definition.

The Development of Research Criteria

At the same time that the DSM-III criteria for ADD/+H and ADD/−H were gaining in recognition, others were attempting to specify research diagnostic criteria (Barkley, 1982; Loney, 1983). My own efforts in this endeavor were spurred on by the rather idiosyncratic and highly variable approach to diagnosis being used in clinical practice; the vague or often unspecified criteria used in published research studies; and the lack of specificity in current theoretical writings on the disorder up to 1980. There was also the more pragmatic consideration that as a young scientist attempting to select hyperactive children for research studies, I had no operational or consensus criteria available for doing so. I therefore set forth a more operational definition of hyperactivity (or ADD/+H), which required not only the usual parent and/or teacher complaints of inattention, impulsivity, and overactivity, but also stipulated that these symptoms had to (1) be deviant for the child's mental age as measured by well-standardized child behavior rating scales; (2) be relatively pervasive within the jurisdictions of the major caregivers in the child's life (parent/home and teacher/school); (3) have developed by 6 years of age; and (4) have lasted at least 12 months (Barkley, 1982).

Concurrently, Loney (1983) and her colleagues were engaged in a series of historically important studies that differentiated the symptoms of hyperactivity or ADD/+H from those of aggression or conduct problems (Loney, Langhorne, & Paternite, 1978; Loney & Milich, 1982). Following an empirical/statistical approach to developing research diagnostic criteria, Loney demonstrated that a relatively short list of symptoms of hyperactivity could be empirically separated from a similarly short list of aggression symptoms. Empirically derived cutoff scores on these symptom ratings by teachers could create these two semi-independent constructs. These constructs proved highly useful in accounting for much of the heterogeneity and disagreement across studies.

Among other things, it became well established that many of the negative outcomes of hyperactivity in adolescence and young adulthood were actually due to the presence and degree of aggression that coexisted with the hyperactivity. Purely hyperactive children were shown to display substantial cognitive problems with attention and overactivity, while purely aggressive children did not. Previous findings of greater family psychopathology in hyperactive children were also shown to be primarily a function of the degree of aggression in the children. Furthermore, hyperactivity was found to be associated with signs of developmental and neurological delay or immaturity, whereas aggression was more likely to be associated with environmental disadvantage and family dysfunction (Hinshaw, 1987; Milich, Loney, & Landau, 1982; Paternite & Loney, 1980; Rutter, 1989; Werry, 1988; Weiss & Hechtman, 1986). The need for future studies to clearly specify the makeup of their samples along these two dimensions was now obvious, and the raging debate as to whether hyperactivity was separate from or merely synonymous with conduct problems was settled by this important research discovery (Ross & Ross, 1982). These findings also led to the demise of the commonplace use of the Conners 10-item Hyperactivity Index to select children as hyperactive, because it was now shown that many of these items actually assessed aggression rather than hyperactivity, resulting in samples of children with mixed disorders (Ullmann et al., 1985).

The drive toward greater clarity, specificity, and operationalization of diagnostic criteria would continue throughout the 1980s. Experts within the field (Quay, 1987; Rutter, 1983, 1989; Werry, 1989) now called upon their colleagues to demonstrate that the symptoms of ADHD could distinguish it from other childhood psychiatric disorders—a crucial test for the validity of a diagnostic entity—rather than continuing simply to demonstrate that ADHD children differed from normal populations. The challenge would not be easily met. Notable advances were the efforts by Eric Taylor (1986a) and colleagues in Great Britain to further refine the criteria and their measurement along more empirical lines. His statistical approach to studying clusters of behavioral disorders resulted in the recommendation (Taylor, 1989) that a syndrome of hyperactivity be valid and distinct from other disorders, particularly conduct problems. This distinction required that the symptoms of hyperactivity and inattention be excessive and handicapping to the children; that the symptoms occur in at least two of three broadly defined settings (e.g., home, school, and clinic); that they be objectively measured rather than subjectively rated by parents and teachers; that they develop before age 6 years and last at least 6 months; and that they *not* include symptoms of autism, psychosis, or affective disorders (i.e., depression, anxiety, mania, etc.).

Efforts to develop research diagnostic criteria for ADHD eventually led to an international symposium on the subject (Sergeant, 1988) and a general consensus that subjects selected for research on ADHD should meet at least the following criteria: (1) reports of problems with activity and attention from at least two independent sources (home, school, clinic); (2) endorsement of at least three of four difficulties with activity and three of four with attention; (3) onset before 7 years of age; (4) duration of 2 years; (5) significantly elevated scores on parent/teacher ratings of these ADHD symptoms; and (6) exclusion of autism and psychosis. The proposed criteria were quite similar to others proposed earlier in the decade (Barkley, 1982), but provided for greater specificity of symptoms of overactivity and inattention and a longer duration of symptoms.

Subtyping of ADD

Also of import was the attempt to identify other useful approaches to subtyping than just those based on the degree of hyperactivity (+ H/ − H) or aggression associated with ADD. A significant though underappreciated line of research by Roscoe Dykman and Peggy Ackerman at the University of Arkansas distinguished between ADD children with and without learning disabilities, particularly reading impairments. Their research (Ackerman, Dykman, & Oglesby, 1983; Dykman, Ackerman, & Holcomb, 1985) and that of others (McGee, Williams, Moffitt, & Anderson, 1989) showed that some of the cognitive deficits (verbal memory, intelligence, etc.) formerly attributed to ADHD were actually more a function of the presence and degree of language/reading difficulties than of ADHD. And, although some studies indicated that ADHD children with reading disabilities did *not* constitute a distinct subtype of ADHD (Halperin, Gittelman, Klein, & Rudel, 1984), the differential contributions made by reading disorders to the cognitive test performance of ADHD children require that subsequent research studies either carefully select subjects with pure ADHD unassociated with reading disability, or at least identify the extent of reading disorders in the sample and partial out their effects on the cognitive test results.

Others in this era attempted to distinguish between "pervasive" and "situational" hyperactivity. The former was determined by the presence of hyperactivity at home and school, while the latter referred to hyperactivity in only one of these settings (Schachar, Rutter, & Smith, 1981). It was shown that pervasively hyperactive children were likely to have more severe behavioral symptoms, greater aggression and peer relationship problems, and poorer academic achievement. The DSM-III-R (American Psychiatric Association, 1987) incorporated this concept into an index of severity of ADHD, and British scientists came to view pervasiveness as an essential criteria for the diagnosis of a distinct syndrome of hyperactivity (see above). However, research appearing at the end of the decade (Costello, Loeber, & Stoutheimer-Loeber, 1989) demonstrated that such group differences were probably due to differences in the source of the information used to classify the children (parents vs. teachers), rather than to actual behavioral differences between the situational and pervasive subgroups. This does not mean that symptom pervasiveness may not be a useful means of subtyping or diagnosing ADHD, but that more objective means of establishing it are needed than just comparing parent and teacher ratings on a questionnaire.

A different and relatively understudied conceptualization was that of subtypes of ADHD created by the presence or absence of significant anxiety/ depression or affective disturbance. Several studies demonstrated that ADHD children with significant anxiety or affective disturbance were likely to show poor or adverse responses to stimulant medication (Taylor, 1983; Voelker, Lachar, & Gdowski, 1983) and would perhaps respond better to antidepressant medications (Pliszka, 1987). To date, the utility of this last subtyping approach remains underinvestigated.

ADD Becomes ADHD

Later in the decade, the DSM-III-R (American Psychiatric Association, 1987; see also Chapter 2) further revised the criteria for defining this disorder, and changed its name to ADHD. These revisions were significant in several respects. First, a single item list of symptoms and a single cutoff score replaced the three separate lists (Inattention, Impulsivity, and Hyperactivity) and cutoff scores in the DSM-III. Second, the item list was now based more on empirically derived dimensions of child behavior from behavior rating scales; the items and cutoff score had also undergone a large field trial to determine their sensitivity, specificity, and power to distinguish children with ADHD from those with other psychiatric disorders and normal children (Spitzer, Davies, & Barkley, in press). Third, the need to establish the symptoms as being developmentally inappropriate for the child's mental age was stressed more emphatically. Fourth, the coexistence of affective disorders with ADHD no longer excluded the diagnosis of ADHD. Finally, and more controversially, the subtype of ADD/−H was removed as a subtype and relegated to a vaguely defined category, Undifferentiated ADD, that was in need of greater research on its merits (Barkley, Spitzer, & Costello, 1990). ADHD was now classified with two other behavioral disorders (Oppositional Defiant Disorder and Conduct Disorder) in a supraordinate category known as the Disruptive Behavior Disorders, in view of their substantial overlap or comorbidity in clinic-referred populations of children.

ADHD as a Motivation Deficit Disorder

One of the most far-reaching and exciting developments in this decade only began to emerge in the latter half of the period. It is not likely to be fully appreciated for at least another decade or more. This was the nascent and almost heretical view that ADHD was not actually a disorder of attention at all. Doubt as to the central importance of attention to the disorder crept in late in the 1970s, as some researchers more fully plumbed the depths of the attentional construct while others took note of the striking situational variability of the symptoms (Douglas & Peters, 1979; Rosenthal & Allen, 1978; Routh, 1978; Sroufe, 1975). As more rigorous and technical studies of attention in ADHD children appeared in the 1980s, an increasing number failed to find evidence of problems with sustained attention under some experimental conditions while observing them under others (see Douglas, 1983, 1988, for reviews; Barkley, 1984; Draeger et al., 1986; Sergeant, 1988; Sergeant & van der Meere, 1989; van der Meere & Sergeant, 1988a, 1988b). These findings, coupled with the realization that both instructional and motivational factors in an experiment played a strong role in determining the presence and degree of ADHD symptoms, led some investigators to hypothesize that motivation may be a better model for explaining the deficits seen in ADHD children (Rosenthal & Allen, 1978; Sroufe, 1975). Following this line of reasoning, others pursued a behavioral or functional analysis of these symptoms; they hypothesized deficits in the stimulus control over behavior, particularly by rules and instructions (Barkley, 1981; Willis & Lovaas, 1977).

I initially raised the possibility that deficits in rule-governed behavior might account for many of the deficits in ADHD, but later amended this to include the strong probability that responses to behavioral consequences might also be impaired and could conceivably account for the problems with rule following (Barkley, 1984, 1990). Others independently advanced the notion that a deficit in responding to behavioral consequences, not attention, was the difficulty in ADHD (Beninger, 1989; Haenlein & Caul, 1987; Prior, 1987; Quay, 1988; Sagvolden, Wultz, Moser, Moser, & Morkrid, 1989; Sergeant, 1988; van der Meere & Sergeant, 1988b). That is, it was now hypothesized that ADHD arises out of an insensitivity to consequences—reinforcement, punishment, or both. This insensitivity was viewed as neurological in origin. Yet this idea was not new, having been advanced some 20 years earlier by investigators studying conduct problem children (see Patterson, 1982, for a review), and somewhat later by Wender (1971) in his classic text on MBD. What were original in these more recent ideas were the greater specificity of their hypotheses and the increased evidence supporting them. Others would continue to argue against the merits of a Skinnerian, or functional, analysis of the deficits in ADHD (Douglas, 1990) and for the continued explanatory value of cognitive models of attention in accounting for the deficits in ADHD children. But at this writing, the disenchantment with an attention or cognitive model of ADHD continues unabated.

The appeal of the motivational model came from several different sources: (1) its greater explanatory value in accounting for the more recent research findings on situational variability in attention in ADHD; (2) its consistency with neuroanatomical studies suggesting decreased activation of brain reward centers and their cortical-limbic regulating circuits (Lou et al., 1984, 1989); (3) its consistency with studies of the functions of dopamine pathways in regulating locomotor behavior and incentive or operant learning (Beninger, 1989); and (4) its greater prescriptive power in suggesting potential treatments for the ADHD symptoms. Whether ADHD will come to be labeled as a motivational deficit is uncertain, but there is little doubt that these new theories, based on the construct of motivation and a more functional analysis of behavior, are radically altering the way in which we conceptualize this disorder.

Other Historical Developments of the Era

The Importance of Social Ecology

The 1980s would also witness considerably greater research into the social-ecological impact of ADHD symptoms on the children, their parents (Barkley, 1989a; Barkley, Karlsson, & Pollard, 1985; Mash & Johnston, 1982), teachers (Whalen, Henker, & Dotemoto, 1980, 1981), siblings (Mash & Johnston, 1983a), and peers (Cunningham, Siegel, & Offord, 1985; Henker & Whalen, 1980). These investigators further explored the effects of stimulant medications on these social systems as well; their findings buttressed the conclusion that ADHD children elicit significant negative, controlling, and hostile or rejecting interactions from others that can be greatly reduced by stimulant medication. From these studies emerged the view that ADHD as a handicapping condition does not rest solely in the child, but in the interface between the child's capabilities and the environmental demands made within the social-ecological context in which that child must perform (Whalen & Henker, 1980). Changing the attitudes, behaviors, and expectations of caregivers, as well as the demands they make upon ADHD children in their care, often results in tremendous changes in the degree to which the ADHD children are disabled by their behavioral deficits.

Improved Research Methodology

Another noteworthy development in this decade was the greater sophistication of research designs attempting to explore the unique features of ADHD relative to other psychiatric conditions rather than just in comparison to the normal state. As Rutter (1983, 1989) has noted repeatedly, the true test of the validity of a syndrome of ADHD would be the ability to differentiate its features from those of other psychiatric disorders of children, such as affective or anxiety disorders, learning disorders, and particularly Conduct Disorder. Those studies that undertook such comparisons in the 1980s indicated that situational hyperactivity was not consistent in discriminating among psychiatric populations, but that difficulties with attention and pervasive (home and school) hyperactivity were more reliable in doing so and were often associated with patterns of neurocognitive immaturity (Firestone & Martin, 1979; Gittelman, 1988; McGee, Williams, & Silva, 1984a, 1984b; Rutter, 1989; Taylor, 1988; Werry, 1988). The emerging interest in comparing ADD/+H and ADD/−H children served to further this line of inquiry by demonstrating that children with one subtype could be distinguished from children with the other (see Chapter 3) and from groups of learning-disabled and normal children (Barkley, DuPaul, & McMurray, in press). Further strengthening the position of ADHD as a psychiatric syndrome was evidence from family aggregation studies that relatives of ADHD children had a different pattern of psychiatric disturbance from relatives of those children with Conduct Disorder or mixed ADHD and Conduct Disorder (Biederman, Munir,

Knee, Armentano, Autor, Waternaux, & Tsuang, 1987; Lahey, Piacentini, McBurnett, Stone, Hartdagen, & Hynd, 1988). Purely ADHD children were more likely to have relatives with ADHD, academic achievement problems, and dysthymia, whereas children with Conduct Disorder had a greater prevalence of Conduct Disorder, antisocial behavior, substance abuse, depression, and marital dysfunction among their relatives. This led to speculations that ADHD has a different etiology from Conduct Disorder. The former may arise out of a biologically based disorder of temperament or a neurocognitive delay; the latter may spring from inconsistent, coercive, and dysfunctional child rearing or child management, frequently associated with parental psychiatric impairment (Patterson, 1982, 1986).

Equally elegant research was done on potential etiologies of ADHD. Several studies on cerebral blood flow revealed patterns of underactivity in the prefrontal areas of the CNS and their rich connections to the limbic system via the striatum (Lou et al., 1984, 1989). This work was replicated by studies using computerized averaging of brain cortical electrical activity (Satterfield, personal communication, 1984). Other studies (Hunt, Cohen, Anderson, & Minderaa, 1987; Rapoport & Zametkin, 1988; S. E. Shaywitz, Shaywitz, Cohen, & Young, 1983; Shekim, Glaser, Horwitz, Javaid, & Dylund, 1987; Zametkin & Rapoport, 1986) on brain neurotransmitters provided further evidence that deficiencies in dopamine, norepinephrine, or both may be involved in explaining these patterns of brain underactivity—patterns arising in precisely those brain areas in which dopamine and norepinephrine are most involved. Drawing these lines of evidence together even further was the fact that these brain areas are critically involved in incentive or motivational learning and response to reinforcement contingencies. More rigorous studies on the hereditary transmission of ADHD were also published (Goodman & Stevenson, 1989), indicating a strong heritability for ADHD symptoms.

Follow-up studies appearing in this decade were also more methodologically sophisticated, and hence more revealing not only of useful predictors of later maladjustment, but of potential mechanisms involved in the differential courses shown within this population (Barkley, Fischer, Edelbrock, & Smallish, in press-a, in press-b; Fischer, Barkley, Edelbrock, & Smallish, in press; Gittelman et al., 1985; Lambert, 1988; Weiss & Hechtman, 1986). These findings are discussed in detail in Chapter 4. Again, neurocognitive delays, the presence and pervasiveness of early aggression, and mother–child conflict were associated with a different, and more negative, outcome in later childhood and adolescence than was ADHD alone (Campbell, 1990; Paternite & Loney, 1980).

There was also a movement during this decade away from the strict reliance on clinic-referred samples of ADHD children to the use of community-derived or epidemiologically based samples. This change was prompted by the widely acknowledged bias that occurs among clinic samples of ADHD children as a result of the process of referral itself. It is well known that children who are referred are often more (though not always the most) impaired, have more numerous comorbid conditions, are more likely to have associated family difficulties, and are skewed toward those socioeconomic classes that value the utilization of mental health care resources. Such biases can create findings that are not representative of the nature of the disorder in its natural state. For instance, it has been shown that the ratio of boys to girls within clinic-referred samples of ADHD children may range from 6:1 to 9:1 and that girls with ADHD within these samples are as likely to be aggressive or oppositional as boys (see Chapter 2). By contrast, in samples of ADHD children derived from community or school-based samples, the ratio of boys to girls is only 2.5:1 and girls with ADHD are considerably less likely to be aggressive than boys. For these and other reasons, a greater emphasis on studying epidemiological samples of children and the rates and nature of ADHD within them (Offord et al., 1989) arose toward the latter half of the 1980s.

Developments in Assessment

The 1980s also witnessed some advances in the tools of assessment in addition to those for treatment. The Child Behavior Checklist (CBCL; Achenbach & Edelbrock, 1983, 1986) emerged as a more reliable, more rigorously developed, and better-normed alternative to the Conners rating scales (Barkley, 1988c). It was widely adopted in research on child psychopathology in general, not just in ADHD, by the end of this period. Other rating scales more specific to ADHD were also developed, such as the ADD-H Comprehensive Teacher Rating Scale (ACTeRS; Ullmann, Sleator, & Sprague, 1984a), the Home and School Situations Questionnaires (Barkley & Edelbrock, 1987; DuPaul, 1990b), the Child Attention Profile (see Barkley, 1988d), and the ADHD Rating Scale (DuPaul, 1990a).

Michael Gordon (1983) developed and commercially marketed a small, portable, computerized device that administered two tests believed to be sensitive to the deficits in ADHD. One was a continuous-performance test (CPT) measuring vigilance and impulsivity, and the other was a direct reinforcement of low rates (DRL) test assessing impulse control. This became the first commercially available objective assessment device for evaluating ADHD children. Although the DRL test showed some promise in early research (Gordon, 1979), it was subsequently shown to be insensitive to stimulant medication effects (Barkley, Fischer, Newby, & Breen, 1988) and was eventually de-emphasized as useful in diagnosis in ADHD. The CPT, by contrast, showed satisfactory discrimination of ADHD from normal groups and was sensitive to medication effects (Barkley et al., 1988; Barkley, DuPaul, & McMurray, 1990b; Gordon & Mettelman, 1988). Although cautionary statements were made that more research evidence was needed to evaluate the utility of the instrument (Milich, Pelham, & Swanson, 1985) and that its false-negative rate (misses of legitimate ADHD children) might be greater than that desired in a diagnostic tool (see Chapter 10), the device had found a wide clinical following by decade's end.

Greater emphasis was also being given to developing direct behavioral observation measures of ADHD symptoms that could be taken in the classroom or clinic; these proved to be more objective and useful adjuncts to the heavy reliance on parent and teacher rating scales in the diagnostic process. Abikoff, Gittelman-Klein, and Klein (1977) and O'Leary (1984) developed classroom observation codes with some promise for discriminating ADHD from normal and non-ADHD children (Gittelman, 1988). Roberts (1979), drawing upon the earlier work of Routh and Schroeder (1976) and Kalverboer (1988), refined a laboratory playroom observation procedure that was found to discriminate ADHD children not only from normal children, but also from aggressive or mixed aggressive–ADHD children (see Chapter 10). This coding system had excellent 2-year stability coefficients. My colleagues and I later streamlined it somewhat (Barkley et al., 1988) for more convenient clinical or classroom use, and we found it to be quite sensitive to stimulant medication effects (Barkley, 1989b; Barkley et al., 1988), to differentiate between ADD/ + H and ADD/ − H children (Barkley, DuPaul, & McMurray, 1990b), and to correlate well with parent and teacher ratings of ADHD symptoms (Barkley, 1989c). Nevertheless, problems with developing normative data and with implementing such a procedure in busy clinic practices remained hindrances to its widespread adoption. These advances in assessment are detailed much more thoroughly in later chapters of this text (see Chapters 9 and 10).

Developments in Therapy

Developments also continued in the realm of treatments for ADHD. Comparisons of single versus combined treatments were more common during the decade (Barkley, 1989a), as was the use of more sophisticated experimental designs (Hinshaw, Henker, & Whalen, 1984a; Pelham, Schnedler, Bologna, & Contreras, 1980) and mixed interventions (Satterfield, Satterfield, & Cantwell, 1981). Several of these developments in treatment require historical mention.

The first was the emergence of a new approach to the treatment of ADHD— cognitive-behavior modification (Camp, 1980; Douglas, 1980a, 1980b; Kendall & Braswell, 1984; Meichenbaum, 1988). Founded on the work of Russian neuropsychologists (Luria, 1966), North American cognitive-developmental psychologists (Flavell, 1970), and early cognitive-behavioral theorists (Meichenbaum, 1977), these approaches stressed the need to develop self-directed speech in impulsive children in order to guide their definition of and attention to immediate problem situations, to generate solutions to these problems, and to guide their behavior as the solutions were performed. Self-evaluation, correction, and consequation at task completion were also viewed as important (Douglas, 1980a, 1980b). Although first reports of the efficacy of this approach appeared in the 1970s (Meichenbaum & Goodman, 1971; Bornstein & Quevillon, 1976), it was not until the 1980s that these initial claims of success with nonclinical populations of impulsive children were more fully tested in clinical populations of ADHD children. The results were disappointing (Abikoff, 1987; Gittelman & Abikoff, 1989). Generally, they indicated some degree of improvement in impulsiveness on cognitive laboratory tasks, but this was insufficient to be detected in teacher or parent ratings of school and home ADHD behaviors; certainly cognitive-behavioral techniques were not as effective as stimulant medication (Brown, Wynne, & Medenis, 1985). Many in the field continued to see some promise in these techniques (Barkley, 1981, 1989a; Meichenbaum, 1988; Whalen & Henker, 1985), particularly when implemented in natural environments by important caregivers (parents and teachers); others ended the decade with a challenge to those who persisted in their support of this approach to provide further evidence for its efficacy (Gittelman & Abikoff, 1989).

I believe that cognitive-behavioral techniques may continue to play a useful role in the management of ADHD children, provided that they are taught to parents and teachers for use in the myriad day-to-day exchanges with the children, and combined with reinforcement methods for the children's displaying self-controlled behavior. For this reason, cognitive-behavioral procedures have been incorporated into the chapters on parent training (Chapters 12 and 14), classroom management (Chapter 15), and social skills training (Chapter 16), as well as in the chapter on family systems (Chapter 13), where parents are encouraged to use such skills themselves.

A second development in treatment was the publication of a specific parent training format for families with ADHD and oppositional children. A specific set of steps for training parents of ADHD children in child behavior management skills was developed (Barkley, 1981) and refined (Barkley, 1987) in this decade. The approach was founded on a substantial research literature (Forehand & McMahon, 1981; Patterson, 1982) demonstrating the efficacy of differential attention and time-out procedures for treating oppositional behavior in children—a behavior frequently associated with ADHD. These two procedures were coupled with additional components based on a theoretical formulation of ADHD as a developmental disorder that is typically chronic and is associated with decreased rule-governed behavior and an insensitivity to certain consequences, particularly mild or social reinforcement. These components included counseling parents to conceptualize ADHD as a developmentally handicapping condition; implementing more powerful home token economies to reinforce behavior, rather than relying on attention alone; using shaping techniques to develop nondisruptive, independent play; and training parents in cognitive-behavioral skills to teach their children during daily management encounters, particularly those involving disruptive behavior in public places (Anastopoulos & Barkley, 1988). The details of this program are set forth in Chapter 12.

Because of the demonstrated impact of parental and family dysfunction on the severity of children's ADHD symptoms, the children's risk for developing Oppositional Defiant Disorder and Conduct Disorder, and the responsiveness of the parents to treatments for the children, clinicians began to pay closer attention to intervening in family systems rather than just in child management skills. Noteworthy among these attempts were the modifications to the above-described parent training program by Charles Cunningham at McMaster University Medical Center (see Chapter 13). Arthur Robin at Wayne State University and the Children's Hospital of Michigan, and Sharon Foster at West Virginia University (Robin & Foster, 1989), also emphasized the need for work not only on family systems but also on problem solving and communication skills in working with the parent–adolescent conflicts so common in families with ADHD teenagers. This approach is set forth in Chapter 14.

A similar increase in more sophisticated approaches occurred in this era in relation to the classroom management of ADHD children (Barkley, Copeland, & Sivage, 1980; Pelham et al., 1980; Pfiffner & O'Leary, 1987; Whalen & Henker, 1980). These developments were based on earlier promising studies in the 1970s with contingency management methods in hyperactive children (Allyon et al., 1975). The details of such an approach are provided in Chapter 15. Although these methods may not produce the degree of behavioral change seen with the stimulant medications (Gittelman-Klein, Abikoff, Pollack, Klein, Katz, & Mattes, 1980), they provide a more socially acceptable intervention that can be a useful alternative when children have mild ADHD and cannot take stimulants, when their parents decline the prescription, or when an adjunct to medication therapy is desired to further enhance academic achievement.

The fourth area of treatment development was that of social skills training for ADHD children. Stephen Hinshaw and his colleagues (Hinshaw et al., 1984a) developed a program for training ADHD children in anger control techniques. This program demonstrated some initial short-term effectiveness in assisting these children to deal with this common deficit in their social skills and emotional control. The procedures are described by David Guevremont in Chapter 16.

Finally, medication treatments for ADHD expanded to include the use of the tricyclic antidepressants, particularly for those ADHD children with characteristics that would contraindicate using a stimulant medication, such as tic disorders, Tourette's syndrome, or anxiety/depression (Pliszka, 1987). The work of Joseph Biederman and his colleagues at Massachusetts General Hospital (Biederman, Gastfriend, Jellinek, & Goldblatt, 1985; Biederman, Baldessarini, Wright, Knee, Harmatz, & Goldblatt, 1989) on the safety and efficacy of the tricyclic medications encouraged the rapid adoption of these drugs by many practitioners, particularly at a time when the stimulants, such as Ritalin, were receiving such negative publicity in the popular media (see below).

Developments in Public Awareness

Several noteworthy developments also occurred in the public forum during the 1980s. Chief and most constructive among these was the blossoming of numerous parent support associations for families with ADHD. Although less than a handful existed in the early 1980s, within 9 years there were well over 200 such associations throughout the United States alone. By 1989, these had organized themselves into national networks and political action organizations known as Children with ADD (CHADD) and ADD Association in the United States and the Foundation for Attention Disorders in Canada. With this greater public/parent activism, initiatives were taken to have state laws and federal laws re-evaluated and, it was hoped, changed to include ADHD as an educational disability in need of special educational services in public schools. A listing of many parent support associations appears in Appendix B.

As noted earlier, when PL 94-142 was passed and implemented in the mid-1970s, it overlooked ADHD in its description of learning or behavioral disorders eligible for mandated special services in public schools—an oversight that led to much parental and teacher exasperation in trying to get educational recognition and assistance for this obviously academically handicapping disorder. Other parents initiated lawsuits against private schools for learning-disabled students for educational malpractice in failing to provide special services for ADHD children (Holland, 1988; Skinner, 1988). At this writing, it is not clear whether state laws will be so amended, particularly in an era concerned with rising taxes and taxpayer revolts against them. Plans are underway to petition the U.S. Congress to amend the federal law as a more efficient means to achieve this end. Supporting this effort was a recent ruling in California that a school district violated the Civil Rights Act when it discriminated against an ADHD child because of his handicap in not providing him with special educational services (Office of Civil Rights, 1989). As should be evident from this text, I am fully supportive of these efforts to obtain special educational resources for ADHD children and adolescents, in view of their tremendous risk for academic underachievement, failure, retention, suspension, and expulsion, not to mention negative social and occupational outcomes (Barkley, Fischer, et al., in press-a, in press-b; Cantwell & Satterfield, 1978; Weiss & Hechtman, 1986).

The Church of Scientology Campaign

Yet with this increased public activism also came, in my view, a tremendously destructive trend in the United States, primarily fueled by the Church of Scientology and its Citizens Commission on Human Rights (CCHR). This campaign capitalized on the media's general tendency to publish alarming or titillating stories uncritically, and on the public's gullibility in regard to such stories. Drawing upon evidence of an increase in stimulant medication use with school children as well as upon the extant public concern over drug abuse, members of CCHR effectively linked these events together to play upon the public's general concern for using behavior-modifying drugs with children. Moreover, reminiscent of the gross overstatement seen in the earlier "reefer madness" campaign by the U.S. government against marijuana, members of CCHR selectively focused on the rare cases of adverse reactions to stimulants and greatly exaggerated both the number and degree of them to persuade the public that these reactions were commonplace. They also argued that massive overprescribing was posing a serious threat to our school children.

By picketing scientific and public conferences on ADHD, actively distributing leaflets to parents and students in many North American cities, seeking out appearances on many national television talk shows, and writing numerous letters to newspapers decrying the evils of Ritalin and the myth of any disorder of ADHD (Bass, 1988; CCHR, 1987; Cowart, 1988; Dockx, 1988), CCHR members and others took this propaganda directly to the public. Ritalin, it was claimed, was a dangerous and addictive drug often used as a chemical straitjacket to subdue normally exuberant children because of intolerant educators and parents and money-hungry psychiatrists (Clark, 1988; CCHR, 1987; Dockx, 1988). Dramatic, exaggerated, or unfounded claims were made that Ritalin could frequently result in violence or murder, suicide, Tourette's syndrome, permanent brain damage or emotional disturbance, seizures, high blood pressure, confusion, agitation, and depression (*The Call,* 1988; CCHR, 1987; Clark, 1988; Dockx, 1988; Laccetti, 1988; Toufexis, 1989; Williams, 1988). It was also claimed that the increasing production and prescription of Ritalin were leading to increased abuse of the drug (*Worcester Telegram and Gazette,* 1987; Cowart, 1988).

Great controversy was said to exist among the scientific and professional practice communities concerning this disorder and the use of medication. No evidence was presented in these articles, however, that ever demonstrated a rise in Ritalin abuse or linked it with the increased prescribing of the medication. Moreover, close inspection of professional journals and conferences revealed that no major or widespread controversy ever existed within the professional or scientific fields over the nature of the disorder or the effectiveness of stimulant medication. Yet lawsuits were threatened, initiated, or assisted by the CCHR against practitioners for medical negligence and malpractice, and against schools for complicity in "pressuring" parents to have their children placed on these medicines (Bass, 1988; Cowart, 1988; Henig, 1988; *Nightline,* 1988; Twyman, 1988). A major lawsuit ($125 million) was also filed by the CCHR against the American Psychiatric Association for fraud in developing the criteria for ADHD (Henig, 1988; *Investors' Daily,* 1987).

So effective was this national campaign by the CCHR, so widespread were newspaper and television stories on adverse Ritalin reactions, and so easily could public sentiment be misled about a disorder and its treatment by a fringe religious group and overzealous popular writers that within 1 year the public attitude toward Ritalin was dramatically altered. Ritalin was now seen as a dangerous and overprescribed drug, and the public came to believe that there was tremendous professional controversy over its use. The minor benefits to come out of this distorted reporting were that some practitioners became more rigorous in their assessments and more cautious in their prescribing of medication. Schools also became highly sensitized to the percentage of their enrollment receiving stimulant medication and encouraged exploration of alternative behavioral means of managing children.

Yet even these few positive effects of this campaign would be greatly outweighed by the damaging effects on parents and children. Many parents would be scared into unilaterally discontinuing the medication with their children without consulting their treating physicians. Others rigidly refused to consider the treatment as one part of their children's treatment plan if recommended, or were harassed into such refusals by well-meaning relatives misled by the distorted Church of Scientology propaganda and media reports. Some ADHD adolescents began refusing the treatment, even if beneficial to them, after being alarmed by these stories. Some physicians stopped prescribing the medications altogether out of concern for the threats of litigation, thereby depriving many children within their care of the clear benefits of this treatment approach. Most frustrating to watch was the unnecessary anguish that this created for parents whose children were already on the medication or were contemplating its use.

The psychological damage this has done to those children whose lives could have been improved by this treatment is incalculable. The meager, poorly organized, and sporatically disseminated response of the mental health professions was primarily defensive in nature (Barkley, 1988f; Weiner, 1988), and as usual was too little, too late to change the tide of public opinion. It will take years to reverse this regression in public opinion concerning ADHD and its treatment by medication. Already, however, there are positive signs that this may be happening, as parent support associations organize themselves better, undertake the education of their local communities about the disorder and its treatments, and attempt to change legislation concerning education of their children.

The Prevailing View at the End of the 1980s

This decade closed with most professionals viewing ADHD as a developmentally handicapping condition that is generally chronic in nature, has a strong biological or hereditary predisposition, and has a significant negative impact on academic and social outcomes for many children. However, its severity, comorbidity, and outcome were viewed as significantly affected by environmental, particularly familial, factors. Growing doubts about the central role of attention deficits in the disorder arose late in the decade, while increasing interest and excitement focused on possible motivational factors or reinforcement mechanisms as the core difficulty in ADHD. Effective treatment was now viewed as requiring multiple methods and professional disciplines working in concert over longer time intervals, with periodic reintervention as required, to improve the long-term prognosis for ADHD. The view that environmental causes were involved in the genesis of the disorder was weakened by increasing evidence for the heritability of the condition and its neuroanatomical localization. Even so, evidence that familial/environmental factors were associated with type of outcome was further strengthened. Developments in treatment expanded the focus of interventions to parental disturbances and family dysfunction, as well as to the children's anger control and social skills. A potentially effective role for the use of tricyclic antidepressant medications was also demonstrated, expanding the armamentarium of symptomatic interventions for helping ADHD children.

Despite these tremendous developments in the scientific and professional fields, the general public became overly sensitized to and excessively alarmed by the increasing use of medication as a treatment for this disorder. Fortunately, the explosive growth of parent support/political action associations for ADHD arose almost simultaneously with this public controversy over Ritalin; at this writing, they promise to make the education of ADHD children a national political priority at the start of this last decade of the 20th century. These associations also offer the best hope that the general public can be provided with a more accurate depiction of ADHD and its treatment. Perhaps now the public can be made to understand that hyperactive, disruptive child behaviors may arise out of a biologically based disability that can be diminished or amplified by the social environment, rather than being entirely due to the simplistic yet pervasive societal view of bad parenting as its cause.

SUMMARY

This chapter has provided an overview of the historical development of the concept of ADHD. The view that emerged at the beginning of the 1900s was one of ADHD as a biologically based disorder of the control of behavior by morals and volitional inhibition; it was seen as little affected by social circumstances. This would evolve over 90 years to a view of ADHD as a biological, often hereditary, predisposition to defects in the regulation of behavior by rules and consequences—defects that could be significantly modulated by social circumstances. Throughout this evolution, the role of behavioral disinhibition/self-regulation has proven a central theme to which theorists of different eras have returned again and again. Along the way, labels changed from "brain damage syndrome" and "organic driveness" to "hyperkinetic impulse disorder" and then on to "ADD," culminating in "ADHD." Although a greater appreciation for the modulating role of the environment on the expression of ADHD symptoms gradually emerged, the view of biological factors as primary in the development of the disorder was never completely displaced. As for prognosis, the disorder was initially viewed as a relatively chronic condition and later came to be seen as one that would be outgrown by puberty; later still, the perspective of ADHD as a chronic developmental disorder re-emerged. Numerous other developments in both professional and public awareness of the disorder occurred throughout the century. At this writing, the stage is set for an explosion in public activism that promises to alter both society's view of the disorder and the manner in which it is handled by the educational system.

As we look ahead, it is easy to see that the last decade of the century will be an exciting if not controversial one. The DSM-IV is due out early in this decade and will probably make some changes to the criteria used to diagnose ADHD; in addition, it should elevate ADD/−H to the status of a separate, unique disorder. Federal and state laws governing the education of ADHD children are also likely to change, and the degree of this change will no doubt hinge more on economic impact than on the actual needs of these children. The availability of parent support associations for ADHD will become commonplace, and some effort to unite these organizations in regard to a national agenda is clearly desirable. Few major breakthroughs are likely to come in the area of treatment as we come to accept the developmentally disabling nature of the disorder; this will be similar to the status of treatments in the fields of mental retardation, autism, and learning disabilities. But a wider availability of existing treatments is to be hoped for, as is their earlier application during the preschool and early elementary years.

One prominent controversy involving society's attitudes cannot be overlooked. A society founded on egalitarian ideals and an economic meritocracy must come to face an emerging paradox about its assumptions concerning child behavior and character development. That paradox lies in the progressively accepted conclusion from our research that disorders of social conduct can have biological and often hereditary origins. In ADHD, deficiencies in behavioral self-regulation arise early in childhood; are chronic in many cases; are amplified by conditions of social disadvantage; and predispose afflicted individuals to a high risk of educational, social, and occupational underachievement and, to a lesser but still significant degree, of antisocial conduct. How such individuals can be expected to compete equally and successfully in an economic meritocracy without special assistance and considerations is the hidden paradox here. A resolution of this paradox that is sufficient to address the problems of ADHD children will not prove an easy one.

2

Primary Symptoms and Conceptualization

The value of a principle is the number of things it will
explain; and there is no good theory of a disease which
does not at once suggest a cure.

—RALPH WALDO EMERSON (1803–82)

A tremendous amount of research has been published on children with Attention-deficit Hyperactivity Disorder (ADHD)—their primary characteristics and related problems, the situational variability of these problems, their prevalence, and their etiologies. It was estimated by 1979 that over 2,000 studies existed on this disorder (Weiss & Hechtman, 1979), and this figure has surely doubled in the past 10 years. I have attempted to cull from this substantial fund of research the information that I believe is most useful for clinical work with these children; this information is described in this chapter. It is surely not the intent of the chapter, or of this book, to provide a critical review of the scientific literature—only to glean from it that which has a direct bearing on the clinical assessment and management of this condition. The clinically useful findings on the primary symptoms of ADHD are reviewed here, along with those pertaining to situational variability and prevalence. A modern reconceptualization of ADHD is also discussed. The associated features and comorbid disorders often seen with ADHD, and the etiologies proposed for the disorder, are reviewed in Chapter 3. The developmental course and outcome of ADHD children are described in Chapter 4. Those findings pertaining to the family interactions of these children and characteristics of their parents are discussed in Chapter 5.

Throughout this chapter and the remainder of this book, the term ADHD is used, although the research on which this discussion is based may have employed the related diagnoses of "hyperactivity," "hyperactive child syndrome," or "Attention Deficit Disorder with Hyperactivity" (ADD/+H). I realize that these terms and the diagnostic criteria used for them in this research are not completely identical. However, I believe that the clinical description of the children studied and the criteria used to select them for study are of sufficient similarity to permit one to argue that they pertain to quite similar groups of children. For gaining a general impression of the disorder and for the clinical purposes of this text, the minor differences that may exist among these groups because of these somewhat different terms and selection criteria do not seem, at least to me, of sufficient import to justify qualifying each finding to be discussed by the manner in which the particular subjects were selected and diagnosed. But in so doing, I fully appreciate that for research purposes such differences among sample selection criteria are quite significant for both qualifying and interpreting one's findings.

PRIMARY SYMPTOMS

ADHD children are commonly described as having chronic difficulties in the areas of inattention, impulsivity, and overactivity—what one might call the "holy trinity" of ADHD. They are believed to display these characteristics early; to a degree that is inappropriate for their age or developmental level; and across a variety of situations that tax their capacity to pay attention, inhibit their impulses, and restrain their movement. As noted in Chapter 1, definitions have varied considerably throughout the history of this disorder, as have the recommended criteria for obtaining a diagnosis. The currently recommended criteria are set forth in Chapter 6, along with guidelines for distinguishing this disorder from other conditions that may be comorbid with it or that present with superficially similar features to it.

Inattention

By definition, children having ADHD display marked inattention, relative to normal children of the same age and sex. However, "inattention" is a multi-dimensional construct that can refer to problems with alertness, arousal, selectivity, sustained attention, distractibility, or span of apprehension, among others (Hale & Lewis, 1979). Research to date suggests that ADHD children have their greatest difficulties with sustaining attention to tasks or vigilance (Douglas, 1983). These difficulties are sometimes apparent in free-play settings, as evidenced by shorter durations of play with each toy and frequent shifts in play across various toys (Barkley & Ullman, 1975; Routh & Schroeder, 1976; Zentall, 1985). However, they are most dramatically seen in situations requiring the child to sustain attention to dull, boring, repetitive tasks (Luk, 1985; Milich, Loney, & Landau, 1982; Ullman, Barkley, & Brown, 1978; Zentall, 1985) such as independent schoolwork, homework, or chore performance.

The problem is not so much one of heightened distractibility, or the ease with which children are drawn off task by extraneous stimulation, although many parents and teachers will describe these children in such terms. Research on the distractibility of ADHD children has been somewhat contradictory on this issue, but in general finds these children to be no more distractible than normal children by extratask stimulation (Campbell, Douglas, & Morgenstern, 1971; Cohen, Weiss, & Minde, 1972; Rosenthal & Allen, 1980; Steinkamp, 1980). The findings for irrelevant stimulation provided within the task are more conflicting, however: Some studies find that such stimulation worsens the performance of ADHD children (Rosenthal & Allen, 1980), while others find no effect (Fischer, Barkley, Edelbrock, & Smallish, in press) or even an enhancing effect on attention (Zentall, Falkenberg, & Smith, 1985). Instead, the problem appears consistently to be one of diminished persistence or effort in responding to tasks that have little intrinsic appeal or minimal immediate consequences for completion (Barkley, 1990). The clinical picture may be different, however, in those situations where alternate, competing activities are available that promise immediate reinforcement or gratification, in contrast to the weaker reinforcement or consequences associated with the assigned task. In such cases, the ADHD child may appear distracted and in fact is likely to shift "off task" in order to engage the highly rewarding competing activity. It is not clear whether this represents true distraction as described above (i.e., the child orients to extraneous stimuli) or behavioral disinhibition (i.e., the child fails to follow rules or instructions when provided with competing, highly rewarding activities). It is my view that the latter is more likely to account for these attentional shifts than is a generalized problem with orienting to extraneous stimuli.

Parents and teachers will often describe these attentional problems in terms such as "Doesn't seem to listen," "Fails to finish assigned tasks," "Daydreams," "Often loses things," "Can't concentrate," "Easily distracted," "Can't work independently of supervision," "Requires more redirection," "Shifts from one uncompleted activity to another," and "Confused or seems to be in a fog" (Barkley, DuPaul, & McMurray, in press; Stewart, Pitts, Craig, & Dieruf, 1966). Many of these terms are the most frequently endorsed items from rating scales completed by these caregivers (see Chapter 9). Studies using direct observations of child behavior find that "off-task" behavior or not paying attention to work is recorded substantially more often for ADHD children and adolescents than learning-disabled or normal children (Abikoff, Gittelman-Klein, & Klein, 1977; Barkley, DuPaul, & McMurray, in press; Luk, 1985; Fischer et al., in press; Ullman et al., 1978). What is not so clear in these studies is whether this deficit in paying attention reflects a primary deficit in sustained attention or is secondary to the problem of behavioral disinhibition described below.

Behavioral Disinhibition

Intertwined with the difficulty in sustained attention is a deficiency in inhibiting behavior in response to situational demands, or impulsivity—again, relative to children of the same mental age and sex. Like "inattention," "impulsivity" is multidimensional in nature (Milich & Kramer, 1985), and it remains unclear which aspects of impulsivity are problematic for ADHD children. Clinically, these children are often noted to respond quickly to situations without waiting for instructions to be completed or adequately appreciating what is required in the setting. Heedless or careless errors are often the result. They may also fail to consider potentially negative, destructive, or even dangerous consequences that may be associated with particular situations or behaviors, and so seem to engage in frequent, unnecessary risk taking. Taking chances on a dare or whim, especially from a peer, may occur more often than is normal. Consequently, accidental poisonings and injuries are not uncommon, and ADHD children may carelessly damage or destroy others' property considerably more frequently than normal children. Waiting their turn in a game or in a group lineup before going to an activity is often problematic for them. When faced with tasks or situations in which they are encouraged to delay seeking gratification and work toward a longer-term goal and larger reward, they often opt for the immediate, smaller reward that requires less work to achieve. They are notorious for taking "short cuts" in their work performance, applying the least amount of effort and taking the least amount of time in performing tasks they find boring or aversive.

When the children desire something to which others control access and they must wait a while to obtain it, as in a parent's promise to eventually take them shopping or to a movie, they may badger the parent excessively during the waiting interval, appearing to others as incessantly demanding and self-centered. Situations or games that involve sharing, cooperation, and restraint with peers are particularly problematic for these impulsive children. They often say things indiscreetly without regard for the feelings of others or the social consequences to themselves. Blurting out answers to questions prematurely, and interrupting the conversations of others, are commonplace. The layperson's impression of them, therefore, is often one of irresponsibility, immaturity or childishness, laziness, and outright rudeness. Little wonder that they experience more punishment, criticism, censure, and ostracism by adults and their peers than do normal children.

The problem of impulsivity is often scientifically defined as a pattern of rapid, inaccurate responding to tasks (Brown & Quay, 1977) such as Kagan's Matching Familiar Figures Test (MFFT; Kagan, 1966). In this task, a child is shown a picture below which are six very similar pictures. The child is to select from among the six that which is identical to the sample. ADHD children are noted to respond more quickly than others on the MFFT and to make more mistakes. Most often, it is their number of errors rather than their rapidity of responding that sets them apart from normal children (Brown & Quay, 1977), but even here recent findings have been conflicting (Fischer et al., in press; Barkley, DuPaul, & McMurray, in pressb; Milich & Kramer, 1985). Impulsivity may also refer to poor sustained inhibition of responding (Gordon, 1979), poor delay of gratification (Rapport, Tucker, DuPaul, Merlo, & Stoner, 1986), or impaired adherence to commands to regulate or inhibit behavior in social contexts (Kendall & Wilcox, 1979). Furthermore, studies that have factor-analyzed ratings of impulsive behavior mixed in with ratings or objective laboratory measures of inattention, overactivity, and oppositional behavior (Achenbach & Edelbrock, 1983; Milich & Kramer, 1985) have failed to differentiate an Impulsivity dimension from that measuring Hyperactivity—that is, overactive children are also impulsive children, and vice versa. This calls into serious question the existence of impulsivity as a separate dimension of behavioral impairment apart from hyperactivity in these children. It also strongly implies that the more global problem of behavioral disinhibition is what unites these two symptoms.

Evidence that behavioral disinhibition, or poor regulation and inhibition of behavior, is in fact the hallmark of this disorder has been accumulating recently from several sources. First, as noted at several points in this chapter, studies have typically shown that it is not inattention that distinguishes ADHD children from children with other clinical disorders or from normal children as much as it is their hyperactive, impulsive, and disinhibited behavior. Second, when objective measures of the three symptoms of ADHD are subjected to a discriminant-function analysis (a statistical method of examining the variables that contribute most to group discrimination), the symptoms of impulsive errors (typically on vigilance tasks) and excessive activity level are typically what best discriminate ADHD children from non-ADHD children (Barkley, DuPaul, & McMurray, in press; Grodzinsky, 1990). A third source of evidence was derived from the field trial (Spitzer, Davies, & Barkley, in press) that tested the sensitivity and specificity of the 14 descriptors now comprising the diagnostic criteria for ADHD in the *Diagnostic and Statistical Manual of Mental Disorders,* third edition, revised (DSM-III-R; see below). These descriptors were rank-ordered by their discriminating power and are presented in the DSM-III-R in descending order. Careful inspection of this rank ordering reveals that again symptoms characteristic of disinhibition, such as poorly regulated activity and impulsivity, are more likely to discriminate children with ADHD from children with psychiatric disorders and normal children. For these reasons, I believe that the evidence available is sufficient to allow us to conclude that behavioral disinhibition rather than inattention is the hallmark of ADHD. In fact, this disinhibition or poor inhibitory regulation of behavior may result in the attention problems often noted in these children. That is, the attention problems may be secondary to a disorder of behavioral regulation and inhibition, rather than being a primary and distinct deficit apart from such disinhibition. This idea is developed further in the concluding section of this chapter.

Hyperactivity

The third primary characteristic of ADHD children is their excessive or developmentally inappropriate levels of activity, be it motor or vocal. Restlessness, fidgeting, and generally unnecessary gross bodily movements are commonplace (Stewart et al., 1966; Still, 1902). These movements are often irrelevant to the task or situation and at times seem purposeless. Parents often describe the problem in such terms as "Always up and on the go," "Acts as if driven by a motor," "Climbs excessively," "Can't sit still," "Talks excessively," "Often hums or makes odd noises," and "Squirmy." Observations of the children at school or while working on independent tasks find that they are out of their seats, moving about the class without permission, restlessly moving their arms and legs while working, playing with objects not related to the task, talking out of turn to others, and making unusual vocal noises (Abikoff et al., 1977; Barkley, DuPaul, & McMurray, in press; Cammann & Miehlke, 1989; Fischer et al., in press; Luk, 1985). Making running commentaries on the activities around them or about others' behavior is not unusual. Direct observations of their social interactions with others also indicate generally excessive speech and commentary (Barkley, Cunningham, & Karlsson, 1983; Zentall, 1985).

Numerous scientific studies attest to these complaints that ADHD children are more active, restless, and fidgety than normal children throughout the day and even during sleep (Barkley & Cunningham, 1979b; Porrino, Rapoport, Behar, Sceery, Ismond, & Bunney, 1983). Again, however, there are many different types of "overactivity" (Barkley & Ullman, 1975; Cromwell, Baumeister, & Hawkins, 1963), and it is not always clear exactly which types are the most deviant for ADHD children. Measures of ankle movement and locomotion seem to differentiate them most reliably from normal children (Barkley & Cunningham, 1979b), but even some studies of wrist activity and total body motion have found them to be different as well (Barkley & Ullman, 1975; Porrino et al., 1983). There are also significant situational fluctuations in this symptom (Jacob, O'Leary, & Rosenblad, 1978; Luk, 1985; Porrino et al., 1983), implying that it may be the failure to regulate activity level to setting or task demands that is so socially problematic in ADHD (Routh, 1978), rather than just a greater-than-normal absolute level of movement. However, it has not been convincingly shown that excessive activity level distinguishes ADHD from other clinic-referred groups of children (Firestone & Martin, 1979; Sandberg, Rutter, & Taylor, 1978; Shaffer, McNamara, & Pincus, 1974). Recent studies suggest that it may be the pervasiveness of the hyperactivity across settings (home and school) that separates ADHD from these other diagnostic categories (Taylor, 1986b). As discussed below, this distinction may have more to do with our sources of information (parents vs. teachers) than with real differences in situational versus pervasive ADHD (Rapoport, Donnelly, Zametkin, & Carrougher, 1986).

As noted above for impulsivity, studies of objective measures or behavior ratings of hyperactivity have usually not found that it forms a separate factor or dimension apart from impulsivity. Typically, studies that factor-analyze behavioral ratings often find that items of restlessness may load on a factor comprising primarily poor attention and organization, while other types of overactivity load on a factor constituting impulsive or disinhibited behavior. This factor, not that of inattention, is what best distinguishes ADHD from other clinical conditions and from the normal state, as noted above. Hence, in our ranking of the importance of these primary symptoms, greater weight should be given to the behavioral class of impulsive and hyperactive characteristics than to inattention in conceptualizing this disorder and its clinical presentation. Again, the poor regulation and inhibition of behavior are the distinctive features of this disorder.

Deficient Rule-Governed Behavior

Although the idea is not yet widely accepted, many have stated that difficulties with adherence to rules and instructions may also be a primary deficit of ADHD children (American Psychiatric Association, 1987; Barkley, 1981, 1982, 1990; Kendall & Braswell, 1984). Care is taken here to exclude poor rule-governed behavior that may stem from sensory handicaps (e.g., deafness), impaired language development, or defiance or oppositional behavior. ADHD children have demonstrated significant problems with compliance to parental and teacher commands (Barkley, 1985a; Whalen, Henker, & Dotemoto, 1980), to experimental instructions in the absence of the experimenter (Draeger, Prior, & Sanson, 1986), and to prohibitions to defer gratification (Rapport, Tucker, et al., 1986). In fact, I have previously argued that most prior research demonstrating impaired attention and impulse control in ADHD children actually demonstrated poor rule-governed behavior, in that all of these studies involved experimenter instructions to subjects (Barkley, 1984, 1990). What the studies actually showed was that ADHD children have problems sustaining responding to experimenter rules and instructions, particularly when the instructions are not repeated or when the experimenter leaves the setting (Douglas, 1983; Draeger et al., 1986). Once again, "rule-governed behavior" is a multidimensional construct having various components, such as "pliance" (compliance to an immediately preceding stated rule) and "tracking" (correspondence over time between a previously stated rule and an individual's behavior), to name a few (Zettle & Hayes, 1983). It remains to be shown which of these are specifically impaired in ADHD children. However, there is little doubt in my mind that poor rule-governed behavior is closely associated with the behavioral disinhibition that is the distinctive feature of ADHD.

Zentall (1985), after reviewing the literature concerning the relationship of setting factors to the expression of ADHD symptoms, has concluded that noncompliance is not the primary difficulty of these children. This line of reasoning is based on the fact that the presence of an adult with them does not always lead to noncompliance, and may even improve their task performance. It is also based on observations that ADHD children may be inattentive and overactive in isolated or free-play settings even where no adults are present. But Zentall apparently has confused the notion of noncompliance or defiance with that of problems with rule-governed behavior, described above. "Defiance" is an active refusal to obey, through verbal or physical resistance or both. As I discuss below, over 60 percent of clinic-referred ADHD children will eventually develop a significant degree of this type of oppositional behavior. In contrast, "rule-governed behavior" refers to the extent to which behavior is under the stimulus control of preceding verbal stimuli that specify contingencies (if-then relations between behavior and consequences). The crux of this construct is whether correspondence exists between a child's behavior and previously stated rules. These rules may have been provided immediately prior to the performance of the desired behavior or may have been previously stated to the child earlier in time. ADHD children may display significant problems with initiating or sustaining responses to commands and rules, either immediately (pliance) or over time (tracking or sustained correspondence), without necessarily verbally refusing to obey or physically resisting the guidance of adults. Moreover, children are expected to adhere to previously stated rules of conduct, whether adults are present or not and whether the situation is free-play or task-oriented. This conceptualization of ADHD is further developed later in this chapter. Suffice it to say here that the fact that ADHD children are more active and inattentive in free-play settings or in the absence of adults does not eliminate the probability that they manifest impairments in rule following in these situations.

In any case, it is quite common clinically to hear these children described as not listening, failing to initiate compliance to instructions, unable to maintain compliance to an instruction over time, and poor at adhering to directions associated with a task. All of these descriptors are problems in the regulation and inhibition of behavior, especially by rules; their failure to develop adequately in ADHD children suggests serious problems with behavioral disinhibition in this disorder.

Greater Variability of Task Performance

Another characteristic that some believe to be a primary deficit in ADHD children is their excessive variability of task or work performance over time. Douglas (1972) noted this problem in observations of ADHD children performing reaction time tasks or serial problem solving, and many others have reported it since. It is a finding repeatedly noted on other tasks as well. One often finds that their standard deviation of performance on multitrial tasks is considerably larger than that seen in normal children. Both the number of problems or items completed and their accuracy of performance change substantially from moment to moment, trial to trial, or day to day in the same setting. Teachers often report much greater variability in homework and test grades, as well as in-class performance, than is seen in normal children. An inspection of the teacher's grade book for an ADHD child is often revealing of this pattern of performance. Similarly, parents may find that their children perform certain chores swiftly and accurately on some occasions, but sloppily if at all on other days.

As some have noted (Kupperman, 1988), the fact that these children have done their work well on a few occasions will be held against them for the rest of their academic careers. They are seen as capable but merely lazy. Yet this excessive variability may in fact be a hallmark of this disorder relative to other behavioral disorders, and that it may even be diagnostic of it. Rather than using such observations to rule out a potentially disabling condition in the children, clinicians may find that this variability in task performance is actually useful for ruling it in.

A Consensus Definition of ADHD

The foregoing discussion suggests that a consensus definition of ADHD might be phrased as follows:

> *Attention-deficit Hyperactivity Disorder is a developmental disorder characterized by developmentally inappropriate degrees of inattention, overactivity, and impulsivity. These often arise in early childhood; are relatively chronic in nature; and are not readily accounted for on the basis of gross neurological, sensory, language, or motor impairment, mental retardation, or severe emotional disturbance. These difficulties are typically associated with deficits in rule-governed behavior and in maintaining a consistent pattern of work performance over time.*

Despite this apparent consensus view of ADHD, evidence is increasingly suggesting that it is the behavioral class of impulsivity and hyperactivity, or poor response regulation and inhibition, that underlies this disorder. A definition based on this view is presented later, in the section of this chapter dealing with a reconceptualization of ADHD.

CONSENSUS DIAGNOSTIC CRITERIA FOR ADHD

At present, the primary characteristics of ADHD and the diagnostic criteria officially developed for clinical use are set forth in the DSM-III-R (American Psychiatric Association, 1987), used primarily in the United States, and the *International Classification of Diseases,* 10th edition (ICD-10; World Health Organization, 1990), used mainly in Europe. The DSM-III-R criteria are presented in Table 2.1, and the ICD-10 criteria are shown in Table 2.2.

The DSM-III-R criteria for ADHD constitute a considerable improvement over those provided in the earlier versions of the DSM (American Psychiatric Association, 1968, 1980) and in the ICD-10 in many respects:

1. The items used to make the diagnosis were selected primarily from factor analyses of items from parent and teacher rating scales; thus, the items had already shown high intercorrelation with each other and validity in distinguishing ADHD from other groups of children (Barkley, Spitzer, & Costello, 1990). This is not the case for ICD-10.

2. In contrast to the DSM-III, the items in the DSM-III-R are no longer clustered within the separate categories or constructs of Inattention, Impul

TABLE 2.1. Diagnostic Criteria for Attention-Deficit Hyperactivity Disorder

A. A disturbance of at least six months during which at least eight of the following are present:
   (1) often fidgets with hands or feet or squirms in seat (in adolescents, may be limited to subjective feelings of restlessness).
   (2) has difficulty remaining seated when required to do so
   (3) is easily distracted by extraneous stimuli
   (4) has difficulty awaiting turn in games or group situations
   (5) often blurts out answers to questions before they have been completed
   (6) has difficulty following through on instructions from others (not due to oppositional behavior or failure of comprehension), e.g., fails to finish chores
   (7) has difficulty sustaining attention in tasks or play activities
   (8) often shifts from one uncompleted activity to another
   (9) has difficulty playing quietly
   (10) often talks excessively
   (11) often interrupts or intrudes on others, e.g., butts into other children's games
   (12) often does not seem to listen to what is being said to him or her
   (13) often loses things necessary for tasks or activities at school or at home (e.g., toys, pencils, books, assignments)
   (14) often engages in physically dangerous activities without considering possible consequences (not for the purpose of thrill-seeking), e.g., runs into street without looking

   Note: The above items are listed in descending order of discriminating power based on the data from a national field trial of the DSM-III-R criteria for Disruptive Behavior Disorders.
B. Onset before the age of seven.
C. Does not meet the criteria for a Pervasive Developmental Disorder.

   Criteria for Severity of Attention-deficit Hyperactivity Disorder:

   Mild: Few, if any, symptoms in excess of those required to make the diagnosis *and* only minimal or no impairment in school and social functioning.

   Moderate: Symptoms or functional impairment intermediate between "mild" and "severe."

   Severe: Many symptoms in excess of those required to make the diagnosis *and* pervasive impairment in functioning at home and school and with peers.

Note. From the *Diagnostic and Statistical Manual of Mental Disorders* (3rd ed., rev., pp. 52–53) by the American Psychiatric Association, 1987, Washington, DC: Author. Copyright 1987 by the American Psychiatric Association. Reprinted by permission.

sivity, and Hyperactivity, with each having a separate cutoff score for determining its diagnostic significance. This polythetic approach to the symptoms of ADHD is more consistent with the dimensional view taken of other psychiatric disorders in the DSM-III-R, and with a similar view taken in more empirical approaches to a taxonomy of childhood disorders (Achenbach & Edelbrock, 1983).

   3. The DSM-III-R avoids clustering particular items underneath a given construct (e.g., Inattention, Hyperactivity, etc.) purely on the basis of committee consensus, as was done in the DSM-III and has been done in the ICD-10. Attempts at factor-analyzing the older DSM-III items have shown that

TABLE 2.2. ICD-10 Diagnostic Criteria for Hyperkinetic Disorders

A. Demonstrable abnormality of attention and activity at HOME, for the age and developmental level of the child, as evidenced by at least three of the following attention problems:
  (1) short duration of spontaneous activities;
  (2) often leaving play activities unfinished;
  (3) over-frequent changes between activities;
  (4) undue lack of persistence at tasks set by adults;
  (5) unduly high distractibility during study, e.g., homework or reading assignment;
   and by at least two of the following activity problems:
  (6) continuous motor restlessness (running, jumping, etc.);
  (7) markedly excessive fidgeting and wriggling during spontaneous activities;
  (8) markedly excessive activity in situations expecting relative stillness (e.g., mealtimes, travel, visiting, church);
  (9) difficulty in remaining seated when required.
B. Demonstrable abnormality of attention and activity at SCHOOL or NURSERY (if applicable), for the age and developmental level of the child, as evidenced by at least two of the following attention problems:
  (1) undue lack of persistence at tasks;
  (2) unduly high distractibility, i.e., often orienting towards extrinsic stimuli;
  (3) over-frequent changes between activities when choice is allowed;
  (4) excessively short duration of play activities;
   and by at least two of the following activity problems:
  (5) continuous and excessive motor restlessness (running, jumping, etc.) in situations allowing free activity;
  (6) markedly excessive fidgeting and wriggling in structured situations;
  (7) excessive levels of off-task activity during tasks;
  (8) unduly often out of seat when required to be sitting.
C. Directly observed abnormality of attention or activity. This must be excessive for the child's age and developmental level. The evidence may be any of the following:
  (1) direct observation of the criteria in A or B above, i.e., not solely the report of parent and/or teacher;
  (2) observation of abnormal levels of motor activity, or off-task behaviour, or lack of persistence in activities, in a setting outside home or school (e.g., clinic or laboratory);
  (3) significant impairment of performance on psychometric tests of attention.
D. Does not meet criteria for pervasive developmental disorder (F84), mania (F30), depressive (F32) or anxiety disorder (F41).
E. Onset before the AGE OF SIX YEARS.
F. Duration of AT LEAST SIX MONTHS.
G. IQ above 50.
 NOTE: The research diagnosis of Hyperkinetic Disorder requires the definite presence of abnormal levels of inattention and restlessness that are pervasive across situations and persistent over time, that can be demonstrated by direct observation, and that are not caused by other disorders such as autism or affective disorders.
 Eventually, assessment instruments should develop to the point where it is possible to take a quantitative cut-off score on reliable, valid, and standardized measures of hyperactive behaviour in the home and classroom, corresponding to the 95th percentile on both measures. Such criteria would then replace A and B above.

they do not cluster into three dimensions the way they are listed in the formal criteria, but in fact form two dimensions: Inattention-Restlessness and Impulsivity-Hyperactivity. The ICD-10 criteria, however, remain clustered under two dimensions, these being Attention Problems and Activity Problems. It is not at all clear whether these items would empirically cluster in this fashion.

4. As was not the case for either DSM-III or ICD-10, the cutoff point in the DSM-III-R was determined in a field trial (Spitzer et al., in press), and so had some empirical basis for its selection.

5. The specification of guidelines in DSM-III-R for establishing the severity of the disorder is important and reflects the research finding that the disorder has a significant range of expression and situational variation in its symptoms (see above). The degree of pervasiveness of the symptoms may be a particularly important indicator of the severity of the disorder, and both DSM-III-R and ICD-10 acknowledge this importance. However, they differ in that ICD-10 requires pervasiveness across situations for the diagnosis to be made, whereas DSM-III-R uses it simply to rate the severity of the disorder. Research shows that this insistence on agreement across home, school, and clinic in ICD-10 would severely restrict the diagnosis to approximately 1 percent or less of the childhood population (Lambert, Sandoval, & Sassone, 1978; Szatmari, Offord, & Boyle, 1989a).

6. Removing the requirement that the presence of affective disorders exclude the diagnosis of ADHD is a significant improvement of the DSM-III-R. Follow-up research clearly shows that ADHD children are not more likely to develop a major affective disorder; thus, when such a disorder is present it should not rule out ADHD, nor should ADHD rule out diagnosing an affective disorder when it is present. ICD-10 continues to labor under the outdated impression that a depressive or anxiety disorder should pre-empt the diagnosis of Hyperkinetic Disorder.

7. The DSM-III-R removed the subtyping of Attention Deficit Disorder with and without Hyperactivity (ADD/+H and ADD/−H). Instead, ADD/+H is now ADHD, while ADD/−H is relegated to a relatively undefined disorder called Undifferentiated ADD. This was said to be necessary because little research was available at the time the DSM-III-R was drafted to indicated whether ADD/−H was a true subtype of ADHD, having the same attention disturbance, or whether it was an entirely separate and distinct disorder. This appears to have been a prudent gesture: Subsequent research, reviewed in Chapter 3, has pointed to ADD/−H as having a different attention disturbance from that in ADHD. ICD-10, by contrast, provides no mention of the existence of this subtype.

However, this review is not intended to suggest that the DSM-III-R criteria cannot be improved. Continuing research on the disorder and its characteristics suggests that the following would further improve the rigor of these criteria in distinguishing children with ADHD from children having other clinical disorders. One problem is that the placement of items into a single list or dimension in DSM-III-R is not as consistent with research findings as it could be. Factor analyses of the 14 items suggest that they form two relatively separate behavioral dimensions, these being Inattention-Restlessness and Impulsivity-Hyperactivity (DuPaul, 1990a). It would therefore seem wise to present these symptoms in two separate lists, each having a separate cutoff score empirically determined in a field trial. Fortunately, this is now underway as part of a field trial test of possible DSM-IV criteria for this disorder. The ICD-11 would do well to follow suit and cluster its items on the basis of research on their interrelations rather than committee consensus.

Another difficulty in both approaches rests in the use of a fixed cutoff score across such a wide age range, from children through adolescents and even adults. It is well recognized that the symptoms of ADHD are present to a considerably greater degree in all preschool children and decline significantly over development into young adulthood. If the goal of a cutoff score is to restrict the diagnosis to a standard level of prevalence—say, the 97th percentile—then a single cutoff score simply will not achieve this aim across development. It will prove overly inclusive at young ages and overly restrictive or exclusive at adolescence and adulthood. The DSM-III-R field trial data in fact show such a problem with the cutoff score of 8 of 14 symptoms, in that the sensitivity and specificity of this cutoff score declined significantly with age (Spitzer et al., in press). More recent studies suggest that a score of 10 of 14 would be more appropriate for preschool-age children (those aged 5 or below), while 8 of 14 remains satisfactory with 6- to 11-year-olds (DuPaul, 1990a). For adolescents, 6 of 14 would be more appropriate, respecting the decline in the prevalence of the ADHD symptoms in the normal population at this age (Barkley, Fischer, Edelbrock, & Smallish, in press-a). Although the ICD-10 acknowledges that eventually some objective measure of hyperactive behaviors should be used with a cutoff score of the 95th percentile, it does not yet apply this cutoff score to its own item listing, nor does it recommend using well-standardized behavior rating scales to assist in this task. Both the DSM and ICD criteria should begin to acknowledge the usefulness of rating scales in the diagnosis of this disorder.

A related problem with the DSM and ICD criteria is their failure to distinguish different cutoff scores for girls and boys. Research on rating scales and in developmental psychopathology has repeatedly shown that the prevalence of these symptoms is strongly related to gender, with girls showing considerably less of these characteristics than boys within community samples. Again, applying a fixed cutoff score will overidentify ADHD in boys and underidentify it in girls. The DSM-IV and ICD-11 should address this oversight by providing separate cutoff scores for boys and girls.

The requirement that the symptoms have lasted at least 6 months in both the DSM-III-R and ICD-10 requires some refinement, especially for use with preschool children. Ample evidence is now available that 3-year-olds with significant symptoms of inattention and hyperactivity have a high likelihood of remission of these concerns within 12 months (Campbell, 1987; see also Chapter 4). However, those whose problems last at least 12 months, or beyond 4 years of age, appear to have a very stable set of behavioral features that is predictive of ongoing ADHD in the later school years. Consequently, the duration of symptoms should be extended to 12 months.

The findings discussed thus far in this chapter indicate that behavioral disinhibition is the hallmark of ADHD, and so clinicians should place greater emphasis on the Impulsivity-Hyperactivity than on the Inattention symptoms in describing the disorder. Because behavioral disinhibition is what discriminates ADHD most clearly from other disorders, meeting a cutoff score for these items should be a first requirement in the diagnostic criteria. Also, the Inattention items are as likely to be diagnosed in children with ADD/−H, who do not have this problem of behavioral disinhibition.

Finally, as discussed in Chapter 3, Undifferentiated ADD or ADD/−H should be provided with its own distinct label and diagnostic criteria apart from ADHD (or Hyperkinetic Disorder in ICD-10), as evidence points to its being a distinct childhood disorder and not a subtype of ADHD.

IS ADHD A CLINICAL SYNDROME?

A troublesome issue for attempts to define ADHD as a disorder or syndrome has been the frequent finding that objective measures of these behaviors do not correlate well with each other (Barkley, in press; Barkley & Ullman, 1975; Routh & Roberts, 1972; Ullman et al., 1978). Typically, for a disorder to be viewed as a syndrome, its major features should be related: The more deviant an individual is on one symptom, the more deviant he or she should be on the other major symptoms. The relatively weak or insignificant correlations among laboratory measures of hyperactivity, inattention, and impulsivity have often been used as evidence against the existence of ADHD as a disorder or syndrome by both scientists (Shaffer & Greenhill, 1979) and social critics (Kohn, 1989; Schrag & Divoky, 1975).

However, these weak relationships may have more to do with the manner in which we define the attention deficit or overactivity problems in ADHD children (Rutter, 1989), and, more likely, with the measures we choose to assess these behaviors. How long a child attends to a classroom lecture may be a very different type of attentional process from that required to perform a vigilance test or that required to search out important from unimportant features in a picture (Barkley, 1988d; Ullman et al., 1978). Similarly, taking adequate time to examine a picture before choosing one identical to it from a number of similar pictures (as in Kagan's MFFT; see above) may be a different type of impulsivity from that seen when children are asked to draw a line slowly, or when they are asked whether they wish to work a little for a small reward now or do more work for a large reward later (Milich &

Kramer, 1985; Rapport, Tucker, et al., 1986). It may be a source of wonder, then, that these types of measures correlate at all with each other.

In contrast, studies that factor-analyze parent or teacher ratings of ADHD symptoms often find that they are highly interrelated (Achenbach & Edelbrock, 1981; Barkley, 1988c, in press; DuPaul, 1990a; Hinshaw, 1987), such that they can be combined into a single dimension (Hyperactivity) or at most two dimensions (Inattention-Restlessness and Impulsivity-Hyperactivity). Similarly, when measures of attention and impulsivity are taken within the same task, as in scores for omission and commission errors on a continuous-performance test, they are highly related to each other (Barkley, 1990; Gordon, 1983). This suggests that the frequent failure to find relationships among various lab measures of ADHD symptoms has more to do with the source or types of measures chosen; their highly limited sampling of behavior (typically 20 minutes or less per task); and their sampling of quite diverse aspects of inattention, impulsivity, or hyperactivity than to a lack of relationships among the natural behaviors of these children.

Furthermore, the fact that such symptoms may not occur to a uniform degree in the same children does not rule out the value of considering ADHD as a syndrome. As Rutter (1977, 1989) has noted, a disorder may not show uniform variation but may still be clinically useful as a syndrome. If such children show a relatively similar course and outcome, their symptoms predict differential responses to certain treatments relative to other disorders, or they tend to share a common etiology or set of etiologies, then it may still be valuable to consider children with such characteristics as having a syndrome of ADHD. I and others (Douglas, 1983; Rutter, 1989; Taylor, 1986b) believe that the evidence supports such an interpretation of ADHD.

More problematic for the concept of a syndrome, however, is whether the defining features of ADHD can discriminate ADHD from other types of psychiatric disturbance in children. The evidence here is certainly conflicting and less compelling (Reeves, Werry, Elkind, & Zametkin, 1987; Werry, Reeves, & Elkind, 1987). Mentally retarded, autistic, psychotic, depressed, conduct-disordered, anxious, and learning-disabled children may show deficits in attention or be overactive. When studies compare such groups, they often find few differences among them on measures of ADHD characteristics (see Werry, 1988, for a review). However, such studies must first take into account the comorbidity of many of these disorders with each other. "Comorbidity" means that children with one disorder have a high likelihood of having a second. Some children may have only one of the disorders, some the other, and many have both. This is often noted with ADHD, Oppositional Defiant Disorder, Conduct Disorder, and learning disabilities. Many studies of this issue have not taken care to choose subjects who have only one of these disorders to compare against those who have "pure" cases of the other disorders. As a result, they compare mixed cases of ADHD with mixed cases of other disorders; this greatly weakens the likelihood that differences among the groups

will emerge. When subjects have been more carefully selected, differences between pure ADHD and other disorders have been more significant and numerous (August & Stewart, 1982; Barkley, DuPaul, & McMurray, in press;
Barkley, Fischer, Edelbrock, & Smallish in press-a; McGee, Williams, & Silva,
1984a, 1984b).

Differences in approaches to defining ADHD can also contribute to the
difficulties in evaluating ADHD as a distinct clinical syndrome. Research in
the 1960s and 1970s was characterized by poorly specified and often subjective criteria for deciding on which subjects would be called hyperactive, or
ADHD, with tremendous discrepancies across studies in these selection criteria (Barkley, 1982). Such criteria guaranteed not only that the studies would
differ greatly in their findings, but also that many would employ subjects of
mixed comorbidity, assuring a very conflicting pattern of results across the
literature. With the development of consensus criteria for clinical diagnosis
(as in the DSM-III and the more recent DSM-III-R) or for research (Barkley,
1982; Sergeant, 1988), and with greater attention to the study of pure cases
of the disorder, better and more critical tests of the notion of ADHD as a
distinct disorder can now be undertaken.

SITUATIONAL AND TEMPORAL VARIATION

As already noted, all of the primary symptoms of ADHD show significant
fluctuations across various settings and caregivers (Barkley, 1981; Zentall,
1984). This can be seen in Figure 2.1, which shows the severity of behavior
problems across a variety of home and public situations as reported by parents of ADHD children. Play alone, washing and bathing, and when fathers
are at home are a few of the situations that are less troublesome for ADHD
children, whereas instances where children are asked to do chores, when parents are on the telephone, when visitors are in the home, or when children
are in public places may be times of peak severity of their disorder.

Figures 2.2 and 2.3 show the mean activity level for 12 hyperactive and 12
normal children monitored during school hours and after school activities on
school days, respectively (Porrino et al., 1983). Again, significant fluctuations
in activity are evident across these different contexts for both ADHD and
normal children, with the differences between them becoming most evident
during school classes in reading and math. Despite these situational fluctuations, ADHD children appear to be more deviant in their primary symptoms
than normal children in most settings; yet these differences can be exaggerated greatly as a function of several factors related to the settings and to the
tasks children are required to perform in them (Zentall, 1985).

Degree of Environmental Demands for Inhibition

Some of the variables determining this variation have been delineated. One
of these—the degree of "structure," or more specifically the extent to which

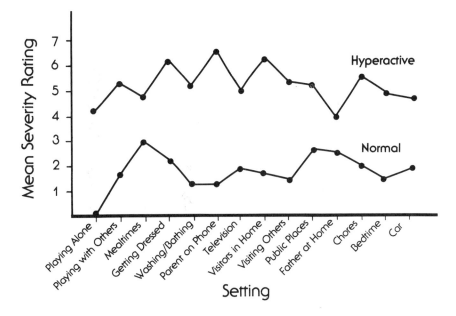

FIGURE 2.1. Mean scores for 30 hyperactive and 30 normal children age 5 to 11 years on the Home Situations Questionnaire.

caregivers make demands on ADHD children to restrict behavior—appears to affect the degree of deviance of these children's behavior from that of normal children. In free-play or low-demand settings, ADHD children are less distinguishable from normal children than in highly restrictive settings (Barkley, 1985a; Jacob et al., 1978; Luk, 1985; Routh & Schroeder, 1976).

Related to this issue of setting demands is the effect of task complexity on ADHD children. The more complicated the task, and hence the greater its demand for planning, organization, and executive regulation of behavior, the greater the likelihood that ADHD children will perform more poorly on the task than normal children (Douglas, 1983; Luk, 1985). Obviously, the symptoms of ADHD are only handicapping when the demands of the environment or task exceed a child's capacity to sustain attention, regulate activity, and restrain impulses. In environments that place few or no demands on these behavioral faculties, ADHD children will appear less deviant and will certainly be viewed by others as less troublesome than in settings or tasks that place high demands on these abilities. As Zentall (1985) has rightly noted in her comprehensive review of setting factors in the expression of ADHD symptoms, we must look closely at the discriminative stimuli in the task and setting to which the children are being required to respond, to gain a better understanding of why these children have so much trouble in some settings and with some tasks than others.

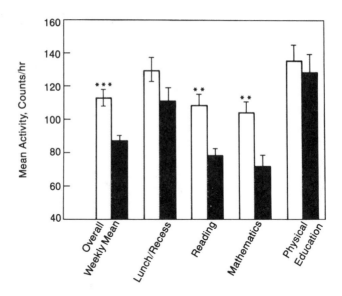

FIGURE 2.2. Mean hourly activity scores and *SEM*s over period of 4 days for 12 hyperactives (open bars) and 12 controls (solid bars) during school hours (baseline week). Asterisks indicate significant differences on two-tailed *t* tests: triple asterisk, *p* < .001; double asterisk, *p* < .01. From "A Naturalistic Assessment of the Motor Activity of Hyperactive Boys" by L. J. Porrino, J. L. Rapoport, D. Behar, W. Sceery, D. R. Ismond, & W. E. Bunney, Jr., 1983, *Archives of General Psychiatry, 40,* 681– 687. Copyright 1983 by the American Medical Association. Reprinted by permission of the authors and publisher.

Behavior Toward Fathers Compared to Mothers

ADHD children appear to be more compliant and less disruptive with their fathers than with their mothers (Tallmadge & Barkley, 1983; Tarver-Behring, Barkley, & Karlsson, 1985). There are several possible reasons for this. For one, mothers are still the primary custodians of children within the family, even if they are employed outside the home; they may therefore be the ones who are more likely to tax or exceed the children's limitations in the areas of persistence of attention, activity regulation, impulse control, and rule-governed behavior. Getting children to do chores and schoolwork, to perform self-care routines, and to control their behavior in public remains predominantly a maternal responsibility and so mothers may be more likely to witness ADHD symptoms than fathers. It would be interesting to examine families of ADHD children in which these roles are reversed, to see whether fathers become the ones reporting more deviance of the children's behavior.

Another reason may be that mothers and fathers tend to respond to inappropriate child behavior somewhat differently. Mothers may be more likely to reason with children, to repeat their instructions, and to use affection as a means of governing child compliance. Fathers seem to repeat their commands

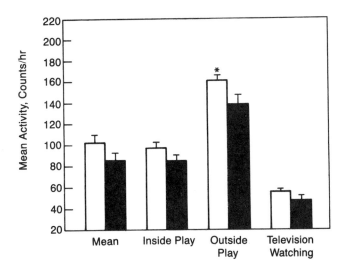

FIGURE 2.3. Mean hourly activity scores and *SEMs* over period of 4 days for 12 hyperactives (open bars) and 12 controls (solid bars), calculated for specific situations during after-school hours (baseline week). Asterisk indicates significant difference ($p < .05$) on two-tailed t tests. From "A Naturalistic Assessment of the Motor Activity of Hyperactive Boys" by L. J. Porrino, J. L. Rapoport, D. Behar, W. Sceery, D. R. Ismond, & W. E. Bunney, Jr., 1983, *Archives of General Psychiatry, 40*, 681–687. Copyright 1983 by the American Medical Association. Reprinted by permission of the authors and publishers.

less, to reason less, and to be quicker to discipline children for misconduct or noncompliance. The larger size of fathers and their consequently greater strength (among other characteristics) may also be perceived as more threatening by children, and hence may be more likely to elicit compliance to commands. For whatever reason, the greater obedience of ADHD children to their fathers than to their mothers is now well established. It should not be construed as either a sign that a child does not actually have ADHD or that the child's problems are entirely the result of maternal mismanagement.

Repetition of Instructions

On tasks where instructions are repeated frequently to the ADHD child, problems with sustained responding are lessened (Douglas, 1980a, 1980b, 1983). Research has shown that when directions for a laboratory task or psychological test are repeated by the examiner, better performance is derived from ADHD children. However, it is not clear whether this is specific to these laboratory tasks and the novel examiner, or can be generalized to activities with routine caregivers. I raise this doubt because, as noted above, it is not uncommon for parents and teachers frequently to complain that repeating their commands and instructions to ADHD children produces little change in compliance.

Novelty and Task Stimulation

ADHD children display fewer behavioral problems in novel or unfamiliar surroundings, or when tasks are unusually novel, but increase their level of deviant behavior as familiarity with the setting increases (Barkley, 1977a; Zentall, 1985). It is not uncommon to find that ADHD children are rated as far better in their behavior at the beginning of the academic year, when they are presented with new teachers, classmates, classrooms, and even school facilities. Their behavioral control, however, usually deteriorates over the initial weeks of school. Similarly, when ADHD children visit with grandparents whom they have not seen frequently, who are likely to provide them with considerable one-to-one attention, and who are unlikely to make numerous demands of their self-control, it seems likely that the children will be at their best levels of behavioral control.

Task stimulation also seems to be a factor in the performance of ADHD children. Research suggests that these children are likely to pay much more attention to colorful or highly stimulating educational materials. than to relatively less stimulating or uncolored materials (Zentall, 1985). Interestingly, such highly stimulating materials may not affect the attention of normal children as much or may even worsen it.

Magnitude of Consequences

Settings or tasks that involve a high rate of immediate reinforcement or punishment for compliance to instructions result in significant reductions in, or in some cases amelioration of, attentional deficits (Barkley, 1990; Barkley, Copeland, & Sivage, 1980; Douglas, 1983; Douglas & Parry, 1983). Few ADHD children seem to demonstrate attention deficits when they play popular video games, such as Nintendo, or when large amounts of money or salient rewards are promised them immediately upon completion of a task. Certainly, differences in activity level between hyperactives and normals while watching television may be minimal or nonsignificant, yet such differences are substantially evident during reading and math classes at school (Porrino et al., 1983). In these instances where ADHD children are engaged in highly reinforcing activities, they may even perform at normal or near-normal levels. However, when the schedule and magnitude of reinforcement are decreased, the behavior of ADHD children may become readily distinguishable from that of normals (Barkley et al., 1980). Such dramatic changes in the degree of deviance of behavior as a function of motivational parameters in the setting has led several scientists to question the notion that ADHD is actually a deficit in attention at all. Instead, they suggest that it may be more of a problem in the manner in which behavior is regulated by its effects or consequences (Barkley, 1990; Draeger et al., 1986; Haenlein & Caul, 1987; Prior, Wallace, & Milton, 1984)—in essence, that ADHD is a motivational deficit rather than an attentional one. This issue is discussed further below in conceptualizing this disorder.

A situational factor related to motivation appears to be the degree of individualized attention being provided to the ADHD child. In one-to-one situations, ADHD children may appear less active, inattentive, and impulsive; in group situations, where there is little such attention, ADHD children may appear at their worst. Some studies, for instance, have found that whether the experimenter sits in the room with a child or not greatly determines whether differences between ADHD and normal children on visual or auditory attention tasks or on attention to arithmetic work will be found (Draeger et al., 1986; Steinkamp, 1980).

Fatigue

Fatigue or time of day (or both) may affect the degree to which ADHD symptoms are exhibited. Zagar and Bowers (1983) observed the behavior of ADHD children in their classrooms and during various problem-solving tasks, and found that they performed significantly better on these tasks when given in the mornings, whereas their classroom behavior was significantly worse in the afternoons. These changes in behavior with time of day did not appear to be a function of boredom or fatigue with the task, as efforts were made to counterbalance the order of administration of the tests across mornings and afternoons. Performance in the afternoon was routinely worse, whether it was the first or second administration of the task. However, there is the possibility that general fatigue, defined simply as time since the last resting or sleeping period, may still explain these results. Similar effects of time of day were noted in the study by Porrino et al. (1983), which monitored 24-hour activity levels across school days and weekends separately. These findings are shown in Figure 2.4 for school days and indicate the hours of 1 P.M. to 5 P.M. to be the peak times of activity for ADHD children.

This is not to say that differences between hyperactive and normal children do not exist in early mornings but emerge only as time of day advances, for this is not the case (Porrino et al., 1983). Normal children show similar effects of time of day upon their behavior, and so hyperactive children appear to be more active and inattentive than normal children, regardless of time of day. It remains true, however, that relatively better performances on tasks and in classrooms by ADHD children may be obtained at some times of the day rather than others. The findings so far suggest that educators would do well to schedule overlearned, repetitive, or difficult tasks that require the greatest powers of attention and behavioral restraint for morning periods, while placing recreational, entertaining, or physical activities in the afternoons (Zagar & Bowers, 1983). Such findings certainly raise serious doubts about the ad-

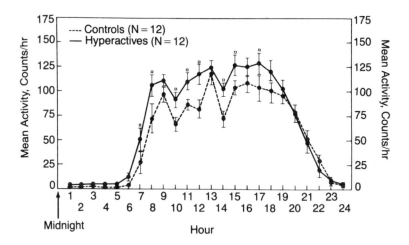

FIGURE 2.4. Mean hourly activity scores and *SEMs* over period of 3–5 days for hyperactives and controls, calculated for typical weekday. Small squares indicate hours during which hyperactives were significantly more active than controls ($p < .05$, by Sheffe procedure after analysis of variance). From "A Naturalistic Assessment of the Motor Activity of Hyperactive Boys" by L. J. Porrino, J. L. Rapoport, D. Behar, W. Sceery, D. R. Ismond, & W. E. Bunney, Jr., 1983, *Archives of General Psychiatry,* 40, 681–687. Copyright 1983 by The American Medical Association. Reprinted by permission of the authors and publisher.

equacy of the practice of scheduling homework periods for ADHD children in late afternoons or early evenings.

Implications for Diagnosis and Management

These situational fluctuations in symptom levels have significant implications for clinical diagnosis of ADHD. It is clear that the disorder is not completely pervasive across all settings. As a result, the previous and common clinical practice of establishing places where the ADHD child can behave "normally" and then ruling out the diagnosis is no longer tenable. Many clinicians have interrogated parents as to how their ADHD children behave while watching television, playing video games, or spending time with their fathers, grand-parents, or babysitters. Having learned that the children are much better be-haved or "normal" in these settings, the clinicians have proceeded to con-clude that such children can not have ADHD because the symptoms are neither persistent nor pervasive. Some have even gone so far as to state that because the children behave better for their fathers (and often better during the office exam with the clinician!), the problem must rest with the mothers' inept man-agement of their children. Such a prejudice against mothers, in fact, is still rather pervasive among laypersons and even some professionals. It is now quite clear that ADHD children show a tremendous variability in their symptom severity across settings, tasks, and time. And, although they are typically more deviant than normal children in their levels of activity and inattention in most settings, the factors within the setting and especially in the demands of the task are highly related to the level of deviance noted (Zentall, 1985). It therefore seems best, in searching for information to assist with the diagnosis, to focus clinical attention more on the ability of ADHD children to sustain attention, regulate activity, control impulses, and follow rules under conditions of tedium (especially boring, repetitive, or protracted work assignments) or under social conditions demanding restraint.

As already noted, these situational changes in behavior and performance can also have some impact on the management of ADHD children. An awareness of the situational or task factors that can enhance performance may greatly empower a parent or teacher to devise methods or schedules of work that best fit with the ADHD child's limited capacities for sustaining attention and regulating activity level. Difficult, complex, or tedious work can be organized into smaller units, provided with greater clarity, assisted by having the child think aloud and talk himself or herself through the task, and enhanced by providing more immediate and salient reinforcers for task completion. Scheduling such activities during morning hours, as suggested earlier, may further enhance task performance. Permitting some motion and talking during task completion, and interspersing periods of restraint with periods of exercise or movement, may also help. These and other suggestions are reviewed in the chapters on parent training and classroom management of this text, but clearly stem from a knowledge of these important situational and task parameters.

PREVALENCE AND SEX RATIO

Because ADHD cannot be strictly defined and precisely measured, its true incidence cannot be accurately determined. Some social critics have used this point to challenge whether a disorder of ADHD exists at all (Kohn, 1989; Schrag & Divoky, 1975). This same problem, however, plagues all psychiatric disorders and even many medical conditions (e.g., Alzheimer's disease, Reye's syndrome, etc.), and yet this hardly makes them clinically useless or fictitious disorders. The consensus of opinion seems to be that approximately 3 to 5% of the childhood population has ADHD (American Psychiatric Association, 1987), but this greatly hinges on how one chooses to define ADHD, the population studied, the geographic locale of the survey, and even the degree of agreement required among parents, teachers, and professionals (Lambert et al., 1978). Estimates vary between 1 and 20% (DuPaul, 1990a; Ross & Ross, 1982; Szatmari et al., 1989a).

Certainly, behaviors similar to the symptoms of ADHD can be found in a large percentage of normal children. In 1958, Rema Lapouse and Mary Monk had teachers evaluate a large sample of school-age children as to the presence of various behavior problems. Their findings revealed that 57% of the boys and 42% of the girls were rated as overactive. Similarly, John Werry and Herbert Quay (1971) also surveyed a large population of school children and found that teachers rated 30% of the boys and 12% of the girls as overactive, 49% of the boys and 27% of the girls as restless, and 43% of the boys and 25% of the girls as having short attention spans.

Critics of the concept of ADHD as a disorder have used such figures to argue that if so many normal children have these features, how can one choose to label some of them as having a clinical or psychiatric disorder (Kohn, 1989; Schrag & Divoky, 1975)? These critics ignore the requirement that the degree of these behavioral characteristics must be developmentally inappropriate for the children's age and sex before it can be considered as clinically deviant or meaningful (American Psychiatric Association, 1987; Barkley, 1981, 1982). In other words, a statistical criterion is applied in which the referred children are compared to their peers in their level of these problematic behaviors, to determine how deviant they are from same-age, same-sex children. The further the children are from their peers in these behaviors, the greater the odds that they will be impaired in their educational and social adjustment and will eventually be diagnosed as having ADHD.

Defining Deviance

A problem here, admittedly, is deciding what cutoff point is needed to determine that children are "developmentally inappropriate" in their behavior. Some have used the criterion of 1.5 standard deviations above the normal mean on parent or teacher rating scales of these ADHD symptoms. However, surveys of large samples of children, such as that done by Ronald Trites and colleagues (Trites, Dugas, Lynch, & Ferguson, (1979) using 14,083 school children, find that this cutoff score can identify an average of 14% of the population as hyperactive. In other studies (see Szatmari et al., 1989a; Taylor, 1986b), estimates can range from less than 1% to over 22% when cutoff scores ranging from 1 to 2 standard deviations above the mean on structured psychiatric diagnostic interviews are used. However, when others have applied the cutoff of two standard deviations above the mean using DSM-III-R symptoms, a more acceptable range of 2 to 9% has been labeled as hyperactive or ADHD (DuPaul, 1990a). Applying a more stringent statistical criterion, such as two standard deviations from the mean, is obviously somewhat arbitrary, but it is in keeping with tradition in defining other conditions (such as learning disabilities and mental retardation) as deviant. It also ensures that an excessive number of children are not being given a psychiatric diagnosis and reserves the diagnosis for the most severely afflicted. When such a stringent criterion as the 97th percentile is applied (two standard deviations above the mean), it does appear to identify a group of children whose ADHD symptoms are not only seriously deviant, but are also stable over as long a time as 8 to 10 years and highly predictive of later maladjustment, particularly in academic adjustment and attainment (Barkley, Fischer, et al., in press-a).

More recently, Szatmari et al. (1989a) have reported the results of a survey of the entire province of Ontario, Canada, in which they found the prevalence of ADHD to be 9 percent in boys and 3.3% in girls. These rates varied somewhat by age for boys: There was a prevalence of slightly more than 10 percent in the 4-to-11 age group, dropping to 7.3% in the 12-to-16 age group. The prevalence for girls, however, did not vary significantly across these age groupings (3.3 vs. 3.4%, respectively). The findings are quite similar to those of the much smaller community survey conducted by DuPaul (1990a), using DSM-III-R symptoms. Overall, then a prevalence of approximately 5 to 6% of children between 4 and 16 years of age are likely to be diagnosed as ADHD.

The Problem of Agreement Among Caregivers

Much is often made by social critics of the fact that the prevalence of ADHD appears to differ significantly as a function of how many people must agree on the diagnosis (Kohn, 1989). The study by Lambert et al. (1978) on this issue is the one most often cited. In this study, parents, teachers, and physicians of 5,000 elementary school children were asked to identify children they considered to be hyperactive. Approximately 5% of these children were defined as hyperactive when the opinion of only one of these caregivers (parent, teacher, physician) was required—a prevalence figure very close to that found both by Szatmari et al. (1989a) in their Canadian survey and by DuPaul (1990a) in the United States. However, this prevalence figure dropped to about 1% when agreement among all three was required. This should hardly be surprising, considering that no effort was made to provide these "social definers" with any criteria for making their judgments or any training in the actual symptoms believed to constitute this disorder. Research routinely finds agreements among people to be low to modest when judging the behavior of another, unless more specific and operational definitions of the behavior being judged and training in the application of the definitions are provided.

It is well established, for instance, that parent and teacher ratings of many different types of child behavior problems are likely to have interrater agreement coefficients of less than .50 (Achenbach, McConaughy, & Howell, 1987). Even fathers and mothers may have agreements of little more than .60 to .70. Certainly, the fact that children behave differently in different situations and with different adults can be a major factor contributing to this lack of agreement. The often subjective judgments required in determining whether a child's behavior occurs "often" or is "deviant" can be another. Undoubtedly, the fleeting or ephemeral nature of behavior and the constant stream of new behaviors or actions of children can create further confusion as to which of these actions should be considered in the judgment. Finally, the use of adult opinions to determine the diagnosis of hyperactivity will always be somewhat confounded by the characteristics and mental status of the adult informant, in addition to the child's actual behavior. As discussed in more detail in Chapter 9 on behavior rating scales, psychological distress, depression, family discord, and social biases can affect the judgments adults make about children, and can therefore add to the lack of agreement among adults about the presence and degree of a child's ADHD. Hence the lack of agreement across caregivers and the variations in the prevalence of ADHD that may arise as a result of it are hardly indictments of the concept of ADHD as a disorder, but apply to many other types of human behavior and virtually all mental disorders.

Culture and Socioeconomic Status

Rates of occurrence of ADHD also fluctuate to a small degree across cultures (O'Leary, Vivian, & Nisi, 1985; Ross & Ross, 1982) and socioeconomic status (SES; Taylor, 1986b; Trites, 1979). This variation in prevalence as a function of SES or geographic area was nicely illustrated in the survey by Trites and colleagues (see Trites, 1979), which is graphically depicted in Figure 2.5. Rates of hyperactivity, defined using the Conners rating scales, varied considerably across the metropolitan area of Ottawa and Hull, Canada, with

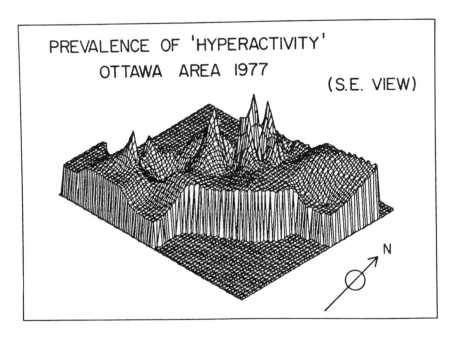

FIGURE 2.5. Prevalence of "hyperactivity" in metropolitan area of Ottawa, Ontario, and Hull, Quebec, Canada, 1977; southeast view. From *Hyperactivity in Children: Etiology, Measurement, and Treatment Implications,* by R. L. Trites, 1979, Baltimore: University Park Press. Copyright 1979 by University Park Press. Reprinted by permission of the publisher.

apparently poorer regions showing higher rates of the disorder. Szatmari et al. (1989a) also found prevalence rates to vary between urban (7.0%) and small urban or rural areas (4.6%).

One reason for such fluctuations may be that women in lower-SES groups are likely to have poorer care and nutrition during their pregnancies and a higher incidence of pregnancy and birth complications. These may affect their children's developing brains and thus predispose the children to a greater risk for ADHD. Second, lower-SES groups are known to have higher rates of family instability, divorce, and parental psychiatric difficulties; these may exacerbate the characteristics of a child with marginal ADHD, so that his or her symptoms are much more prominent. A third explanation may be that a phenomenon known as "social drift" may occur. Children with ADHD may inherit this condition and grow up to have less education than their peers, regardless of their SES level of origin. Upon reaching adulthood, they then drift into a level of employment, and hence a particular SES level, commensurate with their lower educational experience. Given that their condition is hereditary, they are likely to have children with similar problems, thereby inflating the incidence of ADHD within that SES level to which ADHD adults are likely to drift. It is not clear which if any of these explanations accounts for these differences in prevalence across geographic and SES levels. Nevertheless, these differences are relatively minor, and one is likely to find ADHD children coming from virtually all walks of life.

Sex Differences in Prevalence

The prevalence of ADHD is also known to vary significantly as a function of sex of the children being studied. The proportion of males versus females manifesting the disorder varies considerably across studies, from 2:1 to 10:1 (American Psychiatric Association, 1980; Ross & Ross, 1982), with an average of 6:1 most often cited for clinic-referred samples of children. However, epidemiological studies find the proportion to be approximately 3:1 among nonreferred children displaying these symptoms (Szatmari et al., 1989a; Trites et al., 1979).

The considerably higher rate of males among clinic samples of children compared to community surveys seems to be due to referral bias, in that males are more likely than females to be aggressive and antisocial, and such behavior is more likely to get a child referred to a psychiatric center. Hence, more males than females with ADHD will get referred to such centers. In support of this explanation are the following findings: Aggression occurs far more frequently in clinic-referred ADHD children than in those identified through epidemiological sampling (community surveys); hyperactive girls identified in community surveys are often less aggressive than hyperactive boys (see "Sex Differences in the Nature of ADHD," below), but girls who are seen in psychiatric clinics are likely to be as aggressive as boys with ADHD (Befera & Barkley, 1985; Breen & Barkley, 1988). Even so, males remain more likely to manifest ADHD than girls even in community-based samples, indicating that there is a sex-linked mechanism in the expression of the disorder.

Has ADHD Increased in Incidence?

A related issue is the question of whether the incidence of ADHD has increased within the past few decades. The question is difficult to address, as no community surveys of ADHD have been repeated in the same populations or geographic areas over sufficiently long time periods to permit such trends to be evaluated. Some writers (Block, 1977; Ross & Ross, 1982) believe that it may be increasing as a result of increasing cultural tempo or the rate of stimulation and change in a culture. Such speculations based on "tempo," however, are quite difficult to prove scientifically. Others intimate that the more sophisticated and successful life-saving efforts of the medical profession, as seen in neonatal intensive care units, may be increasing the incidence of ADHD by saving babies who would otherwise have died or have been more severely developmentally handicapped. Such logic would suggest that a higher-than-normal incidence of ADHD should be seen in long-term survivors of such intensive care units, and this does appear to be the case. However, this research can be faulted for failing to account for the higher-than-normal association of low SES with babies in these medical units; in other words, it may be the variable of lower SES and not the presence of perinatal complications that accounts for the higher incidence of ADHD. Finally, the actual occurrence of ADHD may not be increasing, while its detection may well be. This may partly stem from a greater awareness on the part of the public about the nature of the disorder, leading to more identification of such children. It could also be due to the trend toward earlier enrollment in preschool for many children, such that their difficulties of inattention, overactivity, and impulsivity will be noticed earlier as well.

SEX DIFFERENCES IN THE NATURE OF ADHD

As noted above, boys are three times more likely to have ADHD than girls, and six to nine times more likely than girls to be seen with ADHD among clinic-referred children. Given these differences in prevalence, one might wonder whether there are differences in the expression of the disorder or its related features between boys and girls. A recent study conducted at Emory University in Atlanta (Brown, Abramowitz, Madan-Swain, Eckstrand, & Dulcan, 1989) evaluated a sample of clinic-referred children diagnosed as having ADHD. They found that girls ($n = 18$) were more socially withdrawn and had more internalizing symptoms (anxiety, depression) than boys ($n = 38$). Other studies based on school-identified hyperactive children have tended to find that hyperactive girls are rated as having fewer behavioral and conduct problems (such as aggressiveness) than hyperactive boys, but usually are not different on any laboratory measures of their symptoms (deHaas, 1986; deHaas & Young, 1984; Pascaulvaca, Wolf, Healey, Tweedy, & Halperin, 1988).

In contrast, two early studies using children referred to pediatric learning and developmental disability clinics suggested that hyperactive girls had lower verbal IQ scores, were more likely to have language disabilities, had a greater prevalence of problems with mood and enuresis, and had a lower prevalence of conduct problems (Berry, Shaywitz, & Shaywitz, 1985; Kashani, Chapel, Ellis, & Shekim, 1979). These studies may have been biased toward finding greater cognitive and developmental problems in their samples because of the source of referrals (learning disorder clinics). Subsequent studies that have used referrals to psychology or psychiatry clinics have found virtually no differences between ADHD boys and girls on measures of intelligence, academic achievement, peer relations, emotional problems, or behavioral disorders (Breen, 1989; Horn, Wagner, & Ialongo, 1989; McGee, Williams, & Silva, 1987). The exception to this was the finding reported by Taylor (1986a, pp. 141–143) that girls referred to a child psychiatry service at Maudsley Hospital in London had a greater degree of intellectual deficits than boys, but were otherwise equivalent in the onset and severity of their hyperactive symptoms. Slight differences have been found in mothers' treatment of their ADHD boys compared to mothers of ADHD girls: Boys received greater praise and direction from their mothers, but boys were less compliant than girls with their mothers' commands (Barkley, 1989b; Befera & Barkley, 1985). No sex differences were noted in the effects of stimulant medication on these interactions (Barkley, 1989b).

In general, ADHD girls within community samples may have fewer conduct problems than boys, but otherwise appear little different from them in their pattern of ADHD symptoms on objective tests. In clinic samples, few sex differences are noted, suggesting that girls who get referred to psychiatric clinics may be as aggressive or conduct-disordered as boys. Sex differences in cognitive performance are not routinely found, and, where they have been, are probably an artifact of the types of clinics from which the children were recruited.

CURRENT CONCEPTUALIZATION OF THE DISORDER

Although numerous studies have consistently demonstrated that ADHD children have deficits in impulse control, attention to tasks, and the regulation of their activity levels, recent reviews question whether these are the fundamental behavioral disturbances in ADHD. The global and multidimensional nature of such constructs as "inattention," "impulsivity," and "overactivity"; the well-demonstrated situational variation in ADHD symptoms; and the lack of testability of many of the theories of ADHD predicted on these constructs have led recent researchers to posit more specific behavioral impairments that may better account for the results of research in this area.

In the first edition of this text (Barkley, 1981) and in a more recent paper (Barkley, 1990), I raised the notion that a behavioral or functional analysis of the primary characteristics of ADHD could prove quite heuristic. Skinner (1953) has presented an analysis of the constructs of attention, impulsiveness, and self-control from this perspective that seems quite useful in understanding what the actual underlying behavioral deficit of ADHD children might be. Skinner proposes that attention itself is not a behavior or response of the individual. Instead, it is a term we use to represent *a relationship* between something in the environment (a discriminative stimulus) and the behavior of the individual. When children look at, orient to, move toward, or manipulate a stimulus in the environment, they are said to be attending to the event or object. Attention, then, is actually a form of stimulus control—a functional relationship between a stimulus or event and a child's response to it. When the relationship between an environmental stimulus and children's behavior is weak, we say that the children are inattentive to that stimulus. When children do not maintain their behavior toward an environmental event for as long as other children do, we say that they have poor sustained attention or poor attention span. When they respond too quickly but incorrectly to the presentation of a stimulus, we say that they are impulsive. And when children show problems with waiting for an event or consequence to occur, we say again that they are impulsive or, more specifically, cannot delay gratification.

Hence, poor attention and impulsivity are not actually behaviors or cognitive faculties of the children, but represent *relationships* between environmental events and child behavior. In particular, they represent temporal relationships among these events. We can therefore no more blame the weakness of these relationships as the problem in ADHD children than we can blame a low correlation coefficient for the failure of two events to covary. Perhaps if we referred to ADHD as "Correlation Deficit Disorder," it would help to illustrate this point and reveal the fallacy of present models of ADHD based on cognitive constructs of attention or impulse control. Blaming a relationship is not helpful in understanding the problem, misses the more crucial aspects of the problem of ADHD, and stifles further analysis by appearing to provide an adequate explanation of the problem. Instead, we should explore these temporal relationships between stimuli and behavior more thoroughly, and in particular should evaluate what other factors are important in conditioning and maintaining these relationships in children.

The Problem of Stimulus Control

From this perspective, the problem of ADHD children is a problem of control of behavior by socially important stimuli. If we are to better understand the nature of ADHD, we must ask why these important stimuli fail to control behavior adequately. Whether stimulus control develops in children is a function of not only the kinds of stimuli we present to them, but primarily the types of consequences we use in training them and the scheduling or arrangement of these consequences. A functional analysis of ADHD symptoms directs our investigation to the kinds of tasks or stimuli to which ADHD children have so much trouble responding, and the types of consequences and their schedules of occurrence under which they cannot maintain persistent responding or effort to these tasks. These are likely to tell us why ADHD children show so much difficulty with these functional relationships between certain stimuli and the socially desired responses to them.

As I have elsewhere indicated (Barkley, 1990), there are many reasons why certain stimuli deemed important by society, such as certain rules, tasks, or events, may fail to adequately control, or set the occasion for, the occurrence of the socially desired responses to these stimuli in ADHD children. These can be summarized as follows: (1) inadequate detection of the stimulus, task, or event by the children (a sensory detection problem); (2) an inability of the children to perform the desired response (as in a physical or motor disability); (3) an inadequate conditioning history (the children have not been properly trained by their caregivers, leading to a lack of skills or knowledge of how to behave); (4) a deficit in the effects of consequences on the children's behavior (those consequences normally used to condition or train normal children are weaker in controlling the behavior of ADHD children); (5) unusually rapid satiation or habituation of the children to these consequences, such that consequences lose their value more quickly in ADHD children (rapid boredom); or (6) a deficiency in the manner in which the schedules of consequences maintain behavior over time (a diminished effectiveness of partial reinforcement schedules to maintain the behavior of ADHD children over time—i.e., persistence of effort toward a task). Unfortunately, these task or setting parameters have not been studied very methodically or rigorously in ADHD children. However, from the information reviewed earlier, we can rule out sensory deficits, physical or motor handicaps, and poor child-rearing skills of parents and teachers as likely sources of this inadequate stimulus control in ADHD children.

Deficient Regulation of Behavior by Rules and Consequences

Different laboratories are beginning to converge on the notion that the manner in which behavior is regulated by its consequences may be the fundamental problem in ADHD. Some hypothesize that ADHD children have higher-than-normal thresholds for arousal by stimulation; as environmental stimulation decreases, hyperactivity and inattention increase as means of compensating for this reduction, so as to maintain an optimal level of central nervous system arousal (Zental, 1985). Others have proposed that thresholds for reinforcement within the brain may be set too high (Haenlein & Caul, 1987). Reinforcers or consequences are therefore less reinforcing or weaker to ADHD children, leading to decreased persistence of responding to tasks.

Compelling but indirect evidence for this view comes from the research on the effects of stimulant drugs on brain reward centers. Such medications appear to lower the threshold for reinforcement, making the individual more sensitive to available reinforcers in the environment; that is, existing reinforcers become more reinforcing and therefore maintain behavior to tasks or stimuli longer than in unmedicated states (see the review by Haenlein & Caul, 1987). Quay (1988) has argued that ADHD may be due to decreased activity in the brain's behavioral inhibition system, such that punishment or its threat fails to inhibit and regulate behavior as well as in normal children. This may explain the symptoms of impulsivity and behavioral disinhibition in ADHD where punishment is used to inhibit or maintain responding. I (Barkley, 1984, 1990) have previously indicated that the problem may rest in several deficits; (1) decreased control by partial schedules of behavioral consequences; (2) rapid habituation or satiation to behavioral consequences, leading to rapid extinction of responding; and (3) diminished regulation of behavior by rules.

Both the first and second of these deficits are similar to the hypotheses of diminished sensitivity to magnitude of consequences by Haenlein and Caul (1987) and diminished inhibition of behavior by threat of punishment by Quay (1988). However, the third deficit requires elaboration here, as it is neither an obvious nor a commonly used construct in the field of child psychopathology. In rule-governed behavior, children's behavior occurs in response to immediately preceding linguistic stimuli and corresponds to that behavior stated in the rule (Skinner, 1953; Zettle & Hayes, 1983). A rule is a contingency-specifying stimulus—a linguistic cue that a particular behavior, if performed, is likely to be followed by a particular consequence. "If you do your homework, you can play with the Nintendo video game for a while" is such a rule. There are different components to rule-governed behavior. "Pliance" refers to behavior that occurs immediately following the presentation of the rule, while "tracking" refers to continued correspondence between behavior and the rule for much longer periods of time after the rule has been presented. Children may recall and subvocally repeat previously presented rules when in future situations in which the original rule giver is absent. We often think of this as a form of self-control. They can also be trained to generate their own rules through the commonly taught steps of problem solving (i.e., "State the problem, generate a list of possible solutions or rules, consider the outcomes for each, select and apply the solution, evaluate its success," etc.), or what Skinner has called "second-order" rules.

It virtually goes without saying that ADHD children have problems with self-control and problem solving, but problems with the other components, especially tracking, seem to be just as troublesome. It is also notable that rule-governed behavior seems important in training children to control impulsive responses and delay gratification. One function of a rule, in fact, is to state the contingency between present behavior and consequences relatively distant in the future. By training children to use rules to control behavior, we free them up from control by the immediate and occasionally spurious consequences associated with impulsive behavior, and bring them under the control of the longer-term consequences of their actions. This is achieved by using socially arranged and often artificial rewards for obeying rules. For these reasons, I have hypothesized that ADHD children have a deficiency in rule-governed behavior relative to their developmental level, along with these other deficits in sensitivity to consequences.

All of these deficits with responding to consequences and rule-governed behavior are believed by their proponents to be neurologically based deficits in ADHD children and are not due to purely environmental or social causes. This is not to say that environmental conditions may not exacerbate (or improve!) the symptoms of ADHD children, but that their problems do not originate in some defect in the environment.

Summary of the Conceptualization

It appears that the primary symptoms of ADHD described earlier can be more heuristically conceptualized as deficits in the functional relationships between child behavior and environmental events than as cognitive constructs or capacities. ADHD is therefore a problem with the stimulus control or regulation of behavioral responses, particularly in the area of behavioral inhibition. Evidence suggests that this deficit in behavioral regulation may stem from one or more of the following impairments: (1) diminished sensitivity to behavioral consequences, (2) diminished control of behavior by partial schedules of consequences, and (3) poor rule-governed behavior. Which of these may prove to be primarily involved in ADHD is not yet clear. However, there is little doubt that present cognitive conceptualizations of ADHD as a problem in attention or impulsivity are losing their explanatory and prescriptive value, and are likely to be replaced by theories founded on motivational deficits rather than on attentional ones.

ADHD Redefined

I have come to view ADHD as follows:

ADHD consists of developmental deficiencies in the regulation and maintenance of behavior by rules and consequences. These deficiencies give rise to problems with inhibiting, initiating, or sustaining responses to tasks or stimuli, and adhering to rules or instructions, particularly in situations where consequences for such behavior are delayed, weak, or nonexistent. The deficiencies are evident in early childhood and are probably chronic in nature. Although they may improve with neurological maturation, the deficits persist in comparison to same-age normal children, whose performance in these areas also improves with development.

These apparently biological deficiencies in the regulation and maintenance of behavior emanate into the social ecology of the child's social interactions in the family, school, and community, resulting in increased controlling responses by caregivers and peers in return. Over time, as these controlling responses meet with little success in managing the ADHD child's behavioral problems, family members, peers, and classmates may come to reject the child, avoiding unnecessary interactions as a means of limiting conflict. In families where other factors (such as parental psychopathology, marital discord, or family hardships) result in inconsistent, unpredictable, coercive, or simply diminished efforts at child management, defiant, oppositional, and aggressive behaviors may increase in the ADHD child. Left untreated, the development of these early antisocial behaviors appears to increase the risk of early and recurrent patterns of delinquent and antisocial conduct in the community that may be maintained into young adulthood (Patterson, 1982; Farrington, Loeber, & van Kammen, 1987). Managed properly, these social interaction conflicts of ADHD children may be maintained at relatively low levels, such that difficulties with school performance may be the primary area of difficulty for ADHD children during adolescence (Paternite & Loney, 1980).

Clinical Implications

The clinical implications of this reconceptualization of ADHD as a motivational disorder are enormous. Only a few of the more significant ones are mentioned here. First, the notion that these are biologically based handicaps in the response of ADHD children to environmental contingencies and consequences should at once direct society to desist from blaming these children for not behaving normally. They are not intentionally lazy, naughty, or simply unwilling to conform. Second, it should also relieve parents and teachers of believing that they are guilty of mismanaging these children. Yet it simultaneously burdens them with the notion that the disorder is relatively permanent and presently incurable.

Third, this view directly specifies the types of environments and tasks in which ADHD children will perform well or even normally (clear, external rules with immediate, salient, and frequent reinforcement) and where they will be most handicapped by their deficits (numerous implicit rules with low reinforcement). The design of prosthetic educational settings and the modification of child management skills and family functioning are seen as straightforward recommendations from this approach. Consequently, this view is highly heuristic and clinically prescriptive in planning interventions for ADHD. Fourth, the relative permanence of the condition argues for much longer interventions and periodic reintervention if treatment gains are to be maintained over time. A corollary of this is that short-term interventions that are withdrawn are likely to result in a rapid return to baseline or pretreatment levels of symptoms. And fifth, assessment procedures must take into account the tremendous variations across settings and caregivers and over time that result from such deficits. Suffice it to say here that these and other implications of this view are woven throughout the chapters on assessment and treatment that follow.

In any case, future conceptualizations of the disorder are likely to rely more heavily on motivational deficiencies with a physiological basis than on attentional deficits in accounting for the behavioral symptoms of ADHD children. These theories provide for more testable hypotheses, coincide better with known neurophysiological effects of drugs used to treat the disorder, offer better explanatory value for the tremendous situational fluctuations seen in ADHD symptoms, and are much more prescriptive of necessary treatments than has been the case for cognitive models of attention deficits in ADHD

SUMMARY

This chapter has described in detail the primary symptoms of ADHD and concluded that behavioral disinhibition, or the inability to adequately regulate behavior by rules and consequences, is the sine qua non of this disorder. Such disinhibition creates difficulties with maintaining attention to tasks, especially in settings where other activities offer competing immediate consequences of a higher magnitude than those inherent in the task assigned to the children. The manner in which the ADHD symptoms may be affected by situational variation, and possible contributors to this variation, have been discussed.

A review of epidemiological studies suggests that the prevalence of the disorder is approximately 3 to 5 percent, and that it occurs in boys almost three times as often as in girls. Despite this sex difference in prevalence, clinical studies suggest that girls and boys referred to clinics are quite similar in their presenting symptoms. However, epidemiological studies imply that in community samples, girls are considerably less likely to manifest aggressive behavior or conduct problems. Evidence for a syndrome of ADHD has been briefly reviewed; the conclusion is that although such evidence is not always consistent, it is sufficiently compelling and clinically useful to permit us to view the disorder as a syndrome. Finally, a reconceptualization of ADHD has been presented that emphasizes biologically based deficiencies in the regulation of behavior by rules and consequences, rather than an attentional deficit, as being the core problems in ADHD.

3

Associated Problems, Subtyping, and Etiologies

I have often said that all of the misfortunes of men spring from their not knowing how to live quietly at home, in their own rooms.

—BLAISE PASCAL (1623–62)

Besides their primary problems with inattention, impulsivity, and overactivity, or inability to regulate their behavior by its consequences, children with Attention-deficit Hyperactivity Disorder (ADHD) may have a variety of other difficulties. Children with ADHD have a higher likelihood of having other medical, developmental, behavioral, emotional, and academic difficulties. Not all ADHD children display all of these problems, but many display them to a degree that is greater than expected in normal children. They are therefore considered to be related or comorbid features, as they are not diagnostic of the disorder when present, nor do they rule out the diagnosis when absent. This chapter describes these frequently associated problems seen in ADHD children and adolescents. It also presents some of the more promising subtyping approaches being proposed in an effort to reduce the heterogeneity of this disorder. Later, the many etiologies or causes proposed for ADHD are discussed.

ASSOCIATED PROBLEMS

Intellectual Development and Academic Performance

Children with ADHD are likely to be behind both normal children and their own siblings in their intellectual development; they score an average of 7 to 15 points below both control groups on standardized intelligence tests (Fischer, Barkley, Edelbrock, & Smallish, in press; McGee, Williams, Moffitt, & Anderson, 1989; Prior, Leonard, & Wood, 1983; Tarver-Behring, Barkley, & Karlsson, 1985). It is not clear whether these differences in scores represent real differences in intelligence or just differences in test-taking behavior (i.e.,

ADHD children may perform more poorly due to their inattention). It is also possible that because these studies often used mixed groups of children having both ADHD and learning disability (LD), the lower intelligence scores in the ADHD groups could be related to the coexisting LD and not to the ADHD per se, as some have suggested (Bohline, 1985). However, in a recent study of ADHD and LD children in our clinic, the LD children without ADHD actually had IQ estimates even lower than those found in the mixed ADHD-LD group, whose IQ estimates were in turn lower than those of the normal control group (Barkley, DuPaul, & McMurray, in press-a). In any case, ADHD children are likely to represent the entire spectrum of intellectual development, with some being gifted while others are normal, slow learners, or even mildly intellectually retarded.

One area of tremendous difficulty for ADHD children is that of their academic performance and achievement. Almost all clinic-referred ADHD children are doing poorly at school, typically underachieving relative to their known levels of ability as determined by intelligence and academic achievement tests. This is believed to be the result of their inattentive, impulsive, and restless behavior in the classroom. Evidence supporting this interpretation comes from numerous studies of stimulant medication with ADHD children that demonstrate significant improvements in academic productivity and sometimes accuracy when the children are taking their medication (Barkley, 1977a; Pelham, Bender, Caddell, Booth, & Moorer, 1985; Rapport, DuPaul, Stoner, & Jones, 1986). Even so, ADHD children are also likely to show performance on standardized achievement tests that is lower than that of their classmates by as much as 10 to 15 standard score points (Barkley, DuPaul, & McMurray, in press; Cantwell & Satterfield, 1978; Fischer et al., in press; Safer & Allen, 1976). This suggests not simply that they are underperforming in school relative to their ability, but that they may have less academic ability than normal classmates. Consequently, it is not surprising to find that up to 40% or more may eventually be placed within formal special educational programs for LD or behaviorally disordered children, and that 23 to 35 percent will have been retained in grade at least once before reaching high school (Barkley, DuPaul, & McMurray, in press; Barkley, Fischer, Edelbrock, & Smallish, in press-a; Brown & Borden, 1986; Munir, Biederman, & Knee, 1987; Szatmari, Offord, & Boyle, 1989b; Stewart, Pitts, Craig, & Dieruf, 1966; Weiss & Hechtman, 1986).

Learning Disabilities

It is presumed that ADHD children are also more likely than normal children to have LD (Safer & Allen, 1976). An LD however, is not simply a failure to do one's work in school, but is typically defined as a significant discrepancy between one's intelligence or general mental abilities on the one hand and one's academic achievement, such as reading, math, spelling, handwriting, or language, on the other. Both intelligence and achievement must be assessed by well-standardized tests. The prevalence rates of LD can vary greatly as a function of how this "significant discrepancy" is defined.

Several different formulas can be applied to define an LD. One such formula, used in past research with Attention Deficit Disorder (ADD) children (Lambert & Sandoval, 1980) is to compare scores on intelligence tests with those on achievement tests for reading and math. An LD is defined as a significant discrepancy between these standard scores. Such a discrepancy can be based on the standard error of both tests or, as is more common, on the differences between them in standard deviations *(SD)*—say, 15 points or one *SD*, where both tests have a mean of 100 and an *SD* of 15. A problem with this "IQ-achievement discrepancy" approach is that it overestimates the prevalence of LD, especially in children performing normally in school and those who are intellectually above average or gifted. Such children may be performing perfectly adequately in school and on achievement tests, but because of higher-than-normal levels of intelligence may have a significant discrepancy between their IQ and achievement test scores (e.g., IQ = 130 while Reading standard score = 100).

A second approach is to define LD as a score falling below 1.5 *SD* from the normal mean on an achievement test (7th percentile). This "achievement cutoff score" approach is less likely to diagnose normal children as LD. But it may diagnose borderline mildly retarded children as such, because their achievement test scores would be consistent with their low IQ scores and place them below this LD cutoff point. A third, more rigorous approach being used in current research is to combine both approaches into a single formula. In this case, LD is defined as both a score below the 7th percentile on an achievement test *and* a significant discrepancy between IQ and achievement on that test. This is called the "combined formula" in this text.

I applied all three approaches to a data set recently collected, which included 42 ADHD and 36 normal children (Barkley, DuPaul, & McMurray, in press). Standard scores from the Wechsler Intelligence Scale for Children—Revised (WISC-R) and the Wide Range Achievement Test—Revised (WRAT-R) were used in calculating the percentage of LD children with each formula. The results are shown in Table 3.1. The percentage of children in each group defined as LD varied considerably with each approach. If the IQ-achievement discrepancy formula was used with the WISC-R Full Scale IQ and the WRAT-R standard scores, where a discrepancy was defined as one *SD*, each group showed a large number of subjects as LD in either reading, spelling, or math. However, over 20, 38, and 35% of the normal children were defined as LD in reading, spelling, or math, respectively, by this approach. Clearly this is not a rigorous approach to defining LD. According to the achievement cutoff score formula, where the 7th percentile served as the cutoff, considerably fewer subjects in each group were defined as LD. Fewer than 3% of the normal children were defined as LD on any measure of achievement by this approach. Finally, when both approaches were combined, the prevalence of LD in each group was reduced somewhat further.

TABLE 3.1. Percentage of Each Subject Group Having
Learning Disabilities (LD) for Reading, Math, and Spelling,
Using Three Different Empirical Definitions of LD

Formula	ADHD	Normal
	Reading	
IQ-achievement discrepancy	40.5	20.6
Achievement cutoff score	21.4	0.0
Combined formula	19.0	0.0
	Spelling	
IQ-achievement discrepancy	59.5	38.2
Achievement cutoff score	26.2	2.9
Combined formula	23.8	0.0
	Math	
IQ-achievement discrepancy	59.5	35.3
Achievement cutoff score	28.6	2.9
Combined formula	26.2	2.9

In summary, the approach used to define LD will greatly determine the prevalence of LD in a sample of ADHD children. Only when the achievement cutoff score approach or the combined formula is used is the prevalence of LD in normal children maintained at a realistic level. According to these more conservative approaches, between 19 and 26% of ADHD children have at least one type of LD, either in math, reading, or spelling.

Speech and Language Development

Although ADHD children do not appear to have a high rate of serious or generalized language delays, they are more likely to have specific problems in their speech development than are normal children. Using community-based samples, many studies have found them to be somewhat more likely to be delayed in the onset of talking in early childhood than normal children (6 to 35% vs. 2 to 5.5%; Hartsough & Lambert, 1985; Szatmari et al., 1989b; Stewart et al., 1966). Other studies, using clinic-referred children, have found no differences in the risk for delayed speech development (Barkley, DuPaul, & McMurray, in press). However, whether speech onset is delayed or not, studies are in general agreement that ADHD children are more likely to have problems with expressive language but not in receptive language, with 10 to 54% having speech problems, compared to 2 to 25% of normal children (Barkley, DuPaul, & McMurray, in press; Hartsough & Lambert, 1985; Munir et al., 1987; Szatmari et al., 1989b).

As noted in Chapter 2, ADHD children are likely to talk more than normal children, especially during spontaneous conversation (Barkley, Cunningham,

& Karlsson, 1983; Zentall, 1989). However, when confronted with tasks in which they must organize and generate speech in response to specific task demands, they are likely to talk less, to be more dysfluent (e.g., to use pauses, fillers such as "uh," "er," and "um," and misarticulations), and to be less proficient in their organization of speech (Hamlett, Pelligrini, & Conners, 1987; Zentall, 1985). Since confrontational or explanatory speech is more difficult and requires more careful thought and organization than spontaneous or descriptive speech, these speech difficulties of ADHD children suggest that their problems are not so much in speech and language per se as in the higher-order cognitive processes involved in organizing and monitoring thinking and behavior, known as "executive processing."

Memory, Executive Processes, and Other Cognitive Abilities

Besides having lower academic achievement in general, as well as a greater prevalence of specific types of LD, ADHD children as a group also tend to be poorer in complex problem-solving strategies and organizational skills (Hamlett et al., 1987; Tant & Douglas, 1982). They also apply less efficient strategies in approaching memory tasks (Voelker, Carter, Sprague, Gdowski, & Lachar, 1989). These difficulties do not appear to be the result of lack of skills or knowledge of how to organize materials or strategies in these tasks; rather, they seem due to lack of effort or use of the strategy during performance of the task itself (Voelker et al., 1989).

Children with ADHD do not have significant memory problems in general, in that they are able to learn and recall information as well as normal children on simple word lists or other memory tasks (Douglas, 1983). Nor do ADHD children have a particularly distinctive profile on standard neuropsychological test batteries (McGee et al., 1989; Schaughency, Lahey, Hynd, Stone, Piacentini, & Frick, 1988). Instead, their problems in task performance arise when they must apply executive strategies in approaching a task. Such strategies are often impulsive, poorly organized, and relatively inefficient (Zentall, 1988). Thus, neuropsychological tests that measure complex problem solving, response inhibition, and sustained effort—believed to be primarily frontal lobe functions—are more likely to reveal differences between ADHD and normal children (Chelune, Ferguson, Koon, & Dickey, 1986; Grodzinsky, 1990; Mariani, 1990).

Studies also show that ADHD children are also less able to communicate the strategies they use to others (Hamlett et al., 1987). Explaining rules one uses to others requires first that one has developed rules for one's own performance and has then organized them in a coherent fashion. As noted earlier, ADHD children have difficulties with various aspects of rule-governed behavior, including problem-solving or self-generating rules, which can interfere with tasks that require rule discovery and communication of those rules to others. Taken together, these findings indicate significant deficits in executive processes—strategies or mechanisms used by individuals to orchestrate or organize and monitor their own thoughts and behavior.

Sensory and Motor Problems

There is no evidence that ADHD children are any more likely than normal children to have difficulties in the development of their hearing, although they may have more otitis media or middle ear infections than normal children (Mitchell, Aman, Turbott, & Manku, 1987). Some have noted greater difficulties in vision for ADHD children, particularly strabismus (Hartsough & Lambert, 1985; Stewart et al., 1966). Even so, the percentage having such visual problems is quite low (19 to 21%). However, others (Barkley, DuPaul, & McMurray, in press-a) have not found any history of visual problems in ADHD children.

Results are conflicting as to whether ADHD children experience a greater risk of delays in walking, with some studies not finding any higher prevalence of this problem (Hartsough & Lambert, 1985), while others have (Mitchell et al., 1987; Szatmari et al., 1989b). Some studies (Hartsough & Lambert, 1985) have found children with ADHD to be somewhat more likely to have delays in the onset of crawling (6.5%) compared to normal children (1.6%). Others have found no greater risk for delays in any areas of motor development (Barkley, DuPaul, & McMurray, in press-a). Nevertheless, as a group, as many as 52 percent of ADHD children compared to up to 35% of normal children are characterized as having poor motor coordination (Barkley, DuPaul, & McMurray, in press-a; Hartsough & Lambert, 1985; Szatmari et al., 1989b; Stewart et al., 1966). This is especially true on tasks requiring fine motor coordination, such as maze drawings or pegboard tasks (McMahon & Greenberg, 1977; Shaywitz & Shaywitz, 1985; Ullman, Barkley, & Brown, 1978).

These children may also manifest more neurological "soft" signs related to gross motor coordination and motor overflow movements during a screening exam, compared to normal and purely LD children (Denckla & Rudel, 1978; Denckla, Rudel, Chapman, & Krieger, 1985; McMahon & Greenberg, 1977; Shaywitz & Shaywitz, 1985). "Motor overflow movements" are unnecessary associated movements when the children are asked to perform very specific muscle group movements (finger flexion, toe tapping, etc.) and are indicative of poor motor inhibition (Denckla & Rudel, 1978). Many ADHD children are notorious for having difficulties with handwriting or penmanship.

Minor Physical Anomalies and Health Problems

It has been repeatedly shown that ADHD children have more minor physical anomalies than normal children (Firestone, Lewy, & Douglas, 1976; Lerer, 1977; Quinn & Rapoport, 1974; Still, 1902). "Minor physical anomalies" are slight deviations in the outward appearance of the child. Such things as an index finger longer than the middle finger; a curved fifth finger; third toe as long or longer than second toe; adherent ear lobes; a single transverse palmar crease; furrowed tongue; greater than normal head circumference; low-seated or soft, fleshy ears; electric, fine hair; two whorls of hair on back of head; eyes placed slightly further apart than normal; and greater skin on nasal side of eyelid, among others, are considered minor anomalies in these studies.

Studies of infants have shown that a higher number of minor anomalies in infancy may be significantly related to the development of behavior problems and specifically hyperactivity at age 3 years (Waldrop, Bell, McLaughlin, & Halverson, 1978). Others, however, have been unable to replicate these findings (Burg, Hart, Quinn, & Rapoport, 1978; Quinn, Renfield, Berg, & Rapoport, 1977; Rapoport, Pandoni, Renfield, Lake, & Ziegler, 1977). Still other studies have noted that the relationship between minor anomalies and hyperactivity may be more specific to boys, whereas minor anomalies are related to overly inhibited and hypoactive behavior in girls (Waldrop, Bell, & Goering, 1976). However, these findings were contradicted by a later study (Jacklin, Maccoby, & Halverson, 1980), and others have found no relationship whatsoever between number of anomalies and behavior (LaVeck, Hammond, & LaVeck, 1980). Thus, while ADHD children may display more of these anomalies, there is little if any consistent relationship between high number of minor anomalies and hyperactive behavior (Firestone et al., 1976; Krouse & Kauffman, 1982).

Some studies have noted a greater incidence of maternal health and pre- and perinatal complications, such as toxemia, pre-eclampsia, postmaturity, and fetal distress, in the pregnancies of ADHD children compared to normal children (Hartsough & Lambert, 1985). However, as many or more studies have not found this to be the case (Barkley, DuPaul, & McMurray, in press-a; Stewart et al., 1966).

Several studies have found ADHD children to have more problems with general health than normal children. Hartsough and Lambert (1985) found 50.9% of hyperactive children to be described as in poor health during infancy, while Stewart et al. (1966) found a prevalence of 24% of their sample to be so described. The figures for control children were 29.2 and 2.7% respectively. The presence of chronic health problems, such as recurring upper respiratory infections, allergies, or asthma, have also been noted more often in hyperactive than in normal children (39 to 44% vs. 8 to 25%) (Hartsough & Lambert, 1985; Mitchell et al., 1987; Szatmari et al., 1989b). Trites, Tryphonas, and Ferguson (1980) also noted more allergies among hyperactive than normal children, but others have not found these differences between groups (Mitchell et al., 1987).

Enuresis, particularly nighttime bedwetting, has been noted to occur in as many as 43% of ADHD children compared to normal children (28%) (Stewart et al., 1966), although two more recent studies did not find this to be the case (Barkley, DuPaul, & McMurray, in press-a; Kaplan, McNichol, Conte, & Moghadam, 1988). Hartsough and Lambert (1985) reported that ADHD children were more likely to have difficulties with bowel training than were normal children (10.1 vs. 4.5%), while Munir et al. (1987) found that 18% had functional encopresis. We were unable to replicate either of these findings, however (Barkley, DuPaul, & McMurray, in press-a). Thus, it is not clear whether ADHD children are more likely to have problems with enuresis or encopresis, but the evidence seems far from convincing to date.

Children with ADHD are considerably more likely to have accidents than are normal children, with up to 46% being described as accident-prone and 15% having had at least four or more serious accidents, such as broken bones, lacerations, head injuries, severe bruises, lost teeth, or accidental poisonings (Hartsough & Lambert, 1985; Mitchell et al., 1987; Stewart et al., 1966). Results for the comparison or normal groups of children in these studies were 11% and 4.8%, respectively. Stewart, Thach, and Friedin (1970) found that 21% of hyperactive children had experienced at least one accidental poisoning, compared to 7.7% for normal children. In a much larger study of more than 2,600 children, Szatmari et al. (1989b) found that 7.3% of ADHD children had had an accidental poisoning while 23.2% had suffered bone fractures, compared to prevalences of 2.6 and 15.1%, respectively, in the control group. However, retrospective and prospective studies generally find a relationship between degree of aggressiveness, not the degree of overactivity, and the likelihood of accidental injury in preschoolers (Davidson, Hughes, & O'Connor, 1988; Langley, McGee, Silva, & Williams, 1983). Since ADHD children are more likely to be aggressive or oppositional, it may be this characteristic that increases their accident proneness, rather than their higher rates of activity level or impulsivity (Langley et al., 1983; Manheimer & Mellinger, 1967). Moreover, accident proneness is moderated by certain parental characteristics, such as degree of monitoring of child behavior and maternal neuroticism (Davidson et al., 1988).

ADHD children have not been found to have any more hospitalizations, greater length of hospital stays, or more surgeries than normal children (Barkley, DuPaul, & McMurray, in press-a; Hartsough & Lambert, 1985; Stewart et al., 1966).

Sleep Problems

Several studies have found children with ADHD to have a higher likelihood of sleeping problems than normal children. Difficulties with time taken to fall asleep may be seen in as many of 56% of ADHD children, compared to 23% of normal children, and up to 39% of ADHD children may show problems with frequent night wakings (Kaplan et al., 1987; Stewart et al., 1966; Trommer, Hoeppner, Rosenberg, Armstrong, & Rothstein, 1988). Over 55% of ADHD children have been described by parents as tired upon awakening, compared to 27% for normal children (Trommer et al., 1988). This higher incidence of sleep difficulties may appear as early as infancy in ADHD children (Stewart et al., 1966; Trommer et al., 1988), with as many as 52% of ADHD children described as such in infancy, compared to 21% of normal children.

Emotional Disturbances

Comorbidity of ADHD with other behavioral and emotional disorders is generally quite common, with up to 44% having at least one other psychiatric disorder, 32% having two others, and 11% having at least three other disorders (Szatmari, Offord, & Boyle, 1989a). As a group, ADHD children are rated as having more symptoms of anxiety, depression, and low self-esteem than normal children or children with LD who do not have ADHD (Bohline, 1985; Breen & Barkley, 1983, 1984; Margalit & Arieli, 1984; Weiss, Hechtman, & Perlman, 1978). This is clearly indicated in Figure 3.1, which shows the typical profile for 26 hyperactive and 26 normal children on the Personality Inventory for Children (Breen & Barkley, 1983).

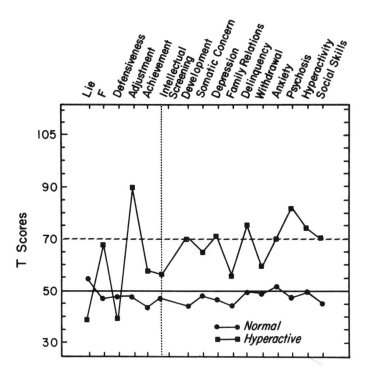

FIGURE 3.1. The profile of T scores for 26 hyperactive and 26 normal boys on the Personality Inventory for Children. From "The Personality Inventory for Children (PIC): Its Clinical Utility with Hyperactive Children" by M. Breen and R. A. Barkley, 1983, *Journal of Pediatric Psychology, 8*, 359–366. Copyright 1983 by Plenum Publishing Corporation. Reprinted by permission of the authors and publisher.

Given this higher occurrence of emotional symptoms in ADHD children, are they more likely to meet full criteria for a diagnosis of other affective or mood disorders? The studies are inconsistent on this issue. One study found that 32% of children with ADHD had a major affective disorder and 27% met criteria for an anxiety disorder (Munir et al., 1987). Szatmari et al. (1989a), in their large epidemiological survey, found that 17% of girls and 21% of boys with ADHD between four and 11 years of age had at least one of these neurotic disorders, while this figure rose to 24% for boys and 50% (!) for girls during the adolescent years. Others have also found that between 20 and 30% of ADHD children have a comorbid anxiety or mood disorder (Jensen, Burke, & Garfinkel, 1988). However, the research findings are not perfectly consistent on this issue, with a few studies not finding a higher incidence of these disorders in ADHD children (Barkley, DuPaul, & McMurray, in press-a) or those followed into adolescence and young adulthood (Gittelman, Mannuzza, Shenker, & Bonagura, 1985; Weiss & Hechtman, 1986). Nevertheless, whether or not ADHD children are more likely to meet the full diagnostic criteria for other affective or mood disorders, they certainly seem more likely to have at least some of the symptoms of such disorders than are normal or other control groups of children.

Greater somatic complaints have also been noted in ADHD compared to normal children (Barkley, DuPaul, & McMurray, in press-a). Complaints of headaches, stomachaches, and vague somatic complaints, as well as complaints related to the aforementioned physical problems (i.e., colds, otitis media, allergies), appear to be more common among ADHD children. Szatmari et al. (1989a) found that as many as 24% of ADHD boys and 35% of ADHD girls between 12 and 16 years met criteria for a Somatization Disorder.

Conduct Problems

It is widely accepted by scientists studying ADHD children that they display a greater degree of difficulties with oppositional and defiant behavior, aggressiveness and conduct problems, and even antisocial behavior than do normal children (see Figure 3.1). Over 65% of clinic-referred samples may show significant problems with stubbornness, defiance or refusal to obey, temper tantrums, and verbal hostility toward others (Loney & Milich, 1982; Stewart et al., 1966). Up to 40% of ADHD children and 65% of ADHD adolescents will meet full diagnostic criteria for Oppositional Defiant Disorder (ODD; Barkley, DuPaul & McMurray, in press-a; Barkley, Fischer, et al., in press-a) as defined in the DSM-III-R (American Psychiatric Association, 1987). These studies indicate that as many as 21 to 45% of ADHD children and 44 to 50% of adolescents will be diagnosed as having the more serious problem of Conduct Disorder (CD) as defined by DSM-III-R guidelines (see also Szatmari et al., 1989a). These disorders are described in more detail in Chapter 6. The most common types of conduct problems are lying, stealing, truancy, and (to a lesser degree) physical aggression.

Some investigators have expressed the belief that ADHD and CD were the same or quite similar disorders (Shapiro & Garfinkel, 1986; Stewart, Cummings, Singer, & deBlois, 1981), but more recent research indicates that relatively pure cases of both can be found and that these disorders are likely to have somewhat different correlates and outcomes (see Hinshaw, 1987, and Werry, 1988, for reviews, and Chapter 4 on course and outcome). Children with CD usually come from backgrounds with greater social adversity and have a higher prevalence of psychiatric disorders among their parents and relatives than do ADHD children without significant conduct problems (McGee, Williams, & Silva, 1984b; Reeves, Werry, Elkind, & Zametkin, 1987; Szatmari et al., 1989b). ADHD children are more likely to have developmental delays and cognitive immaturities than are those with CD (McGee, Williams, & Silva, 1984a; Szatmari et al, 1989b). In cases where children have both disorders, they will display the cognitive immaturities and attention deficits typical of ADHD, as well as a greater likelihood of factors associated with social adversity and family psychiatric problems.

Social Relationships and Attributions

William Pelham and Mary Bender (1982) estimate that over 50% of ADHD children have significant problems in social relationships with other children. Mothers (Campbell & Paulauskas, 1979), teachers (Barkley, DuPaul, & McMurray, in press-a), and peers (Johnston, Pelham, & Murphy, 1985; Pope, Bierman, & Mumma, 1989) report hyperactive children to be significantly more aggressive, disruptive, domineering, intrusive, noisy, and socially rejected than normal children, especially if they are male hyperactives (Milich & Landau, 1982; Pelham & Bender, 1982). The relationships and interactions of ADHD children with their parents are discussed in Chapter 5.

Investigators who have directly observed these peer interactions suggest that the inattentive, disruptive, off-task, immature, and provocative behaviors of ADHD children quickly elicit a pattern of controlling and directive behavior from their peers when they must work together (Clark, Cheyne, Cunningham, & Siegel, 1988; Cunningham & Siegel, 1987; Whalen, Henker, Collins, Finck, & Dotemoto, 1979; Whalen, Henker, Collins, McAuliffe, & Vaux, 1979). In their communication patterns, ADHD children in these studies have been found to talk more but to be less efficient in organizing and communicating information to peers with whom they are asked to work. Morever, despite talking more, the ADHD children are less likely to respond to the questions or verbal interactions of their peers. Hence there is clearly less reciprocity in the social exchanges of hyperactive children with their peers (Cunningham & Siegel, 1987; Landau & Milich, 1988). ADHD children have also been shown to have less knowledge about social skills and appropriate behavior with others (Grenell, Glass, & Katz, 1987).

In general, ADHD children tend to have a more external locus of control than normal children (Linn & Hodge, 1982). That is, they are more likely to view the events that happen to them as outside of their personal control or due to "fate." Those ADHD children who are also aggressive may display an additional tendency to overinterpret the actions of others toward them as actually having hostile intentions, and are therefore more likely to respond with aggressive counterattacks over minimal (if any) provocations (Milich & Dodge, 1984). Such communication problems, skills deficits, attributional biases, and interaction conflicts could easily lead to the ADHD children (especially those who are aggressive) being rejected as playmates by their classmates and neighborhood peers in very short order. Many have noted that it takes very few social exchanges over only 20 to 30 minutes between ADHD and normal children for normal children to find the ADHD children disruptive, unpredictable, and aggressive, and hence to react to them with aversion, criticism, rejection, and sometimes even counteraggression. Certainly they are likely to withdraw from the ADHD children when opportunities to do so arise (Milich & Landau, 1982; Pelham & Bender, 1982; Pelham & Milich, 1984).

SUBTYPING OF ADHD

As can be seen from the foregoing review, the ADHD diagnosis is applied to a heterogeneous group of children believed to have in common the characteristics of developmentally inappropriate levels of inattention, impulsivity, and in some cases overactivity (American Psychiatric Association, 1980, 1987). However, many investigators believe that disturbances in sustained attention, particularly vigilance, characterize all children assigned to this disorder. Despite these apparent commonalities, children so diagnosed are acknowledged to present with a diversity of related psychiatric symptoms, family backgrounds, developmental courses, and responses to treatments. Given this diversity, increasing scientific attention has been paid to identifying approaches to subtyping this disorder into more homogeneous, clinically meaningful subgroups. Such subtyping approaches are clinically useful if they provide important differential predictions about etiologies, developmental courses, outcomes, or responses to therapies between the subtypes. In short, they must show some value beyond the differences that would be expected on the measures on which the subtyping occurred or those measures known to be related to them. Many ways of subtyping ADHD children have been employed. Some have been without much clinical merit, such as sorting ADHD children on the presence or absence of reading disorders (Halperin, Gittelman, Klein, & Rudel, 1984). Others, however, are either promising or have established themselves to be quite clinically useful. These are reviewed below.

Subtyping on Hyperactivity

A controversial subtyping approach is based on the presence and degree of overactivity (American Psychiatric Association, 1980). Children with ADHD are sorted into those having ADD with Hyperactivity (ADD/+H) or ADD without Hyperactivity (ADD/−H). This method of creating subtypes of ADHD was first proposed in the DSM-III, but was later de-emphasized in the DSM-III-R, given the lack of research at that time on the utility of this approach. Several studies found few if any important differences between ADD/+H and ADD/−H children (Maurer & Stewart, 1980; Rubinstein & Brown, 1984). Just as many, however, indicated that ADD/+H children were more aggressive, more rejected by peers, had lower self-esteem, and may be more impaired in cognitive and motor test performance than ADD/−H children (Berry, Shaywitz, & Shaywitz, 1985; King & Young, 1982). In contrast, ADD/−H children were characterized as more anxious, daydreamy, lethargic, and sluggish than ADD/+H children when teacher ratings of classroom adjustment were used (Edelbrock, Costello, & Kessler, 1984; Lahey, Schaughency, Strauss, & Frame, 1984; Lahey, Schaughency, Hynd, Carlson, & Nieves, 1987).

More recent studies have compared these subtypes on more objective tests and measures with mixed results. Carlson, Lahey, Frame, Walker, and Hynd (1987) found ADD/+H children to have poorer peer relationships, with significantly more of them nominated as "least liked" by their peers than ADD/−H children. The latter children, however, received more such nominations than did normal control children. When measures of academic achievement and neuropsychological functions were used, most studies found no important differences between the groups (Carlson, Lahey, & Neeper, 1986): Both groups were found to be more impaired in academic skills and in some cognitive areas than normal control children. However, using a very small sample of both subtypes ($n = 10$), Hynd, Lorys-Vernon, et al. (in press) found the ADD/−H children to have more LD, particularly in math performance, than the ADD/+H children. The ADD/−H children were also slower in a rapid naming task than the ADD/+H children.

Unfortunately, none of these studies have directly addressed the issue of whether ADD/−H and ADD/+H are subtypes of the same type of attentional disorder or whether they represent qualitatively different disorders, despite having similar levels of deviance on teacher rating scales of inattention. This would require a more comprehensive and objective assessment of different components of attention in both groups. In the one study that used four different types of reaction time tasks to study neurocognitive processing, few meaningful differences between the subtypes were obtained (Hynd, Nieves, et al., in press). However, these reaction time tasks do not necessarily evaluate the different components of attention as viewed from neuropsychological models (Mirsky, 1987; Posner, 1987), and so the question as to whether these subtypes have the same type of attentional disturbance remains unanswered.

Several major problems also exist with these past studies. First, many have relied predominantly on teacher ratings both in defining their groups and then in examining differences between groups. Where teacher ratings are used to assign the children into the two subtypes, it is highly likely that differences on teacher ratings of other behaviors will be subsequently found. This is due to the common source of these ratings (i.e., the teacher) and to the generally significant correlations found across most dimensions of behavior rated by the same individual. Hence, such studies have confounded their independent and dependent variables (Lahey et al., 1984, 1987). A similar problem exists where parent ratings are used as both independent and dependent variables. Second, several studies relied on clinicians' judgments, using the DSM-III criteria for determining these two disorders (Berry, et al., 1985; Edelbrock et al., 1984). However, factor analyses of the DSM-III item lists for Inattention, Hyperactivity, and Impulsivity have not found these items to cluster into the same dimensions as they are listed in the DSM-III (Lahey, Pelham, et al., 1988). As a consequence, attempting to subtype children based on these item lists may result in relatively impure subgroups of ADD with respect to whether hyperactivity is actually present or absent in these children. Finally, several of these studies used nonclinical samples of children defined as having ADD only as a result of relatively high scores on teacher rating scales. These scores typically would not be considered clinically deviant. The extent to which their results are representative of clinic-referred children with seriously deviant ADD symptoms is questionable.

In a recently completed study (Barkley, DuPaul, & McMurray, in press-a), we conducted a more comprehensive evaluation of these subtypes of ADD than had been done previously. We used an extensive battery of structured psychiatric interviews; objective measures of child behavior, attention, impulsivity, adaptive behavior, and academic achievement; and the more typical parent and teacher behavior rating scales employed by past research. This project involved four groups of subjects: 42 children in the ADD/+H group, 48 in the ADD/−H group, 16 in the LD group, and 34 in the normal group. All children were between 6 and 11 years of age and were of normal intelligence.

The results generally suggested that both groups of ADD children are at greater risk for a variety of behavioral, social, and emotional problems than are non-ADD LD or normal children. It appears that the presence of serious inattention in both groups is sufficient to predispose them toward greater problems with behavioral, academic, and social adjustment. However, the additional presence of hyperactivity in the ADD/+H subtype is associated with considerably less self-control and greater impulsivity, and markedly worsens the degree of both internalizing and externalizing problems likely to be manifested by ADD children. More importantly, it creates a relatively unique additional risk for serious aggressive or oppositional behavior and antisocial conduct. More than twice as many ADD/+H children as ADD/−H children were diagnosed as having ODD (41% vs. 19%), using DSM-III-R criteria, and more than three times as many were diagnosed as having CD (21% vs. 6%); these differences were obtained despite the fact that all of these children were still within elementary school age and had equivalent levels of inattention. These findings corroborate other studies in showing that the combination of inattention and overactive-impulsive behavior greatly predisposes young children to a higher risk of concurrent and later antisocial conduct (Paternite & Loney, 1980).

As in other past studies (Carlson et al., 1986; Lahey et al., 1984), we found both groups of ADD children to be impaired in their academic adjustment and achievement levels, to have been retained in grade (32% in each group), and to have been placed in special education considerably more than our normal control children (45% vs. 53%). However, we found that ADD/+H children were more likely to have been placed in special classes for behavior-disordered children (emotionally disturbed) than the ADD/−H children (12% vs. 0%), while the latter children were more likely to be in classes for LD children than the ADD/+H children (34% for ADD/+H and 53% for ADD/−H). These differences in class placement do not appear to be the result of actual differences in the rates of LD between these disorders, as we found no such differences when using commonly accepted definitions of LD applied to achievement and intelligence tests as discussed below. Instead, both groups of children had equivalent rates of LD, but the additional problems with conduct and antisocial behavior were likely to result in the ADD/+H children being assigned to the behaviorally disturbed programs rather than the LD programs. Similarly, our ADD/+H children were also more likely to have been involved in individual (51% vs. 32%) and family therapy (32% vs. 13%) than were our ADD/−H or control groups of children.

The results for academic achievement tests were similar to those of Carlson et al. (1986), who also found no significant differences between children with these ADD subtypes, either in their degree of deficits in achievement or in the degree to which achievement scores fell below those expected from intelligence test scores. Both groups of ADD children performed significantly more poorly than normal children on academic achievement tests. We went further in our analysis of these subtypes to determine the prevalence of LD in each as defined by three separate empirical definitions of LD (see "Learning Disabilities," above, for these definitions). Regardless of the manner in which LD was defined, the two ADD groups did not differ in their percentage of LD children, ranging from 19 to 40% in reading, 22 to 59% in spelling, and 22 to 59% in math. The best definition of LD, that combining the IQ-achievement discrepancy formula with the achievement cutoff score formula, indicates that approximately 20% of both groups of ADD children have an LD in reading, spelling, or math.

The findings for the developmental and medical histories of these groups of subjects were somewhat discrepant from those recently reported by Frank and Ben-Nun (1988). We did not find an increased incidence of perinatal and neonatal abnormalities in the ADD/+H group as compared to the ADD/−H group. We did find a greater history of ADD among the paternal relatives and of substance abuse among the maternal relatives of the ADD/+H children than among those of the ADD/−H children, whereas Frank and Ben-Nun (1988) did not find such differences in family histories. Moreover, we noted a significantly greater prevalence of anxiety disorders among the maternal relatives of the ADD/−H than among those of the ADD/+H children, which was not reported by the Frank and Ben-Nun study. This may have been due to considerably smaller sample sizes in their study (21 ADD/+H and 11 ADD/−H) and their use of clinical judgments based on the DSM-III criteria to assign children to groups. As noted above, the use of the older DSM-III criteria may result in a less pure distinction between the subtypes on the symptoms of hyperactivity, given the failure of those hyperactivity items to cluster empirically in the manner in which they are listed in DSM-III. Consistent with our findings, however, were the reports by Frank and Ben-Nun (1988) of no differences between these ADD subgroups in abnormal medical histories or developmental delays.

Unlike several prior studies (Befera & Barkley, 1985; Cunningham, Benness, & Siegel, 1988), we did not find mothers of our ADD/+H children to report themselves as more depressed or to have more marital conflict than mothers of our ADD/−H, LD, or normal control children. Mothers in all three of our clinical groups reported greater levels of interpersonal sensitivity and hostility, as well as general psychological distress, than did mothers of the normal children.

A major interest of our research was whether the ADD/+H and ADD/−H groups of children actually comprise subtypes of an identical problem in attention or whether they are in fact distinctly separate cognitive and psychiatric disorders. The results, albeit tentative, suggest that ADD/−H comprises a different type of attentional disturbance and therefore should not be considered a subtype of ADD/+H (now ADHD). ADD/−H children differed from ADD/+H children in having considerably fewer problems with off-task behavior during a vigilance task; less aggression, impulsivity, and overactivity both at home and at school; and less situational pervasiveness of their conduct problems both at home and at school (Barkley, DuPaul, & McMurray, in press-a). They also had significantly fewer problems in peer relationships than the ADD/+H children and were rated as displaying significantly fewer symptoms of ADHD, with their mean number of such symptoms falling below the recommended cutoff score for that disorder (8 of 14 ADHD symptoms). Even more telling, however, was the finding that ADD/−H children performed considerably worse on the Coding subtest of the WISC-R and on a measure of consistent retrieval of verbal information from memory. The ADD/+H children did not differ from normal subjects on either of these measures. These findings intimate that ADD/−H children may have more of a problem with memory, perceptual-motor speed, or even more central cognitive processing speed, whereas ADD/+H children may manifest more problems with behavioral disinhibition and poor attention to tasks in addition to their overactivity.

We examined a smaller subset of these same subject groups on neuropsychological measures of frontal lobe functions (Barkley, Grodzinsky, & DuPaul, 1990). The ADD/+H children performed considerably worse than ADD/−H children on both the Stroop Color Test and the Hand Movements subtest of the Kaufman Assessment Battery for Children (K-ABC), while ADD/–H children were not different from the normal or LD groups on any frontal lobe measures. These findings, when placed in the context of neuropsychological (Mirsky, 1987) or information-processing (Sergeant & van der Meere, 1989) models of attention, suggest that ADD/–H children may have more trouble with focused attention or speed of information processing (input analysis and retrieval of stored information). In contrast, ADD/+H children may have greater difficulty with sustained attention and impulse control, or motivational parameters involved in the task (resource allocation or maintaining effort).

Such differences in the types of attention affected in these groups of ADD children would be expected to have different neuroanatomical loci (Mirsky, 1987; Posner, 1987). ADD/+H may be a problem in the functional level of prefrontal-limbic pathways, particularly the striatum (Lou, Henriksen, & Bruhn, 1984; Lou, Henriksen, Bruhn, Borner, & Nielsen, 1989), while ADD/–H may involve more posterior associative cortical areas and/or cortical-subcortical feedback loops, perhaps involving the hippocampal system (Heilman, Voeller, & Nadeau, in press; Hynd, Lorys-Vernon, et al., in press; Posner, 1987). Consistent with this notion of different neurological mechanisms underlying these disorders are the preliminary findings of Shaywitz et al. (1986) that small samples of ADD/+H children show a different response than do ADD/–H children in growth hormone and prolactin levels in blood plasma when placed on methylphenidate. The authors imply that ADD/+H may involve a problem with dopamine, while ADD/–H may selectively involve norepinephrine. These neuropsychological and neurochemical hypotheses regarding ADD/–H are quite conjectural at present. Nevertheless, they hint at the possibility of eventually identifying two distinctive attentional disorders in children that corroborate distinctions already being made in the study of normal attentional processes in the basic neurosciences (Mirsky, 1987; Posner, 1987).

These differences between the ADD subtypes in behavior and cognitive test performance are quite consistent with some previous studies (Berry et al., 1985; Carlson et al., 1987; Lahey et al., 1987) in finding ADD/+H children to be more disinhibited and impulsive, conduct-disordered, and socially rejected, while ADD/–H children are more cognitively sluggish, daydreamy, and socially withdrawn. Furthermore, our inspection of the types of inattention items rated by teachers as problematic for these subtypes revealed a different pattern of attentional problems and cognitive styles for each, similar to those found in prior research (Edelbrock et al., 1984; Lahey, Schaughency, Frame, & Strauss, 1985). The ADD/+H children were described as more noisy, disruptive, messy, irresponsible, and immature, while the ADD/–H children were rated as more confused, daydreamy or lost in thought, and apathetic or lethargic.

In general, these results suggest that ADD/+H children have considerably different patterns of psychiatric comorbidity than do ADD/–H children, being at significantly greater risk for other Disruptive Behavior Disorders, academic placement in programs for behaviorally disturbed children, school suspensions, and psychotherapeutic interventions than are ADD/−H children. These patterns of comorbidity, along with the findings of different family psychiatric histories, suggest that these are dissimilar psychiatric disorders rather than subtypes of a shared disturbance in attentional processes. Although an alternative conclusion—that ADD/−H represents simply a milder form of ADD/+H—is possible, our results indicated that 93% of the ADD/+H group met the new DSM-III-R criteria for ADHD, while only 31% of the ADD/−H group did so. Our research also appears to indicate that children with ADD/−H can be distinguished in a number of domains of adjustment and cognitive performance from those with ADD/+H. Not only do they present as having different levels of activity, but they also have quite distinct differences in the kinds of attentional problems they manifest. And, while both groups are equally at risk academically, they are quite different in their social morbidity, with ADD/+H children evidencing considerably greater levels of aggression, oppositional defiant behavior, and conduct problems.

The evidence available to date compels us to begin considering ADD/+H and ADD/−H as separate and unique childhood psychiatric disorders and not as subtypes of an identical attention disturbance. For now, in our own clinic, we have come to label the ADD/+H group as having ADHD, following the currently recommended guidelines in the DSM-III-R, and part of the larger category of Disruptive Behavior Disorders. In contrast, we consider the ADD/−H group as having a "focused attention disorder" involving poor focus of attention/awareness and deficient speed of cognitive processing of information.

A recent survey (Szatmari et al., 1989a) indicates that the prevalences of these two disorders within the population are quite different, expecially in the childhood years (6 to 11 years of age). ADD/−H appears to be considerably less prevalent than ADD/+H. Only 1.4% of boys and 1.3% of girls have ADD/−H, while 9.4% of boys and 2.8% of girls have ADD/+H. These figures change considerably; in the adolescent age groups, where 1.4% of males and 1% of females have ADD/−H, while 2.9% of males and 1.4% of females have ADD/+H. In other words, the rates of ADD/−H remain relatively stable across these developmental age groupings, while ADD/+H, especially in males, shows a considerable decline in prevalence with age. Among all children with either type of ADD, about 78% of boys and 63% of girls will have ADD/+H.

It remains to be seen just how stable the ADD/−H disorder is over development. One recent developmental study of a large sample of clinic-referred children suggests that its stability is quite poor, with none of the children originally diagnosed as having ADD/−H receiving that same diagnosis 4 years later (Cantwell & Baker, 1989). However, this study used the original DSM-III criteria for diagnosis; as discussed above, this may create considerable overlap between the two disorders on the dimension of Hyperactivity. This might help to explain why a large percentage (80%) of those children origi-nally diagnosed as having ADD/−H received a diagnosis of ADD/+H at 4-year follow-up. The sample of ADD/−H children in this study was also quite small ($n = 5$), making the results of the study questionable as to how repre-sentative they are of ADD/−H children. Consequently, this research can hardly be considered a definitive longitudinal study on the outcome of this disorder. More research on the long-term outcome of ADD/−H is to be encouraged.

Unfortunately, at present, little is known about which types of treatment may be more effective with the ADD/−H group, while much is known about the treatment of the ADHD group (see Chapters 12 through 17). Five studies exist on the response of these two types of ADD to different doses of stimu-lant medication. They suggest that both groups generally respond positively to medication, but that a lower dose of medication is sufficient to manage the problems of ADD/−H children, while higher doses appear to be more effective for the ADD/+H children (Barkley, DuPaul, & McMurray, in press−b; Famularo & Fenton, 1987; Saul & Ashby, 1986; Shaywitz, Shaywitz, Jatlow, Seabrechts, Anderson, & Cohen, 1986; Ullmann & Sleator, 1985). More re-search is to be encouraged on the responses of these different disorders to other types of behavioral, educational, and pharmacological interventions.

Subtyping on Aggression

Another, more widely accepted subtyping approach that has already demon-strated considerable clinical significance has been based on aggression (Loney, Kramer, & Milich, 1981; Loney & Milich, 1982). "Aggression" re-fers to oppositional, defiant, stubborn, explosive, hostile, verbally aggressive, and fighting behaviors. Current diagnostic nomenclature refers to children with these symptoms as having ODD (American Psychiatric Association, 1987). This disorder is believed to be highly related to later CD and antisocial be-havior (Barkley, Fischer, et al., in press−a; Reeves et al., 1987) and is viewed by some as an earlier developmental precursor of it. Although these ODD symptoms can certainly occur independently of ADHD, many studies show that they are highly interrelated (Hinshaw, 1987; Shapiro & Garfinkel, 1986), especially in clinic-referred samples. Hence the two disorders appear to over-lap considerably, as noted above in the "Conduct Problems" section, in that children who have one disorder often manifest the other. Yet much evidence has accumulated that shows important differences between children having either disorder alone and those having both ADHD and aggression (ODD or CD) (Hinshaw, 1987; McGee et al., 1984a, 1984b; Werry, 1988).

In general, children with ADHD and aggression display significantly greater levels of physical aggression, lying, and stealing, as well as more rejection by peers, than either purely ADD or purely aggressive children (Loney, Langhorne, & Paternite, 1978; Milich, Landau, Kilby, & Whitten, 1982; Walker, Lahey, Hynd, & Frame, 1987). These children also display different patterns of so-cial attribution (Milich & Dodge, 1984), often viewing others' actions as

intentionally aggressive against them. They are typically rated as more severely maladjusted (McGee et al., 1984b), and have a poorer adolescent and
young adult outcome (Milich & Loney, 1979; Paternite & Loney, 1980),
than children having either disorder alone. Finally, children having both disorders have greater levels of parental and family psychopathology (particularly antisocial conduct and major depressive disorders), as well as greater
social adversity, than do children with either disorder alone (Biederman, Munir, & Knee, 1987; Lahey, Piacentini, McBurnett, Stone, Hartdagen, & Hynd,
1988; Reeves et al., 1987; Szatmari et al., 1989b). Clearly, the use of aggression (ODD or CD) for subtyping of children with ADHD has been of great
scientific and clinical utility.

Existing research suggests that the mechanism for the development and
maintenance of aggression in children may occur as a result of the combination of early negative child temperament (i.e., irritability, quickness to anger,
low frustration tolerance) with disordered parental and family functioning.
The parental psychiatric characteristics contribute to aggressive child behavior by their impact upon parent-child interactions in particular and child rearing
in general (Bond & McMahon, 1984; Jouriles, Pfiffner, & O'Leary, 1988).
For instance, Patterson's (1982) extensive research suggests that the use of
coercion (unpredictable, often noncontingent aversive verbal and physical exchanges) by parents in parent-child interactions leads to the child's acquisition of aggressive behavior as a means of successfully escaping or avoiding
unwanted, tedious, or aversive intrusions from others. Families with greater
parental psychopathology , maternal depression, and marital discord seem
more likely to engage in such coercive exchanges with their children; to reinforce negative and coercive behavior by their children via escape (negative
reinforcement); and to have higher rates of conduct problems with their children, perhaps as a result (Jouriles et al., 1988; Lahey, Piacentini, et al., 1988).
It is therefore easy to see how families with ADHD children who are quick-
tempered, and in which the parents are experiencing personal psychiatric distress or marital discord, can give rise to and maintain aggressive or ODD-
like behavior in those ADHD children through inconsistent, unpredictable,
and aggressive interactions. It is the success of such behavior in fending off
or escaping from such aversive parental (and sibling) intrusions that seems to
reinforce and maintain childhood aggression (Patterson, 1982).

Subtyping on Internalizing Symptoms

Another approach to subtyping ADHD, considerably less studied than the
others described above, is based on the presence and degree of anxiety and
depression in ADD children (often referred to as "internalizing symptoms").
This subtyping model is based on several studies showing that children who
had relatively high ratings of internalizing symptoms were more likely to have
poor or adverse responses to stimulant medication (Taylor, 1983; Pliszka,
1989; Voelker, Lachar, & Gdowski, 1983), and may be more appropriate

for antidepressant medications (Pliszka, 1987). Results of other studies suggest the possibility that, within the broader population of ADHD children, those with internalizing symptoms may have the greater likelihood of mood and affective disorders in later childhood and adolescence. Research shows that some anxiety disorders and depressive symptoms in childhood may evolve into other types of anxiety or mood disorders or even major depressive disorders in later childhood or adolescence (Cantwell & Baker, 1989; Strauss, Lease, Last, & Francis, 1988). However, no studies have specifically examined the stability and differential course of ADHD children with and without significant internalizing symptoms, and so the actual clinical predictive value of this subtyping approach remains unstudied.

Subtyping on Situational versus Pervasive Nature of Symptoms

It is a common observation in clinical practice that some ADHD children show their symptoms primarily at home whereas others show these symptoms primarily at school, and many do in both situations. Considerable differences in opinion have existed between North American and European mental health professionals as to whether the situational (primarily at home or primarily at school) group of ADHD children should be considered to have a psychiatric disorder. Those in North America consider those in either the situational or the pervasive group to have ADHD; Europeans typically restrict the diagnosis of hyperactivity, or ADHD, to those children showing their symptoms pervasively (Schachar, Rutter, & Smith, 1981).

Early research suggested that the situational type of ADHD was primarily associated with other behavioral disorders, such as aggression, and did not manifest as strong a pattern of cognitive impairment, immaturity, or actual ADHD behaviors in school, whereas the pervasive type of ADHD showed such impairments and was more stable over development (Sandberg, Rutter, & Taylor, 1978; Schachar et al., 1981; Schleifer et al., 1975). However, Cohen and Minde (1983), in a study of kindergarten ADHD children, did not find such differences among these subgroups. Even so, they did note that the home-only ADHD children were more likely to have negative parent-child interactions, implying that such children may have more difficulties with oppositional behavior and negative maternal behavior than with just ADHD. A more recent paper by Bourdreault et al. (1988) suggested that situational ADHD may simply be a milder form of ADHD than that seen in the pervasive type of ADHD, having similar but less severe types of cognitive and behavioral impairment. These findings support the view taken in the DSM-III-R that pervasiveness of ADHD symptoms should be used to determine severity of the ADHD condition, rather than whether the disorder exists or not.

However, a recent study (Costello, Loeber, & Stouthamer-Loeber, 1989) indicates that caution must be exercised in using the pervasiveness of symptoms in the diagnosis of ADHD. This distinction, it is noted, is greatly confounded by differences in sources of information (parents vs. teachers) who are well known to have only moderate levels of agreement on the occurrence of most childhood behavior problems, particularly ADHD. And so the comparison of situational versus pervasive ADHD is actually a study of the degree to which parents and teachers agree about the behavior of these children. In fact in a recent epidemiological survey (Szatmari et al., 1989a), only 15 percent of all ADHD children fell into this pervasive or consensus group. Studies are therefore automatically biased toward finding differences between children defined on this basis, because of these known disagreements between such sources or raters. Home-only (parent-identified) ADHD children may be expected to have worse ratings on other parent-completed measures of behavior and adjustment, as compared to school-only or pervasive ADHD children. Similarly, school-only (teacher-identified) ADHD children will be worse on other teacher-completed measures than home-only or pervasive ADHD children. Where the measures are independent of the source used to classify the children, no differences in behavior are likely to be seen. This is precisely what Costello et al. (1989) found and what must be controlled for in future studies of this subtyping approach.

Although the existing research is therefore not especially clear as to the value of subtyping ADHD children by the situations in which they display their characteristic symptoms, it seems clinically useful to continue to view pervasive ADHD as at least a more severe degree of the disorder than situational ADHD, and to begin to allocate greater clinical resources and interventions to this more pervasive group (Szatmari et al., 1989a).

ETIOLOGIES

Since the first edition of this text (Barkley, 1981) was published, considerable research has accumulatead on several promising etiologies for ADHD. Even so, this research continues to be methodologically difficult and is often inconsistent and conflicting in its results. There is little doubt among senior investigators in this field that multiple etiologies may lead to ADHD. Our knowledge of the final common neurological pathway through which these produce their effects on behavior has been significantly increased by converging lines of evidence from cerebral blood flow studies, studies of brain electrical activity using computer-averaging techniques, and studies using neuropsychological tests sensitive to frontal lobe dysfunction. Neurochemical abnormalities that may underlie this disorder are extremely difficult to document with any certainty, but the findings to date also converge on a possible common neurological mechanism for ADHD. Nevertheless, most findings on etiologies are correlational in nature, not permitting direct evidence of causality. For instance, even though parents of ADHD children may smoke tobacco more during their pregnancies, and pregnant women who smoke are more likely to have ADHD, this does not directly prove that smoking causes the ADHD. It is possible that parents of ADHD children, themselves likely to have some manifestations of the disorder, may smoke more than parents of normal children; the genetic relationship between the parents and children may be important here, rather than the smoking itself. Great care needs to be taken, then, in interpreting the results of much of this research.

Neurological Factors

A variety of etiologies have been proposed for ADHD. Brain damage was initially proposed as a chief cause of ADHD symptoms (see Chapter 1); it was suggested to occur as a result of known brain infections, trauma, or other injuries or complications occurring during pregnancy or at the time of delivery. Several studies show that brain damage, particularly hypoxic/anoxic types of insults, are associated with greater attention deficits and hyperactivity (Cruikshank, Eliason, & Merrifield, 1988; O'Dougherty, Nuechterlein, & Drew, 1984). ADHD symptoms also occur more often in children with seizure disorders (Holdsworth & Whitmore, 1974). However, most ADHD children have no history of significant brain injuries, and so such injuries are unlikely to account for the majority of children with this condition.

Some studies have not found a greater incidence of pregnancy or birth complications in ADHD compared to normal children (Barkley, DuPaul, & McMurray, in press-a), while others have found a slightly higher prevalence of unusually short or long labor, fetal distress, low forceps delivery, and toxemia or eclampsia (Hartsough & Lambert, 1985; Minde, Webb, & Sykes, 1968). Nichols and Chen (1981) also found that low birth weight was associated with an increased risk of hyperactivity. Several studies suggest that mothers of ADHD children conceive these children at an age younger than that of mothers of control children, and that such pregnancies may have a greater risk of adversity (Denson, Nanson, & McWatters, 1975; Hartsough & Lambert, 1985; Minde et al., 1968). Since pregnancy complications are more likely to occur among teenage mothers, mothers of ADHD children may have a higher risk for such complications, which may act neurologically to predispose their children toward ADHD. However, the complications that have been noted to date are rather mild and hardly compelling evidence of pre- or perinatal brain damage as a cause of ADHD. Furthermore, large-scale epidemiological studies have generally not found a strong association between pre- or perinatal adversity and symptoms of ADHD once other factors are taken into account, such as maternal smoking and alcohol use (see below) as well as socioeconomic disadvantage, all of which may predispose to perinatal adversity and hyperactivity (Goodman & Stevenson, 1989; Nichols & Chen, 1981; Werner, Bierman, French, Simonian, Connor, Smith, & Campbell, 1968).

No differences in brain structure have been noted on computed tomography (CT) scan analysis (Denckla, LeMay, & Chapman, 1985; B. A. Shaywitz, Shaywitz, Bryne, Cohen, & Rothman, 1983; Thompson, Ross, & Horwitz,

1980), and preliminary findings from studies using the higher-resolution magnetic resonance imaging (MRI) devices have been conflicting (Hynd, personal communication April, 1989; Taylor, personal communication, April 1989). To summarize, reviews of the evidence suggest that fewer than 5 percent of ADHD children have hard neurological findings indicative of actual brain damage (Ferguson & Rapoport, 1983; Rutter, 1977, 1983). Thus, while certain types of trauma, infection, or disease of the central brain may give rise to ADHD, these causes account for a very small minority of the population of ADHD children.

Some (Kinsbourne, 1977) have speculated that ADHD may arise as a result of delayed brain maturation. This theory is quite appealing in view of the immature social behavior displayed by these children; their frequent findings of neuromaturational delay on neurological exam (see Chapter 8); and the consistency between their deficits in attention, impulse control, and self-regulation and the behaviors of younger normal children (Routh, 1978). But there has been no direct neurological evidence submitted in support of such a theory, and so it remains conjectural.

Possible neurotransmitter dysfunctions or imbalances have been proposed, resting chiefly on the responses of ADHD children to differing drugs. Given the findings that normal children show a positive, albeit lesser, response to stimulants (Rapoport, Buchsbaum, Zahn, Weingartner, Ludlow, & Mikkelsen, 1978), evidence from drug responding by itself cannot be used to support a neurochemical abnormality in ADHD. However, some direct evidence from studies of cerebrol spinal fluid in ADHD and normal children indicates decreased brain dopamine in ADHD children (Raskin, Shaywitz, Shaywitz, Anderson, & Cohen, 1984). Evidence from other studies using blood and urinary metabolites of brain neurotransmitters have proven conflicting in their results (S. E. Shaywitz, Shaywitz, Cohen, & Young, 1983; Shaywitz, Shaywitz, Jatlow, Sebrechts, Anderson, & Cohen, 1986; Zametkin & Rapoport, 1986). What evidence there is seems to point to a selective deficiency in the availability of dopamine, but this evidence cannot be considered conclusive at this time. Some evidence suggests that diminished dopamine may play some role in CD (Bowden, Deutsch, & Swanson, 1988) as well, implying that previous differences between ADHD and normal children in this area could have been due to large overlap of CD with ADHD in such samples.

More recently, studies of cerebral blood flow have found diminished perfusion to the striatum and orbital prefrontal regions, more so in the right hemisphere than in the left (Lou et al., 1984, 1989). Such findings, however, have been founded on extremely small sample sizes and used hyperactive children who had significant evidence of neurological disturbance. Even so, the findings are consistent with unpublished evidence collected by James Satterfield (personal communication October 1986) that ADHD children display less electrical activation in their prefrontal and frontal-limbic regions, again more on the right side than on the left side.

Certain studies have used neuropsychological tests of frontal lobe functions and have detected deficits on these tests, albeit inconsistently (Conners & Wells, 1986; Chelune et al., 1986; Fischer et al., in press; Grodzinsky, 1990; Heilman et al., in press; Mariani, 1990). Where consistent, the results suggest that disinhibition of behavioral responses is demonstrated by these tests, rather than difficulties with abstract reasoning, response initiation, verbal fluency, perseveration, or other frontal lobe functions. Such findings are more often associated with orbital-frontal and orbital-limbic impairments than with damage to dorsolateral or medial frontal lobe regions (Stuss & Benson, 1986).

These findings point to a central nervous system mechanism in the development of ADHD systems. This is most likely in the connections between the prefrontal areas and the limbic system, especially in the striatum (Heilman et al., in press; Lou et al., 1984, 1989; Zametkin & Rapoport, 1986). These brain areas are known to underlie aspects of response inhibition, inattention, and incentive learning or sensitivity to reinforcement. They are also some of the most dopamine-rich areas of the human brain, and so a hypothesis of selective dopamine depletion would be consistent with these other findings. The findings from neurological studies are also consistent with those from behavioral observations and neuropsychological tests, which show behavioral disinhibition and poor self-regulation of responses to be the hallmarks of ADHD (Conners & Wells, 1986). The inability of ADHD children to actively inhibit behavior as demanded by situations and tasks when the consequences for doing so are weak or delayed, becomes readily apparent in such settings when the children are faced with alternate, competing activities in the environment that offer immediate rewards for responding to them.

Psychophysiological Findings

Numerous studies have measured various psychophysiological functions in hyperactive children and contrasted these findings with those from normal or other control groups. Regrettably, these studies are methodologically poor in many cases, often failed to select for relatively pure cases of ADHD, frequently used such small samples that statistical power to detect findings was deficient, and usually used poor control groups. It is therefore hardly surprising that the findings across studies are quite contradictory (see Conners & Wells, 1986; Hastings & Barkley, 1978; Rosenthal & Allen, 1978; Taylor, 1986b, for reviews). Where positive findings are noted, one cannot be sure whether they are related to the hyperactivity or to the comorbid conditions (LD, CD, etc.) often existing in the hyperactive group.

Most research does not indicate a pattern of general autonomic underarousal in ADHD children. Some studies have found smaller orienting responses on measures of galvanic skin response, as well as more rapid heart rate deceleration in hyperactive children, suggesting a more specific pattern of underreactivity in these children. Equally as many studies, however, have not found such patterns. Several studies examining cortical electrical activation—usually by electroencephalogram (EEG) or averaged evoked responses

(AERs)—have found greater slow-wave EEG activity in some hyperactive children, or smaller amplitude of responses to stimulation with more rapid habituation of the response to the stimulus on AERs. Still, findings for cortical activation are just as conflicting as those for autonomic measures of arousal. At present, there is sufficient evidence to suggest that hyperactive children do not have a pattern of nervous system underarousal. However, the general tendency of the findings tentatively suggests that a type of underreactivity to stimulation may occur in some hyperactive children.

Attempts have been made by some investigators to determine whether various psychophysiological measures could be used to predict the response of hyperactive children to stimulant medication. Despite the optimistic claims by some (Logan, Farrell, Malone, & Taylor, 1988), much of this research has proven contradictory or useless (see Conners & Wells, 1986, for a critique).

Environmental Toxins

In the 1970s and early 1980s, it was popular to view ADHD as resulting from food additives, particularly salicylates, food dyes, and preservatives. This mainly stemmed from the widespread media attention given to Benjamin Feingold (1975) and his claims that over half of all hyperactivity was the result of such substances. However, a substantial amount of subsequent research was unable to support this claim (Conners, 1980; Taylor, 1980). While a small percentage (<10%) of preschool-age children may have shown a slight increase in activity or inattentiveness, no evidence was ever provided either that normal children can acquire ADHD by consuming such substances or that ADHD children are made considerably worse by them.

Interest in this theory has diminished greatly over the past decade, being replaced by the now popular view that refined sugar can cause ADHD (Smith, 1975). In fact, so widely had this idea been accepted by laypersons that in January 1987 "What is sugar?" was offered as the correct question to the answer, "It is the major cause of hyperactivity in North America," on the popular television game show *Jeopardy!*. Despite widespread attention in the lay media to these claims, not a single scientific study has been provided by its proponents to support them. In the past several years, a number of scientifically controlled studies of sugar have been conducted, and these have generally proven negative (see Gross, 1984; Wolraich, Milich, Stumbo, & Schultz, 1985). At this point, continuing claims that dietary substances are a major contributor to ADHD cannot be taken seriously, and the burden of proof that they do must rest with those who would propose such etiologies. Uncontrolled clinical case illustrations will simply not suffice.

Some evidence of a correlational nature exists to show that elevated blood lead levels in children may be associated with a higher risk for hyperactivity and inattention (Baloh, Sturm, Green, & Gleser, 1975; David, 1974; de la Burde & Choate, 1972, 1974; Needleman, Gunnoe, Leviton, Reed, Peresie, Maher, & Barrett, 1979). Also, studies of emotionally disturbed children have

found significant relations between hair lead levels and total number of behavior problems on a teacher rating scale (Marlowe, Cossairt, Moon, Errera,
MacNeel, Peak, Ray, & Schroeder, 1985; Marlowe, Errera, Ballowe, & Ja-
cons, 1983). More recent and more methodologically sophisticated studies
have found a low correlation between blood lead and hyperactivity (Thomson, Raab, Hepburn, Hunter, Fulten, & Laxen, 1989), while others have
found even weaker correlations between blood or dentine lead levels (about
.10 to .19). This relationship is attenuated further (below .10) when other
possible confounding factors are taken into account (Fergusson, Fergusson,
Horwood, & Kinzett, 1988; Gittelman & Eskinazi, 1983; Silva, Hughes,
Williams, & Faed, 1988). Milar, Schroeder, Musak, and Boone (1981) found
no differences in either parent ratings of hyperactivity or playroom observations of behavior between children with moderately elevated lead burden and
those without such a lead burden. At present, there is enough evidence to
show that body lead levels are associated to a very small degree with hyperactivity and inattention in a general population of children. However, ADHD
children often show minimal if any increase in their body lead burdens. Body
lead is therefore unlikely to be a major cause of ADHD in children, despite
its significance as a public health concern (Taylor, 1986b).

Cigarette smoking during during pregnancy has also been shown to be
greater in mothers of ADHD children than control children (Denson et al.,
1975; Streissguth et al., 1984). Data from longitudinal studies of a large sample of pregnancies indicated that maternal cigarette smoking was significantly
associated with the degree of hyperactivity and inattention in the children of
those pregnancies (Nichols & Chen, 1981; Streissguth et al., 1984). These
studies also found that these mothers smoked more outside of this pregnancy
period and that their husbands also smoked more than those in the normal
control groups. Thus, both direct and ambient cigarette smoke exposure is
higher in ADHD children during pregnancy, and this may be associated with
anoxic injury to the brain. Again, these results are correlational and cannot
prove that it is the maternal cigarette smoking that is causal of the children's
ADHD. Given the evidence of a genetic link in ADHD, the parents of these
children are also more likely to have ADHD. It may be that ADHD is associated with greater adolescent and adult smoking, but that the genetic relationship between ADHD parent and ADHD child rather than the parents'
greater smoking explains this link. One simply cannot determine the causal
direction in this research.

A similar situation exists between maternal alcohol consumption during
pregnancy and hyperactivity in the offspring. Research indicates that children
born to alcoholic mothers are more likely to have problems with hyperactivity and inattention (Bennett, Wolin, & Reiss, 1988; S. E. Shaywitz, Cohen,
& Shaywitz, 1980). The amount of alcohol consumed appears to be directly
proportional to the degree of inattention in the offspring at age 4 years
(Streissguth et al., 1984). Again, correlation does not imply causation, although teratogenic effects of alcohol on the developing brain seem likely.

Nevertheless, as with smoking, we find that ADHD children are more likely to consume alcohol than normal children as they enter adolescence and young adulthood. Again, given the greater likelihood that their own parents had ADHD and that these parents may also have drifted toward greater alcohol consumption (Cunningham et al., 1988), it may be that the greater alcohol use is but a marker for the genetic relationship between parental ADHD characteristics and offspring risk for ADHD.

In the mid-1970s, a photographic engineer proposed that cool-white fluorescent lighting emitted certain soft X-rays and radio frequencies that could cause children to become hyperactive. Since many public schools use such lighting in classrooms, it was argued that this lighting increased the activity levels of children in these classrooms and could even make some clinically hyperactive. Mayron, Ott, Nations, and Mayron (1974) reported the results of comparing normal children exposed to standard cool-white fluorescent lighting and broad-spectrum fluorescent lamps. They claimed that children exposed to the broad-spectrum lighting showed significant reductions in hyperactivity, relative to children exposed to the standard cool-white lamps. The study was quite poorly designed and seriously methodologically flawed, however. Subsequently, O'Leary, Rosenbaum, and Hughes (1978) attempted to replicate these findings using considerably improved methodology; clinically hyperactive children rather than normal children; direct behavioral observations of classroom activity and attention, as well as teacher ratings of behavior; and a sophisticated reversal design in which the same children were exposed to alternating weeks of cool-white lamps and the full-spectrum lighting. No effects of lighting condition were found.

Side Effects of Medications

There is some evidence that the medications used to treat seizure disorders, particularly phenobarbital and Dilantin, are likely to result in increased problems with inattention and hyperactivity in children taking these medications (Committee on Drugs, 1985). It has been estimated that between 9 and 75% of children given phenobarbital are likely to develop hyperactivity or have any pre-existing ADHD symptoms worsened by this drug (Committee on Drugs, 1985; Wolf & Forsythe, 1978). However, a more recent study suggests that while such symptoms are more common in children treated with phenobarbital, few if any of these children meet full clinical criteria for ADHD (Brent, Crumrine, Varma, Allan, & Allman, 1987). Instead, more of the children treated with this medication are likely to be diagnosed as depressed or irritable. Considering that very few ADHD children are taking these medications, such drugs cannot be considered to be a major cause of ADHD in the population. It would still be advisable, however, for clinicians working with ADHD children with epilepsy to be cautious about the possibility that certain types of anticonvulsants could worsen such a pre-existing condition.

Some clinical anecdotal evidence has suggested that theophylline, a medication used in treating asthma and certain allergies, may cause inattention and hyperactivity as side effects. This is not to say that these effects reach degrees that could be considered to warrant a diagnosis of ADHD, but that they may sufficiently predispose a child on these medications to be somewhat poorer at paying attention in school, or may make the symptoms of a child who already has ADHD even worse.

Genetic Factors

One of the most exciting areas of research on etiologies has been the role of hereditary transmission of symptoms across generations. For many years, evidence has existed showing higher rates of psychopathology—particularly depression, alcoholism, conduct problems, and hyperactivity—among the biological relatives of ADHD children versus those of normal children or those of adopted hyperactive children (Biederman, Munir, 1987; Cantwell, 1975; Morrison & Stewart, 1971, 1973a). McMahon (1980) has noted a number of methodological problems in these studies that raise doubts about interpreting them as evidence for an hereditary cause of ADHD. Also, as Lahey, Piacentini, et al. (1988) have recently shown, many of these adult psychiatric disorders are more closely associated with CD in children than with ADHD. Since these studies probably contained mixed cases who had both hyperactivity and CD, the results may reflect the familial association of psychiatric disorders in CD children and not necessarily in hyperactive children. Lahey, Piacentini, et al. (1988) did find a higher prevalence of ADHD even among the relatives of the pure ADHD children who were without CD. Other studies indicate that between 20 and 32 percent of parents and siblings of ADHD children also have the disorder (Biederman, Munir, et al., 1986; Deutsch et al., 1982; Safer, 1973). Such research suggests a genetic predisposition to the disorder.

Twin studies have shown greater concordance for inattention and overactivity between identical than between fraternal twins (O'Conner, Foch, Sherry, & Plomin, 1980; Willerman, 1973), further suggesting some role for genetics in the transmission of these characteristics in families. However, these studies used populations of normal children rather than clinically hyperactive children, and so the generality of their findings to the disorder of ADHD is limited. In a study by Lopez (1965), four identical (monozygotic) twin pairs were compared to six fraternal (dizygotic) twin pairs where one twin in each dyad was hyperactive. The results indicated complete concordance for hyperactivity among the monozygotic twins, but only a 17% concordance rate among the dizygotic twins. Heffron, Martin, and Welsh (1984) also reported a perfect concordance for hyperactivity among three monozygotic twin pairs in which one was hyperactive, as we did (Cunningham & Barkley, 1978) for one monozygotic pair. Although these findings clearly support an hereditary mechanism for hyperactivity, the small sample sizes in both studies and different sex compositions of the monozygotic versus dizygotic twin pairs in the Lopez study greatly limit the conclusions that can be drawn from their results.

Most recently, in the largest study of twin pairs reported to date, Goodman and Stevenson (1989) evaluated the heritability of hyperactivity among 127 monozygotic and 111 dizygotic twin pairs. Concordance for clinically diagnosed hyperactivity was found to be 51% among the monozygotic twins and 33% among the dizygotic pairs. The authors estimate that the heritability for the traits of hyperactivity, or ADHD, is 30 to 50%, indicating that genetic factors play a significant role in this disorder. Common environmental factors accounted for between 0 and 30% of the variance in ADHD symptoms in this sample, arguing against any theory attributing hyperactivity to entirely environmental factors (such as poverty, overcrowding, chaotic family style, pollution, or food additives).

Environmental and Psychosocial Factors

A few environmental theories of ADHD have been proposed (Block, 1977; Willis & Lovaas, 1977) but have not received much support in the available literature. Willis and Lovaas (1977) claimed that hyperactive behavior is the result of poor stimulus control, as discussed in Chapter 2, but that this poor regulation of behavior is due to poor parental management of the children. In support of this theory, studies of the parent-child interactions of hyperactive children clearly show that these parents are more likely to give commands to their children, to be more negative toward them, and in some instances to be less likely to respond to the social initiatives of their children toward them than are mothers of normal children (Barkley, Karlsson, & Pollard, 1985; Campbell, 1973, 1975; Cunningham & Barkley, 1979; Tallmadge & Barkley, 1983). However, these studies also show that the hyperactive children are less compliant, more negative, and less able to sustain their compliance to parental commands than are normal children. It is unclear what the direction of effects are in these interactions (i.e., whether the mother causes the child's problems or the child's problems cause the mother's negative reactions).

To analyze these interactions further, several investigators evaluated the effects of stimulant medication and placebo on these mother-child interactions and found that the medications resulted in significant improvements in child hyperactivity and compliance. There was a corresponding reduction in mothers' use of commands, direction, and negative behavior when the children were on medication, indicating that the negative behavior of the mothers appeared to be in response to the difficult behavior of these children (Barkley & Cunningham, 1979a; Barkley, Karlsson, Strzelecki, & Murphy, 1984; Barkley, Karlsson, Pollard, & Murphy, 1985; Cunningham & Barkley, 1978; Humphries, Kinsbourne, & Swanson, 1978). Further supporting this view were the findings from the large study of hyperactivity in twins by Goodman and Stevenson (1989). They also found that mothers' use of criticism and their general malaise in parenting were associated to a small but significant degree with ADHD symptoms. But these factors accounted for less than 10 percent of the variance in these symptoms in this population. They are therefore not viewed as a major contributor to the occurrence of these symptoms in children.

Taken together, these findings suggest that the overly critical, commanding, and negative behavior of mothers of hyperactive children is most likely a reaction to the difficult, disruptive, and noncompliant behavior of these children rather than a cause of it. This is not to say that the manner in which parents attempt to manage their children's ADHD behavior cannot exacerbate it or serve to maintain higher levels of conflict between mothers and children over time. Studies have shown that the continuation of hyperactive behavior over development, and especially the maintenance of oppositional behavior in these children, are related in part to parents' use of commands and criticism (Barkley, Fischer, Edelbrock, & Smallish, in press-b; Campbell, 1987, 1990; Campbell & Ewing, in press).

As discussed in Chapter 1, Block (1977) has proposed that an increase in "cultural tempo" in Western civilization may account for the prevalence of hyperactivity in these countries. Precisely what is meant by "cultural tempo" is not operationally defined, nor is evidence presented to suggest that underdeveloped or Eastern cultures have less hyperactivity than do more developed or Western cultures. While intriguing, this theory and its modification by Ross and Ross (1982) remain speculative and would seem to be almost scientifically untestable.

Summary of Possible Etiological Factors

Most investigators in this area endorse a biological predisposition to the disorder, much like that of mental retardation, in which a variety of neurological etiologies (e.g., pregnancy and birth complications, acquired brain damage, toxins, infections, and heredity) can give rise to the disorder through some disturbance in a final common pathway in the nervous system. In the case of ADHD, it would seem that hereditary factors play the largest role in the occurrence of these symptoms in children. It may be that what is transmitted genetically is a tendency toward dopamine depletion in, or at least underactivity of, the prefrontal-striatal-limbic regions and their rich interconnections. The condition can be exacerbated by pregnancy complications, exposure to toxins, or neurological disease, and by social factors (such as environmental and family adversity, dysfunctional child rearing and management, or educational environment). Cases of ADHD can also arise without a genetic predisposition to the disorder, provided the child is exposed to significant disruption or neurological injury to this final common neurological pathway; however, this would seem to account for a small minority of ADHD children. By contrast, little if any evidence supports the notion that ADHD can arise purely out of social or environmental factors, such as poverty, family chaos, diet, or poor parent management of children.

CONCLUSION

This chapter has briefly reviewed the conditions that appear to be comorbid with ADHD, potentially useful subtyping approaches, and the evidence for etiologies of ADHD. Most common among the comorbid conditions are problems with school underachievement, oppositional defiant behavior, antisocial conduct, and LD. Disturbances in executive mental functions, especially those involved in response inhibition under conditions of delayed or low reinforcement, are commonplace and frequently lead to poorly organized and disruptive behavior when performing tasks requiring persistence of effort.

Approaches to subtyping reviewed here have suggested that the subtype of ADD/−H probably represents a distinct childhood disorder with a different impairment in attention from that seen in children with ADD/+H, and so should not be considered a subtype of ADHD. The division of ADHD children into those with and without aggression is highly useful in predicting outcome and family dysfunction. ADHD children with higher levels of internalizing symptoms, particularly anxiety, are also useful to distinguish, if only in predicting their response to stimulant medication. The utility of the subtyping approach based on pervasiveness of ADHD across situations, however, remains to be convincingly demonstrated.

Etiologies for ADHD have also been reviewed, and the findings suggest strong evidence for a genetic mechanism of inheritance, while brain injuries may account for a small percentage of ADHD children. Neurological studies are converging on the conclusion that a dysfunction in the orbital-limbic pathways of the frontal area (and particularly the striatum) is the probable impairment that gives rise to the primary features of ADHD, particularly its behavioral disinhibition and diminished sensitivity to behavioral consequences or incentive learning.

4

Developmental Course and Adult Outcome

> What is already passed is not more fixed than the certainty that what is future will grow out of what has already passed, or is now passing.
>
> —George B. Cheever (1807–90)

As discussed in Chapter 2, the symptoms of Attention-deficit Hyperactivity Disorder (ADHD) appear to arise relatively early in childhood, with the mean age of onset being between 3 and 4 years (Barkley, Fischer, Edelbrock, & Smallish, in press-a; Barkley, Fischer, Newby, & Breen, 1988) and ranging between infancy and 7 years. While a few cases may develop after age 7 years, these would seem to be either cases where the disorder is acquired secondary to an obvious neurologically compromising event (such as trauma or hypoxic injury), or cases where the children may have had their ADHD characteristics for quite some time, but these do not interfere with their academic or social functioning until later childhood. The latter situation seems to occur in very bright or gifted ADHD children whose superior intellect seems to allow them to pass through the early grades of school without difficulty because they do not need to apply much effort to be successful. As the work at home and school increases in length and complexity, and greater demands for responsibility and self-control are made in later childhood, such ADHD children are now handicapped by their deficits. Once again, the interface between environmental demands and children's capabilities—discussed throughout this text—seems important in determining the degree to which the children's ADHD characteristics will prove socially discernible or disabling throughout their development.

This chapter discusses the developmental course and outcome of ADHD children as revealed by many different follow-up studies, including my own recent research in this area. The discussion begins with factors that appear to be associated with risk for and early emergence of the disorder and that may eventually prove to be early predictors of ADHD.

FACTORS ASSOCIATED WITH RISK FOR DEVELOPING ADHD

Certain parental characteristics have been noted to be associated with ADHD in children, as described above. Studies in this area imply that parents with depression, alcoholism, Conduct Disorder (CD), and antisocial behavior may be more likely to have children with ADHD (Cantwell, 1975; Morrison & Stewart, 1973a). However, these disorders may be more likely to be associated with subsequent risk in their children for aggression and antisocial behavior than ADHD. Certainly, ADHD in the parents and relatives of children would appear to be an important marker for increased risk of the disorder (Barkley, DuPaul, & McMurray, in press-a; Deutsch et al., 1982). Having a hyperactive sibling may also be a predictor of higher risk of hyperactivity among other children in the family (Nichols & Chen, 1981). Goodman and Stevenson (1989) estimate this risk to be approximately 13 to 17% for female siblings and 27 to 30% for male siblings, regardless of whether the hyperactive proband is male or female. In short, families with an existing history of ADHD among their relatives, especially the immediate parents and siblings, are more likely to have hyperactive children than are those families without such familial disorders. Other family risk factors associated with the early emergence and persistence of ADHD symptoms have been low maternal education and socioeconomic status (SES), and single parenthood or father desertion (Nichols & Chen, 1981; Palfrey, Levine, Walker, & Sullivan, 1985).

Several studies have shown that pregnancy complications and problems at time of delivery are more likely to have occurred with ADHD children than normal children (Hartsough & Lambert, 1985; Minde, Webb, & Sykes, 1968; Nichols & Chen, 1981). As noted in Chapter 3, this is not to say that such factors are the cause of the children's hyperactivity, but that where such factors exist they may at least be predictive of later hyperactivity. In their large epidemiological study, Nichols and Chen (1981) found that the following pregnancy factors, in decreasing order of importance, were predictive of later hyperactivity in children: number of cigarettes smoked per day, maternal convulsions, maternal hospitalizations, fetal distress, and placental weight. Hartsough and Lambert (1985) found an association between young motherhood as well as poor maternal health and hyperactivity in the children. Alcohol consumption during pregnancy is also associated with later attention deficits in children, as discussed in Chapter 3. For whatever reason, these factors appear to be associated with a higher risk for ADHD among the children born of such pregnancies.

Certain neonatal and infancy variables have been studied for their association with ADHD. Delayed motor development, smaller head circumference at birth and at 12 months of age, meconium staining, neonatal nerve damage, primary apnea, and low birth weight, among others, were found by Nichols and Chen (1981) to be predictive of later hyperactivity to a low but significant degree (regression weights below .19). Greater health problems and delayed motor development have also been found by others to be associated with a higher risk for early and persistent ADHD symptoms (Hartsough & Lambert, 1985; Palfrey et al., 1985). The early emergence of excessive activity level, short durations of responding to objects, low persistence of pursuing objects with which to play, strong intensity of response, and demandingness in infancy are more often found in ADHD than in normal or other clinical control groups of children (Barkley, DuPaul, & McMurray, in press-a; Hartsough & Lambert, 1985). These factors also predict the persistance of these behavioral problems into the preschool years (Campbell, 1990; McInerny & Chamberlin, 1978; Palfrey et al., 1985).

During the preschool period (ages 2 to 5 years), it appears that the appearance of early and persistent problems with social interaction with peers, excessive activity, inattention, and emotional difficulties such as aggression or fearfulness and social withdrawal are associated with preschool ADHD (Palfrey et al., 1985; Prior, Leonard, & Wood, 1983). In particular, negative temperament appears to be an important risk factor. "Temperament" refers to early and relatively persistent personality characteristics of children, such as activity level; intensity or degree of energy in a response; persistence or attention span; demandingness of others; quality of mood (i.e., irritability or quickness to anger or other display of emotion); adaptability or capacity to adjust to change; and rhythmicity or the regularity of sleep/waking periods, eating, and elimination. These temperamental variables have been noted above in discussing infant predictors of ADHD and appear to be equally significant as predictors in these preschool years. These characteristics, especially overactivity, high intensity, inattention, negative mood, and low adaptability, are also predictive of a continuation of both ADHD symptoms and aggression or conduct problems by the time of entry into formal schooling (Buss, Block, & Block, 1980; Campbell, 1990; Earls & Jung, 1987; Fagot, 1984; Fischer, Rolf, Hasazi, & Cummings, 1984; Garrison, Earls, & Kindlon, 1984; Halverson & Waldrop, 1976; Palfrey et al., 1985). In addition, they are predictive of greater reading and academic achievement delays, and greater use of special educational services, by second grade (Palfrey et al., 1985). This same set of variables is further predictive of a significantly greater risk for psychiatric diagnosis, particularly for the DSM-III-R Disruptive Behavior Disorders, by adolescence (Lerner, Inui, Trupin, & Douglas, 1985). Certainly, children whose inattentive-hyperactive symptoms are sufficiently severe to warrant a diagnosis of ADHD in childhood are quite likely to continue to receive this diagnosis up to 5 to 8 years later (Barkley, Fischer, et al., in press-a; Beitchman, Wekerle, & Hood, 1987).

However, several studies also indicate that while early negative temperament may continue to predict ongoing negative temperament, it is a relatively weak predictor by itself of later clinically significant levels of psychological or behavioral problems in children (Cameron, 1978; Carey & McDevitt, 1978; Chamberlin, 1977). Greater power of prediction in these studies is achieved by combining these temperamental variables with knowledge of parental characteristics, especially psychiatric ones and those related to management of the child. Campbell (1990) found that the existence of a negative, critical, and commanding style of child management by mothers of children with preschool hyperactivity was also associated with the persistence of hyperactivity by ages 4, 6, and 9 years. Others (Cameron, 1977; Earls & Young, 1987) also found that prediction of behavioral problems in childhood was greatly enhanced by considering parent psychiatric distress, hostility, and marital discord in addition to preschool temperament. Thus, it appears that child temperament, while an important early risk factor, can be moderated or exacerbated by a particular caregiver environment, and that knowledge of the caregiver and home environment can enhance prediction of later behavioral problems such as ADHD.

Taken together, these findings suggest that it is possible to identify children at risk for developing an early and persistent pattern of ADHD symptoms prior to their entrance into kindergarten and perhaps even as early as 4 years of age. A combination of child and parental variables seems the most useful. The following factors would appear to be useful as potential predictors of the early emergence and persistence of ADHD in children: (1) family history of ADHD; (2) maternal smoking and alcohol consumption and poor maternal health during pregnancy; (3) single parenthood and low educational attainment; (4) poor infant health and developmental delays; (5) the early emergence of high activity level and demandingness in infancy; and (6) critical/directive maternal behavior in early childhood. Some studies have examined factors that may be protective against the development of ADHD or its persistence from early childhood to school age. These include (1) higher maternal education; (2) better infant health; (3) higher cognitive ability and perhaps language skills, particularly in the child; and (4) greater family stability (see Campbell, 1987, 1990; Palfrey et al., 1985; Weithorn & Kagen, 1978).

PRESCHOOL ADHD CHILDREN

Many studies indicate that preschool-age children are likely to be rated as inattentive and overactive by their parents. In their follow-up study of children from birth to second grade, Palfrey et al. (1985) found that up to 40% of these children had sufficient problems with inattention by age 4 years to be of concern to their parents and teachers. Yet this and other studies (Campbell, 1990; Campbell & Ewing, in press) show that the vast majority of these concerns remit within 3 to 6 months. Even among those children whose problems may be severe enough to receive a clinical diagnosis of ADHD, only 48% will have this same diagnosis by later childhood or early adolescence. This suggests that significant inattention and overactivity by age 3 to 4 years, by themselves, are not indicative of a persistent pattern of ADHD into later childhood or adolescence in at least 50 to 90% percent of those children so characterized. Palfrey et al. (1985) noted that approximately 5% of their total sample of children, or about 10% of those with parent or teacher concerns about inattention, eventually developed a pattern of persistent inattention that was predictive of behavior problems, low academic achievement, and need for special educational services by second grade. Campbell's (1990) research also showed that among difficult-to-manage 3-year-olds, those whose problems still existed by age 4 years were much more likely to be considered clinically hyperactive, and to have difficulties with their hyperactivity as well as conduct problems, by ages 6 and 9 years. Therefore, both the degree of ADHD symptoms *and* their duration determine which children are likely to show a chronic course of their ADHD symptoms throughout later development. This research also suggests that the duration of 6 months for symptoms of ADHD recommended in the DSM-III-R is inadequate for preschool-age children. A duration of 12 months appears both more rigorous and more useful in making predictions about the stability of ADHD behavioral patterns in preschool-age children.

Children with this durable pattern of ADHD in this age group are described by their parents as restless, always up and on the go, acting as if driven by a motor, and frequently climbing on and getting into things. They are more likely to encounter accidental injuries as a result of their overactive, inattentive, impulsive, and often fearless pattern of behavior. "Childproofing" the home at this age becomes essential to reduce the risk of injury or poisoning, as well as to protect family valuables from the often vigorous and destructive pattern of play shown by many of these children. Persistent in their wants, demanding of parental attention, and often insatiable in their curiosity about their environment, ADHD preschoolers pose a definite challenge to the parenting skills of their mothers. Such children require far more frequent and closer monitoring of their ongoing conduct than do normal preschoolers; at times, they have to be tethered to allow parents to complete necessary household functions that require their undivided attention. Those ADHD children with excessive moodiness, quickness to anger, and low adaptability and rhythmicity, as described in the discussion of temperament above, are likely to prove the most distressing to their mothers. Noncompliance is common, and at least 30 to 60% are actively defiant or oppositional, especially if they are boys. While temper tantrums may be common occurrences even for normal preschoolers, their frequency and intensity are often exacerbated in ADHD children. Mothers of these children are likely to find themselves giving far more commands, directions, criticism, supervision, and punishment than do mothers of normal preschoolers (Barkley, 1988e; Battle & Lacey, 1972; Campbell, 1990; Cohen, Sullivan, Minde, Novak, & Helwig, 1981). Although the mothers of ADHD preschoolers are likely to report feeling competent in their sense of knowing how to manage children, this will progressively decline as these children grow older and parents find that the typical techniques used to manage normal children are less effective with ADHD children (Mash & Johnston, 1983c). The coexistence of additional difficulties, such as sleep problems, toilet training difficulties, and/or motor and speech delays, in a small percentage of ADHD children is likely to further tax the patience and competence of many of their parents. No wonder, then, that parents of preschool ADHD children report their lives to be much more stressful in their parental roles than that reported by mothers of normal preschoolers *or mothers of older ADHD children* (Mash & Johnston, 1982, 1983c).

Should such a child happen to have a mother whose own mental health is compromised by psychiatric problems, such as depression, anxiety, or hysteria, or whose marriage is in trouble, the combination of negative child temperament with a psychologically distressed caregiver could be potentially explosive and increase the risk of physical abuse to the child. This same situation may also arise where the father of this child is alcoholic, antisocial, or highly aggressive within the family. Research indicates that this combination of parent and child characteristics is a strong predictor of children's later developing significant aggressive behavior and Oppositional Defiant Disorder (ODD; see Chapter 5).

Placement of these children in day care, an increasingly common practice for preschool children in our society, is likely to bring additional distress as day care personnel begin to complain about the children's disruptive behavior, aggression toward others in many cases, and difficulties in being managed. Such children are often noted to be out of their seats, wandering the classroom inappropriately, disrupting the play activities of other children, excessively demanding during peer interactions, and especially vocally noisy and talkative (Campbell, Schleifer, & Weiss, 1978; Campbell, Schleifer, Weiss, & Perlman, 1977; Schleifer et al., 1975). It is not uncommon to find that the more active and aggressive among these ADHD children are actually "kicked out" of preschool; so begins the course of school adjustment problems that afflict many of these children throughout their compulsory educational careers. Other ADHD children, especially those who are not oppositional or aggressive, who are milder in their level of ADHD, or who are intellectually brighter, may have few or no difficulties with the demands of a typical day care or preschool program. This is especially so if it is only a half-day program a few days each week.

Difficulties in obtaining babysitters for their ADHD children, especially the more severely ADHD and oppositional among them, will be reported by mothers of children at this age during clinical interviews. This may result in a greater restriction of time available for both socializing with other adults and carrying out the typical and necessary errands within the community needed to care for a household. For single parents of ADHD children, these limitations may prove more frequent and distressing, as there is no other adult with whom to share the burden of raising such children.

THE ADHD CHILD IN MIDDLE CHILDHOOD

Once ADHD children enter school, a major social burden is placed upon them that will last at least the next 12 years of their lives, will be the major area of impact from their handicapping condition, and will create the greatest source of distress for many of them and their parents. The abilities to sit still, attend, listen, obey, inhibit impulsive behavior, cooperate, organize actions, and follow through on instructions, as well as to share, play well, and interact pleasantly with other children, are essential to negotiating a successful academic career beyond those cognitive and achievement skills needed to master the curriculum itself. It is not surprising that the vast majority of ADHD children will have been identified as deviant in their behavior by entry into formal schooling, particularly first grade. Parents will not only have to contend with the ongoing behavioral problems at home noted in the preceding section, but will now have the additional burden of helping their children adjust to the academic and social demands of school. Regrettably, these parents must also tolerate the complaints of many teachers who see the children's problems at school as stemming entirely from home problems or poor child-rearing abilities in the parents.

Often at this age, parents must confront decisions about whether to retain the children in kindergarten because of "immature" behavior and/or slow academic achievement. The fact that many schools now assign homework, even to first-graders, adds an additional demand on both the parents and the children to accomplish these tasks together. It is not surprising to see that homework time becomes another area in which conflict now arises in the family. For those 20 to 25% of ADHD children likely to have a reading disorder, these will soon be noted as the children try to master the early reading tasks at school. Such children are doubly handicapped in their academic performance by the combinations of these disabilities. Those who will develop math and writing disorders often have these problems go undetected until several years into elementary school. Even those without a comorbid learning disability (LD) will almost certainly be haunted by their highly erratic educational performance over time: Some days they perform at or near normal levels of ability and accomplish all assignments, while other days they fail quizzes and tests and do not complete assigned work. Disorganized desks, lockers, coat closet spaces, and even notebooks are highly characteristic of these children, forcing others to step in periodically and reorganize their materials to try to facilitate better academic performance.

At home, parents often complain that their ADHD children do not accept household chores and responsibilities as well as other children their age. Greater supervision of and assistance with these daily chores and self-help activities (such as dressing, bathing, etc.) are common and lead to the perception that these children are quite immature. While temper tantrums are likely to decline, as they do in normal children, ADHD children are still more likely to emit such behavior when frustrated than do normal children. Relations with siblings may be tense as the siblings grow tired of and exasperated at trying to understand and live with such disruptive forces as their ADHD brothers or sisters. Some siblings will develop resentment over the greater burden of work they often carry compared to their hyperactive siblings. Certainly, the greater time these ADHD children receive from their parents is often a source of jealousy on the part of their siblings, especially those who are younger than the ADHD children. At an age where other children are entering extra-curricular community and social activities, such as clubs, music lessons, sports, and Boy or Girl Scouts, ADHD children are likely to find themselves barely tolerated in these group activities or outright ejected from them in some cases. Parents frequently find that they must intervene in these activities on behalf of their children to explain and apologize for their behavior and transgressions to others, to try to aid the children in coping better with the social demand, or to defend their children against sanctions that may be applied for their unacceptable conduct.

An emerging pattern of social rejection will have appeared by now, if not earlier, in over half of all ADHD children because of the poor social skills described in Chapter 3. As Ross and Ross (1976) have aptly described, even when an ADHD child displays appropriate or prosocial behavior toward others, it may be at such a high rate or intensity that it elicits rejection by and avoidance of the child in subsequent situations, or even punitive responses from his or her peers. This can present a confusing picture to the ADHD child attempting to learn appropriate social skills. This high rate of behavior, vocal noisiness, and tendency to touch and manipulate objects more than is normal for age combine to make the ADHD child overwhelming, intrusive, and even aversive to others. By late childhood, and for obvious and varied reasons, it is common to find many ADHD children developing feelings of low self-esteem about their school and social abilities. Yet many will place the blame for these difficulties on their parents, teacher, or peers because of their limited self-awareness.

By later childhood and preadolescence, these patterns of academic, familial, and social conflicts will have been well established for many ADHD children. At least 30 to 50% are now likely to develop symptoms of CD and antisocial behavior between 7 and 10 years of age (Barkley, Fischer, et al., in press-a). The most common among these are lying, petty theivery, and resistance to the authority of others. At least 25% or more may have problems with fighting with other children. Bragging or boasting about fictitious accomplishments, cheating others at games or in schoolwork, and in some cases truancy from school may also be seen. ADHD children who have not developed some comorbid psychiatric (ODD or CD), academic (LD and under-achievement), or social disorder by this time will be in the minority. Those who remain purely ADHD are likely to have the best adolescent outcomes, experiencing problems primarily with academic performance and eventual educational attainment. For others, an increasing pattern of familial conflict and antisocial behavior in the community may begin to appear or worsen where it had already existed. Such conflicts often prove particularly recalcitrant to treatment. The majority of ADHD children (60 to 80%) by this time will have been placed on a trial of stimulant medication, and over half will have participated in some type of individual and family therapy (Barkley,

DuPaul, & McMurray, in press-a; Barkley, Fischer, et al., in press-a). Approximately 30 to 45% will also be receiving formal special educational assistance for their academic difficulties by the end of sixth grade.

ADOLESCENT OUTCOME OF ADHD CHILDREN

Despite a decline in their levels of hyperactivity and an improvement in their attention span and impulse control, 70 to 80% of ADHD children are likely to continue to display these symptoms into adolescence to an extent inappropriate for their age group. As Ross and Ross (1976) have indicated, the adolescent years of ADHD individuals may be some of the most difficult because of the increasing demands for independent, responsible conduct, as well as the emerging social and physical changes inherent in puberty. Issues of identity, peer group acceptance, heterosocial dating and courtship, and physical development and appearance erupt as a new source of demands and distress with which the ADHD adolescent must now cope. Sadness, depression in a minority of cases, poor self-confidence, diminished hopes of future success, and concerns about school completion may develop.

Follow-up studies published during the past 17 years have done much to dispel the notion that the disorder is typically outgrown by the adolescent years. These studies have consistently demonstrated that many children diagnosed as hyperactive in childhood continue to display their symptoms to a significant degree in adolescence and young adulthood (Brown & Borden, 1986; Thorley, 1984; Weiss & Hechtman, 1986). In general, these studies indicate that between 30 and 50% of these children continue to be impaired by their symptoms in adolescence or to meet DSM-III diagnostic criteria for Attention Deficit Disorder with Hyperactivity (Gittelman, Mannuzza, Shenker, & Bonagura, 1985; Lambert, Hartsough, Sassone, & Sandoval, 1987). As discussed below, my own research indicates this to be a substantial underestimate of the true prevalence of ADHD in hyperactive children followed to adolescence. As many as 25 to 35% of these adolescents display antisocial behavior or CD, and up to 58% have failed at least one grade in school (Brown & Borden, 1986). Other studies have clearly shown these children to be significantly behind matched control groups in academic performance at follow-up (Lambert et al., 1987; Weiss & Hechtman, 1986). Research has been less consistent in documenting whether hyperactive children are at greater risk for substance abuse than normal children upon reaching adolescence, with some finding a greater occurrence of both alcohol and drug abuse (Blouin, Bornstein, & Trites, 1978; Hoy, Weiss, Minde, & Cohen, 1978; Loney, Kramer, & Milich, 1981), while others find it only for drug use (Gittelman et al., 1985; Minde, Lewin, Weiss, Lavigueur, Douglas, & Sykes, 1971; Weiss & Hechtman, 1986). Most studies have followed groups of clinically diagnosed hyperactive children. Where epidemiologically derived samples have been used, rates of antisocial behavior, academic failure, and continuation of the symptoms of ADHD remain higher than in matched normal samples, but less than half those reported in the clinical samples (Lambert et al., 1987).

A significant limitation of many of these studies, particularly those initiated in the early 1970s, was the lack of consensus criteria for the diagnosis of hyperactivity. Many of these early studies relied exclusively on the referral of the child based on parental or teacher complaints of hyperactivity, and clinical diagnosis, as the primary inclusion criteria. None of these studies used standardized child behavior rating scales to establish a cutoff score for the degree of deviance of their subjects in ADHD symptoms. Considering that many normal children may have parent or teacher complaints of inattentiveness, hyperactivity, or impulsivity (Achenbach & Edelbrock, 1981), it is likely that previous studies have been overly inclusive, permitting many children with borderline or marginal ADHD characteristics to be included in their samples. This could result in the outcome of the hyperactive sample being considerably more positive and having much higher remission rates than would have been the case had more rigorous research selection criteria been employed, as is now customary in many studies. All of the studies cited above were begun, and many completed, prior to the publication of consensus diagnostic criteria for Attention Deficit Disorder in the DSM-III (American Psychiatric Association, 1980) or ADHD in the DSM-III-R (American Psychiatric Association, 1987), leading to tremendous variation across studies in their selection criteria.

A more detailed picture of the adolescent outcome of ADHD children has emerged in a recent outcome study (Barkley, Fischer, Edelbrock, & Smallish, in press-a, in press-b; Fischer, Barkley, Edelbrock, & Smallish, in press) of a large sample of ADHD and normal children followed prospectively 8 years after their initial evaluation. Unlike the samples in past studies, the clinic-referred children diagnosed as hyperactive in the present study fulfilled a set of rigorous research criteria designed to select a sample of children who were truly developmentally deviant in their symptoms relative to same-age normal children. These criteria are discussed in Chapter 6.

The initial sample comprised 158 hyperactive children and 81 normal children between 4 and 12 years of age. A total of 123 hyperactive children and 66 normal children were located and agreed to be interviewed and complete our questionnaires, either in person, or by telephone (interview) and mail (rating scales). This represents a total of 78% of the original sample for hyperactive children and 81% for the normal group. These recruitment rates compare favorably to the prospective follow-up studies by Lambert et al. (1987) and Gittelman et al. (1985), in which the average recruitment rate was between 72 and 85%, and are considerably higher than those in most of the earlier follow-up studies (see Brown & Borden, 1986, for a review). In the hyperactive group, 12 of the subjects (9.7%) were female and 111 were male, while in the normal group 4 of the subjects (6.1%) were female and 62 were male.

Comorbidity for Other Disruptive Behavior Disorders

We examined the rates of the occurrence of the Disruptive Behavior Disorder diagnoses in both groups of children. We also calculated the number of symptoms within each disorder that represented two standard deviations above the mean (97th percentile) for the normal adolescents. We did so because the DSM-III-R cutoff scores for these disorders were based on field trials of primarily elementary-age children, in whom one would expect a greater occurrence of the ADHD characteristics and a lesser degree of CD symptoms within the normal population at that age range. Since these symptoms are known to vary considerably with age, it is likely that the cutoff scores may be overinclusive for some age groups while being underinclusive for others.

We found that the vast majority of our hyperactive subjects (71.5%) met the current DSM-III-R criteria for ADHD, with a mean number of 9 symptoms versus only 1.5 in the control group. Furthermore, when the cutoff of two standard deviations above the normal mean is used to make the diagnosis for ADHD, the cutoff score must be adjusted downward to 6 rather than 8 of 14 symptoms. Using this norm-referenced cutoff score resulted in a larger percentage of the hyperactive group (83.3%) being eligible for a diagnosis of ADHD in adolescence. The mean age of onset for the subjects' ADHD symptoms was 3.7 years. Over 59% of the hyperactive group met DSM-III-R criteria for a diagnosis of ODD as compared to 11% of the control group, and this rate did not change appreciably when the cutoff score of two standard deviations from the normal mean was substituted as the diagnostic cutoff point (5 or more symptoms). Approximately 43% of the hyperactive group qualified for a diagnosis of CD using DSM-III-R criteria, as compared to only 1.6% of the control group. Again, readjusting the symptom cutoff score based on the two-standard-deviation mark for the normal control group results in a lowering of the cutoff score from 3 symptoms to 2; this led to a much larger percentage of the hyperactive group being diagnosed as having CD (60%). These results indicate that the cutoff scores chosen for the DSM-III-R are too high for the disorders of ADHD and CD when used to diagnose adolescents. The use of the recommended cutoff scores results in the exclusion of 12 to 17% of the hyperactive children who are truly statistically deviant from normal children (>97th percentile) in their number of symptoms for these conditions but who do not meet present DSM cut points. The mean age of onset for ODD was 6.7 and for CD was 6.0 years.

In Table 4.1, we report the relative rates of occurrence for each of the DSM-III-R symptoms within each of the three Disruptive Behavior Disorders. Among the ADHD symptoms, it seems that difficulties with attention and instruction following were the most problematic for this group at outcome. Among the ODD symptoms, arguing and irritable or touchy manner were the most frequent. As one might expect, the occurrence for each symptom of CD was considerably less than for these other two disorders; however, in all but four of these symptoms, the rate in the hyperactive group was still signif-

TABLE 4.1. Prevalence of Disruptive Behavior Disorder Symptoms at Outcome

Diagnosis/symptom	Hyperactives (%)	Normals (%)
Attention-deficit Hyperactivity Disorder		
Fidgets	73.2 *	10.6
Difficulty remaining seated	60.2 *	3.0
Easily distracted	82.1 *	15.2
Difficulty waiting turn	48.0 *	4.5
Blurts out answers	65.0 *	10.6
Difficulty following instructions	83.7 *	12.1
Difficulty sustaining attention	79.7 *	16.7
Shifts from one uncompleted task to another	77.2 *	16.7
Difficulty playing quietly	39.8	7.6
Talks excessively	43.9 *	6.1
Interrupts others	65.9 *	10.6
Doesn't seem to listen	80.5 *	15.2
Loses things needed for tasks	62.6 *	12.1
Engages in physically dangerous activities	37.4 *	3.0
Oppositional Defiant Disorder		
Argues with adults	72.4 *	21.1
Defies adult requests	55.3 *	9.1
Deliberately annoys others	51.2 *	13.6
Blames others for own mistakes	65.9 *	16.7
Acts touchy or easily annoyed by others	70.7 *	19.7
Angry or resentful	50.4 *	10.6
Spiteful or vindictive	21.1	0.0
Swears	40.7 *	6.1
Conduct Disorder		
Has stolen without confrontation	49.6 *	7.6
Has run away from home overnight at least twice	4.9	3.0
Lies	48.8 *	4.5
Has deliberately engaged in fire setting	27.6 *	0.0
Truant	21.1 *	3.0
Has broken into home, building, or car	9.8	1.5
Has deliberately destroyed others' property	21.1 *	4.5
Physically cruel to animals	15.4 *	0.0
Has forced someone into sexual activity	5.7	0.0
Has used a weapon in a fight	7.3	0.0
Initiates physical fights	13.8	0.0
Has stolen with confrontation	0.8	0.0
Physically cruel to people	14.6 *	0.0

Note. Adapted from "The Adolescent Outcome of Hyperactive Children Diagnosed by Research Criteria, I: An 8 Year Prospective Follow-up Study" by R. A. Barkley, M. Fischer, C. Edelbrock, and L. Smallish, in press, *Journal of the American Academy of Child and Adolescent Psychiatry.* Copyright 1990 by Williams & Wilkins. Reprinted by permission.
* $p < .01$ by chi-square

icantly greater than that seen in the normal adolescents. Only running away, sexual assault, and theft involving confronting a victim were not significantly different.

Auto Accidents

Prior research (Weiss & Hechtman, 1986) suggests that hyperactive adolescents have a higher incidence of automobile accidents than normal adolescents. In our sample, 17 of the 123 hyperactives (13.8%) had driver's licenses, with an equal percentage of normal children (9 of 66, or 13.6%) also having licenses. Among those teens with licenses, 46% of the hyperactives and 33% of the controls had experienced at least one auto accident. This difference between groups was not statistically significant. However, five of the hyperactives who did not have licenses had an auto accident while driving, while none of the controls had done so. Our failure to find a significantly greater number of auto accidents in our hyperactive group probably stems from the fact that many of our adolescents had not yet reached the age at which they could drive.

Substance Use and Abuse

Previous research has been equivocal concerning whether the rates of substance use and abuse among hyperactive adolescents differ from those among normal adolescents. In Table 4.2, we present the rates of occurrence for eight specific categories of substance use. It can be seen that cigarette and alcohol use were the only categories of substance use that significantly differentiated the hyperactive and normal teenagers, according to teens' self-reports. A previous follow-up study by Gittelman et al. (1985) found that the differences between hyperactive and normal teens in substance use at outcome were primarily accounted for by those hyperactive teens who had received a diagnosis of CD. We separated our subjects into those who were purely hyperactive and those who were both hyperactive and CD. The former had no greater use of cigarettes, alcohol, or marijuana than normal subjects. However, the mixed hyperactive-CD subjects used these substances at a rate of two to five times that of the pure hyperactives or normals.

Academic Outcome

The academic outcome of the hyperactive adolescents was considerably poorer than that of the normal adolescents, with at least three times as many hyperactive subjects having failed a grade (29.3 vs. 10%). Almost 10% of the hyperactive sample had quit school at this follow-up point, compared to none of the normal sample. The mean numbers of grade retentions (0.33 vs. 0.11), suspensions (3.69 vs. 0.35), and expulsions (0.14 vs. 0.02) were also significantly greater within the hyperactive than normal group. We also found that

TABLE 4.2. Illicit Substance Use at Outcome as Reported by Mothers and Adolescents for Hyperactive and Normal Groups, and for Hyperactive Subjects Subgrouped as to the Presence or Absence of Conduct Disorder (CD) as Diagnosed by DSM-III-R Criteria

Measure	Entire samples (%)		Hyperactives (%)	
	Hyperactives	Normals	w/CD	w/o CD
By mothers' report				
Cigarettes	48.8	30.3	65.2**	32.2
Alcohol	41.5	22.7	54.3	29.0
Marijuana	15.4	7.6	28.3**	4.8
Hashish	0.0	1.5	0.0	0.0
Cocaine	0.8	0.0	2.2	0.0
Stimulants	1.6	0.0	4.3	0.0
Sedatives	0.8	0.0	2.2	0.0
Tranquilizers	1.6	0.0	2.2	1.6
Heroin	0.0	0.0	0.0	0.0
Hallucinogens	0.0	0.0	0.0	0.0
By adolescents' report				
Cigarettes	48.0*	26.7	63.6**	35.7
Alcohol	40.0	21.7	57.7	33.9
Marijuana	17.0	5.0	27.3	8.9
Hashish	7.0	1.7	11.4	3.6
Cocaine	4.0	0.0	9.1	0.0
Stimulants	6.0	0.0	4.5	7.1
Sedatives	2.0	0.0	4.5	0.0
Tranquilizers	1.0	0.0	2.3	0.0
Heroin	0.0	0.0	0.0	0.0
Hallucinogens	2.0	1.7	4.5	0.0

Note. Adapted from "The Adolescent Outcome of Hyperactive Children Diagnosed by Research Criteria, I.: An 8 Year Prospective Follow-up Study" by R. A. Barkley, M. Fischer, C. Edelbrock, and L. Smallish, in press, *Journal of the American Academy of Child and Adolescent Psychiatry.* Copyright by Williams & Wilkins. Reprinted by permission.
* $p < .02$ by chi-square analysis.
** $p < .01$ by chi-square analysis.

the levels of academic achievement on standard tests were significantly below normal on tests of math, reading, and spelling, falling toward the lower end of the normal range (standard scores between 90 and 95).

We again examined whether the presence of CD at follow-up within the hyperactive group accounted for these greater-than-normal rates of academic failure. The results indicated that while hyperactivity alone increased the risk of suspension (30.6% of pure hyperactives vs. 15.2% of controls) and dropping out of school (4.8% of pure hyperactives vs. 0% of controls), the additional diagnosis of CD greatly increased these risks (67.4% were suspended and 13% dropped out). Moreover, the presence of CD accounted almost entirely for the increased risk of expulsion within the hyperactive group, in that the pure hyperactive group did not differ from the normals in expulsion rate (1.6% vs 1.5%), whereas 21.7% of the mixed hyperactive-CD group had been expelled from school. In contrast, the increased risk of grade retention in the hyperactives was entirely accounted for by their hyperactivity, with no further risk occurring among the mixed hyperactive-CD group.

Treatment Received

The extent of various interventions received in the ensuing 8 years since initial evaluation and their durations for both groups are shown in Table 4.3. Not surprisingly, more ADHD children had received medication, individual therapy, group therapy, and special educational services than normal children. As for the duration of treatment among those receiving it, the hyperactive children had received substantial periods of stimulant medication treatment (mean of 36 months), individual and family therapy (means of 16 and 7 months, respectively), and special educational assistance for learning, behavioral, and speech disorders, (means of 65, 59, and 40 months, respectively) during the past 8 years. This pattern is very similar to that found by Lambert et al. (1987) in their follow-up of 58 hyperactives and controls.

Conclusions and Integration with Past Research

The results of this follow-up study are consistent with those of many other adolescent outcome studies in finding hyperactive children to be at substantially higher risk for negative outcomes in the domains of psychiatric, social, legal, academic, and family functioning than a control group of normal children followed concurrently (Brown & Borden, 1986; Thorley, 1984; Weiss & Hechtman, 1986). In contrast to other studies that followed hyperactives into adolescence, however, the present research found a substantially greater number of hyperactive children with negative outcomes in many of these domains of functioning than had been previously demonstrated. Our rates for continuing psychopathology were somewhat higher than the rates of 68% having ADHD at some time since age 13 years in the Gittelman et al. (1985) adult outcome study, and considerably higher than the 43% continuing to be hyperactive in the Lambert et al. (1987) study. Nevertheless, the rates are equal to those found in the Mendelson, Johnson, and Stewart (1971) retrospective study, in which between 71 and 84% of the subjects continued to manifest the symptoms of overactivity, inattention, and impulsivity. In any case, our findings make it clear that when rigorous criteria are used to diagnose children as hyperactive or ADHD (Barkley, 1981, 1982), they select a group of children whose symptom deviance remains highly stable over time (8 years), with the vast majority of them (over 80%) continuing to have this disorder into adolescence.

Yet the research of Weiss and Hechtman (1986) suggests that while present, these primary ADHD symptoms are not the major concerns of either

TABLE 4.3. Treatment History of the Hyperactive and Normal Groups at Outcome

Type of treatment	Hyperactives	Normals
Medication		
Methylphenidate (%)	80.5**	0.0
Duration (mos.)	36.1**	0.0
D-amphetamine (%)	3.3	0.0
Duration (mos.)	1.1	0.0
Pemoline (%)	19.5**	0.0
Duration (mos.)	2.6	0.0
Tranquilizers (%)	1.6	0.0
Duration (mos.)	0.1	0.0
Other psychotropic drugs (%)	14.6	3.0
Duration (mos.)	0.4	3.0
Individual psychotherapy (%)	63.4**	13.6
Duration (mos.)	16.3**	2.0
Group psychotherapy (%)	17.9*	4.5
Duration (mos.)	1.8	0.1
Family therapy (%)	49.6**	24.2
Duration (mos.)	7.2**	1.4
Inpatient psychiatric treatment (%)	9.8	1.5
Duration (mos.)	0.3	0.03
Residential psychiatric treatment (%)	8.9	0.0
Duration (mos.)	1.9	0.0
Foster care (%)	4.9	0.0
Duration (mos.)	1.7	0.0
Special educational services		
Learning disability classes (%)	32.5**	3.0
Duration (mos.)	65.5	48.0
Behavior disorder classes (%)	35.8*	6.1
Duration (mos.)	59.1	37.5
Speech therapy (%)	16.3**	1.5
Duration (mos.)	40.2**	6.0
Biological mother received therapy (%)	46.3	28.8
Biological father received therapy (%)	21.1	13.6
Biological mother and father received marital therapy (%)	30.9	19.7

Note. Adapted from "The Adolescent Outcome of Hyperactive Children Diagnosed by Research Criteria, I.: An 8 Year Prospective Follow-up Study" by R. A. Barkley, M. Fischer, C. Edelbrock, and L. Smallish, in press, *Journal of the American Academy of Child and Adolescent Psychiatry.* Copyright by Williams & Wilkins. Reprinted by permission.

* $p < .02$ by chi-square analysis.
** $p < .01$ by chi-square analysis.

parents or adolescents at outcome. Instead, poor schoolwork, social difficulties with peers, problems related to authority (especially at school), and low self-esteem are major concerns at this developmental stage. Our results discussed below lend considerable credence to these concerns. A review of the concerns of parents of children with ADHD, however, would probably indicate that the first three of these concerns are the primary reasons they also seek clinical services for their children. Social conflict within the family is likely to be listed as the fourth concern of these childhood years. This suggests to me that at any stage in the course of development, the concerns of parents of ADHD children will stem primarily from the impact of the children's deficits on their functioning in the school, in the family, and within the peer group, and not from the ADHD symptoms per se. Only later in development is one likely to see the impact of the ADHD symptoms on personal satisfaction and self-acceptance, and so problems such as low-self-esteem may then emerge as significant concerns of the adolescent or young adult with ADHD. Once again, it appears that where the ADHD symptoms are not disabling to the individuals themselves, they are of considerably less concern to the caregivers of ADHD children than where they are proving especially handicapping in meeting environmental expectations.

The rates of antisocial behavior and CD in our study were also higher than those seen in most follow-up studies. Most previous studies of adolescent outcome have found between 22 and 30% of their hyperactives engaging in antisocial acts (see Brown & Borden, 1986, for a review; Huessy, Metoyer, & Townsend, 1973; Mendelson et al., 1971; Zambelli, Stam, Maintinsky, & Loiselle, 1977). Gittelman et al. (1985) reported that 45% of their sample had met DSM-III criteria for CD at some time since age 13 years. Our results are similar to those of Gittelman et al. (1985) in finding that 43% of our hyperactives could be diagnosed as having CD according to the more recent DSM-III-R criteria. The most common antisocial acts were stealing, thefts outside the home, and fire setting. Mannuzza, Gittelman, Konig, and Giampino (in press) have recently shown that this subgroup of hyperactives is at substantial risk for later criminal activities in adulthood, and that it is this adolescent antisocial behavior and not ADHD that accounts for this risk of later criminality.

Like many other follow-up studies, ours found a significantly higher rate of academic performance problems in our hyperactives as compared to the control group. Our hyperactives were three times more likely to have failed a grade or been suspended, and over eight times more likely to have been expelled or dropped out of school, than the normal controls at adolescent outcome. Our rates for truancy were comparable to those (17%) reported in other follow-up studies (Mendelson et al., 1971). Even so, the level of grade repetition was only half that found in previous follow-up studies (56 to 70%; Ackerman, Dykman, & Peters, 1977; Mendelson et al., 1971; Minde et al., 1971; Stewart, Mendelson, & Johnson, 1973; Weiss, Minde, Werry, Douglas, & Nemeth, 1971).

I do not believe this indicates that our hyperactive subjects were performing better academically than those in other studies. As many or more of our adolescents had been suspended or expelled from school as in prior studies, and they were doing poorly on standardized achievement tests relative to normal children (Fischer et al., in press). Instead, I believe this may be due in part to the availability of federally mandated special educational services for children in our follow-up study; such services were not available before 1977, by which time most of the other follow-up studies into adolescence had been completed. At least a third of our hyperactive subjects had received some form of special educational assistance through either LD or behavior disorders programs. Although our children may have been doing as poorly academically as those in other studies, the recommendation that a child be retained in grade as the solution to this problem may be less frequently made, now that there is a greater array of special educational services to manage the problem.

Our findings for substance use are consistent with those of several previous follow-up studies. We found that a significantly greater number of hyperactives had smoked cigarettes or marijuana, whereas Hartsough and Lambert (1985) found only cigarette use to be greater in hyperactive than normal adolescents. Borland and Heckman (1976) also found more of their hyperactives to be smoking cigarettes than their brothers at follow-up. All of this certainly points to a higher-than-normal risk for cigarette use among hyperactives in adolescence. Blouin et al. (1978), in a retrospective study, found that 57% of hyperactives versus 20% of the controls had used alcohol at least once per month. Weiss and Hechtman (1986) also found somewhat more of their hyperactives, as teenagers, to have used nonmedical substances (particularly alcohol) than their control subjects. With the exception of the study by Hartsough and Lambert (1985), there is some consistency across studies in finding hyperactives to be at somewhat higher risk for alcohol use in adolescence than normal children.

Predictors of Adolescent Outcome

Several follow-up studies of hyperactive children have examined the degree to which certain childhood and family characteristics at study entry predict the adolescent outcomes of hyperactive children (Barkley, Fischer, et al., in press-b; Lambert et al., 1987; Paternite & Loney, 1980; Weiss & Hechtman, 1986). No single predictor, by itself, seems especially useful in prophesizing the outcome of ADHD children. The combination of several factors is important in such an exercise, with the following predictors appearing to be useful.

First, the SES of the family and general level of intelligence of the child are positively related to outcome, especially to academic outcome, eventual educational attainment, and level of employment. Family SES is also related to the severity of ADHD symptoms at outcome, with children from lower SES levels having significantly higher degrees of ADHD. Second, the degree to which children experience peer relationship problems predicts the degree to which they will experience interpersonal problems in adulthood. Third, the degree of aggressiveness and conduct problems in childhood predicts a poorer outcome in many different domains of adjustment, including poorer educational adjustment and attainment, poorer social relationships, and increased risk for substance abuse. As expected, childhood aggression is also related to adolescent delinquency and antisocial offenses. Fourth, the degree to which parental psychopathology is present in the families of ADHD children is associated with an increased risk of psychiatric and emotional problems in the ADHD children themselves by late adolescence. Fifth, the degree of conflict and hostility in the interactions of parents with their ADHD children is significantly associated with the degree to which these conflicts, as well as generally aggressive behavior, are present in adolescence. And sixth, the degree of ADHD in childhood is related only to the degree of academic attainment in adolescence.

To date, research has not found the type or extent of childhood intervention to have much impact on the adolescent or young adult outcome of ADHD children. However, the multimodal treatment study of Satterfield, Satterfield, and Cantwell (1980, 1981) suggests that a combination of medication, special education, parent counseling and training in child management, classroom consultation, and individual counseling of the children may, if maintained over several years into early adolescence, alter the prognosis for ADHD children. This seems particularly true for those with early aggression and hence a tendency toward later antisocial behavior.

ADULT OUTCOME

Only a few studies have followed samples of hyperactive children into adulthood. This research is nicely summarized in the excellent text by Weiss and Hechtman (1986). Where appropriate, the results from the more recent follow-up study of Gittelman et al. (1985) are noted.

Psychiatric Status

The results of research to date suggest that problems with behavior in general and ADHD symptoms specifically continue for 50 to 65% of these children as they achieve adulthood. Although many ADHD children are employed and self-supporting in adulthood, their general level of educational attainment and SES are below those of control children or even their own siblings. Antisocial behavior is likely to be troublesome for at least 20 to 45% of these children upon reaching adulthood, and as many as 25% will qualify for a diagnosis of adult Antisocial Personality—a pattern of repetitive antisocial behavior beginning in early adolescence.

These cases of antisocial conduct overlap considerably with the 12% who are likely to have a Substance Abuse Disorder (Gittelman et al., 1985). The most abused substances in Gittelman et al.'s sample appeared to be nonprescription drugs, rather than alcohol. Although ADHD subjects in early adulthood were no more likely at the follow-up assessment to be using or abusing drugs than controls, over the preceding 5-year period ADHD individuals were more likely to report episodes of alcohol or marijuana abuse or addiction than were control subjects. They were also more likely to have tried hallucinogens. At the 5-year follow-up, these differences between ADHD and control subjects were no longer significant, suggesting that what tendency toward greater substance use there is in ADHD young adults lessens with time. One problem with these statistics is that they are highly dependent upon the time and place where the follow-up study occurs. As a result, studies from large metropolitan areas are likely to find considerably greater drug use and criminality than those done with subjects in rural areas. Considering the increase in both drug use and crime between the 1960s and 1970s, studies begun in the early 1960s, as many of those reviewed by Weiss and Hechtman (1986) were, are likely to indicate less substance use or abuse than those begun in the 1970s or later. Thus, great caution is required in extrapolating these figures to current ADHD adults.

Only 11% of ADHD children as adults are free of any psychiatric diagnosis, function well, and have no significant symptoms of their disorder. However, only a third of normal control children are functioning this well in adulthood, and so this means of judging adult outcome must be considered "supernormality" (Weiss & Hechtman, 1986, p. 74). Approximately 79% of ADHD children, as adults, complain of difficulties with neurotic symptoms (such as anxiety, sadness, somatic complaints, or other internalizing features), and 75% report interpersonal problems—versus about 51 and 54%, respectively, of control subjects. The incidence of psychotic disorders in ADHD children at adulthood is no greater than that for the normal control group. Sexual adjustment problems have been described by as many as 20% of the ADHD group in adulthood, a figure eight times greater than that of the control group (i.e., 2.4%). The results of the Weiss and Hechtman (1986) study suggest that almost 10% will have attempted suicide within the past 3 years and about 5% will die from either suicide or accidental injury. Both percentages are considerably greater than those seen in control groups, where none of the subjects have experienced these events.

Academic Attainment

The trends toward lower academic achievement and ability, and more grade retentions, suspensions, and expulsions, that are evident in the adolescent years increase; by adulthood, the percentages of ADHD children having difficulties in these areas are even greater than those percentages noted in adolescence, and of course, greater than those of control subjects. Over 30% will drop out and never complete high school, as compared to fewer than 10% of control children. Approximately 5% will go on to complete a university degree program, as compared to over 41% of control children.

Antisocial Behavior

As adults, individuals with a prior history of ADHD have been found to have a greater likelihood of contacts with the police and courts, primarily for traffic offenses (18% vs. 5% for controls). However, problems with theft and non-prescription sale of drugs may occur in a significant minority of subjects. Approximately 20% of ADHD children have committed acts of physical aggression toward others in adulthood within the past 3 years, compared to 5% of control children. It is fair to say that the vast majority of ADHD individuals are not antisocial in adulthood, but that a small number (perhaps 25%) are and that they display a persistent pattern of such conduct over time.

Employment Functioning

Results from past studies suggest that, as adolescents, ADHD individuals are no different in their job functioning from normal adolescents. However, these findings need to be qualified by the fact that most jobs taken by adolescents are unskilled or only semiskilled and that they are usually part-time. As ADHD children enter adulthood and take on full-time jobs that require skilled labor, independence of supervision, acceptance of responsibility, and periodic training in new knowledge or skills, their deficits in attention, impulse control, and regulating activity level, as well as their poor organizational and self-control skills, could begin to handicap them on the job. The findings from the few outcome studies that have examined job functioning suggest that this may be the case. Although ADHD adults are likely to be employed full-time, are completely self-sufficient (financially independent of their families), and are upwardly mobile (increasing in economic status with time), the quality of their work adjustment differs significantly from that of normal control subjects in adulthood. ADHD adults are likely to have lower SES than their brothers or control subjects in these studies, and to move and change jobs more often; however, they also have more part-time jobs outside of their full-time employment. Employers have been found to rate ADHD adults as less adequate in fulfilling work demands, less likely to be working independently and to complete tasks, and less likely to be getting along well with supervisors. They also do more poorly at job interviews than do normal individuals. ADHD adults report that they are more likely to find certain tasks at work too difficult for them. Finally, ADHD adults are more likely to quit their jobs, as well as to be laid off from work, relative to control subjects. In general, ADHD adults appear to have a poorer work record and lower job status than normal adults.

Social Skills

Weiss and Hechtman (1986) are the only investigators to date to have studied the social skills of ADHD adults followed prospectively from childhood. Their findings indicate greater social skills and interaction problems for ADHD adults, particularly in the areas of heterosocial skills (male-female interactions) and assertion. It should not be surprising then to note that the greater self-esteem problems of ADHD children noted in adolescence continue, and may even worsen as they reach adulthood.

Physical Stature

A few studies of children with ADHD have suggested that they may be smaller and have a younger bone age than normal children of the same chronological age. Furthermore, because many ADHD children have taken stimulant medication and this has been believed to retard growth in some children, it is important to examine the physical outcome of ADHD children upon their reaching adulthood. Unfortunately, few studies have done so. Those that have did not find the eventual height and weight of ADHD children to be any different from those of control children, regardless of whether the ADHD subjects had taken stimulant medication (Weiss & Hechtman, 1986).

Predictors of Adult Outcome

Again, the study by Weiss and Hechtman (1986) is the only one yet to report on potential predictors of adult outcome in a prospectively followed group of ADHD children. Their results suggest that predictors of adolescent outcome are useful in predicting adult outcome as well. The emotional adjustment of ADHD adults was related to the emotional climate of their homes, particularly the mental health of family members, in childhood and to the emotional stability and intelligence of the ADHD subjects themselves. It is important to note here that emotional stability as measured in this study was highly related to childhood aggression, making these results consistent with those for predictors of adolescent outcome, where childhood aggression was highly related to many aspects of adolescent adjustment. Friendships in ADHD adults were also related to the early emotional climate of the home. Academic attainment (number of grades completed) was best predicted by a combination of factors, these being childhood intelligence, hyperactivity, child-rearing practices, SES of the parents, and the emotional climate of the home. The employment functioning of these ADHD adults was significantly related to their childhood intelligence estimates and their relationships with adults.

Earlier antisocial behavior was significantly associated with a greater number of firings from jobs, and, in combination with earlier hyperactivity and relationships with adults, was significantly associated with general work record as rated by current employers. The likelihood of committing criminal offenses in adulthood was most strongly associated with childhood emotional instability (aggression), and to a lesser degree with intelligence, hyperactivity, SES, mental health of family members, emotional climate in the home, and parental overprotectiveness in child rearing. Not surprisingly, these same factors were associated with the likelihood of later nonmedical drug use.

In general, no single childhood factor is likely to be of much use in predicting the adult adjustment of ADHD individuals. However, the combination of child cognitive ability (intelligence) and emotional stability (aggression, low frustration tolerance, greater emotionality) with family environment (mental health of family members, SES, emotional climate of home) and child-rearing practices provides for considerably more successful prediction of adult outcome. As Whalen and Henker (1980), among others (Paternite & Loney, 1980), noted a decade ago, both the current childhood adjustment and the long-term outcome of ADHD children result from the interplay of the child's characteristics with the social ecological context. Focusing on either of these to the exclusion of the other, as in family functioning on the one hand or degree of childhood ADHD on the other, is unlikely to prove useful in predicting the adult adjustment of ADHD individuals.

CONCLUSION

In this chapter, the developmental course and outcome of ADHD children is described, with particular attention paid to both the adolescent and young adult status of these children. A number of promising early predictors of risk for ADHD in early childhood have been noted; chief among these seem to be a family history of ADHD and the emergence of difficult temperament in the preschool years. High activity levels and demandingness in the child, when coupled with maternal psychological distress and family dysfunction, are highly related to the persistence of ADHD into later childhood and to the development of oppositional behaviors. Throughout their development, ADHD children are at greatest risk for academic problems in both their skill development and behavioral adjustment. Their second greatest risk is for antisocial conduct, which itself becomes a strong predictor of adolescent substance abuse and later adult criminality. As adults, they are likely to be underachieving in their occupational settings and having problems with working independently of supervision. A small but significant minority, perhaps 25%, become persistently antisocial in adulthood.

Although most ADHD children continue to have symptoms of their disorder well into adolescence and adulthood, the majority have adjusted to their symptoms and have made a satisfactory adult adjustment. In order to predict the outcome of these children, a combination of variables must be considered; chief among these are family SES and childhood intelligence, followed by childhood aggression and poor parental management of child behavior. Parent psychiatric disturbances along with family dysfunction are also related to outcome, particularly the development of ODD and later Antisocial Personality. The best outcome seems to be associated with milder ADHD symptoms and higher intelligence in childhood, coupled with well-adjusted parents and a stable family environment. Until very recently, the availability of various treatments for ADHD has had little significant impact on its course and outcome.

5

The Families of ADHD Children

> Happy are the families where the government of parents
> is the reign of affection, and obedience of the children the
> submission of love.
>
> —Francis Bacon (1561–1626)

Sometimes it is necessary to state the obvious. This is particularly so when it comes to the fact that children with Attention-Deficit Hyperactivity Disorder (ADHD) exist as an integral part of a multilevel social system. Traditionally, our theories, assessment, and treatment of these children often focus so heavily on their behavioral characteristics that we forget this important point. No one can fully appreciate the disorder—its causes, impairments, course, and outcome—without recourse to this social ecology and the dynamic interplay across its levels of action. The very diagnosis, in fact, hinges upon our understanding this point. The reports of others within this social network are what determine which children get referred, diagnosed, and treated. The prognosis of ADHD surely involves the social ecology as well. This is illustrated nicely in the discussion of the multivariate predictors of outcome of ADHD in Chapter 4. To understand who becomes ADHD, who stays ADHD over development, which ADHD children develop additional comorbid conditions, which will fare well despite these problems, and which will fare poorly in adulthood requires reference to a multivariate world. Hence, knowing that children have ADHD is of limited value in making any prognostications or prescriptions for them without first referring to the various contexts in which they interact, the people with whom they interact, and the contexts and people that in turn act upon them.

The important levels of analysis in this social ecology have been nicely discussed in the exceptional writings of Carol Whalen and Barbara Henker (1980) and their students and colleagues over the past decade. These levels are best conceptualized in my view as a series of concentric rings, beginning with the physical and neurological level at the center and proceeding outward to the neuropsychological, behavioral, immediate social-familial, and ultimately the socioeconomic levels of analysis. These are discussed in greater detail in Chapter 7 in describing my approach to the assessment of ADHD children. Suffice it to say here that one extremely important level of this analysis is the family environment in which these children find themselves. More specifically, the impact they produce upon their families, the effects their families have upon them, the manner in which their behavior is managed by parents, and the psychological integrity of those parents are absolutely crucial to understand in a thorough analysis of ADHD. It is the purpose of this chapter to discuss what is known about the family life of these children and to extract from it the clinically important details for the understanding and management of them.

No scientist is without prejudice in constructing a theoretical framework in which to understand nature, and I am certainly no exception to this observation. My view of these families is best conceptualized as a behavioral-systems approach—an approach well articulated in the writings of Eric Mash and Leif Terdal (1988). It is inherently empirical, based as much as possible on the results of scientific studies and observations of these families. It is not as cerebral, literary, or frankly glitzy as other models of family functioning, but it is surely practical. My understanding of these families is a combination of the theories of Richard Bell and Lawrence Harper (1977) on the reciprocal effects of children and parents on each other; Gerald Patterson (1982) on the functional relations occurring in these family exchanges; and Robert Wahler (1976) and Jean Dumas (1986) on the manner in which distal social and contextual variables produce effects on the proximal and immediate social exchanges between parents and children. These theories are interwoven throughout not only the present analysis but also the chapters on treatment that follow, especially those on parent training (Chapters 12 and 13) and treating family systems (Chapter 13).

The importance of appreciating the social-familial context in understanding ADHD children draws support from several lines of reasoning. First, the social interactions of these children with and reactions from their parents and siblings have been shown to be different from those in normal families; they are inherently more negative and stressful to all members. This creates an important source of consequences for the behavior of ADHD children, as well as models for vicarious learning of social conduct and its rules. Despite the view taken here that ADHD has a strong biological/hereditary predisposition to its development, not even the most ardent advocate of this view could deny the powerful effects these social consequences must produce on the expression of ADHD behaviors.

Second, evidence abounds that the parents and siblings of ADHD children are more likely to be experiencing their own psychological distress and psychiatric disorders than are those of normal children. These disturbances surely affect the management and rearing of ADHD children in unique ways that seem to have long-lasting effects for the adolescent and adult outcomes of these children.

And third, while many clinicians endorse a "family systems" view in their clinical practice, these views are notorious for being grounded solely in theories that are rarely subjected to scientific analysis or incorporated into practice. Holding such views, a number of clinicians ignore the overwhelming evidence of strong reciprocal effects in these family interactions; they focus primarily if not exclusively on the impact of parental behavior on the children, while missing the substantial effects produced by these children on their parents and family life in general. Many child clinicians, even those with family systems views, continue to scrutinize the parents of ADHD children for even the slightest flaw upon which to build their clinical case against these parents as being the root cause of the problems within these family systems. Such views are inherently one-sided and unfair, certainly untrue, and perhaps even damaging to the adjustment of these children if interventions are founded upon them.

I first examine some of the findings from the empirical literature on the family interactions of ADHD children, and next discuss the parental psychiatric disorders and psychological distress noted in families of ADHD children. I then present an overview of an integrated model for conceptualizing these findings that has proven of considerable use to me and others, both in research and in provision of clinical services to these families.

PARENT-CHILD INTERACTIONS

Over the past 15 years, a significant number of scientific studies have appeared on the manner in which ADHD children interact with their parents and the reactions of parents to them. I have also devoted much of my own scientific research to understanding these interaction patterns and their modification by various treatments. Space regrettably permits but a cursory overview here of the many details of these studies.

The Interactions of ADHD Children with Their Mothers

In the first studies to use direct observations of the behavior of mothers with their ADHD children, Campbell (1973, 1975) found that hyperactive boys initiated more interactions with their mothers during task completion. The children also spoke more frequently toward their mothers and requested more help with the task from them than normal children did with their mothers. The mothers of hyperactive children showed higher levels of involvement with their children, giving more suggestions, approval, and disapproval, as well as more directions concerning impulse control. The more complex and difficult the tasks assigned to the children became, the more obvious and significant these behavior patterns between hyperactive children and their mothers became.

In a series of studies, my colleagues and I have evaluated a variety of child characteristics for their effects on mother-child interactions in families with ADHD and normal children. In the first studies, we demonstrated that hyperactive children were less compliant, more negative, more off task, and less able to sustain compliance to maternal directives than were normal children; in turn, their mothers were more commanding and negative, and less responsive to positive or neutral communications from their children, than mothers of normal children (Cunningham & Barkley, 1979). These results are shown in Tables 5.1 and 5.2. We also found, as did Campbell, that hyperactive children talked more frequently during these exchanges (Barkley, Cunningham, & Karlsson, 1983).

Subsequently, we showed that these interaction conflicts were partly a function of the age of the ADHD children (Barkley, Karlsson, & Pollard, 1985; Barkley, Karlsson, Strzelecki, & Murphy, 1984), with younger children having far more mother-child conflicts than older children in both ADHD and normal families. It appears that with maturation and the corresponding improvement in ADHD symptoms, the degree of conflict seen in these inter-

TABLE 5.1. Behavioral Observations during the Free-Play Setting for 20 Hyperactive and 20 Normal Children

| | Free-play percentages | | | | |
| | Normal | | Hyperactive | | |
Behavioral measure	$\overline{X}$	SD	$\overline{X}$	SD	t
Interaction					
Mother initiates	54.3	13.1	37.4	16.3	−3.59**
Child responds	83.9	15.6	93.9	6.9	2.63*
Mother questions	15.4	7.9	16.5	8.6	0.42
Child answers	96.1	6.8	92.3	11.1	−1.32
Child initiates	67.7	18.4	61.0	15.2	−1.26
Mother responds	91.8	8.3	67.3	12.8	−7.21***
Child questions	7.7	4.6	6.4	6.3	0.72
Independent play					
Child plays independently	29.9	19.3	35.2	16.7	0.92
Mother encourages play	53.2	10.5	22.5	13.4	−5.60***
Mother controls/interrupts play	6.1	8.5	28.0	19.2	4.67***
Mother observes play	40.8	24.4	47.7	25.3	0.88
Control/compliance					
Mother commands	10.2	11.6	21.5	15.4	2.61*
Child complies	90.5	16.0	57.6	24.3	−5.05***
Compliance duration[a]	1.6	1.6	1.1	0.9	−1.14
Mother rewards compliance	16.0	31.6	9.5	24.1	−0.73

Note. From "The Interactions of Normal and Hyperactive Children with Their Mothers in Free Play and Structured Tasks" by C. E. Cunningham and R. A. Barkley, 1979, Child Development, 50, 217–224. Copyright 1979 by the Society for Research in Child Development. Reprinted by permission of the authors and publisher.
[a]Number of 15-second coding intervals.
*p<.05.
**p<.01.
***p<.001.

TABLE 5.2. Behavioral Observations during the Task Setting for 20 Hyperactive and 20 Normal Children

| | Task percentages | | | | |
| | Normal | | Hyperactive | | |
Behavioral measure	$\overline{X}$	SD	$\overline{X}$	SD	t
Control/compliance					
Mother commands	21.3	11.3	40.8	18.7	5.46**
Child complies	95.4	8.9	70.5	18.9	−5.33**
Compliance duration[a]	9.0	4.3	5.0	5.6	−2.55*
Mother rewards compliance	9.1	6.5	4.3	5.1	−2.60*
Mother attends to compliance	30.2	13.9	11.9	8.2	−5.04**
Contingent reward ratio	1.0	2.8	.7	28.3	−3.85**
Interaction					
Mother initiates	32.8	12.2	17.3	6.7	−4.96**
Child responds	92.2	18.4	92.3	16.4	0.02
Mother questions	6.2	3.1	7.2	5.9	0.71
Child answers	91.7	23.8	93.1	22.8	0.18
Child initiates	11.6	12.7	10.7	12.1	0.22
Mother responds	95.9	11.5	56.4	39.4	−4.31**
Child questions	2.4	3.1	2.8	2.0	0.55

Note. From "The Interactions of Normal and Hyperactive Children with Their Mothers in Free Play and Structured Tasks" by C. E. Cunningham and R. A. Barkley, 1979, *Child Development*, 50, 217–224. Copyright 1979 by the Society for Research in Child Development. Reprinted by permission of the authors and publisher.
[a]Number of 15-second coding intervals.
*p<.05.
**p<.001.

actions lessens significantly. These age-related declines in conflict are graphically depicted in Figure 5.1. This figure shows that as the children's ability to comply increased with age, the degree to which mothers issued commands declined. This applied to both hyperactive and normal children. However, even at the older age levels, more maternal commands and child negative or noncompliant behaviors were found in the ADHD families than in the normal families. Similar results were reported by Mash and Johnston (1982) in comparing younger and older hyperactive children. This pattern even appears to extend downward into the preschool age groups of ADHD children (Barkley, 1988e; Campbell, Breaux, Ewing, Szumowski, & Pierce, 1986; Cohen, Sullivan, Minde, Novak, & Keene, 1983) as well as upward into adolescence (Barkley, Fischer, Edelbrock, & Smallish, in press-b). It seems that despite improvements in ADHD behavior and parent-child conflicts with age, ADHD children continue to have more problems in their parent-child interactions than normal children well into adolescence.

As in the Campbell (1973, 1975) studies cited above, the setting for the interactions also appears to be important, with greater conflict occurring in task situations than in free play across all of our studies and appearing to

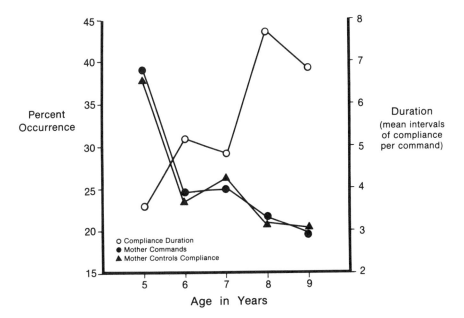

FIGURE 5.1. Duration of child compliance and percentage of mother commands and mother control of child compliance for five age levels of hyperactive and normal children (combined). This illustrates the decline in mothers' controlling behavior for both groups of children as a function of improvements in duration of compliance with increasing age of the children. Data are from "Effects of Age on the Mother–Child Interactions of Hyperactive Children" by R. Barkley, J. Karlsson, and S. Pollard, 1985, *Journal of Abnormal Child Psychology, 13,* 631–638.

increase as task difficulty for the child increases (for instance, compare Table 5.1 to Table 5.2). In contrast, the sex of the child has little effect on these interactions, with both ADHD boys and girls showing generally similar patterns of aversive mother-child interactions, while differing significantly from normal boys and girls (Barkley, 1989b; Befera & Barkley, 1985; Breen & Barkley, 1988). These patterns of conflict show up, although to a lesser degree, in comparing mother-child interactions of ADHD children with those of their normal siblings (Tarver-Behring, Barkley, & Karlsson, 1985). Other studies of ADHD children with their siblings have also documented significantly greater conflict in these interactions than that seen between normal children and their siblings (Mash & Johnston, 1983a). Again, interaction conflicts are more negative in younger than in older ADHD children.

How Does ADHD Affect Family Interactions?

What is it about ADHD children that seems to predispose their family interactions toward greater conflict? The answer cannot be asserted with certainty, but an obvious starting place is the ADHD symptoms themselves. The inattentive, impulsive, and overactive behavior patterns of ADHD children often conflict with the demands of parents to sustain performance on certain tasks. This automatically predisposes ADHD children toward greater non-compliance with instructions from others and greater difficulty in sustaining that compliance until the task is completed. Combine this with the behavioral disinhibition of these children—their tendency to gravitate off task to whatever else is more immediately reinforcing—and it seems highly probable that they will elicit greater direction, control, suggestion, encouragement, and ultimately anger from those responsible for seeing that the children's work gets done.

Since free play is likely to demand less sustained attention and allows ADHD children greater freedom to shift across activities with few significant consequences, their behavior will elicit far less control from adults during these situations. However, if this play involves cooperation with peers or siblings, adhering to rules of a game or social etiquette, inhibiting frustration when losing at the game, and waiting one's turn, conflicts will arise even in such modified free-play situations, as was found by Mash and Johnston (1983a) in the sibling interactions of ADHD children. In short, by virtue of their primary behavioral disabilities, ADHD children are assured of greater conflict with others, especially when task or setting demands exceed their behavioral capacities in the deficit areas.

But even where task demands are not excessive, the greater rates of behavior, activity, and vocalization emitted by ADHD children and their greater intrusiveness compared to normal children are likely in and of themselves to be perceived as aversive by others who must remain around them for extended periods of time. Such behavioral excess will probably trigger controlling responses from others in an effort to lessen the level of noise and disruption created by the ADHD child (Barkley, 1985b; Bell & Harper, 1977).

Teasing Out the Direction of Effects in Mother-Child Interactions

But if this research literature finds the parents of ADHD children to be more directive and negative with their children, how can we be sure that it is not the parents' method of handling the ADHD children that is causing the conflicts? Evidence that the direction of effects, or causal avenue, in these interactions is from ADHD child to parent rather than the reverse comes from several different sources. First, research on the interactions of ADHD children with other adults and children outside the family, such as teachers and peers, shows that they very quickly elicit similar negative, controlling, and generally directive behavior from others when they interact with them (Cunningham & Siegel, 1987; Whalen, Henker, & Dotemoto, 1980). Second, when ADHD children are placed on stimulant medication, the behavior of their mothers toward them changes significantly: The mothers' frequencies of commands, disapproval, and control diminish to levels similar to those of normal parents in many cases (Barkley & Cunningham, 1979a; Cunningham & Barkley, 1978; Barkley et al., 1984; Humphries, Kinsbourne, & Swanson, 1978).

This was nowhere more powerfully demonstrated to me than in a series of single-case experiments conducted with Charles Cunningham over a decade ago (Cunningham & Barkley, 1978), while we were both in training at the University of Oregon Health Sciences Center. In this study, we were fortunate to evaluate two hyperactive identical twins as part of a double-blind, placebo-controlled study of the effects of methylphenidate (Ritalin) on the mother-child interactions of these children. Each child was studied off medication, then on medication, and then on placebo during separate phases of the study. Formal, systematic observations of the mother-child interactions of these boys were recorded separately for each mother-twin dyad. The results are shown in Figure 5.2.

It is readily apparent that during the phases when medication was administered to these children, child compliance with mother's directives was considerably improved, and this resulted in a decline in the number of commands issued by the mother. The mother's encouragement of play also increased with medication, while her intrusiveness or control over the children's play declined. She proved more responsive to the children's interactions when they were on medication and more rewarding or approving of their compliance during these phases compared to the placebo phases. The results offer a striking testimonial to the effects medication can have on some ADHD children, as well as to the tight reciprocal feedback system that exists between mother and child behaviors. As the behavioral characteristics of one member of the dyad are altered (with medication, in this instance), the behavior of the other member is immediately altered as well in clear response to these changes in the first.

Similar changes with medication have also been demonstrated in the behavior of peers and teachers toward ADHD children (Cunningham, Siegel, & Offord, 1985; Whalen et al., 1980). If the parents of ADHD children were really the major cause of the conflict, medicating their children should produce few effects on the parents' behavior or few declines in the conflicts; this is hardly the case. This does not rule out the possibility that how parents, and others, choose to react to and manage ADHD children may not itself exacerbate these conflicts. It only shows that they do not appear to be the primary cause of them.

These parent-child or child-sibling interactions may escalate into even greater conflicts and aggression in some families. The reasons for this are discussed later in this chapter. Certainly, combining a taxing child with a parent who is already in psychological distress or has personal psychiatric symptoms—parental problems more likely to be seen in parents of ADHD children—can readily worsen the situation, as described further below. In like fashion, the greater prevalence of ADHD and conduct problems in siblings of ADHD

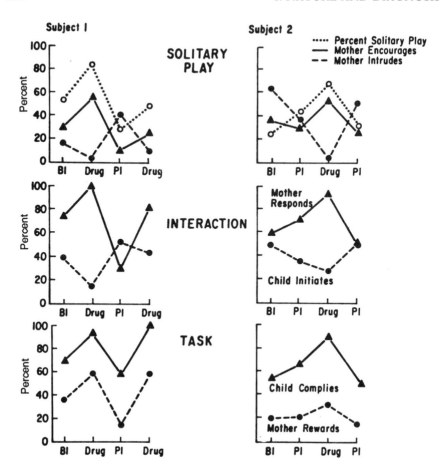

FIGURE 5.2. Selected behavioral measures for Subjects 1 and 2 on baseline (B1), drug, and placebo (P1) sessions. Solitary play and interaction measures were derived from the free-play periods. Task measures were calculated from the structured task situations. From "The Effects of Ritalin on the Mother-Child Interactions of Hyperkinetic Twin Boys" by C. E. Cunningham and R. A. Barkley, 1978, *Developmental Medicine and Child Neurology, 20,* 634–642. Copyright 1978 by Spastics International Medical Publications. Reprinted by permission.

children can further exacerbate the child-sibling conflicts noted in past research, placing even greater stress on the parents' efforts to manage their children.

A Possible Hierarchy of Parental Reactions to Child Misconduct

Although there is little research on the issue, I have noted clinically that parents may move through a hierarchy of efforts to control their ADHD children's disruptive behavior as attempts to use normal management techniques fail or have only partial success. The evidence here is purely anecdotal, but it suggests that parents initially seem to try to ignore or withhold attention from their children when these disinhibiting behaviors are shown. Perhaps they do this for the same reason parents of normal children do—in the belief that some of these behaviors are merely attention-getting in their function, and so ignoring them should diminish their occurrence. But the ADHD child's behavior is not merely the result of bids for attention, and so these techniques are unlikely to succeed. As the disruptive behavior of these children continues little abated or even intensified, parents are likely to begin to issue frequent commands and directives, especially those aimed at impulse control in the children. These commands are often restrictive in that they call for a reduction in what the children are doing. Parents will find themselves having to repeat these commands frequently, as the initial directives produce little change in the behavior of the ADHD children.

At some point, parental frustration and exasperation may result in the parents' issuing threats with these repeated directives, in an effort to motivate the ADHD children to listen and obey. Where this approach fails, as it often does, parents may then move to the use of physical disciplining or other forms of punishment (loss of privileges or time out) to exert control over the children's unruly behavior. However, at this juncture, some parents may simply acquiesce to the children's recalcitrant behavior if the initial command involved task performance rather than behavioral inhibition. They acquiesce, in that they may accomplish the command themselves if it involves performing some chore or task, or simply leave the requested task undone. If the children have begun to comply but the quality of compliance is poor, parents may assist the children in doing the chore. Over time, parents may not start at the beginning of this hierarchy when controlling their ADHD children, but may proceed straight to the level of management that has produced some partial success. This could readily lead to a parent's immediately invoking intense negative reactions toward a child or even using harsh physical discipline for the initial displays of even minimal disruptive behavior. Other parents will continue their pattern of acquiescence, always helping the children perform whatever tasks the children have difficulty completing or are initially resistant to performing. Still other parents will stop issuing as many commands for performing chores, having found it easier simply to do the work themselves rather than enter into conflict with the children.

Again, there is only anecdotal evidence to support this assertion, but I have clinically witnessed some parents who appear to have reached such a severe state of failure in their children's management that they could best be described as being in a state of parenting "learned helplessness." In this condition, parents make no or minimal efforts to give or enforce commands to their children, leaving them in essence to do as they please. This seems to be a final state for parents—the culmination of a long history of difficult interactions with their children, in which few if any tactics have proven effective. Along the way, I have noticed such parents becoming progressively disengaged from their ADHD children, monitoring their behavior less and less and confronting transgressions far less often. Ultimately, they exert little if any supervision over their children. The learned helplessness seen in these extreme cases is to be viewed as a result of the parents' inability to effect change in the children's behavior in spite of all previous efforts to cope. It is not uncommon at this point to find mothers reporting greater feelings of depression, low self-esteem in their role as parents, and little satisfaction with or involvement in their caretaker responsibilities. In parents who are already disposed toward depression by other factors, the development of parenting learned helplessness may proceed rather rapidly toward this state of disengagement. In some cases, such parents may vacillate between complete disengagement from and severe overreaction to their children's transgressions, depending upon their state of depressed mood and irritability at the time.

The Interactions of ADHD Children with Their Fathers

The next issue explored in research in our laboratory was the effect of certain parental characteristics on the parent–child interactions of ADHD children. We evaluated differences in interaction patterns between mothers and fathers of ADHD children, as compared to those of mothers and fathers of normal children (Tallmadge & Barkley, 1983). Again, significant differences were noted between parent–child interactions involving ADHD children and those involving normal children, but few differences occurred as a function of sex of the parent, and no interaction between the parents' sex and the subject groups (normals vs. hyperactives) was found. Within the ADHD group, children were noted to be less negative and off task with their fathers than with their mothers. Unlike parents in the normal group, mothers and fathers of ADHD boys increased their commands and negative behavior as task demands moved from free play to work accomplishment; this was associated with increased negative and off-task behaviors by their children.

The reasons why fathers should have fewer difficulties with their ADHD children than mothers have not been completely established, but there are several likely explanations. One probably has to do with the amount of time each parent spends interacting with the ADHD child, especially in regard to work or chore performance. Mothers remain the primary caretakers of children in our society, even if they work outside the home. The parent who taxes the behavioral deficits of the ADHD child more often is clearly going to be the one who will have more conflicts with that child. Another reason is that mothers appear to rely somewhat more on reasoning and use of affection in gaining children's compliance with instructions, while fathers may reason less, repeat their commands less, and institute punishment for noncompliance more quickly. When these sex differences in normal parent management of children occur with an ADHD child who has major difficulties with rule-governed behavior, that parent relying more on reasoning and rules is likely to face more problems with compliance to commands. One also cannot rule out the fact that the greater physical size and strength of the father may be sufficiently intimidating to the ADHD child, such that he elicits greater compliance to his requests.

It is not uncommon to see problems in the marital relationship develop out of these discrepancies in child behavior toward each parent. I have encountered fathers who either do not believe that their children have any problems or refuse to admit that the problems are actually as serious as the mothers report them to be. In some cases, the fathers may believe that their wives are overly sensitive to what they themselves label as merely normal childhood exuberance in boys. In others, the fathers believe that their wives are simply too permissive and unwilling to discipline the children. This can sometimes lead to the insistence by the fathers that their wives, not their children, are in need of professional assistance. A similar scenario is sometimes seen in the pediatrician's office. Here the male physician has no difficulty managing the ADHD child about whom the mother may so bitterly complain, resulting in the mother being labeled as hysterical and incompetent in her management of the child. It is time for fathers and male professionals to realize that children, especially ADHD children, do show differences in the actual manner in which they respond to their mothers compared to their fathers. This does not necessarily implicate flaws in the mother's caretaking abilities or an excessive sensitivity to normal child behavior. Insisting that a father undertake a family experiment and assume greater responsibility for the day-to-day custodial responsibilities of the ADHD child for a while can often make this point more clearly than any degree of reasoning by the clinician.

The Interactions of ADHD Adolescents with Their Mothers

Much of the research on parent-child interactions to date has focused upon ADHD children between 3 and 11 years of age. Recently, however, some studies have begun to examine these interaction patterns in adolescents with ADHD. In my own lab, we have followed a large sample of ADHD children and matched normal children into their middle to late adolescent years, and evaluated mother-adolescent interactions during a neutral discussion period and a conflict discussion period. We also had both mothers and teens rate the types and degree of conflict they experienced in their homes with each other (Barkley, Fischer, et al., in press-b). Although we examined differences between our hyperactive and normal groups on these measures, we also subdivided the hyperactive subjects into those adolescents who did not meet criteria for ADHD at outcome, those who had only ADHD at outcome, and those who also had ADHD with Oppositional Defiant Disorder (ODD). We did so because past research suggests that much of the conflict in parent-child interactions of ADHD children is primarily due to that subgroup who are aggressive, or have ODD (Tallmadge, Paternite, & Gordon, 1989).

Ratings of Home Conflicts

When we inspected those rating scales assessing communication problems and conflicts in the mother-adolescent interactions, they revealed several surprising results. Although the mothers reported more negative communication and interactions with their hyperactive adolescents than the control mothers, the hyperactive adolescents did not rate their communications with their mothers or fathers (where present) as more negative than those of the normal control teenagers. Similarly, on the Issues Checklist (see Chapter 9), mothers of hyperactive adolescents rated themselves as having more conflicts (or issues involving anger), as well as more intense and angry discussions about these issues with their adolescents, than did mothers of the control teenagers. In contrast, the hyperactive adolescents did not rate themselves as having any more conflicts or more angry discussions with their mothers than did the normal control adolescents. To summarize, although mothers of hyperactives perceived their interactions with their teenagers as being more negative and angry and involving more issues of conflict than mothers of normals, the hyperactives did not rate these same interactions as more negative or conflict-ridden than did normal teens.

This could be due to the hyperactive teens' possibly having less self-awareness than normal teens as to how their behavior affects others. But I believe that other findings intimate that the hyperactive adolescents were probably underreporting the degree of disagreements at home. The hyperactive teens were observed to use more negative behaviors than the normals during neutral discussions with their mothers and to talk less with their mothers during the conflict discussions. They were also found to have significantly more retentions, suspensions, and expulsions at school; to be reported by teachers to have greater behavior problems at school; to have been involved in more illicit substance use; and to have been involved in more antisocial behavior in their communities by their own report than the normal children (Barkley, Fischer, Edelbrock, & Smallish, in press-a). All of these difficulties would be grounds for more parent-adolescent disputes in families of the hyperactives than in families of the normal teenagers. Even so, it is still possible that some degree of exaggeration may exist in these maternal reports of conflicts, given the findings (noted below) that mothers' reports of conflicts at outcome were most closely associated with their reports of their own psychological distress on the Symptom Checklist 90, Revised (SCL-90-R) and their use of more commands and insults during conflict discussions, rather than with any teen behaviors. Similarly, the teens' reports of conflicts at outcome were associated with maternal negative behavior during interactions and maternal psychological distress. It is therefore likely that while hyperactive teens remain deviant from normal in their conduct, they underreport the degree of conflicts they have with parents at home. Their mothers, particularly if they are more psychologically distressed, may in turn overreport these conflicts.

When the subgroups of hyperactive adolescents were examined on these ratings of interaction conflicts, they revealed the same pattern, except that those in the ADHD-ODD subgroup were rated by their mothers as having significantly more conflicts with them than adolescents in the other three groups. In this case, however, the subgroup having no ADHD or ODD was not found to be different from normals, while the two ADHD subgroups did differ from normals on these same measures. A linear effect seemed evident on the measures as a function of number of psychiatric disorders at outcome: The more psychiatric disorders an adolescent had, the greater were the conflicts at home.

Observations of Mother-Teen Interactions

The results from our observations of these mothers and adolescents, using the Parent-Adolescent Interaction Coding System (PAICS; see Chapter 10) behavior categories for both the neutral and conflict discussions, are shown in Table 5.3. This table shows the percentage of occurrence of each of the six behavior categories in each discussion for mothers and teens. Our results indicated that the mothers of these two groups of subjects did not differ in their behavior toward their adolescents during the neutral discussion. However, the hyperactive adolescents were found to use more commands/put-downs toward their mothers and to talk less with their mothers during this

TABLE 5.3. Adjusted Means for the Behavioral Observation Categories for Mothers and Adolescents in Both Neutral and Conflict Discussions for Hyperactive and Normal Subjects

| | | | | Hyperactive subgroups | | | |
Measure	Normals	Hyper-actives	$p<$	No ADHD, no ODD	ADHD, no ODD	ADHD-ODD	Cont.
			Neutral discussion				
Mother categories							
Commands/puts down	1.75	8.21	NS	10.50	3.08	10.11	4>1,3; 1<2,4
Defends/complains	0.74	1.29	NS	1.57	0.61	1.56	NS
Problem-solves	21.96	19.87	NS	23.53	17.97	18.62	4<2
Facilitates	32.72	31.56	NS	24.68	35.53	31.05	NS
Defines/evaluates	10.41	10.16	NS	12.16	10.09	9.74	NS
Talks	32.42	28.90	NS	27.56	32.72	28.90	NS
Adolescent categories							
Commands/puts down	1.07	4.63	.01	2.32	2.57	6.21	4>1,2,3; 1<4
Defends/complains	5.60	8.66	NS	10.70	4.95	10.22	NS
Problem-solves	21.24	23.60	NS	24.00	25.39	21.98	NS
Facilitates	23.27	21.62	NS	22.06	20.40	20.81	NS
Defines/evaluates	11.18	9.37	NS	8.87	9.66	9.44	NS
Talks	37.65	32.11	.05	32.05	37.05	31.36	NS
							(con't)

TABLE 5.3. (*cont.*)

Measure	Normals	Hyper-actives	$p<$	No ADHD, no ODD	ADHD, no ODD	ADHD-ODD	Cont.
				Hyperactive subgroups			
			Conflict discussion				
Mother categories							
Commands/puts down	13.54	22.90	.01	24.57	15.88	27.31	4>1,3; 1<2,4
Defends/complains	4.27	6.73	.05	9.15	5.23	7.13	4>1; 1<2,4
Problem-solves	10.45	9.45	NS	10.86	10.04	11.65	NS
Facilitates	34.40	31.08	NS	24.41	34.55	30.41	NS
Defines/evaluates	10.69	8.75	NS	8.68	10.05	7.69	NS
Talks	26.64	21.09	.01	23.16	22.62	19.24	4<1; 1>4
Adolescent categories							
Commands/puts down	7.47	10.43	NS	9.02	6.76	12.00	NS
Defends/complains	27.97	32.85	NS	36.07	31.77	35.49	NS
Problem solves	7.07	8.47	NS	6.38	11.42	7.58	NS
Facilitates	14.89	16.30	NS	15.68	16.88	15.07	NS
Defines/evaluates	10.56	7.50	.05	6.15	7.75	8.13	NS
Talks	32.04	24.46	.01	26.73	25.42	21.75	4<1; 1>3,4

Note. Column headings under the hyperactive subgroups are as follows: No ADHD, no ODD ($n=17$) for subjects who had neither ADHD or ODD at outcome; ADHD, no ODD ($n=24$) for subjects who had ADHD but not ODD; and ADHD-ODD ($n=47$) for subjects who had both ADHD and ODD. One-way multivariate analysis of covariance (MANCOVA) results for comparison of the normal and hyperactive subjects on each measure were as follows: neutral discussion mother categories, $F=1.65$, not significant; neutral discussion adolescent categories, $F=2.61$, $p<.05$; conflict discussion mother categories, $F=2.29$, $p<.05$; conflict discussion adolescent categories, $F=2.62$, $p<.05$. One-way analyses of covariance (ANCOVAs) were used with the measures on which a significant multivariate F was obtained. In both MANCOVAs and ANCOVAs, the covariates of child's age, child's IQ, and mother's education were used. The "$p<$" column gives significance levels for the univariate comparisons on each measure where a significant multivariate F was obtained. MANCOVAs were then used to compare the three subgroups of hyperactive subjects on each measure. Where results were significant, ANCOVAs were conducted on each measure. Subsequently, pairwise contrasts were used for only those contrasts of interest, which were the ADHD-ODD group against the other three groups and the normal group against the three hyperactive subgroups. The results of these contrasts are shown in the column marked "Cont." In this column, 1 = normals; 2 = no ADHD, no ODD; 3 = ADHD, no ODD; and 4 = ADHD-ODD. An NS indicates that the ANCOVA or MANCOVA was not statistically significant for this measure, and so pairwise contrasts were not performed. From "The Adolescent Outcome of Hyperactive Children Diagnosed by Research Criteria: III. Mother-Child Interactions, Family Conflicts and Maternal Psychopathology," by R. A. Barkley, M. Fischer, C. S. Edelbrock, and L. Smallish, in press, *Journal of Child Psychology and Psychiatry.* Copyright by Pergamon Press. Reprinted by permission.

discussion than did the normal adolescents. In contrast, during the conflict discussion, both the mothers and the adolescents in the hyperactive group differed significantly from the normal subjects in their interactions. The mothers of the hyperactives used more commands and putdowns, were more defensive and complaining, and did less general talking with their teens than did the mothers in the normal group.

Again, the three hyperactive subgroups were compared with one another and the control group. We found that mothers of the combined ADHD-ODD group gave more commands than either the controls or the ADHD-only subgroup. The mothers of the combined ADHD-ODD subgroup also used less problem-solving behavior than those in the no-ADHD, no-ODD subgroup, but not compared to mothers of the normals or the pure-ADHD subgroup; this finding is difficult to interpret. The finding noted above—that hyperactive adolescents gave more commands/putdowns to their mothers in this neutral discussion—appeared to be entirely due to the combined ADHD-ODD subgroup. None of the other hyperactive subgroups were found to differ from normals on this measure, but they were significantly less likely to use this behavior than the combined ADHD-ODD subgroup.

During the conflict discussion, mothers of the combined ADHD-ODD subgroup once again used more commands/putdowns and defending/complaining with their adolescents than mothers of the ADHD-only and control groups, who were not found to differ from each other on these measures. Also, only mothers in the combined ADHD-ODD group were found to do less general talking with their teens than mothers in the normal group. Similarly, adolescents in the combined ADHD-ODD group engaged in less general talk than normals, but in this instance the ADHD-only subgroup also displayed less of this behavior. In general, the results suggest again that where differences between hyperactive and normal subjects are found in mother-adolescent interactions, they are due in most cases to the combined ADHD-ODD group. This suggests that the presence of ODD greatly increases the occurrence of parent-adolescent conflict.

Our findings were also recently replicated in a study by Robin, Kraus, Koepke, and Robin (1987). These investigators found significant deficits in the communication and problem-solving skills of ADHD families, compared to those families with normal or nondistressed adolescents. Families with ADHD adolescents experienced greater anger during their conflicts, more disengagement from each other, and repeated disputes over school issues and issues pertaining to siblings than nondistressed families who did not have ADHD teens. Parents in ADHD families were more likely to adhere to rigid beliefs about their teens' bids for autonomy and to attribute misbehavior in their teens to malicious intention. For their part, the ADHD teens were more likely to see their parents' rules as unfair and unduly restrictive.

Relationship of Mother-Child Interactions to Mother-Teen Interactions 8 Years Later

Since we had observations on our adolescents and their mothers that had been taken 8 years earlier, we chose to correlate the observations we had taken of these families in childhood with those observations at adolescent outcome (Barkley, Fischer, et al., in press-b). We were quite surprised to discover significant relationships between child interactions observed 8 years earlier during free play and task performance, and interactions of these same dyads at adolescent follow-up during the neutral and conflict discussion periods. Given that the observations at both time points were quite brief (15 minutes or less) and different coding systems were employed, it was unexpected to find that many of the behavioral categories from childhood correlated significantly with similar categories used at adolescence.

The extent to which mothers interacted with and were responsive to their children during free play 8 years earlier was significantly and positively related to their degree of talk and facilitation with their adolescents, and negatively related to their adolescents' use of defensiveness and complaining, during the neutral discussion period at follow-up. Moreover, the greater the mothers' facilitation of play in childhood was, the more they were facilitative of their adolescents' problem-solving discussions and the more talkative they were with their teens at adolescent outcome. Mothers' commanding and negative behavior in free play with their children was, in like fashion, related to their level of commands as well as to their teens' defensiveness and complaints at follow-up. Hence, both maternal positive and negative or controlling behaviors during free or unstructured exchanges with their children are unusually stable over this developmental span and are related to adolescent positive and negative behaviors, respectively, at outcome. Child behavior in free play, in contrast, was generally not related to later adolescent behavior at outcome in the neutral discussion.

A somewhat different picture emerged for the stability of mother and child behaviors from the childhood task period to the conflict discussion at adolescent outcome. Again, we found that positive maternal behaviors, such as interaction and praise, were related to positive maternal behaviors at adolescence, such as talking and facilitating, respectively. These positive behaviors of mothers at study entry were also negatively related to both negative maternal behaviors and adolescent negative behaviors during conflict discussion at follow-up. Mothers' use of commands, however, was no longer associated with degree of directiveness at outcome, as it was in the relationships between free play and the neutral discussion noted above. Child noncompliance, on the other hand, was now found to have some significant association with both adolescent and mother behavior at outcome. This was particularly true for off-task behavior by the children during task performance; this predicted greater maternal directiveness, less maternal talking, and greater adolescent directiveness and insults during conflict discussion at outcome.

In summary, the interactional problems of mothers and children during task performance in childhood are significantly stable over development and related to their interactional conflicts during conflict discussions at adolescence. Noncompliant children continue to be more difficult with their parents and to elicit more negative parental behavior in adolescence. Less rewarding and facilitating mothers of young children are likely to remain so into adolescence and are more likely to elicit more negative adolescent behaviors. The reciprocal, bidirectional nature of these conflictual interactions over time is well supported by these findings.

PARENTAL PSYCHIATRIC PROBLEMS

A number of studies have examined parents of ADHD children to determine whether they show any greater signs of psychological distress, or even a greater risk of psychiatric disturbance, than is seen in parents of normal children. In view of the evidence discussed in Chapter 3 concerning the hereditary predisposition to the disorder, such a higher prevalence of psychiatric problems in parents would certainly be expected.

Parenting Stress

There is no question that parents of ADHD children, especially mothers, experience greater stress in their role as caretakers of these children than do mothers of normal children (Breen & Barkley, 1988). Such stress seems to be particularly acute in mothers of young ADHD children. This was elegantly documented in a study by Mash and Johnston (1983c), which assessed parents' perceptions of their own self-esteem as parents, as well as their stress in raising ADHD and normal children. Two age groups were used within each of these subject groups, these being 3- to 6-year-olds and 7- to 10-year-olds. Mothers of ADHD children reported significantly lower levels of parenting self-esteem and markedly higher levels of depression, self-blame, and social isolation than did mothers of normal children. Parenting stress was considerably higher in the mothers of the younger ADHD children than in the older ADHD group. These findings for maternal depression have been documented in other studies as well (Befera & Barkley, 1985; Cunningham, Benness, & Siegel, 1988). Interestingly, Mash and Johnston found that the lower mothers' ratings of parenting self-esteem were, the higher these mothers' ratings of their ADHD children's behavior deviance were. Greater degrees of parenting stress were also positively correlated with greater ratings of behavioral deviance in the ADHD children.

Obviously, the extent to which parents view their children as deviant may be only partly a function of the children's actual level of behavioral problems and partly due to factors affecting the mothers' psychological well-being. But these parental perceptions of deviance are likely to guide parental reactions to child behavior in some situations (Mash & Johnston, 1983b), with the result that some parents of ADHD children will significantly overreact to their children's relatively minor disruptive or negative behavior. Even so, in a review of this literature, Mash and Johnston (in press) have concluded that the major source of parenting stress comes from the primary characteristics of ADHD in the children and its disruptiveness to others, rather than from nonchild sources in the family.

Besides problems with parenting stress, self-esteem, and depression, parents of ADHD children are more likely to report a significantly greater number of stress events not associated with parenting (Barkley, Fischer, et al., in press-b). One such source of distress is in the marital relationship of these parents.

Parents of ADHD children are more likely to have marital disturbances than those of normal children (Befera & Barkley, 1985; Cunningham et al., 1988). These findings are not always evident in some studies, however (Barkley, DuPaul, & McMurray, in press-a; Mash & Johnston, 1983c), and may be related to the proportion of ADHD children in the sample who also have ODD (Barkley, Fischer, et al., in press-b). As I describe below, whether ODD is found in ADHD children seems to be due in part to the degree of marital dysfunction and parental psychiatric problems within the families of these children. Nevertheless, we have found that over an 8-year follow-up period, families of ADHD children are three times more likely to experience separation and/or divorce of the biological parents than are families of normal children (54% vs. 15%; Barkley, Fischer, et al., in press-a).

Some studies have found that the parents of ADHD children also report fewer contacts with extended family members and, when such contacts occur, report them to be less helpful (Cunningham et al., 1988). Extended family contacts and affiliations with adult friends are important sources for emotional support, as well as for acquiring information about appropriate methods of dealing with child management problems. Where these contacts are fewer and less helpful, parents of ADHD children may experience a form of social isolation that is detrimental both to their caretaking abilities with their children and to their own emotional well-being.

Psychiatric Disorders

Almost 20 years ago, reports were appearing that biological parents and extended relatives of hyperactive children were more likely to have had hyperactivity themselves in childhood (Morrison & Stewart, 1971, 1973a), with 5% of the mothers and 15% of the fathers reporting this problem (vs. 2% in the control group). More recent studies have corroborated these earlier and less sophisticated studies, and indicate that biological parents of ADHD children are themselves more likely to have ADHD, or at least some of the residual characteristics of the disorder (Alberts-Corush, Firestone, & Goodman, 1986; Deutsch et al., 1982; Singer, Stewart, & Pulaski, 1981). However, the prevalence of ADHD in the parents in these later studies is even higher than originally suspected. In general, it seems that 15 to 20% of the mothers and 20 to 30% of the fathers of ADHD children may also have ADHD themselves. This greater risk of ADHD is also seen among the biological siblings of ADHD children, where approximately 26% may have the disorder. In general, the risk of ADHD among the first-degree biological relatives of ADHD children is between 25 and 33% (Biederman et al., 1986, 1989; Biederman, Munir, & Knee, 1987).

Parents of ADHD children are also more likely to experience a variety of other psychiatric disorders, the most common of which appear to be conduct problems and antisocial behavior (25 to 28%), alcoholism (14 to 25%), hysteria or affective disorder (10 to 27%), and learning disabilities (Cantwell, 1972; Morrison, 1980; Morrison & Stewart, 1971, 1973b; Singer et al., 1981).

Even if they are not abusing alcohol, parents of ADHD children consume more alcohol than those of normal children (Cunningham et al., 1988). Biederman, Munir, and Knee (1987) and Biederman et al. (1989) have also reported a higher prevalence of affective disorders, particularly Major Depression, among the parents and siblings of ADHD children (27 to 32%) as compared to control children (6%).

Family Psychiatric Disturbance and Child Conduct Problems

In 1983, August and Stewart suggested that the greater incidence of antisocial behavior and alcoholism among first-degree relatives of ADHD children was primarily associated with the incidence of conduct problems and antisocial behavior among ADHD children. ADHD children free of these comorbid conduct problems often had only a greater history of ADHD and learning disorders among their relatives. Hence, the greater family histories of alcoholism and antisocial behavior are associated only with antisocial behavior in children, not with ADHD (Stewart, deBlois, & Cummings, 1980). These findings have been replicated in more recent studies (Biederman, Munir, & Knee, 1987) in which 46% of the first-degree relatives of ADHD children with comorbid ODD or Conduct Disorder (CD) also had ODD, CD, or Antisocial Personality Disorder, as compared to only 13% of the relatives of pure ADHD children.

A recent study by Lahey, Piacentini, et al., (1988) nicely illustrates this relationship. The findings from this study are shown in Tables 5.4 and 5.5; they make a compelling case for the familial association of antisocial behav-

TABLE 5.4. Comparison of Mothers' DSM-III Diagnosis and Antisocial Behavior for Child's Diagnostic Group

Mother's diagnosis (%)	CD $(n=14)$	CD + ADD/H $(n=23)$	ADD/H $(n=18)$	Clinic control $(n=30)$	χ^2 for CD effect	p
Major Depression	50.0	30.43	22.2	16.7	3.86	.05
Dysthymia	21.4	26.1	11.1	3.3	5.63	.05
Manic Episodes	7.1	0.0	0.0	3.3	0.04	NS
Generalized Anxiety	28.6	13.0	16.7	6.7	1.36	NS
Obsessive-Compulsive	14.3	0.0	0.0	0.0	2.73	NS
Somatization	7.1	4.3	0.0	0.0	2.73	NS
Antisocial Personality	7.1	8.7	0.0	0.0	4.03	.05
Alcohol Abuse	7.1	4.4	5.6	0.0	0.68	NS
Drug Abuse	14.3	4.4	5.6	0.0	1.70	NS
History of fighting	14.3	30.4	0.0	0.0	13.06	.001
Arrested	7.1	27.3	0.0	0.0	10.48	.001
Prison sentence	7.1	21.7	0.0	0.0	8.37	.005

Note. From "Psychopathology in the Parents of Children with Conduct Disorder and Hyperactivity" by B. B. Lahey, J. C. Piacentini, K. McBurnett, P. Stone, S. Hartdagen, and G. Hynd, 1988, *Journal of the American Academy of Child and Adolescent Psychiatry, 27,* 163–170. Copyright 1988 by Williams & Wilkins. Reprinted by permission of the first author and the publisher.

TABLE 5.5. Comparison of Fathers' DSM-III Diagnosis and Antisocial Behavior for Child's Diagnostic Group

Father's diagnosis (%)	CD ($n = 14$)	CD + ADD/H ($n = 21$)	ADD/H ($n = 18$)	Clinic control ($n = 30$)	χ^2 for CD effect	p
Major Depression	16.7	4.8	11.1	16.7	0.55	NS
Dysthymia	8.3	0.0	0.0	20.0	2.22	NS
Manic Episodes	0.0	0.0	5.6	10.0	2.90	NS
Somatization	0.0	0.0	0.0	0.0	—	—
Antisocial Personality	38.5	52.4	5.6	16.7	12.11	.001
Alcohol Abuse	15.4	28.6	5.6	10.0	3.68	.05
Drug Abuse	15.4	23.8	0.0	6.7	5.49	.05
History of fighting	14.3	57.1	11.8	17.2	6.36	.01
Arrested	14.3	72.7	16.7	24.1	7.52	.01
Prison sentence	7.7	50.0	11.1	17.2	4.24	.05

Note. From "Psychopathology in the Parents of Children with Conduct Disorder and Hyperactivity" by B. B. Lahey, J. C. Piacentini, K. McBurnett, P. Stone, S. Hartdagen, and G. Hynd, 1988, *Journal of the American Academy of Child and Adolescent Psychiatry, 27,* 163–170. Copyright 1988 by Williams & Wilkins. Reprinted by permission of the first author and the publisher.

ior and affective disorders in relatives with antisocial behavior in ADHD children. When all of these studies are taken together, they suggest a somewhat linear relationship between the severity of aggressive and oppositional behavior in ADHD children and the degree of antisocial behavior, alcoholism, and affective disorders among their parents and extended relatives. In other words, ADHD children with little or no aggressive behavior are likely to have a considerably smaller incidence of these psychiatric disorders among their parents than those with ADHD and ODD. However, children in the latter group are likely to have less of these problems in their parents than do children with ADHD and CD (a more severe form of ODD), who have the highest rates of these disorders among all of the ADHD subgroups.

It should now be obvious from the literature reviewed in the first section of this book that aggression, or hostile and defiant behavior, in ADHD children is an important characteristic to be clinically identified. It is strongly associated with more extreme and more widespread dysfunction in the various domains of childhood adjustment; it is highly predictive of lower academic attainment, more school suspensions and expulsions, greater substance use and abuse, more frequent and repetitive conduct problems and antisocial behavior, and probably poorer occupational attainment and adjustment than are seen in ADHD children who are not significantly aggressive. Its existence also now appears to be substantially a function of family and parental dysfunction and social adversity. Given its importance in ADHD, it is worth trying to understand what factors may lead to its development and maintenance in ADHD children. Perhaps this will point the way toward what can be clinically done about it.

A MODEL FOR THE DEVELOPMENT OF AGGRESSION IN ADHD CHILDREN

Research in ADHD has not focused upon the mechanisms by which aggression arises in some children while not in others, nor on how it serves to affect outcome. However, a potentially useful explanation can be derived by combining the findings from three separate areas of research: (1) the literature on aggression in other childhood populations (Patterson, 1982); (2) the findings on the parent-child interactions of families with ADHD children, described above; and (3) the research on parental psychopathology in families of ADHD children, just discussed.

The findings from the first source strongly indicate that aggressive behavior in children is closely associated with certain types of child management methods, parental psychopathology (particularly maternal depression), and marital discord (Brody & Forehand, 1986; Hops et al., 1987; Jouriles, Pfiffner, & O'Leary, 1988; Panaccione & Wahler, 1986; Webster-Stratton, 1988; Webster-Stratton & Hammond, 1988). These parental disturbances have been shown to be precisely those that are more common among the parents, as well as the extended relatives, of children with ADHD than among those of normal controls. Moreover, these parental problems also predict adolescent outcome, particularly delinquency, almost as well as they do childhood aggression (Hechtman, Weiss, Perlman, & Amsel, 1984) in ADHD children. Combining these findings suggests the following: Childhood aggression in ADHD children may be a *marker variable* for three parent/family variables (child management methods, parental psychopathology, and marital distress) that contribute more strongly to negative outcomes than just aggressive child behavior itself. Intervening strictly at the level of childhood aggression, therefore, will probably not produce as much impact on later adolescent outcome because such interventions fail to address directly the parental disturbances that predispose children toward these later negative outcomes.

Research on the adolescent outcome of ADHD children indicates that a fourth parental variable, paternal aggressive and antisocial behavior, is also associated with later CD and antisocial acts in these children (Barkley, Fischer, et al., in press-a; Lahey, Piacentivi, et al., 1988). Given that aggression in childhood is a precursor to adolescent CD (see below; see also Loney & Milich, 1982; Milich & Loney, 1979; Farrington, Loeber, & van Kammen, 1987), one would expect to see paternal aggression and antisocial behavior, in addition to maternal depression and marital discord, directly associated with early aggression in ADHD children.

The Link Between Parental Disorders and Child Misconduct

The mechanism by which these parental psychiatric factors are associated with or lead to aggression in ADHD children is also not well studied. Again, more extensive research in other areas of child psychopathology, especially child defiance, provides a probable pathway. It is the manner in which such parents manage child behavior, particularly child noncompliance (Jouriles et al., 1988; Panaccione & Wahler, 1986; Webster-Stratton, 1988), that may be the key. Substantial research by Patterson (1982) and Wahler (1980) has shown that parents of aggressive and noncompliant children are more likely to use aggressive behavior, indiscriminate aversiveness, and submissiveness or acquiescence toward their children during management encounters. Their children, in turn, are more likely to escape from these aversive initiatives and the task demands of their parents by using hostile and defiant behavior in response. The successful escape or avoidance of such parental interactions and demands provides negative reinforcement of the children. This increases the probability that hostile and defiant behavior will be used again in subsequent parent-child interactions when tedious, unwanted, or aversive demands are made on the children. In short, how parents manage the usual bouts of child defiance may result in an escalation of such "garden variety" episodes of child oppositional behavior to serious, clinical levels of aggression (Patterson, 1976).

The process by which this happens may be glacially slow, as Patterson describes, but through hundreds of negative parent-child encounters each week it moves inexorably toward the cementing of aggressive and antisocial behaviors in a child's repertoire. This course will become increasingly difficult to alter over the child's development as a result of this substantial and socially pernicious learning history. A factor that may predispose children within these families to even greater risk of oppositional and defiant behavior is early childhood temperament, particularly those elements of temperament related to hyperactivity, impulsiveness, persistence in demands, and quickness to anger (see Chapter 4; see also Buss, 1981; Patterson, 1982; Webster-Stratton & Eyberg, 1982).

The sequence of parent-child aversive/coercive exchanges described above would appear to provide the possible causal mechanism linking negative child temperament on the one hand, and parental psychiatric and marital distress on the other, to aggression in ADHD children. Relevant evidence for such a mechanism comes from several studies of depression in mothers. Maternal depression appears to produce at least three different levels of effects on maternal caretaking activity. The first is on maternal perceptions of child behavioral deviance and maladjustment. Depressed women rate their children as more deviant than objective assessments of the children warrant, perhaps because of their reduced tolerance for child misconduct (Brody & Forehand, 1986; Webster-Stratton & Hammond, 1988). This would be consistent with Beck's (1967) findings that cognitive distortions in depressed patients lead to reduced tolerance for others' behavior. It is also in agreement with Mash and Johnston's (in press) model of parenting stress in mothers of ADHD children, where maternal beliefs and attitudes are a major factor determining such stress.

The second level of influence is on the actual behavior of depressed mothers toward their children. Depressed women are more critical, disapproving, and aversive and less positive in interactions with their children (Hops et al., 1987; Webster-Stratton, 1988; Weissman et al., 1984). Their initiation of attack behaviors against others is often indiscriminant and not always contingent on the children's immediately preceding behavior. Psychologically distressed parents are therefore more likely to provide inconsistent management of "garden variety" types of child defiance.

This causal path from maternal mood to maternal behavior toward children was revealed in an elegantly designed experiment by Jouriles, Murphy, and O'Leary (1989). Mothers of 40 boys aged 3 to 6 years were exposed to alternating positive and negative mood induction conditions; each parent experienced both mood manipulations. Direct observations of mother-child interactions were conducted across all conditions. The findings indicated that following the negative mood induction condition, mothers reduced their positive statements toward their children and engaged in less verbal interaction with them. Children in these conditions became less compliant with maternal commands. The opposite occurred following the positive mood induction: Maternal positive statements toward children increased, as did general verbal interactions. Child compliance was also better within these conditions. One could hypothesize from these findings that negative maternal mood reduces the available social reinforcement for ongoing positive child behaviors, resulting in a decline in child prosocial behavior and compliance to the mother's commands. This study further suggests that maternal affect is the mechanism by which distal or contextual family events that occur considerably earlier in the day or even week may produce effects on later parent-child interactions.

The third level of effects of parental depression or distress is on children's behavior via their interactions with depressed mothers, as already noted above. Research by Hops et al. (1987) found that the children of depressed mothers were more likely to emit aggressive behavior toward the mothers, which appeared to result in immediate reductions in mothers' dysphoric affect. Conversely, mothers' dysphoric affect was likely to result in immediate but temporary suppression of child and paternal aggression toward them. The researchers speculate that both maternal dysphoric affect and child aggression function to negatively reinforce temporary, immediate suppressions in these behaviors in each other, while acting in the long run to actually increase their future probability of occurrence.

These findings suggest that children who are temperamental and quick to respond to such attacks with aggressive or hostile counterattacks are more likely to find their behavior negatively reinforced with the successful escape from further attacks or unwanted demands by others. Child aggressive/defiant behavior consequently escalates and is maintained at higher levels within these aggressive families. The observation that siblings of aggressive children are also more likely to manifest such aggressive behavior within these family systems only provides further opportunities for chains of attack-counterattack-withdrawal sequences to further strengthen child aggressive behavior.

That ADHD children within these families may acquire these antisocial skills more rapidly than non-ADHD children may simply have to do with their higher rate of initiating behaviors toward others, especially behaviors that others find disruptive or aversive. Depression need not be the only maternal condition that can predispose family systems toward these aggressive exchanges. General psychological distress, antisocial personality, affective and anxiety disorders, or hysteria could lead to similar parent-child exchanges. In short, to the degree that parental psychological distress, whatever its source, has an impact upon parental management of child behavior, altering the consequences that parents provide for both prosocial and aggressive behavior, the risk that ADHD children will develop defiant and aggressive behavior correspondingly increases.

Other studies show that marital discord may function in a similar manner to alter parent perceptions and management of child misbehavior, and thereby to increase child defiant and aggressive behavior in a family (Bond & McMahon, 1984; Emery, 1982; Jouriles, Barling, O'Leary, 1987; Christensen, Phillips, Glasgow, & Johnson, 1983). The combination of both maternal depression/distress and marital discord results in even higher rates of both perceived child deviance and actual parent-child conflict and child aggression than either parent variable alone (Hops et al., 1987; Webster-Stratton, 1988). Certainly, both maternal depression and marital discord are not completely independent of each other; thus each is likely to be found to some degree when the other is present, and the two are likely to interact in their effects on child aggression (Emery, Weintraub, & Neale, 1982).

Research (Wahler, 1980; Dumas, 1986) has also shown that rates of aversive mother-child interactions may be increased even further in families where depressed mothers experience a greater degree of aversive interactions with other adults (e.g., spouses/boyfriends, relatives, and case workers). On days when mothers have more aversive exchanges with other adults, they are more likely to use aversive behavior with their children than on days of fewer or no such aversive exchanges with others (Dumas, 1986). Within families of ADHD children, such aversive yet distal setting or contextual events may be father aggression and antisocial behavior and degree of marital verbal and physical aggression. Both father antisocial behavior and marital discord occur more often in ADHD than in normal families. Recent research indicates that at least 30% of all marriages are likely to involve some violence between partners over the life of the marriage (Straus, Gelles, & Steinmetz, 1980), and that among maritally distressed couples this percentage is likely to be considerably higher. Such violence in marriages has been linked to considerably greater levels of aggression in clinic-referred children, especially if it is witnessed by the children, than in nonviolent clinical families (Jouriles et al., 1987).

It is highly likely, therefore, that marital discord, maternal depression/distress, paternal antisocial behavior, and marital aggression will be significantly interrelated in the families of some ADHD children. It is precisely this subgroup of ADHD children that is likely to acquire serious aggressive conduct. Yet it must be said that few studies of marital discord and child maladjustment have attempted to partial out the contributions of marital violence from those of general marital distress (Jouriles et al., 1987). Furthermore, past research in this area has also not examined the degree to which general aggressiveness and antisocial conduct in fathers serve as contributors to child aggression in ADHD. Such research is to be strongly encouraged.

Drawing together these separate lines of research seems to suggest the following link among ADHD, parent psychopathology, and aggression. If maternal depression/distress results in inconsistent and noncontingent management of child noncompliance, then childhood aggression should be considerably more prevalent in ADHD children with such depressed mothers than in ADHD children without them. Similarly, marital discord will also be found to correlate with child aggression and defiance during parent-child interactions. Where *both* maternal depression and marital discord are present in the mothers of ADHD children, even higher rates of childhood defiance and aggression should be seen than in families where mothers are only depressed or only maritally distressed. Since single parents appear to have more aggressive child behavior than married parents of clinic-referred families (Horne, 1981), it will also be important in future research to examine the impact of this factor apart from that of depression on aversive mother-child interactions in ADHD families. This is especially pertinent to families of ADHD children because their divorce rate is more than three times that of the average population during a fixed period of time, as noted above. Social isolation or insularity in single mothers is an especially strong moderating variable in the degree of child aggressiveness, and so this requires separate assessment in any research on marital status and child aggression (Dumas & Wahler, 1985). Finally, paternal antisocial behavior and marital aggression within married ADHD families may serve as additional indirect or contextual influences that increase rates of aversive mother-child interactions and child aggression beyond those attributable to maternal depression or general marital distress.

Further Evidence for the Model

I am aware of only one study that has evaluated the relationship between these parental factors and aggressive behavior specifically in ADHD children, and this examined the role of marital discord and marital aggression (Prinz, Myers, Holden, Tarnowski, & Roberts, 1983). Quite surprisingly, it found no relationship between marital discord and parent or teacher ratings of aggression. Yet marital aggression was weakly related to parent ratings of hyperactive and aggressive behavior. This is quite inexplicable, given the substantial research linking these variables in other populations, as well as our own pilot studies (see below) intimating such a relationship. These enigmatic results clearly demand a replication study with a much larger sample.

This theoretical formulation of aggression in ADHD children may also explain why interventions for ADHD aimed only at the level of child behavior are unlikely to alter long-term outcome in aggressive ADHD children. Without concentrating on the moderating variables of parental psychological distress and marital discord, such interventions have a low likelihood of success. Training in effective child behavior management skills must therefore be combined with treatments of the maternal distress, such as cognitive-behavior/problem-solving therapies; of the marital discord, as in communication training/conflict resolution approaches; and of the paternal aggression, as in Rosenbaum's (1983) approach to maritally violent men—all as dictated by the particulars of the family case. The use of psychopharmacology as an adjunct to these other therapies may be necessary in some cases to address the more serious forms of maternal or paternal affective disturbance.

It seems plausible that the causal direction in this relation, at least initially, is more likely to be from maternal depressed affect to child aggression than vice versa in ADHD children. This is not to say that ADHD in children cannot cause mild maternal depression, as it surely can. But the subsequent response of these parents to gambits of child defiance is what may cause such defiance to escalate to clinical levels of child aggression. If so, it seems possible to directly reduce the level of maternal depression and to dissect its effects on child aggression by using antidepressant medication as the "psychopharmacological scalpel." One could then examine the degree to which such changes in maternal mood are associated with reductions in difficult mother-child interactions, and in both maternal perceptions and actual rates of childhood aggression. This same type of research was used (see above) to tease out the direction of effects in parent-child interactions of ADHD children: Stimulant medication was used to alter the ADHD children's behavior, and the effects of this altered behavior on parental behavior was examined. It could be applied here to tease out the direction of effects between maternal depression and child aggression. I know of no research, either in the ADHD literature or in the depression literature, that has directly examined the effects of antidepressant medication on mother-child interactions in depressed women. One might expect that reduction in depression achieved by antidepressants should then result in reductions in maternal negative behavior, in greater approval and positive affect, and in more consistent management of child behavior during mother-child interactions if the above hypotheses are correct. This should result in reductions in child defiance and aggression. Research is to be strongly encouraged that evaluates the effects of antidepressant medication on maternal affect, as well as on marital and family functioning and on the mother-child interactions of depressed mothers of ADHD children, to test this causal mechanism directly.

It will be important in this research to distinguish between maternal perceptions of childhood aggression and observed child aggressive behaviors displayed during family interactions. Maternal depression, marital distress, and maternal isolation result in higher maternal ratings (perceptions) of child aggression (Brody & Forehand, 1986; Dumas & Wahler, 1985; Webster-Stratton, 1988), as well as higher actual rates of maternal criticism and aversiveness during mother-child interactions (Jouriles et al., 1988; Webster-Stratton & Hammond, 1988). However, it is not clear whether children of such mothers actually display higher rates of aversiveness toward their mothers, as the results have proven inconsistent (Dumas & Wahler, 1985; Hops et al., 1987; Griest, Wells, & Forehand, 1979; Webster-Stratton, 1988). Moreover, maternal ratings of aggression are weakly if at all related to direct observations of aggression (see below); but, as noted above, they are strongly correlated with other maternal characteristics such as depression and marital discord. Some of the weakness in the correlation of maternal ratings and direct observations is clearly due to considerable differences in measurement approaches (i.e., ratings collapsed over months vs. observations taken for 30 to 60 minutes). Even so, stronger correlations ought to be seen than those already observed if these variables are in fact related to each other. At the very least, these conflicting results indicate that studies that employ only one or the other of these types of measures of child aggression are likely to come to quite different conclusions about variables related to aggression. Investigators will therefore need to employ both types of measures to avoid this pitfall.

Although past studies of maternal depression and child misbehavior have frequently referred to these mothers as "depressed," this does not refer to actual clinical levels or diagnoses of Major Depression or any of the related depressive disorders (e.g., Dysthymia, Bipolar Disorder, etc.), as no formal diagnostic criteria for depression were either taken or employed in subject selection. Depression has been primarily assessed through a rating scale, often the Beck Depression Inventory (BDI), and many studies have used a low cutoff score (10 or higher out of a possible 60). It would seem more appropriate to refer to mothers so classified as "unhappy," "sad," "distressed," or at best "mildly depressed." Even so, a large body of research indicates that even mild levels of depression or unhappiness in mothers are strongly associated with higher maternal ratings of child maladjustment and observations of greater maternal aversiveness in child management.

I noticed in my earlier studies that mothers of ADHD children rated themselves as more depressed and their marriages as more distressed than did mothers of normal children. This led me to wonder about the relationship of these parent characteristics to both maternal ratings of child aggression and actual conflicts in parent-child interactions. To address this issue my colleagues and I collected parent self-ratings of depression and marital discord in a study of subtypes of ADHD, discussed in Chapter 3 (Barkley, DuPaul, & McMurray, in press-a). An analysis of the relationship between these ratings and maternal ratings of aggression on the Child Behavior Checklist was undertaken to see whether in fact maternal depression and marital discord were actually related to maternal ratings of childhood aggression in ADHD, as hypothesized above. Mothers were subdivided into maritally distressed and nondistressed groups, using the Locke-Wallace Marital Adjustment Test (MAT) recommended score of 85 or below for distress. The results indicated that the mean aggression rating for ADHD children (hyperactive subgroup) of maritally distressed mothers ($n = 17$) was 78 (mean T score of 50 and SD of 10 for normals), while that for nondistressed mothers ($n = 43$) was 65. Another way of expressing this relationship was to calculate the percent of ADHD children receiving clinically significant aggression ratings (T score > 70) as a function of the marital distress groupings. In the maritally nondistressed group, 26% of the ADHD children were rated as clinically aggressive; in the maritally distressed group, the risk more than doubled to 65%. So far, the results supported the model hypothesized above.

We then divided these same mothers into those who were depressed ($n = 13$) or nondepressed ($n = 46$), using the recommended cutoff score of 10 or higher on the BDI, indicating at least mild depression (scores of 18 or higher are usually used to diagnose clinical levels of depression, and very few of these mothers had such scores). The mean child aggression rating for the depressed group was 80 versus 67 for the nondepressed group. Of the nondepressed group, 32% of the children had clinically significant ratings of aggression (T score > 70), while the risk doubled to 64% in the children of the depressed group. When these groups were sorted into a 2×2 design (with vs. without depression and with vs. without marital distress), an even more striking relationship appeared. Depressed/distressed mothers gave the highest mean child aggression ratings (mean of 92), while the nondepressed/distressed and depressed/nondistressed ratings gave lower but still deviant aggression ratings (means of 72 and 73, respectively). The lowest ratings were for the nondepressed/nondistressed group (mean of 67.5).

These findings corroborate the hypotheses noted above that marital distress and maternal depression are both risk factors for perceptions of serious aggression in children; they also extend these findings to specifically diagnosed ADHD children, and indicate that both parent characteristics may contribute some unique variance to the problem. Unfortunately, we have not yet analyzed the results from observations of the mother-child interactions of the children in this study to permit a determination of whether these parent variables are related to actual maternal behavior and child aggression, or just to maternal perceptions (ratings) of such.

However, I have analyzed the effects of these variables on the interactions of mothers with their hyperactive adolescents to see whether maternal depression and marital discord are related to actual parent-teen conflicts. In this research, described above (see "The Interactions of ADHD Adolescents with Their Mothers"), we followed up many of the children in our original large-scale studies of mother-child interactions (123 hyperactives, or 80% of our original sample) over a period of 8 years. We found that even as teenagers (with a mean age of 15 years), they continued to have significantly greater problems in parent-teen interactions, as measured both by separate parent and teen ratings of conflict and by direct observations of parent-teen interactions during conflict discussions (Barkley, Fischer, et al., in press-b).

One approach to addressing the issue of the degree of relationship between maternal distress/marital discord and actual mother and child behaviors is to correlate measures of both. The entire sample of hyperactive and normal adolescents was collapsed into a single group for this purpose, because the groups were not originally formed on the basis of these conflict and interaction measures, and there was considerable overlap between the groups in their interaction patterns. We therefore computed correlations between selected rating scales of these maternal characteristics and the behavioral observations of mothers and teens during the conflict discussion. We used the BDI, the MAT, and selected scales from the SCL-90-R that appeared to have some bearing on interpersonal conflict (see Chapter 9 for a review of these scales). Complete data were available for 156 subjects on all scales except the MAT, on which data for only 133 subjects were available, due to the large number of single parents in the sample. These findings are shown in Table 5.6. To reduce the likelihood of Type I errors, given the large number of correlations, only those having a $p < .01$ are considered statistically significant.

The results indicated that maternal depression, as rated on the BDI or the SCL-90-R, was significantly and positively associated with the likelihood of mothers' use of commands/putdowns and negatively associated with the use of general talk during the conflict discussion. Similarly, the less satisfied mothers were with their marriages, the greater was their use of both commands/putdowns and defending/complaining, and the less they used facilitative behavior and general talk. Mothers' reports of interpersonal hostility from the SCL-90-R were associated with more commands/putdowns and less defining/evaluating and general talk, while increased maternal paranoia was related to increased commands/putdowns and less facilitative and defining/evaluating behavior by mothers during conflict discussion with their teens. Finally, the General Severity Index of the SCL-90-R was positively associated with commands/putdowns and negatively related to mothers' use of general talk. In general, the more depressed mothers were, the more discordant they reported their marriages to be, the more hostile they perceived their relations with others to be, and the greater their psychological distress, the more negative and directive behavior and the less positive and facilitating behavior they used during problem-solving discussions with their adolescents.

These maternal characteristics were also associated to a similar degree with certain adolescent behaviors, particularly defending/complaining, during the conflict discussion. As shown in Table 5.6, greater maternal depression, marital discord, and maternal psychopathology were significantly related to greater teen use of defending/complaining and lesser teen use of defining/evaluating and general talk. Mothers who reported more paranoia on the SCL-90-R also had teens who used more defending/complaining and less facilitation during these problem-solving discussions.

These relationships of actual mother and adolescent behavior during conflict discussions with mothers' self-reports of marital problems and psychological distress at outcome reveal a pattern quite similar to that seen in the other studies noted above on aggression and hyperactivity (Brody & Forehand, 1986; Dumas, 1986; Jouriles et al., 1988; Mash & Johnston, 1983c).

TABLE 5.6. Relationship of Maternal Self-Reports of Marital Discord and Psychopathology to Observations of Mother-Adolescent Interactions during the Conflict Discussion for Hyperactive and Normal Subjects Combined

Behavior category				Maternal ratings				
	BDI	MAT	OC	IS	DEP	HOS	PAR	SEV
Mother								
Commands/puts down	.20*	−.31**	.29**	.16	.26**	.32**	.21*	.28**
Defends/complains	.02	−.25*	.11	.04	.13	.08	.10	.11
Problem-solves	−.13	.03	−.12	−.01	−.07	−.20*	−.07	−.10
Facilitates	−.11	.18	−.12	−.09	−.12	−.09	−.16	−.09
Defines/evaluates	−.08	.16	−.11	−.07	−.04	−.21*	−.17	−.11
Talks	−.06	.24*	−.23*	−.11	−.25*	−.17	−.04	−.23*
Teen								
Commands/puts down	.06	−.27**	.10	.04	.12	−.03	.03	.10
Defends/complains	.19	−.29**	.26**	.24*	.32**	.23*	.23*	.28**
Problem-solves	−.04	.01	−.11	−.10	−.08	−.08	−.01	−.09
Facilitates	−.19	.21*	−.13	−.06	−.11	−.06	−.20*	−.09
Defines/evaluates	−.15	.29**	−.08	−.09	−.15	−.16	−.14	−.14
Talks	−.06	.25*	−.22*	−.19	−.29**	−.21*	−.11	−.25*

Note. Results are for 156 subjects for all scales except the MAT, on which complete data were available for 133 subjects. BDI, Beck Depression Inventory; MAT, Locke-Wallace Marital Adjustment Test; OC, SCL-90-R Obsessive Compulsive scale; IS, SCL-90-R Interpersonal Sensitivity scale; DEP, SCL-90-R Depression scale; HOS, SCL-90-R Hostility scale; PAR, SCL-90-R Paranoia scale; and SEV, SCL-90-R General Severity Index.
* $p < .01$.
** $p < .001$.

Mothers' use of directive and negative behaviors during interactions with their teenagers were significantly associated not only with their reports of their adolescents' behavior problems and interaction conflicts at home, but also with their own self-reports of depression, marital discord, and psychological distress. Thus, as in prior research, both maternal perceptions of adolescent conduct problems and actual maternal negative behavior during interactions with their teenagers are associated with maternal psychological maladjustment. Like Mash and Johnston (1983b, 1983c) in their studies of younger hyperactive children, we also found that the degree of negative and controlling behavior exhibited by teens in our study was related to these maternal reports of personal and marital distress.

In summary, it appears that while mother and adolescent negative behaviors during conflict interactions are closely related to their reports of conflicts at home, especially maternal reports of these conflicts, they are also related to the degree of distress reported by mothers in themselves and their marriages. Our prospective data and those of Campbell and Ewing (in press) indicate that both maternal perceptions of child misconduct and actual maternal controlling behavior in early childhood are more predictive of later childhood and adolescent conduct problems and aggression than is actual child behavior.

Another approach to addressing the issue of the association of maternal depression and marital discord to aggression in ADHD children is to subdivide the ADHD children into groups based on the presence or absence of both marital discord and maternal depression, resulting in a 2×2 design as described above. For the purposes of this discussion, I subdivided the 79 families of these ADHD teens in which the parents were currently married into a 2×2 design with vs. without depression and with vs. without marital distress), using the same criteria noted above. As described above, we observed several behaviors of both parents and teens during conflict discussions, and collected both mother and teen ratings of conflicts at home. Given that three of the four cells contained quite small samples (n's = 8 to 15), statistical power in the analysis is quite low, and so only trends ($p < .15$) in the data can be discerned. The means (percentage of occurrence) for each group on each measure are shown in Table 5.7, along with the results of the two-way analysis of covariance (ANCOVAs) using child age, child IQ, and maternal education as covariates. Results for the Issues Checklist rating scale are raw mean scores. Mean severity was rated on a scale from 1 ("mild") to 5 ("hot"). Below each measure is indicated the significance level of any results, followed by an M if a mean effect for marital distress was found, a D if a main effect for depression was found, and an $M \times D$ for any significant interaction.

For mothers, the results suggest that maternal depression and marital distress interact in unique ways, depending upon the measure examined. Both factors separately increased maternal defensive and complaining behavior during conflict discussions, but where both were present, complaining was lower than where only marital distress existed without depression. Maternal depres-

TABLE 5.7. Observations of Mother and Adolescent Behavior in ADHD Adolescents as a Function of Marital Distress and Maternal Depression

Measure	No distress		Distress	
	Not depressed	Depressed	Not depressed	Depressed
Mother (%)				
Commands/puts down	18.6	32.7	28.1	28.9
Defends/complains ($p < .09$, D×M)	4.9	8.1	10.1	7.5
Problem-solves ($p < .05$, D, D×M)	11.2	4.3	9.9	9.3
Facilitates ($p < .12$, D × M)	35.0	25.7	25.3	28.8
Defines/evaluates	8.9	6.6	8.9	6.6
Talks	21.3	22.8	17.9	18.9
Adolescent (%)				
Commands/puts down ($p < .08$, M, D)	6.3	11.9	15.1	13.6
Defends/complains ($p < .05$, M, D)	30.1	36.0	36.4	50.5
Problem-solves	8.5	6.5	8.9	8.0
Facilitates ($p < .01$, D)	19.0	8.3	15.2	7.6
Defines/evaluates ($p < .05$, M)	9.7	9.0	5.1	4.3
Talks ($p < .01$, M)	26.5	28.3	19.8	14.6
Issues Checklist				
Mother about teen				
No. of conflicts	19.4	20.6	21.7	20.1
Mean severity	2.3	2.6	2.5	2.4
Teen about Mother				
No. of conflicts ($p < .12$, D)	11.1	13.5	11.5	15.8
Mean severity ($p < .05$, D)	1.9	2.3	1.7	2.4

Note. The information in parentheses below each measure indicates the results of the 2×2 (marital distress × maternal depression) analyses of variance. A "$p <$" indicates the level of statistical significance for any main effect or interaction term. D, main effect for depression; M, main effect for marital distress; D × M, interaction of depression with marital distress.

sion was also associated with less use of problem-solving remarks and less facilitative behavior (remarks that encourage problem solving in the other person). However, marital discord was also associated with reduced facilitative behavior, whether or not depression was also present. Interestingly, mothers' ratings of the number of conflicts with their teens did not differ across the four groups. However, in comparison to norms on the scale, the ratings of all four groups were considerably higher for both number of conflicts and mean intensity of them.

For the adolescents, both marital discord and maternal depression were separately associated with increases in negative behavior and reductions in positive ones, but did not interact with each other. Both maternal depression and marital distress were associated with increased insults and putdowns by the teens, as well as with their display of defensive and complaining comments. The latter teen behavior was especially elevated within the group of mothers who were both depressed and distressed. An example of reciprocity between mother and teen behavior in these interactions is clearly shown in the category of teen facilitative behavior, where a main effect for maternal depression was associated with reduced facilitation. As noted above, "facilitation" refers to remarks by one person that encourage problem-solving behavior in the other. The reduced teen facilitation parallels the reduced problem-solving behavior among the depressed mothers. Marital distress but not maternal depression was associated with reduced levels of defining/evaluating and general talking by the teens with their mothers. "Defining/evaluating" refers to remarks that help either to further clarify the problem under discussion (defining) or to evaluate the consequences of solutions being discussed. In contrast, only maternal depression was associated with teens' ratings of their conflicts with their mothers. ADHD teens with depressed mothers reported more conflicts and more intense conflict discussions than those with nondepressed mothers.

Conclusions Regarding the Model

In summary, these pilot data suggest both separate and interactive effects for marital discord and maternal depression on the behavior of mothers with their ADHD adolescents. The effects seem to be somewhat dependent on both the individuals and the measures under study. However, these results clearly contradict those of the only other study to examine the impact of marital distress/violence on aggression in ADHD children (Prinz et al., 1983). That study found no relationship between ratings of marital discord/aggression and ratings of aggression in the children—results completely at odds with a substantial body of research on these factors in non-ADHD populations. Our results are generally consistent with that body of research, and imply that those findings may be extrapolated to understanding mechanisms associated with aggression in specifically diagnosed ADHD children.

Combining our preliminary findings supports the model described earlier—that maternal depression and marital discord seem to be related to maternal perceptions (ratings) of child aggression in ADHD, as well as to actual parent behavior toward the children and the children's response. However, these maternal perceptions of aggression are not as strongly related to the children's actual aggressiveness during parent-child interactions. The findings suggest that depressed/distressed mothers have altered perceptions of child misconduct and perhaps less tolerance for that which occurs. Such mothers also use excessive disapproval, irritability, and aversiveness, and less approval and positive behavior, in their interactions with their children than would nondistressed mothers to the same behaviors. Their children, however, are also more aversive in their interactions with their mothers, as shown in our pilot analyses of our parent-teen interaction data.

I have elsewhere attempted to evaluate whether these negative parent-child interactions in ADHD children are more a function of the children's ADHD symptoms or the parent's methods of management (see "Teasing Out the Direction of Effects in Mother-Child Interactions," above). We were able to dissect the direction of effects in these interactions through the use of double-blind, placebo-controlled crossover experiments with methylphenidate. In a series of studies, we repeatedly showed that methylphenidate given to the children resulted in significant reductions in child negative and off-task behavior, as well as increases in both contingent and sustained compliance (Barkley, 1988e, 1989b; Barkley & Cunningham, 1979a; Barkley, Karlsson, Pollard, & Murphy, 1985; Barkley et al., 1984; Cunningham & Barkley, 1978). We also demonstrated corresponding decreases in mothers' use of commands and negatives, but less consistently did we find increases in mothers' approval or positive attention. Schachar, Taylor, Weiselberg, Thorley, and Rutter (1987) recently affirmed these findings by showing that methylphenidate increased maternal warmth and affection and decreased maternal criticism and directiveness in ADHD children. However, medication did not change family cohesiveness, efficiency of parental coping, or consistency of interpersonal interactions. Yet these latter family factors seem to be involved in maintaining child aggressive behavior and determining child outcome.

FOUR STAGES IN THE EVOLUTION OF CONDUCT PROBLEMS

Available evidence suggests that aggressive or oppositional child behavior, once developed, may progress to more serious forms of antisocial conduct. Edelbrock (1989) has proposed a useful and empirically based taxonomy of child conduct problems that may help to clarify the relationship between oppositional behavior and more severe symptoms of CD or antisocial symptoms. In this model, based on an evaluation of 307 clinically referred children, four clusters of conduct problems are aligned along a single dimension. These clusters appear to be developmental stages in the progression of conduct problems from minor to serious; from within the home to the school and then to the community; and from overt, public acts to more covert, deceitful, and intentionally hidden transgressions. These clusters or stages are shown in Table 5.8.

The first cluster or stage is best summarized as "oppositional" and represents behaviors used in resisting demands made by others, especially within the home. It does not correspond to any psychiatric diagnosis, but is often referred to in the literature of noncompliance as "simple oppositional behav-

TABLE 5.8. Edelbrock's Developmental Stage Theory of Childhood Conduct Problems

Stage	Behaviors
Stage 1	Argues, brags, demands attention, disobeys at home, and/or is impulsive.
Stage 2	Includes Stage 1 behaviors; in addition, is cruel, disobeys at school, screams, has peer problems, fights, sulks, swears, and/or lies/cheats.
Stage 3	Includes Stages 1 and 2 behaviors; in addition, is destructive, threatens people, attacks people, has bad friends, and/or steals at home.
Stage 4	Includes Stages 1–3 behaviors; in addition, engages in vandalism, runs away, is truant, uses alcohol/drugs, steals outside the family, and/or sets fires.

Note. Adapted from *Childhood Conduct Problems: Developmental Considerations and a Proposed Taxonomy* by C. S. Edelbrock, 1989, unpublished manuscript, University of Massachusetts Medical Center, Worcester. Reprinted by permission of the author.

ior" or as an "adjustment reaction with conduct problem features." From this stage, some children may progress to a pattern of behaviors best labeled as "hostile/offensive" that involves attacks against others, either verbally or physically. This stage corresponds nicely to the diagnosis of ODD from the DSM-III-R. The third stage represents a more serious form of the second, wherein attacks become of a more severe magnitude of harm to others, destructiveness occurs, and the child drifts into hanging around with others who also get into trouble. This stage has been called "aggressive/destructive" and corresponds to the diagnosis of CD in the DSM-III-R. Perhaps it should be called "Type I CD" to distinguish it from the next stage. The fourth stage represents the most serious of conduct problems and comprises a pattern of covert antisocial acts such as fire setting, truancy, stealing, and vandalism. This has been called the "delinquent stage" by Edelbrock, and also corresponds to the diagnosis of CD as well as early Antisocial Personality Disorder, if the individual is 18 or older. Perhaps it should be known as "Type II CD" when the individual is under 18 years of age.

As the severity across stages increases, the relative prevalence of each within the population declines, and the threshold of items or behaviors needed for the individual to be placed in that stage (i.e., to be considered deviant at that stage) also declines. In other words, a pattern of five to nine oppositional behaviors may be needed for a child to be deviant for age as a preschooler and to be placed in the oppositional stage, while only one or two of the delinquent symptoms need be present for an adolescent to be equally as deviant and to be placed in the delinquent stage.

Edelbrock's model has substantial empirical support from research on developmental psychopathology (Achenbach & Edelbrock, 1978, 1981); the follow-up studies of both aggressive and hyperactive children (Patterson, 1982; Weiss & Hechtman, 1986); and the field trials from the DSM-III-R, which suggested precisely this linkage between ODD and CD (Spitzer, Davies, & Barkley, in press).

What determines this progression over development? The research by Patterson (1982) and many others suggests, as noted above, that the shift from the simple "garden variety" noncompliance seen in normal children to more serious levels of defiance (Stage 1) probably occurs as a result of a combination of negative child temperament and coercive parent-child interactions that involve inconsistent and often noncontingent consequences for defiance. The escalation of coercive behaviors within this family interaction pattern over time as a function of negative reinforcement and the hundreds of weekly "training" interactions within the family probably account for the movement into subsequent stages.

The transition across stages to more serious antisocial acts within the community (from Stage 2 to Stage 4), however, has much to do with the degree of parental monitoring of the aggressive child. Where such children are left to wander with little supervision, they are most likely to engage successfully in both overt and especially covert or clandestine antisocial acts. This failure to monitor child behavior properly may arise, as noted above, from a pattern of learned helplessness in the parent in which disengagement from the child is occurring, combined with parental depression or general psychological distress that itself detracts from such monitoring. Certainly, the progression from less serious conduct problems to more serious ones can occur rapidly in some children while taking years to occur in others. Some studies have shown that the presence of ADHD in children with early oppositional behavior is likely to lead to a more rapid acquisition of more serious forms of antisocial behavior—a more rapid progression through these stages—than in cases where ADHD is absent or less severe.

CLINICAL IMPLICATIONS

From this increasing wealth of research on the families of ADHD children, a number of implications for clinical practice seem evident:

1. The clinical assessment of ADHD children must incorporate measures that assess not only child behavior and adjustment, but also parent-child interactions, parental psychological status, and marital functioning, if a thorough picture of the social-ecological fabric of ADHD children is to be obtained.

2. Reference must be made to the developmental context in which the findings from this assessment were obtained. The manner in which these levels of the social-ecological system have interacted to result in the family as it now presents must be appreciated. Fault finding within such reciprocal sys-

tems is often difficult and needlessly judgmental. One can identify those problems within the family that seem primarily attributable to separate child and parent characteristics without the witch-hunt atmosphere that sometimes occurs in such clinical assessments. Great compassion and empathy are far more useful both in discovering these sources of maladjustment and in understanding their direction of effects.

3. In counseling the parents of ADHD children, it will be necessary to separate the causes and mechanisms for the children's ADHD from that of hostile and defiant behavior, ODD, or CD. The former is clearly a developmental disorder of behavioral disinhibition associated with neuromaturational immaturity and having a strong hereditary predisposition. Parents therefore cannot be held responsible for this developmental disorder. The ODD or CD, however, is likely to arise within and be maintained by family characteristics, particularly parental psychiatric factors and conditions of social adversity. These permit the modeling of aggressive social exchanges with others, as well as the success of "garden variety" aggression in escaping both these attacks and unwanted task demands made by others. Consequently, parents can and should be held accountable (not blamed!) for these circumstances and should be strongly encouraged to accept this responsibility and seek mental health services to change them. The treatments for ADHD and for ODD or CD are obviously distinct.

4. The clinical treatment of ADHD when it coexists with ODD or CD must involve more comprehensive interventions that focus, as needed, on parental beliefs and attitudes, psychological distress, communication and conflict resolution skills, and family systems, rather than simply using medication or training parents in child management skills alone. Training in child management, when provided, must concentrate on the inconsistent and often noncontingent use of social consequences within these families and on increasing the availability of rewards and incentives for prosocial conduct. It must also strive to increase parental involvement, and particularly monitoring of child behavior both at home and in the neighborhood, if it is to prevent the escalation to more serious stages of antisocial behavior. My coauthors and I describe exemplar programs for each of these approaches in the section of this text dealing with treatment.

5. The families of children with both ADHD and ODD or CD are likely to require more frequent and periodic monitoring (via follow-up visits and periodic reintervention as the case dictates) than families of children with other types of childhood psychological disorders, if a significant impact is to be made on long-term outcome.

SUMMARY

In this chapter, I have reviewed the results of research on the parent-child interactions of ADHD children, as well as on the aggregation of psychiatric disorders among the biological relatives (especially parents) of these children. This research suggests that ADHD children and adolescents pose significant management problems for their parents as a result of their developmental disability in behavioral disinhibition and inattention. These ADHD children are more likely to have parents who have ADHD as well. Among that subgroup of ADHD children who are also significantly aggressive, or hostile and defiant, there is also a considerably greater prevalence of antisocial conduct, affective disorders (such as Major Depression), alcoholism, and hysteria among their parents and extended relatives. Such findings intimate that the development of aggressive behavior and later antisocial conduct in ADHD children is associated with and is perhaps a function of these parental psychological disturbances.

Borrowing from Patterson's (1982) model of child aggressive behavior, I have proposed a theoretical model to account for the mechanisms by which such parental distress creates or exacerbates early aggression in ADHD children and contributes to its maintenance over development. I have hypothesized that these parent psychiatric symptoms have an impact upon parental mood. This negative parental mood results in an increased perception of the deviance of behavior in their ADHD children; it also increases the occurrence of negative behaviors initiated toward these children. Such distressed parents also decrease their levels of positive statements and general social interactions with their children. These parental behaviors result in increased child negative behaviors and decreased compliance with parental commands via the frequent coercive exchanges that occur within these families. To the degree that such behavior serves to help a child reduce and subsequently avoid future negative attacks by the parent or unwanted demands for task performance, the child's behavior will escalate due to negative reinforcement. The hundreds of such negative parent-child exchanges weekly culminate over time in the entrenchment of serious hostile, defiant, and antisocial behavior within ADHD children's behavioral repertoire. This pattern, when combined with reduced parental monitoring of child behavior in the community, creates a high risk for adolescent social maladjustment, criminality, academic failure, and even substance abuse. Simply treating ADHD children's aggressive behavior will therefore prove inadequate. Treatments must also address the parental and marital factors that give rise to these negative parent-child interactions and the reduced child monitoring, if they are to prove even partially effective in reducing these significant developmental risks posed by early aggression in ADHD children.

6

Differential Diagnosis

> It is the close observation of little things which is the se-
> cret of success in business, in art, in science, and in every
> pursuit in life. Human knowledge is but an accumulation
> of small facts, made by successive generations of men—
> the little bits of knowledge and experience carefully trea-
> sured up and growing at length into a mighty pyramid.
>
> —SAMUEL SMILES (1812–1904)

One of the most important goals of a clinical assessment is reaching a proper diagnosis in view of the presenting problems of the case. Simply cataloguing the child's behavioral and cognitive deficiencies and excesses, of course, can lead almost by itself to certain decisions regarding appropriate treatment. Reaching a proper diagnosis, however, allows the clinician to bring to bear on the case the wealth of previous clinical and research literature that has accumulated on groups of children with the same diagnosis. This literature may then point the way to other treatments or their contraindications, to information about the course and outcome of the disorder, and to potential etiologies of it. A diagnosis may also be required in order for the child in question to gain legitimate access to certain types of treatment, such as stimulant medication, or educational resources, such as special educational placement.

This process of diagnosis is accomplished mainly through the differentiation of the condition from other potentially applicable disorders—the process of differential diagnosis. It is not enough simply to know the criteria for the diagnosis of Attention-deficit Hyperactivity Disorder (ADHD); the clinician must also be able to distinguish its symptoms from other psychiatric conditions that may bear a superficial resemblance to them. Furthermore, it is now accepted in research and clinical practice that children may and often do have multiple disorders coexisting with their ADHD at the time of initial clinical presentation. Clinicians would previously attempt to grapple with which of these was the primary disorder and which were secondary to it (stemming from it), usually in the belief that establishing and then treating the primary disorder might lead to amelioration of the secondary disorders, perhaps without intervention specifically for them. This is no longer viewed as quite so necessary, given the available research evidence in developmental psychopathology that a case can have several primary disorders, each of which is less likely to be secondary to the others and which will probably require separate treatment. Such coexisting or comorbid disorders, when they occur with ADHD, may certainly interact with and exacerbate each other, result in a different developmental course and adolescent or adult outcome, have a somewhat different pattern of etiologies, and even have a different response to treatment than pure ADHD alone. Knowledge of the conceptualizations of other disorders that are likely to initially resemble ADHD or to coexist with it, and of their diagnostic criteria, is therefore essential to proper clinical diagnosis.

In this chapter, I briefly discuss a number of childhood and adolescent disorders that either have a high probability of being seen in conjunction with ADHD or at times may have some superficial resemblance to it. A few additional disorders are briefly mentioned because ADHD is sometimes believed in clinical practice to be a "masked" form of these other disorders, such as anxiety or depression. The diagnostic criteria for many of these disorders, where such consensus criteria exist, are also presented. I rely primarily upon the consensus criteria for these disorders set forth in the current version of the *Diagnostic and Statistical Manual of Mental Disorders* (American Psychiatric Association, 1987), known as the DSM-III-R, because they are the most current and were established in quasi-experimental field trials. The reader should understand, however, that these criteria are undergoing review, revision, and retesting in new field trials as of this writing, and that these revisions will appear in DSM-IV some time in the early 1990s.

I have chosen not to include a discussion of complex tic disorders or Gilles de la Tourette's syndrome here because they rarely occur in children with ADHD. However, over 70 percent of children who have Tourette's syndrome are likely to have ADHD, and so clinicians should not be completely unfamiliar with the nature of and criteria for the diagnosis of Tourette's syndrome. The interested reader is referred to my own review of this disorder (Barkley, 1988b) or the excellent texts by Shapiro, Shapiro, Bruun, and Sweet (1978) or Cohen, Bruun, and Leckman (1988).

THE DISRUPTIVE BEHAVIOR DISORDERS

Three childhood and adolescent disorders coexist with a sufficiently high probability that they are seen as related or overlapping disorders. These are ADHD, Oppositional Defiant Disorder (ODD), and Conduct Disorder (CD). Research has indicated that parent and teacher ratings of the symptoms of these disorders correlate highly with each other (Hinshaw, 1987), but represent somewhat separate or semi-independent dimensions of psychopathology. Because of the substantial relationship to each other, they are now clustered into a supraordinate diagnostic category known as the Disruptive Behavior Disorders. They are so named because all of them are disruptive of social situations, impinging substantially on the social conduct, activities, and rights of those around them. In this sense, they are socially intrusive and bothersome to others. This is in contrast to the anxiety or affective disorders, for instance, or the Specific Developmental Disorders (learning disabilities, or LD), which are considerably less socially disruptive for others and primarily impose upon the adjustment of only the afflicted individual.

Attention-Deficit Hyperactivity Disorder

The essential features of ADHD have been described in detail in Chapter 2 and consist of developmentally inappropriate degrees of inattention, impulsivity, and overactivity. In my view, the essence of the disorder consists of behavioral disinhibition and poor self-regulation. These behavioral difficulties arise early (often in the preschool years) and appear to be relatively chronic over time, such that 70 to 80 percent of children so diagnosed in their early to middle childhood will continue to meet criteria for this diagnosis in adolescence. Up to 50 to 70 percent may continue to manifest the disorder into adulthood.

The DSM-III-R guidelines for diagnosing ADHD are listed in Table 2.1 of Chapter 2. The 14 descriptors in that table are listed in descending order of discriminating power, based on data from the national field trial of these criteria for the DSM-III-R (see Spitzer, Davies, & Barkley, in press). It is recommended that a symptom be endorsed only if it occurs considerably more frequently than in most people of the same mental age. This is essential, as noted in Chapter 2, because a large minority of normal children are often described as having these characteristics, particularly during their early childhood or first years of elementary school. Unfortunately, no guidelines are provided as to how to determine whether each symptom is developmentally inappropriate. Using the ADHD Rating Scale (see Chapter 9) can help to some degree with this determination, as each characteristic is rated by the parent or teacher of the child on a 4-point scale ("not at all," "just a little," "pretty much," and "very much"). Items endorsed with the two highest ratings ("pretty much" and "very much") are considered to be developmentally inappropriate for the purpose of diagnosis. Another approach to this dilemma is for the clinician to stipulate to the parent or teacher during the interview that in reviewing each of these characteristics, he or she is seeking to know whether they occur much more often than typically seen in normal children.

The criterion that 8 of 14 descriptors be endorsed in order to apply the diagnosis is based upon a field trial, which showed that this score achieved the greatest classification rate of ADHD children from other childhood disorders. However, clinicians should be aware that the large majority of children in this field trial were between 6 and 12 years of age and that a significant effect of age was noted on the classification rate or sensitivity of the cutoff score. That is, the cutoff score was not as sensitive or specific to ADHD in the older age groups as it was in the young ones. This is in keeping with the results of our own follow-up study of ADHD children described in Chapter 4 (Barkley, Fischer, Edelbrock, & Smallish, in press-a), where it was noted that a cutoff of 6 of 14 symptoms was actually at the 97th percentile for age (two standard deviations above the normal mean). The cutoff score of 8 of 14 is far too stringent and results in a failure to classify adolescents who are clinically and statistically deviant. I would therefore strongly encourage clinicians evaluating adolescents for ADHD that the cutoff be adjusted downward to 6 of 14 in determining the diagnosis.

The opposite problem probably exists in evaluating preschool-age children. Normal children within this age group (2–5 years) are considerably more likely to manifest these behavioral descriptors, and so logic would dictate that a higher cutoff score would be needed to achieve the same statistical criterion of the 97th percentile and thus to be considered deviant. Although there is no research on preschool-age children at present to suggest what this cutoff score should actually be, research on the ADHD Rating Scale by George DuPaul (1990a) at our clinic suggests that 10 of 14 symptoms would place a 5-year-old at the 97th percentile for age. Perhaps we should adopt this cutoff score for younger children as well, so as to avoid excessively diagnosing ADHD among preschoolers.

The DSM-III-R provides guidelines for establishing the severity of ADHD. These are based upon a combination of the pervasiveness of the symptoms across situations and the number of symptoms being endorsed. The disorder is considered mild if a case has few, if any, symptoms beyond the cutoff score required for diagnosis and there is minimal or no impairment in school or social functioning. Such a case may also be considered situational; that is, the child manifests the symptoms only at home or only at school, as discussed in Chapter 2. The disorder is considered severe if many symptoms occur in excess of the cutoff score and they are pervasive in their impairment of functioning at home and school and with peers. Moderate ADHD exists when the case falls somewhere between these two extremes.

It is recommended that children having a Pervasive Developmental Disorder (e.g., Autistic Disorder) not be considered for a diagnosis of ADHD, as virtually all of these children have disturbances in the three primary areas of ADHD. It is believed that adding the label of ADHD to this more severe and profound developmental disturbance adds little to clinical decision making about the management of the case. One could also make the same argument for adding a diagnosis of ADHD to any diagnosis of severe or profound mental retardation.

In making the differential diagnosis of ADHD, the DSM-III-R recommends that clinicians take care in making judgments about children who are from inadequate, disorganized, or chaotic home environments, because such children may appear to have difficulties with attention and goal-directed behavior that are secondary to these environmental factors. In such cases, disentangling what is a primary characteristic or disability inherent in the child from that which is secondary to the environment can be difficult or impossible. However, I am aware of no research showing that ADHD is a likely sequela of poorly organized or functioning family environments. Many ADHD children are likely to have families that appear more negative, stressed, and disorganized by virtue not only of the impact of the children's ADHD on the families, but also of the greater likelihood of ADHD and other psychiatric disorders in the parents of ADHD children. Research evidence to date suggests that such environments are far more likely to have an influence on whether ODD or CD develops in conjunction with the ADHD than on creating the ADHD itself. This is not to say that such a chaotic environment may not exacerbate the manifestation of ADHD symptoms in such a child, but that the family environment is not likely to have solely created the ADHD. Attempting to tease out these causal influences is both unnecessary and futile. It is my opinion that where children meet the criteria for ADHD, they should receive the diagnosis regardless of the status of their home environment. How severe their ADHD may be, or at least how severe their parents view it as being, may be influenced to some degree by the extent of parental psychological distress and family turmoil present in particular cases.

Some children may acquire ADHD secondary to an obvious, documented, and significant neurologically compromising event (head trauma, infection, hypoxic injury, etc.). Where this occurs, I recommend that such cases be labeled as "acquired ADHD," provided that the children meet all of the other criteria set forth here apart from age of onset. Such cases, in my experience, differ in several important respects from the more common type of ADHD discussed in this text. First, the children may show more severe symptoms during the immediate posttraumatic recovery period. Second, they may show a lessening or complete amelioration of their symptoms over development, such that they come closer to normal or premobid levels of functioning. And, third, they may show a poorer response to stimulant medication treatment than children with the more common "idiopathic" or "developmental" type of ADHD described here.

In addition to the DSM-III-R criteria and the recommended adjustments, I consider it imperative that the following additional criteria be applied in making the diagnosis of ADHD. This is done to add greater rigor to the diagnostic process, so as to ensure that the diagnosis is not excessively or inappropriately applied. These additional criteria are as follows:

1. A score on a well-standardized child behavior rating scale, completed by parents or teachers, of these ADHD symptoms that places the child above the 93rd percentile (1.5 standard deviations above the mean) for children of the same age and sex. Such a criterion helps to correct for the lack of important adjustments for age and sex of the child in the DSM-III-R criteria, as noted above. It also helps to base the diagnosis on larger samples of norma-

tive data than were available in the DSM-III-R field trial. As recommended in Chapter 9, the Child Behavior Checklist for parents and teachers can be used to establish this developmental deviance of symptoms. Other rating scales that can be used in this same manner are reviewed in Chapter 9 and Appendix A.

2. Comparison of the score on this rating scale to that for the chronological age group consistent with the child's *mental age,* for any child whose IQ is estimated to be below 78 to 80 (approximately 1.5 standard deviations below the mean). The three primary symptoms of ADHD are known to vary as a function of mental or developmental age. The DSM-III-R makes it clear that such mental age adjustments are important in clinical judgment about cases of possible ADHD. Yet it provides no guidelines for how to determine this, other than a single cutoff score to be applied across all ages and mental levels. By using a rating scale and correcting for mental age, the clinician can achieve a relatively crude statistical adjustment for this problem.

3. A duration of symptoms of at least 12 months. This is especially important in evaluating preschool-age ADHD children. As discussed in Chapter 4, as many as 45 percent of children will at some point have concerns raised about their attention span during their preschool years. Such concerns are often transient: Fewer than 10 percent of these children, or 5 percent of the total population, have persistent concerns raised about their deviant attention and activity level beyond 12 months after onset of the concern. This research implies that a criterion of 6 months for duration of symptoms is far too liberal, especially when evaluating preschool-age children. However, where children's ADHD characteristics have lasted at least 12 months, it appears to represent a relatively stable and chronic pattern of disability in keeping with the view of ADHD as a developmental disorder.

4. A score on either the Home Situations Questionnaire—Revised or the School Situations Questionnaire—Revised (see Chapter 9) that places the child above the 93rd percentile in the pervasiveness of his or her inattention. This criterion requires that the child demonstrate a relatively pervasive pattern within a setting (e.g., home or school) in the number of situations in which the problems with sustained attention appear. This is in contrast to the earlier distinction in which pervasiveness was defined as being across home and school settings.

These relatively rigorous and specific diagnostic criteria, when combined with those from the DSM-III-R, are quite clinically useful in identifying a group of children whose ADHD symptoms are developmentally deviant, pervasive across situations, and developmentally stable. They are therefore useful in deriving a reliable and valid diagnosis, as well as in justifying the means by which the diagnosis was achieved to parents, other professionals, or agency and court representatives who may have a need to know the grounds on which the diagnosis is based. And it certainly provides an answer to the social critics who would argue, "Since many normal children show some of these characteristics, how can professionals diagnose any child as ADHD?"

Clinicians should not overlook the utility of taking a careful family history of psychiatric disorders among the parents and extended families of ADHD children (i.e., siblings, aunts, uncles, and grandparents). Research suggests that children who have ADHD alone with no other Disruptive Behavior Disorder seem more likely to have the disorders of ADHD among their fathers and perhaps other male relatives, and ADHD and Dysthymia among their mothers and perhaps other female relatives. Where psychoses, schizophrenias, or bipolar disorders are noted, this is a significant indication, as ADHD children are no more likely than normal children to have such a family history. Clinically, this dictates that the child being evaluated receive more careful scrutiny for signs of risk for or early emergence of these disorders, or for a thought disorder or "multiplex developmental disorder" (see below).

Oppositional Defiant Disorder

Upwards of 65 percent of children with ADHD are likely to develop sufficient levels of oppositional behavior that they qualify for a comorbid diagnosis of ODD (Barkley, DuPaul, & McMurray, in press-a; Barkley, Fischer, et al., in press-a). To primary caregivers, the symptoms of these disorders can often be both confused and confusing, as discussed in Chapter 5. It is essential that clinicians understand both the nature of and diagnostic criteria for both disorders, as they are distinct in their clinical presentation, likely etiology, developmental course and outcome, and types of treatments.

Oppositional or noncompliant behavior is a fairly common characteristic of preschool-age children. Refusing to obey, whining, or temper tantrums, as seen in such children, is not in and of itself sufficient for them to be diagnosed as having ODD. Instead, clinicians might better consider this as "simple oppositional behavior," or perhaps as a V code for mother–child interaction problems in the DSM-III-R guidelines. Forehand and McMahon (1981) describe these noncompliant children quite nicely and offer a successful parent training program for them.

In contrast, as noted in the DSM-III-R, the essential feature of ODD is a recurring pattern of negativistic, hostile, and defiant behavior that has become developmentally stable (at least for 6 months). I would clarify this by adding that this pattern is a combination of two elements, these being mood and behavior toward others: (1) negative, hostile, and angry mood with (2) defiant, argumentative, and resistant conduct in opposition to demands made by others, particularly caregivers (parents and teachers). Either can occur separately and not result in this diagnosis, as in Dysthymia or Major Depression in the case of the former, or simple oppositional behavior (as above) in the case of the latter. It is their combination that seems to be so virulent and so developmentally devastating.

As with ADHD, the symptoms must be present to a degree that is excessive or deviant for the child's mental age. The four stages of conduct problems described by Edelbrock (1989) and reviewed in Chapter 5 are worth recalling here, as they explain the link between early oppositional behavior and later ODD or CD. As this model notes, the oppositional behavior is most often seen in the home environment, especially during the preschool years. It is far more likely to be noted by mothers than by fathers, but can be seen in interactions with both caregivers. It may not emerge in the school environment until middle childhood in many cases, but in others it may be present even in preschool settings. The pattern of hostile and defiant behavior is most evident in interactions with adults and peers the children know well, and may not appear at all with strangers or with clinicians during office evaluations. When questioned about their conduct, it is not uncommon for such children or adolescents to see their behavior as justifiable in response to unreasonable demands made upon them by others. Over time, this disorder evolves from oppositional behavior toward parents to hostile and aggressive behavior toward others, to antisocial acts within the community, and finally to covert, clandestine criminal behavior as in CD (see below).

The pattern of behavior seen in ODD has been referred to in the research literature as "aggression" or as "conduct problems"; however, as noted above, I believe that "hostile/defiant" is a better term. Physical aggression toward others may not necessarily be present for the child to receive this diagnosis or for the pattern to be developmentally significant. And the term "conduct problem" is easily confused in the literature with the more formal diagnosis of CD (see below). Factors that may be associated with the development and maintenance of this behavior pattern are discussed in Chapter 5. Probably the greatest single body of research on this disorder has been accumulated by Gerald Patterson at the Oregon Social Learning Center (see Patterson, 1982). This and other research suggests that this pattern of behavior often emerges during the preschool years, primarily toward mothers, but can be witnessed in interactions with other family members as well. However, because the majority of preschool-age children, especially 2- to 3-year-olds, manifest oppositional behavior, it may not be judged as abnormal by caregivers until 5 or 6 years of age, when most normal children have remitted in this pattern of behavior toward others. Consequently, the reported age of onset as a disorder by caregivers is likely to be between 6 and 7 years of age, on average (Barkley, Fischer, et al., in press-a), even though signs of the pattern have emerged earlier in childhood.

ODD is more common in males than in females and shows a relatively high degree of stability over development (Hinshaw, 1987; Patterson, 1982). It is most severe within the home, especially during the childhood years, but may become equally as severe in school in some children by adolescence. A pattern of negative and coercive behavior is often seen among other family members besides just the afflicted child. In addition, there is a higher incidence of marital problems and personal emotional or psychiatric problems among the parents, and greater social disadvantage of the family, than is seen in normal children or then in children with pure ADHD (Werry, Reeves, & Elkind, 1987). Over time, ODD is likely to be associated with low self-esteem, low frustration tolerance, temper outbursts, poor peer relations, and eventually poor school performance. A large subset of these children, perhaps 60 percent, will go on to develop CD (see below) as well. If so, a greater risk for tobacco and alcohol use and abuse exists, as well as for use of other nonprescription and illicit substances (see Barkley, Fischer, et al., in press-a; McMahon & Wells, 1989; Patterson, 1982).

The DSM-III-R criteria for ODD are listed in Table 6.1. As with the criteria for ADHD, these symptoms are listed in descending order of their discriminating power, based on the field trial conducted on the Disruptive Behavior Disorders for DSM-III-R. Again, each item must be developmentally inappropriate to be endorsed, but again no guidelines are offered for making this determination. And, because these symptoms are likely to be more prevalent in the normal population during the preschool years, I would recommend again that adjustments for using the cutoff score be made when evaluating this age group of children so as to avoid excessive diagnosing (say, six or seven of nine symptoms). Our study on adolescents, however, suggests that five of nine is an adequate cutoff score for placing a teenager at the 97th percentile for age (Barkley, Fischer, et al., in press-a); thus no adjustment to these criteria is necessary for this age group, as is the case for ADHD. The DSM-III-R field trial also found no effect of age upon the sensitivity or specificity of these criteria (Spitzer et al., in press). The guidelines for determining severity of ODD are identical to those used for ADHD, as described above.

TABLE 6.1. DSM-III-R Diagnostic Criteria for Oppositional Defiant Disorder

---

A. A disturbance of at least six months during which at least five of the following are present:
  (1) often loses temper
  (2) often argues with adults
  (3) often actively defies or refuses adult requests or rules, e.g., refuses to do chores at home
  (4) often deliberately does things that annoy other people, e.g., grabs other children's hats
  (5) often blames others for his or her own mistakes
  (6) is often touchy or easily annoyed by others
  (7) is often angry and resentful
  (8) is often spiteful or vindictive
  (9) often swears or uses obscene language
  . . . .
B. Does not meet the criteria for Conduct Disorder, and does not occur exclusively during the course of a psychotic disorder, Dysthymia, or a Major Depressive, Hypomanic, or Manic Episode.

Note. From the *Diagnostic and Statistical Manual of Mental Disorders* (3rd ed., rev., pp. 57–58) by the American Psychiatric Association, 1987, Washington, DC: Author. Copyright 1987 by the American Psychiatric Association. Reprinted by permission.

In addition to these criteria, I would add a set of more rigorous conditions for making the diagnosis, as I have done with ADHD above: (1) a score on a well-standardized behavior rating scale of aggression or conduct problems completed by parents or teachers that places the child above the 93rd percentile for age and sex; (2) a score on the original Home and School Situations Questionnaires that places the child above the 93rd percentile for age and sex in the pervasiveness of his or her symptoms; and (3) a duration of symptoms of 12 months, especially when dealing with a preschool-age child. It is not yet clear whether ODD symptoms vary as a function of mental age, as in ADHD, although they do manifest some changes over development. I recommend correcting for mental age in ADHD, because it represents a disorder of neuromaturational immaturity that is therefore likely to be associated with variations in mental development. Such variation needs to be excluded as the cause of ADHD, because the disorder is thought to represent a significant discrepancy between behavioral inhibition or self-regulation on the one hand and intellectual development on the other. ODD is more likely to be a pattern of negative mood or temperament combined with a learned pattern of opposition to direction from others (Taylor, 1986a; Werry, Elkind, & Reeves, 1987; Werry, Reeves, & Elkind, 1987). Clearly, more research on this issue is warranted. Until then, and because symptoms of ODD seem to be less likely to be affected by mental age and are more associated with environmental factors, adjusting for mental age in the case of developmentally slow or retarded children does not seem to me to be as necessary as it is for ADHD.

Conduct Disorder

In childhood, it appears that approximately 20 to 30 percent of ADHD children will begin to manifest sufficient signs of antisocial behavior to receive a diagnosis of CD (Barkley, DuPaul, & McMurray, in press-a). However, by adolescence, between 40 and 60 percent will be so diagnosed (see Chapter 4). The vast majority of those children who receive a diagnosis of CD will also be diagnosed as having ODD. In accordance with Edelbrock's model, this indicates that a large subset of ODD children develop a comorbid CD or pattern of antisocial behavior toward others, and that almost all CD children have had or still have ODD (McMahon & Wells, 1989; Spitzer et al., in press).

The DSM-III-R indicates that the essential feature of this disorder is "a persistent pattern of conduct in which the basic rights of others and major age-appropriate societal norms or rules are violated" (p. 53). It is typically pervasive: It is as likely to occur in school, in the community, or with peers as much as it does in the home setting. It differs from ODD in that physical aggression is a far more common act in CD individuals, as are physical destructiveness and confrontation of others during criminal activities. Combined with this pattern of direct antisocial acts toward others is a pattern of covert, clandestine antisocial behaviors, such as breaking and entering, stealing, truancy, running away from home, and cheating; these are typically associated with lying to cover up some of these covert acts. This represents the fourth stage in the evolution of conduct problems in children as described by Edelbrock (1989).

Three types of CD are recognized in the DSM-III-R, although there is considerable debate over the validity of these subgroups: Group Type (CD occuring as a group activity with peers), Solitary Aggressive Type (physically aggressive behavior occuring in isolation from a peer group), and Undifferentiated Type. The last of these does not overlap with either of the other types and is said to include the majority of CD individuals.

A number of other problems are viewed as related features of CD. Poor school performance; a greater occurrence of school suspensions and expulsions; and greater tobacco, alcohol, and illicit drug use and abuse are commonly associated conditions. Precocious sexual activity, venereal disease, and teenage pregnancy are also more common associated conditions than is normal for age. The risk of suicidal gestures is greatly increased in the presence of CD in an adolescent. Many of the symptoms of ODD will be present, as noted above, but the diagnosis of CD is said to pre-empt the use of the diagnosis of ODD, given that over 95 percent of CD children have ODD. A pattern of antisocial behavior and psychiatric disturbance, particularly Major Depression, substances abuse, and Antisocial Personality Disorder, is more commonly seen in families of CD cases.

Although many of the descriptors or symptoms of CD are associated with the adolescent age range, the mean age of onset for CD among ADHD children has been shown to be in middle childhood, typically between 6 and 8 years of age (Barkley, Fischer, et al., in press-a; McMahon & Wells, 1989). This earlier onset is often associated with a more persistent pattern of CD than in a later-onset group. In some cases, ODD is actually a developmental precursor to the later development of CD. However, in other cases, the two disorders are reported by parents to have developed relatively close in time, raising questions as to why some children develop only ODD while others develop ODD and CD almost simultaneously. Patterson (1982) has suggested that parental monitoring may have much to do with this, as parents who poorly monitor the activities of their ODD children are likely to find CD symptoms developing quickly within these children. Others have suggested that the combination of ADHD symptoms with ODD is far more likely to accelerate the development of CD than is the presence of ODD alone (Farrington, Loeber, & Van Kammen, 1987). This accounts for the earlier onset of CD within the ADHD population than is normally seen in CD cases without ADHD.

The diagnostic criteria for CD as recommended in the DSM-III-R (American Psychiatric Association, 1987) are given in Table 6.2. As with the other Disruptive Behavior Disorders, these symptoms are listed in descending order of their discriminating power, based on the national field trial data for the

TABLE 6.2. DSM-III-R Criteria for Conduct Disorder

A. A disturbance of conduct lasting at least six months, during which at least three of the following have been present:
    (1) has stolen without confrontation of a victim on more than one occasion (including forgery)
    (2) has run away from home overnight at least twice while living in parental or parental surrogate home (or once without returning)
    (3) often lies (other than to avoid physical or sexual abuse)
    (4) has deliberately engaged in fire-setting
    (5) is often truant from school (for older person, absent from work)
    (6) has broken into someone else's house, building, or car
    (7) has deliberately destroyed others' property (other than by fire-setting)
    (8) has been physically cruel to animals
    (9) has forced someone into sexual activity with him or her
    (10) has used a weapon in more than one fight
    (11) often initiates physical fights
    (12) has stolen with confrontation of a victim (e.g., mugging, purse-snatching, extortion, armed robbery)
    (13) has been physically cruel to people
                          . . . .
B. If 18 or older, does not meet criteria for Antisocial Personality Disorder.

Note. From the *Diagnostic and Statistical Manual of Mental Disorders* (3rd ed., rev., p. 55) by the American Psychiatric Association, 1987, Washington, DC: Author. Copyright 1987 by the American Psychiatric Association. Reprinted by permission.

DSM-III-R. The cutoff score appears to be appropriate for most age ranges of children and adolescents, although our follow-up study (Barkley, Fischer, et al., in press-a; see Chapter 4) found that 2 of these 13 symptoms were sufficient to meet the 97th percentile for age in a group of normal adolescents. A problem with these criteria is that there are few descriptors that would apply to children in the preschool years or early elementary grades. This gives the impression that CD arises in later childhood and adolescence, when in fact there may be earlier developmental forms of the disorder. Certainly, as noted earlier, signs of ODD are often seen in the childhood years of CD cases. Items from child behavior rating scales that load on a dimension known as Delinquent or Conduct Disorder (see Chapter 9 and Appendix A) and that may indicate the earlier form of this disorder have to do with lying, stealing at home, frequent obscene language, fire setting within the home, taking the possessions of other children from their homes or school classrooms, physical fighting with other children, and early shoplifting. Within the preschool years, unprovoked aggression, threats of severe aggression or retaliation to other children, and frequently taking play materials of others—not to mention the signs of ODD—may be indicators of a significant risk for later CD.

A carefully taken family history of psychiatric disorders can, once again, assist with the differential diagnosis of both CD and ODD. Unlike children with simply ADHD, children with both ADHD and ODD or CD are considerably more likely to have a family history of CD, Antisocial Personality Disorder, substance abuse, and Major Depression among their parents or extended families.

Conclusions about the Disruptive Behavior Disorders

It should be clear from these descriptions that ADHD, ODD, and CD are not synonymous with one another. Evidence exists to show that children can have any of these disorders alone, but that they are more often likely to occur in combination with each other. Some evidence also exists to show that where ADHD exists in the presence of these other disorders (especially CD), it is likely to be associated with an earlier onset of the other disorders and a more persistent, stable pattern of antisocial behavior. Many investigators of these disorders have reached a consensus that ADHD is likely to be an early-onset disorder of cognitive or neuromaturational development pertaining to the ac-quisition of adequate attention span, impulse control, and regulation of activ-ity level. ODD and CD, by contrast, are likely to reflect problems perhaps with early negative temperament and certainly with family and social adver-sity. And so, where early ADHD is noted in the presence of disorganized, chaotic, and psychiatrically disturbed family situations, the risk for subse-quent ODD and CD would seem to be especially high.

ATTENTION DEFICIT DISORDER WITHOUT HYPERACTIVITY (UNDIFFERENTIATED ATTENTION DEFICIT DISORDER)

In Chapter 3, I have discussed the results of research on Attention Deficit Disorder without Hyperactivity (ADD/−H) as a presumed subtype of ADHD, reaching the conclusion that it appeared to be a unique psychiatric disorder distinct from ADHD. ADD/−H was renamed Undifferentiated Attention Def-icit Disorder (UADD) in the DSM-III-R. Minimal criteria were provided for its diagnosis. Essentially, the committee drafting these criteria felt that insuf-ficient research evidence existed at that time to guide their deliberations, and so little information was provided about the disorder. Since then, as discussed in Chapter 3, substantial research has accumulated to suggest that UADD constitutes a different type of attention deficit—one probably involving fo-cused attention and cognitive processing speed, rather than sustained atten-tion and impulse control. Cognitively, children with UADD appear somewhat sluggish in responding to tasks; often have their awareness focused on inter-nal events rather than external demands; and are typically much slower in completing pencil-and-paper tasks, such as the Coding subject on the Wechs-ler Intelligence Scale for Children—Revised (WISC-R). They also have con-siderably greater inconsistency in memory recall, particularly on verbal tasks. In their behavioral presentation, they are viewed by many as daydreamy, confused or lost in thought, apathetic or unmotivated, and at times slow-moving. They frequently stare. They are less active, by definition, than ADHD children and apparently less disruptive of others' activities. *They do not show a pattern of behavioral disinhibition, and hence are not impulsive, intrusive, or unable to delay gratification to a degree that is abnormal for their mental age.* Consequently, these children are rarely socially aggressive or opposi-tional and defiant, and so they probably have somewhat better social accep-tance than ADHD children. Their social acceptance, however, is not neces-sarily normal, as they do appear to be more socially neglected or overlooked, whereas ADHD children appear to be more rejected.

The distinctive patterns of behavioral presentation of UADD and ADHD are illustrated in Figures 6.1 and 6.2, which show the Child Behavior Profiles from the Child Behavior Checklist parent and teacher forms, respectively. It is readily apparent that the pattern of disruptive, aggressive, and antisocial behavior that characterizes the ADHD group is much less evident in the UADD group.

In their academic performance and achievement, UADD children are likely to be as impaired as are ADHD children. They are often described as under-achieving, or working below tested levels of academic and intellectual ability;

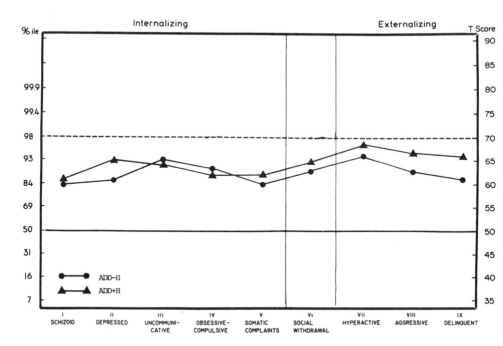

FIGURE 6.1. The Child Behavior Profile for 48 children with Attention Deficit Dis-order without Hyperactivity (ADD/−H) and 42 children with Attention Deficit Dis-order with Hyperactivity (ADD/+H), based on parent ratings on the Child Behavior Checklist.

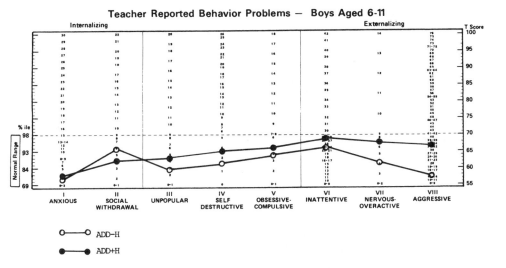

FIGURE 6.2. The Child Behavior Profile for 48 children with ADD/−H and 42 children with ADD/+H, based on teacher ratings on the Child Behavior Checklist—Teacher Report Form.

moreover, as many as 25 to 35 percent may have additional LD in reading, math, writing, or language—comorbidities similar to those between ADHD and LD

Within the DSM-III-R, the description of UADD is as follows:

> This is a residual category for disturbances in which the predominant feature is the persistence of developmentally inappropriate and marked inattention that is not a symptom of another disorder, such as Mental Retardation or Attention-deficit Hyperactivity Disorder, or of a disorganized and chaotic environment. Some of the disturbances that in DSM-III would have been categorized as Attention Deficit Disorder without Hyperactivity would be included in this category. Research is necessary to determine if this is a valid diagnostic category and, if so, how it should be defined. (American Psychiatric Association, 1987, p. 95).

The earlier DSM-III had provided more specific criteria than this (see Chapter 1), essentially requiring that these children meet the cutoff scores of three of five items in the category of Inattention and three of six items in the category of Impulsivity. The children, however, could not meet the criteria in the category of Hyperactivity. While these criteria are considerably more operational than the later DSM-III-R description of the disorder, they are not particularly valid in view of subsequent research on children with UADD. When ratings from the symptom lists from DSM-III are submitted to factor or cluster analysis, they do not load or intercorrelate in the same manner as they are listed within each symptom of the DSM-III. Some items under Hyperactivity cluster with those of Inattention while others cluster with Impulsivity, yielding a two-factor solution, Inattention-Restlessness and Impulsivity-Hyperactivity. And so use of the DSM-III criteria for ADD/-H, or UADD, would not necessarily lead to a relatively pure group. Some mildly hyperactive children could fall within this group, particularly those who are inattentive and impulsive but whose activity symptom is primarily fidgeting rather than gross motor overactivity.

Another problem with these criteria is their requirement that children be impulsive but not hyperactive. This is most unlikely to occur clinically because of the substantial interrelationship between Impulsivity and Hyperactivity items (they actually load on the same factor in statistical analyses). Moreover, as research has indicated, children with UADD or ADD/-H are not typically impulsive. Finally, the DSM-III cutoff scores are not based on any empirical data, but simply on committee consensus. Hence we do not know whether the requirement of three of five Inattention items or three of six Impulsivity items is really the best cutoff in terms of sensitivity, specificity, and the power to discriminate this group from other clinical disorders. For these reasons, I cannot recommend the use of the older, albeit more specific, criteria for ADD/-H from the DSM-III.

For the time being, the most useful approach to diagnosing this condition would be a relatively empirical one based on well-standardized rating scales with items measuring Inattention and Hyperactivity. Children scoring significantly deviant on scales measuring Inattention, but within the normal range on scales assessing Hyperactivity, would be diagnosed as having ADD/-H or UADD. Several scales are useful in this regard, these being the Child Attention Profile (CAP), the ADHD Rating Scale, or the ADD Evaluation Scale (ADDES) described in Chapter 9, and the ADD-H Comprehensive Teacher Rating Scale (ACTeRS) or the Swanson, Nolan, and Pelham (SNAP) rating scale described in Appendix A. Requiring that a child place 1.5 or 2 standard deviations above the mean on the Inattention scale and within 1 standard deviation of the mean on the Hyperactivity scale would be both clinically useful and empirically based. It was this approach that we used in our research on ADD/-H, described in Chapter 3 (Barkley, DuPaul, & McMurray, in press-a).

Teachers appear to be somewhat better than parents at making this distinction between inattentive and hyperactive symptoms, particularly when using behavior rating scales. Studies often find that when ratings of these symptoms are factor-analyzed, those from parents yield a single dimension, representing both inattentive and overactive symptoms, while those from teacher ratings yield two separate dimensions representing these symptoms. Teachers are apparently more adept at making this distinction in symptoms, perhaps because of the nature of academic work and the related behaviors demanded of the children in the classroom as opposed to the home setting. An exception to this is the ADHD Rating Scale (see Chapter 9), which yields separate Inattention-Restlessness and Impulsivity-Hyperactivity factors, or scales, for both parent and teacher ratings when the DSM-III-R symptom list is used in a rating scale format.

There now seems to be sufficient evidence about additional characteristics of these children that could be used to further refine the differential diagnosis of UADD or ADD/-H as opposed to ADHD. In addition to the empirical approach just described, clinicians would do well also to look for evidence of developmentally inappropriate degrees of the following disturbances in attention, which are less characteristic of ADHD children:

1. Often daydreams or is "lost in a fog"
2. Is frequently "spacey" or internally preoccupied
3. Is often confused or lost in thought
4. Often appears to be apathetic or unmotivated
5. Frequently is sluggish or slow-moving
6. Often stares

In addition, clinicians should exclude children who are unusually impulsive, noisy, disruptive, irresponsible, or aggressive. Recall that the essential feature of ADD/-H is not behavioral disinhibition, but a primary deficit in focused attention and perceptual processing speed. Children with ADD/-H frequently display poor performances on the Coding subtest of the WISC-R, with scores of 7 or lower (one or more standard deviations below the mean), and on measures of consistent retrieval of verbal information, such as the Wisconsin Version of the Selective Reminding Test (Newby, 1989). They typically perform within the normal range on the number correct and on the number of commission errors on a vigilance or continuous-performance test, and may have borderline or even low-normal scores for number of omission errors on this test. Consequently, in our clinic at least, we have come to think of these children as having a "focused attention disorder" rather than one of sustained attention or vigilance. As recommended in the DSM-III-R, clinicians should take care to exclude other conditions, such as ADHD, psychosis, autism, and especially anxiety disorders, as my clinical experience and some research evidence suggest that anxious children may display similar attentional problems.

The family history of psychiatric disturbance may also aid in the differential diagnosis of UADD from ADHD. Our research suggests that parents and extended relatives of children with ADHD seem more likely to have not only ADHD, but oppositional/conduct problems and substance abuse, than relatives of children with UADD. UADD children appear more likely to have relatives with LD and anxiety disorders. Where family histories suggest an unusual prevalence of psychoses, schizophrenia, or major mood disorders, clinicians should take care to evaluate the children more carefully for signs related to these disorders. Children with UADD seem to have no greater occurrence of such disorders in their families or of symptoms of such disorders in themselves.

SPECIFIC DEVELOPMENTAL DISORDERS

As discussed in Chapter 3, ADHD children are considerably more likely than normal or control groups of children to display associated problems with academic achievement skills, language, and motor-coordination. Approximately 20 to 25 percent will have significant delays in the development of math, reading, or spelling, and 10 to 30 percent may have problems with language. Parents of ADHD children also describe their children as being less coordinated, on average, than those of normal children. Clinicians must therefore be familiar with the criteria used to diagnose these conditions in ADHD children.

The DSM-III-R refers to the various types of LD as Specific Developmental Disorders. They are distinguished by inadequate development in specific academic skills areas, such as reading, math, spelling, and writing, as well as in the prerequisite cognitive areas of language, speech, and motor skills. These delays are not due to intellectual retardation or to lack of educational opportunity. A child may have as many of these disorders as are applicable. The diagnosis is based upon comparisons of the child's performance on standardized achievement tests or tests of the specific developmental abilities (e.g., speech, motor skills) with performances on intellectual tests that include both verbal and nonverbal (spatial-mechanical) abilities.

Much has been written about LD children, and no attempt is made here to review it other than to provide a cursory mention of the various disorders and the criteria used to diagnose them. Each of the skill disorders is defined by a pattern of performance on a well-standardized test of that skill area that falls makedly below the level expected on the basis of the person's schooling and intelligence, as measured by an individually administered, well-standardized IQ test. Visual and hearing impairments are to be excluded as primary causes of the condition. The disorder is diagnosed only where it results in a significant impairment with academic achievement or activities of daily living. The following are considered to be academic skill disorders: (1) Developmental Arithmetic Disorder; (2) Developmental Expressive Writing Disorder; (3) and Developmental Reading Disorder. In addition, several disorders of speech and language are also defined in the DSM-III-R as falling within the Specific Developmental Disorders category, these being Developmental Articulation Disorder, Developmental Expressive Language Disorder, and Developmental Receptive Language Disorder. Finally, a Developmental Coordination Disorder is defined as a motor skills deficit wherein one's performance in daily living skills requiring motor coordination is markedly impaired relative to one's age and intelligence, and this impairment is not due to a known physical abnormality such as cerebral palsy, hemiplegia, or muscular dystrophy.

Although these definitions seem relatively simple and straightforward, they lack any precise indication of what is meant by a "significant discrepancy" between performance in the skill area and the person's age and intelligence. This problem has been noted in Chapter 3, where three different formulas for calculating a significant discrepancy are discussed. As I have shown in that chapter, the prevalence of a particular type of LD or Specific Developmental Disorder is greatly a function of which formula is applied. The most rigorous and acceptable definition that does not overdiagnose LD in normal or mentally retarded children is the following: (1) Performance in the academic or developmental skill area 1.5 standard deviations or more below the mean on a well-standardized, individually administered test of that skill, combined with (2) a discrepancy of at least 15 standard score points (1 standard deviation) between the standardized score on the skills test (mean standard score of 100 and standard deviation of 15 points) and the standardized score on the intelligence test.

Clinicians should take note, however, that this definition may not be completely consistent with how their particular state and the school district in which the child resides defines a language disability or LD. Hence, while this definition may be quite adequate for clinical diagnosis, it may not gain access for the child to special educational resources unless the state and district criteria are also met.

It should be clear from this discussion that ADHD is not a Specific Developmental Disorder or LD as these disorders are currently defined, but that there may be some overlap, or comorbidity, of these two types of disorders. ADHD could be defined as a Specific Developmental Disorder if one chose to define ADHD as a significant discrepancy between a child's performance on a well-standardized measure of attention and the child's age and intelligence. Such a definition, however, would have to incorporate delays in impulsivity and regulation of activity level to be fully consistent with the current consensus view of ADHD. The diagnostic criteria for ADHD come precariously close to just such a definition. Should standardized tests of attention become available that are valid for ADHD, it would be possible for ADHD to be included in the federal definition of LD in Public Law 94-142 (see Chapter 15), as some parent associations for ADHD would hope. But given that well-standardized, widely available, sufficiently valid tests of these neurocognitive abilities underlying ADHD do not yet exist, the behavioral definition of ADHD given above, along with the use of the more subjective measures of parent and teacher rating scales, will have to suffice for now.

The differences in behavioral patterns between ADHD and LD children are readily evident in Figure 6.3, which shows the profiles from the Personality Inventory for Children for these two groups of children. Greater elevations on scales related to hyperactivity, aggression, delinquency, family problems, and general behavioral severity are obvious for the ADHD group.

ANXIETY DISORDERS OF CHILDHOOD AND ADOLESCENCE

Many clinicians have asked me how one can distinguish between primary ADHD and ADHD that is secondary to an anxiety disorder. I believe that

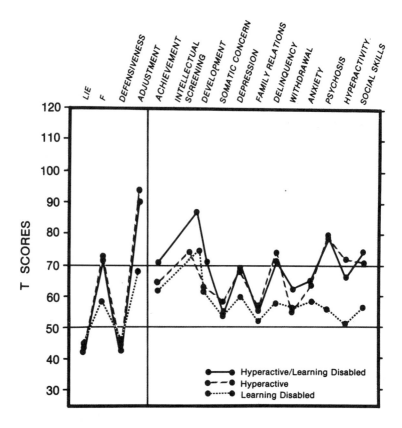

FIGURE 6.3. Meat *T* scores for learning-disabled, hyperactive, and hyperactive/learning-disabled children on the Personality Inventory for Children. From "Psychological Adjustment of Learning Disabled, Hyperactive, and Hyperactive/Learning Disabled Children as measured by the Personality Inventory for Children" by M. Breen and R. A. Barkley, 1984, *Journal of Clinical Child Psychology, 13,* 232–236. Copyright 1984 by Lawrence Erlbaum Associates. Reprinted by permission of the authors and publisher.

this question arises from a psychodynamic formulation of both disorders, or certainly of anxiety disorders. I do not hold such a view of either disorder, and so the answer seems to me at least to be obvious and simple. ADHD is always a primary disorder when the presenting complaints meet all of the diagnostic criteria and when autism and severe or profound mental retardation have been excluded. It is like any other specific neuropsychological or neuromaturational impairment or delay in a child's cognitive functioning—say, a language disorder or a reading disability. It is a specific delay in the triad of symptoms relative to one's mental age and is likely to be of neurological origin. Because it is probably neurological and hereditary in its initial predisposition, I do not see it as possibly arising out of or secondary to some psychic conflict or psychodynamic turmoil within the child. Conceived of in this way, it need not be considered a secondary condition to anything.

The idea of ADHD as a "masked" anxiety disorder simply has no evidence supportive of it in the existing research literature. That ADHD can be frequently seen in conjunction with family distress, parental marital and psychiatric problems, hostile child management methods by parents, and a chaotic home life, as well as with low self-esteem, poor peer relations, and academic failure in the child, should not deceive one into thinking that it arises *because* of these distressing aspects of the child's life. There is some evidence, in fact, to show that some of these family factors can arise *secondary* to the child's ADHD. Moreover, many studies, especially follow-up studies, of ADHD children do not show a greater prevalence of diagnoses of anxiety disorders. The exception may be Somatization Disorder, but this can be easily accounted for on the basis of the numerous medical and health problems often seen in conjunction with ADHD. And so where symptoms of anxiety are seen in conjunction with ADHD, both are best viewed, at least for now, as primary and comorbid conditions. The causes of each are likely to be quite different, and certainly their treatments must be so. Nevertheless, some mention of the types and nature of the childhood anxiety disorders is given below, merely to acquaint the young, inexperienced practitioner with their distinguishing features and to make it readily apparent why they are not at all similar to or "masked" by symptoms of ADHD.

The DSM-III-R recognizes several different types of anxiety disorders in childhood and adolescence. The specific criteria for each are not listed here, since they are seldom seen in conjunction with ADHD, but clinicians should certainly be familiar with them (see American Psychiatric Association, 1987, pp. 58–65). However, so clinically pervasive is the belief that such disorders may give rise to ADHD that a brief description of each is provided below. In any of these disorders, ADHD is not described as a frequently associated, predisposing, or resultant condition in the DSM-III-R or in any other scholarly text on the subject. I think it is time for clinical practitioners to come up to date with this view. The interested reader is referred to the excellent texts on anxiety disorders by Morris and Kratochwill (1983) and Gittelman (1986), and the superb reviews by Barrios and O'Dell (1989) and Barrios and Hartmann (1988).

What all of these disorders have in common, obviously, is that anxiety is a major or predominant characteristic of the clinical presentation. What distinguishes them is the apparent focus of or precipitant to the anxious behavior in many cases.

Separation Anxiety Disorder

A diagnosis of Separation Anxiety Disorder requires that excessive anxiety have been present for at least 2 weeks and that it occur in conjunction with separation from those to which the child is attached. The reaction must be excessive for the child's mental age. Physical complaints (stomachaches, nausea, headaches, etc.) are commonly associated with the anxious reaction, as are morbid fears of an accident or illness befalling those to whom the child is attached when he or she is separated from them. Fear of the dark is apparently a common associated phobia, and depressed mood may also be frequently seen. The onset of the disorder is before age 18, and the exclusion of a Pervasive Developmental Disorder or any of the psychotic disorders is required.

Avoidant Disorder of Childhood or Adolescence

Avoidant Disorder has as its predominant characteristic excessive "shrinking" or withdrawing from contact with unfamiliar people that is of sufficient severity to interfere with the child or adolescent's social relationships and daily functioning and that has lasted for at least 6 months. Consequently, social withdrawal, embarrassment, and timidity, as well as lack of assertiveness, poor self-confidence, and poor heterosocial activity, are commonly noted when the child is in the company of strangers; even muteness may be seen in its more extreme form. It is often seen in conjunction with other anxiety disorders.

Overanxious Disorder

Overanxious Disorder is an excessive or unrealistic and relatively pervasive anxiety that has lasted at least 6 months. The child may display excessive or unrealistic worry about future events, past behavior, or his or her competence in various areas of adaptive functioning (e.g., athletic, academic, social, etc.). Somatic complaints (e.g., headaches or stomachaches) may be seen, as in Separation Anxiety Disorder. The child may also display excessive self-consciousness, need for reassurance about various concerns, and feelings of tension or inability to relax.

Once again, taking a careful family history of psychiatric disorders among parents, siblings, and extended family members may further assist with differential diagnosis of ADHD as opposed to this or any of the other anxiety disorders. Children with anxiety disorders are unlikely to have the more frequent family history of ADHD, aggression/ODD/CD, substance abuse, and Antisocial Personality Disorder seen in children with ADHD, especially those with comorbid ODD or CD. Clinically anxious children are more likely to have a family history of anxiety disorders, parental introversion, and possibly mental illness (e.g., psychoses, mood disorders, or the schizophrenias; Werry, Reeves, & Elkind, 1987).

Conclusions about the Anxiety Disorders

At present, the research evidence available suggests that ADHD is not typically associated with any of the childhood or adolescent anxiety disorders, and that these disorders rarely have ADHD as an associated, pre-existing, or resultant condition. Excessive anxiety, in whatever form, is simply not typical of the vast majority of ADHD children. Anxious children may be restless, fidgety, and less able to concentrate, but they do not show the persistent and pervasive pattern of behavioral disinhibition, hyperactivity, and poor sustained attention from early childhood so typical of ADHD. Moreover, they are rarely impulsive and "externalizing" or acting out in their behavior, whereas the vast majority of ADHD children are so. They are often neglected by their peers if they have peer problems at all, whereas ADHD children are frequently rejected outright by their peer group. Anxious children are also unlikely to show patterns of abnormality or neuromaturational delays on formal tests of impulsivity, motor development, or executive processes. A pattern of anxiety disorders, social withdrawal, and parental overprotectiveness is more often seen in their families than in those of ADHD children (Werry, Elkind, & Reeves, 1987; Werry, Reeves, & Elkind, 1987; Gittelman, 1986).

Consequently, where excessive anxiety is seen as a comorbid feature, care should be taken to establish the form, nature, and type of the anxiety disorder, but time should not be wasted pursuing needless "chicken and egg" questions as to whether the ADHD is secondary to the anxiety or causal of it. From the point of view of diagnosing ADHD, the utility of establishing a coexisting anxiety disorder or just excessive anxiety in general is that it predicts a greater risk of an adverse reaction to stimulant medication (see Chapter 17) and that it is likely to require additional treatments beyond those typically used to treat the ADHD alone.

DEPRESSION OR MOOD DISORDERS

There is considerable conflict over whether ADHD children have more depressive or mood disorders than normal children. Some studies do find that ADHD children have higher ratings on scales measuring depression than those of normal children, while many others do not, especially when ADHD subjects are compared to clinical control groups of children. A few studies by Biederman and colleagues (Biederman, Faraone, Keenan, Knee, & Tsuang, 1989; Biederman, Menir, Knee, et al., 1987) have found a higher prevalence of Major Depression among a group of clinic-referred ADHD children, but we have not found such an association (Barkley, DuPaul & McMurray, in press-a). Follow-up studies have been consistent in showing that affective or depressive disorders are not more common in adolescence or young adulthood in ADHD individuals (Barkley, Fischer, et al., in press-a; Gittelman, Mannuzza, Shenker, & Bonagura, 1985; Weiss & Hechtman, 1986). At present, it seems best to view the depressive disorders as having a low likelihood of association with ADHD. Where present, they should certainly be viewed and treated as equally primary or comorbid conditions, rather than viewing one as secondary to the other. The presence of serious depression is viewed by some as a contraindication for stimulant medication treatment, as these drugs may exacerbate feelings of sadness or dysphoria. Others would at least urge caution in using a stimulant with a depressed ADHD child for the same reasons, although the stimulants have been noted clinically to improve some cases of depressed affect in ADHD children.

"Depression" as a symptom, however, refers to sad affect (Kazdin, 1989); this may certainly punctuate the life of the typical ADHD child periodically, particularly as regards his or her lack of peer acceptance and school failure. Low self-esteem is frequently noted in older ADHD children and adolescents, and is felt retrospectively about their childhood by ADHD individuals in adulthood. Diagnosing such children as having an Adjustment Reaction with Mixed Mood or Depressed Mood may be more appropriate, as this mild disturbance in affect is likely to arise from the numerous psychosocial stressors experienced throughout the development of ADHD children and their families.

However, where the depressed or irritable mood is more serious and persistent, a diagnosis of Dysthymia may be appropriate. The DSM-III-R criteria for this disorder are given in Table 6.3. It should be clear from the table that some adolescents with ADHD may qualify for this diagnosis. The risk for the disorder is higher in ADHD children, as there is often a greater history of this disorder within the immediate family members (over 20 percent in some studies; see Chapter 5), especially if the children have comorbid CD. In cases where both ADHD and Dysthymia are evident, both should be diagnosed,

TABLE 6.3. DSM-III-R Diagnostic Criteria for Dysthymia

A. Depressed mood (or can be irritable mood in children and adolescents) for most of the day, more days than not, as indicated either by subjective account or observation by others, for at least two years (one year for children and adolescents)
B. Presence, while depressed, of at least two of the following:
   (1) poor appetite or overeating
   (2) insomnia or hypersomnia
   (3) low energy or fatigue
   (4) low self-esteem
   (5) poor concentration or difficulty making decisions
   (6) feelings of hopelessness
C. During a two-year period (one year for children and adolescents) of the disturbance, never without the symptoms in A for more than two months at a time.
D. No evidence of an unequivocal Major Depressive Episode during the first two years (one year for children and adolescents) of the disturbance.

. . . .

E. Has never had a Manic Episode or an unequivocal Hypomanic Episode.
F. Not superimposed on a chronic psychotic disorder, such as Schizophrenia or Delusional Disorder.
G. It cannot be established that an organic factor initiated and maintained the disturbance, e.g., prolonged administration of an antihypertensive medication.

Note. From the *Diagnostic and Statistical Manual of Mental Disorders* (3rd ed., rev., p. 232) by the American Psychiatric Association, 1987, Washington, DC: Author. Copyright 1987 by the American Psychiatric Association. Reprinted by permission.

TABLE 6.4. DSM-III-R Diagnostic Criteria for Major Depressive Episode

A. At least five of the following symptoms have been present during the same two-week period and represent a change from previous functioning; at least one of the symptoms is either (1) depressed mood, or (2) loss of interest or pleasure. (Do not include symptoms that are clearly due to a physical condition, mood-incongruent delusions or hallucinations, incoherence, or marked loosening of associations.)
  (1) depressed mood (or can be irritable mood in children and adolescents) most of the day, nearly every day, as indicated either by subjective account or observation by others
  (2) markedly diminished interest or pleasure in all, or almost all, activities most of the day, nearly every day, as indicated either by subjective account or observation by others of apathy most of the time
  (3) significant weight loss or weight gain when not dieting (e.g., more than 5% of body weight in a month), or decrease or increase in appetite nearly every day (in children, consider failure to make expected weight gains)
  (4) insomnia or hypersomnia nearly every day
  (5) psychomotor agitation or retardation nearly every day (observable by others, not merely subjective feelings of restlessness or being slowed down)
  (6) fatigue or loss of energy nearly every day
  (7) feelings of worthlessness or excessive or inappropriate guilt (which may be delusional) nearly every day (not merely self-reproach or guilt about being sick)
  (8) diminished ability to think or concentrate, or indecisiveness, nearly every day (either by subjective account or as observed by others)
  (9) recurrent thoughts of death (not just fear of dying), recurrent suicidal ideation without a specific plan, or a suicide attempt or a specific plan for committing suicide
B. (1) It cannot be established that an organic factor initiated and maintained the disturbance
  (2) The disturbance is not a normal reaction to the death of a loved one (Uncomplicated Bereavement)
C. At no time during the disturbance have there been delusions or hallucinations for as long as two weeks in the absence of prominent mood symptoms (i.e., before the mood symptoms developed or after they have remitted).
D. Not superimposed on Schizophrenia, Schizophreniform Disorder, Delusional Disorder, or Psychotic Disorder NOS [not otherwise specified].

Note. From the *Diagnostic and Statistical Manual of Mental Disorders* (3rd ed., rev., pp. 222–223) by the American Psychiatric Association, 1987, Washington, DC: Author. Copyright 1987 by the American Psychiatric Association. Reprinted by permission.

and consideration of a trial of antidepressant medication may be appropriate.

As a disorder, "depression" often refers to a constellation of behaviors in addition to sad affect; these include a loss of interest in activities, feelings of worthlessness and guilt, sleep disturbances, changes in weight and appetite, psychomotor agitation or retardation, fatigue, diminished ability to concentrate or indecisiveness, and suicidal ideation (Kazdin, 1989). These symptoms occur to a more severe and persistent degree than is seen in Dysthymia. The DSM-III-R criteria for Major Depressive Episode are given in Table 6.4. These criteria include several symptoms that superficially could be viewed as related to ADHD, these being sleep problems, poor concentration, and psychomotor agitation. However, the clinical manifestation of these features is often very different in the depressed individual than in the ADHD child or adolescent. Fewer than 30 percent of ADHD children have sleep problems, and these typically involve excess bids for extra attention at bedtime and early rising, rather than the serious insomnia and hypersomnia seen in Major Depressive Episode. The poor concentration of the ADHD individual is highly situational, often appearing primarily in settings of tedium or low intrinsic reinforcement in the task, but being excellent for activities that typically interest the individual. In Major Depressive Episode, the poor concentration indicates not rapid boredom with the task, but excessive preoccupation with one's thoughts, indecisiveness, and poor awareness of one's surroundings. It is as likely to occur during interesting as during uninteresting tasks, and is associated with a loss of interest in previously pleasurable activities—something not seen in ADHD. The psychomotor agitation seen in Major Depressive Episode is not of the persistent quality of that seen in ADHD, and rarely if ever has the early onset in the preschool years often noted in ADHD. Instead, it is more episodic, being punctuated by periods of psychomotor retardation—something else that is rarely if ever noted in ADHD. And so, despite superficial resemblances in a few symptoms, these are quite distinct disorders, and where both are present they should be diagnosed and separately treated.

Manic–depression, or Bipolar Disorder, is often viewed as a more severe type of depressive disorder and is considerably less frequently diagnosed in children than is Major Depressive Episode or ADHD. Children diagnosed as having Bipolar Disorder often show periods of hyperactive behavior, particularly during episodes of the manic cycle in their disorder, and are highly likely to be aggressive and antisocial. However, the vast majority of ADHD children do not meet criteria for Bipolar Disorder. Nevertheless, many children with Bipolar Disorder are likely to meet the criteria for ADHD. Clinicians should therefore have some knowledge of the criteria used to diagnose a bipolar illness and should contrast these with the criteria for ADHD.

The criteria for Bipolar Disorder, Mixed, from the DSM-III-R are as follows (American Psychiatric Association, 1987, p. 226): First, the current (or most recent) episode should involve the full symptomatic picture of both Manic and Major Depressive Episodes, except that the duration requirement of 2 weeks for depressive symptoms is waived; the symptoms should be intermixed or rapidly alternating every few days. Second, depressive symptoms, when these are prominent, should last at least a full day. The symptoms for Major Depressive Episode are noted above; those for Manic Episode are given in Table 6.5. It can be seen from this table that three problems seen in ADHD children may overlap with the items for Manic Episode, these being the sleep disturbance, talkativeness, and distractibility. However, as is obvious from the discussion of Major Depressive Episode, the qualitative expression of these symptoms is often quite different in this disorder than in ADHD. More im-

TABLE 6.5. DSM-III-R Diagnostic Criteria for Manic Episode

A. A distinct period of abnormally and persistently elevated, expansive, or irritable mood.

B. During the period of mood disturbance, at least three of the following symptoms have persisted (four if the mood is only irritable) and have been present to a significant degree:
   (1) inflated self-esteem or grandiosity
   (2) decreased need for sleep, e.g., feels rested after only three hours of sleep
   (3) more talkative than usual or pressure to keep talking
   (4) flight of ideas or subjective experience that thoughts are racing
   (5) distractibility, i.e., attention too easily drawn to unimportant or irrelevant external stimuli
   (6) increase in goal-directed activity (either socially, at work or school, or sexually) or psychomotor agitation
   (7) excessive involvement in pleasurable activities which have a high potential for painful consequences, e.g., the person engages in unrestrained buying sprees, sexual indiscretions, or foolish business investments

C. Mood disturbance sufficiently severe to cause marked impairment in occupational functioning or in usual social activities or relationships with others, or to necessitate hospitalization to prevent harm to self or others.

D. At no time during the disturbance have there been delusions or hallucinations for as long as two weeks in the absence of prominent mood symptoms (i.e., before the mood symptoms developed or after they have remitted).

E. Not superimposed on Schizophrenia, Schiziphreniform Disorder, Delusional Disorder, or Psychotic Disorder NOS.

F. It cannot be established that an organic factor initiated or maintained the disturbance. . . .

Note. From the *Diagnostic and Statistical Manual of Mental Disorders* (3rd ed., rev., p. 217) by the American Psychiatric Association, 1987, Washington, DC: Author. Copyright 1987 by the American Psychiatric Association. Reprinted by permission.

portantly, it is the presence of a significant mood disturbance and its cycling nature that so readily discriminates manic-depression from ADHD.

The differential diagnosis of ADHD and manic-depression can sometimes be difficult, however, especially if the child is presenting clinically at the time of a manic episode in the course of the disorder. Nieman and DeLong (1987) have shown that these disorders can be readily discriminated by reference to comorbid psychotic and aggressive symptoms. Manic children are likely to have a long-standing history of depression, considerably greater emotional maladjustment, and evidence of psychotic symptoms or significant disturbances in thinking and mood (see below). Many are highly asocial or even schizoid in their social relations—social patterns not typical of ADHD children. Furthermore, their levels of aggression are likely to be considerably more deviant than those characteristic of ADHD children of that age group. These patterns of behavior are evident in Figure 6.4, which demonstrates the differences in profiles on the Personality Inventory for Children between ADHD children and children with mania. Finally, as noted earlier, a well-taken fam-

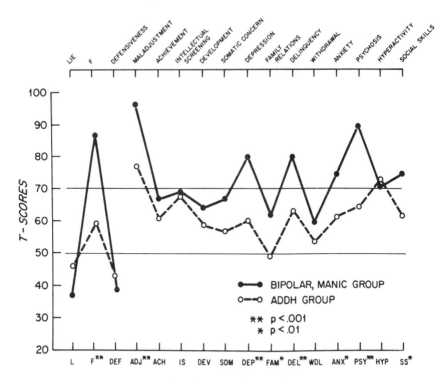

FIGURE 6.4. Mean T scores for ADHD (abbreviated here as ADDH) and bipolar, manic groups of children on the Personality Inventory for Children. From "Use of the Personality Inventory for Children as an Aid in Differentiating Children with Mania from Children with Attention Deficit Disorder with Hyperactivity" by G. W. Nieman and R. DeLong, 1987, *Journal of the American Academy of Child and Adolescent Psychiatry, 26,* 381–388. Copyright 1987 by Williams & Wilkins. Reprinted by permission of the authors and publisher.

ily history of psychiatric disturbance can be invaluable, as ADHD children are not very likely to have a greater prevalence of manic-depression or psychotic disorders, while children with mania are highly likely to have such relatives.

MIXED THOUGHT AND AFFECTIVE DISORDERS (MULTIPLEX DEVELOPMENTAL DISORDER)

Children who manifest oddities or peculiarities in the development of thinking, affect, and social interaction that are insufficient to meet criteria for the more severe disorders of autism, psychosis, schizophrenia, or even manic-depression are a tremendously understudied group. Previously, they have been labeled as having DSM-III-R Schizotypal or Schizoid Personality, or atypical

Pervasive Developmental Disorder, but many experienced clinicians recognize the inadequacy of these labels and diagnostic criteria for this group of children. Most recently, Cohen (1989) has referred to them as having "multiplex developmental disorder" (MDD), while in our clinic they have simply been referred to as having thought disorders. Certainly, they are rare in epidemiological samples—probably almost as rare as children with autism or childhood psychosis. No adequate follow-up studies have been published on this group of children, but those few that have followed children diagnosed as having Schizotypal Personality have noted a greater incidence of schizophrenia, Borderline Personality Disorder, and major mood disorders such as manic-depression among a sizeable minority of these children. Many continue to be socially eccentric, peculiar, and emotionally labile at outcome, even though they do not qualify for formal psychiatric diagnoses.

And yet these children will be occasionally seen in clinical settings, and especially in tertiary care psychiatric settings, because of the confusion and puzzlement they create among primary medical, educational, and mental health providers. Superficially, at least, many present with symptoms of ADHD and with scores on rating scales of ADHD that are considerably deviant. This can easily deceive the clinician, particularly one conducting a cursory assessment, into concluding that such children merely have ADHD. It is my opinion and that of my colleagues that distinguishing ADHD from MDD or thought disorder is one of the most difficult differential diagnoses to make. Should a stimulant medication be given to such a child, the mistake in diagnosis may often be readily apparent: The child's affective symptoms, thinking, and even social oddities may be considerably exacerbated, sometimes to the point of becoming a psychotic episode. But this is not always so, as a few of these children have been known to show greater attention and less behavioral disinhibition on stimulants, yet their eccentricities remain unchanged. However, a more careful interview (such as that described in Chapter 8) can often reveal considerably greater evidence of odd and peculiar social and emotional problems as well as disturbances in thinking, which are simply not characteristic of ADHD children. And so, while this condition rarely occurs in conjunction with ADHD in children, its frequent misdiagnosis as ADHD when it is seen in the clinic and the negative consequences that can stem from such faulty diagnosis compel me to review it here in some detail.

Development of a Rating Scale for MDD

Regrettably, absolutely no consensus diagnostic criteria exist for this group of children to guide the clinician. As a result, David Dinklage and David Guevremont in our clinic set about developing a rating scale that might serve as the basis for selecting MDD children for a research project to study them. The first draft of the scale is shown in Figure 6.5.

Several steps went into developing the items. First, a review of the scant literature on this disorder was conducted to search for potential items. Sec-

Child's name: _____   **Sex:** M F

Race: _____   **Date of birth:** _____

This form was filled out by: _____

Below is a list of behaviors. For each item, please circle 2 if the item is very true or often true of your child. Circle 1 if the item is somewhat or sometimes true. If the item is not true of your child, circle 0. Please answer <u>all</u> items as well as you can, even if some do not seem to apply to your child.

0 = NOT TRUE	1 = SOMEWHAT OR SOMETIMES TRUE	2 = VERY TRUE OR OFTEN TRUE

0 1 2   1. "Misses the point" or main idea in conversation
0 1 2   2. Rambling speech—one idea is not connected to the next
0 1 2   3. Refers to self in the third person (e.g., uses own name instead of "I" or "me")
0 1 2   4. Makes odd noises/talks in odd voices
0 1 2   5. Obsessive interest in narrow or atypical topic or event (e.g., death, the supernatural, anatomy, fantasy characters)
0 1 2   6. Makes irrelevant comments
0 1 2   7. Insists on sticking to unusual routines
0 1 2   8. Lacks interest in toys or uses toys in an unusual manner
0 1 2   9. Strong attachments to inanimate objects
0 1 2   10. Unusual aversions to neutral objects or situations (e.g., will not wear certain materials, refuses to walk up a certain stairway)
0 1 2   11. Engages in repetitive or stereotypic behavior (e.g., shakes or flaps hands, repeatedly touches hair or other material)
0 1 2   12. Extreme reactions to minor inconveniences or irritations
0 1 2   13. Difficulties dealing with change in daily schedule or routines
0 1 2   14. Marked lack of concern for appearance
0 1 2   15. Lacks social discretion (e.g., comments on people's behavior in public without concern for their reaction or feelings)
0 1 2   16. Acts as if other people were not in the same room
0 1 2   17. Poor judge of other people's reactions or feelings
0 1 2   18. Reveals overly personal detail to acquaintances or strangers
0 1 2   19. Lacks interest in peers
0 1 2   20. Makes poor eye contact with others
0 1 2   21. Does not appreciate personal space (e.g., stands too close or talks with back to person)
0 1 2   22. Mood changes quickly without apparent reason
0 1 2   23. Describes the details of an event but misses the meaning or importance of it
0 1 2   24. Sits, stands, or walks in odd postures
0 1 2   25. Attributes meaning to events that are simply a coincidence
0 1 2   26. Believes others are talking about him/her when others are speaking softly among themselves
0 1 2   27. Overly suspicious of others
0 1 2   28. Confuses the sequence in which events occurred when describing them

(con't)

0	1	2	29. Lacks compassion when others are hurt or finds it humorous
0	1	2	30. Laughs or cries for little apparent reason
0	1	2	31. Attends to background or distant sound that others would ignore
0	1	2	32. Excessively preoccupied with violent stories, TV shows, or weapons
0	1	2	33. Confuses the causes of events or fails to understand how events cause other events
0	1	2	34. Draws excessively detailed pictures
0	1	2	35. Dislikes being held or touched
0	1	2	36. Keeps a diary or journal of rambling thoughts or random ideas
0	1	2	37. Speaks in half-thoughts or incomplete phrases without concern for whether others can understand or follow his/her ideas
0	1	2	38. Gets angry for little apparent reason
0	1	2	39. Has unusual fears not typical for his/her age group (e.g., afraid to take shower or put head under the water after 6 years of age)
0	1	2	40. Hoards worthless objects that have no apparent meaning or value
0	1	2	41. Speaks in excessively loud or soft voices
0	1	2	42. Overreacts to pain (e.g., bumps leg and screams or cries excessively)
0	1	2	43. Exhibits ritualistic behavior (e.g., has to line up toys in a particular order after using them)
0	1	2	44. Spends an unusual amount of time fantasizing
0	1	2	45. Mouths or chews objects
0	1	2	46. Seems to be extremely naive for his/her age (e.g., believes anything he/she is told)
0	1	2	47. Does not respond to the initiations of other children
0	1	2	48. Picks nose, skin, or other parts of the body
0	1	2	49. Makes bizarre statements
0	1	2	50. Interacts with acquaintances and strangers in a similar manner
0	1	2	51. Hits or bites self
0	1	2	52. Repeats certain acts over and over
0	1	2	53. Lacks modesty for his/her age

FIGURE 6.5. Children's Atypical Development Scale (CADS). Reprinted by permission of the developers, David Guevremont and David Dinklage.

ond, a group of four experienced clinicians was then convened to consider these items and to generate further items. And finally, a review of the charts of 20 such children was undertaken to look for clinical comments, interview notes, and the like that could suggest further items. This resulted in a 53-item list. Each item can be answered 0 ("not true"), 1 ("somewhat or sometimes true"), and 2 ("very true or often true").

The scale was then administered to parents of 23 children with diagnoses of atypical Pervasive Developmental Disorder or "thought disorder" and 20 matched ADHD children. These were children of normal intelligence who did not have autism, psychosis, or Asperger's syndrome. Two control groups of

TABLE 6.6. Results of a Pilot Study to Develop a Rating Scale for Multiplex Developmental Disorder

1. Misses the point or main idea in a conversation (43 vs. 15%)
2. Rambling speech—one idea is not connected to the next (35 vs. 5%)
6. Makes irrelevant comments (48 vs. 10%)
7. *Insists on sticking to unusual routines (57 vs. 0%)*
9. Strong attachments to inanimate objects (43 vs. 5%)
11. *Engages in repetitive or stereotypic behavior (e.g., shakes or flaps hands, repeatedly touches hair or other material) (65 vs. 0%)*
12. *Extreme reactions to minor inconveniences or irritations (65 vs. 30%)*
13. *Difficulties dealing with change in daily schedule or routines (61 vs. 15%)*
14. Marked lack of concern for appearance (43 vs. 15%)
15. *Lacks social discretion (e.g., comments on people's behavior in public without concern for their reaction or feelings) (65 vs. 10%)*
17. *Poor judge of other people's reactions or feelings (61 vs. 15%)*
19. Lacks interest in peers (39 vs. 5%)
20. Makes poor eye contact with others (39 vs. 5%)
22. *Mood changes quickly without apparent reason (55 vs. 30%)*
23. Describes the details of an event but misses the meaning or importance of it (39 vs. 5%)
29. Lacks compassion when others are hurt or finds it humorous (39 vs. 0%)
30. *Laughs or cries for little apparent reason (57 vs. 20%)*
31. *Attends to background or distant sound that others would ignore (57 vs. 5%)*
33. *Confuses the causes of events or fails to understand how events cause other events (61 vs. 10%)*
37. Speaks in half-thoughts or incomplete phrases without concern for whether others can understand or follow his/her thoughts (35 vs. 5%)
38. Gets angry for little apparent reason (48 vs. 30%)
39. Has unusual fears not typical for his/her age group (e.g., afraid to take a shower or put head under the water after 6 years of age) (35 vs. 5%)
40. Hoards worthless objects that have no apparent meaning or value (35 vs. 10%)
41. Speaks in excessively loud or soft voices (48 vs. 25%)
44. Spends an unusual amount of time fantasizing (35 vs. 5%)
46. *Seems to be extremely naive for his/her age (e.g., believes anything he/she is told) (57 vs. 10%)*
48. Picks nose, skin, or other parts of the body (48 vs. 20%)
49. Makes bizarre statements (35 vs. 10%)
52. Repeats certain acts over and over (35 vs. 5%)
53. Lacks modesty for his/her age (48 vs. 10%)

Note. The percentages given here indicate the proportion of parents in the MDD and ADHD groups, respectively, who endorsed these items. Items were included in the table if they were endorsed by at least 35 percent of the MDD parents; items endorsed by more than 50 percent of these are italicized. Results are reprinted with permission of David Guevremont and David Dinklage, the principal investigators in this study.

LD ($n = 12$) and normal ($n = 12$) children were also used. The results are shown in Table 6.6. The results of this pilot study confirm Cohen's conclusions that MDD children have disturbances in thought, affect, and social conduct that are very different from those in ADHD, LD, or normal children. Chief among these were the items shown in Table 6.6, endorsed as 2 ("very true or often true") for at least 35 percent of the MDD group. These items were endorsed for considerably less of the ADHD groups, and for few or none of the controls. Parentheses compare MDD to ADHD groups. Items italicized in the table were endorsed by more than half of parents in the MDD group, and therefore seem to be the most distinguishing features of MDD as compared to ADHD. They also might eventually serve as the basis for the development of formal diagnostic criteria for MDD.

Essential Features of MDD

I offer here a set of personal guidelines that have proven quite clinically useful and that are in agreement with Cohen's (1989) suggestions for discriminating MDD from other childhood disorders. Many of these observations are also derived from the small pilot project by David Guevremont and David Dinklage described above.

In the differential diagnosis of thought disorder or MDD, the clinician probes for evidence of *odd and peculiar behavior or symptoms* within at least three of the following five domains of development: thinking, affect, social, sensory, and motor. This is not to say that ADHD children do not have problems in several of these domains, for they do, as described in Chapter 3. However, their behavior is often immature or like that of younger normal children, whereas that of MDD children is odd, atypical, and not at all like that of younger children (or, for that matter, any age group of normal children).

Disturbances in Thinking

Developmentally atypical symptoms within this domain are common and should probably be viewed as essential to the diagnosis of the disorder. MDD children manifest odd, peculiar, and even eccentric patterns of thinking that bear a striking resemblance to the thinking problems seen in the schizophrenic disorders, but to a considerably weaker degree (they are not sufficient for a diagnosis of psychosis). Although ideas may be occasionally bizarre, hallucinations and delusions are frankly absent. Instead, MDD children show patterns of loose thinking that is mildly disorganized at times but not necessarily incoherent or unintelligible. They may skip across ideas while speaking without providing adequate transitions, may utter half-thoughts of ideas, and may respond to questions from others with answers irrelevent to the topic of the question. Confusion in the temporal order of events being narrated, as well as the causal connection between events, may sometimes be observed. Unusual fascinations and preoccupations sometimes exist. The children's speech may be excessively detailed when describing an event, and they may often fail to get to the point of their explanation.

MDD children often misperceive the intent of others' actions and behaviors toward them, frequently injecting excessive meaning into what others say or do. This overinterpretation of events or finding significant meanings in minor affairs can even occur with spurious or coincidental social or physical events.

Vaguely formed ideas of reference are sometimes seen in older children with MDD; for example, they may believe that what other children are discussing out of hearing range is about them. At other times, they may as often miss the intended meaning of others' comments, intonations, or gestures, and as a result do not seem to be "with it." Abstract ideas, double entendres, or subtle meanings seem very difficult for these children to detect in the behavior and conversations of others. This concreteness of ideas may also be seen in academic work as well. Such cognitive distortions are not typical of ADHD children. Staring, daydreaming, and episodes of intense pensive thought or internal preoccupations are not uncommon, such that MDD children's awareness seems detached from ongoing external events.

Disturbances in Affect

MDD children are frequently likely to have odd, peculiar, or atypical patterns of emotional expression that may be almost as important as the difficulties in thinking. The crux of the disability in affect, it seems to me, is that feelings are often dissociated from the ongoing situational context. Emotions may be quickly triggered by minor or trivial events and grossly exaggerated in their degree, while little if any emotion may be forthcoming in social contexts where it is natural and expected. Consequently, these children may be observed to laugh or cry, or express hatred, anger, or extreme sadness, for little or no apparent reason. These feelings may arise quickly, with no apparent warning, and just as quickly disappear, leaving the children acting as if nothing odd had transpired in their feelings at all. Either extreme fascination with or extreme aversion to violent acts as seen in movies or television may sometimes be seen. At other times, when others known to the children suffer injuries or tragic events, they may appear bland or completely unmoved by the emotionally moving events, or may show the opposite reaction to that deemed socially appropriate (e.g., laughing at another's injury or misfortune). The feeling of empathy is often difficult for these children.

Because of the labile, capricious, and unpredictable nature of emotional expression in MDD children, their parents and peers find it confusing to know how to act around them, as they never really know what may set the children off on the next emotional burst. It is possible that some of these children are manifesting an early form of Bipolar Disorder, and this certainly needs to be carefully considered clinically (see above). But for many others the pattern of moodiness is not cyclical or alternating simply between manic and depressive poles of emotion, but seems to be a more pervasive disturbance of most or all dimensions of affect. It is the grossly situationally inappropriate and odd pattern of these feelings that readily distinguishes MDD from ADHD. ADHD children may be overly emotional, quick to anger, or low in frustration tolerance, but their affect is rarely considered odd, peculiar, or divorced from reality. Exaggerated in their expressions, perhaps; detached and capricious, hardly.

Disturbances in Social Functioning

The third area of disturbance, that of social functioning, is witnessed almost as often as the other two; in Cohen's (1989) conceptualization of MDD, these three form the "holy trinity" of features of it. Again, the distinguishing character of MDD in the social domain is its odd, peculiar, and utterly atypical quality. ADHD children may be socially assertive, aggressive, and disruptive, and often are quite immature, but rarely are they viewed as strange, odd, weird, or peculiar in their social conduct by others. MDD children, in contrast, are often seen by others, especially peers, as strange indeed. They often may display no interest in making and maintaining friendships with others or initiating social contacts; in this respect, they are much like schizoid personalities. Their play, hobbies, or other interest may be somewhat odd and often socially isolated. They have few if any close friends, often by choice, and it is very hard to motivate them to seek out frequent social contacts or develop friendships because of their apathy and lack of motivation concerning social relations.

When interacting with others, MDD children may violate accepted norms of social exchange, as in standing too close or too far from others; showing no effort at eye contact; inappropriately touching others; displaying peculiar mannerisms during interactions; and initiating, changing topics in, or terminating conversations with others in peculiar ways. In younger children, wandering away during the middle of cooperative games or conversations with others without comment can occur. During verbal social exchanges, the thinking difficulties noted above may come into play, making the children seem goofy, awkward, clumsy, or simply strange in their conduct, thoughts, and interests. They are often seen by parents as indiscreet in the information they divulge to others, often revealing close, confidential family matters to utter strangers.

MDD children sometimes seem to misperceive their own social status, believing themselves to be liked by others and to have some friends or even loving relationships with members of the opposite sex that either do not exist or exist at a mere fraction of the closeness level perceived by these children. This can frequently lead to considerable social troubles or contacts with authorities in school. They may say or do things based on these distorted social perceptions that suggest a closeness or intimacy they simply do not have with the other party. In adolescence, obsessions with others, especially members of the opposite sex, can sometimes develop to the point where they harass the objects of their intense interests.

A lack of concern for their appearance is not infrequently noted in MDD children by their parents. Poor dental and body hygiene, and a lack of interest in necessary self-care routines, may be seen long past the age where older children or early adolescents have begun to take personal initiative for these routines. Clothing is sometimes chosen and worn without any regard for its social acceptability, but merely its functional value. Repeatedly wearing dirty garments, lack of concern for use of deodorants, and little or no attention to hair care or style may develop in some older MDD children to the extent that classmates or school authorities must comment to them or their parents about taking action to deal with these problems.

Disturbances in Sensory Perception

Distortions or odd, peculiar, or eccentric perceptions within sensory domains are not as commonly witnessed as the three primary disturbances; some MDD children show none of these sensory characteristics at all. Others, however, seem likely to have unusual sensory reactions. Sometimes they may fail to detect obvious, loud, or important sensory stimuli, while at other times they may overreact or overattend to minor sensory input. Trouble in distinguishing the signal from the noise in sensory input seems at times to typify their sensory reactions. They may completely unattend to loud noises on one occasion but may overreact, sometimes painfully, to equally loud noises on other occasions. Some may be unusually bothered by touch or physical contact with others, appearing to be tactilely hypersensitive or defensive. A few MDD children my colleagues and I have seen are distressed by contact with water, especially submersion of their heads during a bath or shower, while a few others show unusual withdrawal or fearful reactions to bright lights, bold colors, or busy patterns. Out of these peculiar sensory perceptions may develop certain ritualistic behaviors of preferences that are equally peculiar. These sensory-perceptual disturbances seem to mimic (to a very weak degree) the perceptual inconstancies seen in autistic children. A penchant for excessive detail may be seen in their artwork or written stories as much as in their verbal narratives, described earlier. Parents report that some of these children seem to focus on the minor details of the environment, often missing or showing diminished interest in the important elements of a context.

Disturbances in Motor Behavior

As is the case with sensory-perceptual oddities, some though by no means the majority of MDD children display peculiarities in motor behavior. These may be displays of odd posture, manner, gait, or carriage while sitting, standing, or walking. They may stand and slouch in an odd posture, walk hunched over or near walls of hallways as if in a paranoid or protective fashion, or stride with odd rhythm or peculiar motion. Others may show repetitive, purposeless motions such as stereotypies. Again, the types of motor oddities are similar to those seen in autism or the childhood psychoses, but are considerably less severe, frequent, or disruptive to the children's daily functioning.

Conclusions about MDD

It is our custom in our clinic to view children who have disturbances in at least three of these five domains to have a thought disorder or MDD. This of course assumes that the children do not meet criteria for Pervasive Developmental Disorders, for psychoses or schizophrenia, or for the major affective disorders. We have frequently noticed that parents will be far more aware of these symptoms than teachers. Also, academic achievement or even classroom performance may be little if at all impaired. Other than the social withdrawal or aloofness and excessively detailed and concrete thinking shown by these children, school personnnel may be blissfully unaware of the unpredictable and confusing behaviors of these children that parents must contend with at home.

One tipoff that a clinician may be contending with such a case is when parent rating scales of child psychopathological symptoms (such as the Child Behavior Checklist) show that the majority of items have been endorsed, many to the extreme degree. Such ratings may show that the child is certainly deviant on symptoms of ADHD, but rendering this diagnosis from such ratings alone would be a gross presumption. A second useful source of information is once again the family history of psychiatric disturbance. It is our experience that MDD children have a considerably higher prevalence of schizophrenia, other psychoses, and the major affective disorders than either ADHD or normal children. Where such a history is recorded, the clinician would do well to probe very carefully in the five developmental domains described above to ensure that the case is not MDD masquerading superficially as ADHD.

SUMMARY

Children with ADHD are highly likely to have other associated or comorbid disorders. In this chapter, I have attempted to review the diagnostic criteria and differential diagnostic features of not only ADHD but also these other disorders. Substantial attention has been devoted to ODD and CD because of their considerably greater comorbidity with ADHD than any other disorders. Criteria for ADD/−H or UADD have been proposed in view of the lack of current consensus criteria for this unique childhood condition. It now seems likely that this disorder represents a separate, distinct childhood psychiatric condition from ADHD rather than being a subtype of it.

A small but still sizeable minority of ADHD children are likely to have problems with one or more of the different types of LD or Specific Developmental Disorders, and so these have been briefly discussed. Although anxiety disorders and depression are relatively rare in ADHD children, I have discussed their nature here as well because of the common clinical misconception that ADHD may be a "masked" form of these other disorders. And, lastly, I have attempted to discuss the guidelines clinicians might wish to use in distinguishing a rare but clinically significant group of children who are often misdiagnosed as having ADHD, but who have far greater disturbances in thinking, social, and affective domains of development—children with thought disorders or MDD.

PART II

ASSESSMENT

Through every rift of discovery some seeming anomaly drops out of the darkness, and falls, as a golden link, into the great chain of order.

—Edwin Hubbell Chapin (1814–80)

7

Clinical, Developmental, and Biopsychosocial Considerations

TERRI SHELTON AND RUSSELL A. BARKLEY

> Marshall thy notions into a handsome method.—One will carry twice more weight packed up in bundles, than when it lies flapping and hanging about his shoulders.
>
> —THOMAS FULLER (1608–61)

The process of assessment is a critical factor in the diagnosis and treatment of any behavior disorder, and this is no less the case with Attention-deficit Hyperactivity Disorder (ADHD). Viewed as a developmental disorder of attention span, impulse control, activity level, and rule-governed behavior, which begins in early childhood and has multiple etiologies, ADHD is complex, and the assessment process and subsequent treatment must reflect both the developmental nature of the disorder and its complexity.

Two recently emerging trends in the conceptualization and treatment of childhood psychopathology have bearing on the assessment of ADHD. First, there is a growing awareness of the need for a systems perspective and a consideration of individual differences. The translation of this perspective into assessment means that several levels of analysis (i.e., genetic, neurological, neuropsychological, behavioral, familial, and broader social factors) must be examined. Second, there must be an integration of traditional clinical approaches with knowledge of developmental principles. Because of the complexity of most childhood behavior disorders, and of ADHD in particular, decisions about referral, assessment, diagnosis, and treatment must be evaluated within a developmental and social context. Adaptational difficulties that lead to referral frequently reflect developmental and/or situationally inappropriate or exaggerated expressions of behavior that may at times occur in children not referred (Achenbach & Edelbrock, 1981). Thus, as Mash (1989) notes, "decisions are best made based on a consistently applied theoretical framework, well-established research findings, relevant to both normal and deviant child and family functioning, empirically documented treatment procedures, and operational rules that are sensitive to the realities and changing demands of clinical practice" (p. 4). An appreciation of both the biopsychosocial factors and the developmental context provides such a conceptual framework for designing and administering an assessment battery, interpreting results, and translating these into treatment recommendations.

THE BIOPSYCHOSOCIAL PERSPECTIVE

The need for the biopsychosocial perspective is clearly applicable to the assessment of ADHD. In this model, the various levels of analysis or functioning are analogous to a series of concentric circles, with the innermost circle representing the biological level of functioning, surrounded by the successive levels of cognitive or neuropsychological functioning, behavioral-environmental interactions, social-familial functioning, and finally the socioeconomic or sociopolitical level. Impairments in functioning at any level may have an impact upon the functioning of adjacent levels, which then may create spillover or radiating effects into other levels of this model. Generally, disturbances at inner levels of functioning are believed to radiate outward to the larger, adjacent circles that encompass them. However, these effects may also radiate inward toward lower or more biological levels of functioning in some cases. For instance, certain socioeconomic factors, such as a parent's layoff from employment, may result in an acute change in the family's ability to afford safe, decent housing. This stressor may then radiate inward in the model: The family's subsequent choice of housing—say, an older, dilapidated apartment—may then expose the child daily to leaded paint in the environment. This increases the subsequent risk of lead poisoning. Should such poisoning occur, it has an impact upon the neurological integrity of the child. These changes in neurological integrity then radiate back outward to affect cognitive and neuropsychological functioning, behavior, and so on. Clearly, transactions may occur in either direction across these levels of functioning. Despite this interplay among biological, psychological, and social factors, each level is considered separately here, merely to highlight its relative importance for the assessment of ADHD.

Biological Factors

At the first level of the child's functioning stand the child's physical integrity; genetic predispositions toward various behavioral classes, such as depression, anxiety, or even ADHD; and especially the neurological integrity of the central nervous system, as this is the final common pathway for all behavior. A number of findings from the literature on ADHD suggest that the biological level is an important level of analysis in assessing ADHD children. Certain early biological factors have been identified as placing a child at risk for ADHD. Although the link is still controversial, there is some evidence that maternal smoking may be related to later ADHD (Denson, Nanson, & McWatters, 1975; Nichols & Chen, 1981). More clearly established is the link between excessive alcohol use during pregnancy and fetal alcohol syndrome, as well as the less severe manifestation in fetal alcohol effects. Hyperactivity has been found to be among the behaviors associated with this syndrome, as well as mental retardation and/or learning difficulties (Jones, Smith, Ullenland, & Streissguth, 1973; S. E. Shaywitz, Cohen, & Shaywitz, 1980). Other prenatal and perinatal factors such as anoxia should be examined. While the relationships between these prenatal factors are at present correlational and not clearly causative, they should be considered as part of a global assessment.

Other theories have suggested that environmental toxins may contribute to ADHD. For example, some evidence of a correlational nature exists that elevated blood lead levels in children may be related to excessive activity and inattention (David, 1974; de al Brude & Choate, 1972, 1974; Gittelman & Eskinazi, 1983). Although these factors are thought to explain ADHD for only a small percentage of children, the impact of elevated lead levels on learning suggests that this issue should likewise be addressed in a comprehensive ADHD evaluation.

Because of the pervasiveness of the deficits associated with ADHD, along with variability in performance across children, studies, tasks, and occasions, many have proposed that there are generic underlying deficits. Disruptions in the central nervous system, such as possible neurotransmitter dysfunctions or imbalances, have been proposed as causing ADHD. The findings of decreased cerebral blood flow, frontal lobe deficits on neuropsychological tests, and various psychophysiological findings intimate some central nervous system mechanism in the development of ADHD symptoms (Anastopoulos & Barkley, 1988; Chelune, Ferguson, Koon, & Dickey, 1986; Hastings & Barkley, 1978; Lou, Henriksen, & Bruhn, 1984). While an inclusion of some of these assessments may not be practical in routine ADHD evaluations (e.g., cerebral blood flow studies), a consideration of neuropsychological characteristics may comprise a "second-level" assessment where more specific information is needed about a child's ability and risk for learning disability (LD).

An increased number of minor physical anomalies (Firestone & Prabhu, 1983; Fogel, Mednick, & Michelsen, 1985) and neuromaturational "soft" signs (e.g., poor balance, impaired fine motor coordination, clumsiness) also have been associated with ADHD. While identification of these is not essential for establishing the diagnosis of ADHD, some attention should be devoted to them, given their potential impact on the child's social and academic competence.

Cognitive/Neuropsychological Factors

The second level of functioning or analysis in the biopsychosocial model is concerned with the functional status of the central nervous system as it pertains to neuropsychological and developmental competencies of the child. Deficits in executive processes, rule-governed behavior, and behavioral inhibition constitute the essence of ADHD, and therefore mark this level of analysis as being imperative in assessment of the ADHD child.

The child's individual differences and certain psychological/intellectual characteristics are important factors in the way in which ADHD manifests itself, and thus should be part of the ADHD evaluation. There is broad intraindividual variability across tasks and situations among children with ADHD (Whalen, Henker, & Hinshaw, 1985). Therefore, in addition to assessing whether or not a child can accomplish or complete a task, the clinician should examine other factors as well. Individual differences in the style of problem solving; manner of approaching the task; the ability to develop a strategy and to translate that strategy into action; compensatory skills a child uses to help maintain his or her attention or to avoid the task (e.g., self-distracting behaviors); the ability to shift set; and the attributions the child makes for his or her success and failure are all factors that influence the child's academic performance and social interactions.

In the testing situation, note must be made not only of the child's compensatory skills, but of the motivational strategies provided by the examiner to obtain the child's cooperation. Along with this, it should be clear whether the examiner's goal is to obtain the child's "best" or "average" performance. Other individual differences and psychological factors, such as whether the child has taken any medication, should be noted as well.

As mentioned, there is inherent variability in the ADHD child's performance, depending on the test stimulus (e.g., poorer performance if the task is overly familiar; Zentall, 1986). As Ross and Ross (1982) summarize:

> If the attributes of the task are sufficiently powerful—for example, novel, exciting, visually focusing to mobilize the child's cognitive energy—and he possesses the requisite task competencies, then he will perform at a level appropriate for his IQ score. . . . He also attends closely to television programs, movies, and to the passing scene while riding in an automobile for relatively long periods. In these situations his cognitive energy is to a great extent being mobilized for him: in the first case by a compelling adult and in others by an attention directing presentation. (p. 220)

Other factors affecting performance and the degree to which ADHD compromises the child's abilities may include the child's task preferences, the child's temperament or mood, and whether the child performs better in the morning or afternoon. Assessing these factors can be helpful not only in reconciling conflicting data in the assessment, but, perhaps more importantly, in making program recommendations.

The child's cognitive abilities are perhaps the key neuropsychological factors to be assessed or examined within the ADHD evaluation. Not only is this necessary for the diagnosis itself, to determine that the child's behavior is inappropriate when compared to other children of the same mental age, but the information is important for treatment and prognosis as well. For example, children with ADHD who are very bright may be performing at grade level. If their behavior is not disruptive, they may not come to the attention of the classroom teacher. However, if an intellectual assessment reveals that the children have superior intellectual abilities, then performing at grade level is clearly not in line with these skills, and some type of academic intervention should be investigated. Likewise, a child with ADHD who has above-average intellectual abilities may have a better prognosis than a child with low-average skills because of the ability to generate and use compensatory strategies.

Some children with ADHD may be having difficulty with a particular subject in school because they perceive it as boring (e.g., learning multiplication tables). However, others may have difficulty, not because of interest, but because of specific deficits in skills required for that task (e.g., auditory memory). For example, the interaction of visual-motor problems with the ADHD characteristics of distractibility and the inability to persist may impede a child's development of handwriting skills. Some children with ADHD do have some type of LD, although the percentage is relatively small (i.e., approximately 25%, with estimates varying depending on the definition of LD). These children present particular challenges, not only for assessment but for classroom intervention. While clearly the ADHD and LD interact, multiple intervention strategies are needed, and care must be taken not to ignore one or the other difficulty.

As mentioned elsewhere (Chapter 3), ADHD often occurs in conjunction with other behavior disorders. An evaluation of these psychological factors is imperative. The assessment of the co-occurrence of difficulties such as conduct problems helps to identify those children at risk for antisocial difficulties in the future (Thorley, 1984; Weiss & Hechtman, 1986). It is also important in examining the appropriateness of the addition of stimulant medication to the treatment package and may help to organize treatment goals by priority. For example, the primary treatment goal for the adolescent who has not only ADHD but a history of stealing and aggression as well is likely to be amelioration of the conduct problems, because of the importance of these behaviors for the safety of the individual and others, their impact on family interaction, and their effects on the prognosis for future psychological adjustment.

Finally, the ADHD evaluation should consider the child's *positive* psychological and individual characteristics as well. The child with ADHD is likely to demonstrate difficulties in a number of areas, and it is easy to devote the majority of the assessment to the identification of these deficits. However, the child's strengths as well as weaknesses should be evaluated. Information from the fields of developmental disabilities and early intervention indicate that this competency-oriented or enablement model, as opposed to the deficit-oriented medical model (e.g., Dunst, Trivette, & Deal, 1988), is more likely to encourage an active participation on the part of parents and the child in remedying the difficulties. Furthermore, highlighting the child's strengths not only serves to identify a basis for the development of compensatory strategies, but also may help to improve the child's self-esteem.

Behavioral and Environmental Factors

At the next level of the biopsychosocial model, one examines the immediate, molecular interactions of the child's neuropsychological and behavioral functioning with the social environment. How well is the child able to meet demands made by caregivers and others in the environment? What consequences accrue to the child as a result? How sensitive is this child to this ongoing stream of social interactions, which provide literally hundreds of learning trials daily that shape and mold the child's behavioral repertoire? These are all issues to consider at this level of analysis.

ADHD is not qualitatively different from normal behaviors; rather, it is the presence of extreme levels of impulsivity, distractibility, activity, and so on. Therefore, it is important to assess not just the child's individual differences—the presence or absence of the behaviors; their frequency, intensity, and chronicity—but the social context in which these behaviors occur (Campbell, 1990). This social context includes specific task and situational parameters, as well as interactions with parents, teachers and peers.

Task and Situational Parameters

The impact of situational characteristics on the variability in the ADHD child's task performance has been noted. However, these variables can be easily overlooked in a traditional assessment. For example, the way in which the teacher structures the classroom affects the child's performance. A preschooler with ADHD may have difficulty in an open or Montessori-style classroom if the expectations or demands are not clear or if the child is not assisted in the transition from one learning center to another. For the child with ADHD who is receiving some resource room assistance, the number and timing of transitions from the regular classroom to the resource room may affect the child's level of attention and cooperation. As transitions are often difficult for the child with ADHD, expecting the child (particularly a young child) to make the transition from one classroom to another several times a day may be problematic. The difficulty and interest level of the task are likewise important to assess; the reinforcement schedule that is operating in the home or school environment is a factor as well. Numerous studies have documented that changes in these variables can exacerbate or diminish the severity of the ADHD symptoms (Douglas & Parry, 1983; Parry & Douglas, 1983; Draeger, Prior, & Sanson, 1986). Knowledge of the way in which the child receives feedback can help the clinician not only to assess the presence or absence of ADHD and its severity, but also to identify areas for intervention.

Other general aspects of the physical environment should be assessed if at all possible, such as through a school observation. For instance, in a classroom, the space, comfort, level of distraction, noise, and student-teacher ratio can affect the performance of all children, but children with ADHD may be particularly sensitive to these variables.

Social Interaction

A child with ADHD is at risk for problematic interactions with parents, teachers, and peers because of the characteristics of ADHD. The importance of these interactions in the child's development necessitates that the child's competencies as well as the responses of others in these areas be assessed in some way. The child's and family's coping reactions and the possible breakdown in adaptation yield important information for both diagnosis and treatment (Cicchetti & Braunwald, in press; Tronick & Gianino, 1986; Zeitlin, Williamson, & Rosenblatt, 1987).

Previous research indicates that although some of the parent-child interaction is dependent on the reciprocal influences of the child's and the family's characteristics (Bell & Harper, 1977; Sameroff & Chandler, 1975), some of the ADHD child's qualities may in fact contribute to the more negative behaviors evidenced by both parents and teachers. Because the child with ADHD has difficulty with rule-governed behavior, adults—whether they be teachers (e.g., Whalen, Henker, Dotemoto, 1980) or parents (e.g., Campbell, Breaux, Ewing, Szumowski, & Pierce, 1986)—may begin to use more controlling tactics to try to curb the behavior. The resultant interaction can be a spiral of increasing oppositional and negative behavior on the part of the child, and increasingly controlling and potentially aggressive behavior on the part of the adults (see Chapter 5). Examining the interaction through interviews, analogue situations where behavior is coded during a particular task, or direct observation in the classroom provides important information about the applicability of a diagnosis of ADHD, as well as clarifying behaviors and situations to be targeted for future intervention.

Children with ADHD have problematic interactions not only with adults but with peers as well. Difficulties in taking turns, shifting from one activity to another before completing the first one, and not following the rules or directions are just some of the ADHD characteristics that can impede a child's social competence. In sociometric studies, children with ADHD consistently receive negative ratings from peers (deHaas, 1986; Johnston, Pelham, & Murphy, 1985; Whalen, Henker, Dotemoto, & Hinshaw, 1983). This is particularly problematic, given the observation that many children with ADHD are socially "busy"; they seek friends and engage in the same amount of prosocial activity as normal children, but in ineffective ways (Cunningham, Siegel, & Offord, 1985; Grenell, Glass, & Katz, 1987; Mash & Johnston, 1982). Given the importance of peer interaction in the overall development of children, this area of a child's social environment should be included as part of the ADHD assessment and, where possible, in treatment.

Social-Familial Factors

The next level of functioning to be considered in our model requires an appreciation of what some have thought of as social-contextual factors or distal influences on social interactions and family functioning. These have to do with broader and often more amorphous social influences, such as the psychological integrity of the parents and siblings and the degree to which psychiatric difficulties are present, the well-being of the marriage, and the types of stressors that may occur within daily family life—all of which can produce effects on the quality of caregiving in general toward the child, and specifically on the manner in which child behavior is to be managed.

Research findings suggest modest to moderate associations between ADHD and various dimensions of psychosocial and familial factors. However, in the families of children who have both ADHD and Conduct Disorder (CD), there are considerably higher rates of depression, alcoholism, conduct problems, and hyperactivity among first-degree relatives (Biederman, Munir, Knee, Armentano, Autor, Waternaux, & Tsuang, 1987; Cantwell, 1975; Lahey, Piacentini, McBurnett, Stone, Hartdagen, & Hynd, 1988); there is also considerably greater marital turmoil. These findings do not unequivocally suggest a causal link between these parent and family factors on the one hand and either ADHD or CD on the other. Nevertheless, the suggestion of a genetic predisposition is obvious and increasingly substantiated as more research is conducted. Moreover, the serious impact of adult psychopathology and marital disharmony on children certainly influences the course and outcome of the disorder.

An assessment of these factors is also important in planning treatment. For example, a treatment recommendation of parent training (see Chapters 12 and 13) may not be an appropriate first intervention for parents who are having significant marital problems, with one partner experiencing depression. It may be more prudent and successful to work with the child's teacher, as well as to suggest recommendations addressing the marital and adult psychological problems. Also, given the relatively higher percentage of parents of children with ADHD who have ADHD themselves, it may be difficult for parents with ADHD characteristics to follow consistently the rules of a behavior management program or to assist their children in organizing their homework when they themselves have difficulty with organization.

While the investigation of these factors can provide important information for both the treatment and prognosis of the child with ADHD, care must be taken in how the assessment is presented and conducted. Because the child is the "identified patient" referred for assessment, parents may be somewhat reluctant to provide information about an area that they believe has no bearing on the child or one that may be particularly embarrassing for them (e.g., past history of LD, current marital difficulties). Explaining the reasons behind the rating scales or interview questions and their applicability to the child's outcome, as well as providing assurance of confidentiality, can support family members in sharing this valuable information.

Finally, the child's characteristics must be interpreted within the context of parental and adult perceptions of the behavior; in other words, the examiner must note not only what behavior is reported, but how the behavior is perceived, interpreted, and labeled. For example, do the child's parents view the behavior as problematic, or are they just following the referral of another concerned party (e.g., a teacher)? Conversely, parents may identify concerns that are not shared by other adults in the child's social environment. This lack of concordance often brings into question the validity of parent and/or teacher report. Some clinicians may take the perspective that if the behavior is not viewed by them directly during the assessment or not documented on a single aspect of the child's performance (e.g., the Distractibility factor on the Wechsler Intelligence Scale for Children—Revised [WISC-R]), then the diagnosis of ADHD is not applicable. However, research supports the inherent variability in performance among children with ADHD. Many of the characteristics of the testing situation (e.g., one-on-one situation, consistent and frequent feedback, novel task demands, frequently changing tasks of short duration) may diminish the demonstration of the ADHD characteristics that are clearly evident in more frequently occurring environments, such as the classroom. Moreover, many professionals, especially in the fields of developmental disability and early intervention (e.g., Dunst et al., 1988), have supported the validity of parent report. They point out that if the parent perceives a problem, then there is in fact a problem in the parent-child interaction. While the problem may not be ADHD, and the perceptions of the parents and teacher (not the child) may form the focus of the intervention, the perspective of parents and teachers cannot be ignored.

Socioeconomic and Sociopolitical Factors

Although they occupy a less well-defined and more amorphous, indirect level of influence, socioeconomic and sociopolitical factors are of substantial import in the adjustment of ADHD children. The parents' levels of education, their type of employment, the income this provides to the family, and its stability, among other socioeconomic factors, dictate the resources that are likely to be available for dealing with the health, developmental, educational, and behavioral problems often seen in ADHD children. Cultural, ethnic, and religious factors play a role at this level of adjustment, in that they may dictate what perspective is to be taken toward a child's behavioral and academic problems, how seriously they are to be viewed, and what approaches are deemed acceptable for use in remediating these problems. The degree to which parents and extended family members involve themselves in child care and what their roles are to be are likewise often explicitly or implicitly dictated by these cultural factors.

Sociopolitical factors are also of interest at this level. The city, state, and even country in which the child and family reside, the types of social services provided by their government, and the degree of financial support society may provide its less well-functioning members are just a few of these factors that have some impact on the functioning of the ADHD child and his or her family. Even the school district where the family resides will greatly determine what eligibility conditions must be met to obtain special educational services, the types and quality of those services, and even the manner in which behavioral disorders will be viewed by the school personnel.

These "megainfluences" that operate at a macrosystem level are not always easily quantified or assessed in any systematic or straightforward way, yet they can hardly be ignored. For instance, it is easy for professionals like us to state that the adequate assessment of the ADHD child must be multi-method and rely on multiple sources of information, and that treatment must be a combination of psychological, educational, and medical interventions. However, in rural areas, such as on Native American reservations in the Southwest, it may be almost impossible to employ multiple methods of assessment across multiple sources when one is the only physician or school psychologist available to provide services to ADHD children. Moreover, the lack of trained psychologists or social workers who can implement behavioral technologies such as parent training, classroom behavior management, and marital communication and problem-solving therapy—much less double-blind, placebo-controlled trials of medication—precludes the ability to provide the multimodal, rigorously monitored treatments so frequently recommended by authorities in this field. Certainly the experts' ubiquitous dictum never to use medication as the sole intervention with ADHD children will and perhaps should go unheeded in such circumstances, as the local professional struggles to provide the highest quality of care he or she can with the limited tools of the trade available to that community.

In short, the biopsychosocial model that we advocate for use with the assessment of ADHD children requires that some attention be given to evaluating influences operating at each level of functioning within the model, if a thorough and useful appreciation of the child and social context is to result. However, we acknowledge that the extent to which this ideal is carried out in practice must depend upon the constraints of reality in particular professional settings.

DEVELOPMENTAL CONSIDERATIONS

Concurrent with the increased interest in a biopsychosocial perspective is the growing emphasis on incorporating developmental considerations into the design, conduct, and interpretation of the assessment of childhood behavior disorders (Campbell, 1990; Edelbrock, 1984; Mash, 1989; McMahon & Peters, 1985). Although the clinical/traditional psychiatric and developmental approaches to child psychopathology are not necessarily incompatible, there are important differences. Historically, the assessment, treatment, and study of childhood behavior disorders have not included both perspectives. Developmental research was not always linked to clinical research or practice. Similarly, clinicians and researchers did not always look to the body of developmental literature for a conceptual framework; rather, attempts were made to extend adult models and theories of psychopathology downward to child populations. Even when a difference was acknowledged between adults and children, some assessment instruments were designated as being for "children" of broad or unspecified age, disregarding the impact of gender or the differences among girls and boys of various ages.

As we have noted in the preceding section on the biopsychosocial perspective, a consideration of individual differences and the context in which the child functions necessarily implies a consideration of developmental factors such as the child's chronological age; level of cognitive and adaptive development; age of onset and chronicity of symptoms; family background; and social factors. The application of a developmental framework to the understanding of ADHD can be reflected in (1) the referral process, (2) the choice of an assessment battery and focus of the evaluation, (3) the interpretation of the findings and diagnosis, (4) the prognosis, (5) treatment, and (6) general aspects of the assessment process and interpretation with specific age groups.

Referral

Developmental factors come into play before the assessment process begins. Which child is referred and at what point are dependent on the child's age and gender and the interaction of these factors with parental and adult expectations and attributions for behavior. For example, the proportion of boys versus girls manifesting ADHD varies considerably across studies, from 4:1 to 9:1 (American Psychiatric Association, 1987), with an average of 6:1 being most frequently cited. However, in community samples, the proportion is reported to be approximately 3:1 among nonreferred children displaying these symptoms (American Psychiatric Association, 1987; Trites, Dugas, Lynch, & Ferguson, 1979). The discrepancy in the two estimates reflects the increased frequency with which males are referred for mental health services.

There is variability in the degree to which behavior is interpreted as abnormal, depending on age and gender. Thus, what is symptomatic at one age may not be at another. For example, aggression in a toddler may not be as much a matter for concern as aggression in an older adolescent. What may be viewed as "typical boy behavior" or the "terrible twos" may be seen as deviant in a girl or older child, respectively.

Choice of Assessment Battery

Developmental factors should be considered in the choice of the specific instruments to be used in the evaluation. Because of the importance of age and gender in the interpretation of findings, instruments must have appropriate normative data. Another consideration in the choice of an assessment battery is the degree to which self-report is used. Self-report can be a valuable adjunct in the assessment of an adolescent with ADHD, but may be more difficult to obtain and of questionable validity in a preschooler. The focus of the evaluation and the perspectives assessed will also vary according to the child's age. The evaluation of the younger child may involve evaluating the perceptions of just the parents and perhaps a day care worker. However, the evaluation of an adolescent might include an interview with the individual, self-report measures, ratings from parents, and ratings from more than one teacher. The situations where an elementary-school-aged child with ADHD may evidence difficulties may be very different from those for an adolescent, and these different settings and the perspectives of varying informants must be considered.

A developmental approach also considers the importance of historical antecedents or developmental precursors in the choice of instruments to assess ADHD. Because the current DSM-III-R criteria for ADHD (American Psychiatric Association, 1987) require that the behavioral difficulties have an onset before the age of 7 years, the assessment of ADHD in preschoolers requires measures that can be used at this age, along with appropriate normative data. Likewise, the assessment of ADHD in an older child requires the inclusion of a thorough interview with the child's parent or guardian, and possibly with the child (depending on his or her age), in order to establish the presence of the behavioral difficulties at or before age 7.

A developmental approach recognizes that change is inherent in any child's behavior. Thus, the ADHD evaluation may need to include instruments that can be administered over time, that have high test-retest reliability, and that include developmental norms, in order to determine whether the problem behaviors represent ADHD or a transient developmental phase that will improve with time alone.

Interpretation of Results and Diagnosis

The fact that change is inherent in any child's behavior creates a particular problem in the assessment of ADHD in preschoolers (e.g., Campbell, 1990; Trad, 1989; Zentall, 1985). Although the DSM-III-R requires that the behavioral difficulties be present for at least 6 months, many clinicians and researchers are questioning whether this is sufficient to ensure that ADHD is not overdiagnosed in young children (see Chapter 6; see also Campbell, 1990; Rutter & Shaffer, 1980). Problems inherent in the application of DSM-III-R criteria to childhood behavior disorders in general have been noted by Campbell (1990) and others (Guevremont, DuPaul, & Barkley, in press-a). Because of the frequency with which the behavioral difficulties characterizing ADHD occur in preschoolers, it may be prudent to increase the number of behavioral symptoms necessary for the ADHD diagnosis in this age group. As Campbell (1990) and others (Shelton & Barkley, in press) note, the danger of the diagnosis may outweigh the benefits, and the ADHD diagnosis should be used cautiously with children under the age of 5. In these instances, a descriptive approach may be more helpful in obtaining needed services for the children and in targeting behaviors for intervention without adding the potential stigma of a diagnostic label that may prove inaccurate in the future. Conversely, many (see Chapter 6) have suggested that the need to evidence 8 out of the 14 diagnostic criteria may result in underdiagnosing adolescents with ADHD. Thus, the diagnostic criteria may need to be adjusted depending on the child's age to account for the differing representation of symptoms naturally occurring in children as a whole. Chapter 6 has suggested that using 10 symptoms for preschoolers and 6 symptoms for adolescents may more accurately assess the presence or absence of ADHD in these age groups.

Adaptations in diagnostic criteria may need to be considered on individual tests as well. For example, the criteria for distractibility or vigilance in a continuous-performance task for adolescents may need to be different from the criteria for first-graders, because of the developmental changes in attention that occur with age, regardless of ADHD. Even though this problem may be addressed through normative data, the actual task requirements (e.g., length of vigilance task) may need to be adjusted to avoid the possibility that a test no longer differentiates individuals because of the lack of difficulty for a particular age group.

As we have mentioned earlier in considering individual differences, the child's developmental age must be considered in the diagnosis of ADHD. Children with mental retardation or developmental delay often evidence many of the features of ADHD because of their delay. However, the additional diagnosis of ADHD can be made only if the relevant symptoms are excessive for the child's *mental* age (American Psychiatric Association, 1987).

The frequency of the co-occurrence of ADHD with other behavioral difficulties (e.g., Oppositional Defiant Disorder in young children) also has developmental implications. A developmental approach to assessing childhood psychopathology recognizes the potential for age and gender differences in the *patterning* of behaviors. For example, Achenbach and Edelbrock (1978) found in the factor analyses of data obtained from the Child Behavior Checklist that certain behavioral difficulties tended to cluster together at certain ages but not at others. Their findings suggest that behavioral problem scales constructed for one age group may yield misleading inferences when applied to other groups. This is particularly applicable in the diagnosis of ADHD. Because the prevalence estimates for many of the individual defining symptoms of ADHD are high among the general population (e.g., overactivity and restlessness), the frequency, intensity, and chronicity of *clusters* of symptoms must be considered within a developmental and social context when defining the disorder (Rutter & Garmezy, 1983).

Developmental considerations are applicable with respect not only to the assessment of the child, but to the assessment of parent and teacher reports and interpretations of those findings. For example, a parent's perspective on his or her child's behavior can be influenced by whether he or she is a first-time parent who may have a scanty reference base for "typical boy behavior."

Prognosis

The consideration of developmental factors is important not only in the diagnosis of ADHD, but in the prognosis for the child as well. As mentioned earlier, several familial and broader social factors (e.g., degree of psychopathology among parents) affect prognosis. In addition, the age of onset, chronicity of symptoms, and co-occurrence of other symptomatology are important. For example, although one should certainly be concerned about a child's increased noncompliance, aggression, and school failure, the prognosis is quite different if the difficulties have developed over the past few months during the parents' divorce than it would be if these difficulties have been long-standing and observed in a variety of situations.

Inclusion of a developmental perspective in the assessment of ADHD implies knowledge not only of normal child development, but of the developmental course of childhood behavior problems as well. Further study is needed, but the identification of the prognostic significance of behavioral problems and the co-occurrence and patterning of other behavioral and familial problems (e.g., ADHD and CD) will be helpful in determining the priority of treatments, and in identifying those children at greatest risk for serious difficulties in the future.

Treatment

These general developmental considerations are applicable to treatment as well. The applicability and success of interventions will vary as a function of the child's age and cognitive-developmental level as well as social factors. Thus, the primary recipients of the intervention for a preschooler with ADHD symptoms will most likely be the child's parents and preschool teacher. Problem-solving strategies, such as cognitive self-instruction, are likely to be more appropriate for school-age children (Kendall, Lerner, & Craighead, 1984). Behavioral interventions in preschoolers are likely to focus on parents as the "change agents" and to target the attainment of self-help skills. Interventions with adolescents, such as the development of new patterns and skills of communication among family members, will need to involve the adolescents themselves more actively (Robin, 1981).

Impact of Developmental Perspective on Specific Age Groups

A specific application of one developmental theory—Erikson's theory of the stages of psychological development—illustrates the way in which a child's age and the demands of the social environment affect the manifestation of ADHD and thus its assessment and treatment across ages.

According to Erikson (1963), an individual's personality develops as a function of one's historical and cultural past and is constantly subject to change. He proposed that personality organization occurs in a sequence of phases, the "eight stages of man." Each phase presents the individual with a challenge, a turning or choice point in development. The importance of the developmental perspective in the assessment of ADHD is illustrated through an examination of these challenges operating during the toddler, elementary school, and adolescent ages.

Toddler and Preschool Age

In young children, the primary challenge is to acquire a sense of autonomy while combating a sense of doubt and shame. A successful outcome of this stage is a realization of will. The normal conflicts between parents and toddlers are likely to be intensified when a toddler has ADHD. The high frequency of overactivity, the short attention span, and the oppositionality that normally characterize this age group are likely to be exacerbated. Because of the frequency with which ADHD symptoms occur in this age range, it may be difficult to (1) differentiate normal parent-child conflict from oppositional defiant behaviors and (2) to diagnose the presence of ADHD. The fact that many of the assessment instruments typically used to assess ADHD do not have norms for preschoolers or may have task requirements beyond their abilities further compounds the problem. However, the child's approach to developmental assessments can be quite helpful. For example, on the Peabody Picture Vocabulary Test, the latency to first response and whether a 3-year-old considers all the choices before pointing to a picture can provide some information about impulsive responding, similar to the information obtained on the Matching Familiar Figures Test. Furthermore, this type of information is easily translated into recommendations for classroom instruction.

The settings in which the child's ADHD characteristics are most obvious may be varied. Although some toddlers are in preschool, most of these settings are not structured and a child's difficulties in following rules, sitting still, or completing boring, routine tasks may not be as obvious as later in elementary school or in the home, where the parents are struggling with the child over self-help skills. Daily activities such as getting out of bed, getting dressed, eating, going to bed, and toileting are potential battlegrounds for the toddler with ADHD. Similarly, the toddler with ADHD struggles to achieve a sense of autonomy with peers. However, low frustration tolerance, difficulty in taking turns, high activity level, and high inattention do not aid the toddler with ADHD in negotiating these early social compromises.

Thus, conflicts over daily routines and difficulties with aggression or behavioral immaturity in peer interaction are often identified by the parents of young children with ADHD, whereas the teachers may not observe any problematic behavior, or in some cases may attribute the behavior to social immaturity. Although some discrepancy between parent and teacher reports at this age is not totally unexpected, given the differences in environmental demands, attributing the behavior to social immaturity alone can be problematic if in fact a child does have ADHD. For example, the 5-year-old with behavioral or social immaturity may benefit greatly from starting kindergarten a year late or repeating the kindergarten year, without any additional educational assistance. However, if the difficulties are due to ADHD and not just to a transient delay in the acquisition of skills, retention alone will be insufficient. As one mother commented, "Using that reasoning, he will have to repeat each grade twice in order to learn the material necessary to graduate."

The interaction of the child's developmental and ADHD characteristics can affect the actual process of assessment. Because preschool children are less attentive and more impulsive than older children in general, the preschool child with ADHD will be especially inattentive. Therefore, it is important to have all testing materials organized and easily available to maximize the child's attention to the tasks. Furthermore, the total length of the assessment may need to be adjusted for the preschooler. Evaluations may need to occur over several sessions, perhaps with one session for the parent interview, another for direct testing with the child, and a third reserved for feedback and discussion of treatment recommendations.

The same determination of will that characterizes the preschooler's interaction with parents may be manifested in the testing situation. Refusing to complete tasks, to cooperate, or to inhibit "silly" behavior may arise. The examination is likely to proceed more smoothly when the expectations for behavior are communicated clearly at the beginning of the evaluation.

Some preschoolers may be especially wary of strangers and may refuse to be separated from their parents for the evaluation. A decision must be made as to whether forcibly removing the parent, which may well cause distress, is more likely to yield representative results than is having the parent present for the direct testing of the child, which will also affect results. Obviously the decision will vary on a case-by-case basis, but the information needs to be incorporated in the interpretation of the findings.

Elementary School Age

The developmental/psychological challenge for children in elementary school is to achieve a sense of initiative and a realization of purpose. While parent-child interaction is important, there is an increased attention to one's capabilities, often measured in terms of school performance or athletic abilities. This can be particularly problematic for the child with ADHD, where difficulties with "initiative" itself are common.

Many children with ADHD go undiagnosed until this point. As mentioned, the flexibility and acceptance of overactivity and inattention that characterize some preschools may conceal a child's difficulties. However, in elementary school, these behaviors are not as acceptable. At this age, children are required to follow rules and routines that are designed to facilitate the functioning of the group rather than tailored to the children's individual needs or preferences (Campbell, 1990; Ross & Ross, 1982), and thus difficulty with rule-governed behavior becomes evident among children with ADHD. A thorough developmental history can be very helpful in identifying the onset of these concerns and in helping the family and the child to understand why difficulties have arisen at this point. These difficulties may be subtle, such as mild disruptive behaviors during unstructured activities (e.g., recess, in the halls), or more obvious, such as failure to finish assigned tasks. Bright children with ADHD may have little difficulty in first through third grades, mastering the rote material despite their inability to devote full attention to the curriculum. However, they may begin to show increasing academic underachievement when entering fourth grade, as the curriculum in most schools shifts at this point from memorization of rules to the application of basic principles in new situations. The degree of independent work also increases; this often presents a problem for the child with ADHD, who often needs the motivation that the presence of an adult provides. Thus, a thorough analysis of the child's academic achievement and his or her intellectual and developmental abilities, as well as the current academic demands, is important.

The child's emerging sense of competence and self-esteem is particularly at risk at this age, given that he or she may not perform well in comparison to peers. Children with ADHD may have difficulty participating in sports. Trouble taking turns, not following instructions, ignoring rules, and inattention, as well as possible visual-motor or gross motor difficulties (which occur more often in children with ADHD), do not enhance athletic ability, particularly in group sports (e.g., playing outfield in baseball). Difficulties in peer interaction, once thought to be a transient phase of early childhood, begin to be viewed by adults and peers as an enduring characteristic. Adult-supervised activities and careful choice of sports (e.g., one in which the child, not only the parent, has interest; action-oriented activities, such as playing infield as opposed to outfield) can be helpful.

Finally, the attributions the child makes for his or her difficulties are important to assess, as are self-esteem and social competence. Often at this age, the child is old enough to be aware of the difficulties, but not old enough to understand the subtleties of ADHD. For example, many children with ADHD will acknowledge that they think they are "stupid." How else can they explain why everyone else in the class can finish their papers and they cannot? Although individual play therapy has not been shown to be helpful in reducing the effects of ADHD, it may be helpful for a child to meet with a school counselor or other therapist to explore these attributions.

Adolescence

In adolescence, the goal is to achieve a sense of identity while fending off a sense of inferiority. A successful accomplishment of this stage is a realization of competence. To accomplish this goal, there is a resurgence in autonomy, with a concomitant decline in parental influence and decreased supervision by any one teacher, and increasing responsibility for one's sexual conduct, school and family chores, and behavior in the community (e.g., driving responsibly). However, many of these emerging desires, typical developmental challenges, and social demands will immediately conflict with the ADHD adolescent's delays in judgment, persistence, self-awareness, and goal-directed behavior; perhaps as many as 75% of adolescents with ADHD will continue to evidence problems in school, home, or community adjustment (e.g., Weiss & Hechtman, 1986).

The focus of the conflict, and perhaps of assessment and treatment, often shifts from academic problems to more intense family conflicts centered around the adolescent's failure to accept responsibility for behavior, to complete routine tasks and assignments, and to obey rules. In addition, approaches that may have been somewhat successful in the past (e.g., time out) must be changed, and in some cases both parents and adolescents must learn new skills (e.g., communication strategies) in order to negotiate the inequity among the adolescents' characteristics, the environmental demands, and the developmental challenges of this age.

Other developmental considerations include an awareness of the developmental course of ADHD. While adolescents do not "outgrow" ADHD, sedentary fidgetiness often replaces excessive gross motor activity. Furthermore, the settings in which fidgetiness is most likely to occur may decrease. For example, it may be easier for the adolescent with ADHD to sit still, knowing that he or she will change classes every 45 minutes as opposed to having to sit in the same seat all day. Thus, the diagnosis of ADHD in adolescence should not be ruled out simply because of the absence of overtly inappropriate levels of activity.

In adolescence, there is often a decrease in the involvement of any one particular adult, whether parent or teacher, in the individual's life. Therefore, information about the adolescent's performance and behavior should be obtained from multiple informants wherever possible. This is particularly true of those children who receive their educational instruction from more than one teacher, as is most probably the case in high school as well as for those receiving special educational assistance. As mentioned, a lack of concordance between ratings often occurs. However, variability in performance can be important not only in diagnosing ADHD, but also in yielding important information about areas in need of intervention and about environmental characteristics that tend to increase the adolescent's positive and compensatory behaviors.

Because of their increased ability for introspective thought as well as more developed verbal skills, many older adolescents can provide valuable information about their own perspective on their behavioral difficulties. The information can be obtained through interview or self-report measures. Some assurance of confidentiality should be included when obtaining self-reports from adolescents. For example, if behavioral ratings are obtained prior to the evaluation, many adolescents may be hesitant to answer items honestly and may minimize their difficulties if they feel that their parents will view their responses prior to the evaluation. Conversely, some adolescents, particularly those having oppositional tendencies, may exaggerate their behavior difficulties if they know that their parents will be aware of their responses. As with the separation issue in preschoolers, the validity of the adolescent's self-report is difficult to determine, but the manner in which the information is obtained should be specified.

Consideration of "Goodness of Fit"

In addition to the differences that the child's age and gender make in the assessment of ADHD, two other concepts in child development literature—those of temperament and goodness of fit—illustrate the application of a developmental as well as a systems perspective in the assessment of ADHD. "Temperament," or "behavioral style," refers to the *how* of behavior, as opposed to its content, topography, or motivation. Although there are many conceptualizations of this construct, the most widely recognized and used system in clinical research and practice derives from the work of Thomas, Chess, and their associates in the New York Longitudinal Study (Thomas, Chess, Birch, Hertzig, & Korn, 1963; Thomas & Chess, 1977; Thomas, Chess, & Birch, 1968). Thomas and Chess noted that temperamental characteristics, even those associated with the "difficult child" (e.g., arrhythmic, withdrawing, nonadaptable, intense, and negative), did not lead inevitably to behavioral problems. Rather, it was the "goodness of fit"—the interaction of the environmental demands, expectancies, and supports with the child's characteristics—that was the determining factor. It is, therefore, the relationship between temperament and the environment that has implications for functioning, rather than the nature of either one alone. Optimal development is thought to occur when there is a match or compatibility between the capacities and characteristics of the individual on the one hand and the demands and expectations of the environment, especially in the family, on the other. This model has been used not only in temperament research, but in the conceptualization of normal and atypical child development (Greenspan, 1981; Kagan, 1971; Murphy, 1981; Stern, 1977).

Although early research suggested that children "outgrow" ADHD in puberty, more recent studies continue to demonstrate that children with ADHD have difficulties with inattention, impulsivity, and to some extent hyperactivity well into adolescence and adulthood (Mannuzza, Gittelman, Bonagura, Konig, & Shenker, 1988; Weiss & Hechtman, 1986). Therefore, ADHD is in many ways a type of developmental disability, beginning in early childhood and persisting across time and situations. But, as with any disability, what determines whether ADHD becomes a "handicapping" condition is this "goodness of fit" or match between the environmental demands and the child's capabilities.

Children and adolescents with ADHD are particularly at risk for a mismatch between their abilities and the demands made by parents, teachers, and peers. As mentioned, most adolescents are expected to gradually achieve a sense of competence, but this goal and the demands of the environment in meeting this goal conflict with the abilities of the adolescent with ADHD. Thus, the ADHD evaluation must include an assessment not only of the child's or adolescent's abilities (e.g., sustaining attention for homework, intellectual abilities, social skills), but also a recognition of the current environmental demands and developmental challenges. For example, one may want to assess a child's capacity for sustained attention in a one-on-one situation versus a larger classroom, or on a "boring" task versus one that has intrinsic interest for the child. An evaluation of the greater social environment would include an assessment of parental expectations and attributions for the child's difficulties; available supports; current demands by family, school, and peers; and the adaptational strategies used by the child and adults to address these challenges.

An application of this framework to treatment suggests that the goal of treatment is to improve the "goodness of fit." Thus, specific interventions may be targeted at (1) enhancing the child's capabilities and/or (2) adjusting the environmental demands. For example, one may improve the goodness of fit by providing the child with coping strategies such as social skills training or cognitive self-instructional techniques, so that he or she is better able to meet the current demands. Another intervention may involve changing the conceptualization of behavior in others with whom the child or adolescent with ADHD interacts. What may be developmentally appropriate for an individual without ADHD (e.g., 1 hour of homework for 10- to 12-year-olds; driving independently for adolescents) may have to be reduced, reversed, or even forestalled for a period of time until greater maturity permits the individual with ADHD to meet these challenges successfully. This adjustment often requires significant reframing of the expectations of parents, teachers, and others (see Chapters 12 and 13), as well as an appreciation of ADHD as a developmental disability. Statements such as "He should be able to sit still," "He ought to be dressing himself without my standing over him," or "Other children her age are interested in these activities" may need to be examined closely to determine their appropriateness, given the child's ADHD. Interventions might include adjusting the amount of in-class, individual work; arranging for the child to be in a classroom with a smaller teacher-student ratio; and teaching the parents additional behavioral strategies that provide the child with more consistent, frequent, immediate, and tangible feedback about his or her behavior. Thus, assessment and intervention must examine both aspects of the reciprocal interaction: the child's characteristics or capabilities, and the environment, including both demands and supports.

GENERAL ASSESSMENT CONSIDERATIONS

The importance of instrument selection in assessment is obvious but bears repeating. In addition to the factors mentioned previously, the choice should be based upon the child's characteristics (such as chronological age and apparent behavioral and development functional levels), the nature of the difficulties, and the purpose of the assessment. If "assessment" can be defined as gaining information that facilitates decision making, then a critical aspect is the purpose of the assessment and the type of decision being made. In some cases the goal may be screening, to identify those children in need of further assessment. In others the purpose may be to confirm or disconfirm the diagnosis. The assessment may be "descriptive"—documenting the child's status or current capabilities, establishing a baseline, or identifying relevant problems for intervention. It may also be "prescriptive," where the assessment is used for treatment planning and/or evaluation of the effectiveness of the intervention. Finally, the evaluation may be designed for research and/or epidemiological studies. While many assessment tools can be used for a variety of purposes, a decision theory approach using some guiding framework (Cronbach & Gleser, 1965) in instrument selection is likely to provide the most appropriate information, particularly when one is assessing a complex disorder such as ADHD.

There are numerous ways to incorporate both the biopsychosocial and developmental perspectives into the assessment of ADHD. While one may develop a standard battery, including a variety of measures from multiple perspectives, others have suggested that a decision-making or problem-solving model (e.g., Evans & Meyer, 1985; Herbert, 1978; Kanfer & Schefft, 1988) may be helpful in designing a thorough assessment approach that is responsive to the changing diagnostic criteria for ADHD as well as to the child's evolving development and social milieu. Kanfer and Saslow's (1969) S-O-R-K-C model has served as the framework for many behavioral assessment models and has applicability in the evaluation of ADHD.

In the S-O-R-K-C model, S (stimulus) refers to antecedent events; O (organism) refers to biological conditions; R (response) refers to observed behaviors; K (contingency) refers to schedules or contingency-related conditions; and C (consequence) refers to events that follow R. Included in the model are seven specific areas to be assessed that are helpful in making treatment recommendations. These include (1) an initial analysis of the problem situation; (2) clarification of the problem situation, which examines the conditions under which the problem occurs; (3) a motivational analysis, in which incentive and aversive conditions are determined; (4) a developmental analysis, in which biological, sociological, and behavioral changes relevant to the problem behavior are specified; (5) an analysis of self-control, where the situations, limitations, and strategies of self-control are examined; (6) an analysis of social relationships, including problems in interaction with significant others as well as social resources; and (7) an analysis of the social-cultural-physical environment, in which norms, settings, and environmental expectations are identified. Although this model may be too thorough, particularly if one's purpose is screening, it does provide a mechanism whereby the biopsychosocial and the developmental perspectives can be combined.

Another general consideration in assessment is the way in which results are interpreted. The availability of appropriate normative data is important, and many instruments assessing childhood psychopathology are norm-referenced. These tests are particularly helpful in evaluating the applicability of diagnostic criteria. However, instruments that are criterion-referenced may be appropriate at times. In these tests, a child's individual scores are evaluated in terms of specific objectives or tasks that are accomplished or failed. As opposed to norm referencing, where the child's performance or difficulties are compared to those of a larger population of children who have some shared characteristic (e.g., age), criterion-referenced tests compare the child's present or future performance against his or her *own* performance. An advantage of criterion-referenced instruments is the ease with which the information can be used to develop treatment interventions. Other approaches that are often utilized in developmental/educational evaluations and that may prove helpful in the development and evaluation of interventions include profile analysis (Simeonsson, 1986); goal attainment scaling (Simeonsson, Cooper, & Scheiner, 1982); and the assessment of interactive competencies (Dunst & McWilliam, 1988) based on a developmental model. Thus, different decisions require different instruments and subsequently different assessment strategies.

Other general considerations include the following: (1) the length of the assessment; (2) available settings (e.g., access to observation); (3) cost, including the monetary and emotional cost to the child and family; (4) equipment and training required to administer the test; and (5) the instrument's psychometric characteristics, such as reliability and validity. Because of the need to consider the child's environment, the ecological validity of certain measures becomes paramount. Another factor is the "bandwidth-fidelity dilemma." This refers to balancing the need to assess a child's characteristics in a number of areas, but perhaps with less accuracy or "fidelity," against obtaining information in a single area with relatively high accuracy (Conger, 1974; Conger & Lipshitz, 1973). Thus, if one is primarily interested in screening, a narrow bandwidth and higher fidelity might be preferred in instrument selection. Conversely, description and treatment planning would suggest giving priority to wide bandwidth, with a possible decrease in fidelity.

CONCLUSION

The very nature of ADHD demands a consideration of biopsychosocial and developmental factors in both assessment and treatment. The primary problem areas of sustained attention, impulsivity, overactivity, and poor rule-governed behavior reflect the multidimensionality of the disorder and necessitate a multitrait assessment approach. Because of the comorbidity of ADHD with other difficulties, such as LD, CD, and oppositional behaviors, an evaluation must consider these individual psychological factors. The problem behaviors must be inappropriate when compared to those of other children of the same mental age, so these behaviors must be assessed within a developmental context, using assessment instruments that have appropriate normative data. Also, the chronic nature of ADHD suggests that the problematic behaviors must be examined in the context of maturational changes. This requires a knowledge of the way the disorder typically manifests itself across these ages and the co-occurrence of ADHD with other problems; assessment measures must be selected to cover the needed ages and range of behaviors. The cross-situational and pervasive nature of ADHD, and its variability depending on task demands, require a consideration of the perspectives of a number of individuals (e.g., the child, parents, teachers, and peers) as well as an examination of the environmental demands. Finally, the greater prevalence of psychiatric difficulties in parents of children in ADHD and the importance of the role of parents in evaluation and treatment of these children necessitate a consideration of familial factors as well.

As Mash (1989) notes, "assessment and treatment must attempt to ascertain complex interactions between and among external events, perceptions, and cognitive appraisals of such events, internal conditions (e.g., values, physical status, personality traits), external resources for coping (e.g., social support), decision-making processes, and preferred coping strategies" (p. 9). As the definition of ADHD continues to be refined, the specific aspects of assessment must change as well. The current status of the field, however, strongly suggests that professionals must rely on several methods of assessment, utilize several different sources of information from different settings, and interpret the data obtained within both a biopsychosocial and a developmental perspective.

8

Clinical Interviews and the Medical Examination

Opinion is that high and mighty dame which rules the
world, and in the mind doth frame distastes or likings;
for in the human race, she makes the fancy various as the
face.

—JEREMIAH BROWN HOWELL (1772–1822)

Probably the three most important components in a comprehensive evaluation of the client who has Attention-deficit Hyperactivity Disorder (ADHD)
are the clinical interview, the medical examination, and the completion and
scoring of behavior rating scales. This applies as much to adults presenting
for evaluation of their own ADHD symptoms as to children or adolescents
brought by their parents for evaluation of suspected ADHD. In this chapter,
I describe the details of conducting clinical interviews with parents, teachers,
and children/adolescents in cases where the children or adolescents are being
presented for evaluation of ADHD. I also briefly discuss the essential features
of the medical examination of ADHD children and issues that need to be
addressed by that exam. An in-depth discussion of the use of behavior rating
scales appropriate for use with these children and adolescents follows in Chapter
9 (see also Appendix A). Where it is feasible, I also recommend supplement-
ing these two components of the evaluation with objective assessments of the
ADHD symptoms, such as with psychological tests of attention or direct behavioral observations. These methods of assessment are discussed in Chapter
10. I have provided six examples of evaluations that include all three of these
components in Chapter 11.

INFORMATION OBTAINED AT TIME OF REFERRAL

At the point when a child is referred for services, some important details can
be gleaned by telephone interview with the mother. The form used to take
referrals at our ADHD clinic at the University of Massachusetts Medical Cen-

ter is shown in Figure 8.1. Besides noting demographic information, it also obtains a brief overview of the reasons for the referral, to aid the clinician in determining whether the referral is appropriate to his or her practice. This form also allows for some initial procedures to be set in motion. In particular, it is important at this point to do the following: (1) obtain any releases of information needed to permit reports of previous professional evaluations to be sought; (2) contact the child's treating physician for further information on health status and medication treatment, if any; (3) obtain the results of

Child's Name _____ **Date** _____

Date of Birth _____ **Age** _____ **Grade** _____

Previously seen at Clinic? _____ Patient No. _____

Mother's Name _____ Father's Name _____

Marital Status _____ Custody _____

Address _____

Home Phone _____ Work Phone _____ (Mom/Dad)

Insurance _____

Child's School _____

Address _____

Teacher's Name _____

Referred By: _____

Referred For:

Evaluation
Drug Trials
Parent Training
Social Skills
School Consultation

Currently being seen by: _____

Previously diagnosed by: _____

Currently taking medication for behavior problems?   Yes   No

If yes, what and dosage? _____

- -

Disposition: _____

_____

Forms sent out: _____

Appointment Date: _____

Psychologist: _____

FIGURE 8.1. Referral information.

the most recent Public Law 94-142 evaluation from the child's school, or have the parent initiate one immediately if school performance concerns are part of the referral complaints; (4) mail out the packet of parent and teacher behavior rating forms to be completed and returned before the initial appointment, being sure to include the written release-of-information permission form with the school forms; and (5) obtain any information from social service agencies that may be involved in providing services to this child.

The form we use in our ADHD clinic for gaining initial demographic information on a child referral is shown in Figure 8.2. This is often mailed out in advance of the initial evaluation, along with child behavior rating scales, and returned prior to or at the time of the first appointment. It contains essential information about the child, family members, parental employment, marital status, family physician, and school placement. The name of the professional who may have initiated the referral should also be determined, along with whether or not copies of the final report should be sent to this individual and whether copies of his or her reports can be obtained for this evaluation.

INTERVIEW PROCEDURES

Interviewing is both an art and a science; it involves techniques not easily acquired from a mere reading of the passages that follow, nor simply from a desire to help others. Careful and thorough training in this process is essential. Those wishing to read more on clinical interviewing are referred to the excellent texts by Benjamin (1969) and Edinburg, Zinberg, and Kelman (1975), as well as chapters on the subject by Bierman (1983) and Morganstern (1976), among others.

Parent Interview

The parental interview is an indispensable part of the evaluation of children and adolescents presenting with concerns about ADHD. No adult is more likely to have the wealth of knowledge about, history of interactions with, or sheer time spent with a child than is a parent. In addition, although parental reports are often criticized for their unreliability or low level of agreement with teachers' reports ($r = .28$; Achenbach, McConaughy, & Howell, 1987), parents' reports can be improved simply by making questions much more specific to the information needed to assess and treat ADHD. The agreememt of reports between parents is more satisfactory ($r = .60$), albeit moderate in degree; this suggests that disagreements between teachers and parents may have much to do with the different situations in which they observe children and the different degrees of familiarity with the children (Achenbach et al., 1987) than with a lack of veracity in their reports about the children.

Child's Name _____ **Birth Date** _____ **Age** _____

Address _____
          Street   City   State   Zip

Home Phone _____ Work Phone _____ Father/Mother
                                                    (Circle One)

Child's School _____ Teacher's Name _____

School Address _____
                        Street   City   State   Zip

School Phone _____ Child's Grade _____

Is Child in Special Education? YES NO If so, what type? _____

Father's Name _____ Age _____ Education _____
                                                          (in years)

Father's Place of Employment _____

Type of Employment _____ Annual Salary _____

Mother's Name _____ Age _____ Education _____
                                                          (in years)

Mother's Place of Employment _____

Type of Employment _____ Annual Salary _____

Is this child adopted? YES NO If so, age when adopted? _____

Are the parents named above married? _____ Separated? _____ Divorced? _____

Child's Physician _____

Physician's Address _____
                        Street   City   State   Zip

Physician's Telephone Number _____

List all other children in the family:

          Name   Age   School Grade
_____   _____   _____
_____   _____   _____
_____   _____   _____
_____   _____   _____

FIGURE 8.2. Child and family information.

Purposes

The parental interview often serves several purposes. First, it establishes a necessary rapport among the parents, the child, and the examiner that will prove invaluable in enlisting parental cooperation with later aspects of assessment and treatment. Second, the interview is an obvious source of highly descriptive information about the child and family, revealing each parent's particular views of the child's apparent problems and narrowing the focus of later stages and components of the evaluation. Third, it can readily reveal the degree of distress that the child's problems are presenting to the family, especially the parent being interviewed; it can also indicate the overall psychological integrity of the parent. Hypotheses as to the presence of parental personality or psychiatric problems (e.g., depression, hysteria, hostility, marital discord, etc.) may be revealed that will require further evaluation in subsequent components of the assessment and consideration in formulating treatment recommendations.

A fourth purpose is that the interview may begin to reveal significant aspects of the parent–child relationship, should the child be permitted to remain within the clinic room during the parental interview. Provided that this is feasible and acceptable to the parent, the child can be allowed to play in the same room while the examiner is speaking with the parent. Notes can then be made of the manner in which the parent and child interact with each other in this context. Since ADHD children often present problems for their parents when they are speaking with others, such as when the parents are on the telephone or have visitors to their homes, similar interaction problems may arise while a parent speaks with the examiner. If a room with a one-way mirror is available to permit later observations of parent–child interactions, then the interview can be conducted within this room to allow adequate habituation of the child to the novel aspects of this room, in hopes of making these later observations more representative of parent–child interactions at home. While making such behavioral notations during the interview, the examiner must be careful not to overinterpret these data, as office behavior of ADHD children is often far better than that observed at home (Sleator & Ullmann, 1981). Such observations merely raise hypotheses about potential parent–child interaction problems that can be explored in more detail with the parent toward the end of this interview, as well as during later direct behavioral observations of parent and child during play and task performance together. At the end of this portion of the interview, the examiner would do well to inquire of the parent just how representative the child's immediate behavior is of that seen at home when the parent must speak with other adults in the child's presence.

The presence of the child during the parental interview, however, presents thorny issues for the evaluation to which the examiner must be sensitive. Some parents will be less forthcoming about their concerns and the details of their children's specific problems when the children are present; they may not wish to overly sensitize or embarrass the children unnecessarily, or to create another reason for arguments to occur at home about the nature of the children's problems. Others will be heedless of these potential problems posed for their children by this procedure, making it even more imperative that the examiner review these issues with them before beginning the evaluation. And still other parents may use their children's presence to humiliate the children further in public over their deficiencies or the distress they have created for their families by behaving the way they do. Suffice it to say here that the examiner must consider whether the advantages created by having a child present are outweighed by these potential negative effects with each particular family, and should review the issues with each parent before starting the interview.

A fifth purpose of the initial parent interview is that it can help to focus the parent's perceptions of the child's problems on more important and more specific controlling events within the family. Parents often tend to emphasize historical or developmental causes of a global nature in discussing their children's problems, such as what they did or failed to do with the children earlier in development that may have led to this problem (e.g., placing a child in infant day care, an earlier divorce, a child's diet in earlier years, etc.). The interactional interview discussed later can serve to shift the parents' attention to more immediate antecedents and consequences surrounding child behaviors, thereby preparing the parents for the initial stages of parent training in child management skills.

A sixth purpose of the interview is to formulate a diagnosis and develop treatment recommendations. Although diagnosis is not always considered necessary for treatment planning (a statement of the child's developmental and behavioral deficits is often adequate), the diagnosis of ADHD does provide some utility in terms of predicting developmental course and prognosis for the child (see Chapter 5), determining eligibility for some special educational placements (see Chapter 15), and predicting potential response to a trial of stimulant medication (see Chapter 17). Many child behavior problems are believed to remit over short periods of time in as many as 75% of the cases. However, ADHD is a relatively chronic condition, warranting much more cautious conclusions about eventual prognosis and preparation of the family for coping with these later problems.

The seventh and last purpose that a parental interview may serve is sheer catharsis, especially if this is the first professional evaluation of the child or if previous evaluations have proven highly conflicting in their results and recommendations. Ample time should be provided to allow parents to ventilate this distress, hostility, or simply frustration. It may be helpful to note at this point that many parents of ADHD children have reported similarly distressing, confusing, or outright hostile previous encounters with professionals and educators about their children, not to mention well-intentioned but overly enmeshed or misinformed relatives. Compassion and empathy for the plight of the parents at this point can often result in a substantial degree of rapport with and gratitude toward the examiner and a greater motivation to follow subsequent treatment recommendations. At the very least, parents are likely to feel that they have finally found someone who truly understands the nature of their children's problems, the distress they have experienced in trying to assist the children, and the recommendations that may be necessary to do something about them.

The suggestions that follow for interviewing parents of ADHD children are not intended as rigid guidelines, only as areas that clinicians should consider. Each interview will obviously differ according to individual child and family circumstances. Generally, those areas of importance to an evaluation include child-related information; school-related information; information about parent-child interactions; and details about the parents, other family members, and community resources that may be available to the family.

Information About the Child

The interview should begin with an explanation of the procedures to be undertaken as part of this evaluation and the time it is expected to take. If it has not been discussed already, the projected cost of the evaluation and the manner in which the fee is to be handled (i.e., insurance, self-pay, etc.) should be addressed. Some clinicians at this point may feel comfortable in discussing with parents the limitations that laws place on their promise of confidentiality of information, particularly those requirements pertaining to reports of child neglect or abuse. Other clinicians prefer to wait until further in the interview when discussing parent management of the child, while still others may address the subject only after information that points to abuse has been divulged. At this point, many states require that the information be reported to the relevant state social service agency. This last approach brings with it a serious risk of destroying rapport with the examiner and parental feelings of having been deceived or even entrapped. No doubt, motivation for subsequent treatment with this therapist is jeopardized or tainted in many of these cases, such that a referral to another professional for treatment may be in order. There is no adequate rule of thumb for when to address this issue with parents, but it seems that the general clinical trend is toward full disclosure of these limits at the outset of the interview.

The interview progresses to a review of the parents' initial concerns about the child—what brings them to the clinic at this time. These details, along with the other information about the child and family mentioned below, can be recorded on a structured psychological interview such as that provided at the end of this chapter in Appendix 8.1 and currently used in our own ADHD clinic. The advantage to such a format is that it prompts the examiner to inquire about a variety of details needed to assess the child and family without relying exclusively on memory or habit, or memorizing all of the symptom lists of the DSM-III-R childhood diagnoses that may be relevant to a particular case. Each parental concern can be assigned to a general problem area (home behavior, peer relations, school performance, community conduct, etc.) and listed on the form, with specific details recorded under each general problem area. Parents are given ample time and repeated prompts to discuss all of the concerns that have brought them to the clinic at this time. Some parents require great encouragement and prompting, as they are unaccustomed to disclosing personal or intimate information about themselves or their children. Others may be extremely chatty, disorganized, detailed, or unfocused, given the likelihood that at least 20% of these parents have ADHD themselves, so that much structuring and redirection from the examiner may be needed.

Parents of ADHD children are likely to state initially that the children can't finish work they are assigned, don't listen to instructions, are careless in their work habits, can't sit still when necessary, and require substantial if not constant supervision. Restlessness, distractibility, low frustration tolerance, difficulties in organizing work, and excessive talking may also be described. Poor impulse control, such as inability to wait in line or take turns in a game, blurting out answers to questions or making indiscreet comments, doing things without thinking, and inability to work for delayed but larger rewards are likewise fairly typical of ADHD children. Oppositional behavior, defiance, stubbornness, and physical and verbal aggressiveness may also be reported in a large majority of ADHD children. Often, asking about recent examples of each concern can elucidate more helpful details. Home and school problems should be noted separately on the interview form, as their nature, implications, and interventions may be different, depending on which setting is involved. Making this distinction will also serve to guide the types of questions that may be involved in the subsequent interview with the child's teacher.

In discussing parental concerns, the examiner should focus on the more specific situations in which problem behaviors occur, the antecedent events that may serve to provoke them (if any), the frequency with which they are occurring (i.e., daily, weekly, monthly, etc.), and the manner in which the parents have chosen to manage them in the past. It is well worth inquiring as to differences between parents in their management approaches to the child's problems, as these often contribute to greater marital conflict, which may require separate treatment from that to address the child's problems. It is essential that parents be questioned about the history of these concerns, the point in development at which they arose, their duration, and any episodes of their remission; these are integral criteria to the diagnosis of ADHD, as well as other childhood psychiatric diagnoses.

If these problems are of long-standing duration, why are the parents seeking the clinician's assistance now? This question may reveal much about parental motivation for treatment, about other family stressors that have recently arisen to make the child's problems unendurable, or about demands being made on the parents by other social agents (teachers, social workers, etc.) to obtain assistance for the child. This naturally leads to questions about the types of previous professional assistance the family has obtained and whether it is possible for the clinician to contact these professionals for further details on the child and family. Finally, it is always worth asking what the parents believe has led their child to develop these problems, as this will indicate what types of parental misperceptions may need to be corrected during the parent counseling to follow the evaluation (see Chapter 11).

I find it helpful at this point to take out the behavior rating scales that have been completed by the parents and review the items they have endorsed. If there are any problems endorsed on the scales but not mentioned by the parents in the interview, this serves as an excellent time to gain further information as to why the parents endorsed the items as they did. Similarly, inspection of the teacher-completed behavior rating scales can suggest areas of inquiry about school adjustment that parents may have overlooked in divulging their concerns.

The examiner should then review with the parents whether the child manifests any problems within a number of broad developmental domains. I have customarily divided these into physical health, sensory, motor, language, thinking, intellect, academic achievement, self-help, social, emotional, and familiar relationship domains. Questioning about impairments, developmental delays, oddities, or unique strengths within these areas is not only essential to a careful differential diagnosis, but will greatly assist the clinician in formulating the list of treatment recommendations for the parents.

Within the sensory domain, one obviously needs to inquire about the intactness of vision, hearing, and touch. In the motor domain, the child's skill in gross motor and fine motor areas of development should be briefly explored, particularly as they may pertain to self-help, athletic, and academic demands being made on the child. Is the child delayed in walking, balance, hopping, skipping, running, climbing, or bike riding within the gross motor domains? Does he or she have problems with buttoning, zipping, dressing, bathing, eating, drawing, copying, or writing in the fine motor area? The importance of inquiring about odd or peculiar reactions or habits of the child in each of these areas has been noted in Chapter 6, particularly in discriminating ADHD from the more serious thinking or affective disorders of childhood. Does the child show odd mannerisms, stereotypies, postures, or ritualistic displays? In addition, difficulties with nervous tics or mannerisms, compulsive behaviors, or other signs of tic disorders or Tourette's syndrome should be reviewed at this point, as their presence will weigh against using stimulant medications for such children (see Barkley, 1988b, for further information on Tourette's syndrome).

The clinician should briefly review the child's receptive, expressive, and written language abilities, along with a more careful inquiry into the nature of any thinking problems the child may display; looseness of ideas, speaking in half-thoughts, odd or bizarre comments, answers that are irrelevant to the topic of a question or conversation, atypical fascinations, excessively detailed speech, excessive circumlocution, inability to get to the point of a narrative, and so forth. ADHD children rarely have problems in these areas, while children with thinking disorders (e.g., Schizoid, Schizotypal, or Borderline Personality Disorder, atypical Pervasive Developmental Disorder, or "multiplex developmental disorder"; see Chapter 6) are much more likely to manifest them. As noted in Chapter 17, looseness of thought or psychotic-like thinking processes are contraindications to the use of stimulant medication even if ADHD symptoms are also present. In this area, it is also helpful to inquire about the child's degree of self-awareness, particularly about his or her ADHD symptoms, peer problems, family difficulties, academic troubles, or other problems. It is common for ADHD children to have significant limitations in self-awareness, often underreporting the degree of distress they present to others as well as the extent of their rejection by others.

Concerning intelligence, parents are asked to provide an assessment of the child's developmental level relative to other children they have known. Then parents can be asked about specific delays in reading, math, spelling, writing, and other academic subjects, as well as organizational problems the child may have in approaching schoolwork and homework. These should be followed by questions about the child's self-help skills, such as dressing, feeding, toileting, bathing, and other elements of self-care. Any sleeping problems should be discussed, because ADHD children have a 30% chance or more of having such sleep disturbances as late sleep onset, frequent night waking, early rising, or nightmares; these may require further medical evaluation or even treatment. Certainly, where they are present to a significant degree, their likelihood of proving of further stress to parents beyond the child's daytime behavioral problems deserves acknowledgment by the clinician. Also, inquiry should be made as to the types of chores and responsibilities the child is asked to do and how well these are accomplished, especially without supervision in the case of an older child.

The child's general emotional demeanor can then be reviewed, with attention to excessive, exaggerated, or grossly inappropriate affective displays. ADHD children are often quick to frustration and anger, and are likely to be somewhat exaggerated in their emotional reactions, but these reactions are invariably related to environmental events. Where parents provide evidence of situationally inappropriate affect that is entirely out of context or detached from environmental events, greater probing should be done to discern the possibility of one of the aforementioned thinking disorders or a childhood affective disorder, such as Overanxious Disorder, Major Depression, or Bipolar Disorder. Laughing, anger, hatred, silliness, crying or sadness, or explosive hostile outbursts for no apparent reason are not typical of ADHD children and may suggest a different, possibly serious comorbid psychopathological condition. Equally significant is the child's failure to react to common emotion-provoking stimuli—to express concern over harm or injury to others, pleasure at his or her own or others' successes, or empathy with others who have failed at something, are ill, or are undergoing stressful life events. Certainly the absence of or extreme vacillations in affection towards family members should be noted. Excessive levels of anxiety or depression when revealed in this manner are important, as they generally contraindicate stimulant medication therapy for such children.

Given the frequent difficulties ADHD children have in social relations with peers, some time should be devoted to discussing the child's social skills. How many friends does he or she have? Of what ages? How does the child treat classmates and neighborhood peers? How easily is he or she accepted into peer groups? Is the child interested in seeking out playmates and friend-ships? How age-appropriate are his or her play interests? These are all areas for exploration. Other relevant questions include the following: How do other adults who have cared for this child view the child's social skills? What ef-forts to correct these social deficits have been previously attempted? And does the child belong to any organized, structured peer groups (Boy or Girl Scouts, athletic teams, school clubs, church groups, etc.)? Again, ADHD children are more likely to be active, loud, impulsive, aggressive, or even oppositional in their peer relations and to have fewer friends as a result. But rarely are they odd, peculiar, distant, aloof, or grossly out of context in their interactions or utterly uninterested in making or keeping friends. These latter eccentricities may, again, be harbingers of a more serious affective or thinking problem. Not only may such a problem contraindicate stimulant medication, but it may require unusual and creative efforts at tailoring behavioral interventions for the child. Social acceptance, moreover, has been repeatedly shown to pre-dict later social acceptance in adulthood; where difficulties in this area are present, they will warrant some efforts at social skills remediation as dis-cussed in Chapter 16.

Lastly, in this review of developmental domains, the examiner should in-quire about family relationships. How well does this child relate to siblings and parents? Which parent carries the brunt of the custodial and training work with the child? To whom is the child likely to turn for guidance or comfort when distressed? These are some questions that can be revealing of significant information needed for treatment formulation. In single-parent families, are there extended relatives who provide relatively frequent custo-dial care to the child (grandparents, aunts, uncles, in-laws, etc.)? If so, what are their relationships with the child like? If the child is from a divorced family, what are custody arrangements like? How hostile are the visitation exchanges? To what degree are the child and any siblings subjected to these hostilities? How involved is the other parent going to be in this referral, eval-uation, and subsequent treatment recommendations? The answers to these and other questions in this domain will prove crucial to decisions about the success of parent training, medication, and even educational recommenda-tions. They may also indicate the possibility of some legal or court involve-ment by the examiner if custody issues are soon to be reopened by the par-ents.

This review of developmental domains is then followed with a review of the checklists of symptoms that are part of the criteria for many child psy-chiatric disorders that may coexist with ADHD. These are also provided in the structured interview form in Appendix 8.1 and include the symptoms not only of ADHD, but also of Oppositional Defiant Disorder, Conduct Disor-der, Overanxious Disorder, Separation Anxiety Disorder, Major Depression, and Dysthymia. Familiarity with the DSM-III-R criteria for each of these dis-orders is important, as each has different cutoff scores, ages of onset, dura-tion of symptoms, and exclusionary criteria. Furthermore, the clinician must take care in reviewing each symptom list to periodically remind the parents that he or she is trying to determine whether these behaviors occur excessively for the child's age. Many of these behaviors occur in normal children, but what distinguishes the disordered from the normal child is the degree and severity of the symptoms relative to same-age norms.

This review of the litany of the child's problems can overwhelm some parents and certainly leave the impression that the examiner is only interested in the child's weaknesses. The examiner should therefore take care at this juncture to inquire about strengths of the child in each of the domains described above, as these may be quite useful in planning subsequent interventions. The examiner can also use this opportunity to inquire about possible interests, privileges, and rewards that the child enjoys; these can serve later in establishing the reinforcement programs that are crucial in child behavior management training with parents.

A careful review of the child's developmental and medical history should then be undertaken. As noted in Appendix 8.1, questions can focus on the mother's health during the pregnancy, the term of the pregnancy, whether any medications or other substances (alcohol, cigarettes, caffeine) were taken, complications of the delivery and immediate postnatal period (respiratory distress, convulsions, severe jaundice, infection, etc.), and congenital abnormalities that may have required treatment. If the child was adopted, what is known of the biological parents, particularly health and psychiatric problems, as well as the mother's pregnancy? The ages at which the child crawled, sat, walked, talked, and was toilet-trained can be used to gauge the possibility of developmental delays in motor and language domains that may require greater attention during this evaluation.

Any significant or unusual illnesses, accidents, or surgeries during early childhood should be noted. ADHD children are known to have more frequent colds, upper respiratory infections, otitis media, and allergies than normal children. Any of these conditions, as well as other chronic or recurring medical illnesses, can have an impact upon the child's psychological adjustment, exacerbating existing ADHD symptoms. If the child has any chronic medical illnesses that require treatment (diabetes, epilepsy, allergies, etc.), they should be noted, along with the types of treatments being used. Some treatments for these conditions, such as theophylline for asthma and Dilantin or phenobarbital for seizures, are known to create symptoms like ADHD as side effects or to exacerbate them where they are pre-existing conditions.

Questions about early infant and toddler temperament should also be ventured and will probably reveal that the child was quite active from an early age, often insistent on having his or her own way about many things, and often quite irritable and quick to anger. If the child has a history of treatment with psychoactive medication, it should be recorded, along with the types, doses, and durations of treatment with each medication. Sometimes this reveals a pattern of inappropriate medication or, more often, poor attention to dosage, such that an inadequate trial of medication occurred. This could lead to the possibility of a reconsideration of these medications if necessary. Finally, when was the child last seen by a physician for a physical examination, and were any abnormalities noted?

School-Related Information

The interview should then progress to a consideration of the child's history of schooling. These days, many children are likely to have had day care or preschool experiences, and these should be discussed. What kind of preschool program was the child involved in, and how often? More importantly, what behavioral or developmental problems may have been noted by the school staff? Many ADHD children have difficulties adjusting to the demands of preschool routines, and their teachers complain that they are overactive, inattentive, impulsive, and generally hard to manage. Delays in fine and gross motor skills may be noted, and as many as 30% may have mild language delays as well. The age at which the child began kindergarten, what school, and the child's progression through subsequent grades and schools should be recorded, as should any significant behavioral, learning, or social problems at each of these grade levels. In addition, what types of special educational evaluations and placements has the child previously received, and when was the last multidisciplinary team evaluation (PL 94-142) conducted on this child? If such an evaluation has not been done, it should be initiated immediately in the case of any ADHD child with significant academic problems; eligibility for any formal special educational services will be contingent upon the findings of this evaluation, and it may take as long as 3 to 4 months to be completed.

One should also ask about what specific concerns the child's teachers are raising that may be different from or in addition to those the parents have mentioned. Has the child repeated a grade, been suspended, or been expelled? ADHD children have at least a 30% chance of one or more grade retentions by high school, and those who are defiant or conduct-disordered have a high probability of some suspensions or expulsions. Has truancy been problematic, and if so, how has it been handled? Lastly, it is important to inquire about the nature of the relationship that presently exists between the parents and school—is it collegial, supportive, or adversarial? Has communication been open and reasonably clear, or limited and hostile? This can greatly assist the examiner in preparing for contacts with the school staff during subsequent calls or school visits. Written permission should then be obtained to contact the school for further information if it has not been previously received.

Information about the Parents and Family

As Chapter 5 has shown, families of ADHD children are frequently stressed, chaotic, or (in a substantial minority of cases) outright dysfunctional. Information about the parents and family context can be of great assistance not only in differential diagnosis, but also in appreciating the etiological mechanisms for some of the child's coexisting problems. For instance, oppositional or defiant behavior often arises in the context of parent and family turmoil, and especially where maternal depression, marital discord, and maternal and paternal antisocial behavior exist. Moreover, such information will weigh heavily in planning treatment recommendations, as they have direct bearing on parental ability and motivation to participate in some treatments, particularly parent training, family therapy, or other parent-focused interventions.

Inquiry can begin with the ages, educational levels, and occupations of each parent and progress to a consideration of any potential psychiatric, learning, developmental, or chronic medical problems the parents have experienced or are now experiencing. I also like to inquire about whether the parents' own parents and siblings displayed any significant learning, psychiatric, or developmental problems, as certain types of these are more common in the families of ADHD children. This can be done again using the interview format in Appendix 8.1, where a matrix of psychological disorders is available for each parent's own relatives as well as other children in the immediate family. The types of family psychopathology may also suggest avenues for pursuing a more careful differential diagnosis of the child. For instance, families of ADHD children have no greater incidence of psychosis in their relatives. Where such disorders are reported, greater care in discussing thinking, affective, social, and other domains of the child's adjustment may need to be taken, to be sure that the clinician is not mistaking early-emerging signs of a thinking or mood disorder for ADHD. Moreover, a family history of serious tic disorders or Tourette's syndrome indicates that an ADHD child may be at a greater risk for such symptoms, especially if subsequently given stimulant medication.

Some discussion at this point is essential as to the status of the marriage of the parents, its degree of satisfaction or discord, and (if discordant) the nature of the discord. Have there been prior separations, divorces, or remarriages of either parent? Have the parents sought counseling for any marital problems that exist? If so, from whom; what type of treatment was involved; and how long were they in therapy? Marital discord seems to play a critical role in the development and maintenance of oppositional and aggressive child behavior in ADHD children, apparently because of its impact on the day-to-day management tactics used by parents with these children. The marriage, then, may prove to be the first area on which intervention will be subsequently focused, as any other child-focused treatments may be hampered by the existence of marital discord.

Parents can then be questioned about the extent of their social activities outside the marriage. Past research has shown that the degree of isolation, especially of mothers, from other socially supportive agents (friends, neighbors, extended family, etc), as well as the number and level of negative or aversive exchanges with other adults outside the family, is highly related to the degree of perceived child behavior problems and to success in subsequent parent training programs (Dumas, 1986; Wahler, 1980). When insularity or isolation is problematic, treatment may first have to address this problem before other interventions are likely to be successful.

I then proceed to a discussion of the siblings in the immediate family and any psychological, educational, developmental, or other problems these siblings may be having. Some studies indicate that as many as 30% of the siblings of ADHD children are also experiencing learning and behavioral problems; these can further stress a family system and require attention from the examiner during treatment planning.

Information on Parent-Child Interactions

In those cases where defiance or oppositional behavior appears to coexist with ADHD, and this may be true for as many as 65% of clinic-referred children and teens, some time needs to be taken to further pursue the nature of parent-child interactions. Parents of ADHD children, particularly those who are aggressive or defiant, are likely to use more commands, reprimands, and negative comments with their children. In turn, their children are less likely to comply with commands and more likely to use negative, defiant, and oppositional behavior with their parents (see Chapter 5). This information is indispensable to the planning of subsequent child behavior management training (Chapter 12), family therapy (Chapter 13), or parent-adolescent training (Chapter 14); such interventions need to be tailored to the needs of each particular family. With parents of a child aged 2 to 5 years, I proceed to undertake a separate interview using the format set forth in Table 8.1, which covers the situations in which the parent and child have conflicts, the manner in which parent and child react to each other in each situation, and the frequency/severity of the conflict. This format is adapted from that originally developed by Constance Hanf at the University of Oregon Health Sciences Center and has proven extremely useful in subsequently designing parent training interventions for these families.

For children aged 5 to 12 years, or where time restricts this more thorough interview of parent-child interactions, the examiner can review the parents' responses to the Home Situations Questionnaire (completed before the appointment) and select several of the most severely conflictual situations with which to pursue the nine follow-up questions shown in the right side of Table 8.1. Since the nature of the interaction is likely to prove quite similar across situations (see Chapter 5) in these instances of oppositional child behavior, it is necessary to review only a few of them to gain sufficient appreciation for the dynamics or social learning mechanisms taking place in these encounters. The most likely situations in which oppositional behavior may arise with ADHD children are shown on the left side of Table 8.1. These seem to be when the parent is on the telephone, when visitors are in the home, when the family is visiting others, when parent and child are in public places such as

TABLE 8.1. Parental Interview Format

Situations to be discussed with parents	Follow-up questions for each problematic situation

General—overall interactions
Playing alone
Playing with other children
Mealtimes
Getting dressed in morning
During washing and bathing
While parent is on telephone
While watching television
While visitors are in your home
While visiting others' homes
In public places (supermarkets,
    shopping centers, church, etc.)
While mother is occupied with
    chores or activities
When father is at home
When child is asked to do chores
At bedtime
Other situations
	1. Is this a problem area? If so,
	    then proceed with questions 2 to
	    9.
	2. What does your child do in this
	    situation that bothers you?
	3. What is your response?
	4. What does the child do next?
	5. If the problem continues, what
	    will you do next?
	6. What is usually the outcome of
	    this interaction?
	7. How often do these problems
	    occur in this situation?
	8. How do your feel about these
	    problems?
	9. On a scale of 0 to 9 (0 = no
	    problem; 9 = severe problem),
	    how severe is the problem to
	    you?

Note. Adapted from interview used by C. Hanf, Oregon Health Sciences University, 1976. From *Hyperactive Children: A Handbook for Diagnosis and Treatment* by R. A. Barkley, 1981, New York: Guilford Press. Copyright 1981 by The Guilford Press. Reprinted by permission.

stores and church, and when the child is asked to do chores or homework. Playing alone, watching television or playing video games, washing and bathing, and times when the father is at home are likely to be considerably less problematic for ADHD children. Those settings most troublesome for adolescents with ADHD are discussed in Chapter 14.

The nature of the interaction that transpires between an oppositional child and parent has been discussed in Chapter 5 and is known as "coercion." As previously described, it comprises a series of escalating negative verbal exchanges between parent and child that may ultimately culminate in the child's escape from or avoidance of unwanted demands made by other family members. Readers wishing a greater knowledge of these mechanisms are encouraged to read Patterson's (1982) text, *Coercive Family Process.*

In the case of adolescents, families will have completed the Issues Checklist before the appointment, or should do so at this point in the interview. This rating scale, discussed in Chapter 9, provides a thorough overview of the types of conflicts that parents and ADHD teens may be experiencing. Reviewing the responses can then provide further areas of exploration for this interview, especially as to how parents are presently dealing with the conflicts, the types of incentives and discipline they employ, and their consistency and collaboration in following through on their management efforts. It is particularly useful to discuss how the parents approach the resolution of a conflict with the adolescent, as we have found that dictatorial or one-sided (parental) decision making around conflicts is often part of the dysfunction in the parent-adolescent relationship. The types of difficulties parents may have in their communication and problem-solving skills with ADHD adolescents, and treatment of these difficulties, are discussed in Chapter 14.

Child Interview

Depending upon the child's age and intellectual level, some time in the assessment must be given to interviewing the child and making informal observations of his or her appearance, behavior, and gross developmental skills. The child interview serves much the same purposes as the parental interview, as discussed above. Building rapport, clarifying perceptions of current problems, revealing the status of current parent-child relations, providing an opportunity for catharsis, and assisting with differential diagnosis and treatment planning are as much a basis for interviewing the child as the parents. Moreover, the credibility of the entire evaluation from the view of the parents often hinges on how much time has been devoted by the examiner to directly studying the child.

The examiner must be careful, however, not to place too much emphasis on the significance of some of the information obtained in this component of the evaluation, for several reasons. First, informal observations of the child's conduct during the interview may be quite unrepresentative of the child's behavior in more naturalistic surroundings. Research indicates that most ADHD children rarely misbehave during such one-to-one office evaluations (Costello et al., 1988; Sleator & Ullmann, 1981), so that normal conduct in the office does not exclude the likelihood that the children actually have ADHD. Yet many clinicians choose to place greater weight on their own observations of the children than on the reports of parents or teachers; this often results in misdiagnosis of the children as normal or in blaming of the mothers' management of the children as the major basis for the children's misconduct toward their mothers at home. I have found it quite helpful to acknowledge to parents the fact that ADHD children are often well behaved during the initial evaluation and to tell them not to worry about it, as I will rely on multiple sources of information in reaching an impression and diagnosis about the children. This well set parents at ease, contribute to greater rapport with the examiner, and reassure parents that the examiner trusts their reports of their children's problems in other settings. Parents often feel that they will be accused of contriving their children's problems or perhaps exaggerating them if their children act normally during this office visit. Moreover, some parents may even come to question their own competence as parents when they once again witness how well the children can behave for strangers, in contrast to the conflicts they have at home with these children.

Second, casual observations of children's developmental abilities, such as walking, posture, fine motor manipulation during toy play, language, affect, or social skills, may also not accurately assess the children's performance in these developmental domains in their natural environments. Particularly for young children, shyness, muteness, or refusal to perform requested activities may not be at all indicative of the children's actual behavior elsewhere. As with informal behavioral observations, deficits or aberrations noted during the exam may have some significance, although even these need to be verified through more objective and representative means of assessment. However, where normal performances are witnessed, these may not necessarily indicate that a child is without deficiencies in these developmental domains. In cases where either casual observation of the child or the parent or teacher interview suggests developmental delays, then the child should be scheduled for thorough and objective developmental testing.

Finally, caution must also be applied in the case of children's reports of information about themselves, their current adjustment, their families, and especially their emotional status. Research and developmental theory both suggest that children are not particularly reliable in the reporting of information about themselves, either over time or in relation to the reports of others about them. Agreements between children and other informants usually average about .22 (Achenbach et al., 1987). Reliability does increase with age (Bierman, 1983; Edelbrock & Costello, 1984), however, suggesting that more time may be fruitfully spent with older children in obtaining self-reports of information about their adjustment. This is not to say that children are completely unreliable—only that what reports they give should be used to raise clinical hypotheses, which must then be verified through other, more reliable means. The more specific and publicly observable the event is that a child is being asked to report on, the greater is the likelihood that the report may prove reliable and hence valid. The more introspective and subjective the event, such as feelings or preferences, the less reliable, stable, or even valid the report is likely to be. Thus, it is highly advantageous for the examiner to speak briefly with the parents following this child interview, so as to check out the veracity of his or her own observations and the child's self-reports with the parents' own observations of the child.

I find it useful to begin the child interview with questions about why the child feels he or she is visiting the clinic today and what the parents may have told him or her about the reason for the visit. This may reveal misperceptions about the rationale for the evaluation (e.g., "Am I going to get a physical exam or a shot?"), which can be quickly corrected. Explaining the procedure that is to be followed in the evaluation can also be helpful at this point. I then proceed to a discussion of neutral topics with the child to set him or her at ease, such as favorite hobbies, television shows, sports, or pets.

With sensitivity, I then progress to questioning the child about any behavior problems or conflicts the child feels he or she may be having at home and the nature of these. This is followed with specific questions about where the child attends school, who his or her teachers are, the types of subjects the child is taking in school, and which he or she likes most. I then ask whether the child believes he or she is doing poorly in any subjects and what reasons he or she feels may explain any such difficulties. Behavior problems in the classroom are then discussed, along with the types of discipline the child may have experienced in his or her current classes for any such misconduct. The child's perceptions of social acceptance by peers at school are then discussed; I take care to note any particularly difficult relationships the child may presently have with others. I then refer back to my notes from the parental interview and question the child about his or her perceptions of any other problems the parents have reported (e.g., bedwetting, lying, stealing, etc.).

This is followed with an effort to get the child to formulate those problems that the child would like to see changed or improved. The results may, at times, be different from the priority given to problems by the parents, yet the child's version may be as legitimate a rendering of the situation as that of the parents. Using the "three wishes" method may assist a young child in thinking along these lines. I do this by telling the child that I wish to play a game with him or her in which I pretend to be a magician or sorcerer who can grant the child's every wish. I will grant three wishes that the child can use to improve anything about himself or herself, the family, schooling, or peer relations. The child is then prompted to consider these wishes briefly and then to report his or her desires for change.

Obviously, great delicacy and diplomacy are required in this portion of the interview so as not to appear accusatory, offended, or displeased with the child, but instead to appear concerned, inquisitive, and desirous of being of help. At some point, if a child discloses without solicitation that he or she is "hyperactive" or "ADD," I will take advantage of this moment to inquire as to how the child learned of this, what this label means in his or her opinion, why the child thinks he or she is this way, and what the child feels may need to be done to help him or her. Otherwise, I do not use this label in the child's interview, preferring to wait until the diagnostic process is completed to discuss the implications of this label with the child. This is often done either at the completion of the evaluation and parent feedback conference or as the first session in parent/family counseling (see Chapter 12).

For older ADHD children, typically 8 years of age or more, one may wish to obtain their own reports on the degree of difficulty they have with the 14 items making up the DSM-III-R criteria for ADHD. Using the ADHD Rating Scale described in Chapter 9 can be a useful way of structuring a child's responses to these 14 items. However, our recent follow-up research, described in Chapter 4, found that the validity of ADHD adolescents' self-reports of their symptoms was quite low. They often underreported not only their own symptoms, but their degree of family conflicts as well. So great care must be taken not to place too much weight on these findings. ADHD children are notorious for underreporting their difficulties and are likely to do so in this aspect of the interview as well.

Some examiners may find it helpful during this interview, particularly for young children, to allow them to play, draw, or simply wander about the office. Using an incomplete-sentences format may also help to begin to focus such children on their own feelings about their problems. Once again, due caution must be applied when interpreting both the behavioral observations made and the responses of a child to these unstructured or semistructured activities in the office.

I then close the interview with a return to a discussion of some neutral topics with the child, so as to diminish any affective arousal that may have been engendered by this conversation on the child's problems and deficiencies. At this point, I may briefly reinterview the parents about any hypotheses or observations of concern raised during the child's interview, or proceed directly to any objective testing of the child, after which I will further interview the parents.

In conducting these interviews, it is equally important to pay attention to the style and quality of the children's reponses and not just to their content. ADHD children frequently are unaware of or are less sensitive to their difficulties, the problems they pose for others, and the implications of these problems for their immediate adjustment. Many view others as the cause of their current dilemmas and have little appreciation for the roles they have played in creating the current crises. Since reflection is often deficient in these children, their responses are more likely to be impulsive, distorted, or fabricated. They may be based more on spur-of-the-moment feelings or on a desire to please the examiner than the responses of normal children, and this may add to the unreliability of their self-reports. For instance, it is commonplace to hear ADHD children describe themselves as having many friends at school or home, in striking contrast to their parents' reports that the children are virtually friendless or outright rejected by their peer group. Similarly, ADHD children may report that their school performance is adequate, when in fact they may be on the verge of retention or transfer to a special educational classroom because of their underachievement, learning disabilities, or disruptive classroom conduct.

In the case of older ADHD children or adolescents, signs of depression, low self-esteem, or antiauthoritarian behavior may be seen and should be carefully noted. Defiance or opposition to the evaluation, direct hostility toward the parents during the evaluation, or outright refusal to cooperate with the interview are sometimes seen and have direct implications for therapy with these families (see Chapter 14). Conducting a second attempt at speaking with such an adolescent at a later appointment, when the teen is not so stubborn, defensive, or agitated, may be a useful means of proceeding with this portion of the evaluation. When cooperative, these adolescents provide a somewhat more reliable picture of their current adjustment than would younger ADHD children, especially concerning their current affective adjustment, activities outside the home, social adjustment, sexual activities, illicit or illegal actions, and potential substance abuse.

Parent-Child Structured Psychiatric Interviews

Besides the traditional interviews typically used in clinical practice, structured psychiatric interviews have also come to be used in some major university clinics and teaching hospitals for the assessment of psychopathological symptoms in children. Many of these interviews were developed from classification systems, such as the DSM-III, and provide an extensive item list that the examiner uses to query the respondent. Such interviews may yield more precise and quantifiable information about the various problems of ADHD children. Those employed in research on ADHD have been the Schedule for Affective Disorders and Schizophrenia for School-Age Children (K-SADS;) (Puig-Antich & Chambers, 1978), the Diagnostic Interview for Children and Adolescents (DICA; Herjanic, Brown, & Wheatt, 1975), the Interview Schedule for Children (Kovacs, 1982), the Child Assessment Schedule (Hodges, Me-Knew, Cytryn, Stern, & Kline, 1982), and the Diagnostic Interview Schedule for Children (DISC; Costello, Edelbrock, Kalas, Kessler, & Klaric, 1982). These structured interviews can be employed with both parents and children and scored to yield the various diagnoses that may apply to a given case. Their limitations, however, are numerous (Edelbrock & Costello, 1984), not the least of which is their being immediately outdated by the publication of the DSM-III-R (American Psychiatric Association, 1987). Many of these scales have now been revised or modified to take into account the changes in items and criteria in the DSM-III-R. These versions too may be short-lived, given that DSM-IV is now in preparation and promises to change these diagnostic criteria again. Furthermore, normative data are not available for most scales, making them difficult to use clinically for determining the actual statistical deviance of a child from his peer group on these instruments. At present, such interview schedules may be most useful for research rather then clinical practice.

Achenbach and McConaughy (1989) have recently developed the Semistructured Clinical Interview for Children (SCIC), appropriate for ages 6 to 11 years. The SCIC provides information on seven broad areas of development and adjustment: (1) activities, school, and friends; (2) family relations; (3) fantasies; (4) self-perception and feelings; (5) parent-reported problems; (6) cognitive tasks (a reading recognition and math test); and (7) screening for fine and gross motor problems. Open-ended questions and probes may be used, as well as play with toys to set the child at ease during the interview. Throughout the interview, notes are also kept of the child's behavior, using a separate observation form. Both the interview and self-report form are then scored and plotted on a profile containing eight scales that were empirically derived using a clinical sample of 108 referred children. These scales are Inept, Unpopular, Anxious, Withdrawn-Depressed, Inattentive-Hyperactive, Resistant, Family Problems, and Aggressive.

One advantage to this interview form is that it is not tied to any particular version of the DSM or other psychiatric taxonomies, and so is unlikely to become immediately outdated with the next revision of such a classification system. (This can also be a disadvantage, though, in that the child's responses do not immediately map onto currently accepted diagnostic criteria for childhood disorders.) Another advantage is its reliance on empirically established scales, such that items are clustered on those scales with which they are most highly associated, rather than on the more arbitrary symptom lists that are believed to be associated with particular psychiatric disorders. Finally, the use of a structured observation form for rating the child's behavior during the 1- to 1½-hour interview and testing allows clinical observations to be cast in a more quantifiable form, which can then be compared against those ratings obtained from the parent and teacher report forms of the Child Behavior Checklist (see Chapter 9), from which many of these behavioral items were taken. The SCIC interview and observation forms can be obtained from Thomas Achenbach, PhD, Department of Psychiatry, University of Vermont, 1 South Prospect St., Burlington, VT 05401.

Parent-Adolescent Structured Psychiatric Interviews

Various structured psychiatric interviews have been developed to quantify information regarding symptomatology, using specific criteria for childhood and adolescent disorders. Typically, these interviews include standard lists of symptoms presented to the parent or adolescent, with specific guidelines for follow-up questioning and recording of responses (Edelbrock & Costello, 1984). Several structured interviews incorporate DSM-III diagnostic criteria for a wide range of childhood disorders, including Attention Deficit Disorder with Hyperactivity. Among those that have separate formats for questioning adolescents and their parents are the K-SADS (Puig-Antich & Chambers, 1978), the DICA (Herjanic et al., 1975), and the DISC (Costello et al., 1982). Other interview formats have been developed solely for use with adolescents and include items related to ADHD symptomatology, most notably the Teenager or Young Adult Schedule (TOYS; Gittelman & Mannuzza, 1985), a modified version of the National Institute of Mental Health (NIMH) Diagnostic Interview Schedule (Robins, Helzer, Croughan, & Ratcliff, 1981).

These structured interviews vary with respect to time for completion, range of item coverage, and degree of training required by the interviewer. Their advantage lies chiefly in their standardization of questions to be addressed during interviews. Yet several factors limit the usefulness of information provided by these measures. Although they possess a certain degree of face validity, their actual construct, concurrent, and predictive validities remain to be documented (Edelbrock & Costello, 1984). In addition, since many of these interviews were based on DSM-III diagnostic criteria, they are now limited by that system's reliability and validity. Some structured interviews have been changed in accordance with the revisions of DSM-III-R, but these new forms will now require further reliability and validity studies. Moreover, as noted above, the appearance of DSM-IV within the next few years will require that these interviews once again be revised. Thus, while above-named instruments may be helpful in conducting research, their use in the clinical assessment of adolescents with ADHD is premature, given the dearth of knowledge regarding their psychometric properties.

Teacher Interview

Next to parents, few other caregivers will have spent more time with ADHD children than their teachers, particularly if the children are of elementary age. Their opinions of the children are a critical element of the evaluation of ADHD and should be solicited and respected. If personal interviews are not possible, as they often are not, then examiners should initiate telephone contact with the teachers. In my view, obtaining teacher rating scales is not a substitute for personal discussion with the teachers. The teacher interview serves much the same purposes as the parent and child interviews, as described above.

Obviously, the teachers should be questioned about a child's current academic and behavioral problems in the school setting. Reports of excessive restlessness, vocal noisiness, inattention to work, underachievement, and noncompliance with class rules are commonplace. Relations with classmates should be discussed and will probably reveal problems of avoidance or rejection, particularly if the ADHD child is also aggressive. Problems with immature, silly, disruptive, or impulsive behavior are likely to be noted in situations involving limited or no supervision (during recess, lunch, or special assemblies; while in hallways or bathrooms; or on the bus). Lying, petty thievery, and physical fighting may be reported in a minority of children in whom antisocial behavior has developed. Care should be taken to get information as to the parameters of these problems, their frequency of occurrence, whether antecedent events have been identified that precipitate them, and what the teachers are currently doing to manage them. The child's performance within each academic subject should be briefly discussed, and the examiner should inquire whether the child has received a multidisciplinary team evaluation as part of his or her rights under PL 94-142. If not, the teachers should be asked whether such an evaluation should be initiated so as to obtain additional special educational resources for the child.

It is also useful to ask about previous communications between the parents and teachers about the child and how positive, cooperative, or unsupportive the parents have proven. Sometimes teachers may reveal information that is of relevance to judging parental motivation for further treatment, parental misperceptions about the nature of the child's problems or what resources the school does or does not have available to help, and parental uncooperativeness with previous reasonable plans for intervention by the school staff. It is also possible that this discussion may reveal similar problems with the uncooperativeness, insensitivity, or naiveté of the school personnel themselves in previously managing the child's problems.

THE PEDIATRIC MEDICAL EXAMINATION

It is essential that children being considered for a diagnosis of ADHD have a complete pediatric physical examination. However, in the past such examinations have often been brief, relatively superficial, and as a result often unreliable and invalid for achieving a diagnosis of ADHD or identifying other comorbid behavioral, psychiatric and educational conditions (Costello et al., 1988; Sleator & Ullmann, 1981). This is often the result of ignoring the other two essential features of the evaluation of ADHD children, these being a thorough clinical interview (as reviewed above) and the use of behavior rating scales (see Chapter 9). It is imperative that adequate time be allotted to accomplishing these components of the evaluation, so that these children and adolescents can be properly diagnosed and treated. If this is not possible, then the physician is compelled to conduct the appropriate medical examination but withhold the diagnosis until the other components can be accomplished by referral to another mental health professional.

The features of the pediatric examination and the issues that must be entertained therein are described below. For previous reviews of this exam, I am indebted to my medical colleagues, Drs. Sally and Bennett Shaywitz (Shaywitz & Shaywitz, 1984) of Yale University Medical School, and Dr. Mary B. McMurray (McMurray & Barkley, in press) of the University of Massachusetts Medical Center.

The Medical Interview

Most of the contents of an adequate medical interview are identical to those described above for the parent interview. However, greater time will obviously be devoted to a more thorough review of the child's genetic background, pre- and perinatal events, and developmental and medical history, as well as to the child's current health, nutritional status, and gross sensory-motor development. Taking the time to listen to the parents' story and the child's feelings, and to explain the nature of the disorder, is one of the most important things a physician can offer a family. In this way, the evaluation process itself can often be therapeutic.

One major purpose of the medical interview that distinguishes it from the more psychological one described above is its focus on differential diagnosis of ADHD from other medical conditions, particularly those that may be treatable. In rare cases, the ADHD may have arisen secondary to a clearly biologically compromising event, such as severe Reye's syndrome, hypoxic-anoxic event (such as near-drowning or severe smoke inhalation), significant head trauma, or central nervous system infection or cerebral-vascular disease. The details of such an event should be obtained, as well as the child's developmental, psychiatric, and educational status prior to the event and significant changes in these domains of adjustment since the event. Ongoing treatments related to such an event should also be documented. In other cases, the ADHD may be associated with significant lead or other metal or toxic poisonings that will require treatment in their own right.

It is also necessary to determine whether the child's conduct or learning problems are related to the emergence of a seizure disorder. As many as 20% or more of epileptic children may have ADHD as a comorbid condition, and up to 30% may develop ADHD or have it exacerbated by the use of phenobarbital or Dilantin as anticonvulsants (Wolf & Forsythe, 1978). In such cases, changing to a different anticonvulsant, if possible, may greatly reduce or even ameliorate the attentional deficits and hyperactivity of such children.

A second purpose of the medical exam is to thoroughly evaluate any co-existing conditions that may require medical management. In this case, the child's ADHD is not seen as arising from these other conditions but as being comorbid with it. As noted in Chapter 3, ADHD is often associated with higher risks not only for other psychiatric or learning disorders, but also for motor incoordination, enuresis, encopresis, allergies, otitis media, and somatic complaints in general. A pediatric evaluation will be desirable or even required for many of these comorbid conditions. For instance, the eligibility of the child for physical or occupational therapy at school or in a rehabilitation center may require a physician's assessment and written recommendation of the need for such. And, although most cases of enuresis and encopresis are not due to underlying physiological disorders, all cases of these elimination problems should be evaluated by a physician before nutritional and behavioral interventions are begun. In some of these cases, medications may be prescribed to aid in their treatment even though the problems are "functional" in origin, as in the use of oxybutynin or imipramine in the treatment of bedwetting. Certainly children with significant allergies or asthma will require frequent medical consultation and management of these conditions, often by specialists who appreciate the behavioral side effects of medications often used to treat them. Theophylline, for example, is increasingly recognized as affecting children's attention span and may exacerbate a pre-existing case of ADHD. For these and other reasons, the role of the physician in the evaluation of ADHD should not be underestimated, despite overwhelming evidence that by itself the medical exam is inadequate to serve as the basis for a diagnosis of ADHD.

A third purpose of the medical examination is to determine whether physical conditions exist that are contraindications for treatment with medications. For instance, a history of high blood pressure or cardiac difficulties warrants careful consideration about a trial on a stimulant drug, given the known pressor effects of these drugs on the cardiovascular system. Some children may have a personal or family history of tic disorders or Tourette's syndrome; this would dictate caution in trying this child on stimulants, in view of their greater likelihood of bringing out such movement disorders or increasing the occurence of those that already exist. These examples merely illustrate the myriad medical and developmental factors that need to be carefully assessed in considering whether a particular ADHD child is an appropriate candidate for drug treatment.

Physical Examination

In the course of the physical examination, height, weight, and head circumference require measurement and comparison to standardized graphs. Hearing, vision, and blood pressure should be screened. Findings suggestive of hyper- or hypothroidism, lead poisoning, anemia, or other chronic illnesses obviously need to be documented and further workup pursued. The formal neurological examination often includes testing of cranial nerves, gross and fine motor coordination, eye movement, finger sequencing, rapid alternating movements, impersistence, synkinesia, and motor overflow, as well as testing for choreiform movements and tandem gait tasks. The exam is often used to look for signs of previous central nervous system insult or of a progressive neurological condition. Abnormalities of muscle tone, or a difference in strength, tone, or deep tendon reflex response between the two sides of the body, should be noted. The existence of nystagmus, ataxia, tremor, decreased visual field, or fundal abnormalities should be determined and further investigation pursued where such abnormalities are found. This should be followed by a careful neurodevelopmental exam for the following areas: motor coordination, visual-perceptual skills, language skills, and cognitive functioning. While these tests are certainly not intended to be comprehensive or even moderately in-depth evaluations of these functions, they are invaluable as quick screening methods for relatively gross deficiencies in these neuropsychological functions. Where deficits are noted, follow-up with more careful and extensive neuropsychological, speech and language, motor, and academic evaluations may be necessary to document their nature and extent. Some physicians may want to employ more standardized neurological exams (David, 1989), or neuromaturational test batteries, such as the Pediatric Early Elementary Examination (PEEX) and the Pediatric Examination of Educational Readiness at Middle Childhood (PEERAMID; Levine, 1985; Levine & Rappaport, 1983)

Routine physical examinations of ADHD children are frequently normal and of little help in the diagnosis of the condition or its management. One certainly needs to rule out, however, the rare possibility of visual or hearing deficits that may give rise to ADHD-like symptoms. Also, on physical inspection, ADHD children may have a greater number of minor physical anomalies, such as an unusual palmar crease, two whorls of hair on the head, increased epicanthal fold, hypertelorism, or other such anomalies of outward appearance. Studies are conflicting on whether such findings occur more often in ADHD, but certainly they are nonspecific to it, being found in other psychiatric and developmental disorders. Shaywitz and Shaywitz (1984) state that examining for these minor congenital anomalies may only be beneficial where the suspicion of maternal alcohol abuse during pregnancy exists, so as to determine the presence of fetal alcohol syndrome. Small palpebral fissures and midfacial hypoplasia with growth deficiency are supportive of this diagnosis. Finally, given the considerably greater distress ADHD children present to their caregivers, their risk of being physically abused would seem to be higher than normal. Greater attention by the physician to other signs of abuse during the examination is therefore required.

The routine examination for growth in height and weight is also often normal, although one study reported a younger bone age in children with minimal brain dysfunction, including hyperactivity. (Schlager, Newman, Dunn, Crichton, & Schulzer, 1979) Nevertheless, where a trial on a stimulant drug is contemplated, accurate baseline data on physical growth, heart rate, and blood pressure will be needed against which to compare data subsequently obtained during the drug trial or during long-term maintenance on these medications.

Similarly, the routine neurological examination is frequently normal in ADHD children. These children may display a greater prevalence of neurological "soft" signs suggestive of immature neuromaturational development, but again these are nonspecific for ADHD and can often be found in learning-disabled, psychotic, autistic, and retarded children, not to mention a small minority of normal children. Such findings are therefore not diagnostic of ADHD, nor does their absence rule out the condition (Reeves & Werry, 1987). Instead, findings of choreiform movements, delayed laterality development, fine or gross motor incoordination, dysdiadochokinesis, or other soft signs may suggest that a child requires more thorough testing by occupational or physical therapists and may be in need of some assistance in school with fine motor tasks or adaptive physical education.

ADHD children may also have a somewhat higher number of abnormal findings on brief mental status examinations or screening tests of higher cortical functions, especially those related to frontal lobe functions (e.g., sequential hand movement tests, spontaneous verbal fluency tests, "go–no go" tests of impulse control, etc). Where these are found, I believe that more thorough neuropsychological testing may be useful in further delineating the nature of these deficits and providing useful information to educators for making curriculum adjustments for these children. In come cases, findings on brief mental status exams may have more to do with a coexisting learning disability than with ADHD. Where problems with visual-spatial-constructional skills or simple language abilities are noted, they are most likely signs of a comorbid learning disorder, as they are not typical of ADHD children generally. It is often the case that these brief mental status exams are normal. This does not necessarily imply that all higher cortical functions are intact, as these screening exams are often relatively brief and crude methods of assessing neuropsychological functions. Most sensitive and lengthier neuropsychological tests may often reveal deficits not detected during a brief neurological screening or mental status exam. Even so, the routine assessment of ADHD children with extensive neuropsychological test batteries is also likely to have a low yield. It should be undertaken only where there is a question of coexisting learning or processing deficits that require further clarification, and even then tests should be selected carefully to address these specific hypotheses.

Laboratory Tests

A number of studies have used a variety of physical, physiological, and psychophysiological measures to assess potential differences between ADHD children and other clinical or control groups of children. Although some of these have demonstrated differences, such as reduced cerebral blood flow to the striatum or diminished orienting galvanic skin responses in ADHD children (see Chapter 3), none of these laboratory measures are of value in the diagnostic process as yet. Parents, teachers, or even other mental health professionals are sometimes misled by reports of such findings or by the conclusion that ADHD is a biologically based disorder, and frequently ask for medical tests to be done on their children to confirm the diagnosis. At this moment, no such lab tests exist. Consequently, laboratory studies, such as blood work, urinalysis, chromosome studies, electroencephalograms (EEGs), averaged evoked responses, magnetic resonance imagining (MRI), or computerized axial tomograms (CT scans), should not be used routinely in the evaluation of ADHD children. Only where the medical and developmental history or the physical exam suggests that a treatable medical problem (such as a seizure disorder) exists, or that a genetic syndrome is a possibility, would these laboratory procedures be recommended; such cases are quite rare.

Where ADHD children are being placed on the stimulant drug Cylert (pemoline), then routine liver function studies need to be done at baseline and again periodically during the use of this drug because of an apparently greater risk of hepatic complications from this medication. This is not the case for the more popular stimulants, Ritalin (methylphenidate) or Dexedrine (*d*-amphetamine). Blood assays of levels of stimulant medication have so far proven unhelpful in determining appropriate dosage, and therefore are not recommended as part of routine clinical titration and long-term management of these medications. The use of the tricyclic antidepressants for treating ADHD children, especially those with greater anxiety or depressive symptoms, will require that a baseline routine electrocardiogram be done and then repeated several weeks after beginning drug treatment, given the greater potential for changes in cardiac rhythm and cardiotoxicity of these drugs. Whether blood levels of the tricyclics are useful in titrating them for maximum clinical response is debatable at this time, because there is little standardized information to serve as a guide in the matter.

SUMMARY

Interviews with parents, children/adolescents, and teachers form an indispensable component in the evaluation of ADHD. Despite their problems at times with reliability, they provide a wealth of useful information for differential diagnosis and treatment planning that simply cannot be obtained by any other means. Throughout these interviews, the clinician must allocate sufficient time to explore the necessary topics with each informant, in order to provide as thorough a picture of a child as needed for a satisfactory differential diagnosis, to develop a hierarchy of the important targets for intervention, and to begin selecting a series of treatment approaches and their priority for implementation. A 20- to 30-minute initial interview will simply not suffice! Those professionals whose case load limits them to such cursory assessments of child psychological disorders should frankly not undertake the process. They should view their task instead as screening for potential problems and then making referrals to those professionals skilled and interested in providing the time needed to make a satisfactory assessment of these children. The average length of time devoted to interviewing parents, child, and teachers in an initial assessment is often $2\frac{1}{2}$ hours; this figure does not include formal behavioral observations and psychological testing of the child, or obtaining and scoring the parent and teacher rating scales. Furthermore, interviewing is both a skill and an art, requiring great sensitivity not only to the content areas to be discussed, but also to potential hidden agendas behind the seeking of the evaluation. Appreciation of the current emotional climate of the family is essential, as is a sensitivity to the potential for shame, humiliation, or guilt that can be engendered in the process of submitting oneself or one's child to this evaluative and judgemental process. Certainly the art of social persuasion needed to obtain as factual a presentation of the child's problems as possible is an essential ingredient in this process. Interviewing is therefore at its best in the hands of those professionals well trained in its use, where it can be seen to be a veritable therapeutic and educational tool beyond its purposes of simply obtaining information.

APPENDIX 8.1

ADHD CLINIC PARENT INTERVIEW

Name of Child _____ **Interview Date** _____

Interviewer _____ **Informant** _____

Patient No. _____

Reason for Referral:

Referral Source:

Parental Objectives:

I. DEVELOPMENTAL FACTORS
A. Prenatal History

1. How was your health during pregnancy?

Good ___ (1)
Fair ___ (3)
Poor ___ (5)
DK ___

2. How old were you when your child was born?

Under 20 ___ (1)
20–24 ___ (2)
25–29 ___ (3)
30–34 ___ (4)
35–39 ___ (5)
40–44 ___ (6)
Over 44 ___ (7)
DK ___

Do you recall using any of the following substances or medications during pregnancy?

3. Beer or wine
   (1) Never
   (2) Once or twice
   (3) 3–9 times
   (4) 10–19 times
   (5) 20–39 times
   (6) 40+ times

4. Hard liquor
   (1) Never
   (2) Once or twice
   (3) 3–9 times
   (4) 10–19 times
   (5) 20–39 times
   (6) 40+ times

5. Coffee or
   other caffeine (Cokes, etc.)
   Taken together, how many times?
   (1) Never
   (2) Once or twice
   (3) 3–9 times
   (4) 10–19 times
   (5) 20–39 times
   (6) 40+ times

6. Cigarettes
   (1) Never
   (2) Once or twice
   (3) 3–9 times
   (4) 10–19 times
   (5) 20–39 times
   (6) 40+ times

7. Did you ingest any of the following substances?
   ___ Valium (Librium, Xanax)
   ___ Tranquilizers
   ___ Antiseizure medications (e.g., Dilantin)
   ___ Treatment for diabetes
   ___ Antibiotics (for viral infections)
   ___ Sleeping pills
   ___ Other (please specify: _____)

B. Perinatal History

8. Did you have toxemia or eclampsia?

No ___ (0)
Yes ___ (1)
DK ___

9. Was there Rh factor incompatibility?

No ___ (0)
Yes ___ (1)
DK ___

10. Was (s)he born on schedule?

8 mos. or earlier __ (1)
Term 8–10 mos. __ (2)
10 mos. __ (3)
DK __

11. What was the duration of labor?

Under 6 hr __ (1)
7–12 hr __ (2)
13–18 hr __ (3)
19–24 hr __ (4)
Over 24 hr __ (5)
DK __

12. Were you given any drugs to ease the pain during labor?
Name: _____

No __ (0)
Yes __ (1)
DK __

13. Were there indications of fetal distress during labor or during birth?

No __ (0)
Yes __ (1)
DK __

14. Was delivery   Normal?

No __ (0)
Yes __ (1)

Breech?

No __ (0)
Yes __ (1)

Caesarian?

No __ (0)
Yes __ (1)

Forceps?

No __ (0)
Yes __ (1)

Induced?

No __ (0)
Yes __ (1)

15. What was the child's birth weight?

2 lb– 3 lb 15 oz __ (1)
4 lb– 5 lb 15 oz __ (2)
6 lb– 7 lb 15 oz __ (3)
8 lb– 9 lb 15 oz __ (4)
10 lb–11 lb 15 oz __ (5)
DK __

16. Were there any health complications following birth?

No __ (0)
Yes __ (1)
If yes, specify: _____

C. Postnatal Period and Infancy

17. Were there early infancy feeding problems?

No __ (0)
Yes __ (1)

18. Was the child colicky?

No __ (0)
Yes __ (1)

19. Were there early infancy sleep
pattern difficulties?

No __ (0)
Yes __ (1)

20. Were there problems with the   No — (0)
    infant's responsiveness (alertness)?   Yes — (1)

21. Did the child experience any health problems during infancy?
                                                           No — (0)
                                                           Yes — (1)

22. Did the child have any congenital problems?
                                                           No — (0)
                                                           Yes — (1)

23. Was the child an easy baby? By that, I mean did (s)he cry a lot? Did (s)he follow
    a schedule fairly well?
                                               Very easy — (1)
                                               Easy   — (2)
                                               Average   — (3)
                                               Difficult — (4)
                                               Very diff. — (5)

24. How did the baby behave with other people?
                             More sociable than average   — (1)
                             Average sociability   — (2)
                             More unsociable than average — (3)

25. When (s)he wanted something, how insistent was (s)he?
                                    Very insistent   — (1)
                                    Pretty insistent   — (2)
                                    Average   — (3)
                                    Not very insistent — (4)
                                    Not at all insistent — (5)

26. How would you rate the activity level of the child as an infant/toddler?
                                               Very active — (1)
                                               Active   — (2)
                                               Average   — (3)
                                               Less active — (4)
                                               Not active — (5)

D. Developmental Milestones

27. At what age did (s)he sit up?   3–6 mos.   — (1)
                                               7–12 mos.   — (2)
                                               Over 12 mos. — (3)
                                               DK   —

28. At what age did (s)he crawl?   6–12 mos.   — (1)
                                               13–18 mos. — (2)
                                               Over 18 mos. — (3)
                                               DK   —

29. At what age did (s)he walk?   Under 1 yr — (1)
                                               1–2 yr   — (2)
                                               2–3 yr   — (3)
                                               DK   —

30. At what age did (s)he speak single words (other than "mama" or "dada")?

9–13 mos.	__ (1)
14–18 mos.	__ (2)
19–24 mos.	__ (3)
25–36 mos.	__ (4)
37–48 mos.	__ (5)
DK	__

31. At what age did (s)he string two or more words together?

9–13 mos.	__ (1)
14–18 mos.	__ (2)
19–24 mos.	__ (3)
25–36 mos.	__ (4)
37–48 mos.	__ (5)
DK	__

32. At what age was (s)he toilet-trained?
    (Bladder control)

Under 1 yr	__ (1)
1–2 yr	__ (2)
2–3 yr	__ (3)
3–4 yr	__ (4)
DK	__

33. At what age was (s)he toilet-trained?
    (Bowel Control)

Under 1 yr	__ (1)
1–2 yr	__ (2)
2–3 yr	__ (3)
3–4 yr	__ (4)
DK	__

34. Approximately how much time did toilet training take from onset to completion?

Less than 1 mo.	__ (1)
1–2 mos.	__ (2)
2–3 mos.	__ (3)
More than 3 mos.	__ (4)

II. MEDICAL HISTORY

35. How would you describe his/her health?

Very good	__ (1)
Good	__ (2)
Fair	__ (3)
Poor	__ (4)
Very poor	__ (5)

36. How is his/her hearing?

Good	__ (1)
Fair	__ (2)
Poor	__ (3)

37. How is his/her vision?

Good	__ (1)
Fair	__ (2)
Poor	__ (3)

38. How is his/her gross motor coordination?

Good	__ (1)
Fair	__ (2)
Poor	__ (3)

39. How is his/her fine motor coordination?

Good	__ (1)
Fair	__ (2)
Poor	__ (3)

40. How is his/her speech articulation?

Good __ (1)
Fair __ (2)
Poor __ (3)

41. Has he had any chronic health problems (e.g., asthma, diabetes, heart condition)?

No __ (0)
Yes __ (1)

If yes, please specify _____

42. When was the onset of any chronic illness?

Birth __ (1)
0–1 yr __ (2)
1–2 yr __ (3)
2–3 yr __ (4)
3–4 yr __ (5)
Over 4 yr __

43. Which of the following illnesses has the child had?
(For the following, No = 0; Yes = 1)

Mumps __
Chicken pox __
Measles __
Whooping cough __
Scarlet fever __
Pneumonia __
Encephalitis __
Otitis media __
Lead poisoning __
Seizures __
Other diseases __
(specify) __

44. Has the child had any accidents resulting in the following?
(No = 0; Yes = 1)

Broken bones __
Severe lacerations __
Head injury __
Severe bruises __
Stomach pumped __
Eye injury __
Lost teeth __
Sutures __
Other (specify) __

45. How many accidents?

One __ (1)
2–3 __ (2)
4–7 __ (3)
8–12 __ (4)
Over 12 __ (5)

46. Has he ever had surgery for any of the following conditions?
(No = 0; Yes = 1)

Tonsillitis __
Adenoids __
Hernia __
Appendicitis __
Eye, ear, nose, & throat __

Digestive disorder	—
Urinary tract	—
Leg or arm	—
Burns	—
Other	—

47. How many times?

Once	— (1)
Twice	— (2)
3–5 times	— (3)
6–8 times	— (4)
Over 8 times	— (5)

48. Duration of hospitalization?

One day	— (1)
One day + night	— (2)
2–3 days	— (3)
4–6 days	— (4)
1–4 weeks	— (5)
1–2 mos.	— (6)
Over 2 mos.	— (7)

49. Is there any suspicion of alcohol or drug use?

No	— (0)
Yes	— (1)
DK	—

50. Is there any history of physical/sexual abuse?

No	— (0)
Yes	— (1)
DK	—

51. Does the child have any problems sleeping?

None	— (0)
Difficulty falling asleep	— (1)
Sleep continuity disturbance	— (2)
Early morning awakening	— (3)

52. Is the child a restless sleeper?

No	— (0)
Yes	— (1)
DK	—

53. Does the child have bladder control problems . . . at night?

No — (0)
Yes — (1)

If yes, how often? _____
If yes, was (s)he ever continent? _____
during the day? No — (0)
Yes — (1)
If yes, how often? _____
If yes, was (s)he ever continent? _____

54. Does the child have bowel control problems . . . at night?

No — (0)
Yes — (1)

If yes, how often? _____
If yes, was (s)he ever continent? _____
during the day? No — (0)
Yes — (1)
If yes, how often? _____
If yes, was (s)he ever continent? _____

55. Does the child have any appetite control problems?

Overeats   __ (1)
Average   __ (2)
Undereats __ (3)

III. TREATMENT HISTORY

56. Has the child ever been prescribed any of the following:
(No = 0; Yes = 1) (Duration coded in months)

Ritalin	__	Anticonvulsants	__
Duration of use	__	Duration of use	__
Dexedrine	__	Antihistamines	__
Duration of use	__	Duration of use	__
Cylert	__	Other prescription drugs	__
Duration of use	__	Duration of use	__
Tranquilizers	__	Specify:	_____
Duration of use	__		

57. Has the child ever had any of the following forms of psychological treatment? If so, how long did it last?

Individual psychotherapy   __
Duration of therapy   __
Group psychotherapy   __
Duration of therapy   __
Family therapy with child   __
Duration of therapy   __
Inpatient evaluation/Rx   __
Duration of inpatient stay   __
Residential treatment   __
Duration of placement   __

IV. SCHOOL HISTORY

Please summarize the child's progress (e.g., academic, social, testing) within each of these grade levels:

Preschool

Kindergarten

Grades 1 thru 3

Grades 4 thru 6

Grades 7 thru 12

58. Has the child ever been in any type of special educational program, and if so, how long?

Learning disabilities class	—
Duration of placement	—
Behavioral/emotional disorders class	—
Duration of placement	—
Resource room	—
Duration of placement	—
Speech & language therapy	—
Duration of therapy	—
Other (please specify)	—
Duration	—

59. Has the child ever been:

Suspended from school	—
Number of suspensions	—
Expelled from school	—
Number of expulsions	—
Retained in grade	—
Number of retentions	—

60. Have any additional instructional modifications been attempted?

None	—	(0)
Behavior modification program	—	(1)
Daily/weekly report card	—	(2)
Other (please specify)	—	(3)

V. SOCIAL HISTORY

61. How does the child get along with his/her brothers/sisters?

Doesn't have any	—	(0)
Better than average	—	(1)
Average	—	(2)
Worse than average	—	(3)

62. How easily does the child make friends?

Easier than average	—	(1)
Average	—	(2)
Worse than average	—	(3)
DK	—	(4)

63. On the average, how long does your child keep friendships?

Less than 6 months	—	(1)
6 months–1 year	—	(2)
More than 1 year	—	(3)
DK	—	

VI. CURRENT BEHAVIORAL CONCERNS

Primary concerns   Other (related) concerns

64. What strategies have been implemented to address these problems?
    (Check which have been successful)

    | | | Rewards | ___ (4) |
    | Verbal reprimands | ___ (1) | Physical punishment | ___ (5) |
    | Time out (isolation) | ___ (2) | Acquiescence to child | ___ (6) |
    | Removal of privileges | ___ (3) | Avoidance of child | ___ (7) |

65. On the average, what percentage of the time does your child comply with initial
    commands?

    | 0–20% | ___ (1) |
    | 20–40% | ___ (2) |
    | 40–60% | ___ (3) |
    | 60–80% | ___ (4) |
    | 80–100% | ___ (5) |

66. On the average, what percentage of the time does your child eventually comply
    with commands?

    | 0–20% | ___ (1) |
    | 20–40% | ___ (2) |
    | 40–60% | ___ (3) |
    | 60–80% | ___ (4) |
    | 80–100% | ___ (5) |

67. To what extent are you and your spouse consistent with respect to disciplinary
    strategies?

    | Most of the time | ___ (1) |
    | Some of the time | ___ (2) |
    | None of the time | ___ (3) |

68. Have any of the following stress events occurred within the past 12 months?

    | Parents divorced or separated | ___ (1) |
    | Family accident or illness | ___ (2) |
    | Death in family | ___ (3) |
    | Parent changed job | ___ (4) |
    | Changed schools | ___ (5) |
    | Family moved | ___ (6) |
    | Family financial problems | ___ (7) |
    | Other (please specify) | ___ (8) |

VII. DIAGNOSTIC CRITERIA

69. Which of the following are considered to be a significant problem at the present
    time? (0 = No; 1 = Yes)

    | Fidgets | ___ |
    | Difficulty remaining seated | ___ |
    | Easily distracted | ___ |
    | Difficulty awaiting turn | ___ |
    | Often blurts out answers to questions before they have been completed | ___ |
    | Difficulty following instructions | ___ |
    | Difficulty sustaining attention | ___ |
    | Shifts from one activity to another | ___ |
    | Difficulty playing quietly | ___ |
    | Often talks excessively | ___ |
    | Often interrupts or intrudes on others | ___ |
    | Often does not listen | ___ |

Often loses things   —

Often engages in physically dangerous activities   —

TOTAL FOR ADHD = __ (8 or more)

70. When did these problems begin? (Specify age): _____

71. Which of the following are considered to be a significant problem at the present time. (0 = No; 1 = Yes)

Often loses temper   —
Often argues with adults   —
Often actively defies or refuses adult re-
quests or rules   —
Often deliberately does things that an-
noy other people   —
Often blames others for own mistakes   —
Is often touchy or easily annoyed by
others   —
Is often angry or resentful   —
Is often spiteful or vindictive   —
Often swears or uses obscene language   —

TOTAL for Oppositional Defiant Disorder = __ (5 or more)

72. When did these problems begin? (Specify age): _____

73. Which of the following are considered to be a significant problem at the present time? (0 = No; 1 = Yes)

Stolen without confrontation   —
Run away from home overnight at least twice   —
Lies often   —
Deliberate fire-setting   —
Often truant   —
Breaking and entering   —
Destroyed others' property   —
Cruel to animals   —
Forced someone else into sexual activity   —
Used a weapon in a fight   —
Often initiates physical fights   —
Stolen with confrontation   —
Physically cruel to people   —

TOTAL for Conduct Disorder = __ (3 or more)

74. When did these problems begin? (Specify age): _____

75. Which of the following are considered to be a significant problem at the present time? (0 = No; 1 = Yes)

Unrealistic and persistent worry about
possible harm to attachment figures   —
Unrealistic and persistent worry that a
calamitous event will separate the
child from attachment figure   —
Persistent school refusal   —
Persistent refusal to sleep alone   —
Persistent avoidance of being alone   —
Repeated nightmares re: separation   —
Somatic complaints   —

Excessive distress in anticipation of
separation from attachment figure ___

Excessive distress when separated from
home or attachment figures ___

TOTAL for Separation Anxiety Disorder = ___ (3 or more)

76. When did these problems begin? (Specify age): _____

77. Which of the following are considered to be a significant problem at the present
time? (0 = No; 1 = Yes)

Unrealistic worry about future events ___
Unrealistic concern about appropriate-
ness of past behavior ___
Unrealistic concern about competence ___
Somatic complaints ___
Marked self-consciousness ___
Excessive need for reassurance ___
Marked inability to relax ___

TOTAL for Overanxious Disorder = ___ (4 or more)

78. When did these problems begin? (Specify age): _____

79. Which of the following are considered to be a significant problem at the present
time? (0 = No; 1 = Yes)

*Depressed or irritable mood most of day,
nearly every day ___
*Diminished pleasure in activities ___
Decrease or increase in appetite assoc.
with possible failure to make weight
gain ___
Insomnia or hypersomnia nearly every
day ___
Psychomotor agitation or retardation ___
Fatigue or loss of energy ___
Feelings of worthlessness or excessive
inappropriate guilt ___
Diminished ability to concentrate ___
Suicidal ideation or attempt ___

TOTAL for Major Depressive Episode (items 3–9) = ___ (5 or more)

80. When did these problems begin? (Specify age): _____

81. Which of the following are considered to be a significant problem at the present
time? (0 = No; 1 = Yes)

*Depressed or irritable mood for most of the day × 1 yr ___
Poor appetite or overeating ___
Insomnia or hypersomnia ___
Low energy or fatigue ___
Low self-esteem ___
Poor concentration or difficulty making decisions ___
Feelings of hopelessness ___
Never without symptoms for > 2 mos. over a 1-yr period ___

TOTAL for Dysthymia (items 2–7) = ___ (2 or more)

82. When did these problems begin? (Specify age): _____

VIII. OTHER CONCERNS

83. Has the child exhibited any of the symptoms below? (0 = No; 1 = Yes)

Stereotyped mannerisms   —
Odd postures   —
Excessive reaction to noise or fails to react to loud noises   —
Overreacts to touch   —
Compulsive rituals   —
Motor tics   —
Vocal tics   —

TOTAL = __

(NOTE: The remaining questions in this section are optional.)

84. Has the child exhibited any symptoms of thought disturbance, including any of the following: (0 = No; 1 = Yes)

Loose thinking (e.g., tangential ideas, circumstantial speech)   —
Bizarre ideas (e.g., odd fascinations, delusions, hallucinations)   —
Disoriented, confused, staring, or "spacey"   —
Incoherent speech (mumbles, jargon)   —

TOTAL = __

85. Has the child exhibited any symptoms of affective disturbance, including any of the following: (0 = No; 1 = Yes)

Excessive lability w/o reference to environment   —
Explosive temper with minimal provocation   —
Excessive clinging, attachment, or dependence on adults   —
Unusual fears   —
Strange aversions   —
Panic attacks   —
Excessively constricted or bland affect   —
Situationally inappropriate emotions   —

TOTAL = __

86. Has the child exhibited any symptoms of social conduct disturbance, including the following? (0 = No; 1 = Yes)

Little or no interest in peers   —
Significantly indiscreet remarks   —
Initiates or terminates interactions inappropriately   —
Qualitatively abnormal social behavior   —
Excessive reaction to changes in routine   —
Abnormalities of speech   —
Self-mutilation   —

TOTAL = __

IX. FAMILY HISTORY

87. How long have you and the child's father (mother) been married? (Please note whether the child was the product of 1st, 2nd, etc. marriage.)

Never were married __ (0)
Separated __ (1)
Divorced __ (2)
Widowed __ (3)
Married for __ years __ (4)

88. How stable is your current marriage?

Stable __ (1)
Unstable __ (2)

NOTES

PATERNAL RELATIVES

	Self	Mother	Father	Siblings				Total
				Bro	Bro	Sis	Sis	
Problems with aggressiveness, defiance, & oppositional behavior as a child								
Problems with attention, activity, & impulse control as a child								
Learning disabilities								
Failed to graduate from high school								
Mental retardation								
Psychosis or schizophrenia								
Depression for greater than 2 weeks								
Anxiety disorder that impaired adjustment								
Tics or Tourette's								
Alcohol abuse								
Substance abuse								
Antisocial behavior (assaults, thefts, etc.)								
Arrests								
Physical abuse								
Sexual abuse								

0 = Negative; 1 = Positive

MATERNAL RELATIVES

	Self	Mother	Father	Siblings Bro	Bro	Sis	Sis	Total
Problems with aggressiveness, defiance, & oppositional behavior as a child								
Problems with attention, activity, & impulse control as a child								
Learning disabilities								
Failed to graduate from high school								
Mental retardation								
Psychosis or schizophrenia								
Depression for greater than 2 weeks								
Anxiety disorder that impaired adjustment								
Tics or Tourette's								
Alcohol abuse								
Substance abuse								
Antisocial behavior (assaults, thefts, etc.)								
Arrests								
Physical abuse								
Sexual abuse								

0 = Negative; 1 = Positive

SIBLINGS

	Brother	Brother	Sister	Sister	Total
Problems with aggressiveness, defiance, & oppositional behavior as a child					
Problems with attention, activity, & impulse control as a child					
Learning disabilities					
Failed to graduate from high school					
Mental retardation					
Psychosis or schizophrenia					
Depression for greater than 2 weeks					
Anxiety disorder that impaired adjustment					
Tics or Tourette's					
Alcohol abuse					
Substance abuse					
Antisocial behavior (assaults, thefts, etc.)					
Arrests					
Physical abuse					
Sexual abuse					

0 = Negative; 1 = Positive

9

Behavior Rating Scales

> General observations drawn from particulars are the jewels of knowledge, comprehending great store in a little room.
>
> —JOHN LOCKE (1632–1704)

An essential component of the evaluation of children with Attention-deficit Hyperactivity Disorder (ADHD), second only to the interviews discussed in Chapter 8, is the use of well-standardized behavior rating scales. Several types of rating scales that I have found to have utility in assessing ADHD symptoms in children and adolescents, as well as assessing parental characteristics and marital satisfaction, are described below. In view of the greater likelihood of psychological distress, psychopathology, and marital discord with the parents of ADHD children and the impact of these difficulties upon treatment planning and implementation, I consider parent self-report scales to be almost as important in the evaluation of ADHD children as are those scales commonly completed by parents and teachers about the ADHD children. I have therefore reviewed several parent self-report scales that we have found useful in our clinical evaluations of ADHD children and their families. The reader wishing to see how these child and parent rating scales are used in an evaluation is referred to Chapter 11, where six cases examples are provided.

NATURE AND FUNCTION

Since child behavior rating scales have ascended to so important a place in the evaluation of ADHD children, it is useful to have an understanding of the characteristics and properties of such scales and the assumptions that underlie their use. This should result in a greater appreciation for the merits and limitations of these instruments, and greater insight into their clinical interpretation.

Essential Requirements

One of the most commonly employed methods for objectifying people's opinions about themselves or children in their care is to quantify their responses in behavior rating scales or questionnaires and to develop normative data on those responses. No other area of psychopathology has spawned more rating scales than the study of conduct problems and hyperactivity in children. The best of these for use with ADHD children are reviewed below under the heading "Parent and Teacher Rating Scales." A separate section deals with self-report rating scales which ADHD adolescents may complete about themselves concerning their behavioral adjustment and family conflicts, and with parent self-report measures concerning their own psychological adjustment and marital satisfaction.

Before these scales are reviewed, it is worth remembering that a clinically useful scale should meet certain standards other than the fact that some expert in the field has created or recommended it. These psychometric properties are as follows:

1. The scale should have items that are worded so as to make it clear to the respondent what is being rated. The more specific and operational the content of the item, the greater its reliability will be.

2. The scale should have enough items pertaining to the psychological or behavioral construct(s) of interest to be an adequate sampling of the domain of this construct and to be reliable as a measure of it. It should not have so many as to be inordinately time-consuming and hence discouraging to those asked to complete it. Some scale developers have apparently overlooked this requirement and developed scales containing several hundred items that can take up to an hour to complete. There is no evidence that the yield from such scales is so much better than that of shorter scales of the same construct(s) as to justify this extra time from respondents.

3. The answer format provided for the items should have a sufficient range to allow for a representative sampling of the range of frequency of the symptom or construct within the population of interest. Simple "yes-no" formats rarely permit this finer discrimination of frequency or severity that may be necessary to discriminate clinical from normal populations. The descriptors attached to these ranges of responses (i.e., "not at all," "just a little," etc.) should be made as clear as possible regarding the level of frequency or severity to which they refer. To the extent that they are vague and open to differing interpretations, the reliability of the scale will be reduced.

4. The item should have some "face validity"; that is, its content should reflect the construct(s) of interest. This does not guarantee that the scale actually assesses the construct. The latter quality, known as "construct validity," must be empirically established (see next paragraph).

5. The scale should demonstrate validity in assessing the construct of in-

terest. That is, it should correlate significantly with other measures of the same construct(s) taken by other means or from other sources. Rating scales for ADHD symptoms vary considerably in the degree to which they have demonstrated this type of validity. Related to this concept is the notion of "concurrent validity" or "ecological validity"—the scale must be significantly related to measures of the behaviors or constructs of interest taken in the natural setting in which the problem is known to exist. It is not surprising to find that even the best rating scales of ADHD correlate only moderately (.30 to .50) with actual observations of ADHD symptoms taken in home or classroom settings (Barkley, 1989c).

6. Another psychometric requirement of rating scales related to construct validity is "discriminant validity." In other words, does the scale discriminate between samples of subjects that are known to have more or less of this particular behavior or symptom? In the case of ADHD, many rating scales have been able to show that they can discriminate ADHD groups from normal and non-ADHD clinical samples, which is why they are so highly recommended as part of the assessment process.

7. It is quite helpful clinically if the scale can demonstrate some "predictive validity," in that it correlates significantly with the same scale or other comparable measures taken at some later time in development. For instance, it has been frequently shown that childhood ratings of aggression or conduct problems in ADHD children are significantly related to adolescent ratings of parent-child conflicts as well as delinquency as much as 8 years after initial assessment (Barkley, Fischer, Edelbrock, & Smallish, in press-b).

8. Rating scales should also have acceptable levels of reliability both over time and between raters. In the former case, ratings taken at one point in time should correlate significantly with those taken by the same individual on the same scale at some point in the relatively immediate future (usually several weeks to months); this is known as "test-retest reliability." This is particularly relevant when one is attempting to assess a behavior or symptom that is believed to be relatively stable or chronic over time, such as ADHD. Agreement between raters, known as "interrater reliability," is also desirable, in that it shows that two raters assessing a person at the same time can agree on the presence and degree of the behavior or construct being rated. Where these types of reliability are poor, validity of the scale will also be poor.

9. Finally, it would be very beneficial to clinical practice for scales to demonstrate some "prescriptive utility." This refers to the ability of a scale to predict a person's differential response to subsequent treatments. Until relatively recently, most rating scales of ADHD have not been of much value in this respect. However, several recent studies suggest that unusually high ratings on rating scales assessing anxiety and depression are predictive of adverse responses to stimulant medication in ADHD children (Voelker, Lachar, & Godowski, 1983; Taylor, 1986b), while high ratings on scales assessing inattention predict a positive response to these medications (Barkley, 1976; Taylor, 1983).

Underlying Assumptions

Cairns and Green (1979) have described a number of important assumptions underlying the use of behavior rating scales. Clinicians should keep these in mind as they attempt to judiciously interpret these sources of information about children:

1. The informant shares with the clinician some common understanding of the attribute or behavior to be rated. The more abstract the concept, the greater the discrepancy that may exist between what the clinician intends to have rated and what the informant actually rates.

2. The informant shares an understanding of which behaviors of the child actually represent the attribute on the scale. Behaviors that are relevant to a given scale item may vary due to developmental, situational, or demographic variables; it is assumed that the rater and clinician share a similar perception of which aspects of these behaviors are to be considered in responding to the item.

3. The rater is capable of extracting from the "stream of everyday life activities" of the child those behaviors relevant to the quality or attribute being rated. The informant must decide not only whether the attribute being rated has occurred, but whether that occurrence qualifies for inclusion in the item being rated.

4. The informant and clinician share the same concept of the reference points for the scaling along which the item is to be rated. The informant and clinician may or may not share the same perception of the base rates of the behavior being rated, and hence the perception of what constitutes such scale anchor points as "just a little" or "very much." Interrater reliability of scales depends greatly upon this shared understanding of scale reference points. For instance, Ross and Ross (1982) provided college-educated mothers with the four response choices from the Conners Parent Rating Scale, along with three items from the scale, and asked these mothers how many times within the past month their children would have had to show the behavior in that item for them to use each point on the response scale ("not at all," "just a little," "pretty much," "very much"). The resulting responses were surprisingly varied. Frequencies of behavior for the response of "not at all" ranged from 0 to 15, for "just a little" from 1 to 120, and for "very much" from 5 to 300. One cannot always assume, then, that rater and clinician share the same notion of quantity or quality of behavior reflected in an item's response scale.

The extent to which most or all of these assumptions are met for particular rating scales, populations of raters or of children, or types of psychopathology is open to considerable question. Clinicians should therefore take care not to base their clinical impressions entirely upon scores on a behavior rating scale, but should weigh and balance this information against that received from other sources and informants.

Related Issues

The validity or reliability of child behavior rating scales can also be compromised by numerous other conceptual or practical problems in their construction, use, or interpretation. One is the nature of those sources of variation contributing to the ratings on a scale. Many clinicians interpret scale findings as if they represented only the actual behavior of the children being rated. However, various characteristics of the informants—their education, intelligence, emotional status at the time the ratings were conducted, and tendency toward response biases—all contribute to some degree to the particular ratings on a scale. Other sources of variation come from the manner in which the scale has been constructed, the specificity of its wording, the time period over which the ratings are to be made, and the breadth of response scaling provided, as well as those factors (developmental, demographic, contextual, etc.) creating actual situational variation in a child's behavior.

Many scale developers have employed various types of factor analyses to create subscales, which are then labeled as reflecting certain constructs or dimensions of child behavior (e.g., Aggression, Social Withdrawal, etc.). However, those interpreting such subscale scores or dimensions must consider that they only partially reflect the actual child behaviors they are meant to represent. Factors derived from these analyses depend heavily upon the type, nature, content, and number of items entering the analyses; their scaling; their situation specificity; the informants from whom the ratings were obtained; and the nature of the sample on which the ratings were made. As a result, such factors may or may not represent real dimensions of child behavior, but they undoubtedly reflect more than simply child behavior, given the assumptions and issues already noted (Mischel, 1973). It is essential, therefore, that research establish the construct validity of these subscales by anchoring them to measures of the same constructs taken by other means before they can be interpreted as truly reflecting those qualities or attributes of child behavior. To some degree, this has been done with some of the scales used with ADHD children; the evidence, although reasonably satisfactory, is far from perfect.

Advantages over Other Measures

Despite the problems inherent in the use and interpretation of rating scales, they offer numerous advantages over other methods and, for these reasons, will increasingly be used in research in child psychopathology (see Edelbrock & Rancurello, 1984; Mash & Terdal, 1981; McMahon, 1984; O'Leary, 1981). Some of the many advantages are that ratings (1) have the capability of gathering information from informers with many years of experience with the child across diverse settings and circumstances; (2) permit the collection of data on behaviors that occur extremely infrequently and are likely to be missed by *in vivo* measures; (3) are inexpensive to administer and require little time to complete; (4) may have normative data for establishing the statistical deviance of child behavior ratings; (5) exist in a variety of forms focusing on a diversity of dimensions of child psychopathology; (6) incorporate the opinions of significant people in the child's natural environment who are responsible for the care, management, and ultimately the therapeutic treatments a child will receive; (7) filter out situational variation, thereby focusing on the most stable and enduring characteristics of the child; and (8) permit quantitative distinctions to be made concerning qualitative aspects of child behavior that are often difficult to obtain through direct observational methods.

Clinical Benefits

Many rating scales of ADHD do not meet all (or even most) of the psychometric requirements described earlier, although they have a considerably better base of empirical support than when the first edition of this text was published (Barkley, 1981). What, then, are the advantages to employing rating scales in clinical practice? There are many, as noted above, but a few require elaboration here. First, most rating scales for ADHD now have adequate normative data that permit clinicians to determine the degree of deviance of a particular child within the population of same-age and same-sex children. This is essential to the diagnosis of ADHD. Many ADHD characteristics occur to some degree in normal children, particularly preschoolers, and so some method of determining whether the reports of a parent or teacher indicate that a child is truly deviant is required. Rating scales provide one method, albeit imperfect, for assessing deviance.

Second, rating scales can be a convenient means for collapsing information about a child across situations and lengthy time intervals into units of information of value to diagnosis. It would be almost impossible and certainly unwieldy to collect direct observations of children over diverse settings and several months for clinical purposes. For cost-effectiveness, then, rating scales are hard to beat.

Third, ratings can provide a convenient means for assessing dimensions of child behavior that are hard to quantify by other means. Certain features of affect or the disruptive quality of a child's behavior are not easily assessed directly or are sufficiently subjective as to preclude their objective measurement. Yet it is often these qualitative features that are crucial to a thorough clinical appreciation of a child's current adjustment. The actions of important caregivers in the lives of ADHD children are often based upon these subjective impressions, whether or not they accurately reflect the children's actual behavior in a situation. To understand these perceptions of other adults, clinicians must obtain their opinions and contrast them against the typical views of normal children by these same types of caregivers. Rating scales are superior in providing these assessments.

And fourth, rating scales provide a convenient means for evaluating a person's response to clinical interventions. Most research on treatments for ADHD children now employs parent and teacher ratings as one means of monitoring the children's reaction to the treatments under study. Many clinicians are beginning to do the same. This seems especially important in obtaining information from teachers during trials on medication, as the peak therapeutic effects of the drugs occur during school hours, and ADHD children are often medicated because of concerns about school performance. And yet surveys suggest that clinicians rarely obtain such information from teachers (Gadow, 1981), probably in large part because of the inconvenience of doing so. The brevity, widespread availability, and convenience of rating scales for both clinicians and teachers, however, should now make their inclusion mandatory in the clinical assessment and drug treatment of ADHD children.

Nevertheless, it must not be forgotten that rating scales are merely quantified opinions and can be subject to the same biases as can anyone's opinions of another; thus, they should not be the only means of assessing ADHD children. Moreover, rating scales fail to assess certain antecedent and consequent events surrounding a child's behavior that may be of substantial importance to determining why the problem behavior occurs, when and where it does, and thereby how to manage it effectively. And so, while rating scales offer tremendous benefits to the clinical evaluation and management of ADHD children, their interpretation requires clinical sensitivity and careful judgment.

PARENT AND TEACHER RATING SCALES

A number of parent and teacher rating scales of child behavior are now reviewed. I have found these particular scales to be the most useful in the clinical evaluation of ADHD children. A more comprehensive review of other rating scales that have been used in research and practice with ADHD children is provided in Appendix A. The structure, scaling, factorial content, and procedure for obtaining each scale are briefly presented, along with an indication of whether data on various forms of reliability and validity are available. Indications of "Yes" or "No" after each category of reliability and validity serve only to note that information of this sort was or was not available in the literature when I conducted this review. It does not indicate the adequacy of those findings. Whether or not normative data are available is also specified, along with the ages of the children for whom those data are appropriate. A brief commentary then follows, providing more specific information on reliability and validity of the scale (if available), and addressing the strengths or weaknesses of the scale for clinical use with ADHD children.

Parent Rating Scales

CHILD BEHAVIOR CHECKLIST *(CBCL; Achenbach & Edelbrock, 1983)*

Developers: Thomas M. Achenbach, Ph.D., and Craig S. Edelbrock, Ph.D.

Where to obtain: Thomas M. Achenbach, Ph.D., Department of Psychiatry, University of Vermont, Burlington, VT 05401

Copyrighted: Yes

Items: 138   Scaling: 0–2   *Ages:* 4–16 years

Completion Time: 15–20 minutes   *Scoring Software:* Yes

Reliability Information Available:

Test-Retest: Yes   *Interrater:* Yes   *Internal Consistency:* Yes

Validity Information Available:

Construct: Yes   *Discriminant:* Yes   *Concurrent:* Yes

Predictive: Yes   *Treatment-Sensitive:* Yes

Normative Data: Yes (2–16 years; $n = 1,300$)

Factors Assessed: (dependent on age) Social Withdrawal, Depressed, Immature, Somatic Complaints, Sex Problems, Anxious–Schizoid, Aggressive, Delinquent, Hyperactive, Uncommunicative, Obsessive-Compulsive

Bibliography: Yes, see manual

Comments

Clinicians interested in employing this scale should thoroughly peruse the manual (Achenbach & Edelbrock, 1983), from which most of the information on reliability and validity was obtained. The 138 items on the CBCL are broken down into 20 items that assess Social Competence and 118 items that comprise the Behavior Problems scale. The Social Competence scale generates three scores: Activities (sports, hobbies, etc.), Social (organizations, friendships, etc.), and School (performance, problems, etc.). These are then plotted on one of six profiles, depending on the age (4–5 years, 6–11 years, and 12–16 years) and sex of the child. This is a highly unique and informative aspect of this scale, relative to others that provide little or no such information on social competence.

The remaining 118 items comprise the Behavior Problems scale. Factor analyses of the responses to these items for 2,300 clinic-referred children again revealed different sets of factors for males and females and for three separate age groupings (4–5 years, 6–11 years, and 12–16 years). The profiles generated for each grouping consist of eight or nine factors. Norms for the factor scales were collected on 1,300 normal children who were well stratified regarding socioeconomic class and ethnic composition. The percentage of children receiving a positive endorsement by each item is reported in Achenbach and Edelbrock (1981). The developers suggest that parents completing the scale have at least a fifth-grade reading level, while linguistic analysis of the items indicates a mean reading complexity level of 8.2 (Harrington & Follett, 1984).

Reliability information from the manual indicates 1-week test-retest coefficients of .95 (Behavior Problems) and .99 (Social Competence) by the intraclass computation method. Test-retest coefficients over a 3-month interval were .84 (Behavior Problems) and .97 (Social Competence). Pearson coefficients ranged from .61 to .96 across factors and age × sex groupings. Stability coefficients of .53 for clinicians' reports and .59 for mothers' reports over a 6-month period have been noted. Estimates of stability over 3 months, 6 months, and 18 months are reported in the manual. Interparent agreement on a clinic-referred sample of children was .978 for Social Competence and .985 for Behavior Problems. Across factors, the range of agreement between parents was .26 to .78 for the Behavior Problems scale and .44 to .81 on the Social Competence scale. Satisfactory interparent agreements were also reported by Mash and Johnston (1983c).

Although less research exists on the CBCL than on the Conners scales or the Behavior Problem Checklist because of its more recent development, this situation is quickly changing. Large numbers of currently ongoing research projects are using the CBCL, and so ample published research on the validity of the scale will be forthcoming very soon. Concurrent validity has been established by demonstrating significant correlations of like factors between the CBCL and (1) the Conners scales and the Revised Behavior Problem Checklist (see manual and Kazdin & Heidish, 1984; Mash & Johnston, 1983c); (2) the Werry-Weiss-Peters Activity Rating Scale (Mash & Johnston, 1983c); and (3) a semistructured psychiatric interview, the Diagnostic Interview Schedule for Children—Parent Report (Costello & Edelbrock, 1985). The CBCL has shown adequate discriminant validity in distinguishing between clinic-referred and nonreferred children (see manual), hyperactive and normal children (Barkley, 1981; Edelbrock, 1984; Mash & Johnston, 1983c), children of maritally distressed and nondistressed mothers (Bond & McMahon, 1984), depressed and nondepressed children (Seagull & Weinshank, 1984), adopted and nonadopted children (Brodzinsky, Schecter, Braff, & Singer, 1984), and maltreated and control children (Salzinger, Kaplan, Pelcovitz, Samit, & Krieger, 1984). The instrument has shown some usefulness in screening for psychopathology in a primary care pediatric setting (Costello & Edelbrock, 1985), and in assessing changes in conduct problems following a parent training program in child management skills (Webster-Stratton, 1984). Research has also been done developing profile typologies for a variety of childhood disorders (Edelbrock &Achenbach, 1984).

There can be little doubt that this is the most well-developed, empirically derived behavior rating scale currently available for assessing psychopathology and social competence in children. The item content is sufficiently broad to capture the majority of internalizing or externalizing disorders, to assess social competence, and to evaluate a diversity of psychopathological disturbances likely to present in clinical practice. The developers respect the fact that different types of psychopathology exist for the different sexes at different age levels of children, and provide for this in the scoring of the instrument. The availability of an equally well-developed Teacher Report Form for the CBCL (see below), as well as a Youth Self-Report Form, further recommends the use of these scales as standard components of a thorough evaluation of ADHD children.

A CBCL profile based on 60 hyperactive children is shown in Figure 9.1. It indicates that as a group ADHD children display high elevations on many of the scales, but particularly on the Hyperactive, Aggressive, Delinquent, and Obsessive-Compulsive scales. The elevation on the Aggressive scale reflects the fact, noted in Chapter 2, that aggressive or oppositional defiant behavior is often associated with ADHD and so would be expected to be high in this mixed sample of ADHD children. Similarly, the elevation on the Delinquent scale also reflects the greater comorbidity of Conduct Disorder or antisocial behavior with ADHD. While at first surprising, the elevation on the Obsessive-Compulsive scale does not really reflect greater neuroticism in ADHD children. Instead, the higher score on this scale is due to the loading of several items pertaining to inattentive and hyperactive behavior ("staring,"

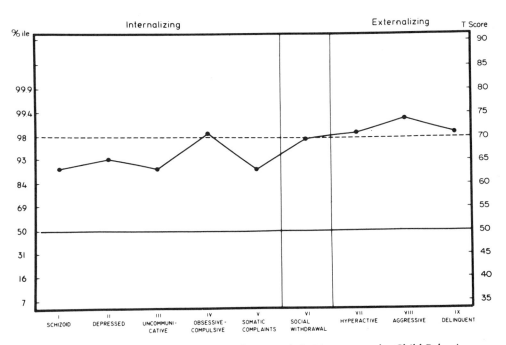

FIGURE 9.1. Profile for 60 hyperactive boys aged 6–11 years on the Child Behavior Profile, based on parent ratings from the Child Behavior Checklist. From *Hyperactive Children: A Handbook for Diagnosis and Treatment* by R. A. Barkley, 1981, New York: Guilford Press. Copyright 1981 by The Guilford Press. Reprinted by permission of the publisher.

"daydreaming," "confused or seems to be in a fog," and "talks too much"), as well as sleep problems, which are known to occur in at least 30 percent of ADHD children. Examples of profiles from six clinical cases having different diagnoses are given in Chapter 11.

CONNERS PARENT RATING SCALE—Revised (CPRS-R; Goyette, Conners, & Ulrich, 1978)

Developer: C. Keith Conners, Ph.D.

Where to Obtain: C. Keith Conners, Ph.D., Department of Psychiatry, Duke University Medical Center, Durham, NC 27710

Copyrighted: Yes

Items: 48   *Scaling:* 0–3   *Ages:* 3–17 years

Completion Time: 5–10 minutes   *Scoring Software:* Yes

Reliability Information Available:

Test-Retest: No   *Interrater:* Yes   *Internal Consistency:* No

Validity Information Available:

Construct: Yes   *Discriminant:* No   *Concurrent:* No

Predictive: No   *Treatment-Sensitive:* Yes

Normative Data: Yes (ages 3–17 years; $n = 570$)

Factors Assessed: Conduct Problems, Learning Problems, Psychosomatic, Impulsive-Hyperactive, and Anxiety

Bibliography Available: Yes, from developer

Comments

There are three versions of the Conners Parent Rating Scale (CPRS) currently in common use: (1) the original 93-item scale (Conners, 1970); (2) the 48-item revised version (CPRS-R; Goyette et al., 1978); and (3) the 10-item Abbreviated Symptom Questionnaire (ASQ). The original 93-item version and the 10-item abbreviated scale are reviewed in Appendix A. Conners revised the original CPRS in 1978, reducing the number of items to 48 and slightly rewording those that were retained to simplify administration and interpretation. Those items assessing internalizing or neurotic disorders appear to have been greatly reduced in number, making the revised scale more useful for assessing conduct problems (aggression, hyperactivity, etc.) as opposed to the more internalizing disorders (depression, psychosomatic disorders, etc.). Hence, the CPRS-R would seem most useful where a brief evaluation of conduct problems or hyperactivity is of interest.

Normative data on the scale are reported in the paper by Goyette et al. (1978) for boys and girls aged 3 to 17 years, and are also available from the developer. Where normative data are important, clinicians may wish to use this version over the original, as the norms are provided for a wider age range of subjects and are broken down by sex. Ratings between mothers and fathers were not found to differ significantly, with agreement ranging between .46 and .57 across the five factors. Not unexpectedly, agreement between the parent and teacher ratings was somewhat lower, ranging between .33 and .45. Test-retest reliability information could not be located for this scale. Nevertheless, it would appear prudent to assume that this scale will demonstrate the same practice effects as the original scale, making it important for the CPRS-R to be administered at least twice before use in any protocol assessing treatment effects.

The validity of the CPRS-R has not been as well studied as that of the original scale. Given the similarity of items assessing conduct problems between the two scales, data on the validity of the externalizing factors (such as Hyperactive-Immature and Conduct Disorder) for the original scale would appear to be applicable to the comparable factors (Impulsive-Hyperactive and Conduct Problems) on the revised version. Recent research has shown the scale to be sensitive to stimulant drug effects (Barkley, Fischer, Newby, & Breen, 1988), parent training in child management (Pollard, Ward, & Barkley, 1983), and self-control training of hyperactive children (Horn, Ialongo, Popovich, & Peradotto, 1984). However, the CPRS-R would not seem as useful for the initial assessment and diagnosis of ADHD as the CBCL (reviewed above), given its limited length and item coverage as well as its smaller normative sample. Instead, it would be more appropriate for evaluating treatment effects—say, during a stimulant medication trial, or before and after parent training in child behavior management.

EYBERG CHILD BEHAVIOR INVENTORY (ECBI; Eyberg, 1980)

Developer: Sheila M. Eyberg, Ph.D.

Where to Obtain: Sheila M. Eyberg, Ph.D., Department of Clinical Psychology, University of Florida, Box J-165, JHMHC, Gainesville, FL 32610

Copyrighted: Yes

Items: 36   *Scaling:* 1–7   *Ages:* 2–12 years

Completion Time: 10 minutes   *Scoring Software:* Yes

Reliability Information Available:

Test-Retest: Yes   *Interrater:* Yes   *Internal Consistency:* Yes

Validity Information Available:

Construct: Yes   *Discriminant:* Yes   *Concurrent:* Yes

Predictive: No   *Treatment-Sensitive:* Yes

Normative Data: Yes (ages 2–7 and 13–16 years; n's = 512 and 102)

Factors Assessed: Conduct Problems/Oppositional Behavior

Bibliography: Yes, 19 references, from developer

Comments

The ECBI is a short rating scale designed to record parent reports of child-hood behavioral problems, particularly oppositional behavior and conduct disorders (Eyberg & Ross, 1978). Two scores are obtained: an Intensity score, reflecting the sum of the ratings (1–7) across all items, and a Problem score, comprised of the number of items endorsed as problems by the parent. While normative data are available (Eyberg & Robinson, 1983; Robinson, Eyberg, & Ross, 1980), the samples are more representative of lower- to lower-middle-income groups, and the older age group (13–16 years) is quite small and comprised disproportionately of females (63%). Furthermore, despite initial reports of significant effects of sex on the norms, the normative data are not broken down by sex but by age alone. Factor analyses (Eyberg & Robinson, 1983; Robinson et al., 1980) suggest that the scale is predominantly assessing conduct problems. However, other factors were discovered but not reported, making interpretation of the scale and its comparison to other rating scales difficult. Computer software for scoring the scale can be obtained from Holtum, Robinson, and Eyberg (1984).

Reliability information has been reported in several papers. Test-retest coefficients over 21 days were .86 for the Intensity score and .88 for the Problem score (Robinson et al., 1980). Interparent agreement on ratings for eight adolescents was found to be .79 (Eyberg & Robinson, 1983). Internal-consistency coefficients of .98 and split-half reliabilities of .90 to .94 have been reported (Eyberg & Robinson, 1983; Robinson et al., 1980).

The validity of the scale has been primarily established through the afore-mentioned factor-analytic studies, as well as those documenting adequate discrimination among normal, conduct problem, neglected, and other clinic-referred children (Aragona & Eyberg, 1981; Eyberg & Robinson, 1983; Eyberg & Ross, 1978; Robinson et al., 1980). The scores have been found to relate significantly to direct observational measures of noncompliance and negative parent-child interactions, as well as of child activity level and temperament (Robinson & Eyberg, 1981; Webster-Stratton & Eyberg, 1982). The scale has been shown repeatedly to be sensitive to treatment effects of parent training in child behavior management skills (Eyberg & Robinson, 1982; Eyberg & Ross, 1978; Packard, Robinson, & Grove, 1983; Webster-Stratton, 1984).

In summary, where the clinician desires a scale measuring child conduct problems and oppositional behavior, particularly for evaluating the effects of parent training programs, this scale appears quite useful. Its narrowness of item content, however, limits its use where a broad assessment of child psychopathology is desired.

HOME SITUATIONS QUESTIONNAIRE (HSQ; Barkley, 1987)

Developer: Russell A. Barkley, Ph.D.

Where to Obtain: Russell A. Barkley, Ph.D., Department of Psychiatry, University of Massachusetts Medical Center, 55 Lake Avenue North, Worcester, MA 01655

Copyrighted: Yes

Items: 16   *Scaling:* 0–9   *Ages:* 4–18 years

Completion Time: <5 minutes   *Scoring Software:* No

Reliability Information Available:

Test-Retest: Yes   *Interrater:* Yes   *Internal Consistency:* Yes

Validity Information Available:

Construct: Yes   *Discriminant:* Yes   *Concurrent:* Yes

Predictive: Yes   *Treatment-Sensitive:* Yes

Normative Data: Yes (ages 4–16 years; $n = 1,060$)

Factors Assessed: Social Interaction, Oppositional-Unfocused, Oppositional-Focused, Self-Engaged Situations

Bibliography: Yes (see Barkley & Edelbrock, 1987)

Comments

The previously reviewed rating scales serve to identify *what* type of problems a child or adolescent may be having. The HSQ was designed to evaluate *where* children and adolescents may be exhibiting their problem behaviors (i.e., situational variation of behavior disorder). The scale is shown in Figure 9.2. Parents are asked to indicate whether their child or adolescent displays behavior problems in each of 16 situations around the home and in public. If a problem is present, the severity is rated using a scale from 1 ("mild") to 9 ("severe"), yielding two scores: the number of problem settings and the mean severity rating. The most common problem settings and their mean severity ratings for ADHD children have been shown in Chapter 2 (see Figure 2.1) for 30 hyperactive and 30 normal children. These indicate that hyperactive children have fewer problems during play alone or when the father is at home, but have substantial difficulties when parents are on the phone, when company is at the home, or when they are asked to do chores.

Three additional factor scores can also be calculated for the HSQ factors noted above. Normative data were collected by Breen and Altepeter (1990) and are available for children from ages 4 to 18 years; these are shown in Table 9.1. The HSQ provides a situational profile that can be quite useful in designing contingency management interventions as part of parent training (see Barkley & Edelbrock, 1987). Among children, it has been found to be sensitive to the effects of both parent training and stimulant medication interventions (Barkley, Karlsson, Pollard, & Murphy, 1985; Barkley et al., 1988; Pollard et al., 1983). The scale also readily discriminates ADHD adolescents from normal adolescents, and childhood ratings are predictive of ongoing conflicts in parent-child interactions up to 8 years later in adolescence (Barkley, Fischer, et al., in press-b). One significant problem with this scale is that it confounds ratings of conduct problems with those of ADHD, so that it is

HOME SITUATIONS QUESTIONNAIRE

Child's Name _____ **Date** _____

Name of Person Completing This Form _____

Instructions: Does your child present any problems with compliance to instructions, commands, or rules for you in any of these situations? If so, please circle the word Yes and then circle a number beside that situation that describes how severe the problem is for you. If your child is not a problem in a situation, circle No and go on to the next situation on the form.

Situations	*Yes/No* (Circle one)		*If yes, how severe?* Mild (Circle one) Severe
Playing alone	Yes	No	1 2 3 4 5 6 7 8 9
Playing with other children	Yes	No	1 2 3 4 5 6 7 8 9
Mealtimes	Yes	No	1 2 3 4 5 6 7 8 9
Getting dressed/undressed	Yes	No	1 2 3 4 5 6 7 8 9
Washing and bathing	Yes	No	1 2 3 4 5 6 7 8 9
When you are on the telephone	Yes	No	1 2 3 4 5 6 7 8 9
Watching television	Yes	No	1 2 3 4 5 6 7 8 9
When visitors are in your home	Yes	No	1 2 3 4 5 6 7 8 9
When you are visiting someone's home	Yes	No	1 2 3 4 5 6 7 8 9
In public places (restaurants, stores, church, etc.)	Yes	No	1 2 3 4 5 6 7 8 9
When father is home	Yes	No	1 2 3 4 5 6 7 8 9
When asked to do chores	Yes	No	1 2 3 4 5 6 7 8 9
When asked to do homework	Yes	No	1 2 3 4 5 6 7 8 9
At bedtime	Yes	No	1 2 3 4 5 6 7 8 9
While in the car	Yes	No	1 2 3 4 5 6 7 8 9
When with a babysitter	Yes	No	1 2 3 4 5 6 7 8 9

---------------------------- For Office Use Only ----------------------------

Total number of problem settings _____ Mean severity score _____

FIGURE 9.2. The Home Situations Questionnaire. From *Defiant Children: A Clinician's Manual for Parent Training* by R. A. Barkley, 1987, New York: Guilford Press. Copyright 1987 by The Guilford Press. Reprinted by permission of the publisher.

not a pure measure of either. For now, it seems best to use the original HSQ where assessment of general behavior problems (especially oppositional or aggressive behavior) is of interest, and to use the revised version (HSQ-R) where a more refined assessment of attention deficits is of interest (see below).

TABLE 9.1. Norms for the Home Situations Questionnaire (HSQ)

Age groups (in years)	n	Number of problem settings	Mean severity
Boys			
4–5	162	3.1 (2.8)	1.7 (1.4)
6–8	205	4.1 (3.3)	2.0 (1.4)
9–11	138	3.6 (3.3)	1.9 (1.5)
Girls			
4–5	146	2.2 (2.6)	1.3 (1.4)
6–8	202	3.4 (3.5)	1.6 (1.5)
9–11	142	2.7 (3.2)	1.4 (1.4)

Note. Table entries are means with standard deviations in parentheses. From *Factor Structures of the Home Situations Questionnaire (HSQ) and the School Situations Questionnaire (SSQ)* by M. J. Breen and T. S. Altepeter, 1990, unpublished manuscript, Winneconne Public Schools, Winneconne, WI. Reprinted by permission of the author.

HOME SITUATIONS QUESTIONNAIRE—REVISED (HSQ-R; DuPaul, 1990b)

Developers: George J. DuPaul, Ph.D., and Russell A. Barkley, Ph.D.

Where to Obtain: George J. DuPaul, Ph.D., Department of Psychiatry, University of Massachusetts Medical Center, 55 Lake Avenue North, Worcester, MA 01655

Copyrighted: No

Items: 14   *Scaling:* 0–9   *Ages:* 6–12 years

Completion Time: <5 minutes   *Scoring Software:* No

Reliability Information Available:

Test-Retest: Yes   *Interrater:* No   *Internal Consistency:* Yes

Validity Information Available:

Construct: Yes   *Discriminant:* Yes   *Concurrent:* Yes

Predictive: No   *Treatment-Sensitive:* Yes

Normative Data: Yes (ages 6–12 years; $n = 581$)

Factors Assessed: Self-Care/Public Settings, Chore/Social Settings

Bibliography: No

Comments

The HSQ-R is a recent revision of the original HSQ, designed to assess specific problems with attention and concentration across a variety of home and public situations. As such, it is a more refined measure than the HSQ where the pervasiveness of attention problems is of interest, as it is in the diagnosis of ADHD. The scale is shown in Figure 9.3. DuPaul (1990b) has collected normative data for a relatively equal number of boys and girls between the ages of 6 and 12 years. These norms are shown in Table 9.2. Four scores can

HOME SITUATIONS QUESTIONNAIRE—REVISED

Name of Child _____ **Date** _____

Name of Person Completing This Form _____

Does this child have problems paying attention or concentrating in any of these situations? If so, indicate how severe these attentional difficulties are.

Situations	*Yes/No* (Circle one)		*If yes, how severe? (Circle one)* Mild Severe
While playing alone	Yes	No	1 2 3 4 5 6 7 8 9
While playing with other children	Yes	No	1 2 3 4 5 6 7 8 9
Mealtimes	Yes	No	1 2 3 4 5 6 7 8 9
Getting dressed	Yes	No	1 2 3 4 5 6 7 8 9
While watching TV	Yes	No	1 2 3 4 5 6 7 8 9
When visitors are in your home	Yes	No	1 2 3 4 5 6 7 8 9
When you are visiting someone else	Yes	No	1 2 3 4 5 6 7 8 9
At church or Sunday school	Yes	No	1 2 3 4 5 6 7 8 9
In supermarkets, stores, restaurants, or other public areas	Yes	No	1 2 3 4 5 6 7 8 9
When asked to do chores at home	Yes	No	1 2 3 4 5 6 7 8 9
During conversations with others	Yes	No	1 2 3 4 5 6 7 8 9
While in the car	Yes	No	1 2 3 4 5 6 7 8 9
When father is home	Yes	No	1 2 3 4 5 6 7 8 9
When asked to do school homework	Yes	No	1 2 3 4 5 6 7 8 9

Office Use Only: No. of problems _____ Mean severity _____

FIGURE 9.3. The Home Situations Questionnaire—Revised. From *The Home and School Situations Questionnaires—Revised: Normative Data, Reliability, and Validity* by G. J. DuPaul, 1990, unpublished manuscript, University of Massachusetts Medical Center, Worcester. Reprinted by permission of the author.

be obtained from the scale: the number of problem settings, the mean severity score, and the two factor scores noted above. The scale has been shown to have satisfactory test-retest reliability and to correlate significantly with other parent-completed rating scales of hyperactivity, such as the CPRS-R and the ADHD Rating Scale described below (DuPaul, 1990a). Given that the original HSQ was quite sensitive to treatment effects, this one is likely to prove so as well, especially in evaluating the effects of stimulant medication. Studies are underway now to evaluate this property of the scale.

TABLE 9.2. Means and Standard Deviations for the HSQ-R by Age and Gender

Age	Number of problem settings	Mean severity	Factor 1	Factor 2
		Girls		
6 (n=45)				
M	4.49	3.02	11.62	6.33
SD	3.82	1.88	15.02	9.19
7 (n=70)				
M	4.37	3.13	13.11	5.75
SD	4.13	1.75	16.74	9.86
8 (n=51)				
M	4.39	3.08	13.25	6.33
SD	3.82	1.67	16.28	10.97
9 (n=52)				
M	4.62	3.16	13.58	8.45
SD	4.41	1.81	17.21	13.87
10 (n=45)				
M	3.56	2.99	11.87	5.74
SD	4.19	1.79	18.40	10.96
11 (n=34)				
M	2.03	3.40	6.15	3.46
SD	2.71	2.16	10.52	6.68
12 (n=21)				
M	3.19	3.15	11.43	6.00
SD	4.11	2.08	18.78	14.40
		Boys		
6 (n=54)				
M	5.44	3.39	17.46	9.10
SD	3.60	1.81	17.94	13.41
7 (n=42)				
M	3.76	3.09	13.46	7.96
SD	4.32	1.89	21.00	14.58
8 (n=37)				
M	5.19	3.61	18.43	11.36
SD	4.50	1.85	20.97	15.45
9 (n=33)				
M	4.42	3.69	15.68	7.91
SD	4.12	1.95	18.20	12.31
10 (n=41)				
M	5.15	3.17	14.95	8.78
SD	4.64	1.84	17.54	11.40
11 (n=36)				
M	4.67	3.05	13.22	8.82
SD	4.70	1.80	17.76	14.89
12 (n=20)				
M	4.00	3.86	17.29	5.41
SD	3.23	1.84	18.37	8.47

Note. From *The Home and School Situations Questionnaires—Revised: Normative Data, Reliability, and Validity* by G. J. DuPaul, 1990, unpublished manuscript, University of Massachusetts Medical Center, Worcester. Reprinted by permission of the author.

Teacher Rating Scales

CHILD BEHAVIOR CHECKLIST—TEACHER REPORT FORM (CBCL-TRF; Edelbrock & Achenbach, 1984)

Developers: Craig S. Edelbrock, Ph.D., and Thomas M. Achenbach, Ph.D.

Where to Obtain: Thomas M. Achenbach, Ph.D., Department of Psychiatry, University of Vermont, Burlington, VT 05401

Copyrighted: Yes

Items: 126   *Scaling:* 0–2   *Ages:* 6–16 years

Completion Time: 15–20 minutes   *Scoring Software:* Yes

Reliability Information Available:

Construct: Yes   *Interrater:* No   *Internal Consistency:* Yes

Validity Information Available:

Construct: Yes   *Discriminant:* Yes   *Concurrent:* Yes

Predictive: No   *Treatment-Sensitive:* No

Normative Data: Yes (ages 6–16 years; *n* = 1,100)

Factors Assessed: (dependent on age and sex) Anxious, Social Withdrawal, Unpopular, Self-Destructive, Obsessive-Compulsive, Inattentive, Nervous-Overactive, and Aggressive; ratings of school performance are also provided

Bibliography: Yes, see manual (Achenbach & Edelbrock, 1986)

Comments

This checklist is quite similar in format and item content to the parent report form described above. In place of the Social Competence scale on the parent form, an Adaptive Functioning scale has been developed, reflecting the child's work habits, level of academic performance, degree of teacher familiarity with the child, and general happiness of the child. The Behavior Problems scale, like that for the parent, comprises a number of factor-analytically developed subscales spanning a broad range of child psychopathology. There are six different factorial profiles (three age groupings by sex), respecting the changing nature of psychopathology across the developmental span of childhood and adolescence. This is a major advantage of this scale over other teacher rating scales, in addition to the excellent normative data available for addressing questions of statistical deviance.

Test-retest reliability was reported to average .89 across the various scores from the measure (range .74 to .96) over a 1-week period (Edelbrock & Achenbach, 1984). For a 2-month interval, the mean coefficient was .77 (range .63 to .88), while stability coefficients over a 4-month period ranged between .25 and .82 (mean .64); these findings indicate satisfactory test-retest reliability as well as stability of the scores over longer periods. As with most scales, stability of the Internalizing scales was generally lower than that of the Externalizing scales. The term "Internalizing" in reference to scales is used to represent the broad band factor that includes scales assessing Anxiety, Depression, Obsessive–Compulsive, and Uncommunicative. "Externalizing" refers to those scales assessing conduct problems such as Hyperactivity, Aggression, and Delinquency. However, significant declines were noted in six of the eight Behavior Problems scale scores over the 4-month interval—a finding of import for studies wishing to measure changes in ratings due to treatment. Interteacher agreements have not yet been reported for this scale; parent-teacher agreements have ranged between .29 (Anxious) and .61 (Nervous-Overactive) (Edelbrock, personal communication, August 1984).

Due to its more recent development, the CBCL-TRF has limited information on its various types of validity, compared to the parent report form described earlier. Nevertheless, what research has been done suggests great promise for this rating scale. Significant correlations between scores on the Behavior Problems scale and those obtained by direct classroom observations have been obtained (Edelbrock, personal communication, August, 1984; Reed & Edelbrock, 1983), and the factor scores correlate well with their equivalents on the Conners Teacher Rating Scale (Edelbrock & Reed, 1984). The Inattentive scale, as well as several items from the Adaptive Functioning scale, has also been found to significantly differentiate clinic-referred children with DSM-III Attention Deficit Disorder (ADD) from those referred for other problems, and to further differentiate the subtypes of ADD with and without hyperactivity (ADD/+H and ADD/−H; see Chapter 2; Edelbrock, Costello, & Kessler, 1984; Kazdin, Esveldt-Dawson, & Loar, 1983). Another recent study (Harris, King, Reifler, & Rosenberg, 1984) noted significant differences between learning-disabled children and those with emotional disabilities on four of the eight subscales from the Behavior Problems scale. The use of the Behavior Problems scale as a measure of treatment effects has not yet been accomplished.

In summary, the CBCL-TRF is still in the process of validation, but offers great promise as an equally useful counterpart to the parent report form of the CBCL, on which more research has been done. As a measure of general psychopathology in children, as well as of the more commonly found specific dimensions of maladjustment, the scale appears to be quite useful. Its method of development and standardization are without equal within the various scales available for teacher reports of child behavior problems. The availability of the parent report form, the Youth Self-Report Form (see below), and the Direct Observation Form (see Chapter 10) of the CBCL further recommends its adoption for research, particularly where multiple informants and sources of information are of interest. With further research on its interrater agreement with teachers and its construct, discriminant, and concurrent validity, this scale should offer great utility to clinicians wishing a broad yet conveniently administered method of assessment for child psychopathology, profile analysis of subtypes of psychopathology, and treatment outcome.

CONNERS TEACHER RATING SCALE—REVISED (CTRS-R; Goyette et al., 1978)

Developer: C. Keith Conners, Ph.D.

Where to Obtain: C. Keith Conners, Ph.D., Department of Psychiatry, Duke University Medical Center, Durham, NC 27710

Copyrighted: Yes

Items: 28   *Scaling:*   0–3   *Ages:*   3–17 years

Completion Time: 5–10 minutes   *Scoring Software:*   Yes

Reliability Information Available:

Test-Retest: Yes   *Interrater:*   No   *Internal Consistency:*   No

Validity Information Available:

Construct: Yes   *Discriminant:*   No   *Concurrent:*   Yes

Predictive: No   *Treatment-Sensitive:*   Yes

Normative Data: Yes (ages 3–17 years; $n = 383$)

Factors Assessed: Conduct Problems, Hyperactive, Inattentive-Passive

Bibliography: Yes, from developer

Comments

There are at least four versions of the Conners Teacher Rating Scale (CTRS) in current use: (1) the original version (Conners, 1969, 1973); (2) the revised form (CTRS-R; Goyette et al., 1978); (3) the Abbreviated Symptom Questionnaire (ASQ), or Hyperactivity Index (see Goyette et al., 1978); and (4) the Iowa Conners Teacher Rating Scale (Loney & Milich, 1982). These scales vary primarily in the number of items of the original scale they have retained. The ASQ has also been called the Abbreviated Teacher Rating Scale (ATRS). The revised version is reviewed here; the other three versions are discussed in Appendix A.

   In 1978, the original 39-item scale was reduced to 28 items, producing the CTRS-R. Most of the items retained are similar to those on the original scale, with some slight rewording, and the response scaling for each item remains the same. The scale and its psychometric properties and norms are available in the report by Goyette et al. (1978). Test-retest reliability coefficients over a 1-week period were found to be .97 for the total score; no information on interrater (teacher) agreement or internal-consistency coefficients could be located for this revised version. Parent-teacher agreement has ranged from .33 to .45 across factors (Goyette et al., 1978), which is not surprising in view of the different situations and behaviors being rated by each adult.

   Information on the validity of the revised version is less, given its relatively recent development. However, given the comparability of the factors with their counterparts on the original scale, the revised version is likely to prove as valid and useful for assessing externalizing or conduct problem symptoms as the original. The factors from the revised version correlate well with comparable factors from the CBCL-TRF (Edelbrock & Reed, 1984). Like the original scale, the revised version has also proven useful in assessing behavioral changes in hyperactive children due to stimulant medication (Barkley et al., 1988).

The CTRS-R appears most useful as a quick screening measure for conduct problems and hyperactivity, but not especially useful for evaluating internalizing, neurotic, depressive, and anxious symptoms. It is therefore not recommended for use in the initial assessment or diagnosis of ADHD children because of the limited number of items dealing with hyperactive and inattentive behavior, the limited normative data, and the lack of items pertaining to internalizing symptoms. The CBCL-TRF is preferable for these purposes. The CTRS-R is likely to find its greatest value in assessing stimulant drug effects, or other treatment effects, where the convenience of teacher completion of the scale is paramount. Once again, however, clinicians must be aware of potential practice effects on the scale over repeated administration; the guidelines set forth for the original scale should be followed.

SCHOOL SITUATIONS QUESTIONNAIRE (SSQ; Barkley, 1987)

Developer: Russell A. Barkley, Ph.D.

Where to Obtain: Russell A. Barkley, Ph.D., Department of Psychiatry, University of Massachusetts Medical Center, 55 Lake Avenue North, Worcester, MA 01655

Copyrighted: Yes

Items: 12   *Scaling:*   0–9   *Ages:*   4–11 years

Completion Time: <5 minutes   *Scoring Software:*   No

Reliability Information Available:

Test-Retest: Yes   *Interrater:*   No   *Internal Consistency:*   Yes

Validity Information Available:

Construct: Yes   *Discriminant:*   Yes   *Concurrent:*   Yes

Predictive: No   *Treatment-Sensitive:*   Yes

Normative Data: Yes (ages 4–11 years; $n = 615$)

Factors Assessed: Social Interaction, Focused Attention, and Novel Activities Situations

Bibliography: Yes (see Barkley & Edelbrock, 1987)

Comments

The SSQ, like the HSQ (described above), was designed to evaluate *where* children may be exhibiting their problem behaviors (i.e., situational variation of behavior disorder). The scale is shown in Figure 9.4. Teachers are asked to indicate whether the child displays behavior problems in each of 12 situations around the classroom and in other school settings. If a problem is

SCHOOL SITUATIONS QUESTIONNAIRE

Child's Name _____ **Date** _____

Name of Person Completing This Form _____

Does this child present any behavior problems for you in any of these situations? If so, indicate how severe they are.

Situations	*Yes/No* (Circle one)		Mild				*If yes, how severe?* (Circle one)				Severe
While arriving at school	Yes	No	1	2	3	4	5	6	7	8	9
During individual deskwork	Yes	No	1	2	3	4	5	6	7	8	9
During small-group activities	Yes	No	1	2	3	4	5	6	7	8	9
During free-play time in class	Yes	No	1	2	3	4	5	6	7	8	9
During lectures to the class	Yes	No	1	2	3	4	5	6	7	8	9
At recess	Yes	No	1	2	3	4	5	6	7	8	9
At lunch	Yes	No	1	2	3	4	5	6	7	8	9
In the hallways	Yes	No	1	2	3	4	5	6	7	8	9
In the bathroom	Yes	No	1	2	3	4	5	6	7	8	9
On field trips	Yes	No	1	2	3	4	5	6	7	8	9
During special assemblies	Yes	No	1	2	3	4	5	6	7	8	9
On the bus	Yes	No	1	2	3	4	5	6	7	8	9

---------------------------- For Office Use Only ----------------------------

Total number of problem settings _____ Mean severity score _____

FIGURE 9.4. The School Situations Questionnaire. From *Defiant Children: A Clinician's Manual for Parent Training* by R. A. Barkley, 1987, New York: Guilford Press. Copyright 1987 by The Guilford Press. Reprinted by permission of the publisher.

present, the severity is rated using a scale from 1 ("mild") to 9 ("severe"). Two scores are yielded: the number of problem situations and the mean severity rating. Three additional factor scores can also be calculated for those factors noted above. Normative data were collected by Breen and Altepeter (1990) for children from ages 4 to 11 years; these are shown in Table 9.3.

The SSQ provides a situational profile that can be quite useful in designing behavioral interventions in the classroom (see Barkley & Edelbrock, 1987). It has been found to be sensitive to the effects of stimulant medication interventions (Barkley et al., 1988). The scale also readily discriminates ADHD from normal children (Barkley, DuPaul, & McMurray, in press-b). As with the HSQ, however, a significant problem with this scale is that it confounds ratings of conduct problems with those of ADHD, so that it is not a pure measure of either. For now, it seems best to use the original SSQ where as-

TABLE 9.3. Norms for the School Situations Questionnaire (SSQ)

Age groups (in years)	n	Number of problem settings	Mean severity
Boys			
6–8	170	2.4 (3.3)	1.5 (2.0)
9–11	123	2.8 (3.2)	1.9 (2.1)
Girls			
6–8	180	1.0 (2.0)	0.8 (1.5)
9–11	126	1.3 (2.1)	0.8 (1.2)

Note. Table entries are means with standard deviations in parentheses. From *Factor Structures of the Home Situations Questionnaire (HSQ) and the School Situations Questionnaire (SSQ)* by M. J. Breen and T. S. Altepeter, 1990, unpublished manuscript, Winneconne Public Schools, Winneconne, WI. Reprinted by permission of the authors.

sessment of general behavior problems (especially oppositional or aggressive behavior) is of interest, and to use the revised version (SSQ-R) where a more refined assessment of attention deficits is of interest (see below).

SCHOOL SITUATIONS QUESTIONNAIRE—REVISED (SSQ-R; DuPaul, 1990b)

Developers: George J. DuPaul, Ph.D., and Russell A. Barkley, Ph.D.

Where to Obtain: George J. DuPaul, Ph.D., Department of Psychiatry, University of Massachusetts Medical Center, 55 Lake Avenue North, Worcester, MA 01655

Copyrighted: No

Items: 8 *Scaling:* 0–9 *Ages:* 6–12 years

Completion Time: <5 minutes *Scoring Software:* No

Reliability Information Available:

Test-Retest: Yes *Interrater:* No *Internal Consistency:* Yes

Validity Information Available:

Construct: Yes *Discriminant:* Yes *Concurrent:* Yes

Predictive: No *Treatment-Sensitive:* Yes

Normative Data: Yes (ages 6–12 years; n = 490)

Factors Assessed: Not yet determined

Bibliography: No

Comments

The SSQ-R is a revision of the original SSQ, designed to assess specific problems with attention and concentration across a variety of school situations. It is therefore of benefit when a more refined measure than the SSQ is desired for establishing the pervasiveness of attention problems, as it is in the diagnosis of ADHD. The scale is shown in Figure 9.5. DuPaul (1990b) has collected normative data for a relatively equal number of boys and girls between

SCHOOL SITUATIONS QUESTIONNAIRE—REVISED

Name of Child _____

Name of Person Completing This Form _____

Does this child have problems paying attention or concentrating in any of these situations? If so, indicate how severe these attentional difficulties are.

Situations	Yes/No (Circle one)		Mild			If yes, how severe? (Circle one)				Severe	
During individual deskwork	Yes	No	1	2	3	4	5	6	7	8	9
During small-group activities	Yes	No	1	2	3	4	5	6	7	8	9
During free-play time in class	Yes	No	1	2	3	4	5	6	7	8	9
During lectures to the class	Yes	No	1	2	3	4	5	6	7	8	9
On field trips	Yes	No	1	2	3	4	5	6	7	8	9
During special assemblies	Yes	No	1	2	3	4	5	6	7	8	9
During movies, filmstrips	Yes	No	1	2	3	4	5	6	7	8	9
During class discussions	Yes	No	1	2	3	4	5	6	7	8	9

Office Use Only: No. problems _____ Mean severity _____

FIGURE 9.5. The School Situations Questionnaire—Revised. From *The Home and School Situations Questionnaires—Revised: Normative Data, Reliability, and Validity* by G. J. DuPaul, 1990, unpublished manuscript, University of Massachusetts Medical Center, Worcester. Reprinted by permission of the author.

ages 6 and 12 years. These norms are shown in Table 9.4. Two scores can be obtained from the scale: the number of problem settings, and the mean severity score. The scale has been shown to have satisfactory test-retest reliability and to correlate significantly with other parent-completed rating scales of hyperactivity, such as the CTRS-R and the ADHD Rating Scale described below (DuPaul, 1990a). Since the original SSQ was quite sensitive to treatment effects, this one will probably prove so as well, particularly in evaluating the effects of stimulant medication. Studies are underway now to evaluate this property of the scale.

CHILD ATTENTION PROBLEMS (CAP) (Barkley, 1988d)

Developers: Craig S. Edelbrock, Ph.D.

Where to Obtain: Craig S. Edelbrock, Ph.D., Department of Psychiatry, University of Massachusetts Medical Center, 55 Lake Avenue North, Worcester, MA 01655

Copyrighted: Yes

Items: 12   *Scaling:* 0–2   *Ages:* 6–16 years

Completion Time: <5 minutes   *Scoring Software:* No

TABLE 9.4. Means and Standard Deviations for the SSQ-R by Gender and Age

Age	Girls		Boys	
	Number of problem settings	Mean severity	Number of problem settings	Mean severity
6 (*n* = 42)				
M	2.84	3.47	2.12	4.82
SD	3.26	2.01	3.10	2.30
7 (*n* = 78)				
M	2.40	3.50	3.30	3.85
SD	2.94	1.91	3.17	2.00
8 (*n* = 90)				
M	2.12	3.02	2.50	3.14
SD	2.59	1.36	2.80	1.41
9 (*n* = 78)				
M	2.79	3.81	3.49	4.23
SD	3.13	1.72	3.38	1.98
10 (*n* = 78)				
M	2.32	3.18	2.98	3.56
SD	2.80	1.93	3.08	1.68
11 (*n* = 88)				
M	2.00	2.99	3.86	4.01
SD	2.62	2.00	3.11	2.56
12 (*n* = 36)				
M	2.06	3.01	3.70	3.37
SD	2.64	2.03	2.94	2.01

Note. From *The Home and School Situations Questionnaires—Revised: Normative Data, Reliability, and Validity* by G. J. DuPaul, 1990, unpublished manuscript, University of Massachusetts Medical Center, Worcester. Reprinted by permission of the author.

Reliability Information Available:

Test-Retest: No   *Interrater:* No   *Internal Consistency:* Yes

Validity Information Available:

Construct: Yes   *Discriminant:* Yes   *Concurrent:* Yes

Predictive: No   *Treatment-Sensitive:* Yes

Normative Data: Yes (ages 6–16 years; *n* = 1,100)

Factors Assessed: Inattention and Overactivity

Bibliography: No

Comments

The CAP profile was developed by Edelbrock primarily for assessing stimulant drug effects. Items that tap only the dimensions of Inattention and Overactivity were selected from the CBCL-TRF. Five items loading on the Overactivity scale and the seven loading on the Inattention scale were chosen to create this brief instrument. The scale is shown in Figure 9.6. Normative data

CHILD ATTENTION PROBLEMS

Child's Name _____   **Child's Age** _____

Filled Out by _____   **Child's Sex** [ ] M [ ] F

Directions: Below is a list of items that describe pupils. For each item that describes the pupil *now* or *within the past week,* check whether the item is *Not True, Somewhat* or *Sometimes True,* or *Very* or *Often True.* Please check all items as well as you can, even if some do not seem to apply to this pupil.

	Not True	Somewhat or Sometimes True	Very or Often True
1. Fails to finish things he/she starts	[ ]	[ ]	[ ]
2. Can't concentrate, can't pay attention for long	[ ]	[ ]	[ ]
3. Can't sit still, restless, or hyperactive	[ ]	[ ]	[ ]
4. Fidgets	[ ]	[ ]	[ ]
5. Daydreams or gets lost in his/her thoughts	[ ]	[ ]	[ ]
6. Impulsive or acts without thinking	[ ]	[ ]	[ ]
7. Difficulty following directions	[ ]	[ ]	[ ]
8. Talks out of turn	[ ]	[ ]	[ ]
9. Messy work	[ ]	[ ]	[ ]
10. Inattentive, easily distracted	[ ]	[ ]	[ ]
11. Talks too much	[ ]	[ ]	[ ]
12. Fails to carry out assigned tasks	[ ]	[ ]	[ ]

Please feel free to write any comments about the pupil's work or behavior in the last week.

Administration
The CAP was designed to be completed by teachers or teacher aides on a weekly basis.
Scoring
Each item is scored 0 for *Not True,* 1 for *Somewhat* or *Sometimes True,* or 2 for *Very* or *Often True.* Total Score is the sum of all 12 items (range: 0–24). Upper limit of the normal range is 15 for boys, 11 for girls. Inattention is the sum of items 1, 2, 5, 7, 9, 10, & 12 (range: 0–14). Upper limit of the normal range is 9 for boys, 7 for girls. Overactivity is the sum of items 3, 4, 6, 8 & 11 (range 0–10). Upper limit of the normal range is 6 for boys, 5 for girls.

FIGURE 9.6. Child Attention Problems scale. From C. S. Edelbrock. University of Massachusetts Medical Center, Worcester. Reprinted by permission.

TABLE 9.5. Normative Cutoff Points For the Inattention, Overactivity, and Total Scores for the Child Attention Profile

Cutoff points	Total (1,100)[a]	Boys (550)	Girls (550)
	Inattention[b]		
Median	1	2	0
69th percentile	3	4	2
84th percentile	6	7	5
93rd percentile	8	9	7
98th percentile	11	12	10
	Overactivity		
Median	0	1	0
69th percentile	1	2	1
84th percentile	4	4	2
93rd percentile	6	6	5
98th percentile	8	8	7
	Total score		
Median	2	4	1
69th percentile	6	7	4
84th percentile	10	11	8
93rd percentile	14	15	11
98th percentile	19	20	16

Note. From C. S. Edelbrock, Dept. of Psychiatry, University of Massachusetts Medical Center, Worcester. Reprinted by permission.
[a] Numbers in parentheses are sample sizes.
[b] The inattention score is the sum of items 1, 2, 5, 7, 9, 10, and 12. The Overactivity score is the sum of items 3, 4, 6, 8, and 11. Table entries are raw scores that fall at or below the designated percentile range. The 93rd percentile is the recommended upper limit of the normal range. Scores exceeding this cutoff are in the clinical range. All scores are based on teacher reports.

for this 12-item scale are available, based on scores obtained from 1,100 children of both sexes from ages 6 through 16 years; these are shown in Table 9.5. Although many of its properties (e.g., test-retest reliability, concurrent and predictive validity) have yet to be investigated, it has been shown to be quite sensitive to stimulant drug effects in several recently completed drug studies (Barkley, McMurray, Edelbrock, & Robbins, 1989; Barkley, DuPaul, & McMurray, in press-b). Moreover, the CAP appears useful in the classification of ADD children into the subtypes ADD/+H and ADD/−H (Barkley, DuPaul, & McMurray, in press-a). Unlike that of the CTRS-R, the CAP's Inattention subscale is relatively "pure" and not confounded by items related to conduct, affective disturbance, or overactivity.

ACADEMIC PERFORMANCE RATING SCALE (APRS; DuPaul, Rapport, & Perriello, 1990)

Developer: George J. DuPaul, Ph.D.

Where to Obtain: George J. DuPaul, Ph.D., Department of Psychiatry, University of Massachusetts Medical Center, 55 Lake Avenue North, Worcester, MA 01655

Copyrighted: No

Items: 19   *Scaling:* 1–5   *Ages:* Grades 1–6

Completion Time: <5 minutes   *Scoring Software:* No

Reliability Information Available:

Test-Retest: Yes

Interrater: No   *Internal Consistency:* Yes

Validity Information Available:

Construct: Yes   *Discriminant:* Yes   *Concurrent:* Yes

Predictive: No   *Treatment-Sensitive:* Yes

Normative Data: Yes (grades 1–6; $n = 247$)

Factors Assessed: Learning Ability, Academic Performance, Impulse Control, and Social Withdrawal

Bibliography: No

Comments

The APRS was developed in 1989 to complement other teacher rating scales, which are inadequate for evaluating a child's academic productivity and accuracy in the classroom. The scale is brief and convenient, and has adequate psychometric properties for use with children in grades 1 through 6. The scale is shown in Figure 9.7, and its normative data are displayed in Table 9.6. It can be scored to yield four scores derived from factor analysis of the scale items: Learning Ability, Academic Performance, Impulse Control, and Social Withdrawal. The scale has quite satisfactory test-retest reliability and internal consistency, and its scores correlate significantly with those on other teacher ratings of behavior. It also correlates with test scores from standardized academic achievement tests given annually to children, as well as with actual calculations of academic productivity and accuracy taken in the children's classrooms. The value of the scale seems to be in the assessment of the first two scores, which are not available on any other teacher rating scales. Its brevity also recommends it for use in evaluating the effects of stimulant drug dosages on academic accuracy and productivity, especially when balanced against the information obtained on the Social Withdrawal factor.

ACADEMIC PERFORMANCE RATING SCALE

Student _____ Date _____

Age _____ Grade _____ Teacher _____

For each of the below items, please estimate the above student's performance over the *past week*. For each item, please circle *one* choice only.

1. Estimate the percentage of written math work *completed* (regardless of accuracy) relative to classmates.	0–49% 1	50–69% 2	70–79% 3	80–89% 4	90–100% 5
2. Estimate the percentage of written language arts work *completed* (regardless of accuracy) relative to classmates.	0–49% 1	50–69% 2	70–79% 3	80–89% 4	90–100% 5
3. Estimate the *accuracy* of completed written math work (i.e., percent correct of work done).	0–64% 1	65–69% 2	70–79% 3	80–89% 4	90–100% 5
4. Estimate the *accuracy* of completed written language arts work (i.e., percent correct of work done).	0–64% 1	65–69% 2	70–79% 3	80–89% 4	90–100% 5
5. How consistent has the quality of this child's academic work been over the past week?	Consistently Poor 1	More Poor Than Successful 2	Variable 3	More Successful Than Poor 4	Consistently Successful 5
6. How frequently does the student accurately follow teacher instructions and/or class discussion during *large-group* (e.g., whole class) instruction?	Never 1	Rarely 2	Sometimes 3	Often 4	Very Often 5
7. How frequently does the student accurately follow teacher instructions and/or class discussion during *small-group* (e.g., reading group) instruction?	Never 1	Rarely 2	Sometimes 3	Often 4	Very Often 5
8. How quickly does this child learn new material (i.e., pick up novel concepts)?	Very Slow 1	Slow 2	Average 3	Quickly 4	Very Quickly 5
9. What is the quality or neatness of this child's handwriting?	Poor 1	Fair 2	Average 3	Above Average 4	Excellent 5

10. What is the quality of this child's reading skills?	Poor	Fair	Average	Above Average	Excellent
	1	2	3	4	5
11. What is the quality of this child's speaking skills?	Poor	Fair	Average	Above Average	Excellent
	1	2	3	4	5
12. How often does the child complete written work in a careless, hasty fashion?	Never	Rarely	Sometimes	Often	Very Often
	1	2	3	4	5
13. How frequently does the child take more time to complete work than his/her classmates?	Never	Rarely	Sometimes	Often	Very Often
	1	2	3	4	5
14. How often is the child able to pay attention without you prompting him/her?	Never	Rarely	Sometimes	Often	Very Often
	1	2	3	4	5
15. How frequently does this child require your assistance to accurately complete his/her academic work?	Never	Rarely	Sometimes	Often	Very Often
	1	2	3	4	5
16. How often does the child begin written work prior to understanding the directions?	Never	Rarely	Sometimes	Often	Very Often
	1	2	3	4	5
17. How frequently does this child have difficulty recalling material from a previous day's lessons?	Never	Rarely	Sometimes	Often	Very Often
	1	2	3	4	5
18. How often does the child appear to be staring excessively or "spaced out"?	Never	Rarely	Sometimes	Often	Very Often
	1	2	3	4	5
19. How often does the child appear withdrawn or tend to lack an emotional response in a social situation?	Never	Rarely	Sometimes	Often	Very Often
	1	2	3	4	5

FIGURE 9.7. The Academic Performance Rating Scale. From *Teacher Ratings of Academic Performance: The Development of the Academic Performance Rating Scale* by G. J. DuPaul, M. Rapport, and L. M. Perriello, 1990, unpublished manuscript, University of Massachusetts Medical Center, Worcester. Reprinted by permission of the authors.

TABLE 9.6. **Means and Standard Deviations for the Academic Performance Rating Scale by Grade and Gender**

Grade	Total score	Learning Ability	Impulse Control	Academic Performance	Social Withdrawal
			Girls		
Grade 1 (*n* = 40)					
M	67.02	27.15	21.05	33.98	16.83
SD	16.27	8.41	4.46	8.49	4.83
Grade 2 (*n* = 45)					
M	72.56	29.89	22.59	36.46	18.26
SD	12.33	6.44	3.91	6.22	4.37
Grade 3 (*n* = 42)					
M	72.10	28.62	23.00	35.93	18.77
SD	14.43	6.85	4.92	7.34	3.82
Grade 4 (*n* = 38)					
M	67.79	27.29	22.15	33.32	17.41
SD	18.69	8.57	5.27	9.28	5.08
Grade 5 (*n* = 44)					
M	73.02	29.39	23.58	37.00	18.31
SD	14.10	6.90	4.07	6.43	4.44
Grade 6 (*n* = 31)					
M	74.10	30.13	23.00	36.74	19.17
SD	14.45	7.28	4.31	7.09	3.71
			Boys		
Grade 1 (*n* = 42)					
M	71.95	30.19	22.86	35.52	17.88
SD	16.09	7.22	5.02	8.85	4.50
Grade 2 (*n* = 44)					
M	67.84	28.44	20.79	33.80	16.64
SD	14.86	7.11	4.59	8.43	5.10
Grade 3 (*n* = 49)					
M	68.49	28.39	20.90	34.71	17.67
SD	16.96	7.31	5.47	9.08	4.73
Grade 4 (*n* = 40)					
M	69.77	28.50	21.78	34.36	18.40
SD	15.83	7.51	4.90	8.40	4.21
Grade 5 (*n* = 34)					
M	63.68	26.00	19.86	32.09	16.56
SD	18.04	8.15	5.17	9.83	5.15
Grade 6 (*n* = 38)					
M	65.24	26.64	20.08	33.22	16.78
SD	12.39	6.52	3.86	6.39	4.05

Note. From *Teacher Ratings of Academic Performance: The Development of the Academic Performance Rating Scale* by G. J. DuPaul, M. Rapport, and L. M. Perriello, 1990, unpublished manuscript, University of Massachusetts Medical Center, Worcester. Reprinted by permission of the authors.

Scales for Parents or Teachers

ADHD RATING SCALE (DuPaul, 1990a)

Developer: George J. DuPaul, Ph.D.

Where to Obtain: George J. DuPaul, Ph.D., Department of Psychiatry, University of Massachusetts Medical Center, 55 Lake Avenue North, Worcester, MA 01655

Copyrighted: No

Items: 14   *Scaling:*   0–3   *Ages:*   6–12 years

Completion Time: <5 minutes   *Scoring Software:*   No

Reliability Information Available:

Test-Retest: Yes   *Interrater:*   No   *Internal Consistency:*   Yes

Validity Information Available:

Construct: Yes   *Discriminant:*   Yes   *Concurrent:*   Yes

Predictive: No   *Treatment-Sensitive:*   Yes

Normative Data: Yes (ages 6–12 years; $n = 765$ for parents, $n = 551$ for teachers)

Factors Assessed: Inattention-Restlessness and Impulsivity-Hyperactivity

Bibliography: No

Comments

The ADHD Rating Scale was developed by DuPaul (1990a) to assess the 14 symptoms of ADHD from the diagnostic criteria in the DSM-III-R (American Psychiatric Association, 1987). It is highly useful, as it provides a direct rating of the essential symptoms of the disorder from both parents and teachers, and has substantial normative data for each gender that are based on both parent and teacher reports. The scale can be used to supplement parent and teacher interviews of these diagnostic items and can provide a more rigorous estimate of the cutoff score for a child. Scores of 2 or higher are considered to be inappropriate for a child's developmental level, and a quick count of the number of items with such scores can determine whether the child exceeds the 8 of 14 criteria recommended by the DSM-III-R. However, based on the norms gathered by DuPaul (1990a), the 8-of-14 figure appears to be satisfactory for girls but too liberal for boys, resulting in overidentification of ADHD in the population. This suggests that different cutoff scores for boys and girls should be used. A cutoff of 10 of 14 seems more appropriate for boys, based on these data.

Three scores are calculated for the scale: total score, Inattention-Restlessness, and Impulsivity-Hyperactivity. The rating scale is shown in Figure 9.8, and the norms for the scale for parents and teachers are shown in Tables 9.7 and 9.8, respectively. The scale has been shown to discriminate ADHD children from learning-disabled and normal children, as well as to differentiate children with ADD/+H from those with ADD/−H (Barkley, DuPaul, & McMurray, in press-a). It has also been shown to be sensitive to stimulant drug effects (Barkley, DuPaul, & McMurray, in press-b).

ADHD RATING SCALE

Child's Name _____ **Age** _____ **Grade** _____

Completed by _____

Circle the number in the *one* column which best describes the child.

	Not at all	Just a little	Pretty much	Very much
1. Often fidgets or squirms in seat.	0	1	2	3
2. Has difficulty remaining seated.	0	1	2	3
3. Is easily distracted.	0	1	2	3
4. Has difficulty awaiting turn in groups.	0	1	2	3
5. Often blurts out answers to questions.	0	1	2	3
6. Has difficulty following instructions.	0	1	2	3
7. Has difficulty sustaining attention to tasks.	0	1	2	3
8. Often shifts from one uncompleted activity to another.	0	1	2	3
9. Has difficulty playing quietly.	0	1	2	3
10. Often talks excessively.	0	1	2	3
11. Often interrupts or intrudes on others.	0	1	2	3
12. Often does not seem to listen.	0	1	2	3
13. Often loses things necessary for tasks.	0	1	2	3
14. Often engages in physically dangerous activities without considering consequences.	0	1	2	3

FIGURE 9.8. The ADHD Rating Scale. From *The ADHD Rating Scale: Normative Data, Reliability, and Validity* by G. J. DuPaul, 1990, unpublished manuscript, University of Massachusetts Medical Center, Worcester. Reprinted by permission of the author.

ATTENTION DEFICIT DISORDERS EVALUATION SCALE (ADDES; McCarney, 1989)

Developer: Stephen B. McCarney, Ed.D.

Where to Obtain: Hawthorne Educational Services, P.O. Box 7570, Columbia, MO 65205

Copyrighted: Yes

Items: 46 (parent), 60 (teacher)   *Scaling:* 0–4   *Ages:* 4–18 years

Table 9.7. Means and Standard Deviations for Parent-Completed ADHD Rating Scale by Gender and Age

Age	Boys			Girls		
	Total	Factor I	Factor II	Total	Factor I	Factor II
6 years ($n=113$)						
M	13.71	8.54	8.08	11.50	7.18	6.56
SD	9.66	6.58	5.70	9.51	6.42	5.44
7 years ($n=117$)						
M	13.69	8.96	7.69	10.65	6.67	5.83
SD	11.89	8.06	6.90	8.95	5.72	5.08
8 years ($n=108$)						
M	16.21	10.70	8.96	10.92	6.92	5.77
SD	10.97	7.60	6.01	8.71	5.97	4.72
9 years ($n=94$)						
M	14.08	9.19	7.65	11.23	7.26	5.93
SD	10.40	7.11	6.08	9.27	6.34	4.96
10 years ($n=105$)						
M	13.71	9.65	6.73	10.68	6.64	5.66
SD	10.22	7.75	5.25	10.18	6.39	6.01
11 years ($n=80$)						
M	13.91	9.22	7.34	7.34	4.63	3.63
SD	11.69	8.08	6.58	9.25	6.06	4.90
12 years ($n=52$)						
M	15.34	10.79	7.21	7.70	5.22	3.65
SD	10.72	7.59	5.57	10.15	6.42	5.69

Note. From *The ADHD Rating Scale: Normative Data, Reliability, and Validity* by G. J. Du-Paul, 1990, unpublished manuscript, University of Massachusetts Medical Center, Worcester. Reprinted by permission of the author.

Completion Time: 15 minutes   *Scoring Software:* Yes

Reliability Information Available:

Test-Retest: Yes   *Interrater:* Yes   *Internal Consistency:* Yes

Validity Information Available:

Construct: Yes   *Discriminant:* No   *Concurrent:* Yes

Predictive: No   *Treatment-Sensitive:* No

Normative Data: Yes (ages 4–18 years; $n=4,876$)

Factors Assessed: Inattention, Impulsivity, and Hyperactivity

Bibliography: No

Comments

The ADDES is a recently developed and commercially marketed scale expressly for use with parents (and teachers) of ADHD children. It has the largest normative sample of any published rating scale for use with this disorder, and appears to have a larger item content with regard to the three

TABLE 9.8. Means and Standard Deviations for Teacher-Completed ADHD Rating Scale by Gender and Age

Age	Boys			Girls		
	Total	Factor I	Factor II	Total	Factor I	Factor II
6 years (*n* = 55)						
M	12.04	7.88	6.19	8.69	5.83	4.31
SD	12.17	7.60	6.64	9.88	5.97	5.87
7 years (*n* = 89)						
M	13.46	8.41	7.17	10.47	7.12	5.40
SD	11.52	7.58	7.65	11.37	7.36	6.10
8 years (*n* = 102)						
M	10.81	6.52	6.00	8.54	6.00	3.86
SD	9.94	6.23	5.94	9.36	6.21	5.26
9 years (*n* = 89)						
M	13.46	8.17	7.34	9.67	5.85	5.21
SD	12.41	7.51	7.09	10.22	6.26	6.13
10 years (*n* = 84)						
M	11.82	7.67	5.82	7.44	5.15	3.34
SD	10.46	6.98	5.92	8.44	6.10	4.44
11 years (*n* = 96)						
M	13.98	8.93	6.90	7.18	4.36	3.78
SD	13.25	7.81	7.71	9.29	5.71	5.51
12 years (*n* = 36)						
M	12.10	7.05	6.50	7.19	4.75	3.31
SD	8.12	5.55	4.54	8.14	5.22	4.32

Note. From *The ADHD Rating Scale: Normative Data, Reliability, and Validity* by G. J. Du-Paul, 1990, unpublished manuscript, University of Massachusetts Medical Center, Worcester. Reprinted by permission of the author.

symptoms of ADHD as well. Considerable attention was given to national representation of the normative sample, making this a finely developed instrument for assessing ADHD. Internal consistency was found to be .97 for the entire scale; test-retest reliability was also excellent, exceeding .89 for each of the three scales. The interrater reliability of the scales ranged from .81 to .90 across all age levels. The scales have been shown to correlate to a significant degree with those from the ADD-H Comprehensive Teacher Rating Scale (ACTeRS; see Appendix A).

An intervention manual comes with the kit and lists a variety of behavioral and educational strategies that can be used to improve the primary symptoms of ADHD. Educators are likely to find the scale quite useful because these recommendations are phrased in such a way as to fit neatly into formal individual education plans (IEPs) for ADHD children. The major drawback to the scale at this time is the utter lack of any published scientific research on its merits. A further deficiency, it seems, is that the scales were not developed by factor or cluster analysis or some other empirical means to evaluate the dimensions of behavior reflected in the items. Factor analyses of similar scales, such as those of the ADHD Rating Scale (see above), often reveal only two dimensions of behavior (Inattention-Restlessness, Hyperactivity-Impulsivity) rather than the three reported for this scale. There is little doubt that this scale can discriminate ADHD from normal children, but its relationship to other scales and particularly to more objective measures of ADHD awaits demonstration.

Considering that the item content of the ADDES is similar to that of other rating scales of ADHD symptoms, although it has more items, it is likely to have relatively satisfactory relationships to these other measures. Its sensitivity to treatment, however, awaits demonstration. Many of the recommendations for IEPs derived from the scale scores are fairly straightforward, and common-sense recommendations for dealing with inattentive, impulsive, or disruptive behavior in the classroom. But they have not been put to the test by the scale developer in any rigorous scientific field studies. Such a rating scale is unlikely to replace the CBCL as a general screening instrument for psychopathology in children because of its narrow item content. However, it may prove to be a better instrument than many of the very brief, specialty scales for ADHD—such as the Conners scales, the CAP, and the ADHD Rating Scale (noted above), as well as those described in Appendix A—because of its larger item set for assessing the three dimensions of ADHD symptoms. Its merits remain to be more fully evaluated.

OTHER RATING SCALES FOR CLINICAL USE

Measures of Conflict in Families with ADHD Adolescents

Conflict Behavior Questionnaire (CBQ; Robin & Foster, 1989)

The CBQ is designed to assess the degree of conflict and quality of communication in the parent-teen relationship. This is important when evaluating adolescents with ADHD, as their families may be at higher risk for interpersonal conflict than the normal population (Thorley, 1984; Weiss & Hechtman, 1986). Parents and teens complete parallel forms of the CBQ, wherein they are asked about their interactions with each other over the past several weeks. Each version contains 70 true-false statements regarding either the respondent's appraisal of the other's behavior (e.g., "My mom doesn't understand me") or of the nature of their interactions (e.g., "We joke around often"). Two scores are generated: Appraisal of the Adolescent (or Parent) and Appraisal of the Dyad. Several briefer versions of the CBQ are also available (see Robin & Foster, 1989).

Normative data on distressed and nondistressed families are available for determining the relative level of distress an identified family may be experiencing (Robin & Foster, 1989). The CBQ has demonstrated internal consistency (Prinz, Foster, Kent, & O'Leary, 1979), with low to moderate test-retest reliability over a 6- to 8-week span (Robin & Foster, 1989). Given the volatile nature of parent-teen conflict, this temporal instability is not surprising. CBQ scores have been shown to discriminate distressed from nondistressed families and to be sensitive to the effects of a behavioral family therapy program employing problem-solving/communication training (Robin & Foster, 1989). They have also been found to correlate with behavioral observation measures of interaction conflicts in families of ADHD adolescents (Barkley, Fischer, et al., in press-b).

Issues Checklist (IC; Robin & Foster, 1989)

The IC is a list of 44 common issues that may lead to parent-adolescent conflict. The scale is shown in Figure 9.9. It can be used in conjunction with the more global CBQ to delineate specific conflictual issues. Adolescents and

ISSUES CHECKLIST

☐ Adolescent ☐ Adolescent
☐ Mother *with* ☐ Mother
☐ Father ☐ Father

Name: _____ **Date:** _____

Below is a list of things that sometimes get talked about at home. We would like you to look carefully at each topic on the left-hand side of the page and decide whether the *two of you together* have talked about that topic *at all* during the last 2 weeks.

If the two of you together have discussed it during the last 2 weeks, circle *Yes* to the right of the topic.

Go down this column for all pages.

If the two of you together have *not* discussed it during the last 2 weeks, circle *No* to the right of the topic.

Now, we would like you to go back over the list of topics. For those topics for which you circled *Yes*, please answer the two questions on the right-hand side of the page.
1. How many times during last 2 weeks did topic come up?
2. How hot are the discussions?

Go down this column for all pages.

Topic			How many times?	How hot are the discussions?					
				Calm		A little angry		Angry	
1. Telephone calls	Yes	No		1	2	3	4	5	
2. Time for going to bed	Yes	No		1	2	3	4	5	
3. Cleaning up bedroom	Yes	No		1	2	3	4	5	
4. Doing homework	Yes	No		1	2	3	4	5	
5. Putting away clothes	Yes	No		1	2	3	4	5	
6. Using the television	Yes	No		1	2	3	4	5	
7. Cleanliness (washing, showers, brushing teeth)	Yes	No		1	2	3	4	5	

Go down this column for all pages.   Go down this column for all pages.

Topic			How many times?	How hot are the discussions?				
				Calm		A little angry		Angry
8. Which clothes to wear	Yes	No		1	2	3	4	5
9. How neat clothing looks	Yes	No		1	2	3	4	5
10. Making too much noise at home	Yes	No		1	2	3	4	5
11. Table manners	Yes	No		1	2	3	4	5
12. Fighting with brothers or sisters	Yes	No		1	2	3	4	5
13. Cursing	Yes	No		1	2	3	4	5
14. How money is spent	Yes	No		1	2	3	4	5
15. Picking books or movies	Yes	No		1	2	3	4	5
16. Allowance	Yes	No		1	2	3	4	5
17. Going places without parents (shopping, movies, etc.)	Yes	No		1	2	3	4	5
18. Playing stereo or radio too loudly	Yes	No		1	2	3	4	5
19. Turning off lights in house	Yes	No		1	2	3	4	5
20. Drugs	Yes	No		1	2	3	4	5
21. Taking care of records, games, toys, and things	Yes	No		1	2	3	4	5
22. Drinking beer or other liquor	Yes	No		1	2	3	4	5
23. Buying records, games, toys, and things	Yes	No		1	2	3	4	5
24. Going on dates	Yes	No		1	2	3	4	5
25. Who should be friends	Yes	No		1	2	3	4	5
26. Selecting new clothing	Yes	No		1	2	3	4	5
27. Sex	Yes	No		1	2	3	4	5
28. Coming home on time	Yes	No		1	2	3	4	5
29. Getting to school on time	Yes	No		1	2	3	4	5
30. Getting low grades in school	Yes	No		1	2	3	4	5
31. Getting in trouble in school	Yes	No		1	2	3	4	5
32. Lying	Yes	No		1	2	3	4	5
33. Helping out around the house	Yes	No		1	2	3	4	5
34. Talking back to parents	Yes	No		1	2	3	4	5
35. Getting up in the morning	Yes	No		1	2	3	4	5

Go down this column for all pages.   Go down this column for all pages.

Topic			How many times?	How hot are the discussions?				
				Calm		A little angry		Angry
36. Bothering parents when they want to be left alone	Yes	No		1	2	3	4	5
37. Bothering teenager when he/she wants to be left alone	Yes	No		1	2	3	4	5
38. Putting feet on furniture	Yes	No		1	2	3	4	5
39. Messing up the house	Yes	No		1	2	3	4	5
40. What time to have meals	Yes	No		1	2	3	4	5
41. How to spend free time	Yes	No		1	2	3	4	5
42. Smoking	Yes	No		1	2	3	4	5
43. Earning money away from house	Yes	No		1	2	3	4	5
44. What teenager eats	Yes	No		1	2	3	4	5

Check to see that you circled Yes or No   Tell interviewer you are finished.
for every topic. Then tell the interviewer
you are finished.

FIGURE 9.9. The Issues Checklist. From *Negotiating Parent-Adolescent Conflict* by A. L. Robin and S. L. Foster, 1989, New York: Guilford Press. Copyright 1989 by The Guilford Press. Reprinted by permission of the authors and publisher.

their parents complete identical checklists, wherein they are asked to indicate whether a particular issue (e.g., drugs, curfew) has been discussed over the past 4 weeks. Each respondent is also asked to rate the anger intensity of discussions on a 5-point scale (i.e., from "calm" to "angry") and to estimate the frequency of such discussions. Three scores are obtained: the total number of issues discussed, the mean anger intensity level of issues endorsed, and the weighted average of the frequency and anger intensity level of endorsed issues (i.e., anger per discussion).

Data from a large number of "distressed" and "nondistressed" families have been aggregated by Robin and Foster (1989) to demonstrate the IC's ability to discriminate between these two groups. These norms are available in Table 9.9. The test-retest reliability of the IC is adequate for parent report over short time spans (Robin & Foster, 1989), while stability coefficients are lower for adolescent self-report. This is not entirely unexpected, since it is designed to assess relatively volatile behavior over a short time period. IC scores have been shown to be sensitive to the effects of problem-solving/com-

TABLE 9.9. Norms for the Issues Checklist

	Distressed			Nondistressed				
	n	$\bar{x}$	SD	n	$\bar{x}$	SD	t	r_{pbs}[a]
Maternal quantity	124	22.55	7.35	68	17.83	7.07	3.62**	.25
Maternal anger intensity	124	2.42	0.46	68	1.70	0.45	11.43**	.64
Maternal anger intensity × frequency	124	2.29	2.15	68	0.83	1.08	5.21**	.35
Adolescent-mother quantity	96	20.68	7.59	68	18.46	7.25	1.88*	.15
Adolescent-mother anger intensity	96	2.34	0.63	68	1.77	0.49	6.20**	.44
Adolescent-mother anger intensity × frequency	96	1.93	1.81	68	0.84	0.86	4.60**	.40
Paternal quantity	60	18.38	5.05	38	11.64	4.63	6.61**	.60
Paternal anger intensity	60	2.18	0.60	38	1.82	0.57	2.93*	.29
Paternal anger intensity × frequency	60	2.39	0.64	38	1.94	0.59	3.46**	.33
Adolescent-father quantity	38	13.60	5.54	14	10.71	4.65	1.71*	.24
Adolescent-father anger intensity	38	2.40	0.76	14	1.75	0.64	2.80*	.37
Adolescent-father anger intensity × frequency	38	2.72	0.95	14	1.88	0.69	2.97*	.39

Note. From *Negotiating Parent-Adolescent Conflict* by A. L. Robin and S. L. Foster, 1989. New York: Guilford Press. Copyright 1989 by The Guilford Press. Reprinted by permission of the authors and publisher.
[a]r_{pbs} = point-biserial correlation between the particular score and group membership (distressed vs. nondistressed).
*$p < .05$.
**$p < .001$.

munication training (Foster, Prinz, & O'Leary, 1983; Robin, 1981). They also discriminate ADHD from normal adolescents, although only on the parents' report form (Barkley, Fischer, et al., in press-b). ADHD adolescents do not report their family interactions to be any more conflictual than normal adolescents do, suggesting a significant deficit in self-awareness in the ADHD teens. The IC appears to be highly useful in delineating the sources of parent-teen conflict, creating a hierarchy to establish the priority of treatment goals on the basis of intensity of individual conflict areas, and determining the discrepancy between parent and adolescent report. It can also be repeated periodically throughout family therapy to determine the effectiveness of therapy in reducing these conflicts.

Adolescent Self-Report Measures

Although ratings completed by parents and teachers are essential components of the assessment process, they may have less validity for adolescents than for children, due to the altered nature of relationships between the adolescents and these observers as compared to those of younger children. For this reason, it is essential to obtain self-report ratings from teenagers, especially in regard to the presence of more covert emotions (e.g., depression) or actions (e.g., substance use). Such measures also have the advantage of collecting information from one of the more important respondents (i.e., the identified patient) in an evaluation. The use of the CBQ and IC to address teen perceptions of interactions with parents has been discussed above. Several additional self-report measures are available, of which those most commonly employed with ADHD adolescents are reviewed below.

Child Behavior Checklist—Youth Self-Report (CBCL-YSR; Achenbach & Edelbrock, 1987)

The CBCL-YSR measure is quire similar in item content and format to the teacher and parent versions of the CBCL discussed above, except that the items are worded in the first person. It is designed to be completed by children and adolescents from 11 to 18 years old, with responses resulting in profiles for two separate scales: Competence and Behavior Problems. The Competence scale is comprised of two subscales (i.e., Activities and Social), wherein scores are plotted on a profile containing normative data. The Behavior Problems scale contains 112 items, of which 16 are designed to tap social desirability (e.g., "I like to help others"). The remaining 96 items are scored to yield factor scale scores, which are then plotted on a profile containing the normative data. Factor analyses resulted in similar broad-band dimensions of Internalizing and Externalizing disturbance across gender. Different narrow-band factors (e.g., Depressed, Delinquent, Aggressive) were obtained for each sex. Most of the narrow-band factors have clear counterparts in the teacher and parent versions of the CBCL. Interestingly, items related to ADHD (e.g., "I have trouble concentrating") do not account for enough variance to comprise a separate factor and are included in the "Other Problems" category. Thus, the CBCL-YSR may be more useful as a screening measure for symptomatology frequently *associated* with ADHD (e.g., aggression, depression) than for ADHD per se.

Normative data were collected on 686 nonreferred children and adolescents in a manner similar to that used for the parent and teacher versions of the CBCL. Test-retest reliability coefficients among samples of both referred and nonreferred children are quite satisfactory for a self-report measure and indicate greater stability among older adolescents (Achenbach & Edelbrock, 1987). Both scales of the CBCL-YSR significantly discriminate referred from nonreferred adolescents (Achenbach & Edelbrock, 1987). It is useful in discriminating adolescents with ADHD from normal teenagers (Fischer, Edelbrock, Barkley, & Smallish, 1990), but its sensitivity to treatment effects has not yet been studied.

Measures of ADHD Symptoms

Two brief questionnaires have recently been developed to assess the frequency and severity of ADHD symptoms reported by adolescents. Both the

ADD-H Adolescent Self-Report Scale (Conners & Wells, 1985) and the Self-Evaluation (Teenager's) Self-Report (Gittelman, 1985b) involve the teenager's rating the frequency of various ADHD symptoms on a 4-point Likert scale (i.e., similar to the Conners rating scales). Many items on the latter scale were derived directly from the CPRS. While both measures appear potentially useful for both diagnosis and treatment evaluation, neither normative data nor information regarding their psychometric properties are currently available, and thus their clinical usefulness is limited. Moreover, the items on both scales are based on the DSM-III criteria for ADD, and are outdated now that the revised DSM-III-R item set is available.

Measures of Internalizing Symptoms

Given the higher risk of affective or emotional disturbance among adolescents with ADHD than among their normal counterparts, it is often necessary to include questionnaires tapping internalizing symptomatology in the initial evaluation battery. For instance, the results of parent, teacher, and/or general self-report (e.g., CBCL-YSR) ratings may indicate the presence of possible depression or anxiety symptoms. More specific self-report measures such as the Beck Depression Inventory (Beck, Ward, Mendelson, Mock, & Erbaugh, 1961), the Reynolds Adolescent Depression Scale (Reynolds, 1987), or the Manifest Anxiety Scale (Taylor, 1951) may be necessary as a supplement to the CBCL-YSR in such cases.

Limitations of Self-Report Measures

The reliability and validity of self-report instruments, especially when employed with children or adolescents, are typically inferior to the psychometric properties of rating scales completed by parents or teachers (Achenbach & Edelbrock, 1987). The limited evidence for their ability to discriminate ADHD from non-ADHD teenagers further limits their use in clinical settings. However, when employed in a multimethod, multi-informant assessment battery, they may provide valuable information regarding self-perceptions of internalizing and externalizing symptomatology that may not be available from other sources. While the results of such ratings may not be helpful for diagnostic purposes, they may be clinically useful in providing leads for further assessment and in assessing a teenager's motivation to participate in treatment.

Parent Self-Report Measures

Beck Depression Inventory (BDI; Beck et al., 1961; Beck, 1967)

The BDI is a 22-item scale frequently used in research to assess degrees of sadness and depression in subjects. Each item has four possible responses, and items are scored on a 0-to-3 scale. The psychometric properties of the scale are satisfactory (Beck, Steer, & Garbin, 1988). The scale is undoubtedly the most widely used measure of depression in adults and is valuable in a clinical assessment of either the parents of ADHD children or ADHD adults. Not only does the scale reveal degrees of depression that may warrant clinical intervention, but the scores may have to be considered in interpreting parents' ratings of child behavior, as parental depression has been shown to result in parents' reporting higher scores on scales assessing oppositional behavior in children than objective indices of child behavior would warrant (see Chapter 5). The scale can be obtained from the Psychological Corporation, Dallas, Texas.

Symptom Checklist 90–Revised SCL-90-R; Derogatis, 1986

The SCL-90-R is a brief rating scale of various psychiatric symptoms for adults. Results are scored against normative data to yield standard scores for eight scales (Anxiety, Phobia, Paranoia, Depression, etc.) and a General Severity Index. It was used to gather data on parents of ADHD adolescents in our follow-up studies discussed in Chapter 4, and seems clinically useful either in screening parents of ADHD children or in assessing ADHD adults for the same reasons given above. The scale can be obtained from Leonard Derogatis, Ph.D., Department of Psychiatry, Johns Hopkins University Medical School, Baltimore, MD 21205.

Locke-Wallace Marital Adjustment Test (MAT; Locke & Wallace, 1959)

The MAT is a commonly used brief rating scale of marital satisfaction. It is shown in Figure 9.10, along with instructions for its scoring and interpretation. It is used clinically to screen for marital difficulties in the families of ADHD children. Such difficulties may have an impact on how distressing the parents rate the behaviors of ADHD children, and so must be used in interpreting the scores from parent-completed rating scales of ADHD children (see Chapter 5). Marital difficulties may also predict greater problems in child behavior management training of such parents (Dumas, 1986).

Parenting Stress Index (Abidin, 1986)

The Parenting Stress Index is a 120-item scale which assesses different aspects of child behavioral problems as well as parenting stress. The scale yields scores for the domains of Parent Characteristics, Child Characteristics, and Life Stress. The scale has been used extensively in child clinical research on parenting stress, and an extensive bibliography on this research is available from the scale developer. Some of the six child subscales are redundant with those from the CBCL, for instance, but several of these subscales are unique to this instrument, such as Acceptability to Parent and Reinforcing to Parent, which

Name _____ **Date** _____

1. Check the dot on the line scale below which best describes the degree of happiness, everything considered, of your present marriage. The middle point, "happy," represents the degree of happiness which most people get from marriage, and the scale gradually ranges on one side to those few who are very unhappy in marriage, and on the other, to those few who experience extreme joy or felicity in marriage.

Very						
unhappy			Happy			Perfectly happy

State the approximate extent of agreement or disagreement between you and your mate on the following items by checking a box for each item:

	Always Agree	Almost Always Agree	Occasion-ally Disagree	Frequently Disagree	Almost Always Disagree	Always Disagree
2. Handling family finances						
3. Matters of recreation						
4. Demonstrations of affection						
5. Friends						
6. Sex relations						
7. Conventionality (right, good, proper conduct)						
8. Philosophy of life						
9. Ways of dealing with in-laws						

10. When disagreements arise, they usually result in:

☐ husband giving in ☐ wife giving in ☐ agreement by mutual give and take

11. Do you and your mate engage in outside interests together?

☐ all of them ☐ some of them ☐ very few of them ☐ none of them

12. In leisure time, do you genereally prefer:

☐ to be "on the go" ☐ to stay at home

Does your mate generally prefer:

☐ to be "on the go" ☐ to stay at home

13. Do you ever wish you had not married?

   ☐ Frequently   ☐ Occasionally   ☐ Rarely   ☐ Never

14. If you had your life to live over, do you think you would:

   ☐ marry the same person   ☐ marry a different person   ☐ not marry at all

15. Do you confide in your mate:

   ☐ almost never   ☐ in some things   ☐ in most things   ☐ in everything

FIGURE 9.10. The Locke-Wallace Marital Adjustment Test. A score of less than 84 is felt to signify maladjustment (places an adult in the bottom 4% of the normative sample). From "Short Marital Adjustment and Prediction Tests: Their Reliability and Validity," by H. J. Locke and K. M. Wallace, 1959, *Journal of Marriage and Family Living, 21,* 251–255. Copyright 1959 by the National Council on Family Relations. Reprinted by permission of the authors and publisher.

obviously focus more on parent-child relations than do other rating scales. Similarly, some of the parent subscales are redundant with those from the SCL-90-R and the MAT (see above), but a few are also unique, such as Unattached to Child, Feel Incompetent in Parental Role, Social Isolation, and Health Problems. It is the Life Stress scale that is particularly useful and unique to this inventory and likely to be of most benefit in clinical situations. I have found the scale to be somewhat cumbersome for parents in our clinical practice when given with the other scales used above. Having the parent complete it while he or she waits during the child's interview and testing may reduce this problem. A computer software program for scoring is available.

The instrument was normed on 534 parents, primarily white, whose children ranged in age from 1 month to 19 years. Most of the children, however, were under 5 years of age, and the normative sample is clearly not representative of the U.S. population, raising serious questions about the applicability of the scale to later childhood or adolescent populations and the interpretation of its scores outside the racial and economic background of the sample. The appropriateness of the scale for fathers is also in doubt. Even so, for mothers, especially those with preschool-age children, the scale is likely to prove quite valuable as a measure of parenting stress. Reliability information on the scale suggests that it is excellent. Until a better normative sample is available, however, caution must be used when employing the scale for diagnosis and when interpreting its findings (Doll, 1989). The scale can be obtained from Richard R. Abidin, Ph.D., Pediatric Psychology Press, 2915 Idlewood Drive, Charlottesville, VA 22901.

Parenting Practices Scale (Strayhorn & Weidman, 1988)

The Parenting Practices Scale is a 34-item scale that assesses the extent to which parents use practices commonly taught in most behavioral parent training programs and considered to be the most effective skills in managing child behavior problems. The scale has satisfactory reliability and internal consistency, and correlates well with other scales of child behavior problems. It also provides more information on the parents' use of specific types of behavior management tactics with their children over longer time intervals than can be conveniently obtained via parent interview (see Chapter 8) or by direct observational measures (see Chapter 10). Normative data are lacking, however, making the scale useless for determining the degree of deviance of a parent's child management practices. However, for monitoring change within a parent before, during, and after parent training, the scale has utility (Strayhorn & Weidman, 1988). The scale can be obtained from Joseph Strayhorn, M.D., Western Psychiatric Institute and Clinic, 3811 O'Hara St., Pittsburgh, PA 15213.

SUMMARY AND CONCLUSIONS

Numerous rating scales obviously exist for the clinical assessment of ADHD children and their families. Choosing among them can be difficult, but the choice is essentially dependent upon the purposes of the evaluation itself. If a general clinical and diagnostic *assessment of an ADHD child (ages 2–11)* is the intent, then the following scales would seem most useful, in my opinion:

CBCL (parent and teacher versions)
ADHD Rating Scale (parent and teacher versions)
HSQ-R
SSQ-R
APRS

Where one's purpose is more specific—say, a further assessment of oppositional behavior—then additional rating scales, such as the original HSQ and SSQ and the ECBI, might be of help.

If the intent is *evaluation of an ADHD adolescent,* these scales would seem helpful, in my view:

CBCL (parent and teacher versions)
ADHD Rating Scale (parent and teacher versions)
CBCL-YSR
CBQ
IC

Again, these can be supplemented with additional, more specific scales where there is interest in more detailed ratings of a particular dimension of behavior—say, the Reynolds Adolescent Depression Scale for depression.

If one's intent is *evaluation of a child's or adolescent's response to medication* for ADHD, these scales have been used in our clinic:

CPRS-R and CTRS-R
ADHD Rating Scale
HSQ-R (to age 12)
SSQ-R (to age 12)
APRS (grades 1–6)
Side Effects Rating Scale (see Chapter 17)

If the purpose is *evaluation of the effects of parent training* in child/adolescent behavior management, the following appear to be useful:

CPRS-R or ECBI (for ADHD children)
HSQ (for ADHD children)
Parenting Practices Scale (for ADHD children)
CBQ (for ADHD teens)
IC (for ADHD teens)

However, as noted earlier, these scales should be given twice before using them to assess treatment effects, because of known practice effects on most of them that result in apparent improvement in scores. In other words, the questionnaires should be given at the initial assessment and then again just before undertaking treatment; this second administration should be used as the baseline score against which to judge treatment efficacy.

In clinical evaluations, the *assessment of parent adjustment* might include the following:

SCL-90-R
MAT
Parenting Practices Scale
CBQ (for parents of ADHD teens)
IC (for parents of ADHD teens)

Great sensitivity and diplomacy must be used, however, in assessing parents of children and adolescents referred for evaluation, as it may not be immediately obvious to the parents why they are being evaluated. I generally explain to the parents as part of the initial interview why parent and family adjustment are important aspects to assess in evaluating a child. I then provide them with these scales to complete while they are waiting during their child's interview and testing. They should not simply be mailed out in advance of any appointment with a terse statement saying to complete and return the forms, as many parents will find this puzzling and even offensive. School personnel may be even less justified in employing these scales as part of an educational evaluation of an ADHD child, given that the school is not likely to undertake parent training in child management, family therapy, or psychological intervention with the parents, based upon the findings from the scale. Parents are also likely to take umbrage at the fact that highly sensitive information about them is being retained in their child's school file.

Where disagreements across informants are found in using these scales, these should not be used to immediately dismiss the veracity of any informant's reports. Instead, they often provide clinically valuable information, either about the child's actual situational variation in behavior or about the informant's perspective relative to how others view the child. For instance, disagreements between parent and teacher ratings are common, and correlations between these sources of reports rarely exceed .50 in most research studies. This is the result not only of obvious differences in the demands made on children in each setting and the types of people with whom they are being asked to interact, but also of the obvious differences in background and training of these different informants in child behavior and development. Such disagreements, by themselves, should never be used to rule out a diagnosis of ADHD. They must be balanced against other findings reviewed above, such as the degree of experience of each informant with the child, the state of psychological adjustment or distress of the informant, and even known prejudices the informant may have about the purposes to which the ratings are to be put in the evaluation. Similarly, disagreements between parents' ratings and a youth's self-reports may reflect naiveté by the parents about the teen, as in the case of the teen's internalizing symptoms or feelings, or limited self-awareness by the teen, as in the case of the severity of conflicts with the parents. Other details of the case must be used to tease out the precise meanings of these disagreements among sources of reports, but there is no doubt that the disagreements can suggest clinically useful information.

In summary, the use of rating scales has risen to the level of an essential component in the evaluation of ADHD children and their families. Despite their ease of administration and scoring, great care and sensitivity must be used in the proper clinical application of these scales. Their utility is considerable in the assessment process, but one must never forget that they are mere quantifications of the opinions of people. They are therefore prone to the same biases as are any opinions of people about themselves or others. Their role is to complement, not to replace, other sources of information about the person obtained through other (possibly more objective) means.

10

Tests and Observational Measures

To behold is not necessarily to observe, and the power of
comparing and combining is only to be obtained by education. It is much to be regretted that habits of exact observation are not cultivated in our schools; to this deficiency may be traced much of the fallacious reasoning
and the false philosophy which prevails.

—KARL WILHELM HUMBOLDT (1767–1835)

In the decade since the first edition of this text appeared (Barkley, 1981),
substantial progress has been made in developing more objective means of
assessing Attention-deficit Hyperactivity Disorder (ADHD) symptoms in children, as well as in evaluating the properties of those tests and measures already in existence. Most of these instruments, however, have still not reached
the stage where they can be recommended for widespread clinical use in evaluating ADHD children, because of poor standardization, limited normative
data, or lack of information on their psychometric properties (see Chapter 9
for a discussion of these properties). The reader interested in a review of
laboratory measures used with hyperactive children is referred to the excellent reviews by Virginia Douglas (Douglas, 1983; Douglas & Peters, 1979).
But a few measures have been standardized, normed, and evaluated for these
properties. These measures are described below, along with their clinical advantages and disadvantages. Suffice it to say here that the most useful among
them at this point in time seem to be vigilance or continuous-performance
tests (CPTs) and direct, systematic behavioral observations of ADHD symptoms in the home or classroom (or, if this is not feasible, in a clinic playroom
setting). Several other measures are reviewed that are not yet ready for clinical adoption, but have been used frequently enough in research to be familiar
to many and so require some comment here. The use of objective measures
in the evaluation of ADHD children is illustrated in the six clinical cases
described in Chapter 11.

LABORATORY TESTS AND MEASURES

Several clinic-based tests of sustained attention and impulsivity have recently been standardized for use in evaluating symptoms of ADHD. Their potential as reliable and valid components of a multimethod assessment battery is great, in part because they are not as tainted by those biases that can arise in the use of methods relying on personal opinions (i.e., interviews and rating scales). Normative data can be readily collected for most laboratory measures, and standardized administration procedures can increase the reliability of their use in clinical settings. The most promising of these measures for use with ADHD children and adolescents are reviewed under the headings of the constructs they are purported to assess.

Vigilance and Sustained Attention

Continuous-Performance Tests

One of the most widely studied laboratory measures of vigilance or attention span with the ADHD population is the CPT (Rosvold, Mirsky, Sarason, Bransome, & Beck, 1956). Many variations of the CPT are available (e.g., visual, auditory); however, the most common one requires the youngster to observe a screen while individual letters or numbers are projected onto it at a rapid pace (typically one per second). The child is told to respond (e.g., to press a button) when a certain stimulus or pair of stimuli in sequence appears. The scores derived from the CPT are the number of correct responses, number of target stimuli missed (omission errors), and number of responses following nontarget or incorrect stimuli (commission errors). The latter score is presumed to tap both sustained attention and impulse control, while the two former measures are believed to assess sustained attention only (Sostek, Buchsbaum, & Rapoport, 1980). This method has been shown to be one of the most reliable for discriminating ADHD from normal children (Douglas, 1983) and is sensitive to stimulant drug effects among ADHD children and adolescents (Coons, Klorman, & Borgstedt, 1987; Garfinkel, Brown, Klee, Braden, Beauchesne, & Shapiro, 1986). However, the clinical use of this technique is limited due to the lack of a standardized procedure, dearth of normative data, and an often unwieldy apparatus.

Several computer software programs for similar tasks are available for use with personal computers (see Conners, 1985a; Klee & Garfinkel, 1983). Unfortunately, research on the ability of CPT software programs to discriminate children with ADHD from their normal counterparts or to detect stimulant drug effects is limited. Nevertheless, these software programs offer some promise of eventually yielding clinically useful, objective, convenient, and inexpensive measures of sustained attention for ADHD children and adolescents.

One CPT that has been developed recently for clinical assessment purposes is that of the Gordon Diagnostic System (Gordon, 1983), shown in Figure

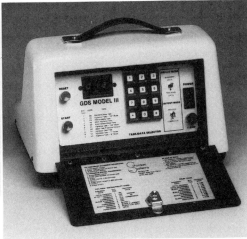

FIGURE 10.1. The Gordon Diagnostic System. *Left:* Button-press device used by child. *Right:* Task/data selector.

10.1. This is a portable, solid-state, childproofed computerized device that administers a 9-minute vigilance task, wherein the child must press a button each time a specified, randomly presented numerical sequence (e.g., a 1 followed by a 9) occurs. Normative data are available based on more than 1,000 children aged 3 to 16 years. Gordon's CPT has been found to have satisfactory test-retest reliability (Gordon & Mettelman, 1988), to correlate modestly but significantly with other laboratory measures of attention (Barkley, 1989c), to discriminate ADHD from normal children (Barkley, DuPaul, & McMurray, in press-a; Gordon, 1988; Grodzinsky, 1990; Mariani, 1990), and to be sensitive to moderate to high doses of stimulant medication (Barkley, Fischer, Newby, & Breen, 1988; Barkley, DuPaul, & McMurray, in press-b; Rapport, DuPaul, Stoner, & Jones, 1986). Of all of the measures of attention used in laboratory studies, this is the only one that has enough available evidence on its psychometric properties and sufficient normative data to be adopted for clinical practice.

However, as Gordon rightly cautions, no score on a vigilance task such as this should be the sole determinant of a diagnosis of ADHD. This is especially important, given that there is roughly a 15 to 35% false-negative rate (i.e., legitimate ADHD children scoring normal on the test) with this type of instrument (Gordon, Mettelman, & DiNiro, 1989; Trommer, Hoeppner, Lorber, & Armstrong, 1988). The false-positive rate of the instrument, however, is excellent, with only 2% of normal children being classified as ADHD (Gordon et al., 1989). Like rating scales, the test provides one source of information to be integrated with other sources in reaching a final diagnostic decision.

Cancellation Tasks

Several paper-and-pencil versions of CPT tasks have been used as methods of assessing attention. These tasks typically involve having the child scan a series of symbols (letters, numbers, shapes) presented in rows on sheets of paper. The child is typically required to draw a line through or under the target stimulus with a pencil. One such task that has shown promise in discriminating ADHD from normal children is the Children's Checking Task, developed by Margolis (1972). The task consists of a series of 15 numerals per row, printed in 16 rows on a page. There are seven pages to the task. A tape recorder reads off the numbers in each row, and the child is required to draw a line through each number as it is read. Discrepancies between the tape and the printed page are to be circled by the child. There are seven discrepancies between the tape and printed pages. The task takes about 30 minutes to complete. Scores are derived for errors of omission (missed discrepancies) and errors of commission (numbers circled that were not discrepancies). Brown and Wynne (1982) found that the task discriminated groups of ADHD and reading-disabled children. The task correlates modestly but significantly with other measures of attention (Keogh & Margolis, 1976), often to a larger degree than any of the other laboratory measures (see Barkley, 1989c). Perhaps this is because it is somewhat similar to the accuracy demands made during work that children must do in the classroom. Nevertheless, its sensitivity to ADHD symptoms requires more research and replication of these initially promising results before it can be recommended for clinical practice.

Freedom from Distractibility Factor of the WISC-R

Factor analysis of the Wechsler Intelligence Scale for Children—Revised (WISC-R; Wechsler, 1974) by Kaufman (1975) demonstrated that the 12 subtests can be reduced to three factors: Verbal, Spatial Construction, and Freedom from Distractibility. This last factor has been widely touted as a measure of attention and distractibility in children, and has been adopted by many as a clinical measure of ADHD. This factor consists of the scores on the Arithmetic, Digit Span, and Coding subtests and is called Freedom from Distractibility "because of research with hyperactive children showing that drug therapy leads to decreased distractibility and improved memory and arithmetic skills in these youngsters" (Kaufman, 1980, p. 179). Scores on this factor have been found to correlate to a low but significant degree with other tests of attention (Klee & Garfinkel, 1983). Evidence is conflicting, however, as to whether the test can adequately discriminate groups of ADHD from normal or reading-disabled children (Brown & Wynne, 1982; Milich & Loney, 1979). We have recently found that this factor was unable to distinguish children with Attention Deficit Disorder with hyperactivity (ADD/+H) from ADD children without hyperactivity (ADD/−H), or from learning-disabled and normal children (Barkley, DuPaul, & McMurray, in press-a). These subtests appear to assess short-term memory, facility with numbers, perceptual-motor speed, visual-spatial skills, and arithmetic calculation. Consequently, poor performances on this factor do not indicate in any straightforward way that deficits in attention account for them. Moreover, a number of investigators have urged caution in interpreting these subtests as measures of distractibility, believing the label to be oversimplified and misleading (Ownby & Matthews, 1985; Stewart & Moely, 1983). *I do not recommend that this factor be used in assessing attention or in establishing evidence for or against a diagnosis of ADHD.*

Impulse Control

Three laboratory-based methods for assessing impulsivity among children with ADHD are potentially useful in clinical evaluations. As described above, commission errors on a CPT are presumed to measure this behavioral dimension. In addition, the Matching Familiar Figures Test (MFFT) has a lengthy history of use in research studies investigating impulse control in normal and disturbed children and adolescents.

Originally developed by Kagan (1966), this match-to-sample test involves the examiner presenting a picture of a recognizable object to the youngster, who must choose the identical matching picture from among an array of six very similar variants. The test includes 12 trials, with scores derived from the mean time taken to the initial response (latency) and the total number of errors (incorrectly identified pictures). A longer version of the MFFT employing 20 stimulus trials (MFFT-20) has been developed (Cairns & Cammock, 1978); this version is purported to have greater reliability among older children and adolescents (Messer & Brodzinsky, 1981). Unfortunately, more recent research on the original test has often failed to find significant differences between ADHD and normal children (Barkley, DuPaul, & McMurray, in press-a; Fischer, Barkley, Edelbrock, & Smallish, in press; Milich & Kramer, 1985). It has also shown conflicting and often negative results in detecting stimulant drug effects in ADHD children (Barkley, 1977b; Barkley, DuPaul, & McMurray, in press-a). Furthermore, norms for the adolescent population are not currently available for either version of this measure, thus limiting their use as diagnostic measures. *Consequently, I do not endorse this instrument for use in clinical practice in making diagnostic decisions about ADHD children.*

A third measure of impulse control is the Delay Task, also developed by Gordon (1983), and part of the Gordon Diagnostic System discussed above (see Figure 10.1). This test utilizes a differential reinforcement of low rates (DRL) paradigm, in which the child sits before the portable, computerized device shown in Figure 10.1a and is told to wait a while before pressing the large blue button on the front panel of the device. The child is told that if he or she has waited long enough, a point will be earned when the button is finally pushed. If the child presses the button too early, he or she must wait a while before pushing the button again. Cumulative points are scored on a digital counter on the face of the device. The child is not informed of the actual delay required to earn reinforcement (6 seconds). The test lasts 8 minutes and has normative data for more than 1,000 children. Initial evidence (Gordon & McClure, 1983; McClure & Gordon, 1984) indicated that the test discriminated groups of ADHD from non-ADHD and normal children, correlated significantly with parents and teacher ratings of hyperactivity and other lab measures of impulsivity, and had adequate test-retest reliability (Gordon & Mettelman, 1988). However, others (Barkley et al., 1988) have not found the task to be sensitive to stimulant drug effects in ADHD children and it correlates poorly if at all with ratings of hyperactivity by parents and teachers. At this time, the task requires more research on its clinical utility before it can be adopted for clinical assessments of ADHD.

Neuropsychological Functions

As noted in Chapter 2, current views of ADHD hold that it is likely to involve some impairment of the prefrontal cortex and/or the connections between the prefrontal and limbic motivational systems. This suggests that neuropsychological measures of frontal lobe functions may be useful in assessing ADHD children. In fact, the vigilance tasks described above are often found to be sensitive to frontal lobe injuries and, as already noted, have some sensitivity to ADHD symptoms as well. Other neuropsychological tests that have been used with ADHD children are described here.

Wisconsin Card Sort Test

The Wisconsin Card Sort Test (Grant & Berg, 1948) is one of the most commonly used measures of adult frontal lobe dysfunction (Lezak, 1983). It involves an examiner presenting a series of cards with various colored geometric shapes and numbers of shapes on them. The subject is to sort these cards based upon a categorizing rule known only to the examiner (color, number, shape). The examiner gives the subject feedback after each effort to sort the cards, indicating whether the sort is correct or incorrect. From this feedback, the subject must deduce the categorizing rule as quickly as possible to limit the number of sorting errors. After a certain number of such trials, the examiner shifts the sorting rule to a different category, and the subject must again deduce the rule from the limited feedback provided. Norms for children were reported by Chelune and Baer (1986). Test-retest reliability appears to be satisfactory (Lezak, 1983). Chelune, Ferguson, Koon, and Dickey (1986) reported significant differences between ADHD and normal children on this particular test. However, subsequent efforts have failed to replicate these findings (Fischer et al., in press; Grodzinsky, 1990), and so *the test is not recommended for clinical use in diagnosing ADHD children.*

Stroop Word-Color Association Test

The Stroop Word-Color Association Test (Stroop, 1935) is a timed test measuring the ability to suppress or inhibit automatic responses. Children must read the names of colors, although the names are printed in a different-colored ink from the color specified in the name (e.g., the word "red" is printed in blue ink). Test-retest reliability is well established, as is sensitivity to frontal lobe functions in adults (Lezak, 1983). The test has been found in a recent study by a doctoral student in my lab to discriminate ADHD from normal children (Grodzinsky, 1990) and ADD/+H from ADD/−H children (Barkley, Grodzinsky, & DuPaul, 1990). The test may therefore eventually hold some value in clinical testing of ADHD children. Its sensitivity to discriminating ADHD children probably rests in its assessment of impulsivity.

Hand Movements Test

The Hand Movements Test, a subtest of the Kaufman Assessment Battery for Children (Kaufman & Kaufman, 1983), is a well-standardized and normed test for children based on a traditional measure of frontal lobe function in adults. Children are presented with progressively longer sequences of three hand movements that they must imitate. The test has acceptable reliability and normative data and has been shown by two doctoral students in my laboratory to readily discriminate ADHD from normal children (Grodzinsky, 1990; Mariani, 1990) and ADD/+H from ADD/−H children (Barkley, Grodzinsky, & DuPaul, 1990). Its sensitivity to ADHD may rest in the well-known fine motor coordination difficulties often seen in these children as well as in their inattention to the task itself, especially as sequences of movements become progressively longer.

Limitations of Laboratory Measures and Psychological Tests

Although the apparent objectivity of laboratory measures is highly appealing, their limitations often tend to be overlooked. Many laboratory measures continue to lack adequate information concerning their psychometric properties (e.g., reliability, validity, sensitivity and specificity). Others do not have adequate samples of normative data to permit their use as measures of behavioral deviance. Both of these limitations, however, are readily overcome by additional research.

One limitation not so handily addressed is the inability of laboratory tests to capture information regarding the antecedents and consequences of the child's or adolescent's behavior. Such contextual information may have great clinical value in elucidating the controlling variables related to the person's presenting problems. In a behavioral or functional analysis of ADHD symptoms, understanding these environmental parameters is crucial in designing behavioral interventions to address the referral concerns. Another limitation not so easily remedied is the high level of inference required in interpreting the results of these laboratory measures. To what extent do these laboratory measures actually capture the behaviors of interest to referring agents and/or critical to predicting treatment response? Claiming that a poor score on a 9-minute vigilance task reflects inattention or impulsivity requires a significant inferential leap from a limited sample of behavior to a broad cognitive construct. Incorporating direct behavioral observation measures along with these laboratory tests may overcome this problem.

DIRECT OBSERVATIONAL PROCEDURES

Informal or unsystematic behavioral observations of a child in the clinical setting or during testing can be useful in developing impressions of the child's physical appearance, language, and other developmental areas, as discussed in Chapter 8 on interviews. However, attempting to draw diagnostic conclusions about ADHD from clinic behavior with an examiner is not recommended, as such behavior has often been shown to be quite atypical of the child's behavior with other caregivers in natural settings. This is also true of using observations of child behavior during psychological testing of children in the school setting (Glutting & McDermott, 1988). However, systematic, formal behavioral observations in natural settings or in clinic analogue situations can be useful in the diagnosis and assessment of ADHD children. The most useful of these assessment methods are reviewed below.

Where to Observe?

Assuming that direct observations of child behavior are feasible, where should they occur in order to be of greatest utility? Some have argued that the home or school settings of ADHD children are the best contexts in which to gather information on the children, and it is hard to quibble with this argument. Such observations have the greatest likelihood of capturing the actual behavior of the children that is of such importance and concern to their caregivers. Unfortunately, such observations can be quite expensive to make, and many insurance companies will not reimburse the private practitioner for these types of out-of-office procedures. But if one works within a school system or for a social service agency that typically employs home visits as part of a family evaluation, then these direct observations can be far more practical and clinically rich in information.

Where natural observations are not possible, observations in a clinic playroom equipped with a one-way mirror and a sound monitoring system can be considerably less costly and of some value in the assessment process. A major question that arises from clinic "analogue" observations is whether the behavior so witnessed is typical of the child's behavior in more natural settings. In other words, are the observations ecologically valid? Several steps can be taken to maximize the likelihood of observing typical child behaviors. Furnishing the clinic room so that it looks similar to an average home family room may help—for example, using a sofa, armchairs, bookshelves, a toy box, and even a television and telephone. Also, the nature of the tasks assigned to the children should approximate those given at home or school that typically elicit the ADHD symptoms or other behaviors of interest to the clinician.

We have found that it is better to place the child in the room alone when the purpose is to assess ADHD behaviors, to see how well the child works independently of supervision. Where defiant and oppositional behavior are of interest, then having the mother present in the room with the child and requiring her to give the instructions or tasks to the child is essential. It should be kept in mind, though, that it will be difficult to evaluate ADHD symptoms during these interactions, as they will be confounded with defiance toward the mother. Ideally, observing the child alone while he or she is performing work and then again later with the mother during chore performance can be the most useful. Allowing the child adequate time to habituate to the room can help to enhance the child's comfort with the surroundings, and hence to increase the likelihood that more typical behaviors will be observed. This can be achieved by conducting the parent and child interviews in this same clinic room, thereby providing about 2 hours of habituation before the systematic behavioral observations begin. Research suggests that where such steps are taken, the behaviors recorded do correlate to a significant and meaningful degree with behavioral observations and ratings taken in the natural environment (Barkley, 1989c). However, the degree of this relationship is low to moderate ($r = .20$ to $.50$), suggesting that the behaviors in the clinic are not completely accurate representations of those at home or school. Caution must be used in their interpretation.

Where clinic observations are to be used, I customarily do not permit either parent into the observation room during the formal observation period. Having one parent in the observation room and the other in the playroom being observed with the child can often lead to discomfort on the part of the observed parent, and thereby may further reduce the representativeness of these observations. Also, such situations provide an opportunity for the observing parent to converse with the examiner, distracting the examiner from a more fine-grained observation of the child's behavior in the room or from valuable reflection about the information obtained so far in the evaluation. If the child is made aware of a parent's observation from the adjoining room, this can further inhibit the child from displaying more typical forms of behavior at times, making the observation devoid of much ecological validity.

If observations are to be taken in the home, then the observer may wish to consult the guidelines given below for such home visits. For those conducted in the classroom, several precautions are worth noting. Chief among these is the need to protect the identity of the student being observed, so as not to create any greater social stigma than an ADHD child may already be suffering. Remaining unobtrusive in the classroom and pretending to observe all of the children and class activities can contribute to this aim. The examiner should also remind the teacher not to divulge the purpose of the visit at the time the school visit is scheduled.

A second precaution is to ensure that the observation coincides with a time when the target child is engaged in a task likely to elicit the ADHD symptoms or other behaviors of interest. I have found times when independent seatwork is being assigned to be especially useful for these observation visits. Third, making several visits is likely to yield information more representative of the child's typical class conduct than is a single, brief observation. Finally, as with observations at home, it is useful to observe the interactions of the adult in charge of the setting—in this case, the teacher—with the target child, so as to evaluate what role these antecedents and consequences may play in further eliciting or maintaining disruptive child behavior at school. This need not be done systematically, but through clinical observations and notes on the margins of the coding form being used for the child's behavior.

ADHD Symptoms

Behavioral Coding in Natural Settings

Behavioral observations obtained from natural settings (e.g., the classroom) provide a wealth of information regarding the frequency, severity, antecedents, and consequences of ADHD symptoms. Various recording methods have been specifically developed for this purpose, including the Hyperactive Behavior Code (Jacob, O'Leary, & Rosenblad, 1978) and the Classroom Observation Code (Abikoff, Gittelman-Klein, & Klein, 1977). Each of these systems requires observers to classify behaviors into a variety of categories (e.g., "daydreaming," "aggression", using interval sampling procedures. The developers have found these methods to discriminate children with ADHD from their normal classmates and to correlate highly with teacher ratings on the Conners Teacher Rating Scale (CTRS).

Behavioral Coding in Analogue Settings

Since clinicians often do not have the luxury of obtaining *in vivo* observations, behavioral coding systems (Roberts, 1979) have also been developed for use in analogue (e.g., clinic playroom) settings. Such systems have been found to discriminate ADHD children from those who are purely aggressive, those who are both ADHD and aggressive, and a group of psychiatric control children (Milich, Loney, & Landau, 1982). Typically, these observations are conducted by using a clinic room equipped with a one-way mirror, wherein the youngster is observed while seated at a desk and attempting to complete a task, such as a large set of mathematics problems. The system has been modified for use with adolescents by playing rock music on a nearby cassette tape player during the task to serve as a possible distractor (Fischer et al., in press). This situation lasts 15 minutes, during which the examiner records the initial occurrence of five behavioral categories (e.g., "off task," "fidgets," "vocalizes") during each 15- to 30-second interval. The choice of intervals depends on the degree of behavior one wishes to sample. More frequent observations ought to be used where possible, as they sample a greater number of behaviors during a fixed period of observation. Separate scores (percentage of occurrence) can be derived and examined for each measure or collapsed to yield a total ADHD behavior score (total percentage of occurrence). The number of task problems completed and those completed accurately are also recorded. These measures have been found to discriminate ADHD from normal children (Breen, 1989; Mariani, 1990) and are sensitive to drug and dose effects of stimulant medication (Barkley et al., 1988; Barkley, DuPaul, & McMurray, in press-b).

In the ADHD Behavior Coding System that I have developed, the child or adolescent is observed during performance of independent academic work (the Restricted Academic Situation). The child is placed alone in a clinic playroom and provided with a packet of math problems to complete. The child is told to complete as many math problems as possible, not to leave his or her chair at the table, and not to touch any toys. Math problems are selected from six available difficulty levels to be well within the child's math grade level at school. Toys are provided on a bookshelf in the playroom. The situation lasts 15 minutes, and the child's behavior can be scored at this time or videotaped for later coding. Behavior is scored using five behavioral categories: "off task," "fidgets," "out of seat," "vocalizes," and "plays with objects." The definitions for these are shown in Table 10.1. Every 15 to 30

TABLE 10.1. Conducting the Behavioral Observations during the Restricted Academic Situation

This task is designed to observe and record symptoms of ADHD during individual academic work, such as that which might be given as homework or in-class deskwork to a child. The task involves the following procedures:

In-Clinic Observations

1. Place the child in a playroom containing toys, a small work table and chair, a one-way mirror, and an intercom. Let the child play for 5 minutes as a habituation period.

2. Enter the room and tell the child that you now have some schoolwork for him or her to do. Tell the child to sit at the small table, stay in the chair, and complete the packet of math problems. Tell the child not to play with any toys and not to leave the seat during this work time; you will be back in a while to see how much work he or she has done. Be sure to give the child a set of math problems at a difficulty level well below the child's current grade. We typically use a set that is one grade level below that grade in which the child is currently placed.

3. Leave the playroom, enter the observation room, and begin coding the child's behavior using the procedures described below. After 15 to 20 minutes, end the coding session.

TABLE 10.1. (*cont.*)

In-School Observations

Observe the child in his or her regular classroom for 15 to 20 minutes when the child has been given academic work to do alone at his or her desk. You can either have the teacher give work that is from a current assignment or take in a set of math problems you have specially constructed for this exercise. In any case, be sure the child has been given enough work to occupy 15 to 20 minutes. Have the teacher tell the child to go to his or her desk, complete the assigned packet of work, and stay in the seat. Then begin to observe and record the child, using the procedures below.

For a normative comparison, ask the teacher to point out an average child in that classroom and code that child's behavior during individual deskwork for the same period of time.

To increase the validity of your school observations, take several observations over several days to increase the sampling of child behavior.

Coding Instructions

It is helpful to make a tape recording that contains cues for the beginning of each 30-second interval of observation. This tape can simply say, "Begin 1" and then 30 seconds later "Begin 2," and so on for the 30 observation intervals. We use 30-second intervals over a 15-minute observation period, but others have used 15- or 20-second coding intervals over 20 minutes or more of observation to increase the sensitivity of the measure. When the tape sounds the beginning of a coding interval, observe the child and place a check mark next to any of the behavior categories that occur, using the column marked for that coding interval (1, 2, 3, . . .). When the next interval begins, move to the next column and again place a check beside any of the behavior categories that occur. Once a behavior has been checked during an interval, it cannot be checked again until the next interval.

At the end of the observation period, calculate the percentage occurrence of each behavior category by dividing the number of check marks for that category by the total number of recording intervals. You should also calculate the number of math problems completed and the percentage completed correctly.

Definitions

1. *Off task:* This category is checked if the child interrupts his or her attention to the tasks to engage in some other behavior. Attention is defined as visually looking at the task materials. If the child breaks eye contact with the math problems, then he or she is coded as off task.

2. *Fidgeting:* Any repetitive, purposeless motion of the legs, arms, hands, buttocks, or trunk. It must occur at least twice in succession to be considered repetitive, and it should serve no purpose. Examples include swaying back and forth, kicking one's legs back and forth, swinging arms at one's side, shuffling feet from side to side, shifting one's buttocks about in the chair, tapping a pencil or finger repeatedly on the table, and so on.

3. *Vocalizing:* Any vocal noise or verbalization made by the child. Examples: speech, whispering, singing, humming, making odd mouth noises, clicking one's teeth, and so on.

4. *Plays with objects:* Touching any object in the room besides the table, chair, math problems, and pencil. The child may touch his or her own clothing without being considered to play with an object. However, touching toys, walls, light switches, curtains, or any other object in the room is coded in this category.

5. *Out of seat:* Any time the child's buttocks break contact with the flat surface of the seat.

seconds, the coder checks on the coding sheet whether any of the five behavior categories were observed. The coding sheet is shown in Figure 10.2. This coding procedure yields 30 to 60 possible occurrences for each of the five behavior categories. The scores are the percentage of occurrence of each category and a total percentage of occurrence for all behavior categories (total ADD behaviors). Intercoder agreement in previous studies using this coding system was .77 to .85.

It is unlikely that normative data could be developed that would be clinically useful for such an observation system. The rates of these behaviors would probably vary as a function of the size of the particular room being used for the observations, the types of math problems given to the child, the types of toys available for play in the room, and other contextual variables. Instead, it would seem more appropriate that clinicians wishing to use such an in-clinic observation system collect a sample of norms on local children using their particular playroom, furnishings, and tasks. The lack of norms, however, would not preclude the use of this coding system within a child's natural school classroom. In this instance, the other normal children in the class could serve as a normative reference point, providing better control over potentially confounding variables than could any effort to norm such a procedure. In this case, the clinician should observe the child while he or she is performing independent deskwork. After recording the child's behavior for 15 to 20 minutes, the clinician can then ask the teacher to point out a typical child in this classroom, and the clinician can now observe this child using the same behavioral coding system. For greater rigor, the clinician may wish to alternate coding of the ADHD child and the normal child every 15 to 30 seconds and to take several observations across several days to ensure greater representativeness of the data so obtained. Such observations are likely to prove as useful as (or more useful than) any other sources of information in the evaluation, because they directly assess the actual ADHD symptoms of concern to the child's teacher. Such in-class observations correlate highly with teacher ratings of ADHD symptoms, as well as with measures of academic accuracy and productivity (DuPaul, 1990c).

Behavioral Coding during Testing

It is instructive to assess the presence of ADHD symptoms during the Gordon CPT task described above, using this type of behavioral observation system. We have shown that such observations may be as sensitive to discriminating ADHD children from other diagnostic groups as are the CPT scores themselves (Barkley, DuPaul, & McMurray, in press-a).

Child Behavior Checklist—Direct Observation Form (CBCL-DOF)

Achenbach (1986) has developed a form for scoring direct observations of children in group or classroom settings that is comparable to the items con-

RESTRICTED ACADEMIC SITUATION CODING SHEET

Interval #:	1	2	3	4	5	6	7	8	9	10	11	12	13	14	15
Off task															
Fidgeting															
Vocalizing															
Plays w/obj.															
Out of seat															

Interval #:	16	17	18	19	20	21	22	23	24	25	26	27	28	29	30
Off task															
Fidgeting															
Vocalizing															
Plays w/obj.															
Out of seat															

Interval #:	31	32	33	34	35	36	37	38	39	40	Total
Off task											/40
Fidgeting											/40
Vocalizing											/40
Plays w/obj.											/40
Out of seat											/40

Total: /200

Child's Name: Coder Initials:

_____   _____

Date:

_____

Week #	Initial	Wk 1	Wk 2	Wk 3	Wk 4

Comments:

FIGURE 10.2. Coding sheet for the Restricted Academic Situation.

tained on the parent and teacher report forms of the CBCL (see Chapter 9). It is recommended that children be observed on three or more occasions for at least 10 minutes or more on each. The observer completes the scale after each observation and takes the average of the observations for that particular setting. Scores are obtained for mean time on tasks, total problems, and total Internalizing and Externalizing symptoms. In addition, scores on six scales developed from factor analysis of the 96-item pool can also be obtained, these being Withdrawn-Inattentive, Nervous-Obsessive, Depressed, Hyperactive, Attention-Demanding, and Aggressive. Norms are based on 287 children observed in classroom settings. The observation system has adequate interobserver reliability and concurrent and discriminant validity (McConaughy & Achenbach, 1988; McConaughy, Achenbach, & Gent, 1988).

The advantages of this observational system are numerous. First, a much wider array of both internalizing and externalizing symptoms can be assessed than is typical of other observational systems described above. Second, it is the only system with normative data for elementary-age children for classroom observations. Third, its scales were empirically developed, and so provide an impression of precisely how a variety of behaviors cluster in their natural occurrence. And finally, it has been shown to discriminate among various types of child psychiatric disorders and their behavioral profiles (McConaughy et al., 1988). This system would seem to have great merit for both research and clinical use in assessing a broad range of behavioral characteristics in school settings. School personnel should be encouraged to adopt such a system as part of their standard evaluation of children for consideration for special education, rather than relying so heavily on traditional projective methods of assessing behavior and personality.

Parent-Child Interactions

Over 60% of clinic-referred ADHD children also display problems with oppositional and defiant behavior. When feasible, it can be clinically useful to take observations of a child's interactions with his or her parent; these not only can establish the child's deviance, but also can provide evidence as to what procedures the parents are using that will require modification during child behavior management training. Several coding systems are available, and these are described below.

Observations of Mother-Child Interactions during Tasks

Several procedures have been developed for recording mother-child interactions in clinic playroom settings. The one we have used most often in our research is the Response Class Matrix, which was described in detail in the first edition of this text (Barkley, 1981) and has been recently reviewed elsewhere (Mash & Barkley, 1987). However, the system is sufficiently compli-

min.	1 Par.	Child	Par.	2 Par.	Child	Par.	3 Par.	Child	Par.	4 Par.	Child	Par.	5 Par.	Child	Par.
1	C R R	Cpy	A	C R R	Cpy	A	C R R	Cpy	A	C R R	Cpy	A	C R R	Cpy	A
	R R R	Ncpy		R R R	Ncpy		R R R	Ncpy		R R R	Ncpy		R R R	Ncpy	
	R R R	Neg	PNeg	R R R	Neg	PNeg	R R R	Neg	PNeg	R R R	Neg	PNeg	R R R	Neg	PNeg
2	C R R	Cpy	A	C R R	Cpy	A	C R R	Cpy	A	C R R	Cpy	A	C R R	Cpy	A
	R R R	Ncpy		R R R	Ncpy		R R R	Ncpy		R R R	Ncpy		R R R	Ncpy	
	R R R	Neg	PNeg	R R R	Neg	PNeg	R R R	Neg	PNeg	R R R	Neg	PNeg	R R R	Neg	PNeg
3	C R R	Cpy	A	C R R	Cpy	A	C R R	Cpy	A	C R R	Cpy	A	C R R	Cpy	A
	R R R	Ncpy		R R R	Ncpy		R R R	Ncpy		R R R	Ncpy		R R R	Ncpy	
	R R R	Neg	PNeg	R R R	Neg	PNeg	R R R	Neg	PNeg	R R R	Neg	PNeg	R R R	Neg	PNeg
4	C R R	Cpy	A	C R R	Cpy	A	C R R	Cpy	A	C R R	Cpy	A	C R R	Cpy	A
	R R R	Ncpy		R R R	Ncpy		R R R	Ncpy		R R R	Ncpy		R R R	Ncpy	
	R R R	Neg	PNeg	R R R	Neg	PNeg	R R R	Neg	PNeg	R R R	Neg	PNeg	R R R	Neg	PNeg
5	C R R	Cpy	A	C R R	Cpy	A	C R R	Cpy	A	C R R	Cpy	A	C R R	Cpy	A
	R R R	Ncpy		R R R	Ncpy		R R R	Ncpy		R R R	Ncpy		R R R	Ncpy	
	R R R	Neg	PNeg	R R R	Neg	PNeg	R R R	Neg	PNeg	R R R	Neg	PNeg	R R R	Neg	PNeg
6	C R R	Cpy	A	C R R	Cpy	A	C R R	Cpy	A	C R R	Cpy	A	C R R	Cpy	A
	R R R	Ncpy		R R R	Ncpy		R R R	Ncpy		R R R	Ncpy		R R R	Ncpy	
	R R R	Neg	PNeg	R R R	Neg	PNeg	R R R	Neg	PNeg	R R R	Neg	PNeg	R R R	Neg	PNeg
7	C R R	Cpy	A	C R R	Cpy	A	C R R	Cpy	A	C R R	Cpy	A	C R R	Cpy	A
	R R R	Ncpy		R R R	Ncpy		R R R	Ncpy		R R R	Ncpy		R R R	Ncpy	
	R R R	Neg	PNeg	R R R	Neg	PNeg	R R R	Neg	PNeg	R R R	Neg	PNeg	R R R	Neg	PNeg
8	C R R	Cpy	A	C R R	Cpy	A	C R R	Cpy	A	C R R	Cpy	A	C R R	Cpy	A
	R R R	Ncpy		R R R	Ncpy		R R R	Ncpy		R R R	Ncpy		R R R	Ncpy	
	R R R	Neg	PNeg	R R R	Neg	PNeg	R R R	Neg	PNeg	R R R	Neg	PNeg	R R R	Neg	PNeg
9	C R R	Cpy	A	C R R	Cpy	A	C R R	Cpy	A	C R R	Cpy	A	C R R	Cpy	A
	R R R	Ncpy		R R R	Ncpy		R R R	Ncpy		R R R	Ncpy		R R R	Ncpy	
	R R R	Neg	PNeg	R R R	Neg	PNeg	R R R	Neg	PNeg	R R R	Neg	PNeg	R R R	Neg	PNeg
10	C R R	Cpy	A	C R R	Cpy	A	C R R	Cpy	A	C R R	Cpy	A	C R R	Cpy	A
	R R R	Ncpy		R R R	Ncpy		R R R	Ncpy		R R R	Ncpy		R R R	Ncpy	
	R R R	Neg	PNeg	R R R	Neg	PNeg	R R R	Neg	PNeg	R R R	Neg	PNeg	R R R	Neg	PNeg

Abbreviations: Par. = parent; C = parent original command; R = parent repeat command; Cpy = compliance within 10 seconds; Ncpy = noncompliance (failure to comply in 10 seconds); Neg = child negative behavior; A = parent approval and praise; PNeg = parent negative behavior.

FIGURE 10.3. Coding sheet for recording mother-child interactions. From *Defiant Children: A Clinician's Manual for Parent Training* by R. A. Barkley, 1987. New York: Guilford Press. Copyright 1987 by The Guilford Press. Reprinted by permission of the publisher.

cated and the training of behavior coders sufficiently lengthy and time-consuming that I do not recommend its adoption for most clinical practices.

The approach we have used instead for clinical purposes is a modified version of the parent-child coding system developed by Forehand and McMahon (1981). The system we employ is described in detail in another text of mine (Barkley, 1987). The coding form is set forth in Figure 10.3, and behavioral definitions are shown in Table 10.2. The clinical situation we employ is designed to assess oppositional and defiant behavior in children during task performances with their mothers, and also to record parental behaviors during these interactions. Each mother-child dyad is placed in an observation room in which toys are available for play. A videotape player may be used

TABLE 10.2. Recording Observations of Parent-Child Interactions

Coding Instructions

Provide the parent with a list of tasks to do with the child. [Some suggestions for tasks are listed elsewhere in this chapter.] Observe the parent and child for 10 minutes. During this time, record their behavior using the scoring sheet that follows. Instructions for scoring are provided below.

Behavior Categories and Definitions

The following definitions apply to each of the behavioral categories provided on the coding sheet for recording parent-child interactions.

Original Command (C)

In this category are direct commands or statements that contain imperatives or indirectly stated or implied commands that may be stated as interrogatives. Examples include the following:

- Imperatives
  Come here and . . .
  Let me . . .
  Put this . . .
  I want you to . . .
  Stop that!
  No! (when used to get the child to stop doing something)
  Now you are to . . .
- Interrogatives
  Will you hand me . . . ?
  Why don't you . . . ?
  Shall we . . . ?
  Can you . . . ?
  Would you . . . ?

In general, a statement is considered a command if it states or implies that an action is required from the child to start something, stop something, or change to doing something else.

Repeat Command (R)

This is any repetition of a command previously given by the parent where no new command has been given by the parent between the original command and its repetition. If the parent gives a new command, gives a different command, and then goes back to repeat the first command, each of these would be scored as original commands (C), not as a repetition of a command. Examples:

- "Pick up the crayon. . . . Pick it up! I said, pick up that crayon!" (This would be scored as an original command [C], then two repeat commands [R] on the coding sheet.)
- "Pick up the crayon. . . . Get me that block. . . . Now, go back and pick up that crayon like I told you to do." (This would be scored as three original commands [C], since a different command was placed between the first command and its repetition.)

Child Compliance (Cpy)

This category is scored when the child's behavior is in direct response to the parent's command and fulfills the action required by the parent. Any degree of compliance, from approximation to full compliance, is scored in this category. Even if the child is having a tantrum, as long as he or she has begun to comply with what was requested by the parent, the child is scored as having complied with the command. Compliance

TABLE 10.2. (*cont.*)

is scored only if it is initiated within 10 seconds of the original command given by the parent and is scored only once to that original command. Compliance to repeat commands is not scored.

Child Noncompliance (Ncpy)
This category is scored if the child fails to initiate compliance to a parent's command within 10 seconds after the original command was given.

Child Negative (Neg)
This category is scored if the child engages in verbal or nonverbal behavior that conveys refusal, anger, or discouragement in direct response to a parent's original command (C) or a repeat command (R). Examples are saying "No!" to a parent's command, whining, hitting, kicking, saying "I don't want to," pushing, throwing things, pulling away sharply from the parent's grasp, throwing tantrums, crying, swearing or name-calling at the parent, or displaying other negative reactions to the parent's interactions. The category can be scored only once during a command—repeat command sequence. Once the parent shifts to a new original command (C), the category can be scored again.

Parent Approval (A)
This category contains both verbal and nonverbal actions that convey parental approval, encouragement, or acceptance of the child's activities. Clearly, some judgment is required as to the context and emotional tone of these remarks or gestures. In general, when these responses follow the completion of an activity by the child, they are scored as praise. Examples:

- Verbal: OK, Good, That's fine . . . , I like it when you . . . , Terrific!, That was very nice . . . ,
- Nonverbal: Pat on the back, hug, kiss, clapping for child's performance, gestures of approval such as the thumbs-up sign, winking at child.

Parent Negative (PNeg)
This category includes both verbal statements and nonverbval actions conveying discouragement, nonacceptance, or disapproval of the child's activities. Again, some judgment is required concerning the context and emotional tone accompanying the gesture or action. Examples:

- Verbal (direct)
    "No, don't do that . . . !"
    "Stop!"
    "Quit that . . . !"
    "You're a bad boy/girl."
    "That's all wrong . . ."
    "That's not right . . ."
    "I don't like that . . ."
- Verbal (indirect)
    "You're acting like a baby . . ."
    "You'd better watch it or . . ."
    "[Child's name]!!!" (in negative tone)
- Nonverbal
    Spank
    Hit
    Pinch
    Yank at child
    Shove child

Shaking head "no"
Raising hand in threatening gesture
Shaking a finger at child in disapproval

Sometimes, parents may issue a repeat command with a threat, such as "If you don't pick up those toys, I'll spank you!" This would be scored as parent negative (PNeg) rather than as a repeat command (R).

Scoring

1. *Number of parent's commands per minute.* Count all of the circled Cs on the coding sheet and divide by the number of minutes of coding time.
2. *Number of repeat commands per original command.* Count all of the Rs circled on the coding sheet and divide by the number of Cs (commands).
3. *Child compliance percent.* The number of Cpys circled on the coding sheet divided by the number of Cs circled.
4. *Percentage of child negatives.* The number of Negs circled on the coding sheet divided by the number of Cs.
5. *Percentage of parent approvals.* The number of As circled on the coding sheet divided by the number of Cs.
6. *Percentage of parent negatives.* The number of PNegs circled on the coding sheet divided by the number Cs.

Coding

Use a tape recorder with a cassette tape that has been recorded with the verbal cue of "Begin minute 1 . . . Begin minute 2 . . . ," etc., to mark the beginning of each minute. Use the row of the coding sheet corresponding to each minute of observation for recording parent-child interactions in that minute. A coding form contains enough rows for 10 minutes of observation. Since at least 10 minutes of observation are recommended, one form will be used. Each row contains five rectangles and each rectangle corresponds to interactions surrounding each original command issued by the parent. The rectangles are numbered at the top of each column of the coding sheet. This allows space for recording up to five original commands issued by the parent per minute.

When the observations begin, start coding in row 1, the first column (rectangle). Circle a C if the parent gives a command and Cpy if the child begins to comply within 10 seconds of that command or Ncpy if the child fails to begin compliance within 10 seconds. The 10-second interval is determined simply by having the coder count slowly to approximate the time (i.e., "one-one thousand, two-one thousand," etc.). A stop watch can be used for more accurate measurement but is not usually necessary. Circle Rs for all repeated commands. Circle As if the parent provides praise or approval to the child during this interaction or PNegs if disapproval is expressed by the parent. As soon as the parent issues a new command, move to the next column (or rectangle) to the right and begin coding all interactions in this block until another new command is given, at which point move to column 3 and begin coding in this block. When the tape recorder announces the beginning of a new minute, move down to row 2 and begin coding again in column 1 (first rectangle in this row). The next command given by the parent, even if it is a repetition of one given in the previous minute, is scored as an original command. Follow this same procedure for each minute of coding.

In general, remember to move across columns to mark the start of each original command and to move down the rows to begin each new minute of coding.

to play a series of cartoons on a television monitor to further provoke child misbehavior.

After 5 minutes of free play to allow for habituation to the room, the mother is given seven tasks to do with her child. These are as follows: (1) The child must put all of the toys back in their boxes; (2) the child must place all the toys and boxes back on the book shelf; (3) the child must pick up scraps of paper on the floor and put them in the trash can; (4) the child must sit at a table with the mother and sort a deck of pinochle cards, separating jacks and kings from the deck; (5) the child must make a copy of a set of geometric designs, using a pencil and paper; (6) the mother and child must negotiate a maze on the face of an Etch-A-Sketch together, with mother using one control knob and child using the other; and (7) the child must take just one toy, sit at the table and play, and not bother the mother while she reads a magazine. Other sets of commands one may wish to have the mother give the child during this session are shown in Table 10.3.

The interactions can be coded live or videotaped. The observation period lasts for 10 to 15 minutes. A coder scores the child's behavior, using the following categories during each minute: each new command given, whether the child begins complying or not in 10 seconds, the number of times each new command is repeated by the mother, mother praises, child negative behavior (refusals, whines, cries, etc.), and mother negative behavior (yelling, threats, discipline).

Observations of Parent-Adolescent Interactions

A plethora of research has demonstrated the considerable conflicts present in the interactions of preadolescent ADHD children with their parents (see Chapter 5; see also Barkley, 1985a). Evidence is now available that such conflicts continue into adolescence in many ADHD children (Barkley, Fischer, Edelbrock, & Smallish, in press-b). Robin and Foster (1989) have developed a clinic analogue communication task, which we have found to be quite helpful in the clinical assessment of parent-teen interactions.

The parent and adolescent are asked to engage in a problem-centered discussion involving three topics: a neutral discussion (e.g., where to go on vacation), a current list of disagreements, and then a positive discussion (e.g., the most positive characteristics of the other discussant). The topics of disagreement are obtained through selection of the five issues with the "hottest" ratings (highest intensity × frequency product scores) on the parental and adolescent Issues Checklists (see Chapter 9). The discussions can be observed informally, with notes being taken of the nature of the communication styles of parent and adolescent. In some clinics where equipment is available, either audio- or videotaping of the interaction for later analysis and coding can be done from behind a one-way mirror. Such tapes may also prove of benefit for illustrating family communication patterns during therapy.

These discussions may be analyzed using simple global behavioral codes

TABLE 10.3. Three Separate Lists of Commands for Mothers to Give during Playroom Observations of Mother-Child Interactions

SET #1	*SET #2*
1. Stand up, please.	1. Come here and let me fix your shirt (dress).
2. Open the door.	2. Close the door.
3. Give me one of those toys.	3. Put this toy in the box (mother holds box of Legos or Tinker Toys).
4. Put all the toys back in their boxes.	4. Put all of the toys on the coffee table.
5. Put the chairs under the table.	5. Empty that wastebasket into the other one.
6. Pick up the paper behind the black line.	6. Fold the clothes and put them back in the box neatly.
7. Walk the black line slowly, heel to toe.	7. Walk the black line slowly, heel to toe.
8. Put all of the toys on the coffee table.	8. Take off your shoes.
9. Take off your shoes.	9. Draw the designs three times (a set of geometric designs is provided).
10. Sit over there at the work table.	10. Do all the math problems (problems are provided).
11. Draw these designs three times.	11. Do the Purdue Pegboard (provided and explained to parent).
12. Do all the math problems.	12. Move everything off the coffee table and dust it.
13. Bring the black line through the maze on the Etch-A-Sketch.	13. Stack the magazines neatly on the coffee table.
14. Move all the toys off that table and dust it.	14. Put the toys back on the table.
15. Put your shoes on.	15. Put your shoes on.

SET #3

1. Pick up all the toys and put them in their boxes.
2. Sit down here and draw these geometric designs.
3. Sit down here and do all the math problems.
4. Let's draw a line through the maze on the Etch-A-Sketch (mother gets one knob and child gets the other).
5. Let's build a house together out of the Lego blocks.

Note. From *Hyperactive Children: A Handbook for Diagnosis and Treatment* by R. A. Barkley, 1981, New York: Guilford Press. Copyright 1981 by The Guilford Press. Reprinted by permission of the publisher.

(positive, negative, or neutral) for each participant or a more detailed frequency-based code, such as the Parent-Adolescent Interaction Coding System (PAICS; Robin & Foster, 1989). The PAICS codes the verbal behavior of a parent-teen dyad, employing six mutually exclusive categories ("Puts down/commands," "defends/complains," "facilitates," "problem-solves," "defines/evaluates," and "talks"). The PAICS has been found to generate adequate interobserver agreement and to discriminate between distressed and nondistressed families (Robin & Foster, 1989). It also discriminates between ADHD and normal adolescents (Barkley, Fischer, et al., in press-b). However, considerable coder training is required, making it quite unwield for most clinical situations. Regardless of the specific code employed, observation of communication among dyads in a conflictual situation provides fruitful data for both initial assessment and monitoring of treatment progress.

Observations of Mother-Child Interactions in the Home

Some professionals may have the opportunity to take observations of child behavior in the home, particularly as part of their activities within a department of mental health or social services, where such home visits are more common than in clinical practice. When this is feasible, direct, systematic observations of children's behavior, particularly during interactions with parents, can be highly informative. For recording observations of mother and child behaviors during home visits, one can use the systems already described above for parent-child and parent-adolescent interactions in the clinic. As an alternative, one could also use the Family Observation Schedule (FOS) developed by Dadds, Sanders, and Behrens (1987) for recording aggressive and aversive behaviors of parents and children in research on marital discord and child behavior problems.

The FOS uses nine behavioral codes for parent behavior and five for child behavior. The definitions for these codes are shown in Table 10.4. A time-sampling procedure is used, in which behavior is observed for 25 seconds, followed by a 15-second recording period for coders to complete scoring all behaviors occurring in that interval. This 25-second observe/15-second record procedure is repeated throughout the observations taken during the home visit (unstructured time, interactive play, academic homework, and chore performance). A tape recorder with earplug is used to cue the observer as to when each observe and record interval begins. The scores are calculated for each behavior category as a percentage of total intervals of observation in which that category occurred. Three summary score measures are also derived (parent positive, parent aversive, and child aversive) by collapsing relevant parent and child behavior categories into these global categories. Two home visits are recommended across a 2-week period, averaging the scores across these visits to arrive at the final measures.

This coding system has been shown to have satisfactory interrater reliability, to be sensitive to differences in parent and child behaviors between families with and without marital discord, and to be sensitive to changes in par-

TABLE 10.4. Behavioral Categories and Definitions for the Family Observation System

Parent Behavior Categories (9 categories)

1. *Praise:* Praise or approval offered to the child by the parent. This can be verbal praise indicating approval of a specific act, general praise or approval, such as "I like you", or nonverbal approval such as a thumbs up sign, applause, a wink, a kiss, a light pat on the head, or clearly visible smile.

2. *Contact-Neutral:* Any contact deemed to be nonaversive; that is, not causing or having the potential to cause pain or discomfort. Code instances of clearly physical affection under praise above.

3. *Contact-Aversive:* Any contact causing, or having the potential to cause, pain or discomfort in the child, such as spanking, cuffing the child, grabbing the child by the arm and yanking them, pinching so as to inflict discomfort, pulling the child by the ear, grasping the child at the back of the neck, etc.

4. *Question-Neutral:* Any nonaversive request for information from the child.

5. *Question-Aversive:* Any request for information deemed aversive due to content or voice tone, such as yelling, barking, anger, or visible irritation with the child while asking the question.

6. *Instruction-Neutral:* Any verbal command or direction presented nonaversively. A command directs a child to initiate a behavior or to stop a behavior.

7. *Instruction-Aversive:* Any verbal command presented aversively, such as with accompanying anger, loud voice tone, hostility, or clear irritation with the child.

8. *Social Attention-Neutral:* Any nonaversive interaction, verbal or nonverbal, that cannot clearly be scored in another category above. This can be conversation and description or nonverbal as in exchanging an object with the child.

9. *Social Attention-Aversive:* The same as social attention above except that it is presented aversively as defined by negative, angry, or irritated tone of voice or by a clear hostile gesture toward the child.

Child Behavior Categories (6 categories)

1. *Noncompliance:* Fails to initiate compliance with a specific instruction within 5 seconds but without verbal refusal.

2. *Defiance/Refusal:* Child verbally refuses to obey a command or instruction, such as saying "No!", or "I am not going to do it!", or "I won't!".

3. *Complains:* Any instance of verbal complaining involving whining, screaming, crying, or displays of temper that do not include verbal refusal or an aversive command (below).

4. *Aversive Commands:* Any instance of instruction directed toward another person by the child that is judged to be aversive, unpleasant, or demanding in tone of voice. Examples: "You give me that now!", "Fix my dinner!", "I told you to leave me alone!", or "Go away!"

5. *Physical Negative:* Any actual or threatened (gesture) physical attack or damage to another person or destruction of an object, as in slapping, pinching, punching, hitting, kicking, or scratching, or forcibly throwing an object, stamping or kicking an object, or pounding an object with one's fist.

6. *Other Negative:* Any other inappropriate behavior that cannot be classified above, such as teasing or taunting another, humiliating or insulting someone, swearing, violating a family rule, or deliberately ignoring someone.

Note. Adapted from "Marital Discord and Child Behavior Problems: A Description of Family Interactions During Treatment" by M. R. Dadds, M. R. Sanders, and B. C. Behrens, 1987, *Journal of Clinical Child Psychology, 16,* 192–203. Copyright 1987 by Lawrence Erlbaum Associates. Reprinted by permission of the authors and publisher.

ent and child behaviors as a function of parent training in child management (Dadds, Sanders, & Behrens, 1987; Dadds, Schwartz, & Sanders, 1987; Sanders, Dadds, & Bor, 1989). I have chosen to review this coding system over many others used in research, because it is relatively easy to train coders to use, has behavior categories quite relevant to the behavioral constructs of interest to ADHD and oppositional children (maternal and child aggressive/aversive behaviors), has proven convenient for use in home observations, and is sensitive to treatment effects.

Several modifications are recommended to the original system for home application. First, the instructions for coding can be modified such that a 20-second observe/10-second record procedure is employed, rather than the 25-second observe/15-second record method used in the original article. This is done to permit two observation intervals per minute instead of one, thereby increasing the opportunities to record important ongoing behaviors of parent and child. Second, we have made some behavioral categories more specific in their definitions than those provided in the original article, with these amendments taken from the Response Class Matrix (Mash, Terdal, & Anderson, 1973; see Barkley, 1981). And third, we have changed the category of "child noncompliance" such that it is subdivided into active, verbal "defiance/refusal" and the more passive "noncompliance," in which the child fails to initiate compliance but is otherwise not actively vocally resisting direction.

To create a coding form, the clinician can type the 14 behavior codes along the left side of a sheet of paper and create 30 columns across the top to permit 15 minutes of recording on each page. Multiple copies of these pages can be used for lengthier coding sessions. A tape recorder should be used that has an earpiece. A tape is constructed to indicate the beginning of each observe–record interval. For instance, it states "Begin 1" to mark the beginning of the observation period, followed in 20 seconds by the word "Record 1." After 10 seconds, the tape indicates "Begin 2," followed in 20 seconds by "Record 2." The tape follows this sequence repeatedly for up to 90 intervals (45 minutes) or longer as needed.

The home observer, as noted earlier, should make two home visits to a family within a 2-week period. A visit can be scheduled for a time in mid- to late afternoon on a weekday, typically following the child's return home from any school program. The observation can last for 60 to 90 minutes each visit and should be subdivided into a 15- to 45-minute observation of natural interactions as they happen in the home and three structured 15-minute situations, each coded separately. Upon arrival, the observer should instruct the mother in the procedures to be followed in the four situations to be observed. The observer can then find a place within the home from which to conveniently view the family's activities while remaining as unobtrusive as possible.

For "unstructured time," mothers can be asked to carry out their routine activities with the following restrictions: Television, outgoing phone calls, and visitors will not be allowed, and incoming calls will be briefly handled. Mother and child can be asked to remain within sight of the observer. This can last 15 to 45 minutes. For "interactive play," the mother can be asked to play for 15 minutes with the child (using toys, a board game, or an activity of the child's choosing) and remain within one room of the home (e.g., family room, living room, kitchen). For "academic homework" the mother can be given a packet of math problems, selected to be below the child's math grade level from the Wide Range Achievement Test—Revised (WRAT-R). The mother is to instruct the child to come and sit at the kitchen table and do the packet of math problems. We have constructed six different levels of math packets with four different yet equivalent sets at each difficulty level for use in our clinic playroom or for home observation. As an alternative, one might construct a lengthy version of the Coding subtest from the WISC-R (Wechsler, 1974), as this would eliminate any interference with task performance due to poor or limited math ability. This situation can last 15 minutes. Finally, during "chore performance," the mother can be given a list of five commands similar to the ones we have mothers use in our clinic observations (see "Observations of Mother-Child Interactions during Tasks," above). Other commands may be used that are specific to the home setting (e.g., the child must help the mother set the table in preparation for dinner that evening). This situation can also last 15 minutes.

At the end of the observation period, a wealth of clinically useful information will have been obtained about the mother's and child's style of interacting with each other, skills in negotiating cooperative tasks and conflicts, and extent of negative or coercive behaviors that each may employ in their interactions. This information can then serve as the basis for tailoring standard parent training or family therapy programs (see Chapters 12 to 14) to the characteristics of this particular family, or for making recommendations to other social service agencies that may be involved with this family. The behavioral coding system can also be repeated periodically for assessing change in these parent-child interactions as a function of treatment.

Advantages and Limitations of Behavioral Observations

The use of direct observational procedures—recording behavior in the natural environment or in analogue settings structured to elicit behaviors representative of those occurring outside of the clinic—can overcome many of the limitations described above for laboratory measures. Such observations, especially when taken in the natural environment, involve a far lower level of inference in interpreting their findings and often use categories or dimensions of behavior that more closely approximate the behaviors of concern to referring agents (e.g., parents and teachers) than do laboratory tests. Of course, the ecological validity of clinic-based analogue observations must be established empirically by demonstrating their relationship to behavior in natural environments. Observational measures are also quite valuable in monitoring behavioral changes elicited by both drug and behavioral interventions.

Certain limitations do exist with these measures, however. Many variables of research interest may not be readily translated into easily codable categories (e.g., anxiety, low self-esteem, locus of control) or may not have standard coding systems developed for them. Moreover, where coding systems already exist, some necessitate extensive training in the use of relatively complex behavioral categories, thus limiting their utility for most practitioners. Furthermore, the resources necessary to use such observational systems in clinic settings, (e.g., observation mirrors, trained behavioral coders, videotaping equipment) may limit their widespread clinical use.

Analogue observations may be particularly limited in their representativeness by factors such as the artificiality of the clinic setting. A further problem arises from the lack of adequate normative data for most of these measures, making them somewhat less useful for determining the statistical deviance of child behaviors necessary in rendering a diagnosis. The development of local norms through the assessment of clinic-referred and matched controls might be one way of counteracting this limitation.

In the classroom one could employ a method of yoked controls, wherein an average child in the ADHD child's classroom is also observed and used as a comparison standard against which to judge the deviance of the ADHD child's behavior. Of course, variability across school settings would make such standardization very difficult; however, it is not impossible, especially given the success of the CBCL-DOF in doing so. However, for adolescents, the problem is considerably more complex. The fact that middle and high school students spend relatively short periods of time (45 to 60 minutes) in multiple classrooms with multiple teachers on a daily basis, not to mention the potentially greater risk of social stigma from such observations, makes direct observations of these age groups of students almost impossible.

Finally, systematic behavioral observations can lead to reactivity effects, in which the process of observing itself leads to changes in the subject's behaviors, so that they are not as representative of the subject's typical behaviors in that setting. While this can be limited to some degree by making the observation process as unobtrusive as possible, it can never be completely eliminated and must be weighed in the final interpretation of any such behavioral data.

Despite these limitations, direct and systematic behavioral observations can often provide information that is quite valuable in delineating target behaviors for treatment, that is not easily obtainable through other means, and that is less subject to the biases plaguing more traditional interview or rating scale methods of assessment. While a diagnosis of ADHD should never be based solely on this type of information, these behavioral observations—when combined with parent, child, and teacher interviews and rating scales—can add greater validity, integrity, and rigor to the clinical diagnostic process than could these other sources of information alone.

COST-EFFECTIVENESS OF CLINICAL ASSESSMENTS

One often overlooked issue in evaluating ADHD children is the typically exorbitant expense the families and/or insurance carriers have to bear for these evaluations. Professionals may become quite cavalier in this regard when insurance coverage or other third-party reimbursement is available to families, sometimes racking up expenses that can total over $1,000 for information that is of little incremental utility beyond that obtained from parent and teacher interviews and several child behavior rating scales. Care should be taken to select only those procedures that are likely to yield information *not* already available through other means, that have incremental value (i.e., they contribute directly to the decisions that must be made about the child), and yet that do not exceed the means of the family. Using up a child's entire annual mandated insurance benefits for mental health within a single assessment will preclude that child from readily obtaining the mental health treatments that may be needed subsequently. It is my experience that approximately 3 to 4 hours are more than adequate to evaluate the typical ADHD child. (This figure does not include the time that may be required to do more extensive assessment of learning disabilities or neuropsychological functioning in the minority of cases where this may be indicated, or to conduct classroom or home observations where these are deemed appropriate and feasible.)

Professionals who are operating outside of public school systems are professionally and ethically obligated to inform families of the availability of psychometric evaluations of intelligence, achievement, speech and language, and motor development for free through their local public school under Public Law 94-142. Some parents may be ignorant of their right to this resource and should be informed about this service at the time of their referral. Others may choose not to avail themselves of this service because of the frequent delays (up to 90 days) in obtaining such evaluations, or because they wish to have complete control over the information that is revealed in the assessment. Some parents are in fact seeking a second opinion to that provided in the public school's evaluation of their children. In any case, parents should always be provided with the information on how to obtain these public school assessments.

11

Integrating the Results of an Evaluation: Six Clinical Cases

> The improvement of the understanding is for two ends;
> first, our own increase of knowledge; secondly, to enable
> us to deliver that knowledge to others.
>
> —JOHN LOCKE (1632–1704)

In this chapter, I present the results of six actual clinical cases seen at the Clinic for Attention-deficit Hyperactivity Disorder (ADHD) at the University of Massachusetts Medical Center. These cases have been chosen to represent the most common disorders likely to present to such a clinic: ADHD alone; ADHD with Oppositional Defiant Disorder (ODD); ADHD with ODD and Conduct Disorder (CD); ADHD with mood/thinking disorder; Attention Deficit Disorder without Hyperactivity (ADD/−H); and learning disability (LD) without ADHD. The cases have been chosen to illustrate the type of evaluations conducted in our clinic and to demonstrate the manner in which information is integrated to result in both a clinical diagnosis (or multiple diagnoses) and treatment recommendations.

Our clinic utilizes a multimethod, multi-informant assessment approach like that recommended in the foregoing chapters on assessment. First, it incorporates a diagnostic interview with the parents, a brief interview with the child, and a telephone interview with the child's primary teacher (see Chapter 8). As part of this interview, the revised Vineland Adaptive Behavior Scale is sometimes employed where there is an indication from the developmental history or current behavioral status that the child may be significantly below his or her chronological age level in the areas of adaptive functioning assessed by this structured interview (Socialization, Communication, and Daily Living domains).

Parents also complete the Child Behavior Checklist (CBCL), the Home Situations Questionnaire (HSQ), and the Conners Parent Rating Scale—Revised (CPRS-R), discussed in Chapter 9. Parents are typically also requested to complete the Locke-Wallace Marital Adjustment Test (MAT), as a quick screen for potential marital disharmony, and the Symptom Checklist 90—Revised (SCL-90-R), as a screening scale for parental personal distress and psychopathology. We have recently added the Parenting Stress Index as an additional parent self-report measure in our clinical evaluations, but this was not available for those cases described below. All of these parent self-report scales are described in Chapter 9. Teachers are requested to complete the Teacher Report Form of the Child Behavior Checklist (CBCL-TRF), the Child Attention Problems scale (CAP), the ADHD Rating Scale, the School Situations Questionnaire (SSQ), and the Conners Teacher Rating Scale—Revised (CTRS-R), all of which are discussed in Chapter 9. The parent and teacher Conners scales are not used for diagnosis, as they are redundant with the CBCL parent and teacher scales. Instead, we use these initial Conners ratings as a baseline score in case the child may begin a course of medication treatment, in which the Conners scales will be used as repeated measures across treatment weeks.

Up to 30 percent of the children evaluated in our clinic are administered the Wechsler Intelligence Scale for Children—Revised (WISC-R) and the Wide Range Achievement Test—Revised (WRAT-R), where a suspicion exists that the children may have a coexisting LD in addition to their behavioral problems, or where parents or school staff wish to have a brief assessment of the children's current academic achievement status. We do not consider this a comprehensive assessment of LD, but a screening for major areas of academic deficiencies, which can then be followed up with more extensive academic and neuropsychological testing, as needed.

At the time these cases were seen, all of the children in our ADHD clinic were administered the vigilance test from the Gordon Diagnostic System and Kagan's Matching Familiar Figures Test (MFFT). We no longer employ the latter test because of its poor and often unreliable sensitivity to problems of impulsivity in ADHD children. Children were also observed while performing math problems alone in a furnished clinic playroom, known as the Restricted Academic Situation. All of these procedures have been described in Chapter 10.

Many of the children evaluated at our center receive a pediatric examination, particularly where it appears that a trial of medication is likely to be subsequently recommended. This procedure has been discussed in Chapter 8.

CASE 1: ADHD ALONE

John, aged 9, was referred to our clinic by his parents for an evaluation of possible ADHD. He had been previously diagnosed as having ADD by a university hospital clinic in a nearby state, and had been treated with *d*-amphetamine (Dexedrine). His parents were seeking a second evaluation in order to determine the current status and severity of John's ADHD symptoms after several years of various therapies, and, more importantly, to provide advice on educational interventions for John in his current school district.

The parental interview and medical examination revealed that John was the product of a problematic pregnancy and was born approximately 1 month prematurely. He was described as an extremely active baby *in utero*. Delivery was uncomplicated; however, he went into respiratory distress several minutes after delivery and was in critical condition for 8 or 9 days. It was presumed at the time that he had contracted a lung infection. John was colicky as an infant and exhibited projectile vomiting. He also experienced some difficulties establishing a sleep pattern, as he was described as "needing a lot of movement." His infant and early childhood temperament was reported to be somewhat more difficult than average. Developmental milestones such as walking, speech, and bowel and bladder control were all achieved at typical ages.

John's medical status was essentially normal at the time of the referral. He experienced some mild color blindness as well as poor fine and gross motor skills. He had no significant history of accidental poisoning, head injuries, lead poisoning, surgery, significant illnesses, or hospitalization. He had been treated with *d*-amphetamine at 5 milligrams (mg) once per day for 6 months in the year prior to the current evaluation. His parents described significant behavioral improvements from the medication, but questioned its possible growth suppression effects, since there had been a significant reduction in John's appetite at noontime with the medication. More recently, and more briefly, John had been placed on methylphenidate (Ritalin) to determine whether it would produce fewer anorexic effects. John initially received 5 mg twice daily, which was increased to 7.5 mg twice daily. He reportedly became quite "spacey," staring excessively, and his ADHD symptoms were actually exacerbated. He was not returned to any medication at this point and remained off medication for his evaluation at our clinic.

John was the oldest child in the family and resided with his biological parents and a younger sister who was 6 years of age. His father was college-educated and worked in real estate, while his mother had a master's degree in speech and language therapy and worked within this field. The parents reported some marital difficulties at the time of this evaluation. A review of the family psychiatric history indicated that the mother believed that she and her sister probably had had significant attention deficits without hyperactivity as children, and that both had LD. Her father did not graduate from high school, and her mother had experienced episodes of depression that lasted longer than 2 weeks. Although uncertain, there was the suggestion that her sister had experienced a Somatization Disorder. John's father reported that he had probably had ADHD as a child and that his own father had been quite aggressive, defiant, and stubborn, especially during childhood. His father had also experienced alcohol abuse sufficient to interfere with his daily functioning. John's sister was said to be developing well, with no evidence of psychiatric disorder.

John was currently attending a fourth-grade program and had been receiving special educational services for half of his school day through an LD placement over the past 3 years. Both the parent and teacher interviews indicated that these educational services were focusing primarily on organizational skills, reading instruction, and fine motor skills. John had also been receiving speech and language therapy for the past several months. Previously, John had received therapy through an occupational therapist and adaptive physical education because of his gross and fine motor delays. An earlier neurological evaluation when John was 5 years old had indicated evidence of ADHD as well as significant fine and gross motor incoordination. A special educational evaluation at age 6 years revealed average intelligence, with above-average verbal abilities and normal spatial-mechanical (nonverbal) skills. John had not received any individual, family, or group therapy.

In a review of symptoms of various childhood psychiatric disorders, John's parents reported that he had exhibited problems with inattentive, distractible, impulsive, and restless behavior since 4 or 5 years of age. They endorsed 9 of the 14 symptoms of ADHD as being developmentally inappropriate. John's teacher reported similar difficulties in school at the time of this evaluation. John was also reported to exhibit negative emotional reactions to parental discipline or reprimands, but his parents felt that these were secondary to his frustration with learning in school and to his ADHD characteristics. The parents were quite concerned about John's low self-esteem as a result of his failure experiences in school. John did not meet criteria for any other psychiatric disorder, including ODD, CD, affective or anxiety disorders, or difficulties with thinking. Although no motor or vocal tics were reported for John, his parent CBCL indicated a repetitive yawning movement with his lower jaw that appeared to be a nervous mannerism. There was no evidence of any psychosocial stressors acting upon John at the present time, although it was not clear to what extent his parents' marital difficulties might be affecting his behavioral adjustment.

Our interview with John found him to be a polite, handsome young man who sat throughout the interview, but frequently looked about the office and seemed more interested in materials on the office wall and bookshelf than in the interview topics. He was somewhat fidgety while seated, though not overly active. He described a close relationship with both his parents and his younger sister, but felt that the sister often came into his room uninvited and took his toys for play without permission. He felt that his only difficulties at home were in getting homework accomplished, which he hated. His view of school was that the work was boring and some of it was quite difficult for him, especially reading and writing. He felt that he was not as smart as the other children in school, nor could he play sports as well as the other boys. His view of school was that it was hopeless to try to finish his work because he never had adequate time. He had one close friend with whom he played at recess; he would like to have others, yet his efforts to get them to play with him were often spurned.

The pediatric medical exam revealed a child of average height and weight for age. Vision and hearing were normal. Cranial nerves were grossly intact.

Muscle tone was normal in all extremities, as were deep tendon reflexes. John evidenced mild awkwardness at tandem gait testing and heel walking, with some arm posturing being evident. Mild motor impersistence was apparent. There was clumsiness in finger opposition testing. John was quite impulsive in executing tasks from the brief mental status exam. Penmanship was immature and poorly organized. Drawing and copying of geometric designs were executed hastily and with many minor errors. Digit span was average, but simple mental calculation of arithmetic problems seemed mildly delayed. Throughout the exam, John was quite active and fidgety, asking numerous questions about the procedures and talking incessantly. The conclusion was of a child of normal health with no specific neurological abnormalities but with evidence of neuromaturational immaturity.

The results of the parent and teacher rating scales, psychological testing, and behavioral observations are shown in Table 11.1. Results from the parent-completed CBCL indicated significant elevations in hyperactive, inattentive, and impulsive behavior (the Hyperactive scale), as well as difficulties with peer relationships (the Social Withdrawal scale). A significant elevation on the Depressed scale corroborated the parents' reports in the interview of concerns related to John's increasingly poor self-esteem. There was no indication of significant conduct disturbance, aggressive behavior, somatic complaints, or anxiety disturbance. John's clinically significant score on the scale labeled Obsessive-Compulsive is typically seen in ADHD children; it reflected parental concerns about John's frequent staring, daydreaming, excessive talking, and sleep problems. All of these difficulties exceeded the 96th percentile for John's age and sex.

The HSQ ratings indicated behavioral problems with John that were mild and involved five situations in the home; the most difficult of these occurred when John was asked to do homework. Ratings on the CPRS-R indicated

TABLE 11.1. Assessment Results for a Case of ADHD in a 9-Year-Old Boy

CBCL-Parent		CBCL-TRF	
Scale	Percentile	Scale	Percentile
Anxious-Schizoid	91	Anxious	69
Depressed	96*	Social Withdrawal	95*
Uncommunicative	91	Unpopular	87
Obsessive-Compulsive	99*	Obsessive-Compulsive	96*
Somatic Complaints	80	Self-Destructive	80
Social Withdrawal	99*	Inattentive	97*
Hyperactive	99*	Nervous-Overactive	97*
Aggressive	82	Aggressive	69
Delinquent	69		

HSQ		SSQ	
Number of problem settings: 5		Number of problem settings: 3	
Mean severity rating: 2.2		Mean severity rating: 3.4	

CPRS-R

Factor	Raw score
Conduct Problems	4
Psychosomatic	1
Anxiety	3
Impulsive-Hyperactive	7*
Learning Problems	8*
Index	12

Vineland Adaptive Behavior Scale

Domain	Standard score
Communication	66*
Daily Living	70*
Socialization	83

WISC-R

Subtest	Scale score
Information	14
Similarities	15
Arithmetic	8
Vocabulary	17
Comprehension	13
Digit Span	10
Picture Completion	17
Picture Arrangement	10
Block Design	14
Object Assembly	10
Coding	9

Verbal IQ:	113
Performance IQ:	113
Full Scale IQ:	114

CTRS-R

Factor	Raw score
Conduct Problems	10
Inattentive-Passive	20*
Hyperactive	17*
Index	8

ADHD Rating Scale (Teacher)

Total score: 32*

Number of symptoms rated >2: 10*

CAP

Factor	Percentile
Inattention	98*
Overactivity	98*

WRAT-R

Subtest	Percentile
Reading	16
Spelling	14
Arithmetic	47

Gordon vigilance test

Number correct: 35*
Number of omissions: 10*
Number of commissions: 23*

MFFT

Mean time to respond: 7.5 seconds
Number incorrect: 17*

Restricted Academic Situation

Behavior	Percent occurrence
Off task	87*
Fidgets	73*
Vocalizes	28
Plays with objects	8
Out of seat	16
Math problems done (*n*)	29*
Math accuracy (%)	91

Note. CBCL, Child Behavior Checklist; CBCL-TRF, Child Behavior Checklist—Teacher Report Form; HSQ, Home Situations Questionnaire; SSQ, School Situations Questionnaire; CPRS=R, Conners Parent Rating Scale—Revised; CTRS-R, Conners Teacher Rating Scale—Revised; CAP, Child Attention Problems; WRAT-R, Wide Range Achievement Test—Revised; MFFT, Matching Familiar Figures Test. An asterisk indicates a clinically significant elevation (>95th percentile or <5th percentile).

clinically significant scores only on the Impulsive-Hyperactive and Learning Problems factors. As others have noted, the Conners Hyperactivity Index (see Appendix A) is heavily weighted with items reflecting aggression and conduct problems, and has only four items that load on the Impulsive-Hyperactive factor. Hence, the Index is less likely to detect cases of pure ADHD as opposed to mixed ADHD-ODD.

Teacher ratings for John on the CBCL-TRF revealed clinically significant levels (greater than 97th percentile) on the Inattentive, Nervous-Overactive, Social Withdrawal, and again the Obsessive-Compulsive scales. The last-mentioned scale elevation was primarily the result of frequent staring and confusion or mental fogginess, as was also noted on the parent CBCL, rather than significant neurotic symptoms. Teacher ratings on the SSQ fell within the normal range but did point to mild difficulties with behavior during class lectures, individual deskwork, and special assemblies. On the CTRS-R, John received clinically significant scores only on the Inattentive-Passive and Hyperactive factors, but not on other factors. Teacher ratings on the ADHD Rating Scale, which assesses the DSM-III-R symptoms of ADHD, showed that 10 of 14 symptoms were given scores of 2 or higher ("pretty much" or "very much"), which would be considered developmentally inappropriate for age and sufficient for a diagnosis of ADHD. John's scores on the CAP, which we use to differentiate ADD/−H from ADHD, indicated significant elevations on both the Overactivity and Inattention items. Our conclusion, then, was that John most likely had a case of ADHD in which all of the hyperactive symptoms were developmentally deviant but in which problems with aggression or oppositional behavior were not clinically significant.

John's teacher also completed the Academic Performance Rating Scale (APRS; see Chapter 9), which indicated that John was performing his math work at school with 80 to 100% accuracy but only 40% productivity. The accuracy of written language assignments was somewhat lower, falling between 60 and 80%, while productivity was again below the 60% level. John's neatness was rated as often poor. Such findings of low productivity scores in the face of higher accuracy levels are common in ADHD. The somewhat lower accuracy score in language arts probably reflected John's demonstrated LD in this area.

John was administered the WISC-R and WRAT-R, and these results also appear in Table 11.1. John's Full Scale IQ (114) fell within the above-average range, as did his Verbal and Performance IQ scores. They represented a significant increase in intellectual estimates over those average scores achieved at testing several years earlier. This improvement may have been due to both the use of stimulant medication and the special educational services provided to him over the past few years. No significant areas of weakness were apparent on any subtest scores. Scores on the WRAT-R suggested significant discrepancies between intellectual estimates and academic achievement in reading and spelling: His Reading score was at the 16th percentile, and his Spelling score was at the 14th percentile. These scores were consistent with DSM-III-

R criteria for Specific Developmental Disabilities in reading and spelling. Arithmetic performance fell within the normal range at the 47th percentile.

Parental responses to the Vineland Adaptive Behavior Scale indicated significant discrepancies between John's adaptive skills and his intellectual ability. John fell below the 3rd percentile for age in the Communication and Daily Living domains, and fell below the 15th percentile in Socialization. Such discrepancies are common in ADHD children, who possess the intellectual capability needed for normal adaptive performance, but whose ADHD symptoms are likely to interfere with daily demonstrations of these capacities.

John exhibited consistent problems with attention to task and poor impulse control during several of the objective measures of these symptoms. On the Gordon Diagnostic System vigilance test, his total correct score fell within abnormal limits, as did his score for the number of omission errors. However, his errors of commission were considerably more frequent, reflecting serious problems with impulsivity. Performance on the MFFT also reflected a fast, inaccurate pattern of responding, indicative of cognitive impulsivity. John's score for number incorrect was above the 97th percentile for his age; this is considered to be a clinically significant elevation. John was then observed for 15 minutes while he performed math problems selected to be well within his arithmetic ability level. During this Restricted Academic Situation, John was observed to be off task 89% of the time. Scores for a small sample ($n = 36$) of normal children in our clinic indicate an average off-task performance of 47% ($SD = 20$). John was also noted to be significantly fidgety, displaying this behavior during at least 73% of the observation period. Again, we have found normal children to average 27% ($SD = 25$) for this behavioral code. In addition, John was able to complete only 29 of these simple math problems during this time, although his accuracy rate was 91%. Most children in John's age group are able to complete over 100 simple math problems during this same time period. This difficulty in completing independent math work despite normal math achievement (see WRAT-R scores above) and a normal accuracy score (91%) indicates that the major problem for John was the interference of his inattentiveness with the demands of this independent task, not a problem with math skills.

The rating scales completed by the parents about themselves and their marriage revealed several clinically significant bits of information. First, the score of 50 on the Locke-Wallace MAT was considerably below the cutoff score of 84 or lower used to signify dysfunctional marriages, indicating severe marital disharmony. And second, the mother's ratings about herself on the SCL-90-R showed that she endorsed 46 items at a mean of 1.5 (range 0 to 4). The pattern of these responses suggested mild yet potentially significant elevations of scales related to depression, and to a lesser degree anxiety and interpersonal problems. The father's ratings of himself on the SCL-90-R indicated no significant clinical elevations on any scales.

Our clinical impression from these multiple sources of information was that John was a 9-year-old boy with a chronic history of difficulties with inattention, impulsiveness, and restlessness, as well as academic achievement problems. John's hyperactivity was considered mild relative to that of most ADHD children; it consisted primarily of restlessness rather than significant gross motor overactivity, such as moving about a room frequently, climbing on things, and frequently being out of seat when asked to remain seated. His inattention and impulsivity were far more deviant. John manifested a sufficient number and severity of symptoms to warrant a diagnosis of ADHD. His behavioral symptoms had developed at approximately 4 to 5 years of age, and so he also met the criteria for age of onset and duration of symptoms for this diagnosis. We also concluded that John carried an additional diagnosis of Specific Developmental Reading Disorder (an LD), as reflected in his poor reading and spelling performances.

Many recommendations were made to the family; they are very briefly summarized below:

1. Education of the parents via reading materials, a clinical videotape, and one to two sessions of counseling concerning the nature of ADHD, its course, and its outcome. Referral to our local parents' support association for ADHD children was also made. Chapter 12 describes this type of counseling and its goals.

2. A return to the use of *d*-amphetamine at a low dose with closer monitoring of height and weight gain, use of the medication only on school days, and greater attention to calorie intake for John at home; otherwise, a trial on methylphenidate at a higher dose than that tried previously. John had only been on this medication for 3 days at a low dose. It is not uncommon for children to have mild side effects on initial introduction to this medication, which dissipate within 14 days. Also, research suggests that some children may be mildly exacerbated by low doses but display significant behavioral improvement at moderate to higher doses. We recommended a double-blind, placebo-controlled trial of three dose levels (5, 10, and 15 mg twice daily) if methylphenidate were to be tried again. See Chapter 17 for a description of this procedure.

3. Continued placement within the LD program at school, with additional modifications to deal with John's ADHD symptoms. A consultation was scheduled with John's teacher to discuss a number of recommendations like those described in Chapter 15.

4. Short-term training of the parents (four sessions) in several child behavior management methods found useful in assisting ADHD children with compliance and chore performance at home. Several sessions of the parent training program described in Chapters 12 and 13 were adapted for this family. It was not felt that they required more extensive parent training, as John did not have significant oppositional or defiant behavior—unlike many ADHD children, for which the more extended versions of parent training are intended.

5. Development of a home-based reinforcement program for school performance, using a daily school behavior report card (see Chapter 15).

6. Brief family follow-up visits after the parents' completion of parent training, every 3 months for the subsequent year and then every 6 months or as needed thereafter. John's medication would, of course, be monitored by his pediatrician on a more frequent basis.

7. Short-term marital therapy to assist the parents with clarifying and addressing the current issues within their marriage that were proving problematic.

8. Additional individual therapy for John's mother to address her mild but signifiant personal psychological distress.

We often find that such recommendations for parents to receive treatment for themselves occur in 30 to 50% of our clinical referrals. This is hardly surprising, in view of the significant familial genetic relationships in many psychiatric disorders, and specifically ADHD. Such parents are likely to be continuing to struggle with their own ADHD symptoms in some cases or with affective or marital difficulties in others.

CASE 2: ADHD WITH OPPOSITIONAL DEFIANT DISORDER

Larry, aged 7 years and 11 months, was referred to our clinic by his mother for assessment of problems related to inattentive, impulsive, and restless behavior. Larry resided with his biological parents and four siblings, who were considerably older than he, ranging in age from 20 to 28 years. His mother was 47 and his father was 35 years of age. This was his mother's second marriage, with these older children having come from her first marriage. Larry attended a second-grade program in school, with special placement in a program for behavior-disordered children for most of the school day.

Larry's difficulties with ADHD behaviors reportedly developed between 3 and 4 years of age. In addition, his mother complained of difficulties with Larry's interactions with other children: He was quite overcontrolling of others, to the point where few children chose to play with him any more. The pregnancy was complicated only by the mother's use of cigarettes (one pack per day) and very occasional alcohol use. His medical history indicated that he had experienced chronic ear infections and a bout of pneumonia before 1 year of age, requiring two separate hospitalizations for treatment. He also had asthma in early childhood, but this appeared to be less troublesome for him now. Between 3 and 4 years of age, he had been afflicted with scarlet fever. Developmental milestones were all achieved within normal age ranges. Larry was described as an unusually active baby and toddler who could be very insistent about his demands on others. He had not been treated with stimulant medication or any psychological services prior to this evaluation, except for his special educational placement beginning 1 year earlier. Larry had been suspended from school twice because of fighting with other students.

During a review of childhood psychiatric symptoms, Larry's mother endorsed 11 of 14 ADHD symptoms as being developmentally inappropriate. She also reported him to have six of the nine symptoms of ODD to a significant degree for his age, including frequent temper outbursts, arguing with adults, often deliberately annoying others, blaming others for his own mistakes, and frequently refusing to obey adult requests or rules (primarily with his mother). No symptoms of CD were endorsed, nor did Larry meet criteria for any other childhood psychiatric condition.

The family psychiatric history was significant on the maternal side: One of the mother's brothers had been significantly aggressive as a child; another brother had experienced LD in school; and her father, two brothers, and a sister had all failed to graduate from high school. One brother had also experienced a bout of depression lasting longer than 2 weeks. This same brother had been alcoholic and had been arrested once for antisocial behavior. On the father's side of the family, it was reported that he had been significantly aggressive and oppositional as a child, was frequently truant from school, and hated to attend it. He failed to graduate from high school, but later obtained a General Equivalency Diploma (GED). Larry's father's mother might have experienced problems with anxiety sufficient to impair daily functioning, but the father was uncertain of this. He mentioned that his own father had engaged in antisocial behavior, such as thefts and assaults on others. The four older siblings of Larry's immediate family also had a higher-than-normal rate of psychiatric problems. One brother had been seriously defiant and aggressive in childhood, had many symptoms characteristic of ADHD as well as LD, and failed to graduate from high school. This brother also had problems with antisocial conduct. A second brother also failed to graduate from high school, had problems with alcohol and substance abuse, and had engaged in antisocial behavior sufficient to result in several arrests. A sister also failed to complete high school but did obtain a GED later. Such a family psychiatric history is not uncommon in ADHD children manifesting ODD, and places them at high risk for later CD.

The telephone interview with Larry's teacher revealed that she had significant concerns about his aggressive behavior toward other children and his outright defiance of her authority in the classroom. She also noted problems with inattention, impulsivity, and restless, overactive behavior, but felt that these were less impairing of his current class adjustment than was his aggressive, oppositional behavior. Larry was said to have no friends at school and to be considered a bully, even within a class for children with serious behavioral problems. She felt that he might have significant academic achievement delays, but this was difficult to determine because of his refusal to do even the simplest of assignments. Distinguishing which academic problems were due to a disability and which to his defiance was quite problematic.

Throughout the brief child interview with Larry, he was quite fidgety and restless, moving about the examiner's office and exploring various toys and office equipment. His answers were often given quickly and without reflection. He reported having no problems at home of which he was aware, but complained that his older siblings frequently picked on him, fought with him, and teased him. He also described frequent verbal arguments between his parents, as well as being yelled at often for not doing what he was told at home. At school, he reported that he had numerous friends but disliked going to school nonetheless. He complained of being punished often at school, but that this was due to other children's teasing him, pushing him, or taking his things. He felt he was performing normally in his schoolwork, in striking contrast to his teacher's reports of both poor academic work and social rejection by his peers. As with many ADHD children, Larry's self-awareness appeared quite limited, and he viewed many of his difficulties as being the result of others' intrusions on him.

The pediatric medical examination conducted by our consulting staff pediatrician revealed a well-developed child of average height but at the 90th percentile in weight. General examination was unremarkable. Hearing and vision were normal. Neurodevelopmental examination was notable for some choreiform movements of the upper extremities and marked motor overflow with synkinesia on rapid alternating movements. There was some arm posturing during tandem gait testing. Cranial nerves were intact. Muscle strength and tone were normal, but there was evidence of motor impersistence. Brief mental status testing revealed problems with digit span and left-right discrimination. Copying of geometric designs was done impulsively and with significant careless mistakes. He was quite fidgety and talkative throughout the exam, asking many questions unrelated to the matters at hand. The conclusion was that Larry had a "classic" case of ADHD, with evidence of neurodevelopmental immaturity but no specific gross neurological abnormality. The need to explore further for possible LD was noted in view of poor performance in drawing and copying skills, digit span, and right-left discrimination.

The results of the parent and teacher rating scales and psychological testing are shown in Table 11.2. Larry's mother completed the CBCL, which indicated clinically significant problems on the Hyperactive, Aggressive, Delinquent, Social Withdrawal, and Obsessive-Compulsive scales (all above the 97th percentile). Again, elevation on the last scale was due to frequent daydreaming, sleep problems, and excessive speech as well as tiredness. On the HSQ, Larry was rated as being significantly problematic in 8 of 14 situations with a mean severity score of 5.9, placing him above the 95th percentile in the severity score. His scores on the CPRS-R were clinically significant on the Impulsive-Hyperactive, Learning Problems, and Psychosomatic factors. The score on the Conduct Problems factor exceeded the 93rd percentile, being of borderline clinical significance. Like that of many ADHD-ODD children, Larry's Hyperactivity Index score was significantly elevated above the 97th percentile.

Teacher ratings also revealed significant behavioral problems in a number of areas. On the CBCL-TRF, Larry obtained scores in the clinically significant range on the Inattentive, Nervous-Overactive, Aggressive, Obsessive-Compulsive, and Unpopular scales, as well as scores above the 80th percentile on the Social Withdrawal and Self-Destructive scales. Larry reportedly posed problems for his teacher in 8 of 12 school situations on the SSQ, with a severity rating quite beyond that seen in normal children. He had clinically elevated scores on all of the CTRS-R factor scores, and scored above the 98th percentile on both the Inattention and Overactivity scales of the CAP. Larry's teacher endorsed 13 of 14 ADHD symptoms on the ADHD Rating Scale as being developmentally inappropriate (scores of 2 or higher). On the APRS, teacher ratings indicated that Larry completed less than 40 percent of his assigned work in math and language arts and that his accuracy rate was below 60% on most assignments. His approach to work was careless, impul-

TABLE 11.2. Results for A Case of Mixed ADHD and ODD in a 7-Year-Old Boy

| CBCL-Parent | | CBCL-TRF | |
Scale	Percentile	Scale	Percentile
Anxious-Schizoid	80	Anxious	69
Depressed	91	Social Withdrawal	94
Uncommunicative	92	Unpopular	95*
Obsessive-Compulsive	99*	Obsessive-Compulsive	98*
Somatic Complaints	71	Self-Destructive	84
Social Withdrawal	99*	Inattentive	99*
Hyperactive	99*	Nervous-Overactive	95*
Aggressive	99*	Aggressive	95*
Delinquent	97*		

HSQ		SSQ	
Number of problem settings: 8		Number of problem settings: 8	
Mean severity rating: 5.9*		Mean severity rating: 5.8*	

| CPRS-R | | CTRS-R | |
Factor	Raw score	Factor	Raw score
Conduct Problems	13	Conduct Problems	14*
Psychosomatic	10*	Inattentive-Passive	18*
Anxiety	4	Hyperactive	19*
Impulsive-Hyperactive	11*	Index	22*
Learning Problems	10*		
Index	15*		

| Vineland Adaptive Behavior Scale | | ADHD Rating Scale (Teacher) | |
| | | Total score: 39* | |
Domain	Standard score	Number of symptoms rated >2: 13*	
Communication	90	CAP	
Daily Living	77*	Factor	Percentile
Socialization	77*		
		Inattention	98*
		Overactivity	98*

WISC-R			WRAT-R	
Subtest	Scale score		Subtest	Percentile
Information	11		Reading	14
Similarities	15		Spelling	2*
Arithmetic	8		Arithmetic	30
Vocabulary	16			
Comprehension	9		Gordon vigilance test	
Digit Span	6		Number correct: 36	
Picture Completion	11		Number of omissions: 9	
Picture Arrangement	12		Number of commissions: 7	
Block Design	12			
Object Assembly	16		MFFT	
Coding	8		Mean time to respond: 15.3 seconds	
			Number incorrect: 20*	

Verbal IQ: 110
Performance IQ: 112
Full Scale IQ: 111

Restricted Academic Situation

Behavior	Percent occurrence
Off task	97*
Fidgets	27
Vocalizes	53*
Plays with objects	63*
Out of seat	23
Math problems done (*n*)	30*
Math accuracy (%)	100

Note. See Table 11.1 for abbreviations. An asterisk indicates a clinically significant elevation (>95th percentile or <5th percentile).

sive, and often poorly organized. In general, Larry manifested significant and pervasive problems with both ADHD and aggressive/oppositional behavior at school.

Larry was found to be functioning within the high-average range of intelligence on the WISC-R. The only significantly low subtest score was found on Digit Span. Scores on the WRAT-R subtests indicated low-average performance in Reading and Arithmetic and significantly impaired performance in Spelling. These achievement scores were significantly lower than those expected for a child of this intellectual ability. These indicated that Larry probably had significant LD, particularly in written language expression and to a somewhat lesser degree in simple word attack skills, besides having ADHD and ODD. The results for the Vineland scale indicated that Larry placed within the lower normal range on the Communication domain but within the impaired range (below the 5th percentile) on the Daily Living and Socialization domains. This pattern is not uncommon for ADHD children and once again shows that despite adequate intellectual skills, these children manifest significant impairments in performance of daily living skills, self-help responsibilities, and social conduct.

Larry's performance on the Gordon Diagnostic System vigilance test was within the normal range on all scores. This was surprising, given his parent and teacher reports of significant inattention and impulse problems; however, this occurs in 20 to 30% of children with ADHD. This false-negative rate indicates that scores on a vigilance test by themselves are not adequate for diagnosing ADHD. Where normal, they may shed little clinical light on whether the child actually has normal or abnormal attention and impulse control. On the MFFT, Larry obtained an error score above the 97th percentile for his age, indicating significant impulsivity. Behavioral observations taken during the Restricted Academic Situation found Larry to be off task 97% of the time, playing with objects and vocalizing over 50% of the time, and completing only 30 math problems within this time limit, far below that completed by most normal children. His accuracy score was 100%, however, for those problems he attempted.

The parents completed rating scales pertaining to their own adjustment. The Locke-Wallace MAT indicated serious marital discord, with a score of only 37 (scores of 84 or lower, as noted earlier, are indicative of marital dysfunction). Neither parent reported significant problems on any scales of the SCL-90-R, with only 10 items being endorsed to a mild degree by the mother and 9 by the father. This seemed somewhat unusual, given their significant marital problems, as well as the family history of psychiatric troubles in most of the siblings and on both sides of the extended family. It might suggest underreporting of personal problems, although this could not be determined simply from the scores themselves.

The results of this evaluation clearly indicated that Larry had ADHD as well as ODD and was experiencing LD in reading and language arts. The ODD symptoms were quite likely related to the family genetic history of conduct problems, combined with significant marital disharmony, family turmoil, and poor child management methods being used at home. The significant intrafamily modeling of antisocial behavior also probably contributed to this child's current levels of aggressive behavior toward others.

The following treatments were recommended for Larry:

1. Education and counseling on the nature of both ADHD and ODD symptoms, their course, and likely outcomes, particularly stressing the high risk of this child for later CD if left untreated. Parents were provided with reading materials and several sessions of counseling on this information, and were also referred to the local parents' support association for ADHD.

2. A 10-week course of child behavior management training, identical to that described in Chapter 12, to help the parents deal with Larry's serious defiant behavior.

3. A trial of methylphenidate. We subsequently assisted Larry's pediatrician in completing a double-blind, placebo-controlled trial of three doses of medication. Consequently, Larry was placed on 7.5 mg of methylphenidate given twice daily and used on both school days and weekends. At this writing, Larry is followed periodically by his private physician for management

of the medication. We have recommended a repetition of the double-blind, placebo-controlled evaluation in 1 year.

4. Continued placement within the behavioral disorders program at school. However, we emphasized the coexisting and significant learning problems noted in our evaluation, and further recommended consultation from the LD program for Larry's teacher so as to address his achievement deficits and not simply his behavioral problems. Larry's current teacher was relatively sophisticated in behavior management methods, but we reviewed with her some of the in-class techniques described in Chapter 15.

5. Marital therapy for the parents through our outpatient clinic, because of the significant marital discord evident in this evaluation.

6. Later, participation by Larry in a social skills training group at our clinic with five other boys of similar age. Many of the methods described in Chapter 16 were employed.

CASE 3: ADHD WITH CONDUCT DISORDER

Sean was a 15-year-old adolescent who had been followed by me for 8 years because of his ADHD and ODD behaviors. He was originally evaluated at age 7 years because of significant problems with completing academic work at school and serious oppositional behavior at home. He was also reported to have been significantly overactive, impulsive, and inattentive. These problems were said to have arisen at about 3 years of age. Sean scored above the 97th percentile on the Impulsive-Hyperactive and Conduct Problems factors of the CPRS-R, and on the Hyperactive and Aggressive scales of the CBCL. He was also rated as posing behavioral problems in 11 settings on the HSO, with a mean severity rating of 5.4. Teacher ratings placed Sean above the 97th percentile on the Nervous-Overactive, Inattentive, and Aggressive scales of the CBCL-TRF and on the comparable scales of the CTRS-R.

At that time, he resided with both of his parents and a sister who had epilepsy, microcephaly, and severe LD. Sean's medical examination at age 7 was completely normal. His developmental and medical history had also been uneventful. Sean was diagnosed then as having both ADHD and ODD. He was found to be of above-average intelligence, with no evidence of significant academic delays or LD. His mother was noted to be mildly depressed, and there was significant marital discord due to the father's marital infidelities as well as his failure to assist with the management of the children.

During the intervening 8 years, Sean and his parents had participated in a variety of psychological and medical therapies for his disorders. In most cases, Sean and his mother attended sessions aimed at managing his oppositional behavior at home; his father's interest in treatment was only occasionally sufficient for him to attend the sessions. Sean had been placed on medication, but remained on it for only 1 month because of significant side effects. His parents had been referred repeatedly for marital counseling, but the father's refusal to attend many of the sessions often led to discontinuation of treatment by the therapist until the father showed sufficient motivation to re-enter treatment. Sean's mother often threatened to separate from the father, but never took steps to do so. In general, the family atmosphere was often tense, bitter, and filled with much arguing among family members. Therapy with our clinic had terminated 3 years prior to this re-evaluation, due to poor parental follow-up on the treatment recommendations.

At the time of this re-evaluation, Sean continued to reside with his parents and sister. He was completing a 10th-grade program at a local high school and was about to be retained in this grade for the coming academic year. Sean was still not receiving any special educational services, despite his serious behavior problems at school, because he did not display any significant LD. In the past 3 years, Sean had been suspended from school seven times and expelled once because of fighting and misconduct at school. He had skipped school on at least eight known occasions. The threat of grade retention, as well as the escalation of arguments at home to physical fights between the father and Sean, had prompted the mother to return to the clinic for further services.

The structured psychiatric interview conducted with Sean's mother found her to endorse 13 of the 14 ADHD symptoms from the DSM-III-R, with only distractibility remaining unendorsed. A total of seven of the nine items for ODD were also endorsed as being significantly problematic, including frequent arguing with adults, refusal to obey, acting touchy and annoyed, swearing, and acting spiteful and vindictive. These problems had existed since at least 3 to 4 years of age and were a major reason for the original referral to our clinic. For the CD items, 8 of the 13 items were described as significant by Sean's mother, including stealing, frequent lying, truancy, deliberate destruction of others' property, forcing his sister to have intercourse with him, using a weapon in a fight at school, often physically fighting with others, and cruelty toward others. Many of these difficulties were reported to have arisen within the past 18 to 24 months. The parents had chosen not to initiate criminal charges against Sean for the rape of his sister, for fear that he would be sent to a juvenile detention facility until he was 18 years of age.

Further inquiry about Sean's conduct revealed that he had engaged in substance abuse, primarily glue sniffing and misuse of other inhalants. By his own report, he was smoking cigarettes frequently and using alcohol occasionally. Sean's mother reported that he had been involved in several incidents of disorderly conduct in the neighborhood but had never been arrested for these. He had, however, been arrested twice, once for shoplifting and once for possession and use of a weapon in a fight with another teenager. Physical fighting with other teens and with Sean's father occurred sporadically but did not lead to police involvement.

The results of the rating scales completed by Sean's mother are shown in Table 11.3. On the CBCL, significant clinical elevations were noted on all scales, with unusually high elevations (greater than 3 standard deviations) on the three Externalizing scales of Delinquent, Aggressive, and Hyperactive. Interestingly, a significant number of symptoms of anxiety were also endorsed on this evaluation. These had not been present to such a degree on initial evaluation; they included frequent worrying, appearing anxious, and numerous somatic complaints (e.g., dizziness, headache, and stomach pains). On the HSQ, Sean was rated as posing management problems in 14 of the 16 settings, with an average rating of 7.1. This is a seriously deviant rating, exceeding the 99th percentile for age in the number and severity of conduct problems at home. All factors on the CPRS-R were also above the 97th percentile. Sean was rated on the Issues Checklist as having significant conflicts with his parents in 21 of the 44 potential conflict areas, with arguments occurring an average of two to three times per week for most of these issues. Both the number of conflicts and anger intensity scores were clinically deviant

TABLE 11.3. Assessment Results for A Case of Mixed ADHD, ODD, and CD in a 15-Year-Old Adolescent

CBCL-Parent		CBCL-TRF
Scale	Percentile	Unavailable
Anxious-Schizoid	99*	
Uncommunicative	99*	
Obsessive-Compulsive	99*	
Somatic Complaints	99*	
Immature	99*	
Hostile-Withdrawal	99*	
Hyperactive	99*	
Aggressive	99*	
Delinquent	99*	

HSQ		SSQ
Number of problem settings:	14*	Unavailable
Mean severity rating: 7.1*		

CPRS-R		CTRS-R
Factor	Raw score	Unavailable
Conduct Problems	23*	
Psychosomatic	6*	
Anxiety	8*	
Impulsive-Hyperactive	12*	
Learning Problems	12*	
Index	27*	

Vineland Adaptive Behavior Scale		ADHD Rating Scale (Parent)
Domain	Standard score	Total score: 40*
		Number of symptoms rated
Communication	105	>2: 13*
Daily Living	77*	CAP
Socialization	87*	Unavailable

(*cont.*)

TABLE 11.3. Assessment Results for A Case of Mixed ADHD, ODD, and CD in a 15-Year-Old Adolescent (*continued*)

WISC-R			WRAT-R	
Subtest	Scale score		Subtest	Percentile
Information	12		Reading	55
Similarities	15		Spelling	56
Arithmetic	9		Arithmetic	47
Vocabulary	16			
Comprehension	9		Gordon vigilance test	
Digit Span	9		Number correct: 42	
Picture Completion	12		Number of omissions: 3	
Picture Arrangement	11		Number of commissions: 7*	
Block Design	13			
Object Assembly	14		MFFT	
Coding	9		Mean time to respond: 8.9 seconds*	
			Number incorrect: 9*	
Verbal IQ: 114				
Performance IQ: 112			Restricted Academic Situation	
Full Scale IQ: 113				Percent
			Behavior	occurrence
			Off task	20*
			Fidgets	23*
			Vocalizes	0
			Plays with objects	0
			Out of seat	0
			Math problems done (*n*)	100
			Math accuracy (%)	95

Note. See Table 11.1 for abbreviations. An asterisk indicates a clinically significant elevation (>95th percentile or <5th percentile).

for age. However, it is necessary to view the degree of deviance of these ratings with some caution, as Sean's mother continued to rate herself as mildly depressed on the Beck Depression Inventory and SCL-90-R, and the Locke-Wallace MAT indicated serious marital problems (score of only 39).

Sean's math and English teachers failed to return the packet of rating scales sent to them; since it was approaching the end of the academic year, these questionnaires were never obtained.

On the Youth Self-Report form of the CBCL, Sean reported himself to be having significant elevations on the scales related to depression, aggression, and delinquency. Sean endorsed a number of items pertaining to problems with concentrating, impulsiveness, and restlessness, as well as many somatic complaints. He endorsed 16 of the 44 items on the Issues Checklist as being areas of conflict between him and his parents, but rated them as occurring less than once a week and being of mild intensity; these reports conflict with the more numerous and heated conflicts reported by his mother. Sean also reported that he had never engaged in any sexually inappropriate conduct, despite his mother's reports of his having raped his older sister. When challenged with this information, he stated that he had had intercourse with her as an act of kindness, because he knew she would never have a boyfriend and thought she ought to experience what sex was like.

Sean and his mother were observed during a 10-minute neutral discussion period and a 15-minute conflict discussion period, as described in Chapter 10. Throughout both situations, Sean was openly disrespectful and hostile toward his mother and frequently swore at her. He would alternate between refusing to discuss the topics with her and screaming at her how stupid she was and how dumb this evaluation was. He often stated that most of his problems were the result of his parents' being unfair to him and restricting him from liberties all his other friends had been granted. On every attempt to discuss a problem or conflict, Sean would often respond with defensive and whiny comments and offered no constructive solutions to their disagreements. His mother would frequently speak quietly, almost meekly toward him; at the slightest flash of anger, she would typically shift to a different topic or sit quietly for a few moments to allow Sean to cool off before trying to discuss a different problem area with him. The observations suggested severe communication problems in this dyad, with poor problem-solving skills, a weak parental coalition on setting limits with Sean, and minimal attempts to employ consequences for managing Sean's rule infractions.

Sean was administered a battery of psychological tests, the results of which appear in Table 11.3 as well. The WISC-R revealed a Full Scale IQ of 113, with both Verbal and Performance scores falling within this range (above average) and no evidence of deficits on any of the subscales. On the WRAT-R, Sean performed within the average range, with all scores being relatively consistent with his intellectual abilities. On the Gordon vigilance test, Sean achieved a score for commission errors that was below the 5th percentile for his age, indicating significant problems with impulsivity. His omission score and number correct were within the normal range. On the MFFT-20, Sean's speed of responding was abnormally fast and his number of errors was high, again consistent with significant impulsivity. Sean was observed working alone in a clinic playroom while he performed math problems and listened to rock music. He was noted to be off task and fidgety at least 20% of the time, but evidenced no other ADHD behaviors during this time. These scores are consistent with our observations of other ADHD teenagers who, at this age, have problems primarily with inattention and restlessness but not with gross motor overactivity.

The results of this evaluation continued to support a diagnosis of ADHD and ODD as well as a significant CD that had emerged within the past 2 to 3 years. Sean's family life continued to be tumultuous and explosive, with frequent arguments and at times physical confrontations between Sean and his parents. Sean was on probation for his arrests for fighting and shoplifting, and had been informed by the juvenile courts that any further arrests would result in his being placed in juvenile detention. We recommended the following to the family:

1. A return by Sean's parents to marital therapy, to attempt to address their serious marital problems.

2. A course of problem-solving and communication training for Sean and his parents, as described in Chapter 14.

3. Referral of Sean to a child psychiatrist for consideration of a trial on an antidepressant.

4. A conference with Sean's high school teachers at the beginning of the next academic year, to alert them to Sean's behavioral problems, ADHD, and poor organizational abilities, as well as to institute a daily school report card for behavior and a daily assignment notebook to be verified by each teacher for correctness.

5. Individual counseling for Sean to attempt to deal with his symptoms of low self-esteem, mild depression, and mild anxiety.

Two weeks following the evaluation, before any of these interventions could be initiated, Sean was involved in a fight with another adolescent in which the adolescent was stabbed and critically wounded. He was arrested and placed at the state juvenile correctional facility.

CASE 4: ADHD WITH THOUGHT/MOOD DISTURBANCE

Fay, aged 11 years and 11 months was referred to our clinic by her adoptive parents because of significant problems with inattention, restlessness, and poor organizational skills at school and noncompliance and emotional behavior at home. She was attending a fifth-grade program and was not yet receiving any special educational assistance. Fay had been adopted at 5 years of age; she currently resided with her adoptive parents and two older brothers, 14 and 16 years of age, who were also adopted but not of the same parentage as Fay.

Fay's mother was concerned about her behavior even at age 5 years when she was adopted. Fay was even then a quite restless, overactive, and impulsive child, who had considerable problems with obeying instructions and completing requested tasks. Fay also had significant problems with expressing her feelings and often withdrew from other family members. She was seen as considerably more moody than other children her age and would often keep to herself for several weeks at a time, remaining detached from family activities as much as the parents would permit her. Fay's mother was very puzzled, as there was often little or no environmental precipitant to Fay's moods, anger, or social withdrawal.

Fay was also said to have serious problems with organization, both at home and at school. This was quite evident in her household chores and approach to homework, as well as in her school papers. Her mother, a teacher, attempted to assist her, but Fay would often refuse such assistance and become angry or mute during these attempts at assistance with her homework. The mother-daughter relationship was quite frustrating and tense as a result. Fay was often more compliant with her father, who had assumed most of the reponsibility for getting Fay to do homework.

The parents believed that Fay had an extremely low opinion of herself, which was often further diminished by the parents' need to confront her about her frequent lies, fabricated stories, and taking possessions from other family members without permission. Fay was said to view herself as a "bad adopted child" who did not belong in this family. Recently, Fay had begun to talk about her feelings of being adopted and to ask many questions about her biological mother. However, her parents' efforts to discuss these feelings with her were often met with anger, hurt feelings, or simply withdrawal.

A review of various developmental domains with Fay's mother suggested that Fay had significant problems with fine motor skills, especially in handwriting. Gross motor skills were reportedly normal, and Fay was said to enjoy many sports. No difficulties with sensory development or language skills were described. However, in speaking, she often confused the names of things (e.g., saying "grapes" for "strawberries") and was overly detailed in her descriptions of events, often losing track of the purpose of the narrative. Her train of thought was often easily disrupted. Fay had problems remembering details of events or information given by others, according to her parents, and often interjected comments into conversations that had little to do with the topic at hand. As for her emotional status, Fay, as noted above, was frequently moody, sad, and withdrawn, while at other times she appeared to be bland or aloof in her affect. She was quick to anger and often went into a rage over trivial frustrations in her life. She had a fear of being alone and often commented that others would break into their home if she were left by herself. Socially, Fay was quite gullible and very much a follower. She had occasionally gotten into fights with peers over minor disagreements, but otherwise had friends both at home and school. Although she was able to conduct most self-care routines without assistance, she had to be monitored frequently by her parents, as she showed little regard for her personal hygiene.

During the portion of the interview concerning child psychiatric symptoms, Fay's mother described Fay as having all of the 14 symptoms of ADHD and noted that these were present when she came to live with them. Fay was also reported to have seven of the nine symptoms of ODD. Some of the items for Major Depression were endorsed, but not sufficiently to justify this diagnosis. Although she did not meet sufficient criteria for any anxiety disorder, excessive worry and anxiety were reported by her parents.

Very little information was known about Fay's early developmental and medical history, except that she was neglected and quite possibly abused. Her biological mother had been diagnosed as having Bipolar Disorder and had been treated frequently in both outpatient and inpatient programs for her emotional problems. Nothing was known about Fay's biological father.

Fay's adoptive mother was 41 at the time of the evaluation and was working as a school teacher. Her husband was 42 years of age and was also employed as a teacher. Both parents held master's degrees in the educational field. Both of the other children in the family were reported to be developing normally, without LD or psychiatric disorders. The parents' marriage was reported as excellent and often was a source of strength for Fay's mother in dealing with Fay's behavior problems.

In school Fay was described by her teacher as having considerable problems with attention to tasks, organizing her work, and remaining seated during class lectures. These problems had been evident since first grade. A year earlier, Fay had been tested by a school psychologist and found to have no significant deficits in her academic achievement skills. Some mild problems with visual-motor coordination were noted, but these were felt at that time to be insignificant in creating her school performance problems; these were mainly attributed to Fay's ADHD symptoms. No special educational services were recommended. Fay's parents and teacher were concerned about her moving into a middle school setting the next year, where she would have six different teachers and no special assistance, and would be required to be more personally responsible and organized than now.

The interview with Fay found her to be quite shy and uncooperative with the evaluation. She rarely answered the examiner's questions, and when she did used very short phrases. She made little eye contact throughout the evaluation. Fay would not spontaneously divulge information about her home or family life. She was fidgety and restless during the interview, but remained seated throughout the time. There was no indication of significant language problems, but thinking and affect could not be properly assessed due to her uncooperativeness. She acknowledged that she had friends at home and school, but refused to discuss much about her play or social activities. She felt that she was doing well at school, contrary to her teacher's reports, but that she struggled to get homework done. She expressed some anger at her mother for forcing her to do her homework.

The pediatric medical examination was conducted by our consulting pediatrician and was essentially normal.

The results of the behavior rating scales and psychological testing are shown in Table 11.4. The parent ratings on the CBCL revealed significant clinical elevations on almost every scale except that of Sex Problems. Highest elevations were on the Hyperactive scale (greater than 4 standard deviations), but quite severe ratings were seen on all other scales, which all placed Fay at least three or four standard deviations above the mean for her age and sex. Reports on the HSQ revealed significantly pervasive behavior problems of considerable severity. Four of the five factor scores on the CPRS-R were in the abnormal range for age.

On the teacher rating scales, Fay was described as considerably less deviant. Scores on all CBCL-TRF scales fell within the normal range, but there was a borderline significant elevation on the Depressed scale, and ratings on the Nervous-Overactive, Inattentive, and Aggressive scales were at the high end of normal. As noted in Chapter 6, this is often the case with children who have significant thinking or mood disorders; the symptoms of these are far more evident at home than in the structured environment of school. However, scores on the CTRS-R indicated a significant elevation on the Inattentive-Passive factor. Fay was said to have problem behaviors in 4 of the 12 settings on the SSQ, most of which pertained to attention to small-group discussions and class lectures as well as completing independent deskwork. These were noted to be of mild severity. On the ADHD rating scale, the teacher endorsed only 4 of the 14 ADHD symptoms as developmentally in-

TABLE 11.4. Assessment Results for a Case of ADHD with Mood/Thinking Disturbance in an 11-Year-Old Girl

CBCL-Parent		CBCL-TRF	
Scale	Percentile	Scale	Percentile
Anxious-Schizoid	96*	Anxious	69
Depressed	99*	Social Withdrawal	70
Somatic Complaints	99*	Unpopular	84
Sex Problems	69	Depressed	90
Social Withdrawal	99*	Self-Destructive	70
Cruel	99*	Inattentive	87
Hyperactive	99*	Nervous-Overactive	87
Aggressive	99*	Aggressive	87
Delinquent	99*		

HSQ	SSQ
Number of problem settings: 9	Number of problem settings: 4
Mean severity rating: 6.1	Mean severity rating: 2.0

CPRS-R		CTRS-R	
Factor	Raw score	Factor	Raw score
Conduct Problems	4	Conduct Problems	8
Psychosomatic	6*	Inattentive-Passive	10*
Anxiety	6*	Hyperactive	4
Impulsive-Hyperactive	9*	Index	10
Learning Problems	10*		
Index	16*		

Vineland Adaptive Behavior Scale		ADHD Rating Scale (Teacher)	
Domain	Standard score	Total score: 18	
		Number of symptoms rated >2: 4	
Communication	95*	CAP	
Daily Living	70*	Factor	Percentile
Socialization	85		
		Inattention	93*
		Overactivity	84*

(*cont.*)

TABLE 11.4. (*cont.*)

| WISC-R | | | WRAT-R | |
Subtest		Scale score	Subtest	Percentile
Information		10	Reading	75
Similarities		14	Spelling	55
Arithmetic		7	Arithmetic	63
Vocabulary		12		
Comprehension		18	Gordon vigilance test	
Digit Span		10	Number correct: 44	
Picture Completion		11	Number of omissions: 1	
Picture Arrangement		8	Number of commissions: 0	
Block Design		8		
Object Assembly		9	MFFT	
Coding		10	Mean time to respond: 13.5 seconds	
			Number incorrect: 9	
Verbal IQ:	113			
Performance IQ:	93		Restricted Academic Situation	
Full Scale IQ:	104			Percent
			Behavior	occurrence
			Off task	4
			Fidgets	30
			Vocalizes	0
			Plays with objects	0
			Out of seat	0
			Math problems done (*n*)	117
			Math accuracy (%)	94

Note. See Table 11.1 for abbreviations. An asterisk indicates a clinically significant elevation (>95th percentile or <5th percentile). The CBCL parent and CBCL-TRF profiles are not similar to those for boys shown in previous tables, because these instruments have different factor scales for girls.

appropriate, yet endorsed all of the symptoms as occurring to some degree ("just a little"). On the APRS, Fay was rated below the 40th percentile in production of work and below the 60th in work accuracy. Her organizational skills were rated as consistently poor, and her work was often sloppy and illegible.

The results for the WISC-R placed Fay within the normal range for Full Scale IQ, but within the above-average range in Verbal abilities. The 20-point difference between Verbal and Performance IQ was statistically significant for her age ($p < .10$) and suggested clinically and educationally significant impairment in Fay's visual-spatial-mechanical skills. A relative weakness was also noted on the Verbal Arithmetic scale. Fay's performance on the WRAT-R indicated average academic performance in all areas, but very poor handwriting while accomplishing the Spelling test. On the Vineland scales, Fay performed in the normal range in the Communication domain, but placed in the low-average range in Socialization. Impaired performance was noted in Daily Living.

On the Gordon vigilance task and the MFFT, all scores were within the normal range. Observations of Fay while doing math problems in our Restricted Academic Situation all fell within the normal range. Fay was also given several specialized neuropsychological tests, which found her to be impaired in fine motor coordination and agility and in sequential processing of information, but within the normal range in verbal and nonverbal memory.

Both adoptive parents completed the SCL-90-R and the Locke-Wallace MAT. The results indicated no significant psychopathology or psychological distress in either parent, and an excellent marital relationship.

In general, it was our opinion that while Fay met criteria for ADHD and ODD, primarily based on information from the home, she was also experiencing significant attention and organizational problems at school. She had no clear-cut LD as traditionally defined. However, she had mild impairments in spatial-mechanical skills and more significant impairments in fine motor coordination; these could have contributed to these organizational problems and difficulties completing assignments, beyond the contribution made by her inattention. Certainly Fay was manifesting signs of a significant mood disorder with some mild disturbances in thinking. Given the biological mother's history of manic-depression, Fay was viewed as being at high risk for the emergence of a major depressive disorder in her own development. It was also felt that Fay was having significant personal problems dealing with her adoption and that these, along with her significant behavioral and mood problems, were contributing to a strained mother-daughter relationship at this time.

The following were recommended to address these problems:

1. Referral to a child psychiatrist for consideration of a trial on antidepressant medication. It was recommended that Fay be tapered off her medication for allergies; these contained theophylline, which is known to affect attention and mood in some children. Thereafter, she was to be considered for a trial on a tricyclic antidepressant, depending on her response to the other recommendations made below. (She would eventually not be placed on this medication, based on a relatively positive response to these other changes in her family life and schooling.)

2. A consultation with Fay's school staff and sharing of the neuropsychological test results with them. This convinced them to provide Fay with LD assistance through a resource room for an hour each day, to assist her with completion of assignments, organizational skills, and penmanship. In addition, Fay's teacher was asked to reduce the length of assignments where possible so as not to overtax Fay's writing abilities, and to permit Fay to elaborate orally upon her written answers to some educational tasks.

3. Six sessions of child behavior management training, to help the parents address Fay's noncompliance and moodiness at home. As part of this program, they were counseled not only on the nature of ADHD, but also on the nature of Fay's affective/thinking disturbance and her higher risk for a continuation of these difficulties into adolescence. They were also cautioned about

the possible development of Bipolar Disorder, given her family history of this disorder.

4. Individual psychotherapy for Fay, to further explore and (we hoped) to address her apparent significant concerns about her adoption and her relationship with her adoptive mother. It is not always clear in such cases whether children's difficulties in accepting their adoption are contributing to their affective disturbance or vice versa. It is possible within such cases that children with biological predispositions toward depressive illness attribute their moodiness and episodes of depression to social and familial causes within their environment that may not actually be causal of their depressive disorder. Hence, there is a need to explore these issues further with a skilled child therapist.

5. Hiring a tutor to work with Fay on her homework assignments at least twice weekly, so as to remove the parents from this responsibility, which was straining their relationship with Fay.

A year later, at the time of this writing, Fay is being considered for admission to a short-term child inpatient unit because of a deterioration in her mood. She has lately become considerably more depressed, anhedonic, and socially withdrawn. Suicidal ideation has begun to occur that requires more intensive study than can be done on an outpatient basis. Her irritable moods at home have also resulted in significant conflict with her siblings and adoptive parents. She will now begin a trial on antidepressant medication.

CASE 5: ATTENTION DEFICIT DISORDER WITHOUT HYPERACTIVITY

Robert was 7 years and 8 months old at the time of his referral to our clinic by his parents, who were concerned about receiving a second opinion as to his ADD. He had been seen previously by a child neurologist who raised this possibility with them. At the time of referral, Robert was attending an ungraded language-based school program. He was residing with his biological parents and a younger brother, aged 4 years.

The initial parental interview indicated that the parents were primarily concerned about Robert's difficulties with sustaining attention, following through on instructions and rules, and distractibility. These problems were said to have developed at about 5 years of age, or possibly earlier. No problems with defiance or aggressiveness were reported, nor were symptoms of a significant mood or thought disorder described.

A review of Robert's developmental and medical history indicated that the pregnancy was full-term and uncomplicated, with the mother being in good health throughout. Delivery was uncomplicated although Robert was quite small for dates, weighing 5 pounds, 8 ounces at birth. He was said to have had some minor shaking movements shortly after delivery, but these ceased quickly, and no further evidence of potential seizures was noted. In infancy, Robert had difficulties sleeping consistently through the night and often experienced apparent colic. He was a difficult baby, by his mother's report, often crying for little reason and difficult to console. Motor and language milestones were met at normal ages, and bowel and bladder control were achieved uneventfully. However, Robert's level of language complexity and language comprehension were always points of concern for his parents.

At clinical presentation, Robert's health was reported to be excellent. No sensory deficits were noted. Motor skills were fair, according to the parents. There was no history of treatment with psychoactive medication. Robert began a preschool program 2 days a week at age 4 years and apparently did well. However, early in his kindergarten year, Robert's teacher noted that he was not able to learn as quickly as other children. A school evaluation resulted in his immediate placement into an LD program, where he received language-based instruction and speech and language therapy several times per week. He was also provided with occupational therapy twice weekly, due to fine motor impairments.

The review of childhood psychiatric symptoms with the parents indicated that Robert met 5 of the 14 criteria for ADHD, these being predominantly items pertaining to poor attention and often losing things necessary for work. No difficulties with behaviors related to ODD or CD were endorsed, nor did Robert have any symptoms of anxiety or depressive disorders. In fact, his affect was described as usually bland or flat, but occasionally punctuated by an irritable outburst with minimal provocation. He was reported to get along well with other children, but to prefer play with somewhat younger children within his neighborhood.

A review of the family psychiatric history found that the mother had experienced significant learning problems in school, as had one of her brothers. On the father's side of the family, one sister of his had failed to graduate from high school, and a second had a history of anxiety disorder and was now being treated for anorexia nervosa. No other psychiatric disorders were reported among the relatives on either side. Robert's younger sibling was developing normally, with no evidence of psychiatric disturbance.

The brief interview with Robert revealed a small child for his age who was somewhat shy and reluctant to speak with the examiner. His gait and locomotion seemed somewhat awkward and clumsy. Although no speech articulation problems were evident, the level of vocabulary seemed considerably below that of a normal youngster of this age. Robert's language complexity was apparently delayed, as evidenced in short lengths of spoken utterances and relatively simple vocabulary. A word-finding problem existed, with Robert manifesting significant pauses in the middle of phrases as he evidently searched for what he wanted to say. He described satisfactory relationships with his other family members and acknowledged enjoying school, where he had several close playmates. No signs of significant affective or thought disturbance were noted during this time. Throughout the interview, Robert was considerably slower than average in responding to questions, at times appearing to apply considerable effort to understand and process the questions. At other times, he seemed "spacey"; for example he had to ask that some questions be repeated due to his inattention. His responses were equally slow to be processed and expressed, as noted above. Spontaneous speech was quite below normal. The general impression was of a quite immature youngster both physically and cognitively, who was substantially more daydreamy, slow-moving, and easily confused than the average child.

A pediatric medical examination of Robert by our staff pediatrician revealed a boy of average height but at the 15th percentile in weight. Visual acuity was normal, as was hearing on a brief audiological exam. No minor physical abnormalities were noted, and Robert seemed in good health. Neurological examination revealed grossly intact cranial nerve function and good muscle tone in all extremities. Deep tendon reflexes were normal bilaterally. Neurodevelopmental exam demonstrated significant motor overflow movements, as well as synkinesia and difficulties with motor impersistence. Tandem gait was only fair both forwards and backwards, as was heel walking. Eye tracking was noted to be smooth. Finger opposition was observed to be awkward. Right-left discrimination on self was normal for age but on others was delayed. Poor printing skills were evident on brief testing of writing, and his drawing of geometric designs was quite primitive. It was concluded that this healthy child had no specific neurological abnormalities, but significant evidence of immature neurodevelopmental status.

The parents and teacher completed the standard battery of child behavior rating scales, the results of which are shown in Table 11.5, along with findings from psychological testing and direct behavioral observations. Given the significant evidence of intellectual delay noted below, Robert's ratings were compared to children of similar mental rather than chronological age in scoring those rating scales where such specific age norms were available. This was done to control for the possible influence of generalized developmental delay on these ratings, especially those pertaining to inattention, hyperactivity, and impulsivity. Results from the parent-completed CBCL revealed essen-

TABLE 11.5. Assessment Results for A Case of ADD/−H in a 7-Year-Old Boy

CBCL-Parent		CBCL-TRF	
Scale	Percentile	Scale	Percentile
Anxious-Schizoid	69	Anxious	97*
Depressed	69	Social Withdrawal	99*
Uncommunicative	76	Unpopular	84
Obsessive-Compulsive	69	Obsessive-Compulsive	90
Somatic Complaints	76	Self-Destructive	95*
Social Withdrawal	69	Inattentive	97*
Hyperactive	95*	Nervous-Overactive	93
Aggressive	69	Aggressive	69
Delinquent	69		

HSQ

Number of problem settings: 4
Mean severity rating: 1.0

CPRS-R

Factor	Raw score
Conduct Problems	3
Psychosomatic	0
Anxiety	3
Impulsive-Hyperactive	1
Learning Problems	5*
Index	7

Vineland Adaptive Behavior Scale

Domain	Standard score
Communication	66*
Daily Living	72*
Socialization	88

WISC-R

Subtest	Scale score
Information	6
Similarities	12
Arithmetic	6
Vocabulary	9
Comprehension	8
Digit Span	6
Picture Completion	7
Picture Arrangement	7
Block Design	10
Object Assembly	7
Coding	3*

Verbal IQ:	87
Performance IQ:	78
Full Scale IQ:	82

SSQ

Number of problem settings: 3
Mean severity rating: 2.3

CTRS-R

Factor	Raw score
Conduct Problems	5
Inattentive-Passive	18*
Hyperactive	4
Index	13

ADHD Rating Scale (Teacher)

Total score: 21
Number of symptoms rated >2: 6

CAP

Factor	Percentile
Inattention	98*
Overactivity	69

WRAT-R

Subtest	Percentile
Reading	0.6*
Spelling	1.0*
Arithmetic	0.4*

Gordon vigilance test

Number correct: 32*
Number of omissions: 13*
Number of commissions: 5

MFFT

Mean time to respond: 12.5 seconds
Number incorrect: 27*

Restricted Academic Situation

Behavior	Percent occurrence
Off task	73*
Fidgets	37
Vocalizes	20
Plays with objects	7
Out of seat	23
Math problems done (n)	32*
Math accuracy (%)	80

Note. See Table 11.1 for abbreviations. An asterisk indicates a clinically significant elevation (>95th percentile or <5th percentile).

tially normal scores on all scales except the Hyperactive scale, which was at the 95th percentile. Inspection of the specific scale items contributing to this elevation revealed positive endorsements on items pertaining to acting immature, poor concentration, confusion and daydreaming, speech difficulties, and poor school performance. Ratings on the CPRS-R were similarly normal except for the Learning Problems Factor, which was at the 98th percentile. Scores on the HSQ indicated very mild behavior problems in only four home situations. These scores were within the normal range for mental age. Those areas endorsed as mildly problematic were getting dressed, washing, doing homework, and occasionally playing with other children.

Teacher ratings on the CBCL-TRF indicated clinical elevations on the Inattentive, Anxious, Social Withdrawal, and Self-Destructive scales. The rating on the Nervous-Overactive scale was at the 93rd percentile. Again, it is helpful to inspect the nature of the items that contribute to significant scale elevations, especially where such elevations are not evident on other scales or parent ratings. Ratings on the Anxious scale were apparently elevated due to endorsements on items indicating shyness, self-consciousness, and secretiveness, as well as occasional worrying and mild fearfulness in making mistakes. The elevation on the Self-Destructive scale was due essentially to endorsements of items pertaining to clumsiness, mild fears, and strange behavior ("Can't really laugh or relax, seems tense"). On the Nervous-Overactive scale, significant hyperactivity was not reported, but mild fidgeting was. The scale elevation was mainly the result of 2-point responses on the items of hoarding objects and messiness. Ratings on the CTRS-R revealed significant elevations on the Inattentive-Passive Factor only. Similarly, only the Inattention subscale of the CAP was significantly deviant for mental age (98th percentile). On the ADHD Rating Scale, 6 of the 14 symptoms were endorsed with scores higher than 2 (developmentally inappropriate); all of these pertained to problems with inattention and losing things needed for work. These reports were quite consistent with those ADHD symptoms endorsed by the parents during their interview. Scores on the SSQ indicated mild behavior problems in three school settings, these being during free play, in the hallways, and in the bathroom. These scores were within the normal range for mental age. On the APRS, the teacher reported that less than 60% of math and language arts work was being completed, but that what work was done was generally 80% accurate.

Parents' answers to the Vineland scale disclosed significant problems in Communication and Daily Living, but low-average levels of performance in the Socialization domain. However, these standard scores were quite consistent with Robert's measured intelligence, described next.

Robert's performance on the WISC-R placed his overall intelligence toward the lower end of the low-normal range. Verbal IQ was somewhat higher but still within the low-normal range, while Performance IQ was within the borderline range of mental retardation. Robert's performance showed substantial scatter across subtests, with an extremely low score on Coding (a measure of perceptual-motor speed of copying as well as short-term memory), but an average to above-average score on Similarities (a measure of verbal abstract reasoning). Academic achievement skills assessed by the WRAT-R found that Robert was impaired in all areas, with standard scores significantly below even his low-average intellectual estimates (Reading = 58, Spelling = 64, and Arithmetic = 56). All of these scores were below the 1st percentile for age. These results indicate a significant delay in academic achievement—a delay even greater than would be expected for a child of low-normal intelligence.

The tests of attention and impulsivity indicated borderline to abnormal performance on the total correct and number of omissions scores of the Gordon vigilance task, but normal commission errors. This indicated to us a pattern of significant inattention without evidence of impulsivity or disinhibition. However, the score on the MFFT for errors was significantly abnormal (98th percentile). Although this would be traditionally interpreted as evidence of impulsivity, it is well known that performance on this test is highly correlated with intelligence. In the face of a normal score on commission errors and no parent or teacher complaints of impulsivity, we chose to view this score as an artifact of the child's obvious intellectual delays. Behavioral observations of Robert during the Restricted Academic Situation indicated an abnormal score only on the category "off task." Robert's performance on the math problems task given during this observation was consistent with teacher reports. Only 32 of these simple problems were completed, but at an 80% accuracy level. Again, most normal children accomplish more than 100 problems during this 15-minute observation period.

Robert's parents completed the SCL-90-R about themselves, the results of which were within the normal range. Thus, there was no evidence of significant psychopathology in either parent. Ratings of the marriage indicated an excellent relationship (score of 138 on the Locke-Wallace MAT).

It was our impression that Robert was a child of low-average intelligence with neuromaturational immaturity and significant delays in academic achievement, even beyond what would be accounted for on the basis of his intellectual delay. In addition, substantial evidence pointed to a significant problem with inattention, despite adjusting his scores on parent and teacher rating scales for his mental delays by comparing him to children of younger chronological age but equivalent mental age on these scales. There was no evidence of significant hyperactivity or impulsivity, although mild restlessness did exist. Such minor restlessness is not inconsistent with ADD/−H, as teacher ratings of that symptom cluster with inattention rather than hyperactivity items when factor-analyzed. Thus, we diagnosed Robert as having both ADD/−H and Specific Developmental Disorders in reading, math, and written expression. The following were recommended to the parents:

1. Two sessions of counseling to educate the parents about the nature of ADD/−H as a distinct condition from ADHD. What the parents might have heard from others about ADHD might not apply to Robert. That is, not

being aggressive or impulsive and not showing behavioral disinhibition, Robert would be considerably less likely to develop conduct problems and difficulties with antisocial behavior in later adolescence than children with ADHD. And, given his proneness to shyness, mild anxiety, and secretiveness, he might be at somewhat greater risk for an anxiety disorder than is typically seen in normal or even ADHD children. His greatest risk, however, was clearly in the area of academic achievement.

2. Retention of Robert within his self-contained, ungraded, language-based special education classroom for one more year before considering him for transfer to a more traditional LD program. Speech and language therapy as well as occupational therapy should, of course, continue.

3. A consultation with the child's school district, to educate them about the nature of ADD/−H and share with them the opinions in paragraph 2 above. Several methods for improving attention and organization in the classroom were shared with the teacher during this consultation, including the use of the Attention Trainer (see Chapter 15), which we have found to be of substantial value to children with this diagnosis. In addition, breaking assignments into smaller units, providing a timer for structuring these assignments, and teaching Robert self-instruction techniques to use while working were felt to be beneficial to his completing assigned work.

4. A trial on stimulant medication, even though Robert was not considered to be hyperactive. The results of our research on drug responding in children with ADD/−H indicate that they often respond well to medication, but require much less medication to achieve this response than do ADHD children. Although somewhat shy and withdrawn, Robert was not viewed as so anxious that a stimulant medication trial would be contraindicated. A double-blind, placebo-controlled trial on methylphenidate did in fact reveal a remarkably positive response at just 5 mg b.i.d. (twice daily), with no greater improvement at 10 mg b.i.d. and a marked increase in staring, daydreaming, and irritability at this dose. Further deterioration in attention and mood occurred at 15 mg b.i.d. On 5 mg b.i.d., Robert showed normal performances on the vigilance task, a 60% decline in off-task behavior during the Restricted Academic Situation, a 25% increase in work productivity, and an improvement in work accuracy to 92%. Teacher ratings of inattention fell within the normal range at this dose level.

CASE 6: LEARNING DISABILITIES WITHOUT ADHD

Gregory was referred for evaluation by his mother due to concerns about his impaired academic performance. He was 7 years, 3 months of age at the time of referral and resided with his biological parents and an older sister, aged 10 years. He attended a first-grade program but was receiving additional assistance in a resource room for LD.

Greg's developmental and medical history reflected a normal full-term pregnancy and delivery, complicated only by Rh incompatibility. Greg weighed a healthy 8 pounds, 9 ounces at birth. His infancy was reported as uneventful for medical or developmental problems. Subsequent motor and language milestones were achieved at normal ages, and bowel and bladder control occurred at $2\frac{1}{2}$ years of age without problems. Health at the time of evaluation was excellent, with no evidence of hearing or visual disturbance or motor incoordination. The pediatric medical examination at this time was completely normal, indicating a healthy child with no evidence of neuromaturational difficulties. There was no history of any psychological or psychiatric intervention for Greg.

During the parental interview, Greg's mother reported her concern to be that Greg was not reading as well as he should for his age. She had requested an evaluation at school, which corroborated her concerns about reading. This resulted in Greg's receiving LD assistance for reading and spelling through a resource room program, while remaining in regular education classes for all other subjects. However, Greg's first-grade teacher had noted some difficulties with paying attention in school. This led his mother to seek our services for evaluation of possible ADHD.

The review of childhood psychiatric symptoms indicated an endorsement of only 3 of the 14 symptoms of ADHD as being developmentally inappropriate; these were problems with following through on instructions, shifting from one activity to another too often, and often losing things necessary for work. No symptoms of inattention, overactivity, or impulsivity were reported. No signs of ODD or CD were described, nor were there any signs of affective or anxiety disorders or significant thinking disturbance. Greg was, however, described as unusually self-conscious, especially about his reading problem and receipt of special tutoring at school. There had been a recent death in the family of an uncle with cancer; Greg had been unusually close to this relative.

The family psychiatric history revealed that neither of the mother's parents had graduated from high school, but there were no psychiatric disorders on her side of the family. On the paternal side, the father reported having significant learning problems when he was in school. Also, he felt that his father and a brother and sister had also had significant reading problems during their own formal education. His mother and father had also failed to complete high school. Greg's older sister was reported to be developing normally, with no signs of learning problems or psychiatric disturbance.

The interview with Greg found him to be a pleasant, compliant, soft-spoken child. He was cooperative with the interview and revealed no signs of significant language, motor, sensory, affective, or thinking disorders. He reported close, affectionate relations with his family members, and satisfactory relations with other neighborhood children and his classmates. In describing his school adjustment, he noted that he typically enjoyed school, but was very unhappy at having to leave his regular classes to attend the LD resource room for his reading. He felt that other children might see him as "stupid" and different from them because of his need for these services. He responded in the affirmative when asked whether he worried about having to leave his class each day for these special services.

The child behavior rating scales and results of psychological testing are shown in Table 11.6. The results of the parent rating scales revealed normal scores on all scales except the Depressed scale on the CBCL and the Anxiety and Learning Problems scales of the CPRS-R. The elevation on the Depressed scale of the CBCL resulted from the affirmative endorsement of items related to being self-conscious, occasionally being worried, having a poor self-image, and being secretive. Greg was described as presenting mild behavioral problems in 7 of the 16 home situations on the HSQ, but this was within the normal range for his age. None of the scores on the various teacher rating scales were clinically elevated. The teacher endorsed only 1 item from the

TABLE 11.6. Assessment Results for a Case of Reading/Spelling Disorder without ADHD in a 7-Year-Old Boy

CBCL-Parent		CBCL-TRF	
Scale	Percentile	Scale	Percentile
Anxious-Schizoid	93	Anxious	69
Depressed	95*	Social Withdrawal	69
Uncommunicative	84	Unpopular	69
Obsessive-Compulsive	69	Obsessive-Compulsive	69
Somatic Complaints	69	Self-Destructive	69
Social Withdrawal	69	Inattentive	69
Hyperactive	69	Nervous-Overactive	69
Aggressive	69	Aggressive	69
Delinquent	69		

HSQ		SSQ	
Number of problem settings:	7	Number of problem settings:	0
Mean severity rating:	3.0	Mean severity rating:	0.0

CPRS-R		CTRS-R	
Factor	Raw score	Factor	Raw score
Conduct Problems	5	Conduct Problems	0
Psychosomatic	0	Inattentive-Passive	0
Anxiety	7*	Hyperactive	0
Impulsive-Hyperactive	0	Index	2
Learning Problems	7*		
Index	2		

Vineland Adaptive Behavior Scale		ADHD Rating Scale (Teacher)	
Domain	Standard score	Total score: 1	
		Number of symptoms rated >2: 0	
Communication	50*	CAP	
Daily Living	87	Factor	Percentile
Socialization	90	Inattention	69
		Overactivity	69

WISC-R			WRAT-R	
Subtest		Scale score	Subtest	Percentile
Information		11	Reading	8*
Similarities		10	Spelling	7*
Arithmetic		8	Arithmetic	32
Vocabulary		8		
Comprehension		11	Gordon vigilance test	
Digit Span		7	Number correct: 36	
Picture Completion		14	Number of omissions: 9	
Picture Arrangement		10	Number of commissions: 7	
Block Design		10	MFFT	
Object Assembly		12	Mean time to respond: 15.3 seconds	
Coding		8	Number incorrect: 20*	

Verbal IQ:	97	
Performance IQ:	105	
Full Scale IQ:	101	

Restricted Academic Situation

Behavior	Percent occurrence
Off task	27
Fidgets	7
Vocalizes	53*
Plays with objects	3
Out of seat	7
Math problems done (*n*)	99
Math accuracy (%)	100

Note. See Table 11.1 for abbreviations. An asterisk indicates a clinically significant elevation (>95th percentile or <5th percentile).

ADHD rating scale, and this was not rated as developmentally inappropriate (≥ 2).

On the Vineland interview concerning adaptive behavior, Greg's mother reported significant problems in the Communication domain, primarily due to poor reading and writing skills. Daily Living and Socialization domain scores were normal.

Greg's scores on the WISC-R were within the average or normal range in both Verbal and Performance domains. On the WRAT-R, however, his performance in Reading and Spelling was significantly poor (below the 8th percentile), and his Arithmetic performance was somewhat weak for age, being in the low-normal range. His performance in Reading and Spelling was 1.5 standard deviations below average and below levels considered normal based on intellectual testing. There was clear evidence here of a reading disability with associated spelling disorder.

On the Gordon vigilance test, Greg's performance was normal on all three scores. However, performance on the MFFT was abnormal. Observations of Greg while performing math problems during the Restricted Academic Situation fell within the normal range for all behaviors except vocalizing. Greg frequently whispered to himself while doing his math problems. His math productivity and accuracy during this task were quite satisfactory.

Greg's parents completed the SCL-90-R, with all scores placing within the normal range. There was a mild, marginally significant elevation on scales related to interpersonal sensitivity on the mother's reports. The marital relationship was reported as good to excellent on the Locke-Wallace MAT.

Our conclusion was that Greg was a boy of average intelligence with a significant reading/spelling disorder, likely of familial/hereditary origin. There was no evidence of ADHD or other significant psychopathology. However, we viewed Greg as a socially sensitive child who was having difficulties accepting his disability and need for special educational services. What minimal inattention was occurring at school seemed to us secondary to his self-consciousness about going out of his class for special education and fears of social teasing and ostracism from peers because of his leaving class for these services. We therefore recommended the following to his mother:

1. Continuation of the special education program for reading problems. However, we recommended that Greg's teacher try to minimize the act of his leaving the classroom by not drawing extra attention to this event. Moreover, we felt it would be useful for Greg's special education teacher to speak with him about his disability and the fact that many other children in school received such services, so as to emphasize that he was not unique in this respect. If necessary, Greg was to meet weekly with a school psychologist to discuss his feelings about his disability and to desensitize him to his fears about social rejection because of them. There existed no objective evidence that Greg was in fact being teased or losing friends because of his need for special class services.

2. Formal individual psychotherapy, using cognitive-behavioral therapy techniques and self-esteem-building exercises, if the measures recommended in paragraph 1 should fail to assuage Greg's self-consciousness over his disorder and correct his low self-esteem.

3. Continuation of instruction, albeit through private sources, in reading/spelling skills during the summer months, so as to preclude any regression in these areas while Greg was not in school.

4. Counseling for Greg's parents about the nature of Greg's LD, its likely biological origin, and the need to keep expectations reasonable for Greg's school performance in view of this disability. The need to downplay the disability and to emphasize Greg's strengths socially, athletically, and in other areas of school achievement was stressed.

CONCLUSIONS

These six cases illustrate the most common types of referrals to clinics that specialize in evaluating children with ADHD. They also illustrate one approach to the multimethod clinical assessment of such children. While others may prefer to use somewhat different interview formats, rating scales, and psychological tests from those employed in our clinic, the important aspect of the evaluation is that it rely on multiple sources of information about the child from multiple respondents (parents, teachers, clinician) across a wide range of settings (home, school, clinic, community), and employ multiple assessment instruments (interviews, ratings, tests, informal and formal direct behavioral observations). Each source, respondent, and method of assessment tends to balance out the types of errors that can be inherent in the others, ensuring that the integrated results will provide a more valid picture of the child's current adjustment than could any source or method alone. A sampling of the types of recommendations likely to be made in these cases has also been provided. These categories of recommendations receive considerable attention in subsequent chapters.

In general, our approach to assessment is in keeping with the views of Mash and Terdal (1988) that assessment and treatment are closely intertwined and constantly ongoing activities in clinical practice. Although they are artificially separated in this text for ease of presentation, it should be evident that decisions about treatment are constantly being raised and evaluated for appropriateness by the clinician throughout each step of the assessment process and are not left to the end of the evaluation. Similarly, assessment is an integral part of treatment, with baseline information being collected prior to treatment and then obtained periodically and formally throughout the treatment process.

Our diagnostic and treatment decision making follows a relatively straightforward set of steps:

1. Document the major concerns of the referral sources and probe for indications of developmental deviance in these complaints, as well as indications of the veracity of the complaints.

2. Begin to cluster the referral concerns into areas of developmental competence (sensory, motor, language, intellect, executive processes, social, emotional, etc.) and areas of ecological significance for the child (home, school, community).

3. Contrast the findings in these domains and situations with consensus criteria and guidelines for the diagnosis of childhood psychiatric and developmental disorders, such as those of the DSM-III-R. Begin to note all that seem pertinent to the case.

4. Rank-order the apparent disorders and developmental concerns into a hierarchy of importance for this particular case, as this will naturally guide which interventions need to be started immediately and which may come later.

5. Note the unique aspects of this particular case: child characteristics, parental characteristics, family functioning and stressors, and community resources that may or may not be available to assist with the case.

6. Begin listing the treatments that seem appropriate to each area of disorder, dysfunction, or developmental delay.

7. Consider potential aspects of the case that contraindicate the treatments being considered or are likely to hamper their implementation.

8. Assess the resources available to this child that can specifically address these treatment recommendations.

9. Note any uncertainties about the case and the information being provided from various sources and instruments. Consider how best to address these inconsistencies or uncertainties. Contrasting redundant measures of a particular ability or skill derived from different sources against each other is one approach. Employing additional assessment methods may be another. Testing the veracity of the source or method against other sources or methods is a third. A referral to a specialist is in order when these uncertainties fall outside one's domain of professional competence.

10. Note any legal or ethical dilemmas that arise from the information being gathered in the assessment, and begin considering how best to address them. Consultations with professional colleagues are highly recommended in such instances. Legal counsel may also sometimes be advisable.

11. Take special care to highlight sensitive information that may not be appropriate to share with others working with the child in the natural setting, and discuss with parents the concerns about protecting this type of information. For instance, the knowledge of family psychiatric disorders is very helpful in differential diagnosis, but does not need to be part of a report to be placed in a school file or other loosely protected record.

12. Once treatments are undertaken, consider what criteria are to be met for treatment to be terminated, at least for the time being. ADHD children have so many coexisting difficulties in many cases that they can wind up in endless treatment or psychotherapy unless it is clear what is to be achieved, so that these often expensive interventions can be terminated at some point.

Certainly other activities occur in the integration of information from an assessment. The list above merely highlights certain significant procedures and issues that apply to most cases. Above all, the professional style in the assessment and diagnosis is crucial: it must be one of serving humanely, diplomatically, sensitively, and compassionately the cases to be evaluated. Excessive moralizing, overly judgmental attitudes, and a condescending or humiliating style toward cases assure poor rapport with families and children, diminished motivation by them to comply with treatment, and a higher risk of hurting one's own practice or even being sued for malpractice. Above all, where doubt in one's judgment about aspects of a case exists, whether in diagnosis, prognosis, or treatment, it should be expressed openly, honestly, without apology, and with suggestions as to how (if possible) it might be addressed. It should go without saying that a coping, problem-solving, hypothesis-testing, humble clinician who can honestly say at times, "I am not sure," is a far more effective professional in these cases than a brash, rigid, overconfident, closed-minded, and arrogant one. It is at those times we are so certain in our judgments that we may be most mistaken. Despite what we may know about ADHD, and it is considerable, there is much about it that we do not know. As a consequence, no integration of clinical findings from an assessment is perfect or complete. Surprises will certainly abound for those clinicians who devote their practices to these children and their families.

PART III

TREATMENT

Existence was given us for action. Our worth is determined by the good deeds we do, rather than by the fine emotions we feel.

—Elias L. Magoon (1810–86)

12

Counseling and Training Parents

ARTHUR ANASTOPOULOS and RUSSELL A. BARKLEY

> If I were asked what single qualification was necessary for one who has the care of children, I should say patience— patience with their tempers, with their understandings, with their progress. It is not brilliant parts or great acquirements which are necessary for teachers, but patience to go over first principles again and again; steadily every day; never to be irritated by wilful or accidental hindrance.
>
> —Francis de S. Fenelon (1651–1715)

Parent training and parent counseling are two of the most commonly recommended treatment services offered through the Attention-Deficit Hyperactivity Disorder (ADHD) Clinic at the University of Massachusetts Medical Center. Most often they are delivered together in the context of an 8- to 12-session cognitive-behavioral treatment program, which may be used either with individual families or with several families in a group therapy format.

The original version of this program first appeared in Barkley's 1981 text, *Hyperactive Children: A Handbook for Diagnosis and Treatment.* A modified version was described in great detail in the 1987 text by Barkley, *Defiant Children: A Clinician's Manual for Parent Training.* Although the current program is fundamentally similar in nature to these earlier versions, additional clinical experience and parent feedback have led to further revisions, which we believe represent significant improvements.

In this chapter we discuss the parent counseling and training program that we currently employ. We begin this discussion by presenting our rationale for utilizing this particular combination of treatment strategies. Thereafter, we provide a detailed description of the manner in which we implement the program with clinic-referred ADHD children and their families.

RATIONALE

Although we have always recognized the therapeutic value of parent training and parent counseling, our appreciation of their role in the clinical management of ADHD children has increased a great deal in recent years. Several factors have helped shape our thinking on this matter. In part, our current perspective has been influenced by the lessons that clinical experience has taught us. Recent shifts in how we conceptualize ADHD at a theoretical level have come into play as well. Also affecting our thinking is the clinical research literature, where preliminary empirical evidence supporting the use of these interventions has been reported. Further discussion of these matters is presented below.

Clinical Considerations

In Chapter 17 it is noted that stimulant medication therapy is by far the most commonly employed treatment strategy in the clinical management of ADHD children. In brief review, stimulant medications have been shown to be highly effective in bringing about significant improvements in attention span, impulse control, and physical restlessness in a large percentage of ADHD children (Taylor, 1986a). Increases in child compliance with parent and teacher requests (Barkley, 1988e), as well as decreases in child aggressive behavior and conduct problems (Hinshaw, Henker, & Whalen, 1984b), have also been reported.

Taken at face value, these findings might lead some individuals to conclude that stimulant medication therapy alone is sufficient for bringing about desired changes in the behavior of ADHD children. To the extent that this is a valid conclusion, there would be little reason to incorporate parent training/counseling strategies (or any other intervention strategies, for that matter) in the clinical management of ADHD children. Such an assumption, however, is clearly in error. As our clinical experience has repeatedly demonstrated, there are several limitations in using stimulant medication therapy with ADHD children, which in part provide a rationale for employing parent training/counseling.

For example, while stimulant medications can lead to significant improvements in behavior for a large percentage of ADHD children, as many as 20% to 30% of the school-age population, and an even higher percentage of the preschool population, may not show a favorable response. Even when a favorable response is obtained, a small percentage of ADHD children may exhibit undesirable side effects, which may be of sufficient magnitude to rule out an ongoing stimulant medication regimen. In sum, there are many ADHD children for whom stimulant medication therapy is not a viable treatment option. For this segment of the population, therefore, alternative treatment approaches, such as parent training, must be incorporated.

Even when ADHD children show a favorable medication response in the absence of significant side effects, there are additional reasons why this treatment approach alone cannot meet all of their clinical management needs. For instance, clinical use of stimulant medication does not automatically provide parents with improved parenting skills, with which they may respond to medication-induced improvements in child behavior. Of additional concern is that these improvements in child behavior generally are not maintained when medication is not being taken. Thus, it is far more difficult for parents to manage ADHD children during late afternoons and early evenings, when the therapeutic benefits of stimulant medication are diminishing. Similar management problems may arise during weekends and school vacations, which are often designated as drug-free holidays. To the extent that parents spend time with their children when medication is not being used, it becomes necessary for them to rely upon other means of handling their behavioral difficulties. One such means, of course, is through the use of specialized child management skills, which may be derived from the parent training program. Independent of whether or not stimulants are clinically effective, many parents maintain a strong preference not to use any medication for child behavior management purposes. In recent years such antimedication preferences have been on the increase (see Chapter 1 for a discussion). While it is a clinician's responsibility to inform parents of his or her professional opinion regarding the potential benefits of medication, ultimately the parents must decide whether or not to proceed with such a recommendation. When parents express a preference not to employ stimulant medication, other treatment approaches must be employed. In clinical situations like this, many parents are relatively more comfortable addressing their child's ADHD difficulties through parent training strategies.

Additional justification for initiating parent training/counseling stems from a consideration of the fact that the problems of ADHD children are seldom limited to the core ADHD symptoms themselves. As noted in earlier chapters, ADHD children frequently exhibit other types of psychosocial difficulties, such as aggression, oppositional defiant behavior, conduct disturbance, academic underachievement, diminished self-esteem, depression, peer relationship problems, enuresis, and encopresis. Because many of these problem areas cannot be managed through stimulant medication therapy, they must be addressed by other means. For many ADHD children, parent training/counseling is often used for this purpose.

The oppositional defiant or noncompliant behavior of ADHD children is an especially appropriate target for parent training/counseling. There are several reasons for this. As noted by Patterson (1982), noncompliant child behavior is extremely pervasive. Of further concern is that it can lead to more serious behavioral difficulties, such as repetitive lying, stealing, and other chronic violations of societal rules. At times it may hinder the behavioral treatment of other clinical difficulties, such as enuresis or encopresis. In combination with ADHD, it is a significant predictor of later maladjustment during adolescence and young adulthood. In short, noncompliance is a serious behavioral complication that can affect many areas of a child's psychosocial functioning. As such, it must be targeted for treatment, along with whatever ADHD difficulties may be present. Although this admittedly can be quite challenging, the parent training portion of our program is well suited to meeting this challenge. And because noncompliance is so pervasive in nature, its successful management can lead to numerous improvements in overall psychosocial functioning.

Another matter of clinical importance is that the problems of ADHD children can place a tremendous strain upon family functioning. Traditional parenting techniques, which may work well for normal siblings, frequently are rendered ineffective when applied to ADHD children. Not only is the normal parenting process disrupted; often, so too are parent-child relations, sibling relations, marital relations, and/or parental personal functioning. When these sorts of family problems arise, they must be dealt with directly. One way of doing so is through parent training/counseling.

There are times, of course, when the reported problems of ADHD children are experienced primarily in the school setting, rather than at home. Under these circumstances, there might be reason to question the need for parent training/counseling. Based on our clinical experience with this population, we believe that these intervention strategies can still serve a useful therapeutic purpose. For example, parents who are keenly aware of ADHD and its management are generally in a better position to work with teachers in a cooperative and collaborative fashion. This can be especially beneficial when classroom contingency management techniques are employed. As ADHD children are promoted from one grade to the next, they sometimes are assigned to teachers who are unfamiliar with ADHD. When this occurs, informed parents can share their knowledge of ADHD and its management with the new teachers, thereby providing some degree of continuity from one academic year to the next. On occasion, serious differences of opinion between parents and school personnel may arise with respect to the need for classroom modifications or special education services. In these conflict situations, informed parents can be more effective advocates on behalf of their ADHD children, or at the very least, can work closely with a state-appointed child advocate.

As is evident from the preceding discussion, there are many commonly encountered clinical situations that provide a basis for including parent training/counseling in the overall clinical management of ADHD children. Additional justification for implementing this particular combination of intervention strategies may be derived from a consideration of the following theoretical points.

Theoretical Considerations

In recent years important clinical and empirical evidence has emerged, potentially signaling a shift in the way that ADHD is conceptualized and labeled. More specifically, it has been postulated that the behavior problems of ADHD children may stem more from an underlying motivational deficit, rather than from a deficit in core attentional processes (see Chapter 2).

Much of the impetus for conceptualizing ADHD as a motivational disorder comes from the observed variability in ADHD symptomatology across situations. For example, parents commonly report that ADHD children *can* pay attention to certain activities, such as Nintendo games, or sit still in certain situations, such as watching *Sesame Street* or some other favorite television program. To many individuals this is quite confusing; they may believe that a child either has an attention deficit or does not. Such confusion presumably stems from the commonly held assumption that ADHD is ever-present—that is, a type of all-or-none phenomenon. Clinicians who work closely with ADHD children know that nothing could be further from the truth. Unlike a severe hearing loss or other types of physical disabilities, ADHD is a condition whose behavioral symptoms vary a great deal as a function of the situational demands placed upon the child.

To the extent that this motivational-deficit hypothesis is valid, it has direct bearing on how parents might manage the home behavior problems of ADHD children. More specifically, it suggests that parents must provide ADHD children with ongoing external motivation, which they seem to require in order to overcome their difficulties in situations that they do not find intrinsically interesting. One way this may be accomplished is through home-based applications of specialized contingency management techniques. These, of course, may be learned through participation in the parent training portion of the treatment program, which is described later in this chapter.

For many families, parental acquisition of specialized contingency management techniques is sufficient for bringing about desired changes in the home behavior of ADHD children. For a significant portion of the ADHD population, however, this intervention alone may not be enough. As mentioned earlier, some parents may be experiencing depression, anxiety, health problems, or other types of personal distress. Marital tensions, financial strains, and other psychosocial stressors may exist as well. To the extent that these circumstances are present, parents must direct much of their time and energy to coping with these difficulties. In the process of doing so, parental attention is necessarily diverted away from parenting responsibilities. Under these conditions, efforts to teach them specialized contingency management techniques often fall short. For this reason individual, marital, and/or family counseling services must be provided either prior to or during ongoing parent training efforts.

Even in families that are relatively free from such complications, there are additional reasons why parent training alone may be insufficient for meeting their home management needs. For example, learning of a child's ADHD diagnosis can be a stressful experience for many parents. Such stress frequently can stem from parental misconceptions of ADHD. Or, like that of parents who learn for the first time of a child's lifelong chronic illness, it may result from parental difficulties in accepting what they perceive to be a defective child, who deviates from their hopes and expectations. Regardless of their basis, such difficulties in adjusting to the ADHD diagnosis can interfere a great deal with parental efforts to manage child behavior.

Inaccurate parental perceptions of child behavior can also impede parent training. Not infrequently, parents may be discouraged and view their child's behavior as unchangeable. In many cases they may have tried unsophisticated forms of behavior management and come to the conclusion that "nothing works." Or they may misinterpret much of their child's misbehavior as acts of intentional malice and insist on using harsh disciplinary strategies as punishment. Because ADHD children frequently display inappropriate behavior, parents may inadvertently begin to anticipate and to focus their attention exclusively upon negative child behavior; in the process, they may lose sight of any prosocial behavior that may occur. As a result of such difficulties, parents may develop negative feelings toward their child. They may also develop a negative outlook on their child's future, often viewing it as hopeless.

Inaccurate self-perceptions may also come into play for parents of ADHD children. For example, when told of their child's ADHD diagnosis, the parents may automatically assume that they are in some way directly responsible. Or as sometimes happens, one spouse may blame the other for the child's difficulties. In either case, such assumptions about the etiology of ADHD are often accompanied by strong feelings of parental guilt. These in turn may interfere with parent training efforts. Of additional concern is that many parents routinely report that they have been repeatedly unsuccessful in managing their children's behavior. Such experience often leads to self-perceptions of inadequacy in the parenting role. In some cases parenting self-esteem may even diminish to the point where parents no longer perceive themselves to be in control of their children. When such negative self-appraisals occur, parental motivation to try recommended child management techniques is often quite low.

In sum, parents' perceptions of themselves, of their children, and of the ADHD diagnosis itself can be highly inaccurate at times. Such inaccuracies are frequently accompanied by negative feelings, such as guilt, diminished self-esteem, sadness, and/or hopelessness. When these emotional complications arise, they can seriously interfere not only with the normal parenting process, but also with parental efforts to acquire specialized child management skills through participation in the parent training program.

For these reasons, additional parent counseling may be needed. In order to understand what type of counseling may be best suited to meeting these needs, it is first necessary to consider another theoretical point of view. Specifically, we are referring to the theoretical premises that serve as a foundation for employing cognitive therapy strategies. Although an extensive discussion of these premises is clearly beyond the scope of this text, a brief overview is provided to clarify their relevance to ADHD children and their parents. Readers interested in acquiring additional information about cognitive therapy are encouraged to consider other sources (Beck, Rush, Shaw, & Emery, 1970; Freeman, Simon, Beutler, & Arkowitz, 1981).

A central premise of cognitive therapy is that the way we think about ourselves and the world around us affects the way that we feel and behave. In many situations our perceptions of reality are inaccurate, due to what are known as cognitive distortions or errors in thinking. Several types exist. For example, we may jump to faulty conclusions when predicting the future or when trying to read someone else's mind. Or we may take a limited amount of information and overgeneralize from it. Another common cognitive distortion is all-or-none thinking—that is, the tendency to interpret circumstances in either-or, black-and-white terms. When we repeatedly engage in these sorts of thinking errors, they can lead to inaccurate perceptions of ourselves and of the world around us. These in turn may contribute to the emergence and/or maintenance of negative feelings and maladaptive behaviors.

Of what clinical relevance are these theoretical premises for ADHD children and their parents? Perhaps the best way to begin answering this question is through case illustration. During a routine feedback session, the parents of a recently diagnosed 10-year-old boy admitted that they had very little interest in pursuing our recommendation to participate in the parent training/counseling program. After all, they previously had worked with another mental health professional who had given them ongoing parenting advice, which they did not find to be especially helpful. Thus, they had come to the conclusion that "nothing works" for their child, which left them feeling quite discouraged. It was respectfully called to their attention that they might be overgeneralizing from this limited therapeutic experience. Upon further questioning, it became clear that the child management techniques that they had been using were quite different from those available through our parent training/counseling program. Because they had not yet tried our approach, it remained possible that it might be effective in bringing about the kinds of changes in their child's behavior that they desired. Then again, it might not. Not until they put this hypothesis to test would it be possible to evaluate its validity. After these parents were counseled in this manner, they became more receptive to giving the parent training/counseling program a try. Much to their delight, the child management skills that they eventually acquired were highly successful in bringing their child's home behavioral difficulties under better control. This in turn seemed to ease some of the parenting stress that they had felt for so long.

This clinical situation, of course, is just one of the many ways in which cognitive therapy strategies might be utilized in the counseling that is done with parents of ADHD children. Numerous other examples of how this approach can be applied are provided in a later section of this chapter. For the time being, let it suffice to say that cognitive therapy strategies are often well suited to correcting parents' faulty perceptions of themselves, of their children, and of the ADHD diagnosis. As such, they frequently can serve to increase a parent's willingness to employ specialized contingency management techniques and/or to facilitate a parent's psychological adjustment to having an ADHD child.

In summarizing this theoretical discussion, we would like to emphasize the following points. First and foremost, our conceptualization of ADHD has recently shifted in the direction of viewing it as a motivational disorder. This provides us with a theoretical rationale for teaching parents specialized contingency management techniques, which may be used to motivate ADHD children to do the things that they are disinclined to do. Second, in order to use such techniques most effectively, parents should possess an accurate understanding of how ADHD affects their child and his or her behavior. Their assumption, of course, underlies our reasoning for routinely counseling them about this disorder. And finally, because many parents experience negative feelings and/or lack the motivation necessary to acquire specialized child management tactics, they must often be counseled about such matters. Working from the assumption that these difficulties can stem from faulty parental perceptions of themselves and of their ADHD children, we have systematically incorporated cognitive therapy strategies (e.g., cognitive restructuring) into the counseling that we provide.

Despite the logical appeal of this reasoning, it should be remembered that any theory must be supported by evidence. And while our clinical experience certainly provides such support, it is limited by its subjective nature. Just as in other fields of science, the availability of objective evidence, obtained from carefully controlled research, is a necessary condition for assessing the validity of our theoretical assumptions. With this in mind, it therefore becomes necessary to ask the question: Is there empirical support for employing parent training/counseling in the clinical management of ADHD children?

Empirical Support

Within the child clinical research literature are direct and indirect sources of empirical evidence that have bearing on the question above. The direct evidence comes from investigations that have evaluated the efficacy of parent training/counseling specifically within ADHD populations. The indirect evidence may be found in studies that have employed somewhat different parent training approaches, either with ADHD children or with children manifesting other types of behavior disorders. Each of these is discussed below.

Somewhat surprisingly, parent training/counseling interventions have not been researched extensively within the ADHD population. In contrast with the hundreds of studies that have been published on the use of stimulant medication therapy, no more than 10 parent training/counseling investigations have been reported. Among these, only two were conducted in a manner consistent with the parent training/counseling procedures outlined in the earlier texts (Barkley, 1981, 1987). In both studies, however, significant improvements in child behavior were obtained following parental participation in the treatment program (Pisterman, McGrath, Firestone, & Goodman, 1988; Pollard, Ward, & Barkley, 1983). In the other published reports, similar behavioral parent training programs were investigated, but in none of these was parent counseling systematically incorporated into the treatment regimen (Bidder, Gray, & Newcombe, 1978; Dubey, O'Leary, & Kaufman, 1983; Firestone, Kelly, Goodman, & Davey, 1981; Gittelman-Klein et al., 1976; Henry, 1987; Horn, Ialongo, Popovich, & Peradotto, 1987; Pelham et al., in press). Despite this major procedural difference, these related investigations generally were consistent in demonstrating that parent training can bring about significant improvements in child behavior.

Taken together, these results suggest that behavioral parent training, either alone or in combination with parent counseling, can be therapeutically beneficial to ADHD children and their families. Above and beyond this statement, however, it is difficult to draw conclusions pertaining to more specific clinical matters. For example, the available research does not provide a basis for assessing the separate and joint contributions of parent training and parent counseling. Nor does it provide any clinical guidelines for determining which ADHD children and their families are best suited to receiving this type of intervention.

Such matters remain unclear for several reasons. First of all, none of the available research in this area was completed in the context of a systematic program of research on parent training/counseling. Instead, each of the studies cited above was conducted independently by different researchers. Further complicating the situation are numerous methodological inconsistencies across investigations, as well as methodological shortcomings within some of the reported studies. For example, surprisingly few studies defined their ADHD populations by means of commonly employed diagnostic criteria, such as those available in any of the *Diagnostic and Statistical Manuals of Mental Disorders,* published by the American Psychiatric Association. In those that did, little attempt was made to control for the presence of co-occurring behavioral and/or emotional complications. Several investigations were limited by extremely small sample sizes. Many studies also failed to incorporate checks on the degree to which therapists adhered to the intended treatment regimen. Some chose not to include direct observational measures in their assessment of targeted parent-child interactions, while others omitted follow-up assessments as a way of gauging the stability of treatment gains over time.

In view of these methodological concerns, it would seem prudent to defer any final judgment on the overall therapeutic effectiveness of parent training/counseling with ADHD children until further direct research is completed. In making this statement, we are in no way suggesting that clinicians should refrain from using this treatment approach. On the contrary, we believe that there is a sufficient amount of preliminary support for conducting such interventions. We would also contend, however, that additional research, which is systematic in nature and methodologically sound, must still be conducted for us to understand more completely the full impact of this treatment approach.

Until such studies are completed, it may be useful to consider a related area of research that has indirect bearing on this situation—that is, the studies that have employed similar parent training approaches with noncompliant, oppositional defiant, and conduct-disordered children (Forehand & McMahon, 1981; McMahon & Wells, 1989). In a series of related investigations, Forehand and his associates repeatedly demonstrated that their behavioral parent training program was highly effective in bringing about significant improvements not only in targeted noncompliant and defiant behaviors (McMahon & Forehand, 1984), but also in nontargeted behaviors, such as aggression (Wells, Forehand, & Griest, 1980). Such treatment gains generalized readily from the clinic setting to the natural home environment (Webster-Stratton, 1984), and typically remained quite stable over time, often being maintained up to 4 years following termination of treatment (Forehand, Wells, & Griest, 1980). Of additional importance for the purposes of the present discussion is that various modifications to the basic Forehand program enhanced the generalization and/or maintenance of treatment gains. This included, for example, therapeutic efforts to increase parental knowledge of the social learning principles underlying the program (McMahon, Forehand, & Griest, 1981). Also reportedly enhancing treatment outcome were procedures that targeted various aspects of general family functioning, such as parent perceptions of child behavior, marital adjustment, and parental personal adjustment (Griest, et al., 1982).

As will become evident shortly, the parent training component of our treatment program is in many respects similar to the Forehand approach. This similarity, of course, is by no means a coincidence, as both programs were greatly influenced in their development by Hanf's (1969) two-stage behavioral program for child noncompliance. Additional overlap would certainly seem to exist with respect to the populations targeted by these two approaches. As noted earlier, ADHD children frequently exhibit noncompliant and oppositional defiant behavior patterns, which were the focus of the investigations conducted by Forehand and his associates. To the extent that these two approaches share common ground, the above-cited research findings lend support, albeit indirectly, to the efficacy of our parent training/counseling program for ADHD children and their families.

In summary, we introduced this section of the chapter by asking a simple question: Is there empirical support for employing parent training/counseling in the clinical management of ADHD children? Our answer to this question is, of course, anything but simple. There is a limited, but not conclusive, amount of direct evidence providing preliminary support for using these treatment strategies. Indirect support may be gleaned from the extensive body of related research that has examined the efficacy of behavioral parent training with children manifesting associated behavioral difficulties. Before we can draw more definitive empirical conclusions, additional research is needed. Until this is completed, however, we believe that the available empirical evidence, in combination with our previously stated theoretical convictions and clinical experience, provides us with sufficient justification for continuing to use this particular treatment program.

OVERVIEW OF THE PARENT TRAINING PROGRAM

Having presented our clinical, theoretical, and empirical reasoning, we are now in a position to discuss our clinical application of the parent training/ counseling program. We begin by reviewing our clinical criteria for making referrals. This is followed by a discussion of various clinical and stylistic considerations that apply to all phases of treatment. After briefly summarizing our therapeutic objectives, we then present a detailed description of the specific steps that we take in implementing the complete program.

Prior to beginning this discussion, however, we should point out two important qualifications. First, although this treatment approach can be used either with individual families or with several families in a group therapy format, our description of it pertains primarily to its application with individual families. Upon completing this, we comment briefly upon its modified use with groups of families. Second, it is important to bear in mind that many features of the current program have been discussed in great detail in an earlier text (Barkley, 1981), as well as in a recently published clinician's manual (Barkley, 1987). Given the availability of this latter publication in particular, our objective in writing this portion of the chapter is not to provide the equivalent of a clinician's manual. We do, however, present summary descriptions of the procedures that have been previously covered. In addition, we focus detailed attention upon the procedural refinements that we have recently made. By presenting information in this way, we hope that readers will gain a better understanding of the framework that guides us in our clinical application of this program.

Selection Criteria

A diagnosis of ADHD in and of itself is not sufficient grounds for referring a particular child and family to the parent training/counseling program. Additional child, parent, and/or family characteristics must be taken into account as part of the clinical decision-making process.

One of the simplest criteria to assess is the chronological age of the identified child. In most cases children must be between 3 and 11 years of age in order for their parents to be considered for the program. Although referrals are presently limited in this way, we should point out that we are nearing the completion of a research project, the results of which will serve to clarify whether a modified version of this same program is suitable for use with adolescents from 12 to 17 years of age.

These age guidelines, of course, presume a relatively close correspondence between a child's chronological age and mental age. When a significant discrepancy exists, this can affect the referral process. for instance, an ADHD child whose mental age falls below 3 years is not very likely to benefit a great deal from his or her parents' participation in the complete treatment program. At the other end of the continuum, an ADHD teenager whose mental age lies below 12 years may in fact be an appropriate referral.

In addition to these chronological and mental age considerations, the identified child's diagnostic status must be taken into account. Such information is routinely derived from the multimethod assessment battery that has been described in Part II. Although a diagnosis of ADHD is a necessary condition for referral, it is by no means sufficient on its own. The severity of the ADHD diagnosis also comes into play, as do the presence and severity of various co-occurring conditions.

In our experience, the complete treatment program is often ideally suited to meeting the clinical management needs of ADHD children who also display significant oppositional defiant behavior or conduct problems. Even when these associated behavioral complications are absent, the program may still be beneficial to children whose ADHD is moderate to severe in intensity. In cases where the ADHD may be extremely severe, however, it may first be necessary to consider placing the children on a trial of stimulant medication. So as to avoid confounding the outcome of such therapeutic trials, participation in the parent training/counseling program is temporarily postponed. Once it has been determined that a child will or will not continue to receive stimulant medication therapy, parent training/counseling services may be employed at that point. For those children who show a favorable response to stimulants, continued use of such medication generally makes their behavior easier to manage, thereby facilitating parental efforts to employ recommended parent training skills.

The presence of other serious behavioral complications, such as extreme aggressiveness and violence, can also affect the timing of parental participation in the program. In such a situation it may initially be necessary to manage the child in a residential setting away from home. As the child's extreme behaviors are brought under better control, portions of the parent training/ counseling program may be started and practiced during weekend home visits. Upon discharge, continuation of the program may then serve to facilitate the child's transition back into the home.

For those ADHD children whose ADHD difficulties are mild and who do not exhibit oppositional defiant behavior or related problems, implementation of the complete treatment program may not be the most efficient means of meeting their clinical management needs. Nevertheless, their psychosocial circumstances may still be enhanced either by the parent counseling portion of the program or by parental acquisition of select contingency management skills (e.g., a home token system) that address their motivational deficits. Other ADHD children for whom the complete program may initially be inappropriate are those who are also experiencing significant depression, anxiety, or other sorts of emotional difficulties. In many cases like this, the children's emotional complications are independent of the ADHD and clearly of greater clinical concern. For this latter reason in particular, they must often be addressed first. Once such difficulties are resolved, however, it may then be appropriate to initiate parent training/counseling services.

Referral to the program is, of course, not just a function of the child's characteristics. Numerous parent characteristics enter into the clinical decision-making process as well. Perhaps the most important of these is the parents' ability to tolerate the child's deviant behavior. While some parents are able to cope satisfactorily with even the most severe child behavior problems, others are highly distressed by much milder child difficulties. For this reason their referral for parent training/counseling depends a great deal on their perceived need for such services. There are times, of course, when parents do not perceive such a need, and yet it is our professional opinion that they might indeed benefit from the program. This occurs most often among parents who, although they have control over their child's behavior, are experiencing a great deal of stress in maintaining such control. In such situations, we frequently advise parents to participate in the program. By doing so, parents gain access to more efficient child management techniques and coping strategies, which in turn reduces the stress that they experience in their parenting role.

Another basis for referral arises when parental differences of opinion exist with respect to various child management issues. For example, a husband and wife may differ a great deal in their interpretation of their child's ADHD, or they may seriously disagree over how to manage his or her behavior. Joint participation in the treatment program affords them an opportunity for acquiring a common base of ADHD knowledge, from which they may also employ more consistent child management strategies. This can serve to reduce marital tensions related to child management, and to facilitate parental efforts to gain control over their child's problem behaviors.

In situations where marital tensions stem from areas other than child management issues, referral to the program may not be appropriate at first. There are several reasons for this. Some parents may be so preoccupied with their troubled marital circumstances that they are unable to commit the time and energy necessary for meeting the increased parenting responsibilities required by the treatment program. Or, as sometimes happens, parents are so unwilling to compromise with each other that they are unlikely to agree upon using recommended parent training strategies. When such serious complications exist, parents are advised to begin receiving marriage counseling, either prior to or concurrent with their participation in the parent training/counseling program. As might be expected, failure to do so greatly jeopardizes the outcome of any subsequent treatment that may be rendered on behalf of a child.

Marital difficulties are not the only circumstance affecting the timing of parental participation in the program. One or both parents may be depressed, anxious, or affected by other types of medical or psychological difficulties, the primary cause of which is not their ADHD child. Because coping with such personal distress may necessarily divert parental attention away from meeting routine parenting responsibilities, many parents may find it difficult to put forth the effort necessary to benefit from participation in the parent training/counseling program. For this reason it is often necessary to direct them to appropriate medical and/or mental health professionals to begin addressing their concerns. Such assistance can occur either prior to or during their participation in parent training/counseling.

In addition to these personal and marital issues, parents of ADHD children may be facing external stresses and strains that are not readily under their control. This might include, for example, sudden financial strains resulting from a recent job loss, or ongoing stresses pertaining to the daily care of a chronically ill relative. Although such complications may not require ongoing professional assistance, these too may still affect the timing of when parents decide to become involved in the treatment program.

As a rule, parental levels of education and intelligence are not major factors in deciding whether or not to refer a family for parent training/counseling. In extreme cases, however, they may need to be taken into account. For example, parents with borderline to mildly delayed intellectual functioning may not be able to implement recommended child management strategies, or to understand fully the counseling objectives of the program. While this of course can happen, we do not automatically assume it to be the case. Instead, we generally try to implement the program at a pace commensurate with the parents' learning style. If after a few sessions it becomes clear that this is not working, then we may ask parents to have a close friend or relative accompany them during subsequent treatment sessions. Once properly informed, such individuals frequently are in an excellent position to communicate important therapeutic information and to ensure that recommended treatment strategies are used correctly within the home setting.

Another commonly encountered clinical situation that affects referral decisions is when the ADHD child and/or other members of the family are already receiving mental health services. Before starting our parent training/counseling program, we generally contact the professional providing treatment (with the family's consent, of course). Once the therapeutic nature and intent of such services are clarified, a decision is made as to whether or not participation in parent training/counseling is at cross-purposes with the existing treatment. If it is, then we generally advise against doing both treatments simultaneously, leaving it up to the parents to decide which type of therapeutic assistance they will pursue. If no apparent conflict exists, we initiate the program, but thereafter monitor the situation periodically to ensure that no conflict arises.

Although it is not usually an exclusionary factor, the number of parents likely to be attending treatment sessions may also enter into the referral de-cision-making process. In two-parent families, the presence of both parents is highly desirable but not always feasible, due to job schedule conflicts, child caretaking responsibilities, and so forth. Instead of automatically restricting such families from the program, we generally allow for one-parent partici-pation. In many cases this can be an acceptable arrangement, as long as the parent not in attendance is understanding, cooperative, and supportive of the treatment process. An additional reason for allowing one-parent participation is that several methods exist for getting around this sort of problem. For example, the parent in attendance may take detailed session notes or audi-otape the session. Such recorded information may then be shared and dis-cussed with the absent parent later at home.

This completes our review of the clinical criteria that we employ in making referrals to the parent training/counseling program. What should be evident by now is that the referral process is not a simple or straightforward matter. On the contrary, numerous psychosocial circumstances must be taken into account to ensure that this form of treatment is clinically appropriate for referred ADHD children and their families.

Clinical and Stylistic Considerations

Before outlining the specific steps that comprise the complete parent training/counseling program, we must first discuss a number of general clinical and stylistic considerations that pertain to all facets of treatment.

For instance, despite the availability of a detailed outline (Barkley, 1981) and a treatment manual (Barkley, 1987), this is by no means a simple inter-vention that can be implemented in a "cookbook" fashion. On the contrary, it requires certain minimum levels of clinical expertise. Being well versed in current ADHD research findings is an especially critical qualification for cli-nicians to possess, in light of the increasing number of talks, magazine arti-cles, newspaper stories, and television presentations on the Ritalin contro-versy (see Chapter 1), as well as other aspects of ADHD. Clinicians lacking such knowledge are very likely at some point in time to encounter parents who themselves possess a great deal of ADHD knowledge. And if by chance these same clinicians should respond to sophisticated parent questioning in an unsatisfactory manner, parental confidence in their expertise may diminish significantly. This, of course, may eventually interfere with any subsequent therapeutic efforts.

It is also necessary to bear in mind that the parent training portion of the treatment program is fundamentally behavioral in nature, and that the coun-seling portion routinely incorporates cognitive therapy strategies. Thus, ex-perience in using various child behavior therapy strategies, especially contin-gency management techniques, is highly desirable. So too is expertise in using various cognitive therapy techniques, such as cognitive restructuring. This is not to suggest that clinicians of other theoretical orientations should refrain from employing the program. On the contrary, they are encouraged to do so, provided that they become relatively familiar with the behavioral and cognitive principles of the program. As with other treatment approaches, however, the more skilled clinicians may be in using these cognitive-behavioral strategies, the more likely it is that they will be able to handle the difficult management and adjustment issues that parents of ADHD children frequently present.

Being cognitive-behavioral in nature, the treatment program routinely and systematically incorporates the use of highly specific between-session assignments, which are generally carried out within the home setting. Such assignments serve in part to facilitate parents' acquisition of various observational and monitoring techniques pertinent to their child's behavior. Of additional clinical significance is that they increase the likelihood that acquired parenting skills will generalize from the clinic, where they are learned, to the home setting. Between-session assignments may also serve as a vehicle for indirectly accessing clinically relevant thoughts and feelings, which parents may experience in the process of employing recommended child management tactics. Such information may then be used for cognitive restructuring purposes or for any other aspect of the counseling that is done with parents.

Because satisfactory completion of between-session assignments is a critical factor in the outcome of the program, clinicians must take steps to ensure that this occurs. One such step is to send parents home with written handouts, which summarize important in-session and between-session information. At times it may also be appropriate to have them audiotape treatment sessions. Such recorded information may then be reviewed as often as necessary to clarify clinical points pertinent to the between-session assignment. Should insurmountable problems arise in implementing a particular assignment, parents can also contact therapists by telephone to solve problems prior to their next regularly scheduled treatment session.

At the start of every session, time is set aside for reviewing parental efforts to carry out between-session assignments. Special attention is typically focused upon those assignments related to parental implementation of recommended child management strategies. Refinements in the parents' application of such strategies are made as necessary. When clinicians begin to sense that parents have acquired a certain level of skill mastery, therapeutic attention is shifted to the next treatment step. In this regard the parent training portion of the program follows a building-block model, with each step dependent upon successful completion and mastery of the preceding step. Use of such a model affords clinicians ample flexibility in proceeding with treatment at a pace meeting the needs of individual children and their parents.

Successful progress through the treatment program also requires close collaboration and cooperation between parents and clinicians. Several clinical and stylistic considerations must be taken into account in achieving this goal. As should be the case in other treatment approaches, clinicians must convey to parents a sense of genuine understanding, caring, respect, and support. At the same time they must present therapeutic information in ways that are clear and easy to understand. Everyday language should be employed, rather than professional jargon, which may be confusing to many parents. For similar reasons, daily life experiences, commonly encountered by ADHD children and their families, should be used as a context for illustrating clinical points that need to be made. Given that parenting ADHD children can be a very trying and stressful experience, it is sometimes helpful as well to incorporate humor into the sessions. Not only does this allow parents a welcome moment of relief, it can also help them understand and remember clinical information more effectively.

A Socratic style of questioning is also routinely used throughout treatment to foster close collaboration and cooperation. Such questioning generally makes it easier for clinicians to avoid succumbing to professional lecturing, which some parents may find disrespectful and condescending. It also forces parents to become more actively involved in the treatment process. By responding to questions that lead to therapeutically desirable solutions, parents gain a sense of having reached such solutions on their own. This in turn often serves to increase parenting self-esteem and to decrease parental dependence on clinicians. Such decreased dependence, of course, increases the likelihood that treatment gains will generalize across situations, even when they have not specifically been covered in treatment. Decreased dependence on the therapist can also increase the chances that treatment gains will remain stable after the active portion of the parent training/counseling program is completed.

Although implementation of these clinical and stylistic considerations can facilitate the therapy process, it does not necessarily guarantee a successful outcome. Even with ongoing clinical supervision, some parents may continue to experience child management difficulties. Such difficulties frequently stem from complications that parents encounter in practicing recommended treatment strategies. This might include, for example, family illnesses or job schedule changes that arise unexpectedly and interfere with parent training efforts. As long as these sorts of complications are not chronic in nature, their impact on the treatment program is minimal, and therefore they do not need to be addressed as a clinical issue. If on the other hand they occur more regularly, then it may become necessary to postpone completion of the treatment program until after such complications have been resolved.

Forgetfulness, procrastination, and even adult ADHD symptoms can also contribute to parental difficulties in practicing recommended parenting skills. When these sorts of problems arise, clinicians may wish to impose contingencies upon parents as a way of increasing their motivation to incorporate prescribed child management tactics. Withholding treatment sessions until greater compliance is achieved is one method for dealing with this kind of difficulty. Another useful method for promoting greater parental compliance is a breakage-fee system (Patterson, 1982). In this system parents leave a predetermined, fixed sum of money with the therapist. Specified amounts are then returned to parents when satisfactory compliance with between-session assignments occurs. Whenever noncompliance occurs, however, money is mailed to a political group or organization intensely disliked by the parents. Generally speaking, this approach works quite well in motivating parents who agree to its use.

As noted earlier in this chapter, parents who maintain negative perceptions of themselves and of their ADHD children may also find it difficult to employ recommended treatment strategies. To the extent that this occurs, parent counseling should be initiated to help them identify the basis of their faulty thinking. Once this is clarified, alternative perceptions should be generated and put to the test. Presumably this will lead parents to more accurate appraisals of themselves and of their children, which eventually should serve to facilitate their implementation of prescribed home management strategies.

There are times, of course, when parental difficulties in utilizing specialized child management techniques are not related to improper motivation or to faulty perceptions. Instead, they may be the result of parenting skill deficiencies. An especially effective way of pinpointing such deficiencies is through clinic-based observations of parent-child interactions. More specifically, parents may be asked to implement the intervention strategy in question while being observed through a one-way mirror. This allows the clinician to identify any problems that parents may be having in using a particular technique. Feedback about such problems may then be given to parents after the session is completed. Or the clinician may choose to demonstrate the proper application of the strategy with the child, and then ask the parents to try it once again before they depart. In an extension of this approach, parents may also be asked to wear a "bug-in-the-ear" device while being observed. This device allows clinicians to provide discreet feedback, which parents may then use immediately to facilitate their management of their child. As might be expected, such close clinical supervision is usually highly effective in bringing about desired improvements in targeted parenting skills.

Use of these supervisory tactics does not have to be limited to problem situations. In some cases they may be employed throughout all phases of treatment to enhance parental acquisition of all child management techniques that are part of the program. For many clinicians, however, this may not be a feasible option, because they do not have access to one-way mirrors or bug-in-the-ear devices. Should these resources not be available, other therapeutic strategies may be utilized to enhance parental learning of new child management procedures. For example, clinicians may include in-session modeling and role-playing exercises as part of their therapeutic contact with parents. In addition, they may choose to amplify clinical points by representing them pictorially or graphically, either on a chalkboard or on a piece of paper; the latter may then be taken home for review.

Treatment Objectives

Having completed our discussion of the various clinical and stylistic considerations that permeate all phases of treatment, we are now in a position to

outline the overall therapeutic objectives of our parent training/counseling program. One of the program's most important goals is to increase parental knowledge and understanding of ADHD, primarily through didactic instruction. An equally important objective of the program is to provide parents with ongoing clinical supervision in the use of specialized contingency management techniques, which may be used to address the motivational deficits and/or noncompliant behavior displayed by ADHD children. A third objective is to facilitate parental adjustment to having an ADHD child, primarily through the use of cognitive therapy strategies. Cognitive therapy strategies may also be used to achieve a fourth goal, which is increasing parental compliance with the prescribed treatment regimen. And finally, in the process of meeting these four objectives, it is the overall purpose of this treatment program to provide parents with coping skills that will lead to happier and less stressful lives, both for themselves and for their ADHD children.

SPECIFIC TRAINING STEPS

Although it generally can be completed within 8 to 12 sessions, the parent training/counseling program does not confine clinicians to a specific number of treatment sessions that must be followed inflexibly. Instead, it allows them to guide parents through treatment in a step-by-step fashion, taking as many sessions as necessary to bring about desired therapeutic change. With this in mind, we now begin discussing the specific 10 steps that make up the complete intervention program.

Step 1: Program Orientation and Review of ADHD

The overall objectives of the first step are (1) to acquaint parents with the mechanics of conducting the treatment program, (2) to begin increasing their knowledge of ADHD, and (3) to begin addressing any faulty perceptions that they may have about themselves or about their children.

The session typically starts with parents' providing a brief update on their status since the completion of the diagnostic evaluation. If necessary, additional assessments are done to evaluate the emergence of any new child behavior problems and to provide a more accurate baseline against which future therapeutic changes may be gauged. Having completed the updating process, we next explain the rationale and purpose of the training program, as well as its sequence of training steps. Matters pertaining to confidentiality and billing are covered at this time as well.

Following this orientation to the program, we begin discussing the topic of ADHD by reviewing its history, its numerous label changes, its core symptoms, the currently accepted clinical criteria used to formulate its diagnosis, and its prevalence rates in both clinic and general populations. Also covered are many of the commonly encountered associated features of ADHD, such as oppositional defiant behavior, aggressiveness, academic underachievement,

social skills deficits, emotional immaturity, and atypical physical characteristics, all of which set these children apart from other children in the general population. Currently available information about adolescent and adult outcomes is presented as well; this is generally followed by a discussion of the immediate and extended families of ADHD children. Various types of assessment devices are described, primarily in the context of the multimethod assessment battery presented earlier.

Attention is then directed to the causes of this disorder. Although it is recognized that the etiology of ADHD is multidimensional, emphasis is placed upon the view that, for most children, ADHD is a biologically based, inborn temperamental style that predisposes them to be inattentive, impulsive, and physically restless, as well as deficient in their capacity for rule-governed behavior (Anastopoulos & Barkley, 1988; Wender, 1987). Alerting parents to this theoretical bias helps to set the stage for later therapeutic efforts to create a prosthetic home environment that allows ADHD children to develop compensatory skills for coping with this chronic and pervasive behavioral disability. And finally, an extensive review of available treatment approaches is given, with emphasis placed upon the need for utilizing a multidimensional clinical management approach. Also emphasized during this review of treatment procedures is the notion that ADHD is, in many cases, a lifelong condition that is coped with or compensated for, rather than ultimately cured.

In presenting this information, it has been our experience that we need to keep it as brief as possible. Doing so allows parents to focus more attentively upon the main points that need to be made. We have also found it helpful to limit excessive reference to summary statistics and percentages obtained from the ADHD population as a whole. As so many parents have so frankly stated, they are not interested in facts and figures that have little to do with their child. In essence, the more that we relate the presentation to parents' particular child, the more likely it is that the parents will grasp the clinical and theoretical points we wish to make.

Recognizing that we cannot possibly cover everything that parents want to know, we conclude our ADHD presentation by giving them an opportunity to ask questions. Not uncommonly, this enables us to identify and to clarify points of confusion, often stemming from discrepancies that exist between what the parents have just learned and what they may have learned previously from TV, magazines, and so forth. Should parents feel overwhelmed by the sheer volume of new ADHD information, we remind them that processing of such information will occur gradually over time. Should they wish to facilitate their acquisition of such knowledge, they are also alerted to the availability of pertinent texts (Barkley, 1981; Ingersoll, 1988; Wender, 1987) and encouraged to review a videotaped presentation on the topic. Similar materials are recommended for review by their child's teachers and relatives, if parents so desire.

Prior to concluding this session, we encourage parents to voice their emotional reactions to what they have just heard. This, of course, begins the

formal counseling portion of the treatment program. Should parental feelings of shock, guilt, sadness, or anger be expressed, therapeutic attention is directed to clarifying the nature of such emotions. In particular, an attempt is made to identify the presence of any faulty perceptions that may in part underlie the negative emotional reactions.

Parental guilt is an especially common reaction, stemming from the belief that faulty parenting has somehow caused the ADHD problem. One way to deal with this is as follows. If there are siblings in the family, parents are asked to explain why it is that their parenting is successful with these children and not with the ADHD child. This serves to clarify that the problem may be more a function of the child's temperamental style than of their own parenting style. Support for this alternative viewpoint is then provided by means of reviewing pertinent ADHD findings. Additional evidence is accumulated over the course of treatment, as parents discover that specialized child management tactics can be effective.

Anxiety over their child's future is another common emotional reaction. In dealing with this concern, we respectfully point out to parents that they may be overgeneralizing from the ADHD diagnosis alone, not to mention making a negative future prediction. We therefore remind them that many other psychosocial factors enter into any future predictions. Thus, outcomes other than the negative ones that they may fear are possible. We also call their attention to the fact that any attempts at predicting the future are probability statements, rather than certainties. To the extent that we can alter these probabilities, we will. Thus, instead of automatically assuming that their child's future is bleak, they should concentrate their energies on doing the things necessary to make their child's prognosis more favorable.

In addition to having parents verbalize their emotional reactions to the ADHD presentation, we ask them to state their expectations for treatment outcome. Such expectations are often unrealistic in the sense that changes in their child's behavior are expected to occur in a rapid, continuous fashion. As an alternative to this viewpoint, we propose that therapeutic change occurs in a gradual, variable manner. Thus, when new behavior problems arise well into the treatment process, parents are reminded that this is just a normal part of the up-and-down therapeutic process, rather than a sign of regression to pretreatment levels of functioning. In addition to this type of cognitive restructuring, we encourage parents to view such setbacks as opportunities for learning. In this context parental efforts to implement recommended treatment strategies can be viewed as practice attempts that lead to skill refinement. For most parents this is a much less threatening and more constructive premise to adopt throughout their participation in the program.

Quite obviously, the counseling that is done in this first step of the program is seldom sufficient for completely resolving parental adjustment difficulties. From a cognitive therapy point of view, additional evidence is usually needed to restructure long-standing negative parental perceptions, which presumably contribute to such adjustment difficulties. This evidence, therefore, is routinely collected and called to parents' attention over the course of the treatment. In this regard the cognitive therapy or counseling that is done with parents may be viewed as an ongoing, process-oriented therapeutic tool.

Step 2: Understanding Parent-Child Relations and Principles of Behavior Management

The objectives of the second step are twofold: to provide parents with a four-factor model for understanding deviant child behavior and to increase parental knowledge of behavior management principles as they apply to ADHD children.

After reviewing carryover concerns from the previous session, we provide parents with a conceptual framework for understanding deviant parent-child interactions and their therapeutic management. Initially, the theoretical views of Bell (Bell & Harper, 1977) and Patterson (1976) are introduced in general terms. In this context, parents are alerted to four major factors that, in various combinations, can contribute to the emergence and/or maintenance of children's behavioral difficulties.

The first of these factors is a child's characteristics. Prominent among these is the youngster's inborn temperamental style, which encompasses general activity level, attention span, impulse control, emotionality, sociability, responsiveness to stimulation, and habit regularity. After checking with parents as to whether they detected early signs of temperamental difficulties in their own child, we next point out how such difficulties can frequently bring the child into conflict with his or her environment. In a similar vein, the potential behavioral complications of various physical characteristics and/or developmental disabilities are brought into the discussion.

Along with the child's characteristics, a like number and variety of parent characteristics are cited as circumstances that can place children at risk for behavioral difficulties. Additional attention is directed to the goodness of fit between various child and parent characteristics.

Stresses impinging upon the family are recognized as well. In particular, parents are taught several ways in which family stress can contribute to the emergence and/or maintenance of behavioral difficulties: by altering parental perceptions of the child, by altering the child's emotional well-being directly, and/or by preoccupying parents to the point that they become highly variable and inconsistent in their disciplinary approach.

Finally, situational consequences—that is to say, the way that parents respond to the child's behavior when it occurs—are discussed. Unlike the first three factors of this model, situational consequences are recognized as being much more under the control of parents and other adults. Pointing this out provides a clear rationale for targeting modification of situational consequences as a major focus of the parent training program.

Having presented the four-factor model, we go on to describe in greater detail how situational consequences affect the emergence, maintenance, and/

or exacerbation of children's behavioral difficulties. In this context parents are first taught that children generally misbehave or exhibit noncompliance either to gain positive consequences or to avoid unpleasant or boring situations. A useful way to illustrate this latter situation is to discuss the manner in which a cycle of multiple parental requests, following multiple instances of child noncompliance, generally leads to escalating emotions and coercive interactions, not to mention an increased likelihood of further noncompliance from the child.

At this point in the session we have also found it helpful to provide parents with an overview of general behavior management principles as a way of preparing them for later coverage of specific behavioral techniques. This overview may be introduced with a discussion of how antecedent events, as well as consequences, can be altered to modify children's behavior. Additional attention may then be focused upon different types of reward and penalty strategies; the need for using such consequences in combination; and the advantages of dispensing them in a specific, immediate, and consistent fashion.

Much as we have done in the theoretical portion of this chapter, we then point out that the behavior management needs of ADHD children are somewhat different from those of other children. In particular, we review the various situational variables and feedback conditions that can affect their behavior and performance (see Chapter 2). Thereafter, we provide practical suggestions for incorporating these modified behavior management principles successfully. For example, because ADHD youngsters become bored easily and quickly, we advise parents to use consequences that are particularly salient and meaningful, and to change such consequences periodically to keep them interesting and motivating for their child.

Inevitably at this point in the discussion, some parents may state, "I've tried that before and it doesn't work." Others may claim, "I don't think that you should have to reward kids for things that they're supposed to do." Such assumptions must be respectfully challenged, clarified, and reframed in order to maintain parental interest in trying the specific treatment strategies recommended later in the program.

This concludes Step 2. To increase parental understanding of the information and concepts covered in this step, we generally ask parents to complete a between-session assignment pertaining to the following: a profile of their child's characteristics, a profile of their own characteristics, and an inventory of family stresses (see Barkley, 1987). On a less formal basis we also ask them to begin observing their parenting efforts in the context of the above-discussed behavior management principles.

Step 3: Enhancing Parental Attending Skills

The therapeutic intent of the third step is to begin teaching parents positive attending and ignoring skills in the context of a special playtime exercise.

As was the case in the previous step, this step begins with a careful review of any carryover concerns, as well as a review of the assigned homework. Thereafter, we begin a discussion of the importance of attending positively not only to children but to adults as well. After noting that many ADHD children generally engage in fewer behaviors that elicit any type of positive parental response, we go on to point out that many parents of ADHD children tend to interact less with them. When parent-child interactions do occur, they often can be quite corrective, directive, coercive, and unpleasant in nature. As might be expected under such conditions, most ADHD children are even less willing to behave in a compliant manner.

It is precisely for these reasons that we introduce the notion of "special time." Unlike other types of special time, which simply involve setting aside time with the child, special time in this program requires that parents must remain as nondirective and as noncorrective as possible. This is accomplished in the following manner. Parents first set aside a daily time period, usually 15 to 20 minutes on average, for interacting with their child. Ideally this should be scheduled in the absence of major time pressures or other types of interference. During special time the child is allowed to decide what to do, within broad limits of course. Parents must refrain from asking too many questions and avoid the temptation to suggest alternative play or interaction approaches. While continuing to observe their child in this manner, they must try to narrate the ongoing play activities in positive terms, while ignoring any mildly inappropriate behavior that may arise.

After hearing the description of this procedure, some parents may claim "I already do this with my child." Again, the specifics of what they actually do must be contrasted with the specifics of what is being recommended. In the process of doing so, it is usually most beneficial to emphasize the unique nondirective and noncorrective features of this technique.

Those who have ever tried this approach to special time are well aware of how difficult it is. This too is called to the attention of parents for the purpose of setting realistic expectations for its implementation. Despite this type of difficulty, proper application of special time generally improves parental attending skills and frequently can lead to more pleasant and desirable parent-child relations.

To assist parents in their efforts to practice this technique between sessions, we give them a written handout outlining the details of the procedure (see Barkley, 1987). As always, we also remind them to contact us by telephone for assistance, should any unforeseen problems arise.

Step 4: Paying Positive Attention to Appropriate Independent Play and Compliance; Giving Commands More Effectively

The fourth step involves three new objectives: (1) to extend positive attending skills to appropriate independent play, (2) to extend positive attending skills to child compliance with simple parental requests, and (3) to teach parents more effective methods of communicating commands.

At the start of this step we review parental efforts to employ special time and suggest refinements for its continued use in the future. Parent and child emotional reactions to special time are discussed as well.

Once it is clear that parents have become sufficiently comfortable with and adept at using positive attending strategies, it becomes possible to expand their use to other situations. Many children, especially those with ADHD, become disruptive when parents are engaged in home activities, such as talking on the telephone, preparing dinner, or visiting with company. After calling attention to the fact that parents generally do not hesitate to interrupt an ongoing activity to address disruptions, we routinely pose the following questions: Should parents stop what they are doing to attend positively to children when they are engaged in independent play that is not disruptive? Most parents do not think so, citing the "let sleeping dogs lie" philosophy as their rationale. This assumption is first examined from a cognitive therapy perspective—specifically, in terms of the fact that it is an example of jumping to conclusions (in this case, a negative future outcome). Parents are then asked how certain they are that dispensing positive attention in this manner will be disruptive. Most often they state that they are pretty sure, but not 100%. While acknowledging that parents might in fact be correct in their prediction, we also point out that they may not be. Until their "sleeping dogs" philosophy is put to empirical test against our alternative hypothesis, neither can be confirmed or disconfirmed. Additional justification for putting these competing assumptions to test may be inferred from our previous review of general behavior principles. More specifically, we explain that when appropriate independent play is ignored, this decreases its probability of occurring, thereby increasing the likelihood that various disruptive behaviors will develop inadvertently. If it is attended to positively, however, independent play is much more likely to reappear in the future. Recognizing that initial parental attempts to reinforce appropriate independent play may at first be disruptive, we also remind parents that children eventually become accustomed to this change in parental response. This then leads to gradual improvements in their tendency to behave appropriately while their parents are busy.

Positive attending skills may also be applied to parental command situations. Although most parents have little trouble pointing out the various ways in which ADHD children do not comply with their requests, it is much harder for them to identify request situations that elicit compliance. Some even get to the point of believing that their child "does nothing that I ask him (or her) to do." While it is certainly true that ADHD children are frequently noncompliant, it is equally important for parents to recognize an unintentional tendency on their part to ignore instances of compliance when they occur. In cognitive therapy terms, parents are selectively attending to the negative aspects of their child's responses to their requests. In behavior therapy terms, they are discouraging compliance through their ignoring, and encouraging noncompliance through their attention to it.

To help parents deal with this situation more effectively, we initially point out the overgeneralization in their thinking. More specifically, we highlight the fact that all of their commands are not equal. Some, such as "Do your homework," have a low probability of eliciting child compliance, whereas others, such as "Please turn on the television," have a much higher probability. Upon careful review of their home life, most parents begin to see more clearly that they frequently do ignore many high-probability compliance opportunities. Thus, it is inaccurate for them to conclude that their child *never* complies.

Against this background, we point out the importance of paying more positive attention to their child whenever they catch him or her being compliant. In addition, we advise them to set the stage for practicing their use of such positive attending skills, by having them issue brief sequences of simple household commands that have a high probability of eliciting compliance from their child. Over time this should lead to a gradual increase in the child's overall compliance with parental requests, including those of relatively low probability.

The final topic of discussion for this step in the training program is the manner in which commands are given. Verbal and nonverbal parameters of how parents communicate commands to children are examined. This includes coverage of the following recommendations: that parents only issue commands they intend to follow through on; that commands take the form of direct statements rather than questions; that commands be relatively simple; that they be issued in the absence of outside distractions, and only when direct eye contact is being made with the child, so as to increase the likelihood of the child's attending to such instructions; and that commands be repeated back to the parents, so as to give them an opportunity to clarify any misunderstanding before the child responds.

Like all other steps in this training program, this session ends with a specific request for parents to practice these techniques prior to the next session. To assist them in doing so, we give them written handouts on paying attention to independent play, on paying attention to compliance, and on giving commands more effectively (see Barkley, 1987).

Step 5: Establishing a Home Token System

The establishment of a reward-oriented home token system is the major focus of the fifth step. Such a system serves to provide ADHD children with the external motivation they need to complete parent-requested activities that may be of little intrinsic interest.

Following review and refinement of the therapeutic skills practiced since the previous sessions, we embark upon a discussion of one of the more difficult aspects of the training program—that is, setting up a home token system. Such a system is utilized in part because positive attending and ignoring strategies are often insufficient for managing ADHD children, who generally require more concrete and meaningful rewards. Having discussed this rationale, we introduce the token system by asking parents to generate two lists: one list of daily, weekly, and long-range privileges that are likely to be interesting and motivating to the child; another list of daily and weekly chores and/or household rules. Later at home, parents may wish to incorporate input from the child as to any other items that should be included in these lists.

Point values are then assigned to each list. For children 8 years old and under, plastic poker chips are used as tokens in a manner similar to that employed by Christophersen, Barnard, and Barnard (1981): Earned poker chips are collected and stored in a home "bank" that a child has set aside specifically for that purpose. For 9- to 11-year-old children, points are used in place of chips and are monitored in a checkbook register or some other type of notebook of interest to a youngster. Generally speaking, children can earn predetermined numbers of poker chips or points for complying with initial parent requests and for completing assigned tasks, which previously may have been left incomplete due to lack of interest or motivation in doing them. In addition, parents can dispense bonus chips or points for especially well-done chores or independent displays of appropriate behavior. At no time, however, should chips or points be taken away for noncompliance in this phase of the training program. Instead, encountered noncompliance should be handled in the same way that parents have dealt with such situations previously.

Parental motivation, which may have been quite high up until now, may begin to waver for several reasons. Some parents may once again tell us, "I've done something like this before and it doesn't work." As described earlier, cognitive therapy strategies may be used to correct this type of faulty thinking, which has the potential to interfere with parental efforts to institute a home token system. Another potentially self-defeating assumption that parents may express is "I don't think my child will go along with this." When this is stated, it becomes necessary to discuss the issue of who is in charge—parent or child? In the context of such a discussion, parental control is framed as a constructive responsibility, one that children may not like or appreciate immediately, but nevertheless one that is ultimately in their best interests. When they look at it in this light, most parents are at the very least willing to give the home token system a try.

Having made sure that parents fully understand the working mechanics of this token system, we provide them with an extensive written handout summarizing this phase of the program. This, of course, serves as a useful reminder of what to do as they practice this technique at home prior to the next sessions. In addition, we remind parents to call immediately for consultation, should any complications arise.

Step 6: Review of Home Token System; Using Response Cost

The therapeutic goal of the sixth step is primarily refinement of the home token system, which includes the addition of response cost strategies for minor noncompliance.

During the initial portion of this step, we carefully review parental efforts to implement the home token system. Because problems inevitably arise, we set aside most of this session for review purposes. Confusion is clarified where needed, and suggestions for increasing the effectiveness of this system are made as well.

Following this discussion, we introduce the notion of "response cost," which represents the first time in the treatment program that a penalty or punishment approach has been considered for use. More specifically, we instruct parents to begin deducting chips or points for noncompliance with one or two particularly troublesome requests or violations of household rules. Thus, not only does the ADHD child fail to earn chips or points that would have resulted from compliance; previously earned chips or points are now also removed from the bank for displays of noncompliance. The number of chips or points lost is equal to the number of chips or points that would have been gained, had compliance occurred. For many ADHD children, who over the past week have learned how to expend minimal effort to get the privileges that they desire, adding a response cost component to their token system often increases their overall level of compliance with parental requests, because they now have the additional incentive of trying not to lose what they have already earned. We routinely caution parents to avoid getting into punishment spirals, whereby so many chips are taken away that a debt is incurred. As a rule, we advise parents not to employ response cost more than twice in a row for the same noncompliant behavior. If needed, backup penalties, such as time out, can be employed instead. Furthermore, parents need to take steps to ensure that a child's token reserves do not approach a zero balance, which might diminish his or her interest in the program. If the balance gets low, parents must dispense bonus tokens for any display of appropriate child behavior, whether or not it happens to be on the list.

Unlike the other steps of the program, this step does not include a handout for parents to take home for review. Should problems arise, parents are expected to call for assistance prior to the next session.

Step 7: Using Time-Out from Reinforcement

Time-out strategies for dealing with more serious forms of child noncompliance are the focus of the seventh treatment step.

After reviewing the home token system, with an emphasis on parental efforts to handle noncompliance by means of response cost, we introduce the notion of using "time-out from reinforcement," or simply "time-out." Although most types of noncompliance will continue to be handled via response cost, we encourage parents to identify one or two especially resistant types of noncompliance that may become the targets of time-out. Once these are identified, attention is focused upon the mechanics of implementing the time-out procedure. Like the token system, time-out is a rather difficult technique to employ. Its use must be explained very carefully and thoroughly before parents are asked to practice it at home. After giving an overview of the procedure, we generally model its application. This will include, of course, attention to the following points:

After a parental request is made and the child fails to comply within approximately 5 seconds, parents must adopt a firm facial expression and body posture, and issue a firmly stated warning, such as "If you don't do as I asked, then you are going to sit in that chair." If after 5 more seconds the child fails to comply, parents announce even more sternly, "You didn't do as I asked, so you must now sit in that chair." All child attempts to avoid going to the chair, such as bargaining or requests to relieve sudden attacks of hunger or thirst, must be ignored. Having escorted the child to the chair, parents then announce with clear conviction, "You are to stay in that chair and remain quiet until *I* tell you when you can come out." Unlike many other variations of the time-out procedure, this particular application does not give control over the child's release either to the child ("Stay there until you're ready to come out") or to the clock ("You must stay there for 10 minutes"). Instead, control is clearly within the domain of the parent.

Three main conditions must be met prior to releasing the youngster from the time-out chair. First, the child must serve a minimum amount of time, generally equal in minutes to the number of years in his or her age. Once this condition is met, parents may approach the time-out chair only when the child has been quiet for a brief period of time. This, of course, avoids the problem of inadvertently dispensing parental attention for inappropriate behavior. Next, parents must reissue the request or command that initially led the youngster to be placed into time-out. In cases where the child does not comply with the reissued directive, the entire three-step time-out cycle is repeated as many times as is necessary, until compliance is achieved. When compliance finally is achieved, parents are to thank the child in a neutral manner for doing what was asked; no tokens are dispensed, however. A few moments later, parents should look for an opportunity to praise the child in a more meaningful way with chips or points. In so doing, parents balance out their prior use of punishment.

In addition to covering these facets of time-out, we routinely address other aspects of this procedure, such as where to place the time-out chair (e.g., in a dining room or other places in the home that can be supervised easily). Likewise, it is important to cover what types of backup strategies may be employed in the event that the child decides to leave the chair. These may include, for example, response cost, privilege removal, grounding, and/or physical restraint.

More so than any of the other procedures in this program, time out is a strategy that usually has been tried previously in one form or another. Thus, many parents have firm beliefs about its use. These biases or assumptions, which are often overgeneralizations, must be elicited and clarified via Socratic questioning. Thereafter, whatever overgeneralization exists will need to be addressed by cognitive restructuring techniques. Failure to do so runs the risk that parents will not be properly motivated to incorporate this treatment strategy in the manner in which it is intended. This in turn may increase parental frustration and diminish any further interest in participation in the program.

At the end of this session, we give parents a written handout on time-out as a reminder of the many complicated steps involved in using these techniques. More so than in other sessions, we urge parents to call for assistance as needed prior to the next session.

Step 8: Extending Time Out to Other Misbehavior; Managing Children's Behavior in Public Places

The goals of the eighth step are to begin extending parental use of time out to other problem areas and, more generally, to begin expanding use of the entire home-based program to settings outside the home.

Initially, we review parental efforts to incorporate time-out strategies into the ongoing home management system. Refinements are suggested as needed. Provided that this has gone fairly well and provided that parents feel comfortable with its use, we encourage them to begin using time-out for other types of major noncompliance or rule violations. If they have not reached this level of comfort and mastery, we simply ask them to make necessary refinements and to continue targeting the same sources of noncompliance that were identified previously.

At this point in the treatment program, parental expertise in using home-based strategies is usually quite satisfactory. For this reason parents are now ready to begin generalizing their newly acquired skills to problematic settings outside the home. Among the many problematic outside settings often identified by parents are grocery stores, department stores, movie theaters, restaurants, and churches. Disciplinary strategies previously employed in public places are reviewed and analyzed in terms of their overall ineffectiveness.

Against this background, we next emphasize the importance of anticipating such problems in public. Along with anticipating their likely occurrence, we advise parents to establish a clear plan for dealing with them, prior to entering a predictably problematic public situation. This may be accomplished by parental adherence to the following steps: First, parents must review with their child their expectations for his or her behavior in this setting. Next, they must establish some incentive for compliance with these rules. Finally, they must specify what types of punishment will be applied, should noncompliance with these rules ensue. Of equal importance to the success of this plan is to have the child state his or her understanding of these rules and consequences prior to entering the public situation. This allows parents an opportunity to clarify any misunderstanding on the part of the child that may result from confusion or from inattentiveness.

Generally speaking, modified versions of the strategies used successfully within the home are incorporated into this plan. These may include, for example, dispensing poker chips for ongoing compliance with parental requests such as "Stay close, don't touch, don't beg," or removal of poker chips for noncompliance with these same requests. Modified versions of time-out may also be employed by parents, using quiet, out-of-the-way public areas for this purpose.

In contrast with their eagerness to try out various home management techniques, many parents are much less enthusiastic about experimenting with these techniques in public places. The perceived threat of public embarrassment is often cited. After all, "What will people think?" The mind-reading aspects of this particular situation are highlighted as the basis for their jumping to such a conclusion. Alternative viewpoints of what people might think, and the relative importance of what others think when it pertains to their child's welfare, are discussed. Addressing parental perceptions of this situation in this manner generally makes it possible to reduce their uneasiness and to increase their motivation for trying such a new and challenging approach.

Having been acquainted to this aspect of the training program, parents are asked to practice these procedures on at least two separate occasions prior to the next session. For the purpose of reminding them later, a written handout on the topic of managing difficult child behavior in public places is distributed at the end of the session.

Step 9: Handling Future Behavior Problems

After reviewing and fine-tuning parental efforts to employ newly acquired child management skills in public places, we take time to review all previously covered aspects of the training program. As needed, we make suggestions for increasing parental effectiveness in using any given procedure. Parental feedback about the training program may be elicited at this time as well. Such comments often serve as a backdrop against which handling of future behavior problems may be discussed.

Recognizing the potential for inaccuracies, we explore with parents what they believe may be problematic for them in the future. In a similar vein we encourage them to contemplate how they might handle such problematic situations. Attention is also directed to the various ways in which many parents slip away from adherence to this program. While some degree of slippage or departure from the protocol is acceptable and to be expected, too much may lead to increased behavioral difficulties. For this reason we review how parents may run a check on themselves to ascertain where fine-tuning of their specialized child management skills is required. A written handout summarizing this self-check system is distributed at this time.

We use the final portion of this session as an opportunity to begin addressing follow-up and/or termination issues. In addition to agreeing upon an appropriate booster session date, we try to determine whether any other type of clinical disposition is in order. On a fairly regular basis this might include a discussion of various school-related issues.

In addition to giving parents general school management suggestions, we frequently cover the mechanics of setting up a daily report card system (see Chapter 15). In this system teachers monitor specific classroom behaviors (e.g., stays in seat, finishes assigned tasks) by providing ratings on an index card, which is sent home on a daily basis. These teacher ratings are then converted into either token gains or losses, proportional to the quality of behavior and performance displayed by the child that day. One major advantage to using home-based consequences in this system is that they are consistently more meaningful and effective than stickers, extra recess, or other types of consequences typically available in school. Another significant advantage is that it imposes very little burden on classroom teachers, who must also direct their time and energy to meeting the needs of other students in the class. Of more general importance is that the daily report card system incorporates many of the behavior management principles specific to ADHD children. For example, implicit in its use is an attempt to provide extremely specific, immediate, and frequent feedback, all of which should serve to facilitate classroom performance.

If needed, parents are given a handout summarizing the mechanics of using this system. And if they wish, school consultation visits may be scheduled to address classroom management concerns directly with school personnel.

Step 10: Booster Session

Although any length of time may be deemed acceptable, it is customary to meet with parents for a booster session approximately 1 month after conducting Step 9. During this session we generally readminister pertinent rating scales and questionnaires, which serve as indices of any posttreatment changes that may have occurred. Further review and refinement of previously learned intervention strategies is conducted as well. Also established at this time is a mutually agreed-upon final clinical disposition. If desired, this may include scheduling of additional booster sessions.

INDICUAL VERSUS MULTIFAMILY
GROUP CONSIDERATIONS

The preceding discussion of the parent training/counseling program is based upon clinical contact that may occur with individual families, rather than with parent groups. To our knowledge, there is no clear-cut empirical evidence to suggest that either mode of intervention is superior to the other. For this reason, the decision to participate in either an individual or group treatment format is often based largely on parental preference.

Because some parents are uncomfortable talking about their children's behavioral difficulties in front of others, they may wish to receive parent training/counseling services on an individual family basis. The individual family format is also often better suited to meeting the needs of intellectually slow parents or parents with mild psychiatric difficulties, both of whom may require close supervision of their efforts to acquire new parenting skills. In addition, a somewhat atypical ADHD presentation can often be managed more effectively on an individual family basis, because therapists have greater flexibility to tailor their therapeutic suggestions to the individual needs of the child. Finally, scheduling constraints may dictate a course of individual treatment, especially when work or vacation schedules make it difficult for parents to adhere to the relatively rigid schedule of the multifamily group format.

For many other parents, the multifamily group format is desirable, in part because it affords them the opportunity to meet others like themselves; this allows for much-needed mutual understanding and support. This can be especially valuable for single parents, whose friends and extended family members may not be as understanding or supportive. In addition, the multifamily group format provides numerous opportunities for parents to learn from one another, as well as from the therapist. From the clinician's point of view, delivering this type of group treatment is tremendously cost-effective. Not only does it reduce therapist time demands; it also enables the therapist to meet the clinical needs of a larger segment of the ADHD population. This can be especially important when the demands of a clinical case load become too great.

When using a group format, clinicians basically follow the same treatment outline that was described earlier. At the same time, however, they must be prepared to deal with potential parental adjustment difficulties in ways that are not too embarrassing or too personal. If they become so, then an individual session outside of the group setting may need to be scheduled to address such concerns. Similarly, clinicians must be ready to handle, as delicately as possible, any occurrences of parental noncompliance with the treatment regimen, especially if other parents in the group are proceeding smoothly through the program. Again, an additional individual session may be necessary to deal with this sort of complication. When such complications become chronic, consideration must sometimes be given to discontinuing group participation in favor of an individual format, which is better suited to handling such circumstances.

BENEFITS

In our earlier review of the pertinent clinical research literature, we concluded that there is preliminary support for utilizing parent training/counseling with ADHD children and their families. Such support stems primarily from a consideration of the improvements in targeted child behavior that have been consistently reported across studies. While this is, of course, a significant finding in and of itself, our clinical experience has repeatedly demonstrated that the therapeutic benefits of parent training/counseling very often go beyond this domain. As might be expected, parental knowledge and understanding of ADHD generally increase a great deal following parent training/counseling. So too does parental expertise in using specialized child management skills to address the motivational deficits, as well as the noncompliant behavior, of ADHD children. Newly acquired parenting skills can also facilitate the behavioral management of other problem areas, such as enuresis or encopresis, which often accompany ADHD difficulties.

Along with these direct benefits, a number of indirect family benefits may occur. For example, many parents report significant improvements in the behavior of siblings, as a result of their modified use of these same parenting strategies with the siblings. In some cases, they may also report feeling reduced personal and family stress levels. Marital tensions stemming from child management issues frequently are lessened. As a function of improved parenting effectiveness, many parents begin to view themselves more positively in their parenting roles; over time this can enhance parenting self-esteem. Likewise, because ADHD children encounter more frequent positive reinforcement from their parents, they too may feel happier and more confident. In addition to feeling better about themselves, many parents and children also begin to like each other even more so than before. Overall family functioning may become less stressful as well, with siblings and ADHD children generally interacting more cooperatively. On a less frequent basis, improvements in a child's home behavior may be accompanied by improvements in school behavior and academic performance. To the extent that daily report cards and other classroom management strategies are employed directly, additional improvements in school functioning may occur as well.

While such benefits are indeed impressive, it should be remembered that our awareness of them comes to us primarily through our subjective clinical experience, which may of course be affected by our theoretical biases. Being limited in this way, our clinical impressions by themselves are insufficient for attesting to the validity and reliability of such outcome changes. Therefore, additional empirical support must be established. Unfortunately, many of the outcome changes that we have consistently observed have not yet been put to empirical test. When such research is eventually conducted, however, it is our expectation that adequate support will be found.

SUMMARY AND CONCLUSIONS

We began this chapter by discussing how our clinical experience, our theoretical views, and the currently available research findings have provided us with a rationale for employing parent training/counseling with ADHD children and their families. We followed this with a review of the clinical criteria that guide us in making referrals for this type of treatment. Thereafter, we highlighted numerous clinical and stylistic considerations that must be taken into account throughout all phases of this intervention. After outlining the program's overall objectives, we then presented a detailed description of the 10 therapeutic steps that make up the complete treatment protocol. Next, we briefly addressed the advantages and disadvantages of delivering this type of treatment in an individual family format versus a multifamily group format. And finally, we highlighted many of the direct and indirect benefits that we frequently observe following parent participation in the complete treatment program.

Before concluding, we would like to emphasize several points. First of all, it is clearly evident from our clinical experience that multiple treatment strategies must be used in combination to address the wide range of psychosocial difficulties that ADHD children frequently display. Because the parent training/counseling program is well suited to addressing many of these difficulties within the home setting, it frequently can be an integral part of the ongoing clinical management of ADHD children. It should not, however, be implemented routinely for all ADHD children. Instead, as discussed earlier, it should be incorporated into a multimodal treatment plan only after careful consideration is given to its overall clinical appropriateness.

Another point that we would like to emphasize is the multifaceted nature of this treatment approach. Although it bears a resemblance to other behavioral parent training programs (e.g., that of Forehand & McMahon, 1981), the parent training/counseling program that we now employ encompasses many other distinctive treatment components. This includes, for example, the didactic manner in which parental knowledge of ADHD is increased. In this regard one of our major objectives is to teach parents that ADHD is in large part an inborn biological temperamental predisposition, which parents and children must learn to cope with over time, rather than cure. Another distinctive feature is the degree to which cognitive therapy strategies are incorporated into the counseling portion of the program. This, of course, stems from our belief that parents' faulty perceptions of themselves and of their children can interfere with their implementation of the program, and in some cases with their psychological adjustment to having ADHD children. And perhaps the most distinctive aspect of the program is the manner in which its procedures reflect the view that ADHD is primarily a motivational disorder. In this context, parents learn to alter situational variables and to employ specialized contingency management techniques—not just to address the noncompliant behavior of ADHD children, but also to provide them with the external incentives that they seem to require to overcome their motivational deficits, which presumably underlie many of their behavioral difficulties.

13

A Family Systems Approach to Parent Training

CHARLES E. CUNNINGHAM

> The father and mother of an unnoticed family, who in
> their seclusion awaken the mind of one child to the idea
> and love of goodness, who awaken in him a strength of
> will to repel temptation, and who send him out prepared
> to profit by the conflicts of life, surpass in influence a Na-
> poleon breaking the world to his sway.
>
> —WILLIAM ELLERY CHANNING (1780–1842)

While the diagnosis of Attention-deficit Hyperactivity Disorder (ADHD) emphasizes the child's problems with sustained attention, activity level, and impulse control, it is the impact of these difficulties on the child's social relationships that often prompts parents to seek professional assistance. As noted
in Chapter 2, the ADHD child often behaves in a poorly regulated manner,
is difficult to manage during daily tasks, fails to complete chores, and may
prove overtly oppositional or noncompliant. Moreover, the ADHD child is
more likely to encounter serious conflicts with peers (Cunningham & Siegel,
1987) or adults in a position of authority. The child's failure to follow rules
or anticipate consequences greatly increases the risk of serious personal injuries (Szatmari, Offord, & Boyle, 1989b). In response to these difficulties, parents adopt a more controlling, less positive response to child management
(Cunningham & Barkley, 1979; Mash & Johnston, 1982; Barkley, Karlsson,
& Pollard, 1985; Barkley, Karlsson, Strzelecki, & Murphy, 1984), which
may compound and perpetuate the child's difficulties (Patterson, 1982). Parents understandably report great frustration, a lower sense of confidence (Mash
& Johnston, 1983c), and a reduced sense of personal control over the child's
behavior (Sobol, Ashbourne, Earn, & Cunningham, 1989).

Chapter 12 has presented a parent training program that is effective in
improving both the child management skills of parents and child behavior in

ADHD children. Although that program's emphasis on parent-child interactions will prove useful for relatively well-functioning families, there is an emerging consensus that effective training with more problematic children may need to be conducted with reference to a wider family and community framework (Griest & Wells, 1983; Mash, 1984). This "systems" perspective implies that parent-child relationships will influence and be affected by structural and transactional relationships within the child's nuclear family, extended family, and community (see Chapter 7).

Several lines of evidence suggest that a more systemic approach may be particularly useful with families of ADHD children. First, during the course of the child's development, families of ADHD children will be confronted with a substantially larger number of behavioral, developmental, and educational problems than those of normal children. The time, logistical demands, and energy required to cope with these difficulties places an enormous burden of stress on all aspects of marital and family functioning (Emery, 1982; Epstein, Bishop, & Levine, 1978). The systems-oriented program described here, therefore, is designed to develop the problem-solving skills, collaborative approaches to management, and supportive communication that should allow families to cope effectively with the stress imposed by an unusually difficult ADHD child.

Second, while referrals to training programs are often prompted by child management difficulties, parents of ADHD children frequently report problems in related areas of individual, marital, or family functioning. These include lack of confidence in parenting skills (Mash & Johnston, 1983c); depression (Cunningham, Benness, & Siegel, 1988; Befera & Barkley, 1985; Breen & Barkley, 1988); and less frequent, less helpful contacts with extended family members (Cunningham et al., 1988). Social isolation (Wahler, 1980), marital conflict, family dysfunction, and parental depression may negatively bias parental perceptions of child behavior (Griest, Wells, & Forehand, 1979; Webster-Stratton, 1988), adversely affect parental management (Mash & Johnston, 1983c; Panaccione & Wahler, 1986), and reduce the effectiveness of parenting programs (McMahon, Forehand, Griest, & Wells, 1981). This program's emphasis on family functioning may therefore be particularly useful with more problematic couples.

Third, from 40 to 60% of ADHD children also evidence significant oppositional or conduct problems (Szatmari, Boyle, & Offord, 1989a). From a parenting perspective, it is often the ADHD child with Oppositional Defiant Disorder or Conduct Disorder who is most problematic to manage (Barkley, Fischer, Edelbrock, & Smallish, in press-b). Moreover, those ADHD children with Conduct Disorder or Oppositional Defiant Disorder are the ones at greatest risk for longer-term social and emotional disorders (Weiss & Hechtman, 1986). Epidemiological evidence suggests that whereas ADHD is linked primarily to developmental correlates, conduct problems are associated with an increased odds of marital conflict and family dysfunction (Szatmari et al., 1989a). A parenting program that strengthens dimensions of family functioning linked to the development and maintenance of conduct problems may therefore prevent the emergence of or reduce the severity of the problems presented by this very difficult subgroup of ADHD children.

In summary, the distress experienced by parents of ADHD children; the complex relationships among parenting stress, child management strategies, and child behavior; the correlation between marital conflict or family dysfunction and conduct problems; and the prospective longitudinal links between family variables and longer-term adjustment all make it necessary to approach the task of building parenting skills within a systemic framework. The program described here, therefore, utilizes the task of parenting skill development as a context in which key dimensions of family functioning may be strengthened.

BACKGROUND OF THE TRAINING PROGRAM

Three-Dimensional Structure and Process

The parenting program has goals along three interrelated dimensions: (1) improvements in parenting skills, (2) improvements in family functioning, and (3) the development of rationales supporting the importance of each of the parenting and family systems skills developed. The structure and therapeutic processes of this program, therefore, are based on an integration of principles, techniques, and therapeutic goals from social-learning-based parenting programs, family systems theory and therapy, and social-cognitive psychology. Parents will have an opportunity to develop strategies for improving relationships via play and conversation, avoiding escalating conflicts, encouraging children to plan and rehearse solutions to difficult situations, encouraging cooperative prosocial behavior, establishing limits, and enforcing these with effective consequences. Formulating, mastering, implementing, and maintaining these parenting skills requires—and this program provides a context for developing—effective problem-solving skills, balanced child management responsibilities, and increased supportive communication. Finally, the commitment to each parenting and family systems goal may be enhanced by providing the couple with an opportunity to devise personal rationales.

Social-Learning-Based Parent Training Programs

The parenting component of this program is based on the social learning approach developed by Connie Hanf (Hanf & Kling, 1973) at the University of Oregon Health Sciences Center, and is similar to the program presented in Chapter 12 of this volume (see also Barkley, 1987). Although this program incorporates the role-playing and skill-building strategies introduced by Hanf, a less didactic approach to the training process has been developed. In contrast to parent training programs that introduce new skills via modeling and direct instruction, this program incorporates a variation of coping-modeling procedures (Kazdin, 1974; Meichenbaum, 1971; Sarason, 1975), in which (1) videotaped role players display exaggerated versions of common child management errors; (2) parents identify the errors modeled, discuss their consequences, develop alternative strategies, and formulate supporting rationales; (3) the therapist models the couple's solution; and (4) parents rehearse the strategy via role-playing exercises, clinic practice with the ADHD child (and siblings), and daily homework assignments.

There are several advantages to this approach. First, the exaggerated videotaped model simplifies complex child management problems, highlights errors, and depicts longer-term consequences that may be less evident in daily interaction. The ensuing discussion promotes a more comprehensive understanding of child behavior problems. Second, formulating alternative strategies and devising supporting rationales should enhance commitment to new ideas and adherence to homework goals (Greenwald & Albert, 1968; Janis & King, 1954; King & Janis, 1956). Third, a sometimes humorous display of exaggerated parenting errors seems to distance problems and to elicit less defensiveness and resistance than do more didactic modeling and instructional strategies (Patterson & Forgatch, 1985). Fourth, developing solutions to complex problems is likely to promote a sense of personal competence and control. Finally, these discussions allow the therapist to build and the parents to experience a more collaborative, step-by-step approach to child management problem solving.

Cognitive and Social-Psychological Contributions

Since successful parent training often requires a shift in firmly established expectations and beliefs regarding child behavior, discipline, and family relationships, this program has incorporated a number of principles from cognitive and social-psychological models of attitude change (Leary & Miller, 1986). Attributional research, for example, suggests that parental explanations regarding the causes of children's misbehavior exert an important impact on both emotional and disciplinary responses, and may pose a serious impediment to change. Although therapists may easily present persuasive evidence supporting new approaches, social-psychological research suggests that optimal shifts in attitudes and behavior will be obtained when parents devise their own solutions and rationales (Leary & Miller, 1986). The coping-modeling procedures used in this program, therefore, allow parents to explore the consequences of common child management errors and assumptions, to formulate alternative strategies, and to develop supporting rationales.

In this model, parents formulate rationales according to several attributional perspectives. Social learning attributions, for example, encourage parents to consider the lessons taught by a particular management strategy. Relational/communicative attributions help to make clear and to address the messages that a parent's management strategies may communicate to the ADHD child or other family members. Reframing management strategies from this perspective often elicits affective responses that motivate change via cognitive and social learning techniques. Short-term versus long-term attributions encourage parents to anticipate the probable course set in motion by a particular strategy. This is particularly important in countering expectations regarding immediate change with the assumption that, while progress will be slow and at times inconsistent, sustained use of a strategy may foster longer-term improvements, prevent further deterioration, or prevent secondary sequelae. Finally, effort attributions encourage parents to decide whether, given the lessons taught, the likely course of change, and the relational message communicated by a particular strategy, their efforts to master and implement it are justified.

In addition to recommendations regarding the design of the therapeutic process, cognitive and social-psychological models suggest a number of targets for the training program. Effective child management requires that parents regulate their own thoughts and emotions. Parents, for example, often find their efforts to disengage from upwardly escalating arguments compounded by incorrect causal attributions ("He's doing this to get at me"), unrealistic expectations ("Six-year-olds should never talk to their parents in that tone of voice"), or attributions regarding their ability to control their feelings ("I can't stand this any more"). In this program, therefore, parents develop cognitive strategies to cope with counterproductive thoughts.

Finally, because the problems of many ADHD children reflect deficits in self-regulation (Barkley, in press; Douglas, 1983), this program includes both a group designed to teach children simple self-control strategies and parenting strategies to prompt and reinforce the ADHD children's planning and self-regulatory efforts.

Contributions from Family Systems Theory

This program's systemic goals are derived from two models: the McMaster Model of Family Functioning (Epstein et al., 1978) and the structural models of Minuchin (Minuchin, 1974). Although this program does not represent a comprehensive approach to intervention with families of ADHD children, it does address several dimensions of family functioning that are integral to successful child management. These include an effective approach to the solution of child management problems, a more balanced distribution of child management responsibilities, and more supportive communication among family members.

While families of ADHD children without oppositional or conduct problems often do not evidence major deficits in family functioning (Cunningham et al., 1988; Szatmari et al, 1989b), the long-term task of managing an ADHD child may erode a family's coping skills. This program, therefore, is designed to enhance those dimensions of family functioning needed to deal more effectively with the task of raising an ADHD child.

TABLE 13.1. Outline of Training Program for Parents of 4- to 12-Year-Olds

I. Preliminary multidisciplinary assessments
II. Screening/contracting session
III. Parent training curriculum
   Session 1: Problem solving
   Session 2: Attending to play and conversation
   Session 3: Balancing attending among siblings
   Session 4: Rewards
   Session 5: Planned ignoring
   Session 6: Transitional strategies
   Session 7: When-then contingencies
   Session 8: Planning ahead for uninterrupted parental activities
   Session 9: Planning for a telephone call
   Session 10: Planning for a visitor
   Session 11: Time out from positive reinforcement
   Session 12–14: Generalizing skills to selected problems
   Session 15: Maintaining gains/closing
IV. Monthly booster sessions

A FAMILY-SYSTEMS-ORIENTED PARENTING PROGRAM

Preliminary Assessments

Table 13.1 provides an overview of the parent training program. Prior to participation in the program, each family receives an interdisciplinary assessment designed to provide a formal diagnosis, formulations regarding variables that are influencing the child's behavior problems, and a comprehensive management plan. This battery includes measures of the child's intellectual and academic skills; pediatric assessments to rule out contributing medical conditions; and individual, marital, and family assessments as indicated.

Assessment for Parent Training

General Assessment Goals

The screening interview is designed to explore parental concerns regarding the child and to determine how the couple manages child behavior problems. Since this program will approach parenting from a family systems perspective, the interview also examines the behavior of other children in the family and determines how the parents (1) divide child management responsibilities, (2) approach the solution of child behavior problems, and (3) provide supportive communication to each other. The therapist will outline the program and help the couple determine whether this approach will be of assistance.

Context of the Assessment

While many therapists conduct interviews that include all family members, I prefer an initial discussion that provides the couple with an opportunity to explore their concerns without children present. Interviews with the children and the family as a whole may be conducted later.

Preinterview Questionnaires

Prior to the interview, parents complete the Child Behavior Checklist (Achenbach & Edelbrock, 1983), the Home Situations Questionnaire (Barkley & Edelbrock, 1987), a measure of parenting confidence, the Beck Depression Inventory (Beck, Rush, Shaw, & Emery, 1979), and either the Locke-Wallace Marital Adjustment Test (Locke & Wallace, 1959) or the McMaster Family Assessment Device (Epstein, Baldwin, & Bishop, 1983). These questionnaires, in conjunction with the multidisciplinary assessments, parent questionnaires, and teacher reports completed during the initial assessment phase, provide the background information necessary to conduct a detailed, efficient intake interview (see Chapters 7–11).

Beginning the Screening Interview

The therapist should outline the goals of the screening session and begin with an open-ended overview of parental concerns. While schools often refer families to parenting programs, epidemiological studies indicate that many parents of ADHD children do not experience the level of difficulty reported by teachers (Szatmari et al., 1989a). These families may be less interested in parenting skills and home behavior and more interested in problems at school. Moreover, problems may have subsided, the child may have been placed on stimulant medication, or new problems may have emerged.

Assessing Child Behavior and Parenting Strategies

To establish a balanced working alliance with both father and mother, it is helpful to begin by noting that because the mother and father may have different views regarding the child's behavior, may manage the child differently, and may elicit different responses from the child, this interview will explore each parent's unique perspective. Next, the therapist should conduct a detailed exploration of selected situations from the Home Situations Questionnaire (Barkley & Edelbrock, 1987). It is informative to review situations where parents agree that the child is unusually difficult, proceed to situations in which the father and mother report different levels of difficulty, and finish with typically problematic situations that the family manages well. This overview will provide insight into parental views regarding normal and abnormal behavior, suggest situational factors influencing the child's behavior, reveal differences in the views or strategies adopted by the mother and father, contrast successful and unsuccessful strategies, and allow a balanced discussion of the family's strengths and weakness.

The discussion of each situation should begin with an open-ended question regarding the child's behavior (e.g., "How do things go when you're getting your child ready for school in the morning?") Parents should describe a recent situation; estimate the frequency, duration, and intensity of the problem; and consider historical factors that may have been associated with its onset. Specific problems, for example, are often linked to stressful events in family life, whether these are normal (e.g., birth of siblings, start of school) or unusual (e.g., moves, financial difficulty, or illness in a family member). The therapist should reflect the emotional impact of each situation and explore parental explanations regarding the child's behavior. Attributions or beliefs that modulate emotional reactions and disciplinary responses should be noted.

Next, the therapist should review the range of strategies each parent has adopted in an effort to manage the problem (e.g., "That sounds like a very frustrating situation. How have you tried to deal with it?"). The effectiveness of each strategy should be explored via open-ended questions such as "How does your child respond?"

Finally, the couple should identify the most promising strategy and explore its advantages according to the four-level attributional model described above. For example, the therapist may ask, "Of the strategies you've tried, which makes the most sense?"

Although the role-playing and rehearsal exercises discussed later provide an ongoing opportunity to observe parenting skills, clinic observations and home visits constitute a potentially important source of information (see Chapter 10). However, these are time-consuming methods that may not elicit problematic transactions and are limited by the absence of standardized settings and norms.

Assessing Roles

Determining who manages the child's behavior in different situations, performs child care tasks, and relates to professionals provides important information regarding the couple's distribution of child management responsibilities.

Assessing Problem-Solving Skills

The therapist should determine *how* the strategies used in each situation were developed (e.g., "How did you decide to manage mealtimes this way?"). It is helpful to explore (1) when and where the parents discuss child management problems, (2) how frequently these discussions occur, (3) and how effectively the parents work together. The couple may be asked to discuss the solution of problems during the course of the interview or to formulate solutions to a standard set of written child management problems (Johnston, Cunningham, & Hardy, 1988).

Assessing Communication Skills

The screening interview provides an opportunity to observe communicative transactions, prompt feedback, and explore communication at home. After each situational review, for example, therapists should ask parents to give feedback as to "how your husband/wife handles this problem." If responses are consistently negative, the therapist should provide a more structured prompt to identify the *most successful* components of the spouses approach: "What's best about your husband/wife's approach to this situation?" Asking "Were you aware that your husband/wife felt this way? How does your spouse usually let you know?" will provide additional information regarding communication at home.

Since the ADHD child can be a tremendous source of stress, the therapist should explore the family's approach to affective communication. At points in the interview where the therapist reflects emotional responses to a particular problem, for example, it is useful to determine whether one spouse was aware of the feelings the other spouse experienced, how these feelings were communicated, and the other spouse's response to these communicative efforts. For example, "Mary, it sounds like you were feeling quite discouraged/angry/worried. John, were you aware of this at the time? How does Mary let you know? Mary, how does John respond?"

Presenting the Parenting Program

To allow an informed decision regarding participation, the therapist should provide an overview of the goals, requirements, and probable outcomes of the program. I present an educational rationale, drawing parallels to courses with which the couple is familiar. For example,

> "This course is designed to help parents develop the more specialized strategies needed to cope with a particularly challenging child. During the course of the child's development, an emphasis will be placed on problem-solving skills and approaches to child management that are useful in a variety of situations. Like most courses, this program begins with a review of simple strategies that many parents use effectively. While some strategies discussed may be unnecessary at this time, they may prove useful as children mature or new problems emerge. Over sessions, the course shifts from simple play and conversational skills to more specialized strategies and difficult situations. Because solutions to complex problems will be based upon the skills acquired in earlier sessions, it is important that all strategies be mastered."

The details of the program should then be reviewed. These should include the starting date, time, and place of the program. The therapist should describe the training process and discuss expectations regarding attendance and homework. Finally, many parents and referral sources expect unrealistically rapid and sustained improvement in a child's temperament and behavior. If newly acquired strategies are evaluated according to unattainable objectives, these will be abandoned as ineffective. The therapist should therefore present conservative predictions regarding the course and magnitude of change, and emphasize the importance of attending consistently, participating actively in discussions and skill-building exercises, and completing homework assignments.

Once this review has been completed, the therapist and the couple should determine whether participation in the program is indicated. This type of program is most useful when parents need to develop new skills, to fine-tune or apply existing skills more consistently, to eliminate counterproductive strategies or cognitions, to resolve disagreements regarding management, or simply to develop more confidence in their parenting skills. This program will be less useful if parents insist on immediate improvement; if problems occur primarily at school; or if behavior problems are secondary to *severe* marital conflict, family dysfunction, parental psychopathology, or abuse. In such cases, this type of program may be an important component of a more comprehensive intervention, but other approaches to treatment should be considered.

Finally, parents should weigh the time commitment against the longer-term course over which (modest) gains may be anticipated. While parents may decide to participate during the session, the opportunity to make this decision independently at home seems to increase commitment, diminish resistance, and reduce dropouts, which are commonly encountered in parent training programs (Patterson & Forgatch, 1985).

Structure of Parents' Sessions

Table 13.2 outlines the structure of individual parent training sessions. With the exception of Sessions 1 and 15, all sessions are conducted according to this general framework.

Outlining the Session

Each session begins with a brief social period, allowing one couple to raise concerns that need to be discussed (Step 1). The therapist then provides an

TABLE 13.2. Structure of Individual Parent Training Sessions

Step 1. Introductory social phase
Step 2. Therapist outlines session plan
Step 3. Each parent reviews homework successes
Step 4. Parents troubleshoot videotaped coping model
Step 5. Therapist models couple's solution
Step 6. Each parent role-plays solution with therapist
Step 7. Each parent practices solution with child/siblings
Step 8. Couple formulates homework goals

overview of the goals for the session (Step 2), which include (1) a review of homework assignments, (2) a troubleshooting exercise in which the couple will develop solutions to a common child management problem, (3) role playing to rehearse new strategies, (4) practice with the child, and (5) time to establish homework goals.

Reviewing Homework (Sessions 2–15)

Problem-solving and self-monitoring homework sheets should be reviewed (Step 3). Each spouse should give a detailed description of a situation in which the strategies developed in the preceding session were executed *successfully*. Parents should be encouraged to focus on successful follow-through on homework goals rather than short-term improvements in child behavior. The therapist should summarize the situation, label key strategies, and organize these into a logical management sequence. Next, parents should review their *rationale* for this strategy. According to the attributional model presented above, parents might consider the social learning basis of the strategy ("What lesson were you teaching?"), the long-term impact of the strategy ("If you used this consistently for the next several years, what differences might you expect?"), or the relational/communicative content of the strategy ("What are you really telling your child by _____?"). Finally, parents might consider whether the long-term benefits of this strategy justify the effort required to implement it. While attributional discussions should increase commitment and adherence (Leary & Miller, 1986), the limited time available needs to be balanced across the session's problem-solving, role-playing, and rehearsal exercises. Attributional discussions, therefore, should be restricted to one or two dimensions per parent.

Troubleshooting Videotaped Errors

In Step 4, the couple will formulate solutions to videotaped examples of common parenting errors. The couple should begin by reviewing the approach to problem solving formulated in Session 1. The therapist may wish to outline this "PASTE" model on a chalkboard: (1) *P*ick a soluble problem; (2) generate *A*lternative solutions, paraphrasing each other's proposals; (3) evaluate the strengths and weaknesses of each suggestion and *S*elect the best alternative; (4) *T*ry it out; and (5) *E*valuate outcome. The therapist then plays a brief videotape depicting a situational encounter between parents and children that is a common source of problems (Barkley & Edelbrock, 1987). The role-playing parents featured on the tape make exaggerated versions of common child management errors. The errors are selected to focus discussion on key components of a more general management strategy. Each tape depicts both fathers and mothers modeling each error and illustrates the error's emotional and behavioral impact.

Next, the therapist should prompt the couple to (1) identify parenting errors on the tape and (2) discuss the consequences of each according to the attributional model described above. For example, what lessons might an error inadvertently teach, what message is communicated, or what is the error's long-term impact? The therapist should encourage balanced participation by asking for each spouse's perspective regarding different errors.

Next, the couple should generate alternative approaches to each error. The therapist should prompt detailed descriptions of promising strategies and restate, summarize, and organize parental suggestions into a cohesive approach. The couple should evaluate each alternative according to selected questions from the attributional model outlined above. Again, to facilitate a balanced discussion, the therapist should solicit both spouses' perspective regarding each suggestion.

If parents fail to identify important errors or strategies the therapist might (1) replay the tape, prompting a discussion of key parent-child sequences; (2) replay the tape in a series of antecedent-consequent steps (child behavior, parent response, etc.); (3) role-play a clearer or more exaggerated version of the error; (4) role-play contrasting positive and negative alternatives; or (5) simply present open-ended questions (e.g., "How would you respond if _____?"). The parents should then formulate a solution, supporting rationale, and final summary of the overall strategy.

Modeling Proposed Solutions

Next, the therapist re-enacts the scenario, modeling the solution proposed by the parents (Step 5). This observational learning opportunity increases the likelihood that parents will execute the strategy successfully in subsequent role-play exercises. On most sessions, one parent should be asked to play the role of a child. As some parents may be inclined to confront the therapist with a worst-case child behavior scenario, the child's role should be defined carefully.

Role-Playing Proposed Solutions

In Step 6, each parent should review the strategies he or she will be practicing and rehearse it in a brief (e.g., 2-minute) exercise with the therapist playing the role of a child. The therapist should ensure success by playing a manageable child who responds positively to the parent's efforts. As parental skill and confidence increase, the therapist should role-play the more challenging behaviors parents will encounter at home. The role-playing parent should be allowed to repeat this exercise until the skill is mastered. The other spouse should then have an opportunity to complete the exercise.

Role-playing frequently reveals strategies that the couple did not discuss during troubleshooting exercises. The therapist should label and describe the strategy, prompt an attributional discussion, and facilitate an exchange of feedback.

Practice with Child/Siblings

Each parent is then given an opportunity to practice newly formulated strategies in a short analogue with the ADHD child and any siblings (Step 7). This consolidates new skills prior to their application at home, increases confidence, and enhances parents' commitment to the solution (Leary & Miller, 1986). This exercise also familiarizes the child and siblings with new strategies and provides children with an opportunity to practice solutions they have formulated in their own group. The therapist should prompt a review of the strategies to be used in the role play, seat the spouse behind a one-way mirror, and select a child or children from the group room. The therapist should describe the situation and prompt the child to devise a plan. A prosocial prompt ("How can you help out?") seems to elicit the most cooperative response. Note that during the group sessions, children will have reviewed this type of situation, identified errors, formulated a strategy and rehearsed its application, and practiced a plan. The child should be rewarded for devising a plan and escorted into the room.

The acquisition of skills in this situation can be enhanced by the use of a "bug-in-the-ear" FM transmitter. This provides a reinforced model for the observing spouse; it also allows the therapist (or spouse) to reward positive parenting responses, label strategies that were not discussed during the troubleshooting exercise, and prompt the application of specific skills. Before returning to the group room, the child should be prompted to evaluate his or her performance and provide an appropriate self-reward. The parents and therapist should then reassemble to review the analogue.

Homework Assignments

Finally, each parent should identify specific situations to which the strategies developed in the session might be applied (Step 8). Parents should be encouraged to (1) describe the homework proposal in considerable detail, (2) devise a strategy for reminding themselves to implement these changes, and (3) identify and formulate solutions to obstacles that might prevent them from following through. The couple is assigned a written homework project to (1) discuss more detailed plans regarding the strategies developed in the session; (2) identify situations in which strategies might be applied; (3) monitor application by each parent; and (4) complete a reading from Patterson's (1968) text *Living with Children* which provides a background in social learning principles (McMahon, Forehand, & Griest, 1981).

Improving Family Functioning

Training sessions provide a context in which the therapist may accomplish the systemic goals of the program. The structure and process of each training session as described above prompt positive shifts in the way many couples approach the solution of child management problems, distribute child care and management responsibilities, and communicate regarding both the instrumental and affective dimensions of child management. Behavioral and social-psychological models suggest a number of strategies by which the therapist may increase parental commitment to following through on these changes. Several useful approaches are outlined below.

Prompting and Fading

After each parent's homework review, role-playing exercise, and practice session with the child or children, the other spouse should be prompted to identify those strategies that were used most effectively "John, I'd like you to think back through the role play and give Jan some feedback on each of the strategies you thought she handled well"). Once this type of descriptive positive feedback is exchanged comfortably, the therapist should fade the prompts by gradually reducing the amount of detail provided in each instruction. This should be accomplished in an errorless fashion (Terrace, 1974), so that, at each step, the feedback provided by the spouse is positive. A parent who is less experienced or less comfortable communicating in this manner often directs comments regarding the spouse to the therapist. As parents' skill and comfort increase, they should be encouraged to speak directly to each other. Again, these prompts should be faded from detailed instructions to more subtle gestures.

Enhancing Commitment to Change via Attributional Discussions

The couple's commitment to new communication, role allocation, or problem-solving strategies may be enhanced by (1) labeling transactions that represent approximations to important systems goals, and (2) prompting an attributional discussion of the advantages of this approach. These discussions might begin with open-ended prompts (e.g., "You've been giving each other a lot of positive feedback in these sessions. Why does this make sense for you?") or social learning attributional prompts (e.g., "How does this affect your husband/wife's management of your son/daughter?"). On other occasions the therapist might explore relational/communicative ("What are you really telling your husband/wife/family when you take the time to sit down together and discuss problems?"), long-term ("If you consistently solved problems as a couple over the years, what difference would it make for your family?") or effort ("Is it worth the time and effort for you to _____?") attributions. It is helpful to ask the spouses to provide feedback to one another regarding these assumptions: "Is he/she right?" or "What's it like to hear that from your husband/wife?"

The different levels of the family system (child, siblings, couple, family), in combination with the four types of attributional prompts discussed (social learning, relational/communicative, short-term vs. long-term, or effort) provide a variety of perspectives from which the couple may formulate rationales supporting important changes. Although each discussion should be limited to one or two attributional perspectives, additional time should be allocated to those that elicit particularly productive responses.

Troubleshooting

Providing the couple with an opportunity to troubleshoot videotaped examples of common errors in problem solving, roles, or communication represents an alternative approach to building the marital skills needed to manage ADHD children effectively. This approach is used particularly in Session 1, where couples identify problem-solving errors, discuss their consequences, generate an alternative approach, and formulate supporting rationales.

Prompting Generational Transfer

Finally, most parenting strategies are applicable to interactions with other members of the family, extended family, or community (e.g., "It sounds like this makes sense with children. Does it apply to adults?"). Attending and conversational skills, strategies for balancing time and attention, coping skills for ignoring minor annoyances or avoiding escalating arguments, giving compliments, and planning solutions to potential problems may all prove useful in a variety of contexts.

Formulating Systemic Homework Goals

If the couple states a commitment to important systemic goals, these should be included in their weekly homework assignment. The couple should be encouraged to formulate a detailed plan as to how specific changes might be implemented, to anticipate obstacles, to consider ways of reminding themselves, and to monitor their success. These projects should be included in each session's homework review.

CURRICULUM FOR PARENTS' SESSIONS

The curriculum of the parent training program has been outlined in Table 13.1. This section summarizes the strategies discussed in each session, suggests themes for coping-modeling scenarios, and outlines the homework assignment. A more detailed presentation of possible scenarios is available (Cunningham, 1989). Each session is conducted within the general framework discussed above. The curriculum begins with problem solving, moves to simple play and conversational approaches, and progress to increasingly complex planning strategies that incorporate the skills acquired in early sessions. This curriculum sequence is based on several assumptions. First, problem-solving skills developed in Session 1 may be rehearsed, mastered, and transferred to the different problems encountered in each subsequent session's troubleshooting exercises. Moreover, the basic skills acquired in early sessions are reviewed and rehearsed in later role playing, practice, and homework exercises. Successes encountered in early sessions build the confidence needed to confront the more difficult skills and problems dealt with in later sessions. Finally, attending, balanced attending, and reward sessions provide parents with the skills needed to enhance their relationship with the ADHD child prior to tackling oppositional behavior and conduct problems.

Session 1: Problem Solving

Goals

In the first session, parents formulate an approach to the solution of child management problems that is very similar to the model presented by Arthur Robins in Chapter 14. This typically includes (1) selecting optimal times and locations for problem solving, (2) identifying problems and establishing priorities, (3) solving one manageable problem at a time, (4) generating alternative solutions, (5) paraphrasing the spouse's suggestions, (6) evaluating alternatives, (7) selecting the best approach, (8) compromising in the event of disagreement, and (9) evaluating outcome. This is often summarized on the chalkboard as a "PASTE" model (see "Troubleshooting Videotaped Errors," above).

Coping-Modeling Scenarios

The errors illustrated in the videotaped coping-modeling scenarios include (1) attempting to solve problems at rushed chaotic times, (2) discussing problems in extremely vague language, (3) dealing with several problems simultaneously, (4) failing to listen carefully, (5) cutting off or rejecting proposals, (6) failing to compromise, (7) failing to determine whether a solution actually worked, and (8) engaging in generalized personal criticism.

Modeling and Role-Playing Exercises

After the therapist had modeled the problem-solving steps suggested by the couple, the spouses should be asked to apply these to the solution of a simple problem. To ensure success, the couple should proceed through this exercise in a slow, step-by-step sequence. Before beginning the exercise the therapist should prompt the couple to review the PASTE (or alternative) approach to problem solving. As each step is completed, the therapist should interrupt the exercise, label the step, prompt the couple to review the next step, and allow the discussion to proceed. When a consensus regarding a solution has been reached, each spouse should be prompted to identify those strategies used by the other spouse which were most helpful. The therapist should encourage an attributional discussion of selected problem-solving skills and assign a more difficult problem. Prompts to rehearse steps that have been mastered should be faded as the couple proceeds through subsequent problems.

Homework Assignment

Parents should complete a written assignment to (1) list times and places that would be most conducive to effective problem solving, and (2) determine how frequently these discussions should be scheduled. Several problem-solving homework discussions should be arranged to facilitate continued practice. The couple should rehearse the general approach prior to each homework exercise and record the details of the problem-solving discussion (time, place, problem, alternatives, solution, implementation, and evaluation date).

Session 2: Attending to Play and Conversation

Goals

The second session introduces strategies for attending to play, conversation, and prosocial behavior that are similar to those discussed in Chapter 12. Depending upon the developmental level of the child, parents typically suggest (1) quiet interested watching/listening, (2) nonverbal displays of interest, (3) naming objects, (4) describing actions, (5) labeling feelings and prosocial behaviors, (6) asking questions that are closely related to the child's play or conversation, and (7) repeating or summarizing the child's statements. In addition to their socially reinforcing and relational effects, naming, describing, reflective questions, and expansions of the child's utterances are thought to serve important language-teaching functions (Hoff-Ginsberg, 1987).

Coping-Modeling Scenarios

Specific errors presented in the coping-modeling scenarios include (1) physically violating the child's personal space, (2) directing the child's activity, (3) pre-empting the child's problem-solving efforts, (4) interrupting play and conversation with unrelated questions, (5) shifting the conversational focus from child's to parent's interests, and (6) engaging in unwarranted criticism. The concept of personal space provides a useful structural frame of reference for considering other dimensions of family life.

Homework

Parents discuss and list (1) ways of attending to child behavior, (2) situations in which attending strategies might be applied, and (3) behaviors that might be attended to. Each parent should identify a different situation in which to practice attending strategies each day and should record the situation, child, and strategies used. The reading assignment for the week should be Chapters 1 and 2 from *Living with Children* (Patterson, 1968).

Session 3: Balancing Attending among Siblings

Goals

In the third session parents (1) balance attention to the target child and siblings, (2) develop strategies for attending simultaneously to two children by addressing comments to both children simultaneously (e.g., "You've *both* built some great things with the Legos"), and (3) reinforce prosocial transactions between siblings (quiet parallel play, cooperative activity, turn taking, sharing, helping, problem solving, and compromising). At a more systemic level, the concept of balance provides a frame of reference via which parents may consider family structure and transactions (e.g., "You've concluded that it's important to balance time between children. Are there other areas of family life where it's important to maintain a balance?").

Coping-Modeling Scenarios

The coping-modeling scenarios allow parent to explore the impact of an inequitable distribution of (1) physical proximity and contact, (2) time, and (3) attention strategies among siblings.

Homework

Parents should list (1) different situations in which balanced attending strategies might be used, (2) ways of simultaneously attending to two or more children, and (3) prosocial transactions that should be reinforced. Each parent should apply balanced attending strategies in at least one new situation each day and should monitor this assignment. Chapters 3 and 4 from *Living with Children* should be completed.

Session 4: Rewards

Goals

In the fourth session, parents develop more specific strategies for verbally or nonverbally rewarding prosocial behavior. Parents will learn to reward positive behavior immediately, deliver rewards frequently, and prevent satiation by developing a variety of effective rewards.

Coping-Modeling Scenarios

Errors depicted in the coping-modeling scenarios include failing to reward positive behaviors, rewarding behaviors very infrequently, and rewarding behaviors after a long delay.

Homework

Parents list (1) ways of rewarding positive behavior, (2) situations in which rewards need to be used more frequently, and (3) specific behaviors which should be rewarded. Each parent should identify a different situation in which to practice reward strategies each day and monitor the situation, child, and strategies used. The reading assignment for the week should be Chapters 1 and 2 from *Living with Children.*

Session 5: Planned Ignoring

Goals

Parents will develop strategies for (1) ignoring minor problems, (2) ignoring or disengaging from upwardly escalating coercive episodes, and (3) using thoughts (cognitions) that allow them to cope more effectively with potentially explosive situations (e.g., "It's important that he learn that he cannot get his way by throwing tantrums").

Coping-Modeling Scenarios

The coping-modeling videotape is composed of several short scenes in which (1) parents attend to and reinforce inappropriate behaviors; (2) a negative parental response (e.g., nagging, pleading, yelling, or criticizing) to provocative comments escalates a disruptive episode (Patterson, 1982); or (3) counterproductive parental cognitions (e.g., "He's just doing this to get me; I can't stand this any more") precipitate an emotional overreaction.

Homework

The couple should list (1) behaviors for each child that might be ignored, (2) situations in which ignoring might be applied, and (3) examples of coping cognitions. Each parent should identify at least one situation daily where ignoring strategies might be practiced and monitor their completion of this assignment. Chapters 5 and 6 of *Living with Children* should be completed.

Session 6: Transitional Strategies

Goals

Parents formulate strategies for (1) obtaining the child's attention and presenting instructions, (2) preparing the child in advance for potentially problematic transitions (e.g., "In a few minutes it will be time to _____"), (3) ignoring initial protests, and (4) rewarding follow-through.

Coping-Modeling Scenario

The coping-modeling videotape consists of a series of brief scenarios that include the following errors: (1) failing to obtain the child's attention, (2) presenting overly complex instructions, (3) presenting transitional commands abruptly without warning, (4) attending to minor protests and provoking confrontation, and (5) failing to reward successful follow-through of a command.

Homework

Parents will list situations to which transitional strategies might be applied, use this strategy at least once daily, and monitor its application.

Session 7: When-Then Contingencies

Goals

Parents explore the "Premack principle," which is that the completion of less rewarding tasks is reinforced by allowing the child to participate in more rewarding activities (e.g., "*When* you complete your homework, *then* you can watch televisions"). Finally, parents consider the relative effectiveness of when-then statements presented in pleading, firm/neutral, or negative tones of voice.

Coping-Modeling Scenarios

The coping-modeling scenarios (1) show parents allowing children to participate in highly rewarding activities before completing less interesting tasks, and (2) illustrate the potentially counterproductive effects of negative when-then statements (e.g., "If you don't _____, then you won't _____").

Homework

Parents should list (1) reinforcing activities that their child enjoys each day; (2) daily tasks that they would like the child to complete; and (3) sequences in which *when* the child completes a task he or she can *then* engage in a rewarding activity. To encourage more balanced application of this strategy, different lists should be constructed for each child of appropriate age in the family. Each parent should identify and monitor the application of when-then strategies in at least one situation daily. Chapters 7 and 9 from *Living with Children* should be completed.

Session 8: Planning Ahead for Uninterrupted Parental Activities

Goals

In Session 8, parents develop a strategy for dealing more directly with the ADHD child's self-regulatory deficits. This approach should improve behavior in situations where the child responds impulsively because of unfamiliarity with or inability to regulate behavior according to rules and consequences. Parents typically formulate an approach that includes (1) sitting down with the child at a positive time well in advance of new, complex, or repeatedly problematic situations; (2) describing the situation to the child (e.g., "I have some reading I have to do tonight"); (3) prompting the child to formulate a plan (e.g., "What could you do to help out?"); (4) reinforcing planning; (5) prompting the child to rehearse the plan *immediately* prior to the target situation (e.g., "It's time to do my reading. What were you going to do to help?"); (6) reinforcing review; (7) reinforcing successful follow-through; (8) ignoring minor errors; (9) prompting the child to review the plan as necessary; and (10) as behavior improves, fading prompts and reinforces for planning and review, and shifting reinforcers to a less frequent variable schedule.

For children with more limited language and mediational skills, parents may (1) anticipate difficult situations, (2) present simple instructions, (3) prompt the child to restate the instruction, (4) prompt the child to repeat the instruction immediately prior to the target situation, (5) reinforce repetition and follow-through, (6) ignore minor errors, and (7) repeat the sequence as needed.

Coping-Modeling Scenarios

To formulate this strategy, parents troubleshoot a series of short videotaped scenarios. In addition, since this is a complex strategy, the therapist may elect to help parents refine a proposal by using *contrasting role plays* that model alternative (positive and negative) approaches to particular steps. The first coping-modeling scenario depicts (1) complex, multiple-step commands; (2) negative tone of voice and nonverbal gestures; (3) long intervals separating the instructions and the task; and (4) the absence of reminders or prompts to review rules and consequences. Next, two approaches to planning ahead may be contrasted: stating parental expectations (e.g., "I have reading for my course. I want you to play quietly and not interrupt me") versus prompting the child to formulate a plan ("I have some reading for my course. What could you do to help out?"). After this, the parents can proceed to a more subtle contrast of alternative approaches to reviewing plans: (1) *parent* reviewing versus parent prompting *child* to review, and (2) parent prompting child to review *rules* versus reviewing *plans*.

After each contrasting role play, the therapist should prompt the couple to consider the advantages and disadvantages of each alternative according to the four-level attributional model presented above.

The next tape depicts a parent planning successfully and prompting rehearsal but failing to (1) reinforce successful follow-through of commands, or (2) ignore minor errors or interruptions. The therapist should summarize by verbally modeling the components of the strategy that the parents have formulated at this point.

The final segment depicts parents who fail to fade the planning and prompted rehearsal strategies in situations that the child has mastered.

Homework

The couple should list all of the possible situations to which planning ahead might be applied. Each parent should practice and record the application of this strategy in at least one situation each day. Parents should also complete Chapter 16 from *Living with Children* which introduces a simple point system.

Session 9: Planning for a Telephone Call

Goals

Session 9 allows parents to rehearse and extend the planning strategies developed in Session 8 to a more complex situation in which both parent and child are distracted by a telephone conversation. Parents will develop an additional strategy for *publicly rewarding* the child by commenting positively regarding the child's behavior to another adult.

Coping-Modeling Scenarios

The sequence of tapes repeats the errors depicted in the Session 8 scenarios and presents an additional error: publicly criticizing the child.

Homework

Parents should list situations, other children, or groups of children to which planning strategies may be applied. Special attention should be placed on situations where the child may be allowed to overhear himself or herself being spoken about positively. Each parent should select at least one situation in which to practice this strategy each day (parents may wish to ask friends, relatives, or spouses to call at a prearranged time). Note that parents may wish to plan together with the child. Parents interested in additional readings on point systems should be assigned Appendix B from Barkley's (1981) text, which presents a more complex point system, or the more detailed handout on the home point system from *Defiant Children* (Barkley, 1987).

Session 10: Planning for a Visitor

Goals

Session 10 extends planning and prompted rehearsal strategies to a more difficult situation in which the parent is occupied in conversation with a visitor. Visitors are salient distracters who pose considerable difficulty for ADHD children and their parents (Barkley & Edelbrock, 1987). This analogue provides parents with a general approach for dealing with other adults (relatives, babysitters, or teachers) who may inadvertently encourage disruptive behavior. Parents typically elect to (1) apply the planning and prompted rehearsal strategies developed in Sessions 7 and 8; (2) inform the visiting adult about their goals for the child and the strategies they are using (e.g., "We're trying to teach John not to interrupt, so we won't encourage him when he does"), and (3) give the visitor suggestions regarding how he or she might assist the parent.

Coping-Modeling Scenarios

The role-playing parent correctly models all of the strategies developed in the preceding sessions. These include prompting the child to formulate a plan at a neutral time well in advance of the visit, prompting the child to rehearse the plan when the visitor knocks on the door, rewarding the child for following the plan, commenting positively to the visitor regarding the child's efforts, ignoring minor errors, and prompting the child to review the plan when more major interruptions occur. With the exception of several very minor interruptions, which the parent ignores, the child responds well to these strategies. The visitor, however, attends to minor disruptive behaviors or interruptions that escalate in frequency and intensity.

Homework

The parents should list the situations, children, and other adults to which this planning strategy might be applied and practice its application. Chapter 8 from *Living with Children*, which introduces time-out procedures, should be completed.

Session 11: Time Out from Positive Reinforcement

Goals

In Session 11 parents formulate a time-out strategy for situations when children refuse to comply with important commands or engage in behaviors which cannot be ignored. Time-out includes a group of strategies in which misbehavior temporarily terminates access to rewarding activities. Examples often include placing the child in a chair, corner, or bedroom, or removing a privilege. According to this strategy, parents (1) get the child's attention; (2) present firm, simple, instructions; (3) reinforce compliance; (4) provide a warning if the child fails to comply within approximately 10 seconds; (5) implement time-out if the child fails to comply with the warning; (6) ignore disruptive behaviors; (7) terminate the time-out after 2 to 5 minutes (or an appropriate interval for privileges) and 30 seconds of quiet behavior (Hobbs & Forehand, 1975; Hobbs, Forehand, & Murray, 1978); and (8) repeat the original command. Parents who have read Patterson's (1968) Chapter 8 in preparation for this session often elect to impose 1-minute extensions if the child refuses to comply with time-out. This program does not, however, advocate intrusive procedures such as spankings or incarceration in locked rooms.

Coping-Modeling Scenarios

Errors include (1) pleading with the child to comply, (2) repeated vague warnings, (3) attending to disruptive behavior in time-out (e.g., arguing with the child) (4) terminating time-out in response to tantrums or disruptive behavior, (5) failing to repeat the original command when time-out is terminated, or (6) failing to reward compliance following time-out.

Homework

Parents should discuss whether they will use time-out procedures, the types of time-out procedures that might be appropriate for different children in the family, the logistics of using that procedure (place, duration, response to refusals) the behaviors to which they will apply time-out, and how they will inform the child regarding its use. After these discussions are complete, they should begin applying and monitoring the use of time-out.

Sessions 12–14: Generalizing Skills to Selected Problems

Sessions 12–14 allow the couple to consolidate and generalize new strategies by applying them to outstanding problems at home or school. Parents should select a problem that might be managed using the strategies developed in the program, review the problem-solving (PASTE) approach developed in Session 1, and use this to formulate solutions. The therapist should model the strategies proposed; allow the couple to rehearse the strategy; and, if an appropriate clinic analogue can be developed, allow the couple to practice the solution with the ADHD child and siblings. Parents should establish homework goals, monitor application, and review the outcome on the following session. For generalization sessions, the therapist may select supplementary readings that will be of assistance.

Session 15: Closing

In the closing session, the couple should be encouraged to review those strategies that have contributed most to improved child behavior and positive parent-child relationships. To enhance commitment to the continued use of these skills, the therapist should prompt the couple to review explanations of why these strategies are important. Next, the couple should review helpful approaches to problem solving, communication, or the distribution of child management responsibilities and formulate supporting explanations. Finally, the parents should anticipate obstacles that might prevent effective maintenance and consider solutions. If significant management difficulties persist, the therapist may wish to schedule additional problem-solving sessions or identify therapeutic alternatives. Finally, to evaluate the effectiveness of the program, father and mother should independently complete the battery of questionnaires used prior to treatment.

Optional Sessions and Readings

The general set of strategies developed during the program will allow parents to formulate solutions to a wide range of child management problems. In selected cases, however, it may be helpful to develop sessions addressing specific problems with which an individual family has particular difficulty. In these instances the therapist should devise coping-modeling scenarios illustrating unique dimensions of the problem, prompt a troubleshooting discussion, provide the couple with an opportunity to rehearse the strategy in a simulated setting, and encourage the development of homework goals. Examples have included point systems, behavior at school, resolving conflict with adolescents, dealing with extended family members, or managing behavior in public places.

Modifications for Single-Parent Families

Modifications of this program have been used successfully with groups of four to six single parents. Although videotape analogues should depict single-parent families, the structure and process of individual sessions and the content of the respective analogues are similar to those used with couples. To allow all members of the group to participate in discussions, role-playing exercises, and rehearsal sessions with their children, sessions should be extended to 2 hours. The systemic issues discussed in these groups typically include balancing the needs of parent and child; communicating effectively with other caretakers (babysitters, former spouse, teachers); and developing networks that provide personal support, assistance, and a vehicle for collaborative problem solving. Leaders should facilitate a consensus regarding solutions and prompt members to give one another positive descriptive feedback following homework, role playing, and rehearsal exercises. Effective

TABLE 13.3. Outline of Children's Group Program

Session 1: Introduction
Session 2–5: Selected prosocial skills
Session 6–8: Behavior at home
Sessions 9–14: Selected home/school problems
Session 15: Closing
Monthly booster sessions

problem-solving and communicative transactions should be labeled, and members should formulate supporting rationales. To rehearse problem-solving and communication skills and to encourage the development of personal networks, homework assignments might include phone calls or meetings between group members.

CHILDREN'S GROUP

Rationale

Table 13.3 outlines the group for 4- to 12-year-old children that runs concurrently with parenting sessions. These groups may be composed of siblings, children from individual couples whose sessions are scheduled simultaneously, children and siblings from different families participating in small groups, or children from single-parent groups. This group allows children to (1) formulate, rehearse, and apply their own solutions to the problems being solved by parents; (2) improve their understanding of peer and parent-child relationships, (3) increase their commitment to change, (4) build the skills needed to solve problems collaboratively with parents and teachers and (5) familiarize themselves with the types of point systems that parents and teachers may implement. Concurrent parent and child programs focusing on the solution of similar problems encourage children to respond more positively to parental efforts to apply newly acquired management skills. Parents, in turn, may promote generalization by prompting and reinforcing the general strategies and more specific solutions that children develop.

Structure and Process

Session 1

The structure of children's group sessions is summarized in Table 13.4. In Session 1, the leader encourages children to discuss reasons for attending the group, establish personal goals, and consider potential benefits. The leader provides an overview of the group program and describes the sessional schedule of activities. Next, the leader prompts group members to formulate rules governing their behavior during the session (e.g., "What should we do when

TABLE 13.4. **Structure of Individual Children's Group Sessions**

Step 1. Introductory social phase
Step 2. Leader outlines session plan
Step 3. Participants review/formulate rules for session
Step 4. Participants review homework successes
           (Leader awards points[a])
Step 5. Participants troubleshoot videotaped (or other) coping model
           (Leader awards points[a])
Step 6. Leader role-plays group solution
Step 7. Each participant role-plays solution with leader
           (Leader awards points[a])
Step 8. Participants practice solution with parents or peers
           (Leader awards points[a])
Step 9. Participants exchange points for reinforcers
Step 10. Members establish homework goals

[a]Points may be lost for specified infraction at any time.

someone has an idea/wants to speak/is talking/is practicing new skills/etc.?") and to design lists or pictorial reminders. The therapist should introduce a token system that allows tokens or points to be earned for following rules, solving problems, completing homework, and the like (or lost for agreed-on infractions). Tokens or points are to be exchanged according to a menu of in-session reinforcers.

Reviewing Homework

At the beginning of Sessions 2 and of each subsequent session, there is a brief introductory social phase (Step 1). The leader then outlines the session plan (Step 2), and prompts the group to review the rules formulated in the preceding session and to formulate solutions to new problems that may have emerged (Step 3). Next, each describes situations in which the strategies formulated in the preceding session were applied successfully (Step 4).

Troubleshooting

The leader presents a videotaped role play, live role play, or doll analogue depicting a problem with parents, siblings, and peers (Step 5). As in the sessions for parents, tapes present exaggerated examples of common errors and illustrate potential consequences. Sessions 2 through 5 focus on developmentally appropriate prosocial skills such as turn taking, sharing, joining, cooperation, helping, or conversation. Sessions 6 through 8 target the same situations discussed by parents: behavior when parents are occupied, talking on the phone, entertaining visitors, or giving instructions. Sessions 9 through 14 deal with additional problems identified by the parents, siblings, teachers, or therapist.

The leader prompts the group to (1) identify errors in the role play, (2) discuss the immediate and longer-term consequences of each error, (3) suggest alternative approaches, (4) evaluate each alternative by considering short- and longer-term social and emotional consequences, and (5) reach a consensus regarding the best alternative. Finally, points should be awarded for good problem solving.

Modeling and Rehearsing Solutions

Next, the leader models or presents a videotaped enactment of the solution proposed by the group (Step 6). Each member should then be prompted to verbally rehearse the skills to be practiced and to apply these in a brief exercise with the therapist acting the role of a sibling, peer, parent, or teacher (Step 7). The leader prompts and reinforces key responses during the role play, encourages children to evaluate their own performance, and asks group members to identify strategies that the role player executed most successfully. Finally, points should be awarded for participation and approximations to successful performances.

The therapist should arrange in-session activities that allow the children to rehearse the strategies developed (Step 8). These may include games that require turn taking, special toys that should be shared, tasks that allow older siblings to help younger siblings, and opportunities to compliment one another. The leader should prompt members to apply new skills, fade prompts as skill improves, and award points for successful follow-through. It is during this stage of the program that individual children or groups of siblings will be interacting with parents. The therapist should prompt children to formulate a plan for the specific analogue that the parents will be conducting and to rehearse the plan just prior to entering the room with their parents.

Exchanging Points for Reinforcers

The group should now have an opportunity to exchange points earned during the homework review, problem solving, role playing, and rehearsal exercises (Step 9).

Formulating Homework Assignments

Finally, the therapist should prompt each child to formulate a specific plan as to how the strategies developed during the session might be applied at home or school. To facilitate adherence, children should devise reminders such as small pictures or notes, determine where these might be placed, and (where developmentally appropriate) use simple self-monitoring procedures. Parents and teachers should be encouraged to prompt children to review their homework plans, assist in posting reminders, and reward successful follow-through.

BOOSTER SESSIONS

Graduates of the parenting program are encouraged to attend monthly 2-hour booster sessions in which parents (1) review useful strategies, (2) discuss previously effective strategies that need to be reintroduced, (3) present situations that have been managed successfully, (4) formulate solutions to new problems, (5) discuss useful community resources, and (6) invite speakers on topics of interest.

OUTCOME

My colleagues and I have recently completed a 3-year randomized trial comparing the effectiveness of systems-oriented and standard parent training programs for families with ADHD children with and without conduct problems. Although the data analysis is still in progress, preliminary observations suggest that most participants evidence improvements in child management skills and parenting confidence. Parents consistently report planning ahead and when-then strategies to be the most useful skills acquired during the program. At a more systemic level, many couples evidence an improvement in collaborative problem solving, supportive communication, and shared management responsibility. Mothers (and less frequently fathers) show improvements in Beck Depression Inventory scores, and in some cases marital adjustment scores are higher. While child behavior in situations to which parents apply newly developed strategies and general conduct problem scores also improve, improvements on measures of primary ADHD symptoms are modest. The approach to children's groups used here has been examined with several different populations (Clark, Cunningham, & Cunningham, in press; Cunningham, Clark, Heaven, Durrant, & Cunningham, in press), but its contribution to the parenting program merits further study. Finally, despite promising short-term outcomes, clinical experience suggests that booster groups are critical to longer-term maintenance for many families.

This program assumes that allowing parents to formulate their own solutions to child management problems, enhancing commitment via attributional strategies, and improving key dimensions of family functioning will enhance outcome. Nonetheless, this type of parent training program appears to yield similar outcomes in both maritally distressed and nondistressed families (Brody & Forehand, 1985; Oltmans, Broderick, & O'Leary, 1977). Moreover, simply including fathers does not appear to improve the effectiveness of parent training programs (Adesso & Lipson, 1981; Firestone, Kelly, & Fike, 1980; Martin, 1977). Nonetheless, parents consider the opportunity to work jointly on both parenting and systems goals to be an extremely important component of the program. Moreover, interventions combining parent training with the types of strategies that this program employs to improve problem solving, communication, and conflict resolution do enhance outcome for discordant families (Dadds, Schwartz, & Sanders, 1987).

CONCLUDING COMMENTS

This approach to the management of the ADHD child combines principles and techniques from social-learning-based parent training programs, social-cognitive psychology, and family systems theory. It has, with minor modifications, been used successfully with a wide range of developmental problems (Cunningham, 1989). Although the effectiveness of this approach may be inferred from studies of related programs (Forehand & McMahon, 1981; Pisterman et al., 1987; Pollard, Ward, & Barkley, 1983), controlled clinical trials are needed to examine the program's overall effectiveness and to determine the relative contribution of the social learning, cognitive-attributional, and systemic components of the model to outcomes in various domains for different family and diagnostic subtypes.

14

Training Families with ADHD Adolescents

ARTHUR L. ROBIN

> Youth is the period of building up in habits, and hopes,
> and faiths.—Not an hour but is trembling with destinies;
> not a moment, once passed, of which the appointed work
> can ever be done again, or the neglected blow struck on
> the cold iron.
>
> —JOHN RUSKIN (1819–1900)

Adolescence is a challenging developmental period for families since children are undergoing exponential physiological, cognitive, behavioral, and emotional changes. The normal problems of adolescence are magnified exponentially for the individual with Attention-deficit Hyperactivity Disorder (ADHD) and the family, because the core symptoms and associated features of ADHD interfere with successfully mastering the developmental tasks of adolescence. As a result, ADHD teens encounter academic failure, social isolation, depression, and low self-esteem, and become embroiled in many unpleasant conflicts with their families.

Parents encounter a variety of home management problems with their ADHD adolescents, including the normal problems of adolescence and many specific to ADHD. Many of these problems relate to noncompliance around the house and school-related issues such as homework. Table 14.1 illustrates the responses of 65 mothers of young ADHD adolescents (87% boys, 13% girls; mean age = 13.4) to the Home Situations Questionnaire (HSQ), one measure of the situations in which home management problems arise. The mothers completed the HSQ prior to the initial diagnostic visit to the Children's Hospital of Michigan Attention Deficit Disorder (ADD) Clinic. Mothers most frequently reported problems at home with their ADHD adolescents concerning school, homework, chores, playing with others, when the mothers were on the telephone, bedtime, and in public places. Situations such as playing

TABLE 14.1. Home Situations Questionnaire as Rated by Mothers of Young ADHD Teens (*n* = 65)

Situations	Percentage responding yes	Mean intensity (SD)
At school	82	4.5 (2.0)
Homework	82	5.0 (2.0)
Doing chores	78	4.2 (1.9)
Playing w/others	60	3.6 (1.9)
Mother on phone	56	3.1 (1.6)
Bedtime	46	3.3 (1.9)
In public	45	3.2 (1.9)
Others visiting	41	3.5 (1.8)
At meals	35	3.4 (2.3)
In car	32	3.5 (1.8)
Visiting others	30	3.5 (1.8)
Watching TV	27	3.2 (1.4)
Dressing	18	3.6 (1.7)
With sitter	18	4.4 (1.6)
Washing	16	0.5 (0.5)
Playing alone	7	0.1 (2.8)

alone, washing, dressing, and watching television were relatively infrequently reported as problems. Interestingly, although the intensity of the problems was higher for school, homework, and chores than for the remaining situations, intensity did not vary by situation as much as frequency did.

Further clinical assessment of the types of home problems summarized in Table 14.1 usually reveals an underlying conflict between the adolescent's desire to make his or her own decisions about chores, homework, or whatever the issue may be, and the parents' desire to retain decision-making authority; that is, specific disputes reflect independence-related themes. Such conflicts take the form of unpleasant verbal exchanges characterized by shouting, yelling, name calling, and other hurtful and coercive communication styles.

THEORY

A comprehensive biobehavioral–family systems model is helpful in understanding the factors that determine the degree of conflict concerning home management issues experienced by the family with an ADHD adolescent. Within this model, my colleagues and I postulate that the biological/genetic factors underlying ADHD interact with the developmental tasks of adolescence and environmental/family contingencies to influence the frequency and intensity of home management problems. Teenagers are expected to accomplish five major developmental tasks: (1) individuate from their parents; (2)

adjust to sexual maturation; (3) develop new and deeper peer relationships; (4) form a self-identity; and (5) plan for a career. Parent-teen relations undergo radical restructuring punctuated by periodic perturbation and conflict as adolescents become more independent, necessitating a shift from a more authoritarian to a more democratic parental decision-making structure and communication process.

We (Robin & Foster, 1989) have outlined how three major dimensions of family relations determine the degree of clinically significant conflict likely to occur as teenagers individuate from their parents: (1) deficits in problem-solving and communication skills, (2) cognitive distortions, and (3) family structure problems. Families who are unable to solve problems through a process of mutual problem definition, brainstorming alternative solutions, solution evaluation and negotiation, and careful implementation planning are likely to develop excessive independence-related disputes. When a family also communicates in an accusatory, defensive, or sarcastic manner, members become enraged and act based upon hot emotions rather than cool logic, precluding rational problem solving.

Cognitive distortions are unreasonable expectations and malicious attributions that elicit angry affect and sidetrack solution-oriented communication. A parent, for example, may fear the ruinous consequences of giving too much freedom to an adolescent; may demand unflinching loyalty or obedience; or may incorrectly attribute innocent adolescent behavior to malicious, purposeful motives. An adolescent may jump to the conclusion that the parents' rules are intrinsically unfair and likely to ruin any chance of having fun in peer relations, and may feel that teenagers should have as much autonomy in decision making as they desire. In crisis situations unreasonable beliefs color judgment and add emotional overtones to behavioral reactions. A father who demands obedience, is concerned about ruination, and believes the adolescent is purposely misbehaving will have a difficult time, for example, remaining rational at 2:00 A.M. when his daughter comes home 2 hours past the agreed-upon curfew. If the daughter thinks that her father's midnight curfew is unfair because it prevents her from ever having any fun with her friends, and feels that her father has no right to dictate her curfew, she will also be less than rational. Such unrealistic cognitive reactions mediate emotional overreactions which spur continued conflict.

Family structure problems are difficulties in the organization of the family. All families have a hierarchy or "pecking order," and in Western civilization parents are typically in charge of children. Adolescence is a transitional period when parents are supposed to be upgrading the children's status in the hierarchy, culminating in an egalitarian relationship between adult children and their parents. It is easy for a coercive child to overwhelm the parents, and by adolescence the child may have too much power in the family—a situation we call "hierarchy reversal." As a result, the parents are unable to work as a team to establish and set rules and limits. Sometimes one parent and the adolescent may also take sides against the other parent, forming a cross-generational coalition. Parental disciplinary control is diluted, facilitating inappropriate adolescent behavior since the adolescent can successfully appeal to one parent to stop the other from punishing acting-out behavior. Two family members may place the third in the middle of a conflict, forcing the third to take sides. This pattern, called "triangulation," often occurs with an ADHD adolescent when the father comes home to find that the mother and son have had a major battle earlier that afternoon. Mother and son both turn to the father, presenting their sides of the argument and appealing for support, and the father is triangulated or caught in the middle. Sometimes the father will side with his wife, but other times with his son. Each of these structural problems may result in a "divide and conquer" situation, where the adolescent can continue to engage in some antisocial or inappropriate behavior because the parents are not able to work well as an executive team in setting and enforcing limits.

To these three factors of skill deficits, cognitive distortions, and family structure problems we must add the biologically determined characteristics of ADHD—inattention, impulsivity, and hyperactivity—as determinants of home-based problems in families with ADHD adolescents. Inattention spurs increased conflict by making it difficult for the ADHD adolescent to stay on task when resolving conflicts during family discussions; to carry out agreements with parents; and to complete schoolwork, chores, or other responsibilities. It is also very easy for parents to attribute failure to complete a task to malicious motives or to conclude that the adolescent is not meeting parental expectations, spurring cognitive distortions. Parents often have a very difficult time distinguishing between "defiance" and "inattention" as explanatory factors when teenagers do not follow their instructions. Impulsivity spurs increased conflict because impatient adolescents agitate their parents and engage in coercive attempts to avoid punishment and obtain freedom. When ADHD adolescents become hyperexcitable in disagreements with their parents, it is very difficult for them to shift gears and calm down, spurring speedy escalation of the conflict. The poor frustration tolerance, wide mood swings, and failure to consider the consequences of an action that are adolescent expressions of ADHD impulsivity lead to explosive outbursts, frequent arguments, and physical confrontations between ADHD adolescents and their parents. Motoric hyperactivity, when it persists during adolescence, is often misinterpreted as "disrespectful behavior" by parents with high expectations for obedience and perfection, leading them to lash out at the teenagers; this creates a backlash that sets in motion an escalating chain of negative communication.

Individual psychopathology in the parents, such as depression, substance abuse, anxiety, personality disorders, or schizophrenia, add even more complexity and stress to the home-based problems of the ADHD adolescent. As the genetic basis for ADHD is becoming more widely known and accepted, therapists are diagnosing many of the parents of ADHD children as having ADHD themselves. The stress of having two or more distractible, hot-tem-

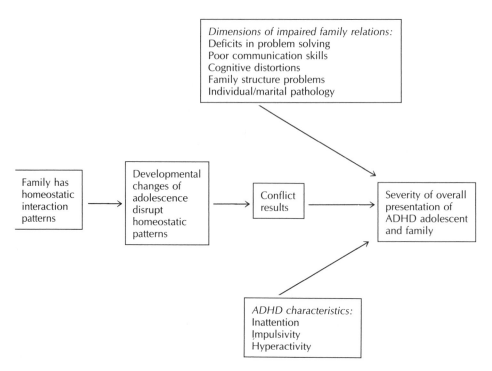

FIGURE 14.1. A biobehavioral–family systems model of ADHD.

pered, impulsive, restless members in a single family exponentially raises the probability of clinically significant conflict. Finally, extrafamilial factors such as the school and peer environments have an impact upon the overall family relationships.

Figure 14.1 summarizes this biobehavioral–family systems model. Prior to the adolescence of its children, a family has developed a homeostatic pattern or system of "checks and balances" regulating its members' interactions. The developmental changes of adolescence disrupt homeostatic patterns, spurring an acute period of "normal parent-teen conflict" between ages 12 and 14. Most families emerge from this stage with new homeostatic patterns and methods of resolving home-based conflicts. Deficits in problem solving, poor communication skills, cognitive distortions, family structure problems, and individual/marital pathology promote clinically significant conflict during early adolescence. These five factors interact with the adolescent's biologically based degree of inattention, impulsivity, and hyperactivity to create a clinical presentation of severe, moderate, or mild ADHD with or without associated Oppositional Defiant Disorder or Conduct Disorder. The issues listed in Table 14.1 become the arena in which these interacting patterns are played out.

INTERVENTION

A multidimensional intervention approach is essential for home management of the ADHD adolescent. A family with an ADHD adolescent typically arrives at the therapist's office in a state of acute crisis: The teenager is failing in school and often about to be expelled for disruptive behavior; the parents and adolescent are having major arguments and fights over school- and home-based defiance and disobedience; the teenager is angry and depressed, sometimes suicidal; and the parents are depressed, angry, and most importantly "burned out" from a life of daily combat with a defiant, disobedient youth. External agencies such as the police have also often been involved for truancy, runaway attempts, or other antisocial behaviors committed by the teenager in the community. Often, the acute crisis is the culmination of many years of struggling to socialize a difficult child who does not appear to have learned from repeated punishments or other consequences. No one has understood why the adolescent always failed to "work up to potential" or "act mature." The therapist must stabilize the acute crisis and begin a more long-term intervention. Table 14.2 outlines the stages of this multidimensional intervention.

TABLE 14.2. Phases of Intervention for ADHD Adolescents

    I. Engagement/family ADHD education (2–3 sessions).
        A. Assess presenting problems in family session.
            1. Home-based, independence-related conflicts.
            2. School-related problems.
            3. Deficits in problem solving/communications.
                a. Observe and comment upon behavior in session.
                b. Obtain description of recent argument at home.
            4. How out-of-control and antisocial is the adolescent? Will restoration of parental control need to be done early in treatment?
        B. Shape a shared view of the problem.
            1. Reframe individualistic problems in interactional terms.
            2. Note contribution of biologically based ADHD characteristics to all of the problems, defusing blame and malicious attributions.
        C. Individual session with the adolescent.
            1. Deepen rapport through discussion of teenager's interests, hobbies, peer issues.
            2. Assess adolescent's degree of oppositionality to directives coming from the therapist.
            3. Help define goals for change that are of interest to the adolescent through Socratic discussion, not lecture.
        D. Session with the parents.
            1. Assess "burnout" and motivation to work for change.
            2. Assess marital relations and stresses placed upon the marriage by the adolescent.
            3. Assess whether parents have ADHD.
            4. Define parental goals for change.

(cont.)

TABLE 14.2. (*cont.*)

  E. Family ADHD education.
   1. Explain ADHD as a lifelong, biologically based handicap interacting with family, school, and personality variables.
   2. Review normal adolescent development.
   3. Explain how ADHD compromises normal adolescent development.
   4. Reframe school failure and home conflict in more benign terms.
   5. Debunk common myths about ADHD and its treatment.
  F. Build a therapeutic contract in a family session.
   1. Review goals—improve school performance, decrease defiant behavior at home, improve problem-solving and communication skills, change beliefs and cognitions, and any teen goals.
   2. Set time limit for therapy—15 to 20 sessions.
   3. Establish policies for attendance, fees, scheduling, cancellations, etc.

II. Address medication issues (1–2 sessions).
  A. Provide accurate information about stimulant medication.
   1. Medication as coping technique for symptoms of inattention, poor task persistence, and impulsive behavior.
   2. Use metaphor of needing glasses for a visual handicap to explain the need for medication for an attentional handicap.
  B. Help the family members outline the advantages and disadvantages of medication.
   1. Have them make a list of pros and cons.
   2. Treat the adolescent's objections to medication seriously and address them.
   3. Help them decide whether the advantages outweigh the disadvantages.
  C. Locate a physician skilled with teenagers and ADHD.
  D. Meet individually with the adolescent to assess and respond to resistance to medication.
  E. Start stimulant medication and monitor regularly.

III. Restore parental control (2–3 sessions).
  A. Does the teenager engage in severe, antisocial behaviors that adults are not stopping?
  B. If yes, pinpoint these behaviors—aggression, destruction, severe verbal abuse, severe noncompliance.
  C. Use strategic-structural family techniques to build a strong parental coalition.
  D. Identify a "bottom line"—some source of extrafamilial control for the parents to invoke if they cannot control the teen (police, juvenile justice system, foster care, mental hospital).
  E. Break the severe behaviors into components.
  F. Ask the parents to reach an agreement about rules and consequences for each component of the antisocial behavior. Be flexible as to whether the adolescent is present during this discussion.
  G. Anticipate adolescent "escape" from parental consequences and plan to circumvent it.
  H. Persist in pushing for a strong parental coalition and carrying out of consequences until the adolescent's behavior comes under better control.

IV. Behavioral study skills for improving school performance (2–3 sessions).
  A. What are the academic/study deficits?
   1. Does the adolescent have the ability to succeed in school? IQ testing may be needed.

   2. Does the adolescent attend to the tasks? Medication may be needed.
   3. Does the adolescent understand the material? Tutoring or special education may be needed.
   4. Does the adolescent participate in class and cooperate with the teacher? A home-school report system may be needed for monitoring and motivation.
   5. Does the adolescent complete homework?
      a. Does the adolescent know the assignments? A written assignment sheet may be needed.
      b. Is the adolescent organized? Does he or she have correct materials, put long-term tasks on a calendar, etc.?
      c. Does the adolescent have a quiet place and regular time to do homework?
      d. Does the adolescent stick with homework?
      e. Do parents enforce and monitor homework compliance?
      f. Does the adolescent hand in completed assignments?
   B. Use stimulus and consequence control techniques to correct these deficits.

V. Teach problem-solving and communication skills (6–7 sessions).
   A. Introduce the steps of problem solving.
      1. Define the problem.
      2. Generate alternative solutions.
      3. Evaluate and decide upon a mutually acceptable solution.
      4. Plan to implement and consequate the solution.
      5. Verify the outcome at the next session.
   B. Problem-solve one issue per session.
      1. Begin with moderate-intensity issues.
      2. Move later to more intense issues.
      3. Use instructions, modeling, rehearsal, and feedback to teach these skills.
   C. Assign homework to implement the solutions and practice problem solving during family meetings.
   D. Introduce communication training (third session of this phase of treatment).
      1. Review family handout of negative communication.
      2. Ask for illustrations of each negative communication habit in the family.
      3. Suggest and rehearse alternative, positive communication behaviors.
   E. Target one or two negative communication behaviors per session.
      1. Use feedback, modeling, and behavior rehearsal to correct targeted behaviors whenever they are emitted.

VI. Address beliefs and attributions—cognitive restructuring (2–3 sessions).
   A. Reframe inappropriate attributions.
   B. Introduce steps of cognitive restructuring—major beliefs.
      1. Provide a rationale linking behavior, cognitions, and affect.
      2. Identify the inappropriate cognition.
      3. Provide a logical challenge to it.
      4. Suggest an alternative cognition.
      5. Develop an "experiment" to disconfirm the unreasonable cognition.

VII. Provide individual therapy to teen.
   A. Optional component—often segments of sessions under earlier sections of the outline are done individually with the adolescent.
   B. Supportive psychotherapy.
   C. Anger control/self-control techniques.

(cont.)

TABLE 14.2. (*cont.*)

    D. Coping with depression, low self-esteem.
    E. Peer relationship, sexuality issues.

VIII. Disengagement/termination phase (1–2 sessions).
    A. Review previous skills.
    B. Anticipate future crises and prepare family to cope with them.
    C. Increase time interval between last few sessions.
    D. Establish framework for follow-ups.

Treatment Overview

Engaging the family in treatment while assessing the problems is the initial step of intervention. The engagement process begins when the diagnosis of ADHD is made. For the first time in many years the family now has a non-blaming, logically consistent cognitive framework for understanding what appeared to be a "bad kid" or "bad parents" or "incompetent teachers." As the diagnosis is made, the family must be engaged in an ongoing therapeutic process, while the therapist also assesses relevant interaction patterns, skill deficits, cognitive distortions, and family structure problems. Family education about ADHD is an intrinsic part of this early engagement/assessment phase of intervention because education plus emotional support help the family to accept the diagnostic information and realize that they are not to blame for all of the trouble that has taken place. Acceptance of ADHD as a physically handicapping condition made better or worse by home and school environmental factors usually leads to discussion of the use of stimulant medication in order to correct the adolescent's handicapped attentional process and to enhance impulse control. At this stage, the therapist must help the family find a knowledgeable physician who understands adolescents to prescribe and monitor stimulant medication. If the adolescent is exhibiting aggression or severe conduct-disordered behavior, the therapist must also quickly move to restore adult authority over the youth—using a combination of behavioral contracting and strategic-structural family therapy techniques—before any other progress can be achieved.

School success becomes the next major target. Medication is usually a necessary but not sufficient condition for academic success; the therapist must conduct a task analysis of the factors contributing to poor grades, and provide remediation in the form of behavioral study skills training and/or recommendations for special education services to help shape appropriate academic behaviors in the classroom and at home. As the adolescent improves in school, the family is ready for problem-solving/communication training, a behavioral–family systems approach to parent-teen conflict resolution. The therapist teaches the family members steps of problem solving and modifies negative communication habits and inappropriate cognitions. Homework assignments are given to promote generalization of newly acquired skills to the natural environment. In the later phases of treatment, the therapist may conduct individual psychotherapy with the adolescent, focusing on depression, peer relationships, sexuality, and individuation issues. By this time, the parents may begin to realize that they too have ADHD, and may ask the therapist for help with personal and/or marital issues.

The initial burst of therapy usually takes from 15 to 20 sessions, spaced over 4–6 months. Afterwards, the therapist leaves the family with the "dental checkup metaphor' of ADHD follow-up: Just as we go to the dentist twice a year for an examination, cleaning, and checkup, the ADHD teenager needs a "check" of the status of ADHD-related problems several times a year. Just as the dentist intervenes to correct any problems that are noted—recurrences of old problems or new difficulties—the therapist helps the teen and parents cope with a breakdown in the use of previously learned coping techniques or helps them to overcome new difficulties that have arisen.

In the following sections, each "module" of this multidimensional intervention is reviewed.

Engagement and Family ADHD Education

Since the formal process of diagnosing ADHD through the use of interviews, rating scales, and tests has been discussed in Chapters 8 to 10, the present discussion begins with the next step, following presentation of the diagnosis to the family. The first two or three sessions following the initial ADHD diagnosis usually constitute the engagement phase of therapy. In the first session, my colleagues and I begin by seeing the adolescent together with the parents, then conclude the session with a brief individual adolescent interview. In the second and third sessions, we see the couple together and then the parents and adolescent together, respectively. The goals of the initial family session are to collect information regarding family interaction patterns, establish rapport, shape a shared view of the problem as an interaction of biology and environment, and dispel myths about ADHD through family ADHD education. The therapist opens by giving each family member a turn to express the problem in his or her own terms. As their stories unfold, the therapist reacts to both the content of their statements and the communication style of the family in the session. The therapist must carefully reframe individualist presentations of problems in biobehavioral-interactional terms, in order to shape a shared view of the problem conducive to accepting the family-based intervention that will follow.

An excerpt from the initial session with Matthew Cohen (not his real name), aged 16, and his parents illustrates how we shape a shared view of the problem in biobehavioral-interactional terms:

THERAPIST: So what are the major problems at home?

MRS. COHEN: Matthew's bad temper. He gets really angry for no good reason. Then he curses, yells, and is totally out of control.

MATTHEW: You're full of it, Mom! I don't do that! You're just a nag!

THERAPIST: Wait a minute, Matt. I know you feel strongly about this, but I have to check out something with your mother first. Give me a play-by-play description of a recent temper outburst.

MRS. COHEN: Last night. All I did was ask nicely did he have homework, and he cursed me right out.

THERAPIST: How did you ask, and what happened next?

MRS. COHEN: I said, 'Don't you have homework?' He said, 'No,' and I said, 'Come on, your teacher says she always gives homework. Tell us the truth.' And . . .

MATTHEW: See, there she goes bugging me and thinking I'm always lying.

THERAPIST: Matthew, I know you feel strongly. And I can see how when your mom puts you on the spot about homework, you come out slugging.

MRS. COHEN: Doc, you got it. He actually ended up pushing and hitting me last night.

THERAPIST: So, when you say that Matt loses his temper easily, you are talking about something between you and Matt, not just Matt. You ask nicely first. He doesn't answer. So you turn the screws a bit and press him, suggesting he is lying or holding back on you. He clobbers you back. We are looking at a sequence of communication between the two of you, not just one person losing his temper, right?

MRS. COHEN: I guess so, but it's his ADHD that makes him do it, not my question.

MATTHEW: There she goes again, with that ADHD shit! Next she's going to tell you about Ritalin, the miracle drug."

THERAPIST: Matt, sounds like you get pretty mad and sarcastic when your mom blames your ADHD for everything. Mrs. Cohen, a person with ADHD is like a tightly stretched guitar string. The string can break if you pluck it too hard, but it must be plucked to break. Matt may be more likely to explode because of his biology, but it still takes your statement to set him off. And with the guitar, if you pluck the string just right, you can make beautiful music. You and Matt have the potential to get along with more harmony, even if his ADHD makes him like the tight string. This is a two-person problem. We need to change how you two communicate, not just Matt and not just Mom.

The therapist reframed the mother's individualistic presentation of her son's bad temper as biologically based in terms of an interactional process characterized by veiled maternal provocations eliciting negative adolescent counterattacks; the biological tendency toward impulsivity was presented as a catalyst fueling the adolescent's split-second counterreaction. The guitar metaphor was designed to make vivid the interactional interpretation of Matt's problems. A therapist repeatedly engages in this type of reframing in order to prepare parents and adolescents for a family-based skill training intervention aimed at changing interaction patterns, taking into account biological limitations.

During the remainder of the first family interview, the therapist pinpoints the issues of dispute and begins to assess the deficits in problem solving and communication, as well as the cognitive distortions. The therapist collects information both by asking direct questions and by commenting on observed interactions in the session, inquiring whether such patterns commonly occur at home. In the individual interview with the adolescent, the primary goals are deepening rapport; dispelling common myths about therapy; and helping the adolescent to realize that there may be benefits to be gained from participating in therapy, in terms of improved school performance, fewer adults getting on his or her case, and additional freedoms to be obtained.

In the second and third sessions, we focus on family ADHD education. Families with ADHD adolescents come to therapy with many blameful, malicious attributions. Teachers and school personnel have often reinforced these negative attributions about the adolescent by telling the parents that he or she has not worked up to potential, is unmotivated, acts disruptive, and is antisocial. The therapist needs to explain the diagnosis of ADHD to the family, emphasizing that it is a biologically based handicap of inattention, impulsive control, and restlessness, and that the adolescent's problems are, to a certain extent, beyond his or her ability to control. However, it is important to add that biology interacts with environment, such that the extent to which the adolescent has difficulty with concentration, impulse control, and responsivity to consequences depends on family and school training over many years. The adolescent is not to be excused from responsibilities because of a biological handicap, but rather helped to cope with his handicap in order to maximize his or her ability to meet responsibilities. A memorable example that helps emphasize this point can be given of a situation where an ADHD adolescent runs through a red light and causes an accident while driving. The police and insurance company will not excuse the adolescent from responsibility for the accident because of biologically based distractibility, but after the consequences of the accident are faced, the adolescent needs help to reduce distractibility in the future. The parents may be less angry if they understand the role of biologically based distractibility while nonetheless holding the adolescent responsible for his or her inappropriate driving behavior.

Family ADHD education also involves setting reasonable expectations for the adolescent and debunking common myths about ADHD. It is reasonable for parents to expect the ADHD adolescent to strive for academic and social success, and to fulfill basic responsibilities in the home and family. It is unreasonable for parents to expect perfection or flawless performance, particularly in the areas of chores and schoolwork. As parents are helped to understand that ADHD involves delays in general development, such that the adolescent may look and act younger than his or her chronological age, the social immaturity and interest in preadolescent games and peer relations become more understandable. We provide this education through discussion, presentation of videotaped lectures, and prescription of books to be read by the family.

The engagement phase of therapy ends with the formulation of a therapeutic contract outlining the goals of therapy, a time frame, scheduling and attendance policies, homework policies, fees, and the like. The goals follow naturally from the discussion of the last few sessions—ameliorating ADHD symptoms that interfere with school success and home relations, improving school performance, reducing conflict at home through better problem solving and more positive communication, and correcting faulty perceptions and unreasonable cognitions about family life and ADHD. Readers interested in a more detailed account of the engagement process and the family assessment interviews should consult Robin and Foster (1989) and Foster and Robin (1988).

Stimulant Medication

Whether or not medication will be prescribed is determined in the next session. If medication is to be prescribed, it is important to begin it early in the overall therapy, in order to have time to titrate the dose and maximize the synergistic potential of medication plus behavioral skill training. The clinical use of stimulant medication is discussed in detail in Chapter 17. When prescribing medication with adolescents, the physician must pay particular attention to the following factors: ensuring an adequate dose level, carefully titrating morning and afternoon doses to correspond with particular academic activities, establishing clear-cut criteria for evaluating outcome, minimizing side effects, and adjusting timing to provide adequate length of medication coverage throughout the day. I have all too commonly been asked to evaluate ADHD adolescents who are reportedly "medication nonresponders," only to find that the physician prescribed 5 mg of Ritalin to a 150-pound adolescent at 7:00 A.M. and 3:00 P.M. When the mother returns to the physician 3 months later to complain that there has been no improvement in her son's report card and no decrease in conflict at home, it is concluded that Ritalin "doesn't work"! In this chapter, the focus is not on the basic technical skills of using medication with teenagers, but rather on how to present the use of medication to an adolescent.

Most ADHD adolescents resist taking stimulant medication, whether or not they had positive experiences with it during their younger years. During a time of identity exploration marked by a fierce desire to be different from their parents but carbon copies of their peers, adolescents do not want to do anything that makes them feel different from their friends. Nor do they wish to follow regimens that they perceive as imposed by adults, whether parents or physicians. They believe they know what is best for themselves, and look upon medication as a source of "external control" from which they need to "individuate." Teenagers who have taken Ritalin as younger children often complain that the medication calms them down too much—or, as one athletic youngster said, "Ritalin takes away my killer instinct." What they mean is that they enjoy being wild and impulsive, which medication curbs. They also often attribute a variety of extraneous somatic complaints to Ritalin, even though most of these bear little relation to the psychostimulant. Thus, their resistance stems from basic developmental needs, as well as a history of poor parent-child relations.

A sensitive professional must present the use of stimulant medication to an adolescent within a context that takes these developmental factors into account. The traditional, "Doctor knows best," authoritarian presentation often backfires. A Socratic approach that treats the adolescent as an independent decision maker who needs to perceive the advantages of stimulant medication before agreeing to take it is preferable. The following excerpt from a session with an adolescent illustrates this approach:

DR. JONES: I understand that things are pretty rotten at school. Tell me about it.

BILL: Yeah. I'm getting lousy grades. And the teachers get on my case about talking out.

DR. JONES: How would you like your grades to be?

BILL: C's, B's, but at least passing.

DR. JONES: From all our past talks, it seems like keeping your mind on the work in school and at homework time has been tough, right?

BILL: Sure has. School's so boring, I can't make myself study, even if I want to. And all the noise in class bugs me.

DR. JONES: This is all part of the ADHD thing we've talked about before. Your body won't let your mind stay with things, through no fault of yours. Say, I've got an idea I'd like to run by you. You and I both wear glasses. When we take our glasses off, what happens?

BILL: Things look foggy.

DR. JONES: Right! We need glasses to see clearly. We don't choose to need glasses. That's the way our bodies and eyes are, right?

BILL: I guess so.

DR. JONES: ADHD is similar. You didn't choose to have trouble with concentrating and thinking before acting. You body is just that way. I don't have any glasses for concentration, but I do know of a medication called Ritalin, which acts on your concentration like glasses do on your eyes.

BILL: What do you mean? I'm not taking any smart pills! Only retards need that.

DR. JONES: You feel like I think you're a retard because I'm suggesting medication?

BILL: All my friends make fun of those special ed. kids on the bus who take pills at lunch.

DR. JONES: Bill, you have plenty of smarts. Remember, how I explained that you got a high score on the IQ tests?

BILL: Yeah.

DR. JONES: And as for kids making fun of you, no one is going to know about the pills unless you tell. By the way, does wearing glasses make you or I retards?

BILL: I guess not.

DR. JONES: OK. Fact is, I can't drive a car without my glasses because I might get in an accident. People with ADHD concentration problems might get in accidents unless they do something to pay attention better.

BILL: You think Mom might let me take driver's ed. if I take this Ritalin stuff?

DR. JONES: I don't know. But I honestly can make a stronger case with your parents for anything that requires concentration—driver's ed., a new school, things like that—if I know you are dealing with this ADHD thing.

BILL: Won't I get hooked on this stuff? Like dope? And won't I feel weird? There was some guy on TV who said Ritalin takes away your sex drive.

DR. JONES: Good questions. Not at all. You don't get addicted to Ritalin. You don't feel much different; in fact, your teachers and parents may see more change than you. And believe me, Ritalin does nothing to your sex drive. That's bull.

BILL: When do I start these pills? Can we talk to my mom about driving today?

Dr. Jones first established that Bill wished to improve his school performance, and that increased concentration was essential. Then he used the analogy of visual impairment to provide a rationale for stimulant medication. When Bill objected, he empathized with Bill's concerns but provided accurate information about Ritalin. By linking concentration to driving, he suggested a possible reinforcer for compliance with a medication regimen. Bill reached a decision that the advantages outweighed the disadvantages, particularly as he realized that good concentration might result in privileges such as driving. Professionals must help the adolescent suggest a goal for change linked to the use of medication, take the time to listen to the adolescent's concerns about stimulant medication, create an empathetic context for the provision of accurate information, and then help the adolescent weigh the advantages versus the disadvantages of the medication. In the course of providing information about medication, it is often helpful to cite anecdotal and quantitative data about past experiences of other adolescents with stimulant medication. For example, when adolescents express concern about the side effects of Ritalin, we often report the following data concerning the percentage of 52 successively referred ADHD adolescents at the Children's Hospital of Michigan ADD Clinic who reported side effects at the first return visit after starting Ritalin (mean daily dose = 25.8 mg; range = 10 to 60 mg): (1) decrease in appetite, 34%; (2) trouble falling asleep, 23%; (3) stomachache, 23%; (4) headache, 10%; (5) sadness, 8%; (6) getting more hyper, 8%; and (7) motor tics/twitches, 2%. Such data suggest a relatively low percentage of overall side effects.

If the adolescent persists in refusing to take the medication, other interventions should be explored. Imposing medication upon a teenager without informed consent is not only ineffective but also unethical. The adolescent will find a way to avoid the pills. As one adolescent recently told me, "I hated the Ritalin so much that on the way to school I ate five candy bars to undo the effect of the pills."

Restoring Parental Control

Whenever possible, my colleagues and I prefer to work first on school success and conflict resolution/communication skills, and then to target problems in family structure. However, some ADHD adolescents present to the therapist with such severe oppositional and/or conduct-disordered behavior that they will successfully resist or sabotage all of the other components of treatment until their acting-out behavior is modified. These are the adolescents with histories of aggressive behavior since early childhood or extreme hyperactivity persisting even into adolescence. At the time they arrive for therapy, their parents have very little real control over any of their behaviors. Often, other adults do not have any control over them either. These teenagers tell the therapist that they do not plan to cooperate and have outsmarted many previous therapists. They have acquired powerful repertoires of coercive behavior that reliably function to cause their parents and teachers to back down in discipline and/or limit-setting situations. In terms of family structure problems, the hierarchy of "parent in charge of child" is completely reversed, with the adolescents dictating to their parents, as well as to teachers and other adults.

The therapist must relate to these adolescents in an extremely assertive manner, making it clear that while their opinions will be valued and listened to, there will be certain ground rules for decent interpersonal conduct. Such ground rules usually include the following: (1) There is to be no physical violence during the session or at home; (2) there is to be no vile language during the session; and (3) everyone has a turn to express his or her opinion but only one person at a time talks. The therapist helps model control for the parents by enforcing these ground rules strictly during the sessions. The therapist moves to re-establish parental control by strengthening the parental coalition and teaching the parents to work as a team in setting limits and enforcing consequences. The power of extrafamilial sources of control such as the juvenile justice system, the police, and the inpatient mental health system can be used to back up parental authority. A "bottom line" for antisocial, illegal, and aggressive behavior must be set, with a clear specification of extrafamilial consequences if the adolescent crosses this line. For example, in a family where the adolescent physically assaults the parents, the therapist and parents may agree that the police will be called, charges will be brought, and the adolescent will spend some time in a juvenile lockup if assaultive behavior occurs. In a family where the adolescent chronically and repeatedly violates all of the household rules concerning curfew, smoking, participation in chores, and the like, the parents may decide that at a certain point the teenager must leave home and go to a foster home for a period of time.

When the bottom line is set, the therapist meets individually first with the adolescent, then with the couple. In the session with the adolescent, the therapist has the adolescent project the positive and negative consequences of "crossing the bottom line" and being removed from the house. Graphic descriptions of juvenile settings and foster homes, with careful comparison of the material advantages and disadvantages of the adolescent's own home versus the extrafamilial setting, are given. The therapist is careful not to preach to the adolescent, but rather to develop a Socratic discussion of these points. It is important for the therapist to indicate that the adolescent must choose what is best for him or her, not the therapist and not the parents.

In the meeting with the couple, the therapist begins the process of asking the parents to reach an agreement about appropriate limits and consequences for severe acting-out behavior. Usually, the couple needs a lot of support and direction from the therapist to accomplish this task since they have been unable to reach effective agreements in the past, and feel extremely "burned out" by the time of this session. The spouses often have very different styles of relating to the adolescent—one overinvolved and emotional, and the other disengaged and harsh—and the adolescent has often been able to take advantage of these differences to "divide and conquer," transforming disciplinary efforts into marital disputes. The therapist should break the severe antisocial behaviors down into small components and help the parents reach agreements to work as a team in exercising effective control over one component at a time. As each component is targeted for change, the parents are helped to anticipate all of the adolescent's possible "escape routes" to avoid compliance and close them off.

When a plan of action for controlling antisocial behavior has been reached, the therapist asks the parents to present it assertively to the adolescent in a family session, empathizing with the adolescent's anger but insisting upon the necessity for implementing the plan. At the next session, the therapist reviews the effectiveness of the plan, helps the parents make adjustments, responds to reasonable suggestions from the adolescent for modifications, and then moves on to additional components of antisocial behavior in a similar fashion.

Case Examples of Restoring Parental Control

Successful effort versus an unsuccessful effort to restore parental control are contrasted in two clinical cases. In the Nordon family, 14-year-old Andrew was having impulsive temper tantrums at home, during which he engaged in destructive behavior toward his father's property or aggressive behavior toward his mother and sister. Seemingly minor provocations set off Andrew's tantrums. When his father refused to take him to the store to purchase a Halloween costume, Andrew squirted a bottle of mustard on his father's $400 suit, ruining it. When his mother refused to give him his favorite dessert, he threw a bottle of pop at her, making a hole in the wall. He terrorized his sister constantly, randomly punching her, pulling her hair, and stealing her money and possessions. Mr. and Mrs. Nordon disagreed vehemently with each other about how to handle their son. Mr. Nordon favored physical punishments ("the belt"), while his wife was afraid that Andrew and his dad would hurt each other if her husband used too many spankings. She tried to "reason" with her son, and in fact stood between her husband and son to prevent physical confrontations. Aside from reasoning, she did nothing to consequate tantrums. The couple argued constantly about Andrew's tantrums, which occurred four to five times per week.

When the therapist met with the couple, they agreed that the "bottom line" would be to call the police and press charges in the event of assaultive behavior, and to require financial restitution in the case of destruction of property. They had a very difficult time, though, in reaching an agreement about how to respond at the time of each impulsive episode. Mr. Nordon insisted upon the necessity for physical punishment, and his wife insisted upon doing nothing except having a quiet discussion with her son at a later time. Each parent rigidly accused the other of perpetuating Andrew's tantrums. Andrew expressed some guilt over the effects of the tantrums on his family, but minimized their intensity and claimed he could control them at any time. He objected to his parents' "stupid" rules and perceived his destructive behavior as "getting even." Mrs. Nordon also punished her husband for hitting her son by withdrawing sexually from him for a week following each episode. However, she did this subtly, developing headaches or other somatic symptoms rather than directly refusing to have sexual relations. By the end of the week, he would move out of their bedroom and sleep on the couch in the living room.

The therapist pushed the parents to reach a number of agreements for controlling components of Andrew's tantrums. First, the father agreed to refrain from physical violence toward his son if his wife would be verbally assertive in telling Andrew to get in control or go to his room for 30 minutes until he calmed down during a tantrum. The implementation of this agreement was fraught with perils since Mrs. Nordon either "forgot" to be assertive or despite prior rehearsal responded to her son in a "mousy manner." Mr. Nordon would at first exercise restraint, but by the third time his wife refused to assert herself, he resorted to physical punishment. Only when her husband actually stood by and coached her every statement was Mrs. Nordon able to begin to respond to her son assertively.

After a month of the therapist's pushing the parents to refine and implement their agreement, Mrs. Nordon began to assert herself. An episode where Andrew hit and taunted his sister so intensely that she huddled in the corner sucking her thumb and crying hysterically was the turning point for Mrs. Nordon. She "realized" how tyrannical her son was and began to crack down. Mr. Nordon was incredulous, but strongly supported his wife. Within 3 more weeks, the tantrums had diminished from four or five to one or two per week. Andrew attributed the change in his behavior to his own "willpower," a fantasy that the therapist did not challenge. The couple was again having regular intimate relations, a change that strengthened their general resolve to work as a team. Strategic family therapists might wonder about the role of Andrew's tantrums in helping the couple avoid sexual relations; whatever this connection, from a behavioral–family systems viewpoint therapy needed to focus directly upon Andrew's behavior and his parents' responses to it.

In the second case, 17-year-old Jimmy Selby had a history of drug and alcohol use, stealing radar detectors to support his drug habit, aggression toward his parents and peers, extreme hyperactivity, school expulsion and failure, and destruction of property. The symptom of hyperactivity had not diminished as he entered adolescence, and his parents had little control over him at the time of therapy. He was taking 20 mg of Ritalin twice a day on school days; this was the highest dose he would agree to take, and as his mother said, "At least he can stop moving long enough for me to talk to him on medication." As was the case with the Nordons, Mrs. Selby was more lenient than her husband. She tried to give her son every chance to improve, attributing much of his severe misbehavior to his ADHD. Mr. Selby basically concluded that "Jimmy is a bad kid" and either screamed, hit, or withdrew.

The couple agreed that the "bottom line" would be declaring Jimmy ungovernable and turning him over to the juvenile authorities for placement in a foster home or a residential treatment center. The first concrete issue around which the therapist pushed the couple to agree upon consequences was Jimmy's habit of stealing his father's tools, which then turned up in local pawn shops. After much debate, they agreed that if any tool was missing, Jimmy would be assumed responsible and would lose the use of the family car for one weekend. The agreement was enforced for 2 weeks; then it broke down when the father lost his temper and struck his son over a missing tool. The father avoided the next two therapy sessions with "out-of-town business trips." The mother felt sorry for Jimmy when he was suspended from school for making lewd remarks to the principal's daughter on school grounds, and let him use the car.

When the father returned for several sessions, the therapist again pushed the parents to reach agreements concerning consequences for oppositional behavior. They concurred that Jimmy should not bring a "beeper" to school (to contact his drug pusher friends), should only use the car for transportation to and from school, and should pay his father back for the missing tools out of his paycheck from a part-time job. The therapist attempted to get the father to take an active role in the enforcement of these agreements, but most of the load fell on the mother's shoulders. Meanwhile, she "hid" another series of Jimmy's misbehaviors from her husband (and the therapist), including chronic curfew violations, failing grades in school, and repeated in-school detentions for verbally abusing teachers. She was afraid that her husband would be "too hard on the boy." Eventually, her husband happened to answer a phone call from school and discovered what was happening. He was furious at his wife and again failed to attend therapy sessions.

By this time, Mrs. Selby was completely "burned out." Jimmy continued to protest that he was "innocent" and everyone was "framing him." The mother told the therapist that she did not have the strength to continue and would seriously consider placement out of the home for Jimmy. Since therapy has terminated, however, she has been unable to summon the courage to file for placement, and at this writing the drama continues unabated. She appears to fear that her son will pay his drug pusher friends to burn down the family home and murder her if she contacts the police. Her husband comes and goes from the house as if Jimmy did not exist, and Jimmy does whatever he wants.

In the Selby case, the therapist was unable to maintain the involvement of the father in supporting his wife in dealing with a difficult adolescent. The adolescent had the stamina to "wear down" both parents, who entered therapy already "burned out." The therapist could not convince the parents to exercise the bottom line of invoking external authorities. Jimmy had little or no remorse or conscience about his antisocial behavior. By contrast, Andrew felt badly about the effect of his tantrums on his family, even though he was unable to control them. The Nordons also expressed some affection for each other, while the Selbys related with cold hatred, clearly decreasing their motivation to change. Both adolescents had been diagnosed as having ADHD since age 7, and both were on Ritalin during the course of therapy. The differences between family members' overall degree of warmth/caring and their abilities to experience empathy and understanding of another's social perspective seemed to be the variables that facilitated or detracted from their responsivity to the therapist's attempt to restore parental control.

Behavioral Study Skills Training

Most families coming for therapy with their ADHD adolescents consider school success to be their highest-priority goal. While many school-related problems can be resolved through the use of the problem-solving steps taught to the family in the next phase of therapy, these techniques take a number of weeks to master. There are a number of straightforward behavioral study skills techniques that the therapist can teach to the adolescent and parents in several sessions; these often result in immediate improvement in school performance. These techniques are usually taught in family sessions so that the parents can help the adolescent implement them at home.

First, the therapist helps the adolescent analyze logically the point at which academic performance breaks down. In order to achieve academic success, a student must (1) have the level of intellectual ability and prerequisite academic skills necessary to do the assigned work in his or her current educational placement; (2) attend classes; (3) understand how the grade is determined in each class (e.g., what objectives are to be learned); (4) listen and understand new material taught during the classes; (5) participate in classroom activities; (6) take down the important points from lectures in his or her notes; (7) complete daily and long-term homework assignments and turn them in on time; (8) read the texts and other books; (9) prepare for tests and quizzes effectively; and (10) take tests and quizzes effectively. Since many teachers base grades in part upon "attitude," "effort," or "behavior," the student must also have a good relationship with the teachers and be reasonably polite, cooperative, and compliant in class. Poor grades may be the result of a breakdown for the ADHD adolescent in any one or more of these areas. The therapist reviews each area with the family and attempts to pinpoint where academic performance is breaking down. As the problem areas are identified, skill acquisition, stimulus control, or motivational systems are taught to correct the problem.

If there may be a problem in the area of overall ability or learning style, a full learning disabilities workup will be recommended, with possible recommendations for special education. If truancy has been a problem, the family is helped to specify clear-cut consequences for truant behavior. Difficulty in understanding teacher expectations and grading systems is a common source of adolescent confusion; in this case, the therapist helps the adolescent prepare to ask the teachers for concrete objectives and clear-cut information about how much each component of the class counts in the grades. When listening in class is the major problem, stimulant medication is often the solution, since we know of no behavioral intervention that has as potent a direct impact upon the attentional process.

However, before concluding that the problem is in listening and paying attention, the therapist must rule out the possibility that the work is too hard or easy for the adolescent, producing boredom or frustration that is misinterpreted as "inattention." Difficulties with note-taking skills can be addressed through formal note-taking training courses, which teach skills for selecting the main points from a lecture (Robin, Fox, Martello, & Archable, 1977); through the use of tape recorders to supplement written notes; or through teaching the student how to obtain the necessary information from books. Because of perceptual-motor delays, many ADHD adolescents cannot write as fast as their peers while listening to the teacher. Teachers need to adjust the extent to which note taking is essential to such adolescents' success by helping them find alternative methods to acquire the necessary factual material.

With regard to test-taking skills, here too the therapist can give useful hints based on general behavioral principles. For example, many ADHD students perseverate on the first difficult test item they encounter, becoming frustrated and running out of time before they can complete the test. They can be taught to check their negative emotional reaction to difficult items through coping self-instructions ("It's only one item; I am going to skip it and not worry; I'll come back to it later"), to move on to the easier items, and to return to the difficult items if they have time at the end.

Their parents may need to help them practice these behaviors at home in a "mock" test situation. Many teenagers do not consider whether they are studying for the types of items on the test. Multiple-choice items require study focused on recognition tasks, while essay items require study emphasizing practice in writing paragraphs in response to hypothetical test questions. Sometimes the therapist may decide it is appropriate to request that an ADHD adolescent be permitted to take certain tests untimed—a request I have made a number of times for the Scholastic Aptitude Tests.

Homework is usually the most serious school-related problem that parents bring up. Many parents question whether they ought to be involved in helping middle and high school students complete homework. They feel or have been led to believe that students "should" be responsible for their own homework and must learn to "sink or swim." In the abstract, students should be responsible; however, ADHD students usually are not responsible, in part due to their biologically based handicap. So we tell parents that, practically speaking, they need to remain involved with their adolescents in regard to homework if they wish to see them succeed as students, whatever their own philosophical inclination may be. Of course, the degree of involvement may change with time and proper training.

The therapist first must assess whether the adolescent reliably knows what has been assigned and tracks on a calendar when assignments are due. Bringing home written assignment sheets initialed by teachers and establishing daily review by parents are usually the most reliable ways to correct "forgetfulness" of assignments. If the assignment sheet does not come home, parents need to specify a punishing consequence. At home, the family needs to establish guidelines for when and where to do homework; a well-lit desk in the adolescent's bedroom without the television or radio blaring, daily from 7:00 to 8:00 P.M., would be an example of a positive setting. It is usually necessary for at least one parent to be present in the house during the designated homework time to monitor compliance with the conditions. All too often, parents are out of the home when the teenagers do homework; conditions are less than optimal if parents are not present to monitor. While parents should not have to stand over an adolescent to facilitate homework completion, it is important for parents to review the homework to determine its completion and give suggestions for improvement. Parents may also be able to help some adolescents study for examinations through verbal rehearsal of the material.

If there are substantial difficulties with disruptive behavior in the classroom as well as academic performance, the therapist may choose to establish a weekly home-school report card or behavioral contract. This intervention is discussed in Chapter 15 in more detail and is not covered here.

We have found that it usually takes two or three sessions to help an adolescent begin to "clean up the school act" through the kind of behavioral study skills interventions outlined here. As things are beginning to fall into place with schoolwork, then the therapist moves on to deal with other home-based conflicts. We have also found that failure to attend to school performance issues early in treatment may result in premature termination of therapy since academic success is such a high-priority goal. Since it is relatively easy and nonthreatening to intervene in this arena, the study skills interventions also serve to deepen the family's faith in the therapist and demonstrate to the adolescent that change is possible without tremendous emotional upheaval.

Problem-Solving/Communication Training

After the therapist has educated the family about ADHD, established an effective medication regimen, restored parental control over antisocial acting-out behavior, and helped the adolescent "clean up the school act," the family is usually ready for problem-solving/communication training (PSCT). Prior to this phase of intervention, the therapist has been providing direct solutions to presenting problems through didactic information, referral for medication, parental action, and academic change. Now the therapist shifts gears to teaching "process skills" so that the family members can learn how to provide their own solutions to problems and cope with their own negative interactions in the future.

Conflicts between the ADHD adolescent and the parents over a variety of rules and regulations represent the most common home problem presented to clinicians. Since developmental research has suggested that democratic parenting approaches are more effective than either autocratic or permissive approaches in fostering responsible adolescent individuation (Conger, 1973), it is important to teach conflict resolution skills that involve mutual discussion and decision making by the parents and the adolescent. In the heat of battle, most parents and adolescents become emotionally charged, communicating to each other in reciprocally accusatory, defensive, and hurtful ways. Thus, improving communication becomes a complementary goal to teaching democratic conflict resolution skills. We (Robin & Foster, 1989) have developed and researched an intervention to accomplish these two goals—PSCT. Barkley (1990) has successfully applied this intervention to ADHD adolescents in a large outcome study comparing PSCT, contingency management, and structural family therapy.

Families are taught to follow the four-step model of problem solving in Table 14.3 when discussing a parent-child disagreement. First, each family member *defines the problem* by making a clear, short, nonaccusatory "I-

TABLE 14.3. Problem-Solving Outline for Families

I. Define the problem.
 A. Tell the others what they do that bothers you and why. "I get very angry when you come home 2 hours after the 11 P.M. curfew we agreed upon."
 B. Start your definition with an "I"; be brief, be clear, and don't accuse or put down the other person.
 C. Did you get your point across? Ask the others to paraphrase your problem definition to check whether they understood you. If they understood you, go on. If not, repeat your definition.

II. Generate a variety of alternative solutions.
 A. Take turns listing solutions.
 B. Follow three rules for listing solutions:
  1. List as many ideas as possible.
  2. Don't evaluate the ideas.
  3. Be creative; anything goes, since you will not have to do everything you list.
 C. One person writes down the ideas on a worksheet (see Figure 14.2).

III. Evaluate the ideas and decide upon the best one.
 A. Take turns evaluating each idea.
  1. Say what you think would happen if the family followed the idea.
  2. Vote "plus" or "minus" for the idea and record your vote on the worksheet next to the idea.
 B. Select the best idea.
  1. Look for ideas rated "plus" by everyone.
  2. Select one of these ideas.
  3. Combine several of these ideas.
 C. If none are rated "plus" by everyone, negotiate a compromise.
  1. Select an idea rated "plus" by one parent and the teen.
  2. List as many compromises as possible.
  3. Evaluate the compromises as described in steps III-A and III-B.
  4. Reach a mutually acceptable solution.
  5. If you still cannot reach an agreement, wait for the next therapy session.

IV. Plan to implement the selected solution.
 A. Decide who will do what, where, how, and when.
 B. Decide who will monitor the solution implementation.
 C. Decide upon the consequences for compliance or noncompliance with the solution.
  1. Rewards for compliance: Privileges, money, activities, praise.
  2. Punishments for noncompliance: Loss of privileges, groundings, work detail.

statement," which pinpoints the others' actions that are problematic and why. As each person gives his or her definition, the therapist teaches the others to verify their understanding of the definition by paraphrasing it to the speaker. This phase ends with a statement by the therapist acknowledging that there may be several different "problems" defined, but that if all agreed on the same definition, there would be no disagreement.

Second, the family members take turns *generating a variety of alternative solutions* to the problem. Three rules of brainstorming are enforced by the therapist to facilitate free exchange of ideas: (1) List as many ideas as possible—quantity breeds quality; (2) don't evaluate the ideas, since criticism stifles creativity; and (3) be creative, since just saying something doesn't mean a person will have to do it. The therapist has the family members take turns recording the ideas on a worksheet. At first, the adolescent may be asked to record the ideas, a strategy that helps maintain a minimal level of attention to the task. Usually, parents and adolescents begin by suggesting their original positions as solutions. Gradually, new ideas emerge. If the atmosphere is very tense or the family runs out of ideas, the therapist may suggest ideas too, but usually the therapist suggests outlandish ideas to lighten the atmosphere and spur creativity. When the therapist judges that there are one or two "workable" ideas (i.e., ideas that may achieve mutual acceptance), then the family is asked to move to the next phase of problem solving.

Third, the family is asked to *evaluate the ideas and decide upon the best one*. They take turns evaluating each idea, projecting the consequences of implementing it and rating it "plus" or "minus." The therapist teaches family members to clarify each other's projections of the consequences of particular ideas, but to refrain from critical crosstalk that could sidetrack the discussion. The ratings are recorded in separate columns for each member on the worksheet. Here the therapist prompts members to consider carefully whether the ideas address their perspectives on the original problem. When the ideas have all been rated, the family reviews the worksheet to determine whether a consensus was reached (all "plus") for any ideas. Surprisingly, a consensus is reached about 80% of the time. The family then selects one of the ideas rated positively by everyone, or combines several such ideas into the solution.

If a consensus was not reached on any idea, the therapist teaches the family negotiation skills. The therapist looks for the idea on which the family came closest to a consensus, and uses it as a catalyst for generating additional alternatives and conducting further evaluations, in order to spur agreement to a compromise position. A great deal of emphasis is placed upon analyzing the factors impeding parents and child from reaching agreement and addressing these factors. Often, cognitive distortions underlie intransigence in reaching a consensus, and these factors must be addressed (following suggestions to be made later in this chapter) before a consensus can be reached.

During the fourth phase of problem solving, the family *plans to implement the selected solution and establishes the consequences for compliance versus noncompliance*. They must decide who will do what, when, where, and with what monitoring to make the solution work. With ADHD adolescents in particular, establishing clear-cut consequences for compliance versus noncompliance is very important, since we know that performance deteriorates in the absence of regular structure and immediate consequences. It is important to provide prompts for performing behaviors related to the solution, reinforcement for successful task completion, and punishment for noncompliance. Occasionally, a home token economy may be useful if reinforcement is needed for a number of solutions. Common reinforcers have included extensions on bedtime or curfew, extra telephone privileges, video games and movies, money, or access to the family car. Common punishers have included work detail around the house, groundings, and loss of video games or other privileges. With regard to prompts, they must be salient and timely since the natural distractibility and forgetfulness that are part of ADHD make it difficult for teenagers to remember effortful tasks. For example, if the adolescent needs to remember to take the trash out on Tuesday and Thursday evenings, the mother might post a bright sign as a reminder earlier those afternoons and give one verbal reminder as the evening begins. Figure 14.2 illustrates a completed worksheet for a problem with chores.

Problem-solving skills are taught through the use of instructions, modeling, behavior rehearsal, and feedback. The therapist briefly introduces problem

---

Name of Family: The Johnsons   **Date:** 11/25/89

Topic: Household Chores

Definitions of the Problem:
    Mom: I get upset when I have to tell Allen 10 times to take out the trash and clean up his room.
    Dad: It bothers me to come home and find the trash still in the house and Allen's records and books all over his room, with my wife screaming at him.
    Allen: My parents tell me to take out the trash during my favorite TV show. They make me clean up my room when all my friends are out having fun.

Solutions and Evaluations:	Mom	Dad	Allen
1. Do chores the first time asked	+	+	−
2. Don't have any chores	−	−	+
3. Grounded for 1 month if not done	−	+	−
4. Hire a maid	+	−	+
5. Earn allowance for chores	+	+	+
6. Room cleaned once by 9 P.M.	+	+	+
7. Parents clean the room	−	−	+
8. Close the door to room	+	−	−
9. Better timing when asking Allen	+	+	+
10. One reminder to do chores	+	+	+

Agreement: <u>Nos. 5, 6, 9, 10.</u>

Implementation Plan: By 9 P.M. each evening Allen agrees to clean up his room, meaning books and papers neatly stacked and clothes in hamper or drawers. Doesn't have to pass "white glove test." Will earn extra $1.00 per day on allowance if complies with no reminders or one reminder. By 8 P.M. on Tuesdays, Allen agrees to have trash collected and out by curb. Will earn $2.00 extra if complies. Punishment for noncompliance: Grounding for the next day after school. Dad to monitor trash; Mom to monitor room.

FIGURE 14.2. Example of a completed problem-solving worksheet.

solving at the beginning of this phase of treatment and helps the family select an issue of moderate intensity for discussion. Moderate-intensity issues are better than "hot" issues in the early stages of training since the family can concentrate on skill acquisition without excessive anger. The Issues Checklist, which has been discussed in Chapter 9, may be used to help pinpoint topics for problem solving. Topics with an intensity score of 2 or 3 on the Issues Checklist are considered moderate. The therapist gives instructions and models, then guides the family to rehearse each step of problem solving. As family members emit each problem-solving behavior, the therapist gives them feedback, successively approximating criterion responses by prompting them to restate their point in an improved fashion. Negative communication is interrupted and redirected rather than corrected in order to facilitate completion of the discussion.

At the end of the discussion, the family is asked to implement the solution at home and report back to the therapist next week. If the solution was effectively implemented, the therapist praises the family and begins a new problem-solving discussion. Otherwise, the reasons for failure are analyzed, and the problem is again discussed to reach a more effective agreement. Generalization of problem solving is programmed by having the family establish a regular meeting time, during which accumulated problems are solved or components of problem solving are practiced.

After two sessions of problem-solving practice, the therapist introduces communication training by distributing a copy of Table 14.4 and reviewing these common negative communication patterns with the family. The therapist asks the family to recall recent occurrences of any negative communication habits that apply to them. The incidents are reviewed, with the therapist identifying who said what to whom and what the impact on the victim was, as well as the relationship between the perpetrator and the victim. The therapist is careful to note how negative communication not only produced bad feeling and a counterattack, but also sidetracked the discussion away from effective problem solving. Thus, the hurtful effects of negative communication are identified, and the reciprocal escalation of negative interchanges can be highlighted. Any examples that occur during the session become prime material for discussion. Next, the therapist points out alternative, more constructive methods for communicating negative affect, disagreement, criticism, and generally telling another person one cares about that one finds their behavior unacceptable. Family members are asked to rehearse specific positive communication interchanges that apply to them. The therapist is careful to emphasize that he or she is not urging family members to suppress their feelings and hide their anger, but rather to express their legitimate affect with intensity but nonhurtful specificity.

Following this overview of communication skills, the therapist pinpoints one or two negative communication patterns per session and intervenes to change them. Whenever the negative pattern occurs, the therapist directly stops the session, gives feedback about the occurrence of the negative com-

TABLE 14.4. Family Handout on Negative Communication

Check if your family does this:	More positive way to do it:
1. __ Call each other names.	Express anger without hurtful words.
2. __ Put each other down.	"I am angry that you did _____"
3. __ Interrupt each other.	Take turns; keep it short.
4. __ Criticize all the time.	Point out the good and bad.
5. __ Get defensive when attacked.	Listen carefully and check out what you heard—then calmly disagree.
6. __ Give a lecture/big words.	Tell it straight and short.
7. __ Look away, not at speaker.	Make good eye contact.
8. __ Slouch or slide to floor.	Sit up and look attentive.
9. __ Talk in sarcastic tone.	Talk in normal tone.
10. __ Get off the topic.	Finish one topic, then go on.
11. __ Think the worst.	Keep an open mind. Don't jump to conclusions.
12. __ Dredge up the past.	Stick to the present.
13. __ Read each other's mind.	Ask the other's opinion.
14. __ Command, order.	Ask nicely.
15. __ Give the silent treatment.	Say it if you feel it.
16. __ Throw a tantrum, "lose it."	Count to 10; take a hike; do relaxation; leave room.
17. __ Make light of something serious.	Take it seriously, even if it is minor to you.
18. __ Deny you did it.	Admit you did it, but say you didn't like the way you were accused.
19. __ Nag about small mistakes.	Admit no one is perfect; overlook small things.

Your "Zap Score" (total no. of checks) __

munication, and asks the family to "replay the scene" using more constructive communication methods. Such corrections are often frequent during this phase of intervention. To be effective, the therapist must wield a "velvet sledgehammer," coming down consistently on each instance of the inappropriate behavior, but landing with aplomb. In order to program generalization, the family is assigned homework to practice positive communication skills in daily interchanges and at family meetings. Family members are taught how to correct each other's communication without spurring excessive antagonism, extending the "velvet sledgehammer" approach to the home.

Experience has suggested a number of special considerations when applying PSCT to ADHD adolescents and their parents. First, the therapist must maintain the adolescent's attention during crucial moments of each session— a more than trivial task with many ADHD teens. Keeping comments brief, bringing the adolescent into the discussion at crucial moments and addressing the remainder of the comments to the parents, and talking in an animated manner are three useful hints for the therapist.

Second, some 12- to 14-year-old ADHD adolescents are not able to understand the concepts of problem solving or may not be ready emotionally and/or developmentally to assume responsibility for generating and negotiating solutions. Repeated difficulty in defining problems or generating solutions is a sign of such a deficit, along with general silliness or social immaturity. In such cases, the therapist can rely more upon behavioral contracting by having the parents take charge of establishing the contingencies and mainly consult the adolescent about the reinforcers. Alternatively, the therapist can simplify the steps of problem solving to a level that the immature adolescent can process; for example, the parents may generate a list of alternative solutions and boil them down through evaluation to three options, which are then presented to the adolescent for a "vote."

Third, ADHD family members may have such "short fuses" due to their biologically based impulsivity that they often explode at each other during the sessions. The therapist should follow our (Robin & Foster, 1989, pp. 219–221) advice for maintaining session control—interrupting "runaway chains" as soon as they start, establishing nonverbal cues for "having the floor," teaching anger control and relaxation techniques, and being as directive as necessary to control the session.

Fourth, ADHD adolescents can be so impulsive and distractible that their parents feel the need to correct everything they do or say, creating an endless series of issues and negative communication patterns. Such adolescents are not typically aware of how their behavior "drives their parents up a tree" and react strongly, spurring endless conflict. The therapist must build upon the advice given during the earlier ADHD family education phase of treatment: The parents need to realize that an adolescent does not choose to be this way and cannot help some of the forgetful, counterintuitive behavior. Parents need to learn to "pick their issues wisely," deciding what to take a stand on and what to ignore. For example, fidgety/restless adolescent behavior during family discussions is best reframed as due to a biological tendency and then ignored, rather than treated as "another sign of disrespect for authority." By contrast, impulsive name calling may be in part biologically based but cannot be ignored since it creates hurtful feelings and fuels coercive, escalating negative communication cycles.

The therapist usually sequences PSCT over six to seven sessions. The first two sessions typically involve problem-solving discussion, followed by a communication training session. The fourth and fifth session involve continued problem-solving training with correction of negative communication habits. Intense issues are handled in these sessions. The sixth and seventh sessions include a great deal of emphasis on troubleshooting the use of the skills at home, and preparing the family to continue their use without the therapist's guidance.

Cognitive Restructuring

As the family acquires problem-solving and communication skills, the therapist begins to identify cognitive distortions that interfere with parent-adolescent relations at home. Cognitive distortions may be broad underlying assumptions or "beliefs" that individuals have about their relationships, specific expectations pertaining to certain interactional events, or attributions that individuals have as they interpret the outcomes of interactional events (Epstein, Schlesinger, & Dryden, 1988; Robin & Foster, 1989). Cognitive distortions may also refer to the processes by which individuals interpret events rather than the content alone of their interpretations. Beck, for example, has developed a typology of difficulties in logical reasoning. A parent who concludes from a single curfew infraction that his daughter is totally irresponsible and disobedient may be "overgeneralizing," while a mother who overreacts to a single D on a report card with three C's and two B's may be engaging in "arbitrary inference."

We find it useful to distinguish for training and intervention purposes between specific cognitive distortions that are expressed during problem-solving discussions, and other therapeutic activities and pervasive underlying belief themes that may be the source of the specific cognitive distortions. Specific cognitive distortions are situationally based cognitions such as believing an adolescent is wasting the parents' money by forgetting to turn the lights off, or fearing an adolescent will become a drug addict by going to a rock concert without a parent. The therapist can often deal with these specific distortions through reframing. "Reframing" refers to providing a neutral to positive connotation for a remark attributed to negative motives. Yelling and screaming may be reframed as "really getting in touch with feelings." Failing to follow rules and disobeying may be reframed as "due to ADHD, which is a physical problem." Forgetting to complete chores or homework can be reframed as "ADHD-related forgetfulness helped along by the effortful nature of the tasks, which no teens like to do." Parental overprotection may be reframed as "deep caring and concern."

Parents often ask the therapist whether to treat forgetfulness and/or failure to follow instructions as disobedience deserving punishment or as biologically based inattention that should be excused. Since it is usually impossible to determine the "truth," we advise parents to assume that ADHD-related biological factors are playing a role in an adolescent's behavior pattern, but nonetheless to hold the adolescent accountable for the action. We teach the parents not to jump to the malicious conclusion that the adolescent is purposely neglecting responsibilities, but to give the adolescent the benefit of the doubt. This type of reframing is done throughout all of the phases of therapy, and is essential to fostering positive parent-adolescent interactions since the ADHD adolescent inevitably continues to engage in forgetful actions that aggravate parents.

TABLE 14.5. Steps of Cognitive Restructuring

I. Present a cognitive mediational rationale.
  A. Events evoke extreme cognitions.
  B. Extreme cognitions mediate angry affect.
  C. Angry affect mediates negative communication and arguments.
  D. Use imaginal exercises to present the rationale.

II. Review common unreasonable beliefs (Table 14.6).
  A. Ask them to give examples of ruination, malicious intent, obedience/perfectionism, etc., from recent family life.
  B. Teach them to discriminate reasonable from unreasonable expectations in these areas.
  C. Help them brainstorm more reasonable cognitions for identified situations.
  D. Plan for how they can self-monitor their tendencies to jump to unreasonable conclusions in conflict situations.

III. Target an unreasonable belief for correction.
  A. Stop the session when the discussion evokes the extreme belief. Likely times are these:
    1. Failure to reach a negotiated agreement.
    2. Sabotage of the implementation of a previous agreement.
    3. Clear statement of belief: "He never obeys," "If she doesn't do her homework, she doesn't appreciate all the money I spend on private school."
  B. Clearly label the extreme belief and its impact upon the ongoing interaction.
  C. Provide a logical challenge to the belief, with tact.
    1. Find a "loophole" in the reasoning.
    2. "Blow up" the belief to absurd proportions.
    3. Point to evidence that contradicts the belief.
  D. Suggest alternative, more reasonable beliefs.
    1. Family members brainstorm.
    2. Therapist suggests.
  E. Outline an "experiment" to "test" the reasonable versus the unreasonable beliefs.
    1. Normative survey.
    2. Trial run of a solution consistent with the reasonable belief.
    3. Archival data collection—library, etc.
  F. Assign the experiment as homework.

    The therapist may cope with major cognitive distortions through applying the steps of cognitive restructuring outlined in Table 14.5. First, a rationale is given to explain the connection among behavior, thoughts, feelings, and interactions. For example, family members may be asked to close their eyes and imagine that the teenage daughter has come home 2 hours past curfew. The parents are asked to imagine how disobedient their teen has been, and how disrespectful and unappreciative it was to disregard a rule that already was stretched to the limit to give the teenager as much freedom as reluctant parents can tolerate. The adolescent is asked to imagine how unfair and embarrassing it was to have to leave the party early, how much parental rules are ruining peer relations, and how upset the teen was to see the other girls at the party nonverbally suggesting to her boyfriend that he return to them after "dumping" her at home with her overprotective parents. Then the therapist inquires about all family members' affect at that moment, noting the strong anger and frustration they express. The therapist comments upon the sequence of environmental event (A), extreme thought (B), and angry affect (C), teaching the ABC model of emotions. Finally, the therapist inquires about the likely outcome of a problem-solving discussion when everyone is so emotionally aroused. Family members usually agree that a "bloodbath" would ensue rather than a logical problem-solving discussion because of the hostility and anger. This imaginal exercise saliently introduces cognitive restructuring.

Second, the therapist reviews common unreasonable beliefs with the family by distributing Table 14.6 to them. The family is taught the constructs of ruination, malicious intent, obedience/perfectionism, appreciation/love, unfairness, and autonomy, and asked to reconstruct recent interactions that exemplify these belief themes. The therapist conducts discrimination training by contrasting extreme versus nonextreme forms of the beliefs, using the situations supplied by the family. For example, if the mother states that she fears the ruinous consequences of the adolescent's failing to complete his homework, the therapist might point out,

> "There are several ways you can think about this. You might think, 'If Bill doesn't get his math homework done, he will fail math, fail ninth grade, fail to graduate, get a lousy job, and end up an unhappy adult.' On the other hand, you might think, 'So he gets an F on his math homework. What's the worst thing that can happen? He could get a lower grade. Didn't I ever fail to get my homework done? I survived, and he will too.' How would you feel with each way of thinking?"

The therapist Socratically helps the mother to recognize what is reasonable and logical versus unreasonable and illogical. As family members generate more reasonable ways of thinking about problem situations, they are prompted to self-monitor and correct their thoughts at home.

A great deal of emphasis is placed upon self-monitoring and correcting high-frequency cognitions that are associated with common ADHD-related issues, such as forgetfulness, not following instructions, and disorganization—particularly when a chain of ADHD-related behaviors occurs rapidly. For example, Bill may come home from school, race in the door like a human dynamo, get mud on the carpet, leave his wet coat on the sofa, leave the milk out and cookie crumbs on the counter after his snack, tease his little sister and pull the dog's tail, leave the light in the bathroom on, and race upstairs with a pounding step to play Nintendo after telling his mother he has no homework and he doesn't remember what he did in school that day. Halfway up the steps, Bill may remember he promised to call his girlfriend, and come racing back down the steps, then grab the telephone without any explanation, putting his feet on the furniture and acting oblivious to his by now screaming mother. Even after reviewing Table 14.6 and recognizing that Bill

TABLE 14.6. Common Unreasonable Beliefs

Parents

I. Ruination: "If I give my teen too much freedom, he (she) will ruin his (her) life, make bad judgments, and get in serious trouble."

Examples: 1. Room incompletely cleaned: "He will grow up to be a slovenly, unemployed, aimless, worthless welfare case."
2. Home late: "She could get hurt out late. She could get pregnant, addicted to drugs, and become an alcoholic."
3. Homework incomplete: "He will never graduate from high school, will never get into a good college, will not get a good job, and won't be able to support himself. He will be a drain on us forever."

II. Malicious intent: "My teen misbehaves purposely to hurt me."

Examples: 1. Forgetting to turn the lights off: "She's trying to make me go broke."
2. Talking disrespectfully: "He's talking that way to get even with me."
3. Playing stereo loud: "She's blasting that stereo just to get on my nerves."

III. Obedience/perfectionism: "My teen should always obey me and behave like a saint."

Examples: 1. Doesn't follow directions: "He can't even take out the trash without me bugging him 10 times. What disrespect/disobedience! If I did this to my dad, I would have been dead meat."
2. Acting hyper around relatives: "At her age she should be able to sit still and act mature."

IV. Appreciation/love: "My teenager should spontaneously show love and appreciation for the great sacrifices I make."

Examples: 1. "Look what I got after all I've done for you. You don't care about me. You're selfish."
2. "What do you mean you want more allowance? After all the money I give you and all the things I buy, you should be perfectly happy."

Adolescents

I. Unfairness/ruination: "My parents' rules are totally unfair. I'll never have a good time or any friends. My parents are ruining my life with their unfair rules."

Examples: 1. Curfew: "Why should I have to come home earlier than my friends? That's unfair. I'll never have any friends."
2. School: "Mrs. Jones is unfair. She always gives me a hard time. She has it in for me. She's the reason I'm failing math."

II. Autonomy: "My parents have no right to tell me what to do."

Examples: 1. Smoking: "It's my body. I can do whatever I want with it. You have no right to interfere."
2. Chores: "I don't need any reminders. I can get it all done by myself."

III. Appreciation/love: "My parents would let me do whatever I want if they really cared about me."

Examples: 1. "If my parents really loved me, they would let me use the car and go to the concert."
2. "Sally's mother buys her all those designer clothes. Her parents really love her. Mine hate me and want me to look ugly."

is not maliciously attacking her, Bill's mother may have difficulty taking this chain of behaviors in stride without having extreme thoughts about disobedience, disrespect, and malicious intent. Parents need multiple practice trials at cognitive restructuring, along with a skill-oriented plan, to cope with such common runaway chains of ADHD-driven adolescent behavior.

Third, the therapist targets one unreasonable belief theme at a time for modification. When that theme arises during the therapy session, the therapist stops the discussion and probes the family members to bring out the unreasonable belief. Often, failure to reach a negotiated agreement, excessive anger about an adolescent behavior out of proportion to the "offense," or sabotage of solution implementation are tipoffs that unreasonable beliefs are mediating interactions. As the family members articulate, with strong therapist direction, their extreme thinking, the impact upon the family is explored. Are parents polarized in their position on an issue because of excessive adolescent complaints of injustice? Is an adolescent very angry because of unreasonable parental demands for expressions of caring and appreciation? Is an impulsive, distractible teenager refusing to complete and hand in his or her homework even more because a perfectionistic parent insists that it be rewritten until it is perfectly neat?

When the family members perceive the deleterious impact of the extreme thinking upon their relations, the therapist provides a logical challenge to the beliefs, with tact. A loophole in logic may be apparent; only one exception challenges the rule. The faulty thinking may be "blown up" to absurd proportions, or evidence that contradicts the idea may be pointed out. Family members are asked to brainstorm alternative ways of thinking about the situation, and to devise an "experiment" to "test" out the reasonable versus the unreasonable belief. The therapist helps the family design and conduct the experiment, carefully examining the results at the next session.

For example, consider a father who is very angry because his son shows no appreciation for all of the money that has been spent to help him succeed in school (e.g. books, school clothes, supplies, computers, tutoring, and therapy), and is further frustrated at the "disrespect and disobedience" his son shows by acting restless and bored whenever the topic of appreciation is broached (e.g. the father gives a lecture). The therapist might begin by pinpointing the extreme belief: "So you are saying adolescents should always express deep appreciation for their parents' sacrifices, and it is a sign of extreme disobedience and disrespect when an ADHD teen with a biological handicap of self-control who has never sat still for more than 10 minutes fidgets while his dad lectures to him for a half-hour about his lack of caring." As the therapist and family begin to examine this proposition, they may be asked whether they can find any examples of overgeneralization, arbitrary inference, or other logical errors in the statement. The therapist might ask the adolescent how much appreciation his friends express to their parents, and ask the parents how much appreciation their most highly valued friends' children express. The alternative proposition that "Even though adolescents love and appreciate their parents, they rarely express it, and this is the result of their normal desire to individuate from their parents" might be presented for discussion. In order to "test out" these alternatives, the family might be asked to (1) read a book on normal adolescent development; (2) do a "normative survey" (e.g., ask five friends who are relatively satisfied with their children how many times per day appreciation is expressed); and (3) have the adolescent "off the record" tell his parents how appreciative he really is, and why it is difficult to express it often, particularly when his peers are present. Similar strategies might be applied to the father's reasoning about the disrespect and disobedience.

These strategies for cognitive restructuring are continued for the remainder of therapy, with homework assignments for family members to catch each other's faulty thinking and suggest corrections.

Individual Therapy

Although most of the goals of a home-management-oriented intervention for the ADHD adolescent are best accomplished through family-oriented sessions, there are times when individual sessions with the adolescent are helpful. Issues related to self-esteem, depression, and sexuality are often handled best in individual sessions, where the adolescent may feel free to share his or her feelings more openly than in the parents' presence. The therapist can also teach anger control techniques efficiently in individual sessions (Feindler & Ecton, 1987), and a variety of behavioral self-control techniques may also prove useful in helping ADHD adolescents to change their own study skills and social behaviors (Brigham, 1988).

Concluding Phase of Therapy

The initial burst of home-management-oriented family intervention with the average ADHD adolescent and his or her parents comes to a conclusion after 15–20 sessions. By this time, parental control has been restored, the adolescent has mastered improved study skills, the family members have acquired positive communication and effective problem-solving skills, and many of their extreme cognitions have begun to change. Crises continue to occur, but (one hopes) the family should be able to weather these storms through the use of these newfound skills and attitudes. Typically, there has been little long-term personality change in family members, but rather behavioral and attitudinal change in their interactions and interpretations of each other's behaviors. Either the family members hint that they no longer need to attend therapy regularly, or the therapist notices that they do not have many issues to bring up.

Therapy is gradually faded out by increasing the intervals between the last few sessions to 3, 4, and 6 weeks. In these final sessions, the therapist reviews previously acquired problem-solving skills, checks up on the continued success of solutions implemented throughout therapy, and helps the family to anticipate and plan to cope with upcoming events. When therapy ends, the family is left with an open invitation to return as needed. They are asked to contact the therapist for a 12-month follow-up, and given the idea that with further developmental changes, new ADHD-related problems are likely to recur, necessitating "booster sessions."

SUMMARY

In this chapter I have tried to give the practitioner a feel for the type of biobehavioral–family systems intervention that is needed to address the home management issues of the ADHD adolescent. The intervention integrates PSCT, a family-based program originally developed for parent-teen conflict regardless of formal diagnosis (Robin & Foster, 1989), with medication and behavioral study skills training. Modifications in each of these programs to deal with the special considerations of ADHD in adolescence have been incorporated into the overall protocol presented here. Recent research has begun to delineate the family relationship problems of the ADHD adolescent (see Chapter 5), and to examine the effectiveness of at least the PSCT portions of the treatment program with an ADHD population (Barkley, 1990). Clearly, much additional research evaluating the entire treatment package outlined here, and further delineating the family problems associated with ADHD, is needed.

The interventions outlined in this chapter should be regarded as a starting point for such research as well as clinical practice. As the practitioner experiments with clinical variations on the strategies presented here, it is suggested that the major developmental differences between adolescents and younger children be kept in mind. ADHD adolescents, like all adolescents, think they know all of the answers and do not typically wish to have our help. The democratically oriented, problem-solving-based interventions that have been discussed are based upon the notion of developing a collaborative relationship with the adolescent rather than a dictatorial, authoritarian approach, which is more appropriate for younger ADHD children.

15

Educational Placement and Classroom Management

LINDA J. PFIFFNER and RUSSELL A. BARKLEY

> Education does not mean teaching people to know what
> they do not know; it means teaching them to behave as
> they do not behave.
>
> —JOHN RUSKIN (1819–1900)

Children with Attention-deficit Hyperactivity Disorder (ADHD) may exhibit a wider range of problems in the classroom than in any other setting. Inattention, impulsivity, and overactivity, the cardinal symptoms of ADHD, translate into a variety of classroom behavior problems including difficulty in staying seated, paying attention, working independently, and following directions and rules. ADHD children are also often disruptive and interrupt class lessons and quiet work periods. They also tend to be very disorganized and have great difficulty in keeping track of their academic materials (e.g., books, paper, pencils) and assignments.

In addition to problems stemming from the core symptoms, children with ADHD frequently exhibit a myriad of associated problems that may have an even more debilitating effect on school performance. Given their high rates of off-task and disruptive behavior, it is not surprising that ADHD children experience frequent academic problems ranging from failure to complete work and poor grades to significant underachievement, grade retentions, suspensions, and expulsions (see Chapters 3 and 4). In addition, these children exhibit a high incidence of specific learning disabilities (Cantwell & Satterfield, 1978; see Chapter 3).

More than half of all hyperactive children also have significant problems of an oppositional nature (Hinshaw, 1987). These problems run the gamut from defiance, tantrums, and refusal to follow class rules to more serious violations of social norms including stealing, fighting, lying, truancy, and destruction.

Seriously disturbed peer relations are also prominent among ADHD children. Despite their apparent interest in establishing interpersonal contacts, their attempts to interact with peers are typically high-rate, intrusive, and often negative. As a reflection of their lack of success in the social arena, these children are consistently rejected by their peers on sociometric indices (Milich & Landau, 1982).

Teachers frequently respond to the challenging problems exhibited by children with ADHD by becoming more interactive and commanding (e.g., Campbell, Endman, & Bernfield, 1977). Over time, teachers may become frustrated in working with these difficult children and become less positive and more negative in their interactions as well. Although the impact of these predominantly negative interactions on long-term functioning is not well understood, such interactions may further exacerbate poor academic and social achievement, reduce the children's motivation and self-esteem, and ultimately result in school failure. On the other hand, a positive teacher-student relationship may not only improve academic and social functioning in the short term, but may also increase the likelihood of long-term success. For instance, adults who had been hyperactive as children have reported that a teacher's caring attitude, extra attention, and guidance were "turning points" in helping them overcome their childhood problems (Weiss & Hechtman, 1986).

Given the range and significance of ADHD children's difficulties at school, a great need exists for effective school interventions. The purpose of this chapter is to review and describe the success of behavioral and cognitive-behavioral interventions in treating ADHD children in the classroom. It is important to point out that these interventions are intended to maximize children's likelihood for success, and are not intended to cure or normalize their problems. Although the interventions can have a powerful and positive impact, the refractory nature of ADHD symptomatology makes it likely that these children will continue to experience at least some difficulty in their academic and social endeavors.

TREATMENT TARGETS

Disruptive, off-task behaviors are probably the most salient problems exhibited by ADHD children in the classroom. As a result, it is not surprising that these problems have been the focus of numerous intervention studies. Off-task behaviors have been readily modified with a variety of behavioral techniques. However, improvement in classroom deportment is often not paralleled by improvement in academic functioning, suggesting that on-task behavior may be necessary but not sufficient for academic progress. As a result, many researchers have questioned the practice of limiting the focus of intervention to classroom behavior and have instead targeted academic measures. The results of these studies have demonstrated not only significant improvement in academic performance but also improvement in children's behavior, although the latter was not directly targeted for the intervention. Focusing solely on academic performance appears to be insufficient, however, since children's behavior does not always improve when academic performance is the target for intervention. In addition, undesirable behavior is necessary to target directly when it occurs during nonacademic school periods (such as recess and lunch), and when it is of an especially severe nature (as in the case of aggression, stealing, or destruction).

More recently, the poor peer relations of ADHD children have been targeted for intervention. In these programs, contingencies have been placed on children's use of appropriate social skills such as sharing, cooperating, and initiating play with other children. Preliminary studies, finding improvement in these skills, point to the utility of directly targeting these problem areas (see Chapter 16).

In sum, effective management programs should directly target the areas in which change is desired (e.g., deportment, academic problems, social skills). The identification of target areas in individual cases will probably require a functional analysis. Such an analysis requires several steps. First, the behavior in question should be pinpointed and carefully defined so that the teacher is able to monitor the behavior reliably. Next, the antecedents and consequences to the behavior in the natural environment should be identified. Antecedents that set the occasion for problem behavior may include difficult or challenging work, a teacher direction or negative consequence, or disruption from another child.

These antecedent events need not immediately precede the problem behavior to be important in this analysis. Distal events, or those occurring minutes to hours before the target behavior, may have some role to play in increasing the probability of disruptive behaviors. For instance, arguments or fights with other family members at home or with other children on the bus ride to school may alter certain affective states (e.g., anger, frustration), which may make the occurrence of aggressive or defiant behavior upon arrival at school more probable.

Consequences that follow and maintain problem behavior may include teacher or peer attention, or withdrawal of a task or teacher request. Identification of such antecedents and consequences should help isolate features in the classroom environment or teacher interactions requiring change. It is also important to identify appropriate classroom behaviors that can replace the problem behavior. For example, staying seated may be identified as an appropriate behavior to replace wandering around the class. If positive alternative behaviors are not taught and only problem behavior is targeted for intervention, children may simply replace one problem behavior with another.

INTERVENTION ISSUES

Although the aforementioned discussion implies that the initial targets of intervention are the child's disruptive and poorly regulated behaviors, this is hardly the case. The actual initial target of intervention is the teacher's knowledge of and attitude toward the disorder of ADHD. For we have found that where teachers have a poor grasp of the nature, course, outcome, and causes of this disorder and misperceptions about appropriate therapies, attempting to establish behavior management programs within that classroom will have little impact. As with parent training, then, the initial step in classroom management is educating teachers about the disorder. This is done by providing brief reading materials similar to those mentioned in Chapters 12 and 13. We also have made a videotape that summarizes the disorder which many consumers have found to be more convenient to their busy schedules than reading the materials we provide. In either case, some means of providing information to educators about ADHD is a critical first step.

A variety of behavioral interventions have been utilized to modify classroom behavior. The primary interventions include teacher- and peer-administered consequences, home-based consequences, cognitive-behavioral interventions, and modification of factors related to academic tasks and the classroom environment. Each of these strategies is described and evaluated below in terms of its usefulness with ADHD children.

The specific intervention selected is ideally based on a functional analysis of the problem behavior as described above. However, classroom resources and teacher characteristics often play important roles in the final selection of an intervention. To be successful, most teacher-based behavioral programs require accurate record keeping, close monitoring of the child, and administration of a range of rewards and/or negative consequences. Although teachers of small classes may have little difficulty in implementing such procedures, they can be quite time-consuming and impractical for a teacher of a class of up to 40 students to implement. Therefore, these programs may require simplification, as well as tailoring to the routine of individual classes, before they can be implemented successfully.

It is also important to note that teachers vary in their ability and motivation to implement behavioral programs according to their training, experience, and beliefs about the educational process. In some cases, intensive training in behavioral procedures may be required. Additional "booster" sessions following training may also be necessary in order to maintain a teacher's use of the procedures. Teachers who adhere to a nondirective approach to education are often averse to using behavioral approaches out of concern that these approaches are too mechanistic and fail to foster a child's natural development and motivation to learn. In some cases, these beliefs may be altered through the success of a behavioral program. In other cases, such beliefs may greatly impede the effective use of behavioral programs and a transfer to an alternative teacher with a behavioral orientation may prove to be beneficial. In such a case of poor teacher motivation, or a case where teacher philosophy greatly conflicts with the necessary interventions for an ADHD child, parents are encouraged to be assertive in pressing the school administrators for either greater teacher accountability or a transfer to another classroom or school rather than waste a year of an ADHD child's education.

The involvement of a consulting therapist is often useful in order to help plan the intervention and train the teacher and parents in its effective implementation. Weekly or biweekly meetings are typically scheduled among teacher, parent, and therapist in order for the therapist to provide instruction and coaching in behavioral management as well as continual monitoring and evaluation of the program. It is advisable that older children (e.g., ages 7 and older) be included during some of these meetings to help set goals and determine appropriate and valuable rewards. Involving the children in this way often enhances their motivation to participate and be successful in the program. During these meetings, behavioral contracts delineating the details of the programs are often written and signed by parent, teacher, and child. Contracts can help maintain the consistent use of the program over time; emphasize the different roles of teacher, parent, and child in the program (e.g., the teacher's role in monitoring child behavior, the parent's role in dispensing rewards, and the child's role in engaging in appropriate target behaviors); and also give the program a more formal appeal.

Overall, the importance of a close collaboration among members of the treatment team cannot be overemphasized. However, successful collaboration may be thwarted in several ways. Parents of ADHD children often have a long history of conflictual interactions with school personnel. In some cases, parents may feel that the school system is failing to address their children's needs. For instance, parents whose children are in mainstream classes may be frustrated when the children's teachers are unable to implement an intensive behavioral program. Some parents may also have unrealistic expectations that the school should cure their children's problems. In cases where parents are having few if any difficulties at home, they may believe that inadequate teaching or management are causing their children's difficulties at school.

On the other hand, teachers may believe that problems of ADHD are due to emotional problems stemming from conflictual family relationships or that medication is indicated because of the disorder's presumed biological origin. In either case, some teachers may believe that changing their interactions will have little impact on the children. Other teachers may resent altering their teaching style if they believe this suggests that their own behavior is causing the children's problems. Because antagonism on a parent's or teacher's part will probably undermine any intervention, these problems need to be addressed. A consulting therapist may help mediate these problems by providing information regarding the nature of ADHD and its causes as well as information regarding the role of behavioral interventions (including both their strengths and limitations) in the treatment of ADHD. If need be, a change in classrooms can be requested when a teacher is reluctant to try any special management programs with an ADHD child.

As noted in Chapter 5, the psychological status of parents must be considered in evaluating the veracity and severity of parental reports about the disruptive behavior of ADHD children. It seems that a similar state of affairs exists in the evaluation of teacher complaints about ADHD children. There is little reason not to believe that affective status, degree of psychological distress, and extent of other stressors in the life of the teacher play some role in the teacher's level of tolerance for the ADHD child's behavior, the teacher's perceptions and reports of the child's degree of behavioral deviance to others, and the teacher's cooperation in behavioral intervention programs for the child. Although formal assessment of teachers' psychological integrity is not an acceptable aspect of the evaluation of ADHD children, clinicians and educators must be sensitive to the possible role these factors play in the degree of problems an ADHD child is having in a particular classroom and attempt to informally assess them as appropriate.

In many cases, behavioral interventions are used in conjunction with pharmacological approaches to treat ADHD children's school problems. Since recent research documents superior effects with combined as compared to single interventions for some children (Pelham & Murphy, 1986), it may be prudent to consider using medication to treat the school problems of some ADHD children (see Chapter 17).

Whether or not medication is used, a number of general principles apply to the classroom management of ADHD children. These stem from the model presented earlier (see Chapter 2) according to which ADHD is primarily an impairment in the regulation of behavior by its consequences and by rules. These principles apply as much to classroom management as they do to parent training in child management at home (see Chapters 12 and 13). This conceptualization of ADHD requires the following:

1. Rules and instructions provided to ADHD children must be clear, brief, and often delivered through more visible and external modes of presentation than is required for the management of normal children. Stating directions clearly, having the children repeat them out loud, having the children utter them softly to themselves while following through on the instruction, and displaying sets of rules or rule prompts (e.g., stop signs, big eyes, big ears for "stop, look, and listen" reminders) prominently throughout the classroom are essential to proper management of ADHD children. Relying on the children's recollection of the rules as well as upon purely verbal reminders is often ineffective. Externally represented rules, therefore, are more influential at regulating behavior than are internally represented ones.

2. Consequences used to manage the behavior of ADHD children must be delivered more swiftly and immediately than is needed for normal children. Delays in consequences greatly degrade their efficacy with ADHD children. As we note throughout this chapter, the timing and strategic application of consequences with ADHD children must be more systematic and are far more crucial to their management than with normal children.

3. Consequences must be delivered more frequently, not just more immediately, to ADHD children in view of their motivational deficits. This means that feedback for ongoing task performance must be delivered more often if the children are to use such feedback to shape and regulate behavior toward

the task or instruction. Behavioral tracking, or ongoing adherence to rules after the rule has been stated and compliance initiated, appears to be problematic for ADHD children. Frequent feedback or consequences for rule adherence seem helpful in maintaining appropriate degrees of tracking to rules over time.

4. The consequences used with ADHD children must often be of a higher magnitude, or more powerful, than those needed to manage the behavior of normal children. The relative insensitivity of ADHD children to response consequences dictates that those chosen for inclusion in a behavior management program must have sufficient reinforcement value or magnitude to motivate these children to perform the desired behaviors. Suffice it to say, then, that mere occasional praise or reprimands are simply not enough to manage ADHD children effectively.

5. Appropriate and often richer incentives or motivational parameters must be provided within a setting or task to reinforce appropriate behavior before punishment can be implemented. This means that punishment must remain within a relative balance with rewards or it is unlikely to succeed. It is therefore imperative that powerful reinforcement programs be established first and instituted over 1 to 2 weeks before implementing punishment in order for the punishment, sparingly used, to be maximally effective. Often ADHD children will not improve with the use of response cost or time-out if the availability of reinforcement is low in the classroom and hence removal from it is unlikely to be punitive. "Positives before negatives" is the order of the day with ADHD children. When punishment fails, this is the first area that clinicians, consultants, or educators should explore for problems before instituting higher magnitude or more frequent punishment programs.

6. Those reinforcers or rewards that are employed must be changed or rotated more frequently with ADHD than with normal children, given the penchant of the former for more rapid habituation or satiation to response consequences, apparently rewards in particular. This means that even though a particular reinforcer seems to be effective for the moment in motivating an ADHD child's compliance, it is likely that it will lose its reinforcement value more rapidly than with a normal child over time. Reward menus in classes, such as those used to back up token systems, must therefore be changed periodically (say, every 2 to 3 weeks) to maintain the power or efficacy of the program in motivating appropriate child behavior. Failure to do so is likely to result in the loss of power of the reward program and the premature abandonment of token technologies based on the false assumption that they simply will not work any longer. Token systems can be maintained over an entire school year with minimal loss of power in the program provided that the reinforcers are changed frequently to accommodate to this problem of habituation. Such rewards can be returned later to the program once they have been set aside for a while, often with the result that their reinforcement value appears to have been improved by their absence or unavailability.

7. Anticipation is the key with ADHD children. This means that teachers

must be more mindful of planning ahead in managing ADHD children, particularly during phases of transition across activities or classes, to ensure that the children are cognizant of the shift in rules (and consequences) that is about to occur. It is useful for a teacher to take a moment to prompt a child to recall the rules of conduct in the upcoming situation, repeat them orally, and recall that the rewards and punishments will be in the impending situation *before* the child enters that activity or situation. "Think aloud, think ahead" is the important message to educators here. Following a three-step procedure similar to that used in parental management of ADHD children in public places (see Chapter 12) can be effective in reducing the likelihood of inappropriate behavior. As noted below, by themselves such cognitive self-instructions are unlikely to be of lasting benefit; however, when combined with contingency management procedures they can be of considerable aid to the classroom management of ADHD children.

With these seven principles in mind, the creative educator or consultant can readily devise an effective management program for the ADHD child in the classroom.

TEACHER-ADMINISTERED INTERVENTION STRATEGIES

Teacher-administered positive and negative consequences are the most commonly used behavioral interventions with ADHD children in the classroom. Positive consequences usually include positive teacher attention (e.g., praise), tokens, and tangible rewards. Commonly used negative consequences consist of ignoring, verbal reprimands, response cost, and time-out. Although these procedures are discussed separately, most classroom management programs involve a combination of these interventions. In fact, clinically significant improvement in classroom behavior and academic performance is likely to accrue only with a combination of different strategies.

Positive Consequences

Positive Teacher Attention

Praise and other forms of positive teacher attention, such as a smile, nod, or pat on the back, are some of the most basic management tools in a teacher's armamentarium. Positive attention is valued by most children, including hyperactive children, and numerous studies document positive effects of such attention on appropriate classroom conduct. Similarly, withdrawal of teacher attention contingent upon undesirable behavior (i.e., ignoring) tends to decrease that behavior, especially when it is maintained by teacher attention (e.g., calling out).

Although these procedures may seem unusually simplistic, the systematic and effective use of teacher attention in this manner requires great skill. In general, praise appears to be most effective when it specifies the appropriate behavior being reinforced and when it is delivered in a genuine fashion (see O'Leary & O'Leary, 1977). The latter may be facilitated by use of a warm tone of voice and varied content appropriate to the developmental level of the child. Praise is also more effective when it is delivered as soon as possible following the appropriate behavior. It is this *strategic* timing in the application of teacher attention contingent upon appropriate child conduct that is so crucial to its being effective as a behavior change agent.

Effective ignoring requires complete withdrawal of teacher attention. This procedure is most appropriate to use for nondisruptive minor motor and nonattending behaviors intended to gain teacher attention. Although ignoring can be very effective, the use of this procedure with annoying, somewhat disruptive behavior can be very difficult. Even an occasional verbal or non-verbal response (e.g., a glance) can maintain the behavior. In addition, when problem behavior is initially ignored, it often becomes worse before it im-proves since the child whose behavior is being ignored often attempts to gain the teacher's attention in any way he or she can. In these cases, it is important that ignoring be consistent in order to prevent the child from learning that an escalation of the problem behavior will eventually gain the teacher's atten-tion. It should be noted, however, that ignoring is generally not effective in modifying problem behavior that is not maintained by teacher attention. Ig-noring is also contraindicated in cases of aggression or destruction. It is our considered opinion that most child behavior problems of ADHD children are not purely bids for teacher attention and so this strategy alone is unlikely to result in dramatic changes in the behavior of these children.

The simultaneous use of praise and ignoring often increases the efficacy of both procedures. Thus, appropriate behavior (e.g., sitting in seat) that is in-compatible with ignored behavior (e.g., wandering around the class) should be consistently praised. In addition, one of the most powerful uses of teacher attention for modifying problem behavior capitalizes on the positive spillover effects of positive attention. In this procedure, the teacher ignores the disrup-tive student and praises the student(s) who are working quietly. The behavior of the problem student often improves as a result, presumably due to the vicarious learning that has occurred through this modeling procedure and the child's desire for teacher attention.

Requiring teachers to increase their monitoring of ongoing child behavior and to readily consequate the occurrence of ongoing appropriate behavior may be easier said than done. The considerable demands on teacher time and attention in the average classroom often compete with the teacher's ability to monitor the activities of all children and intervene immediately. In particular, it may be difficult to watch for what seems like relatively modest appropriate behavior in ADHD children, especially when normal children perform such behaviors with minimal attention for doing so. To assist teachers with re-membering to attend to and reinforce ongoing appropriate child conduct, several cue or prompt systems can be recommended. One such system involves placing large "smiley face" stickers around the classroom in places where the teacher may frequently glance, such as toward the clock on the wall. When these are then subsequently viewed, they serve to cue the teacher to remember to check out what the ADHD student is doing and to attend to it if it is at all positive.

A second system relies on tape-recorded cues. A soft tone can be taped onto a 90-minute or 120-minute cassette so that it occurs at random intervals. This tape is then played throughout the class time with the children. Whenever the tone is emitted, the teacher is to note briefly what the ADHD child is doing and provide a consequence to the child (praise, token, or response cost) for the behavior at that point in time. We recommend that the tape initially contain relatively frequent tone prompts for the first 1 to 2 weeks, which can then be faded to less frequent schedules of prompts over the next several weeks. We recommend that these be variable-interval prompts so that they occur relatively randomly on the tape. This tape can play openly to the class or can be used with a pocket-size tape player, such as a Sony Walkman, with an earpiece for private monitoring by the teacher.

Such a system can then be converted to a self-monitoring program for second-grade-level or older ADHD students by providing the children with small white file cards on their desks. Each card is divided down the middle to form two columns, with a plus sign ($+$) or smiley face over the top of the left column and a minus sign ($-$) or frowning face over the right column. The teacher then instructs the children that whenever they hear the tone, if they are doing as instructed for that activity, they can award themselves a hash mark in the plus column. If they were not obeying instructions or were off-task, they must place a hash mark in the minus column. The teacher's job at the sound of the tone is to rapidly scan the classroom and note the ADHD child's behavior, then note whether the child is delivering the appropriate consequence to himself or herself. Such scanning for honesty can be further aided by using two separate cards for pluses and minuses, with the plus card taped to the left corner of the child's desk and the minus card taped to the right corner. The program can also be made more effective by having an easel at the front of the classroom with a list of five or so rules that should be followed during that class period (i.e., the five rules for deskwork might be "Stay in seat, stay on-task, don't space out, don't bug others, do your work"). The teacher can then refer to the set of rules in force at that particular class period or activity when the activity begins and can flip to the appropriate chart at that time, calling the children's attention to these rules.

A third system for prompting strategic teacher attending and monitoring is to have the teacher place 10 or so Bingo chips in his or her left pocket that must be moved to the right pocket whenever positive attention has been given appropriately to the ADHD child. The goal is eventually to move all 10 chips to the right pocket by the end of that class period.

Overall, the systematic use of contingent praise and ignoring can be a powerful management tool and should be a mainstay in any classroom program. In addition, once the skills are learned, they generally do not require any more time or resources than procedures the teacher is currently using. Often, teachers of hyperactive children are spending a great deal of time attending to negative behavior. This procedure simply involves a teacher's altering his or her pattern of interaction from attending to negative to attending to positive behaviors. Again, it is the timing of the attention that is so important to its success in managing behavior.

Tangible Rewards and Token Programs

Despite the utility of praise and ignoring, these procedures, while necessary for success, are often not by themselves sufficient with ADHD children. Wender (1971) and others (see Chapter 2) have theorized that ADHD children evidence a diminished response to positive reinforcement or to consequences in general. Recent research supports this theory (e.g., Douglas, 1985) and suggests that ADHD children may have an elevated reward threshold, which reduces the magnitude of reward they experience (e.g., Haenlein & Caul, 1987). In addition, ADHD children have been shown to perform as well as non-ADHD children with continuous reinforcement, but perform significantly worse with a partial schedule of reinforcement (Douglas & Parry, 1983). Thus, as noted earlier, ADHD children seem to require more frequent and more powerful reinforcement. A variety of more powerful rewards, often in the form of special privileges, can be utilized to modify classroom performance. These activities may include helping the teacher, extra recess, special games, computer time, and art projects. Some tangible or backup rewards are distributed on a daily basis, while longer periods (e.g., weekly) of appropriate behavior or academic functioning may be required for more valuable rewards.

A study conducted by Pfiffner, Rosen, and O'Leary (1985) found that the contingent use of very frequent praise (e.g., six praise statements per child per hour) coupled with special activities and privileges (e.g., songtime, posting work on a "superstar" board, reading comic books, special recess activities, positive note home, stickers, running errands for the teacher) was much more effective than an approach consisting primarily of praise. In this study, the special activities and privileges were provided several times during the school day, contingent on academic and behavioral performance. The addition of an individualized reward program, wherein children selected their own rewards each day from a reward menu, proved to be particularly effective in maintaining high rates of on-task behavior and academic productivity. The individualized reward program also greatly reduced the need for negative consequences.

Token reinforcement systems have also been widely used with great success to modify behaviors of ADHD children (see Pfiffner & O'Leary, in press). These systems involve the distribution of tokens (e.g., poker chips, stars) or

points contingent upon appropriate behavior. Children typically accumulate tokens or points throughout the day and later exchange their earnings for desired backup privileges, activities, or tangible objects (e.g., food, small toys). Backup rewards are typically assigned a purchase value so that rewards can be matched to the number of tokens or points earned. As we describe later, some programs also include a response cost component wherein children lose points for inappropriate behavior.

The identification of powerful backup consequences is critical for program success and may be achieved in a number of ways. For instance, teachers may interview children regarding the kinds of activities or other rewards they would like to earn. As indicated earlier, children's compliance with token programs may be greater when they have provided input regarding the rewards to be used. Potential reinforcers may also be identified through observation of the high-rate behaviors emitted by a child. For instance, Legos may be an effective reward for a child who spends much of his or her free time playing with Legos. That is, the child will probably improve his or her behavior if Lego play is made available only as a reward for appropriate behavior. In some cases, rewards available at school may not be sufficiently powerful to alter a child's behavior. Home-based reward programs, discussed in a subsequent section, may be considered in those cases. It is also possible to have parents provide a favored toy or piece of play equipment from home to the teacher for contingent use in the classroom as part of a classroom token or reward system. One very powerful reinforcer at this writing is access to video games, such as Nintendo. Having such a video game (either the larger systems or the newer hand-held models) can greatly enhance the power of a class reward program when children can earn time on the video game for accurate and timely completion of classwork and adherence to classroom rules of conduct. We have been successful in approaching local civic clubs (Rotary Club, Civitans, Lions Club, Knights of Columbus, etc) to donate the equipment to a particular classroom or at least to partially offset its expense by providing presentations to them on the seriousness of classroom behavioral problems and the critical need for such reinforcers in the management of disruptive (and normal!) children. Otherwise, soliciting each parent of a child in that classroom to donate a mere $3.00 or so is often adequate to purchase these systems for reinforcement of child behavior.

When a teacher is in doubt as to what privileges to place on a token system menu for a particular child, it is often helpful to have the child construct the menu with the teacher's assistance. Where this is not helpful, then monitoring the manner in which the child spends free time activities over the next-week may suggest what privileges or activities are especially rewarding to that particular child.

Token programs can be individual or group-based. In individual programs, children earn tokens and backup positive consequences contingent on their own behavior. In group programs, all class members earn rewards based on the behavior of one or more of their classmates. Individual and group programs appear to be equally effective, although they may be most useful in different situations. For instance, when only one child is evidencing a problem or the behavioral goals for several children are very dissimilar, individual contingency programs may be indicated. On the other hand, group programs may be particularly useful when peer contingencies are competing with teacher contingencies (e.g., when peers reinforce disruptive students by laughing or joining in on their off-task pursuits). In some group programs, the performance of an ADHD student serves as the criterion for distribution of rewards to the class. In other cases, tokens or points are dispensed to each child in the classroom, including the ADHD child, contingent upon the occurrence of the appropriate behavior of any student. A variation of this procedure involves the use of team contingencies. In these programs, children are divided into competing teams and earn or lose points for their respective team, depending on their behavior. The team with the greatest number of positive points or fewest negative points earns the group privileges.

Group programs targeting all students' behavior have the advantage of not singling out ADHD children. Given the concern that some teachers have about possible stigmatization or undue attention to problem children receiving treatment, this procedure may be preferable. This may also be the treatment of choice when there is concern that children not involved in treatment may increase their misbehavior in order to be a part of the program and receive reinforcement. It should be noted, however, that concerns of stigmatization and escalation of problem behavior have not been substantiated in research studies. When using group contingencies, however, teachers should take care to minimize possible peer pressure and subversion of the program by one or more children. Powerful reward-only programs may be effective in this regard.

Token programs targeting academic functioning have proven successful in improving performance in both academic and behavioral domains. For example, in a widely cited study, Allyon, Layman, and Kandel (1975) investigated the effects of a token reinforcement system on three diagnosed hyperactive children after they had been withdrawn from medication. The token system involved the children's earning checks recorded on an index card for each correct academic response. The checks were exchanged for a large array of backup reinforcers (e.g., candy, free time, school supplies, picnics in the park) later in the day. The purchase price of backup reinforcers ranged from 1 to 75 checks. Discontinuation of medication resulted in a dramatic increase in inappropriate and disruptive behavior across all three children. Subsequent implementation of the token program sharply increased math and reading scores and reduced disruptive behavior to a level similar to that observed on medication.

Robinson, Newby, and Ganzell (1981) evaluated the effects of an innovative token reward system, targeting both academic performance and cooperative peer tutoring, on the academic performance of 18 disruptive hyperactive boys. Tokens were issued for successful completion of four tasks: two that involved learning to read and using new vocabulary words in sentences and two that involved teaching these tasks to another student. When tokens had been earned for completion of each of these four tasks, they were exchanged for 15 minutes of play on a pinball machine or electronic "pong" game, both of which were located in the classroom. Additional game time was earned whenever a child passed a unit skills test. This token intervention program dramatically increased task completion and performance on the school district's standardized weekly reading exams. Although no specific contingencies were established for nonacademic behavior, the contingencies for academic performance and peer tutoring resulted in a reduction in disruptive behavior. This study is particularly noteworthy for demonstrating that it is possible to design a powerful token program with a class of hyperactive boys that can be successfully administered by a single teacher.

The success of token programs in these and numerous other studies, and the utility of these programs with a wide range of problem behavior, have led to their widespread use in school settings. Tokens are portable so they can be administered in any situation and can usually be distributed immediately following desirable behavior. Token programs also tend to be very powerful because a wide range of backup rewards can be used to avoid satiation of any one reward. However, appropriate and realistic treatment goals are critical for the success of the program. In many typical classrooms, rewards are often reserved for exemplary performance. While this practice may be sufficient for some children, it is unlikely to improve the performance of children exhibiting severe attentional and behavioral problems. Regardless how motivated such a child may be initially, if the criterion for a reward is set too high, the child will rarely achieve the reward and will probably give up trying. To prevent this occurrence, rewards should initially be provided for approximations to the terminal response and should be set at a level that ensures the child's success. For instance, a child who has a long history of failing to complete work should be required to complete only a part, not all of his or her work, in order to earn a reward. Similarly, a child who is often disruptive throughout the day may initially earn a reward for exhibiting quiet, on-task behavior for only a small segment of the day. As performance improves, more appropriate behavior can be shaped by gradually increasing the behavioral criteria for rewards.

The nature in which token systems are constructed and implemented will certainly change as a function of the age of the ADHD children with whom they are to be used. We have found that tangible tokens, such as poker chips, are very important in managing young children (4- to 7-year-olds); points, numbers, or hash marks on a card can be used with older children (through high school). Also, with preschool or kindergarten age children, the plastic chips when awarded may actually serve as distractors and become objects of play or overly excite the children, if within their field of vision/reach. To counteract this, we have often used small fabric pockets that are pinned to the children's clothing on their backs. When tokens are dispensed, the teacher reaches to a child and slips the token in the child's "knapsack" along with a light affectionate squeeze to the shoulder. Several times each day, the pockets are removed and emptied and the children can exchange their tokens for various classroom privileges.

Negative Consequences

Ignoring

Ignoring, as discussed previously, is often used as one of the first interventions for mild misbehavior, especially in cases when children's misbehavior is maintained by teacher attention. Ignoring is not simply the failure to monitor child behavior but is the *contingent withdrawal* of teacher attention upon the occurrence of inappropriate child behavior. However, the use of ignoring alone or in conjunction with praise is often ineffective in shaping or maintaining high rates of on-task behavior and work productivity with ADHD children (Rosen, O'Leary, Joyce, Conway, & Pfiffner, 1984). Even in the context of a powerful reward program, ignoring may not be sufficient (e.g., Pfiffner & O'Leary, 1987). In these cases, additional negative consequences appear to be not only effective, but also necessary with ADHD children. In fact, negative consequences may be more important than praise for maintaining appropriate behavior (e.g., see Acker & O'Leary, 1987; Rosen et al., 1984).

Reprimands

The verbal reprimand is probably the most frequently used negative consequence in the classroom. However, the effectiveness of reprimands appears to vary, depending upon a number of parameters associated with the delivery style. A series of studies investigating these parameters were conducted by S. G. O'Leary and her colleagues at Point of Woods Laboratory School, a full-day educational program, with eight second- and third-grade children referred from regular classes because of inattention, overactivity, and conduct problems. In the first of these studies, Rosen et al. (1984) compared two multiple-component reprimands, one labeled "prudent" and the other labeled "imprudent." Prudent reprimands were immediate, unemotional, and brief, and were consistently backed up with time out or loss of a privilege for repeated noncompliance. Imprudent reprimands were delayed, long, and emotional, and concrete backup consequences were not utilized. The results strongly supported the superior effects of prudent reprimands.

Subsequent studies have examined the effects of a variety of individual parameters of negative consequences, including length, timing, consistency, and intensity (see Pfiffner & O'Leary, in press). Short reprimands appear to be more effective than long reprimands (e.g., a lecture), possibly because less attention is paid to children when a short reprimand is delivered. ADHD children also appear to respond more favorably to negative consequences delivered early in the sequence of misbehavior. This appears to be particularly true in cases where peer attention is maintaining off-task behavior. With regard to consistency of feedback, mixing positive and negative feedback for inappropriate behavior appears to be particularly deleterious. For example, children who are sometimes reprimanded for calling out, but other times responded to as if they had raised their hands, are apt to continue if not to increase their calling out. Reprimands also appear to be more effective when delivered with eye contact and in close proximity to the child. In addition, children respond better to teachers who deliver consistently strong reprimands at the outset of the school year (immediate, brief, firm, and in close proximity to the child) than to teachers who gradually increase the severity of their discipline over time.

In sum, reprimands appear to be most effective when they are consistent, immediate, brief, delivered in close proximity to the child, and of sufficient intensity at the outset. These dimensions may be particularly critical with hyperactive children, who may be sensitive to these stylistic features. However, verbal reprimands are not always sufficient. More powerful backup consequences, including response cost and time out, may be necessary in these cases.

Response Cost

Response cost involves the loss of a reinforcer contingent upon inappropriate behavior. Lost reinforcers can include a wide range of privileges and activities. Response cost has often been used to manage the disruptive behavior of ADHD children in the context of a token program. This procedure involves the children's losing tokens for inappropriate behavior in addition to earning them for appropriate behavior. Similar to reward-only token programs discussed earlier, this procedure is convenient and readily adapted to a variety of target behaviors and situations. Furthermore, response cost has been shown to be more effective than reprimands with ADHD children and can also increase the effectiveness of reward programs.

Rapport, Murphy, and Bailey (1982) compared the effects of response cost with those of stimulant medication on the behavior and academic performance of two hyperactive children. In the response cost procedure, the teacher deducted 1 point every time she saw a child not working. Each point loss translated into a loss of 1 minute of free time. An apparatus was placed at each child's desk to keep track of point totals. One child's apparatus consisted of numbered cards that could be changed to a lesser value each time a point was lost. The teacher had an identical apparatus on her desk where she kept track of point losses. The child was instructed to match the number value on his apparatus with that of the teacher's on a continual basis. The second child had a battery-operated electronic "counter" with a number display. The teacher decreased point values on the display via a remote transmitter.

Both response cost procedures resulted in increases in both on-task and academic performance, which compared favorably with the effects of stimulant medication. The immediacy with which consequences could be delivered in either procedure (the teacher was able to administer a consequence even when she was some distance away from the child) probably contributed to their efficacy. In addition, these procedures are particularly noteworthy for their practicality and ease of administration.

To aid in making the implementation of classroom token systems as convenient as possible, Michael Gordon has marketed the Attention Trainer® (available from Gordon Systems, DeWitt, NY.) This device is displayed in Figure 15.1 and was invented and field-tested in the aforementioned study by Rapport et al. (1982). A small plastic box containing a display counter on the face of the box and a red light on top is placed on the child's desk during individual work periods. The box is turned on and each minute a point is awarded to the child on the counter display. It is assumed that the child is on-task and following rules during this time. The teacher carries a small transmitter during this class time. If the child is observed to be off-task, not working, or disruptive, the teacher simply presses a button on the transmitter, and the red light is triggered on the child's box. A point is simultaneously deducted from the face of the counter. We have found this system to be highly useful for both children with Attention Deficit Disorder with hyperactivity (ADD/+H) and those without hyperactivity (ADD/−H; see Chapter 3). Although some teachers initially believe that such a device may result in negative social stigma or excessive peer attention, we have never found this to be the case. Encour-

FIGURE 15.1. The Attention Trainer®. (Available from Gordon Systems, 301 Ambergate Rd., DeWitt, NY 13214.)

aging the teachers to try the device for a few days is more than sufficient to convince them that this negative social reaction does not typically happen. Thereafter, they are often ardent supporters of using the device, frequently loaning it to other teachers who witness its use and effectiveness. The device can be faded out for use over 4 to 6 weeks and replaced by a less intensive class token system or self-monitoring program (such as the tone prompt system described above) or by a home-school report card (described below).

As with other punishment procedures, however, the use of response cost has met with concern regarding possible adverse effects including escalation of problem behavior, dislike of the teacher, or avoidance of school. However, several studies comparing response cost and reward procedures do not support such concerns. Response cost involving the contingent loss of tokens that had been distributed "for free" at the outset appears to be just as effective as reward procedures involving the receipt of tokens contingent on appropriate behavior (e.g., Sullivan & O'Leary, in press). In addition, teachers' and children's attitudes toward response cost programs appear to be as positive as those toward reward programs. It should be noted, however, that teachers may tend to be more positive with children when implementing a reward procedure. This may be due to the emphasis in these programs on tracking positive child behavior. Similarly, teachers implementing cost programs may be more critical, due to the emphasis in these programs on tracking negative child behavior. Therefore, a special effort should be made to continue monitoring and praising appropriate behavior when cost programs are in effect. It is also advisable that when rewards and response cost are used together, the opportunity to earn tokens should be greater than the possibility of losing them. The need for frequent costs will be greatly reduced by targeting appropriate behaviors judiciously (i.e., those that are incompatible with the inappropriate behaviors). As with any behavioral procedure, the effectiveness of such programs depends on the selection of appropriate behavioral goals that afford the child success. In all cost programs, care should be taken to avoid the use of unreasonably stringent standards that lead to excessive point or privilege losses.

Time-Out

Time out from positive reinforcement (i.e., "time-out") is frequently recommended for hyperactive children who are particularly aggressive or disruptive. This procedure involves the withdrawal of positive reinforcement contingent upon inappropriate behavior. Several variations of time-out are used in the classroom including removal of materials, removal of adult or peer attention, or removal of the student from the classroom situation. The last procedure, often referred to as "social isolation," usually involves placement in a small empty room (i.e., "time-out room") for short periods of time (e.g., 2 to 10 minutes).

Social isolation has been increasingly criticized over the years due to ethical concerns and difficulty with implementing the procedure correctly. Thus, less restrictive time-out procedures have been utilized. In these procedures, a child is not isolated or removed from the class but is removed from the area of reinforcement or the opportunity to earn reinforcement. This may involve having the child sit in a three-sided cubicle or sit facing a dull area (e.g., a blank wall) in the classroom. In other cases, children may be required to put their work away (which eliminates the opportunity to earn reinforcement for academic performance) and their heads down (which reduces the opportunity for reinforcing interaction with others) for brief periods of time. Another time-out procedure, implemented by Kubany, Weiss, and Sloggett (1971), involves use of a "good-behavior clock." In this procedure, rewards (e.g., penny trinkets, candy) are earned for both a target child and the class when the child has behaved appropriately for a specified period of time. A clock runs whenever the child is on-task and behaving appropriately, but is stopped for a short period of time when the child is disruptive or off-task. Kubany et al. (1971) found dramatic decreases in a hyperactive student's disruptive behavior as a result of this procedure.

Most time-out programs set specific criteria that must be fulfilled prior to release from time-out. Typically, these criteria involve the child's being quiet and cooperative for a specified period during time-out. In some cases, extremely disruptive hyperactive children may fail to comply with the standard procedure, either by refusing to go to time-out or not remaining in the time-out area for the required duration. To reduce noncompliance in these cases, children may earn time-off for complying with the procedure (i.e., the length of original time-out is reduced). Alternatively, refusal to follow time-out rules may result in the length of the original time-out's being increased for each infraction, or the child may be removed from the class to serve the time-out elsewhere (e.g., in another class, or in the principal's office). Failure to comply with time-out may also be consequated with a cost procedure. For instance, activities, privileges, or tokens may be lost for uncooperative behavior in time-out. One strategy that may be particularly effective for reducing noncompliance to time-out involves children staying after school to serve their time-out when they are not cooperative in following time-out rules during school hours. The use of this procedure, however, depends on the availability of personnel to supervise the children after school.

Overall, time-out appears to be an effective procedure for reducing aggressive and disruptive actions in the classroom, especially when they are maintained by peer or teacher attention. Time-out may not be effective in cases where inappropriate behavior is due to a desire to avoid work or be alone, since in these cases time-out may actually be reinforcing. It is important that time-out be implemented with minimal attention from teacher and peers. In cases where a child's problem behavior consistently escalates during time-out and requires teacher intervention (e.g., restraint) to prevent harm to self, others, or property, alternative procedures to time-out may be indicated. Procedural safeguards and appropriate reviews are important to ensure that time-out is used in an ethical and legal way (see Gast & Nelson, 1977).

Suspension

Suspension from school (usually from 1 to 3 days) is sometimes used as punishment for severe problem behavior. However, it is recommended that this procedure be used with caution. Many children may find staying at home or going to day care more enjoyable than being in school, which can thereby undermine the effectiveness of the procedure. In addition, suspension is contraindicated in cases where parents do not have the appropriate management skills needed for enforcement or in cases where parents may be overly punitive or abusive.

Minimizing Adverse Side Effects

Despite the overall effectiveness of negative consequences, adverse side effects may occur if they are used improperly. O'Leary and O'Leary (1977) offer several guidelines to minimize possible adverse side effects. First, punishment should be used sparingly. Teachers who frequently use punishment to the exclusion of positive consequences may be less effective in managing children's behavior due to a loss in the teachers' reinforcing value and/or due to the children having satiated or adapted to the punishment. Excessive criticism or other forms of punishment may also cause the classroom situation to become aversive. As a result, a child may begin to avoid certain academic subjects by skipping classes, or to avoid school in general by becoming truant. Frequent harsh punishment may even accelerate a child's overt defiance, especially in cases where a teacher inadvertently serves as an aggressive model. When negative consequences are used, children should be taught and reinforced for alternative appropriate behaviors incompatible with inappropriate behaviors. This practice will aid in teaching appropriate skills as well as decrease the potential for the occurrence of other problem behaviors. In addition, punishment involving the removal of a positive reinforcer is usually preferable to punishment involving the presentation of an aversive stimulus. Use of the latter method, as exemplified by corporal punishment, is often limited for ethical and legal reasons.

Maintenance and Generalization

Despite the substantial success of teacher-administered behavioral interventions, little evidence exists that treatment gains persist once the programs are terminated. Furthermore, the improvements wrought by contingency management programs in one setting (e.g., reading class) often do not generalize to settings in which the programs are not in effect (e.g., math class, recess).

Technologies are currently being developed to improve the probability that treatment gains will transfer to other school settings as well as across academic years. One procedure involves implementing programs in all the settings in which behavioral change is desired. Maintenance of treatment gains may also be facilitated by withdrawing the classroom contingency programs gradually. For example, a study conducted by Pfiffner and O'Leary (1987) found that the abrupt removal of negative consequences, even in the context of a powerful token program, led to dramatic deterioration in class behavior. However, when negative consequences were gradually removed, high on-task rates were maintained. Gradual withdrawal of contingency programs may be accomplished by reducing the frequency of feedback (e.g., fading from daily to weekly rewards) and by substituting natural reinforcers (e.g., praise, regular activities) for token rewards. One particularly effective procedure for fading management programs involves varying the range of conditions or situations in which contingencies are administered, in order to reduce the child's ability to discriminate when contingencies are in effect. The less the discriminability of the changes in contingencies when one is fading a program, the more successful fading appears to be.

Self-management skills such as self-monitoring and self-reinforcement (to be described in a subsequent section) have also been taught in order to improve maintenance of gains from behavioral programs and to help prompt appropriate behavior in nontreated settings. Although these procedures have been found to improve maintenance following withdrawal of token programs, they are not effective in the absence of teacher supervision, and little evidence exists to suggest that they facilitate generalization across settings.

Continued development of programs to enhance maintenance and generalization of teacher-administered interventions appears to be critical for children's long-term success in school. Nevertheless, specially arranged interventions for ADHD children may be required across school settings and for extended periods of time over the course of their education, given the developmentally handicapping nature of their disorder.

PEER-ADMINISTERED CONTINGENCIES

The disruptive and intrusive behavior of ADHD children often prompts their peers (both ADHD and non-ADHD) to respond in ways that promote and/ or maintain the problem behavior. On the one hand, peers may reinforce a display of clowning behavior with smiles and giggles. On the other hand, peers may retaliate against provocative teasing or intrusiveness and thus further perpetuate the problem. As discussed previously, group contingencies are often effective in counteracting peer reinforcement of inappropriate behavior. However, studies show that peers can also intervene directly to produce desirable changes in their disruptive classmates.

One of the most powerful ways peers can intervene is by ignoring disruptive, inappropriate behavior. Peers can also increase their classmates' appropriate behavior through praise and positive attention. A common example of this effect occurs during sports events when team members cheer and congratulate one another for successful plays. However, peers can also be encouraged to praise one another for other accomplishments or appropriate behavior, such as being a good sport, getting a high grade on an exam (or accepting a low grade without a tantrum), contributing to a class discussion, or helping another student. Peer-monitored token programs in which peers monitor child behavior and distribute tokens to deserving students have also been successful when conducted under teachers' supervision.

In order to promote peers' use of reinforcement and ignoring, it is necessary that teachers reward their efforts. In some cases, praise is sufficient. However, with ADHD children, ignoring and positive attention will be reinforced more effectively with tangible rewards or with tokens in a token economy. Serving as a peer monitor or dispenser of reinforcers appears to be a particularly powerful reward and children will often purchase the privilege of distributing rewards with tokens they have earned.

The use of peers as "behavior modifiers" may be advantageous for several reasons. First, since teachers are unable to continually observe every student's behavior, peers may be better able to monitor their classmates' behavior and therefore better able to provide accurate, immediate, and consistent reinforcement. Second, training children to alter their interactions with peers not only improves peer behavior, but also directly improves the behavior of the children implementing the intervention. This would seem particularly beneficial for ADHD children who are at such a great risk for poor peer relations. Third, peer reinforcement systems may facilitate generalization, since peers may function as cues for appropriate behavior in multiple settings. Fourth, peer-mediated programs may be more practical and require less time than traditional teacher-mediated programs.

Despite these advantages, peer-mediated programs are successful only to the extent that peers have the ability and motivation to learn and accurately implement the program. Peers may be overly lenient and reward too liberally because of peer pressure, fear of peer rejection, or more lenient definitions of misbehavior. On the other hand, children may use the program in a coercive or punitive fashion. Due to these concerns, it is advisable that peers not be involved in implementing punishment programs such as response cost. In addition, when peers are utilized as change agents, they should be carefully trained and supervised and contingencies should be provided for accurate ratings.

HOME-BASED CONTINGENCIES

Home-based contingency programs have been effective in modifying a wide range of problems at school. Due to their high cost-effectiveness and involvement of both teacher and parents, they are often one of the first interventions used. In general, these programs involve the provision of contingencies in the home based on the teacher's report of the child's performance at school. Teacher reports usually consist of either a note or a more formal report card delineating the target behavior(s) and a rating for each behavior. Teacher reports are typically sent home on a daily basis. In some cases, notes are sent home only when a child has met the behavioral or academic goals for that day. In other cases notes are sent home on both "good" and "bad" days. As children's behavior improves, the daily reports can readily be faded to twice weekly, biweekly, monthly, and finally to the reporting intervals typically used in the school. A variety of home-based programs may be developed and individualized for each child. Target behaviors may include both behavior and academic performance. Targeting inadequate academic performance may be especially effective since some home-based programs targeting only academic performance have resulted in improvements in both academic and social behaviors. Examples of target behaviors include completion of all (or a specified portion of) work, staying in assigned seat, following teacher directions, and playing cooperatively with others. Negative behaviors (e.g., aggression, destruction, calling out) may also be included as target behaviors to decrease. In addition to targeting in-class performance, homework-related activities may also be included. ADHD children often have difficulty in remembering to bring home assignments, completing the work, and then returning the completed work to school the next day. Each of these areas may be targeted in a note-home program.

The number of target behaviors may vary from as few as one to as many as seven or eight. Targeting very few behaviors may be indicated when a program is first being implemented (to maximize the child's likelihood of success), when few behaviors require modification, or in cases where teachers have difficulty monitoring many behaviors. The daily ratings of each target behavior may be global and subjective (e.g., "poor," "fair," "good") or more specific and objective (e.g., frequency of each behavior or the number of points earned or lost for each behavior). We recommend including at least one or two positive behaviors that the child is currently reliably displaying, so that the child will be able to earn some points during the beginning of the program.

Typically, children are monitored throughout the school day. However, in order for some success to be achieved with particularly high-rate problem behaviors, children may initially be rated for only a portion of the day. As behavior improves, ratings may gradually include more periods/subjects until the children are being monitored throughout the day. In cases where children attend several different classes taught by different teachers, programs may involve some or all of the teachers depending upon the need for intervention in each of the classes. When more than one teacher is included in the program, a single report card may include space for all teachers to sign, or different report cards may be used for each class and organized in a notebook for a child to carry between classes.

The success of the program requires a clear, consistent system for translating teacher reports into consequences at home. Some programs involve rewards alone; others incorporate both positive and negative consequences. Some studies suggest that a combination of positive and negative consequences may be more effective than rewards alone. However, in cases where parents tend to be overly coercive or abusive, reward-only programs are preferable.

One advantage of home-based programs is that a wide variety of contingencies can be utilized. At a minimum, praise and positive attention should be provided whenever a child's goals are met. With ADHD children, however, tangible rewards or token programs are often necessary. For example, a positive note home may translate into TV time, a special snack, or a later bedtime. A token economy or response cost program may also be utilized, in which a child earns points for positive behavior ratings and loses points for negative ratings. Both daily rewards (e.g., time with parent, special dessert, TV time) and weekly rewards (e.g., movie, dinner at a restaurant, special outing) may be utilized.

Overall, home-based reward programs can be as effective as (if not more effective than) classroom-based programs, but may be particularly effective when used in conjunction with classroom-based programs. Daily reports seem particularly well suited for ADHD children, since they often benefit from more frequent feedback than is usually provided at school. These programs also afford parents more frequent feedback regarding their child's performance than would normally be provided; this can prompt parents when to reinforce a child's behavior, as well as when behavior is becoming problematic and requires more intensive intervention. In addition, the type and quality of reinforcers available in the home are typically far more extensive than those available in the classroom—a factor that may be critical with hyperactive children, as reviewed earlier. Aside from these benefits, note-home programs generally require considerably less teacher time and effort than a classroom-based intervention. As a result, teachers who have been unable to implement a classroom management program may be far more likely to implement a note-home program.

Despite the impressive success of note-home programs, the effectiveness of such a system depends on accurate assessment of child behavior by the teacher as well as consistent and contingent consequences at home. In some cases, children may attempt to subvert the system by failing to bring home a report, forging a teacher signature, or failing to get certain teacher signatures. To discourage this practice, missing notes or signatures should be treated the same way as "bad" reports (e.g., a child fails to earn points, or privileges or points are revoked). In cases where parents may be overly punitive or lack skills to follow through with consequences, their implementation of appropriate consequences should be closely supervised (possibly by a therapist), or

DAILY STUDENT RATING CARD

NAME ______________________ DATE __________

Please rate this child in each of the areas listed below as to how he performed in school today using ratings of 1 to 5. 1 = excellent, 2 = good, 3 = fair, 4 = poor, 5 = terrible or did not work.

	CLASS PERIODS / SUBJECTS					
AREA	1	2	3	4	5	6
participation						
class work						
handed in homework						
interaction with other children						
teacher's initials						

Place comments on back if needed:

FIGURE 15.2. A daily school report card for controlling ADHD behavior at school, used with a home-based token reward system.

other adults (e.g., school counselors, principal) may implement the program.

We now describe several types of home-based reward programs that rely on daily school behavior ratings. One example is shown in Figure 15.2. This card lists four areas of potentially problematic behavior with ADHD children. Columns are provided for up to six different teachers to rate a child in these areas of behavior or for one teacher to rate the child multiple times across the school day. We have found that more frequent ratings are more effective forms of feedback to children and more informative to their parents. The teacher initials the bottom of the column after rating the child's performance during that class period to guard against forgery. Where getting the correct homework assignment home is a problem for some ADHD children, the teacher can require the child to copy the homework for that class period on the back of the card before completing the ratings for that period. In this way, the teacher merely checks the back of the card for accuracy of copying the assignment and then completes the ratings on the front of the card. For particularly negative ratings, we also encourage teachers to provide a brief explanation to the parents of what resulted in that negative mark. The teachers rate the children using a 5-point system.

The child takes a new card to school each day, or these can be kept at school and a new card given out each morning, depending upon the parents' reliability in giving the card out each day. Upon returning home, a parent immediately inspects the card; discusses the positive ratings first with the child; and then proceeds to a neutral, business-like (not angry!) discussion with the child about any negative marks and the reason for them. The child is then asked to formulate a plan for how to avoid getting the negative mark tomorrow (parents are to remind the child of this plan the next morning before the child departs for school). The parent then awards the child points for each positive rating on the card and deducts points for each negative mark. For instance, a young elementary-age child may receive five chips for a 1, three for a 2, and one chip for a 3, while being fined three chips for a 4 and five chips for a 5 on the card. For an older child, the number of points assigned might be 25, 15, 5, −15, and −25, respectively, for these marks on the card. The chips or points are summed, the fines are subtracted, and the child may then spend chips on activities from a home reward menu.

A similar card system was devised for an aggressive ADHD child who was having problems with interactions with others during school recess periods each day. This card, shown in Figure 15.3, was to be completed by the recess monitor during each recess period, inspected by the teacher when the child returned to the classroom, and then sent home for use as described above in a home point system. The teacher was also instructed to use a "think aloud, think ahead" procedure with the child just prior to the child's exiting the class for recess. In this procedure, she reviewed the rules for proper recess

---

Name _____   **Date** _____

Please evaluate this child in the following areas of behavior during free or unstructured school time, especially during *recess*. Using a rating of 1 = excellent, 2 = good, 3 = fair, 4 = poor, please place a number beside each behavior listed below for each recess or free-time period this child is observed each day.

Free Time/Recess

	#1	#2	#3	#4
1. Keeps hands to self; does not push, shove, pinch, or touch others wrongly	—	—	—	—
2. Does not fight with other children (hitting, kicking, biting) or try to provoke them by tripping them, shoving them, or taking their things	—	—	—	—
3. Follows rules	—	—	—	—
4. Tries to get along well with other children	—	—	—	—
Other comments:				

FIGURE 15.3. A daily school report card for controlling aggressive behavior at recess, used with a home-based reward system.

behavior with the child, noted their existence on the card, and directed the child to give the card immediately to the recess monitor. As these cards illustrate, virtually any child behavior can be targeted for intervention via these monitoring/rating systems.

COGNITIVE-BEHAVIORAL INTERVENTIONS

Cognitive-behavioral interventions were originally developed in order to directly treat the impulsive, unorganized, and unreflective manner in which hyperactive children approach academic tasks and social interactions. With their emphasis on the development of self-control, it was thought that cognitive-behavioral therapies would result in better maintenance and generalization of behavioral improvement than that achieved with traditional behavioral interventions.

A variety of different classroom-based cognitive-behavioral strategies have been utilized with hyperactive children. These include behavioral self-control techniques such as self-monitoring and self-reinforcement as well as more comprehensive procedures. Behavioral self-control strategies focused on self-monitoring and self-reinforcement involve children's monitoring and evaluating their own academic and social behavior and rewarding themselves (often with tokens or points) on the basis of those evaluations. Training typically involves teaching children how to observe and record their own behavior and how to evaluate their behavior to determine whether they deserve a reward. Occurrences of appropriate as opposed to inappropriate behavior are usually monitored, and children often keep written records of their ratings. Accuracy of child ratings is usually assessed by comparing these ratings against the teacher's records.

Self-monitoring and self-reinforcement were first implemented in order to maintain gains in classroom behavior established through token reinforcement programs. For example, Turkewitz, O'Leary, and Ironsmith (1975) gradually transferred control of a token reinforcement program from the teacher to the children by teaching children to evaluate and reward their own behavior. Accuracy of children's self-evaluations was taught by rewarding children depending upon the extent to which their ratings matched the teacher's ratings. Results showed that children's appropriate classroom behavior was maintained as they assumed primary responsibility for evaluating and reinforcing their own behavior.

Hinshaw, Henker, and Whalen (1984b) extended the use of self-monitoring and self-reinforcement to children's peer interactions. They utilized a training program similar to Turkewitz et al.'s (1975) "Match Game" to teach children to self-evaluate and self-reward their cooperative interactions with peers. In this procedure, trainers first taught children behavioral criteria for a range of ratings by modeling various behaviors (e.g., paying attention, doing work, cooperative behavior) and rating the behaviors on a scale from 1 to 5 points (e.g., 1 = "pretty bad," 5 = "great!"). Thereafter, children participated in role plays followed by naturalistic playground games in which trainers rated each child's behavior on the 1-to-5 scale and instructed children to monitor and rate their own behavior using the same scale. Children were encouraged to try to match the trainer's ratings. Initially, children were given extra points for accurate self-evaluations regardless of the actual point value of their behavior. However, once children learned the procedure, they were rewarded only when their behavior was desirable *and* matched the trainers' ratings. Results of this study revealed that reinforced self-evaluation was more effective than externally administered reinforcement in reducing negative and increasing cooperative peer contacts on the playground.

Many cognitive training programs involve teaching children self-instructional and problem-solving strategies in addition to self-monitoring and self-reinforcement. The self-instructional program introduced by Meichenbaum and Goodman (1971), or a variant of this program, is often utilized. This program involves teaching children a set of self-directed instructions to follow when performing a task. Self-instructions include defining and understanding the task or problem, planning a general strategy to approach the problem, focusing attention on the task, selecting an answer or solution, and evaluating performance. In the case of a successful performance, self-reinforcement (usually in the form of a positive self-statement, such as "I really did a good job") is provided. In the case of an unsuccessful performance, a coping statement is made (e.g., "Next time I'll do better if I slow down") and errors are corrected. At first, an adult trainer typically models the self-instructions while performing a task. The child then performs the same task while the trainer provides the self-instructions. Next, the child performs the task while self-instructing aloud. These overt verbalizations are then faded to covert self-instructions. Reinforcement (e.g., praise, tokens, toys) is typically provided to the child for following the procedure as well as selecting correct solutions.

A variety of training tasks have been utilized ranging from a host of psychoeducational tasks (e.g., reproducing designs, following sequential instructions, concept problems) to academic and/or social relationship tasks. Studies show that the use of training tasks similar to the area(s) in which improvement is desired is most successful. For instance, the use of academically related tasks seems to facilitate generalization from the training sessions to academic performance in the classroom more than does the use of psychological tasks, such as maze performance. Similarly, training regimens that focus primarily on cognitive problem solving with psychoeducational or academic tasks have failed to show the same degree of improvement in children's social behavior as that found when social interactions are the focus of the training. In addition, children's improvement in these comprehensive programs appears to occur most consistently when external or self-reinforcement is provided for accurate and positive self-evaluations in conjunction with self-instructional training. In fact, when programs are effective, it may be more a result of reinforcement than of self-instructions.

A multicomponent self-control training program, including both behavioral self-control and self-instructions, was examined in a study conducted by Barkley, Copeland, and Sivage (1980) with six 7- to 10-year-old hyperactive boys. The study was conducted in an experimental classroom, which children attended in the afternoon after attending their regular class in the morning. Self-instructional training was provided in small- and large-group activities, with training tasks including both academic and social problems. Tokens were distributed for accurate performance of the self-instruction procedure. During individual seatwork, children self-monitored and recorded their on-task behavior at intervals signaled by a prerecorded tone. Specifically, whenever children heard the tone, they evaluated their behavior with respect to the posted classroom rules (e.g., staying in seat, working quietly). If they had been following the rules, they recorded a check mark on an index card kept at their desk. Initially, the tone sounded on a variable 1-minute schedule, but was faded to a variable-interval 5-minute schedule. Accurate reports, defined as matching observers' reports, were rewarded with tokens that could be exchanged for privileges.

Results are shown in Figures 15.4 and 15.5. They revealed that on-task behavior improved during individual seatwork, pointing to the efficacy of the self-monitoring and reinforcement procedures. The frequent use of these procedures was most effective (i.e., 1-minute rating intervals) and older children profited more from the procedure than did younger children. In contrast, training in self-instruction did not reduce misbehavior during the group lessons. This finding was probably due to the lack of contingencies for appropriate behavior during this time. In addition, behavioral improvements made during individual seatwork did not generalize to the regular classroom. Thus, the effectiveness of self-monitoring and self-reinforcement seemed to be limited to the context in which they were taught and where contingencies were in effect for their use.

Social problem solving and stress inoculation, two additional cognitive-behavioral interventions, have been applied toward improving the peer interactions of ADHD children. For instance, Hinshaw, Henker, and Whalen (1984a) utilized these interventions to enhance ADHD children's ability to control their anger in response to peer provocation. The treatment began with instruction in problem-solving skills and self-instructional strategies applied to academic and fine motor tasks. Problem-solving skills were then extended to interpersonal conflict situations. This portion of training involved children's generating and evaluating solutions to vignettes of interpersonal problems. The children also practiced self-control skills during role plays of interpersonal problems (e.g., meeting a new boy, playing a competitive game). The final treatment procedure involved training in stress inoculation and social problem-solving skills to be used in coping with verbal taunting and

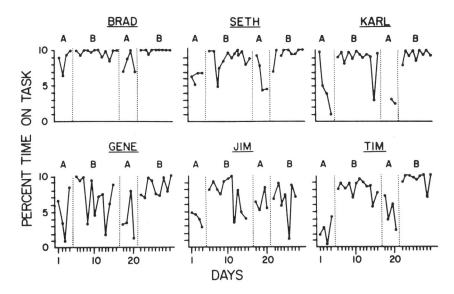

FIGURE 15.4. The percentage of time on task (× 10) during individual work time for each of six hyperactive boys across baseline (A), treatment (B), and reversal (A) phases. The graphs are in order of highest to lowest mental age (MA) (upper left to lower right) for the boys: Brad (MA = 10 years, 2 months); Seth (MA = 10 years, 1 month); Karl (MA = 8 years, 6 months); Gene (MA = 8 years, 1 month); Jim (MA = 6 years, 9 months); and Tim (MA = 6 years, 6 months). From "A Self-Control Classroom for Hyperactive Children" by R. A. Barkley, A. Copeland, and C. Sivage, 1980, *Journal of Autism and Developmental Disorders, 10,* 75–89. Copyright 1980 by Plenum Publishing Corporation. Reprinted by permission.

provocation from peers during a brief group interaction. Stress inoculation procedures involved monitoring internal cues related to anger and aggression and developing and practicing selected self-control coping strategies under increasingly greater provocation from peers. Self-control strategies included such response as ignoring, initiating calm conversation with peers, looking out the window, counting to 10, or reading a book. This cognitive-behavioral treatment resulted in greater self-control and greater use of effective coping strategies than a control treatment focusing on social problem solving (without practice), perspective taking, and enhancement of empathy. However, it was not known whether the positive effects found during the staged situation would generalize to more naturalistic peer interactions.

Despite these promising results, many other studies fail to show positive effects of treatment (see Abikoff, 1985, for a review). Overall, the effects of cognitive-behavioral therapies are not as strong, as durable, or as generalizable as was once expected. Treatment gains usually are not maintained after the cognitive-behavioral procedures are withdrawn and rarely generalize to settings in which the procedures have not been implemented. Limited effects may be the result of failing to individualize treatment to the specific deficits

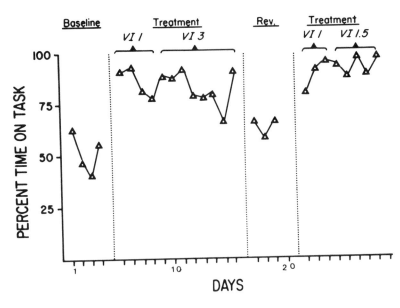

FIGURE 15.5. Mean percentage of time spent on task by six hyperactive boys during all treatment conditions. From "A Self-Control Classroom for Hyperactive Children" by R. A. Barkley, A. Copeland, and C. Sivage, 1980, *Journal of Autism and Developmental Disorders, 10,* 75–89. Copyright 1980 by Plenum Publishing Corporation. Reprinted by permission.

of the child. The lack of generalization to academic and behavioral measures and to nontreated school settings found in many studies may be due to the brevity of the training (often only a few hours), and to little or no overlap between the skills taught during training and the requirements of the classroom or playground. Improved generalization may require training children in all settings in which self-control is desirable and training individuals in these settings (e.g., teachers, recess monitors) to encourage children's application of the skills.

Cognitive-behavioral treatments have also not been shown to be superior to traditional behavioral programs or to enhance the effects of behavioral programs on a consistent basis. In addition, cognitive-behavioral interventions frequently require an excessive amount of time and resources to implement properly. Trained experimenters or teachers are necessary to teach the children the procedures. Supervision of children's self-monitoring and evaluation is also required to ensure honest reports, since without supervision children become increasingly lenient in their self-evaluations and inappropriate behavior increases.

In light of these issues, the value of the widespread use of these procedures with ADHD children remains to be seen. It is our opinion that cognitive-behavioral techniques are most likely to be useful when they are taught directly to a child's caregivers (parents and teachers) for use within the myriad day-to-day interactions with that child, rather than having the child formally practice these skills in individual sessions in a clinic or outside of the classroom. A simple cognitive training strategy will therefore be necessary if it is to be conveniently implemented by the parents or teachers. One such approach is the "think aloud, think ahead" method mentioned above. Another is the "STAR" program where children learn to Stop, Think ahead about what they have been asked to do, Act or do the requested task while talking to themselves about the task, and Review their results. However, children must be adequately reinforced for displaying self-control skills in order to maintain this type of behavior—the training alone is insufficient.

CLASSROOM STRUCTURE AND TASK DEMANDS

A variety of factors related to the structure of the classroom environment, classroom rules, and the nature of task assignments have been recommended for modification in order to improve hyperactive children's school functioning. Early efforts focused on procedures to reduce stimulation in the classroom (i.e., minimal stimulation programs). These procedures were based on the premise that excessive distractibility was causing the problems of inattention exhibited by hyperactive children. Teachers were advised to remove as many visual distracters (e.g., colorful pictures and posters, brightly colored clothing and jewelry) and auditory distracters from the classroom as possible. In some cases, children were placed in desks facing a corner or wall; in other cases, three-sided cubicles were utilized to reduce exposure to distracting stimuli. Research evaluating these programs has generally not found that they lead to improvement in classroom behavior or academic performance of hyperactive children. Other investigators, proposing that traditional classrooms are too restrictive for hyperactive children, have advocated the use of classrooms that afford a greater degree of freedom and flexibility. However, this approach has also not been supported empirically.

Nevertheless, several specific features of the classroom environment may warrant modification when working with hyperactive children. Probably one of the most common classroom interventions involves moving the hyperactive child's desk away from other children to an area closer to the teacher. This procedure not only reduces the child's access to peer reinforcement of his or her disruptive behavior, but also allows the teacher to monitor the child's behavior better. As a result, the teacher can provide more frequent feedback which, as discussed earlier, is necessary with many ADHD children. It may also be beneficial for ADHD children to have individual and separated desks. When children sit very near one another, attention to task often decreases because of the disruptions that occur among children. Altering seating arrangements in this manner may sometimes be as effective as a reinforcement program in increasing appropriate classroom behavior.

Physically enclosed classrooms (with four walls and a door) are often recommended for hyperactive children over classrooms that do not have these physical barriers (i.e., "open" classrooms). An open classroom is usually noisier and contains more visual distractions since children can often see and hear the ongoing activities in nearby classes. In light of research showing that noisy environments are associated with less task attention and higher rates of negative verbalizations among hyperactive children (Whalen, Henker, Collins, Finck, & Dotemoto, 1979), open classrooms appear to be less appropriate for ADHD children.

It is also advisable that the classroom structure be well organized and predictable, with the posting of a daily schedule and classroom rules. Posted feedback charts regarding children's adherence to the classroom rules may also facilitate program success. In some cases, we have found the use of "nag tapes" to be particularly helpful in making rules more "externalized" and more effective in controlling child behavior. This involves tape-recording a set of reminders for the child ("Stay on task, don't space out, do your work, don't bug others," etc.) that are randomly interspersed on the audiotape. Obviously, they should be not so frequent as to disrupt the child's work. We often try to use the child's father as the voice on the tape, to capitalize on the somewhat greater compliance of ADHD children to their fathers than their mothers. When the child is about to do deskwork, he or she takes out a small portable tape recorder, plugs in an earpiece so the tape does not distract other students, and turns on the tape. The child then proceeds to do his or her work, while the tape is simultaneously providing reminders to remain on task. However, the efficacy of these types of procedures will depend greatly on their being combined with consistent methods of rule enforcement and the contingent use of rewards and punishments.

The following additional changes to classroom structure and curriculum are likely to prove beneficial to the management of ADHD children:

1. As with all children, academic tasks should be well matched to ADHD children's abilities. Increasing the novelty and interest level of the tasks through use of increased stimulation (e.g., color, shape, texture) seems to reduce activity level, enhance attention, and improve overall performance (Zentall, Falkenberg, & Smith, 1985).

2. Varying the presentation format and task materials (e.g., through use of different modalities) also seems to help maintain interest and motivation. When low-interest or passive tasks are assigned, they should be interspersed with high-interest or active tasks in order to optimize performance. Tasks requiring an active (e.g., motoric) as opposed to a passive response may also help hyperactive children to channel their disruptive behaviors into constructive responses (Zentall & Meyer, 1987).

3. Academic assignments should be brief (i.e., accommodated to the child's attention span) and feedback regarding accuracy of assignments should be

immediate. Short time limits for task completion should also be specified and may be enforced with the use of external aids such as timers.

4. Children's attention during group lessons may be enhanced by delivering the lesson in an enthusiastic yet task-focused style, keeping it brief, and allowing frequent and active child participation.

5. Interspersing classroom lecture or academic periods with brief moments of physical exercise may also be helpful, so as to diminish the fatigue and monotony of extensive academic work periods (e.g., jumping jacks by the desk, a quick trip outside the classroom for a brisk 2-minute run or walk, forming a line and walking about the classroom in a "conga line" fashion, etc.).

6. Teachers should attempt to schedule as many academic subjects during morning hours as possible, leaving the more active, nonacademic subjects and lunch to the afternoon periods. This is suggested in view of the progressive worsening of ADHD children's activity levels and inattentiveness over the course of the day (see Chapter 2).

7. Whenever possible, classroom instructions should be supplemented with direct-instruction (e.g., DISTAR) drill of important academic skills, or, even better, with computer-assisted drill programs. ADHD children are considerably more attentive to these types of teaching methods than to mere lectures.

MANAGING ACADEMIC PROGRAMS WITH ADHD ADOLESCENTS

All of the recommendations above apply as much to adolescents with ADHD as to children. However, implementing these recommendations becomes considerably more difficult with adolescents because of the increased number of teachers involved in high school; the short duration of the class periods with each; the greater emphasis on individual self-control, organization, and responsibility for completing assignments; and the frequent changes that occur in class schedules across any given week. All of this is likely to result in a dramatic drop in educational performance in many ADHD children after they enter high school. There is little or no accountability of teachers or students at this level of education unless the students' behavioral offenses become sufficiently heinous to attract attention or unless their academic deficiencies are grossly apparent. It is very easy for the average ADHD adolescent to "fall through the cracks" at this stage of education unless he or she has been involved with the special educational system before entering high school. Those who have will have been "flagged" as in need of continuing special attention. But most ADHD adolescents will not be in special education and so are likely to be viewed merely as lazy and irresponsible. It is at this age level that educational performance becomes the most common reason ADHD adolescents will be referred for clinical services (see Chapter 4).

Dealing with large educational institutions can be frustrating for parent, clinician, and ADHD teenager alike. Even the most interested teacher may have difficulties mustering sufficient motivation among his or her colleagues to help an ADHD adolescent in trouble at school. Below we have listed a number of steps that can be attempted to manage poor educational performance and behavioral adjustment problems in middle and high school. To the degree that other methods described above can also be implemented, so much the better.

1. A Public Law 94-142 evaluation of the adolescent should be immediately initiated, if one has not been done before or has not been done within the past 3 years (federal law requires a re-evaluation every 3 years a child is in special education). Special educational services will not be forthcoming until this evaluation is completed, and this can take up to 90 days or longer in some districts. The sooner it is initiated, the better.

2. ADHD adolescents invariably require counseling on the nature of their handicapping condition. Although many have certainly been previously told by parents and others that they are "hyperactive" or have ADHD, many of them still have not come to accept that they actually have a disability. In our opinion, this counseling is not intended to depress the individuals over what they cannot do, but to help them accept that they have certain limitations and to find ways to prevent their disability from creating significant problems for them. Such counseling is difficult, requiring a sensitivity to the adolescents' striving to be independent and to form their own opinions of themselves and their world. It often takes more than a single session to succeed in this endeavor but patience and persistence can pay off. Our approach is to stress the concept of individual differences: Everyone has a unique profile of both strengths and weaknesses in mental and physical abilities, and each of us must adjust to them. We often confide about our own liabilities and use humor to get the adolescent to see that they are not the only ones who have weaknesses. It is how we accept and cope with our weaknesses that determines how much they limit our successes in life. And yet we have personally sat at many school meetings where parents, teachers, school psychologists, and private tutors all had gathered to offer assistance to ADHD teenagers, only to have the teens refuse the offers while promising that they could turn things around on their own. Until ADHD adolescents accept the nature of their disorder, they are unlikely to fully accept the help that may be offered them.

3. If ADHD adolescents have been on medication previously and responded successfully, they should be counseled on the advantages of returning to the medication as a means of both improving their school performance and obtaining those special privileges at home that may be granted as a result of such improved performance. (See Chapter 14 for an example of such counseling with a teenager about medication.) Many adolescents are concerned about others' learning that they are on medication. They can be reassured

that only they, their parents, and the physician are aware of this and that no one at school need know unless the teenagers expose it. Therapists should be prepared in many cases, however, for ADHD adolescents to want to "go it alone" without the medication, believing that with extra applied effort they can correct the problem.

4. It is often essential that a team meeting be scheduled at the beginning of each academic year, and more often as needed, at an ADHD teen's school. The teachers, school psychologist, guidance counselor, principal, parents, *and the adolescent* are to be present. The therapist should take a handout describing ADHD to give to each participant (the chapter on ADHD by Barkley, 1989a, can be circulated as a condensed reading on the disorder and its treatments). The therapist should briefly review the nature of the adolescent's disorder and stress the need for close teamwork among the school, parents, and teen if the teen's academic performance is to be improved. The teachers should describe the current strengths and problems of the teen in their classes and make suggestions as to how they think they can help with the problem (e.g., being available after school a few days each week for extra assistance; reducing the length of written homework assignments; allowing the teen to provide oral means of demonstrating that knowledge has been acquired rather than relying on just written, time test grades; developing a subtle cueing system to alert the teen as to when he or she is not paying attention in class without drawing the whole class's attention to the fact; etc.). It is at this conference that the teen is asked to make a public commitment as to what he or she is going to strive to do to make school performance better. Once plans are made, the team should agree to meet again in 1 month to evaluate the success of their plans and troubleshoot any problem areas. Future meetings may need to be scheduled depending upon the success of the program to date. At the least, meetings twice a year are to be encouraged even for a successful program, so as to monitor progress and keep the school attentive to the needs of this teen. The adolescent always attends these meetings.

5. A daily home-school report card should be introduced as described above. These are often critical for teens more than any other age group; they give a teen and his or her parents daily feedback on how well the teen is performing in each class. Again, the back of the card can be used to record daily homework assignments, which are verified by each teacher before completing the ratings on the card and initialing the front of the card. In conjunction with this, a home point system must be set up that includes a variety of desired privileges the teen can purchase with the points earned at school. Such things as telephone time, use of the family car, time out of the home with friends, extra money, clothes, musical tapes and compact discs, and special snacks kept in the house can be placed on the program. Points can also be set aside in a savings book to work toward longer-term rewards. It should be recalled, however, that the daily, short-term, immediately accessible privileges and not these longer-term rewards are what give the program its motivational power, and the reward menu should not contain too many long-term rewards. Once

the adolescent is able to go for 3 weeks or so with no score of 4 or 5 (negative ratings) on the card, then the card is faded to a once- or twice-per-week schedule of completion. After a month of satisfactory ratings, the card can either be faded out or reduced to a monthly rating. The adolescent is then told that if word is received that grades are slipping, the card system will have to be reinstated.

6. The school should be encouraged to provide a second set of books to the family, even if a small deposit is required to do so, so that homework can still be accomplished even if a book required for homework is forgotten by the teen and left in his or her locker.

7. One of the teen's school teachers, the homeroom teacher, a guidance counselor, or even a learning disabilities teacher should be asked to serve as the "case manager." This person's role is to meet briefly with the teen three times a day for just a few minutes to help keep him or her organized. The teen can stop at this person's classroom or office at the start of school, at which time the manager checks to see that the teen has all the homework and books needed for the morning's classes. At lunch, the teen checks in again with this manager who sees that the teen has copied all necessary assignments from the morning classes, helps him or her select the books needed for the afternoon classes, and then sees that he or she has the assignments to be turned in that day for these afternoon classes. At the end of school, the teen checks in again with the manager to be sure that he or she has all assignments and books needed to go home for homework. Each visit takes no more than 3 to 5 minutes; however, interspersed as they are throughout the school day, these visits can be of great assistance in organizing the teen's schoolwork.

8. All parties should consider whether getting a private tutor for the teen may be beneficial. Many parents find it difficult to do homework with their teens or to tutor them in areas of academic weakness. The teens often resist these efforts as well, and the tension or arguments that can arise may spill over into other areas of family functioning even after the homework period has passed. Where this is the case and a family can afford it, hiring a tutor to work with a teen even twice a week can be of considerable benefit to both improving the teen's academic weaknesses and "decompressing" the tension and hostility that arises around homework in the family.

9. The therapist should insist that the parents set up a special time each week to do something alone with this teen that is mutually pleasurable, so as to provide opportunities for parent-teen interactions that are not task-oriented, school-related, and fraught with the tensions that work-oriented activities can often bring with ADHD teens. This can often contribute to keeping parent-teen relations positive and counterbalance the conflicts that school performance demands frequently bring to such families.

EDUCATIONAL PLACEMENT

As reviewed earlier, a wide range of behavioral interventions have been shown to be effective in improving the classroom performance of hyperactive children. However, many of the programs described above are designed to be implemented by teachers of small classes who are well trained in behavioral procedures. In order to be implemented in mainstream classes, many of these programs may require the assistance of a classroom aide, or modification in terms of reduced time and resources (e.g., less frequent teacher monitoring and/or delivery of rewards). Teachers of mainstream classes may also require extensive training in behavior modification. Although intensive classroom programs are often not feasible in large classes, home-based programs are usually recommended, since they are often both practical and powerful.

In many cases, these procedures are sufficient, especially for children with mild to moderate ADHD symptoms or for children whose attentional and behavioral problems are controlled with pharmacological interventions. However, in other cases, especially when children have severe ADHD symptoms and accompanying problems of opposition, aggression, and/or learning disabilities, these simplified procedures are inadequate and alternative educational placements may be necessary (e.g., special education, private school). Ideally, these placements should include classes with a small student-teacher ratio that are taught by teachers with expertise in behavior modification. These factors will enable teachers to provide the intensive one-to-one instruction necessary, as well as the continuous monitoring, feedback, and use of intensive behavioral programs that appear necessary to maximize these children's success.

Special Educational Services

Obtaining special educational services that offer such classes for ADHD children is often a difficult process. Many ADHD children do not qualify for special educational services according to the guidelines specified in PL 94-142. Clinicians need to keep in mind that diagnostic criteria for ADHD do not correspond in any direct way to eligibility criteria in federal and state laws governing placement within special educational programs. When ADHD children do qualify, they are often assigned to classes containing children with very different problems from their own (e.g., severe emotional disturbances or learning problems). Such placements often depend on the type of problem comorbid with the ADHD. For instance, ADHD children who are particularly aggressive and defiant are likely to be placed in programs for emotionally disturbed children, while those with coexisting learning disabilities but minimal aggression are likely to wind up in learning disability resource rooms. Certainly, ADHD children with significant speech and language or motor development problems are likely to receive language interventions, occupational and physical therapy, and adaptive physical education provided that these developmental problems are sufficient to interfere with academic performance. The ADHD child without these comorbid conditions is likely to be eligible for little special education in most states. Efforts are now underway by national parent support associations to force states and the federal government to reconsider the eligibility criteria for special services. Any change is likely to come after much debate and may be contingent upon the need to limit any cost that opening special education programs to another handicapped population would entail for school districts.

In the meantime, it is essential that clinicians be very familiar with the federal guidelines for special education, as well as with their own specific state guidelines and any particular local district guidelines. In addition, clinicians should become acquainted with the directors of special education within the school districts from which their clients most commonly come, so as to know their criteria for special education placement and be able to advocate knowledgeably for the children in their practice. The phrase "You are only as good as your Rolodex" is a truism in dealing with educational placements for ADHD children as well as locating resources within the private sector, such as private schools, formal and informal tutoring programs, and special summer camps for behavioral problem children. Sometimes the clinician will be contacted to give a "second opinion" on a case because of conflict between parents and school staff over the nature and extent of the child's problems and his or her eligibility for services. It is in such cases that clinicians must determine the precise nature of the school district's eligiblity criteria and select assessment methods for addressing these criteria that are acceptable within school district policies.

It is also important that clinicians understand the principle of the "least restrictive environment" as it applies to decisions regarding special educational placement. PL 94-142 makes it clear that special services are to be provided in such a way that handicapped children may interact with nonhandicapped peers as much as possible. Hence, school districts are likely to err in the direction of placing ADHD children in the least restrictive environment necessary to manage the academic and behavioral problems—that is to say, in the program that provides the greatest contact with normal students. Some teachers are not always in agreement with this, preferring that even children with mild ADHD be removed to special educational settings, rather than having to adjust their own classroom curriculum and behavioral management style to accommodate the maintenance of these children in regular education. Parents may be equally biased toward special education believing that the smaller class sizes, better-trained teachers, and greater teacher attention are to be preferred over regular education. School districts are likely to resist these pressures so as not to violate the rights of the children to the least restrictive environment or risk legal action for doing so. Parents may find this frustrating, but must be helped to understand the philosophy behind this placement bias and its basis in law.

An Exemplary Program for ADHD Children

Only a few school-based treatment programs specifically serving ADHD children exist. One program, exemplary for specifically targeting the diverse needs of ADHD children, has been developed by James Swanson at the University of California–Irvine in collaboration with the Orange County Department of Education (UCI-OCDE). This program has been modeled after the summer programs developed by William Pelham at Washington State University, Florida State University, and the University of Pittsburgh, and by Barbara Henker, Stephen Hinshaw, and Carol Whalen at the University of California–Los Angeles.

The UCI-OCDE year-round program serves ADHD children in kindergarten through fifth grade. (For a full description, see Swanson et al., in press.) A full-day educational curriculum (approximately 12–15 children per class) and a comprehensive clinical program are provided to children over the course of approximately 1 year. The clinical component includes many of the techniques described above. First, an intensive behavior modification program based on a token economy is provided in the classroom. Children, working independently and in small groups, earn points every 30 minutes throughout the school day in the following areas: getting started, completing assignments, appropriate interaction with peers and adults, following instructions, and cleaning up. Points are tallied throughout the day and are exchanged for daily rewards (e.g., computer video games, Legos, games). Reward choices are dependent on the percentage of points earned (e.g., earning 90% of points results in choice of computer games, Legos, or any reward activity; earning 80% or better provides choice of a board game or art supplies; earning below 80% provides paper and pencil only). Weekly rewards (e.g., special outings, cooking, movies) are also earned, depending on the number of points accumulated over the course of the week. Teachers initially administer the point system. After demonstrating success with the system, children learn to self-monitor, self-evaluate, and self-reinforce their own performance. Once children learn to evaluate their behavior accurately, teacher feedback is gradually reduced.

The second clinical component involves parent participation in a 6-week parent training class and weekly individual therapy sessions. This training focuses on the principles and techniques of behavior modification and includes development of an individual home program to address problems at home and to reinforce successful performance at school. Parent participation facilitates consistency across settings and promotes generalization of in-school gains to the home environment.

Social skills training is a third component and is delivered to the children in daily group sessions. This training focuses on teaching children the skills necessary to interact successfully with their peers and adults. Instruction, role plays, and *in vivo* practice during cooperative and competitive group games are used to teach a wide variety of social skills. Children's performance is monitored and reinforced by social skills counselors through the point system. Children are also taught to self-evaluate and reward their performance during social skills sessions. As their social behavior improves, the children are rewarded with increased privileges and counselor feedback is gradually reduced. Generalization of appropriate social skills to the playground and classroom is facilitated by involving the playground supervisors and classroom teachers in social skills training sessions, so that they reinforce children's use of these skills in each of these environments.

After meeting academic, behavioral, and social goals in the program, children are transferred back to their home schools. To facilitate a successful return to the home school, children may attend a transition school. At this school, advanced social skills groups are conducted, and classroom behavioral programs are established to facilitate transfer of learning. Individualized home-based reinforcement programs targeting school behaviors are typically implemented during the transition process.

The UCI-OCDE combined clinical and educational program appears to hold much promise in the treatment of ADHD children. Development and evaluation of this and other multifaceted school-based treatment programs may be important not only for serving these children, but also for preventing the development of more serious antisocial problems as the children enter adolescence and adulthood.

SUMMARY

This chapter has reviewed a variety of behavior management methods that, when used in combination, can lead to substantial improvement in the classroom deportment, academic performance, and peer relations of ADHD children. Manipulation of teachers' attention (e.g., praising appropriate behavior and ignoring inappropriate behavior) is the basic ingredient in all interventions, but when used alone is usually not sufficient. ADHD children seem more responsive to frequent and powerful incentives such as tangible rewards or token economies. Prudent reprimands, backed up with a loss of privileges or time-out for severe behavior, are also necessary to reduce inappropriate disruptive behavior. Group contingencies and peer-administered consequences may be especially useful with ADHD children, since they may improve peer status in addition to behavioral and academic performance. Integrating schools and home contingencies is particularly useful to facilitate consistency and generalization across settings. Although recent studies show some success with cognitive-behavioral interventions, particularly in the area of social skills, the expectation that these interventions would result in greater maintenance and generalization than traditional approaches has not been realized. We therefore recommend that they be integrated with the teaching styles of the child's teacher for use in day-to-day exchanges, rather than taught in formal, one-to-one sessions outside of school.

The success of these procedures often depends on the ability of the teacher to monitor child behavior frequently, provide immediate feedback, and provide backup consequences (when needed) on a consistent basis. When these techniques are used in mainstream classes, practical issues often necessitate modifications and an emphasis on home-based contingencies. In cases requiring more intensive interventions, small classes with specialized programs designed to address the behavioral, academic, and social needs for ADHD children may be required.

The generalization and maintenance of treatment gains have thus far been elusive. Although the development of more sophisticated technologies may improve maintenance and generalization, the pervasive and durable problems exhibited by ADHD children seem to necessitate individualized, broadly based, long-term interventions. The effectiveness of these interventions requires not only a range of appropriate techniques, but also a high level of rapport and cooperation among those individuals working with the children, including school personnel, parents, and consultants. Moreover, the success of these interventions is undoubtedly a function of the ability of the treatment team to maintain a high level of optimism, enthusiasm, and energy throughout their work with these children.

Acknowledgment: Special thanks are extended to James Swanson and Cheryl Rosenau for their review of an earlier version of this chapter.

16

Social Skills and Peer Relationship Training

DAVID GUEVREMONT

> In poverty and other misfortunes of life, true friends are a
> sure refuge.—The young they keep out of mischief; to the
> old they are a comfort and aid in their weakness, and
> those in the prime of life they incite to noble deeds.
>
> —ARISTOTLE (382–322 B.C.)

Peer rejection in childhood is a devastating experience, associated with subjective feelings of loneliness, low self-esteem, poor schoolwork, juvenile delinquency, and dropping out of school. Research in the past 25 years has also shown longer-term outcomes to be poor for children without friends, including occupational difficulties, alcoholism, psychiatric hospitalizations, and antisocial behavior. Although it has long been acknowledged that most ADHD children experience interaction problems with their parents and teachers, during the past 10 years researchers and clinicians have become keenly aware of the significant social problems these children encounter in their peer relations. It is estimated that as many as 50 to 60% of ADHD children experience some form of social rejection from their peer group.

It is not clear that poor peer relations in childhood directly cause later life problems; it is equally plausible that the same factors contributing to social problems in childhood are responsible for maladjustment in later life. Such factors could easily be underlying personality disorders or even Attention-deficit Hyperactivity Disorder (ADHD). Nonetheless, most experts agree that positive relationships with peers in the childhood years provide a critical buffer against stress as well as psychological and psychiatric problems. Although there is probably no single factor that adequately explains why some children develop poor peer relationships, it is not uncommon for rejected children to display a higher rate of negative, aggressive, and/or self-centered behavior than accepted peers, coupled with deficient prosocial skills. It is reasonable to assume that the same inherent constitutional factors that contribute to parent-child interaction problems place the ADHD child at risk for developing poor peer relationships.

In this chapter, a social skills intervention program is described based on my colleague's and my assumptions about the mechanisms and processes related to peer rejection in ADHD children. Before describing the program, I briefly highlight some of the behavioral and social characteristics of the socially rejected ADHD children for whom the program is designed.

BEHAVIORAL CHARACTERISTICS OF SOCIALLY REJECTED CHILDREN

A relatively large literature exists describing the behavioral and social characteristics of socially rejected children. Rejected children are generally identified as those whom most children least like to play or interact with among their peers. Rejected children are actively disliked by their peers. Peer rejection is quite stable over time, with approximately 45% remaining rejected 1 year later and as many as 30% maintaining their rejected status for up to 4 years. Moreover, rejected children tend to maintain their social status across transitions into new peer groups.

Naturalistic observation studies conducted in classroom and free-play settings have highlighted the behavioral and social styles of socially rejected children. For example, in the preschool years, children who are rejected by their peers engage in higher rates of aggression, rough-and-tumble play, and solitary play, and initiate interactions in a more hostile or teasing manner, than do popular preschoolers. There is some evidence that preschool-age hyperactive children's social behavior is characterized by a considerable amount of aggressiveness, attempts to dominate peers, and destructive behavior. Behavioral irregularity and emotional immaturity, such as abrupt mood changes and temper tantrums, make their social behavior somewhat unpredictable for teachers and peers, further hindering the development of acceptance by peers. Thus, even by 4 or 5 years of age, many ADHD children are viewed by parents and teachers as relating more poorly than other children with their peers (see Chapters 3 and 4).

During the early elementary school years, peer rejection is associated with disruptive classroom behavior, physical and verbal aggression, arguing, noisy or obnoxious behavior, and initiating interactions in a disruptive manner—characteristics commonly associated with the behavior of many preadolescent ADHD children. Classroom inattention, distractibility, and hyperactivity have also been strongly linked to peer rejection. In fact, comparisons of aggressive boys with those who are both aggressive and hyperactive/inattentive have found that only the latter group may be at high risk for peer rejection. It is clear, then, that social rejection is the product not only of one's peer interactions, but of a larger class of behavior that is inappropriate to the specific situational norms and expectations. Finally, some researchers have noted that, in addition to the higher rates of negative behavior displayed by rejected children, many show age-inappropriate and highly immature development of prosocial skills. Not surprisingly, many ADHD children tend to gravitate toward younger children, perhaps because they are allowed to dominate social activities. Others begin to associate and relate better with older youths who may be more tolerant of their immaturities.

In contrast to the large research literature that exists on younger children's peer relations, little research has explored the social behaviors associated with adolescent peer rejection. The few studies that have been conducted suggest that verbal aggression, property violations, disruptiveness, and annoying or bothersome behaviors continue to be associated with peer rejection. Interestingly, ADHD adolescents report spending significantly more of their spare time alone or with younger children than do normal teenagers, who report spending most of their free time with same-age peers. Common social behaviors associated with peer acceptance and rejection among preschoolers, elementary-age children, and adolescents are shown in Table 16.1.

TABLE 16.1. Behavioral Correlates of Social Acceptance and Rejection

Acceptance	Rejection
Nurturance giving, positive interactions, parallel play, friendly approach, sharing	Aggression, hyperactivity, rough-and-tumble play, solitary activity, destructiveness, teasing, hostile initiations, provocative actions, excessive talking, demanding and domineering, taking others' toys
Elementary school	
Positive initiations, reciprocal exchanges, asking questions, social conversation, cooperative group behavior, giving compliments, skillful entry into peer dyads, interaction with popular children, saying "yes" to requests, on-task classroom behavior, tidy and attractive appearance, sharing, initiating games, controlled affect when angry	Verbal and physical aggression, disruptive attempts to enter play groups, off-task behavior, lack of cooperation in groups, negative classroom behavior, rule violations, bothersome and "noisy" behavior, arguing, self-centered or attention-getting behavior, indiscreet remarks about others, quickness to anger
Adolescence	
Conversation, loyalty, unsolicited gift giving, offering help, commitment, genuineness, cheerfulness, friendliness, enthusiasm	Disruption, snobbish behavior, rule violations, aggression, property violations, annoying behavior, excluding others from activities, poor heterosocial skills, cruelty, lying, stealing, impulsive social comments, immature interests

OVERVIEW OF SOCIAL SKILLS TRAINING

Social skills training programs have been developed in the past 15 years in an attempt to directly alter the peer relations and longer-term outcomes of children who are socially rejected or isolated from their peer group. More recently, a few training programs have been examined specifically for ADHD children. Although there exist countless approaches and commercially available packages to teach children social skills, most have in common at least two goals: (1) to increase the children's awareness and sensitivity of how their social behavior affects others (social knowledge); and (2) to teach new prosocial behaviors believed to be deficient in the children's social repertoire (skill acquisition).

There have been far too few systematic outcome studies to permit any final conclusions to be drawn about the efficacy of these treatment efforts. Nonetheless, the clinical research literature suggests that the two most basic goals of social skills training are often accomplished. That is, children who have received training become more knowledgeable about appropriate and inappropriate social behavior and many learn the specific social skills targeted in the intervention. Despite some rather promising outcomes, however, it is often been the case that participants' social behavior does not change in their natural environments. That is, skillful behavior performed in the actual training setting often does not generalize to the children's natural environment. Moreover, even when the newly learned social skills are used in natural settings such as school, the social status of the children often does not change. Thus, the unliked children may continue to be rebuffed by peers despite their use of more appropriate interpersonal behaviors.

Before dismissing social skills training altogether as a viable treatment option for rejected children, it is important to consider that social skills training programs have rarely included active strategies or comprehensive attempts to (1) promote generalization to the natural environment or (2) directly influence the social status of the trained children. It has now become clear that programs that are narrow in scope and that do not actively address issues of generalization and social status are not likely to have a positive impact on the children's immediate or longer-term peer relationships.

During the past 3 years, my colleagues and I have developed a social skills training interaction program aimed specifically at the types of social problems and skills deficits common among ADHD children, particularly preadolescent boys. The program consists of three interrelated components: (1) social skills and cognitive-behavioral training, (2) generalization programming, and (3) strategic peer involvement. We consider these latter two portions of the intervention (generalization programming and peer involvement) to be absolutely necessary to the success of the program. Thus, in addition to traditional social skills training procedures, active interventions in the natural environment using behavior change agents (e.g., parents and teachers) and behavior management procedures are absolutely essential to support changes in social behavior and promote improvements in social status.

The program that I describe here was initially conducted in 12 sessions at our clinic. More recently, we have conducted school-based skills training so as to enhance generalization and peer involvement. We have extended the length of the program to 20 to 25 sessions. It is too early to draw conclusions on the overall effects of the program; it has not been formally tested with rigorous scientific methods. Nonetheless, initial observations and feedback have been positive. Before describing some of the practical and clinical issues involved in the three-stage training program, I turn briefly to some of the assessment issues involved in screening and identifying candidates for the treatment.

ASSESSMENT OF SOCIAL COMPETENCE: SCREENING AND IDENTIFICATION

There are a number of methods for obtaining information about an individual child's social status and relative social strengths and weaknesses. Interviews, behavior rating scales, sociometrics, structured role-playing, and direct observation methods represent the most common of these. The latter three methods have primarily been used in research because they require considerable time and special resources to carry out. In clinical practice, interviews and behavior rating scales are usually sufficient for selecting children for a social skills training program. The essential goals of our initial assessments are to (1) obtain an estimate of the children's social status; (2) gather information about specific problematic social behaviors (e.g., does not share, tries to bully others); and (3) screen referrals that may be inappropriate for the group (i.e., because of extreme antisocial behavior, serious language or developmental handicaps, acute depression or anxiety, etc.).

The most reliable and valid method for determining a child's social status is the use of sociometric measures. Sociometrics are procedures that directly involve children in rating their peers' social competence. Peer nominations, for example, have each child in a classroom select three children that they "like the most" and three that they "like the least." The number of positive nominations received is an index of popularity, while the number of negative nominations received is an index of social rejection. These assessment methods are usually unavailable to the clinician because they are impractical and because ethical concerns (e.g., confidentiality) often restrict their use.

Our primary reason for desiring information on social status is to ascertain whether a child is identified as socially rejected or neglected. There exists a group of socially neglected children with peer relationship problems who tend to be withdrawn and isolated. The withdrawn ADHD child will frequently correspond with the diagnostic subtype of Attention Deficit Disorder without hyperactivity, where anxious or depressive symptoms may exist. Our training program has been tailored more for the socially rejected ADHD child who displays a high level of disruptive, obnoxious, or aggressive behavior. Social skills training with the anxious and withdrawn ADHD child will obviously be quite different.

A brief interview with the parent, child, and teacher is usually sufficient for determining a child's general rate of social interactions with peers, reciprocity with others (e.g., sharing, taking turns), ability to resolve conflicts with other children, number of friends, and duration of friendships. The child's perspective on his or her social status and friendships should be interpreted cautiously, although it may be possible to assess the degree of subjective distress associated with peer relations. Clinicians should also note that parents have often been found to be poor judges of the quality of their children's peer relationships. Classroom teachers, on the other hand, will undoubtedly have had greater opportunity to observe a child in a variety of situations with same-age peers and probably have a good sense of the child's general social status within the classroom. We have found teacher interviews quite reliable in our selection of children who are primarily rejected and aggressive as opposed to socially withdrawn.

Interviews can be easily supplemented with standardized rating scales that provide information about the statistical deviance of a child's behavioral adjustment (Barkley, 1988a). It is useful to use at least two rating scales: one that provides information on general childhood psychopathology, and one that specifically taps social skills. The Child Behavior Checklist (CBCL; parent and teacher versions; see Chapter 9) will do nicely for assessing general psychopathology. A child's status on the Aggressive and Delinquent dimensions of this scale can be compared to scores on the Social Withdrawal and Anxious scales. Obviously, normal scores on Internalizing dimensions and abnormally high scores on Externalizing dimensions correspond to the socially rejected, somewhat aggressive group that we seek. The opposite profile (i.e., abnormally high scores on Internalizing scales and normal scores on Externalizing scales) may reflect the neglected social status group that will require a different approach to social skills training (e.g, increasing peer contacts and desensitization of social anxiety). The CBCL also allows for a global screening of social adjustment through items on the Social Competence scale.

To elucidate some of the more specific social strengths and weaknesses of an individual child, it is useful to administer a social skills teacher rating scale. Information that is then obtained about specific social behaviors allows therapists to control the homogeneity of the group and develop vignettes and exercises for training purposes that reflect actual social problems of group members. Teacher ratings of children's social behavior correlate quite highly with peer sociometrics and information obtained through direct observation. Two teacher social skills rating scales that we have found useful are the Matson Evaluation of Social Skills with Youngsters (MESSY), developed by John Matson and his colleagues (Matson, Rotatori, & Helsel, 1983), and the Taxonomy of Social Situations for Children (TOPS), developed by Ken Dodge and his colleagues (Dodge, McClaskey, & Feldman, 1985).

The MESSY is a 64-item, 5-point teacher rating scale (there is also a self-report version) covering a range of prosocial (e.g., "plays by the rules of a game") and negative (e.g., "always wants to be first") social behaviors characteristic of preadolescent children. Although the MESSY requires further work to elucidate its psychometric and normative properties, test-retest reliabilities are adequate, and initial factor analyses revealed Inappropriate/Impulsiveness and Appropriate Social Skills dimensions. Thus, it is possible to evaluate social strengths and weaknesses with the MESSY.

The TOPS is a 44-item, 5-point rating scale designed to identify the presence and severity of children's social difficulties across six social areas: Peer Group Entry, Response to Provocation, Response to Failure, Response to Success, Social Expectations, and Teacher Expectations. A total score and scores on each of the six factors can be compared to normative data on second- through fourth-graders. The TOPS is useful for identifying common problem situations as well as providing information on a child's common response to these situations. The TOPS has both high internal consistency and test-retest reliability and differentiates socially rejected from nonrejected children.

PRACTICAL ISSUES IN SOCIAL SKILLS TRAINING

Before describing the social skills training program that we have used with preadolescent ADHD children, it is important to consider the numerous practical and logistical issues in conducting such a training program. I now highlight some of the more salient considerations.

Characteristics of the Group

Although some degree of social skills training can be conducted on an individual basis, most experts agree that a group format holds a number of advantages. First, peer modeling and active practice of social skills with peers under the supervision of the clinician are only possible in a group. Although some degree of role playing with an adult clinician may be possible, this somewhat artificial experience may be quite different from real-life peer interactions. Second, social skills training groups can provide a rich supply of real-life examples from participants' actual experiences. Third, group formats can function to provide a degree of social support to participants, who may experience limited success or ostracism in other peer group formats. And fourth, corrective feedback or positive acknowledgment from peers can be a powerful tool in shaping behavior.

Clinicians should consider three additional issues in developing a social skills group: (1) group size, (2) ages and gender of participants, and (3) degree and severity of ADHD symptoms and associated behavior problems of group members.

Group Size

The actual size of the group may vary according to the ages of the children, the number of trainers participating, and the nature and severity of behavioral problems of group members. Generally speaking, however, we have found that group training with ADHD children cannot be successfully accomplished with more than eight children and that the ideal group consists of four to six children. Where eight or more children are involved, at least two trainers will almost always be required, and even then we have found it extremely difficult to carry out session-by-session goals in a timely fashion. Undoubtedly, among the greatest challenges clinicians will face in conducting social skills training groups with ADHD children are the time and energy required simply to manage general behavior and maintain attention. With groups larger than six, we have found ourselves dedicating as much as 50% of training sessions to managing behavior. Issues related to maintaining control of behavior and attention are discussed later.

Age and Gender Considerations

When one is considering the age range of children to participate in a group, common sense and developmental considerations dictate that participants' ages be within 2 years of one another (e.g., 8 to 10, 12 to 14). This helps assure the children are functioning at a similar level with respect to cognitive development and that they share common social experiences. Moreover, our experiences and those coming from other laboratories have led us to question whether very young ADHD children benefit from social skills training groups at all, particularly training groups that are not dominated by a "hands-on" behavior management package in the children's school setting. In general, for children between the ages of 4 and 7, classroom-based programs that include a social skills curriculum would appear to have a greater chance of success. Several of these programs have been developed as ongoing classroom-wide curricula, such as the "Think Aloud" program of Bonnie Camp and May Bash (1981) for socially aggressive youngsters.

With preadolescents, same-gender groups are almost routinely preferred by the children and are consistent with social-developmental needs—namely, that interactions and friendships occur with same-gender peers. The same generally holds true of ADHD early adolescents (e.g., 12- to 13-year-olds), most of whom are more immature in their social development. With older adolescents, mixed-gender groups may be appropriate, depending on the preference and needs of group members.

Severity of Problems

A pivotal issue in developing a social skills group for ADHD children is that of the degree and severity of ADHD symptoms and associated behavior problems of group members. All group members will show significant levels of inattention, impulsivity, and poor self-control, and in most cases hyperactivity. A large percentage will also have problems in complying with rules and instructions, as well as oppositional or defiant behavior. It is challenging enough to manage the behavior of one ADHD child in a group of normal children. Obviously, creating a group that contains five or six of these children will result in special problems.

We have found two ways of alleviating some of the problems with conducting social skills training groups with ADHD children. The first is careful selection of participants according to the degree and severity of problems that they display. For example, in a group of six, it is generally advisable to reserve several slots for children showing mild patterns of aggressive or oppositional defiant behavior. These children are frequently those who display poor social relations primarily because of immaturity or social awkwardness, rather than high levels of disruptive or acting-out behavior. The remaining members of the group would be divided between ADHD children with moderate forms of behavioral and/or social disturbances and those with more severe behavior problems. Because of the benefits of more appropriate peer models as well as practical problems in managing a group, clinicians are cautioned against selecting a group where the majority display significant patterns of oppositional or aggressive behavior.

A second potential solution to this problem is to form a more general social skills group, reserving two or three slots for children who, in addition to having peer relationship problems, also carry a diagnosis of ADHD. At the very least, this may free up some of the time needed to simply maintain attention. Finally, we generally ask parents of children taking medication to consult with the children's physicians about whether there are contraindications for using the medication during the group. As a general rule, a child's ability to benefit from the skills training program may be enhanced while the child is on medication.

Trainer Qualifications

Perhaps the most important qualifications for those running social skills training groups for ADHD children are knowledge of and practice in behavior management. A thorough background in basic behavior management procedures is necessary because skillful management of the group is a prerequisite to teaching social skills. In the past, we have conducted groups for eight boys using two trainers highly skilled in the use of behavior management strategies, and have still come across regular problems in smoothly meeting session goals. It goes without saying that knowledge of the basic characteristics of

ADHD is essential to a full appreciation of the group's special management needs.

An additional qualification is a broad-based knowledge of the social skills literature, particularly that which pertains to the selection of skills for different developmental levels. Finally, clinicians should be well versed in basic instructional and teaching procedures, such as modeling, role playing rehearsal, and coaching with children. A description of these training procedures in the context of social skills training can be found in Michelson, Sugai, Wood, and Kazdin (1983).

Length of Training

When we first began running social skills training groups for ADHD boys, we offered the service for 10 sessions of 75 minutes each. Several problems with conducting such a short-term training program became apparent. First, it generally takes several sessions for group members to become comfortable with one another, and early sessions often lack participation and spontaneity. Second, ADHD children are clearly not one-trial learners, and it takes several sessions before the group rules and consequences begin to influence behavior. Third, clinicians should anticipate that the special characteristics of this population (e.g., inattention, disruptiveness) will often result in session goals only being partially met. Fourth, and perhaps most important, short-term training may result in very poor generalization to more natural social situations. Repetition, practice, and the solidifying of skills through high rates of reinforcement both within and outside of the training setting dictate that a lengthier training format be developed. There is some research to support what may appear to be obvious: Lengthier training programs result in greater skill acquisition and generalization. Based on research findings and our own clinical experience, it is suggested that a minimum of 18 to 20 sessions be used. In addition, sessions that run over 60 minutes may result in increased off-task behavior; therefore, clinicians may wish to spend between 30 and 40 minutes in actual training exercises and leave another 10 to 15 minutes for departure transitions.

Behavior Management Issues

It is imperative that therapists carefully prepare a behavior management system to be used in the social skills training sessions. Without such a system, a large amount of time will be spent in attempting to correct misbehavior or excessive inattentiveness. Behavior management principles for parents, described in Chapters 12 and 13, can be adapted to the group. Group rules and expectations for behavior should be established early on, written and posted, and reviewed at each session. Consequences should also be clearly stated in advance.

We have found it necessary to divide training sessions into brief 5-minute intervals so that consequences and feedback may be delivered frequently and relatively immediately throughout the session. Feedback and consequences delivered at the end of the session will be insufficient. At the end of each interval, points or tokens are given to participants who have followed group rules adequately and participated cooperatively. Alternately, participants' names can be written on a board and stars placed beside the names at the end of each interval of cooperative behavior. Obviously, tokens and stars are not awarded to children whose behavior has been unacceptable during the interval. Tokens or stars are exchanged at the end of the group for small rewards. We have used snacks, such as popcorn, as the rewards. As a rule, participants must earn greater than 70% of the possible tokens or stars to earn a snack.

We have also found it useful to introduce occasional "special" rewards. This simply involves awarding a special prize as a bonus to a group member whose behavior or participation has been exemplary in a given session. No previous announcement is made about the availability of the special reward until the session is coming to an end. We try to use these bonus rewards in about one-third of the sessions, although in no predictable order. We have found individual contingencies to be much more potent than group contingencies. The one exception to this is that participants may earn a "group treat" such as a pizza party after a specified number of points, stars, or tokens is accumulated by the whole group.

Finally, therapists are also advised to specify sanctions for grossly inappropriate behavior. We have used brief 2- to 3-minute time-outs for repetitive rule violations or acts of physical or verbal aggression. Needless to say, one of the best strategies for reducing misbehavior is for therapists to make sure that sessions are highly structured and fast-paced, and that participants remain actively involved in the various phases of training.

A SOCIAL SKILLS TRAINING PROGRAM FOR ADHD CHILDREN

The four major skills covered in the ADHD social skills training portion of the intervention program are (1) social entry, (2) conversational skills, (3) conflict resolution and problem solving, and (4) anger control. This program has been derived from clinical research on the common social skills deficit of ADHD and socially rejected children, and from the work of several investigators who have empirically tested various components of this training program in their individual laboratories.

Session 1: Introduction and Orientation

The initial session is designed to (1) provide a general orientation to the group; (2) introduce the participants to one another; (3) review goals and activities that the group will engage in; and (4) introduce the rules and behavior management system. No social skills training occurs during the initial session.

Most children enter the group with limited information about why they are here or what the group specifically involves. Often parents will have provided their children with a variety of reasons for attending the program, some of which may be inaccurate. We have found it useful to tell the children that they will be meeting with one another once a week to have fun and learn about ways to make and keep friends. At this point, we have found that many of the children are reluctant to acknowledge that they have social problems; some may not be fully aware of the extent of their social difficulties. Therefore, clinicians may wish to refrain from pointing out to the group members that they have been specifically referred for the group because of their peer relationship problems. After a degree of rapport between group members and therapists has been established, participants are usually more willing to admit to and discuss their difficulties (and possibly their distress) regarding peer relations. Generally speaking, the timing of such a discussion is better left to Session 3 or 4. It is important to emphasize to the group that meetings are going to be fun and lively, pointing out the variety of activities that they will be involved in as well as the rewards that can be earned.

After some of the purposes and activities of the group have been highlighted, participants are asked to identify themselves. To elicit humor and facilitate group members' recall of others' names, they are also asked to name their favorite foods. The members are told to listen carefully because they will be asked to see how many names and favorite foods of other group members they can remember. This exercise is continued until each group member and the therapists have had an opportunity to try to recall names and foods. Each session begins with the same exercise until it is clear that participants are familiar with one another's names.

A group name is selected by participants during the first session to provide the group with a cooperative task and begin to develop a sense of group cohesion. First, each child is asked to select a name, which is written on a blackboard. Usually, group names describe sport teams (e.g., "Giants") or television characters (e.g., "Teenage Mutant Ninja Turtles"). Unless a clearly inappropriate name is selected we generally include all responses from the group. On occasion, children will select names that contain either inappropriate words or comments (e.g., one child selected the "Hyperactive Fruitcakes" for the group name). Group members then vote on one name and the majority vote determines the name of the group. The group is then given markers and a large roll of paper to individually draw pictures that they think represent the name of the group. This poster is hung on a wall at each session.

The final part of the first session is devoted to introducing the group to the rules and management system that will be employed at each session. Active participation of group members is sought in establishing why rules are necessary. With few exceptions, we have found the children quite capable of articulating a variety of reasons for having rules and contributing to what the group rules should be. Therapists should try to keep the number of rules down to a minimum of three or four, with at least one of the rules specifying that physical or verbal aggression will not be tolerated. The monitoring system and consequences are then specified in detail.

It is especially important to end the first session on a positive note. We generally reserve 10 to 15 minutes for a popcorn party or provide some type of snack. Therapists should be cautioned against allowing this period to become too unstructured. Instead, it is useful to provide an activity in conjunction with the snack. In our groups, we end each of the sessions with a similar snack period and structured game. Finally, we have found it useful to have children leave the training room one at a time or in pairs rather than dismissing them as a group. This helps to ensure a controlled departure, which otherwise can be quite unruly.

Sessions 2–4: Social Entry Skills

Prior to the second session, therapists may want to construct small business-like cards with the group name that participants have selected written on one side and the three or four group rules written on the reverse. This helps to externalize rules and increase their salience while, at the same time, reinforcing the notion of group membership. The second session can then begin with each member receiving his or her card and a review of the group rules and consequences.

Beginning with the second session, each group meeting follows a general sequence of activities. This sequence is depicted in Table 16.2.

Most of Sessions 2 through 4 is devoted to the first social skill to be trained: social entry.

TABLE 16.2. The General Sequence of Activities Followed During Each Social Skills Training Session

---

 1. Review of group rules and behavior management system.
 2. Introduction, rationale, and group discussion of social skill.
 3. Verbal instruction on the performance of the skill; step-by-step components are discussed and posted on a blackboard or sign.
 4. Modeling by the therapists; participants observe the therapists acting out each of the steps involved in performing a social skill.
 5. Role playing between a therapist and one participant; the therapist and a single group member participate in a brief role play.
 6. Coaching and feedback; the therapists provide verbal feedback to each child and offer suggestions through verbal instruction and further modeling.
 7. Child-to-child role playing; child dyads are formed to practice the social skills while therapists and other group members provide feedback.
 8. Videotaping; child-to-child role plays are recorded and reviewed while further feedback is provided.
 9. Summary of the skills focused on during the session.
10. Assignment of homework.
11. Delivery of consequences.

Background and Description

"Social entry" refers to the behavioral skills needed to successfully initiate or join the ongoing interactions of another child or group of children. Using observational data from both school and analogue laboratory settings, research has demonstrated that socially rejected children, in comparison to popular children, characteristically employ less successful tactics when trying to initiate interactions. For example, popular children tend to approach unfamiliar peers gradually, hovering on the periphery as though information were being collected about the other children and their activities. Popular children are also more likely to verbally initiate contact with others with non-self-centered comments, such as questions. Socially rejected children are equally likely to approach their peers; however, in contrast to popular children, rejected children are more likely to initiate contact with disruptive, obnoxious, or self-centered behaviors (e.g., "I know how to play that"). Our clinical experience suggests that these types of ineffective strategies are characteristic of the social behavior of many ADHD children. They may be by-products of impulsivity and/or deficient social knowledge and skills.

Overview

Social entry or initiation can usually be introduced and practiced in two to three sessions. However, ongoing feedback on initiation behaviors can be provided through the entire skills training program. Therapists should be prepared to provide a rationale about the importance of initiation strategies. We have found it particularly useful to model in an exaggerated fashion the behaviors associated with unsuccessful attempts to initiate contact with another person. For example, a volunteer from the group may be asked to play the role of a new boy at school during recess. The volunteer is asked to sit at a table and play with a toy. A therapist asks group members to pretend that he or she (the therapist) is another child about to meet the other boy for the first time. The therapist then demonstrates two or three initiation approaches, each characterized by disruptive or self-centered behavior. Different children can play the role of the new child at school and describe their reactions to being "greeted" in such a way. Prompts and questions from the therapist (e.g., "What do you think the new boy would be thinking?", "What behaviors make you think that?") may be necessary to facilitate the discussion.

The discussion then turns to the types of initiation behaviors that are likely to be more successful. A list of "Do's and Don'ts" can be written on a board as they are generated by the group members and therapists. Several key behaviors are emphasized. First, the successful entry excludes disruptive initiations. It is necessary to focus on both the quality of the behavior used to initiate interactions and the timing or situational appropriateness of initiations. It is pointed out that knowing what the other child or children are doing will make it easier to tell whether or not an initiation is likely to be disruptive. Participants are asked to think of examples where initiating an interaction with another child may be disruptive or inappropriate. Common examples (e.g., while another child is doing classroom seatwork, when someone is talking) are discussed. The second key behavior that is emphasized is making initial verbal responses to a peer or group of peers. Once again, group members should be kept active by having them discuss verbal strategies that are likely to be effective and ineffective. Ineffective strategies include self-centered and domineering statements, bragging, teasing, and criticism; effective strategies might include asking questions, making neutral comments about the activity, complimenting, and requesting permission to join the activity.

After the rationale and instructions are provided, training should then turn to role-playing and coaching of social entry skills. It is important to begin with very brief, highly structured, dyadic practice scenarios. Many socially rejected and ADHD children are able to interact reasonably well in one-on-one situations. Larger-group and unstructured conditions, on the other hand, often lead to deterioration in behavior. A therapist may wish to ask at first for one volunteer and to conduct role-plays with a single child while other group members observe. As children become comfortable with the mechanics of role-playing and adequate in demonstrating appropriate social entry skills, it may then be possible for the therapist to stop participating in the role-play and allow two children to interact together.

The brief role-plays that we begin with (some of which may be as brief as 10 seconds) usually involve one child playing with a toy or engaging in a "staged" play activity. A second child is asked to show how he or she might initiate an interaction with the other child, using strategies that were covered earlier. After each brief role-play, feedback is provided, emphasizing the "good" strategies that were performed. It is useful to have group members identify what specific entry strategies were used during the role-play. Each group member should be encouraged to participate in the role-plays and have the opportunity to play both the active and "staged" roles.

The difficulty level of practice scenarios should be increased very gradually. Initially, the number of children participating in a particular role-play can be increased from two to three. For example, two children can engage in a "staged" play activity while a third child attempts to enter the dyad using appropriate initiation tactics. To increase the difficulty level further, lengthier role-plays should be developed. Children involved in the "staged" play activity can follow basic scripts describing the roles they are to take. The roles generally involve stumbling blocks for the boy attempting to initiate and join the ongoing dyad, such as having the dyad ignore initial greetings and requests. We have found it useful to prepare brief scripts beforehand by writing them down on index cards and having role-play participants select them from a box randomly. The scripts are designed to vary the nature of the social entry experiences, come closer to approximating real-life instructions, and provide a more challenging exercise than was provided by brief dyadic role-plays. The scripts can be developed by the therapists in advance, although it is also useful to generate ideas for scripts with group members. It is critical to keep them relatively short and simple.

Coaching and feedback are used extensively during and after role-plays. Although clinic and agency resources will determine the availability of equipment, we have found videotaping of role-plays quite useful. After several role-plays have been performed, a brief period of time is devoted to watching taped scenes; the therapist playing the tape stops it on occasion to provide feedback or to ask questions of participants about various social-interactional behaviors. The taping is helpful in maintaining interest and provides a form of visual feedback unavailable via verbal instructions alone. It is not uncommon for a few participants to express some reluctance about being videotaped early on. Within a brief period of time, however, all group members are usually comfortable with the taping. With careful supervision we also will occasionally allow participants to have turns operating the camera or "directing" a role-play activity.

Sessions 5–7: Conversational Skills

One of the most basic social behaviors that appears to be deficient in many ADHD children is interpersonal reciprocity. From an early age, this is seen in the context of the children's domineering and bossy behavior with peers. During the late childhood and early adolescent years problems with reciprocity become more noticeable in the context of poor communication skills. We spend three or more sessions providing instruction on basic conversational skills since this is a major source of interaction with the peer group during the elementary school-age years, and perhaps a pivotal vehicle for developing close friendships.

Background and Description

Studies examining the social interactions of ADHD boys with normal peers show that the ADHD children initiate verbal interactions more frequently than normal children. Normal children, in turn, are more responsive to the ADHD children's initiations. When normal children initiate verbal interactions or ask questions of ADHD boys, however, ADHD boys are more likely to ignore them. Thus, although more talkative, ADHD boys are also less responsive and reciprocal.

Moreover, studies by Carol Whalen and her colleagues (Whalen, Henker, Collins, McAuliffe, & Vaux, 1979) have found ADHD boys to be less likely than normal boys to adjust their social communication behaviors to the changing demands of the situation. In a "Space Flight" game, one child in each dyad played the role of Mission Control (the message sender) while the other played the role of the Astronaut (the message receiver). Although the behaviors of ADHD boys was appropriate when serving as Mission Control, they were more intrusive in their communications than normal boys while playing the role of the Astronaut, issuing significantly more statements of disagreement. Normal children were also more likely to request feedback or confirmation when in the role of the receiver (Astronaut) than hyperactive boys.

It is clear from these studies that ADHD children do not modulate their social communication behaviors in accordance with the task or situational demands. Reviews of ADHD children's social communication skills have suggested four deficits; (1) inability to shift roles between giving and receiving information in dyadic interactions, (2) increased inappropriate and/or disagreeable verbal interchanges, (3) inefficient conversation, and (4) greater difficulty staying on task.

Overview

Beginning at about Session 5, attention is turned to social communication skills—a logical extension of social entry skills covered in previous sessions. Whereas social entry skills are designed to enhance successful initiations with others, conversational skills begin to address the ADHD child's ability to maintain social interaction and perhaps to develop and solidify friendships. Research on conversation training with socially rejected children has produced encouraging findings.

Following an approach used by Landau and Milich (1988) to assess social communication skills, we have found it useful to employ a game-like task called "TV Talk Show" to introduce basic communication skills and begin to provide opportunities for role playing and coaching. Later, more naturalistic conversational tasks are used in an attempt to parallel real-life experiences. In the TV Talk Show task, one child serves as the "host" whose task it is to interview the "guest." The host is told that he or she must talk with the guest, with the following goals: (1) to make the guest feel welcome; (2) to learn about some of the guest's interests; and (3) to provide the guest with information about his or her (the host's) own interests.

Children are arranged in dyads, and each dyad is videotaped for 3 minutes during the mock interview. After all group members have had a chance to participate in at least one videotaping, the tape is reviewed and discussed with group members. Positive social communication behaviors are acknowledged, and awkward and difficult scenes are discussed. It has been our experience that 3 minutes in the interviewing exercise is quite long initially. It may be necessary to gradually increase the length of time as participants become more competent with the task.

Three verbal skills, two content areas, and several nonverbal behaviors are emphasized during training. The verbal skills are (1) questioning—asking others about themselves; (2) self-expression—sharing information about oneself; and (3) leadership bids—giving help, suggestions, invitations, and feedback. Content areas are (1) sharing the conversation (vs. monopolizing it) and (2) maintaining the correct role as host or guest and staying on-task. Nonverbal behaviors upon which feedback is provided include (1) eye contact and (2) body orientation (e.g., facing the other child). Training consists primarily of direct instruction, modeling of correct behaviors, active coaching by the therapists while children rehearse and participate in role-plays, and verbal and videotaped feedback on performance.

Positive and negative communication behaviors are written on a board or large sign, noting the "Do's" (e.g., "Ask questions") and "Don'ts" (e.g., "Hogging the show"). Positive and corrective feedback is provided to dyads on an immediate and ongoing basis initially. After participants begin to acquire the basic communication skills, feedback is postponed until the end of a 3-minute videotaping. At this point, feedback is provided both by the therapists and by group members, who are asked to comment on what the dyad did well and what areas they could try to improve on.

Depending on the progress group members have made using the TV Talk Show exercise, therapists will eventually want to move on to practicing conversational skills using a more naturalistic format. We usually begin by providing dyads with a topic to use in a 3- to 5-minute conversation. The TV Talk Show game is no longer used at this point. Topics include such areas as favorite toys, games, and activities; liked and disliked TV shows; and summer plans. To enhance the diversity of practice experiences, dyads are eventually directed to engage in a conversation without being provided a topic by a therapist. Instead, it is important for dyads to generate their own topics of shared interest and be able to maintain the conversation for at least several minutes.

Finally, since peer group activities often include three or more children, the final training tasks involve extending conversational exercises to three or more children. The same training sequence is usually required: Therapists should begin with highly structured topics that are provided to children beforehand, and gradually move toward more naturalistic conditions in which triads or larger groups are required to generate their own conversational topics. Although coaching and feedback continues to be provided, therapists should begin to fade their prompts and provide feedback on a less immediate basis.

Sessions 8–10: Conflict Resolution and Problem Solving

It has long been observed that socially incompetent children, particularly those who tend to be aggressive and impulsive, are poorer at solving problems than are socially competent children. More specifically, children who have problems with their social relationships tend to think of fewer solutions to problems, fail to accurately anticipate the consequences to their actions, and articulate less sophisticated and sequential plans for implementing solutions to these problems. Poor problem-solving abilities and impulsive responses to social conflicts often characterize the social behavior of ADHD children.

Background and Description

Social problem solving is considered a cognitive-behavioral skill that involves a careful and reflective style of thinking about and responding to problems and conflicts. This part of the program borrows heavily from the early work of George Spivack and Myrna Shure (1974), and from the programmatic research of Philip Kendall (Kendall & Braswell, 1984) and John Lochman (Lochman & Curry, 1986) and their colleagues, using cognitive-behavioral treatment procedures with impulsive and aggressive preadolescents. It has been our experience that these cognitive-behavioral skills are not, in and of themselves, sufficient to alter actual social behavior. What they do provide is a systematic and reflective approach to considering behavioral alternatives—an approach that is often lacking in ADHD children. Moreover, this problem-solving approach is carried into future sessions, where we introduce anger control training.

Although different models of social problem solving exist, most have in common the following steps: (1) problem identification—accurately identifying the nature of the problem and formulating a goal: (2) alternative thinking—the ability to generate multiple potential solutions when faced with a interpersonal conflict; (3) consequential thinking—the ability to foresee immediate and longer-term consequences of a particular action; and (4) means-ends thinking—the ability to plan a series of specific actions to attain a goal while recognizing potential obstacles. The main objective of problem-solving training is to encourage a reflective style of thinking with the goal of increasing social behavior likely to result in favorable consequences, both short- and long-term.

Overview

We include several sessions of problem-solving skills training in our social skills program for ADHD children with an emphasis on solving social problems and conflicts. Before beginning problem-solving training, therapists should prepare a large number of vignettes and scenarios containing common social conflict situations by writing them on index cards. Examples of problem vignettes are provided in Table 16.3.

Initially, the vignettes are developed by the therapists. Later, group members should be encouraged to raise actual conflicts that they have experienced with their peers. Each of the steps of problem solving should be posted on a sign. The actual steps are taught through extensive use of cognitive modeling. Because problem solving is primarily a set of cognitive skills, therapists must rely on, and actively encourage, overt self-statements to model the reflective thinking process. Problem-solving self-statements might include "What is the problem that I have to solve"?, "I have to stop and think of as many solutions as I can," and "What would probably happen if I decided to do that?" Therapists should use an active dialogue of these self-statements to illustrate

TABLE 16.3. Example Vignettes Used in Problem-Solving Training

"You just came in from recess. It is very hot outside and you're thirsty. There is a long line of other kids waiting to get a drink at the water fountain. You have waited in line for several minutes. Just as it's your turn to get a drink, another boy in your class cuts in front of you."

"A few of the other kids you sometimes hang around with call you over. There are no adults around, and one of the teachers left a stopwatch on the desk. The other boys ask you to get it for them. When you refuse, they dare you and call you 'chicken.' They tell you that if you don't get it for them no one will hang around with you any more."

"You come to school one day after getting a haircut. Another boy in your class starts to laugh at you and make fun of the way your hair looks. Soon he has got other kids teasing you and calling you names."

"You have just finished working on a math assignment and you finished all of the problems. As you walk up to your teacher's desk to show him the work you have completed, another boy bumps into you and your math paper is torn."

"Five boys are playing basketball. You would like to play too. You only know one of the boys, and you're not sure whether they will let you join in."

"While you are sitting in your classroom, your teacher has to leave the room for a minute. She tells your class that none of you are to leave your seats and that if you do you will not be able to go out for recess. Although you did not leave your seat, another boy in your class tells the teacher that you did when she returns."

---

the steps involved in the process, as well as the reflective approach to solving the problem.

Initially, therapists may wish to read a problem vignette like those shown in Table 16.3 and model each of the problem-solving steps, verbalizing aloud problem-solving self-statements. Participants should then discuss the rationale and potential benefits of using such a problem-solving approach and the negative consequences associated with not thinking ahead. This discussion should highlight the problem associated with impulsive decision making in terms of immediate and long-range consequences. Particular emphasis is given to how various decisions influence peer relationships and friendships. Participants are then encouraged to practice using problem-solving steps as a group. One child might be called upon to randomly select and read an index card containing a problem vignette. A therapist then leads the group through each of the problem-solving steps by having group members define the problem, generate alternatives, discuss potential consequences, and plan a course of action. It will be necessary to use a blackboard to write down each of the solutions generated by the group.

Early on, it is probably best to allow any and all solutions so as to encourage creative brainstorming. It is therefore necessary to expect inappropriate, unrealistic, and/or aggressive solutions to be generated during alternative thinking exercises. This will lead into consequential thinking exercises where the potential consequences of the various solutions are reviewed. In situations where participants are poor at foreseeing or anticipating realistic consequences, therapists will need to correct misconceptions or distortions by pointing to what actually occurs in participants' daily lives. Very soon after beginning problem-solving training, generating aggressive or grossly inappropriate solutions should be discouraged, while realistic or prosocial solutions alone are encouraged. There has been recent evidence that the quality of solutions children are able to generate is a more critical predictor of social adjustment than is the quantity of solutions generated.

Soon after group members have begun to show some level of acquisition of the problem-solving steps and process, didactic teaching methods should be augmented with active role-playing and perhaps videotaping as a means of making these cognitive skills more concrete and less conceptual. Problem vignettes may be acted out by having participants play different roles in a conflict situation. For example, one child may be told that he or she needs to go to a table and draw a picture. When that child arrives at the table, there is only one crayon, and it is being used by another child. The child (as well as other group members) is again guided through each of the problem-solving steps, including the development of a sequential plan and a backup plan prior to attempts at acting out the chosen solution.

Sessions 10–14: Anger Control Training

Many (if not the majority of) ADHD children display problems with aggression and emotional control, which are probably contributing factors to poor peer relationships. Our clinical experience has suggested that not only are they often shunned by other children because of their high rate of disruptive or annoying behavior, but many of these children may become the butt of scapegoating, teasing, and provocations. This in turn may result in anger-induced retaliatory action on the part of the ADHD children, such as verbally or physically aggressive behavior, which may in turn contribute to the cycle of peer rejection.

Background and Description

With this unfortunate social cycle of peer conflicts in mind, Stephen Hinshaw, Barbara Henker, and Carol Whalen (1984a) have developed an anger control training program for ADHD boys, using principles and procedures derived from cognitive-behavioral therapy, and more particularly from stress inoculation procedures. In stress inoculation, an individual (1) learns to identify external events (e.g., being teased) and internal events (e.g., thoughts, muscle tension) associated with emotional arousal; (2) is armed with a variety of coping skills to use in the presence of the stressful event; and (3) actively practices using the coping skills while being exposed to controlled levels or degrees of stress. Several empirical investigations of Hinshaw et al.'s anger control training program have produced positive results.

We have incorporated portions of this anger control training in the social skills program, devoting anywhere from three to six sessions to teaching the cognitive-behavioral strategies. In the Hinshaw et al. program, anger control training is preceded by general cognitive-behavioral training in problem solving and self-instruction. The social skills training model described here is comparable; problem-solving skills will have been covered in previous sessions. These strategies set the stage for the self-control approach used in anger control—namely, an emphasis on "stopping and thinking" before acting and the use of a reflective sequence for approaching conflicts. A second critical reason for having a number of more general social skills and cognitive-behavioral training sessions prior to introducing anger control is the need to have developed rapport between therapists and group members, a trusting atmosphere within the group, and a well-defined behavior management system. This is necessary, in part, because realistic anger-inducing provocation exercises are used for the purpose of practicing anger self-control.

For this reason, anger control training with young aggressive children is a sensitive undertaking requiring sufficiently trained therapists and a well-controlled environment. Some investigators have questioned whether some of the exercises employed, in fact, justify teasing or whether they further scapegoat rejected children. Therapists will need to carefully judge the clinical utility, and potential side effects, of these exercises before proceeding. Moreover, unless group members are confident that the therapists can maintain control, these exercises will be highly artificial and void of the intense affect that occurs in real life, which may be necessary for learning and mastering anger control skills. Therapists are therefore advised to introduce anger control training in the later stages of the social skills program, after some of these aforementioned prerequisite issues have fallen into place.

Overview

In the initial session of anger control training, participants are oriented to the general nature of anger. In particular, we (1) discuss common external signs of anger; (2) begin to identify internal (cognitive, effective, physiological) events associated with anger; and (3) think about potential or common consequences to becoming angry. Participants are asked to discuss incidents and situations that often evoke anger. Each group member is asked to volunteer one real-life experience in which he or she became angry and perhaps acted on this anger. We find that the participants usually begin by describing incidents that involve interactions with parents and siblings. It is therefore necessary to ask directly, "What are some things that make you angry at school or at other kids?" Routinely, incidents involving teasing, name calling, or physical provocations are mentioned, and each of these is written by a therapist on a blackboard.

The group members are then asked to imagine what happens to them when they are extremely angered. Therapists should try to highlight several characteristic responses involving thoughts, affect, and physiological reactions (e.g., muscles get tight, face turns red). The more familiar members become with these symptoms of anger, the more likely it is that they will be able to use coping skills quickly enough to prevent a loss of control. Finally, the therapists will want to turn to a discussion of the consequences of anger. It is usually best to begin by having participants describe what usually happens to them when angered, both in terms of their own behavioral reactions (e.g., "I threw everything off my desk") and the subsequent reactions of others (e.g., "I got into trouble," "They kept on teasing me"). It is crucial to point out both short-term and common long-term consequences of frequent anger episodes; group members are not likely to be fully aware of some of the latter. For example, while short-term consequences of anger (e.g., hitting in response to name calling) may successfully terminate the provocation of another child, the longer-term consequences may include increased risk for peer rejection, punitive responses of adult authority figures, and less opportunity to encounter positive social reinforcement for prosocial behavior.

After a thorough introduction to anger, the remainder of the sessions are devoted to learning and practicing coping skills and prosocial alternatives to anger-induced behavior. As mentioned, this involves not only direct instruction and discussion, but also active practice while being exposed to anger-inducing situations. Participants are told that they are going to begin to learn how to use self-control when they are angry by learning a variety of coping behaviors. Each group member is asked to identify peer-related provocations that personally evoke anger or arousal. Therapists will want to ask for volunteers who will share names, phrases, or types of teasing that really "get to them." Again, these should be written down on a blackboard. The therapists should explain that the reason for doing this is that the group members will later practice calling one another these names, so that each one can begin to learn some ways of showing and practicing self-control.

It is not uncommon for several group members to be reluctant about sharing the most derogatory names or insults leveled against them by peers, particularly when they involve attention to some physical flaw (e.g., overweight, short stature). There are several ways of handling this. First, it may be sufficient to rely on peer and therapist modeling to encourage the sharing of information by an initially reluctant group member. Second, the group should be reminded that they must not use these names against other group members in later sessions or outside of sessions because this would be a violation of group trust. Third, the therapists may want to suggest some common derogatory names and assess whether or not they would be anger-evoking enough to use in training coping skills.

Before teasing exercises are formally introduced, it will be necessary to spend an entire session or more practicing coping skills. Five general steps are practiced during coping skills training: (1) considering behavioral alternatives when angry; (2) identifying internal cues associated with anger; (3) using coping self-statements to control anger; (4) having a specific plan or plans for responding to anger-inducing provocations; and (5) developing a backup plan if one becomes too angry despite having a specific plan.

The first coping skill employs problem solving. Social problem-solving skills, of course, have been covered in previous sessions; the basic steps involved in problem solving should be reviewed. Then the group can be asked to list a number of potential courses of action when one is being teased or called names; all the answers are written on a blackboard. The group next is asked to evaluate each potential solution on the basis of immediate and longer-term consequences. Therapists are cautioned against persuading participants away from any retaliatory course of action (e.g., "Calling him names back"), as it may be appropriate to retaliate in some instances. The goal is to elucidate options so that alternatives to "fighting back" or losing control of one's temper may become more salient. Each participant should begin to generate a list of possible alternatives to use when angered.

The second coping skill is becoming more sensitive to internal cues of anger. Since this has been covered during the initial introductory sessions of anger control training, it will be sufficient to review common cognitive, affective, and physiological responses to anger. For most participants, it will be much easier to reflect on their internal anger cues once active anger-inducing exercises are begun. Coping self-statements (also introduced in a previous session), the third skill, are again discussed, and participants are asked to think about statements they could say to themselves that might help them control their anger. Therapists should be prepared to model a variety of statements during role plays with each other (assuming that two therapists are available). For example, while one therapist directs derogatory statements at the other (e.g., "You don't know how to play soccer to save your life," "You're the worst player on the team"), the target therapist should verbalize out loud self-statements that both reflect his or her internal state (e.g., "He's really starting to get to me," "I can feel my heart beating faster") and attempts to control the anger (e.g., "I have to relax," "I'm just going to ignore him").

For some children, it is necessary to provide visual imagery strategies (in addition to self-statements) to be used during coping. Arthur Robin and colleagues (Robin, Schneider, & Dolnick, 1976) have developed the "turtle technique" to help young emotionally disturbed and hyperactive children control anger. Children are taught to play "turtle" when angered by "going into their shell" and protecting themselves from verbal assaults. Relaxation training procedures are taught in conjunction with visual imagery. Depending on the age of group members, therapists may wish to include a relaxation training session and provide visual imagery techniques as part of coping skills training.

Next, participants will need to select between one and three plans for responding to provocations. Specific plans may include such strategies as ignoring, counting to 10, looking out the window, thinking about something else, or walking away. Each participant will need to select plans that he or she feels will be personally appropriate. Finally, each member is also asked to select a "backup" plan to be used if the first plan does not seem to be working. It is important to point out to participants that their self-control plans are not going to terminate the teasing and name calling. Instead, their goals should be to learn to tolerate the teasing and control their anger until the entire teasing session is over. It might also be pointed out that, in real life, other children may reduce their teasing or other provocation once they discover that it no longer elicits an angry response.

Prior to beginning the teasing or provocation exercises, each group member should be able to state (1) a self-control plan (i.e., the behavioral strategy to use in the provocation); (2) a number of coping self-statements he or she will use to control anger; and (3) a backup plan. After each of the coping skills is discussed and extensively modeled by the therapists, it is time to begin introducing teasing exercises so that participants may practice and refine coping skills while being exposed to anger-inducing situations. Initially, this will involve one group member playing the role of the teaser and another playing the role of the one being teased. At a later time, this exercise will be expanded into the "teasing circle," where three or four members of the group stand in a circle around another group member and use names and derogatory comments that were previously determined to elicit anger. Participants are told that it will only be a game, and that group members do not really mean the words but are giving practice using self-control to each other.

The goal is to make the teasing exercises stressful but not ruthless. As a rule, there should be as little adult intervention as possible. Two exceptions to this rule are (1) if an individual child becomes too upset or tearful (something that we have not had happen in any of the numerous groups we have run) or (2) if any acts of physical aggression occur. Participants are informed that they should try to get the target child upset but that no touching, spitting, kicking, or throwing items is allowed. The same prohibitions with respect to physical aggression apply to the child being teased. Generally speaking, teasing sessions should go on for approximately 1 minute, giving the child being teased ample time to experience stress and practice coping skills. Each child should have several opportunities to be teased in dyadic interactions before participating in the group "teasing circle," as this is likely to be considerably more stressful.

Therapists should allow both participants in each dyad several minutes to prepare for their role, such as reviewing coping strategies on the part of the child being teased and reviewing derogatory names on the part of the teaser. Thirty seconds of teasing is usually sufficient during the dyadic teasing exercises, and name calling and teasing by other group members are discouraged. The therapists may have to join in on the teasing to establish the tone and the intensity of the taunting. This is usually less necessary during the "teasing circle" exercise, which lasts 1 minute and involves several or all group members.

We have found videotaping especially instructive during teasing exercises, because it may be difficult if not impossible to give direct feedback to participants during these exercises. When the 1-minute exercise is taped, therapists can not only provide feedback to participants about their self-control behaviors, but may also question the child being teased about internal anger cues and the use of covert self-statements. For example, participants may be asked to tell how they knew that they were beginning to get upset or angry, or to describe what they were thinking or saying to themselves at various points in the exercise. Such feedback sessions may begin to enhance the participants' awareness of these covert events which, in turn, may assist them in early recognition of emotional arousal.

The same strategies are then applied during the "teasing circle" exercise which involves three to five children forming a circle around the child to be teased and using verbal taunts. Participants are praised enthusiastically by the therapists for using coping skills and controlling anger. Following a teasing exercise, group members are also encouraged to compliment the child being teased for displaying self-control. It is critical to end sessions that involve teasing exercises with low-intensity and pleasurable activities so that participants leave the group with pleasant feelings. We use a brief relaxation exercise to end anger control sessions, reminding participants of their promise never to use the derogatory names against one another after sessions have ended.

GENERALIZATION PROGRAMMING

As noted earlier in this chapter, clinicians involved in social skills training with children cannot sit by and passively expect generalization of skills to the natural environment. Active and extensive generalization programming is an absolute necessity when conducting social skills training, as in the program described above. Generalization-programming strategies can be divided into two categories: within-training strategies and environmental support.

Within-Training Strategies

Within-training strategies are procedures and practices conducted during the course of training to increase the chances of skills being learned and over-learned, such that they begin to be used outside of the training context. Six strategies may be used in training to promote generalization: (1) increasing training length; (2) using real-life scenarios and training vignettes; (3) using multiple exemplars and diverse training experiences; (4) incorporating self-monitoring homework exercises; (5) focusing on relevant and pivotal skills; and (6) having booster sessions. These are described further below.

1. The length of training appears to be a critical factor if meaningful behavior change is desired in clinic-referred children. In our most recent social

skills training efforts, the program is carried out at least once a week for almost an entire school year. Contrast this with more traditional social skills training groups, which would typically run for 8 to 10 sessions. As one might intuitively expect, more is better when it comes to skills training intervention with ADHD children. Longer training allows for ample repetition and mastery of the skills, as well as integration of different skills and increased opportunity for practice and rehearsal.

2. A second strategy involves using training exercises and vignettes that reflect actual social problems and experiences of group participants. Highly hypothetical situations created by adults often hold little relationship to children's actual social experiences. Careful attention to developing real-life scenarios on the basis of participants' reports, as well as the reports of significant others, will help to ensure that training exercises are meaningfully related to children's social experiences.

3. Related to this is the need to use multiple exemplars rather than a narrow range of social situations or social response options in the course of training. The clinical research literature has strongly suggested that the diversity of examples used in training will increase generalization in nontraining settings. When participants are exposed to a narrow or highly focused range of situations, examples, scenarios, or social behaviors, the effects of training tend to be highly focused. Diversity can also be achieved by ascertaining that participants have opportunities to play multiple roles during training exercises and to rehearse social interactions in dyads, small groups, and larger-sized groups.

4. A fourth strategy that we have incorporated in training is the use of self-monitoring by participants. Participants should begin to monitor, record, or in some way describe their actual use of social skills on a regular basis while they are in their natural environments. Self-monitoring strategies "force" participants to actively consider and (we hope) to use a particular social skill outside of the training setting. We have used special Logs that are completed on a daily basis by participants and reviewed at the next session. The Log can be completed by a child at any point in the day that a specific skill is used. The Log that we use is a notebook measuring $8\frac{1}{2}$ by 6 inches, containing questions about whether a particular skill was used, in what context, and how effective it was. Figure 16.1 depicts a page from the Problem-Solving Log, used during the weeks that we teach problem-solving skills.

Stickers are placed on each page that has an entry. Two stickers are awarded when the Log entry is signed by a parent or teacher, verifying the authenticity of the Log entry. For a specified number of stickers, participants can earn small prizes (e.g., McDonald's gift certificates). Although it may be difficult to verify the accuracy of these self-reports, the act of simply completing these Logs appears to enhance participants' consideration and possibly deployment of trained behaviors in nontraining settings.

5. A fifth training strategy, which at the outset seems obvious, is to train relevant skills. The term "relevant" as used here refers to social behaviors

YOUR DAILY PROBLEM-SOLVING LOG

Date: _____

Describe the problem: _____
_____
_____

Did you try to use problem solving?   Yes   No

What solutions did you think about using? _____
_____
_____
_____

What solution did you try? _____
_____

How did it work?

1	2	3	4
Not at all	Just a little bit	Pretty well	Great

Initials _____

FIGURE 16.1. A sample page from the "problem-solving log" used to promote generalization of problem-solving skills.

that are age-appropriate, pivotal (as opposed to incidental) to the child's social adjustment, and likely to be "trapped" by natural reinforcers in the environment. A number of social behaviors that become the focus of social skills interventions, although desirable, may be relatively unimportant in changing social status. Social behaviors such as making appropriate eye contact or saying "thank you" might be viewed as enhancement skills rather than as crucial to the child's peer relations. For this reason, therapists may wish to consider those social behaviors that correlate most strongly with peer acceptance and have the greatest likelihood of evoking reciprocal and reinforcing responses from others. With socially rejected children, some of the more relevant skills include those that are designed to decrease aggressive and disruptive behavior.

6. Booster sessions to promote greater generalization and durability of trained skills should be considered a useful within-training strategy. These booster sessions are of most value when some form of feedback is available to the therapists regarding participants' social accomplishments and social problem areas during the period between sessions. New problems that have arisen as well as previous difficulties can be discussed through group problem solving, and new behavioral strategies can be practiced and rehearsed as needed.

Continued contact with group members also provides them with some degree of accountability for their own progress and accomplishments, possibly enhancing motivation to carry out strategies covered during sessions. Finally, booster sessions serve the purpose of reinforcing a sense of belonging and group cohesiveness, which is obviously weak at best with short-term or terminal groups.

Environmental Support

The second category of generalization programming consists of directly engineering environmental support for the skills and behaviors learned in social skills training. Stated succinctly, if the natural environment does not prompt and reinforce social behaviors practiced within training sessions these behaviors are not likely to occur in nontraining settings or will be short-lived. Although contact and cooperative efforts with parents and school personnel may be somewhat difficult for many clinicians, they are indispensable if generalization is desired.

The three primary goals of this type of environmental programming are to (1) increase appropriate skills through various prompts; (2) develop programs to directly reinforce trained skills in the natural environment and to decelerate negative and/or inappropriate social behavior through sanctions and punishment; and (3) teach children to self-recruit reinforcement for their deployment of targeted social skills. Research has shown that it is insufficient to increase the prosocial behavior of rejected children without also decreasing inappropriate behaviors if status in the peer group is to be changed. Thus, it is critical that negative social behaviors be reduced while more positive interactions are promoted.

Enhancing environmental support requires therapists to communicate, consult with, and actively work with parents and teachers, since the home and school will be the primary breeding grounds for the development, and ultimately the modification, of social behaviors and peer interactions.

1. Probably the most basic environmental support strategy involves making salient the social rules and adaptive skills that have been previously taught in the social skills group. Posters, signs, and cue cards listing social rules and desirable behaviors can be posted at home and in the classroom and reviewed at regular intervals. These strategies help to externalize social rules, and may serve to prompt and remind participants to use skills at home and school that they have learned during social skills training sessions.

2. Although prompts and reminders may set the stage for the use of appropriate social skills, this will most invariably be insufficient. Recall that ADHD children are more contingency-shaped than they are rule-governed. Ultimately, the performance of skills acquired in social skills training will be a direct function of the contingencies established in home and school settings to support the use of these new skill. There are several ways in which to develop this environmental support. First, parents and teachers should be

made aware of the specific session-by-session goals and should be given a description of the particular skills covered during each session. The more detailed the descriptions of these skills the better. We have used a weekly handout for parents and teachers to provide them with this information.

In addition to communicating with parents and teachers about the social skills we cover during each session, an organized and systematic behavior management system (preferably at both home and school) should be established. To achieve this, our social skills training program requires parental involvement. Therapists should consider meeting with parents of group participants as regularly as once a month. Consultation with classroom teachers on a regular basis is also necessary.

A structured contingency management system might include (1) monitoring and recording two pivotal prosocial skills (e.g., sharing) and two maladaptive social behaviors (e.g., aggression); (2) a structured reward system for engaging in the prosocial behaviors being monitored; (3) opportunities for bonuses for "special" behaviors or appropriate social behaviors not specifically monitored; and (4) sanctions, fines, and a specified punishment hierarchy for engaging in maladaptive social behaviors. Such a system needs to be coordinated across home and school settings and to be implemented with the same rigor and consistency as other behavior management programs introduced at home or in the classroom. As with any incentive approach used with ADHD children, careful attention must be paid to the immediacy and salience of reinforcers as well as to the need for periodic rotation of reinforcers to prevent habituation or satiation.

3. Children can be taught to actively recruit adult and peer reinforcement and attention for appropriate social behaviors, particularly those that are currently the focus of training. Unfortunately, negative behaviors such as aggression or disruptiveness are often more conspicuous in rejected children, whereas occurrences of appropriate behavior may go unnoticed by others. To combat this phenomenon, children themselves can be instructed to inform relevant adults (and in some cases, peers) when they have engaged in an appropriate targeted prosocial behavior. Incentives are made available for each case of reporting on such prosocial activity. Initially, it is probably wise for adult behavior change agents to disperse a high rate of reinforcement for such reports, even without strong confirmation of their authenticity. Later, greater attempts can be made to confirm such reports after this strategy has become reasonably well developed in a child's repertoire. Several studies have demonstrated that children can cue adults to attend to and reinforce their appropriate behavior, enhancing the generalization of treatment effects.

STRATEGIC PEER INVOLVEMENT

As previously stated, teaching new social skills and promoting their use in the natural environment frequently do not translate into changes in peer social status. Thus, a child previously rejected by peers who skillfully attempts to initiate an interaction with peers may continue to be rebuffed because of reputational biases, which are well established and extremely difficult to alter. Under such circumstances, prosocial behaviors are likely to be short-lived. It now seems imperative that efforts be directed toward not only changing social behavior, but enhancing social status within the peer group.

This is clearly a difficult task, and one that therapists working out of clinic settings may have limited control over. Nonetheless, the clinical impact of social skills training with rejected children may be minimal if actual peer relationships are not altered. Four strategies for addressing peer involvement are (1) peer involvement in training, (2) improved general classroom behavior, (3) use of peer tutors, and (4) home-based friendship building. These are described below.

1. Karen Bierman and her colleagues (Bierman & Furman, 1984) have provided encouraging findings related to altering peer social status. The main strategy responsible for social status changes in these investigations was incorporating peers into the training exercises. It has long been noted that group cooperative efforts, under the structured guidance of adults, can result in children getting along better and liking each other more. This is in direct contrast to what is traditionally done in clinic social skills training programs where children are recruited from various neighborhoods and school systems as strangers and have no contact outside of the training program. In other words, children are rarely trained with their actual peer group. Perhaps the most straightforward solution to this problem is to develop school-based social skills training or to recruit and accept referrals for a group from a single classroom or grade level at a particular school. Although this may be logistically inconvenient, the promising outcomes of such a training program seem to warrant serious consideration.

2. A second strategy that may have a positive impact on peer perceptions of rejected children is to include interventions that, in addition to skill training, attempt to modify problematic and disruptive classroom behavior. Recall that behavioral correlates of peer rejection include general inappropriate behavior and not simply problematic peer interactions. Many ADHD children will display disruptive or bothersome behavior in the classroom. Failure to attend to this dimension of problem behavior may seriously compromise social skills training efforts (see Chapter 15).

3. The use of peer tutors has been widespread in educational interventions, usually resulting in benefits for both the tutors and the children receiving tutoring. Recently, we have begun to train socially competent children to work with their socially rejected peers. The goal of these efforts is simply to get the tutor to reintegrate the rejected child into the larger peer group's activities, not to "force" the tutor to become friends with the rejected child. Strategies basically consist of teaching tutors to initiate interactions with rejected children and incorporate them into activities of the larger peer group. Needless to say, such efforts need to be carried out with extreme clinical

sensitivity and considerable adult supervision. When combined with social skills training and behavior management procedures, our initial attempts at this type of adjunctive intervention appear to have been successful.

4. Most clinicians at one time or another have probably recommended to parents of rejected or friendless children that they involve their children in community group activities such as Boy or Girl Scouts or sport teams in attempts to foster their social competence. Unfortunately, many rejected children will quickly re-establish their social status within these large community groups, thus experiencing further rejection. It now seems more judicious to recommend peer involvement in the context of (1) small-group, highly structured peer activities, (2) activities under the supervision of adults, and (3) noncompetitive activities.

For example, after children have participated in our social skills program, we may encourage their parents to seek peer contact for the children through community programs that offer a low to intermediate difficulty level in which to interact or share activities successfully with other children. Sport teams or other large groups usually provide somewhat unstructured and competitive activities with a moderate level of difficulty for successfully adjusting to group norms. Instead, structured children's programs such as arts-and-crafts activities and swimming lessons, or dyadic contacts arranged by parents, are usually preferable.

With respect to the latter, parents might encourage a child to invite a single peer over to watch a special video movie, and might provide desirable snacks for the children. While such peer contact is not likely to be highly interactive (and may be similar to a parallel play activity engaged in by younger children), it at least gives the rejected child the opportunity to share pleasant contact with a same-age child. This is clearly not a solution to altering social skills deficits. Nonetheless, helping these children to develop at least one close dyadic friendship in which nonconflictual social interactions can be engaged in may be the best therapy of all.

CONCLUSIONS

ADHD children are at high risk for peer rejection. This appears to be due to their tendency to display a relatively high rate of immature, bothersome, or even aggressive behavior while also showing problems in their social maturation, particularly with respect to prosocial skills. In addition, many of these children display negative behavior outside of peer interactions, such as disruptive classroom behavior, that further estranges them from their peer group. These early problems with peer relations frequently result in low self-esteem, loneliness, and even depression in the rejected children. Moreover, the risk for maladjustment in later life appears to be significantly increased by poor childhood social relations.

In this chapter, I have described a three-stage social skills intervention program designed for socially rejected ADHD preadolescents: (1) training in social entry, conversational, conflict resolution, and anger control skills; (2) generalization programming; and (3) strategic peer involvement. It is argued that short-term skills training approaches alone, without consideration for the generalization of these skills to the natural environment or active efforts to promote changes in peer status, are likely to be of little benefit. Longer-term multifaceted programs, using natural therapeutic sources and behavior change agents (e.g., parents, peers), are indispensable to creating meaningful behavior change.

17

Medication Therapy

GEORGE J. DUPAUL and RUSSELL A. BARKLEY

> The command of one's self is the greatest empire a man
> can aspire unto, and consequently, to be subject to our
> own passions is the most grievous slavery. He who best
> governs himself is best fitted to govern others.
>
> —FRANCIS BACON (1561–1626)

Psychostimulant medication is the most common treatment for children with Attention-deficit Hyperactivity Disorder (ADHD). More children receive medication (primarily Ritalin or its generic form, methylphenidate) to manage ADHD than any other childhood disorder—over 600,000 children annually, or between 1% and 2% of the school-age population (Safer & Krager, 1983). In the past, the majority of these children were between 6 and 10 years of age; however, more recently, there has been a significant increase in the prescription of these medications for teenagers with ADHD (Safer & Krager, 1988). More research has been conducted on the effects of stimulant medications on the functioning of children with ADHD than any other treatment modality for any childhood disorder. Numerous studies have clearly demonstrated medication-induced, short-term enhancement of the behavioral, academic, and social functioning of the majority of children being treated. Alternatively, the use of psychotropic drugs with this population continues to be controversial given their behavior-modifying properties and associated side effects.

Despite the widespread use of stimulant medications and our extensive knowledge base regarding assessment of their effects, they are all too frequently improperly prescribed and monitored by practicing clinicians. For example, Gerald Solomons (1973) reported in a study conducted at the University of Iowa Hospitals that only 55% of the ADHD children receiving stimulants were "adequately" monitored—the minimal criterion for "adequacy" being merely two telephone contacts between family and physician in a 6-month period. Although this situation has certainly improved, Ken Gadow (1981) surveyed a large sample of pediatricians and found that surprisingly few of them employed even the most rudimentary objective measures (e.g., teacher rating scales) in monitoring drug response. Many states have now passed legislation requiring that prescriptions for stimulants such as Ritalin and Dexedrine only be written for a 1-month supply and that each prescription be renewed in writing. These regulations have indirectly compelled monthly contacts between physicians and families, so that the probability of a regular review of children's drug responding and possible side effects is presumably increased.

Many special-interest groups, such as the Church of Scientology and its Citizens Commission on Human Rights, have tried to capitalize on the inadequacies of prescription and monitoring of stimulant medications, in an effort to influence public opinion against the use of this treatment with ADHD children (see Chapter 1 for a discussion). In contrast, as this chapter highlights, many medications have been found to be significantly effective in the management of ADHD and associated behavior problems. When used properly, they are beneficial to many of these children and are certainly more cost-effective than their psychoeducational alternatives. Nevertheless, they are not a panacea for treating ADHD, nor should they be the sole form of therapy for these children. It is our position that one of the greatest benefits of stimulant therapy is the possibility that it will maximize the effects of concurrently applied treatments (e.g., behavior modification, academic tutoring). Furthermore, as the previous chapters have shown, children with ADHD exhibit a plethora of physical, cognitive, academic, behavioral, and social difficulties, and it would be ludicrous to assume that medication alone will manage these myriad problems effectively. It is the purpose of this chapter to summarize the research findings on the use of psychotropic medications in treating ADHD and to suggest guidelines for their clinical use. We primarily discuss the central nervous system (CNS) stimulants as these are the most commonly employed and widely investigated class of medications for this population; however, the use of alternative medications is also briefly surveyed. This chapter is not intended as a review of the research literature as many excellent publications are available on this topic.

HISTORY OF STIMULANT MEDICATION USE
WITH CHILDREN

The first reported use of stimulant drugs with behavior problem children is typically credited to Charles Bradley (1937), although, in an earlier issue of another journal, there is a report by Matthew Molitch and August Eccles (1937) on the use of psychostimulants with a similar group of children. Bradley employed amphetamine (Benzedrine) with children on an inpatient residential care ward and noted dramatic improvement in their conduct and school performance. There were few further studies of stimulant medication use with children until the late 1950s and early 1960s, when Bradley's work seems to have been rediscovered by clinicians. This increase in drug use at this time was probably associated with the discovery, marketing, and widespread use of phenothiazines with adults, as well as with the release of methylphenidate for commercial use in 1957.

The use of these drugs with ADHD children was given impetus by the positive reports of Eisenberg (1966), Laufer, Denhoff, and Solomons (1957), and later Conners (1966) on the efficacy of these compounds in improving children's behavior as measured through parent and teacher opinion and rating scales. Given these positive reports and the lack of information on possible long-term deleterious effects, the use of these medications increased to such an extent that over 150,000 children were taking them for behavior management by 1970. At this point, a major controversy developed over a report in the *Washington Post* (Maynard, 1970) stating that 5% to 10% of the children in the Omaha, Nebraska school system were being given stimulants to control their classroom behavior. The report was erroneous; however, it prompted a congressional investigation that served indirectly to spawn numerous scientific investigations into the specific effects of stimulants on various measures of cognitive, academic, and behavioral functioning in children. Although these investigations revealed many positive effects of pharmacotherapy, they also highlighted possible short- and long-term side effects about which clinicians should be concerned.

Today, despite several highly critical books and articles appearing in the lay literature (see Chapter 1), the use of stimulant medication is increasing and is seen by many as the treatment of choice for ADHD. Among the stimulants, Ritalin is by far the most widely prescribed, representing over 90% of the stimulant medication market. Its popularity increased further with the introduction of Ritalin-SR in the early 1980s, thereby providing a sustained-release alternative with a longer duration of therapeutic effect. Since publication of the first edition of this book (Barkley, 1981), the number of research investigations on the various effects of these medications has virtually doubled. The literature is voluminous with respect to the short-term effects of these medications; however, distressingly few well-controlled studies have been conducted regarding their long-term efficacy. Of course, the same state of affairs exists for our knowledge regarding alternative treatment modalities (e.g., behavioral, educational). Overall, the class of stimulant medications continues to be the most commonly employed treatment for ADHD.

PHARMACOLOGICAL ASPECTS
OF STIMULANT MEDICATIONS

Psychostimulant medications are so named because of their ability to increase the arousal or alertness of the CNS. Given their structural similarity to certain brain neurotransmitters, they are considered sympathomimetic compounds. The three most commonly employed CNS stimulants are *d*-amphetamine (Dexedrine), methylphenidate (Ritalin), and pemoline (Cylert). Other stimulant compounds (e.g., caffeine, deanol) are not discussed here given that they have not been found to be as effective as the CNS stimulants and are not typically used clinically.

The primary mode of action of *d*-amphetamine is believed to be that of enhancing catecholamine activity in the CNS, probably by increasing the availability of norepinephrine and/or dopamine at the synaptic cleft, although this remains a matter of some debate. Methylphenidate is a piperidine derivative with structural and pharmacological properties similar to *d*-amphetamine, although its specific mode of action is less clearly understood. It may be that methylphenidate has a greater effect on dopamine activity than on other neurotransmitters, but this remains speculative at this time. Pemoline is similar in function to the other CNS stimulants, though it has minimal sympathomimetic effects and is structurally dissimilar. The specific mechanism of action of pemoline is not understood at this time. For all of these medications, the actual locus of action within the CNS remains speculative with some suggesting that brain stem activation is the primary locus, while others postulate midbrain or frontal cortex involvement. More recent studies of cerebral blood flow have shown that activity in the area of the striatum and the connections between the orbital-frontal and limbic regions is enhanced during stimulant medication treatment (Lou, Henriksen, & Bruhn, 1984; Lou, Henriksen, Bruhn, Borner, & Nielsen, 1989). Further research regarding these parameters is certainly necessary.

All of the psychostimulants are easily taken orally, are rapidly absorbed from the gastrointestinal tract, and cross the blood-brain barrier easily. *D*-amphetamine achieves peak plasma levels in children within 2 to 3 hours, with a plasma half-life between 4 and 6 hours (with substantial interindividual variability). The behavioral effects of this compound appear to peak between 1 and 2 hours postingestion and to dissipate within 4 to 5 hours. About 30% to 50% of the drug is excreted unchanged. Methylphenidate has a plasma half-life of between 2 and 3 hours and is entirely metabolized within 12 hours, with almost none of the drug appearing in the urine. As with *d*-amphetamine, the peak behavioral effects occur within 1 to 2 hours and are dissipated within $3\frac{1}{2}$ to 5 hours after oral ingestion. The plasma half-life of sustained release methylphenidate has been found to range between 2 and 6 hours, with a peak plasma level reached within 1 to 4 hours. Behavioral effects of this preparation appear to peak within about 3 hours, with continued efficacy until 8 hours postingestion. Considerable interindividual variability exists with respect to these parameters, however. Pemoline appears to have a shorter half-life with children (i.e., 7 to 8 hours) than with adults (i.e., 11 to 13 hours) and reaches peak plasma levels 1 to 4 hours postingestion. Within 24 hours, 75% of the dose seems to be excreted in the urine. The time-response characteristics of its behavioral effects have not been well documented.

CLINICAL EFFECTS: SHORT-TERM

There are many excellent scientific reviews of the clinical effects of stimulant medications on children with ADHD, some of which are listed in the reference section. It is not our intention to review research studies in detail or to debate their methodological weaknesses. As noted earlier, there is a voluminous research literature in this area; however, many of the studies contain one flaw or another in their definitions of ADHD, procedures, experimental designs, dependent measures, and data analyses. Nonetheless, the general trends in these studies can be mentioned here and their implications for clinical practice assessed.

In a comprehensive review of the literature conducted some years ago (Barkley, 1977b), it was concluded that the stimulant medications as a group led to an average improvement rate of between 73% and 77% among patients treated. In addition, several studies reported improvement rates in the range of 39% for placebo effects. Clearly, stimulant drugs are judged by parents, teachers, and physicians to produce effects on behavior much greater than the effects of placebos. Alternatively, a notable minority of treated children (i.e., between 23% and 27%) evidenced no change or iatrogenic effects. Thus, it should not be automatically assumed that all ADHD children respond positively or in the same manner to these medications. These results should be clarified by the fact that, in most cases, the measures of "improvement" were solely the opinions of those who worked with the children; few if any objective measures were employed to support the impressions. Since that time, more objective data have been gathered with regard to the short-term effects of these medications across a number of specific areas, as summarized below.

Physiological/Psychophysiological Effects

Minimal research has been conducted on the physiological or metabolic effects of stimulants with ADHD children. The earlier studies in this area have been thoroughly reviewed in a paper by Hastings and Barkley (1978). What has been done suggests that amphetamines may decrease growth hormone, at least temporarily, while methylphenidate may increase growth hormone. Amphetamines may also increase the amount of free fatty acid in plasma. There is so little research in this area that these suggestions must remain speculative until they can be further tested and replicated.

Many more studies have evaluated the effects of CNS stimulants on various psychophysiological measures, but many of these results are inconclusive (See Hastings & Barkley, 1978; Rosenthal & Allen, 1978 for reviews). Heart rate, as well as systolic and diastolic blood pressure, may be increased by these medications; however, these effects appear to be moderated by a number of factors. For instance, higher dosages of stimulants are linearly related to increasing levels of heart rate, and these effects are dependent upon both the initial (i.e., premedication) heart rate and the time course of the medication. Changes in cardiovascular functioning are considered mild and are probably outweighed by other daily physiological stresses (e.g., digestion). Heart rate variability is reduced by methylphenidate, as is heart rate deceleration to a reaction time task. The latter result is consistent with changes in cognitive functions such as attention span and concentration. In all studies, cardiovascular effects of stimulants are subject to a great deal of interindividual variability, thus compromising any conclusions based on group-level data.

The stimulants appear to heighten the background electrical activity of the CNS and to increase its sensitivity to stimulation, as measured in studies using electroencephalograms (EEGs) and auditory and visual evoked potentials (Cantwell & Carlson, 1978). These findings may be loosely construed as suggesting that the stimulants heighten excitatory brain mechanisms, while enhancing those responsible for inhibition. This probably results in the improvements in concentration, motor coordination, and impulse control often obtained with these drugs. No evidence exists to suggest that these medications have any significant effects on various aspects of sleep other than the fact that they may produce mild insomnia, as discussed later.

Cognitive Effects

There have been numerous studies of the effects of stimulants on measures of intellect, memory, vigilance, attention, concentration, and learning (See Barkley, 1977b; Gadow, 1985). A plethora of studies have found that these drugs enhance performance on measures of vigilance, impulse control, fine-motor coordination, and reaction time. Furthermore, positive drug effects have been obtained on measures of short-term memory and learning of paired verbal or nonverbal material (Swanson & Kinsbourne, 1979). Performance on both simple and complex learning paradigms appears to be enhanced. In addition, the results of recent investigations have indicated stimulant-related improvements in perceptual efficiency and speed of symbolic or verbal retrieval (both short- and long-term) (Rapport & Kelly, in press). Alternatively, changes in functioning on more traditional measures of cognitive abilities (e.g., intelligence tests) have not been found. Of course, the latter instruments may not be sensitive enough to detect short-term enhancement of cognitive functioning. In general, obtained drug effects on these various tasks are particularly salient in situations that require children to restrict their behavior and concentrate on assigned tasks (Gadow, 1986).

Earlier investigations have suggested that CNS stimulants may result in state-dependent learning (Aman & Sprague, 1974). The information children learn while on the medication may not be easily recalled when they are off the medication, or vice versa. These results have not been replicated, however, and appear to be of small magnitude when they do occur. Nevertheless, the earlier investigations in this area have led some to suggest that children with ADHD should remain on medication during weekends, holidays, and summer vacations so that their learning or retention will not be disrupted. Such a conclusion does not appear warranted, given the lack of replicable support for state-dependent learning; decisions regarding dosage schedules are best made on an individual basis, as discussed later.

Effects on Academic Achievement

In a review conducted in the late 1970s (Barkley & Cunningham, 1978), it was concluded that stimulant medication treatment was associated with minimal improvement in academic performance. Of course, the studies conducted up to that time primarily utilized traditional academic achievement tests (e.g., Wide Range Achievement Test), which have been roundly criticized as measures of intervention outcome given their paucity of items at each grade level and resultant insensitivity to changes over the short term. More recent studies conducted by the independent research teams of Virginia Douglas (Douglas, Barr, O'Neill, & Britton, 1986), and Mark Rapport (Rapport, DuPaul, Stoner, & Jones, 1986) have found methylphenidate-induced improvements in academic productivity and accuracy among large samples of children with ADHD. Instead of standardized achievement tests, these investigations employed written tasks assigned by each child's teacher as the measures of academic performance. Such measures not only are more sensitive to treatment-related change, but also presumably possess greater ecological validity than do standardized achievement tests. Although it remains to be seen whether these short-term improvements in academic performance lead to greater scholastic success in the long run, these results would indicate a high probability of such findings if medication dosage is titrated to academic functioning.

Behavioral Effects

There have been many studies of the effects of stimulant medications on various behaviors of children with ADHD (Barkley, 1977b). These drugs have been shown to have positive effects on the ability of such children to sustain attention to assigned tasks and to reduce their task-irrelevant restlessness and motor activity. In an earlier review of the literature (Barkley & Cunningham, 1979b), stimulants were found to significantly reduce a number of types of activity, especially in structured, task-oriented situations. In many cases, attention to assigned classwork is improved to the extent that the children's behavior appears highly similar to that of their "normal" classmates. Problems with aggression, impulsive behavior, noisiness, noncompliance, and disruptiveness have also been shown to improve with these medications.

Treatment with stimulant medications has been found to significantly improve the quality of social interactions between children with ADHD and their parents, teachers, and peers. For example, studies conducted by Barkley and colleagues have consistently shown that stimulants increase children's compliance with parental commands and enhance their responsiveness to the interactions of others (see Chapter 5). Negative and off-task behaviors are also reduced in compliance situations. In turn, parents and teachers reduce their rate of commands and degrees of supervision over these children, while increasing their praise and positive responsiveness to the children's behavior. Furthermore, independent investigations conducted by Charles Cunningham (Cunningham, Siegel, & Offord, 1985) and Carol Whalen (Whalen, Henker, Buhrmester, Hinshaw, Huber, & Laski, 1989) and their colleagues have indicated positive medication effects on the interactions of ADHD children with their peers across a variety of situations, with concomitant improvements in the degree to which such children are accepted by their peers. These medications do not appreciably decrease the frequency of initiations of appropriate interactions but do significantly reduce aggressive behaviors. The aforementioned findings are important, for they demonstrate that stimulant medications not only directly alter the behavior of children with ADHD, but also indirectly affect the behaviors of important adults and peers toward those children. When the latter changes are obtained, they obviously contribute further to a positive drug response in the children.

Effects on Mood and Emotion

Despite the finding that adults generally report elevations in mood and euphoria when taking stimulant medications, these effects are rarely seen in children. In Barkley's (1976) review of the literature, only one paper reporting such effects was found. Judith Rapoport and her colleagues at the National Institute of Mental Health (Rapoport et al., 1978) compared the effects of d-amphetamine on adults and children. Here, again, adults reported feelings of euphoria, while few, if any, of the children reported such emotions. Some children did report feeling "funny," "different," or dizzy. As Rapoport et al. suggest, it may be that actual developmental differences in response to stimulant medication make adults more likely to experience temporary elevations in mood. It is also possible, however, that children are not as adept at labeling their feelings and thus underreport euphoria (e.g., referring to it as feeling "funny").

In contrast, a number of investigations have found that children may experience various negative moods or emotions in reaction to treatment with stimulants. These are discussed under "Side Effects," below. In most cases, these mood changes are reported to occur as the drugs are "washing out" of the body in late morning or late afternoon. Such reactions also appear to be dose-related and are more prevalent among children treated with higher dosages.

CLINICAL EFFECTS: LONG-TERM

As was the case when the first edition of this book was published (Barkley, 1981), few studies employing rigorous methodology have evaluated the long-term efficacy of stimulant managements (see Rapport & Kelly, in press). Those that have examined the issue have generally found negative results. Children with ADHD who had been on drugs but were off at the time of follow-up were not found to differ in any important respect from those who had never received pharmacotherapy. Hence, no enduring effects of up to 5 years of medication treatment were observed in these studies (Hechtman, Weiss, & Perlman, 1984). Many important shortcomings of long-term outcome investigations have been identified and are not specifically reviewed here. Suffice it to say that the enduring effects of these medications await rigorous examination. Furthermore, the chronic and pervasive difficulties associated with ADHD are probably not going to be permanently eradicated by any single treatment, even one with demonstrated short-term efficacy such as stimulant medication.

PREDICTING THE CLINICAL RESPONSES TO STIMULANTS

Over the years, a variety of factors have been proposed to distinguish children with ADHD who will respond favorably to stimulant medications (responders) from those who will not (nonresponders), including psychophysiological factors, neurological variables, familial characteristics, demographic/sociological factors, diagnostic categories, rating scale scores, psychological profiles, and behavioral characteristics. In reviews conducted by Barkley (1976) and Taylor (1983), those behavioral and psychophysiological measures related to attention span were found to be the best and most reliable predictors of improvement during stimulant drug treatment. Such a finding is hardly surprising, given that stimulants have their primary mode of action on attention span. This conclusion is in keeping with related research which has indicated that the behavioral effects of stimulants may be dependent upon the drug-free rate of the behaviors in question (i.e., they may be rate-dependent). In other words, the greater the inattention of children, the better their reaction to medication (i.e., the more pronounced effect on attention span). The statistical magnitude of such rate-dependent effects has been found to exceed what would be predicted simply on the basis of a regression-to-the-mean artifact.

Some studies have also found that the quality of the relationship between parent and child is a good predictor of drug response: the better the mother-child relationship, the greater the response to medication (Barkley & Cunningham, 1980). This is related to the findings reported earlier that for many children, the medication produces positive changes in the behavior of both the children and their mothers. It may be that mothers who are more appreciative and rewarding of these initial positive changes in their children's behavior while on stimulants produce further gains associated with treatment. In support of this, Barkley and Cunningham (1979a) have obtained results indicating that mothers who were more interactive with their children and more rewarding of child compliance prior to pharmacotherapy had children who exhibited greater positive changes in behavior as result of treatment with medication.

One of the more recent studies to investigate possible predictors of stimulant medication response was conducted by Eric Taylor and colleagues in England (see Taylor, 1986a). In addition to the aforementioned attentional variables, they found that higher levels of restless behaviors (e.g., hyperactivity), poor motor coordination, younger age, and the absence of symptoms of overt emotional disorder predicted better stimulant response among a large sample of children with ADHD. This and similar reports (Voelker, Lachar, & Gdowski, 1983) suggest that children who are more anxious or depressed according to parent and/or teacher ratings (e.g., Conners rating scales) have a poorer response to stimulant medications. For clinical purposes, the current evidence would suggest that the younger, more inattentive, uncoordinated, hyperactive, and devoid of anxiety symptoms a child is, the better the child's response to psychostimulant treatment will be.

DOSE EFFECTS OF STIMULANT MEDICATION

Perhaps the most widely known study of the effects of different dosages of methylphenidate on the functioning of ADHD children was carried out by Robert Sprague and Esther Sleator (1976, 1977) at the University of Illinois. They evaluated medication effects at two dose levels (i.e., 0.3 mg/kg and 1.0 mg/kg) on classroom behavior and ability to perform a simple learning task. Classroom behavior was assessed using the Conners Teacher Rating Scale, while learning was measured by a short-term memory task. The difficulty level of the latter was systematically manipulated. The results of this study are displayed in Figure 17.1 and have led to some controversial interpretations. Performance on the memory task peaked at a dose of 0.3 mg/kg, then declined to placebo levels at the highest dose. However, teacher ratings of behavioral improvement did not reach their peak of improvement until the 1.0 mg/kg level. These results were interpreted by the investigators and others to indicate that a dose necessary to improve classroom conduct will prove detrimental to learning. Furthermore, these results imply that, to the extent that physicians rely on parent and teacher report to titrate dosage, we may be overdosing ADHD children if the true goal of treatment is improved classroom learning. Several other interpretations of these results are possible (e.g., teacher ratings are less sensitive to medication effects than are laboratory tasks); however, the conclusions stated here have been the most popular ones.

Recent investigations that have employed a greater variety of dependent measures and wider dose ranges have shown that conclusions based on Sprague and Sleator's initial results may need to be qualified. For example, Mark Rapport and colleagues (Rapport, Jones, DuPaul, Kelly, Gardner, Tucker, & Shea, 1987) evaluated the individual responses of 42 children with ADHD to several doses (i.e., placebo, 5 mg, 10 mg, 15 mg, and 20 mg) of methylphen-

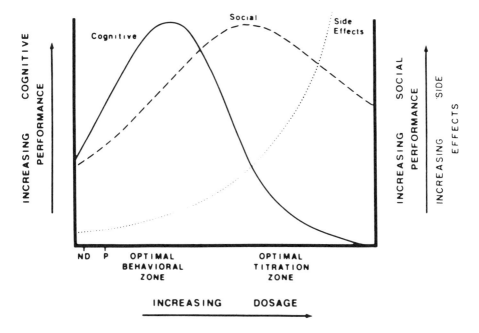

FIGURE 17.1. Theoretical dose-response curves for learning and classroom behavior for methylphenidate. From "Drugs and Dosages: Implications for Learning Disabilities" by R. Sprague and E. Sleator, 1976, in R. Knights and D. Bakker (Eds.), *The Neuropsychology of Learning Disorders*. Baltimore: University Park Press. Copyright 1976 by University Park Press. Reprinted by permission of the authors and publisher.

idate which were administered in a randomly determined sequence. Multiple measures were taken across clinic and classroom settings including performance on a vigilance task, teacher ratings on the ADD-H Comprehensive Teacher Rating Scale (ACTeRS; Ullmann Sleator, & Sprague, 1984a), direct observations of classroom on-task behavior, and efficiency on written academic work (i.e., percentage of work completed correctly or academic efficiency score). At the group level, functioning on all measures was enhanced in a stepwise fashion across doses, reaching a peak at 20 mg. Alternatively, dose-response effects at the individual level were characterized by significant intersubject variability, as shown in Figure 17.2. The response to methylphenidate of individual children could be categorized as follows: (1) improvement related to stepwise increases in dose (Subjects 1 and 2); (2) improvement subject to a "threshold" effect at a moderate (Subject 3) or high (Subject 4) dose; (3) improvement reaching a peak at a moderate dose, with a decrement in performance at higher doses (Subject 5); or (4) improvement inconsistent across doses (Subject 6). These patterns were found to be independent of a child's body weight and to vary across specific measures.

These results, along with those obtained by other research groups, indicate that several factors moderate the dosage effects of methylphenidate and re-

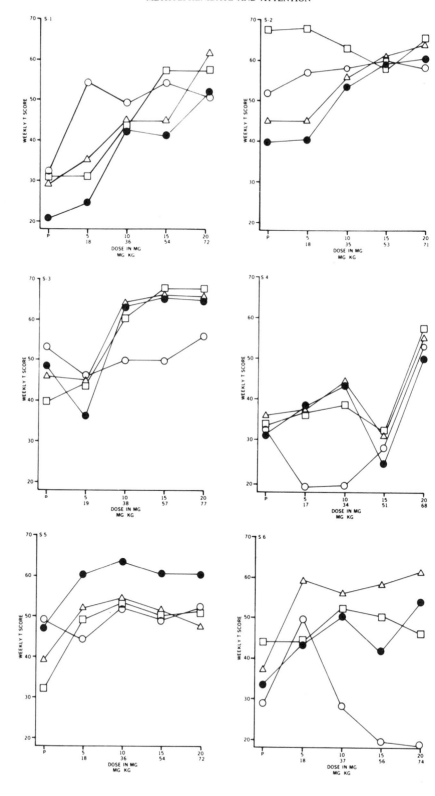

lated medications on the functioning of children with ADHD. First, despite the fact that rather consistent group-level dose-response findings are obtained across studies, these results are highly variable across individual children and must be assessed at the individual level to be clinically useful. Second, dosage effects may vary across areas of functioning, but not necessarily in the systematic fashion suggested by Sprague and Sleator's study. The task specificity of dosage effects also appears to be subject to individual differences. Finally, dosages between 0.3 mg/kg and 1.0 mg/kg have been found to optimize cognitive, academic, and behavioral performance at the group level, thus casting doubt on the notion of low doses being exclusively related to enhancement of learning.

SIDE EFFECTS

A variety of studies have reported on the occurrence of short-term and possible long-term side effects associated with stimulant medication treatment of children with ADHD.

Short-Term Side Effects

In the review of the literature on stimulant medication conducted by Barkley (1977b), 29 studies reported side effects associated with treatment among their subjects. The most common side effects reported were insomnia and decreased appetite, found in 90% and 79% of the studies, respectively. Irritability and weight loss were the next most frequently reported, although they were found in fewer than half of the studies reviewed. Headache and abdominal pain occurred in slightly fewer studies, while the remaining side effects were relatively uncommon. It is worth noting that several of the side effects consisted of negative mood changes (e.g., sadness, proneness to crying, and irritability). As stated previously, adults are more likely to report euphoria, not dysphoria, as a side effect of stimulants.

While the Barkley (1977b) review provides valuable information regarding the prevalence of possible side effects across *studies,* clinicians are typically

← ⎯⎯⎯⎯⎯⎯⎯⎯

FIGURE 17.2. Dose-response curves of the four dependent measures (percentage on task, academic efficiency score, ACTeRS Attention factor score, and continuous-performance test omission errors) for a representative subgroup of six children. Standard (*T*) scores were derived based on the performance of the sample (*n* = 42) aggregated across all conditions (excluding baseline). Improvement on all measures is indicated by an upward movement on the vertical axis. From "Attention Deficit Disorder and Methylphenidate: Group and Single-Subject Analyses of Dose Effects on Attention in Clinic and Classroom Settings" by M. D. Rapport, J. T. Jones, G. J. DuPaul, K. L. Kelly, M. J. Gardner, S. B. Tucker, and M. S. Shea, 1987. *Journal of Clinical Child Psychology, 16*, 329–338. Copyright 1987 by Lawrence Erlbaum Associates, Inc. Reprinted by permission of the first author and publisher.

more interested in the frequency of side effects across *children*. Barkley and colleagues have recently investigated the prevalence of parent- and teacher-reported side effects to two doses (i.e., 0.3 mg/kg and 0.5 mg/kg) of methylphenidate in a sample of 82 children with ADHD (Barkley, McMurray, Edelbrock, & Robbins, in press). The percentages of subjects whose parents indicated the presence of individual side effects are shown in Table 17.1.

TABLE 17.1. Percentage of 82 Subjects Rated by Parents as Displaying Each of 17 Side Effects of Methylphenidate during Each Drug Condition

Side effect	Placebo	Low dose (0.3 mg/kg)	Medium dose (0.5 mg/kg)
Decreased appetite			
Percent	15	52	56
Percent severe	1	7	13
Insomnia			
Percent	40	62	68
Percent severe	7	18	18
Stomachaches			
Percent	18	39	35
Percent severe	0	1	6
Headaches			
Percent	11	26	21
Percent severe	0	1	4
Prone to crying			
Percent	49	59	54
Percent severe	10	16	10
Tics/nervous movements			
Percent	18	18	28
Percent severe	4	7	5
Dizziness			
Percent	4	10	7
Percent severe	0	0	1
Drowsiness			
Percent	18	23	20
Percent severe	1	2	1
Nail biting			
Percent	22	26	29
Percent severe	7	4	9
Talks less			
Percent	16	20	22
Percent severe	1	1	2
Anxiety			
Percent	58	58	52
Percent severe	12	9	7
Uninterested in others			
Percent	18	18	15
Percent severe	0	1	2
Euphoria			
Percent	41	34	43
Percent severe	9	4	7

TABLE 17.1. (*cont.*)

Side effect	Placebo	Low dose (0.3 mg/kg)	Medium dose (0.5 mg/kg)
Irritable			
Percent	72	65	66
Percent severe	18	15	13
Nightmares			
Percent	20	20	21
Percent severe	0	0	3
Sadness			
Percent	43	48	41
Percent severe	5	6	8
Staring			
Percent	40	38	38
Percent severe	2	4	1

Note. "Percent" refers to the percentage of subjects rated 1 or higher in the scale of severity (1 to 9) whereas "percent severe" refers to the percentage of subjects whose severity rating was 7 or higher. From "The Side Effects of Ritalin: A Systematic Placebo Controlled Evaluation of Two Doses" by R. A. Barkley, M. B. McMurray, C. S. Edelbrock, and K. Robbins, in press, *Pediatrics.* Copyright by the American Academy of Pediatrics. Reprinted by permission.

Over half of the sample exhibited decreased appetite, insomnia, anxiousness, irritability, or proneness to crying with both doses of methylphenidate. It should be noted that many of these apparent side effects (especially those associated with mood) were present during the placebo condition and may represent characteristics associated with the disorder rather than its treatment. Also, in most cases the severity of these side effects was quite mild. Stomachaches and headaches were reported in about a third of the subjects, but these were usually of mild severity as well. Thus, clinicians can expect some mild side effects such as insomnia or diminished appetite; however, care should be taken to assess the presence of these during nonmedication conditions, in order to determine their "true" relation to stimulant use.

One side effect that should receive serious attention from clinicians is the possible increase in nervous tics produced by stimulant medications. A number of cases of irreversible Tourette's disorder have also been reported as secondary to stimulant treatment, although these findings are somewhat controversial (Golden, 1974, 1988). Tourette's disorder is a neurological condition comprised of multiple, persistent motor tics and compulsive vocalizations (see Barkley, 1988b). In 60% of the cases, involuntary and compulsive use of obscenities also develops. The disorder typically arises between 4 and 7 years of age; it begins with facial tics and progresses over a period of months or years to tics of the neck, shoulders, arms, trunk, and legs in some cases. This cephalocaudal progression may be somewhat different in each case. Shortly after the initial motor tics develop, repetitive sniffing, throat clearing, coughing, or vocalizations (e.g., guttural sounds, high-pitched noises, barking sounds) may arise. The combination of motor and vocal tics is considered diagnostic although they need not be occurring at the same point in time. It is speculated that the disorder is the result of a hypersensitivity to dopamine within the basal ganglia of the brain. The disorder cannot be cured, but the symptoms can be treated with tranquillizers such as haloperidol (Haldol) or other dopamine antagonists. The disorder typically worsens through adolescence, after which 30% or more of those with the disorder may show improved symptomatology during young adulthood. The rest remain unchanged or show mild worsening of the symptoms. Stress, excitement, anxiety, or the ingestion of stimulant compounds (e.g., caffeine) can temporarily worsen the symptoms.

It has been estimated that fewer than 1% of ADHD children treated with stimulants will develop a tic disorder and that in 13% of the cases stimulants may exacerbate pre-existing tics (Denckla, Bemporad, & MacKay, 1976). While it is not clear whether stimulant medications cause Tourette's disorder in previously unafflicted individuals, these compounds certainly may exacerbate symptoms in patients who already exhibit this disorder. Although the vast majority of such reactions subside once pharmacotherapy is discontinued, a few cases have been reported in the literature where the tics apparently did not diminish in frequency and severity following termination of treatment (Golden, 1988). Therefore, it seems prudent to screen children with ADHD for a personal or family history of tics or Tourette's disorder prior to initiating stimulant therapy, and to proceed cautiously (if at all) with such treatment in those with positive histories. When these medications are used without these risk factors and tics develop, the treatment should be discontinued immediately. Furthermore, the parents should be warned not to have their children treated with stimulants in the future, should they consult other professionals for the children's ADHD.

Another side effect that has been reported, especially for methylphenidate, is a "behavioral rebound" phenomenon. Typically, this is described as a deterioration in behavior (exceeding that which occurs during baseline or placebo conditions) that occurs in the late afternoon and evening following daytime administrations of medication. Charlotte Johnston and colleagues recently (Johnston, Pelham, Hoza, & Sturges, 1988) conducted a rigorous, placebo-controlled study of this apparent phenomenon in a sample of 21 children with ADHD who were treated with two doses (i.e., 0.3 mg/kg and 0.6 mg/kg) of methylphenidate. They found that only about a third of their sample exhibited rebound effects and that the magnitude of these varied considerably across days for individual children. Thus, this phenomenon is not as widespread as believed (once certain biases are controlled for) and even when it does occur, its magnitude across days is highly variable. When we observe such effects occurring for patients in our clinic, several options are available that usually diminish the severity of the rebound. For instance, a child may be administered a lower dosage of medication in the late afternoon (provided that this does not lead to insomnia or loss of appetite at dinnertime), or the noontime dosage may be reduced. In any case, we rarely have to resort to discontinuing the medication entirely because of rebound effects.

There is some debate as to whether stimulant medications can lead to reduced social interactions with other children. For instance, it has been suggested that higher dosages of these drugs can reduce not only negative, aggressive interactions, but prosocial behavior as well. Recent work conducted by Barbara Henker, Carol Whalen, and colleagues at the University of California (Whalen et al., 1987) would indicate that low and moderate doses of methylphenidate do reduce the frequency of aggression and noncompliance in groups of ADHD children, but have no appreciable effect, in either direction, on prosocial or nonsocial behavior. Nevertheless, we have run across isolated cases where parents will comment that a child is no longer "spontaneous" or childlike in his or her behavior, and appears too controlled or socially aloof. In such cases, the dosage may need to be reduced or the medication discontinued.

Each stimulant medication also seems to produce unique side effects. For instance, we have found that a few children will develop allergic skin rashes after a few weeks or more of treatment with pemoline. Ceasing the drug seems to eliminate the rash. Conners and Taylor (1980) reported a similar phenomenon but found that they could return the children to pemoline after the rash had resolved with no recurrence. We have also observed that pemoline tends to increase lip licking, lip biting, and light picking of the finger tips (not the nails). Reducing the dose seems to eliminate the problem. All of the medications can produce temporary symptoms of psychosis at very high doses, or even at smaller doses in very young children (below 3 or 4 years of age).

All of these side effects are clearly dose-related and subject to individual differences. Many of them diminish within 1 to 2 weeks of beginning medication, and all, except possibly the nervous tics, disappear upon ceasing pharmacotherapy. Where side effects persist beyond 1 to 2 weeks of treatment initiation, they can be made more tolerable by a slight lowering of the dose. Alternatively, a trial of a different stimulant medication can be initiated, as some side effects may be unique to the specific stimulant employed. It has been estimated that 1% to 3% of children with ADHD cannot tolerate any dose of stimulant medication.

Long-Term Side Effects

The deleterious effects of using stimulant medications over several years with children have not been well studied. Parents are often quite concerned about children's possible addiction to these drugs or increased risk of abusing other drugs as teenagers. There are no reported cases of addiction or serious drug dependence to date with these medications. Several studies (see Gadow, 1981) have examined the question of whether children on these drugs are more likely to abuse other substances as teenagers than those not taking them. The results suggest that they are not, although more research is needed to rule this out conclusively. Nonetheless, the possibilities are considered quite remote by most investigators in this area. In fact, there is some clinical evidence to suggest that the children on medication frequently dislike it and wish its discontinuance as soon as possible, especially if they are older children or adolescents.

One possible long-term side effect that has been of concern to many clinicians and scientists is the suppression of height and weight gain. Early reports by Safer and Allen and their associates at Johns Hopkins University Medical School (Safer, Allen, & Barr, 1972; Safer & Allen, 1973) indicated that both methylphenidate and d-amphetamine produced this effect. Later studies have found this to be a dose-related phenomenon, to be more prevalent with d-amphetamine, and to occur primarily within the first year of treatment. A rebound in growth or habituation to this effect seems to occur thereafter, and there is no appreciable effect on eventual adult height or weight (Mattes & Gittelman, 1983). This side effect is felt to be secondary to appetite suppression effects of these drugs, although several studies have indicated that stimulants may have some direct effects on growth hormone levels in the blood. Presently, it is believed that suppression in growth is a relatively transient side effect of the first year or so of treatment and has no significant effect on eventual adult height or weight. Furthermore, there is evidence to suggest that if the medication is discontinued at various points in the year (e.g., during summer vacation), a growth rebound will occur. Nonetheless, it behooves the clinician to monitor growth periodically in children receiving stimulant medications.

Although there is no evidence available on either side of the issue, there is some concern as to the effects of chronic stimulant drug use on the development of the cardiovascular system in children. All of the medications reviewed here have some effects on heart rate and blood pressure, although they are relatively mild. The concern, however, is that these children may be at increased risk for cardiovascular problems in middle to late life. At present, follow-up studies have not specifically addressed this important issue.

CLINICAL IMPLICATIONS OF CURRENT RESEARCH

This brief survey of the clinical effects and side effects of stimulant medications suggests the following conclusions about their use in the treatment of ADHD.

1. Between 70% and 80% of children with ADHD appear to exhibit a positive response to CNS stimulants. Primary effects are the improvement of attention span and the reduction of disruptive, inappropriate, and impulsive behavior. Compliance with authority figures' commands is increased, and children's peer relations may also improve, primarily through reductions in aggression. In addition, if the medication is titrated according to changes in academic performance, the latter has been found to be greatly enhanced as well.

2. Although these medications are certainly helpful in the day-to-day management of ADHD, they have not been demonstrated to lead to enduring positive changes after their cessation. Thus, this treatment is not a short-term solution to ADHD, but rather an intervention that must often be employed on a chronic basis to maintain positive effects.

3. The side effects (both short- and long-term) are mild, are often transient, and diminish with reduction or discontinuance of pharmacotherapy. However, children who have a personal or family history of tic or Tourette's disorder should not receive these medications, as these conditions may be exacerbated and possibly irreversible.

4. Despite the lack of established long-term success of these medications, they are significantly useful in managing the behavior of children with ADHD. Although the issue of controlling the behavior of children with drugs is highly controversial, the difficulties these youngsters present to others who must live, work, or attend school with them must not be overlooked. Not only do such children frustrate parents and teachers, but the effects of their disruptive behavior on the ability of their classmates to receive adequate instruction is at times considerable. If medications can temporarily ameliorate these difficulties while reducing the level of ostracism, censure, and punishment that children with ADHD receive, then they are certainly worthwhile in the children's treatment.

5. Stimulant medications are not a panacea for ADHD and should not be the sole treatment employed in most cases. Other therapies focusing on the myriad of social, psychological, educational, and physical problems these children often display will be necessary. Medications do not teach a child anything; they merely alter the likelihood of occurrence of behaviors already in the child's repertoire. The numerous skill deficits with which these children may present will still require attention. Thus, the medication may enhance the efficacy of other interventions by aiding the children to attend and respond to the environment in a more successful fashion. Since these medications are primarily used for classroom conduct and are relatively short-acting, it is the school that reaps their beneficial effects while families must tolerate the side effects (where these exist). Thus, parents will require child management training and other forms of counseling to cope with the children during periods when the medication cannot be used. Each professional must therefore be knowledgeable about the resources within the community that will be necessary to treat the "total child."

FACTORS INFLUENCING STIMULANT MEDICATION USE

It would be idealistic to assume that stimulant medication use is based entirely upon an objective assessment of children's needs and their response to medication. A closer look at the clinical use of pharmacotherapy indicates that several additional factors influence decisions about their use for children with ADHD. A major factor seems to be the availability of other treatments within a given community. Are there other resources for training in child management, special educational assistance, and follow-up support during development? What are these resources, are they affordable to the family in question, and how long will the family have to wait to receive them? Are the professionals providing the services both reputable and effective? The answers to these questions often influence the decision as to whether or not to prescribe drugs.

A second obvious factor is the degree to which the professional whom a family initially contacts knows about and respects other resources. It is disconcerting how many physicians, psychologists, psychiatrists, social workers, and educators are skeptical about or blatantly unaware of the services provided by the other professions in their community for the care and management of children with ADHD.

Another issue influencing pharmacotherapy is that of the educational and socioeconomic level of the parents, and hence their amenability to both drug and nonpharmacological treatments (Brown, Borden, Wynne, Spunt, & Clingerman, 1987). Many forms of intervention and parent training require literate, well-motivated clients who can afford such services. When parents are relatively uneducated and poor, alternatives to medication may be severely limited, regardless of the fairness of the situation. Poor and uneducated parents also tend to view children's health and psychological problems in terms of dealing with crises rather than in terms of prevention. As a result, they are likely to seek help only after a child's problems have become quite serious and may only use treatments that temporarily reduce the "crisis." Thus, when such parents are encountered, medication may be the only viable approach or the only one the parents will utilize if any (Firestone, 1982).

Finally, the severity of a problem at the time of referral may dictate a need for immediate treatment that only medication can effectively provide. Obviously, it requires a well-informed clinician to address these factors adequately and to prevent overreliance on medication simply because it is convenient or because a clinic has a heavy case load.

THE CLINICAL USE OF STIMULANT MEDICATIONS

Suggestions for ways in which to medicate and monitor stimulant use for children with ADHD vary widely. What is offered here is an amalgamation of suggestions from our clinical practice and research, and the advice of other respected scientist/practitioners in this area.

When to Use Medication

Probably the most difficult decision to make in clinical practice is that of when to use medication. The simple diagnosis of ADHD is not an automatic recommendation for drug treatment. Several rules can be followed as aids in this decision, although they are meant only as suggestions that should remain flexible to the needs of the individual child. (See also Cantwell, 1980.)

1. Has the child had adequate physical and psychological evaluations? Medications should never be prescribed if the child has not been directly examined in a thorough manner.

2. How old is the child? Pharmacotherapy is often less effective or leads to more severe side effects among children below the age of 4 and is therefore not usually recommended in such cases.

3. Have other therapies been used? If this is the family's initial contact with the professional, prescription of medication should perhaps be postponed until other interventions (e.g., parent training in child management skills) have been attempted. Alternatively, when the child's behavior presents a severe problem and the family cannot participate in child management training, medication may be the most practical initial treatment.

4. How severe is the child's current misbehavior? In some cases, the child's behavior is so unmanageable or distressing to the family that medication may prove the fastest and most effective manner of dealing with the crisis until other forms of treatment can commence. Once progress is obtained with other therapies, some effort can be made to reduce or terminate the medication, although this is not always possible.

5. Can the family afford the medication and associated costs (e.g., follow-up visits)? Long-term compliance rates are typically poor and may be especially problematic among families of low socioeconomic status. Of course, their ability to afford and their compliance with alternative treatments would also be suspect.

6. Are the parents sufficiently intelligent to supervise the use of the medications and guard against their abuse?

7. What are the parents' attitudes toward pharmacotherapy? Some parents are simply "antidrug" and should not be coerced into agreeing to this treatment, as they will probably sabotage its efficacy.

8. Is there a delinquent sibling or drug-abusing parent in the household? In this case, psychostimulant medication should not be prescribed since there is a high risk of its illicit use or sale.

9. Does the child have any history of tics, psychosis, or thought disorder? If so, the stimulants are contraindicated, as they may exacerbate such difficulties.

10. Is the child highly anxious, fearful, or more likely to complain of psychosomatic disturbances? Such a child is less likely to respond positively to stimulant medications and may exhibit a better response to antidepressant medications.

11. Does the physician have the time to monitor medication effects properly? In addition to an initial assessment of drug efficacy and establishment of the optimal dosage, periodic reassessment of drug response and effects on height and weight should be conducted throughout the year.

12. How does the child feel about medication and its alternatives? With older children and adolescents, it is important that the use of medication be discussed with them and its rationale fully explained. In cases where children are "antidrug" or oppositional, they may sabotage efforts to use it (e.g., refuse to swallow the pills).

Prescribing and Titrating

As noted above, a child should have a thorough evaluation prior to consideration of treatment with stimulant medication. Typically, very young children (i.e., under the age of 4 years) should not be given such medications as a treatment of first choice given the lower probability of a positive response and a higher incidence of side effects. It is generally estimated that children in this age group evidence a 50% response rate, although a recent study conducted by Barkley (1988e) found that over 60% of a sample of 27 preschool children exhibited significant increases in compliance with maternal commands in response to lower doses of methylphenidate. In general, however, very few well-controlled investigations of stimulant effects have been conducted with this age group. Thus, clinicians should exercise extreme caution even when a child in this age group presents with severe ADHD and no contraindications to pharmacotherapy.

If a child is 4 years of age or older, the first choice of medication is usually methylphenidate because of its greater documentation in research, proven efficacy across a wide age range, and greater dose-response information. Since a child's failure to respond to one stimulant does not preclude a positive response to an alternate drug in the same class, we will typically recommend a trial of d-amphetamine or pemoline if a poor response to methylphenidate occurs. In fact, as many as 20% of those who respond poorly to one stimulant are believed to show a positive response to a second one. If the child fails to respond to any of the stimulant compounds, then we will suggest that the physician switch to a tricyclic antidepressant (e.g., desipramine or imipramine), to be discussed later in this chapter. If this too fails, then pharmacotherapy may need to be discontinued for at least 1 year, if not altogether eliminated from consideration. If a child below the age of 6 evidences a poor response to stimulants, we have found that he or she may respond positively in later years (i.e., after the age of 6).

The stimulant medications, their available tablet sizes, and typical dose ranges are displayed in Table 17.2. Fixed dose ranges as opposed to those based on body weight (i.e., mg/kg) are reported, as recent research by Mark Rapport (Rapport, DuPaul, & Kelly, in press) would indicate that gross body weight is not a significant predictor of dose response to methylphenidate. In fact, idiosyncratic response is typically found among children of similar body weights (see Figure 17.2). With methylphenidate, the usual practice is to start a child at a low dose such as 5 mg b.i.d. (i.e., twice per day) and increase the dosage by 5-mg (or 2.5-mg) increments on a weekly basis until therapeutic

TABLE 17.2. Stimulant Medications, Tablet Sizes, and Dose Ranges

Brand name[a]	Manufacturer	Tablet sizes	Dose range[b]
Ritalin (methylphenidate)	CIBA	5 mg 10 mg 20 mg SR, 20 mg[c]	2.5 to 25 mg
Dexedrine (d-amphetamine)	Smith Kline & French	5 mg (tablet and spansule) 10 mg (spansule) 15 mg (spansule) 5 mg/5 ml (elixir)	2.5 to 20 mg
Cylert[d] (pemoline)	Abbott	18.75 mg 37.5 mg 75 mg	18.75 to 112.5 mg

[a]Generic names in parentheses.
[b]Dose range for each administration is provided.
[c]Sustained-release Ritalin (Ritalin-SR) is administered once per day.
[d]Cylert is administered once per day.

effects are reported. The doses used rarely exceed 20 mg b.i.d., because of a possible increase in the severity of side effects. Some investigators (Cantwell & Carlson, 1978) have reported total daily doses of as high as 60 to 70 mg, although we rarely go beyond 30 to 40 mg per day in our clinic.

It is a matter of some controversy as to whether behavioral tolerance develops with chronic administration of stimulant compounds. The few empirical investigations (Winsberg, Mitinsky, Kupietz, & Richardson, 1987) conducted on this subject indicate that failure to maintain clinical response at a given dose is more likely to occur with higher dosages (i.e., 15 mg or 20 mg b.i.d.) after a period of 6 months or more of chronic use. This is by no means a universal phenomenon and each case must be evaluated individually. We usually recommend a re-evaluation of a child's maintenance dose on an annual basis, as discussed below, to determine the necessity of a dosage change.

As Table 17.2 indicates, d-amphetamine is typically given in doses about half those of methylphenidate, presumably due to its greater potency. Pemoline is prescribed and titrated quite differently given that it is a "steady-state" medication. It is generally given only once a day, in the morning. The initial dose is usually 37.5 mg and is titrated upward in 18.75-mg increments every 3 to 5 days until a therapeutic effect is reported. On occasion, a second dose, often half that of the morning dose, may be given at 2:00 P.M. if the morning dose is proving ineffective during the afternoon. This, however, will probably increase the chances of insomnia occurring. Several investigations have indicated that pemoline is slower in achieving its peak effects and in "washing out" of the body than the other stimulants (see Gadow, 1981). Thus, its effects may last 2 to 3 days following its discontinuation.

Both methylphenidate and d-amphetamine are available in short-acting and sustained-release forms. The latter compounds have several advantages such as the preclusion of noontime medication administration at school and greater confidentiality of treatment. However, there is both research and clinical evidence that sustained-release methylphenidate may be less effective than the standard preparation, especially during the first several hours postingestion. For example, Pelham et al. (1987) found Ritalin (10 mg b.i.d.) to be superior to Ritalin-SR (20 mg) in the enhancement of teacher ratings and direct observations of classroom behavior in a sample of ADHD children. In addition, we have found that a number of our clinic patients experience diminished efficacy, particularly during the morning hours, when switching from standard methylphenidate to the sustained-release compound. For these reasons, we are more likely to recommend the shorter-acting forms of these medications except in situations where in-school administration of the drugs is significantly problematic (e.g., no school nurse is available to dispense the medication or teenagers are likely to experience teasing or censure from peers).

In recent years, generic forms of stimulant compounds have been made available as less expensive alternatives to their brand-name counterparts. On paper, a given dose of generic methylphenidate should have similar efficacy to the same dose of Ritalin. Although no systematic investigations of this assumption have been conducted, a significant number of families treated in our clinic have reported a notable dropoff in academic and behavioral performance when they have switched from Ritalin to generic methylphenidate. Thus, whenever parents report a possible "habituation" or "tolerance" effect to a child's maintenance dose, they should be asked whether they recently switched to the generic form of the medication and whether this apparent "habituation" coincided with this change.

Methylphenidate and *d*-amphetamine can be dispensed according to various schedules depending upon the severity of a child's ADHD and associated difficulties. If the medication is used primarily for classroom management, we usually suggest that it be discontinued on weekends, holidays, and summer vacations. When reinitiation of the medication each Monday produces a renewal of side effects exhibited only at the start of each week, we will suggest that the child be kept on one-half or less of the regular dose during the weekend to maintain habituation to side effects. If the child exhibits significant behavioral control difficulties at home as well as school, it is recommended that the child receive medication 7 days a week (with an attempt to discontinue pharmacotherapy during school vacations, when possible). On occasion, we have found it necessary to recommend the use of a three-times-a-day dose schedule with methylphenidate, primarily because its effects may last 3 hours or less with some children. This problem is often discovered in contacts with a child's teachers, who may observe that the morning dose has essentially worn off by 10:30 or 11:00 A.M. and the child is not due for a second dose until noon. In such cases the following schedule may be employed: a breakfast dose at 7:00–8:00 A.M., a second dose at 10:30–11:00 A.M., and a final dose at 2:00–3:00 P.M. Only when the child's behavior problems are exceptionally severe will we recommend a dose closer to the dinner hour due to the increased probability of side effects such as decreased appetite and insomnia at bedtime.

No matter which medication is employed, some common principles (and common sense!) apply. The dose should be the lowest possible and should be given only as many times per day as necessary to achieve adequate management of the child's behavior. In most cases, pharmacotherapy should be discontinued on holidays or summer vacations, unless they are necessary at these times. Titration should be based on objective assessment (as described below) and should start with the lowest possible increments. Sufficient time (e.g., 5 to 7 days) should be allowed for evaluation of the efficacy of each dosage. Parents should never be given permission to adjust the dosage of medication without consultation with the physician. This often leads to overmedication of a child, as the parents may increase the dose every time the child is temperamental, noncompliant, or obstinate. Such occurrences are usually better treated by the altering of parent management styles.

Monitoring Response to Medication

The methods used by practicing clinicians to monitor medication response vary widely in content and quality. Unfortunately, all too frequently, titration of dosage and long-term assessment of efficacy are based solely on the subjective reports of parents, thereby increasing the chances of erroneous decisions. A recent survey of a large national sample of pediatricians conducted by Linda Copeland and colleagues (Copeland, Wolraich, Lindgren, Milich, & Woolson, 1987) indicated that slightly over half of the respondents employed objective teacher and parent rating scales to determine medication efficacy. Although this certainly represents an improvement over previous practice, a large percentage of physicians prescribing stimulant medications do not collect objective data to establish treatment efficacy, optimal dose, or the need for a change in dosage.

Assessing the Initial Trial

Since the response to stimulant medications is often idiosyncratic and dose-specific, it behooves the clinician to collect objective data regarding changes in an ADHD child's behavior across several doses. Under ideal circumstances, a child's optimal dose should be established in the context of a double-blind, placebo-controlled assessment paradigm that includes multiple measures collected across several settings (i.e., home, school, and clinic). This type of evaluation involves not only the aggregation of objective, quantitative data regarding the child's treatment response, but also the use of a placebo control wherein teachers, parents, and children do not know the dosage being administered. This controls for the biases inherent in the collection of some assessment measures (e.g., parent and teacher rating scales). The reader is referred to a recent paper by Barkley, Fischer, Newby, and Breen (1988) to obtain further information about implementing this type of medication evaluation protocol.

Very few physicians have access to the resources and time to conduct elegant, placebo-controlled medication evaluations. Nevertheless, objective data regarding a child's medication response can be collected in a cost-effective fashion through the repeated administration of several parent and teacher rating scales. These measures should be initially administered prior to the onset of treatment to establish baseline levels of performance. Next, parent and teacher ratings should be collected on a weekly basis wherein each week represents a different dosage of the medication. At the conclusion of several weeks of assessment, the clinician should have a wealth of information available to determine whether the child exhibits a positive medication response and which dosage leads to the most significant change with the least side effects.

A wide variety of parent and teacher rating scales are available to assess the ADHD child's attention span, impulse control, activity level, academic performance, and compliance with household and classroom rules. In our clinic, we use multiple measures across sources rather than relying on a single questionnaire from a sole respondent. The parent rating scales that we have found to be the most helpful include the Conners Parent Rating Scale—Revised, the Home Situations Questionnaire, (HSQ), and the ADHD Rating Scale, which have been described in Chapter 9. In addition, parents are given the Stimulant Drug Side Effects Rating Scale shown in Figure 17.3 to assess the quantity and severity of possible side effects. Since children with ADHD tend to display some of these apparent "side effects" prior to receiving medication, it is important to administer this questionnaire during baseline conditions. Some of the more useful teacher rating scales include the Conners Teacher Rating Scale—Revised, the School Situations Questionnaire, (SSQ), the Child Attention Profile, and the ADHD Rating Scale. In addition, it is often helpful for the teacher to complete a weekly Stimulant Drug Side Effects Rating Scale, as he or she may have more of an opportunity to observe any negative effects on mood or social behavior.

Special note must be taken of the high likelihood of practice effects on these rating scales between their first and second administrations. As noted in Chapter 9, many parent and teacher rating scales show significant declines in scores between their first and second administrations even when there has been no intervening treatment. Clinicians who give the scales once, begin drug treatment, and then give them again a week or two later are likely to confuse the drug effects with these practice effects, concluding that the medication or a particular dose of it was helpful when it may not have been. We advise all clinicians using these scales to give them twice before using them in drug trials and to use the *second* administration as the baseline against which to measure changes due to medication trials.

All of the measures mentioned above focus on problem behaviors or situations but do not provide information regarding an increase in the child's

STIMULANT DRUG SIDE EFFECTS RATING SCALE

Name _____ Date _____

Person Completing This Form _____

Instructions: Please rate each behavior from 0 (absent) to 9 (serious). Circle only one number beside each item. A zero means that you have not seen the behavior in this child during the past week, and a 9 means that you have noticed it and believe it to be either very serious or to occur very frequently.

Behavior	Absent									Serious
Insomnia or trouble sleeping	0	1	2	3	4	5	6	7	8	9
Nightmares	0	1	2	3	4	5	6	7	8	9
Stares a lot or daydreams	0	1	2	3	4	5	6	7	8	9
Talks less with others	0	1	2	3	4	5	6	7	8	9
Uninterested in others	0	1	2	3	4	5	6	7	8	9
Decreased appetite	0	1	2	3	4	5	6	7	8	9
Irritable	0	1	2	3	4	5	6	7	8	9
Stomachaches	0	1	2	3	4	5	6	7	8	9
Headaches	0	1	2	3	4	5	6	7	8	9
Drowsiness	0	1	2	3	4	5	6	7	8	9
Sad/unhappy	0	1	2	3	4	5	6	7	8	9
Prone to crying	0	1	2	3	4	5	6	7	8	9
Anxious	0	1	2	3	4	5	6	7	8	9
Bites fingernails	0	1	2	3	4	5	6	7	8	9
Euphoric/unusually happy	0	1	2	3	4	5	6	7	8	9
Dizziness	0	1	2	3	4	5	6	7	8	9
Tics or nervous movements	0	1	2	3	4	5	6	7	8	9

FIGURE 17.3. The Stimulant Drug Side Effects Rating Scale, used to monitor side effects to stimulant medication. From *Hyperactive Children: A Handbook for Diagnosis and Treatment* by R. A. Barkley, 1981, New York: Guilford Press. Copyright 1981 by The Guilford Press. Reprinted by permission of the publisher.

competencies that may be associated with treatment. For this reason, we have found it useful to have teachers complete the Academic Performance Rating Scale discussed in Chapter 9. This questionnaire allows us to obtain valuable information about medication-related changes in the child's academic performance and learning skills. This measure is particularly helpful in titrating the optimal dosage to enhancement of scholastic status rather than solely determining this on the basis of a reduction in problematic behavior.

A Case Illustration

In our clinic, we employ a double-blind, placebo-controlled evaluation for children recommended for stimulant medication. This evaluation includes a variety of parent and teacher rating scales of behavior, side effects, and academic performance, many of which are described above (see also Chapter 9 and Appendix A), as well as a brief objective assessment battery. Specifically, parents complete the HSQ, the ADHD Rating Scale, and the Stimulant Drug Side Effects Rating Scale. Teachers complete the SSQ, the Child Attention Profile or ADHD Rating Scale, the teacher version of the Self-Control Rating Scale, the Academic Performance Rating Scale, and the Stimulant Drug Side Effects Rating Scale. During each drug condition, children are seen for a 45-minute testing session during which they are given the vigilance test from the Gordon Diagnostic System, the Wisconsin Selective Reminding Test, and the Restricted Academic Situation. All of these are described in Chapter 10.

Robert was an 8-year-old ADHD child with Oppositional Defiant Disorder and a learning disability (math) who was initially evaluated in our clinic and recommended for a trial on methylphenidate. He was subsequentedly tested for 1 week each on 5, 10, and 15 mg b.i.d. of methylphenidate and a placebo. All medications and the placebo were placed in identical opaque gelatin capsules by our pharmacy to ensure that the child and parents could not determine the different doses or distinguish medication from placebo without opening the capsules. Neither the parents, the teachers, the child, nor the clinic assistant testing the child knew the order of drug and placebo administration. The findings from this 4-week trial are shown in Table 17.3.

As this table indicates, ratings at home were most improved during the low- and high-dose conditions, although all three doses were associated with a significant increase in the number and severity of behavior side effects. Teacher ratings, it seemed to us, indicated that all three doses were beneficial but that the low dose was as helpful as the moderate and high doses in this respect. Note that side effects at school actually *declined* during the trial, indicating that many of the behaviors thought to be side effects of medication actually predated its administration and may have been helped by medication at school. As noted above, the increase in side effects at home probably accurately reflected true side effects from the medication. On the lab tests, a significant effect was noted on the vigilance test with the high dose seemingly superior to the other doses. In verbal learning and memory, a significant decline was noted on the Wisconsin Selective Reminding Test during the low-dose condition relative to placebo. Neither the moderate nor the high dose resulted in significant improvements on this test compared to placebo. Behavioral observations of Robert performing math problems in the Restricted Academic Situation revealed some significant medication effects for all three doses but the moderate and high doses proved superior to the low dose in this respect.

The anecdotal information obtained from the testing assistant, mother, and teacher during the 4 weeks of the trial is set forth in Table 17.4. These anecdotal comments should indicate the rather idiosyncratic responses that children have to medication in different settings and with different observers. This is why only one observer or only a single lab test should never be used to make decisions about medication. It also indicates the need to systematically monitor medication side effects (e.g., with a rating scale) across all drug conditions. After discussion among the parent, the psychologist, and pedia-

TABLE 17.3. Results of a Stimulant Drug Trial for an 8-Year-Old Boy with ADHD

Measure	Placebo	5 mg	10 mg	15 mg
Parent ratings				
HSQ				
Number of settings	15	12	15	15
Mean severity	6.7	1.0	4.3	3.1
ADHD Rating Scale				
Total score	41	15	24	10
Number of symptoms rated ≥2	14	2	13	0
Stimulant Drug Side Effects Rating Scale				
Number	0	8	10	9
Severity	0	3.1	4.9	1.9
Teacher ratings				
CAP				
Inattention	8	2	2	2
Overactivity	8	1	0	0
SSQ				
Number of settings	4	2	0	0
Mean severity	5.5	1.0	0.0	0.0
TSCRS	47	53	62	56
APRS	55	69	66	65
Stimulant Drug Side Effects Rating Scale				
Number	2	0	1	1
Severity	5.5	1.0	0.0	0.0
Clinic tests/observations				
CPT				
Number correct	34	42	51	58
Omission errors	26	18	9	2
Commission errors	5	6	3	2
Wisconsin Selective Remind-ing Test				
Total recall	62	53	60	58
Long-term storage	53	40	64	59
Long-term retrieval	50	34	54	48
Consistent retrieval	42	18	32	30
Restricted Academic Situation				
Off-task (%)	93	93	27	3
Fidgeting (%)	3	0	3	0
Vocalizes (%)	13	7	57	7
Plays with objects (%)	90	87	0	0
Out of seat (%)	93	67	10	0
Total ADHD behaviors	59	51	19	2
No. of math problems done	5	11	23	17
Percent math correct	20	100	100	94

Note. HSQ, Home Situations Questionnaire; CAP, Child Attention Profile; SSQ, School Situations Questionnaire; TSCRS, teacher version of Self-Control Rating Scale; CPT, continuous-performance test (12-minute version); APRS, Academic Performance Rating Scale.

TABLE 17.4. Anecdotal Comments from a Stimulant Drug Trial for an ADHD Child

Week	Testing assistant	Mother	Teacher
Placebo	Distractible Off task a lot Out of seat a lot Fails to follow in- structions	No change Out of control Uncooperative Much wilder Very fidgety	Difficulty sitting Poor focus on work Messy work Inattentive Restless/runs a lot
5 mg	Tipping chair Squirmy Impulsive Fidgety Off task	More relaxed Stomachache Sadder Very sensitive Improved social interactions	Improved work Completes tasks Less fidgety Better quality of classwork
10 mg	On task more Concentrates More focused Completes work More attentive	Very moody Sensitive Argumentative Irritable Good handwriting	Very focused Good-quality work Stays in seat Good self-control
15 mg	Very attentive More focused More in control Follows directions	Best week Personable Likeable Makes better de- cisions	Focused attention Better use of skill Better handwriting A little less accurate in work

trician, it was decided to use the 15-mg b.i.d. dose with Robert as it clearly produced the best effects at home and school with the fewest side effects. The parents were recommended to participate in our child management training course (see chapter 12) and a visit to the school was planned to institute several of the recommendations discussed in Chapter 15, including a daily school report card. This child was also slated to participate in our social skills training group as described in Chapter 16.

Assessing Maintenance on Medication

Once a child's optimal dosage is established, then the measures described above should be collected periodically throughout the school year to evaluate the need for dosage adjustments or the onset of side effects. The vast majority of the questionnaires need only be readministered every several months or so. However, it is usually a good idea to review items from the Stimulant Drug Side Effects Rating Scale each month when the parents call to obtain another prescription. In addition, at each monthly contact (usually by telephone), a checklist of questions is reviewed with parents to assess continued drug efficacy. This checklist is displayed in Figure 17.4.

1. What dose have you been regularly giving to this child over the past month?

2. Have you noticed any of the following side effects this month?

Loss of appetite/weight loss	Rashes
Insomnia	Dizziness
Irritability in late morning or late afternoon	Dark circles under eyes
Unusual crying	Fearfulness
Tics or nervous habits	Social withdrawal
Headache/stomachache	Drowsiness
Sadness	Anxiety

3. If so, please describe how often and when the side effects occurred.

4. Have you spoken with the child's teacher lately? How is the child performing in class?

5. Did your child complain about taking the medication or avoid its use?

6. Does the drug seem to be helping the child as much this month as it did last month? If not, what seems to have changed?

7. When was your child last examined by the doctor? (If more than 6 mos., schedule the child for a clinic visit and exam.)

8. Have there been problems in giving the child medication at school?

FIGURE 17.4. A checklist of questions to be reviewed monthly with parents of children taking stimulant medication. From *Hyperactive Children: A Handbook for Diagnosis and Treatment* by R. A. Barkley, 1981, New York: Guilford Press. Copyright 1981 by The Guilford Press. Reprinted by permission of the publisher.

When parents call to complain about ineffective doses that were formerly effective, physicians should employ caution in deciding to increase the level of medication. As mentioned above, apparent losses in treatment efficacy can sometimes be associated with a switch to generic or sustained-release forms of the medications. In addition, these behavioral changes may be related to a recent family crisis or uniquely distressing incident. All parents experience days in which, because of stress, illness, or other factors, their level of tolerance for their children's behavior is much lower, leading them to complain. It is not always necessary to increase the dose in such a situation; rather, it may be more helpful simply to listen to the parent in a reflective, supportive manner. It may also be necessary to refer the parent to someone who can deal with the precipitating event. Parents of ADHD children may also be unrealistic in their expectations regarding the amount and consistency of behavioral improvements associated with pharmacotherapy. They should realize that even when medicated, such children will experience their share of "bad days" regardless of the dosage being employed.

If the physician is unable to determine any extraneous factors that may have engendered the complaints, then it may indeed be true that the current dosage has become less effective. Careful questioning of the parent as to the ways in which the child's behavior is different or worse can be useful in making the decision. In addition, the child's teacher should be contacted to ascertain whether similar deterioration in functioning has occurred in the school setting. The parent and teacher questionnaires discussed above should be administered and compared to previously collected data in an effort to specify which behaviors have actually worsened and to quantify the amount of behavioral change. Finally, clinical judgment and experience are crucial in handling these parental complaints effectively without unnecessarily increasing the child's medication.

Approximately every 6 months that a child is on medication, it is advisable to administer a follow-up clinic examination. During this time, height, weight, blood pressure, and heart rate can be recorded to determine potential side effects. Parent and teacher ratings should be collected concurrent with this visit as well. For children receiving pemoline, liver functioning should be checked given the findings that this drug may adversely affect liver functions (Physicians Desk Reference, 1989). Difficulties that continue to plague the child or family can be discussed, and referrals to appropriate professionals can be made as necessary. When parents are called for the appointment by the clinic secretary, they should be encouraged to write down in advance any concerns or questions they might have, so that the visit can be as useful as possible.

Discontinuing Medication

Various investigators have estimated that the average duration of pharmacotherapy appears to be 2 or 3 years (Barkley, Fischer, Edelbrock, & Smallish, in press-a). There are no firm guidelines regarding when to discontinue medication treatment, other than a determination that it no longer seems to be necessary. It was once believed that treatment with stimulants should be discontinued when a child reaches puberty given diminished efficacy and potential for abuse. Over the past several decades, however, empirical investigations have consistently demonstrated that CNS stimulants exert the same beneficial effects on the behavior of teenagers as they do with children. Furthermore, chronic administration of these drugs does not appear to increase the probability of substance abuse.

For the majority of our clinic patients, we will recommend that the continued necessity for medication be re-evaluated on an annual basis. Usually, treatment is discontinued for a short time (e.g., 1 to 2 weeks) and objective measures, such as rating scales, are collected during both medication and nonmedication periods. We suggest that this reassessment take place in the middle of the school year so as to ensure that the child has acclimated to the new classroom and to prevent erroneous decisions being made on the basis of a "honeymoon" effect that may occur during the initial stages of the academic year. If there is no significant difference in the child's behavior when he or she is on or off medication, then treatment may be discontinued for a longer trial period. If there is no appreciable difference with treatment and the child continues to display significant behavioral control difficulties, it may be time to re-evaluate the dosage or switch to a different medication.

Contraindications and Interactions

As stated earlier, children with a history of tics, Tourette's disorder, thought disorder, or psychosis should not be given stimulant medications, for these drugs often exacerbate the symptoms of such disorders (Golden, 1974). Children with high levels of anxiety (e.g., Overanxious Disorder) are also likely to respond poorly to these medications. Furthermore, as also noted earlier, children under 4 years of age tend to be poor responders to stimulant compounds and there are few research studies investigating drug effects and side effects in this age group. There is some controversy over whether stimulants should be given to children with seizures or epilepsy; doubts about the practice are based on the possibility that these drugs may lower seizure thresholds. This phenomenon is rarely if ever seen clinically, however, and it can be avoided by a slight increase in the level of anticonvulsants (Crumrine, Feldman, Teodori, Handen, & Alvin, 1987). Since many children with seizure disorders also present with ADHD symptomatology, the stimulants can be useful in their management if they are judiciously prescribed.

The stimulants can alter the actions of other medications, though such interactions are often not clinically serious or significant. In addition, certain antihistamine medications can inhibit the actions of stimulants, thus reducing the efficacy of the latter. Stimulant medications may antagonize the effects of hypnotic drugs and also increase their toxicity in overdosage. They have also been shown to heighten the activity of antidepressants and monoamine oxidase inhibitors (MAOIs). These compounds may also decrease the efficacy of anticonvulsant drugs, although this remains to be empirically demonstrated. In general, the stimulants have few, if any, serious interactions with other drugs; however, this is not a well-researched area of study.

COMBINED TREATMENT PROGRAMS

One issue that is frequently raised is whether stimulant medication, behavior therapy, or a combination of the two is the best treatment approach to ADHD (see Abikoff & Gittelman, 1985; Barkley, 1989a; Gadow, 1985). For example, some studies using extremely small sample sizes have found that behavior modification can be as effective in managing classroom behavior and enhancing academic productivity as stimulant medication can be (Allyon, Layman, & Kandel, 1975). Currently, most researchers in this area would agree that the combination of the two treatments is superior to either in isolation (see Pelham & Murphy, 1986).

This conclusion is primarily based on the most extensive study conducted to date of this issue (Gittelman-Klein et al., 1980). Sixty-one children with ADHD were randomly assigned to one of three possible treatments: methylphenidate alone, behavior therapy with a placebo, and behavior therapy with methylphenidate. Teacher ratings, direct classroom observations, and global ratings of improvement by parents, teachers, and physicians served as the dependent measures. On the teacher ratings, all treatments produced significant improvements after 8 weeks, but the ratings of the two medication-treated groups were consistently superior to those of the group receiving behavior modification alone, and were indistinguishable from each other. On the direct classroom observations, only the two groups receiving medication showed any significant improvements in their behavior during treatment, whereas little change in the behavior-therapy-alone group was observed in these measures of disruptive behavior. Again, there was no difference in ratings between the two drug-treated groups. Parents' global ratings found all treatments equally effective; teachers found the combined program the most effective, though both treatments used alone were rated as producing improvements in more than 63% of the children treated in each group. Psychiatrists rated 100% of the children in the combined group as improved, as opposed to 81% in the medication-only group and 58% in the behavior-therapy-only group.

Although the Gittelman-Klein et al. study has methodological shortcomings (e.g., integrity of the behavior therapy procedures) that may limit conclusions based on it, the obtained results suggest that behavior therapy alone is not as effective as stimulant medication for the majority of children with ADHD. Clearly, the combination of treatments is superior to either intervention alone. Some may interpret these findings as indicating that behavior therapy programs should only be added to the treatment program if medication is not sufficient; however, as we have stated earlier, relying solely on pharmacotherapy would be doing a child a disservice in the long run.

ALTERNATIVE MEDICATIONS

A wide variety of psychotropic medications have been investigated as possible treatments for ADHD. Other than the CNS stimulants, most of these have been found to be ineffective or no better than placebo. However, some classes of medications, most notably the tricyclic antidepressants, have been found effective in the management of some children with ADHD.

Other Stimulants

The possibility that both deanol (Deaner; Cantwell & Carlson, 1978) and caffeine (Harvey & Marsh, 1978) may be useful in treating ADHD has been suggested. Deanol is an organic salt, 4-(acetylamino) benzoic acid compounded with 2-(dimethylamino)ethanol, that is believed to operate primarily on cholinergic rather than catecholaminergic pathways in the CNS. The little research that exists does not support its efficacy with ADHD children.

Caffeine is a xanthine derivative whose use with ADHD children was the subject of some public attention and support in the early to mid-1970s. At least five or six studies were conducted to compare its efficacy with that of other stimulants (see Gadow, 1981). Some investigations found no effects, and those that did noted the improvements to be greatly inferior to those brought about by the more commonly used stimulants (Reichard & Elder, 1977). At present, caffeine is not seriously considered to have much utility for children with ADHD (Gadow, 1981).

Tricyclic Antidepressants

The antidepressants are slower-acting medications that have been shown to produce behavioral effects similar to those of the stimulants with ADHD children. This is presumably due to their agonistic effects on the noradrenergic system as obtained with the CNS stimulants. Imipramine (Tofranil) and desipramine (Norpramin) have received the most study to date (Donnelly & Rapoport, 1985). Both medications have been found to decrease parent and teacher ratings of inattention, hyperactivity, and aggression among up to 70 percent of ADHD children treated (Riddle, Hardin, Cho, Wolston, & Leckman, 1988). However, neither medication has been found to lead to enhancement of cognitive functioning on laboratory measures (Garfinkel, Wender, Sloman, & O'Neill, 1983) such as continuous-performance tests or paired-associates learning tests. It should be noted that no decrements in cognitive functioning are associated with these medications either. Possible side effects include dry mouth, increases in blood pressure and heart rate, and slowing of intracardiac conduction. For most individuals these side effects are not clinically significant; however, clinicians are advised to closely monitor cardiac functioning on a regular basis, particularly if a child is receiving a dose of 3.5 mg/kg per day or more (Biederman, Baldessarini, Wright, Knee, Harmatz, & Goldblatt, 1989). There is also mounting evidence that desipramine is preferred over imipramine because of its milder side effects and greater levels of positive treatment response (Winsberg, Bialer, Kupietz, & Tobias, 1972).

In the few studies that have directly compared the effects of stimulants and antidepressants, the former have generally been found superior in the enhancement of both behavioral and cognitive functioning (Garfinkel et al., 1983). In fact, youngsters who present with severe aggression may show deterioration in response to chronic treatment with imipramine. Thus, for the vast majority of children with ADHD, stimulant medications remain the medical treatment of choice. However, for youngsters who have not responded to any stimulant medication, desipramine or imipramine may be a viable alternative. Joseph Biederman and colleagues (Biederman, Baldessarini, Wright, Knee, &

Harmatz, 1989) at the Massachusetts General Hospital (1989) have found that approximately 70% of children who are nonresponders to stimulants will exhibit enhanced functioning following treatment with desipramine. In addition, children with ADHD who also exhibit symptoms of anxiety disturbance or depression may respond more positively to antidepressants than to stimulants (Pliszka, 1989). For this subset of youngsters, it may be more prudent to initiate treatment with an antidepressant. The reader who is seriously considering use of these medications with ADHD children is referred to the review article by Pliszka (1987) or the recent paper by Biederman et. al. (1989).

Other Medications

A wide variety of other medications (e.g., neuroleptics, tranquilizers) have been studied as possible treatments for ADHD, with generally negative results (see Zametkin & Rapoport, 1986). On the other hand, several recent investigations have found MAOIs and clonidine to cause significant improvements in the behavioral functioning of children with ADHD. For example, Hunt, Minderaa, and Cohen (1985) found clonidine-induced enhancement of teacher and parent ratings of hyperactivity and conduct problems in 70% of children treated. While these and other initial results are promising, most of the available research has been conducted with small samples and has employed only teacher and parent ratings. Effects on academic performance and cognitive functioning must be studied before these compounds can be considered viable alternatives to stimulant medications. In addition, the magnitude of treatment outcomes associated with alternative medications (MAOIs and clonidine) and CNS stimulants should be directly compared within large samples of ADHD children. Pending the results of such investigations, there appear to be a number of promising alternatives for ADHD children who do not profit from treatment with stimulant medications.

THE ROLE OF NONMEDICAL PROFESSIONALS IN PHARMACOTHERAPY

Pediatricians and child psychiatrists obviously play pivotal roles in the medication treatment of children with ADHD. Other professionals can serve instrumental roles in such treatment by assisting physicians in monitoring medication effects and by administering psychoeducational therapies that can be adjunctive to pharmacotherapy.

School Psychologists and Educators

At first glance, it may seem to school staff members that there are few if any roles that they can play in the drug management of ADHD children. This attitude is misleading, for the role of school personnel can often prove an important one.

1. School psychologists and educators serve an obvious, yet critical, role in the initial diagnosis of ADHD. Families often seek assistance from their pediatricians because of complaints from the school regarding poor classroom behavior. School personnel are second only to parents in the useful information about children with which they can provide physicians, and they are the most important informants when classroom performance is the primary problem. Although physicians of course query the parents for information, they weigh heavily the advice received from school staff in deciding whether or not to medicate such children.

2. The school personnel are also viewed by families as an important source of professional opinion and advice as to whether their children's behavior is deviant, and, if so, where they might best seek help. This is especially true if a child is the only offspring of young parents who are naive about normal child behavior and development. Even when a family recognizes the existence of a behavior problem, it may be the advice and urging of the school that finally prompt the parents to seek medication or other assistance.

3. Once pharmacotherapy is implemented, medical staff will again heavily weigh the school personnel's opinion of a child's drug response in determining the proper dose. In particular, objective ratings and direct behavioral observations can be collected to provide valuable information regarding medication-induced changes in the child's classroom deportment and academic performance. When physicians do not request this information, it is imperative that school staff members contact them with their observations of the child's reactions. Indeed, the school staff should not automatically assume that physicians prescribing such medication will monitor it closely.

4. When the stimulant medication has been properly titrated, school psychologists can greatly assist in identifying residual learning and social skills deficits that will require additional educational programs. As noted above, teachers may be less likely to see these residual problems once children are managed with medication.

5. Finally, school psychologists are in a unique position to implement additional therapies for children with ADHD if medication should prove ineffective, insufficient, or undesirable. Designing behavior modification or education programs and assisting teachers in their implementation are roles that can be filled most effectively by school psychologists. In addition, school psychologists must see that in-service training programs are developed to instruct other staff members and teachers in the uses and abuses of pharmacotherapy in the classroom, as well as alternatives or adjunctive interventions to medication for children with behavior problems.

Child/Pediatric Psychologists

Like educational professionals, child psychologists, especially those trained in pediatric psychology, can play an important role in medication treatment for children with ADHD.

1. Given child or pediatric psychologists' training in evaluation and assessment procedures, they usually have a greater familiarity than do physicians with questionnaires and rating scales best suited to monitoring children's drug responses.

2. Psychologists are also typically trained in the use of direct observational methods for recording home or classroom conduct and social interactions. These methods can prove useful not only in monitoring medication response, but also in suggesting nonpharmacological methods for modifying deviant behavior.

3. The psychologist's background in psychometric testing is often called upon for the assessment of learning or personality problems that pharmacotherapy may or may not affect. Alternative educational, counseling, or psychotherapeutic interventions may be required in addition to medication.

4. Many child psychologists are skilled in training parents in effective child management methods. These methods will be required whether or not pharmacotherapy is used, since the medications are not effective during all the waking hours of children. Parent training has been shown to be as effective as pharmacotherapy for some target behaviors and should be considered before medication for some children with ADHD.

5. When parents manifest personal or marital problems that can interfere with effective drug treatment of their children, child psychologists can provide direct counseling to the parents or refer them to other psychologists more skilled in these problems.

This section clearly suggests that the treatment of children with ADHD, even when stimulant medications are involved, must often be an interdisciplinary matter if broad-spectrum programs are to be designed to address their many adjustment difficulties. Medication alone will not be sufficient to alter the prognosis of these children.

DISCUSSING PHARMACOTHERAPY
WITH PARENTS AND CHILDREN

One of the most critical aspects of pharmacotherapy for children with ADHD, yet one receiving scant attention, is the counseling of parents on the specifics of such a treatment approach. Simply providing the parents with a prescription and telling them to call back in a week or two will not do. Physicians need to take the time to explain the rationale for medication treatment, to discuss its effects and side effects, and to explain carefully how the medication will be titrated (including completion of objective rating scales and obtaining of information from school personnel). It is also important to discuss the probability of a positive response to treatment, results that pharmacotherapy will *not* achieve, and areas in which other therapies will be necessary.

Parents often have many misconceptions and concerns about drug treatment that should be addressed by physicians, such as these: "Are they addictive? How long will my child need them? How will I know what changes to expect? What will we do if the medication does not work? Is my child likely to come to view medication as an acceptable way of handling problems?" Parents obviously need to be cautioned against adjusting the dose without calling their physicians. In addition, the medication should be kept in a safe place, out of reach of children and adults prone to drug abuse. Regardless of the frequency with which physicians must explain medication use to families, it is essential that they remain sensitive to parents' concerns and not deal too glibly with them if the parents are to be an effective part of the medication management team (see Firestone, 1982).

Physicians should also take time to discuss medication treatment with ADHD children. Are the children scared? Do they understand why the medication is being given and what will happen if it works? Are they willing to take medication? What do they think other children will say when they learn of the treatment? While difficult, these and other issues must be addressed with children as parents are typically uncomfortable or unable to discuss this in an appropriate manner. In addition, the children's cooperation with the treatment must be enlisted. One of the more successful methods for explaining the rationale for treatment to children is in terms of personal strengths and weaknesses. We ask children to name activities or attributes in which they think they are better than other children, as well as pointing out that other children in their class may require help for their weaknesses (e.g., tutoring for learning problems, eyeglasses for poor vision). The medication is presented as a form of assistance to address the children's specific weaknesses (i.e., poor attention span, impulsivity, and overactivity). To reduce possible psychological dependence on treatment we further point out that when the medication helps the children, the children are still the ones who are performing the task and making the improvement (i.e., they are responsible for their own behavior).

ETHICAL AND SOCIAL ISSUES IN PHARMACOTHERAPY WITH CHILDREN

It is not the intent of this chapter to provide a lengthy philosophical discourse on the ethical and moral issues attendant to treating deviant behavior in children with psychotropic medications. The reader is referred to Cantwell and Carlson (1978) and Sroufe (1975) for more thorough discussions of these issues. Nevertheless, brief mention of some ethical and social issues is required, as these questions often confront physicians and related professionals at one time or another. In addition to the professionals' understanding of the research literature on stimulant medication, the manner in which these issues are resolved plays a large role in determining the decision to utilize this treatment for individual patients. Some of the more salient issues worthy of consideration are as follows:

1. Have medications become too easily available as a method of treatment? Do professionals frequently overlook other effective treatment approaches because of their inconvenience?

2. How do we resolve the discrepancy between teaching children to "just say no" to drugs and using medications to change their behaviors?

3. Will children with ADHD come to view medicine as the only solution to their social problems?

4. Are there systemic problems in our educational system, which if solved would preclude the need to medicate large numbers of children for ADHD?

5. Are stimulant medications prescribed too frequently due to parent or teacher intolerance (i.e., in cases where children do not present with severe ADHD)?

Although these ethical concerns should be seriously considered by all professionals working with ADHD children, the fact remains that stimulant medications are highly effective in temporarily improving the children's behavioral conduct and classroom performance. Thus, in the majority of cases where medication appears necessary, it is quite beneficial and is an ethically sound treatment.

CONCLUSION

CNS stimulant and, possibly, tricyclic antidepressant medications are highly effective treatments for the symptomatic management of children with ADHD. Stimulant medications appear to exert their primary effects on attention span and impulse control due to their ability to energize inhibitory brain mechanisms. Changes in other behaviors are assumed to be the result of these improvements in attention span and impulsivity. Most children who receive stimulants tend to show improvements in their play, social conduct, and compliance to commands and rules; in turn, these improvements result in a lessening of supervision, reprimands, and punishment from those adults who must frequently interact with them. In addition, the medications also lead to substantial improvements in academic performance, particularly on independent written tasks. Despite strong evidence for the short-term efficacy of pharmacotherapy, changes in the long-term outcome of ADHD children as a result of treatment have not been obtained to date. Although stimulants are quite effective in the day-to-day management of ADHD, other treatments are required to optimize the chances for long-term improvements.

18

Assessment and Treatment of Adults with ADHD

ROBERT KANE, CECILIA MIKALAC, SHELDON BENJAMIN, and RUSSELL A. BARKLEY

It is our own past which has made us what we are. We are the children of our own deeds. Conduct has created character; acts have grown into habits, each year has pressed into us a deeper moral print; the lives we have led have left us such as we are to-day.

—JOHN B. DYKES (1823–76)

Recently, there has been a growing awareness among clinicians of the persistence of symptoms of Attention-deficit Hyperactivity Disorder (ADHD) into adulthood, though few descriptive studies of adult ADHD have been published. Previously, ADHD was seen as a disorder of childhood, and the symptoms were thought to disappear with the onset of puberty (Munoz-Millan & Casteel, 1989). This is certainly not the case any longer, now that follow-up studies have shown that between 30 and 70% of children diagnosed as having ADHD continue to have either the full syndrome or some significant residual symptoms into young adulthood (Barkley, Fischer, Edelbrock, & Smallish, in press-a; Weiss & Hechtman, 1986). The residual symptoms that may be seen in adults vary in type and severity, and cause considerable disruption in the lives of affected individuals (see Chapter 4).

Because ADHD in adults represents a relatively new area of study, this chapter focuses primarily on a potentially useful method of assessment and investigation of adults with ADHD. Issues related to history, differential diagnosis, neuropsychological assessment, and pharmacological and behavioral treatment are also discussed, along with recommendations for future research.

ASSESSMENT

Initial Presentation

Children are often referred to treatment centers for evaluation of ADHD symptoms because of difficulties at school, or parents may initiate contact

TABLE 18.1. Presenting Complaints of Adults Being Evaluated for ADHD

Difficulty in finding and keeping jobs
Performing below level of competence on job
Inability to perform up to intellectual level in school
Inability to concentrate
Lack of organization
Inability to establish and maintain a routine
Poor discipline
Depression, low self-esteem
Forgetfulness or poor memory
Confusion, trouble thinking clearly

because of problems the children have interacting at home or with their peers. Most frequently, however, adults are self-referrals. Complaints vary and depend upon the specific symptoms found troublesome. In our experience, problems related to school, work, or family may lead an adult with ADHD to seek treatment. Frequently, symptoms include difficulty in persevering with and organizing tasks. Patients voice concern over frequent changes in employment and problems in maintaining relationships. They also complain of losing things, of being considered impolite because they frequently interrupt others, and of lack of concentration when reading. Table 18.1 lists major complaints reported by our adult ADHD patients.

Whether or not patients specifically request an evaluation for ADHD depends on their degree of sophistication and prior life experiences. Parents of children being treated for the disorder frequently note that they have problems similar to those of their children. Subsequently, they request evaluation for themselves. In our clinic, newspaper articles about ADHD in adults have elicited recognition and led individuals to seek evaluation. Patients also present to the psychiatric outpatient clinic with ADHD-like symptoms dating back to childhood. These patients are then referred for ADHD evaluation.

Problems presented by patients evaluated in our clinic are consistent with those reported in the literature as characteristic of adult residual ADHD. Data from prospective and retrospective studies describe problems persisting through adolescence and adulthood. Weiss and Hechtman (1986) demonstrated that adults who had been hyperactive children moved more frequently and had significantly more automobile accidents than matched controls. At 10- to 12-year follow-up, Weiss, Hechtman, Perlman, Hopkins, and Wenar (1979) reported academic histories suggesting that ADHD children had completed fewer years of education, had failed more grades, and had produced lower marks than controls. At 10-year follow-up, Weiss, Hechtman, and Perlman (1978) found the behavior of ADHD children to be more impulsive, restless, and immature than that of controls. Sixty-six percent of this sample demonstrated at least one disabling symptom of ADHD at 15-year follow-up (Weiss, Hechtman, Milroy, & Perlman, 1985). Twenty-three percent were diagnosed as having Antisocial Personality Disorder (Weiss & Hechtman, 1986). At 15-

year follow-up, work histories of ADHD children were more problematic than those of matched controls (Weiss et al., 1985).

Gittelman, Mannuzza, Shenker, and Bonagura (1985) followed 101 male adolescents aged 16 to 23 who were diagnosed as hyperactive in childhood. Findings were compared with those of 100 normal children. Information was obtained on 98% of the original sample. The Attention Deficit Disorder with Hyperactivity (ADD/+H) syndrome persisted in 31% of probands in contrast to 3% of controls. Two other conditions distinguished probands from normal controls: Conduct Disorder and substance abuse disorders. Both disorders aggregated significantly with continued symptoms of ADD/+H. These authors replicated their study using 94 hyperactive children and 78 controls (Mannuzza et al, in press). With some variation in percentages, findings were consistent with the initial study.

Mannuzza et al. (1988) used the replication sample to examine the adaptation of probands without evidence of mental disorder at follow-up. They found that ADD/+H probands showed continued difficulties in adjustment. Reported problematic behavior included a high rate of verbal abuse toward teachers, being fired from jobs, and involvement in theft and pranks. Significant differences remained between probands and controls even when a subsample of ADD probands suspected of remitted Conduct Disorder was removed.

Differences in occupational and personal adjustment in later life were reported by Borland and Heckman (1976) between hyperactive children and male siblings. The authors compared 20 adult males with childhood medical histories of hyperactive child syndrome to their nonhyperactive brother. Average age of hyperactives was 30 years; average sibling age was 26 years. Borland and Heckman (1976) concluded that problems in everyday living may result from the persistence of symptoms of hyperactivity into adulthood.

Feldman, Denhoff, and Denhoff (1979) described indications of later life adjustment difficulties for hyperactive children. At follow-up, 91% of the hyperactive children studied were either in school or working. However, compared to sibling controls, they reported lower educational achievement, poorer self-esteem, and increased substance abuse.

One area that has not been explored to any degree is the extent to which adults with ADHD may display characteristics of Oppositional Defiant Disorder (ODD). Typically, these symptoms are not reviewed with adult clients, because they are thought of as comprising a childhood disorder. Furthermore, when Conduct Disorder or Antisocial Personality is present (as is often the case in adults with a childhood history of ODD), either diagnosis precludes the diagnosis of ODD. However, symptoms of ODD are often found in over 65 percent of children with ADHD, not all of whom go on to manifest Conduct Disorder or Antisocial Personality. It is possible that some children or adolescents with ADHD and ODD who do not progress to these more serious disorders may continue to manifest aspects of hostile, defiant, and irritable mood that characterize ODD. Clinicians should use any appropriate V codes from DSM-III-R that apply in these cases but should not over-look the possibility that adult forms of ODD exist and may be differentially associated with ADHD. This possibility is tacitly acknowledged in the Utah Criteria for diagnosing ADHD in adults (discussed below), which include temper outbursts and hostile mood as possible symptoms of ADHD at this age.

Attention problems have been found in adults without a childhood history of hyperactivity, neurological disease, or major psychiatric disturbance. Buchsbaum and colleagues (Buchsbaum et al., 1985) screened 400 college men, using results from a continuous-performance test (CPT). They com-pared men scoring in the highest and lowest 5th percentiles on this test for their results on other cognitive measures; the authors also obtained measures of neurological soft signs, psychopathology, and childhood hyperactivity. Sig-nificant group differences were detected on memory and reaction time mea-sures. Subjects who performed poorly on the CPT also scored lower on other cognitive measures. Poor CPT performers had more neurological soft signs and evidenced evoked potential abnormalities. There was no difference be-tween the groups in the presence of psychopathology. Only 6 of 20 individ-uals in the poor-CPT-performance group reported a history of hyperactivity during childhood. Although the incidence of childhood hyperactivity was greater in the poor CPT performers, it was clear that the presence of attention prob-lems later in life was not tightly linked to childhood hyperactivity, at least as it was self-reported in this sample. Buchsbaum and his colleagues interpreted these findings as supporting the DSM-III diagnosis of Attention Deficit Dis-order without Hyperactivity (ADD/−H).

Several studies support the idea that ADHD is not strictly a disorder of childhood although for some the symptoms may disappear at adolescence. For others, symptoms persist into adulthood and cause considerable prob-lems in adjustment. These problems may be more pronounced when there is also a childhood history of hyperactivity. However, childhood hyperactivity may not be a necessary condition for the persistence of attention disturbances into adulthood.

Clinical Diagnosis

The most difficult clinical problem in assessing and treating adults with atten-tion deficits is differential diagnosis. Adults with attention difficulties may evidence a number of psychiatric problems. This association is twofold. In-dividuals with the diagnosis of ADHD established in childhood are at risk for developing symptoms of affective disorders, substance abuse, intermittent explosive disorder, and antisocial behavior (Biederman et al., 1987; Gomez, Janowsky, Zetin, Huey, & Clopton, 1981; Morrison & Minkoff, 1975; Tar-tar, McBride, Buonpane, & Schneider, 1977). Second, the symptom of dis-turbed attention is associated with many psychiatric disorders. Patients with Borderline Personality Disorder, Antisocial Personality Disorder, agitated depression, hypomania, schizophrenia, substance abuse, alcoholism, or head injury all routinely endorse many, if not all, of the symptoms comprising the DSM-III-R criteria for ADHD (see Chapter 6). Attention difficulties are a known part of the following disorders:

1. Patients with Borderline Personality Disorder have difficulty structuring their lives. They may demonstrate inconsistent work histories and unstable relationships. They may experience flashbacks or psychotic episodes that interfere with cognitive processes, including memory and attention. There may also be concurrent substance abuse.

2. Patients with Antisocial Personality Disorder may have attention difficulty because of subtle neurological deficits or substance abuse. They may have difficulty in recognizing the consequences of and setting limits on their behavior. Some patients with Antisocial Personality Disorder without true attention deficits may report fictitious deficits in order to gain access to methylphenidate, to diminish legal responsibility for their actions, or to obtain disability payments. They may even bring a collaborator to verify their responses.

3. Patients with depression are often inattentive, forgetful, and function poorly on the job. They frequently misplace things. Agitated depression can include hyperactivity and restlessness. Hypomania may closely resemble adult ADHD, especially if mood is only mildly irritable. Hyperactivity, distractibility, impatience, and disorganization are often seen.

4. Schizophrenic patients may be inattentive and distractible. They are frequently disorganized and impatient, and have difficulty completing tasks. They may be restless as a consequence of neuroleptic-induced akathisia.

5. Patients who are intoxicated on or withdrawing from alcohol, cocaine, or other substances also display ADHD symptoms. Frequently they are distractible, fidgety, or inattentive during the interview. They may be impatient and irritable, and have trouble functioning at home, school, or on the job because of substance abuse.

6. Patients with head injuries also may present with the symptoms of ADHD. They are distinguished by time of symptom onset and history of trauma. Head trauma patients may also have more severe cognitive impairment than is typical for ADHD.

7. Medical conditions such as hypo- or hyperthyroidism, renal or hepatic insufficiency, anoxia, or vitamin deficiency may also produce attention deficits. Deficits are sometimes reversible with appropriate medical treatment.

Table 18.2 summarizes the psychiatric and medical conditions associated with attention and organizational deficits. These conditions should be kept in mind while evaluating a patient for possible ADHD, in order to avoid inaccurate diagnosis.

To compound the problem of accurate diagnosis, any of the conditions described above may occur in adult patients who have had childhood ADHD, whether their symptoms have persisted or resolved. Given the frequency of

TABLE 18.2. Conditions That May Include Attention and Organizational Deficits

Psychiatric	Medical
Schizophrenia	Head injury
Bipolar disorder	Dementia
Depression	Delirium
Antisocial Personality Disorder	Chronic obstructive pulmonary disease
Borderline Personality Disorder	Hypothyroidism
Alcohol intoxication or withdrawal	Hyperthyroidism
Other substance abuse disorders	Renal insufficiency
Intermittent explosive disorder	Hepatic insufficiency
Dissociative disorders	Anoxic encephalopathy
Posttraumatic stress disorder	Vitamin deficiency states

these disorders and of ADHD in the general population, the co-occurrence of other disorders requires careful evaluation. The chances of concurrence of ADHD with other disorders may be particularly high in cases of Antisocial Personality Disorder, substance abuse, or brain injury, since childhood ADHD may predispose patients to the development of these other conditions. Even so, a childhood history of ADHD does not eliminate the need for a careful differential diagnosis of adult attention dysfunction from other adult conditions known to be characterized by such dysfunction. Often, it may be indicated to treat the concurrent psychiatric or medical disorder first before assessing the remaining attentional symptoms for the presence of adult ADHD.

Wender, Reimherr, and Wood (1981) propose that the onset of hyperactivity or attentional disturbance must begin and persist from childhood in order for associated psychiatric symptoms to be linked with this disorder. Yet caution is certainly needed in applying this guideline because many adult patients requesting evaluation for ADHD were in school before the disorder was commonly recognized and diagnosed, and may have no documented diagnosis of ADHD as a result. Barkley, Fischer, Edelbrock, and Smallish (in press-b) have shown that adolescents with a well-documented history of ADHD underreport the nature and severity of their symptoms, as well as their conflicts with others. If such underreporting persists into adulthood, and there is reason to believe it may, then relying on a patient's own recollection of whether he or she had ADHD symptoms in childhood may result in ruling out a diagnosis of ADHD when in fact it is appropriate. Women patients with the disorder are particularly less likely to have been diagnosed as having had ADHD in childhood, in view of their lower likelihood of aggressive behavior (see Chapter 2), which would result in a lower chance of their having been referred for psychiatric or special educational services. Combined, these factors make the risk of a false negative concerning the ADHD diagnosis considerably greater with this population.

Accurate diagnosis is of paramount importance when considering treatment. For instance, methylphenidate is likely to worsen psychosis or hypomania and may contribute to further substance abuse in patients predisposed to abuse. Although methylphenidate may be helpful in treatment of depression, the depression usually returns after termination. Because of the side effects, methylphenidate may not be the treatment of choice for depression. The drug is also of no known utility in treating personality disorders. Consequently, a failure to detect these conditions in evaluating adults presenting with attention problems can readily lead to mistreatment.

There are as yet no consensus criteria for making the diagnosis of ADHD or residual ADHD in adults. Efforts have been made to adapt the earlier DSM-III criteria to adult diagnosis; most notable among these is the work by Wender and his colleagues at the University of Utah Medical School. Known as the "Utah Criteria for the Diagnosis of ADD Residual Type," these guidelines stipulate that a patient must have a childhood history, by self-report or parent report, consistent with the criteria for ADD described in Chapter 1. In addition, Wender (personal communication, August 3, 1989) stipulates that an adult must also have shown characteristics #1 and #2 below in childhood, and at least one characteristic from #3 through #6:

1. More active than other children, unable to sit still, fidgetiness, restlessness, always on the go, talking excessively.
2. Attention deficits, sometimes described as "short attention span," characterized by inattentiveness, distractibility, inability to finish schoolwork.
3. Behavior problems in school.
4. Impulsivity.
5. Overexcitability.
6. Temper outbursts.

Wender further stipulates that the first two characteristics described below must also be present in adulthood, as reported either by the patient himself or herself or by others, along with at least two characteristics from #3 to #7:

1. Persistent motor hyperactivity, as manifested by restlessness, inability to relax, "nervousness" (meaning inability to settle down rather than anticipatory anxiety), inability to persist in sedentary activities (e.g., watching movies, TV, reading newspaper), being always on the go, dysphoria when inactive.
2. Attention deficits, as manifested by inability to keep mind on conversation, distractibility (being aware of other stimuli when attempts are made to filter them out); inability to keep mind on reading materials; difficulty in keeping mind on job; frequent "forgetfulness" (often losing or misplacing things, forgetting plans, etc.); "mind frequently somewhere else."
3. Affective lability; usually described as antedating adolescence and in some instances going as far back as the patient can remember. This is manifested by definite shifts from a normal mood to depression or mild euphoria or excitement; depression is described as "down," "bored," or "discontented." Mood shifts usu-

ally last hours to at most a few days and are present without significant physiological concomitants. The shifts may occur spontaneously or be reactive.

4. *Inability to complete tasks.* The subject reports lack of organization in job, running household, or performing schoolwork; tasks are frequently not completed; the subject switches from one task to another in haphazard fashion; there is disorganization in activities, problem solving, and organizing time.

5. *Hot temper, explosive short-lived outbursts.* The subject may report that he or she has transient loss of control and is frightened by his or her own behavior. The subject is easily provoked or constantly irritable. Temper problems interfere with personal relationships.

6. *Impulsivity.* The subject makes decisions quickly and easily without reflection, often on the basis of insufficient information, and frequently to his or her own disadvantage. There is an inability to delay acting without experiencing discomfort. Manifestations include poor occupational performance; abrupt initiation or termination of relationships (e.g., multiple marriages, separations, divorces); antisocial behavior such as joyriding or shoplifting; and excessive involvement in pleasurable activities without recognizing risks of painful consequences (e.g., buying sprees, foolish business investments, reckless driving).

7. *Stress intolerance.* The subject cannot take ordinary stresses in stride and reacts excessively or inappropriately with depression, confusion, uncertainty, anxiety, or anger. Emotional responses interfere with appropriate problem solving. The subject experiences repeated crises in dealing with routine life stresses.

Wender also requires that symptoms of the following DSM-III disorders must be absent: Antisocial Personality Disorder, Major Affective Disorder, Schizophrenia, Schizoaffective Disorder, and Schizotypal or Borderline Personality Disorder. He notes a number of features often associated with ADD in adults, these being marital instability; less academic and vocational success than might be expected on the basis of intelligence and education; alcohol and drug abuse; atypical responses to psychoactive medications; familial history of similar characteristics; and family histories of ADD, alcoholism, drug abuse, Antisocial Personality, and Briquet's syndrome. Finally, the Utah Criteria recommend, although they do not require, a score greater than 12 on the 10-item Conners Abbreviated Rating Scale (see Appendix A) as rated by the patient's mother.

Wender's criteria should be viewed as rough guidelines to follow in evaluating ADHD in adults, but should not be strictly followed for a number of reasons. First, they lack empirical verification at this time and are in many ways founded on the now outdated DSM-III criteria for ADD. Although Biederman, Faraone, Knee, and Munir (1990) have recently found some evidence for the validity of retrospective recall of childhood symptoms of the DSM-III criteria in adult relatives of ADD children, this does not eliminate the numerous problems that plague the DSM-III symptom list (see Chapter 1). It would seem prudent to substitute the DSM-III-R for this first requirement in the Utah Criteria in view of the great overlap in types of items used in both the DSM-III and III-R symptom lists and the more empirical foundation of DSM-III-R, given the field trial on which it is based (Spitzer, Davies, & Barkley, in press). Second, the recommended number of symptoms is not based on any field tests or actual normative data and so it is not known how deviant a patient's behavior must be to actually fulfill these cutoff scores. Third, the inclusion of symptoms pertaining to temper outbursts and hostility toward others actually confounds the diagnosis of ADHD with that of ODD (see Chapter 6). This confounding of ADHD with aggression or ODD has caused numerous problems in the childhood ADHD literature and needs to be avoided in the adult literature where possible. In children at least, about 35% of those with ADHD will not show this pattern of hostile, defiant behavior and irritable mood. Yet it is quite conceivable that such children are still likely to persist in their ADHD symptoms into adulthood. Finally, the inclusion of stress intolerance as a criterion may be confusing the secondary effects of ADHD with its primary symptoms. In our view, these symptoms of stress intolerance should be listed as associated features because they may not always be present; they are not required in either the DSM-III or DSM-III-R childhood criteria; and they may contaminate the criteria with symptoms of Hysterical Personality, Dysthymia, anxiety, or other affective disorders.

In the future, the DSM-IV is likely to include either a separate listing of items for use with adults or, at the very least, a description of how the childhood symptoms should be modified for application to adult diagnosis of ADHD. The DSM-IV committee (Hechtman, personal communication, May 3, 1989) revising the ADHD category is attempting to draft items that reflect attentional problems at work and leisure activities, as well as at school for adults continuing in educational programs. It is also drafting items for impulsivity that reflect the frequency of moves, job changes, quitting of jobs, and other manifestations of impulsivity in adult life. Symptoms of labile mood may also be included especially as they affect relationships as well as dissatisfaction with life circumstances. However, here again a concern must be not to contaminate symptoms of ADHD with those of aggression or hostile and defiant behavior (ODD), as discussed earlier. Some of these draft items (Garfinkel, personal communication, February 5, 1990) are listed below to provide an appreciation for the types of concerns about attention and impulsivity that adult clients may express. However, these should not be viewed as the final DSM-IV criteria, because they are likely to be substantially modified by further committee deliberations and the results of a large-scale field trial planned for 1990–1991.

Draft symptom descriptions for Inattention are as follows:

1. trouble directing and sustaining attention (conversations, lectures, reading instructions, driving)
2. difficulty completing projects, lacks stick-to-it-tiveness
3. easily overwhelmed by tasks of daily living (managing money, paying bills, applying for college, etc.)
4. trouble maintaining an organized living/work place

5. inconsistent work performance
6. lacks attention to detail

Draft symptoms of Hyperactive/Impulsive behavior are as follows:

1. makes decisions impulsively and doesn't anticipate consequences
2. difficulty delaying gratification; seeks out stimulation
3. restless, fidgety
4. makes statements or comments without considering their impact
5. impatient, easily frustrated
6. traffic violations (speeding, running stop signs)

Meanwhile, we have found it useful to employ relatively broad criteria in making a diagnosis of adult ADHD until more empirically based guidelines can be developed. Like Wender, we recommend that evidence of a childhood history of hyperactivity of ADHD be present and that the clinician follow the DSM-III-R guidelines for assistance in making this determination. However, the individual need not meet the strict cutoff score requirements. Instead, we allow great clinical discretion based on the integrity of the sources of information being utilized, the adequacy of historical records that may be available, and the frailty of retrospective recall by both the patient and his or her parents. We also recommend that a rating scale be used to help establish deviance and find the Conners Abbreviated Rating Scale helpful in this respect; again, however, it is not mandatory, in view of the problems known to exist with this 10-item scale as discussed in Appendix A (e.g., it confounds oppositional and aggressive behavior with ADHD) and the lack of norms for use with adults. The ADHD Rating Scale (see Chapter 9) may also prove useful in this regard, although here again normative data are lacking for adults. We are exploring whether the Child Behavior Checklist (CBCL; the original parent form and the Youth Self-Report Form) may be more useful given the greater number of items assessing ADHD on that scale than on the Conners 10-item scale.Comparison of the results on the CBCL Hyperactivity scale (parent form) with the norms for 12- to 16-year-olds would at least provide the clinician with a rough gauge of the adult patient's statistical deviance. Finally, like Wender, we rule out the existence of psychoses, schizophrenia and related disorders, Major Affective Disorder, or Borderline Personality Disorder. However, we do not exclude the diagnosis of Antisocial Personality as up to 25% of ADHD children are likely to meet criteria for this disorder upon reaching adulthood (Gittelman et al., 1985; Weiss & Hechtman, 1986). It is the pattern of presenting symptoms and associated features that is important in diagnosis at this point in the development of this new field, rather than any rigid adherence to specific yet unempirical criteria.

Clinical Assessment

The diagnostic assessment of adult ADHD typically follows the same bio-psychosocial-developmental model outlined in Chapter 7. It begins with a rigorous history. We have found a semistructured interview tailored to the evaluation of ADHD to be useful in substantiating the disorder and in studying associated symptoms and potential commonalities of presentation.

The evaluation should also include the use of behavior rating scales. Rating scales have proven especially useful in the assessment of children with ADHD (see Chapter 9) and hold equal promise for use with adults with ADHD as well. These scales permit the patient and others familiar with him or her to report their observations of behavior collapsed across lengthy time periods that would be otherwise impossible to assess clinically. We believe, therefore, that it is useful to have family members, spouses, or significant others fill out rating forms similar to those completed by the adult patient even though adequate normative data are lacking on such rating scales for adult populations. As a rough gauge of deviance, reports by others about the patient on the CBCL can be compared with the norms for 16-year-olds. A similar approach can be taken with the Conners Parent Rating Scale—Revised, which has normative data to age 17 years. We have also found it beneficial to compare patients' self-ratings with those of others familiar with their behavior as discrepancies may often exist regarding the degree of symptoms present. Consequently, we are reluctant to make the diagnosis of adult residual ADHD and to consider trials of stimulant medication without independent verification of behaviors essential to the diagnosis, in part because of the likelihood that adult patients may underreport or otherwise misrepresent the actual nature of their attentional disturbances.

University of Massachusetts Protocol for Assessment of ADHD Adults

All patients referred to the University of Massachusetts Medical Center (UMMC) for assessment of ADHD are requested to bring someone to the interview who is familiar with their behavior. A parent or spouse is preferred. On arrival, the patients are asked to fill out a number of questionnaires: the Symptom Checklist 90—Revised (SCL-90-R; see Chapter 9); the UMMC ambulatory psychiatry symptom rating scale (Figure 18.1); a checklist of physical complaints, to provide a baseline evaluation against which to assess clinical side effects of medication (Figure 18.2) should such treatment be indicated; and a checklist of 18 symptoms characteristic of adults with ADHD (Figure 18.3), 14 of which are taken from the criteria for ADHD from the DSM-III-R and 4 more from a questionnaire developed by Gittelman (1985a, b).

The time taken to complete the questionnaires is also recorded. Most patients complete these forms within 15 minutes; however, for some patients this part of the process can become quite time-consuming because their attentional or other psychiatric problems may in fact interfere with their attention to this task.

Adequate time must also be budgeted for the initial interview. In our experience, this interview may take $1\frac{1}{2}$ to 2 hours by itself, especially if the patient has obsessive-compulsive features or a schizophrenic-spectrum disor-

Name _____ **Date** _____

Please rate the degree to which you have been experiencing the following problems during the PAST WEEK by making an "X" across each of the following lines:

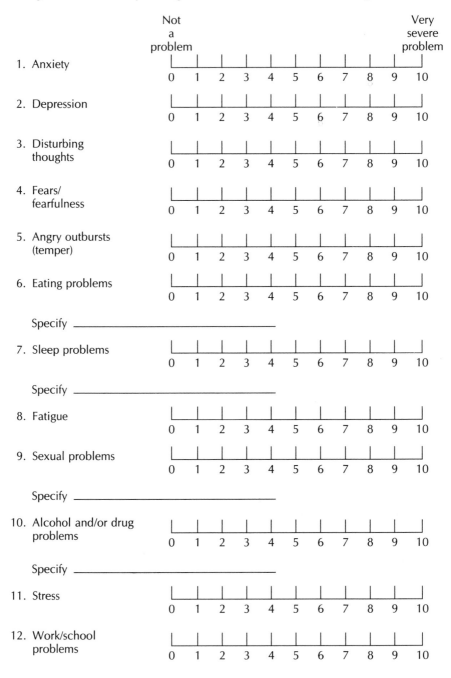

	Not a problem									Very severe problem
	0	1	2	3	4	5	6	7	8	9	10

1. Anxiety

2. Depression

3. Disturbing thoughts

4. Fears/fearfulness

5. Angry outbursts (temper)

6. Eating problems

   Specify _____

7. Sleep problems

   Specify _____

8. Fatigue

9. Sexual problems

   Specify _____

10. Alcohol and/or drug problems

    Specify _____

11. Stress

12. Work/school problems

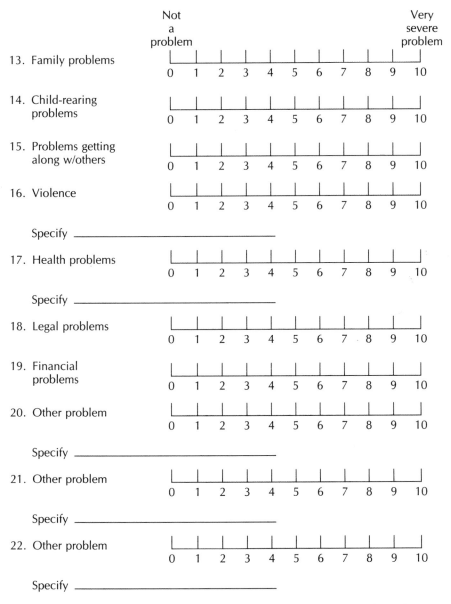

Please circle the numbers of *UP TO THREE* problems that you consider to be your *MAIN* problem(s).

FIGURE 18.1. Self-Rating Symptom Checklist.

Name _____

Date _____

Below is a list of symptoms that some people have. Beside each item indicate how often each is a problem for you.

	Never	Less than 4 times/yr	Less than once/mo.	Less than once/wk	1–3 times/wk	Nearly daily
1. Headaches						
2. Trouble sleeping						
3. Irritable, nervous						
4. Stomach upset						
5. Aches and pains (not backache)						
6. Backache						
7. Rapid heartbeat						
8. Dizziness/ lightheadedness						
9. Vomiting, nausea						
10. Diarrhea						
11. Constipation						
12. Weakness						
13. Tired during the day						
14. Poor appetite						
15. Blurred vision						
16. Dry mouth						
17. Confusion						

FIGURE 18.2. Physical Complaints Checklist.

der. At this same time, the person accompanying the patient is asked to fill out a symptom checklist rating the patient on the same 18 ADHD symptoms on which the patient has rated himself or herself.

The semistructured interview assesses the following: (1) degree of previous knowledge about the diagnostic criteria and treatment of ADHD; (2) current and childhood symptoms, including those associated with ADHD; (3) psy-

Name _____

Date _____

Below is a list of problems and behaviors that some patients have. Beside each item indicate how much of a problem each one is for you in *your* opinion.

	Not at all	Just a little	Pretty much	Very much
1. Physical restlessness				
2. Mental restlessness				
3. Easily distracted				
4. Impatient				
5. "Hot" or explosive temper				
6. Unpredictable behavior				
7. Difficulty completing tasks				
8. Shifting from one task to another				
9. Difficulty sustaining attention				
10. Impulsive				
11. Talks too much				
12. Difficulty doing tasks alone				
13. Often interrupts others				
14. Doesn't appear to listen to others				
15. Loses a lot of things				
16. Forgets to do things				
17. Engages in physically daring activities				
18. Always on the go, as if driven by a motor				

FIGURE 18.3. Patient's Behavior Checklist.

chiatric history, including presence of affective disorder, schizophrenia, or anxiety disorders (including Obsessive Compulsive Disorder); (4) character disorder; (5) presence of substance abuse (including nicotine and caffeine); and (6) detailed social, occupational, and legal history designed to assess degree of functioning. The complete semistructured interview is given in Appendix 18.1.

The interview begins in a general, open-ended fashion. This allows the clinician to assess the patient's coherence and executive functions, including organizational ability, attentiveness, and ability to establish and maintain set. Assessing distractibility may be more difficult since interview rooms are frequently isolated and soundproof. Once this information is gathered, the questions revert to a structured format requiring simple answers. The interview ends with another open-ended task (gathering the occupational history), to provide an additional opportunity to assess the patient's general organizational ability. During the interview, motor behavior and mental status are recorded.

After the interview, the examiner explains the importance of assessment of substance abuse in evaluating attentional dysfunction and asks the patient to submit a urine specimen for toxicology. Continuation of treatment is not affected by the patient's response to this request as some patients may refuse to comply with it. Other patients will have already admitted significant substance abuse during the interview and are not disturbed or offended by the request. A few patients initially deny the abuse but later supply more accurate histories after a positive urine test.

The request for a urine specimen presents an opportunity to measure attention in a scenario resembling a real-life situation. The request is given as part of a three-step command: (1) take the container to the bathroom and obtain the specimen; (2) fill out an ADHD symptom questionnaire; and (3) return to the waiting room when finished. Some patients with serious attention problems have difficulty in following this command.

As in all standard clinical practice, releases are requested for school or medical reports when appropriate. After the interview, if the patient is felt to have contributing neurological factors, a neuropsychiatric examination (including neurological examination, neurodevelopmental screening exam, and detailed mental status assessment) is done. Those patients whose symptoms appear to be consistent with ADHD or other attentional deficits and who are not actively abusing a substance are referred for neuropsychological assessment. On completion of evaluation, the patient returns to discuss treatment options which include no treatment, referral for treatment of concurrent psychiatric illness, or counseling and perhaps medication for the symptoms of the attention deficit.

Neuropsychological Assessment

Although ADHD is a biological disorder, the lesion or lesions producing it have yet to be identified. Some studies have implicated the orbital-frontal region, the limbic pathways, and especially the striatum (see Chapter 3). There are also data suggesting that neuropsychological deficits are part of the disorder (see Chapter 3). In some cases, these deficits may persist into adulthood. As noted earlier, Buchsbaum and his associates demonstrated that college males who performed poorly on a test of sustained attention also did poorly on tests of reaction time, memory, and novel problem solving. However, their subjects were selected on the basis of poor performance on a neuropsychological measure of attention. They were not chosen because of a substantiated history of childhood ADHD.

Wood, Reimherr, Wender, and Johnson (1976) studied 15 adults with longstanding attentional difficulties. Individuals with schizophrenia, primary affective disorder, organic brain syndrome, or mental retardation were excluded. The purpose of this study was to assess the effectiveness of stimulant medication in treating attentional deficits in adults. However, some psychological testing was accomplished. Intellectually, subjects were in the average range: The mean IQ estimated from an abbreviated Wechsler Adult Intelligence Scale (WAIS) was 111. Nevertheless, subjects evidenced difficulty on the written Arithmetic section of the Wide Range Achievement Test (WRAT): Mean score was 80 with a standard deviation of 15. The average score was considerably below expectations in view of their subjects' normal IQ scores and average scores on the Reading and Spelling sections of the WRAT.

These authors attempted to replicate this study with a group of adults who met the operational Utah Criteria for ADD (Wender, Reimherr, & Wood, 1981). The parents of these subjects were given the Conners Abbreviated Rating Scale to complete retrospectively. Psychological test results of subjects who were rated hyperactive as children by their parents were consistent with those reported by the authors in their earlier study. As a group, these individuals had normal IQ scores. However, males evidenced relative problems in academic achievement on the WRAT.

Klee, Garfinkel, and Beauchesen (1986) studied 12 adult males diagnosed in childhood as having ADD. Performances on psychometric tests and responses on behavioral self-report inventories were compared to those of matched controls. Psychometric measures assessed components of attention and impulsivity. The rating scales were modifications of the Conners Teacher Rating Scale (see Chapter 9 and Appendix A). Forms were developed to assess motor activity, concentration, peer relations, mood, temper, organization, and medical problems at the time of administration and during childhood.

Adults diagnosed with ADD as children were found to perform more poorly on some measures of attention than did controls. Specifically, they did less well on the Digit Symbol subtest of the WAIS and made more omission errors on a CPT. They also had lower CPT composite scores, reflecting a combination of commission and omission errors. There was no difference between the groups on self-ratings of current behavior, despite these measured differences on cognitive tests. Significant differences were present on ratings of childhood behavior. The ADD group indicated significantly more childhood behavioral difficulties, consistent with the diagnosis.

Indications from these studies suggest that cognitive inefficiency may persist into adulthood and, in some cases, may be part of adult ADHD. Nevertheless, studies of cognitive deficits associated with adult residual ADHD are few and the type and degree of cognitive impairment continue to warrant investigation. To date, no single battery of tests has been shown to be most effective in studying this disorder. We have developed a protocol for the neuropsychological assessment of adults suspected to have residual ADHD. The protocol is composed of a series of measures thought to be sensitive to cognitive inefficiencies that may be associated with adult ADHD. Specific tests and reasons for selection are described below.

Measures of Attention

Most neuropsychological functions are complex, and that of attention is no exception (Barkley, 1988e). A construct such as attention involves a number of components and individuals deficient in one aspect may not be deficient in others. Recently, Mirsky (1987, 1989) has proposed a model of attention based on factor analysis. It incorporates several different types of attention and includes tests for measurement of each. Mirsky has also suggested anatomical sites where lesions may disrupt a particular type of attention. The localization component is somewhat speculative and relies partially on animal studies.

Mirsky has identified four separate attentional processes: (1) the capacity to focus upon and execute tasks over a short time span; (2) the capacity to encode and mentally manipulate information; (3) the capacity to sustain attention over a longer time period; and (4) the capacity to shift attentional focus flexibly. The neuropsychological test protocol used at UMMC to assess patients with adult residual ADHD uses tests shown by Mirsky to assess these four attentional factors. The tests employed at UMMC and the factors they are believed to assess are listed below:

Focused Attention	Trail Making Tests, Parts A and B
	WAIS-R Digit Symbol subtest
Encoding/Manipulating	WAIS-R Digit Span subtest
	WAIS-R Arithmetic subtest
Sustained Attention	Adaptive Rate Continuous Performance Test
Flexibility	Wisconsin Card Sorting Test

The Trail Making Tests are part of the Halstead-Reitan Neuropsychological Test Battery (Reitan, 1986). The WAIS-R (Wechsler, 1981) is a widely employed instrument in both clinical and neuropsychology. The Wisconsin Card Sorting Test (Heaton, 1981) is used in neuropsychology; it is thought to be sensitive to frontal lobe dysfunction in patients with focal deficits. CPTs are administered less routinely in neuropsychological assessment. However, CPTs are increasingly commercially available and are likely to become more commonplace in such assessments as neuropsychologists become more aware of the need to assess various aspects of attention. The CPT used in our clinic is the Adaptive Rate Continuous Performance Test (Ringholz, 1988, personal communication). It was chosen because it provides a number of measures of vigilance and performance variability in addition to standard scores such as hits, omissions, and false alarms. The CPT by Gordon (see Chapter 10) may also be useful with adults, especially in view of its recently demonstrated sensitivity to ADHD in adolescents (Fischer, Barkley, Edelbrock, & Smallish, in press).

We include an additional measure of attention not used by Mirsky in his factorial model. The Paced Auditory Serial Addition Test (PASAT) was developed by Gronwall (1977; Gronwall & Sampson, 1974; Gronwall & Wrightson, 1981) as a measure of postconcussion effects. The PASAT tests information-processing speed and was used by Gronwall (1977) and her colleagues to assess readiness to return to work following concussion. We include this test in our battery because it assesses novel features of attention. In view of recent findings that the Stroop test (Stroop, 1935) may be sensitive to differences in attention and behavioral inhibition between ADHD and control groups of children (Grodzinsky, 1990), this test may also have some value in testing adults suspected of having ADHD and can be added to this battery.

At this time it is important to note that none of the above-described measures have unequivocally proven themselves to be empirically validated in the discrimination of ADHD from other psychiatric disorders of adulthood. Many have certainly shown some demonstrated sensitivity to attentional deficits in adults with various psychiatric or neurological disorders, but their utility in accurately classifying adults with ADHD against other control groups awaits demonstration. However, a negative score on any test or this set of tests does not rule out the diagnosis of ADHD because these tests are likely to have a significant percentage of false negatives in an adult ADHD population as they do in children with ADHD (see Chapter 10). They are used in our protocol to document possible dysfunctions in various components of attention and not, by themselves, to render the diagnosis of ADHD.

Memory Tests

Parameters important in the assessment of memory include rate of acquisition, stability of recall, and material specificity. Memory deficits associated with ADHD are more apt to be subtle than those associated with structural brain lesions. These deficits may involve an organizational component, especially in retrieval of information. The patient has adequate memory encoding but fails to exercise efficient or well-organized strategies for searching and utilizing memory stores in meeting the demands of the task. To assess these components, we employ the Verbal Selective Reminding Test (Peters & Levin, 1977) and a nonverbal analogue, the Nonverbal Selective Reminding Test (Kane & Perrine, 1985). Selective reminding procedures are sensitive to subtle changes in memory (Peters & Levin, 1977, 1979). When factored with other memory measures, the Verbal and Nonverbal Selective Reminding Tests form independent factors related to verbal recall and nonverbal recognition memory (Kane & Perrine, 1985).

As noted in Chapter 4, Fischer et al. (in press) were unable to demonstrate deficits on a verbal selective reminding test similar to that described above in adolescents with a childhood history of hyperactivity even though over 70% of these subjects continued to meet criteria for ADHD. Barkley, DuPaul, and McMurray (in press-a) also failed to show deficits on a children's version of this verbal memory task in children with well-documented ADHD. However, they did find that children with ADD/−H were significantly impaired in their consistent retrieval of information in long-term storage on this verbal selective reminding test. This implies that deficits of this type on this task may be more indicative of a deficit in focused attention rather than in sustained attention, which is the deficit more likely to be seen in ADHD.

We also employ the Rey-Osterreith Complex Figure Test (Lezak, 1983). The test is given by asking the patient to copy a complex design. Various schemes, such as the use of colored pencils, may be employed to assess the patient's degree of organization in copying the design. Immediately after the patient copies the design, the examiner removes the model and asks the subject to reproduce the design from memory. Twenty minutes later, the examiner again asks the subject to reproduce the design. From this test, measures of organization, constructional ability, immediate recall, and delayed recall are obtained.

Intellectual Level

General intellectual deficits do not appear to be a primary part of the ADHD syndrome. However, studies have noted that ADHD children may score somewhat lower on intelligence tests than control groups of children or even their own siblings (see Chapter 3). It is not clear whether this difference is due to the interference of the attention deficit with the test-taking ability of the ADHD children or actually reflects a real deficiency in intelligence. Nevertheless, when assessing the individual patient, it is important to include a measure of general intellectual level. This is useful in vocational planning and aids in the interpretation of scores obtained on other cognitive measures. We have found the Shipley Institute of Living Scale (Shipley, 1946; Zachary, 1986) helpful. It takes 15 to 20 minutes to administer and produces a reasonable estimate of a patient's WAIS-R Full Scale IQ score. The Shipley Abstraction Quotient measures the degree to which a patient's score on the Abstraction section of the test conforms to predictions based on vocabulary score, age, and level of education.

Academic Achievement Tests

We employ two measures of academic achievement in our battery: the WRAT-R (Jastak & Wilkinson, 1984) and the Nelson-Denny Reading Test (Brown,

Bennett, & Hanna, 1981). The WRAT-R is a brief measure of word reading, spelling, and arithmetic computation. It identifies the presence of learning deficits. The Nelson-Denny assesses both reading rate and comprehension. Individuals with attentional problems may have difficulty with reading comprehension despite intact basic academic skills. However, in view of findings that over 30% of ADHD children have a learning disability (see Chapter 3) and that such disabilities rarely remit completely, it is likely that a significant minority of adults with ADHD may also have an associated learning disability that requires careful assessment in its own right.

Behavioral Observations

As yet, no studies have examined the utility of using systematically recorded behavioral observations of ADHD symptoms with adults with ADHD. However, such observations may actually offer great promise, as they have been shown to be quite sensitive to differences in ADHD behaviors between children with ADHD and various control groups (see Chapter 2). Furthermore, Fischer et al. (in press) found significant differences between adolescents with ADHD and a matched control group on behavioral observations of ADHD symptoms taken while the subjects performed arithmetic problems. There is no reason why observation codes such as those described in Chapter 10 could not be used with adults for recording behavior during task performance, especially when academic work or a CPT is being performed by the adult patient. Future investigations exploring the utility of systematic behavioral observations with adults with ADHD are to be encouraged.

TREATMENT

There is very little information available in the scientific literature to guide the clinical management of ADHD in adults. What little exists pertains to medication treatment, and even this evidence is conflicting. Careful judgment and common sense are therefore essential in approaching the treatment of adults with ADHD. Below we list suggestions that we have followed in treating our ADHD clients, but caution the reader to use them only as the suggestions they are and not as well-proven therapies.

Psychopharmacological Treatments

There is evidence in the literature that pharmacotherapy may be useful in treating some adults with ADHD. Positive results were reported by Wood et al. (1976) for both stimulant and antidepressant medication. Of 15 subjects, 11 were given a double-blind trial of methylphenidate. All subjects received an open trial of pemoline or of a tricyclic antidepressant. A positive response was seen in 8 of the 11 subjects treated with methylphenidate. Improvements noted included decreased nervousness, improved concentration, and better temper control. Eight of the subjects showed a good response to stimulants or tricyclics. Two subjects had moderately favorable responses, and five were unresponsive to pharmacological intervention.

Wender et al. (1981) studied pemoline in treating adults with ADD. Subjects meeting operational criteria for the diagnosis were entered into a random-assignment, parallel, double-blind trial. Active drug was more effective than placebo for patients whose hyperactivity in childhood was rated in the 95th percentile by their parents.

In their review of drug studies with ADHD adults, Wender, Wood, and Reimherr (1985) state that 60% of patients evidence positive symptomatic response to pharmacological intervention. They recommend that drug trials begin with either methylphenidate or *d*-amphetamine.

Clinically, our treatment methods vary and depend upon assessment of the most salient features of a patient's presentation. Primary psychiatric disorders are treated before treatment aimed solely at ADHD is initiated. Patients with depression are treated with a tricyclic antidepressant, usually imipramine or desipramine, since these tricyclics have been reported to be effective in ADHD (see Chapter 17). Individual or group therapy is recommended if indicated. After the depression improves, attention problems and level of functioning are reassessed. If warranted, treatment is then directed at the ADHD symptoms.

Symptoms of hypomania (irritability, hyperactivity, insomnia, impulsivity, etc.) are treated with lithium, especially if there is a family history of affective illness. The trial is easily tolerated and of relatively short duration. Response can be assessed without unduly postponing trials with other medications if these are needed. The treatment sequence protects against committing a patient to an experimental treatment for adult ADHD when an undiagnosed, very common, and easily treatable disorder may be present. If the patient fails to respond to treatment for hypomania, again we revert to the usual protocol for the patient presenting with ADHD alone.

Active substance abuse disorders are referred for treatment. Attentional symptoms are reevaluated when the substance abuse is in full remission. Patients who use marijuana intermittently or who drink moderate amounts of alcohol (a glass of wine per night or two beers per night) are asked to abstain from these substances prior to and during medication treatment. Patients with modest alcohol intake have experienced nearly complete resolution of their ADHD symptoms with abstinence. These individuals have required no further treatment.

Neither methylphenidate nor tricyclic antidepressants have received Food and Drug Administration (FDA) approval for treatment of ADHD in adults. Patients (and often their spouses) are carefully informed of the experimental nature of the treatment and the lack of available data regarding efficacy or adverse effects during long-term use with adults. Common and serious side effects are reviewed with patients. They are asked to avoid using cold medicines that contain stimulants. Documentation of this discussion in each patient's chart is essential.

Many adults have difficulty tolerating regular methylphenidate because of anxiety and restlessness. For this reason, treatment is usually initiated with a sustained-release preparation. Doses range from 20 to 40 milligrams each morning. Many patients take methylphenidate only during the work week, when organizational and attentional skills are most in demand. Parents with young children often continue taking medication through the weekend as they find that child raising also makes demands on attention and organizational abilities. For most patients, the morning dose alone is effective. A few patients take a second dose shortly after lunch to sustain effectiveness through the dinner hour. Methylphenidate is not given after 3 P.M. because of the potential for interference with sleep.

Prior to medication treatment a physical examination is performed by the patient's primary physician, and the following laboratory studies are obtained: an electrocardiogram, a chemistry 12 with liver and renal function tests, a complete blood count with differential and platelet count, thyroid function tests, vital signs, and weight. An Abnormal Involuntary Movements Scale (AIMS; Munetz & Benjamin, 1988) can be administered prior to the medication trial. AIMS results serve as baseline data for measuring the development of abnormal movements, such as tics, during the subsequent drug trial. The Side Effects Rating Scale (see Chapter 17) may also be of some benefit in monitoring these behavioral side effects. Relative contraindications to methylphenidate treatment include the presence of substance abuse, tic disorders, agitated behavior, cardiac disorders, glaucoma, marked anxiety, thought disturbance, and family history of Gilles de la Tourette syndrome. Methylphenidate should be used cautiously in the presence of hypertension since it may exacerbate it. Teratogenic effects of methylphenidate are not clear so it should not be used in women of child-bearing age unless adequate contraception is utilized. A pregnancy test should be done on all female patients of child-bearing age before drug treatment for their ADHD is initiated.

Blood pressure, weight, motor behavior, and liver function are monitored regularly throughout treatment. Periodically the spouse or parent is asked to reassess the level of symptoms seen in the patient during the medication trial. If treatment is effective, striking results ususally occur within the first week or two. After a period of improvement, patients may discontinue their medication, apparently failing to appreciate the magnitude of the untreated problem or its likely persistence. This usually results in sudden re-emergence of symptoms and return to compliance with medication. The spouse or parent is frequently more sensitive to behavioral change than is the patient and this significant other should be included in feedback visits. After the medication routine and follow-up are established, and if the patient has no problematic side effects, visits are spaced to every 3 months. Questionnaires are readministered twice a year.

Some patients are unable to tolerate methyphenidate therapy because of excessive jitteriness, anxiety, or weight loss. Other patients wish to avoid it because of misconceptions about its potentially addictive properties. In these cases, imipramine or desipramine is a reasonable choice for treatment.

A number of agents have been used in the treatment of posttraumatic attention deficits. Dopamine agonists have been tried for behavior initiation problems and for attention/concentration problems following head injury (Gualtieri, 1988). Studied medications include bromocriptine, amantadine, and deprenyl (a monoamine oxidase B [MAO-B] inhibitor that increases the amount of available dopamine). Open trials of pargyline and of deprenyl have shown these agents to have some efficacy in adult ADHD (Wender, Wood, & Reimherr, 1985). In low doses, pargyline is an MAO-B-specific inhibitor. Deprenyl is a complete MAO-B inhibitor.

Psychological Therapies

It is unclear to what extent specific behavioral approaches may augment pharmacological treatment in the adult with ADHD. Since the basis of the disorder is biological, it is unlikely that behavioral therapies will prove sufficient for treatment of the disorder. Nevertheless, the adjunctive role of psychological therapy deserves investigation. Wood (1986) has noted several areas in which psychotherapy might assist the adult with ADHD. Targets for such therapy might include increasing self-esteem, refining interpersonal skills, teaching medication management, and providing vocational assessment and counseling. To this list we would add the teaching of time management and self-organization skills via an individual counseling format, and at times the inclusion of anger-control methods adapted from those discussed in Chapter 16. Adaptation of some of the behavior modification methods and self-control therapies described in Chapter 15 may also be useful, especially for the young adult trying to meet the demands of a college or vocational training program. Frequently, significant others in the life of the ADHD adult must be requested to assist the patient in some of these endeavors, much as parents and teachers of ADHD children are indispensable to helping the children to be more attentive, more compliant, more reflective, and better organized. Moreover, the family systems, problem-solving/communication training, and conflict-negotiating tactics discussed in Chapters 13 and 14 are likely to prove promising, when modified for adult interpersonal conflicts, in addressing the marital, family, and even occupational conflicts experienced by ADHD adults.

A rehabilitation focus similar to that employed with brain-impaired patients might also prove useful. The psychoeducational group model may be best suited for this endeavor. In short, while the earlier chapters on treatment in this volume are specifically intended for children and adolescents, the reader wishing treatment suggestions for ADHD adults should be acquainted with these methods and draw upon them for possible adaptations to working with ADHD adults.

RESEARCH DIRECTIONS

Adult ADHD is a greatly underinvestigated area, requiring additional research related to diagnosis and treatment. Symptoms such as problems with attention, difficulty with organization and self-regulation, and disturbance of mood are not limited to a single psychiatric diagnosis. The need for childhood onset of ADHD symptoms is central to diagnosis in adults. Nevertheless, the relationship of substance abuse, character disorder, impulse control disorder, and affective disorder to the persistence of ADHD into adulthood requires further investigation. It is unclear whether the association of other psychiatric disorders with ADHD reflects a common etiology, or indicates that one disorder predisposes an individual to another. Delineation of this relationship would greatly facilitate appropriate diagnosis and management.

Much of the work on adult ADHD to date has relied on adaptations of rating scales designed for use in diagnosis of childhood ADHD. There is a need for the development and validation of rating instruments for adult ADHD that include items relevant to adult occupational, educational, and social skills. A similar state of affairs exists regarding the use of structured psychiatric interviews for assisting in diagnosis. Current interviews of this type do not typically include symptoms of ADHD; this means that subsections of child diagnostic interviews must be included in these adult interviews to make them useful. Research on the validity of doing so is in great demand.

The efficacy and safety of pharmacological treatments for adult ADHD need much further study. Possible future approval of methylphenidate by the FDA for treatment of adult ADHD hinges on these issues. Reports of efficacy have been encouraging, but studies have suffered from limited sample size and questions concerning differential diagnosis. A similar state of affairs exists regarding the use of tricyclic antidepressants with adults with ADHD.

Further work is also needed to clarify whether there are subtypes of adult ADHD that might influence treatment selection. This includes the admonition that ADD/−H may well exist in adulthood as it does in childhood (see Chapter 2); like its childhood counterpart, adult ADD/−H may well have a very different set of presenting symptoms, course, and response to treatment, not to mention a dysfunction in a different component of attention than occurs in ADHD. Future research in subtyping ADHD would also do well to heed the substantial childhood literature on this subject and explore the utility of subgrouping ADHD adults on the basis of the presence and degree of aggressive symptoms (hostile, defiant behavior) and even antisocial features. Similarly, subtypes based on the presence and degree of internalizing symptoms, such as anxiety and depression, are proving of some use in selecting medications for ADHD children (e.g., stimulants vs. antidepressants; see Chapter 17) and may prove equally useful in selecting treatments for subtypes of adults with ADHD.

Other questions, such as how long to continue treatment and whether behavioral interventions help improve quality of life, also need investigation. Adaptations of the problem-solving/communication training approach described in Chapter 14 by Robin may be useful in providing marital therapy for couples in which one spouse is afflicted with ADHD, especially where hostile and aggressive behaviors are present in the relationship. Similarly, the anger control training program for ADHD children developed by Hinshaw and colleagues (see Chapter 16) might be tested for its utility with ADHD adults who are hampered interpersonally by quickness to anger, irritability, and overemotional behavior in general. The design of behavioral interventions, perhaps even combined with stimulant medication, for reducing the risk of automobile accidents in ADHD adults certainly demands immediate research attention.

CONCLUSION

In this chapter, we have provided an overview of the nature of ADHD in adults as it is currently understood in the limited literature available on the subject. We have also set forth rough guidelines for the clinical assessment and management of this disorder, based upon our preliminary work with a relatively large sample of adults referred to an adult ADHD clinic at our medical center. From the existing (albeit scant) literature on treatment of adults and predominantly from our clinical experience to date, we have attempted to suggest treatment recommendations that may be useful for the adult with ADHD. In doing this, we have stressed the tremendous need for well-controlled research in this area. Nevertheless, it is clear that adults with ADHD do exist and will constitute an increasingly large pool of clients referred to mental health and medical centers for treatment in the future. It is more than timely that clinicians now prepare themselves to contend with what promises to be a sizeable population of new referrals for assessment, differential diagnosis, and management of this personally, socially, educationally, and occupationally disabling condition.

7. When would you say these problems began? (Circle any one)
    1. 0–7 years
    2. 8–12 years
    3. 13–15 years
    4. 16–21 years
    5. 22 to present
8. Now I'm going to ask you some symptoms, and I'd like you to tell me if they were ever more of a problem for you than for other people in your peer group.

Symptom	Yes	No	Now is it: Same	Better	Worse	Comments
a. Fidgetiness or feeling restless						
b. Difficulty remaining satisfied						
c. Being easily distracted						
d. Difficulty waiting your turn						
e. Blurting out answers before the question is completed						
f. Difficulty following through on or completing tasks						
g. Sustaining attention in tasks						
h. Frequently shifting from one task to another						
i. Difficulty doing tasks alone						
j. Talking too much						
k. Interrupting or intruding on others						
l. Not listening to others						
m. Losing important things or forgetting a lot						
n. Engaging in physically daring activities						
o. Always on the go, as if driven by a motor						

APPENDIX 18.1

SEMISTRUCTURED INTERVIEW FOR ADULT ADHD

Name _____   Date _____

Patient No. _____   Time _____

Date of Birth _____   Interviewer _____

Age _____

1. What led you to seek an evaluation for ADHD now?

2. What is your understanding of this disorder?

3. What do you know about the treatment of this disorder?

4. Do you know anyone else who was diagnosed with this disorder?
    1. Yes
    2. No
    3. Not sure
5. If yes, how were they treated for this disorder? (Circle any that apply)
    1. Ritalin or methylphenidate only
    2. Unknown medication or other medication only
    3. Therapy (group or individual) only
    4. Not sure how they were treated
    5. Other
   Comments:

6. What are your greatest concerns about your behavior now?

Symptom	Yes	No	Now is it: Same	Better	Worse	Comments

p. Making decisions too quickly or act- ing too quickly

q. Impatient

9. Did you ever seek treatment for these problems before? (Circle one)

   a. Yes
   b. No

   If yes, when and where did you seek treatment?

   What was the recommended treatment and the outcome?

10. Did your parents ever take you to see anyone about these problems when you were a child or adolescent?

    a. Yes
    b. No
    c. Not sure

11. Did your parents complain that you were difficult to control as a child?

    a. Yes
    b. No
    c. Not sure

    If yes, during what ages did they have this complaint? (Circle all that apply)

    a. 0–7 years   d. 16–21
    b. 8–12   e. 22+
    c. 13–15

12. Now I'm going to ask you some questions about school. What is the highest level of school that you have completed?

    a. 6th grade or less   e. Graduated from high school
    b. 7th or 8th grade   f. 1 or 2 years college
    c. Freshman or sophomore   g. 3 or 4 years college
    d. Junior high school   h. Postgraduate

13. Did you have any trouble starting school in kindergarten or first grade?

14. Did you ever repeat a grade?

    a. Yes
    b. No

    If yes, which grades did you repeat? _____

15. Were you ever in any special classes in school?

    a. Yes
    b. No

    If yes, what kinds of special classes were you in?

16. How would you describe your grades in school?

    a. Average
    b. Better than average
    c. Worse than average

17. What was your best subject in school? _____

18. What was your worst subject in school? _____

19. Did your teachers think you did as well as you could?

    a. Yes
    b. No
    c. Not sure

20. Were you ever truant from school?

    a. Yes
    b. No

If yes, how often and during what grades?

21. Were you ever expelled or suspended from school?

    a. Yes
    b. No

22. Did you ever get in any physical fights at school?

    a. Yes
    b. No

If yes:

    I. During which grades did you get into fights?
        a. K–6th grade
        b. 7th or 8th grade
        c. High school
        d. other

    II. How many times did you get into fights?
        a. One time
        b. Two to five times
        c. Six to ten times
        d. More than ten times

    III. Did you sometimes start the fight?
        a. Yes
        b. No
        c. Not sure

    IV. Did you ever use a weapon in a fight?
        a. Yes
        b. No

23. Did you ever run away from home overnight?

    a. Yes
    b. No

If yes:

    I. How many times did you run away?

      a. Once
      b. Two to five times
      c. Six to ten times
      d. More than ten times

   II. What was the longest duration you ran away from home?
      a. One night
      b. Two to five nights
      c. Six to ten nights
      d. Longer than ten nights

24. Did you ever get in trouble for stealing or damaging property as a child or teen-ager?
    a. Yes
    b. No

25. Have you ever been arrested or in trouble with the law?
    a. Yes
    b. No

26. Do you have a driver's license?
    a. Yes
    b. No

   If yes:

   I. How many traffic tickets (not parking tickets) have you ever gotten?
      a. None
      b. One
      c. Two to three
      d. Four to five

   II. How many car accidents have you ever been in?
      a. None   d. Three
      b. One   e. Four or more
      c. Two

   If no: Why don't you have a driver's license?

27. Do you have problems with your temper?
    a. Yes
    b. No
   If yes, details:

28. Did you ever have any problems with your temper?
    a. Yes
    b. No
    c. Not sure

29. Have you ever lost your temper enough to hurt anyone or damage any property?
    a. Yes
    b. No
    If yes, details:

30. Do other people complain about your temper?
    a. Yes
    b. No
    c. Not sure

31. How would you describe your mood most of the time?
    a. Normal and fairly stable
    b. Anxious or nervous
    c. Depressed, sad, or blue
    d. Labile; mood changes a lot
    e. Other: _____

32. Do you have any problems with your sleep?
    a. Yes
    b. No
    If yes, details:

33. Do you have any problems with your weight?
    a. Yes
    b. No
    If yes, details:

34. Do you ever use any diet preparations?
    a. Yes
    b. No
    If yes, which ones?

35. How much alcohol do you drink *in a week?*
    a. I never drink   d. 5–10 drinks
    b. 0–1 drinks   e. More than 10
    c. 2–4 drinks
    Details:

36. Did you ever drink more heavily?

    a. Yes
    b. No
    If yes, details:

37. Have you ever used any drugs recreationally?

    a. Yes
    b. No

Drug	Used	Freq.

    a. Pot, marijuana, hashish, grass
    b. Amphetamines, stimulants, uppers, speed
    c. Barbiturates, sedatives, downers, sleeping pills, Seconal, Quaaludes
    d. Tranquilizers, Valium, Librium
    e. Cocaine, coke, crack
    f. Heroin
    g. Opiates other than heroin (iodine, Demerol, morphine, methadone, Darvon, opium)
    h. Psychedelics (LSD, mescaline, peyote, DMT, PCP)
    i. Other

38. Do you use any drugs recreationally now?

    a. Yes
    b. No
    If yes, what and how often?

39. Have you ever misused any prescription drugs?

    a. Yes
    b. No
    If yes, details:

Past Psychiatric History

40. Have you ever seen a counselor or psychiatrist before?

    a. Yes
    b. No
    If yes, details:

41. Have you ever been hospitalized for a psychological or psychiatric problem?
    a. Yes
    b. No
    If yes, details:

42. Have you ever had problems with depression?
    a. Yes
    b. No
    If yes, details:

43. Have you ever had any problems with anxiety?
    a. Yes
    b. No
    If yes, details:

Past Medical History
44. Do you have any medical problems currently?
    a. Yes
    b. No
    If yes, details:

45. Have you ever been hospitalized medically?
    a. Yes
    b. No
    If yes, details:

46. Have you ever had any heart problems?
    a. Yes
    b. No
    If yes, details:

47. Have you ever had any liver disease?

     a. Yes

     b. No

     If yes, details:

48. Have you ever had glaucoma?

     a. Yes

     b. No

     If yes, details:

49. Have you ever had any seizures?

     a. Yes

     b. No

     If yes, details:

50. Do you have high blood pressure?

     a. Yes

     b. No

     If yes, details:

51. Are you ever troubled by chest pain or shortness of breath?

     a. Yes

     b. No

     If yes, details:

52. Have you ever had an injury to your head?

     a. Yes

     b. No

     If yes, details:

53. Have you ever lost consciousness?

     a. Yes
     b. No

     I. If yes, what was your first memory afterwards?
     II. Details:

54. Have you ever had encephalitis or a brain infection?

     a. Yes
     b. No
     If yes, details:

55. Have you ever had or do you now have any tics or unusual movements of your body?

     a. Yes
     b. No
     If yes, details:

56. Have you ever had or do you have any vocal tics, or do you make any unusal noises (Tourette's syndrome)?

     a. Yes
     b. No
     If yes, details:

57. Are you right-sided or left-sided (Insert R, L, Amb as appropriate)

     a. Writing _____   c. Throwing _____
     b. Kicking _____   d. Sighting _____

58. Have you ever had any problems with your thyroid gland?

     a. Yes
     b. No
     If yes, details:

Developmental History

59. As far as you know, were there any problems with your mother's pregnancy or delivery of you?

     a. Yes

     b. No

     If yes, details:

60. As far as you know, did you walk, talk, and sit up on time?

     a. Yes

     b. No

     If no, details:

61. Did you have any childhood illnesses?

     a. Yes

     b. No

     If yes, details:

62. Did you have normal relationships with your peers when you were a child?

     a. Yes

     b. No

     If no, details:

Sexual History (For Females Only)

63. Are you sexually active?

     a. Yes

     b. No

64. Are you trying to get pregnant?

     a. Yes

     b. No

65. Do you intend to get pregnant within the next 5 years?

     a. Yes

     b. No

66. Are you using any birth control?

    a. Yes
    b. No

67. Are you currently nursing?

    a. Yes
    b. No

Medications

68. Do you take any medications?

    a. Yes
    b. No

    If yes, details:

69. Do you take any over-the-counter medications?

    a. Yes
    b. No

    If yes, details:

70. (For women) Do you use birth control pills?

    a. Yes
    b. No

Allergies

71. Do you have any allergies to medications?

    a. Yes
    b. No

    If yes, details:

72. Do you have any other allergies?

    a. Yes
    b. No

    If yes, details:

Family History

73. Are there any medical illnesses that run in your family?
    a. Yes
    b. No
    If yes, details:

74. Is there anyone in your family who has had problems with anxiety or depression?
    a. Yes
    b. No
    If yes, details:

75. Is there anyone in your family who has abused alcohol or other drugs?
    a. Yes
    b. No
    If yes, details:

76. Is there anyone in your family who has had any psychiatric illness?
    a. Yes
    b. No
    If yes, details:

77. Is there anyone in your family who has been in trouble with the law?
    a. Yes
    b. No
    If yes, details:

78. Is there anyone in your family who has had seizures or other neurological problems?
    a. Yes
    b. No
    If yes, details:

79. Is there anyone in your family who has had Tourette's syndrome or vocal tics?
    a. Yes
    b. No
    If yes, details:

80. Is there anyone in your family who has a movement disorder or any unusual movements?
    a. Yes
    b. No
    If yes, details:

81. Is there anyone in your family who has had heart problems?
    a. Yes
    b. No
    If yes, details:

82. Is there anyone in your family who has high blood pressure?
    a. Yes
    b. No
    If yes, details:

83. Is there anyone in your family who has had attentional problems?
    a. Yes
    b. No
    If yes, details:

84. Is there anyone in your family who has had learning disabilities?
    a. Yes
    b. No
    If yes, details:

Social History

85. How much do you smoke?

    a. Never smoked
    b. Have quit for more than a year
    c. Have quit for less than a year
    d. Less than half a pack per day (ppd)

    e. Half to one ppd
    f. One to two ppd
    g. Two or more ppd

86. How much caffeine do you drink, including caffeinated tea and soda?

    a. None
    b. 1–2 cups per day
    c. 3–4 cups per day

    d. 5–6 cups per day
    e. 7–10 cups per day
    f. 11+ cups per day

87. Can you tell me your work history, starting as far back as you can remember?

88. Have you served in the military?

    a. Yes
    b. No

    If yes, details (highest rank, special honors, duties, discharge status):

89. What is your current marital status?

    a. Never married
    b. Married
    c. Separated

    d. Divorced
    e. Widowed

90. Are you currently in an intimate relationship?

    a. Yes
    b. No

    If yes, for how long?

    a. Less than 3 months
    b. 3–6 months
    c. 7 months–1 year

    d. 1–5 years
    e. 5–10 years
    f. 10+ years

91. Do you have trouble in your relationships with others?

    a. Yes
    b. No

    If yes, details:

92. How many intimate relationships have you had that lasted more than 3 months?

    a. None   c. Three or four

    b. One or two   d. Five or more

93. I have asked you a lot of questions. Can you think for a minute and tell me if there are any other problems you have that might be related to what you came here for?

A Review of Other Behavior Rating Scales for ADHD Children

Numerous rating scales and checklists exist for use in clinical work with Attention-deficit Hyperactivity Disorder (ADHD) children and adolescents. They range in length from 10 to 600 items and yield from 1 to 33 subscale scores. Item content ranges from highly specific behaviors to highly abstract qualities of personal or social functioning, and from highly specific constructs (e.g. activity level) to broad categories of psychopathology (e.g. externalizing behaviors). They vary in quality, in research available on their psychometric properties, and in the research purposes for which they are best suited. The most clinically useful scales for the assessment of ADHD in children have been reviewed in Chapter 9. However, other scales have been used frequently in research on ADHD and may have some usefulness for clinical work and so these other scales are reviewed here. Much of this information is taken from my earlier review of these rating scales for scientists (Barkley, 1988c).

The structure, scaling, factorial content, and procedure for obtaining each scale are briefly presented, along with an indication of whether data on various forms of reliability and validity are available. Indications of "yes" or "no" after each category of reliability and validity serve only to note that information of this sort was or was not available in the literature when I conducted this review. It does not indicate the adequacy of those findings. Whether or not normative data are available is also specified, along with the ages of the children for whom those data are appropriate. A brief commentary then follows providing more specific information on reliability and validity of the scale (if available), and addressing the strengths or weaknesses of the scale for clinical use.

PARENT RATING SCALES

Conners Parent Rating Scales

There are three versions of the Conners Parent Rating Scale currently in common use: (1) the original 93-item scale (CPRS; Conners, 1970); (2) the 48-item revised version (CPRS-R; Goyette, Conners, & Ulrich, 1978); and (3) the 10-item Abbreviated Symptom Questionnaire (ASQ). The revised version is reviewed in Chapter 9. The others are reviewed below.

ORIGINAL CONNERS PARENT RATING SCALE (CPRS; Conners, 1970)

Developer: C. Keith Conners, Ph.D.

Where to Obtain: C. Keith Conners, Ph.D., Department of Psychiatry, Duke University Medical Center, Durham, NC 27710

Copyrighted: Yes

Items: 93   *Scaling:*   0–3   *Ages:*   6–14 years

Completion Time: 10–15 minutes   *Scoring Software:*   Yes

Reliability Information Available:

Test-Retest: Yes   *Interrater:* No   *Internal Consistency:* No

Validity Data Available:

Construct: Yes   *Discriminant:* Yes   *Concurrent:* Yes

Predictive: Yes   *Treatment-Sensitive:*   Yes

Normative Date: Yes (ages 6–14 years; $n = 683$)

Factors Assessed: Conduct Disorder, Fearful-Anxious, Restless-Disorganized, Learning Problem–Immature, Psychosomatic, Obsessional, Antisocial, Hyperactive-Immature (Conners & Blouin, 1980)

Bibliography: Yes, over 260 references, from developer

Comments

The original CPRS appears to have satisfactory utility where the purpose of evaluation is to briefly assess a broad array of psychopathological symptoms (hyperactivity, depression, aggression, etc.). The majority of items, however, assess conduct problems or externalizing disorders rather than neuroses or internalizing disorders. The scale is widely used and has a substantial research literature concerning its psychometric properties (Conners, 1985b). Two-month test-retest reliabilities have been generally satisfactory, averaging .85, but vary considerably across the factor scores (O'Connor, Foch, Sherry, & Plomin, 1980). Declines in scores from first to second administrations have been reported (Werry & Sprague, 1974) on several of the factors (Hyperactive-Immature, Antisocial, and Learning Problem–Immature) suggesting a possible practice effect comparable to that noted for the teacher version of the rating scale, to be discussed later. It is therefore recommended that the scale be administered twice before use in assessing changes in ratings due to treatment so as to reduce the confounding of the results with this apparent practice effect (see Conners, 1970). Interrater reliability between parents has not been reported for the CPRS. Normative data have been reported by Conners and Blouin (1980).

Factor-analytic studies have also been conducted with speech- and language-impaired children (Mattison, Cantwell, & Baker, 1980). O'Connor et al. (1980) have also reported intraclass correlations on factors derived for a 73-item version of this scale for identical versus fraternal twins; these ranged between .67 and .91 for the former, and between .15 and .56 for the latter. Glow and her colleagues (Glow, 1981; Glow, Glow, & Rump, 1982) have developed an Adelaide (Australia) version of the scale with normative data available on 1,919 children. This slightly modified version also has adequate test-retest reliability and internal consistency.

The original CPRS shows adequate concurrent validity. Research has shown it to correlate significantly with ratings from the Werry-Weiss-Peters Activity Rating Scale (Broad, 1982); the Child Behavior Checklist (Achenbach & Edelbrock, 1983; Mash & Johnston, 1983c); the Behavior Problem Checklist (Arnold, Barnebey, & Smeltzer, 1981; Campbell & Steinert, 1978) and its revised version (Quay & Peterson, 1983); and the Davids Hyperkinesis Index (Arnold et al., 1981). The ratings also correlate significantly with ratings of infant temperament (Weissbluth, 1984), parent-reported stress and self-esteem (Mash & Johnston, 1983c), and the results of semistructured interviews (Hodges, Kline, Stern, Cytryn, & McKnew, 1982). Substantial research supports the discriminant validity of the scale in distinguishing hyperactive from normal children (Prior, Leonard, & Wood, 1983; Ross & Ross, 1976, 1982), clinic- from non-clinic-referred children (Conners, 1970), neurotic from conduct problem clinic-referred children (Conners, 1970), depressed from nondepressed children (Leon, Kendall, & Garber, 1980), and speech- and language-impaired from purely speech-impaired children (Baker, Cantwell, & Mattison, 1980). Studies of various interventions, such as stimulant drugs or dietary management, with hyperactive children have found the scale to be useful in monitoring treatment response (Barkley, 1977b; Cantwell & Carlson, 1978; Harley, Ray, Tomasi, Eichman, Matthews, Chun, Cleelund, & Traisman, 1981). Scores on the various factors of the scale also appear to have some utility in predicting which ADHD children will respond positively or negatively to stimulant drug treatment (Barkley, 1976).

CONNERS ABBREVIATED SYMPTOM QUESTIONNAIRE (ASO; Goyette et al., 1978)

Developer: Same as above

Where to Obtain: Same as above

Copyrighted: Yes

Items: 10   *Scaling:* 0–3   *Ages:* 3–17 years

Completion Time: 3–5 minutes   *Scoring Software:* No

Reliability Information Available:

Test-Retest: No   *Interrater:* Yes   *Internal Consistency:* No

Validity Information Available:

Construct: No   *Discriminant:* Yes   *Concurrent:* No

Predictive: Yes   *Treatment-Sensitive:* Yes

Normative Data: Yes (ages 3–17 years; $n = 570$)

Factors Assessed: Not factor-analyzed

Comments

The ASQ comprises the 10 items of the CPRS most frequently endorsed by parents of hyperactive children; it is often referred to as the Hyperactivity Index. The items were originally believed to measure "core psychopathology" in these children and to provide a convenient means of assessing change in behavior due to treatment (Conners, 1970). Several different versions of the ASQ exist (Ullmann, Sleator, & Sprague, 1985), but Conners recommends that the 10-item index described in the paper on the CPRS-R by Goyette et al. (1978) be used. The ASQ items scored using the template provided by Abbott Laboratories are incorrect, according to Conners, and should not be confused with other versions of the index.

Normative data for the ASQ can be found in the report by Goyette et al. (1978). No test-retest reliability information could be located for the parent version of the ASQ, but interparent agreement (.55 to .71) and parent-teacher agreement (.49) have been reported as satisfactory (Goyette et al., 1978; Mash & Johnston, 1983c). Again, the scale is likely to show declines from first to second administrations in an apparent practice effect and so should be administered at least twice before being used to assess the effects of clinical interventions.

The ASQ has been used extensively for selecting children as hyperactive for research. However, Ullmann et al. (1985) report that the scale actually assesses a mixture of conduct problem and hyperactivity symptoms, and so will result in a mixed sample of conduct problem and hyperactive children when used in this fashion. Considering the importance shown in recent research of distinguishing between purely hyperactive children and those having both hyperactivity and conduct problems (Paternite & Loney, 1980), clinicians interested in assessing only ADHD in a child should not use this scale.

Interestingly, the ASQ has not been found to correlate significantly with actometer measures of activity level taken in a clinical playroom (Barkley & Cunningham, 1980), nor to be predictive of stimulant drug responding in hyperactive children (Barkley, 1976). Significant correlations have been found between parent ASQ ratings in the home and clinic playroom measures of child compliance and mothers' directiveness with hyperactive children (.38 to .48), further supporting the aforementioned point that this scale most likely assesses interaction conflicts and conduct problems in children. This short scale is no longer recommended for clinical use with ADHD children because of the confounding of aggression and hyperactivity items, the confusion over which version a clinician may in fact be using, and the availability of other equally brief scales that assess ADHD symptoms in a purer form.

PERSONALITY INVENTORY FOR CHILDREN (PIC: Wirt, Lachar, Klinedinst, & Seat, 1984)

Developers: Robert D. Wirt, Ph.D., David Lachar, Ph.D., James K. Klinedinst, Ph.D., and Phillip D. Seat, Ph.D.

Where to Obtain: Western Psychological Services, 12031 Wilshire Blvd., Los Angeles, CA 90025

Copyrighted: Yes

Items: 131–600 (four versions)   *Scaling:*   0–1   *Ages:*   6–16 years

Completion Time: 20 minutes to 2 hours.   *Scoring Software:*   Yes

Reliability Information Available:

Test-Retest: Yes   *Interrater:* Yes   *Internal consistency:* Yes

Validity Information Available:

Construct: Yes   *Discriminant:* Yes   *Concurrent:* Yes

Predictive: No   *Treatment-Sensitive:* No

Normative Data: Yes (3–16 years; *n* = 2,390)

Scales: Achievement, Intellectual Screening, Development, Somatic Concern, Depression, Family Relations, Delinquency, Withdrawal, Anxiety, Psychosis, Hyperactivity, and Social Skills

Factors Assessed: Undisciplined/Poor Self-Control, Social Incompetence, Internalization/Somatic Symptoms, and Cognitive Development

Bibliography: Yes, 70 references, from David Lachar, Ph.D., Institute of Behavioral Medicine, Good Samaritan Medical Center, 111 East McDowell Rd., P.O. Box 2989, Phoenix, AZ 85062

Comments

The PIC is not merely a child behavior rating scale, like most others reviewed here; as its name implies, it is an inventory of child personality characteristics. An assumption of most rating scales is that their items and the adult responses thereto are face-valid, representing a generally truthful reporting of the actual characteristics or behaviors described in the item. Such an assumption is not necessarily true of the PIC, as its items were chosen based on how well they discriminated groups of children rather than on their construct validity. In fact, two methods of item development were employed: the Darlington method, where items were selected by how well they correlated with a criterion group, and the rational strategy, where items were nominated by four experienced judges. Nonetheless, the recent revision of the inventory so that it now has factor-analytically based scales makes these scales similar to the others reviewed here; therefore, it is discussed.

Scores for each scale are plotted on a profile and clinical judgments are then based upon the *T*-score elevations of each score. Cutoff scores for determining clinical significance are reported in the paper by Lachar and Gdowski (1979a). The more recent revision of the PIC (Lachar, 1982) contains four possible versions for administration. The first section of 131 items permits scoring of the four factorially developed scales and the Lie scale (one of three validity scales). Completion of the first 280 items permits these factors to be scored, as well as shortened versions of the 12 clinical scales and general adjustment scale. Completion of 420 items permits scoring of all 16 scales plotted on the PIC profile, the four factor scales, and a full critical items list. Should all 600 items be used, all of the possible scales can be scored, including a number of supplemental scales. A sixth- to seventh-grade reading level appears to be necessary for completing the scale (Harrington & Follett, 1984).

Reliability information is reported in the PIC manual (Wirt et al., 1984), with test-retest coefficients for a 15-day interval ranging from .46 to .94 (mean .86) across the scales. Interparent agreement ranges from .21 to .79 (mean .57 to .69), depending upon the study (see manual). Coefficients for internal consistency were −.03 to .86

for the scales and .81 to .92 for the factor-analytically derived scales. Information on validity of the PIC is also reported in the manual and in several more recent reports. Construct validity is difficult to assess, given the method of item development, but appears to be satisfactory for those scales based on factor analysis. The scales significantly differentiate hyperactive, learning-disabled, and normal children (Breen & Barkley, 1983, 1984); learning-disabled and behavior-disordered children (Goh, Cody, & Dollinger, 1984; Porter & Rourke, 1985; Strang & Rourke, 1985); and depressed and nondepressed children (Lobovitz & Handel, 1985). Several of the clinical scales correlate well with parental ratings of children's adjustment to divorce (Kurdek, Blisk, & Siesky, 1981). Profile typologies and actuarial interpretation of the profiles can be found in the report by Lachar, Kline, and Boersma (1986). Some of the PIC scales correlate satisfactorily with parent, teacher, and clinician ratings of child deviance (Lachar & Gdowski, 1979b; Lachar, Gdowski, & Snyder, 1984); the CPRS (Leon et al., 1980); and response to stimulant medication in hyperactive children (Voelker, Lachar, & Gdowski, 1983). Software for computer scoring of profiles is available from the publisher as well as from Greene, Martin, Bennett, and Shane (1981).

The 131-item version of the PIC appears to be the most useful in clinical practice. However, where interest is in assessing family relations, use of one of the longer versions may be of greater value in that it permits scoring of the clinical scale assessing this domain. Nevertheless, several problems exist with the use of this scale in research. The true-false scoring procedure does not yield any specific information on the frequency or severity of the behavior problem or characteristic described in the item. The methods of item development introduce confusion as to just what each item assesses and they preclude the use of the items in epidemiological research. The item length of the original PIC is also problematic; many parents need 1 to 2 hours to complete it. This has been partially rectified by the more recent availability of four different versions of lesser item length. However, the older and perhaps antiquated normative data base, the considerable length of most versions of the scale, and its rather nonempirical approach to item selection render it less satisfactory than the Child Behavior Checklist or other empirically developed scales.

WERRY-WEISS-PETERS ACTIVITY RATING SCALE (WWPARS; Werry & Sprague, 1970)

Developers: John Werry, M. D., Gabrielle Weiss, M. D. and John Peters, Ph.D.

Where to Obtain: John Werry, M.D., Department of Psychiatry, University of Auckland, Auckland, New Zealand (for revised form, see Barkley, 1981)

Copyrighted: No

Items: 22–31   *Scaling:*   0–2   *Ages:*   Not reported

Completion Time: 5 minutes   *Scoring Software:*   No

Reliability Information Available:

Test-Retest: No   *Interrater:*   Yes   *Internal Consistency:*   No

Validity Information Available:

Construct: Yes   *Discriminant:*   Yes   *Concurrent:*   Yes

Predictive: Yes   *Treatment-Sensitive:*   Yes

Normative Data: Yes (ages 1–9 years; $n = 140$)

Factors Assessed: Television, Bedtime/Sleep, Mealtime, Play Behaviors, and Restlessness

Bibliography: No

Comments

Two versions of this scale currently exist: the longer 31-item version of the developers (see Appendix A of Werry & Sprague, 1970) and the modified 22-item version reported by Routh, Schroeder, and O'Tuama (1974), in which school-related items were deleted (see Barkley, 1981). The original WWPARS was developed as a means of quantifying activity level in children, especially as a dependent measure for research in psychopharmacology (Werry & Sprague, 1970). Much debate has occurred over whether the scale actually assesses activity level or some other dimension of child psychopathology, such as situationally inappropriate behavior (see Ross & Ross, 1982, for a discussion). The scale has been employed in numerous studies of hyperactive children as a parent report measure of activity level. The normative data available are for the modified version of the scale (Routh et al., 1974) and are for a small sample of children of above-average intelligence from upper-middle-class families; hence, they are not especially representative of the larger childhood population. Additional normative data for 129 children aged 2 to 5 years were reported by Campbell and Breaux (1983).

No information on test-retest reliability could be located, but interparent agreements of .82 to .90 have been noted (Mash & Johnston, 1983c; Werry, Weiss, Douglas, & Martin, 1966). Validity of the scale has been established in studies demonstrating its ability to discriminate hyperactive from normal and clinic-referred nonhyperactive children (Barkley & Ullman, 1975; Campbell, Schleifer, & Weiss, 1978; Prior et al., 1983; Routh & Schroeder, 1976; Ullman, Barkley, & Brown, 1978) and its significant correlation with actometer measures of activity level in a day hospital setting (Stevens, Kupst, Suran, & Schulman, 1978). However, others have not found parent ratings in the home on the WWPARS to correlate with clinic playroom measures of activity level or attention (Barkley & Ullman, 1975; Routh & Schroeder, 1976; Routh et al., 1974; Ullman et al., 1978). The scale has been found to correlate significantly with the Davids Hyperkinesis Index (Zentall, 1984), the Behar Preschool Behavior Questionnaire (Campbell & Breaux, 1983), and direct observational measures of mother-child interactions in a clinic playroom (Barkley & Cunningham, 1980). Evidence for some predictive validity of the scale was reported by Campbell et al. (1978), who found WWPARS ratings at age $4\frac{1}{2}$ years to be significantly related to ratings on the CPRS at $6\frac{1}{2}$ years of age, and in our laboratory (Barkley & Cunningham, 1980), where the ratings predicted some improvements in mother-child interactions in response to stimulant medication in hyperactive children.

This scale has limited usefulness, being helpful perhaps where parental reports of situationally inappropriate activity are desired. The scale may be of some value in measuring changes in this behavior in response to interventions, as it has been shown to be sensitive to both stimulant drug and parent training programs for hyperactive children (Barkley, 1977a; Dubey, O'Leary, & Kaufman, 1983; Pollard, Ward, & Barkley, 1983). However, the normative data are not satisfactory, making the scale of little value in circumstances where deviance from normal is of interest, as it often is in clinical practice. Moreover, as noted by one of its developers (Werry, 1978, p. 70), the scale appears to be measuring more than simply activity level given its relationship to measures of oppositional behavior and conduct problems reported above. I do not recommend its clinical use at this time.

TEACHER RATING SCALES

Conners Teacher Rating Scales

There are at least four versions of the Conners Teacher Rating Scale in current use: (1) the original Conners Teacher Rating Scale (CTRS; Conners, 1969, 1973); (2) the revised Conners Teacher Rating Scale (CTRS-R; Goyette et al., 1978); (3) the Abbreviated Symptom Questionnaire (ASQ), or Hyperactivity Index (see Goyette et al., 1978); and (4) the Iowa Conners Teacher Rating Scale (Loney & Milich, 1982). These scales vary primarily in the number of items of the original scale they have retained. The ASQ has also been called the Abbreviated Teacher Rating Scale (ATRS). The revised scale is reviewed in Chapter 9. The remaining versions are reviewed below.

ORIGINAL CONNERS TEACHER RATING SCALE (CTRS; Conners, 1969)

Developer: C. Keith Conners, Ph.D.

Where to Obtain: C. Keith Conners, Ph.D., Department of Psychiatry, Duke University Medical Center, Durham, NC 27710

Copyrighted: Yes

Items: 39   *Scaling:* 0–3   *Ages:* Not reported

Completion Time: 5–10 minutes   *Scoring Software:* Yes

Reliability Information Available:

Test-Retest: Yes   *Interrater:* Yes   *Internal Consistency:* Yes

Validity Information Available:

Construct: Yes   *Discriminant:* Yes   *Concurrent:* Yes

Predictive: No   *Treatment-Sensitive:* Yes

Normative Data: Yes (ages 4–12 years; $n = 9,583$)

Factors Assessed: Hyperactivity, Conduct Problem, Emotional-Overindulgent, Anxious-Passive, Asocial, and Daydreams/Attendance Problem

Bibliography: Yes, 260 references, from the developer

Comments

Developed to assess the effects of stimulant drugs in hyperactive children and to aid in differentiating hyperactive from nonhyperactive children (Conners, 1969), the original CTRS has become the most widely used rating scale in research and clinical practice to date. Each of the 39 items is rated on a scale of "not at all," "just a little," "pretty much," and "very much," with these responses assigned credits of 0–3 points, respectively. A total score can be obtained by summing across all items, and factor scores are derived by summing the credits across only those items loading on that factor. The largest sample of normative data was collected on more than 9,500 Canadian children by Trites, Blouin, and Laprade (1982), although smaller samples on normal children are available for the United States (Kupietz, Bialer, & Winsberg, 1972; Ullmann et al., 1985), New Zealand (Sprague, Cohen, & Werry, 1974), West Germany (Sprague, Cohen, & Eichlseder, 1977), Australia (Glow, 1981), French-speaking Canada (Trites & Laprade, 1984), Italy (O'Leary, Vivian, & Nisi, 1985), Great Britain (Taylor & Sandberg, 1984; Thorley, 1983), and Hong Kong (Luk & Leung, 1989). Nevertheless, despite the scale's wide application and the collection of normative samples, the range of ages for these samples remains limited to the elementary school ages (4 to 12 years). Conners recommends that the norms collected by Trites et al. (1982) and the factors derived therefrom be employed as they represent the largest sample available.

Reliability information for the original CTRS has been well established. Test-retest coefficients over a 1-month interval ranged from .70 to .90 across factors (Conners, 1973) and showed satisfactory stability over a 1-year interval, with reliability coefficients ranging from .35 to .57 (Trites, Blouin, Ferguson, & Lynch, 1981). An Australian revision of this scale, the Adelaide version, has also shown excellent stability over a 1-year interval (Glow et al., 1982). Trites et al. (1982) reported interrater (teacher) agreements of .17 to .53 across four of the six factors, with most falling between .44 and .53. Others have found interteacher agreements of .92 for the entire scale with coefficients ranging from .09 to .89 across the factors (Vincent, Williams, Harris, & Duvall, 1977). As with the Trites et al. (1982) study, lower agreements were found for those factors reflecting neurotic or internalizing characteristics and higher agreements for those reflecting conduct problems or externalizing symptoms. Agreements between teachers and trained classroom behavioral observers have also been satisfactory, ranging from .39 to .73 (mean of .51) across the factors (Kazdin, Esveldt-Dawson, & Loar, 1983).

Information on the validity of the scale comes from a multitude of sources, including the original factor-analytic study by Conners (1969) using normal children, and the later work by Trites et al. (1981), Arnold et al. (1981), Glow et al. (1982), O'Leary et al. (1985), Taylor and Sandberg (1984), and Trites and Laprade (1984). Other studies have examined the factor structure of the scale for neurotic and conduct problem children (Conners, 1969), as well as speech- and language-delayed children (Mattison et al., 1980). Various factors from the scale were found to correlate significantly with direct observations of activity level and negative parent-child interactions in the home (Rapoport & Benoit, 1975), in-class behavioral observations and achievement tests (Copeland & Weissbrod, 1978; Lahey, Green, & Forehand, 1980; Kendall & Brophy, 1981), and computerized continuous-performance tests (Klee & Garfinkel, 1983). The concurrent validity of the scale has been frequently demonstrated through findings of significant correlations with other rating scales, including the Behavior

Problem Checklist (Arnold et al., 1981; Campbell & Steinert, 1978), the Davids Hyperkinesis Index (Arnold et al., 1981), and the Child Behavior Checklist (Achenbach & Edelbrock, 1983), among others. Numerous studies attest to the ability of the scale to significantly differentiate various groups of clinic-referred and nonreferred children, such as hyperactive and normal children (Conners, 1969; Sandoval, 1977); conduct problem, normal, and hyperactive children (Taylor & Sandberg, 1984); hyperactive, learning-disabled, and normal children (Ackerman, Elardo, & Dykman, 1979); speech- and language-delayed children (Baker et al., 1980); and other groups of children (King & Young, 1982; Leon et al., 1980; Salzinger, Kaplan, Pelcovitz, Samit, & Krieger, 1984). The scale has also proven quite useful as a measure of treatment effects in studies on stimulant medication (see Barkley, 1977b, and Cantwell & Carlson, 1978, for reviews), dietary manipulations with hyperactive children (Harley et al., 1981), self-control training (Horn, Chatoor, & Conners, 1983), and classroom behavior modification programs (Abikoff & Gittelman, 1984; O'Leary & Pelham, 1978).

There can be little question that where clinicians desire a quick screening measure of psychopathology, particularly conduct problems, the CTRS is a most valuable scale with an enviable record of research on its properties. Although its breadth of item coverage for the neurotic or internalizing disorders is weak, several factors have been found that reflect these dimensions of psychopathology. Those wishing to use the scale to assess treatment effects should be cautious of practice effects, wherein reductions in scores are noted to be significantly lower at the second administration compared to the first, particularly over short time periods (Ullmann et al., 1985; Zentall & Zentall, 1986). Conners suggests that the scale be administered at least twice before pre-post treatment effects are assessed. Where normative data are of importance, the scale appears to have the largest pool of data available for any rating scale for ages 4 to 12 years (Trites et al., 1982).

CONNERS ABBREVIATED SYMPTOM QUESTIONNAIRE (ASQ; Goyette et al., 1978)

Developer: Same as above

Where to Obtain: Same as above

Copyrighted: Yes

Items: 10   *Scaling:*   0–3   *Ages:*   3–17 years

Completion Time: 3–5 minutes   *Scoring Software:*   No

Reliability Information Available:

Test-Retest: Yes   *Interrater:*   Yes   *Internal Consistency:*   No

Validity Information Available:

Construct: Yes   *Discriminant:*   Yes   *Concurrent:*   Yes

Predictive: No   *Treatment-Sensitive:*   Yes

Normative Data: Yes (ages 3–17 years; $n = 383$)

Factors Assessed: Hyperactivity and Conduct Problems

Bibliography: Yes, 260 references, from developer

Comments

This brief 10-item scale was once one of the most frequently used instruments for selecting hyperactive children for research. Clinicians should be aware that at least four versions of this ASQ, or Hyperactivity Index, have been used (Ullmann et al., 1985). The initial 10 items, like those for the parent ASQ described earlier, were believed to reflect the most frequently endorsed items by teachers in rating hyperactive children. However, more recent research suggests that the scale is assessing a mixture of hyperactive *and* conduct problem symptoms and so children selected by this instrument will not be purely hyperactive but a mixed group of hyperactive/conduct-disordered children. Conners recommends that the 10-item index described in the paper by Goyette et al. (1978) be used.

The utility of the ASQ has chiefly been in diagnosing children as hyperactive and in assessing changes in hyperactive and conduct problem behaviors after intervention, particularly stimulant drug therapy. In doing so, the scale has an abundant literature available on its psychometric properties and treatment sensitivity. Normative data for the scale are available in the paper by Goyette et al. (1978). Test-retest reliabilities of .91 to .98 over 1-week intervals (Edelbrock & Reed, 1984; Milich, Loney, & Whitten, 1980), and of .89 over a 2-week interval (Zentall & Barack, 1979), have been found. Interrater agreement for the ASQ with teachers could not be located, but that cited earlier for the same 10-item scale completed by parents has been satisfactory. Agreement between parents and teachers of .49 was reported by Goyette et al. (1978); this is satisfactory considering the differences between home and school settings and the behaviors being rated by these individuals. As with the parent ASQ, validity information has come from research demonstrating significant relationships between the ratings and teacher ratings of impulsivity, laboratory tests of impulse control and distractibility (Brown & Wynne, 1982), teacher records of aggression and hyperactivity, clinic playroom observations of child behaviors, and other rating scales of hyperactivity and conduct problems (Arnold et al., 1981). The scale has proven sensitive to behavioral changes related to stimulant drug treatment (Sprague & Sleator, 1977) and cognitive-behavioral training in self-control strategies with impulsive children (Kendall & Wilcox, 1980; Kendall & Zupan, 1981).

IOWA CONNERS TEACHER RATING SCALE (Loney & Milich, 1982)

Developers: Richard Milich, Ph.D., and Jan Loney, Ph.D.

Where to Obtain: Jan Loney, Ph.D., Department of Psychiatry, Putnam Hall, South Campus, State University of New York at Stony Brook, Stony Brook, NY 11794-8790

Copyrighted: No

Items: 10   *Scaling:* 0–3   *Ages:* Grades 1–5

Completion Time: 3–5 minutes   *Scoring Software:* No

Reliability Information Available:

Test-Retest: Yes   *Interrater:* No   *Internal Consistency:* Yes

Validity Information Available:

Construct: Yes   *Discriminant:* Yes   *Concurrent:* No

Predictive: Yes   *Treatment-Sensitive:* No

Normative Data: Yes (grades 1–5; $n = 608$)

Factors Assessed: Inattention/Overactivity and Aggression

Bibliography: No

Comments

Loney and Milich (1982) selected 10 items from the original CTRS, five of which had high loadings on the Conduct Problem factor and five on the Hyperactivity factor. The items were selected for high divergence, so that each item loaded only on one factor and not the other. This was done to be able to select purely aggressive versus purely hyperactive children. The 10 items use the same response scaling as the CTRS, and separate scores are calculated for the two factors. Normative data are now available on the scale, and the internal consistency of each scale is quite satisfactory (Pelham, Milich, Murphy, & Murphy, 1989). Test-retest reliability of the scales has been shown to be .89 and .86, respectively (Pelham et. al., 1989). The chief use of the scale has been in selecting children as either hyperactive, aggressive, or both. Milich, Roberts, Loney, and Caputo (1980) have reported significant stability of ratings on these two factors over a 2-year period. However, other information on the scale's psychometric properties is lacking. A version for completion by parents was developed by Loney (1984) but has received scant attention in the research literature. The scale would seem useful where a quick, efficient assessment of overactivity and aggression is of clinical interest, as in a trial on stimulant medication.

ADD-H COMPREHENSIVE TEACHER RATING SCALE (ACTeRS; Ullmann, Sleator, & Sprague, 1984a)

Developers: Rina K. Ullmann Ph.D., Esther Sleator, M.D., and Robert L. Sprague, Ph.D.

Where to Obtain: Rina K. Ullmann, Ph.D., Institute for Child Behavior and Development, 51 Gerty Drive, Champaign, IL 61820

Copyrighted: Yes

Items: 24   *Scaling:* 1–5   *Ages:* 5–12 years

Completion Time: 5–10 minutes   *Scoring Software:* No

Reliability Information Available:

Test-Retest: Yes   *Interrater:* Yes   *Internal Consistency:* Yes

Validity Information Available:

Construct: Yes   *Discriminant:* Yes   *Concurrent:* No

Predictive: No   *Treatment-Sensitive:* Yes

Normative Data: Yes (ages 5–12 years; $n = 1,347$)

Factors Assessed: Oppositional Behavior, Attention, Hyperactivity, and Social Problems

Bibliography: No

Comments

This scale was developed for the assessment of children with DSM-III Attention Deficit Disorder (ADD) and for monitoring their response to treatment. The four subscales assessed by the ACTeRS were developed through factor analysis, with the Oppositional Behavior factor accounting for more than 76% of the variance. This factor is quite similar to the Conduct Problem factor on the CTRS and the Aggressive factor on the Teacher Report Form of the Child Behavior Checklist (CBCL-TRF). Normative data for a large sample aged 5 to 12 years are provided in a profile format for easy interpretation of factor scale elevations. However, norms are not reported by age or sex.

Unpublished data are available from Ullmann on the reliability of the instrument. Over a 2-week interval, test-retest coefficients ranged from .68 to .78 for 55 ADD children. Interteacher agreements for 131 children referred for learning disabilities services ranged between .51 to .73. Internal consistency was reported to be .93 to .97 (alpha coefficients).

The construct validity of the scale rests mainly on its development through factor analysis; little research is yet available correlating it with other measures or ratings of these same constructs. Moreover, the use of a normal population on which to base the factor analysis of the scale leaves open to question the applicability of this factor structure to groups of clinic-referred children. The scale has been noted to significantly differentiate ADD from normal and learning-disabled children (Ullmann, 1984; Ullmann, Sleator, & Sprague, 1984b), and has shown some sensitivity to stimulant drug effects (Ullmann & Sleator, 1984a, 1984b) in research with ADD children.

In general, the chief utility of this scale is in the diagnosis of children with ADD, especially in distinguishing those ADD children with and without hyperactivity. It may be particularly useful where stimulant drug treatment is being monitored. Greater research is necessary on the validity of the scale. It is not clear what advantages this scale has over the CTRS (see above), the ADHD Rating Scale (see Chapter 9), or the Child Attention Profile (see Chapter 9), which assess similar factors, which have equally large samples of normative data, and on which there is far greater research on reliability and validity.

SWANSON, NOLAN, AND PELHAM RATING SCALE (SNAP; Swanson & Pelham, 1988)

Developers: James Swanson, Ph.D., Robert Nolan, and William Pelham, Ph.D.

Where to Obtain: William Pelham, Ph.D., Department of Psychiatry, Western Psychiatric Institute and Clinic, 3811 O'Hara Street, Pittsburgh, PA 15231

Copyrighted: No

Items: 23　　*Scaling:* 0–3　　*Ages:* 6–11 years

Completion Time: <5 minutes　　*Scoring Software:* No

Reliability Information Available:

Test-Retest: Yes　　*Interrater:* No　　*Internal Consistency:* Yes

Validity Information Available:

Construct: Yes　　*Discriminant:* Yes　　*Concurrent:* Yes

Predictive: No   *Treatment-Sensitive:* Yes

Normative Data: Yes (ages 6–11 years; $n = 986$)

Factors Assessed: Inattention, Hyperactivity, Impulsivity, Peer Problems

Bibliography: No

Comments

The SNAP checklist was devised to provide a means of collecting quantified teacher ratings on the DSM-III criteria for ADD. In this respect, it is comparable in purpose to the ADHD Rating Scale developed by DuPaul (1990a; see Chapter 9) for the DSM-III-R criteria for ADHD. However, since the revision of the DSM-III criteria, the scale has become outdated, at least for diagnostic purposes.

The developers have reported adequate psychometric properties for the scale. Test-retest reliability over a 2-week period was .69, .78, .92, and .66, respectively, for the subscale scores, with each scale having an average internal consistency of .90. The scale correlates significantly with the ASQ for the CTRS and significantly discriminates ADD from normal children. The normative sample is substantial and appropriate for the elementary grades. Although the factors dealing with ADD symptoms (inattention, hyperactivity, and impulsivity) are less useful now that the DSM has been revised, the Peer Problems scale may still be of some value where this area of adjustment is of interest. Yet, even here, the CBCL-TRF may be of greater utility because of its larger item pool.

MULTI-INFORMANT RATING SCALES

Behavior Problem Checklists

Two versions of the Behavior Problem Checklist presently exist, these being the original (BPC; Quay & Peterson, 1975) and recently revised (RBPC; Quay & Peterson, 1983, 1984) versions. Clinicians should employ the revised version, as Quay is no longer making the original version of the scale available. Nevertheless, the original version is discussed here because of the substantial research on its development, reliability, and validity; because of many similarities between the scales, this research can provide some information on these properties of the new scale.

ORIGINAL BEHAVIOR PROBLEM CHECKLIST (BPC: Quay & Peterson, 1975)

Developers: Herbert C. Quay, Ph.D., and Donald R. Peterson, Ph.D.

Where to Obtain: No longer available

Copyrighted: Yes

Items: 55   *Scaling:* 0–2   *Ages:* Not reported

Completion Time: 10–14 minutes   *Scoring Software:* No

Reliability Information Available:

Test-Retest: Yes   *Interrater:* Yes   *Internal Consistency:* Yes

Validity Information Available:

Construct: Yes   *Discriminant:* Yes   *Concurrent:* Yes

Predictive: Yes   *Treatment-Sensitive:* Yes

Normative Data: Yes (ages 5–13 years)

Factors Assessed: Conduct Problems, Personality Problems, Inadequate-Immature, and Socialized Delinquency

Bibliography: Yes; see Quay (1977)

Comments

The original BPC is one of the most commonly used behavior rating scales in research, second only to the CTRS. It can be completed by parents, teachers, residential treatment center staff, or other informants experienced with a child. The scale identifies broad dimensions of psychopathology based upon orthogonal factors discovered through factor analysis of the ratings on different clinic populations. The fourth factor (Socialized Delinquency) emerged during analyses of data on juvenile offenders and appears to be a less stable factor than the other three. Quay suggests caution in its interpretation. Victor and Halverson (1975) developed two additional scales (Distractibility and Hypersensitivity) for studying normal children. Normative data for children in grades K to 2 (Arnold et al., 1981; Werry & Quay, 1971), 3 to 4 (Schultz, Salvia & Fein, 1974), and 7 to 8 (Quay & Quay, 1965) have been reported, using teachers as informants. A 36-item version of the scale has also been used for which there are norms on 24,997 children (Stone, 1981) for the Conduct Problems and Personality Problems factors only. Data are also available on various clinical populations, such as deaf (Hirshoren & Schnittjer, 1979), visually impaired (Schnittjer & Hirshoren, 1981), institutionalized retarded (Quay & Gredler, 1981), emotionally disturbed (Quay, Morse, & Cutler, 1966), clinic-referred (Lessing & Zagorin, 1971), and learning-disabled (Paraskevopoulos & McCarthy, 1970) children. Norms for Oglala Sioux Indian children were reported by O'Donnell and Cress (1975). These studies and others have provided additional information on the factor structure of the scale with various populations (O'Donnell & Van Tuinan, 1979).

Ample evidence exists to support the reliability of the scale. Test-retest reliability over a 2-week period was found to range between .74 and .93 for teachers (Evans, 1975), and .46 to .70 for dormitory counselors (Kelley, 1981). Stability of the factors over a 2-year interval with normal children was relatively high (range .28 to .74) using teacher ratings (Victor & Halverson, 1975). Interparent agreements between .43 and .83 were noted in several studies (Jacob, Grounds, & Haley, 1982; Noffsinger, 1969; Quay, Sprague, Shulman, & Miller, 1966), depending upon the factor score and the population being used. Not unexpectedly, lower agreements were found for clinic-referred as compared to normal children, and for Inadequate-Immature scores as compared to the other factors. Studies vary as to whether ratings given by mothers differ significantly from those of fathers (Jacob et al., 1982; Speer, 1971). Agreements between teachers have ranged from .22 to .77 (Quay & Quay, 1965; Peterson, 1961), and those between dormitory counselors from .06 to .68 (Kelley, 1981). Information on parent-teacher agreements can be found in the papers by Quay, Morse, and Cutler (1966), Emery and O'Leary (1984), and Touliatos and Lindholm (1981). Ratings have been found to vary as a function of age, grade, sex, race, and social class of the children (Eaves, 1975; Speer, 1971; Touliatos & Lindholm, 1975).

The validity of the BPC is well documented in the reviews by Quay (1966, 1977) and the manual (Quay & Peterson, 1975). Its scales have been found to correlate significantly with measures of activity level (Victor, Halverson, Inoff, & Buczkowski, 1973), recidivism in male criminal offenders (Mack, 1969), peer and teacher ratings of classroom behavior (Harris, Drummond, & Schultz, 1977; Victor & Halverson, 1975), galvanic skin responses (Borkovec, 1970), blood anemia (Webb & Oski, 1973), equivalent factors on the Conners scales (Arnold et al., 1981; Campbell & Steinert, 1978), the Davids Hyperkinesis Index (Arnold et al., 1981), the Bower-Lambert procedures for identifying emotionally handicapped children (Schultz, Manton, & Salvia, 1972), and the Devereaux scales (Proger, Mann, Green, Bayuk, & Burger, 1975). Others have examined the relationship of the scales to marital discord in the parents of the rated children (Emery & O'Leary, 1982, 1984; Porter & O'Leary, 1980). The BPC has been shown to discriminate significantly between various groups of children, including clinic-referred and normal children (Speer, 1971; Sultana, 1974); aggressive, hyperactive, and withdrawn children (Proger et al., 1975); and epileptic, hyperactive, learning-disabled, and normal children (Campbell, 1974). Several studies have used the BPC successfully to evaluate changes following psychotherapy (Askamit, 1974; Brown, 1975; Zold & Speer, 1971) and stimulant medication (Knights & Hinton, 1969; Millichap, Aymat, Sturgis, Larsen, & Egan, 1969).

REVISED BEHAVIOR PROBLEM CHECKLIST (RPBC; Quay & Peterson, 1983, 1984)

Developers: Same as above

Where to Obtain: Herbert C. Quay, Ph.D., Program in Applied Social Sciences, Univerity of Miami, P.O. Box 248074, Coral Gables, FL 33124

Copyrighted: Yes

Items: 89   *Scaling:* 0–2   *Ages:* 5–17 years

Completion Time: 15–20 minutes   *Scoring Software:* No

Reliability Information Available:

Test-Retest: Yes   *Interrater:* Yes   *Internal Consistency:* Yes

Validity Information Available:

Construct: Yes   *Discriminant:* Yes   *Concurrent:* Yes

Predictive: No   *Treatment-Sensitive:* No

Normative Data: Yes (ages 5–17 years; for teachers and mothers)

Factors Assessed: Conduct Disorder, Socialized Aggression, Attention Problems-Immaturity, Anxiety-Withdrawal, Psychotic Behavior, and Motor Tension Excess

Bibliography: Yes; see Quay (1983) and manual (Quay & Peterson, 1983, 1984)

Comments

The expansion of the BPC to 89 items permits a broader assessment of commonly identified dimensions of psychopathology than did the original version. The addition of several items for assessing psychotic behavior increases the utility of the scale for programs dealing with more severely disturbed children. Normative data can be found in the manual for both parent and teacher ratings on large samples of children between kindergarten and grade 12. Those available for parent ratings are based on a smaller sample; additional normative data on parent ratings for a wider age group would be desirable. Although there is less information available on the reliability and validity of this revised version due to its recent development, what is accumulating suggests that the scale will prove as satisfactory in these areas as did the original version. Test-retest coefficients have ranged between .49 and .83. Interteacher agreements have ranged between .52 and .85, while interparent agreements were reported to be between .55 and .93 (Quay & Peterson, 1983, 1984). The scale has been shown to significantly differentiate between clinic-referred and normal children (see manual and Aman & Werry, 1984), and between ADD children with and without hyperactivity (Lahey, Schaughency, Strauss, & Frame, 1984). At present, the Child Behavior Checklist appears to be a better choice for clinical practice until better normative data, particularly for parent reports, become available or unless the clinician is seeking a broader assessment of psychopathology that might include more items pertaining to psychosis.

PRESCHOOL BEHAVIOR QUESTIONNAIRE (PBQ; Behar, 1974)

Developers: Lenore Behar, Ph.D., and Samuel Stringfield, Ph.D.

Where to Obtain: Lenore Behar, Ph.D., 1821 Woodburn Rd., Durham NC 27705

Copyrighted: Yes

Items: 30 *Scaling:* 0–2 *Ages:* 3–6 years

Completion Time: 5–10 minutes *Scoring Software:* No

Reliability Information Available:

Test-Retest: Yes *Interrater:* Yes *Internal Consistency:* No

Validity Information Available:

Construct: Yes *Discriminant:* Yes *Concurrent:* Yes

Predictive: No *Treatment-Sensitive:* No

Normative Data: Yes (ages 3–6 years; $n = 496$, teacher ratings)

Factors Assessed: Hostile-Aggressive, Anxious, and Hyperactive-Distractible

Bibliography: Yes; see Behar (1977)

Comments

This scale was originally developed to identify preschoolers at risk for the development of later emotional problems. Item coverage is limited to the factors noted above with little content dealing with social withdrawal, psychosomatic symptoms, psychotic or obsessive-compulsive behaviors, or learning and cognitive problems. While the normative data available are for teacher reports (see Behar & Stringfield, 1974), recent research has used the scale for assessing parental ratings of child behavior (Campbell & Breaux, 1983). Where establishing the deviance of child behavioral problems in preschool children based upon parental ratings is of interest, use of the Child Behavior Checklist would be more helpful, given the availability of better norms for 4- to 5-year-olds.

Test-retest reliability over a 3- to 4-month period was found to range from .60 to .94, and interrater reliability for teacher ratings was .67 to .84 (Behar & Stringfield, 1974). The scale significantly differentiates hyperactive and normal preschool children (Campbell, Szumowski, Ewing, Gluck, & Breaux, 1982; Prior et al., 1983) as well as normal and emotionally disturbed preschoolers (Behar, 1977). Ratings have been found to correlate significantly with observations of classroom behavior and interactions (Behar, 1977; Rubin & Clark, 1983) and with ratings from the Kohn Problem Checklist and California Preschool Social Competence Scale (Behar & Stringfield, 1974).

Although at the time of its original development (1973) the PBQ was the best rating scale available for preschool children, it has been overshadowed by the development of other rating scales having better normative data and research on their psychometric properties. The CPRS-R now has norms down to age 3 years, while those for the Child Behavior Checklist extends to age 2 years. The latter scale also has broader item coverage, yielding greater information on more dimensions of psychopathology. However, where a short screening instrument of emotional disturbance in preschoolers is desired that uses teacher reports, the scale may continue to be of value, as other teacher rating scales do not have normative data down to age 3 years.

SELF-CONTROL RATING SCALE (SCRS; Kendall & Wilcox, 1979)

Developers: Philip C. Kendall, Ph.D., and Lance E. Wilcox, Ph.D.

Where to Obtain: Philip C. Kendall, Ph.D., Department of Psychology, Temple University, Weiss Hall, Fourth Floor, Philadelphia, PA 19122

Copyrighted: No

Items: 33   *Scaling:*   1–7   *Ages:*   Not reported

Completion Time: 5–10 minutes   *Scoring Software:*   No

Reliability Information Available:

Test-Retest: Yes   *Interrater:*   No   *Internal Consistency:*   No

Validity Information Available:

Construct: Yes   *Discriminant:*   Yes   *Concurrent:*   Yes

Predictive: No   *Treatment-Sensitive:*   Yes

Normative Data: Yes (ages 8–11 years; $n = 110$, teacher ratings)

Factors Assessed: Self-Control Behavior

Bibliography: No

Comments

This scale was developed to assess the narrow constellation of behaviors associated with deficits in self-control in children, and to evaluate changes in this behavior associated with cognitive-behavioral interventions. As such, it seems to have some utility for this purpose, and has shown sensitivity to treatment effects from such interventions (Kendall & Braswell, 1982). Nevertheless, the normative data are quite restricted in sample size and age range, making the scale of little value in establishing statistical deviance of children on this measure. Interrater reliability information is lacking, but test-retest reliability was .84 over a 3- to 4-week interval. Ratings on the scale correlate significantly with the Kagan Matching Familiar Figures Test, Porteus Mazes, teacher ratings on the Child Behavior Checklist, and classroom observations of off-task and disruptive behavior (Kendall, Zupan, & Braswell, 1981; Kendall & Wilcox, 1979). The scale significantly differentiates children referred by teachers for self-control problems from those not so referred (Kendall & Wilcox, 1979), and children referred to mental health clinics from those referred to medical clinics (Robin, Fischel, & Brown, 1984). Research using parent ratings on the scale has been much more limited (see Kendall & Braswel', 1982). A slightly modified version of this scale is available with normative data on 763 children in fourth and fifth grades using teacher ratings (Humphrey, 1982), and on 407 children in first through fifth grades (Work, Hightower, Fantuzzo, & Rohrbeck, 1987).

CONCLUSION

I hope that this review has convinced the reader that ample rating scales exist for the measurement of ADHD symptoms in children. At this time, there seems little need to continue to construct additional scales for ADHD, as some have recently done, because they are quite likely to be redundant with those already in existence. What is needed is additional research on the psychometric properties of those scales already in existence, as well as research on the prescriptive utility of these scales—that is, the extent to which they can predict differential responses to clinical interventions. It is this type of research that will prove of maximum direct benefit to the practitioner and therefore to the ADHD children under his or her clinical care.

APPENDIX B

Parent Support Associations for ADHD

A large number of parent support associations for Attention-deficit Hyperactivity Disorder (ADHD) now exist throughout the United States and Canada. The largest national association is Children with Attention Deficit Disorders (CHADD), which now has over 100 such support associations affiliated with it from almost every state in the United States. Another national organization is Attention Deficit Disorders Association (ADDA). For information on the nearest association, contact the national headquarters of CHADD:

> CHADD
> National Headquarters
> Suite 185
> 1859 North Pine Island Road
> Plantation, FL 33322
> (305) 384-6869

or ADDA at:

> ADDA
> 4300 West Park Blvd.
> Plano, Texas 75093

The Learning Disabilities Association of America also provides support groups for parents of all children with learning problems, not just with ADHD. Information on the nearest chapter can be found by contacting the national organization:

> Learning Disabilities Association of America
> 4156 Library Road
> Pittsburgh, PA 15234
> (412) 341-1515

A national newsletter on ADHD can be obtained from this address:

Challenge
*A Newsletter on Attention-Deficit
Hyperactivity Disorder*
P.O. Box 2001
West Newbury, MA 01985
(508) 462-0495

Additional support associations are as follows:

Alabama

Hyperspace
3603 Eighth Avenue
Birmingham, AL 35222
(205) 328-1717

Arizona

Arizona Council on Behalf of Children and Adults with Attention Deficit Disorders
3881 West Sunny Shadows
Tucson, AZ 85741
or
Place 2502 East Sweetwater
Phoenix, AZ 85032

Arkansas

Learning Disabilities Association of Arkansas
P.O. Box 7316
Little Rock, AR 72216
(501) 666-8777

California

California Association for Children and Adults with Learning Disabilities
17 Buena Vista Avenue
Mill Valley, CA 94941
(415) 383-5242

Colorado

ADDAG
Attention Deficit Disorders Advocacy Group
8091 South Ireland Way
Aurora, CO 80016
(303) 690-7548

Colorado Association for Children and Adults with Learning Disabilities
P.O. Box 32188
Aurora, CO 80041

Delaware

New Castle County Association for Children and Adults with Learning Disabilities
P.O. Box 577
Bear, DE 19701

Florida

ADD-UP
392 Glenbrook Drive
Lantana, FL 33462

PARADE
P.O. Box 954
Fern Park, FL 32730-9998

Georgia

ADD Support Group of Columbus
P.O. Box 7412
Columbus, GA 31908-7412

Hawaii

Hawaii Association for Children and Adults with Learning Disabilities
Room 103
200 North Vineyard
Honolulu, HI 96817

Idaho

ADD Support Group
8420 Holbrook Court
Boise, ID 83704

It All ADDS UP
Pocatello Chapter
5174 Redfish
Chubbick, ID 83202

Illinois

Illinois Association for Hyperactivity and ADD
507 Thornhill Drive
Carol Stream, IL 60188
(312) 653-0222

Indiana
Guidance for Living with ADD (GLADD)
P.O. Box 55613
Indianapolis, IN 46205
(317) 259-1827

Iowa
Attention Deficit Disorder—Understanding Parents (ADD-UP)
3034 Sweetbriar
Iowa City, IA 52242
(319) 351-2520

Support Group for Parents of Children with ADD
5114 Gordon Avenue, N.W.
Cedar Rapids, IA 52405
(319) 396-5239

Kansas
Kansas Association for Children and Adults with Learning Disabilities
P.O. Box 4424
Topeka, KS 66604
(913) 234-9336

Kentucky
ADD Parent Support Group
c/o Our Lady of Peace Hospital
2020 Newbury Road
Louisville, KY 40232
(502) 896-2612

Maine
Special Needs Parent Information Network
P.O. Box 2067
Augusta, ME 04330
1-800-325-0220

Maryland
Attention Deficit Disorder Support Group of Howard County
9222 Mellenbrook Road
Columbia, MD 21045
(301) 992-7550

Massachusetts
New England Attention Disorders Support Group (NEAD)
P.O. Box 82
Northborough, MA 01532
(508) 393-8039

ADD Parent Support Group Network
47 Kristin Road
Plymouth, MA 02360
(508) 746-3959

Michigan
ADD Association of Michigan
P.O. Box 9037
Livonia, MI 48154
(313) 464-8233

Minnesota
Minnesota Association for Children and Adults with Learning Disabilities
#494-N
1821 University Avenue
St. Paul, MN 55104
(612) 646-6136

Co–ADD
The Coalition for the Education and Support of ADD
P.O. Box 242
Osseo, MN 55369-0242
(612) 493-3177

Mississippi
Mississippi Association for Children and Adults with Learning Disabilities
P.O. Box 9387
Jackson, MS 39206
(601) 982-2812

Missouri
Missouri Association for Children and Adults with Learning Disabilities
P.O. Box 3303
2740 South Glenstone
Springfield, MO 65808
(417) 864-5110

Montana
Montana Association for Children and Adults with Learning Disabilities
3024 Macona Lane
Billings, MT 59102
(406) 252-4845

Nebraska
Nebraska Association for Children and Adults with Learning Disabilities
P.O. Box 6464
Omaha, NE 68106
(402) 571-7771

New Hampshire
New Hampshire Association for Children
and Adults with Learning Disabilities
20 Wedgewood Drive
Concord, NH 03307
(603) 224-5872

New Jersey
New Jersey Association for Children and
Adults with Learning Disabilities
P.O. Box 3241
Margate, NJ 08402
(609) 822-4082

New Mexico
ADD Support Group
c/o Mountain Elementary School
2280 North Road
Los Alamos, NM 87544-1798
(505) 662-4367

New York
New York Association for the Learning
Disabled
155 Washington Avenue
Albany, NY 12210
(518) 436-4633

North Carolina
Learning Disabilities Association of North
Carolina
P.O. Box 3542
Chapel Hill, NC 27515-3542
(919) 967-9537

North Dakota
North Dakota Learning Disabilities Association
7 East Central Avenue, #202
Minot, ND 58701
(701) 852-5525

Ohio
Ohio Association for Children and Adults
with Learning Disabilities
2800 Euclid Avenue, #25
Cleveland, OH 44115
(216) 861-6665

Oklahoma
Oklahoma Association for Children and
Adults with Learning Disabilities
3701 N.W. 62nd Street
Oklahoma City, OK 73112
(405) 943-9434

Oregon
Oregon Association for Children and
Adults with Learning Disabilities
Portland State University
PSU Box 751
Portland, OR 97207
(503) 229-4439

Rhode Island
Rhode Island Association for Children and
Adults with Learning Disabilities
P.O. Box 6685
Providence, RI 02904

South Carolina
Piedmont Association for Children and
Adults with Learning Disabilities
P.O. Box 262
Greenwood, SC 29648
(803) 229-7229

South Dakota
South Dakota Parent Connection
P.O. Box 84813
Sioux Falls, SD 57118
(605) 335-8844

Tennessee
Tennessee Association for Children and
Adults with Learning Disabilities
P.O. Box 281028
Memphis, TN 38128
(901) 323-1430

Knoxville Association for Children and
Adults with Learning Disabilities
P.O. Box 23242
Knoxville, TN 37933
(615) 544-3462

Texas
Attention-Deficit Hyperactivity Disorder
Association of Texas
P.O. Box 61592
Houston, TX 77208-1592
(713) 955-3720

Utah
It All ADDS UP/Attention Deficit Disor-
der Foundation
P.O. Box 1082
Sandy, UT 84091-1082
(801) 571-5463

Vermont

Vermont Association for the Learning
Disabled
9 Heaton Street
Montpelier, VT 05602
(802) 223-5480

Virginia

HAAD
106 South Street
Suite 207
Charlottesville, VA 22901

Washington

Washington Association for Children and
Adults with Learning Disabilities
Suite 100
17530 N.W. Union Hill Road
Redmond, WA 98052
(206) 882-0792

Wisconsin

Wisconsin Association for Hyperactive
Children
P.O. Box 1477
Milwaukee, WI 53201-1477
(414) 332-6162

Canada

Foundation for Attention Disorders
Box #339
Station D
Toronto, Ontario, Canada M6P 3J9

Some of the information above was obtained from *Parents Helping Parents,* a directory of support groups for Attention Deficit Disorder, published by CIBA-Geigy Pharmaceuticals, Summitt, NJ.

References

Abidin, R. R. (1986). *The Parenting Stress Index* (2nd ed.). Charlottesville, VA: Pediatric Psychology Press.

Abikoff, H. (1985). Efficacy of cognitive training intervention in hyperactive children: A critical review. *Clinical Psychology Review, 5,* 479–512.

Abikoff, H. (1987). An evaluation of cognitive behavior therapy for hyperactive children. In B. Lahey & A. Kazdin (Eds.), *Advances in clinical child psychology* (Vol. 10, pp. 171–216). New York: Plenum.

Abikoff, H., & Gittelman, R. (1984). Does behavior therapy normalize the classroom behavior of hyperactive children? *Archives of General Psychiatry, 41,* 449–454.

Abikoff, H., Gittelman-Klein, R., & Klein, D. (1977). Validation of a classroom observation code for hyperactive children. *Journal of Consulting and Clinical Psychology, 45,* 772–783.

Achenbach, T. M. (1986). *Manual for the Child Behavior Checklist—Direct Observation Form.* Burlington: University of Vermont, Department of Psychiatry.

Achenbach, T. M., & Edelbrock, C. S. (1978). The classification of child psychopathology: A review and analysis of empirical efforts. *Psychological Bulletin, 85,* 1275–1301.

Achenbach, T. M., & Edelbrock, C. S. (1981). Behavioral problems and competencies reported by parents of normal and disturbed children aged four through sixteen. *Monographs of the Society for Research in Child Development, 46*(1), 1–82.

Achenbach, T. M., & Edelbrock, C. (1983). *Manual for the Child Behavior Checklist and Revised Child Behavior Profile.* Burlington: University of Vermont, Department of Psychiatry.

Achenbach, T. M., & Edelbrock, C. (1986). *Manual for the Teacher Report Form and the Child Behavior Profile.* Burlington: University of Vermont, Department of Psychiatry.

Achenbach, T. M., & Edelbrock, C. (1987). *Manual for the Child Behavior Checklist—Youth Self-Report.* Burlington: University of Vermont, Department of Psychiatry.

Achenbach, T. M., & McConaughy, S. H. (1989). *Semistructured clinical interview for children aged 6–11.* Burlington: University of Vermont, Department of Psychiatry.

Achenbach, T. M., McConaughy, S. H., & Howell, C. T. (1987). Child/adolescent behavioral and emotional problems: Implications of cross-informant correlations for situational specificity. *Psychological Bulletin, 101,* 213–232.

Acker, M. M., & O'Leary, S. G. (1987). Effects of reprimands and praise on appropriate behavior in the classroom. *Journal of Abnormal Child Psychology, 15,* 549–557.

Ackerman, P. T., Dykman, R. A., & Oglesby, D. M. (1983). Sex and group differences in reading and attention disordered children with and without hyperkinesis. *Journal of Learning Disabilities, 16,* 407–415.

Ackerman, P. T., Dykman, R. A., & Peters, J. E. (1977). Teenage status of hyperactive and nonhyperactive learning disabled boys. *American Journal of Orthopsychiatry, 47,* 577–596.

Ackerman, P. T., Elardo, P. T., & Dykman, R. A. (1979). A psychosocial study of hyperactive and learning disabled boys. *Journal of Abnormal Child Psychology, 7,* 91–99.

Adesso, V. J., & Lipson, J. W. (1981). Group training of parents as therapists for their children. *Behavior Therapy, 12,* 625–633.

Alberts-Corush, J., Firestone, P., & Goodman, J. T. (1986). Attention and impulsivity characteristics of the biological and adoptive parents of hyperactive and normal control children. *American Journal of Orthopsychiatry, 56,* 413–423.

Allyon, T., Layman, D., & Kandel, H. (1975). A behavioral-educational alternative to drug control of hyperactive children. *Journal of Applied Behavior Analysis, 8,* 137–146.

Aman, M. G., & Sprague, R. L. (1974). The state dependent effects of methylphenidate and dextroamphetamine. *Journal of Nervous and Mental Disease, 158,* 268–279.

Aman, M. G., & Werry, J. S. (1984). The Revised Behavior Problem Checklist in clinical attenders and nonattenders: Age and sex effects. *Journal of Clinical Child Psychology, 13,* 237–242.

American Psychological Association. (1968). *Diagnostic and statistical manual of mental disorders* (2nd ed.). Washington, DC: Author.

American Psychiatric Association. (1980). *Diagnostic and statistical manual of mental disorders* (3rd ed.). Washington, DC: Author.

American Psychiatric Association. (1987). *Diagnostic and statistical manual of mental disorders* (3rd ed., rev.). Washington, DC: Author.

Anastopoulos, A. D., & Barkley, R. A. (1988). Biological factors in Attention Deficit-Hyperactivity Disorder. *Behavior Therapist, 11,* 47–53.

Aragona, J. A., & Eyberg, S. M. (1981). Neglected children: Mothers' report of child behavior problems and observed verbal behavior. *Child Development, 52,* 596–602.

Arnold, L. E., Barnebey, N. S., & Smeltzer, D. J. (1981). First grade norms, factor analysis and cross correlation for Conners, Davids, and Quay-Peterson behavior rating scales. *Journal of Learning Disabilities, 14,* 269–275.

Askamit, D. L. (1974). *Identification and change in the behavior of students placed in special classes for the emotionally disturbed.* Unpublished doctoral dissertation, University of Nebraska.

Associated Press. (1988). To many, Ritalin is a "chemical billy club." *Worcester Telegram and Gazette,* Jan.

August, G. J., & Stewart, M. A. (1982). Is there a syndrome of pure hyperactivity? *British Journal of Psychiatry, 140,* 305–311.

August, G. J., & Stewart, M. A. (1983). Family subtypes of childhood hyperactivity. *Journal of Nervous and Mental Disease, 171,* 362–368.

Baker, L., Cantwell, D. P., & Mattison, R. E. (1980). Behavior problems in children with pure speech disorders and in children with combined speech and language disorders. *Journal of Abnormal Child Psychology, 8,* 245–256.

Baloh, R., Sturm, R., Green, B., & Gleser, G. (1975). Neuropsychological effects of chronic asymptomatic increased lead absorption. *Archives of Neurology, 32,* 326–330.

Barkley, R. A. (1976). Predicting the response of hyperactive children to stimulant drugs: A review. *Journal of Abnormal Child Psychology, 4,* 327–348.

Barkley, R. A. (1977a). The effects of methylphenidate on various measures of activity level and attention in hyperkinetic children. *Journal of Abnormal Child Psychology, 5,* 351–369.

Barkley, R. A. (1977b). A review of stimulant drug research with hyperactive children. *Journal of Child Psychology and Psychiatry, 18,* 137–165.

Barkley, R. A. (1981). *Hyperactive children: A handbook for diagnosis and treatment.* New York: Guilford Press.

Barkley, R. A. (1982). Specific guidelines for defining hyperactivity in children (Attention Deficit Disorder with Hyperactivity). In B. Lahey & A. Kazdin (Eds.), *Advances in clinical child psychology* (Vol. 5, pp. 137–180). New York: Plenum.

Barkley, R. A. (1984). *Do as we say, not as we do: The problem of stimulus control and rule-governed behavior in children with Attention Deficit Disorder with Hyperactivity.* Paper presented at the Highpoint Conference, Toronto.

Barkley, R. A. (1985a). The social interactions of hyperactive children: Developmental changes, drug effects, and situational variation. In R. McMahon & R. Peters (Eds.), *Childhood disorders: Behavioral-developmental approaches* (pp. 218–243). New York: Brunner/Mazel.

Barkley, R. A. (1985b). The family interactions of hyperactive children: Precursors to aggressive behavior? In D. Routh & M. Wolraich (Eds.), *Advances in behavioral pediatrics* (Vol. 2, pp. 117–150). Greenwich, CT: JAI Press.

Barkley, R. A. (1987). *Defiant children: A clinician's manual for parent training.* New York: Guilford Press.

Barkley, R. A. (1988a). Attention Deficit-Hyperactivity Disorder. In E. Mash & L. Terdal (Eds)., *Behavioral assessment of childhood disorders* (2nd ed., pp. 69–104). New York: Guilford Press.

Barkley, R. A. (1988b). Tic disorders and Tourette's syndrome. In E. Mash & L. Terdal (Eds.), *Behavioral assessment of childhood disorders* (2nd ed., pp. 69–104). New York: Guilford Press.

Barkley, R. A. (1988c). Child behavior rating scales and checklists. In M. Rutter, A. H. Tuma, & I. Lann (Eds.), *Assessment and diagnosis in child psychopathology* (pp. 113–155). New York: Guilford Press.

Barkley, R. A. (1988d). Attention. In M. Tramontana & S. Hooper (Eds.), *Issues in child clinical neuropsychology.* New York: Plenum.

Barkley, R. A. (1988e). The effects of methylphenidate on the interactions of preschool ADHD children with their mothers. *Journal of the American Academy of Child and Adolescent Psychiatry, 27,* 336–341.

Barkley, R. A. (1988f, Fall). Ritalin, Russia, and other ruminations. *Newsletter of Section on Clinical Child Psychology, Division 12, American Psychological Association, 3* (2) p.1.

Barkley, R. A. (1989a). Attention Deficit Hyperactivity Disorder. In E. Mash & R. Barkley (Eds.), *Treatment of childhood disorders* (pp. 39–72). New York: Guilford Press.

Barkley, R. A. (1989b). Hyperactive girls and boys: Stimulant drug effects on mother-child interactions. *Journal of Child Psychology and Psychiatry, 30,* 379–390.

Barkley, R. A. (1989c). The ecological validity of laboratory and analogue assessments of ADHD symptoms. In J. Sargeant & A. Kalverboer (Eds.), *Proceedings of the Second International Symposium on ADHD.* Oxford: Pergamon Press.

Barkley, R. A. (1990). *ADHD adolescents: Family conflicts and their treatment.* Grant from National Institute of Mental Health, MH41583.

Barkley, R. A. (in press). The problem of stimulus control and rule-governed behavior in children with Attention Deficit Disorder with Hyperactivity. In J. Swanson & L. Bloomingdale (Eds)., *Attention deficit disorders* (Vol. 4). New York: Pergamon Press.

Barkley, R. A., Copeland, A. P., & Sivage, C. (1980). A self-control classroom for hyperactive children. *Journal of Autism and Developmental Disorders, 10,* 75–89.

Barkley, R. A., & Cunningham, C. E. (1978). Do stimulant drugs improve the academic performance of hyperkinetic children? A review of outcome research. *Clinical Pediatrics, 17,* 85–92.

Barkley, R. A., & Cunningham, C. E. (1979a). The effects of methylphenidate on the mother-child interactions of hyperactive children. *Archives of General Psychiatry, 36,* 201–208.

Barkley, R. A., & Cunningham, C. E. (1979b). Stimulant drugs and activity level in hyperactive children. *American Journal of Orthopsychiatry, 49,* 491–499.

Barkley, R. A., & Cunningham, C. E. (1980). The parent-child interactions of hyperactive children and their modification by stimulant drugs. In R. Knights & D. Bakker (Eds.), *Treatment of hyperactive and learning disabled children* (pp. 219–236). Baltimore: University Park Press.

Barkley, R. A., & Cunningham, C. E., & Karlsson, J. (1983). The speech of hyperactive children and their mothers: Comparisons with normal children and stimulant drug effects. *Journal of Learning Disabilities, 16,* 105–110.

Barkley, R. A., DuPaul, G. J., & McMurray, M. B. (in press-a). A comprehension evaluation of Attention Deficit Disorder with and without Hyperactivity defined by research criteria. *Journal of Consulting and Clinical Psychology.*

Barkley, R. A., DuPaul, G. J., & McMurray, M. B. (in press-b). Attention Deficit Disorder with and without Hyperactivity: Clinical response to three dose levels of methylphenidate. *Pediatrics.*

Barkley, R. A., & Edelbrock, C. S. (1987). Assessing situational variation in children's behavior problems: The Home and School Situations Questionnaires. In R. Prinz (Ed.), *Advances in behavioral assessment of children and families* (Vol. 3, pp. 157–176). Greenwich, CT: JAI Press.

Barkley, R. A., Fischer, M., Edelbrock, C. S., & Smallish, L. (in press-a). The adolescent outcome of hyperactive children diagnosed by research criteria: I. An 8 year prospective follow-up study. *Journal of the American Academy of Child and Adolescent Psychiatry.*

Barkley, R. A., Fischer, M., Edelbrock, C. S., & Smallish, L. (in press-b). The adolescent outcome of hyperactive children diagnosed by research criteria: III. Mother-child interactions, family conflicts, and maternal psychopathology. *Journal of Child Psychology and Psychiatry.*

Barkley, R. A., Fischer, M., Newby, R., & Breen, M. (1988). Development of a multi-method clinical protocol for assessing stimulant drug responses in ADHD children. *Journal of Clinical Child Psychology, 17,* 14–24.

Barkley, R. A., Grodzinsky, G., & DuPaul, G. J. (1990). *A comprehensive evaluation of Attention Deficit Disorder with and without Hyperactivity: III. Neuropsychological measures.* Manuscript submitted for publication, University of Massachusetts Medical Center, Worcester.

Barkley, R. A., Karlsson, J., & Pollard, S. (1985). Effects of age on the mother-child interactions of hyperactive children. *Journal of Abnormal Child Psychology, 13,* 631–638.

Barkley, R. A., Karlsson, J., Pollard, S., & Murphy, J. (1985). Developmental changes in the mother-child interactions of hyperactive boys: Effects of two doses of Ritalin. *Journal of Child Psychology and Psychiatry, 26,* 705–715.

Barkley, R. A., Karlsson, J., Strzelecki, E., & Murphy, J. (1984). Effects of age and Ritalin dosage on the mother-child interactions of hyperactive children. *Journal of Consulting and Clinical Psychology, 52,* 750–758.

Barkley, R. A., McMurray, M. B., Edelbrock, C. S., & Robbins, K. (1989). The response of aggressive and non-aggressive ADHD children to two doses of methylphenidate. *Journal of the American Academy of Child and Adolescent Psychiatry, 28,* 873–881.

Barkley, R. A., McMurray, M. B., Edelbrock, C. S., & Robbins, K. (in press). The side effects of Ritalin: A systematic placebo controlled evaluation of two doses. *Pediatrics.*

Barkley, R. A., Spitzer, R., & Costello, A. (1990). *Development of the DSM-III-R criteria for the Disruptive Behavior Disorders.* Unpublished manuscript, University of Massachusetts Medical Center, Worcester.

Barkley, R. A., & Ullman, D. G. (1975). A comparison of objective measures of activity and distractibility in hyperactive and nonhyperactive children. *Journal of Abnormal Child Psychology, 3,* 213–244.

Barrios, B. A., & Hartmann, D. P. (1988). Fears and anxieties. In E. J. Mash & L. G. Terdal (Eds.), *Behavioral assessment of childhood disorders* (2nd ed.) (pp. 196–262). New York: Guilford.

Barrios, B. A., & O'Dell, S. L. (1989). Fears and anxieties. In E. J. Mash & R. A. Barkley (Eds.), *Treatment of childhood disorders* (pp. 167–221). New York: Guilford.

Bass, A. (1988, March 28). Debate over Ritalin is heating up: Experts say critics are lashing out for all the wrong reasons. *Boston Globe,* pp. 36–38.

Battle, E. S., & Lacey, B. (1972). A context for hyperactivity in children, over time. *Child Development, 43,* 757–773.

Beck, A. T. (1967). *Depression: Causes and treatment.* Philadelphia: University of Philadelphia Press.

Beck, A. T., Rush, A. J., Shaw, B. F., & Emery, G. (1979). *Cognitive therapy for depression.* New York: Guilford Press.

Beck, A. T., Steer, R. A., & Garbin, M. G. (1988). Psychometric properties of the Beck Depression Inventory: Twenty-five years of evaluation. *Clinical Psychology Review, 8,* 77–100.

Beck, A. T., Ward, C. H., Mendelson, M., Mock, J., & Erbaugh, J. (1961). An inventory for measuring depression. *Archives of General Psychiatry, 4,* 561–571.

Befera, M., & Barkley, R. (1985). Hyperactive and normal boys and girls: Mother-child interaction, parent psychiatric status, and child psychopathology. *Journal of Child Psychology and Psychiatry, 26,* 439–452.

Behar, L. (1974). *Manual for the Preschool Behavior Questionnaire.* Unpublished manuscript, Durham, NC.

Behar, L. (1977). The Preschool Behavior Questionnaire. *Journal of Abnormal Child Psychology, 5,* 265–275.

Behar, L., & Stringfield, S. (1974). A behavior rating scale for the preschool child. *Developmental Psychology, 10,* 601–610.

Beitchman, J. H., Wekerle, C., & Hood, J. (1987). Diagnotic continuity from pre-school to middle childhood. *Journal of the American Academy of Child and Adolescent Psychiatry, 26,* 694–699.

Bell, R. Q., & Harper, L. (1977). *Child effects on adults.* New York: Wiley.

Bender, L. (1942). Postencephalitic behavior disorders in children. In J. B. Neal (Ed.), *Encephalitis: A clinical study.* New York: Grune & Stratton.

Beninger, R. J. (1989). Dopamine and learning: Implications for attention deficit disorder and hyperkinetic syndrome. In T. Sagvolden & T. Archer (Eds.), *Attention deficit disorder: Clinical and basic research* (pp. 323–338). Hillsdale, NJ: Erlbaum.

Benjamin, A. (1969). *The helping interview.* Boston: Houghton Mifflin.

Bennett, L. A., Wolin, S. J., & Reiss, D. (1988). Cognitive, behavioral, and emotional problems among school-age children of alcoholic parents. *American Journal of Psychiatry, 145,* 185–190.

Berry, C. A., Shaywitz, S. E., & Shaywitz, B. A. (1985). Girls with Attention Deficit Disorder: A silent minority? A report on behavioral and cognitive characteristics. *Pediatrics, 76,* 801–809.

Bettelheim, B. (1973). Bringing up children. *Ladies Home Journal,* p. 28.

Bidder, R. T., Gray, O. P., & Newcombe, R. (1978). Behavioural treatment of hyperactive children. *Archives of Disease in Childhood, 53,* 574–579.

Biederman, J., Baldessarini, R. J., Wright, V., Knee, D., & Harmatz, J. S. (1989). A double-blind placebo controlled study of desipramine in the treatment of ADD: I. Efficacy. *Journal of the American Academy of Child and Adolescent Psychiatry, 28,* 777–784.

Biederman, J., Baldessarini, R. J., Wright, V., Knee, D., Harmatz, J. S., & Goldblatt, A. (1989). A double-blind placebo controlled study of desipramine in the treatment of ADD: II. Serum drug levels and cardiovascular findings. *Journal of the American Academy of Child and Adolescent Psychiatry, 28,* 903–911.

Biederman, J., Faraone, S. V., Keenan, K., Knee, D., & Tsuang, M. T. (1989). *Family genetic and psychosocial risk factors in clinically referred children and adolescents with DSM-III Attention Deficit Disorder.* Manuscript submitted for publication, Massachusetts General Hospital, Boston.

Biederman, J., Faraone, S. V., Knee, D., & Munir, K. (1990). Retrospective assessment of DSM-III attention deficit disorder in nonreferred individuals. *Journal of the American Academy of Child and Adolescent Psychiatry, 51,* 102–106.

Biederman, J., Gastfriend, D. R., & Jellinek, M. S. (1986). Desipramine in the treatment of children with attention deficit disorder. *Journal of Clinical Psychopharmacology, 6,* 359–363.

Biederman, J., Munir, K., & Knee, D. (1987). Conduct and Oppositional Disorder in clinically referred children with Attention Deficit Disorder: A controlled family study. *Journal of the American Academy of Child and Adolescent Psychiatry, 26,* 724–727.

Biederman, J., Munir, K., Knee, D., Armentano, M., Autor, S., Waternaux, C., & Tsuang, M. (1987). High rate of affective disorders in probands with attention deficit disorders and in their relatives: A controlled family study. *American Journal of Psychiatry, 144,* 330–333.

Biederman, J., Munir, K, Knee, D., Habelow, W., Armentano, M., Autor, S., Hoge, S. K., & Waternaux, C. (1986). A family study of patients with attention deficit disorder and normal controls. *Journal of Psychiatric Research, 20,* 263–274.

Bierman, K. (1983). Cognitive development and clinical interviews with children. In B. Lahey & A. Kazdin (Eds.), *Advances in clinical child psychology* (Vol. 6, pp. 217–250). New York: Plenum.

Bierman, K., & Furman, W. (1984). The effects of social skills training and peer involvement on the social adjustment of preadolescents. *Child Development, 57,* 230–240.

Birch, H. G. (1964). *Brain damage in children: The biological and social aspects.* Baltimore: Williams & Wilkins.

Blau, A. (1936). Mental changes following head trauma in children. *Archives of Neurology and Psychiatry, 35,* 722–769.

Block, G. H. (1977). Hyperactivity: A cultural perspective. *Journal of Learning Disabilities, 110,* 236–240.

Blouin, A. G., Bornstein, M. A., & Trites, R. L. (1978). Teenage alcohol abuse among hyperactive children: A five year follow-up study. *Journal of Pediatric Psychology, 3,* 188–194.

Bohline, D. S. (1985). Intellectual and effective characteristics of attention deficit disordered children. *Journal of Learning Disabilities, 18,* 604–608.

Bond, C. R., & McMahon, R. J. (1984). Relationships between maternal distress and child behavior problems, maternal personal adjustment, maternal personality, and maternal parenting behavior. *Journal of Abnormal Psychology, 93,* 348–351.

Bond, E. D., & Appel, K. E. (1931). *The treatment of behavior disorders following encephalitis.* New York: Commonwealth Fund.

Borkovec, T. D. (1970). Autonomic reactivity to sensory stimulation in psychopathic, neurotic, and normal juvenile delinquents. *Journal of Consulting and Clinical Psychology, 35,* 217–222.

Borland, B. L., & Heckman, H. K. (1976). Hyperactive boys and their brothers: A 25 year follow-up study. *Archives of General Psychiatry, 33,* 669–675.

Bornstein, P. H., & Quevillon, R. P. (1976). The effects of a self-instructional package on overactive preschool boys. *Journal of Applied Behavior Analysis, 9,* 179–188.

Boudreault, M., Thivierge, J., Cote, R., Boutin, P., Julien, Y., & Bergeron, S. (1988). Cognitive development and reading achievement in pervasive-ADD, situational-ADD, and control children. *Journal of Child Psychology and Psychiatry, 29,* 611–619.

Bowden, C. L., Deutsch, C. K., & Swanson, J. M. (1988). Plasma dopamine-beta-hydroxylase and platelet monoamine oxidase in attention deficit disorder and conduct disorder. *Journal of the American Academy of Child and Adolescent Psychiatry, 27,* 171–174.

Bradley, W., & Bowen, C. (1940). School performance of children receiving amphetamine (benzedrine) sulfate. *American Journal of Orthopsychiatry, 10,* 782–788.

Bradley, W. (1937). The behavior of children receiving benzedrine. *American Journal of Psychiatry, 94,* 577–585.

Breen, M. J. (1986). *Norms for the Home and School Situations Questionnaires.* Unpublished manuscript, Winneconne Public Schools, Winneconne, WI.

Breen, M. J. (1989). ADHD girls and boys: An analysis of attentional, emotional cognitive, and family variables. *Journal of Child Psychology and Psychiatry, 30,* 711–716.

Breen, M. J., & Altepeter, T. S. (1990). *Factor structures of the Home Situations Questionnaire (HSQ) and the School Situations Questionnaire (SSQ).* Unpublished manuscript, Winneconne Public Schools, Winneconne, WI.

Breen, M. J., & Barkley, R. A. (1983). The Personality Inventory for Children: Its clinical utility with hyperactive children. *Journal of Pediatric Psychology, 8,* 359–366.

Breen, M. J., & Barkley, R. A. (1984). Psychological adjustment of learning disabled, hyperactive, and hyperactive/learning disabled children as measured by the Personality Inventory for Children. *Journal of Clinical Child Psychology, 13,* 232–236.

Breen, M. J., & Barkley, R. A. (1988). Child psychopathology and parenting stress in girls and boys having attention deficit disorder with hyperactivity. *Journal of Pediatric Psychology, 13,* 265–280.

Brent, D. A., Crumrine, P. K., Varma, R. R., Allan, M., & Allman, C. (1987). Phenobarbital treatment and major depressive disorder in children with epilepsy. *Pediatrics, 80,* 909–917.

Brigham, T. A. (1988). *Working with troubled adolescents: A self-management program.* New York: Guilford Press.

Broad, J. C. (1982). Assessing stimulant treatment of hyperkinesis by Bristol Social Adjustment Guides. *Journal of Psychiatric Treatment and Evaluation, 4,* 355–358.

Brody, G. H., & Forehand, R. (1985). The efficacy of parent training with maritally distressed and nondistressed mothers: A multimethod assessment. *Behaviour Research and Therapy, 23,* 291–296.

Brody, G. H., & Forehand, R. (1986). Maternal perceptions of child maladjustment as a function of the combined influence of child behavior and maternal depression. *Journal of Consulting and Clinical Psychology, 54,* 237–240.

Brodzinsky, D. M., Schechtner, D. E., Braff, A. M., & Singer, L. M. (1984). Psychological and academic adjustment in adopted children. *Journal of Consulting and Clinical Psychology, 52,* 582–590.

Brown, J. E. (1975). *A comparison of social casework and behavioral contracting with juvenile delinquents on probation.* Unpublished master's thesis, University of Calgary.

Brown, J. I., Bennett, J. M., & Hanna, G. (1981). *The Nelson–Denny Reading Test.* Chicago, IL: Riverside Publishing Co.

Brown, R. T., Abramowitz, A. J., Madan-Swain, A., Eckstrand, D., & Dulcan, M. (1989, October). *ADHD gender differences in a clinic referred sample.* Paper presented at the annual meeting of the American Academy of Child and Adolescent Psychiatry, New York.

Brown, R. T., & Borden, K. A. (1986). Hyperactivity at adolescence: Some misconceptions and new directions. *Journal of Clinical Child Psychology, 15,* 194–209.

Brown, R. T., Borden, K. A., Wynne, M., Spunt, A. L., & Clingerman, S. R. (1987). Compliance with pharmacological and cognitive treatments for attention deficit disorder. *Journal of the American Academy of Child and Adolescent Psychiatry, 26*, 521–526.

Brown, R. T., & Quay, L. C. (1977). Reflection-impulsivity of normal and behavior-disordered children. *Journal of Abnormal Child Psychology, 5*, 457–462.

Brown, R. T., & Wynne, M. E. (1982). Correlates of teacher ratings, sustained attention, and impulsivity in hyperactive and normal boys. *Journal of Clinical Child Psychology, 11*, 262–267.

Brown, R. T., Wynne, M. E., & Medenis, R. (1985). Methylphenidate and cognitive therapy: A comparison of treatment approaches with hyperactive boys. *Journal of Abnormal Child Psychology, 13*, 69–88.

Buchsbaum, M. S., Haier, R. J., Sosteck, A. J., Weingartner, H., Zahn, T. P., Siever, L. J., Murphy, D. L., & Brody, L. (1985). Attention dysfunction and psychopathology in college men. *Archives of General Psychiatry, 42*, 354–360.

Burg, C., Hart, D., Quinn, P. O., & Rapoport, J. L. (1978). Clinical evaluation of one-year-old infants: Possible predictors of risk for the "hyperactivity syndrome." *Journal of Pediatric Psychology, 3*, 164–167.

Burks, H. (1960). The hyperkinetic child. *Exceptional Children, 27*, 18.

Buss, D. M. (1981). Predicting parent-child interactions from children's activity level. *Developmental Psychology, 17*, 59–65.

Buss, D. M., Block, J. H., & Block, J. (1980). Preschool activity level: Personality correlates and developmental implications. *Child Development, 51*, 401–408.

Byers, R. K., & Lord, E. E. (1943). Late effects of lead poisoning on mental development. *American Journal of Diseases of Children, 66*, 471–494.

Cairns, E., & Cammock, T. (1978). Development of a more reliable version of the Matching Familiar Figures Test. *Developmental Psychology, 11*, 244–248.

Cairns, R. B., & Green, J. A. (1979). How to assess personality and social patterns: Observations or ratings? In R. B. Cairns (Ed.), *The analysis of social interactions* (pp. 209–226). Hillsdale, NJ: Erlbaum.

The Call. (1988, March 8), Ritalin linked to bludgeoning death of teenager. p. 3.

Cameron, J. R. (1977). Parental treatment, children's temperament, and the risk of childhood behavioral problems: I. Relationships between parental characteristics and changes in children's temperament over time. *American Journal of Orthopsychiatry, 47*, 568–576.

Cameron, J. R. (1978). Parental treatment, children's temperament, and the risk of childhood behavioral problems: II. Initial temperament, parental attitudes, and the incidence and form of behavioral problems. *American Journal of Orthopsychiatry, 48*, 140–147.

Cammann, R., & Miehlke, A. (1989). Differentiation of motor activity of normally active and hyperactive boys in schools: Some preliminary results. *Journal of Child Psychology and Psychiatry, 30*, 899–906.

Camp, B. W. (1980). Two psychoeducational treatment programs for young aggressive boys. In C. Whalen & B. Henker (Eds.), *Hyperactive children: The social ecology of identification and treatment* (pp. 191–220). New York: Academic Press.

Camp, B. W., & Bash, M. S. (1981). *Think aloud: Increasing social cognitive skills— A problem-solving program for children*. Champaign, IL: Research Press.

Campbell, S. B. (1973). Mother-child interaction in reflective, impulsive, and hyperactive children. *Developmental Psychology, 8*, 341–349.

Campbell, S. B. (1974). Cognitive styles and behavior problems of clinic boys. *Journal of Abnormal Child Psychology, 2,* 307–312.

Campbell, S. B. (1975). Mother-child interactions: A comparison of hyperactive, learning disabled, and normal boys. *American Journal of Orthopsychiatry, 45,* 51–57.

Campbell, S. B. (1987). Parent-referred problem three-year-olds: Developmental changes in symptoms. *Journal of Child Psychology and Psychiatry, 28,* 835–846.

Campbell, S. B. (1990). *Behavior problems in preschoolers: Clinical and developmental issues.* New York: Guilford Press.

Campbell, S. B., & Breaux, A. M. (1983). Maternal ratings of activity level and symptomatic behaviors in a nonclinical sample of young children. *Journal of Pediatric Psychology, 8,* 73–82.

Campbell, S. B., Breaux, A. M., Ewing, L. J., Szumowski, E. K., & Pierce, E. W. (1986). Parent-identified problem preschoolers: Mother-child interaction during play at intake and 1 year follow-up. *Journal of Abnormal Child Psychology, 14,* 425–440.

Campbell, S. B., Douglas, V. I., & Morganstern, G. (1971). Cognitive styles in hyperactive children and the effect of methylphenidate. *Journal of Child Psychology and Psychiatry, 12,* 55–67.

Campbell, S. B., Endman, M., & Bernfield, G. (1977). A three year follow-up of hyperactive preschoolers into elementary school. *Journal of Child Psychology and Psychiatry, 18,* 239–249.

Campbell, S. B., & Ewing, L. J. (in press). Follow-up of hard-to-manage preschoolers: Adjustment at age nine years and predictors of continuing symptoms. *Journal of Child Psychology and Psychiatry.*

Campbell, S. B., & Paulauskas, S. (1979). Peer relations in hyperactive children. *Journal of Child Psychology and Psychiatry, 20,* 233–246.

Campbell, S. B., Schleifer, M., & Weiss, G. (1978). Continuities in maternal reports and child behaviors over time in hyperactive and comparison groups. *Journal of Abnormal Child Psychology, 6,* 33–45.

Campbell, S. B., Schleifer, M., Weiss, G., & Perlman, T. (1977). A two-year follow-up of hyperactive preschoolers. *American Journal of Orthopsychiatry, 47,* 149–162.

Campbell, S. B., & Steinert, Y. (1978). Comparisons of rating scales of child psychopathology in clinic and nonclinic samples. *Journal of Consulting and Clinical Psychology, 46,* 358–359.

Campbell, S. B., Szumowski, E. K., Ewing, L. J., Gluck, D. S., & Breaux, A. M. (1982). A multidimensional assessment of parent-identified behavior problem toddlers. *Journal of Abnormal Child Psychology, 10,* 569–592.

Cantwell, D. P. (1972). Psychiatric illness in the families of hyperactive children. *Archives of General Psychiatry, 27,* 414–427.

Cantwell, D. (1975). *The hyperactive child: Diagnosis, management, current research.* New York: Spectrum.

Cantwell, D., & Baker, L. (1989). Stability and natural history of DSM-III childhood diagnoses. *Journal of the American Academy of Child and Adolescent Psychiatry, 28,* 691–700.

Cantwell, D., & Carlson, G. (1978). Stimulants. In J. Werry (Ed.), *Pediatric psychopharmacology* (pp. 171–207). New York: Brunner/Mazel.

Cantwell, D. P. (1981). Foreward. In R. A. Barkley, *Hyperactive children: A handbook for diagnosis and treatment* (pp. vii–x). New York: Guilford.

Cantwell, D. P. (1985). Hyperactive children have grown up. *Archives of General Psychiatry, 42,* 1026–1028.

Cantwell, E., & Satterfield, J. H. (1978). The prevalence of academic underachievement in hyperactive children. *Journal of Pediatric Psychology, 3,* 168–171.

Carey, W. B., & McDevitt, S. C. (1978). A revision of the Infant Temperament Questionnaire. *Pediatrics, 61,* 735–739.

Carlson, C. (1986). Attention Deficit Disorder without Hyperactivity: A review of preliminary experimental evidence. In B. Lahey & A. Kazdin (Eds.), *Advances in clinical child psychology* (Vol. 9, pp. 153–176). New York: Plenum.

Carlson, C. L., Lahey, B. B., Frame, C. L., Walker, J., & Hynd, G. W. (1987). Sociometric status of clinic-referred children with Attention Deficit Disorders with and without Hyperactivity. *Journal of Abnormal Child Psychology, 15,* 537–547.

Carlson, C. L., Lahey, B. B., & Neeper, R. (1986). Direct assessment of the cognitive correlates of attention deficit disorders with and without hyperactivity. *Journal of Behavioral Assessment and Psychopathology, 8,* 69–86.

Chamberlin, R. W. (1977). Can we identify a group of children at age two who are at risk for the development of behavioral or emotional problems in kindergarten or first grade? *Pediatrics, 59* (Suppl.), 971–981.

Chelune, G. J., & Baer, R. A. (1986). Developmental norms for the Wisconsin Card Sort Test. *Journal of Clinical and Experimental Neuropsychology, 8,* 219–228.

Chelune, G. J., Ferguson, W., Koon, R., & Dickey, T. O. (1986). Frontal lobe disinhibition in Attention Deficit Disorder. *Child Psychiatry and Human Development, 16,* 221–234.

Chess, S. (1940). Diagnosis and treatment of the hyperactive child. *New York State Journal of Medicine, 60,* 2379–2385.

Childers, A. T. (1935). Hyper-activity in children having behavior disorders. *American Journal of Orthopsychiatry, 5,* 227–243.

Christensen, A., Phillips, S., Glasgow, R. E., & Johnson, S. M. (1983). Parental characteristics and interactional dysfunction in families with child behavior problems: A preliminary investigation. *Journal of Abnormal Child Psychology, 11,* 153–166.

Christophersen, E. R., Barnard, S. R., & Barnard, J. D. (1981). The family training program manual: The home chip program. In R. A. Barkley, *Hyperactive children: A handbook for diagnosis and treatment* (pp. 437–448). New York: Guilford Press.

Cicchetti, D., & Braunwald, K. G. (in press). An organizational approach to the study of emotional development in maltreated infants. *Journal of Infant Mental Health.*

Citizens Commission on Human Rights (CCHR). (1987). *Ritalin: A warning for parents.* Los Angeles: Church of Scientology.

Clark, D. (1988, January). [Guest on the syndicated television show *Sally Jessy Raphael*]. New York: Multimedia Entertainment.

Clark, M. L., Cheyne, J. A., Cunningham, C. E., & Siegel, L. S. (1988). Dyadic peer interaction and task orientation in attention-deficit-disordered children. *Journal of Abnormal Child Psychology, 16,* 1–15.

Clark, M. L., Cunningham, L. J., & Cunningham, C. E. (in press). Improving the social interaction of normal children and their autistic siblings using a group problem solving approach. *Child and Family Behavior Therapy.*

Clements, S. D. (1966). *Task Force One: Minimal brain dysfunction in children* (National Institute of Neurological Diseases and Blindness, Monograph No. 3). Rockville, MD: U.S. Department of Health, Education and Welfare.

Cohen, D. (1987). *Tourettes syndrome and Tic Disorders.* New York: Wiley.

Cohen, D. J., Paul, R., & Volkmar, F. R. (1986). Issues in the classification of pervasive and other developmental disorders: Toward DSM-IV. *Journal of the American Academy of Child Psychiatry, 25,* 213–220.

Cohen, N. J., & Minde, K. (1981). The "hyperactive syndrome" in kindergarten children: Comparison of children with pervasive and situational symptoms. *Journal of Child Psychology and Psychiatry, 24,* 443–455.

Cohen, N. J., Sullivan, J., Minde, K., Novak, C., & Helwig, C. (1981). Evaluation of the relative effectiveness of methylphenidate and cognitive behavior modification in the treatment of kindergarten-aged hyperactive children. *Journal of Abnormal Child Psychology, 9,* 43–54.

Cohen, N. J., Sullivan, J., Minde, K., Novak, C., & Keene, S. (1983). Mother-child interaction in hyperactive and normal kindergarten-aged children and the effect of treatment. *Child Psychiatry and Human Development, 13,* 213–224.

Cohen, N. J., Weiss, G., & Minde, K. (1972). Cognitive styles in adolescents previously diagnosed as hyperactive. *Journal of Child Psychology and Psychiatry, 13,* 203–209.

Committee on Drugs, American Academy of Pediatrics. (1985). Behavioral and cognitive effects of anticonvulsant therapy. *Pediatrics, 76,* 644–647.

Conger, A. J. (1974). Estimating profile reliability and maximally reliable composites. *Multivariate Behavioral Research, 9,* 85–104.

Conger, A. J., & Lipshitz, R. (1973). Measures of reliability for profiles and test batteries. *Psychometrike, 38,* 411–427.

Conger, J. J. (1973). *Adolescence and youth: Psychological development in a changing world.* New York: Harper.

Conners, C. K. (1966). The effects of dexedrine on rapid discrimination and motor control of hyperkinetic children under mild stress. *Journal of Nervous and Mental Disease, 142,* 420–433.

Conners, C. K. (1969). A teacher rating scale for use in drug studies with children. *American Journal of Psychiatry, 126,* 884–888.

Conners, C. K. (1970). Symptom patterns in hyperkinetic, neurotic, and normal children. *Child Development, 41,* 667–682.

Conners, C. K. (1973). Rating scales for use in drug studies with children. *Psychopharmacology Bulletin* [Special issue: Pharmacotherapy with children] 9, 24–84.

Conners, C. K. (1980). *Food additives and hyperactive children.* New York: Plenum.

Conners, C. K. (1985a). The computerized continuous performance test. *Psychopharmacology Bulletin, 21,* 891–892.

Conners, C. K. (1985b). *The Conners rating scales: Instruments for the assessment of childhood psychopathology.* Unpublished manuscript, Children's Hospital National Medical Center, Washington, D.C.

Conners, C. K., & Blouin, A. G. (1980). *Hyperkinetic syndrome and psychopathology in children.* Paper presented at the meeting of the American Psychological Association, Montreal.

Conners, C. K., & Rothschild, G. H. (1968). Drugs and learning in children. In J. Hellmuth (Ed.), *Learning disorders* (Vol. 3, pp. 191–223). Seattle, WA: Special Child.

Conners, C. K., & Taylor, E. (1980). Pemoline, methylphenidate, and placebo in children with minimal brain dysfunction. *Archives of General Psychiatry, 37*, 922–932.

Conners, C. K., & Wells, K. C. (1985). ADD-H Adolescent Self-Report Scale. *Psychopharmacology Bulletin, 21*, 921–922.

Conners, C. K., & Wells, K. C. (1986). *Hyperactive children: A neuropsychosocial approach.* Beverly Hills, CA: Sage.

Conrad, P. (1975). The discovery of hyperkinesis: Notes on the medicalization of deviant behavior. *Social Problems, 23*, 12–21.

Coons, H. W., Klorman, R., & Borgstedt, A. D. (1987). Effects of methylphenidate on adolescents with a childhood history of ADD: II. Information processing. *Journal of the American Academy of Child and Adolescent Psychiatry, 26*, 368–374.

Copeland, A. P., & Weissbrod, C. S. (1978). Behavioral correlates of the Hyperactivity factor of the Conners Teacher Questionnaire. *Journal of Abnormal Child Psychology, 6*, 339–343.

Copeland, L., Wolraich, M., Lindgren, S., Milich, R., & Woolson R. (1987). Pediatricians' reported practices in the assessment and treatment of attention deficit disorders. *Journal of Developmental and Behavioral Pediatrics, 8*, 191–197.

Costello, A. J., Edelbrock, C. S., Kalas, R., Kessler, M., & Klaric, S. (1982). *The NIMH Diagnostic Interview Schedule for Children (DISC).* Pittsburgh: Authors.

Costello, E.J., & Edelbrock, C. S. (1985). Detection of psychiatric disorders in pediatric primary care: A preliminary report. *Journal of the American Academy of Child Psychiatry, 24*, 771–774.

Costello, E. J., Edelbrock, C. S., Costello, A. J., Dulcan, M. K., Burns, B. J., & Brent, D. (1988). Psychopathology in pediatric primary care: The new hidden morbidity. *Pediatrics, 82*, 415–424.

Costello, E. J., Loeber, R., & Stouthamer-Loeber, M. (1989). *Pervasive and situational hyperactivity—confounding effect of informant: A research note.* Unpublished manuscript, University of Pittsburgh, Western Psychiatric Institute.

Cowart, V. S. (1988). The Ritalin controversy: What's made this drug's opponents hyperactive? *Journal of the American Medical Association, 259*, 2521–2523.

Cromwell, R. L., Baumeister, A., & Hawkins, W. F. (1963). Research in activity level. In N. R. Ellis (Ed.), *Handbook of mental deficiency.* New York: McGraw-Hill.

Cronbach, L. J., & Gleser, G. C. (1965). *Psychological tests and personnel decisions.* Urbana: University of Illinois Press.

Cruikshank, B. M., Eliason, M., & Merrifield, B. (1988). Long-term sequelae of cold water near-drowning. *Journal of Pediatric Psychology, 13*, 379–388.

Cruickshank, W. M., & Dolphin, J. E. (1951). The educational implications of psychological studies of cerebral palsied children. *Exceptional Children, 18*, 3–11.

Crumrine, P. K., Feldman, H. M., Teodori, J., Handen, B. L., & Alvin, R. M. (1987). The use of methylphenidate in children with seizures and attention deficit disorder. *Annals of Neurology, 22*, 441–442.

Cunningham, C. E. (1989). A family–systems–oriented training program for parents of language–delayed children with behavior problems. In C. E. Schaefer & J. M. Breismeister (Eds.), *Handbook of parent training: Parents as co-therapists for children's behavior problems* (pp. 133–176). New York: Wiley.

Cunningham, C. E., & Barkley, R. A. (1978). The effects of methylphenidate on the mother-child interactions of hyperactive twin boys. *Developmental Medicine and Child Neurology, 20*, 634–642.

Cunningham, C. E., & Barkley, R. A. (1979). The interactions of hyperactive and normal children with their mothers during free play and structured task. *Child Development, 50*, 217–224.

Cunningham, C. E., Benness, B. B., & Siegel, L. S. (1988). Family functioning, time allocation, and parental depression in the families of normal and ADDH children. *Journal of Clinical Child Psychology, 17*, 169–177.

Cunningham, C. E., Clark, M. L., Heaven, R., Durrant, J., & Cunningham, L. J. (in press). The effects of coping modelling problem solving and contingency management procedures on the interactions of LD and ADHD children with an autistic peer. *Child and Family Behavior Therapy.*

Cunningham, C. E., & Siegel, L. S. (1987). Peer interactions of normal and attention-deficit disordered boys during free-play, cooperative task, and simulated classroom situations. *Journal of Abnormal Child Psychology, 15*, 247–268.

Cunningham, C. E., Siegel, L. S., & Offord, D. R. (1985). A developmental dose response analysis of the effects of methylphenidate on the peer interactions of attention deficit disordered boys. *Journal of Child Psychology and Psychiatry, 26*, 955–971.

Dadds, M. R., Sanders, M. R., Behrens, B. C., & James, J. E. (1987). Marital discord and child behavior problems: A description of family interactions during treatment. *Journal of Clinical Child Psychology, 16*, 192–203.

Dadds, M. R., Schwartz, S., & Sanders, M. R. (1987). Marital discord and treatment outcome in behavioral treatment of child conduct disorders. *Journal of Consulting and Clinical Psychology, 55*, 396–403.

David, O. J. (1974). Association between lower level lead concentrations and hyperactivity. *Environmental Health Perspective, 7*, 17–25.

David, R. (1989). *Pediatric neurology for the clinician.* New York: Raven Press.

Davidson, L. L., Hughes, S. J., & O'Connor, P. A. (1988). Preschool behavior problems and subsequent risk of injury. *Pediatrics, 82*, 644–651.

deHaas, P. A. (1986). Attention styles and peer relationships of hyperactive and normal boys and girls. *Journal of Abnormal Child Psychology, 14*, 457–467.

deHaas, P. A., & Young, R. D. (1984). Attention styles of hyperactive and normal girls. *Journal of Abnormal Child Psychology, 12*, 531–546.

de la Burde, B., & Choate, M. (1972). Does asymptomatic lead exposure in children have latent sequelae? *Journal of Pediatrics, 81*, 1088–1091.

de la Burde, B., & Choate, M. (1974). Early asymptomatic lead exposure and development at school age. *Journal of Pediatrics, 87*, 638–642.

Denckla, M. B., Bemporad, J. R., & MacKay, M. C. (1976). Tics following methylphenidate administration. *Journal of the American Medical Association, 235*, 1349–1351.

Denckla, M. B., LeMay, M., & Chapman, C. A. (1985). Few CT scan abnormalities found even in neurologically impaired learning disabled children. *Journal of Learning Disabilities, 18*, 132–135.

Denckla, M. B., & Rudel, R. G. (1978). Anomalies of motor development in hyperactive boys. *Annals of Neurology, 3*, 231–233.

Denckla, M. B., Rudel, R. G., Chapman, C., & Krieger, J. (1985). Motor proficiency in dyslexic children with and without attentional disorders. *Archives of Neurology, 42*, 228–231.

Denson, R., Nanson, J. L., & McWatters, M. A. (1975). Hyperkinesis and maternal smoking. *Canadian Psychiatric Association Journal, 20*, 183–187.

Derogatis, L. (1986). *Manual for the Symptom Checklist 90—Revised (SCL-90R)*. Baltimore: Author.

Deutsch, C. K., Swanson, J. M., Bruell, J. H., Cantwell, D. P., Weinberg, F., & Baren, M. (1982). Over-representation of adoptees in children with the attention deficit disorder. *Behavioral Genetics, 12,* 231–238.

Dockx, P. (1988, January 11). Are school children getting unnecessary drugs? *Woonsocket, RI Sun Chronicle,* p. 15.

Dodge, K. A., McClaskey, C. L., & Feldman, E. (1985). A situational approach to the assessment of social competence in children. *Journal of Consulting and Clinical Psychology, 53,* 344–353.

Doll, E. J. (1989). [*Review of Parenting Stress Index,* 2nd ed.]. *Professional School Psychology, 4,* 307–312.

Dolphin, J. E., & Cruickshank, W. M. (1951a). The figure background relationship in children with cerebral palsy. *Journal of Clinical Psychology, 7,* 228–231.

Dolphin, J. E., & Cruickshank, W. M. (1951b). Pathology of concept formation in children with cerebral palsy. *American Journal of Mental Deficiency, 56,* 386–392.

Dolphin, J. E., & Cruickshank, W. M. (1951c). Visuo-motor perception of children with cerebral palsy. *Quarterly Journal of Child Behavior, 3,* 189–209.

Douglas, V. I, (1972). Stop, look, and listen: The problem of sustained attention and impulse control in hyperactive and normal children. *Canadian Journal of Behavioural Science, 4,* 259–282.

Douglas, V. I. (1980a). Higher mental processes in hyperactive children: Implications for training. In R. Knights & D. Bakker (Eds.), *Treatment of hyperactive and learning disordered children* (pp. 65–92). Baltimore: University Park Press.

Douglas, V. I. (1980b). Treatment and training approaches to hyperactivity: Establishing internal or external control. In C. Whalen & B. Henker (Eds.), *Hyperactive children: The social ecology of identification and treatment* (pp. 283–318). New York: Academic Press.

Douglas, V. I. (1983). Attention and cognitive problems. In M. Rutter (Ed.), *Developmental neuropsychiatry* (pp. 280–329). New York: Guilford Press.

Douglas, V. I. (1985). The response of ADD children to reinforcement: Theoretical and clinical implications. In L. M. Bloomingdale (Ed.), *Attention deficit disorder: Identification, course, and treatment rationale* (pp. 49–66). New York: Spectrum.

Douglas, V. I. (1988). Cognitive deficits in children with attention deficit disorder with hyperactivity. In L. Bloomingdale & J. Sergeant (Eds.), *Attention deficit disorder: Criteria, cognition, and intervention* (pp. 65–82). New York: Pergamon Press.

Douglas, V. I. (in press). Can Skinnerian psychology account for the deficits in attention deficit disorder? A reply to Barkley. In. J. Swanson & L. Bloomingdale (Eds.), *Attention deficit disorders* (Vol. 4). New York: Pergamon Press.

Douglas, V. I., Barr, R. G., O'Neill, M. E., & Britton, B. G. (1988). Dosage effects and individual responsivity to methylphenidate in attention deficit disorder. *Journal of Child Psychology and Psychiatry, 29,* 453–475.

Douglas, V. I., & Parry, P. A. (1983). Effects of reward on delayed reaction time task performance of hyperactive children. *Journal of Abnormal Child Psychology, 11,* 313–326.

Douglas, V. I., & Peters, K. G. (1979). Toward a clearer definition of the attentional deficit of hyperactive children. In G. A. Hale & M. Lewis (Eds.), *Attention and the development of cognitive skills* (pp. 173–248). New York: Plenum.

Draeger, S., Prior, M., & Sanson, A. (1986). Visual and auditory attention performance in hyperactive children: Competence or compliance. *Journal of Abnormal Child Psychology, 14,* 411–424.

Dubey, D. R., & Kaufman, K. F. (1978). Home management of hyperkinetic children. *Journal of Pediatrics, 93,* 141–146.

Dubey, D. R., O'Leary, S. G., & Kaufman, K. F. (1983). Training parents of hyperactive children in child management; A comparative outcome study. *Journal of Abnormal Child Psychology, 11,* 229–246.

Dumas, J. E. (1986). Indirect influence of maternal social contacts on mother-child interactions: A setting event analysis. *Journal of Abnormal Child Psychology, 14,* 203–216.

Dumas, J. E., & Wahler, R. G. (1985). Indiscriminate mothering as a contextual factor in aggressive-opposition child behavior: "Damned if you do and damned if you don't." *Journal of Abnormal Child Psychology, 13,* 1–17.

Dunst, C. J., & McWilliam, R. A. (1988), Cognitive assessment of multiply handicapped young children. In T. D. Wachs & R. Sheehan (Eds.), *Assessment of young developmentally disabled children* (pp. 213–240). New York: Plenum.

Dunset, C. J., Trivette, C. M., & Deal, A. G. (1988). *Enabling and Empowering Families.* Cambridge, MA: Brookline Books.

DuPaul, G. J. (1990a). *The ADHD Rating Scale: Normative data, reliability, and validity.* Unpublished manuscript, University of Massachusetts Medical Center, Worcester.

DuPaul, G. J. (1990b). *The Home and School Situations Questionnaires—Revised: Normative data, reliability, and validity.* Unpublished manuscript, University of Massachusetts Medical Center, Worcester.

DuPaul, G. J. (1990c). *Parent and teacher ratings of ADHD symptoms: Psychometric properties in a community-based sample.* Manuscript submitted for publication, University of Massachusetts Medical Center, Worcester.

DuPaul, G. J., Rapport, M., & Perriello, L. M. (1990). *Teacher ratings of academic performance: The development of the Academic Performance Rating Scale* Unpublished manuscript, University of Massachusetts Medical Center, Worcester.

Dykman, R. A., Ackerman, P. T., & Holcomb, P. J. (1985). Reading disabled and ADD children: Similarities and differences. In D. B. Gray & J. F. Kavanagh (Eds.), *Biobehavioral measures of dyslexia* (pp. 47–62). Parkton, MD: Your Press.

Earls, F., & Jung, K. G. (1987). Temperament and home environment characteristics as causal factors in the early development of childhood psychopathology. *Journal of the American Academy of Child and Adolescent Psychiatry, 26,* 491–498.

Eaves, R. C. (1975). Teacher race, student race, and the Behavior Problem Checklist. *Journal of Abnormal Child Psychology, 3,* 1–9.

Ebaugh, F. G. (1923). Neuropsychiatric sequelae of acute epidemic encephalitis in children. *American Journal of Diseases of Children, 25,* 89–97.

Edelbrock, C. S. (1984). Developmental considerations. In T. H. Ollendick & M. Hersen (Eds.), *Child behavioral assessment: Principles and procedures* (pp. 20–37). New York: Pergamon Press.

Edelbrock, C. S. (1989). *Childhood conduct problems: Developmental considerations and a proposed taxonomy.* Unpublished manuscript, University of Massachusetts Medical Center, Worcester.

Edelbrock, C. S., & Achenbach, T. M. (1980). A typology of Child Behavior Profile patterns: Distribution and correlates in disturbed children aged 6 to 16. *Journal of Abnormal Child Psychology, 8,* 441–470.

Edelbrock, C. S., & Achenbach, T. A. (1984). The teacher version of the Child Behavior Profile: I. Boys aged 6–11. *Journal of Consulting and Clinical Psychology, 52,* 207–217.

Edelbrock, C. S., & Costello, A. (1984). Structured psychiatric interviews for children and adolescents. In G. Goldstein & M. Hersen (Eds.), *Handbook of psychological assessment* (pp. 276–290). New York: Pergamon Press.

Edelbrock, C. S., Costello, A., & Kessler, M. D. (1984). Empirical corroboration of Attention Deficit Disorder. *Journal of the American Academy of Child Psychiatry, 23,* 285–290.

Edelbrock, C. S., & Rancurello, M. D. (1985). Childhood hyperactivity: An overview of rating scales and their applications. *Clinical Psychology Review, 5,* 429–445.

Edelbrock, C. S., & Reed, M. L. (1984). *Reliability and concurrent validity of the Teacher Version of the Child Behavior Profile.* Upublished manuscript, University of Pittsburgh.

Edinburg, G. M., Zinberg, N. E., & Kelman, W. (1975). *Clinical interviewing and counseling: Principles and techniques.* New York: Appleton-Century-Crofts.

Eisenberg, L., (1966). The management of the hyperkinetic child. *Developmental Medicine and Child Neurology, 8,* 593–598.

Emery, R. E. (1982). Interparental conflict and the children of discord and divorce. *Psychological Bulletin, 92,* 310–330.

Emery, R. E., & O'Leary, K. D. (1982). Children's perceptions of marital discord and behavior problems in boys and girls. *Journal of Abnormal Child Psychology, 10,* 11–24.

Emery, R. E., & O'Leary, K. D. (1984). Marital discord and child behavior problems in a nonclinic sample. *Journal of Abnormal Child Psychology, 12,* 411–420.

Emery, R. E., Weintraub, S., & Neale, J. M. (1982). Effects of marital discord on the school behavior of children of schizophrenic, affectively disordered, and normal parents. *Journal of Abnormal Child Psychology, 10,* 215–228.

Epstein, N. B., Baldwin, L. M., & Bishop, D. S. (1983). The McMaster Family Assessment Device. *Journal of Marital and Family Therapy, 9,* 171–180.

Epstein, N. B., Bishop, D. S., & Levine, S. (1978, October). The McMaster Model of Family Functioning. *Journal of Marriage and Family Counseling,* pp. 19–31.

Epstein, N. B., Schlesinger, S. E., & Dryden, W. (Eds.). (1988). *Cognitive-behavioral therapy with families.* New York: Brunner/Mazel.

Erikson, E. H. (1963). *Childhood and society* (2nd ed.). New York: Norton.

Evans, I. M., & Meyer, L. H. (1985). *An educative approach to behavior problems: A practical decision model for intervention with severely handicapped learners.* Baltimore: Paul H. Brookes.

Evans, W. R. (1975), The Behavior Problem Checklist: Data from an inner-city population. *Psychology in the Schools, 12,* 301–303.

Eyberg, S. M. (1980). Eyberg Child Behavior Inventory. *Journal of Clinical Child Psychology, 9,* 22–28.

Eyberg, S. M., & Robinson, E. A. (1982). Parent-child interaction training: Effects on family functioning. *Journal of Clinical Child Psychology, 11,* 130–137.

Eyberg, S. M., & Robinson, E. A. (1983). Conduct problem behavior: Standardization of a behavioral rating scale with adolescents. *Journal of Clinical Child Psychology, 12,* 347–354.

Eyberg, S. M., & Ross, A. W. (1978). Assessment of child behavior problems: The validation of a new inventory. *Journal of Clinical Child Psychology, 7,* 113–116.

Fagot, B. I. (1984). The consequents of problem behavior in toddler children. *Journal of Abnormal Child Psychology 12,* 385–396.

Famularo, R., & Fenton, T. (1987). The effect of methylphenidate on school grades in children with Attention Deficit Disorder without Hyperactivity: A preliminary report. *Journal of Clinical Psychiatry, 48,* 112–114.

Farrington, D. P., Loeber, R., & van Kammen, W. B. (1987, October). *Long-term criminal outcomes of hyperactivity–impulsivity–attention deficit and conduct problems in childhood.* Paper presented at the meeting of the Society for Life History Research, St. Louis.

Feindler, E. L., & Ecton, R. B. (1987). *Adolescent anger control: Cognitive-behavioral techniques.* New York: Pergamon Press.

Feingold, B. (1975). *Why your child is hyperactive.* New York: Random House.

Feldman, S., Denhoff, E., & Denhoff, E. (1979). The attention disorders and related syndromes outcome in adolescence and young adult life. In E. Denhoff & L. Stern (Eds.). *Minimal Brain Dysfunction: A developmental approach* (pp. 133–148). New York: Musson Publishers.

Ferguson, H. B., & Rapoport, J. L. (1983). Nosological issues and biological variation. In M. Rutter (Ed.), *Developmental neuropsychiatry* (pp. 369–384). New York: Guilford Press.

Fergusson, D. M., Fergusson, l. E., Howrood, L. J., & Kinzett, N. G. (1988). A longitudinal study of dentine lead levels, intelligence, school performance, and behaviour. *Journal of Child Psychology and Psychiatry, 29,* 811–824.

Ferrier, D. (1876). *The Functions of the Brain.* New York: Putnam.

Fischer, M., Edelbrock, C. S., Barkley, R. A., & Smallish, L. (1990). *The adolescent outcome of hyperactive children diagnosed by research criteria: IV. Parent, teacher, and youth self-report ratings.* Unpublished manuscript, University of Massachusetts Medical Center, Worcester.

Firestone, P., Kelly, M. J., & Fike, S. (1980). Are fathers necessary in parent training groups? *Journal of Clinical Psychology, 10,* 44–47.

Firestone, P., Kelly, M. J., Goodman, J. T., & Davey, J. (1981). Differential effects of parent training and stimulant medication with hyperactives. *Journal of the American Academy of Child Psychiatry, 20,* 135–147.

Firestone, P., Lewy, F., & Douglas, V. I, (1976). Hyperactivity and physical anomalies. *Canadian Psychiatric Association Journal, 21,* 23–26.

Firestone, P., & Martin, J. E. (1979). An analysis of the hyperactive syndrome: A comparison of hyperactive, behavior problem, asthmatic, and normal children. *Journal of Abnormal Child Psychology, 7,* 261–273.

Firestone, P., & Prabhu, A. N. (1983). Minor physical anomalies and obstetrical complications: Their relationship to hyperactive, psychoneurotic, and normal children and their families. *Journal of Abnormal Child Psychology, 11,* 207–216.

Fischer, M., Barkley, R. A., Edelbrock, C. S., & Smallish, L. (in press). The adolescent outcome of hyperactive children diagnosed by research criteria: II. Academic, attentional, and neuropsychological status. *Journal of Consulting and Clinical Psychology.*

Fischer, M., Rolf, J. E., Hasazi, J. E., & Cummings, L. (1984). Follow-up of a preschool epidemiological sample: Cross-age continuities and predictions of later adjustment with internalizing and externalizing dimensions of behavior. *Child Development, 55,* 1317–1350.

Flavell, J. H. (1970). Developmental studies of mediated memory. In H. W. Reese & L. P. Lipsitt (Eds.), *Advances in child development and behavior* (Vol. 5). New York: Academic Press.

Fogel, C. A., Mednick, S. A., & Michelson, N. (1985). Hyperactive behavior and minor physical anomalies. *Acta Psychiatric Scandinavica, 72,* 551–556.

Forehand, R., & McMahon, R. (1981). *Helping the noncompliant child: A clinician's guide to parent training.* New York: Guilford Press.

Forehand, R., Wells, K. C., & Griest, D. L. (1980). An examination of the social validity of a parent training program. *Behavior Therapy, 11,* 488–502.

Foster, S., Prinz, R., & O'Leary, K. D. (1983). Impact of problem-solving communication training and generalization programming procedures on family conflict. *Child and Family Behavior Therapy, 5,* 1–23.

Foster, S. L., & Robin, A. L. (1988). Family conflict and communication in adolescence. In E. J. Mash & L. G. Terdal (Eds.), *Behavioral assessment of childhood disorders* (2nd ed.) (pp. 717–775). New York: Guilford.

Frank, Y., & Ben-Nun, Y. (1988). Toward a clinical sub-grouping of hyperactive and nonhyperactive Attention Deficit Disorder: Results of a comprehensive neurological and neuropsychological assessment. *American Journal of Diseases of Children, 142,* 153–155.

Freibergs, V. (1965). *Concept learning in hyperactive and normal children.* Unpublished doctoral dissertation, McGill University, Montreal.

Freibergs, V., & Douglas, V. I, (1969). Concept learning in hyperactive and normal children. *Journal of Abnormal Psychology, 74,* 388–395.

Gadow, K. D. (1981). Prevalence of drug treatment for hyperactivity and other childhood behavior disorders. In K. D. Gadow & J. Loney (Eds.), *Psychosocial aspects of drug treatment for hyperactivity* (pp. 13–70). Boulder, CO: Westview Press.

Gadow, K. D. (1986). *Children on medication, Volume 1: Hyperactivity, learning disabilities, and mental retardation.* Boston: Little, Brown & Co.

Garfinkel, B. D., Brown, W. A., Klee, S. H., Braden, W., Beauchesne, H., & Shapiro, S. K. (1986). Neuroendocrine and cognitive responses to amphetamine in adolescents with a history of Attention Deficit Disorder. *Journal of the American Academy of Child Psychiatry, 25,* 503–508.

Garfinkel, B. D., Wender, P. H., Sloman, L., & O'Neill, I. (1983). Tricyclic antidepressant and methylphenidate treatment of attention deficit disorder in children. *Journal of the American Academy of Child Psychiatry, 22,* 343–348.

Garrison, W., Earls, F., & Kindlon, D. (1984). Temperament characteristics in the third year of life and behavioral adjustment at school entry. *Journal of Clinical Child Psychology, 13,* 298–303.

Gast, D. C., & Nelson, C. M. (1977). Timeout in the classroom: Implications for special education. *Exceptional Children, 43,* 461–464.

Gittelman, R. (1985a). Parent questionnaire of teenage behavior (modified Conners). *Psychopharmacology Bulletin, 21,* 923–924.

Gittelman, R. (1985b). Self-evaluation (teenager's) self-report. *Psychopharmacology Bulletin, 21,* 925–926.

Gittelman, R. (Ed.). (1986). *Anxiety disorders of childhood.* New York: Guilford Press.

Gittelman, R. (1988). The assessment of hyperactivity: The DSM-III approach. In

L. Bloomingdale & J. Sergeant (Eds.), *Attention deficit disorder: Criteria, cognition, and intervention* (pp. 9–28). New York: Pergamon Press.

Gittelman, R., & Abikoff, H. (1989). The role of psychostimulants and psychosocial treatments in hyperkinesis. In T. Sagvolden & T. Archer (Eds.), *Attention deficit disorder: Clinical and basic research* (pp. 167–180). Hillsdale, NJ: Erlbaum.

Gittelman, R., & Eskinazi, B. (1983). Lead and hyperactivity revisited. *Archives of General Psychiatry, 40,* 827–833.

Gittelman, R., & Mannuzza, S. (1985). Diagnosing ADD-H in adolescents. *Psychopharmacology Bulletin, 21,* 237–242.

Gittelman, R., Mannuzza, S., Shenker, R., & Bonagura, N. (1985). Hyperactive boys almost grown up. *Archives of General Psychiatry, 42,* 937–947.

Gittelman, R., & Abikoff, H., Pollack, E., Klein, D., Katz, S., & Mattes, J. (1980). A controlled trial of behavior modification and methylphenidate in hyperactive children. In C. Whalen & B. Henker (Eds.), *Hyperactive children: The social ecology of identification and treatment.* (pp. 221–246). New York: Academic Press.

Gittelman-Klein, R., Klein, D. F., Abikoff, H., Katz, S., Gloisten, C., & Kates, W. (1976). Relative efficacy of methylphenidate and behavior modification in hyperkinetic children: An interim report. *Journal of Abnormal Child Psychology, 4,* 361–379.

Glow, R. A. (1981). Cross-validity and normative data on the Conners Parent and Teacher Rating Scales. In K. D. Gadow & J. Loney (Eds.), *Psychosocial aspects of drug treatment for hyperactivity.* Boulder, CO: Westview Press.

Glow, R. A., Glow, P. H., & Rump, E. E. (1982). The stability of child behavior disorders: A one-year test-retest study of Adelaide versions of the Conners Teacher and Parent Rating Scales. *Journal of Abnormal Child Psychology, 10,* 33–60.

Glutting, J. J., & McDermott, P. A. (1988). Generality of test-session observations to kindergartners' classroom behavior. *Journal of Abnormal Child Psychology, 16,* 527–537.

Goh, D. S., Cody, J. J., & Dollinger, S. J. (1984). PIC profiles for learning disabled and behavior-disordered children. *Journal of Clinical Psychology, 40,* 837–841.

Golden, G. S. (1988). The use of stimulants in the treatment of Tourette's Syndrome. In D. J. Cohen, R. D. Bruun, & J. F. Leckman (Eds.), *Tourette's Syndrome & tic disorders: Clinical understanding and treatment* (pp. 317–327). New York: Wiley.

Gomez, R. L., Janowsky, D., Zetin, M., Huey, L., & Clopton, P. L. (1981). Adult psychiatric diagnosis and symptoms compatible with the hyperactive syndrome: A retrospective study. *Journal of Clinical Psychiatry, 42,* 389–394.

Goodman, R., & Stevenson, J. (1989). A twin study of hyperactivity: II. The aetiological role of genes, family relationships, and perinatal adversity. *Journal of Child Psychology and Psychiatry, 30,* 691–709.

Gordon, M. (1979). The assessment of impulsivity and mediating behaviors in hyperactive and non-hyperactive children. *Journal of Abnormal Child Psychology, 7,* 317–326.

Gordon, M. (1983). *The Gordon Diagnostic System.* Boulder, CO: Clinical Diagnostic Systems.

Gordon, M. (1983). *The Gordon Diagnostic System.* DeWitt, NY: Gordon Systems.

Gordon, M., & McClure, F. D. (1983, August). *The objective assessment of Attention Deficit Disorders.* Paper presented at the 91st annual convention of the American Psychological Association, Anaheim, CA.

Gordon, M., & Mettelman, B. B. (1988). The assessment of attention: I. Standardization and reliability of a behavior based measure. *Journal of Clinical Psychology, 44,* 682–690.

Gordon, M., Mettelman, B. B., & DiNiro, D. (1989). *Are continuous performance tests valid in the diagnosis of ADHD/hyperactivity?* Paper presented at the 97th annual convention of the American Psychological Association, New Orleans.

Gould, S. J. (1981). *The mismeasure of man.* New York: Norton.

Goyette, C. H., Conners, C. K., & Ulrich, R. F. (1978). Normative data on Revised Conners Parent and Teacher Rating Scales. *Journal of Abnormal Child Psychology, 6,* 221–236.

Grant, D., & Berg, E. (1948). *The Wisconsin Card Sort Test: Directions for administration and scoring.* Odessa, FL: Psychological Assessment Resources.

Greene, R. L., Martin, P. W., Bennett, S. R., & Shane, J. A. (1981). A computerized scoring system for the Personality Inventory for Children. *Educational and Psychological Measurement, 41,* 233–236.

Greenspan, S. I. (1981). *The clinical interview of the child.* New York: McGraw-Hill.

Greenwald, A. G., & Albert, R. D. (1968). Acceptance and recall of improvised arguments. *Journal of Personality and Social Psychology, 8,* 31–35.

Grenell, M. M., Glass, C. R., & Katz, K. S. (1987). Hyperactive children and peer interaction: Knowledge and performance of social skills. *Journal of Abnormal Child Psychology, 15,* 1–13.

Griest, D. L., Forehand, R., Rogers, T., Breiner, J. L., Furey, W., & Williams, C. A. (1982). Effects of Parent Enhancement Therapy on the treatment outcome and generalization of a parent training program. *Behaviour Research and Therapy, 20,* 429–436.

Griest, D. L., & Wells, K. C. (1983). Behavioral family therapy with conduct disorders in children. *Behavior Therapy,14,* 37–53.

Griest, D. L., Wells, K. C., & Forehand, R. (1979). An examination of predictors of maternal perceptions of maladjustment in clinic-referred children. *Journal of Abnormal Psychology, 88,* 277–281.

Grodzinsky, G. (1990). *Assessing frontal lobe functioning in 6 to 11 year old boys with attention deficit hyperactivity disorder.* Unpublished doctoral dissertation, Boston College.

Gronwall, D. (1977). Paced auditory serial-addition task: A measure of recovery from concussion. *Perceptual and Motor Skills, 44,* 367–373.

Gronwall, D., & Sampson, H. (1974). *The psychological effects of concussion.* Aukland: Oxford University.

Gronwall, D., & Wrightson, P. (1981). Memory and information processing capacity after closed head injury. *Journal of Neurology, Neurosurgery and Psychiatry, 44,* 889–895.

Gross, M. D. (1984). Effects of sucrose on hyperkinetic children. *Pediatrics, 74,* 876–878.

Gualtieri, C. T. (1988). Pharmacotherapy and the neurobehavioral sequelae of traumatic brain injury. *Brain Injury, 2,* 101–129.

Guevremont, D., DuPaul, G. J., & Barkley, R. A. (in press). Diagnosis and assessment of Attention Deficit Hyperactivity Disorder in children. *Journal of School Psychology.*

Haenlein, M., & Caul, W. F. (1987). Attention deficit disorder with hyperactivity: A specific hypothesis of reward dysfunction. *Journal of the American Academy of Child and Adolescent Psychiatry, 26,* 356–362.

Hale G. A., & Lewis, M. (1979). *Attention and cognitive development.* New York: Plenum.

Halperin, J. M., Gittelman, R., Klein, D. F., & Rudel, R. G. (1984). Reading-disabled hyperactive children: A distinct subgroup of Attention Deficit Disorder with hyperactivity? *Journal of Abnormal Child Psychology, 12,* 1–14.

Halverson, C. F., & Waldrop, M. F. (1976). Relations between preschool activity and aspects of intellectual and social behavior at age 7.5 years. *Developmental Psychology, 12,* 107–112.

Hamlett, K. W., Pellegrini, D. S., & Conners, C. K. (1987). An investigation of executive processes in the problem-solving of attention deficit disorder–hyperactive children. *Journal of Pediatric Psychology, 12,* 227–240.

Hanf, C. (1969). *A two stage program for modifying maternal controlling during mother-child interaction.* Paper presented at the meeting of the Western Psychological Association, Vancouver, British Columbia.

Hanf, C., & Kling, J. (1973). *Facilitating parent-child interactions: A two stage training model.* Unpublished manuscript, University of Oregon Medical School.

Harley, J. P., Ray, R. S., Tomasi, L., Eichman, P. L., Matthews C. G., Chun, R., Cleelund, C. S., & Traisman, E. (1981). Hyperkineses and food additives: Testing the Feingold hypothesis. *Pediatrics, 61,* 818–828.

Harrington, R. G., & Follett, G. M. (1984). The readability of child personality assessment instruments. *Journal of Psychoeducational Assessment, 4,* 37–48.

Harris, J. C., King, S. L., Reifler, J. P., & Rosenberg, L. A. (1984). Emotional and learning disorders in 6–12 year old boys attending special schools. *Journal of the American Academy of Child Psychiatry, 23,* 431–437.

Harris, W. J., Drummond, R. J., & Schultz, E. W. (1977). An investigation of relationships between teachers' ratings of behavior and children's personality tests. *Journal of Abnormal Child Psychology, 5,* 43–52.

Hartsough, C. S., & Lambert, N. M. (1985). Medical factors in hyperactive and normal children: Prenatal, developmental, and health history findings. *American Journal of Orthopsychiatry, 55,* 190–210.

Harvey, D. H. P., & Marsh, R. W. (1978). The effects of decaffeinated coffee versus whole coffee on hyperactive children. *Developmental Medicine and Child Neurology, 20,* 81–86.

Hastings, J. E., & Barkley, R. A. (1978). A review of psychophysiological research with hyperactive children. *Journal of Abnormal Child Psychology, 7,* 413–447.

Heaton, R. K. (1981). *A manual for the Wisconsin Card Sorting Test.* Odessa, FL: Psychological Assessment Resources.

Hechtman, L. & Weiss, G. (1986). Controlled prospective 15 year follow-up of hyperactives as adults: Nonmedical drug and alcohol use and antisocial behavior. *Canadian Journal of Psychiatry, 31,* 557–567.

Hechtman, L., Weiss, G., Perlman, R., & Amsel, R. (1984). Hyperactives as young adults: Initial predictors of outcome. *Journal of the American Academy of Child Psychiatry, 23,* 250–260.

Heffron, W. A., Martin, C. A., & Welsh, R. J. (1984). Attention deficit disorder in three pairs of monozygotic twins: A case report. *Journal of the American Academy of Child Psychiatry, 23,* 299–301.

Heilman, K. M., Voeller, K. K. S., & Nadeau, S. E. (in press). A possible pathophysiological substrate of Attention Deficit Hyperactivity Disorder. *Annals of Neurology.*

Henig, R. M. (1988, March 15). Courts enter the hyperactivity fray: The drug Ritalin helps control behavior, but is it prescribed needlessly? *Washington Post,* Health section, p. 8.

Henker, B., & Whalen, C. K. (1980). The changing faces of hyperactivity: Retrospect and prospect. In C. Whalen & B. Henker (Eds.), *Hyperactive children: The social ecology of identification and treatment* (pp. 321–364). New York: Academic Press.

Herbert, M. (1964). The concept and testing of brain damage in children: A review. *Journal of Child Psychology and Psychiatry, 5,* 197–217.

Herbert, M. (1978). *Conduct disorder of childhood and adolescence: A behavioral approach to assessment and treatment.* New York: Wiley.

Herjanic, B., Brown, F., & Wheatt, T. (1975). Are children reliable reporters? *Journal of Abnormal Child Psychology, 3,* 41–48.

Hertzig, M. E., Bortner, M., & Birch, H. G. (1969). Neurologic findings in children educationally designated as "brain damaged." *American Journal of Orthopsychiatry, 39,* 437–447.

Hinshaw, S. P. (1987). On the distinction between attentional deficits/hyperactivity and conduct problems/aggression in child psychopathology. *Psychological Bulletin, 101,* 443–463.

Hinshaw, S. P., Henker, B., & Whalen, C. K. (1984a). Self-control in hyperactive boys in anger-inducing situations: Effects of cognitive-behavioral training and of methylphenidate. *Journal of Abnormal Child Psychology, 12,* 55–77.

Hinshaw, S. P., Henker, B., & Whalen, C. K. (1984b). Cognitive-behavioral and pharmacologic interventions for hyperactive boys: Comparative and combined effects. *Journal of Consulting and Clinical Psychology, 52,* 739–749.

Hirshoren, A., & Schnittjer, C. J. (1979). Dimensions of problem behavior in deaf children. *Journal of Abnormal Child Psychology, 7,* 221–228.

Hobbs, S. A., & Forehand, R. (1975). Differential effects of contingent and noncontingent release from time–out on noncompliance and disruptive behavior of children. *Journal of Behavior Therapy and Experimental Psychiatry, 6,* 256–257.

Hobbs, S. A., Forehand, R., & Murray, R. G. (1978). Effects of various durations of time–out on the non-compliant behavior of children. *Behavior Therapy, 9,* 652–656.

Hodges, K., Kline, L., Stern, L., Cytryn, L., & McKnew, D. (1982). The development of a child assessment interview for research and clinical use. *Journal of Abnormal Child Psychology, 10,* 173–189.

Hodges, K., McKnew, D., Cytryn, L., Stern, L., & Kline, J. (1982). The Child Assessment Schedule (CAS) diagnostic interview: A report on reliability and validity. *Journal of the American Academy of Child Psychiatry, 21,* 468–473.

Hoff-Ginsberg, E. (1987). Why some properties of maternal speech benefit language growth (and others do not). *Society for Research in Child Development Abstracts, 6,* 119.

Holdsworth, L., & Whitmore, K. (1974). A study of children with epilepsy attending ordinary schools: I. Their seizure patterns, progress, and behaviour in school. *Developmental Medicine and Child Neurology, 16,* 746–758.

Holtum, J., Robinson, E. A., & Eyberg, S. M. (1984). *Computer administration and scoring of the Eyberg Child Behavior Inventory.* Unpublished manuscript, Oregon Health Sciences University.

Hohman, L. B. (1922). Post-encephalitic behavior disorders in children. *Johns Hopkins Hospital Bulletin, 33,* 372–375.

Hops, H., Biglan, A., Sherman, L., Arthur, J., Friedman, L., & Osteen, V. (1987). Home observations of family interactions of depressed women. *Journal of Consulting and Clinical Psychology, 55,* 341–346.

Horn, W. F., Chatoor, I., & Conners, C. K. (1983). Additive effects of Dexedrine and self-control training. *Behavior Modification, 7,* 383–402.

Horn, W. F., Ialongo, N., Popovich, S., & Peradotto, D. (1984). *An evaluation of a multi-method treatment approach with hyperactive children.* Paper presented at the 92nd annual convention of the American Psychological Association, Toronto.

Horn, W. F., Ialongo, N., Popovich, S., & Peradotto, D. (1987). Behavioral parent training and cognitive-behavioral self-control therapy with ADD-H children: Comparative and combined effects. *Journal of Clinical Child Psychology, 16,* 57–68.

Horn, W. F., Wagner, A. E., & Ialongo, N. (1989). Sex differences in school-aged children with pervasive attention deficit hyperactivity disorder. *Journal of Abnormal Child Psychology, 17,* 109–125.

Horne, A. M. (1981). Aggressive behavior in normal and deviant members of intact versus mother-only families. *Journal of Abnormal Child Psychology, 9,* 283–290.

Hoy, E., Weiss, G., Minde, K., & Cohen, H. (1978). The hyperactive child at adolescence: Cognitive, emotional, and social functioning. *Journal of Abnormal Child Psychology, 6,* 311–324.

Huessy, H., Metoyer, M., & Townsend, M. (1973). Eight- to ten-year follow-up of children treated in rural Vermont for behavior disorder. *American Journal of Orthopsychiatry, 43,* 236–238.

Humphrey, L. L. (1982). Children's and teachers' perspectives on children's self-control: The development of two rating scales. *Journal of Consulting and Clinical Psychology, 50,* 624–633.

Humphries, T., Kinsbourne, M., & Swanson, J. (1978). Stimulant effects on cooperation and social interaction between hyperactive children and their mothers. *Journal of Child Psychology and Psychiatry, 19,* 13–22.

Hunt, R. D., Cohen, D. J., Anderson, G., & Mineraa, R. B. (1987). Noradrenergic mechanisms in ADDH. In L. Bloomingdale (Ed.), *Attention deficit disorder Vol. 3: New research in attention, treatment, and psychopharmacology* (pp. 129–148). New York: Pergamon Press.

Hunt, R. D., Minderaa, R., & Cohen, D. J. (1985). Clonidine benefits children with attention deficit disorder and hyperactivity: Report of a double-blind placebo crossover therapeutic trial. *Journal of the American Academy of Child and Adolescent Psychiatry, 24,* 617–629.

Hynd, G., Lorys-Vernon, A. R., Semrud-Clikeman, M., Nieves, N., Huettner, M. I. S., & Lahey, B. B. (in press). Attention deficit disorder without hyperactivity (ADD/wo): A distinct behavioral and neurocognitive syndrome. *Annals of Neurology.*

Hynd, G. W., Nieves, N., Conner, R., Stone, P., Town, P., Becker, M. G., Lahey, B. B., & Lorys-Vernon, A. R. (in press). Speed of neurocognitive processing in children with Attention Deficit Disorder with and without Hyperactivity. *Journal of Learning Disabilities.*

Ingersoll, B. (1988). *Your hyperactive child.* Garden City, NY: Doubleday.

Investor's Daily. (1987, November 10). Psychiatrist sued over attention span drug. P. 26.

Jacob, R. G., O'Leary, K. D., & Rosenblad, C. (1978). Formal and informal classroom settings: Effects on hyperactivity. *Journal of Abnormal Child Psychology, 6,* 47–59.

Jacob, T., Grounds, L., Haley, R. (1982). Correspondence between parents' reports on the Behavior Problem Checklist. *Journal of Abnormal Child Psychology, 10,* 593–608.

Jacklin, C. G., Maccoby, E. E., & Halverson, C. F., Jr. (1980). Minor anomalies and preschool behavior. *Journal of Pediatric Psychology, 5,* 199–205.

James, W. (1890). *The principles of psychology* (2 vols.) New York: Henry Holt.

Janis, I. L., & King, B. T. (1954). The influence of role-playing on opinion change. *Journal of Abnormal and Social Psychology, 49,* 211–218.

Jastak, S., & Wilkinson, G. S. (1984). *The Wide Range Achievement Test-Revised: Administration manual.* Wilmington: Jastak.

Jensen, J. B., Burke, N., & Garfinkel, B. D. (1988). Depression and symptoms of attention deficit disorder with hyperactivity. *Journal of the American Academy of Child and Adolescent Psychiatry, 27,* 742–747.

Jeopardy! (1987, January). [Answer and question on hyperactivity]. Los Angeles: KingWorld.

Johnston, C., Cunningham, C. E., & Hardy, C. L. (1988). *A couples' parenting measure.* Poster presented at the annual meeting of the Association for Advancement of Behavior Therapy.

Johnston, C., Pelham, W. E., Hoza, J., & Sturges, J. (1988). Psychostimulant rebound in attention deficit disordered boys. *Journal of the American Academy of Child and Adolescent Psychiatry, 27,* 806–810.

Johnston, C., Pelham, W. E., & Murphy, H. A. (1985). Peer relationships in ADDH and normal children: A developmental analysis of peer and teacher ratings. *Journal of Abnormal Child Psychology, 13,* 89–100.

Jones, K. L., Smith, D. W., Ullenland, C. N., & Streissguth, A. P. (1973). Pattern of malformation in offspring in chronic alcoholic mothers. *Lancet, i,* 1267.

Jouriles, E. N., Barling, J., & O'Leary, K. D. (1987). Predicting child behavior problems in maritally violent families. *Journal of Abnormal Child Psychology, 15,* 165–173.

Jouriles, E. N., Murphy, C. M., & O'Leary, K. D. (1989). Effects of maternal mood on mother-son interaction patterns. *Journal of Abnormal Child Psychology, 17,* 513–526.

Jouriles, E. N., Pfiffner, L. J., & O'Leary, S. G. (1988). Marital conflict, parenting, and toddler conduct problems. *Journal of Abnormal Child Psychology, 16,* 197–206.

Kagan, J. (1966). Reflection-impulsivity: The generality and dynamics of conceptual tempo. *Journal of Abnormal Psychology, 71,* 17–24.

Kagan, J. (1971). *Change and continuity in infancy.* New York: Wiley.

Kahn, E., & Cohen, L. H. (1934). Organic driveness; A brain stem syndrome and an experience. *New England Journal of Medicine, 210,* 748–756.

Kalverboer, A. F. (1988). Hyperactivity and observational studies. In L. Bloomingdale & J. Sergeant (Eds.), *Attention deficit disorder: Criteria, cognition, and intervention* (pp. 29–42). New York: Pergamon Press.

Kane, R. L., & Perrine, K. R. (1985). *Nonverbal Selective Reminding Test.* Unpublished manuscript.

Kanfer, F. H., & Saslow, G. (1969). Behavioral diagnosis. In C. M. Franks (Ed.),

Behavior therapy: Appraisal and status (pp. 417–444). New York: McGraw-Hill.

Kanfer, F. H., & Schefft, B. K. (1988). *Guiding the process of therapeutic change.* Champaign, IL: Research Press.

Kaplan, B. J., McNichol, J., Conte, R. A., & Moghadam, H. K. (1987). Sleep disturbance in preschool-aged hyperactive and nonhyperactive children. *Pediatrics, 80,* 839–844.

Kashani, J., Chapel, J. L, Ellis, J., & Shekim, W. O. (1979). Hyperactive girls. *Journal of Operational Psychiatry, 10,* 145–148.

Kaufman, A. S. (1975). Factor analysis of the WISC-R at eleven age levels between 6.5 and 16.5 years. *Journal of Consulting and Clinical Psychology, 43,* 135–147.

Kaufman, A. S. (1980). Issues in psychological assessment: Interpreting the WISC-R intelligently. In B. Lahey & A. Kazdin (Eds.), *Advances in clinical child psychology* (Vol. 3, pp. 177–214). New York: Plenum.

Kaufman, A. S., & Kaufman, N. L. (1983). *Kaufman Assessment Battery for Children.* Circle Pines, MN: American Guidance Service.

Kazdin, A. E. (1974). Covert modelling, model similarity, and reduction of avoidance behavior. *Behavior Therapy, 5,* 325–340.

Kazdin, A. E. (1989). Childhood depression. In E. J. Mash & R. A. Barkley (Eds.), *Treatment of childhood disorders* (pp. 135–166). New York: Guilford Press.

Kazdin, A. E., Esveldt-Dawson, & Loar, L. L. (1983). Correspondence of teacher ratings and direct observations of classroom behavior of psychiatric inpatient children. *Journal of Abnormal Child Psychology, 11,* 549–564.

Kazdin, A. E., & Heidish, I. E. (1984). Convergence of clinically derived diagnoses and parent checklists among inpatient children. *Journal of Abnormal Child Psychology, 12,* 421–436.

Kelley, C. (1981). Reliability of the Behavior Problem Checklist with institutionalized male delinquents. *Journal of Abnormal Child Psychology, 9,* 243–250.

Kendall, P. C., & Braswell, L. (1982). Cognitive-behavioral self-control therapy for children: A component analysis. *Journal of Consulting and Clinical Psychology, 50,* 672–689.

Kendall, P. C., & Braswell, L. (1984). *Cognitive-behavioral therapy for impulsive children.* New York: Guilford Press.

Kendall, P. C., & Brophy, C. (1981). Activity and attentional correlates of teacher ratings of hyperactivity. *Journal of Pediatric Psychology, 6,* 4541–458.

Kendall, P. C., Lerner, R. M., & Craighead, W. E, (1984). Human development and intervention in child psychopathology. *Child Development, 55,* 71–82.

Kendall, P. C., & Wilcox, L. E. (1979). Self-control in children: Development of a rating scale. *Journal of Consulting and Clinical Psychology, 47,* 1020–1029.

Kendall, P. C., & Wilcox, L. E. (1980). Cognitive-behavioral treatment for impulsivity: Concrete versus conceptual training in non-self-controlled problem children. *Journal of Consulting and Clinical Psychology, 48,* 80–91.

Kendall, P. C., & Zupan, B. A. (1981). Individual versus group application of cognitive-behavioral self-control procedures with children. *Behavior Therapy, 12,* 344–359.

Kendall, P. C., Zupan, B. A., & Braswell, L. (1981). Self-control in children: Further analyses of the Self-Control Rating Scale. *Behavior Therapy, 12,* 667–681.

Keogh, B. K., & Margolis, J. S. (1976). A component analysis of attentional problems of educationally handicapped boys. *Journal of Abnormal Child Psychology, 4,* 349–359.

Kessler, J. W. (1980). History of minimal brain dysfunction. In H. Rie & E. Rie (Eds.), *Handbook of minimal brain dysfunctions: A critical view* (pp. 18–52). New York: Wiley.

King, B. T., & Janis, I. L. (1956). Comparison of the effectiveness of improvised versus nonimprovised role-playing in producing opinion changes. *Human Relations, 9,* 1778–186.

King, C., & Young, R. (1982). Attentional deficits with and without hyperactivity: Teacher and peer perceptions. *Journal of Abnormal Child Psychology, 10,* 483–496.

Kinsbourne, M. (1973). Minimal brain dysfunction as a neurodevelopmental lag. *Annals of the New York Academy of Sciences, 205,* 263–273.

Kinsbourne, M. (1977). The mechanism of hyperactivity. In M. Blau, I, Rapin, & M. Kinsbourne (Eds.), *Topics in child neurology* (pp. 289–307). New York: Spectrum.

Kirk, S. A. (1963). Behavioral diagnoses and remediation of learning disabilities. In *Proceedings of the annual meeting: Conference on exploration into the problems of the perceptually handicapped child* (Vol. 1, pp. 1–7). Evanston, IL.

Klee, S. H., & Garfinkel, B. D. (1983). The computerized continuous performance task: A new measure of attention. *Journal of the American Academy of Child Psychiatry, 11,* 487–496.

Klee, S. H., Garfinkel, B. D., & Beauchesen, H. (1986). Attention deficits in adults. *Psychiatric Annals, 16,* 52–56.

Knights, R. M., & Bakker, D. (Eds.). (1976). *The neuropsychology of learning disorders.* Baltimore: University Park Press.

Knights, R. M., & Bakker, D. (Eds.). (1980). *Treatment of hyperactive and learning disordered children.* Baltimore: University Park Press.

Knights, R. M., & Hinton, G. G. (1969). The effects of methylphenidate (Ritalin) on the motor skills and behavior of children with learning problems. *Journal of Nervous and Mental Disease, 148,* 643–653.

Knobel, M., Wolman, M. B., & Mason, E. (1959). Hyperkinesis and organicity in children. *Archives of General Psychiatry, 1,* 310–321.

Kohn, A. (1989, November). Suffer the restless children. *Atlantic Monthly,* pp. 90–100.

Kovacs, M. (1982). *The longitudinal study of child and adolescent psychopathology: I. The semi-structured psychiatric Interview Schedule for Children (ISC).* Unpublished manuscript, Western Psychiatric Institute.

Krouse, J. P., & Kauffman, J. M. (1982). Minor physical anomalies in exceptional children: A review and critique of research. *Journal of Abnormal Child Psychology, 10,* 247–264.

Kubany, E. S., Weiss, L. E., & Sloggett, B. B. (1971). The good behavior clock: A reinforcement/time out procedure for reducing disruptive classroom behavior. *Journal of Behavior Therapy and Experimental Psychiatry, 2,* 173–179.

Kupietz, S. S., Bailer, I., & Winsberg, B. G. (1972). A behavior rating scale for assessing improvement in behaviorally deviant children: A preliminary investigation. *American Journal of Psychiatry, 128,* 1432–1436.

Kurdek, L. A., Blisk, D., Siesky, A. E. (1981). Correlates of children's long-term adjustment to their parents' divorce. *Developmental Psychology, 17,* 565–579.

Laccetti, S. (1988, August 13). Parents who blame son's suicide on Ritalin use will join protest. *Atlanta Journal*, pp. B1, B7.

Lachar, D. (1982). *Personality Inventory for Children (PIC): Revised format manual supplement*. Los Angeles: Western Psychological Services.

Lachar, D., & Gdowski, C. L. (1979a). *Actuarial assessment of child and adolescent personality: An interpretive guide for the Personality Inventory for Children profile*. Los Angeles: Western Psychological Services.

Lachar, D., & Gdowski, C. L. (1979b). Problem behavior factor correlates of Personality Inventory for Children profile scales. *Journal of Consulting and Clinical Psychology, 47*, 39–48.

Lachar, D., Gdowski, C. L., & Snyder, D. K. (1984). External validation of the Personality Inventory for Children (PIC) profile and factor scales: Parent, teacher, and clinician ratings. *Journal of Consulting and Clinical Psychology, 52*, 155–164.

Lachar, D., Kline, R. B., & Boersma, D. C. (1986). The Personality Inventory for Children: Approaches to actuarial interpretation in clinic and school settings. In H. M. Knoff (Ed.), *The assessment of child and adolescent personality*. New York: Guilford Press.

Lahey, B. B., Green, K. D., & Forehand, R. (1980). On the independence of ratings of hyperactivity, conduct problems, and attention deficits in children: A multiple regression analysis. *Journal of Consulting and Clinical Psychology, 48*, 566–574.

Lahey, B. B., Pelham, W. E., Schaughency, E. A., Atkins, M. S., Murphy, H. A., Hynd, G. W., Russo, M., Hartdagen, S., & Lorys-Vernon, A. (1988). Dimensions and types of attention deficit disorder with hyperactivity in children: A factor and cluster analytic approach. *Journal of the American Academy of Child and Adolescent Psychiatry, 27*, 330–335.

Lahey, B. B., Piacentini, J. C., McBurnett, K., Stone, P., Hartdagen, S., & Hynd, G. (1988). Psychopathology in the parents of children with conduct disorder and hyperactivity. *Journal of the American Academy of Child and Adolescent Psychiatry, 27*, 163–170.

Lahey, B. B. Schaughency, E., Frame, C. L. & Strauss, C. C. (1985). Teacher ratings of attention problems in children experimentally classified as exhibiting attention deficit disorders with and without hyperactivity. *Journal of the American Academy of Child Psychiatry, 24*, 613–616.

Lahey, B. B., Schaughency, E., Hynd, G., Carlson, C., & Nieves, N. (1987). Attention Deficit Disorder with and without Hyperactivity: Comparison of behavioral characteristics of clinic-referred children. *Journal of the American Academy of Child Psychiatry, 26*, 718–723.

Lahey, B. B. Schaughency, E. Strauss, C., & Frame, C. (1984). Are Attention Deficit Disorders with and without Hyperactivity similar or dissimilar disorders? *Journal of the American Academy of Child Psychiatry, 23*, 302–309.

Lambert, N. M. (1988). Adolescent outcomes for hyperactive children. *American Psychologist, 43*, 786–799.

Lambert, N. M., Hartsough, C. S., Sassone, D., & Sandoval, J. (1987). Persistence of hyperactivity symptoms from childhood to adolescence and associated outcomes. *American Journal of Orthopsychiatry, 57*, 22–32.

Lambert, N. M., & Sandoval, J. (1980). The prevalence of learning disabilities in a sample of children considered hyperactive. *Journal of Abnormal Child Psychology, 8*, 33–50.

Lambert, N. M., Sandoval, J., & Sassone, D. (1978). Prevalence of hyperactivity in elementary school children as a function of social system definers. *American Journal of Orthopsychiatry, 48,* 446–463.

Landau, S., & Milich, R. (1988). Social communication patterns of attention deficit-disordered boys. *Journal of Abnormal Child Psychology, 16,* 69–81.

Langley, J., McGee, R., Silva, P., & Williams, S. (1983). Child behavior and accidents. *Journal of Pediatric Psychology, 8,* 181–189.

Lapouse, R., & Monk, M. (1958). An epidemiological study of behavior characteristics in children. *American Journal of Public Health, 48,* 1134–1144.

Laufer, M., & Denhoff, E. (1957). Hyperkinetic behavior syndrome in children. *Journal of Pediatrics, 50,* 463–474.

Laufer, M., Denhoff, E., & Solomons, G. (1957). Hyperkinetic impulse disorder in children's behavior problems. *Psychosomatic Medicine, 19,* 38–49.

LaVeck, B., Hammond, M. A., & LaVeck, G. D. (1980). Minor congenital anomalies and behavior in different home environments. *Journal of Pediatrics, 97,* 940–941.

Leary, M. R., & Miller, R. S. (1986). *Social psychology and dysfunctional behavior.* New York: Springer-Verlag.

Leon, G. R., Kendall, P. C., & Garber, J. (1980). Depression in children: Parent, teacher, and child perspectives. *Journal of Abnormal Child Psychology, 8,* 221–235.

Lerer, R. J. (1977). Do hyperactive children tend to have abnormal palmar creases? Report of a suggestive association. *Clinical Pediatrics, 16,* 645–647.

Lerner, J. A., Inui, T. S., Trupin, E. W., & Douglas, E. (1985). Preschool behavior can predict future psychiatric disorders. *Journal of the American Academy of Child Psychiatry, 24,* 42–48.

Lessing, E. E., & Zagorin, S. W. (1971). Dimensions of psychopathology in middle childhood as evaluated by three symptom checklists. *Educational and Psychological Measurement, 31,* 175–197.

Levin, P. M. (1938). Restlessness in children. *Archives of Neurology and Psychiatry, 39,* 764–770.

Levine, M. D. (1985). *Pediatric examination of educational readiness at middle childhood.* Cambridge, MA: Education Publishing Service.

Levine, M. D. & Rappaport, L. (1983). *Pediatric Early Elementary Examination.* Cambridge, MA: Education Publishing Service.

Lezak, M. (1983). *Neuropsychological assessment.* New York: Oxford University Press.

Linn, R. T., & Hodge, G. K. (1982). Locus of control in childhood hyperactivity. *Journal of Consulting and Clinical Psychology, 50,* 592–593.

Lobovitz, D. A. & Handel, P. J. (1985). Childhood depression: Prevalence using DSM-III criteria and validity of parent and child depression scales. *Journal of Pediatric Psychology, 10,* 45–54.

Lochman, J. E. & Curry, J. F. (1986). Effects of social problem-solving and self-instruction training with aggressive boys. *Journal of Clinical Child Psychology, 15,* 159–164.

Locke, H. J., & Wallace, K. M. (1959). Short marital adjustment and prediction tests: Their reliability and validity. *Journal of Marriage and Family Living, 21,* 251–255.

Logan, W. J., Farrell, J. E., Malone, M. A., & Taylor, M. J. (1988). *Effect of stimulant medications on cerebral event-related potentials.* Paper presented at the 17th national meeting of the Child Neurology Society, Halifax, Nova Scotia.

Loney, J. (1983). Research diagnostic criteria for childhood hyperactivity. In S. B.

Guze, F. J. Earls, & J. E. Barrett (Eds.), *Childhood psychopathology and development* (pp. 109–137). New York: Raven Press.

Loney, J. (1984). *A short parent rating scale for subgrouping childhood hyperactivity and aggression.* Paper presented at the 92nd annual convention of the American Psychological Association, Toronto.

Loney, J., Kramer, J., & Milich, R. (1981). The hyperkinetic child grows up: Predictors of symptoms, delinquency, and achievement at follow-up. In K. D. Gadow & J. Loney (Eds.), *Psychosocial aspects of drug treatment for hyperactivity.* Boulder, CO: Westview Press.

Loney, J., Langhorne, J., & Paternite, C. (1978). An empirical basis for subgrouping the hyperkinetic/minimal brain dysfunction syndrome. *Journal of Abnormal Psychology, 87,* 431–441.

Loney, J., & Milich, R. (1982). Hyperactivity, inattention, and aggression in clinical practice. In D. Routh & M. Wolraich (Eds.), *Advances in developmental and behavioral pediatrics* (Vol. 3, pp. 113–147). Greenwich, CT: JAI Press.

Lopez, R. (1965). Hyperactivity in twins. *Canadian Psychiatric Association Journal, 10,* 421.

Lou, H. C., Henriksen, L., & Bruhn, P. (1984). Focal cerebral hypoperfusion in children with dysphasia and/or Attention Deficit Disorder. *Archives of Neurology, 41,* 825–829.

Lou, H. C., Henriksen, L., Bruhn, P., Borner, H., & Nielsen, J. B. (1989). Striatal dysfunction in attention deficit and hyperkinetic disorder. *Archives of Neurology, 46,* 48–52.

Luk, S. (1985). Direct observations studies of hyperactive behaviors. *Journal of the American Academy of Child Psychiatry, 24,* 338–344.

Luk, S. L., & Leung, P. W. L. (1989). Conners' Teacher Rating Scale—a validity study in Hong Kong. *Journal of Child Psychology and Psychiatry, 30,* 785–793.

Luria, A. R. (1966). *Higher cortical functions in man.* New York: Basic Books.

Mack, J. L. (1969). Behavior ratings on recidivist and nonrecidivist delinquent males. *Psychological Reports, 25,* 260.

Manheimer, D. I., & Mellinger, G. D. (1967). Personality characteristics of the child accident repeater. *Child Development, 38,* 491–513.

Mannuzza, S., Gittelman, R., Bonagura, N., Konig, P. H., & Shenker, R. (1988). Hyperactive boys almost grown up. II. Status of subjects without a mental disorder. *Archives of General Psychiatry, 45,* 13–18.

Mannuzza, S., Gittelman, R., Konig, P. H., & Giampino, T. L. (1989). Hyperactive boys almost grown up: VI. Criminality and its relationship to psychiatric status. *Archives of General Psychiatry, 46,* 1073–1079.

Mannuzza, S., Klein, R., Bonagura, N., Malloy, P., Giampino, T., & Addalli, K. (in press). Hyperactive boys almost grown up: V. Psychiatric status of a replication sample. *Archives of General Psychiatry.*

Margalit, M., & Arieli, N. (1984). Emotional and behavioral aspects of hyperactivity. *Journal of Learning Disabilities, 17,* 374–376.

Margolis, J. S. (1972). *Academic correlates of sustained attention.* Unpublished doctoral dissertation, University of California–Los Angeles.

Mariani, M. A. (1990). *The nature of neuropsychological functioning in preschool-age children with attention-deficit hyperactivity disorder.* Unpublished doctoral dissertation, Boston College.

Marlowe, M., Cossairt, A., Moon, C., Errera, J., MacNeel, A., Peak, R., Ray, J., &

Schroeder, C. (1985). Main and interaction effects of metallic toxins on classroom behavior. *Journal of Abnormal Child Psychology, 13*, 185–198.

Marlowe, M., Errera, J., Nallowe, T., & Jacobs, J. (1983). Low metal levels in emotionally disturbed children. *Journal of Abnormal Psychology, 92*, 386–389.

Martin, B. (1977). Brief family intervention: The effectiveness and importance of including the father. *Journal of Consulting and Clinical Psychology, 45*, 1002–1010.

Marwit, S. J., & Stenner, A. J. (1972). Hyperkinesis: Delineation of two patterns. *Exceptional Children, 38*, 401–406.

Mash, E. J. (1984). Families with problem children. In A. Doyle, D. Gold, & D. Moskowitz (Eds.), *Children in families under stress* (pp. 65–84). San Francisco: Jossey-Bass.

Mash, E. J. (1989). Treatment of child and family disturbance: A behavioral-systems perspective. In E. J. Mash & R. A. Barkley (Eds.), *Treatment of childhood disorders* (pp. 3–36.) New York: Guilford Press.

Mash, E. J., & Barkley, R. A. (1986). Assessment of family interaction with the Response Class Matrix. In R. Prinz (Ed.), *Advances in behavioral assessment of children and families* (Vol. 2, pp. 29–67). Greenwich, CT: JAI Press.

Mash, E. J. & Johnston, C. (1982). A comparison of the mother-child interactions of younger and older hyperactive and normal children. *Child Development, 53*, 1371–1381.

Mash, E. J., & Johnston, C. (1983a). Sibling interactions of hyperactive and normal children and their relationship to reports of maternal stress and self-esteem. *Journal of Clinical Child Psychology, 12*, 91–99.

Mash, E. J. & Johnston, C. (1983b). The prediction of mothers' behavior with their hyperactive children during play and task situations. *Child and Family Behavior Therapy, 5*, 1–14.

Mash, E. J. & Johnston, C. (1983c). Parental perceptions of child behavior problems, parenting self-esteem, and mothers' reported stress in younger and older hyperactive and normal children. *Journal of Consulting and Clinical Psychology, 51* 68–99.

Mash, E. J., & Johnston, C. (in press). Determinants of parenting stress: Illustrations from families of hyperactive children and families of physically abused children. *Journal of Clinical Child Psychology*.

Mash, E. J., & Terdal, L. G. (Eds.) (1981). *Behavioral assessment of childhood disorders*. New York: Guilford Press.

Mash, E. J., & Terdal, L. G. (Eds.) (1988) *Behavioral Assessment of childhood disorders* (2nd ed.). New York: Guilford Press.

Mash, E. J. Terdal, L., & Anderson, K. (1973). The Response Class Matrix: A procedure for recording parent-child interactions. *Journal of Consulting and Clinical Psychology, 40*, 163–164.

Matson, J. L., Rotatori, A. F. & Helsel, W. J. (1983). Development of a rating scale to measure social skills in children: The Matson Evaluation of Social Skills with Youngsters (MESSY). *Behaviour Research and Therapy, 21*, 335–340.

Mattes, J. A. (1980). The role of frontal lobe dysfunction in childhood hyperkinesis. *Comprehensive Psychiatry, 21*, 358–369.

Mattes, J. A. & Gittelman, R. (1983). Growth of hyperactive children on maintenance regimen of methylphenidate. *Archives of General Psychiatry, 40*, 317–321.

Mattison, R. E. Cantwell, D. P., & Baker, L. (1980). Dimensions of behavior in children with speech and language disorders. *Journal of Abnormal Child Psychology,* *8,* 323–338.

Maurer, R. G., & Stewart, M. (1980). Attention Deficit Disorder without Hyperactivity in a child psychiatry clinic. *Journal of Clinical Psychiatry, 41,* 232–233.

Maynard, R. (1970, June 29). Omaha pupils given "behavior" drugs. *Washington Post.*

Mayron, L. M., Ott, J. N., Nations, R., & Mayron, E. L. (1974). Light, radiation, and academic behavior: Initial studies on the effects of full-spectrum lighting and radiation shielding on behavior and academic performance of school children. *Academic Therapy, 10,* 33–47.

McCarney, S. B. (1989). *Attention Deficit Disorders Evaluation Scale (ADDES).* Columbia, MO: Hawthorne Educational Services.

McClure, F. D., & Gordon, M. (1984). Performance of disturbed hyperactive and nonhyperactive children on an objective measure of hyperactivity. *Journal of Abnormal Child Psychology, 12,* 561–572.

McConaughy, S. H., & Achenbach, T. M. (1988). *Practical guide for the Child Behavior Checklist and related materials.* Burlington: University of Vermont, Department of Psychiatry.

McConaughy, S. H., Achenbach, T. M., & Gent, C. L. (1988). Multiaxial empirically based assessment: Parent, teacher, observational, cognitive, and personality correlates of Child Behavior Profile types for 6- to 11-year old boys. *Journal of Abnormal Child Psychology, 16,* 485–509.

McGee, R., Williams, S., Moffitt, T., & Anderson, J. (1989). A comparison of 13 year-old boys with attention deficit and or reading disorder on neuropsychological measures. *Journal of Abnormal Child Psychology, 17,* 37–53.

McGee, R., Williams, S., & Silva, P. A. (1984a). Behavioral and developmental characteristics of aggressive, hyperactive, and aggressive-hyperactive boys. *Journal of the American Academy of Child Psychiatry, 23,* 270–279.

McGee, R., Williams, S., & Silva, P. A. (1984b). Background characteristics of aggressive, hyperactive, and aggressive-hyperactive boys. *Journal of the American Academy of Child and Adolescent Psychiatry, 23,* 280–284.

McGee, R., Williams, S., & Silva, P. (1987). A comparison of girls and boys with teacher-identified problems of attention. *Journal of the American Academy of Child and Adolescent Psychiatry, 26,* 711–717.

McInerny, T., & Chamberlin, R. W. (1978). Is it feasible to identify infants who are at risk for later behavioral problems? The Carey Temperament Questionnaire as a prognostic tool. *Clinical Pediatrics, 17,* 233–238.

McMahon, R. C. (1980). Genetic etiology in the hyperactive child syndrome: A critical review. *American Journal of Orthopsychiatry, 50,* 145–150.

McMahon, R. J. (1984). Behavioral checklists and rating scales. In T. H. Ollendick & M. Hersen (Eds.), *Child behavioral assessment: Principles and procedures* (pp. 80–105). New York: Pergamon Press.

McMahon, R. J., & Forehand, R. (1984). Parent training for the noncompliant child: Treatment outcome, generalization, and adjunctive therapy procedures. In R. F. Dangel & R. A. Polster (Eds.), *Parent training: Foundations of research and practice* (pp. 298–328). New York: Guilford Press.

McMahon, R. J., Forehand, R., & Griest, D. L. (1981). Effects of knowledge of social learning principles on enhancing treatment outcome and generalization in a parent training program. *Journal of Consulting and Clinical Psychology, 49,* 526–532.

McMahon, R. J., Forehand, R. Griest, D. L., & Wells, K. C. (1981). Who drops out of treatment during parent behavioral training? *Behavioral Counseling Quarterly, 1,* 79–85.

McMahon, R. J., & Peters, R. D. (Eds.). (1985). *Childhood disorders: Behavioral-developmental approaches.* New York: Brunner/Mazel.

McMahon, R. J., & Wells, K. C. (1989). Conduct disorders. In E. J. Mash & R. A. Barkley (Eds.), *Treatment of childhood disorders* (pp. 73–134). New York: Guilford Press.

McMahon, S. A., & Greenberg, L. M. (1977). Serial neurologic examination of hyperactive children. *Pediatrics, 59,* 584–587.

McMurray, M. B., & Barkley, R. A. (in press). The hyperactive child. In R. Davids (Ed.), *Pediatric neurology for the clinician.* Norwalk, CT: Appleton-Century-Crofts.

Meichenbaum, D. (1971). An examination of modelling characteristics in reducing avoidance behavior. *Journal of Personality and Social Psychology, 17,* 298–307.

Meichenbaum, D. (1977). *Cognitive behavior modification: An integrative approach.* New York: Plenum.

Meichenbaum, D. (1988). Cognitive behavioral modification with attention deficit hyperactive children. In L. Bloomingdale & J. Sergeant (Eds.), *Attention deficit disorder: Criteria, cognition, and intervention* (pp. 127–140). New York: Pergamon Press.

Meichenbaum, D., & Goodman, J. (1971). Training impulsive children to talk to themselves: A means of developing self-control. *Journal of Abnormal Psychology, 77,* 115–126.

Mendelson, W., Johnson, N., & Stewart, M. A. (1971). Hyperactive children as teen-agers: A follow-up study. *Journal of Nervous and Mental Disease, 153,* 273–279.

Messer, S., & Brodzinsky, D. M. (1981). Three year stability of reflection-impulsivity in young adolescents. *Developmental Psychology, 17,* 848–850.

Meyer, E., & Byers, R. K. (1952). Measles encephalitis: A follow-up study of sixteen patients. *American Journal of Diseases of Children, 84,* 543–579.

Michelson, L., Sugai, D. P. Wood, P., & Kazdin, A. E. (1983). *Social skills assessment and training with children: An empirically based handbook.* New York: Plenum.

Milar, C. R., Schroeder, S. R., Mushak, P., & Boone, L. (1981). Failure to find hyperactivity in preschool children with moderately elevated lead burden. *Journal of Pediatric Psychology, 6,* 85–95.

Milich, R., & Dodge, K. A. (1984). Social information processing in child psychiatric populations. *Journal of Abnormal Child Psychology, 12,* 471–490.

Milich, R., & Kramer, J. (1985). Reflections on impulsivity: An empirical investigation of impulsivity as a construct. In K. D. Gadow & I. Bialer (Eds.), *Advances in learning and behavioral disabilities* (Vol. 3). Greenwich, CT: JAI Press.

Milich, R., & Landau, S. (1982). Socialization and peer relations in hyperactive children. In K. D. Gadow & I. Bialer (Eds.), *Advances in learning and behavioral disabilities* (Vol. 1, pp. 283–339). Greenwich, CT: JAI Press.

Milich, R. S., Laudau, S., Kilby, G., & Whitten, P. (1982). Preschool peer perceptions of the behavior of hyperactive and aggressive children. *Journal of Abnormal Child Psychology, 10,* 497–510.

Milich, R., & Loney, J. (1979). The role of hyperactive and aggressive symptomatology in predicting adolescent outcome among hyperactive children. *Journal of Pediatric Psychology, 4,* 93–112.

Milich, R., Loney, J., & Landau, S. (1982). The independent dimensions of hyperactivity and aggression: A validation with playroom observation data. *Journal of Abnormal Psychology, 91,* 183–198.

Milich, R., Loney, J., & Whitten, P. (1980). *Two-year stability and validity of playroom observations of hyperactivity.* Paper presented at the 88th annual convention of the American Psychological Association, Anaheim, CA.

Milich, R., Pelham, W., Hinshaw, S. (1985). Issues in the diagnosis of Attention Deficit Disorder: A Cautionary note. *Psychopharmacology Bulletin, 22,* 1101–1104.

Milich, R., Roberts, M. A., Loney, J., & Caputo, J. (1980). Differentiating practice effects and statistical regression on the Conners Hyperkinesis Index. *Journal of Abnormal Child Psychology, 8,* 549–552.

Milich, R., Wolraich, M., & Lindgren, S. (1986). Sugar and hyperactivity: A critical review of empirical findings. *Clinical Psychology Review, 6,* 493–513.

Millichap, J. G., Aymat, F., Sturgis, L., Larsen, K. W., & Egan, R. (1969). Hyperkinetic behavior and learning disorders. *American Journal of Diseases of Children, 116,* 235–244.

Minde, K., Lewin, D., Weiss, G., Lavigueur, H., Douglas, V., & Sykes, E. (1971). The hyperactive child in elementary school: A 5 year, controlled followup. *Exceptional Children, 38,* 215–221.

Minde, K., Webb, G., & Sykes, D. (1968). Studies on the hyperactive child. VI. Prenatal and perinatal factors associated with hyperactivity. *Developmental Medicine and Child Neurology, 10,* 355–363.

Minuchin, S. (1974). *Families and family therapy.* Cambridge, MA: Harvard University Press.

Mirsky, A. F. (1987). Behavioral and psychophysiological markers of disordered attention. *Environmental Health Perspectives, 74,* 191–199.

Mirsky, A. F. (1989). The neuropsychology of attention: Elements of a complex behavior. In E. Perecman (Ed.), *Integrating theory and practice in clinical neuropsychology* (pp. 75–91). Hillsdale, NJ: Erlbaum.

Mischel, W. (1973). Toward a cognitive social learning reconceptualization of personality. *Psychological Review, 80,* 252–283.

Mitchell, E. A., Aman, M. G., Turbott, S. H., & Manku, M. (1987). Clinical characteristics and serum essential fatty acid levels in hyperactive children. *Clinical Pediatrics, 26,* 406–411.

Molitch, M., & Eccles, A. K. (1937). Effect of benzedrine sulphate on intelligence scores of children. *American Journal of Psychiatry, 94,* 587–590.

Morganstern, K. P. (1976). Behavioral interviewing: The initial stages of assessment. In M. Hersen & A. Bellack (Eds.), *Behavioral assessment: A practical handbook* (pp. 51–76). New York: Pergamon Press.

Morris, R. J., & Kratochwill, T. R. (1983). *Treating children's fears and phobias: A behavioral approach.* New York: Pergamon.

Morrison, J. (1980). Adult psychiatric disorders in parents of hyperactive children. *American Journal of Psychiatry, 137,* 825–827.

Morrison, J. R., & Minkoff, K. (1975). Explosive personality as a sequel to the hyperactive-child syndrome. *Comprehensive Psychiatry, 16,* 343–348.

Morrison, J., & Stewart, M. (1971). A family study of the hyperactive child syndrome. *Biological Psychiatry, 3,* 189–195.

Morrison, J., & Stewart, M. (1973a). The psychiatric status of the legal families of adopted hyperactive children. *Archives of General Psychiatry, 28,* 888–891.

Morrison, J., & Stewart, M. A. (1973b). Evidence for polygenetic inheritance in the hyperactive child syndrome. *American Journal of Psychiatry, 130,* 791–792.

Munetz, M. R., & Benjamin, S. (1987). How to examine patients using the abnormal involuntary movement scale. *Hospital and Community Psychiatry, 39,* 1172–1177.

Munir, K., Biederman, J., & Knee, D. (1987). Psychiatric comorbidity in patients with attention deficit disorder: A controlled study. *Journal of the American Academy of Child and Adolescent Psychiatry, 26,* 844–848.

Munoz-Millan, R. J. & Casteel, C. R. (1989). Attention-Deficit Hyperactivity Disorder: Recent literature. *Hospital and Community Psychiatry, 40,* 699–707.

Murphy, L. B. (1981). Explorations in child personality. In A. I. Rabin, J. Aronoff, A. M. Barclay, & R. A. Zucker (Eds.), *Further explorations in personality* (pp. 161–195). New York: Wiley.

National Advisory Committee on Hyperkinesis and Food Additives. (1980). New York: Nutrition Foundation.

Needleman, H. L., Gunnoe, C., Leviton, A., Reed, R., Peresie, H., Maher, C., & Barrett, P. (1979). Deficits in psychologic and classroom performance of children with elevated dentine lead levels. *New England Journal of Medicine, 300,* 689–695.

Newby, R. (1989). *The Wisconsin Selective Reminding Test.* Milwaukee: Medical College of Wisconsin.

Nichols, P. L., & Chen, T. C. (1981). *Minimal brain dysfunction: A prospective study.* Hillsdale. NJ: Erlbaum.

Nieman, G. W., & DeLong, R. (1987). Use of the Personality Inventory for Children as an aid in differentiating children with mania from children with attention deficit disorder with hyperactivity. *Journal of the American Academy of Child and Adolescent Psychiatry, 26,* 381–388.

Nightline. (1988). [Segment on Ritalin controversy]. New York: American Broadcasting Company.

O'Connor, M., Foch, T., Sherry, T., & Plomin, R. (1980). A twin study of specific behavioral problems of socialization as viewed by parents. *Journal of Abnormal Child Psychology, 8,* 189–199.

O'Donnell, J. P., & Cress, J. N. (1975). Dimensions of behavior problems among Oglala Sioux adolescents. *Journal of Abnormal Child Psychology, 3,* 163–169.

O'Donnell J. P., & Van Tuinan, M. (1979). Behavior problems of preschool children: Dimensions and correlates. *Journal of Abnormal Child Psychology, 7,* 61–75.

O'Dougherty, M., Nuechterlein, K. H., & Drew, B. (1984). Hyperactive and hypoxic children: Signal detection, sustained attention, and behavior. *Journal of Abnormal Psychology, 93,* 178–191.

Office of Civil Rights. (1989, June 2). Fairfield-Sulsun (CA) unified school district. *OCR/Complaint LOFS, 353* (Suppl. 242), 205.

Offord, D. R., Boyle, M. H., Szatmari, P., Rae-Grant, N., Links, P. S., Cadman, D. T., Byles, J. A., Crawford, J. W., Munroe Blum, H., Byrne, C., Thomas, H., & Woodward, C. (1987). Ontario child health study: Six month prevalence of disorder and rates of service utilization. *Archives of General Psychiatry, 44,* 832–836.

O'Leary, K. D. (1981). Assessment of hyperactivity: Observational and rating methodologies. In S. A. Miller (Ed.), *Nutrition and behavior.* (pp. 291–298). Philadelphia: Franklin Institute Press.

O'Leary, K. D., & O'Leary, S. G. (1977). *Classroom management: The successful use of behavior modification* (2nd ed.). New York: Pergamon Press.

O'Leary, K. D., Pelham, W. E., Rosenbaum, A., & Price, G. H. (1976). Behavioral treatment of hyperkinetic children: An experimental evaluation of its usefulness. *Clinical Pediatrics, 15,* 510–515.

O'Leary, K. D., Rosenbaum, A., & Hughes, P. C. (1978). Fluorescent lighting: A purported source of hyperactive behavior. *Journal of Abnormal Child Psychology, 6,* 285–289.

O'Leary, K. D., Vivian, D., & Nisi, A. (1985). Hyperactivity in Italy. *Journal of Abnormal Child Psychology, 13,* 485–500.

O'Leary, S. G., & Pelham, W. E. (1978). Behavior therapy and withdrawal of stimulant medication in hyperactive children. *Pediatrics, 61,* 211–216.

Oltmans, T. F., Broderics, J. E., & O'Leary, K. D. (1977). Marital adjustment and the efficacy of behavior therapy with children. *Journal of Consulting and Clinical Psychology, 45,* 724–729.

Ounsted, C. (1955). The hyperkinetic syndrome in epileptic children. *Lancet, 53* 303–311.

Ownby, R. L., & Matthews, C. G. (1985). On the meaning of the WISC-R third factor: Relations to selected neuropsychological measures. *Journal of Consulting and Clinical Psychology, 53,* 531–534.

Packard, T., Robinson, E. A., & Grove, D. C. (1983). The effect of training procedures on the maintenance of parental relationship building skills. *Journal of Clinical Child Psychology, 12,* 181–186.

Palfrey, J. S., Levine, M. D., Walker, D. K., & Sullivan, M. (1985). The emergence of attention deficits in early childhood: A prospective study. *Developmental and Behavioral Pediatrics, 6,* 339–348.

Panaccione, V. F., & Wahler, R. G. (1986). Child behavior, maternal depression, and social coercion as factors in the quality of child care. *Journal of Abnormal Child Psychology, 14,* 263–278.

Paraskevopoulos, J., & McCarthy, J. M. (1970). Behavior patterns of children with special learning disabilities. *Psychology in the Schools, 7,* 42–46.

Parry, P. A., & Douglas, V. I. (1976). *The effects of reward on the performance of hyperactive children.* Unpublished doctoral dissertation, McGill University.

Parry, P. A., & Douglas, V. I. (1983). Effects of reinforcement on concept identification in hyperactive children. *Journal of Abnormal Child Psychology, 11,* 327–340.

Pasamanick, B., Rogers, M., & Lilienfeld, A. M. (1956). Pregnancy experience and the development of behavior disorder in children. *American Journal of Psychiatry, 112,* 613–617.

Pascaulvaca, D. M., Wolf, L. E. Healey, J. M., Tweedy, J. R., & Halperin, J. M. (1988, January) *Sex differences in attention and behavior in school-aged children.* Paper presented at the 16th annual meeting of the International Neuropsychological Society, New Orleans.

Paternite, C., & Loney, J. (1980). Childhood hyperkinesis: Relationships between symptomatology and home environment. In C. K. Whalen & B. Henker (Eds.), *Hyperactive children: The social ecology of identification and treatment* (pp. 105–141). New York: Academic Press.

Patterson, G. R. (1968). *Living with children: New methods for parents and teachers.* Champaign, IL: Research Press.

Patterson, G. R. (1976). The aggressive child: Victim and architect of a coercive system. In E. Mash, L. Hamerlynck, & L. Handy (Eds.), *Behavior modification and families* (pp. 267–316). New York: Brunner/Mazel.

Patterson, G. R. (1982). *Coercive family process.* Eugene, OR: Castalia.

Patterson, G. R. (1986). Performance models for antisocial boys. *American Psychologist, 41,* 432–444.

Patterson, G. R., & Forgatch, M. S. (1985). Therapist behavior as a determinant for patient noncompliance: A paradox for the behavior modifier. *Journal of Consulting and Clinical Psychology, 53,* 846–851.

Pelham, W. E. (1977). Withdrawal of a stimulant drug and concurrent behavioral intervention in the treatment of a hyperactive child. *Behavior Therapy, 8,* 473–479.

Pelham, W. E., & Bender, M. E. (1982). Peer relationships in hyperactive children: Description and treatment. In K. D. Gadow & I. Bialer (Eds.), *Advances in learning and behavioral disabilities* (Vol. 1, pp. 365–436). Greenwich, CT: JAI Press.

Pelham, W. E., Bender, M. E., Caddell, J., Booth, S., & Moorer, S. H. (1985). Methylphenidate and children with attention deficit disorder. *Archives of General Psychiatry, 42,* 948–952.

Pelham, W. E., & Milich, R. (1984). Peer relations in children with hyperactivity/attention deficit disorder. *Journal of Learning Disabilities, 17,* 560–567.

Pelham, W. E., Milich, R., Murphy, D. A., & Murphy, H. A. (1989). Normative data on the Iowa Conners Teacher Rating Scale. *Journal of Clinical Psychology, 18,* 259–262.

Pelham, W. E., & Murphy, H. A. (1986). Attention deficit and conduct disorders. In M. Hersen (Ed.), *Pharmacological and behavioral treatments: An integrative approach* (pp. 108–148). New York: Wiley.

Pelham, W. E., Schnedler, R. W., Bender, M. E., Nilsson, D. E., Miller, J., Budrow, M. S., Ronnel, M., Paluchowski, C. & Marks, D. A. (in press). The combination of behavior therapy and methylphenidate in the treatment of attention deficit disorders: A therapy outcome study. In J. Swanson & L. Bloomingdale (Eds.), *Attention deficit disorders* (Vol. 4). New York: Pergamon Press.

Pelham, W. E., Schnedler, R., Bologna, N., & Contreras, A. (1980). Behavioral and stimulant treatment of hyperactive children: A therapy study with methylphenidate probes in a within subject design. *Journal of Applied Behavior Analysis, 13,* 221–236.

Pelham, W. E., Sturges, J., Hoza, J., Schmidt, C., Bijlsma, J. J., Milich, R., & Moorer, S. (1987). Sustained release and standard methylphenidate effects on cognitive and social behavior in children with attention deficit disorder. *Pediatrics, 4,* 491–501.

Peters, B. H., & Levin, H. S. (1977). Memory enhancement after physostigmine treatment in the amnesic syndrome. *Archives of Neurology, 34,* 215–219.

Peters, B. H., & Levin, H. S. (1979). Effects on physostigmine and lecithin on memory in Alzheimer disease. *Annals of Neurology, 6,* 219–221.

Peterson, D. R. (1961). Behavior problems of middle childhood. *Journal of Consulting Psychology, 25,* 205–209.

Pfiffner, L. J., & O'Leary, S. G. (1987). The efficacy of all-positive management as a function of the prior use of negative consequences. *Journal of Applied Behavior Analysis, 20,* 265–271.

Pfiffner, L. J., O'Leary, S. G. (in press). Psychological treatments: School-based. In J. L. Matson (Ed.), *Hyperactivity in children: A handbook.* New York: Pergamon Press.

Pfiffner, L. J., Rosen, L. A., O'Leary, S. G. (1985). The efficacy of an all-positive approach to classroom management. *Journal of Applied Behavior Analysis, 18,* 257–261.

Physicians Desk Reference (1989). Oravell, NJ: Medical Economics Company.

Pisterman, S. J., McGrath, P., Firestone, P., & Goodman, J. T. (1989). Outcome of parent-mediated treatment of preschoolers with Attention Deficit Disorder. *Journal of Consulting and Clinical Psychology, 57,* 628–635.

Pisterman, S. J., McGrath, P., Firestone, P., Goodman, J. T. Webster, I., & Mallory, R. (1987, November). *Compliance outcome of parent-mediated compliance training with preschoolers with attention deficit disorder.* Poster presented at the meeting of the Association For Advancement of Behavior Therapy, Boston.

Pliszka, S. R. (1987). Tricyclic antidepressants in the treatment of children with attention deficit disorder. *Journal of the American Academy of Child and Adolescent Psychiatry, 26,* 127–132.

Pliszka, S. R. (1989). Effect of anxiety on cognition, behavior, and stimulant response in ADHD. *Journal of the American Academy of Child and Adolescent Psychiatry, 28,* 882–887.

Pollard, S., Ward, E. M., & Barkley, R. A. (1983). The effects of parent training and Ritalin on the parent-child interactions of hyperactive boys. *Child and Family Therapy, 5,* 51–69.

Pope, A. W., Bierman, K. L., & Mumma, G. H. (1989). Relations between hyperactive and aggressive behavior and peer relations at three elementary grade levels. *Journal of Abnormal Child Psychology, 17,* 253–267.

Porrino, L, J., Rapoport, J. L., Behar, D., Sceery, W., Ismond, D. R., & Bunney, W. E., Jr. (1983). A naturalistic assessment of the motor activity of hyperactive boys. *Archives of General Psychiatry, 40,* 681–687.

Porter, B., & O'Leary, K. D. (1980). Marital discord and childhood behavior problems. *Journal of Abnormal Child Psychology, 8,* 287–295.

Porter, J. E., & Rourke, B. P. (1985). Socioemotional functioning of learning-disabled children: A subtypal analysis of personality patterns. In B. P. Rourke (Ed.), *Neuropsychology of learning disabilities: Essentials of subtype analysis* (pp. 257–280). New York: Guilford Press.

Posner, M. (1987). *Structures and functions of selective attention* (American Psychology Association Master Lecture Series) Washington, DC: American Psychological Association.

Prechtl, H., & Stemmer, C. (1962). The choreiform syndrome in children. *Developmental Medicine and Child Neurology, 8,* 149–159.

Prinz, R. J., Foster, S. L. Kent, R. N., & O'Leary, K. D. (1979). Multivariate assessment of conflict in distressed and nondistressed mother-adolescent dyads. *Journal of Applied Behavior Analysis, 16,* 91–700.

Prinz, R. J., Myers, D., Holden, E., Tarnowski, K., & Roberts, W. (1983). Marital disturbance and child problems: A cautionary note regarding hyperactive children. *Journal of Abnormal Child Psychology, 11,* 393–399.

Prior, M., Leonard, A., & Wood, G. (1983). A comparison study of preschool children diagnosed as hyperactive. *Journal of Pediatric Psychology, 8,* 191–207.

Prior, M. Wallace, M., & Milton, I. (1984). Schedule-induced behavior in hyperactive children. *Journal of Abnormal Child Psychology, 12,* 227–244.

Proger, B. B. Mann, L., Green, P. A., Bayuk, R. J., Jr., & Burger, R. M. (1975). Discriminators of clinically defined emotional maladjustment: Predictive validities of the Behavior Problem Checklist and Devereaux Scales. *Journal of Abnormal Child Psychology, 3*, 71–82.

Puig-Antich, J., & Chambers, W. (1978). *The Schedule for Affective Disorders and Schizophrenia for School-Age Children.* New York: New York State Psychiatric Institute.

Quay, H. C. (1966). Personality patterns in preadolescent delinquent boys. *Educational and Psychological Measurement, 16*, 99–110.

Quay, H. C. (1977). Measuring dimensions of deviant behavior: The Behavior Problem Checklist. *Journal of Abnormal Child Psychology, 5*, 277–287.

Quay, H. C. (1983). A dimensional approach to behavior disorder: The Revised Behavior Problem Checklist. *School Psychology Review, 12*, 244–249.

Quay, H. C. (1987). The behavioral reward and inhibition systems in childhood behavior disorder. In L. M. Bloomingdale (Ed.), *Attention deficit disorder Vol. 3: New Research in treatment, psychopharmacology, and attention* (pp. 176–186). New York: Pergamon Press.

Quay, H. C. (1988). Attention deficit disorder and the behavioral inhibition system: The relevance of the neuropsychologicl theory of Jeffrey A. Gray. In L. Bloomingdale & J. Sergeant (Eds.), *Attention deficit disorder: Criteria, cognition, and intervention* (pp. 117–126). New York: Pergamon Press.

Quay, H. C., & Gredler, Y. (1981). Dimensions of problem behavior in institutionalized retardates. *Journal of Abnormal Child Psychology, 9*, 523–528.

Quay, H. C., Morse, W. C., & Cutler, R. L. (1966). Personality patterns of pupils in special classes for the emotionally disturbed. *Exceptional Children, 32*, 297–301.

Quay, H. C., & Peterson, D. R. (1975). *Manual for the Behavior Problem Checklist.* Unpublished manuscript, University of Miami.

Quay, H. C., & Peterson, D. R. (1983). *Interim manual for the Revised Behavior Problem Checklist.* Unpublished manuscript, University of Miami.

Quay, H. C., & Peterson, D. R. (1984). *Appendix I to the interim manual for the Revised Behavior Problem Checklist.* Unpublished manuscript, University of Miami.

Quay, H. C., & Quay, L. C. (1965). Behavior problems in early adolescence. *Child Development, 36*, 215–220.

Quay, H. C., Sprague, R. C. Shulman, H. S., & Miller, A. L. (1966). Some correlates of personality disorder and conduct disorder in a child guidance clinic sample. *Psychology in the Schools, 3*, 44–47.

Quinn, P. O., & Rapoport, J. L. (1974). Minor physical anomalies and neurological status in hyperactive boys. *Pediatrics, 53*, 742–747.

Quinn, P. O., Renfield, M., Burg, C., & Rapoport, J. L. (1977). Minor physical anomalies: A newborn screening and 1 year follow-up. *Journal of the American Academy of Child Psychiatry, 16*, 662–669.

Rapin, I. (1964). Brain damage in children. In J. Brennemann (Ed.), *Practice of pediatrics* (Vol. 4). Hagerstown, MD: Prior.

Rapoport, J. L., & Benoit, M. (1975). The relation of direct home observations to the clinic evaluation of hyperactive school age boys. *Journal of Child Psychology and Psychiatry, 16*, 141–147.

Rapoport, J. L., Buchsbaum, M. S., Zahn, T. P., Weingartner, H., Ludlow, C., & Mikkelsen, E. J. (1978). Dextroamphetamine: Cognitive and behavioral effects in normal prepubertal boys. *Science, 199*, 560–563.

Rapoport, J. L., Pandoni, C., Renfield, M., Lake, C. R., & Zielger, M. G. (1977).

Newborn dopamine-beta-hydroxylase, minor physical anomalies, and infant temperament. *American Journal of Psychiatry, 134,* 676–679.

Rapport, J. L., & Zametkin, A. (1988). Drug treatment of attention deficit disorder. In L. Bloomingdale & J. Sergeant (Eds.), *Attention deficit disorder: Criteria, cognition, and intervention* (pp. 161–182). New York: Pergamon Press.

Rapport, M. D., DuPaul, G. J., & Kelly, K. L. (in press). Attention-deficit Hyperactivity Disorder and methylphenidate: The relationship between gross body weight and drug response in children. *Psychopharmacology Bulletin.*

Rapport, M. D., DuPaul, G. J., Stoner, G., & Jones, J. T. (1986). Comparing classroom and clinic measures of attention deficit disorder: Differential, idosyncratic, and dose-response effects of methylphenidate. *Journal of Consulting and Clinical Psychology, 54,* 334–341.

Rapport, M. D., Jones, J. T., DuPaul, G. J., Kelly, K. L., Gardner, M. J., Tucker, S. B., & Shea, M. S. (1987). Attention Deficit Disorder and methylphenidate: Group and single-subject analyses of dose effects on attention in clinic and classroom settings. *Journal of Clinical Child Psychology, 16,* 329–338.

Rapport, M. D., & Kelly, K. L. (in press). Psychostimulant effects on learning and cognitive function in children with attention deficit hyperactivity disorder: Findings and implications. In J. L. Matson. (Ed.), *Hyperactivity in children: A handbook.* New York: Pergamon.

Rapport, M. D., Murphy, H. A., & Bailey, J. S. (1982). Ritalin vs. response cost in the control of hyperactive children: A within-subject comparison. *Journal of Applied Behavior Analysis, 15,* 205–216.

Rapport, M. D., Tucker, S. B., DuPaul, G. J., Merlo, M., & Stoner, G. (1986). Hyperactivity and frustration: The influence of control over and size of rewards in delaying gratification. *Journal of Abnormal Child Psychology, 14,* 191–204.

Raskin, L. A., Shaywitz, S. E., Shaywitz, B. A. Anderson, G. M., & Cohen, D. J. (1984). Neurochemical correlates of attention deficit disorder. *Pediatric Clinics of North America, 31,* 387–396.

Reed, M. L., & Edelbrock, C. (1983). Reliability and validity of the Direct Observation Form of the Child Behavior Checklist. *Journal of Abnormal and Child Psychology, 11,* 521–530.

Reeves, J. C., & Werry, J. S. (1987). Soft signs in hyperactivity. In D. E. Tupper (Ed.), *Soft neurological signs.* New York, NY: Grune & Stratton.

Reeves, J. C., Werry, J., Elkind, G. S., & Zametkin, A. (1987). Attention deficit, conduct, oppositional, and anxiety disorders in children: II. Clinical characteristics. *Journal of the American Academy of Child Psychiatry, 26,* 133–143.

Reichard, C. C., & Elder, T. (1977). The effects of caffeine on reaction time in hyperkinetic and normal children. *American Journal of Psychiatry, 134,* 144–148.

Reitan, R. M. (1986). Theoretical and methodological bases of the Halstead-Reitan Neuropsychological Test Battery. In I. Grant & K. Adams (Eds.) *Neuropsychological assessment of neuropsychiatric disorders* (pp, 3–30). New York: Oxford University.

Reynolds, W. M. (1987). *Reynolds Adolescent Depression Scale.* Odessa, FL: Psychological Assessment Resources.

Riddle, M. A., Hardin, M. T., Cho, S. C., Woolston, J. L., & Leckman, J. F. (1988). Desipramine treatment of boys with attention-deficit hyperactivity disorder and tics: Preliminary clinical experience. *Journal of the American Academy of Child and Adolescent Psychiatry, 27,* 811–814.

Rie, H. E., & Rie, E. D. (Eds.). (1980). *Handbook of minimal brain dysfunctions: A critical view*. New York: Wiley.

Ringholz, G. M. (1988). *Inconsistent attention in chronic survivors of severe closed head injury*. Unpublished Doctoral Dissertation.

Roberts, M. (1979). *A manual for the Restricted Academic Playroom Situation*. Iowa City, IA: Author.

Robin, A. L. (1981). A controlled evaluation of problem-solving communication training with parent-adolescent conflict. *Behavior Therapy, 12*, 593–609.

Robin, A. L., Fischel, J. E., & Brown, K. E. (1984). The measurement of self-control in children: Validation of the Self-Control Rating Scale. *Journal of Pediatric Psychology, 9*, 165–175.

Robin, A. L., & Foster, S. L. (1989). *Negotiating parent-adolescent conflict: A behavioral family systems approach*. New York: Guilford Press.

Robin, A. L., Fox, R. N., Martello, J., & Archable, C. (1977). Teaching note-taking skills to underachieving college students. *Journal of Educational Research, 71*, 81–85.

Robin, A. L., Kraus, D., Koepke, T., & Robin, R. A. (1987, August). *Growing up hyperactive in single versus two-parent families*. Paper presented at the 95th annual convention of the American Psychological Association, New York.

Robin, A. L., Schneider, M., & Dolnick, J. (1976). The turtle technique: An extensive case study of self-control in the classroom. *Psychology in the Schools, 1*, 449–459.

Robins, L. N., Helzer, J. E., Croughan, J., & Ratcliff, K. S. (1981). The NIMH Diagnostic Interview Schedule: Its history, characteristics, and validity. *Archives of General Psychiatry, 38*, 381–389.

Robinson, E. A., & Eyberg, S. M. (1981). The dyadic Parent-Child Interaction Coding System: Standardization and validation. *Journal of Consulting and Clinical Psychology, 49*, 245–250.

Robinson, E. A., Eyberg, S. M., & Ross, A. W. (1980). The standardization of an inventory of child conduct problem behaviors. *Journal of Clinical Child Psychology, 9*, 22–28.

Robinson, P. W., Newby, T. J., & Ganzell, S. L. (1981). A token system for a class of underachieving children. *Journal of Applied Behavior Analysis, 14*, 307–315.

Rosen, L. A., O'Leary, S. G., Joyce, S. A., Conway, G., & Pfiffner, L. J. (1984). The importance of prudent negative consequences for maintaining the appropriate behavior of hyperactive students. *Journal of Abnormal Child Psychology, 12*, 581–604.

Rosenbaum, A. (1983). *Aggress-Less: How to turn anger and aggression into positive action*. New Jersey: Prentice Hall.

Rosenthal, R. H., & Allen, T. W. (1978). An examination of attention, arousal, and learning dysfunctions of hyperkinetic children. *Psychological Bulletin, 85*, 689–715.

Rosenthal, R. H., & Allen, T. W. (1980). Intratask distractibility in hyperkinetic and nonhyperkinetic children. *Journal of Abnormal Child Psychology, 8*, 175–187.

Ross, D. M., & Ross, S. A. (1976). *Hyperactivity: Research, theory, and action*. New York: Wiley.

Ross, D. M., & Ross, S. A. (1982). *Hyperactivity: Current issues, research, and theory* (2nd ed.). New York: Wiley.

Rosvold, H. E., Mirsky, A. F., Sarason, I., Bransome, E. D., & Beck, L. H. (1956). A

continuous performance test of brain damage. *Journal of Consulting Psychology,*
20, 343–350.

Routh, D. K. (1978). Hyperactivity. In P. Magrab (Ed.), *Psychological management*
of pediatric problems (pp. 3–48). Baltimore: University Park Press.

Routh, D. K., & Roberts, R. D. (1972). Minimal brain dysfunction in children: Failure to find evidence for a behavioral syndrome. *Psychological Reports, 31,* 307–
314.

Routh, D. K., & Schroeder, C. S. (1976). Standardized playroom measures as indices
of hyperactivity. *Journal of Abnormal Child Psychology, 4,* 199–207.

Routh, D. K., Schroeder, C. S., & O'Tuama, L. (1974). The development of activity
level in children. *Developmental Psychology, 10,* 163–168.

Rubin, K. H., & Clark, M. L. (1983). Preschool teacher ratings of behavioral problems: Observational, sociometric, and social-cognitive correlates. *Journal of Ab-*
normal Child Psychology, 11, 273–285.

Rubinstein, R. A., & Brown, R. T. (1984). An evaluation of the validity of the diagnostic category of Attention Deficit Disorder. *American Journal of Orthopsychia-*
try, 54, 398–414.

Rutter, M. (1977). Brain damage syndromes in childhood: Concepts and findings.
Journal of Child Psychology and Psychiatry, 18, 1–21.

Rutter, M. (1982). Syndromes attributed to "minimal brain dysfunction" in childhood. *American Journal of Psychiatry, 139,* 21–33.

Rutter, M. (1983). Introduction: Concepts of brain dysfunction syndromes. In
M. Rutter (Ed.), *Developmental neuropsychiatry,* (pp. 1–14). New York: Guilford Press.

Rutter, M. (1988). DSM-III-R: A postscript. In M. Rutter, A. H. Tuma, & I. S. Lann
(Eds.), *Assessment and diagnosis in child psychopathology* (pp. 453–464). New
York: Guilford.

Rutter, M. (1989). Attention deficit disorder/hyperkinetic syndrome: Conceptual and
research issues regarding diagnosis and classification. In T. Sagvolden & T. Archer
(Eds.), *Attention deficit disorder: Clinical and basic research* (pp. 1–24). Hillsdale, NJ: Erlbaum.

Rutter, M., & Garmezy, N. (1983). Developmental psychopathology. In E. M. Heth-
erington (Ed.), *Handbook of child psychology* (4th ed.): Vol. 4. *Socialization,*
personality, and social development. New York: Wiley.

Rutter, M., & Shaffer, D. (1980). DSM-III: A step forward or a step backward in
terms of the classification of child psychiatric disorders? *Journal of the American*
Academy of Child Psychiatry, 19, 371–394.

Safer, D. J. (1973). A familial factor in minimal brain dysfunction. *Behavior Genetics,*
3, 175–186.

Safer, D. J., & Allen, R. P. (1973). Factors influencing the suppressant effects of two
stimulant drugs on the growth of hyperactive children. *Pediatrics, 51,* 660–667.

Safer, D. J., & Allen, R. P. (1976). *Hyperactive children.* Baltimore: University Park
Press.

Safer, D. J., Allen, R. P. & Barr, E. (1972). Depression in growth in hyperactive
children on stimulant drugs. *New England Journal of Medicine, 287,* 217–220.

Safer, D. J., & Krager, J. M. (1983). Trends in medication treatment of hyperactive
school children. *Clinical Pediatrics, 22,* 500–504.

Safer, D. J., & Krager, J. M. (1988). A survey of medication treatment for hyperactive/inattentive students. *Journal of the American Medical Association, 260,* 2256–2258.

Sagvolden, T., Wultz, B., Moser, E. I., Moser, M., & Morkrid, L. (1989). Results from a comparative neuropsychological research program indicate altered reinforcement mechanisms in children with ADD. In T. Sagvolden & T. Archer (Eds.), *Attention deficit disorder: Clinical and basic research* (pp. 261–286). Hillsdale, NJ: Erlbaum.

Salzinger, S., Kaplan, S., Pelcovitz, D., Samit, C., & Krieger, R. (1984). Parent and teacher assessment of children's behavior in child maltreating families. *Journal of the American Academy of Child Psychiatry, 23,* 458–464.

Sameroff, A. J., & Chandler, M. J. (1975). Reproductive risk and the continuum of caretaking casuality. In F. B. Horowitz (Ed.), *Review of child developmental research* (Vol. 4, pp. 187–244). Chicago: University of Chicago Press.

Sandberg, S. T., Rutter, M., & Taylor, E. (1978). Hyperkinetic disorder in psychiatric clinic attenders. *Developmental Medicine and Child Neurology, 20,* 279–299.

Sanders, M. R., Dadds, M. R., & Bor, W. (1989). Contextual analysis of child oppositional and maternal aversive behaviors in families of conduct–disordered and nonproblem children. *Journal of Clinical Child Psychology, 18,* 72–83.

Sandoval, J. (1977). The measurement of hyperactive syndrome in children. *Review of Educational Research, 47,* 293–318.

Sarason, I. G. (1975). Test anxiety and the self disclosing model. *Journal of Consulting and Clinical Psychology, 43,* 148–153.

Satterfield, J. H., Satterfield, B. T., & Cantwell, D. P. (1980). Multimodality treatment. *Archives of General Psychiatry, 37,* 915–919.

Satterfield, J. H., Satterfield, B. T., & Cantwell, D. P. (1981). Three-year multimodality treatment study of 100 hyperactive boys. *Journal of Pediatrics, 98,* 650–655.

Saul, R. C., & Ashby, C. D. (1986). Measurement of whole blood serotonin as a guide for prescribing psychostimulant medication for children with attentional deficits. *Clinical Neuropharmacology, 9,* 189–195.

Schachar, R. J. (1986). Hyperkinetic syndrome: Historical development of the concept. In E. Taylor (Ed.), *The overactive child* (pp. 19–40). Philadelphia: J. B. Lippincott.

Schachar, R. J., Rutter, M., & Smith, A. (1981). The characteristics of situationally and pervasively hyperactive children: Implications for syndrome definition. *Journal of Child Psychology and Psychiatry, 22,* 375–392.

Schachar, R. J., Taylor, E., Weiselberg, M., Thorley, G., & Rutter, M. (1987). Changes in family function and relationships in children who respond to methylphenidate. *Journal of the American Academy of Child and Adolescent Psychiatry, 26,* 728–732.

Schaughency, E. A., Lahey, B. B., Hynd, G. W., Stone, P. A., Piacentini, J. C., & Frick, P. J. (1989). Neuropsychological test performance and the attention deficit disorders: Clinical utility of the Luria-Nebraska Neuropsychological Battery—Children's Revision. *Journal of Consulting and Clinical Psychology, 57,* 112–116.

Schlager, G., Newman, D. E., Dunn, H. G., Crichton, J. U. & Schulzer, M. (1979). Bone age in children with minimal brain dysfunction. *Developmental Medicine and Child Neurology, 21,* 41–51.

Schleifer, M., Weiss, G., Cohen, N. J., Elman, M., Cvejic, H., & Kruger, E. (1975).

Hyperactivity in preschoolers and the effect of methylphenidate. *American Journal of Orthopsychiatry, 45,* 38–50.

Schnittjer, C. J., & Hirshoren, A. (1981). Factors of problem behavior in visually impaired children. *Journal of Abnormal Child Psychology, 9,* 517–522.

Schrag, P., & Divoky, D. (1975). *The myth of the hyperactive child.* New York: Pantheon.

Schultz, E. W., Manton, A. B., & Salvia, J. A. (1972). Screening emotionally disturbed children in a rural setting. *Exceptional Children, 39,* 134–137.

Schultz E. W., Salvia, J. & Fein, J. (1974). Prevalence of behavioral symptoms in rural elementary school children. *Journal of Abnormal Child Psychology, 2,* 17–24

Seagull, E. A. W., & Weinshank, A. B. (1984). Childhood depression in a selected group of low-achieving seventh graders. *Journal of Clinical Child Psychology, 13,* 134–140.

Sebrechts, M. M., Shaywitz, S. E., Shaywitz, D. A., Jatlow, P., Anderson, G. M., & Cohen, D. J. (1986). Components of attention, methylphenidate dosage, and blood levels in children with attention deficit disorder. *Pediatrics, 77,* 222–228.

Sergeant, J. (1988). From DSM-III attentional deficit disorder to functional defects. In L. Bloomingdale & J. Sergeant (Eds.), *Attention deficit disorder: Criteria, cognition, and intervention* (pp. 183–198). New York: Pergamon Press.

Sergeant, J., & van der Meere, J. J. (1989). The diagnostic significance of attentional processing: Its significance for ADDH classification—A future DSM. In T. Sagvolden & T. Archer (Eds.), *Attention deficit disorder: Clinical and basic research* (pp. 151–166). Hillsdale, NJ: Erlbaum.

Shaffer, D., & Greenhill, L. (1979). A critical note on the predictive validity of "the hyperkinetic syndrome." *Journal of Child Psychology and Psychiatry, 20,* 61–72.

Shaffer, D., McNamara, N., & Pincus, J. H. (1974). Controlled observations on patterns of activity, attention, and impulsivity in brain-damaged and psychiatrically disturbed boys. *Psychological Medicine, 4,* 4–18.

Shapiro, A. K., Shapiro, E. Brunn, R. D., & Sweet, R. D. (1978). *Gilles de la Tourette's syndrome.* New York: Raven Press.

Shapiro, B., & Shapiro, E. (1983). *Gilles de la Tourette syndrome.* New York: Raven Press.

Shapiro, S., & Garfinkel, B. (1986). The occurrence of behavior disorders in children: The interdependence of Attention Deficit Disorder and Conduct Disorder. *Journal of the American Academy of Child Psychiatry, 25,* 809–819.

Shaywitz, B. A., Shaywitz, S. E., Byrne, T., Cohen, D. J., & Rothman, S. (1983). Attention deficit disorder: Quantitative analysis of CT. *Neurology, 33,* 1500–1503.

Shaywitz, S. E., Cohen, D. J., & Shaywitz, B. E. (1980). Behavior and learning difficulties in children of normal intelligence born to alcoholic mothers. *Journal of Pediatrics, 96,* 978–982.

Shaywitz, S. E., & Shaywitz, B. A. (1984). Diagnosis and management of Attention Deficit Disorder: A pediatric perspective. *Pediatric Clinics of North America, 31,* 429–457.

Shaywitz, S. E., Shaywitz, B. A., Cohen, D. J., & Young, J. G. (1983). Monoaminergic mechanisms in hyperactivity. In M. Rutter (Ed.), *Developmental neuropsychiatry* (pp. 330–347). New York: Guilford Press.

Shaywitz, S. E., Shaywitz, B. A., Jatlow, P. R., Sebrechts, M., Anderson, G. M., &

Cohen, D. T. (1986). Biological differentiation of Attention Deficit Disorder with and without Hyperactivity: A preliminary report. *Annals of Neurology, 21,* 363.

Shekim, W. O., Glaser, E., Horwitz, E., Javaid, J., & Dylund, D. B. (1987). Psychoeducational correlates of catecholamine metabolites in hyperactive children. In L. Bloomingdale (Ed.), *Attention deficit disorder: New research in attention, treatment, and psychopharmacology* (Vol. 3, pp. 149–150). New York: Pergamon Press.

Shelton, T. L., & Barkley, R. A. (in press). The assessment of Attention Deficit-Hyperactivity Disorder in preschoolers. In D. Willis & J. Culbertson (Eds.), *Testing young children.* Austin, TX: Pro-Ed.

Shipley, W. C. (1946) *Institute of Living Scale.* Los Angeles: Western Psychological Services.

Shirley, M. (1939). A behavior syndrome characterizing prematurely born children. *Child Development, 10,* 115–128.

Simeonsson, R. J. (1986). *Psychological and developmental assessment of special children.* Boston: Allyn & Bacon.

Simeonsson, R. J., Cooper, D. H., & Scheiner, A. P. (1982). A review and analysis of the effectiveness of early intervention programs. *Pediatrics, 69,* 635–641.

Singer, S. M., Stewart, M. A., & Pulaski, L. (1981). Minimal brain dysfunction: Differences in cognitive organization in two groups of index cases and their relatives. *Journal of Learning Disabilities, 14,* 470–473.

Silva, P. A., Hughes, P., Williams, S., & Faed, J. M. (1988). Blood lead, intelligence, reading attainment, and behaviour in eleven year old children in Dunedin, New Zealand. *Journal of Child Psychology and Psychiatry, 29,* 43–52.

Skinner, B. F. (1953). *Science and human behavior.* New York: Macmillan.

Skinner, N. (1988). Dyslexic boy's parents sue school. *Roanoke Gazette,* June 22, 1988.

Sleator, E. K., & Ullmann, R. L. (1981). Can the physician diagnose hyperactivity in the office? *Pediatrics, 67,* 13–17.

Smith, L. (1975). *Your child's behavior chemistry.* New York: Random House.

Sobol, M. P., Ashbourne, D. T., Earn, B. M., & Cunningham, C. E. (1989). Parents' attributions for achieving compliance for attention-deficit-disordered children. *Journal of Abnormal Child Psychology, 17,* 359–369.

Solomons, G. (1965). The hyperactive child. *Journal of the Iowa Medical Society, 55,* 464–469.

Solomons, G. (1973). Drug therapy: Initiation and follow-up. *Annals of the New York Academy of Sciences, 205,* 335–344.

Sostek, A. J., Buchsbaum, M. S., & Rapoport, J. L. (1980). Effects of amphetamine on vigilance performance in normal and hyperactive children. *Journal of Abnormal Child Psychology, 8,* 491–500.

Speer, D. C. (1971). The Behavior Problem Checklist (Peterson-Quay): Baseline data from parents of child guidance and nonclinic children. *Journal of Consulting and Clinical Psychology, 36,* 221–228.

Spitzer, R. L., Davies, M., & Barkley, R. A. (in press). The DSM-III-R field trial for the Disruptive Behavior Disorders. *Journal of the American Academy of Child and Adolescent Psychiatry.*

Spivack, G., & Shure, M. B. (1974). *Social adjustment of young children: A cognitive approach to solving real-life problems.* San Francisco: Jossey-Bass.

Sprague, R. L., Barnes, K. R., & Werry, J. S. (1970). Methylphenidate and thioridazine: Learning, activity, and behavior in emotionally disturbed boys. *American Journal of Orthopsychiatry, 40,* 615–628.

Sprague, R. L., Cohen, M. N., & Eichlseder, W. (1977). *Are there hyperactive children in Europe and the South Pacific?* Paper presented at the 85th annual convention of the American Psychological Association.

Sprague, R., Cohen, M. N., & Werry, J. (1974). *Normative data on the Conners Teacher Rating Scale and Abbreviated Scale.* Unpublished manuscript, University of Illinois.

Sprague, R., & Sleator, E. (1976). Drugs and dosages: Implications for learning disabilities. In R. Knights & D. Bakker (Eds.), *The neuropsychology of learning disorders.* Baltimore: University Park Press.

Sprague, R., & Sleator, E. (1977). Methylphenidate in hyperkinetic children: Differences in dose effects on learning and social behavior. *Science, 198,* 1274–1276.

Sroufe, L. A. (1975). Drug treatment of children with behavior problems. In F. Horowitz (Ed.), *Review of child development research* (Vol. 4, pp. 347–408). Chicago: University of Chicago Press.

Steinkamp, M. W. (1980). Relationships between environmental distractions and task performance of hyperactive and normal children. *Journal of Learning Disabilities, 13,* 40–45.

Stern, D. (1977). *The first relationship.* Cambridge, MA: Harvard University Press.

Stevens, T. M., Kupst, M. J., Suran, B. G., & Schulman, J. L. (1978). Activity level: A comparison between actometer scores and observer ratings. *Journal of Abnormal Child Psychology, 6,* 163–173.

Stewart, K. J., & Moely, B. E. (1983). The WISC-R third factor: What does it mean? *Journal of Consulting and Clinical Psychology, 51,* 940–941.

Stewart, M. A. (1970). Hyperactive children. *Scientific American, 222,* 94–98.

Stewart, M. A., deBlois, S., & Cummings, C. (1980). Psychiatric disorder in the parents of hyperactive boys and those with conduct disorder. *Journal of Child Psychology and Psychiatry, 21,* 283–292.

Stewart, M. A., Cummings, C., Singer, S., & deBlois, C. S. (1981). The overlap between hyperactive and unsocialized aggressive children. *Journal of Child Psychology and Psychiatry, 22,* 35–45.

Stewart, M. A., Mendelson, W. B., & Johnson, N. E. (1973). Hyperactive children as adolescents: How they describe themselves. *Child Psychiatry and Human Development, 4,* 3–11.

Stewart, M. A., Pitts, F. N., Craig, A. G., & Dieruf, W. (1966). The hyperactive child syndrome. *American Journal of Orthopsychiatry, 36,* 861–867.

Stewart, M. A., Thach, B. T., & Friedin, M. R. (1970). Accidental poisoning and the hyperactive child syndrome. *Diseases of the Nervous System, 31,* 403–407.

Still, G. F. (1902). Some abnormal psychical conditions in children. *Lancet, i,* 1008–1012, 1077–1082, 1163–1168.

Stone, B. F. (1981). Behavior problems in elementary school children. *Journal of Abnormal Child Psychology, 9,* 407–418.

Strang, J. D., & Rourke, B. P. (1985). Adaptive behavior of children who exhibit specific arithmetic disabilities and associated neuropsychological abilities and deficits. In B. P. Rourke (Ed.), *Neuropsychology of learning disabilities: Essentials of subtype analysis* (pp. 167–183). New York: Guilford Press.

Straus, M. A., Gelles, R. J., & Steinmetz, S. K. (1980). *Behind closed doors: Violence in the American family.* New York: Anchor Books.

Strauss, A. A., & Kephhart, N. C. (1955). *Psychopathology and education of the brain-injured child: Vol. 2. Progress in theory and clinic.* New York: Grune & Stratton.

Strauss, A. A., & Lehtinen, L. E. (1947). *Psychopathology and education of the brain-injured child.* New York: Grune & Stratton.

Strauss, C., Lease, C., Last, C., & Francis, G. (1988). Overanxious Disorder: An examination of developmental differences. *Journal of Abnormal Child Psychology, 16,* 433–444.

Strayhorn, J. M., & Weidman, C. S. (1988). A parent practices scale and its relation to parent and child mental health. *Journal of the American Academy of Child and Adolescent Psychiatry, 27,* 613–618.

Strecker, E., & Ebaugh, F. (1924). Neuropsychiatric sequelae of cerebral trauma in children. *Archives of Neurology and Psychiatry, 12,* 443–453.

Streissguth, A. P., Martin, D. C., Barr, H. M., Sandman, B. M., Kirchner, G. L., & Darby, B. L. (1984). Intrauterine alcohol and nicotine exposure: Attention and reaction time in 4-year-old children. *Developmental Psychology, 20,* 533–541.

Stroop, J. R. (1935). Studies of interference in serial verbal reactions. *Journal of Experimental Psychology, 18,* 643–662.

Stryker, S. (1925). Encephalitis lethargica—the behavior residuals. *Training School Bulletin, 22,* 152–157.

Stuss, D. T., & Benson, D. F. (1986). *The frontal lobes.* New York: Raven Press.

Sullivan, M. A., & O'Leary, S. G. (in press). Differential maintenance following reward and cost token programs with children. *Behavior Therapy.*

Sultana, Q. (1974). *An analysis of the Quay-Peterson Behavior Checklist as an instrument to screen emotionally disturbed children.* Unpublished doctoral dissertation, University of Georgia.

Swanson, J., & Pelham, W. (1988). *A rating scale for the diagnosis of attention deficit disorders: Teacher norms and reliability.* Unpublished manuscript, University of Pittsburgh, Western Psychiatric Institute.

Swanson, J., Simpson, S., Agler, D., Pfiffner, L., Bender, M., Kotkin, R., Rosenau, C., Mayfield, K., Ferrari, L., Lerner, M., Cantwell, D., & Youpa, D. (in press). *The UCI school-based treatment program for children with ADHD/ODD.* Excerpta Medica International Congress Series.

Szatmari, P., Offord, D. R., & Boyle, M. H. (1989a). Ontario child health study: Prevalence of attention deficit disorder with hyperactivity. *Journal of Child Psychology and Psychiatry, 30,* 219–230.

Szatmari, P., Offord, D. R., & Boyle, M. H. (1989b). Correlates, associated impairments, and patterns of service utilization of children with attention deficit disorders: Findings from the Ontario child health study. *Journal of Child Psychology and Psychiatry, 30,* 205–217.

Tallmadge, J., & Barkley, R. A. (1983). The interactions of hyperactive and normal boys with their mothers and fathers. *Journal of Abnormal Child Psychology, 11,* 565–579.

Tallmadge, J., Paternite, C., & Gordon, M. (1989). *Hyperactivity and aggression in parent–child interactions: Test of a two–factor theory.* Paper presented at Society for Research in Child Development, Kansas City, MO, April.

Tant, J. L., & Douglas, V. I. (1982). Problem solving in hyperactive, normal, and reading-disabled boys. *Journal of Abnormal Child Psychology, 10,* 285–306.

Tartar, R. E., McBride, H., Buonpane, N., & Schneider, D. U. (1977). Differentiation of alcoholics: Childhood history of minimal brain dysfunction, family history, and drinking pattern. *Archives of General Psychiatry, 34,* 761–768.

Tarver-Behring, S., Barkley, R., & Karlsson, J. (1985). The mother-child interactions of hyperactive boys and their normal siblings. *American Journal of Orthopsychiatry, 55,* 202–209.

Taylor, E. A. (1983). Drug response and diagnostic validation. In M. Rutter (Ed.), *Developmental neuropsychiatry* (pp. 348–368). New York: Guilford Press.

Taylor, E. A. (1986a). (Ed.). *The overactive child.* Philadelphia: J. P. Lippincott.

Taylor, E. A. (1986b). Childhood hyperactivity. *British Journal of Psychiatry, 149,* 562–573.

Taylor, E. A. (1988). Diagnosis of hyperactivity—A British perspective. In L. Bloomingdale & J. Sergeant (Eds.), *Attention deficit disorder: Criteria, cognition, and intervention* (pp. 141–160). New York: Pergamon Press.

Taylor, E. A. (1989). On the epidemiology of hyperactivity. In T. Sagvolden & T. Archer (Eds.), *Attention deficit disorder: Clinical and basic research* (pp. 31–52). Hillsdale, NJ: Erlbaum.

Taylor, E. A., & Sandberg, S. (1984). Hyperactive behavior in English school children: A questionnaire survey. *Journal of Abnormal Child Psychology, 12,* 143–156.

Taylor, J. A. (1951). The relationship of anxiety to the conditioned eyelid response. *Journal of Experimental Psychology, 42,* 183–188.

Taylor, J. F. (1980). *The hyperactive child and the family.* New York: Random House.

Terrace, H. (1974). On the nature of nonresponding in discrimination learning with and without errors. *Journal of the Experimental Analysis of Behavior, 22,* 35–45.

Thomas, A., & Chess, S. (1977). *Temperament and development.* New York: Brunner/Mazel.

Thomas, A., Chess, S., & Birch, H. G. (1968). *Temperament and behavior disorders in children.* New York: New York University Press.

Thomas, A., Chess, S., Birch, H. G., Hertzig, M. E., & Korn, S. (1963). *Behavioral individuality in early childhood.* New York: New York University Press.

Thomson, G. O. B., Raab, G. M., Hepburn, W. S., Hunter, R., Fulton, M., & Laxen, D. P. H., (1989). Blood-lead levels and children's behaviour—Results from the Edinburgh lead study. *Journal of Child Psychology and Psychiatry, 30,* 515–528.

Thompson, J., Ross, R., & Horwitz, S. (1980). The role of computed tomography in the study of children with minimal brain dysfuntion. *Journal of Learning Disabilities, 13,* 48–51.

Thorley, G. (1983). *Normative data on the Conners Teacher Questionnaire in two British clinic populations.* Unpublished manuscript, Hospital for Sick Children, Toronto, Canada.

Thorley, G. (1984). Review of follow-up and follow-back studies of childhood hyperactivity. *Psychological Bulletin, 96,* 116–132.

Toufexis, A. (1989, January 16). Worries about overactive kids: Are too many youngsters being misdiagnosed and medicated? *Time,* p. 65.

Touliatos, J., & Lindholm, B. W. (1975). Relationships of children's grade in school, sex, and social class to teachers ratings on the Behavior Problem Checklist. *Journal of Abnormal Child Psychology, 3,* 115–126.

Touliatos, J., & Lindholm, B. W. (1981). Congruence of parents' and teachers' ratings of children's behavior problems. *Journal of Abnormal Child Psychology, 9,* 347–354.

Trad, P. V. (1989). *The preschool child.* New York: Wiley.

Tredgold, A. F. (1908). *Mental deficiency (amentia).* New York: W. Wood.

Trites, R. L. (1979). *Hyperactivity in children: Etiology, measurement, and treatment implications.* Baltimore: University Park Press.

Trites, R. L., Blouin, A. G., Ferguson, H. B., & Lynch, G. W. (1981). The Conners Teacher Rating Scale: An epidemiological inter-rater reliability and follow-up investigation. In K. Gadow & J. Loney (Eds.). *Psychosocial aspects of drug treatment for hyperactivity.* Boulder, CO: Westview Press.

Trites, R. L., Blouin, A. G., & Laprade, K. (1982). Factor analysis of the Conners Teacher Rating Scale based on a large normative sample. *Journal of Consulting and Clinical Psychology, 50,* 615–623.

Trites, R. L., Dugas, F., Lynch, G., & Ferguson, B. (1979). Incidence of hyperactivity. *Journal of Pediatric Psychology, 4,* 179–188.

Trites, R. L., & Laprade, K. (1984). *Traduction et normes pour une version francaise du Conners Teacher Rating Scale.* Unpublished manuscript, Royal Ottawa Hospital.

Trites, R. L., Tryphonas, H., & Ferguson, H. B. (1980). Diet treatment for hyperactive children with food allergies. In R. M. Knight & D. Bakker (Eds.), *Treatment of hyperactive and learning disordered children* (pp. 151–166). Baltimore: University Park Press.

Trommer, B. L., Hoeppner, J. B., Lorber, R., & Armstrong, K. (1988). Pitfalls in the use of a continuous performance test as a diagnostic tool in attention deficit disorder. *Developmental and Behavioral Pediatrics, 9,* 339–346.

Trommer, B. L., Hoeppner, J. B., Rosenberg, R. S., Armstrong, K. J., & Rothstein, J. A. (1988). Sleep disturbances in children with attention deficit disorder. *Annals of Neurology, 24,* 325.

Tronick, E. Z., & Gianino, A. (1986). Interactive mismatch and repair: Challenges to the coping infant. *Zero to Three, 6,* 1–6.

Turkewitz, H., O'Leary, K. D., & Ironsmith, M. (1975). Generalization and maintenance of appropriate behavior through self-control. *Journal of Consulting and Clinical Psychology, 43,* 577–583.

Twyman, A. S. (1988, May 4). Use of drug prompts suit. *Newton Graphic, 28.*

Ullman, D. G., Barkley, R. A., & Brown, H. W. (1978). The behavioral symptoms of hyperkinetic children who successfully responded to stimulant drug treatment. *American Journal of Orthopsychiatry, 48,* 425–437.

Ullmann, R. K. (1984). *Teacher ratings useful in screening learning disabled from attention deficit disordered (ADD-H) children.* Unpublished manuscript, University of Illinois.

Ullmann, R. K., & Sleator, E. K. (1984a). *ADD-H children: Which behaviors are helped by stimulants?* Unpublished manuscript, University of Illinois.

Ullmann, R. K., & Sleator, E. K. (1984b). *Are there really any ADD children? Patterns of ACTeRS' ratings at baseline and on medication.* Unpublished manuscript, University of Illinois.

Ullmann, R. K., & Sleator, E. K. (1985). Attention Deficit Disorder children with and without Hyperactivity: Which behaviors are helped by stimulants? *Clinical Pediatrics, 24,* 547–551.

Ullmann, R. K., Sleator, E. K., & Sprague, R. (1984a). A new rating scale for diagnosis and monitoring of ADD children. *Psychopharmacology Bulletin, 20,* 160–164.

Ullmann, R. K., Sleator, E. K., & Sprague, R. L. (1984b). ADD children: Who is referred from the schools? *Psychopharmacology Bulletin, 20,* 308–312.

Ullmann, R. K., Sleator, E. K., & Sprague, R. L. (1985). A change of mind: The Conners Abbreviated Rating Scales reconsidered. *Journal of Abnormal Child Psychology, 13,* 553–566.

van der Meere, J., & Sergeant, J. (1988a). Focused attention in pervasively hyperactive children. *Journal of Abnormal Child Psychology, 16,* 627–640.

van der Meere, J., & Sergeant, J. (1988b). Controlled processing and vigilance in hyperactivity: Time will tell. *Journal of Abnormal Child Psychology, 16,* 641–656.

Victor, J. B., & Halverson, C. F., Jr. (1975). Distractibility and hypersensitivity: Two behavior factors in elementary school children. *Journal of Abnormal Child Psychology, 3,* 83–94.

Victor, J. B., Halverson, C. F., Jr., Inoff, G., & Buczkowski, H. J. (1973). Objective behavior measures of first and second grade boys' free play and teachers' ratings on a behavior problem checklist. *Psychology in the Schools, 10,* 439–443.

Vincent, J. P., Williams, B. J., Harris, G. E., & Duvall, G. (1977). *Classroom observations of hyperactive children: A multiple validation study.* Paper presented at the 85th annual convention of the American Psychological Association, San Francisco.

Voelker, S. L., Carter, R. A., Sprague, D. J., Gdowski, C. L., & Lachar, D. (1989). Developmental trends in memory and metamemory in children with attention deficit disorder. *Journal of Pediatric Psychology, 14,* 75–88.

Voelker, S. L., Lachar, D., & Gdowski, C. L. (1983). The Personality Inventory for Children and response to methylphenidate: Preliminary evidence for predictive validity. *Journal of Pediatric Psychology, 8,* 161–169.

Wahler, R. G. (1976). Deviant child behavior within the family: Developmental speculations and behavior change strategies. In H. Leitenberg (Ed.), *Handbook of behavior modification and behavior therapy* (pp. 516–545). Englewood Cliffs, NJ: Prentice-Hall.

Wahler, R. G. (1980). The insular mother: Her problems in parent-child treatment. *Journal of Applied Behavior Analysis, 13,* 207–219.

Waldrop, M. F., Bell, R. Q., & Goering, J. D. (1976). Minor physical anomalies and inhibited behavior in elementary school girls. *Journal of Child Psychology and Psychiatry, 17,* 113–122.

Waldrop, M. F., Bell, R. Q., McLaughlin, B., & Halverson, C. F., Jr. (1978). Newborn minor physical anomalies predict short attention span, peer agression, and impulsivity at age 3. *Science, 199,* 563–564.

Walker, J. L., Lahey, B. B., Hynd, G., & Frame, C. (1987). Comparison of specific patterns of antisocial behavior in children with Conduct Disorder with and without coexisting hyperactivity. *Journal of Consulting and Clinical Psychology, 55,* 910–913.

Webb, T. E., & Oski, F. A. (1973). Behavioral status of young adolescents with iron deficiency anemia. *Journal of Special Education, 8,* 153–156.

Webster-Stratton, C. (1984). Randomized trial of two parent training programs for families with conduct-disordered children. *Journal of Consulting and Clinical Psychology, 52,* 666–678.

Webster-Stratton, C. (1988). Mothers' and fathers' perceptions of child deviance: Roles of parent and child behaviors and parent adjustment. *Journal of Consulting and Clinical Psychology, 56,* 909–915.

Webster-Stratton, C., & Eyberg, S. M. (1982). Child temperament: Relationship with child behavior problems and parent-child interactions. *Journal of Clinical Child Psychology, 11,* 123–129.

Webster-Stratton, C., & Hammond, M. (1988). Maternal depression and its relationship to life stress, perceptions of child behavior problems, parenting behaviors, and child conduct problems. *Journal of Abnormal Child Psychology, 16,* 299–315.

Wechsler, D. (1974). *The Wechsler Intelligence Scale for Children—Revised.* New York: Psychological Corporation.

Wechsler, D. (1981). *Wechsler Adult Intelligence Scale-Revised. Manual.* New York: Psychological Corporation.

Weiner, J. (1988). Diagnosis, treatment of ADHD requires skill. *Worcester Telegram and Gazette,* May 14, 1988, 14.

Weiss, G., & Hechtman, L. (1979). The hyperactive child syndrome. *Science, 205,* 1348–1354.

Weiss, G., & Hechtman, L. (1986). *Hyperactive children grown up.* New York: Guilford Press.

Weiss, G., Hechtman, L., Milroy, T., & Perlman, T. (1985). Psychiatric status of hyperactives as adults: A controlled prospective 15 year follow up of 63 hyperactive children. *Journal of the American Academy of Child Psychiatry, 23,* 211–220.

Weiss, G., Hechtman, L., & Perlman, T. (1978). Hyperactives as young adults: School, employer, and self-rating scales obtained during ten-year follow-up evaluation. *American Journal of Orthopsychiatry, 48,* 438–445.

Weiss, G., Hechtman, L., Perlman, T., Hopkins, J. & Wehar, T. (1979). Hyperactives as young adults: A controlled prospective 10-year follow-up of the psychiatric status of 75 children. *Archives of General Psychiatry, 36,* 675–681.

Weiss, G., Minde, K., Werry, J., Douglas, V., & Nemeth, E. (1971). Studies on the hyperactive child: VIII. Five year follow-up. *Archives of General Psychiatry, 24,* 409–414.

Weissbluth, M. (1984). Sleep duration, temperament, and Conners' rating of three-year-old children. *Developmental and Behavioral Pediatrics, 5,* 120–123.

Weissman, M., Prusoff, B., Gammon, G., Merikangas, K., Leckman, J., & Kidd, K. (1984). Psychopathology in the children (ages 6–18) of depressed and normal parents. *Journal of the American Academy of Child Psychiatry, 23,* 78–84.

Weithorn, C. J., & Kagen, E. (1978). Interaction of language development and activity level on performance of first graders. *American Journal of Orthopsychiatry, 48,* 148–159.

Wells, K. C., Forehand, R., & Griest, D. L. (1980). Generality of treatment effects from treated to untreated behaviors resulting from a parent training program. *Journal of Clinical Child Psychology, 9,* 217–219.

Wender, P. H. (1971). *Minimal brain dysfunction in children.* New York: Wiley.

Wender, P. H. (1973). Minimal brain dysfunction in children. *Pediatric Clinics of North America, 20,* 187–202.

Wender, P. H. (1987). *The hyperactive child, adolescent, and adult.* New York: Oxford University Press.

Wender, P. H., Reimherr, F. W., & Wood, D. R. (1981). Attention deficit disorder ('minimal brain dysfunction') in adults: A replication study of diagnosis and drug treatment. *Archives of General Psychiatry, 38*, 449–456.

Wender, P. H., Wood, D. R., Reimherr, F. W. (1985). Pharmacological treatment of attention deficit disorder, residual type (ADD, RT, "Minimal Brain Dysfunction", Hyperactivity in Adults. *Psychopharmacology Bulletin, 21*, 222–231.

Werner, E. E., Bierman, J. M., French, F. E., Simonian, K., Connor, A., Smith, R., S., & Campbell, M. (1968). Reproductive and environmental casualties: A report on the 10-year follow up of the children of the Kauai pregnancy study. *Pediatrics, 42*, 112–127.

Werner, H., & Strauss, A. A. (1941). Pathology of figure-background relation in the child. *Journal of Abnormal and Social Psychology, 36*, 236–248.

Werry, J. S. (1968). Developmental hyperactivity. *Pediatric Clinics of North America, 15*, 581–599.

Werry, J. S. (1978). Measures in pediatric psychopharmacology. In J. S. Werry (Ed.), *Pediatric psychopharmacology* (pp. 29–78). New York: Brunner/Mazel.

Werry, J. S. (1988). Differential diagnosis of attention deficits and conduct disorders. In L. Bloomingdale & J. Sergeant (Eds.), *Attention deficit disorder: Criteria, cognition, and intervention* (pp. 83–96). New York: Pergamon Press.

Werry, J. S., Elkind, G. S., & Reeves, J. C. (1987). Attention deficit, conduct, oppositional, and anxiety disorders in children: III. Laboratory differences. *Journal of Abnormal Child Psychology, 15*, 409–428.

Werry, J. S., & Quay, H. C. (1971). The prevalence of behavior symptoms in younger elementary school children. *American Journal of Orthopsychiatry, 41*, 136–143.

Werry, J. S., Reeves, J. C., & Elkind, G. S. (1987). Attention deficit, conduct, oppositional, and anxiety disorders in children: I. A review of research on differentiating characteristics. *Journal of the American Academy of Child and Adolescent Psychiatry, 26*, 133–143.

Werry, J. S., & Sprague, R. L. (1970). Hyperactivity. In C. G. Costello (Ed.), *Symptoms of psychopathology* (pp. 397–417). New York: Wiley.

Werry, J. S., & Sprague, R. L. (1974). Methylphenidate in children—Effect of dosage. *Australian and New Zealand Journal of Psychiatry, 8*, 9–19.

Werry, J. S., Weiss, G., Douglas, V., & Martin, J. (1966). Studies on the hyperactive child: III. The effect of chlorpromazine upon behavior and learning ability. *Journal of the American Academy of Child Psychiatry, 5*, 292–312.

Whalen, C. K., & Henker, B. (Eds.). (1980). *Hyperactive children: The social ecology of identification and treatment.* New York: Academic Press.

Whalen, C. K., Henker, B., Buhrmester, D., Hinshaw, S. P., Huber, A., & Laski, K. (1989). Does stimulant medication improve the peer status of hyperactive children? *Journal of Consulting and Clinical Psychology, 57*, 5435–5449.

Whalen, C. K., Henker, B., Collins, B. E., Finck, D., & Dotemoto, S. (1979). A social ecology of hyperactive boys: Medication effects in systematically structured classroom environments. *Journal of Applied Behavior Analysis, 12*, 65–81.

Whalen, C. K., Henker, B., Collins, B. E., McAuliffe, S., & Vaux, A. (1979). Peer interaction in structured communication task: Comparisons of normal and hyperactive boys and of methylphenidate (Ritalin) and placebo effects. *Child Development, 50*, 388–401.

Whalen, C. K., Henker, B., & Dotemoto, S. (1980). Methylphenidate and hyperactivity: Effects on teacher behaviors. *Science, 208*, 1280–1282.

Whalen, C. K., Henker, B., & Dotemoto, S. (1981). Teacher response to methylphenidate (Ritalin) versus placebo status of hyperactive boys in the classroom. *Child Development, 52,* 1005–1014.

Whalen, C. K., Henker, B., Dotemoto, S., & Hinshaw, S. P. (1983). Child and adolescent perceptions of normal and atypical peers. *Child Development, 54,* 1588–1598.

Whalen, C. K., Henker, B., & Hinshaw, S. P. (1985). Cognitive-behavioral therapies for hyperactive children: Premises, problems, and prospects. *Journal of Abnormal Child Psychology, 13,* 391–410.

Whalen, C. K., Henker, B., Swanson, J. M., Granger, D., Kliewer, W., & Spencer, J. (1987). Natural social behaviors in hyperactive children: Dose effects of methylphenidate. *Journal of Consulting and Clinical Psychology, 55,* 187–193.

Willerman, L. (1973). Activity level and hyperactivity in twins. *Child Development, 44,* 288–293.

Williams, L. (1988, January 15). Parents and doctors fear growing misuse of drug used to treat hyperactive kids. *Wall Street Journal,* p. 10.

Willis, T. J., & Lovaas, I. (1977). A behavioral approach to treating hyperactive children: The parent's role. In J. B. Millichap (Ed.), *Learning disabilities and related disorders* (pp. 119–140). Chicago: Year Book Medical.

Winsberg, B., Mitinsky, S., Kupietz, S., & Richardson, E. (1987). Is there dose–dependent tolerance associated with chronic methylphenidate therapy in hyperactive children: Oral dose and plasma considerations. *Psychopharmacology Bulletin, 23,* 107–110.

Wirt, R. D., Lachar, D., Klinedinst, J. K., & Seat, P. D. (1984). *Multidimensional description of child personality: A manual for the Personality Inventory for Children, revised 1984.* Los Angeles: Western Psychological Services.

Wolf, S. M., & Forsythe, A. (1978). Behavior disturbance, phenobarbital, and febrile seizures. *Pediatrics, 61,* 728–731.

Wolraich, M., Milich, R., Stumbo, P., & Schultz, F. (1985). The effects of sucrose ingestion on the behavior of hyperactive boys. *Pediatrics, 106,* 675–682.

Wood, D. (1986). The diagnosis and treatment of Attention Deficit Disorder, Residual Type. *Psychiatric Annals, 16,* 23–28.

Wood, D. R., Reimherr, F. W., Wender, P. H., & Johnson, G. E. (1976). Diagnosis and treatment of minimal brain dysfunction in adults. *Archives of General Psychiatry, 33,* 1453–1460.

Woolf, A. D. & Zuckerman, B. S. (1986). Adolescence and its discontents: Attentional disorders among teenagers and young adults. *Pediatrician, 13,* 119–127.

Worcester Telegram and Gazette. (1987). Rise in Ritalin use could mean drug abuse. December 6, 1987, 1L.

Work, W. C., Hightower, A. D., Fantuzzo, J. W., & Rohrbeck, C. A. (1987). Replication and extension of the Teacher Self-Control Rating Scale. *Journal of Consulting and Clinical Psychology, 55,* 115–116.

World Health Organization. (1978). *International classification of diseases* (9th ed.). Geneva: Author.

World Health Organization. (1990). *International classification of diseases* (10th ed.). Geneva: Author.

Zachary, R. A. (1986). *Shipley Institute of Living Scale: Revised manual.* Los Angeles: Western Psychological Services.

Zagar, R., & Bowers, N. D. (1983). The effect of time of day on problem-solving and classroom behavior. *Psychology in the Schools, 20,* 337–345.

Zambelli, A. J., Stam, J. S., Maintinsky, S., & Loiselle, D. L. (1977). Auditory evoked potential and selective attention in formerly hyperactive boys. *American Journal of Psychiatry, 134,* 742–747.

Zametkin, A. J., & Rapoport, J. L. (1986). The pathophysiology of Attention Deficit Disorder with Hyperactivity: A review. In B. Lahey & A. Kazdin (Eds.), *Advances in clinical child psychology* (Vol. 9, pp. 177–216). New York: Plenum.

Zeitlin, S., Williamson, G. G., & Rosenblatt, W. P. (1987). The coping with stress model: A counseling approach for families with a handicapped child. *Journal of Counseling and Development, 43,* 443–446.

Zentall, S. S. (1984). Context effects in the behavioral ratings of hyperactivity. *Journal of Abnormal Child Psychology, 12,* 345–352.

Zentall, S. S. (1985). A context for hyperactivity. K. D. Gadow & I. Bialer (Eds.), *Advances in learning and behavioral disabilities* (Vol. 4, pp. 273–343). Greenwich, CT: JAI Press.

Zentall, S. S. (1986). Effects of color stimulation on performance and activity of hyperactive and nonhyperactive children. *Journal of Educational Psychology, 78,* 159–165.

Zentall, S. S. (1988). Production deficiencies in elicited language but not in the spontaneous verbalizations of hyperactive children. *Journal of Abnormal Child Psychology, 16,* 657–673.

Zentall, S. S., & Barack, R. S. (1979). Rating scales for hyperactivity: Concurrent validity, reliability, and decisions to label for the Conners and Davids Abbreviated Scales. *Journal of Abnormal Child Psychology, 7,* 179–190.

Zentall, S. S., Falkenberg, S. D., & Smith, L. B. (1985). Effects of color stimulation and information on the copying performance of attention-problem adolescents. *Journal of Abnormal Child Psychology, 13,* 501–511.

Zentall, S. S., & Meyer, M. J. (1987). Self-regulation of stimulation for ADD-H children during reading and vigilance task performance. *Journal of Abnormal Child Psychology, 15,* 519–536.

Zentall, S. S., & Zentall, T. R. (1986). Hyperactivity ratings: Statistical regression provides an insufficient explanation of practice effects. *Journal of Pediatric Psychology, 11,* 393–396.

Zettle, R. D., & Hayes, S. C. (1983). Rule-governed behavior: A potential theoretical framework for cognitive-behavioral therapy. In P. C. Kendall (Ed.), *Advances in cognitive-behavioral research* (Vol. 1, pp. 73–118). New York: Academic Press.

Zold, A. C., & Speer, D. C. (1971). Follow-up study of child guidance patients by means of the Behavior Problem Checklist. *Journal of Clinical Psychology, 27,* 519–524.

Index

TOP **10**
SAN DIEGO

PAMELA BARRUS

EYEWITNESS TRAVEL

Left **Hotel del Coronado** Center **Cruiseship liner at San Diego Harbor** Right **Wild Animal Park**

LONDON, NEW YORK,
MELBOURNE, MUNICH AND DELHI
www.dk.com

Reproduced by Colourscan, Singapore
Printed and bound by South China
Printing Co. Ltd, China.

First American Edition, 2005
09 10 9 8 7 6 5 4 3 2 1

Published in the United States by
DK Publishing, 375 Hudson Street
New York, New York 10014

**Reprinted with revisions 2007, 2009
Copyright 2005, 2009 ©
Dorling Kindersley Limited, London
A Penguin company**

ISSN 1479-344X
ISBN 978-0-75664-570-0

Within each Top 10 list in this book, no hierarchy
of quality or popularity is implied. All 10 are, in
the editor's opinion, of roughly equal merit.

We're trying to be cleaner and greener:
- we recycle waste and switch things off
- we use paper from responsibly managed forests whenever possible
- we ask our printers to actively reduce water and energy consumption
- we check out our suppliers' working conditions – they never use child labour

Find out more about our values and
best practices at www.dk.com

Contents

San Diego's Top 10

The information in this DK Eyewitness Top 10 Travel Guide is checked regularly.
Every effort has been made to ensure that this book is as up-to-date as possible at the time of
going to press. Some details, however, such as telephone numbers, opening hours, prices,
gallery hanging arrangements and travel information are liable to change. The publishers
cannot accept responsibility for any consequences arising from the use of this book, nor for
any material on third party websites, and cannot guarantee that any website address in this
book will be a suitable source of travel information. We value the views and suggestions of
our readers very highly. Please write to: Publisher, DK Eyewitness Travel Guides,
Dorling Kindersley, 80 Strand, London, Great Britain WC2R 0RL.

Left **La Jolla** Center **Souvenirs at Tijuana** Right **The Cheese Shop, Gaslamp Quarter**

Left **California Tower, Balboa Park** Right **Catedral de Nuestra Señora de Guadalupe, Tijuana**

Key to abbreviations
Adm admission charge **Dis. access** disabled access

3

SAN DIEGO'S
TOP 10

SAN DIEGO'S TOP 10

⑩ San Diego Highlights

Blessed by a sunny climate that never varies ten degrees from moderate and a splendid setting along the Pacific Ocean, San Diegans can well boast they live the California Dream. Although non-stop outdoor recreation, a vibrant downtown, and world-class attractions keep the city's spirit young, its heart lies in its Spanish beginnings as the birthplace of California.

1 Gaslamp Quarter

Old-fashioned wrought-iron gas lamps lead the way to the hottest scene in town. Rocking nightspots and a dazzling selection of restaurants give life to San Diego's original Victorian downtown *(see pp8–9).*

2 Embarcadero

With its nautical museums, vintage ships, and superb views across a harbor busy with sailboats, ferries, and battleships, the Embarcadero links the city to its ocean heritage *(see pp10–13).*

3 Balboa Park & San Diego Zoo

San Diegans take pride in having one of the finest urban parks in the world. Its famous zoo, fascinating museums, and exquisite gardens offer endless activities *(see pp14–19).*

4 Old Town State Historic Park

The original location and social center of San Diego until 1872, adobe houses, old wood-frame buildings, and artifacts belonging to its pioneer families have been faithfully restored *(see pp22–3).*

5 Coronado

This idyllic community is recognizable throughout the world by the fabulous Hotel del Coronado. Coronado's

white sandy beaches, sidewalk cafés, and oceanfront mansions have enticed visitors for over a century *(see pp24–5).*

La Jolla Bay
La Jolla ⑨
The Muirlands
Pacific Beach
GRAND AVENUE
Mission Beach
Mission Bay
Mission Bay Park
⑧
San Diego River
Ocean Beach
Loma Portal
Point Loma ⑥

Previous pages: **Façade of La Casa del Padre Serra**

6 Point Loma

In 1542, Juan Cabrillo arrived at Ballast Point, claiming California for Spain. Once a whaling, fishing, and leather processing center, stunning homes and marinas now grace Point Loma's waterfront (see pp26–7).

7 Mission San Diego de Alcalá

Father Junípero Serra established this mission in 1769. The first of 21, the mission aimed to Christianize the Native Americans and affirm Spain's presence in California (see pp28–9).

8 SeaWorld

At one of the premiere attractions of Southern California, leaping killer whales, cavorting dolphins, and promenading sea lion divas entertain over four million visitors a year (see pp30–31).

9 La Jolla

Multi-million-dollar seaside villas, boutiques, and elegant restaurants line the streets of this exclusive community, which is also noted for its prestigious biotech and oceanographic research institute (see pp32–3).

10 Tijuana

Only 20 minutes south of San Diego but a whole world away, this famous border town offers great shopping and top-rated restaurants. And yes, striped burros and black velvet Elvis paintings still exist (see pp34–5).

TOP 10 Gaslamp Quarter

A hip nightlife, trendy restaurants, and unique boutiques compete for attention in San Diego's most vibrant neighborhood. Alonzo Horton's 1867 New Town (see p38) seemed doomed to the wrecking ball in the 1970s, but a civic revitalization program transformed the dilapidated area into a showcase destination. By 1980, the Gaslamp Quarter was decreed a National Historic District with its quaint Victorian, Italianate, and Renaissance structures.

Sign for the William Heath Davis House

Gaslamp Quarter street

○ Stop at the Cheese Shop (627 4th Ave) for sandwiches, or at the Ghirardelli Chocolate Shop (643 5th Ave) for a hot fudge sundae.

✿ Parking is difficult at weekends, especially if there's a ballgame over at Petco Park. Take the San Diego Trolley; it stops right at Gaslamp.

• Map J5
• www.gaslamp.org
• William Heath Davis House: 410 Island Ave (619) 233-4692; www.gaslampquarter.org; Open 10am–6pm Tue–Sat, 9am–3pm Sun; Adm $5; Historical walking tours 11am Sat, $10
• Louis Bank of Commerce: 835 5th Ave
• San Diego Hardware: 840 5th Ave
• Old City Hall: 433 G St
• Balboa Theatre: 4th Ave & E St
• Yuma Building: 631 5th Ave
• Keating Building: 432 F St
• Ingle Building: 424 F St
• Lincoln Hotel: 536 5th Ave

Top 10 Features

1. William Heath Davis House
2. Louis Bank of Commerce
3. San Diego Hardware
4. Old City Hall
5. Balboa Theatre
6. Yuma Building
7. Keating Building
8. Ingle Building
9. Lincoln Hotel
10. Wrought-iron Gas Lamps

1 William Heath Davis House

Named after the man who tried but failed to develop San Diego in 1850, the museum is home to the Gaslamp Quarter Historical Foundation. It is the oldest wooden structure in downtown San Diego *(above)*.

2 Louis Bank of Commerce

A bank until 1893, this Victorian structure *(right)* became Wyatt Earp's *(see p39)* favorite bar. It once contained the Golden Poppy Hotel, a notorious brothel. Present-day offices are much tamer.

3 San Diego Hardware

Once a dance hall, then a five-and-dime store, this building housed one of San Diego's oldest businesses, founded in 1892. Though the store relocated in 2006, the original storefront remains.

4 Old City Hall

Dating from 1874, this Italianate building features 16-ft (5-m) ceilings, brick arches, classical columns, and a wrought-iron cage elevator. In 1900, the entire city government would fit inside. Today, the building houses shops and a restaurant.

 Share your travel recommendations on traveldk.com

5 Balboa Theatre

This landmark 1,500-seat theater *(right)* once had water-falls flanking the stage. Notice the beautiful tiled dome on the roof, which is similar to the one on the Santa Fe Depot. The theater reopened in 2008 after extensive renovations.

9 Lincoln Hotel

Built in 1913, the four-story tiled structure features Chinese elements and the original beveled glass in its upper stories. Japanese prisoners were housed here before departing for internment camps during World War II. The Lincoln is now home to low-income residents.

10 Wrought-iron Gas Lamps

Although San Diego's historic district is named after the quaint green wrought-iron gas lamps that line the streets, they run on electricity.

6 Yuma Building

Captain Wilcox of the US *Invincible* owned downtown's first brick structure in 1888. The building *(below)* was named for his business dealings in Yuma, Arizona. Residential lofts with bay windows now occupy its upper levels.

7 Keating Building

Fannie Keating built this Romanesque-style building *(above)* in 1890 in honor of her husband George. It once housed the town's most prestigious offices.

8 Ingle Building

The Hard Rock Café was once known as the Golden Lion Tavern. Note the lion sculptures, the stained-glass windows, and the 1906 stained-glass dome over the bar.

Stingaree District

After its legitimate businesses relocated in the late 19th century, New Town was home to 120 brothels, opium dens, 71 saloons, and gambling halls, some operated by famous lawman Wyatt Earp. It became known as "Stingaree" because one could be stung on its streets as easily as by the stingaree fish in the bay. After police unsuccessfully tried cleaning up Stingaree in 1912, it slowly disintegrated into a slum until rescued by the Gaslamp Quarter Foundation some 50 years later.

If you want to enjoy the architecture, come during the day when the district is less crowded.

🔟 Embarcadero

Ever since Juan Cabrillo sailed into San Diego Bay in 1542 (see p38), much of the city's life has revolved around its waterfront. Pioneers stepped ashore on its banks; immigrants worked as whalers and fishermen; the US Navy left an indelible mark with its shipyards and warships. Tourism has added another layer to the harbor's lively atmosphere. The Embarcadero welcomes visitors with its art displays, walkways, nautical museums, harbor cruises, and benches on which to sit and enjoy the uninterrupted harbor activity.

Embarcadero Marina Park

🍴 For a quick bite, try Anthony's Fishette at 1360 North Harbor Drive. Sandwiches and salads are the best outdoor options.

🚲 Pedicabs are usually available to take you down to Seaport Village.

- Map G3
- Harbor Cruises: 1050 N. Harbor Dr; Narrated tours: 1 hour $18; 2 hours $23; several departures daily
- Santa Fe Depot: 1050 Kettner Blvd
- San Diego Aircraft Carrier Museum: 910 N. Harbor Dr; (619) 544-9600; Open 10am–4pm; Adm adult/child $17/$9

Top 10 Attractions

1. San Diego County Administration Center
2. San Diego Harbor
3. Maritime Museum
4. Piers
5. Santa Fe Depot
6. San Diego Aircraft Carrier Museum
7. Tuna Harbor
8. Seaport Village
9. Embarcadero Marina Park
10. San Diego Convention Center

1 San Diego County Administration Center

Dedicated by President F. Roosevelt, the 1936 civic structure *(above)* looks especially magisterial when flood-lit at night. Enter through the west door and feel free to wander about *(see p44).*

2 San Diego Harbor

One of the greatest attractions of the Embarcadero is watching the bustling harbor, as Navy destroyers, aircraft carriers, ferries, cruise ships, and sailboats glide past. Be a part of the action by taking a harbor cruise.

3 Maritime Museum

Nautical lovers can marvel at *Medea, Star of India (below),* and *Berkeley.* All three vintage ships have been restored to their former glory *(see p42).*

4 Piers

Glistening cruise ships bound for Mexico and the Panama Canal tie up at B Street Pier. Harbor cruises and ferries to Coronado can be caught nearby.

Morning is the least crowded time to visit the Embarcadero.

Santa Fe Depot

The train cars may be modern, but the atmosphere recalls the stylish days of rail travel. The interiors of the Spanish-Colonial style building are resplendent with burnished oak benches, original tiles *(left)*, bronze-and-glass chandeliers, and wonderful friezes depicting Native American themes.

San Diego Aircraft Carrier Museum

The 1,000-ft (305-m) USS *Midway (see pp12–13)*, commissioned in 1945, was once the world's largest warship. Many docents on board are veterans who served on the carrier.

Tuna Harbor

San Diego was once home to the world's largest tuna fleet, with 200 commercial boats. Portuguese immigrants dominated the trade until the canneries moved to Mexico and Samoa. Even today, some tuna boats remain and the US Tuna Foundation still keeps its offices here *(right)*.

Seaport Village

New England and Spanish design blend eclectically in this waterfront area with brilliant harbor views *(above & p49)*.

Embarcadero Marina Park

Relax on one of the grassy expanses to enjoy the excellent views of the harbor and Coronado Bridge. Joggers and bicyclists use the paths around the park *(see p47)*, and on weekends, entertainers and artists demonstrate their work.

San Diego Convention Center

The center was designed along nautical lines to complement the waterfront location, with its flying buttresses, skylight tubes, and rooftop sails.

San Diego & the Military

San Diego has had strong military ties ever since the Spanish built the presidio (fortress) in 1769. Hosting the largest military complex in the world, the military contributes handsomely to the local economy. Their presence is everywhere: Navy SEALS train at Coronado, three aircraft carriers and warships berth in the harbor, and Marines land amphibious tanks along Camp Pendleton. Ship parades and tours are popular events during San Diego's October Fleet Week.

USS *Midway*

🔟 Aircraft Carrier Museum: USS *Midway*

Hangar Deck
The hangar deck stored the carrier's aircraft, with large elevators raising planes up to the flight deck as needed. Now the carrier's entry level, it has audiotour headsets, aircraft displays, a gift shop, café, and restrooms. Don't miss the 24-ft (7-m) Plexiglas model of the *Midway* used by shipbuilders in World War II to construct the carrier.

Island
Sometimes called the Superstructure, ladders take you up to the navigation room and bridge, from where the ship's movements were commanded. The flight control deck oversaw aircraft operations.

Flight Deck
The area of the *Midway's* flight deck is roughly 4 acres (1.6 ha) in size. Additional aircraft are on display here, as well as the entry to the Island. The flight deck was where dramatic take-offs and landings took place – take-offs

Flight deck talk on the USS *Midway*

were from the bow while the angled deck was used for landings.

Aircraft
Nearly two dozen planes and helicopters are on display on the flight and hangar decks. Among the displays are the F-14 Tomcat, which flies at speeds exceeding Mach 2, a F-4 Phantom, and A-6 Intruder. The *Midway* once held up to 80 aircraft of various types.

Galley
The *Midway* could store up to 1.5-million lbs (680,388 kg) of dry provisions and a quarter-million lbs (113,398 kg) of meat and vegetables to feed a crew who ate 13,000 meals daily.

Post Office
The *Midway's* crew often had to wait several weeks at a time for a Carrier Onboard Delivery flight to receive letters from home. The post office was also in charge of the disbursement of money orders.

Berthing Spaces
Sleeping berths for 400 of the 4,500 crew members are displayed on the hangar deck. Beds were too short to be comfortable for anyone over 6 ft (1.8 m), and the accompanying metal lockers could hold barely more than a uniform. Enlisted men were often just out of high school.

Sign up for DK's email newsletter on traveldk.com

8 Arresting Wire & Catapults

Notice the arresting wire on the flight deck. This enabled a pilot to land a 20-ton jet cruising at 150 miles (241 km) an hour on an area the size of a tennis court. A hook attached to the tail of a plane grabbed the wire during landing. Two steam catapults helped propel the plane for take-off.

9 Virtual Reality Flight Simulations

For an additional price, which also includes a briefing, a flight suit, and 30 minutes of flight, you can experience flying a plane by taking the controls of a flight simulator. Also on hand are several standard flight stations, where, for another ticket, you can practice taking off from a carrier.

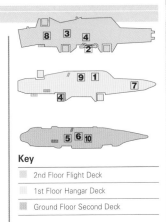

Key

■ 2nd Floor Flight Deck
■ 1st Floor Hangar Deck
■ Ground Floor Second Deck

10 Metal Shop

Located on the mess deck, the metal shop produced metal structures and replicated metal parts for the ship or its aircraft. Self-sufficiency and versatility were the keywords for tours of duty when the ship would be away for months at a time.

Top 10 Midway Statistics

1. Overall length: 1,001 ft, 6 inches (305 m)
2. Width: 258 ft (78.6 m)
3. Height: 222 ft, 3 inches (67.7 m)
4. Full Displacement: 70,000 tons (63,502,932 kg)
5. Number of propellers: 4
6. Weight of each propeller: 22 tons (19,958 kg)
7. Boilers: 12
8. Miles of piping: 200 (322 km)
9. Miles of copper conductor: 3,000 (4,828 km)
10. Ship fuel capacity: 2.23 million gallons (8,441,468 liters)

History of the *Midway*

Commissioned on September 10, 1945, the Midway *was named after the Battle of Midway, which was the turning point for the Allies in the War of the Pacific. She remained the largest ship in the world for ten years, and was the first ship too large to transit the Panama Canal. After the fall of Saigon on April 30, 1975, she saw further action during Operation Desert Storm in 1991, and finished her years of service by evacuating military personnel threatened by the 1991 eruption of Mount Pinatubo in the Philippines. The* Midway *was decommissioned in 1992.*

Launching of the USS *Midway*, 1945

Balboa Park

For over 100 years, Balboa Park has awed San Diegans with its romantic hillside setting, lush landscaping, and splendid architecture. The park's magnificent Spanish architecture dates from the 1915–16 Panama-California Exposition. On weekends, thousands of visitors come to indulge their interests, whether it's for recreation, Shakespeare or art. However, the park is probably best known as the home of the world-famous San Diego Zoo, where almost 4,000 animals and 800 botanical species reside.

Butterfly

Spreckels Organ Pavilion

🍴 **Get lunch at the Japanese Sculpture Garden's Tea Pavilion.**

⭐ **Some parking lots aren't open until 8:30am.**

- *Map L2*
- *www.balboapark.org*
- *House of Hospitality: Open 9am–4pm daily*
- *San Diego Zoo: (619) 231-1515; Open 9am–4pm Sep 5–Jun 23; 9am–9pm Jun 24–Sep 4; Adm adult/child $34/$24; www.sandiegozoo.org*
- *Spreckels Organ Pavilion: (619) 702-8138; Concerts: 2–3pm Sun; 7:30–9pm Mon Jul & Aug*
- *House of Pacific Relations: (619) 234-0739; Open noon–4pm Sun*

Top 10 Attractions

1. Reuben H. Fleet Science Center
2. Casa del Prado
3. Old Globe Theatres
4. El Cid Statue
5. California Building
6. House of Hospitality
7. Spanish Village Art Center
8. San Diego Zoo
9. Spreckels Organ Pavilion
10. House of Pacific Relations

Reuben H. Fleet Science Center
Learn about electricity, digital recording, tornados, and even save Earth from destruction at the interactive Meteor Storm. Catch an IMAX movie or learn some astronomy at a planetarium show *(see p52)*.

Casa del Prado
Rebuilt from a 1915 exposition hall, this Spanish-Colonial building *(above)* is an outstanding structure. Wall reliefs commemorate Father Junipero Serra and Juan Cabrillo. It is now used for community events.

Old Globe Theatres
The Tony-winning Old Globe Theatre *(below)*, Cassius Carter Center Stage, and Lowell Davies Festival Theatre form a cultural resource *(see p50)*.

4 El Cid Statue

Rodrigo Diaz de Vivar, Campeador, better known as the Spanish hero El Cid, overlooks the Plaza de Panama. This 23-ft (7-m) tall bronze sculpture *(right)* was dedicated in 1930 as a symbolic guardian of Balboa Park.

6 House of Hospitality

Modeled on a hospital in Spain, this building was erected in 1915 for the Panama-California Exposition and reconstructed in the 1990s. It is now a visitor's center with helpful staff.

7 Spanish Village Art Center

Richard Requa *(see p39)*, architect of the 1935–36 Exposition, wanted visitors to experience the simple life of a Spanish village. This complex now houses 37 studios where craftspeople and artists display their creations *(below & p43)*.

8 San Diego Zoo

In this zoo *(see pp16–17)*, thousands of animals thrive in recreated natural habitats. Thanks to successful breeding programs and webcams, endangered baby pandas *(below)* are now animal superstars.

5 California Building

Built for the 1915–16 Exposition, this building *(above)* with its 200-ft (61-m) tower has come to represent San Diego's identity. Famous figures of the city's past are represented on the exquisite façade. Inside is the Museum of Man *(see p18)*.

9 Spreckels Organ Pavilion

One of the largest outdoor organs in the world contains 4,530 pipes *(below)*. The metal curtain protecting the organ weighs close to 12 tons. Organ recitals are held every Sunday.

10 House of Pacific Relations

Founded in 1935, these cottages feature cultural ambassadors from 30 countries, who showcase their local traditions and histories.

Balboa Park & World War II

More than 2,000 beds were lined up in Balboa Park's museums to accommodate those wounded in the 1941 Pearl Harbor attack. All buildings were requisitioned for barracks. The park became one of the largest hospital training centers in the world: 600 Navy nurses were stationed at the House of Hospitality, the Globe Theatre became a scullery and the lily pond served as a rehab pool. In 1947, the military returned the park to the city.

→ *Performers at the House of Pacific Relations present ethnic songs and dances every Sunday from March to October.*

Left **Animal show** Right **Gorilla Tropics**

TOP 10 San Diego Zoo

1 Giant Panda Research Station

Four giant panda superstars spend most of their day eating bamboo, oblivious to millions of adoring fans that line up for a glimpse or to watch them via a 24-hour panda cam. Four panda births have occurred at the zoo in the last nine years, most recently female Zhen Zhen in August 2007. She can be seen along with her mother Bai Yum, father Gao Gao, and three-year-old sister Su Lin. The San Diego Zoo has the largest population of endangered giant pandas in the United States.

2 Polar Bear Plunge

In this recreated Arctic tundra habitat, polar bears lounge about and frolic in the chilly water of a 130,000-gallon plunge pool. Sometimes, for a special enrichment treat, zookeepers fill the enclosure with 18 tons of shaved snow

Giant Panda Research Station

for the bears to play in. Don't miss the pool viewing area down below; the bears often swim right up to the window.

3 Scripps Aviary

Inside a massive mesh cage, experience an exotic rainforest with sounds of cascading water and 200 chirping, cawing, and screeching African birds. Sit on a bench amid lush vegetation and try to spot a silvery-checked hornbill or gold-breasted starling.

4 Gorilla Tropics

These Western lowland gorillas romp and climb over wide areas of jungle and grassland. Parent gorillas lovingly tend to their children, while others sit quietly with chins in hand, contemplating the strange creatures on the other side of the glass.

5 Tiger River

A misty, orchid-filled rain-forest is home to the endangered Indo-Chinese tiger. Marvel at these wondrous animals as they sit majestically on the rocks, waterfalls flowing behind them.

Polar Bear Plunge

For the best sightings, keep in mind that the animals feed and are more active in the mornings and late evenings.

This natural habitat was created to resemble their native jungle environment, with steep slopes, logs to climb on, and a warm cave near the viewing window.

Tarantula

Ituri Forest
Meet Jabba, several thousand pounds of hippo, who lives in this re-creation of the Congo River Basin. Jabba shares his jungle home with forest buffaloes, swamp monkeys, and okapis, whose prehensile, long black tongues enable them to grab nearby leaves to eat.

Elephant Mesa
The endangered African and Asian elephants consume up to 125 lbs (57 kgs) of hay and 30 gallons of water a day. Keep your camera ready, as the elephants often toss barrels or scratch their back under a special roller. Asian elephants have dome-shaped backs, while the ears of an African elephant are shaped like the African continent.

Koalas
With names like Koorine and Gidgee, who can resist these cuddly guys? With the largest koala colony outside Australia, the zoo's successful breeding program enables loans to zoos world-wide, and makes financial contributions to habitat conservation programs in Australia.

Reptile House
If it slithers, hisses, or rattles, it's here. Be glad these animals, especially the king cobra, Albino python, and Gila monsters, are behind glass. Cages marked with a red dot indicate the venomous ones.

Children's Zoo

Children's Zoo
Little ones love petting the goats and sheep in the paddock (wash-up sinks are nearby), while older kids squeal with mischievous glee at the tarantulas, black-widow spiders, and hissing cockroaches. The nursery takes care of baby animals whose mothers can't look after them.

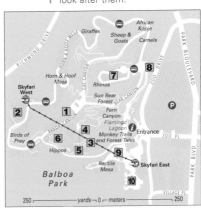

Take the double-deck bus tour first (drivers are fun and informative), and then return to what interests you.

Left **Museum of Art** Center **Museum of Man** Right **Air & Space Museum**

🔟 Balboa Park Museums

1 San Diego Museum of Art
This exceptional collection includes works by old masters and major 19th- and 20th-century artists. Be sure to check out its Asian art collection and temporary exhibitions. ✆ *Map L1 • (619) 232-7931 • Open 10am–6pm Tue–Sun (to 9pm Thu) • Adm • www.sdmart.org*

2 San Diego Museum of Man
Learn about evolution from a replica of a 4-million-year-old human ancestor, and visit the mummy room. Artifacts from the Kumeyaay, San Diego's original inhabitants, and a replica of a huge Mayan monument emphasize the culture of the Americas. ✆ *Map L1 • (619) 239-2001 • Open 10am–4:30pm daily • Adm • www.museumofman.org*

3 San Diego Natural History Museum
Galleries showcase the evolution and diversity of California. Exhibits, guided weekend nature walks, and field trips explore the natural world. ✆ *Map M1 • (619) 232-3821 • Open 10am–5pm daily • Adm • www.sdnhm.org*

4 Timken Museum of Art
The collection includes Rembrandt's *Saint Bartholomew*, and works by Rubens and Bruegel the Elder. ✆ *Map L1 • (619) 239-5548 • Open 10am–4:30pm Tue–Sat; 1:30–4:30pm Sun • Closed Sep • www.timkenmuseum.org*

A portrait by Frans Hals at the Timken Museum

5 Mingei International Museum
The Japanese word *mingei* means "art of the people" and on view here is a display of international folk art. Exhibits include textiles, jewelry, furniture, and pottery. ✆ *Map L1 • (619) 239-0003 • Open 10am–4pm Tue–Sun • Adm • www.mingei.org*

6 Museum of Photographic Arts
Temporary exhibitions featuring the world's most celebrated camera geniuses mix with pieces from the museum's permanent collection. The theater screens film classics. ✆ *Map L1 • (619) 238-7559 • Open 10am–5pm Tue–Sun (to 9pm Thu) • Adm • www.mopa.org*

7 San Diego Historical Society Museum
An alternating collection of old photographs and artifacts that introduce San Diego's early years. ✆ *Map L1 • (619) 232-6203 • Open 10am–5pm daily • Adm • www.sandiegohistory.org*

18

The Best of Balboa Park includes admission to 13 museums, the Japanese Garden, and the zoo; available at the Visitor's Center.

8 San Diego Automotive Museum

Automotive Museum

Discover California's car culture through classic vehicles, rotating themed exhibits, and educational permanent ones. A Racing Hall of Fame honors past giants of the racing world. ✧ *Map L2 • (619) 231-2886 • Open 10am–5pm daily • Adm • www.sdautomuseum.org*

9 San Diego Air & Space Museum

One of the museum's finest planes, the Lockheed A-12 Blackbird spy plane, greets you on arrival. Don't miss the International Aerospace Hall of Fame. ✧ *Map L2 • (619) 234-8291 • Open 10am–4:30pm daily, longer summer hrs • Adm • www.aerospacemuseum.org*

10 San Diego Hall of Champions Sports Museum

The artifacts of San Diego's sports heroes are exhibited here. Inspiring displays cover some 40 sports. ✧ *Map L2 • (619) 234-2544 • Open 10am–4:30pm daily • Adm • www.sdhoc.com*

Top 10 Gardens of Balboa Park

1. Alcázar Gardens
2. Japanese Friendship Garden
3. Botanical Building & Lily Ponds
4. Palm Canyon
5. Casa del Rey Moro
6. Zoro Garden
7. Rose Garden
8. Desert Garden
9. Florida Canyon
10. Moreton Bay Fig Tree

The Mother of Balboa Park

Horticulturalist Kate Sessions needed room to establish a nursery in 1892. She struck a deal with the city of San Diego in which she promised to plant 100 trees a year in the then-called City Park and 300 trees elsewhere in exchange for 36 acres. A 35-year planting frenzy resulted in 10,000 glorious trees and shrubs, shady arbors draped with bougainvillea, and flower gardens that burst with color throughout the year.

Bougainvillea

Alcázar Gardens, inspired by the Alcázar Palace in Seville, Spain

 Free trams help you get around Balboa Park and stop at designated areas.

📖10 Old Town State Historic Park

After Mexico won its independence from Spain in 1821, many retired soldiers created what is now Old Town, laying their homes and businesses around the plaza in typical Spanish style. Through trade with Boston, the town began to prosper. After a fire in 1872 destroyed much of the commercial center, San Diego moved to a "New Town" closer to the bay. Today, you can explore the preserved and restored structures of San Diego's pioneer families.

Canon in Old Town Plaza

Plaza at Old Town

⊙ Head to one of San Diego's most famous Mexican restaurants, Old Town Mexican Café & Cantina *(see p83)*, and watch the ladies make tortillas as you have lunch.

⊘ One-hour walking tours led by park staff leave daily at 11am and 2pm from the Robinson-Rose House.

Many of the park concessionaires sell a lot of kitsch; you'll do better outside the park, or try the lovely shops at Bazaar del Mundo.

• Map N5
• 4002 Wallace St
• (619) 220-5422
• Open 10am–6pm daily

Top 10 Sights

1 Plaza
2 La Casa de Estudillo
3 La Casa de Bandini
4 Seeley Stable
5 San Diego Union Historical Museum
6 Mason Street School
7 Colorado House
8 The Machado-Stewart House
9 Robinson-Rose House
10 Bazaar del Mundo

Buildings in the park

Plaza
Spanish communities used the town plaza for bullfights, political events, executions, and fiestas. Ever since the American flag was raised in 1846, tradition maintains that the Old Town flagpole must be made from a ship's mast.

La Casa de Estudillo
Built by José Estudillo, the Presidio's commander, this 1827 adobe home *(below)* is Old Town's showpiece. Workmen shaped the curved red tiles of the roof by spreading clay over their legs. Thick walls helped support the roof.

La Casa de Bandini
Peruvian Juan Bandini arrived in San Diego in 1819 and became one of its wealthiest citizens. Following business losses, his home was converted into a hotel. It's now home to a Mexican restaurant.

Seeley Stable
Until railroads proved more efficient, Albert Seeley ran a stagecoach business between San Diego and LA. Today, this reconstructed barn houses original carriages and wagons from the Wild West.

Previous pages: **Traditional Victorian houses in the Heritage Park**

San Diego Union Historical Museum

5 This wood-frame house *(above)* was built in New England and shipped down in 1851. Home to the early years of *The San Diego Union*, a faithful restoration depicts the newsroom of the city's oldest newspaper.

Robinson-Rose House

9 Docents are on hand to answer questions at this 150-year-old house which is the headquarters of Old Town *(below)*. Look out for the model of the 1872 Old Town.

BUILT 1853
ROBINSON·ROSE HOUSE

Bazaar del Mundo

10 Vibrant colors and unique shops present the best of Latin America. Andean bands and folk dancers perform amidst Guatemalan weavings and Mexican folk art *(see p82)*.

Mason Street School

6 This one-room school opened in 1865. Its first teacher, Mary Chase Walker, resigned her $65-a-month position when townspeople complained that she had invited a black woman to lunch.

The Machado-Stewart House

8 Jack Stewart married Rosa Machado in 1845 and moved to this adobe home, where the family line continued until 1966. The structure's inevitable deterioration finally compelled them to move.

Colorado House

7 The name Wells Fargo came to symbolize the opening of the American West. At this little museum housed in a former hotel, a restored stagecoach *(right)* is the main exhibit.

First Impressions

In his epic story of early San Diego, *Two Years Before the Mast*, published in 1840, Richard Henry Dana described the town as "a small settlement directly before the fort, composed of about 40 dark-brown-looking huts or houses, and two larger ones plastered." Bostonian Mary Chase Walker, San Diego's first schoolhouse teacher, was more blunt: "Of all the dilapidated, miserable looking places I had ever seen this was the worst."

Coronado

Sometimes described as an island because its village-like atmosphere is far removed from the big city, picturesque Coronado lies on a sliver of land between the Pacific Ocean and San Diego Bay. More retired Navy officers live here than any other place in the US, and although the military presence is high, it's unobtrusive. For over 100 years, visitors have flocked to Coronado to be part of this charmed life. For even with its thriving resorts, restaurants, sidewalk cafés, and unique shops, the village never seems overwhelmed.

Dining alfresco at the Hotel del Coronado

🍴 Enjoy the Hotel del Coronado's ambience by sitting in the Babcock & Story Bar for a drink and tapas.

🕐 Nancy Cobb's excellent historical walking tours depart from Glorietta Bay Inn, 1630 Glorietta Blvd; (619) 435-5993.

• Map C6
• www.coronado visitorcenter.com
• Hotel del Coronado: 1500 Orange Ave; (619) 435-6611; www.hoteldel.com
• Meade House: 1101 Star Park Cir
• Coronado Museum of History and Art: 1000 Orange Ave; (619) 435-7242; Open 9am–5pm Mon–Fri, 10am–5pm Sat–Sun; Suggested adm $4; www.coronadohistory. org
• Ferry Landing Market Place: 1201 First St at B Ave; (619) 435-8895; Open 10am daily, various closing times
• Coronado to San Diego Ferry: (619) 234-4111; Adm $3.50

Top 10 Attractions

1. Hotel del Coronado
2. Coronado Bridge
3. Mansions along Ocean Boulevard
4. Meade House
5. Silver Strand State Beach
6. Orange Avenue
7. Coronado Museum of History and Art
8. Ferry Landing Market Place
9. San Diego Ferry
10. Naval Air Station North Island & the US Naval Amphibious Base

Hotel del Coronado
A San Diego symbol, this 1887–88 Queen Anne wooden masterpiece *(right)* is a National Historic Landmark. This was the first hotel west of the Mississippi to be equipped with electric lights. Don't miss the photo gallery.

Coronado Bridge
Connecting San Diego to Coronado since 1969, this 2.2-mile (3.5-km) span *(below)* has won architectural awards for its unique design. Struts and braces hidden in a box girder give it a sleek look, and its blue color imitates the sky.

Mansions along Ocean Boulevard
Designed by prominent early 20th-century architects Hebbard and Gill, mansions *(above)* dominate Coronado's oceanfront.

Meade House
L. Frank Baum made Coronado his home in 1904 and produced much of his work while living at this charming house, now a private residence.

L. Frank Baum was the author of The Wonderful Wizard of Oz. Published in 1900, it was the first book in his Oz series.

5 Silver Strand State Beach

In 1890, John D. Spreckels *(see p39)* built bungalows and tents along the beach *(above)*. "Tent City" allowed all families to enjoy the once-exclusive beach. Today, anyone can come to dig for clams, beachcomb, and enjoy roasted hot dogs.

9 San Diego Ferry

Before the Coronado Bridge, access was only possible by a long drive around Southern San Diego or via the ferry. The ferry *(below)* is now only for passengers.

10 Naval Air Station North Island & the US Naval Amphibious Base

You might see navy planes flying overhead or Navy SEALS training on Silver Strand Beach. Lindbergh *(see p39)* began his flight across the Atlantic from here.

6 Orange Avenue

Coronado's main shopping street *(right)* is filled with elegant restaurants and sidewalk cafés, as well as a theater and a historical museum. Independence Day and Christmas parades bring residents out to celebrate in true hometown style.

7 Coronado Museum of History and Art

Housed in a distinctive 1910 Neo-Classical bank building, galleries exhibit Coronado's early history. Fascinating photos reveal the initial years of the Hotel del Coronado, Tent City, and the military.

8 Ferry Landing Market Place

Next to the ferry dock is a shopping area surrounded by walkways and benches offering harbor views. The shops sell beachwear, jewelry, souvenirs, and art. This is a handy spot to rent a bike or grab a snack.

The Duke & Duchess of Windsor

When the British King Edward VIII gave up his throne to marry American Wallis Simpson, romantics insisted they originally met at the Hotel del Coronado. In 1920, Wallis Spencer, then married to a naval officer of that name, lived at the hotel. That April, Edward visited Coronado as Prince of Wales. It is unclear whether the future couple actually met; it wasn't until 15 years later that they were formally introduced.

Point Loma

Point Loma was once one of the city's most rough-and-tumble areas. San Diego's first boats were tied up here, followed by the largest whaling operation on the West Coast and leather tanning and tallow production. Today, sailboats and yachts grace the marinas, and the waterfront homes make up some of the most expensive real estate in the city. The Cabrillo National Monument, the third most-visited monument in the US, boasts the most breathtaking views of the entire city.

Inscription at the base of Cabrillo Statue

🅞 At the Cabrillo Monument Visitor Center, some vending machines offer snack food. But if you want to spend the day hiking the trails and exploring the tide pools, bring food and water with you.

🅒 If it's a cloudy day, wait until the sun comes out to visit. Bring binoculars if you can, to enjoy the incredible views.

The San Diego Metropolitan Transit comes out to the monument. Take bus 28 from the Old Town Transportation Center.

• Map A6
• Cabrillo National Monument Visitor Center: 1800 Cabrillo Memorial Drive; (619) 557-5450; Open 9am–5:15pm daily; Adm $5 per vehicle; $3 per person (cyclists and walk-ins); tickets last for seven days

Top 10 Sights

1. Cabrillo Statue
2. Old Point Loma Lighthouse
3. Visitor Center
4. Bayside Trail
5. Military Exhibit
6. Whale Overlook
7. Sunset Cliffs
8. Fort Rosecrans National Cemetery
9. Tide Pools
10. Point Loma Nazarene University

Cabrillo Statue

The actual spot where Cabrillo stepped ashore is on a spit of land downhill at Ballast Point. However, this magnificent statue *(right)* is a worthy tribute to the brave explorer and his men who ventured across uncharted seas to claim new territory for Spain.

Old Point Loma Lighthouse

This Cape Cod-style building *(right)* was completed in 1855. Unfortunately, coastal fog so often obscured the beacon light that another lighthouse, the New Point Loma Lighthouse, had to be built below the cliff.

Visitor Center

Park rangers are on hand to answer questions. Browse through the center's outstanding books about the Spanish, Native Americans, and early California, or enjoy the daily film screenings.

New Point Loma Lighthouse

Bayside Trail

A two-mile (3.2-km) round-trip hiking path winds along an old military defense road. Signs along the way help you identify indigenous plants such as sage scrub, lemonade berry, and Indian paintbrush.

Ballast Point

CABRILLO MEMORIAL DRIVE

Point Loma Ecological Preserve

Military Exhibit
After the 1941 Pearl Harbor attack, many felt that San Diego would be the next target. The exhibit explores how the military created a coastal defense system and the largest gun in the US.

Sunset Cliffs
A path runs along the edge of these spectacular 400-ft (122-m) high cliffs (above), but signs emphatically warn against their instability. Access the beach from Sunset Cliffs Park.

Tide Pools
Now protected by law, starfish, anemones, warty sea cucumbers and wooly sculpins thrive in their own little world.

Point Loma Nazarene University
Once a yoga commune, much of the original architecture of this Christian university (above) is still intact.

Whale Overlook
Pacific gray whales migrate yearly to give birth in the warm, sheltered waters of Baja California before heading back to Alaska for a summer of good eating. January and February are the best times to spot whales (above).

Fort Rosecrans National Cemetery
The southern end of Point Loma belongs to the military installations of Rosecrans Fort. Innumerable crosses mark the graves (below) of 88,000 US veterans, some of whom died at the Battle of San Pasqual in the Mexican-American War.

Juan Cabrillo
After participating in the conquest of Mexico and Guatemala, Juan Cabrillo was instructed to explore the northern limits of the West Coast of New Spain in search of gold, and to discover a route to Asia. He arrived at Ballast Point on September 28, 1542, claimed the land for the crown of Spain and named it San Miguel. Unfortunately, Cabrillo died only a few months later from complications of a broken bone. Spain considered the expedition a failure and left its new territory untouched for the next 225 years.

🔟 Mission San Diego de Alcalá

When Russian fur traders neared California in the 18th century, Spain knew it had to establish a presence in its half-forgotten territory. Founded by Father Junípero Serra in 1769, this was California's first mission. Serra encouraged Native Americans to live here, exchanging work in the fields for religious instruction. Harassment by soldiers and lack of water supplies caused the mission to be moved from its original location in Old Town to this site. In 1976, Pope Paul VI bestowed the mission with the status of minor basilica.

LA CASA DEL PADRE SERRA

Wall engraving at La Casa del Padre Serra

⊘ Food and drinks are not allowed inside the mission.

The San Diego Trolley stops a good three blocks away, so you should drive to the mission if walking is difficult.

- Map E3
- 10818 San Diego Mission Rd
- (619) 281-8449
- www.mission sandiego.com
- Open 9am–4:45pm daily
- Adm $3
- Tote-a-Tape Tours $2
- Church: Mass 7am & 5:30 pm Mon–Fri, 5:30pm Sat, 7am, 8am, 10am, 11am, noon & 5:30pm Sun

Top 10 Sights

1 La Casa del Padre Serra
2 Church
3 Campanario
4 Cemetery
5 Garden Statues
6 Padre Luis Jayme Museum
7 Chapel
8 Gardens
9 Father Luis Jayme Memorial
🔟 El Camino Real

1 La Casa del Padre Serra

The original 1774 adobe walls and beams survived an Indian attack, a military occupation, earthquakes, and years of neglect. Padres lived simply and with few comforts.

2 Church

The width of a mission church was determined by the size of available beams. Restored to specifications of a former 1813 church on this site, the church *(above)* features adobe bricks, the original floor tiles, and wooden door beams.

3 Campanario

This 46-ft (14-m) bell-tower defines California mission architecture. Two of the bells are considered originals, and the crown atop one bell signifies it was cast in a royal foundry.

4 Cemetery

Although it no longer contains real graves, this is considered the oldest cemetery *(below)* in

California. The crosses are made of original mission tiles. A memorial honors Native Americans who died during the mission era.

5 Garden Statues

Four statues of St. Anthony of Padua *(right)*, patron saint of the Indians, Father Serra, St. Joseph, saint of Serra's expedition, and St. Francis oversee the inner garden.

6 Padre Luis Jayme Museum

Artifacts here include records of births and deaths in Father Serra's handwriting, the last crucifix he held, and old photos showing the extent of the mission's dereliction prior to restoration efforts.

9 Padre Luis Jayme Memorial

On November 5, 1775, Indians attacked the mission. A cross *(below)* marks the approximate spot where Kumeyaay Indians killed Jayme, California's first martyr.

10 El Camino Real

Also called the Royal Road or the King's Highway, this road linked the 21 California missions, each a day's distance apart by horseback.

7 Chapel

Taken from a Carmelite monastery in Plasencia, Spain, this small chapel *(below)* features choir stalls, a throne, and an altar dating from the 1300s. The choir stalls are held together by grooves, not nails. The raised seats allowed the monks to stand while singing.

8 Gardens

Exotic plants add to the lush landscaping surrounding the mission *(above)*. With few indigenous Californian plants available, missionaries and settlers introduced plants from all parts of the world, including cacti from Mexico and aloes and bird of paradise from South Africa.

Father Junípero Serra

Franciscan Father Junípero Serra spent 20 years in Mexico before arriving to establish a Spanish presence in California. Crossing the desert in what came to be called the "Sacred Expedition," the appalling conditions of the march left few survivors. But Serra, undeterred, established California's first mission in 1769. He founded nine missions by 1784.

TOP10 SeaWorld

*SeaWorld's great black-and-white whale superstar Shamu is
an identifiable San Diego icon, with 12,000 marine and aquatic
animals serving as his extras. Opened in 1964, SeaWorld has grown into an
internationally acclaimed attraction welcoming four million visitors a year.
It also operates a center for oceanography and marine mammal research,
and rehabilitates stranded and injured animals. Tropically landscaped
grounds and educational exhibits provide respite from the constant action.*

Starfish

*Visitors greeting
SeaWorld's killer whales*

🍴 The Shipwreck Reef
Café offers the widest
food selection in a fun
ship-like setting.

🌟 When you enter,
check the show times
behind the park map
and plan your day
accordingly. Some
presentations and
shows occur only
a few times a day.

Check the website
for discount tickets
and avoid long lines
at the entrance.

• Map B4
• 500 SeaWorld Dr,
Mission Bay
• (619) 226-3901
• Open 10am–5pm daily;
on some weekends and
in summer, opens at
9am and occasionally
closes at 10pm
• Adm adult/child
$61/$51
• Guided tours $12/$42
• Several admission
tickets to SeaWorld and
other Southern California
theme parks available
• www.seaworld.com/
sandiego

Top 10 Attractions

1. Believe!
2. Dolphin Discovery Show
3. Penguin Encounter
4. Risky Rescue
5. Sesame Street Bay of Play
6. Manatee Rescue
7. Wild Arctic
8. Shipwreck Rapids
9. Shark Encounter
10. Journey to Atlantis

1 Believe!
Shamu and fellow killer
whales perform with their
trainers in this amazing
show filled with astonish-
ing choreographed routines
(right). You will be in awe
of these magnificent
animals, right from the
show's start to finish.

2 Dolphin Discovery Show
Atlantic bottlenose dolphins
(below), and two 3,000-lb
(1,361-kg) pilot whales
leap, cavort, and dive to
music. Enthusiastic trainers
dance and dive with them
in this lively and entertaining show.

3 Penguin Encounter
Penguins here live in an
environment that re-cre-
ates conditions in Antarcti-
ca *(above)*. Twice a day,
feeders come out to dis-
cuss penguin habits and
answer your questions.

4 Risky Rescue
Clyde and Seamore
are two sea lions that
dive deep to rescue an
important admiral from
a mystical land.

Wear a hat and use sunblock; the sun can be intense if you're
sitting on the bleachers watching a show.

World of The Sea Aquarium

Flamingo Cove **4**

Forbidden Reef

8

Rocky Point Preserve

1

Skytower Ride

5

9 **6**

Nautilus Pavilion

2

Pets Rule

3

7

Anheuser-Busch Hospitality Center **10**

Entrance

5 Sesame Street Bay of Play

Airbags, nets, and run-through tubes are ideal for active children *(above)*. Take a ride on Elmo's flying fish for fun on an imaginary ocean.

9 Shark Encounter

Learn to differentiate between a male and female shark as you step on a walkway with an underwater view *(below)* of several shark species.

10 Journey to Atlantis

An 8-passenger Greek fishing boat twists and drops unpredictably through mist and special effects while teaching you about the lost city of Atlantis.

6 Manatee Rescue

SeaWorld has rehabilitated several manatees and put them on display until they are ready to be returned to the wild. You can view them in a 200,000-gallon river that re-creates their natural environment.

8 Shipwreck Rapids

If you aren't already wet enough, try a ride on Shipwreck Rapids, a 9-person raft-like inner tube that plunges down rapids and passes under bridges where, for a small fee, others can squirt water at you.

Animal Rescue Programs

Every year hundreds of stranded marine animals are rescued, treated, and released back into the wild by SeaWorld specialists. In 1997 a three-day-old whale weighing 1,500 lb (680 kg) was found off the California coast. Named J.J, the whale spent 15 months in rehabilitation at SeaWorld before she was successfully returned to the ocean. The knowledge gained by staff during the recovery period was shared worldwide.

7 Wild Arctic

Pretend you're on an expedition to the Arctic on a ride that simulates a jet copter landing. Walk past an above- and below-water tank to view white beluga whales and walruses, and don't miss the polar bear *(right)*.

> You might want to carry an extra shirt in case you get wet from the rides and shows.

⑩ La Jolla

Only barren pueblo land in 1886, developer Frank Botsford bought a substantial area in La Jolla which he subdivided. Other real estate developers soon caught on to La Jolla's potential and built stylish resorts. But it wasn't until Ellen Browning Scripps arrived in 1896 with her generous civic endowments that the town developed as a research, education, and art center. Now, La Jolla sits on some of the most expensive real estate in the US. It's no wonder that residents refer to their slice of heaven as the "Jewel."

Torrey Pines State Reserve

🄾 The café at the Museum of Contemporary Art serves good sandwiches and salads.

🄾 Watch the paragliders launch from the Torrey Pines cliffs, or stroll the UCSD campus and its Stuart Collection.

- Map N2
- Museum of Contemporary Art: 700 Prospect; (858) 454-3541; Open 11am–5pm Fri–Tue; 11am–7pm Thu; Adm $10; Free 5–7pm Thu; www.mcasd.org
- Athenaeum Music & Arts Library: 1008 Wall St; (858) 454-5872; Open 10am–5:30pm Tue–Sat (to 8:30pm Wed); www.ljathenaeum.org
- Mount Soledad: Soledad Rd; Open 7am–10pm daily
- Scripps Institution of Oceanography: 8602 La Jolla Shores Dr; www.scripps.ucsd.edu
- University of California, San Diego: 9500 Gilman Dr; (858) 534-2230; www.ucsd.edu

Top 10 Attractions

1. Museum of Contemporary Art
2. Athenaeum Music & Arts Library
3. Ellen Browning Scripps Park
4. Mount Soledad Veterans Memorial
5. Birch Aquarium at Scripps
6. Scripps Institution of Oceanography
7. La Jolla Playhouse
8. Torrey Pines State Reserve
9. Salk Institute
10. University of California, San Diego (UCSD)

Coastal view of La Jolla

1 Museum of Contemporary Art

Only a fraction of more than 3,000 works from every noteworthy art movement since 1950 are on display at this renowned museum *(above)*.

2 Athenaeum Music & Arts Library

Although a membership is required to check out materials from this outstanding collection of music and art, you can attend music performances and visit its art exhibitions.

3 Ellen Browning Scripps Park

Stroll along palm-lined walkways and gaze out over panoramic coastline views *(below)*.

4 Mount Soledad Veterans Memorial

This memorial, erected in 1954 to honor Korean veterans, now honors veterans from all wars. Six walls beneath a 43-ft (13-m) high cross hold 2,400 plaques.

Maps of UCSD are available from the Information Booths at the campus entrances.

5 Birch Aquarium at Scripps

Brilliantly colored underwater habitats educate at this marine museum *(above)*. You'll feel like a scuba diver when viewing sharks swimming in an offshore kelp bed housed in a 70,000-gallon tank. Popular interactive exhibits reveal environmental changes happening now and predictions for the future *(see p53)*.

9 Salk Institute

Jonas Salk founded this institution *(see p44)* for biomedical research in 1960. Its scientists explore gene therapy, AIDS, cancer, and diabetes.

10 University of California, San Diego (UCSD)

Six colleges make up one of the most prestigious public universities *(above)* in the country.

6 Scripps Institution of Oceanography

Leading the way in oceanographic research, this 1903 institute *(right)* is one of the world's largest. A part of UCSD, over 1,000 scientists at 18 centers are developing the latest marine technologies.

7 La Jolla Playhouse

Now part of UCSD's Mandell Weiss Center for the Performing Arts, the Playhouse *(right)* features a state-of-the-art theater, rehearsal halls, and a restaurant *(see p50)*.

8 Torrey Pines State Reserve

At this gorgeous reserve *(see p46)*, hiking trails

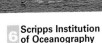

wind past coastal scrub, sculptured sandstone cliffs, wildflowers and woodlands, with stunning views of the Pacific. Guided tours leave from the visitor center.

Mandell Weiss Center

Ellen Browning Scripps

Born in England in 1836, Scripps moved to the US in 1844. She became a teacher, investing her savings in her brother's newspaper ventures, the *Detroit Evening News* and the *Cleveland Press*. Already wealthy, she inherited a vast fortune upon her brother's death in 1900. Scripps spent her last 35 years in La Jolla, giving away millions of dollars for the good of humanity. Her name now adorns countless schools, hospitals, research institutions, and parks.

🔟 Tijuana

The moment you step across "La Linea," as the border is called locally, the sensory assault is overwhelming: vendors, beggars, dust, souvenirs, music, and food smells are just the beginning. Leave the tourist zone and you'll find a city filled with some of the finest restaurants and cultural activities in Mexico and a community characterized by industriousness, resiliency, and resourcefulness.

Mural at Café La Especial

Cathedral de Nuestra Señora de Guadalupe

🍽 **Café La Especial, at Av Revolución & 3rd, #718, offers traditional Mexican fare.**

🗺 **You'll find good maps at the Visitor Information Center.**

- Map E3
- www.tijuanaonline.org
- Centro Cultural de Tijuana: Paseo de los Héroes & Mina, Zona Río; (664) 687-9600
- Frontón Jai Alai: Av Revolución & Calle 7
- Agua Caliente Racetrack: Blvd Agua Caliente 12027
- Catedral de Nuestra Señora de Guadalupe: Calle 2a (Juarez) & Av Niños Heroes
- L.A. Cetto Cava: Av Cañon Johnson 2108; (664) 685-3031; Open 10am–5:30pm Mon–Fri; 10am–4pm Sat
- Museo Foreign Club: Pasaje Constitución 720; Open 8am–4pm daily; Adm US$1
- Museo de Cera: Calle 1, 8281; Open 10am–6pm daily; Adm US$1.50
- Plaza Monumental: Ave Pacifico 1, Playas de Tijuana; (664) 680-1808

Top 10 Attractions

1. Border Crossing
2. Avenida Revolución
3. Centro Cultural de Tijuana (Cecut)
4. Frontón Jai Alai
5. Agua Caliente Racetrack
6. Catedral de Nuestra Señora de Guadalupe
7. L.A. Cetto Cava
8. Museo Foreign Club
9. Museo de Cera
10. Plaza Monumental

Border Crossing

An estimated 60 million people pass through the world's busiest land border every year. While traffic snakes for miles to enter the US, entering Mexico takes less than a minute.

Tourists posing with burros

Centro Cultural de Tijuana (Cecut)

Classical music, dance, and traditional theater are performed here. In the same complex is the outstanding Museo de las Californias.

Avenida Revolución

Bars, pharmacies, and souvenir shops embrace the tourist soul of Tijuana. Have your picture taken on the famous street corner with burros painted to look like zebras – an institution since 1954.

Frontón Jai Alai

Celebrities and the social elite once packed this Moorish palace to watch the fast-playing Jai Alai, a Basque game somewhat like squash. The landmark building *(left)* now hosts concerts and theater events.

➜ *Government-issued photo ID, plus proof of citizenship or a valid passport, is required for re-entry back to the US.*

Agua Caliente Racetrack
Opened in 1929 as the Agua Caliente Spa & Casino, this greyhound racetrack *(above)* is all that's left of the famous complex that once attracted Hollywood celebrities.

Museo de Cera
Tijuana's wax museum presents 86 figures taken from the annals of American and Mexican history, art, and pop culture.

Plaza Monumental
At Plaza Monumental *(above)*, bullfighters from Mexico and Spain come to slay the bull in front of up to 25,000 aficionados Day tours are available from San Diego.

L.A. Cetto Cava
The vineyards of Baja are Mexico's largest, and this winery welcomes visitors for tours. The spotless facility offers dozens of wines for tasting and purchase, as well as wine-related souvenir items.

Museo Foreign Club
Old photos and artifacts will give you a nostalgic look into Tijuana's past. Its founder, William McCain Clauson, is usually on hand. A small art gallery upstairs features the works of various Mexican artists.

Catedral de Nuestra Señora de Guadalupe
Tijuana's oldest church *(above)* has evolved from its humble 1902 origins. Domes top the towers and gold leaf adorns the barrel-vaulted interior.

Tijuana's *Maquiladoras*

Tijuana's population is one of the fastest-growing in Mexico due in part to employment offered by scores of *maquiladora* factories that have sprung up. Taking advantage of low wages and close proximity to the US, workers at these foreign-owned plants assemble electronics, appliances, and TV sets. Wages are higher than elsewhere in Mexico, but so is the cost of living.

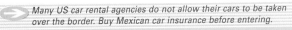

Many US car rental agencies do not allow their cars to be taken over the border. Buy Mexican car insurance before entering.

Left **Statue at Mission de Alcalá** Center **Mission Church** Right **Panama-California Exposition**

Moments in History

1 In the Beginning

A skull discovered in 1929 established human presence in San Diego about 12,000 years ago. The Kumeyaay Indians, present at the time of Cabrillo's landing, lived in small, organized villages. Hunters and gatherers, they subsisted on acorns, berries, and small prey.

2 Discovery by Juan Cabrillo (1542)

Cabrillo *(see p27)* was the first European to arrive at San Diego Bay. The Spanish believed that Baja and Alta California were part of a larger island, "Isla California," named after a legendary land in a popular Spanish 15th-century romance. California became part of the Spanish Empire for the next 279 years.

3 The Spanish Settlement (1769)

Fearing the loss of California, Spain sent an expedition, led by Gaspar de Portolá and Franciscan friar Junípero Serra *(see p29)*, to establish military posts and missions to Christianize the Indians. Disastrous for the Indians, the settlement survived and a city slowly took hold.

4 Mexico Gains Independence (1821)

After gaining independence, Mexico secularized the California missions and distributed their land to the politically faithful. The resulting rancho system of land management lasted into the 20th century. Without Spanish trade restrictions, ports were open to all and San Diego became a center for the hide trade.

Mexican flag

5 California Becomes a State (1850)

The Mexican era only lasted until 1848. One bloody battle between the Americans and Californios *(see p40)* was fought at San Pasqual *(see p41)*. With a payment of $ 15 million and the treaty of Guadalupe Hidalgo, California became part of the US and then later its 31st state.

6 Alonzo Horton Establishes a New City (1867)

Horton realized an investment opportunity to develop a city closer to the water than Old Town. He bought 960 acres for $ 265, then sold and gave lots to anyone who could build a brick house. Property values soared, especially after a fire in 1872 in Old Town. "New Town" became today's San Diego.

7 Transcontinental Railroad Arrives (1885)

Interest was renewed in San Diego when the Transcontinental Railroad finally reached town. Real estate speculators poured in, infrastructure was built, and

Previous pages: **La Jolla coastline**

the future looked bright. However, Los Angeles appeared even more promising, and San Diego's population, which had risen from 5,000 to 40,000 in two years, shrank to 16,000.

Panama-California Exposition (1915–16)

To celebrate the opening of the Panama Canal and draw economic attention to the first US port of call on the West Coast, Balboa Park (see pp14–15) was transformed into a brilliant attraction. Fair animals found homes at the zoo (see pp16–17) and Spanish-Colonial buildings became park landmarks.

California-Pacific Exposition (1935–36)

A new Balboa Park exposition was launched to help alleviate effects of the Great Depression. The architect Richard Requa designed buildings inspired by Aztec, Mayan, and Pueblo Indian themes.

World War II

The founding of the aircraft industry, spurred by the presence of Ryan Aviation and Convair, gave San Diego an enduring industrial base. After Pearl Harbor, the headquarters of the Pacific Fleet moved here. The harbor was enlarged, and hospitals, camps, and housing transformed the city's landscape.

View from Balboa Park, 1916

Top 10 Famous San Diego Figures

1 Father Luis Jayme (1740–75)
California's first martyr died in an Indian attack (see p29).

2 Richard Henry Dana (1815–82)
Author of the 19th-century classic *Two Years Before the Mast*, a historical record of early San Diego (see p23).

3 William Heath Davis (1822–1909)
This financier (see p8) established a new settlement known as "Davis' Folly".

4 Alonzo Horton (1813–1909)
The "Father" of San Diego successfully established the city's present location in 1867.

5 Wyatt Earp (1848–1929)
The gunman (see p8) owned saloons and gambling halls in the Gaslamp Quarter.

6 John D. Spreckels (1853–1926)
A generous philanthropist, businessman (see p25), and owner of Hotel del Coronado.

7 L. Frank Baum (1856–1919)
This author (see p24) lived in and considered Coronado an "earthly paradise."

8 Charles Lindbergh (1902–74)
The first to fly solo across the Atlantic in 1927 (see p25).

9 Theodore Geisel (1904–91)
Best known as Dr. Seuss, he lived and worked in La Jolla.

10 The San Diego Chicken (b. 1953)
The chicken-suited antics of Ted Giannoulas have brought international attention to San Diego sports and events.

> *Dr. Seuss was the author of the children's classics* The Cat in the Hat *and* Green Eggs and Ham.

Left **Victorian houses in Heritage Park** Right **Façade of Mission San Luis Rey de Francia**

TOP 10 **Historic Sites**

1 Ballast Point
In 1542, while Kumeyaay Indians waited on a beach at Ballast Point, Juan Cabrillo *(see p27)* stepped ashore and claimed the land for Spain. In 1803, the "Battle of San Diego Bay" took place here, after Spanish Fort Guijarros fired on an American brig in a smuggling incident.
Ⓢ *Map B6 • Point Loma*

2 Old Town
After Mexico won its independence from Spain in 1821, retired soldiers and their families moved downhill from the presidio, built homes, and opened businesses. An open trade policy attracted others to settle, and by the end of the decade, 600 people lived in Old Town – San Diego's commercial and residential center until 1872.

3 Presidio Hill
Spain established its presence in California atop this hill, and Father Serra founded the first mission *(see pp28–9)* here. During the Mexican-American War in 1846, possession of an earthwork fortress on the hill changed hands three times between the Americans and Californios. Ⓢ *Map P5*

4 Mission San Diego de Alcalá
Originally built on Presidio Hill in 1769, this mission moved up the valley a few years later. The first of 21 missions, it was the

Gaslamp Quarter

birthplace of Christianity in California. It was the only mission to be attacked by Indians. In 1847, the US Cavalry occupied the grounds *(see pp28–9)*.

5 Gaslamp Quarter
Filled with late-19th century Victorian architecture, this premiere historic site was once the commercial heart of Alonzo Horton's *(see pp38–9)* New Town. When development moved north to Broadway, the neighborhood succumbed to gambling halls and brothels. It was revitalized in the 1970s *(see pp8–9)*.

6 Lindbergh Field
San Diego International Airport *(see p85)* is popularly called Lindbergh Field after Charles Lindbergh *(see p39)*, who began the first leg of his trans-Atlantic crossing from here in 1927. The US Army Air Corps drained the surrounding marshland, took over the small airport, and enlarged the runways to accommodate the heavy bomber aircraft manufactured in San Diego during World War II. Ⓢ *Map C5*

The Mexican-Californian ranchers were known as Californios.

7 Border Field State Park

The Mexican-American War concluded with the signing of the Treaty of Guadalupe Hidalgo *(see p38)* on February 2, 1848. A US and Mexican Boundary Commission then determined the new international border between the two countries, with California divided into Alta and Baja. A marker placed in 1851 on a bluff in this park *(see p87)* marks the farthest western point of the new border. ⊗ *Map E3 • (619) 575-3613 • Call for opening hours*

8 San Pasqual Battlefield State Historic Park

On December 6, 1846, an army of volunteer Mexican-Californian ranchers, known as Californios, defeated the invading American army of dragoons in one of the bloodiest battles of the Mexican-American War. Though the Californios won the battle, they subsequently lost the war, and California became part of the US. ⊗ *Map E2 • 15808 San Pasqual Valley Rd, Escondido*

Memorial plaque at San Pasqual Valley

9 Mission San Luis Rey de Francia

Nicknamed the "King of Missions" for its size, wealth, and vast agricultural estates, this mission is the largest adobe structure in California. The Franciscan padres Christianized 3,000 Indians here. After secularization, the mission fell into disrepair and was used for a time as military barracks. Now restored to its former glory, the Franciscan Order administers the mission *(see p95)*.

10 Julian

The discovery of gold in the hills northeast of San Diego in 1870 was the largest strike in Southern California. For five years miners poured into the town of Julian *(see p96)*, which would have become the new county seat if San Diego supporters had not plied the voters of Julian with liquor on election day. The gold eventually ran out, but not until millions of dollars were pumped into San Diego's economy. ⊗ *Map F2*

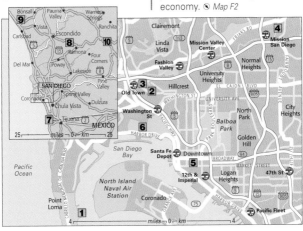

Left *Star of India* at the Maritime Museum Right **Exhibits at the Chinese Historical Museum**

🔟 Museums & Art Galleries

1 Museums of Balboa Park

Housed in stunning structures of Spanish-Colonial, Mayan, and Aztec designs that are architectural treasures in their own right, exhibits at these acclaimed museums constantly change, making Balboa Park *(see pp14–15)* a year-round attraction. Enjoy the exhibits of fine art, photography, aerospace, anthropology, model trains, and much more *(see pp18–19)*.

2 Museum of Contemporary Art

The most important contemporary art trends are presented at this museum. Docent-led tours, lectures, and special family nights make art accessible to all. The museum's flagship facility *(see p32)* is at the former oceanfront home of Ellen Browning Scripps *(see p33)*, with a satellite location downtown *(see pp72–3)*.

Chinese Historical Museum Signs

3 San Diego Maritime Museum

This museum pays tribute to the men and ships that so influenced the history and life of San Diego. Fascinating permanent and temporary exhibitions educate and entertain, while anchored ships can be boarded and explored. 🅝 *Map G3 • 1492 N. Harbor Dr • (619) 234-9153 • Open 9am–8pm Sep–Jun; 9am–9pm Jun–Sep • Adm • www.sdmaritime.com*

4 San Diego Chinese Historical Museum

Artifacts such as ceramics, bone toothbrushes, and old photographs document a fascinating slice of San Diego's history in this Spanish-style building that once served as a Chinese mission. Of note is the ornate bed that once belonged to a Chinese warlord. In the back garden is a koi pond. 🅝 *Map J5 • 404 3rd Ave • (619) 338-9888 • Open 10:30am–4pm Tue–Sat, noon–4pm Sun • Adm • www.sdchm.org*

5 Tasende Gallery

This gallery presents international contemporary artists. Discover the colorful works of Gaudi-influenced artist Niki de Saint Phalle, the pen-and-ink drawings of Mexico's José Luis Cuevas, the bronze sculptures of Britain's Lynn Chadwick, and the surrealist paintings of Chilean Roberto Matta. 🅝 *Map N2 • 820 Prospect St, La Jolla • (858) 454-3691*

6 Alcala Gallery

Early Californian Impressionist art is well represented here by the landscapes of Charles A. Fries, Selden Connor Gile, Maurice Braun, and many others. The gallery also specializes in ancient pre-Columbian art, classical and Asian antiquities, and prints. 🅝 *Map N3 • 950 Silverado St, La Jolla • (858) 454-6610*

7 David Zapf Gallery

This fine arts gallery specializes in San Diego artists. Exhibitions feature paintings, drawings, photography, sculptures, and custom furniture from artists such as Mario Uribe, Gail Roberts, Paul Henry, and Johnny Coleman. The glowing, spiritual landscapes of Nancy Kittredge merit special notice. ⊗ Map H2 • 2400 Kettner Blvd • (619) 232-5004

8 Michael J. Wolf Fine Arts

The oldest gallery in the Gaslamp Quarter features works of emerging US and international contemporary artists. Notice the colorful cubism of Stephanie Clair, the urban landscapes of Luigi Rocca, and the mixed media paintings of Josue Castro, who is inspired by the colors of the Zapotecan culture of Oaxaca. ⊗ Map K5 • 363 5th Ave • (619) 702-5388

9 Fingerhut Gallery

This gallery showcases the etchings and lithographs of masters such as Rembrandt, Chagall, and Picasso. Also featured are the brilliant serigraphs of Jiang, one of the founders of the Hunan school of painting, and works by La Jolla's own Theodore Geisel (see p39). Other artists represented are Georgeana Ireland, Alexander Popoff, Mackenzie Thorpe, and V. Montesinos. ⊗ Map P2 • 1205 Prospect St, La Jolla • (800) 774-2278

Artist at the Spanish Village Art Center

10 Spanish Village Art Center

In a Spanish village-like atmosphere (see p15), adobe houses from the 1935–36 California-Pacific Exposition have been transformed into delightful artists' studios, where you can shop or even take a lesson from the artists. ⊗ Map M1 • (619) 233-9050
• Open 11am–4pm daily
• www.spanishvillageart.com

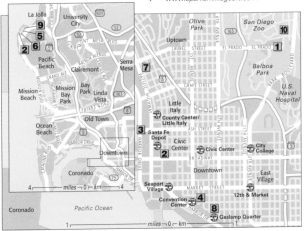

Left **San Diego County Administration Center** Right **Hotel del Coronado**

🔟 Architectural Highlights

1 San Diego County Administration Center

Four architects responsible for San Diego's look collaborated on this civic landmark. What began as a Spanish-Colonial design evolved into a more "Moderne" 1930s style with intricate Spanish tile work and plaster moldings on the tower. ◈ *Map H3 • 1600 Pacific Hwy • Open 8am–5pm Mon–Fri*

2 California Building & Tower

Bertram Goodhue designed this San Diego landmark for the California-Panama Exposition of 1915–16, using Spanish Plateresque, Baroque, and Rococo details. The geometric tile dome imitates Spanish Moorish ceramic work. An iron weather vane in the shape of a Spanish ship tops the 200-ft (61-m) tower *(see p15)*. ◈ *Map L1*

3 Mormon Temple

The temple of the Church of the Latter Day Saints is an ornate, futuristic structure. The golden trumpet-playing angel, Moroni, crowns one of towers and points the way to Salt Lake City. Interiors are closed to the public. ◈ *Map B1 • 7474 Charmant Dr, La Jolla*

4 El Cortez

This landmark was once the tallest building and most famous hotel in

California Building

downtown San Diego. A glass elevator once led to the romantic Sky Room. Ornate Spanish details decorate the reinforced concrete structure, which is now a private condo building. ◈ *Map K3 • 702 Ash St*

5 Hotel del Coronado

Designed by James and Merritt Reid in 1887, this hotel was once the largest in the US to be built entirely of wood. Advanced for its time, the hotel had running bathroom water, telephones, and a birdcage elevator *(see p24)*. ◈ *Map C6*

6 Geisel Library

Named for famed children's author, Dr. Seuss *(see p39)*, and designed by William Pereira, tiers of glass walls are supported by reinforced concrete cantilevers. Filmmakers have used the library as a backdrop for sci-fi television shows. ◈ *Map B1 • UCSD: see p33*

7 Salk Institute

At one of the most famous buildings in San Diego *(see p33)*, twin six-story laboratories comprised of teak panels, concrete and glass stand across from each other, separated by a smooth marble courtyard with a channel of water running down the middle. Note architect Louis Kahn's use of "interstitial" space:

The County Administration Center was designed by Louis Gill, Sam Hamill, Richard Requa, and William Templeton Johnson.

mechanical devices between floors can change laboratory configurations. ◊ *Map B1* • *10010 N. Torrey Pines Rd* • *(858) 453-4100* • *Open 8:30am–5pm Mon–Fri* • *www.salk.edu*

8 Louis Bank of Commerce
Builders of the Hotel del Coronado, the Reid brothers can also take credit for one of the architectural treasures of the Gaslamp Quarter, a stately, four-storey twin-towered Victorian structure *(see p8)*. Built in 1888, it was San Diego's first granite building. Of special merit are the ornate bay windows that project from the façade. ◊ *Map K5*

Three colorful levels at Horton Plaza

9 Horton Plaza
Inside Horton Plaza is a wonderful hodgepodge of bridges and ramped walkways connecting six staggered levels, embellished with towers and cupolas. Its distinctive sherbet color scheme has been copied on many renovation projects throughout San Diego *(see p48)*.

10 Cabrillo Bridge
Built as an entryway to the 1915–16 California-Panama Exposition, this cantilevered and multiple-arched bridge has a 1,500-ft (457-m) span. The best view of the bridge, especially during Christmas, is from the 163 Freeway below. ◊ *Map K1*

Top 10 Public Art Sights

1 Guardian of Water
A 23-ft (70-m) high granite sculpture depicts a pioneer woman. ◊ *Map H3*

2 Horton Plaza Fountain
Flowing water and electric lights were a technological breakthrough in 1909. Bronze plaques honor city notables. ◊ *Map J5*

3 Tunaman's Memorial
A bronze sculpture of three tunamen casting their lines. ◊ *Map B5*

4 Murals at Chicano Park
Pylons of the Coronado Bridge are canvasses for 40 murals exploring Hispanic history. ◊ *Map D5*

5 The Cat in the Hat
The Cat in the Hat looks over Dr. Seuss' shoulder in this bronze sculpture. ◊ *Map B1*

6 Surfhenge
Towering surfboards stand in tribute to the surf gods. ◊ *Map E3* • *Imperial Beach Pier*

7 Woman of Tehuantepec
A 1,200-lb (544-kg) piece of limestone is sculpted into an Indian woman. ◊ *Map L2* • *House of Hospitality*

8 Sun God
A fiberglass bird stretches its wings atop a 15-ft (5-m) concrete arch. ◊ *Map B1*

9 Paper Vortex
A paper airplane is artfully transformed into an Origami crane. ◊ *Map C5* • *San Diego International Airport*

10 Homecoming
A bronze sculpture depicts a sailor, wife, and child in a joyous homecoming embrace. ◊ *Map G4* • *Navy Pier, Harbor Drive*

Left **Balboa Park's Alcázar Garden** Right **Ellen Browning Scripps Park**

TOP 10 Gardens & Nature Reserves

1 Balboa Park

This landmark destination and heart of San Diego offers an array of superb activities. Visit its gardens and museums for inspiration, to play sports, or to watch a concert. Although crowded, Sundays are good days to experience the community at leisure *see pp14–15).*

2 Mission Bay Park

This aquatic wonderland offers every watersport conceivable. You can also bicycle, play volleyball, jog, or nap on the grass. Excellent park facilities include boat rentals, playgrounds, fire rings, and picnic tables. ❧ *Map B3*
• *2688 E. Mission Bay Dr*

Fountain at Balboa Park

3 Ellen Browning Scripps Park

Broad lawns shaded by palms and Monterrey cypress trees stretch the cliffs from La Jolla Cove to Children's Pool *(see p53).* Visitors can walk along promenades that offer a stunning view of the cliffs and beach of Torrey Pines. ❧ *Map N2*

4 Mission Trails Regional Park

At one of the country's largest urban parks, hiking and biking trails wind along rugged hills and valleys. The San Diego River cuts through the middle, and a popular trail leads to the Old Mission Dam. The energetic can hike up Cowles Mountain, San Diego's highest peak at 1,591 ft (485 m). ❧ *Map F3* • *1 Father Junípero Serra Trail*

5 Los Peñasquitos Canyon Preserve

Archeologists discovered artifacts of the prehistoric La Jolla culture in this ancient canyon. You can also explore the adobe home of San Diego's first Mexican land grant family. Between two large coastal canyons, trails lead past woodland, oak trees, chaparral, and a waterfall. ❧ *Map E2* • *12020 Black Mountain Rd*

6 Kate O. Sessions Memorial Park

Named in honor of the mother of Balboa Park *(see p19),* this peaceful spot, with a terrific view of Mission Bay *(see p64),* is a popular picnicking area. Take advantage of the ocean breezes to rediscover kite flying. Walking trails extend 2 miles (3 km) through a canyon lined with native coastal sage. ❧ *Map B3* • *5115 Soledad Rd, Pacific Beach*

7 Torrey Pines State Reserve

A stretch of California's wild coast *(see p33)* offers a glimpse into an ancient ecosystem. Wildflowers bloom alongside hiking trails that lead past rare Torrey pines and 300 other endangered species. Viewing platforms

Torrey Pines State Reserve

overlook sandstone cliffs to the beach below. Spot quail, mule deer, foxes, and coyotes. ® *Map A1 • 12600 N. Torrey Pines Rd • (858) 755-2063 • Open 8am–sunset daily • Adm $8*

Spreckels Park
Named after John D. Spreckels (see p39), who donated the land, the park hosts Sunday concerts during the summer as well as art and garden shows. An old-fashioned bandstand, shady trees, green lawns, and picnic tables complete the picture of a small-town community center. ® *Map C6 • Coronado*

Embarcadero Marina Park
Join the downtown workers for some fresh air and sunshine. Wide grassy areas and benches give you solitude to enjoy the sweeping views of the harbor. During summer, concerts are held on the lawn. ® *Map J6 • Marina Park Way*

Tijuana River National Estuarine Research Reserve
Serene hiking paths meander through fields of wildflowers and native plants. More than 300 species of migratory birds stop by at different times of the year. A visitor center offers information to enhance your visit. ® *Map E3 • 301 Caspian Way, Imperial Beach*

Top 10 Spectacular Views

1 Point Loma
The breathtaking view from the peninsula's end takes in the city, harbor and Pacific Ocean (see pp26–7).

2 Coronado Bridge
Coronado, downtown, and San Diego harbor sparkle both day and night. ® *Map C6*

3 Mount Soledad
San Diego's most glorious view takes in Coronado, Point Loma, downtown, the valleys, and Mission Bay. ® *Map A2*

4 Bertrand at Mr. A's
Planes on approach to Lindbergh Field make dining a visual affair (see p55).

5 Manchester Grand Hyatt San Diego
The 40th-floor lounge offers views of San Diego Bay and Coronado (see p114).

6 Torrey Pines State Reserve
The view down the wind-eroded cliffs and across the Pacific is magnificent.

7 La Valencia Hotel
A drink on the terrace, overlooking vistas stretching to Torrey Pines, makes the world right (see p115).

8 Flying into San Diego
You can almost see what people are having for dinner as you fly in directly over downtown San Diego.

9 Presidio Park
A panoramic view extends from the freeways in Mission Valley below to Mission Bay and the Pacific (see p80).

10 Ferries in San Diego Harbor
On a sunny day nothing beats a ferry ride on the harbor, gazing at the white sailboats against a blue sky.

Horton Plaza

:10: **Stores & Shopping Centers**

Horton Plaza
1 Macy's and Nordstrom department stores serve as anchors to this festive shopping experience, a destination in its own right. Designed as an amusement park for shoppers, ramps lead past staggered shopping levels that hold more than 140 specialty shops, a few restaurants, and movie theaters. The Plaza's landmark is the 1907 Jessop's Clock, a 21-ft (6.4-m) high timepiece with 20 dials that display the time in all parts of the world *(see p71).* ◈ *Map J5*
• *4th Ave & Broadway*
• *(619) 239-8180*

Nordstrom
2 Holding an almost cult-like status among shopping fanatics, "Nordies" remains as popular as ever for its vast clothing selection and impressive shoe department. Belying the plush surroundings, this department store can be quite affordable. Of course, there is always the personal shopper who will help you out in the designer section. The Nordstrom Café is popular for lunch, serving soups, sandwiches, pasta dishes, and salads. ◈ *Map J5 • 103 Horton Plaza*

Le Travel Store
3 Since 1976, travelers Bill and Joan Keller have directed their passion for the road into a one-stop travel shop that offers anything a traveler might desire:

Eagle Creek and Rick Steves luggage and backpacks, an array of packing organizers and travel accessories, and a good assortment of maps and guidebooks.
◈ *Map J5 • 745 4th Ave*

Bookstar
4 For nearly 50 years, the Loma Movie Theater presented Hollywood's greatest epics. In 1990, the theater was transformed into a grand bookstore. Well-stocked shelves sit on various levels as the floor steps down toward the former screen; the original ceiling still exists; and the carpet was specially milled to match the original. ◈ *Map B4*
• *3150 Rosecrans Pl • (619) 225-0465*

Sign at Horton Plaza

The Wine Bank
5 A regular clientele of wine connoisseurs frequent this intimate Gaslamp business. Hundreds of offerings from California and worldwide are found on two floors. Charts of special vintages, wine magazines, and the expertise of wine professionals will help in your selection. Call for the latest wine tasting schedule. ◈ *Map K6*
• *363 5th Ave • (619) 234-7487*

Sport Chalet
6 To participate in San Diego's outdoor life, you might need some sports equipment or active sportswear. This store,

Shops at Seaport Village

well located near Mission Bay, offers everything possible, including rentals of camping equipment, kayaks, waterskis, and tennis racquets, as well as a full-service bike shop. You can also take scuba lessons or book a dive charter boat. ◎ Map B4
• 3695 Midway Dr • (619) 224-6777

Seaport Village
If you're looking for souvenirs or that unusual knick-knack for the shelf, this is the right place. You'll find kites, magnets, gifts for left-handed people, and T-shirts galore. The Village's superb location along San Diego's waterfront will keep you occupied. ◎ Map H5 • 849 W. Harbor Dr • (619) 235-4014 • Open 10am–9pm Sep–May; 10am–10pm Jun–Aug

Girard Avenue & Prospect Street
These intersecting streets in La Jolla are synonymous with upscale shopping and high-end art galleries. If you're seeking an expensive look, chic clothing boutiques and Italian shoe stores will happily oblige. The gorgeous displays in the home decor shops will give you great ideas to take home. In the

breezy arcades, don't miss the one-of-a-kind shops and beach-wear boutiques. ◎ Map N2

Fashion Valley
This ritzy shopping center contains six major department stores, including Neiman Marcus, Saks Fifth Avenue, and Nordstrom, as well as 200 specialty boutiques that carry just about everything. Tiffany & Co., MAC cosmetics, and Louis Vuitton are just a few of the specialty stores found here. The San Diego Trolley conveniently stops in the parking lot. ◎ Map C4 • 7007 Friars Rd

Mission Valley Center
Loehmann's, Nordstrom Rack, and Macy's Home & Furniture are just a few of the stores that carry items seen at higher-priced department stores. Budget shoppers flock to Target, Bed, Bath & Beyond, and more than 150 other stores. Don't confine your shopping to the center: across the street is Saks Off Fifth Avenue's outlet store. ◎ Map D4 • 1640 Camino del Rio N.

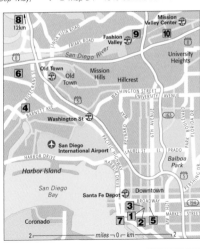

Left **Old Globe Theatres** Right **Posters at La Jolla Playhouse**

🔟 Performing Arts Venues

1 Old Globe Theatres
Approximately 250,000 people annually attend top-rated performances here. Three theaters include indoor performances at the Old Globe, an intimate perspective at the theater-in-the-round Carter stage, and outdoor Shakespeare at the Davies Festival Theatre *(see p14)*. ✎ Map L1 • (619) 234-5623 • Tours 10:30am Sat & Sun • Adm • www.theoldglobe.org

2 Starlight Bowl
The San Diego Civic Light Opera performs summer Broadway shows in this idyllic Balboa Park setting *(see pp14– 15)*. Although under the flight path of San Diego's International Airport, plane-spotters cue the performers when to freeze. Audiences good-humoredly accept the interruptions as part of the experience. ✎ Map L2 • (619) 544-7827 • www.starlighttheatre.org

3 La Jolla Playhouse
Gregory Peck, Mel Ferrer, and Dorothy McGuire founded this acclaimed theater in 1947. All the Hollywood greats once performed here. Now affiliated with UCSD, many plays that debuted here have gone on to win the Tony; the theater itself took America's Outstanding Regional Theater award in 1993. ✎ Map B1 • La Jolla Village Dr at Torrey Pines Rd, UCSD Campus, La Jolla • (858) 550-1010

La Jolla Playhouse sign

4 Lyceum Theatre
Two theaters are part of the San Diego Repertory Theatre complex: the 550-seat Lyceum and the 270-seat Lyceum Space Theatre. Productions run from the experimental to multilingual performances and Shakespeare with a modern slant. In addition, the theater hosts visiting companies and art exhibitions. ✎ Map J4 • 79 Horton Plaza • (619) 544-1000

5 Theatre in Old Town
Only 250 amphitheater-style seats wrap around the stage of this intimate theater housed in an Old Town barn. See dramas, musicals, and comedies such as *The History Boys*, *A Little Night Music*, and *A Christmas Carol*. ✎ Map P5 • 4040 Twiggs St • (619) 337-1525

6 Copley Symphony Hall
Formerly known as the Fox Theatre, a Rococo-Spanish Renaissance extravaganza built in 1929, it was to be destroyed until developers donated it to the San Diego Symphony in 1984. Now brilliantly restored, the hall hosts excellent classical music concerts. ✎ Map K4 • 750 B St • (619) 235-0804

7 Spreckels Theatre
Commissioned by John D. Spreckels *(see p25)*, this Neo-Baroque downtown landmark presents theatrical productions and concerts. Murals, classical

Spreckels Theatre sign

statuary, and an elegant marble lobby give the theater an aura of old San Diego. ✪ *Map J4 • 121 Broadway • (619) 235-9500*

Civic Theatre

If you missed the latest Broadway show, chances are the touring company will perform at this grand theater. Featuring local talent and the world's most acclaimed stars, the San Diego Opera stages five annual productions here. The theater is also home to the California Ballet. ✪ *Map J4 • 1100 3rd Ave • (619) 570-1100*

Coors Amphitheatre

Major pop artists perform from March to October in this acoustically notable open-air amphitheatre. Great sight lines and giant video screens ensure a good view. Seating holds 10,000 people with room on the grass for another 10,000. ✪ *Map E3 • 2050 Entertainment Cir, Chula Vista • (619) 671-3600*

Humphrey's Concerts by the Bay

From May to October, well-known performers of jazz, rock, comedy, blues, folk, and world music perform in an outdoor 1,350-seat amphitheatre next to San Diego Bay. Special packages to Humphrey's Restaurant and Humphrey's Half Moon Bay Inn are available to patrons *(see p117)*. ✪ *Map B5 • 2241 Shelter Island Dr, Shelter Island • (619) 220-8497*

Top 10 Movies Filmed in San Diego

Citizen Kane, 1941
Orson Welles used the California Building *(see p15)* in Balboa Park as Xanadu.

Sands of Iwo Jima, 1949
John Wayne raced up a hill at Camp Pendleton, the setting for the World War II battle.

Some Like It Hot, 1959
The distinctive structure of the Hotel del Coronado *(see p24)* formed a backdrop for Marilyn Monroe, Jack Lemmon, and Tony Curtis.

MacArthur, 1971
San Diego's own Gregory Peck is the general on Silver Strand State Beach *(see p64)*.

The Stunt Man, 1980
This Peter O'Toole film had stuntmen jumping off the roof of the Hotel del Coronado.

Top Gun, 1986
Tom Cruise chatted up Kelly McGillis at the Kansas City Barbecue, currently closed following a fire.

Titanic, 1996
Filmed in an enormous, specially built water tank at Rosarito Beach, Mexico.

Almost Famous, 1999
Nothing much had to be changed from the Volkswagen and Birkenstock look of 1970s Ocean Beach *(see p64)*.

Pearl Harbor, 2000
Kate Beckinsale proved her love for Ben Affleck by coming to bid him goodbye at the San Diego Railroad Museum in Campo.

Traffic, 2000
Along with scenes of San Diego and Tijuana, *Traffic's* car explosion took place in the judges' parking lot of the Hall of Justice.

Left **Miniature town built from lego bricks at Legoland** Right **Roller coaster at Belmont Park**

Children's Attractions

San Diego Zoo
At the renowned San Diego Zoo, kids shriek in delight over the latest creepy-crawly in Bugtown, and build crafts at the animal-themed events. During seasonal holidays and summer, Dr. Zoolittle presents his entertaining science shows. The zoo also offers summer camps and art classes (see pp16–17).

Costumed characters at the zoo

SeaWorld
Kids love to press their faces against glass tanks, inches away from whales, sharks, and manatees. And there's nothing more fun than to be drenched by a performing dolphin (see pp30–31).

Reuben H. Fleet Science Center
Science can be fun for all. At Kid City, children aged 2–5 can play with conveyor belts, air chutes, and colorful foam blocks. Older kids go wild with many hands-on activities. In the Virtual Zone, the Deep Sea Ride plunges 9,000 ft (2,743 m) to ocean depths and encounters a Giant Squid. ◈ Map

M1 • (619) 238-1233 • Open 9:30am–8pm daily (to 9pm Fri) • Adm (free 1st Thu of month) • www.rhfleet.org

Legoland
Children are fascinated by the 30 million plastic bricks fashioned into famous landmarks, life-sized African animals, and landscapes. In Fun Town, kids can drive real electric cars or pilot a helicopter; at the Imagination Zone, they can build race cars and robots. Magicians, ventriloquists, and puppeteers add to the fun. ◈ Map D1 • 1 Legoland Dr, Carlsbad • (877) 534-6526 • Adm

Children's Discovery Center at the San Diego Museum of Man
Located on the museum's second floor, kids dress up as pharaohs and learn about ancient Egypt by building a pyramid, deciphering hieroglyphics, and listening to the god Anubis explain the mummification process. At a re-creation of an archeological dig, children dig through sand for treasure and also learn about dating artifacts (see p18).

Belmont Park
This old-fashioned fun zone keeps the kids entertained for hours. They can take a ride on the Giant Dipper roller coaster, Tilt-a-Whirl, and an antique carousel; enjoy the Bumper Cars; or play in Pirates Cove, an enormous area with slides

Dr. Zoolittle is the wacky resident scientist at San Diego Zoo.

or play in Pirates Cove, an enormous area with slides and tunnels. If the ocean is too cold, try The Plunge, a 175-ft (53-m) indoor pool *(see p60)*. ⓢ *Map A4*
• *3190 Mission Blvd* • *(858) 488-1549*
• *Adm for rides*

Sea Lion-Watching at Children's Pool
Children used to swim at this sheltered cove, but harbor seals and sea lions had much the same idea. The beach is now closed, and children must view the entertaining crowds of marine animals swimming and sleeping from behind a rope. ⓢ *Map N2*
• *Coast Blvd & Jenner St, La Jolla*

Marie Hitchcock Puppet Theatre

Marie Hitchcock Puppet Theatre in Balboa Park
Named after the park's beloved "puppet lady" who delighted audiences with her magical skills, the Balboa Park Puppet Guild entertains kids and adults alike with a wonderful collection of marionettes and hand, rod, and shadow puppets. The Magic of Ventriloquism, Pinocchio, and Grimm's fairytale classics are some of the shows presented. Guest puppeteers are often

featured as well. ⓢ *Map L2*
• *Balboa Park* • *(619) 544-9203* • *Adm*
• *www.balboaparkpuppets.com*

Wild Animal Park
At this park, herds of animals roam freely in enclosures that replicate their natural African habitats. Compatible animals are mixed, allowing you to observe their interactions. Children enjoy the Petting Kraal and seeing the newborns at the Animal Care Center. Those over 8 can accompany their parents on a photo caravan for an encounter with giraffes and rhinos *(see p62)*.

Birch Aquarium at Scripps
Coral reefs, seahorses, octopi, and undulating jellyfish have a high ooh-and-ah factor for kids. The aquarium *(see p33)* presents special hands-on activities, scavenger hunts, craft workshops, and slumber parties throughout the year, among more than 30 tanks filled with brilliantly colored fish. Guided tide-pool adventures for tots, seasonal whale-watching and grunion runs take place off site. ⓢ *Map Q1* • *2300 Expedition Way* • *(858) 534-3474* • *Open 9am–5pm daily* • *Adm*
• *www.aquarium.ucsd.edu*

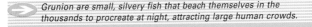

Animals living in harmony at the Wild Animal Park

Grunion are small, silvery fish that beach themselves in the thousands to procreate at night, attracting large human crowds.

Left **Interior of Costa Brava** Right **Rooftop terrace at El Agave Tequileria**

🔟 Restaurants

1 Costa Brava

The aromas of authentic Spanish cooking will fire up your appetite on entering this restaurant. Sit under minimal whitewashed walls at the bar or outside, and savor the best tapas in San Diego. Guitarists, dancers, and satellite feeds of Spanish football entertain on occasion.
Ⓢ *Map B3 • 1653 Garnet Ave • (858) 273-1218 • $$$*

2 Laurel Restaurant & Bar

For an elegant dinner before the theater or symphony, the modern Mediterranean cuisine here is hard to beat. The menu changes according to the season, but you'll always find popular dishes such as duck confit and braised short ribs. The award-winning wine cellar includes some unusual choices from around the world. Ⓢ *Map J1 • 505 Laurel St • (619) 239-2222 • $$$*

3 El Agave Tequileria

Ancient Mexican and Spanish spices and traditions make for a unique Mexican dining experience. Shrimp, sea bass, and the filet mignon prepared with goats cheese and a dark tequila sauce are heavenly. Mole, the distinctive blending of spices, garlic, and sometimes chocolate, is a specialty, as well as 150 tequila selections.
Ⓢ *Map P6 • 2304 San Diego Ave • (619) 220-0692 • $$$*

Cuervo Gold Especial Tequila

4 The Marine Room

Dine on exciting, romantic global cuisine derived from French classics. If you're not that hungry and would like to enjoy the sunset, try hors d'oeuvres in the lounge. Ⓢ *Map P2 • 2000 Spindrift Dr, La Jolla • (866) 644-2351 • $$$$$*

5 The Prado Restaurant

Hand-painted ceilings, glass sculptures, and whimsical artwork adorn this atmospheric restaurant. A large terrace overlooks the gardens of Balboa Park. A variety of margaritas and drinks from around South America complement an excellent cuisine best described as Latin and Italian fusion. Ⓢ *Map L1 • 1549 El Prado, Balboa Park • (619) 557-9441 • $$$*

6 The Fish Market

Take your pick from the "catch of the day" board and settle in at the oyster and sushi bar to await your table. Try for a coveted one on the outside deck directly over the water. You can request your fish be prepared grilled, fried, or Cajun style. A popular display counter offers fish to go. Ⓢ *Map G5 • 750 N. Harbor Dr • (619) 232-3474 • $$$$*

7 Mr. Tiki Mai Tai Lounge

Over a dozen carved Tiki gods welcome you aboard a Polynesian culinary adventure. A wide variety of pupus, crusted

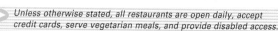

Interior of The Prado Restaurant

mahi mahi, and pineapple pork "pago pago" style, can only be accompanied by a tropical rum drink in a Tiki glass. ◎ *Map K5 • 801 5th Ave • (619) 233-1183 • $$$*

Bella Luna
A loyal clientele proves this is one of the best Italian trattorias in the Gaslamp Quarter. Sidewalk seating offers prime people-watching, but head inside if you prefer a warm, romantic atmosphere in which to enjoy your northern Italian meal. ◎ *Map K5 • 748 5th Ave • (619) 239-3222 • $$$*

Filippi's Pizza Grotto
At this Little Italy favorite, the dim lights, the red-checkered tablecloths and hundreds of Chianti bottles hanging from the ceiling haven't changed in decades. Enter through the Italian deli in front to get to the spaghetti and meatballs and hand-tossed pizzas. ◎ *Map H3 • 1747 India St • (619) 232-5095 • $*

Emerald Chinese Seafood Restaurant
San Diego's best Chinese restaurants are found in Kearny Mesa. The Asian community packs into this large dining room to enjoy lunchtime dim sum and fresh, simple but exquisitely prepared seafood dishes at dinner. ◎ *Map D3 • 3709 Convoy St, Kearny Mesa • (858) 565-6888 • $$$$*

Top 10 Romantic Restaurants

1 Sky Room
Intimate tables and a view of the Pacific complement the sophisticated California cuisine. ◎ *La Valencia Hotel (see p115).*

2 1500 Ocean
Excellent service and elegant presentations at this impressive spot *(see p91)*.

3 Chez Loma
Delicious French cuisine creates the ingredients for romance *(see p91)*.

4 Bertrand at Mr. A's
A dazzling city-view and contemporary cuisine at a local favorite. ◎ *Map K1 • 2550 5th Ave • (619) 239-1377 • $$$$$*

5 Blanca
Contemporary design, romantic lighting, and modern California cuisine. ◎ *Map D2 • 437 S. Highway 101, Solana Beach • (858) 792-0072 • $$$$*

6 Thee Bungalow
Intimate dining rooms in a quiet bungalow. ◎ *Map A4 • 4996 W. Point Loma Blvd • (619) 224-2884 • $$$$*

7 Candelas
Mexican nouvelle cuisine in a hacienda ambience. Seafood is a specialty. ◎ *Map J5 • 416 3rd Ave • (619) 702-4455 • $$$$*

8 The Marine Room
Haute cuisine, candlelight, and soft music arouse the senses *(see p54)*.

9 George's at the Cove
More wedding proposals take place at this superb restaurant than anywhere else in San Diego *(see p101)*.

10 Trattoria Acqua
Enjoy northern Italian cuisine and the sea, and imagine you're on the Riviera. ◎ *Map N2 • 1298 Prospect St, La Jolla • (858) 454-0709 • $$$$*

Left **Interior of La Sala** Right **Façade of Corvette Diner**

TOP 10 Cafés & Bars

1 Café Bassam
An eclectic assortment of paintings, furnishings and antiques decorates the walls of this Bankers Hill café. Order your special brew of espresso or tea and take it to a table to watch the world pass by. Glass jars hold over 100 different types of tea and coffee for sale. ◈ *Map K1 • 3088 5th Ave • (619) 808-3714*

2 La Sala
Sitting in the hotel's lobby lounge amid Spanish mosaics, hand-painted ceilings and murals, red-tiled floors and huge palms is like being in a Spanish palace. Order a drink and gaze out at the ocean; a pianist performs in the evening. On sunny days, take advantage of the outside tables. ◈ *Map N2 • La Valencia Hotel: See p115 • No dis. access*

3 Lestat's Coffee House
Named after the character in Anne Rice's best-selling vampire novels, this café serves excellent coffee and pastries 24 hours a day. In the heart of increasingly hip Normal Heights, local bands entertain in the evening. Bring your laptop to enjoy a free wireless Internet connection. ◈ *Map D4 • 3343 Adams Ave • (619) 282-0437*

4 The Field
Literally imported from Ireland, the wood walls, flooring, decorations, and assorted curios were shipped over and reassembled. Even the bartenders and waitresses are the real thing, not to mention the Guinness. Grab a sidewalk seat on Fifth Avenue or try for a window seat upstairs. The pub food is great, too. ◈ *Map K5 • 544 5th Ave • (619) 232-9840*

5 Top of the Hyatt
Window seats at this bar in the Manchester Grand Hyatt Hotel are at a premium during sunset, when people come to enjoy the breathtaking views of the bay, Coronado, Point Loma, and the jets over Lindbergh Field. Dark woods exude a sedate, plush atmosphere, with drink prices to match *(see p114)*.

6 The Yard House
Whether you'd like a Kona Brewing Fire Rock or a Mad River Jamaican Red Ale, there's definitely a drink for you among the 130 featured beers and ales. Order by the half pint or half yard with some upscale appetizers. Music and TV sports events make the atmosphere young and noisy. ◈ *Map J4 • 1023 4th Ave • (619) 233-9273 • No dis. access*

7 Beach at W Hotel
The ultimate in cool, this spot is the next best thing if you can't make it to the beach. Relax under the stars outside on comfortable banquette seating, order a martini and dig your toes into the heated sand, or go for a Mai Tai in a private, candle-lit cabana. ◈ *Map H4 • 421 W. B St • (619) 398-3100 • No dis. access*

Unless otherwise stated, all restaurants are open daily, accept credit cards, serve vegetarian meals, and provide disabled access.

W Hotel

8 Twiggs Bakery & Coffee House

Enjoy a latte and a snack in this fun café. It's packed all day with neighborhood residents. On the second and fourth Mondays of each month, you'll find live poetry readings being held here. ◈ *Map D4 • 4590 Park Blvd • (619) 296-0616*

9 McP's Irish Pub & Grill

Owned by an ex-Navy SEAL, the pub and its large outside patio are enormously popular with Coronado's military. A pint of Guinness is a good choice to accompany traditional pub grub such as Mulligan stew and corned beef, and the occasional Mexican dish. Enjoy the live local entertainment. ◈ *Map C6 • 1107 Orange Ave, Coronado • (619) 435-5280*

10 Corvette Diner

James Dean photos, neon, and 1950s road-trip artifacts adorn this diner's walls; burgers are named Kookie and Eddie; and a shiny Corvette sits as a shrine in this retro Hillcrest hangout. Libations from the full bar help dull the sensory onslaught. ◈ *Map C4 • 3946 5th Ave • (619) 542-1476*

Top 10 Breakfast Spots

1 Café 222
Try the pumpkin waffles and French toast here. ◈ *Map J5 • 222 Island Ave • (619) 236-9902 • $*

2 Brockton Villa
Start the morning with crêpes, omelets, or a "tower of bagel" (see p100).

3 Crown Room
The room is a living legend, the Sunday feast amazing. ◈ *Map C6 • Hotel del Coronado (see p115).*

4 Hash House A Go Go
Locals vote this the best breakfast spot in town. ◈ *Map C4 • 3628 5th Ave • (619) 298-4646 • No dis. access • $*

5 Hob Nob Hill
Waffles, omelets and pancakes. ◈ *Map J2 • 2271 1st Ave • (619) 239-8176 • $*

6 Broken Yoke Café
Choose from 30 varieties of omelets. ◈ *Map A3 • 1851 Garnet Ave • (858) 270-0045 • $*

7 Kono's Café
Join the line for banana pancakes and breakfast burritos. ◈ *Map A3 • 704 Garnet Ave • (858) 483-1669 • No credit cards • No dis. access • $*

8 Primavera Pastry Café
Croissants and three-egg omelets on sidewalk tables. ◈ *Map C6 • 956 Orange Ave, Coronado • (619) 435-4191 • $*

9 The Cottage
Enjoy the freshly-baked cinnamon rolls and Belgian waffles (see p101).

10 Mission Café
Breakfast is served until 3pm in this funky "Chino-Latino" café. ◈ *Map A3 • 3795 Mission Blvd • (858) 488-9060 • $*

For a key to price categories **see p77**.

Left **Exterior of Bitter End** Right **Interior of Croce's**

Nightlife

The Bitter End

Three floors cater to singles on the move. Upstairs, a replica of a Michelangelo ceiling fresco oversees marble fireplaces, tapestries, and a library. On the ground level, a long mahogany bar serves martinis and drinks of choice, while the downstairs club jams to techno, hip-hop, and retro sounds. ✆ Map K5 • 770 5th Ave • (619) 338-9300 • Cover charge after 9:30 Thu & after 8:30 Fri–Sat

Onyx Room

At this chic basement club, order the cocktail of the month and settle back in a vibrant lounge atmosphere. Upstairs is the Onyx's sister bar Thin, where the "engineered" drinks and atmosphere are the epitome of urban cool. ✆ Map K5 • 852 5th Ave • (619) 235-6699 • Closed Mon, Wed, Sun • Cover charge Thu–Sat

Sevilla

This restaurant-nightclub offers everything Latin. Tango and flamenco dinner shows spotlight

Entrance to the basement club at Onyx

the Spanish restaurant, while instructors teach salsa and samba downstairs. You can practice your moves to the live bands that perform afterwards. The basement becomes a Latin/Euro dance club on Friday and Saturday nights. ✆ Map J5 • 555 4th Ave • (619) 233-5979 • Cover charge

Croce's Jazz Bar & Croce's Top Hat

Ingrid Croce opened Gaslamp's first club in tribute to her late husband, singer/ songwriter Jim Croce, in 1985. The Jazz Bar features traditional, contemporary, and Latin live jazz, while the Top Hat features live R&B bands. However, tables are too close together and service can be indifferent. ✆ Map K5 • 802 5th Ave • (619) 233-3660 • Cover charge

Shaker Room

You'll find a martini to your taste among the 50 house-blended varieties available. Head to the leopard-print loveseats upstairs or enjoy the dance floor. There's happy hour every weekday from 4–7pm, and on the first Friday of the month, "Manicures, Martinis & More" offers fashion, manicures, and drinks for the ladies. ✆ Map K5 • 528 F St • (619) 235-6100 • Cover charge after 8:30 Fri–Sat

Dizzy's

It's all about jazz music at this sparse 1913 warehouse in the Gaslamp Quarter. Dizzy's is located in the San Diego Wine &

Culinary Center, making food and wine readily available. All ages welcome. ◈ Map J5 • 2nd Ave & J St • (858) 270-7467 • Cover charge • www.dizzyssandiego.com

Casbah
7 Underground alternative rock rules at this grungy club. Famous and future bands turn up the decibels every night. Past head-liners have included Alanis Morissette, the Smashing Pumpkins, and Nirvana. ◈ Map H2 • 2501 Kettner Blvd • (619) 232-4355 • Cover charge

Sign for Casbah

Cane's
8 Restaurant by day, happy-hour bar by sunset, and main-stream punk club by night, everyone from Mission Beach's boardwalk packs in and spills onto the rooftop patio overlook-ing the ocean for a good time. ◈ Map A4 • 3105 Ocean Front Walk • (858) 488-1780 • Cover charge

Humphrey's Backstage Lounge
9 Enjoy a variety of live music nightly at this waterfront lounge with an unbeatable view of the bay. Come early for a terrific happy hour. ◈ Map B5 • 2241 Shelter Island Dr • (619) 224-3577 • Cover charge for most bands

Comedy Store
10 Headliners from LA's famous comedy club often perform at this branch. David Letterman, Garry Shandling, and Pauly Shore have all had a go here, as well as the local talent. Sundays are open mike nights. ◈ Map N3 • 916 Pearl St, La Jolla • (858) 454-9176 • Cover charge

Top 10 Gay & Lesbian Venues

1 Spin
Three floors of bars and a dance club with Giant Fridays and Top 40 Saturdays. ◈ Map C4 • 2028 Hancock St • (619) 294-9590

2 Bourbon Street
A piano bar with DJ and a dance floor at weekends and outlandish karaoke. ◈ Map D4 • 4612 Park Blvd • (619) 291-4043

3 The Brass Rail
Dance to Latin or hip-hop at San Diego's oldest gay bar. ◈ Map C4 • 3796 5th Ave • (619) 298-2233

4 Kickers
A gay country-western dance bar. ◈ Map C4 • 308 University Ave • (619) 491-0400

5 Pecs
Gay Harley-Davidson enthusiasts frequent this bar. ◈ Map C4 • 2046 University Ave • (619) 296-0889

6 Universal
Nightclub with two bars, a dance floor, and a restaurant. ◈ Map C4 • 1202 University Ave • (619) 692-1900

7 Number One Fifth Ave
Video bar, pool table, and outdoor patio. ◈ Map C4 • 3845 5th Ave • (619) 299-1911

8 Numbers
Pool tables, dartboards, giant video screens, and two dance floors. ◈ Map D4 • 3811 Park Blvd • (619) 294-7583

9 Rich's
Glam go-go boys and girls dance to electronica. ◈ Map C4 • 1051 University Ave • (619) 295-2195

10 Top of the Park
Piano bar at street level and Friday happy hour on the roof. ◈ Map C4 • 525 Spruce St • (619) 291-0999

Left **Fishing** Right **Horse riding in Cuyamaca State Park**

🔟 Outdoor Activities

Cycling
1 With over 300 miles (483 km) of bikeways, San Diego is one of the most cycle-friendly cities around. Ridelink's map details bike rides around the city and county and is available at tourist offices. ◐ *Ridelink: (619) 237-7665 • Bikes & Beyond: Map C6; 1201 1st St, Coronado; (619) 435-7180*

Sailing & Boating
2 Whether at Mission Bay or the Pacific Ocean, you're bound to see something that floats. You can rent almost any type of boat, complete with a crew, champagne, and hors d'oeuvres. ◐ *Seaforth Boat Rentals: Map B4 • 1641 Quivira Rd, Mission Bay • (888) 834-2628*

Sportfishing
3 Albacore, yellowfin, and dorado are just some of the fish in the offshore waters. Summer and fall are the best months, and half-, full-, and multiple-day trips are all available. A fishing license is not required to fish off the public piers. ◐ *Seaforth Sportsfishing: Map B4 • 1717 Quivira Rd, Mission Bay • (619) 224-3383*

Swimming
4 Nothing beats an ocean dip, though the temperatures seldom exceed 70° F (21° C) even in the summer. Alternatively, you can find swimming pools at most hotels. The Plunge at Mission Beach is a great public pool. ◐ *The Plunge: Map A4 • 3115 Ocean Front Walk • (858) 228-9300 • Adm*

Surfing
5 San Diego's beaches are famous for surfing. The months with the strongest swells are in late summer and fall, ideally under offshore wind conditions. Designated surfing areas can be found at every beach. ◐ *San Diego Surfing Academy: (800) 447-7873*

Golfing
6 With San Diego's perfect climate and amazing views, over 90 public courses and resort hotels offer some of the best golfing in the country. Tee times may be hard to get, so reserve early. The San Diego Convention and Visitors Bureau has a listing of courses. ◐ *San Diego Convention & Visitors Bureau: Map J6 • (619) 236-1212*

Rollerblading
7 Mission Bay and Pacific Beach are the best areas to enjoy the miles of pathway shared by skateboarders and joggers. Some areas of town specifically prohibit skating, so watch out for the signs. ◐ *Mission Beach Club: Map A4 • 704 Ventura, Mission Beach • (858) 488-5050*

Surfers at Swami's Beach, near Encinitas

 Always ask a lifeguard about ocean conditions before plunging into the water.

Rollerblading

Hiking
8 Hiking is available in every environment imaginable. Los Peñasquitos Canyon Preserve and Mission Trails Regional Park offer trails of varying difficulty through their canyons and valleys; the trails of Torrey Pines State Reserve and Tijuana River National Estuarine Research Reserve *(see p47)* pass near the ocean. The San Diego Natural History Museum *(see p18)* hosts guided nature tours.

Horseback Riding
9 Guided horseback rides are available on trails, through parks, and on the beach. The South Bay area offers the only beach where you can take an exhilarating ride on the sand and in the waves. There are also pony rides for children, hayrides, and romantic carriage rides. ⊗ *Happy Trails: Map E3 • 2012A Sunset Ave • (619) 443–3517*
• *www.happytrails-usa.com*

Diving
10 The best spots for diving off the coast are the giant kelp forests of Point Loma and the La Jolla Underwater Ecological Reserve. Common sealife includes lobsters and garibaldi – the official state marine fish. ⊗ *San Diego Ocean Enterprises: Map B2 • 7710 Balboa Ave • (619) 224-3439*

Top 10 Spectator Sports

1 San Diego Chargers
Catch the American Football Conference team at Qualcomm Stadium. ⊗ *Map D3 • (619) 280-2121*

2 San Diego Padres
Petco Park hosts the National League Padres' baseball team. ⊗ *Map K6 • 100 Park Blvd • (877) 374-2784*

3 San Diego State University Aztecs
Take the San Diego Trolley out to Qualcomm Stadium. ⊗ *Map E4*

4 San Diego Gulls Ice Hockey
The Gulls play in the ECHL Premier AA Hockey League. ⊗ *Map B4 • 3500 Sports Arena Blvd • (619) 225-9813*

5 Del Mar Thoroughbred Club
Celebrities and horseracing fans head here. ⊗ *Map D2 • 2260 Jimmy Durante Blvd, Del Mar • (858) 755-1141*

6 Hang gliding/ Paragliding
Hang gliders and paragliders take off from the ocean cliffs north of La Jolla *(see p62)*.

7 San Diego Polo Club
Attend polo matches on Sundays. ⊗ *Map E2 • 14555 El Camino Real, Rancho Santa Fe • (858) 481-9217 • Adm*

8 Golf
Watch the annual golf tournaments at Torrey Pines and La Costa.

9 Mission Bay Park
Mission Bay hosts many boating events. ⊗ *Map B3*

10 Bullfights
Check out the world's leading *toreros* at Plaza Monumental. ⊗ *Map E3 • Playas de Tijuana, Tijuana • (664) 680-1808*

Colorful entrance to Viejas Casino

Offbeat San Diego

1 Paragliding at Torrey Pines

Soar off the spectacular cliffs of Torrey Pines *(see p33)*. In your first lesson, you'll receive basic instructions followed by 20–30 minutes of gliding with your instructor. If you'd like to watch for a while before making that exhilarating plunge, a viewing area and café sit on the cliff's edge. ◈ *Torrey Pines Gliderport: Map A1 • 2800 Torrey Pines Scenic Dr, La Jolla • (858) 452-9858*

2 Movies Before the Mast

In July and August, the Maritime Museum presents nautical-themed movies aboard the 1863 merchant vessel, *Star of India*. Folding chairs are set out on deck, and movies such as *20,000 Leagues Under the Sea* are projected onto a special sail. The gates open at 7pm and there is time to tour the *Star* before the movie *(see p42)*.

3 Rent a Harley Davidson

All of us are born to be wild, so put on your jeans and black leather jacket and rent a bike for a day. You won't be alone: droves of bikers take to the highway, especially on weekends. The backcountry of San Diego County is a prime area for powering a Fat Boy, Road King, or Dyna Wide Glide down the road. ◈ *Rent a Harley-Davidson: Map B4 • 3655 Camino Del Rio West, Suite B • (877) 437-4337*

Roar and Snore at the Wild Animal Park

4 Roar & Snore at San Diego Wild Animal Park

On weekends from May through October, sleep alongside wild animals just as you would in an African game park. Tents that hold up to four persons are provided. Programs include guided discovery hikes and animal encounters, an open-flame grilled dinner, campfire snacks, special late night programs, and a pancake breakfast before a gorgeous sunrise. Reservations are essential *(see p95)*.

5 Gambling at Indian Casinos

Feeling lucky? A dozen tribal casinos promise non-stop Las Vegas-style action and jackpots galore. Starting as a small bingo hall 20 years ago, Indian gaming is now a billion-dollar industry of resort hotels, concert venues, and golf courses. Today, San Diego County has the highest concentration of casinos in the state of California.

Harley-Davidson sign

Thousands of slot machines, video poker, and gaming tables in immense, striking buildings will satisfy the gambler in you. ⊛ *Viejas Casino: Map E2; 5000 Willows Rd, Alpine; (619) 445-5400* • *Barona Resort & Casino: Map E2; 1932 Wildcat Canyon Rd, Lakeside; (888) 722-7662*

6 UFO Spotting in East County

Several San Diego groups take UFO (Unidentified Flying Object) sightings seriously. The best places to spot UFOs are in Borrego Springs and Ocotillo Wells. Given San Diego's strong military presence, that saucer in the sky might well be a secret government mission. ⊛ *Map F1*

7 Hot-Air Ballooning

You can watch or take part in inflating a brilliantly colored balloon. Hop in the basket and begin to float over the valleys and hills with a glass of champagne in hand. Flights leave early in the morning or at sunset. Most hot-air balloon companies have moved recently to Temecula where there are fewer housing developments to impede their landings.
⊛ *California Dreamin': Map E1* • *33133 Vista del Monte Rd, Temecula* • *(800) 373-3359*

8 Biplane Flying

Two of you sit in the front of a beautifully restored 1920s biplane and soar over beaches, golf courses, and houses, while the pilot flies behind. The *Beech Belle*, a restored World War II VIP biplane, is great for that special occasion. If you're looking for an extra thrill, a pilot will put you through aerobatic loops and rolls, or you can take the controls in

Hot-air ballooning

top dog air combat. ⊛ *Barnstorming Adventures: Map E1* • *Montgomery Field* • *(800) 759-5667* • *www.barnstorming.com*

9 Diving at Wreck Alley

Just off Mission Beach is the final resting place for the *Yukon*, a decommissioned Canadian warship, the coastguard cutter *Ruby E*, and a barge, all deliberately sunk to create an artificial reef. A research tower here collapsed on its own, with its dangling wires and protrusions only adding to the otherworldly, ethereal atmosphere. Thousands of invertebrate marine life have taken up residence here. Charter boats will take you out. ⊛ *Map A4*

10 Vintage Train Rides

Operated by the Railway Museum of San Diego, the Golden State Limited departs twice daily on the weekends from the historic Campo train depot, for a pleasant 16-mile (26-km) round trip to Miller Creek. Reserve a spot in the cab of the Diesel-electric locomotive and chat with the engineer and brakeman; you'll even have a chance to toot the horn. ⊛ *Campo Depot: Map F3* • *Hwy 94, Campo* • *(619) 478-9937 (weekends); (619) 465-7776 (weekdays)*

Silver Strand State Beach

Top 10 Beaches

1 Silver Strand State Beach

Between Coronado and Imperial Beach, miles of the "Strand" attracts families with its wide expanses, gentle waves, fire rings, surf fishing, grunion runs *(see p53)* and, unique to San Diego beaches, clamming. The name Silver Strand comes from the tiny silver shells that dot the sand on the oceanside. Pedestrian tunnels lead to the beach on the bayside, where the water is warmer and calmer. *Map E3*

2 Ocean Beach

The laid-back atmosphere of Ocean Beach *(see p85)* attracts locals and some out-of-towners. Surfers usually go out around the pier, and swimmers farther down the beach. There tends to be a strong rip current at the beach, so don't swim out of sight from a lifeguard station. There are plenty of facilities, including showers, picnic tables, and volleyball courts. *Map A4*

Playing volleyball at Ocean Beach

3 Dog Beach

Leashes optional! Your dog can run loose to chase after balls, Frisbees, and other dogs with joyous abandon. The beach is open 24 hours, so you can even come here for a midnight swim. Posts with handy plastic bags help you pick up the after-math. *Map A4 • North end of Ocean Beach at San Diego River*

Sailing at Mission Bay

4 Mission Beach

At this popular beach *(see p97)*, sunburned, sandy bodies vie for space upon the sand, volleyballs and Frisbees fly overhead, and skateboarders and cyclists try to balance drinks and portable MP3 players as they careen down the boardwalk. If the beach scene gets overwhelming, Belmont Park *(see p52)* is just a block away. *Map A4*

5 Mission Bay Beaches

Protected from the waves of the Pacific Ocean, 27 miles (43 km) of shoreline, including 19 miles (30 km) of sandy beaches, coves, and inlets, offer idyllic picnic locations. On sunny days, the water is filled with sailboats, kayaks, waterski-ers, windsurfers, and rowers. Bike paths wind for miles along the shoreline, and wide grassy areas and ocean breezes make flying kites ideal. *Map B4*

Pacific Beach

6 A great beach-going spirit fills the air as skateboarders, joggers, and cyclists cruise the promenade that runs parallel to the beach. People-watching opportunities are endless, since Pacific Beach has a reputation of being the place to hang out. Take a walk out to the Crystal Pier Hotel (see p118), past the bungalows to watch surfers shooting the curl. ◈ Map A3

Crystal Pier Hotel at Pacific Beach

Windansea Beach

7 Legendary among surfers for its shorebreaks, this beach found literary fame as the setting for Tom Wolfe's The Pumphouse Gang. The beach gets a little wider south of the "Shack," a local landmark, but those with small children should still take care. ◈ Map N3

La Jolla Shores

8 A great family beach, but summertime gets crowded as sunbathers, Frisbee-throwers, and boogie-boarders spread out along a broad, sandy white strip lapped by gentle surf. Kellogg Park, which runs alongside part of the beach, is a good picnic area for those who forgot their towels. The La Jolla Underwater Ecological Reserve (see p61) is just offshore, so divers are usually out in the water. ◈ Map Q1

Black's Beach

9 This beach is notorious for its nude sunbathers. Access to the beach, which lies between Torrey Pines State Beach and La Jolla Shores, is either down an unstable 300-ft (91-m) cliff or via a 1-mile (1.6-km) walk along the beach from either the north or south during low tide. Surfers find the southern end of the beach ideal, as well as the

hang-gliders who launch off from the cliffs above. ◈ Map Q1

Torrey Pines State Beach

10 Miles of sandy beaches and secret coves nestle beneath towering sandstone cliffs. During low tide, tide pools offer a glimpse into life under the sea. Torrey Pines is a San Diego favorite because of its lack of crowds, intimacy, and natural beauty. Parking is available at the Torrey Pines State Reserve (see pp46–7) or by the gliderport on top of the cliff. ◈ Map A1

"Shorebreaks" are rough waves that break right on the shore.

65

Left **Cinco de Mayo celebration** Right **Christmas carols at Balboa Park**

Festivals

1 Mardi Gras
Be quick to grab the strings of beads thrown off the floats at the Masquerade Parade. The parade begins in the afternoon at Fifth Avenue, but music and revelry carries on until the early morning. The food booths serve up New Orleans-style Cajun food. ◎ *Gaslamp Quarter • Feb*

2 St. Patrick's Day Parade
A grand parade of marching bands, bagpipes, community organizations, horses, and school groups begins at Sixth and Juniper. Afterwards, an Irish festival takes place at Balboa Park with Irish dancers, lots to eat, green beer, and fun for the entire family. ◎ *Mar*

3 Cinco de Mayo
North of the Mexican border, commemorating the French defeat by Mexican troops is a serious business. Restaurants overflow, Old Town State Historic Park sponsors folkloric ballet performances and mariachi bands, and the Gaslamp Quarter hosts a musical street fair. ◎ *May*

St. Patrick's Day revelers

4 Fourth of July Fireworks & Parades
Nearly every San Diego community has its own July 4th festivities, such as fireworks, surfing contests, parades, and street festivals. Since the ban of home fireworks, commercial fireworks shows are the way to go. The biggest show in the county is held over San Diego Harbor. ◎ *Jul*

5 Lesbian and Gay Parade and Festival
San Diego's gay community hits the streets in celebration of diversity. The parade begins at Fifth Avenue and Laurel in Hillcrest and moves to Balboa Park, where live bands, food booths, and a party atmosphere prevail. Outrageous costumes are the rule of the day. ◎ *End Jul*

6 Halloween Festivals & Haunted Houses
Your worst nightmares may come true at "Frightmare on Market Street", a haunted Victorian building complete with underground catacombs. You might come face to face with Freddy Krueger, the Texas Chainsaw family, and 13 ghosts at the Haunted Hotel. The Haunted Trails of Balboa Park will scare the wits out of you.
◎ *Gaslamp Quarter & Balboa Park • Oct • Adm*

7 Mother Goose Parade
Floats, equestrian units, clowns, marching bands, and drill teams make up only part of the 200 entries in the largest single-

Halloween scarecrow drinking on a porch

day event in San Diego County, attended by about 400,000 people annually. A tradition since 1947, the parade changes its theme every year but always revolves around a celebration of children. ◉ *El Cajon • Sun before Thanksgiving*

Christmas on the Prado
Balboa Park launches the Christmas season by opening its doors to the community. Museums are free after 5pm, carolers sing, and special food booths are set up. The park is closed to traffic, but shuttles reach the outer parking lots. Dress warmly and expect a crowd of over 50,000 people. ◉ *Balboa Park • First Fri & Sat of Dec*

Las Posadas
This is a traditional re-enactment of Mary and Joseph seeking shelter for the Christ child. A candlelight procession begins in Heritage Park, passing by historic homes and businesses that have food set out, and finishing at the plaza in Old Town State Historic Park. ◉ *Mid-Dec*

Boat Parades of Lights
Yachts and sailboats vie for the title of best decorated in Mission Bay and the San Diego Harbor. The best viewing areas for the Mission Bay parade are at Crown Point and Fiesta Island; for the San Diego Harbor Parade, head to the Embarcadero. ◉ *Dec*

Top 10 Fairs & Gatherings

1 Ocean Beach Kite Festival
A kite competition with prizes and demonstrations on the beach. ◉ *Ocean Beach • Mar*

2 Avocado Festival
Special tours, 50 food booths, and awards for best dishes attract huge crowds. ◉ *Fallbrook • Apr*

3 San Diego County Fair
Animals, rides, food, and music. ◉ *Del Mar • Jun • Adm*

4 A Taste of Gaslamp
A self-guided tour passes by restaurants displaying their kitchen samplings. ◉ *Gaslamp Quarter • Jun • Adm*

5 Mainly Mozart Festival
Concerts at San Diego and Tijuana feature works by the wunderkind and his contemporaries. ◉ *Jun • Adm*

6 US Open Sand Castle Competition
Competitors build the most complex and imaginative sand castles. ◉ *Imperial Beach • Jul*

7 Summerfest
Classical music and modern compositions in La Jolla, with artists and ensembles from around the world. ◉ *Aug*

8 Julian Fall Apple Harvest
Music, apple cider, and apple pies in a charming mountain town. ◉ *Mid-Sep–mid-Nov*

9 Cabrillo Festival
Soldiers re-enact the Cabrillo landing, and performers showcase Native American, Aztec, and Mayan dances. ◉ *Cabrillo National Monument • End Sep • Adm*

10 Fleet Week
Navy ship tours and air and sea parades honor the military. ◉ *Oct*

AROUND TOWN

SAN DIEGO'S TOP 10

Left **Balboa Park** Center **Tuna Harbor, Embarcadero** Right **Fountain at Horton Plaza Park**

Downtown San Diego

*S*CARCELY A GENERATION AGO, *one drove through downtown San Diego with the windows rolled up, past derelict tattoo parlors, seedy tenements, and sleazy porn palaces. With vision and dedication, downtown has been transformed into a first-class destination for visitors and a trendy address for residents. Neighborhoods have blossomed with excellent restaurants, art galleries, and festivals; performing arts centers, museums, and a new sports stadium attract visitors by the thousands. The atmosphere is strictly Southern*

Apes at San Diego Zoo

Californian: a blend of urban energy and laid-back priorities. Nowadays, drivers fight for cherished parking spaces and casual strolling is the preferred means of transport. From the edge of the Embarcadero, graced with 19th-century sailing ships, to the beautifully restored Victorian and Italianate buildings of the Gaslamp Quarter, a district straight out of the Wild West and home to trattorias, Irish pubs, and a pulsating nightlife, downtown is a great place to have fun in.

🔟 Sights

1. Gaslamp Quarter
2. Embarcadero
3. Balboa Park & San Diego Zoo
4. Horton Plaza
5. East Village
6. Little Italy
7. Asian Pacific Historic District
8. Museum of Contemporary Art
9. Martin Luther King Promenade
10. Marston House

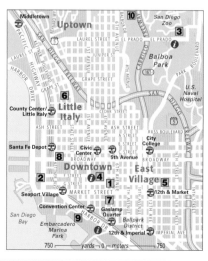

Previous pages: **Colorful house in Hillcrest**

1 Gaslamp Quarter
In the mid-19th century, the Gaslamp Quarter was the heart of a new city, but within 50 years it had fallen prey to gambling halls, opium dens, and houses of prostitution, and within another 50 years, had become a broken-down slum. Now the Gaslamp Quarter sparkles as it looks to a brilliant future. During the day, the gloriously restored historic buildings, each an architectural highlight, attract history buffs and shoppers. By night, crowds line up to dine in fashionable restaurants, listen to music, or sip the latest martini concoction (see pp8–9).

2 Embarcadero
For those arriving by ship or train, the Embarcadero is San Diego's front door. Passengers disembark from gleaming white cruise ships tied up at B Street Pier or pass through a 1915 train depot, eager to enjoy the city's attractions. But unlike most cities, the Embarcadero is an attraction in itself. Pedestrian-friendly walkways pass by historic sailing ships, museums, shopping centers, and parks. Serious and quirky public art works and a splendid harbor

Buildings in the Gaslamp Quarter

filled with maritime life define this lively district (see pp10–11).

3 Balboa Park & San Diego Zoo
Home to the world-famous San Diego Zoo, 15 unique museums, theaters, countless recreational opportunities, and exquisite landscaping, Balboa Park creates an indelible impression. No matter the time of year, vibrant flowers bloom in profusion and pepper tree groves and grassy expanses provide idyllic spots for picnicking. Allow a minimum of a few days to soak in the park's attractions (see pp14–19).

White floss silk tree flower at the Zoo

4 Horton Plaza
When it opened in 1985, developers kept their fingers crossed that this unique shopping center would draw visitors to a declining area and help spearhead a downtown revival. It was an immediate hit – people loved the Plaza's inward-facing design, tiered shopping levels, and the 43 unusual colors of paint on its walls. Covering several city blocks, the plaza features more than 140 shops, movie theaters, and stage productions at the Lyceum Theatre (see p50). Adjacent to Horton Plaza is the Balboa Theatre (see p9), which reopened in 2008 and offers live performances (see p48).

Cyclists along the Embarcadero

5 East Village

Formerly a Victorian village that fell into neglect but survived as a warehouse district and artist colony, this is downtown's newest redeveloped area. Petco Park, the 2004 state-of-the-art baseball stadium and home to the San Diego Padres *(see p61)*, is the neighborhood's major focal point. Check out the 1909 Western Metal Supply building: architects incorporated the vintage building into the stadium's structure. A new Children's Museum of San Diego, shops, restaurants, artists' lofts, and residential high-rises have opened here, with a new main library also planned. *Map L5*

6 Little Italy

One of the more recent neighborhoods to undergo revitalization is also one of San Diego's oldest. Genoese fishing families were the first Italians to settle along the waterfront in the 1860s. Along with Portuguese immigrants, they founded San Diego's prosperous tuna industry. Little Italy, sometimes also known as Middletown, has now become a fashionable address. While retaining its Bohemian character, Italian restaurants, antique and design stores, and hip cafés distinguish its streets. *Map J3*

Little Italy

7 Asian Pacific Historic District

An eight-block area that overlaps part of the Gaslamp Quarter designates the former center of San Diego's Asian community. The Chinese came to San Diego following the California Gold Rush and took up fishing and construction work; others ran opium dens and gambling halls. Filipinos and Japanese soon followed. This is the home of Chinese New Year celebrations, a farmers' market, and an Asian bazaar. Pick up a walking-tour map at the Chinese Historical Museum *(see p42)*, and look out for the Asian architectural flourishes on the buildings you pass by. *Map J5*

8 Museum of Contemporary Art

This two-building downtown location of the museum in La Jolla *(see p32)*, present rotating exhibits from emerging and established contemporary artists, as well as selected pieces from the museum's permanent collection. Marking the entrance is the 18-ft (5.4-m) *Hammering Man at 3,110,527*, a steel and aluminum sculpture by Jonathan Borofsky. The museum also hosts lectures, workshops, and family activities, including the popular "Thursday Night Thing," where the public can meet and mingle with local

---

The Founding of Modern San Diego

When entrepreneur Alonzo Horton arrived in a burgeoning San Diego in 1867, he believed that a new city could prosper in this location. He bought 960 acres and sold and even gave away lots to people. When you walk the Gaslamp Quarter, note the short blocks and lack of alleys, created due to the opinion that corner lots were worth more and alleys only accumulated trash.

artists. Ⓢ Map H4 • 1001 Kettner Blvd • (619) 234-1001 • Open 11am–5pm Wed, Fri–Mon, 11am–7pm Thu • Docent-led tours 6pm Thu, 2pm Sat, Sun

9 Martin Luther King Promenade

Planner Max Schmidt used the idea of functional public art to create this 1/4-mile (0.4-km) promenade along Harbor Drive. Described as a "serape" of colors, textures, and waterworks, the grassy promenade celebrates San Diego's multicultural heritage. Granite stones in the sidewalk bear quotes by civil-rights leader Dr. Martin Luther King. Ⓢ Map H5

10 Marston House

This fine Arts and Crafts house built in 1905 is now open to the public as a museum. The exterior combines elements of Victorian and English Tudor styles, while, the interior offers expansive hallways and intimate living spaces. Adorned with Mission-style furnishings, there are fine pottery, paintings, and textiles by craftsman artisans. The museum is operated by the San Diego Historical Society. Ⓢ Map K1 • 3525 7th Ave • (619) 298-3142 • Open for docent-led tours only: 11am, noon, 1pm, 2pm, 3pm Fri–Sun (additonal tours run at 10am and 4pm June 1–Labour Day) • Adm

Marston House

A Day Walking Around Downtown

Morning

Start at the **Santa Fe Depot**. Walk right on Broadway, cross the RR tracks, and walk two blocks to Harbor Drive. Turn right and head to the **Maritime Museum** (see p42). Check out the exhibits and climb aboard the *Star of India*. Walk back down Harbor Drive to the ticket booth for harbor tours. A narrated harbor cruise brings you close to the naval facilities. Next, spend an hour or so aboard the **USS *Midway*** at the **San Diego Aircraft Carrier Museum** (see pp12–13). Finally, it's time for lunch at **The Fish Market** (see p54).

Afternoon

Continue down Harbor Drive to **Seaport Village** (see p11) and stay on the sidewalk until you reach a crossing. Turn left; walk up the street past the **Manchester Grand Hyatt Hotel**, across Harbor Drive and the trolley tracks. Walk onto the **Martin Luther King Promenade**, which stretches past beautiful downtown apartment revitalizations. At the Convention Center trolley stop, turn left, then left again on J St. On J and 3rd, stop by the **San Diego Chinese Historical Museum** (see p42). Turn left on 3rd and right on Island; you'll pass the historic **Horton Grand Hotel**. At 4th, visit the **William Heath Davis House** (see p8). One block farther is the heart of the **Gaslamp Quarter**. After walking around, treat yourself to a sundae at **Ghirardelli Soda Fountain** at 631 5th Street.

Left **Exterior of Bubbles Boutique** Right **Exterior of San Diego Harley Davidson**

TOP 10 Shopping

1 Vila Moda Boutique
The contemporary womenswear here ranges from casual T-shirts and jeans to formal eveningwear. Vila Moda also sells jewelry, belts, and handbags.
◈ Map K5 • 363 5th Ave • (619) 236-9068

2 San Diego Harley Davidson
At this official boutique, the Harley Davidson logo is emblazoned on everything, including T-shirts, shot glasses, key chains, and kids clothes. ◈ Map H5 • Seaport Village • (619) 234-5780

3 Lucky Dog Pet Boutique
Indulge your dog with a lamb's wool coat, jeweled collar, rawhide shoe chews, and other "essentials and gifts for discriminating canines." ◈ Map J5 • 415 Market St • (619) 696 0364

4 Urban Outfitters
This one-stop clothing shop for the young and trendy never lags behind the latest styles. Their original home accessories with an urban edge are true conversation pieces. ◈ Map K5 • 665 5th Ave • (619) 231-0102

5 Pannikin/Hessian
This magical place is filled with treasures from all over the world, such as festive Rajasthani umbrellas, beaded chairs from Nigeria, Mexican sugar skull molds, countless tea sets, and coffee, tea, and spices. ◈ Map K5 • 675 G St • (619) 239-7891

6 Z Gallery
Here's where you'll find the latest in home decor, dinnerware, and glassware. There are also sofas, beds, and accessories. ◈ Map K5 • 611 5th Ave • (619) 696-8137

7 Bubbles Boutique
Come here for trendy and fun casualwear, luxurious pajamas, hand-crafted bath products, and a great selection of one-of-a-kind gifts and accessories.
◈ Map K5 • 226 5th Ave • (619) 236-9003

8 The Cuban Cigar Factory
Cigar makers roll tobacco from Central America and the Dominican Republic in San Diego's original cigar factory. Aficionados can select from a variety of cigars and admire the humidors on display.
◈ Map K5 • 551 5th Ave • (619) 238-2496

9 Architectural Salvage of San Diego
Head here for Victorian cutglass doorknobs and handles, clawfoot bathtubs, leaded glass, and vintage doors. ◈ Map H3 • 2401 Kettner Blvd • (619) 696-1313

10 Wahrenbrock's Bookhouse
Book collectors will be in heaven at this three-story second-hand bookstore that is jampacked with out-of-print treasures. This is the largest and oldest bookstore in San Diego. ◈ Map K4 • 726 Broadway • (619) 232-0132

Store at San Diego Museum of Man

Museum Shops

1 Mingei International Museum

This store is filled with ethnic clothes, Chinese brushes, Russian dolls, Indian chiming bells, and a good selection of *alebrijes* (see p18).

2 San Diego Museum of Art

Merchandise reflects special exhibits. Wonderful art books, children's books, jewelry, purses, flower pressing kits, and Tibetan chests are for sale. A garden shop sells garden ornaments and bonsai kits (see p18).

3 San Diego Museum of Man

Crafts from around Latin America include carved Peruvian gourds, textiles, Mexican folk art, and three-legged Chilean good luck pigs. There is also a wide assortment of Native American crafts such as silver jewelry (see p18).

4 Museum of Contemporary Art

If you're looking for art gifts with a contemporary edge, you might find them among the select merchandise that relates to the museum's special exhibitions. Always on display are the latest art books and handcrafted jewelry (see pp72–3).

5 Reuben H. Fleet Science Center

Science toys, videos, puzzles, and hands-on games will attract the kids – and you (see p52).

6 Maritime Museum

Gratify your nautical gift needs through a variety of model ships, T-shirts, posters, and prints inscribed with an image of the *Star of India* (see p42).

7 San Diego Art Institute Shop

Juried art shows showcase the work of local artists, whose works often go on sale after being exhibited. This small shop features glass sculptures, porcelain *objets d'art*, hand-painted cushions, and jewelry.
◈ Map L1 • House of Charm, Balboa Park

8 San Diego Chinese Historical Museum

Chinese calligraphy sets, snuff bottles, tea sets, and chops – a type of carved stamp traditionally used to sign one's name – are on sale here (see p42).

9 San Diego Historical Society Museum

If you're interested in the history of San Diego, including haunted locations and biographies of various characters, this museum offers one of the best collections of local history books (see p18).

10 Wyatt Earp Museum & Bookstore

Old photo reprints from Earp's Dodge City and Tombstone gunfighter days and a number of biographies tell the story of Stingaree's most infamous resident. ◈ Map J5 • 413 Market St

Alebrijes *are a type of Mexican folk art from Oaxaca that feature whimsical, painted wooden animals and figurines.*

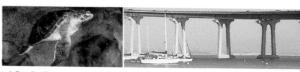

Left **East Pacific green sea turtle** Right **Coronado Bridge**

Cruising the Bay

Museum Vessels of the Embarcadero

The sailing ship *Star of India* dates back to 1863; *Berkeley* used to carry passengers in the Bay Area; and the USS *Midway* features in the Aircraft Carrier Museum (*see pp10–13*).

SPAWAR

The Navy marine mammal facility trains bottlenose dolphins, with their biological sonar, to locate sea mines. ✆ *Map D6*

Cabrillo National Monument

Dedicated to the European discovery of San Diego and Alta California, this monument draws over one million people a year. The statue of Cabrillo is a replica of an original that could not withstand the wind and salt air (*see p26*).

Naval Air Station North Island

Several aircraft carriers tie up here. You can often see high-tech aircraft, submarines, and destroyers take off and land (*see p25*).

Local Marine Wildlife

Seals and sea lions are typical residents of the bay. The endangered East Pacific green sea turtle and the California least tern have protected foraging habitats.

Coronado Bridge

This distinctive bridge links Coronado to San Diego.

Its gradual incline and curve allows cars to maintain speed, and the bridge sits high enough to allow aircraft carriers to pass beneath at high tide (*see p24*).

32nd Street Naval Station

This station provides shore support and living quarters for over 50 naval ships of the Pacific Fleet, and is one of only two major fleet support installations in the country. ✆ *Map D6*

NASSCO Shipyard

The National Steel and Ship-building Company designs and builds US Navy auxiliary ships, commercial tankers, and container ships. It is one of the largest shipyards in the US. ✆ *Map D6*

Naval Amphibious Base

Home to the Navy SEALS and the Navy Parachute Team, the facility has served as an amphibious training base since 1943. The base is responsible for training, maintenance, and crews of the ships of the Pacific Fleet (*see p25*).

Kelp & Seaweed Processing Factory

The kelp forests off San Diego's coast provide valuable resources for Kelco, the largest kelp harvester in California. The company produces 70 different products from kelp, including stabilizers used in everything from salad dressing and ice cream to beer and car wax. ✆ *Map D6*

These are all sights that are pointed out while on a harbor cruise; most cannot be visited.

Sign at The Cheese Shop

Price Categories

Price categories include a three-course meal for one, half a bottle of wine, and all unavoidable extra charges including tax.

$	under $20
$$	$20–$40
$$$	$40–$55
$$$$	$55–$80
$$$$$	over $80

Top 10 Places to Eat

1 Chive
The menu at this hip, contemporary Gaslamp Quarter restaurant offers innovative California fusion cuisine and a variety of small plate options. ◉ Map J5 • 558 4th Ave • (619) 232-4483 • $$$

2 Dakota Grill & Spirits
Exceptional Californian and Southwestern food. Wood-fired pizzas and rib-eye steaks are prepared in an open kitchen. ◉ Map K4 • 901 5th Ave • (619) 234-5554 • $$$$

3 The Grant Grill
Sporting a club-like ambience with modern touches, The Grant Grill offers contemporary California cuisine. Try the crab cake with relish and tangerine sauce. ◉ Map J4 • US Grant Hotel, 326 Broadway • (619) 232-3121 • $$$$

4 Top of the Market
The chichi sister of the Fish Market (see p54). Come here for a window seat, a quieter atmosphere, and seafood prepared with panache. ◉ Map G5 • 750 N. Harbor Dr • (619) 234-4867 • $$$$$

5 Athens Market Taverna
Expect a sensational presentation of classical Greek dishes. The menu relies heavily on fish and meat. ◉ Map J5 • 109 W. F St • (619) 234-1955 • Closed Sun • $$$

6 Red Pearl Kitchen
Chinese and East Asian food is served with flair in this trendy Gaslamp Quarter restaurant. Deep-red walls and contemporary decor add glamour. ◉ Map J5 • 440 J St • (619) 231-1100 • $$$

7 Karl Strauss' Brewery & Restaurant
Try the outstanding burgers, blackened salmon, or baby back ribs. A range of house brews celebrate the local spirit. ◉ Map H4 • 1157 Columbia St • (619) 234-2739 • $$

8 Star of India
A great selection of curries, tandoori-style chicken, lamb, and vegetarian dishes. ◉ Map J5 • 423 F St • (619) 544-9891 • $$

9 The Cheese Shop
Locals line up here for monster-sized custom sandwiches. Roast pork loin and roast beef are special-ties, along with a wide selection of cheese. ◉ Map J5 • 627 4th Ave • (619) 232-2303 • $

10 St. Tropez Bakery & Bistro
Feast on stuffed croissants, crêpes, and well-prepared salads. Save room for utterly delicious pastries. A little wine bar is attached. ◉ Map H4 • 600 W. Broadway/ 1 America Plaza • (619) 234-2560 • $

Unless otherwise stated, all restaurants are open daily, accept credit cards, serve vegetarian meals, and provide disabled access.

77

Left & Center **Belltower & interior of Mission San Diego de Alcalá** Right **Gay poster in Hillcrest**

Old Town, Uptown, & Mission Valley

THIS LONG STRETCH follows the San Diego River from the Mission San Diego de Alcalá to Old Town. Over 200 years ago, Kumeyaay Indians lived in tribal groups within small settlements in the valley. Unknown to them, strangers from the other side of the earth would change their lives forever. Spanish soldiers and Franciscan padres would have their time of glory here, as well as San Diego's pioneer families. Today, the valley itself holds little interest beyond masses of chain motels and shopping centers intersected by a freeway; however, on the bluffs above, you'll find eclectic neighborhoods overflowing with charm, brilliant architecture, and chic restaurants. Tolerance and diversity creates a progressive, Bohemian air, while rising real estate prices have turned simple bungalow homes into showpieces. And San Diego's birthplace is always close by.

10 Sights

1. Old Town State Historic Park
2. Mission San Diego de Alcalá
3. Hillcrest
4. Junipero Serra Museum
5. Heritage Park
6. University of San Diego
7. Whaley House
8. Presidio Park
9. Mormon Battalion Memorial Visitor's Center
10. Mission Hills

Statuette, Mission San Diego de Alcalá

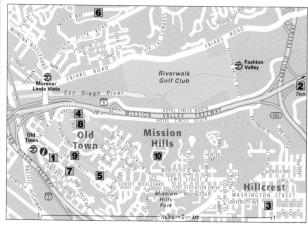

Old Town Plaza, State Historic Park

Old Town State Historic Park

San Diego's first commercial settlement has been either preserved or re-created in this pedestrian-only park. Although much of the town was destroyed in a fire in 1872, prompting the development of a new town center closer to the water, several of the original structures still remain. You can wander into any of Old Town's houses and find museums or concession shops inside, or enjoy one of the park's many Mexican restaurants *(see pp22–3)*.

Mission San Diego de Alcalá

A peaceful enclave among the nondescript strip malls of Mission Valley, the mission's original spirit still lingers in the church and its lovely gardens. The first of California's 21 missions was moved to this permanent site a few years after its founding. Over the years, the structure was rebuilt to suit the needs of the time, transforming it from a simple mission to a fortress with 5- to 7-ft (1.5- to 2-m) thick adobe brick walls. Its famous façade and bell tower have inspired architects to copy the "Mission Style" throughout San Diego *(see pp28–9)*.

Hillcrest

Considered San Diego's first suburb in the 1920s, Hillcrest slowly developed into a residential area, offering a quiet alternative to the bustle of downtown. A trolley stop opened the neighborhood up to thriving businesses, restaurants, and theaters; in the 1940s merchants proudly erected a sign that spanned University Boulevard, proclaiming "Hillcrest" to the world. But fortunes changed, neglect followed, and the sign came down. In the 1970s, the gay and lesbian community took up the revitalization challenge and transformed the community into a hip destination with great restaurants, nightlife, and avant-garde shops. And the sign is back – in neon. ◎ *Map C4*

Junípero Serra Museum

Constructed in 1929 in keeping with the city's Spanish-Colonial heritage, white stucco arches, narrow passages, a red-tile roof, and a stately tower pay tribute to the first mission, which stood near this site. The San Diego Historical Society oversees the museum, which is dedicated to the city's earliest days. Artifacts from ongoing archeological excavations at the presidio, ceramics made by Kumeyaay Indians, clothing, furniture, and a cannon help illustrate the meager life people led. Climb the tower to compare today's view with that of 1929. ◎ *Map P4 • 2727 Presidio Dr • (619) 297-3258 • Open Junday before Labor Day: 10am–4:30pm daily; Labor Day–May: 11am–3pm Mon–Fri, 10am–4:30pm Sat–Sun. Nov–May: closed some weekday mornings • Adm*

Junípero Serra Museum

Heritage Park

5 Downtown's rapid expansion after World War II almost destroyed several Victorian heritage houses and San Diego's first synagogue. The Save Our Heritage Organization rescued and moved these architectural treasures to this specially created park. Of notable interest is the Sherman Gilbert House, once home to art and music patrons Bess and Gertrude Gilbert, who hosted luminaries such as Artur Rubinstein, Anna Pavlova, and the Trapp Family Singers. Bronze plaques describe the houses' former lives. ⬉ *Map P5 • 2454 Heritage Park Row • (619) 291-9784 • Open 9am–5pm daily*

University of San Diego

6 Grand Spanish Renaissance buildings distinguish this independent Catholic university, its design inspired by the university in the Spanish town of Alcalá de Henares. Of exceptional note is the Founders Chapel with its white marble altar, gold-leaf decoration, 14 stained-glass nave windows, and marble floor. The campus is known for the Joan B. Kroc School of Peace Studies and its programs in law, education, nursing, and engineering. ⬉ *Map C4 • 5998 Alcalá Park • (619) 260-4600*

Plaque at Presidio Park

University of San Diego

Apolinaria Lorenzana

In 1800, Apolinaria Lorenzana and 20 orphans arrived from Mexico to be distributed to respectable presidio families. She taught herself to write by copying every written thing she found. She spent her life caring for the mission padres, teaching children and women church doctrine, and tending the sick. Nicknamed La Beata, she was one of the few women to receive a land grant.

Whaley House

7 California's first two-story brick structure also served as San Diego's first courthouse, county seat, and home to Thomas Whaley, who built this house in 1856 over a graveyard and site of a former gallows. Considered one of the most haunted in America, the US Commerce Department declared the house officially haunted in the 1960s. ⬉ *Map P5 • 2482 San Diego Ave • (619) 297-7511 • Open 10am–5pm Mon–Tue, 10am–10pm Thu–Sun; late May–early Sep: 10am–10pm daily • Adm*

Presidio Park

8 Kumeyaay Indians once used this hillside for sacred ceremonies. Site of the original Spanish presidio and mission settlement, a lovely park is all that's left of San Diego's beginnings. The park contains the Serra Museum *(see p79)* and the remaining earthen walls of Fort Stockton, a fortress that changed hands several times during the Mexican-American War, commemorated by bronze monuments, a flagpole, and a cannon. The 28-ft (8.5-m) Serra Cross, constructed from mission tiles, honors Father Junípero Serra *(see p29)*. ⬉ *Map P5*

Mormon Battallion Memorial Visitor's Center

9 Mormon Battalion Memorial Visitor's Center

In July 1846, 500 men, 32 women, and 51 children set out from Council Bluffs, Iowa, on what would be considered one of the longest military marches in history. Six months and 2,000 miles (3,218 km) later, they arrived in San Diego to offer support to the American military garrison during the Mexican-American War. At the Visitor's Center, a volunteer from the Church of Latter-Day Saints will discuss the historic march and Mormon contributions to San Diego and California. ✪ Map P5
• 2510 Juan St • (619) 298-3317
• Open 9am–9pm daily

10 Mission Hills

One of San Diego's most charming and romantic neighborhoods is tucked in the hills overlooking Old Town and San Diego Bay. Tree-lined streets run past architectural jewels built in Craftsman, Mission Revival, Italian Renaissance, and Victorian style. Dating from the early 20th century, homes had to cost at least $3,500, and could not keep any male farm animals. Commercial development was restricted, and only those of Caucasian descent could hold property. Still here is Kate Sessions' 1910 nursery (see p19). ✪ Map Q5 • Mission Hills Nursery: 1525 Fort Stockton Dr

A Walk Around Old Town, Heritage Park, & Presidio Park

Morning

Begin at the **Old Town Transportation Center**. Cross the street and follow the path into **Old Town State Historic Park**. Just to the left is the **Visitor's Center**, where you can pick up a map. Walk along the right side of the Plaza and peek into the Bailey & McGuire Pottery Shop. Follow the signs to the **Casa de Machado-Stewart** and the **Mason Street School** (see p23). Back at the Plaza, visit the **La Casa de Estudillo** (see p22) for the best insight into an upper-class home of early California. From the Plaza's southwest corner, continue out of the State Park. Walk along San Diego Avenue, where you'll find souvenir shops, galleries, and restaurants. Try the **Old Town Mexican Café** (see p83) for lunch.

Afternoon

Cross the street at Conde and backtrack up San Diego Avenue to visit the haunted **Whaley House**. Turn right on Harney Street and walk uphill to **Heritage Park**. Backtrack one block to the **Mormon Battalion Visitor's Center**. Turn right on Juan Street and walk to Mason. You'll see a sign indicating "The Old Presidio Historic Trail". Turn right on Mason, follow the golf course to Jackson, and look for the footpath across the street. You'll parallel Jackson to the left and wind uphill to **Presidio Park**. Across the grass are the ruins of the original presidio, the **Serra Cross**, and the **Serra Museum**.

Left **Original Paw Pleasers** Right **Bazaar del Mundo**

Shopping

Bazaar del Mundo
Lining a lushly landscaped plaza decorated in brilliant colors, quality shops offer Mexican tableware, folk art, Guatemalan textiles, and books. ◎ *Map N5 • 4133 Taylor St • (619) 296-3161*

Circa a.d.
Discover decorating ideas among the exotic home accents, antiques, and teak furniture, mostly from China and Southeast Asia. Planters fill the outside. ◎ *Map N4 • 5355 Grant St • (619) 293-3328*

Babette Schwartz
Come here to find a wacky item to make you the life of the party. The eclectic selection of trendy, funny gifts changes frequently. ◎ *Map C4 • 421 University Ave • (619) 220-7048*

Four Winds Trading Company
This Old Town store specializes in authentic Indian pottery, weavings, jewelry, dreamcatchers, and paintings of Native American themes. ◎ *Map P5 • 2448-B San Diego Ave • (619) 692-0466*

Wear It Again Sam
Vintage clothing includes party dresses, leopard jackets, and Western wear. ◎ *Map C4 • 3823 5th Ave • (619) 299-0185*

Village Hat Shop
If you want to keep the sun off your head, this is the right place: find Panama hats, straw and felt hats, and other imaginative creations on display. ◎ *Map C4 • 3821 4th Ave • (619) 683-5533*

Original Paw Pleasers
If you feel guilty about leaving your dog or cat at home, bribe him or her with a fresh baked treat or liver-flavored ice-cream from this pet bakery. ◎ *Map D4 • 2525 University Ave • (619) 293-7297*

Old Town Market
This festive market offers entertainment and local artisans. The shops sell colorful Mexican goods, including Day of the Dead folk art, textiles, and Talavera ceramics. There are also boutiques that stock Southwestern silver jewelry and gifts. ◎ *Map N5 • 4010 Twiggs St • (619) 260-1078*

Whole Foods
With an emphasis on fresh organic food, you'll find flavorful produce, a great assortment of imported goods, and a deli that specializes in healthy takeout. ◎ *Map C4 • 711 University Ave • (619) 294-2800*

Adams Avenue & Park Boulevard Antique Row
Still untouched by San Diego's urban renewal boom, antique stores, second-hand book and record shops, and retro-clothing boutiques are sprinkled along these streets in east Hillcrest and Normal Heights. ◎ *Adams Ave: Map D4 • Park Blvd: Map D4*

Price Categories

Price categories include a three-course meal for one, half a bottle of wine, and all unavoidable extra charges including tax.

$	under $20
$$	$20–$40
$$$	$40–$55
$$$$	$55–$80
$$$$$	over $80

Yellow Corvette in the Corvette Diner

🔟 Places to Eat

1 Kemo Sabe
If you like to experiment with wild combinations of ethnic flavors, you'll have fun here. It's the Far East meets the American Southwest. ◎ Map C4 • 3958 5th Ave • (619) 220-6802 • $$$$

2 Corvette Diner
Cruise back to the 1950s in this diner decorated with hubcaps, vintage gas station signs, and a yellow Corvette. ◎ Map C4 • 3946 5th Ave • (619) 542-1001 • $

3 Parallel 33
Experience some of the world's most intriguing cuisines, such as the Moroccan b'stilla and Indian lamb braised in curry. ◎ Map C4 • 741 W. Washington St • (619) 260-0033 • Closed Sun • $$$$

4 El Agave Tequileria
Utter culinary magic awaits within one of the first tequilarias in San Diego. Classic Mexican food with French touches make eating here an event (see p54).

5 Café Pacifica
Head to this quiet bungalow for an elegant seafood dinner. Try the signature drink, a Pomerita. ◎ Map P6 • 2414 San Diego Ave • (619) 291-6666 • Limited dis. access • $$$$

6 Chilango's Mexico City Grill
The excellent, authentic Mexican cooking includes mole poblano, a traditional sauce that combines chilies and chocolate served with meat dishes. ◎ Map C4 • 142 University Ave • (619) 294-8646 • $$

7 Old Town Mexican Café & Cantina
Watch the famous "Tortilla Ladies of Old Town." People line up to try the café's grilled pork carnitas and chilaquiles, a delicious tortilla strip casserole. ◎ Map P5 • 2489 San Diego Ave • (619) 297-4330 • $$

8 Crest Café
Butter burgers, veggie baskets, and honey-glazed pork chops are popular items at this old-fashioned diner. ◎ Map C4 • 425 Robinson Ave • (619) 295-2510

9 Bread & Cie
Breads such as anise and black-olive loaf are baked and made into unusual sandwiches. ◎ Map C4 • 350 University Ave • (619) 683-9322 • No credit cards • $

10 Chicken Pie Shop
Seniors and budget-eaters love the hearty food here. Mashed potatoes and gravy accompany tasty chicken pies. ◎ Map D4 • 2633 El Cajon, North Park • (619) 295-0156 • No credit cards • $

Unless otherwise stated, all restaurants are open daily, accept credit cards, serve vegetarian meals, and provide disabled access.

Left **Cabrillo National Monument** Center **Ocean Beach** Right **San Diego International Airport**

Southern San Diego

SOUTH OF SAN DIEGO to the Mexican border, cultures blend irrevocably. Many Mexican citizens live, work in, and send their children to school in communities such as Chula Vista and National City. Likewise, many Americans live in the beach towns south of Tijuana, taking advantage of cheaper housing and medical care. And people flood both ways across the border to shop, to be entertained, and to pursue a livelihood. Vast stretches of empty beaches are protected nature preserves where one can hike and discover abundant wildlife. Beach towns devote themselves to the surf culture, while exclusive Coronado boasts one of the most prized zip codes in the country.

Left **Coronado Bridge** Right **Old Point Loma Lighthouse**

🔟 Sights

1. Coronado
2. Point Loma
3. Tijuana
4. Ocean Beach
5. San Diego International Airport
6. Shelter Island
7. Harbor Island
8. Marine Corps Recruit Depot
9. Border Field State Park
10. Chula Vista Nature Center

Coronado

In the 1880s, two wealthy businessmen, Elisha Babcock, Jr. and Hampton Story, purchased Coronado and set out to build a town. They sold lots, laid streets, and constructed the landmark Hotel del Coronado *(see p115)*. John D. Spreckels *(see p39)* soon bought them out and turned Coronado into a haven for old-money gentry. The military permanently took over much of the peninsula during World War I. The old mansions, resorts, and military base exist harmoniously and give Coronado its unique identity *(see pp24–5)*.

Point Loma

Over one million people a year visit the Cabrillo National Monument at Point Loma. The views are simply mesmerizing, and the peninsula ends at the meeting point of the Pacific Ocean and San Diego Bay. Half the peninsula is occupied by the military, which has prevented over-development. Spend time at Sunset Cliffs Park to experience the wind and sea and perhaps spot a whale *(see pp26–7)*.

Tijuana

During the days of Prohibition, Tijuana used to be the destination of choice for the Hollywood elite and their followers, and for alcohol and gambling. The palatial, Moorish-designed Agua Caliente Casino & Spa *(see p35)* was so popular that it boasted its own landing airstrip for the private planes of the wealthy. Fortunes fell when Mexico declared casino gambling illegal in 1935. US Navy servicemen soon added to Tijuana's reputation at the bars on Avenida Revolución, but nowadays, the city has cleaned up its image considerably. Take the time and you'll find culture and great food in Mexico's fourth largest city *(see pp34–5)*.

Ocean Beach

Unconventional and laid back, OB, as it's locally known, still has a somewhat hippie-like feel from the 1970s. On Newport Avenue, its main thoroughfare, you can still find a few original head shops. But OB is mainly about the beach: on any day of the year, surfers are next to the pier waiting for the next swell; volleyball players are spiking balls over the net; and dogs and their owners are running freely on Dog Beach *(see p64)*.

San Diego International Airport

No matter where you are in San Diego, look up and you'll see a jet soaring dramatically past the downtown high-rises on its final approach to Lindbergh Field *(see p40)* as locals call the airport. A 100 years ago, this area was a muddy wasteland that proved to be an ideal spot for budding inventors and pilots to try out their latest machines. In 1927, Ryan Aviation *(see p39)* designed, produced, and tested on the beach the *Spirit of St. Louis*, the historic plane that Charles Lindbergh piloted solo across the Atlantic. Ⓢ *Map C5*

Street singers in Tijuana

Shelter Island Yacht Harbor in San Diego Bay

6 Shelter Island

Not really an island but a peninsula that juts out into San Diego Bay from Point Loma, the "island" is home to thousands of pleasure boats and a park that stretches along its length. In the 1950s, the city dredged millions of tons of sand and mud from the bay onto a sandbar to create land for marinas and hotels. A number of hotels still have hints of Polynesian themes, a popular style at the time. At the entrance to Shelter Island is the San Diego Yacht Club, the three-time host of the prestigious America's Cup sailing race. ◈ Map B5

7 Harbor Island

Created from 3.5 million tons of mud scooped from the bottom of San Diego Bay, this recreational island is another peninsula that extends into the bay south from the airport. Hotels, restaurants, and marinas take advantage of the gorgeous views across the bay of downtown, Point Loma, and Coronado. Facing the island along the waterfront is Spanish Landing Park, which commemorates the 1769 meeting of the sea and land expeditions of Gaspar de Portolá and Junípero Serra (see p29) which permanently brought the Spanish to California. ◈ Map B5

8 Marine Corps Recruit Depot

Listed on the National Register of Historic Places, the quaint Spanish-Colonial buildings were designed by Bertram Goodhue, architect of several buildings for the Panama-California Exposition in Balboa Park (see pp14–15). The Command Museum displays the history of the Marine Corps in Southern California and the wars in which they fought. Exhibits include photos, paintings, training films, weapons, and a World War II ambulance. ◈ Map B4 • 1600 Henderson Ave • (619) 524-4426 • Open 8am–4pm Mon–Sat (photo ID for Depot; proof of insurance if driving)

Tent City

When John D. Spreckels acquired ownership of the Hotel del Coronado in 1890, he felt the beauty of the area should be available to everyone. He built "Tent City," a makeshift town that catered to the less-well-to-do. Arriving by rail and car, families paid $4.50 a week to live in tents equipped with beds, dressers, and flush toilets. Amenities included carnival booths, Japanese gardens, a library, and children's bull fights. At its peak, the town held 10,000 visitors. The tents came down by 1939, when they could no longer compete with the rising popularity of the roadside motel.

9 Border Field State Park

As the endangered Western snowy plover seeks a place in which to lay her fragile eggs, the green-and-white vehicles of the US Border Patrol swoop down hillsides, lights blazing, in search of the illegal immigrant. An enormous, rusty, corrugated metal fence, which separates the US and Mexico, slices through the park before plunging into the sea. This southern part of the Tijuana River National Estuarine Research Reserve *(see p47)* attracts nature lovers who come to hike, ride horses, picnic on the beach, and birdwatch. On the Mexican side of the fence is a lively Mexican community and bullring *(see p41)*.

10 Chula Vista Nature Center

The center is located in the Sweetwater Marsh National Wildlife Refuge, one of the few accessible salt marshes left on the Pacific Coast. Rent some binoculars and climb to an observation deck to see how many of the 200 bird species that inhabit the refuge you can spot. Or you can also take a self-guided tour along interpretative trails. Children will enjoy petting bat rays and leopard sharks. The parking lot is located near the Baysite/E Street Trolley Station; a free shuttle will take you to the center. Map E3 • 1000 Gunpowder Point, Chula Vista • (619) 409-5900 • Open 10am–5pm Tue–Sun • Adm

Border Field State Park

A Bike Ride Around Coronado

Morning

Begin at **Bikes & Beyond** *(see p60)* at the **Ferry Landing Market Place**. Walk to the sidewalk facing the harbor and enjoy the city view. Pedestrians and joggers also use this sidewalk, so proceed cautiously. Around the corner, you'll face the **Coronado Bridge** *(see p24)*; the bougainvillea-covered walls on the right mark the **Marriott Resort** *(see p114)*. Information boards on the way depict harbor wildlife and a map indicates the various navy yards. Under the bridge, the path turns away from the water. At the street, bear left and cross over. There is no protected bike path, but traffic is light on Glorietta Blvd.

At the marina, the road will fork; take the lower road to the left. Turn right at the stop-light and get off your bike; bike riding is forbidden on Orange Avenue. At 1025 Orange Avenue, **Moo Time Creamery** serves delicious homemade ice cream and smoothies. Walk your bike back to **Hotel del Coronado** *(see p24)* and check out the shops on its lower level *(see p90)*. Leaving the hotel, bear left to Ocean Avenue; the Pacific Ocean is on the left and several 100-year-old mansions on the right. Turn right on Alameda and ride through a typical Coronado neighborhood with Spanish-style houses and bungalows. At 4th, cross the street and walk one block; the **Naval Air Station** will be on your left. Turn right on 1st. It's a straight stretch back to the Market Place.

Left **Shops at Ferry Landing Market Place** Right **Ocean Beach People's Organic Food Market**

TOP 10 Shops

1 Shops at the Hotel del Coronado
You'll find some of the best shopping in Coronado among these extensive shops in the hotel, including women's upscale casual wear, sunglasses, toys, jewelry, and the books of L. Frank Baum *(see p24)*.

2 Bay Books
This independent bookstore has helpful staff, an ample selection of books of local interest and international papers and magazines. ✆ Map C6 • 1029 Orange Ave, Coronado • (619) 435-0070

3 In Good Taste
A store that also operates a catering business, features select gourmet and entertainment items, as well as yummy chocolates. ✆ Map C6 • 1146 Orange Ave, Coronado • (619) 425-8356

4 La Provençale
Fabrics, tablecloths, pillows, purses, and a charming collection of hand-painted eggcups are imported from the South of France. ✆ Map C6 • 1126 Orange Ave, Coronado • (619) 437-8881

5 Kippys
Specializing in "things that glitter," you'll find clothes with lots of sparkles for the rodeo, salsa dancing, or that upcoming pageant. For everyday wear, go for the embellished denim and leather. ✆ Map C6 • 1114 Orange Ave, Coronado • (619) 435-6218

6 Ferry Landing Market Place
Next to the Coronado Ferry dock *(see p25)*, this place offers an eclectic selection of souvenirs, clothing, and galleries. A great farmers' market sets up on Tuesday afternoons. ✆ Map C6

7 Newport Avenue
The main drag through Ocean Beach is chock full of antique shops. Some doorways front malls with dozens of shops inside. Finds range from 1950s retro to Victorian and Asian antiques. ✆ Map B4 • Ocean Beach

8 Ocean Beach People's Organic Food Market
This co-op market has been selling organic, minimally processed natural foods since 1971. For food to go, try the upstairs vegan deli. Non-members are welcome but will be charged a small percentage more. ✆ Map B4 • 4765 Voltaire St • (619) 224-1387

9 Orange Blossoms
Fun, color, and whimsy set the style here. Chic clothing and accessories for women, stylish fashions for girls, and beautiful baby clothes. ✆ Map C6 • 952 Orange Ave, Coronado • (619) 437-8399

10 The Shops at Las Americas
Within walking distance of the border with Mexico, you can stop by this immense outlet center before or after a trip to Tijuana. ✆ Map E3 • San Ysidro

Previous pages: **View of San Diego and the marina**

Price Categories

Price categories include a three-course meal for one, half a bottle of wine, and all unavoidable extra charges including tax.	**$** under $20
	$$ $20–$40
	$$$ $40–$55
	$$$$ $55–$80
	$$$$$ over $80

Hodad's

🔟 Places to Eat

1 1500 Ocean
The elegant atmosphere here is light and airy, as is the distinctive cuisine. There is also a good choice of wines from Southern California's finest vineyards. ⓢ Map C6 • Hotel del Coronado, 1500 Orange Ave • (619) 435-6611 • $$$$$

2 Chez Loma
The luscious French cuisine will put you in heaven. Save with the early-bird special. ⓢ Map C6 • 1132 Loma Ave, Coronado • (619) 435-0661 • Closed Mon • Limited dis. access • $$$$

3 Miguel's Cocina
Colorfully-dressed waitresses serve up enormous plates and lethal margaritas. The enchiladas, tacos, and burritos are hearty. ⓢ Map C6 • 1351 Orange Ave, Coronado • (619) 437-4237 • $$

4 Peohe's
Popular for its views across the bay, fish and classic dishes are served with tropical island flair; desserts are exceptional. ⓢ Map C6 • 1201 1st St, Coronado • (619) 437-4474 • $$$$

5 Clayton's Coffee Shop
Old-fashioned, home-style cooking. A quarter buys three oldies at the jukebox. ⓢ Map C6 • 979 Orange Ave • (619) 435-5425 • No dis. access • No credit cards • $

6 Hodad's
At a beach café devoted to burgers, brews, and surf, soak up the ambience self-described as junkyard Gothic. ⓢ Map A4 • 5010 Newport Ave • (619) 224-4623 • $

7 Point Loma Seafoods
Order the freshest seafood in San Diego. Seafood salads and sushi are popular. ⓢ Map B5 • 2805 Emerson St • (619) 223-1109 • $$

8 Café 1134
This café with a patio offers a selection of sandwiches, wraps, and panini. Breakfast is served all day. ⓢ Map C6 • 1134 Orange Ave, Coronado • (619) 437-1134 • $

9 In-N-Out Burger
This fast food phenomenon relies only on burgers, fries, and drinks. Order "animal style," or "protein style" (a burger wrapped in lettuce). ⓢ Map B4 • 3102 Sports Arena Blvd • (800) 786-1000 • $

10 Mistral
Enjoy memorable California-Mediterranean cuisine while looking out onto the bay. ⓢ Map E2 • Loews Coronado Bay Resort, 4000 Coronado Bay Rd • (619) 424-4000 • $$$$

Unless otherwise stated, all restaurants are open daily, accept credit cards, serve vegetarian meals, and provide disabled access.

91

Left **Souvenirs at Avenida Revolución** Right **Mercado Hidalgo**

Shopping in Tijuana

1 Avenida Revolución
Keep a sense of humor, bargain hard, and remember: what you see is what you get. You may find some lovely folk art, a decent leather purse, and fine silver jewelry *(see p34)*.

2 Plaza Río Tijuana
Anchored by Dorian's department store, this large outdoor mall is the place for inexpensive clothes, shoes, and leather goods, and specialty and service shops. ✆ *Map E3 • Paseo de los Héroes*

3 Mercado de Artesanías
If you're walking over the border, wander through these shops first to get an idea about prices. Treasures exist amid the vast amounts of pottery, glassware, blankets, and baskets. ✆ *Map E3 • Calle 2 & Av Ocampo*

4 Mercado Hidalgo
Strolling through Tijuana's open-air food market is an amazing education in exotic fruits, herbs, and chilies. Indoor shops sell housewares and the largest *piñata* collections ever seen. ✆ *Map E3 • Av Independencia at Blvd Sánchez Taboada*

5 H Arnold
The best folk art shop on Revolución carries a fine selection of *alebrijes*, which cost far more in the US, and Ken Edwards earthenware from Tlaquepaque. ✆ *Map E3 • Av Revolución 1067*

6 Tolán
Although they don't have as much inventory as years past, you can still find glassware, Ken Edwards earthenware, and sculptures by the famed Mexican artist Sergio Bustamente. ✆ *Map E3 • Av Revolución 1471*

7 Plaza Zapato
Over 30 stores are devoted to the sandal, the mule, and the pump. Prices range from inexpensive to the still-affordable. ✆ *Map E3 • Paseo de los Héroes 9415*

8 Plaza Agua Caliente
This upscale shopping mall offers several fine restaurants and many clothing and shoe stores. It is also a center for health and beauty, with day spas, gyms, and specialist treatments. ✆ *Map E3 • Blvd Agua Caliente 4558*

9 Silver
Genuine Mexican silverwork is lovely. By law, it must have four identifying marks: "925," "Mexico," a tax identification number of the company, and the initials of the city of origin. Anything else is fake.

10 Farmacias
The hundreds of pharmacies in Tijuana cater mostly to Americans forced over the border by obscene US drug prices. You must have a prescription and can only bring back a reasonable personal amount.

Price Categories

Price categories include a three-course meal for one, half a bottle of wine, and all unavoidable extra charges including tax.	**$** under $20 **$$** $20–$40 **$$$** $40–$55 **$$$$** $55–$80 **$$$$$** over $80

Café La Especial

🔟 Places to Eat in Tijuana

1 La Diferencia
A charming plant-filled and tiled hacienda offers gourmet choices such as shrimp *chile rellenos*, cactus salad, and seafood. ◈ *Map E3 • Blvd Sánchez Taboada 10611, Zona Río • (664) 634-3346 • $$*

2 Palmazul
Specializing in Baja California cuisine, Palmazul has a frequently changing selection of fresh seafood, poultry, and venison seasoned with the flavors of Baja. ◈ *Map E3 • Blvd Salinas 11154, Col Aviación • (664) 622-9773 • $$*

3 Café La Especial
Since 1952, patrons have eaten the *carne asada* – a thin filet of marinated grilled beef – savory tacos, and enchiladas with gusto. ◈ *Map E3 • Av Revolución 718 • (664) 685-6654 • $*

4 Gypsy's
The influence of artists Antonio Gaudi, Salvador Dali, and Joan Miró is prominent in this little Spanish corner. A plate of tapas and paella go well with a glass of Spanish wine. ◈ *Map E3 • Pueblo Amigo • (664) 683-6006 • $$*

5 Chiki Jai
Spanish Jai Alai players from the Palacio Frontón *(see p34)* appreciated the Basque culinary specialties at this restaurant founded in 1947. Still Spanish-influenced, the food is delicious and well prepared. ◈ *Map E3 • Av Revolución 1388 • (664) 685-4955 • $$*

6 La Casa del Mole
The house specialty is *mole* sauce, which accompanies several meat dishes in this well-regarded restaurant. ◈ *Map E3 • Paseo de los Héroes 1501, Zona Río • (664) 634-6920 • No credit cards • $*

7 La Espadaña
The Spanish Mission-style dining room features mesquite-grilled meats, quail, and chicken filets. Breakfast here is one of the most popular in town. ◈ *Map E3 • Blvd Sánchez Taboada 10813, Zona Río • (664) 634-1488 • $*

8 La Fonda de Roberto
Traditional regional dishes from Mexico are served in this dining room with a courtyard. Entrees include meats with spicy *achiote* sauce, and *chile enogada*. ◈ *Map E3 • Blvd Cuauthémoc Suroeste 2800 • (664) 686-4687 • Closed Mon • $$*

9 La Escondida
A charming old hacienda and garden offers an excellent selection of international and Mexican cuisine, such as baby goat, roasted quail, and Châteaubriand. ◈ *Map E3 • Calle Santa Mónica 1, Las Palmas • (664) 681-4457 • $$*

10 La Cantina de los Remedios
Come here for traditional Mexican food accompanied by tequila or beer. This noisy restaurant has yellow walls, a ceiling mural, and bullfight posters. ◈ *Map E3 • Av Diego Rivera 2476 • (664) 634-3087 • $$*

Unless otherwise stated, all restaurants are open daily, accept credit cards and serve vegetarian meals.

Left **La Jolla's coastal view** Right **Feeding a giraffe at the Wild Animal Park**

Northern San Diego

*S*AN DIEGO'S EXPLOSIVE GROWTH *in the last decade has been concentrated in North County. With plenty of available land, prosperous hi-tech, biotech, commercial, and financial businesses have relocated here and now play a major role in the development of San Diego. Over one million people live in communities with distinct identities and attractions. Neighborhoods vary from the high-end rural estates of Rancho Santa Fe to the more modest housing of Marine Corps families in Oceanside. North County has wide-open spaces, rural charm, and geographical diversity to spare. From Camp Pendleton, travel past vast flower farms, avocado groves, and agricultural fields into mountain wilderness, and finish up in a spectacular desert.*

🔟 Sights

1. SeaWorld
2. La Jolla
3. San Diego Wild Animal Park
4. Mission San Luis Rey de Francia
5. Temecula Wine Country
6. Julian
7. Anza-Borrego Desert State Park
8. Palomar Observatory
9. Pacific Beach
10. Mission Beach

Shipwreck rapids at SeaWorld

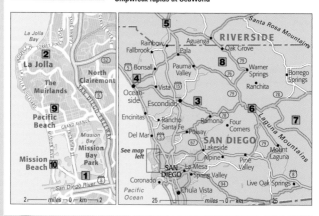

1 SeaWorld
Since 1964, SeaWorld has introduced over 100 million guests to marine life, with more than 35 attractions, exhibits, and shows. The park offers family-oriented thrill rides that compete with the numerous Southern California adventure parks. You can don a wetsuit and enter the dolphin pool in the Dolphin Interaction Program, or participate in Trainer For A Day, where you learn what it takes to be a killer whale and dolphin trainer. SeaWorld also hosts sleepovers, resident, and day camps (see pp30–31).

SeaWorld Adventure Camp complex

2 La Jolla
Spectacular and rich, with a gorgeous location and elegant restaurants and shops, this is an ideal destination. However, La Jollans do not sit around basking in their good fortune. Just north of the village along Torrey Pines Drive, some of the most prestigious research institutions in the world, many underwritten by La Jolla's residents, contribute to the good of humanity. Across the freeway, an area known as the Golden Triangle is a prosperous business and residential district with shops and restaurants (see pp32–3).

3 San Diego Wild Animal Park
Many people prefer the Wild Animal Park to its sister zoo in Balboa Park (see pp16–17). By monorail or a circuitous hiking trail, experience African and Asian animals roaming freely in enormous enclosures that replicate their natural environment. For the ultimate close-up encounter, reserve a spot on the photo caravan where an open-air truck takes you into the animal habitats. A successful breeding program has brought 125 cheetahs, 142 rhinos, and nearly extinct California condors and Arabian oryxes into the world. ◉ Map E2 • 15500 San Pasqual Valley Rd, Escondido • (760) 747-8702 • Open Jan–mid-Jun & mid-Sep–mid-Dec: 9am–4pm daily; mid-Jun–mid-Sep & mid-Dec–Dec 31: 9am–8pm daily • Adm

4 Mission San Luis Rey de Francia
Named after canonized French king Louis IX, this mission was the last to be established in Southern California. Franciscan padres oversaw enormous tracts of land devoted to cattle, sheep, and horses, and a Native American population of 2,800. Relations between the missionaries and the indigenous population were so successful that when Father Peyri was ordered by the Mexican government to return to Spain in 1832, the Native Americans followed him to San Diego Harbor. Today's restored mission offers displays on life and artifacts of the mission era. Still administered by Franciscan friars, the mission offers popular retreats. ◉ Map D1 • 4050 Mission Ave, Oceanside • (760) 757-3651 (ext. 117) • Open 10am–4pm daily • Adm • www.sanluisrey.org

Statue at Mission San Luis Rey de Francia

5 Temecula Wine Country

During the mission days, Franciscan friars recognized that San Diego's soil and climate were ideal for planting grape vines. However, it wasn't until the 1960s that wine was first produced commercially. Now over two dozen wineries stretch across rolling hills studded with oak trees, most of them along Rancho California Road. Wineries offer tastings for a small fee, and many of them operate restaurants and delis. Two of the most popular wineries in the area are Thornton Winery and Callaway Vineyard & Winery. ® Map E1 • Thornton Winery: 32575 Rancho California Rd • (951) 699-0099 • Callaway Vineyard & Winery: 32720 Rancho California Rd • (951) 676-4001

THORNTON WINERY

Thornton Winery logo

6 Julian

When Fred Coleman discovered gold here in 1869, scores of prospectors poured into the region. The boom was over in less than five years, but some stayed in this charming little community surrounded by oak and pine forests high in the Cuyamaca Mountains. Now this designated Historical District is filled with B&Bs, and it is a popular weekend getaway. Julian is also well known for its apple orchards (see p41).

7 Anza-Borrego Desert State Park

Fantastic geological formations, archeological sites, and sweeping desert vistas are only a backdrop for the wildlife found in the largest state park in the continental US. Golden eagles soar above, road-runners dart across the paths, and bighorn sheep dot the mountainsides.

Palomar Observatory at sunset

In springtime, a dazzling array of wildflowers create a magic show of colors across the desert. Stop by the visitor center to pick up a map that marks hiking trails, sites of Native American pictographs, and the park's best viewpoints. ® Map F2

8 Palomar Observatory

High atop one of North County's highest mountains, the dome of the observatory has an otherworldly look. Part of the California Institute of Technology, Palomar is home to the 200-in (508-cm) Hale Telescope, the largest optical instrument of its kind when installed in 1947. Its moving parts weigh 530 tons, the mirror 14.5 tons. Thanks to computer technology, no one "looks"

Brain Power

Beneath San Diego's image of "fun in the sun" is one of the country's most highly educated populations. San Diego has one of the highest PhDs per capita in the nation, 30 percent hold college degrees, and 20 percent of the county's adults are involved in higher education. La Jolla boasts some of the most prestigious research facilities: the Salk Institute, Scripps Research Institute, Scripps Institution of Oceanography, and UCSD.

through the telescope anymore; however, self-guided tours offer a look at the telescope itself; on some Saturdays, there are also docent-led tours. ❧ *Map E1 • 35899 Canfield Road, Palomar Mountain • (760) 742-2119 • Open 9am–4pm daily • Free*

9 Pacific Beach
Residents here enjoy an endless summer climate and an easy-going lifestyle. Life revolves around Garnet Avenue, lined with nightclubs, cafés, late-night restaurants, and shops. The street ends at the 1927 Crystal Pier, a great location to watch surfers, catch a fish, or spend the night in a tiny cottage. Come early to claim a fire ring on the beach and cook up some marshmallows, or bicycle along the boardwalk to Mission Beach *(see p65)*.

10 Mission Beach
The California beach scene struts in full glory along a narrow strip of land filled with vacation rentals and beachwear shops. Skaters, cyclists, and joggers whiz along the Strand, while surfers, volleyball devotees, and sun worshippers pack the sand. Sometimes the streets become so crowded on the Fourth of July weekend that the police have to shut the area down. A block away, Belmont Park *(see p52)* is an old-fashioned fun zone with bumper car rides and a vintage roller coaster *(see p64)*.

Mission Beach

A Walk in La Jolla

Morning

🕐 Begin by looking out the front door of the landmark **Hotel La Valencia** *(see p115)*. Turn left onto Prospect Street and walk past restaurants and art galleries. Before you reach Coast Boulevard, a stairway to the left leads to the **Sunny Jim Cave**. Steps lead through a tunnel into a fascinating, ocean-carved cave, named by L. Frank Baum *(see p39)*. To the left of the entrance a platform overlooks the caves. Continue along Coast Boulevard, admiring views of **Torrey Pines** and **Scripps Pier**. Pass through **Ellen Browning Scripps Park** *(see p46)*. Beyond the end of the park is **Children's Pool** *(see p53)*. Check out the seals and sea lions. Turn left on Cuvier Street and left onto Prospect Street. You'll now be at the **Museum of Contemporary Art** *(see p32)*. Check out the exhibits or have a snack in the café. Louis Gill designed the original museum and the older architecture in this area. Walk back toward the village and peek inside **780 Prospect St**; the cottage dates back to 1904. Cross Prospect at Fay but keep on Prospect. Pass through the Arcade Building to Girard Avenue. Turn right and window-shop along La Jolla's main street.

🛍 Of note is **Warwick's** at 7812, a stationer and bookstore, and **La Jolla Fiber Arts** *(see p99)*. Cross the street at Torrey Pines Road and double back on Girard. Time to enjoy delicious seafood sandwiches and light French entreés at **My Place** *(see p100)*.

Left **Solana Beach** Right **Miniature urban scene at Legoland**

🔟 North County Highway 101

1 Del Mar
The wealthiest community among North County's beach towns, Del Mar is filled with sidewalk cafés, restaurants, and boutiques. ⊗ Map D2

2 Solana Beach
At one of North County's most popular beach towns, Fletcher Cove Beach Park is perfect for swimming and walking. ⊗ Map D2

3 Cardiff-by-the-Sea
Surfers enjoy the reef break at Cardiff, while RV campers kick back at a beachside campground. The San Elijo Lagoon offers hiking trails through an ecological reserve. ⊗ Map D2

4 Encinitas
Voted one of the "Top 10 Surf Towns in the US" by *Surfer* magazine, local highlights include the Self-Realization Fellowship Retreat and Hermitage and the Quail Botanical Gardens. ⊗ Map D2
• Self-Realization Fellowship Retreat and Hermitage: 215 W K St • Quail Botanical Gardens: 230 Quail Gardens Dr • Adm

5 Leucadia
The 21st century hasn't yet hit this sleepy little town with a small beach and a few shops, restaurants, and galleries. ⊗ Map D2

6 The Flower Fields
In spring, the hillsides explode with brilliant-colored blossoms of the giant tecolote ranunculus. The Carlsbad Ranch harvests 6–8 million bulbs for export. ⊗ Map D1
• 5704 Paseo del Norte, Carlsbad • Adm

7 Legoland
This theme park and aquarium is devoted to the plastic brick. Kids enjoy the hands-on activities, rides, and models *(see p52)*.

8 Carlsbad
In the 1880s, Captain John Frazier discovered that the water here had the same mineral content as a spa in Karlsbad, Bohemia. Today, this pretty village still draws visitors with its beaches, resorts, and shops. ⊗ Map D1

9 Oceanside
Town fortunes are tied inevitably with adjoining Camp Pendleton. The California Surf Museum presents a history of the sport. ⊗ Map D1 • California Surf Museum: 223 N. Coast Hwy • (760) 721-6876 • Open 10am–4pm daily

10 Camp Pendleton
Several endangered species and abundant wildlife thrive at the largest US Marine Corps base and amphibious training facility in the country. ⊗ Map D1

Left **La Jolla Fiber Arts** Right **Sign for Cedros Design District**

Shopping

1 Nestlife
This upmarket boutique prides itself on its beautiful accessories for the home, including traditional tableware, fine china, crystal, and linen. ⊛ *Map N3 • 7636 Girard Ave, La Jolla • (858) 454-4200*

2 La Jolla Fiber Arts
Part-gallery with exhibitions and part-retail clothing store, textiles are beautifully crafted into works of art and couture. Tasteful jewelry and accessories coordinate well. ⊛ *Map N3 • 7644 Girard Ave, La Jolla • (858) 454-6732*

3 Ascot Shop
Men who are looking for a quality tailored jacket and conservative casual wear will find a wide selection at this upscale store. ⊛ *Map N3 • 7750 Girard Ave, La Jolla • (858) 454-4222*

4 My Own Space
Dedicated to personal style, this fun shop offers a variety of modern classics and original furnishings, as well as accessories for the home. ⊛ *Map N3 • 7840 Girard Ave, La Jolla • (858) 459-0099*

5 Pilar's Beachwear
There's no excuse to be without a swimsuit. Pilar's large selection of domestic and imported bikinis, one-pieces, and cover-ups, suitable for every age and body type, are in stock. ⊛ *Map A3 • 3745 Mission Blvd, Mission Beach (858) 488-3056*

6 Trader Joe's
This market sells imaginative salads, a wide variety of cheeses, wine, and fun ethnic food that you won't find in a regular supermarket. ⊛ *Map A3 • 1211 Garnet Ave • (858) 272-7235*

7 Carlsbad Premium Outlets
Shop for bargains in one of the most pleasant outlet centers around. The Gap, Bass, Banana Republic, and Jones New York are all here. ⊛ *Map D1 • 5620 Paseo del Norte, Carlsbad*

8 Cedros Design District
This former warehouse district has transformed into a shopping street full of design stores, furnishings, and boutiques. The 100 shops at the Leaping Lotus offer ethnic goods, clothing, and furniture. ⊛ *Map D2 • Cedros Ave, Solana Beach*

9 Del Mar Plaza
Italian home accessories, estate art, and well-known chains such as Banana Republic, and White House/Black Market cater to the discriminating. ⊛ *Map D2 • 1555 Camino Del Mar, Del Mar*

10 Winery Gift Shops
Most wineries in Temecula operate gift shops that stock unusual cookbooks, entertaining supplies, and home decor items. Additionally, many have delis where you can find picnic food to accompany that bottle of wine you just bought. ⊛ *Map E1*

Left **Wild Note Café** Right **Brockton Villa**

🔟 Cafés & Bars

1 Coyote Bar & Grill
Southwestern and Mexican-style appetizers and an extensive tequila menu keep this singles' hunting ground jumping. ◈ *Map D1 • 300 Carlsbad Village Dr, Carlsbad • (760) 729-4695 • $$*

2 Belly Up Tavern
Considered one of the best live music venues in the county, old Quonset huts have been acoustically altered to showcase almost famous and famous bands. ◈ *Map D2 • 143 S. Cedros Ave, Solana Beach • (858) 481-9022 • Adm*

3 Wild Note Café
Come here for lunch: salads and sandwiches are served outside or under ornamented and painted structural beams. Concert-goers from the Belly Up Tavern make dinners hectic. ◈ *Map D2 • 143 S. Cedros Ave, Solana Beach • (858) 720-9000 • $$*

4 Brockton Villa
This historic place offers breakfast, lunch, or dinner, and fabulous views. Choices include crab salad, seafood, and steak. ◈ *Map N2 • 1235 Coast Blvd, La Jolla • (858) 454-7393 • No dis. access • $$$*

5 Pannikin
You can't miss this coffeehouse housed inside a historic Santa Fe Railroad Depot. Grab a beverage and sit upstairs or outside on a shady deck. ◈ *Map D2 • 510 N. Coast Hwy 101, Leucadia • (760) 436-5824 • $*

6 Living Room Coffeehouse
If you're looking for a place to use your laptop, try this hip coffeehouse in upscale La Jolla. Grab a back table to enjoy their million-dollar view. ◈ *Map N2 • 1010 Prospect St • (858) 459-1187 • $*

7 Ruby's Diner
Walk 1,942 ft (591 m) out to the pier's end and reward yourself with a salad, Santa Fe or traditional burger, and a malt at this 1940s-style diner. ◈ *Map D1 • 1 Oceanside Pier, Oceanside • (760) 433-7829 • $*

8 Zinc Café
Great coffee, pastries, and a wide selection of vegetarian dishes make this cozy café a good choice for a shopping break at the Cedros Design Center. ◈ *Map D2 • 132 S. Cedros Ave, Solana Beach • (858) 793-5436 • $*

9 Dudley's Bakery
Boasting an almost cult-like popularity, everyone stops in this bakery and snack shop near Julian. Lines are long to buy loaves of 18 varieties of bread. ◈ *Map E2 • 30218 Hwy 78 & 79, Santa Ysabel • (760) 765-0488 • $*

10 My Place
Come for a casual lunch on the front patio. The fresh fish sandwiches, traditional French niçoise salads, and the crêpes with fresh berries are all popular choices. ◈ *Map N3 • 7777 Girard, La Jolla • (858) 454-3535 • $*

Unless otherwise stated, all restaurants are open daily, accept credit cards, serve vegetarian meals, and provide disabled access.

RESTAURANT · BAR · CAFE

Roppongi

🔟 Places to Eat

1 George's at the Cove
Whether you dine on the terrace or in the dining room, the service, food, and ocean views are always superb. 🔍 Map P2 • 1250 Prospect St • (858) 454-4244 • $$$ (terrace) • $$$$$ (dining room)

2 Osteria Romantica
Authentic Italian cuisine in a cheerful restaurant. Checkered tablecloths, painted chairs, and tile floors create a welcoming atmosphere. 🔍 Map Q2 • 2151 Avenida de la Playa • (858) 551-1221 • $$$

3 Roppongi
Pacific Rim tapas, such as Mongolian shredded duck quesadillas, make this place special. 🔍 Map N3 • 875 Prospect St • (858) 551-5252 • $$$$

4 101 Café
Since its 1928 beginnings as a roadside diner, celebrities and folks just passing through have enjoyed the home-style comfort food. 🔍 Map D1 • 631 S. Coast Hwy, Oceanside • (760) 722-5220 • $

5 The Cottage
At this lovely, quiet 1900s bungalow, the patio is the perfect place to enjoy a light breakfast or lunch. 🔍 Map N3 • 7702 Fay Ave • (858) 454-8409 • $$

6 Girard Gourmet
Select from salads, entrées, and sandwiches. Designer cookies are a specialty. 🔍 Map N2 • 7837 Girard Ave • (858) 454-3321 • $

7 Sushi Ota
Considered the best sushi in town, connoisseurs come for the day's freshest fish transformed into tasty works of art. 🔍 Map B3 • 4529 Mission Bay Dr • (858) 270-5670 • $$$$

8 Rubio's
As the first of a hugely successful Mexican fast-food chain, enjoy the best fish tacos this side of Baja. 🔍 Map B3 • 4504 E. Mission Bay Dr • (858) 272-2801 • $

9 Mille Fleurs
The most acclaimed restaurant in San Diego County is a culinary feast. Fireplaces, fresh flowers, and tapestries complement the exquisite and beautifully presented food. 🔍 Map E2 • 6009 Paseo Delicias, Rancho Santa Fe • (858) 756-3085 • $$$$$

10 Julian Café & Bakery
Home-style cooking in a Western atmosphere attracts locals and weekenders. The food isn't really memorable, but you won't forget the cowboy memorabilia. 🔍 Map F2 • 2112 Main St • (760) 765-2712 • No dis. access • $

Following pages: **Horton Plaza in downtown San Diego**

STREETSMART

SAN DIEGO'S TOP 10

Left **Tourist Office** Right **Gay and lesbian newspaper stands**

Planning Your Trip

Tourist Offices
Multilingual staff at the International Visitors Information Center can answers queries on activities and accommodation, and also sell tickets to attractions. Ask for a copy of the *Official Visitors Planning Guide*. The Mission Bay Visitor Information Center is handy if you're driving on the I-5 and need help with accommodation. The Coronado Visitors Center can give you a map of Coronado and suggest activities in the area.

Media
The *San Diego Reader* is the best source of the latest happenings in town. You'll find restaurant reviews, movies and theater timings, and music events. Free copies can be found throughout the city.

Internet
Websites offer useful information about package vacations, current events, new attractions, city services, transportation, sports, parks, and restaurants in San Diego.

Maps
Maps from the tourist information offices are good for basic sightseeing. To explore San Diego further, Auto Club maps give a good overview, or buy comprehensive street maps of the county published by Thomas Bros.

Visas
For visa information, international travelers should check with their embassy or the US Department of State's website. Canadian citizens only need proof of residence. US and Canadian citizens planning to travel to Tijuana for the day need to have a passport.

Insurance
Be sure to get comprehensive travel insurance before arriving in the US, or you can expect large bills even if you aren't denied medical care. If renting a car, establish what your auto insurer and credit card company covers in case of accident or theft. An auto insurance policy is not valid in Mexico; buy Mexican insurance at the border.

When to Go
San Diego enjoys the most temperate climate in the nation. The rainy season usually begins in December, with a few large storms rolling in by spring. Winter days can be warm and sunny, but ocean temperatures are cold. Summer showers are mild, and offshore breezes ensure pleasant evenings.

What to Take
Casual dress is the rule. Evenings can be cool, so tuck in a sweater or lightweight jacket.

How Long to Stay
Depending on your stamina, San Diego's sights can be covered in a week or less. SeaWorld and the Zoo tend to be exhausting all-day affairs, so plan a light day after your visits. Allow a few days to travel up the coast or around the backcountry.

Traveling with Children
San Diego is a non-stop kids' playground. Hotels welcome families, although some B&Bs are not set up for children. Many of the larger resorts feature kids programs and can supply names of licensed baby-sitters.

Directory

Tourist Offices
• *International Visitors Information Center*: (619) 236-1212
• *Mission Bay Visitor Information Center*: (619) 276-8200
• *Coronado Visitors Center*: (619) 437-8788

San Diego Reader
• www.sandiegoreader.com

San Diego Websites
• www.sandiego.org
• www.sandiego.gov
• www.signonsandiego.com

Auto Club Maps
• AAA office: 2440 Hotel Cir N, Mission Valley

Department of State
• http://travel.state.gov

Share your travel recommendations on traveldk.com

Left **San Diego International Airport, Lindbergh Field** Right **Greyhound Bus**

TOP 10 Getting to San Diego

1 San Diego International Airport – Lindbergh Field

Most flights land at Terminals 1 and 2, with Southwest Airlines located in Terminal 1. Short flights within Southern California operate from the Commuter Terminal. The only non-stop international flights fly to and from Mexico and Canada.

2 Getting into Town

Exiting Terminals 1 and 2, the skybridge links to the Transportation Plaza. Flyer Route 992 is a public bus that departs every 10 minutes and connects with the trolley and Amtrak before continuing up Broadway. Many hotels are only 10 minutes away.

3 Private Shuttles, Taxis, & Limo Services

Door-to-door shuttles are available at the airport's Transportation Plaza. Fares are based on distance and per person. Limo services can meet you in baggage claim. Call ahead to book a pickup to the airport.

4 Aeropuerto Internacional General Abelardo L. Rodríguez – Tijuana

Located 5 miles (8 km) east of downtown, frequent flights link Tijuana to the rest of Mexico. Domestic flights within Mexico are often cheaper than flying internationally from California.

5 Customs

Each person above 21 is allowed one liter of liquor and 200 cigarettes duty free. Citizens may bring in $400 worth of gifts, non-citizens $100. Cash exceeding $10,000 must be declared. Fresh produce, meats, and plants are prohibited.

6 Cruise Ships

All cruise ships moor at B Street Terminal along the Embarcadero on N. Harbor Drive. Ships sail to the Mexican Riviera or do mini-cruises to Ensenada and Catalina.

7 Amtrak Trains

Amtrak's Pacific Surfliners arrive at the historic Santa Fe Depot. About eleven trains travel daily to and from Orange County and Los Angeles, and several continue on to Santa Barbara.

8 Greyhound Buses

Greyhound buses operate 24 hours, are air conditioned, cheap, and cover the entire US and most of Canada. There are direct connections to LA, Las Vegas, and Phoenix, and buses from downtown to Tijuana's central bus terminal.

9 Car

From Los Angeles, I-5 passes along coastal towns, heads into downtown, and continues to the international border. Shortly before La Jolla, I-5 splits with I-805, re-connecting at the border. If coming from the east, I-8 passes through Mission Valley and ends just past SeaWorld. I-15 from Las Vegas serves inland San Diego County.

10 McClellan-Palomar Airport

This airport is useful if visiting North County. Some 30-miles (48-km) north of downtown, United Express flies shuttles to and from Los Angeles, and America West Express connects with Phoenix. Parking is free for up to two weeks.

Directory

Airports
- San Diego International Airport: (619) 400-2900
- Tijuana International Airport: (664) 607-8200
- McClellan-Palomar Airport: (760) 431-4646

Shuttles, Taxis, & Limo Services
- Cloud 9 Shuttle: (800) 974-8885 toll free
- Yellow Cab of San Diego: (619) 234-6161
- La Costa Limousines: (888) 299-5466 toll free

Amtrak Buses
- Santa Fe Depot: 1050 Kettner Blvd; (800) 872-7245

Greyhound Buses
- 120 W. Broadway; (619) 239-3266

Taxis charge by the car, so for three or four people a taxi may be cheaper than the airport shuttle.

Left **Detail of trolley sign** Center **Taxi** Right **Cyclists on Embarcadero**

🔟 Getting Around San Diego

Trolley

Inexpensive and fun, this light-rail system has three lines. The Blue line travels between Old Town, downtown, and San Ysidro. The Orange line is handy for the Gaslamp Quarter, the Convention Center, and Seaport Village. The Green line travels between Old Town and Santee. Tickets are available at station vending machines, and are good for buses too.

Buses

Buses connect with the North County Transit District, which serves coastal and inland San Diego County. Fares are payable in exact change as you board. The Transit Store offers maps and the *Way to Go!* brochure, which details how to reach sights by bus.

The Coaster

A regional rail service runs between downtown and Oceanside, stopping in Old Town, Sorrento Valley, Solana Beach, Encinitas, Carlsbad, and Oceanside. Trains run Monday to Saturday. Buy tickets at a vending machine and validate them before boarding.

Ferry

A fun way to travel to Coronado is on the San Diego–Coronado Ferry. It takes passengers and bicycles only. Buy your ticket at the San Diego Harbor Excursion Dock or the Ferry Landing Market Place in Coronado. Ferries leave San Diego at 9am and run hourly until 9pm, Sun–Thu, and an hour later on Friday and Saturday.

Cars

You won't need a car if you're only visiting downtown, but it's essential to get quickly around the rest of the city. A few car rental agencies have cars you can drive into Mexico. Don't forget to buy additional insurance at the border.

Taxis

Taxis don't cruise for fares. You can usually find one in front of large hotels, the airport, or some shopping centers. Rates are clearly posted on the taxi door; distances in San Diego can make some trips an expensive proposition.

Harbor Cruises

San Diego Harbor Excursion offers several ways to tour the harbor. One- and two-hour narrated trips cover the harbor, Shelter Island, Point Loma, Coronado Bridge, and more. Sunday brunch, dinner, nature and whale-watching cruises are also available.

Limousines

For a touch of luxury, limousines can be hired for one-way and round-trip transfers, or for the entire day. Drivers can provide you with good insider information.

Excursions

Old Town Trolley Tours circle Old Town, Seaport Village, Horton Plaza, Balboa Park, the Zoo, and Coronado. You can get on or off all day; the full circuit takes two hours. Gray Line San Diego offers narrated tours of the city, as well as day trips to Southern California theme parks and Mexico.

San Diego Water Taxi

On-call water taxis will transport you to locations around the harbor. They run from 3 to 10pm daily.

Directory

MTS Trolley & Buses
• (619) 231-1466; www.transit.511sd.com

Taxis, Limousines & Water Taxis
• San Diego Cab: (619) 226-8294 • Yellow Cab: (619) 234-6161 • Coronado Cab: (619) 435-6211
• La Costa Limousine: (888) 299-5466 toll free
• San Diego Water Taxi: (619) 235-8294

Harbor Cruises
• San Diego Harbor Excursion: 1050 N. Harbor Dr; (619) 234-4111

Excursions
• Old Town Trolley Tours: (619) 298-8687
• Gray Line San Diego: (800) 331-5077

Left **Cars queue up at the Mexico-Tijuana border** Right **Lifeguard vehicles**

🔟 Things to Avoid

1 Driving Frustrations
Morning and afternoon rush hour on Interstates is an appalling exercise in futility. A 30-minute drive on the I-5 can take hours. Ask someone at your hotel how to time things, and know your directions well. Parking in Mission Beach or La Jolla can be next to impossible in the summer.

2 Car Theft
San Diego's proximity to the Mexican border makes car theft a concern. Even if your car is found across the border, the paperwork to bring it back is a nightmare. Neighborhoods prone to theft include Pacific Beach, San Ysidro, and Mission Valley.

3 Driving Without Insurance in Mexico
If your car is stolen while over the border, your US car insurance won't cover it. If you are in any way associated with an accident, your vehicle will be impounded and you will be arrested until liability is sorted out. Protect yourself by buying a policy before driving over the border.

4 Narcotraficantes
Narcotraficantes, or drug smugglers, thrive along the border with the local drug cartel. A clampdown in Tijuana resulted in open conflict between drug dealers and law enforcement in early 2008. Visit the US State Department website (http://tijuana.usconsulate.gov) for current travel conditions. Visitors to Mexico should use common sense and limit explorations to popular tourist areas when travel advisories are in place.

5 Sun
Slather on the sunscreen during the day and be sure to take a hat whenever you're outdoors, especially at SeaWorld and the Zoo. California has one of the country's highest incidences of skin cancer; no surprise since people pursue outdoor activities year round.

6 High Surf
Dangerous riptides can occur along the coastal beaches; ask the lifeguards about swimming conditions at an unfamiliar beach. Posted green flags indicate safe swimming, yellow mean caution, and red flags denote hazardous surf. If you are caught in a riptide, don't try to swim directly to shore; let the current carry you down the coast until it dies out, and then swim in.

7 Water Contamination
Ocean waters are generally clean, except after a heavy storm. Accumulated and untreated runoff from miles away washes down storm drains and empties into the ocean, and sewer leaks are common. Especially hard-hit beaches are Imperial Beach and Border Field State Park. There are signs indicating safety levels of the water.

8 Smoking
Smoking is forbidden inside any public enclosed area, including restaurants and bars, although a few establishments have designated smoking patios. The city of San Diego has banned smoking on beach boardwalks, seawalls, and piers; some communities are trying to forbid smoking on streets and beaches. It's possible to spend your entire vacation in San Diego without smelling a single cigarette.

9 Panhandlers
Like any major city, San Diego has its share of panhandlers, most of whom are not aggressive. Downtown has the largest concentration, followed by the beach towns, including La Jolla.

10 Crime
San Diego is a safe city; most petty crime is limited to theft and car break-ins. Common sense prevails: don't walk around late at night; don't leave valuables inside your car; and don't give an angry salute to a driver who's cutting you off.

The San Diego Union-Tribune *publishes beach pollution reports on its weather pages.*

Left **San Diego Museum of Art, Balboa Park** Right **Rose Garden at Balboa Park**

🔟 Budget Tips

1 Airline Deals
When flying into Southern California, consider an open-jaw ticket, with which you can fly into Los Angeles and depart from San Diego. Two good budget airlines are Southwest Airlines and JetBlue.

2 Hotel Discounts
Discounts are offered to Auto Club members, military personnel, corporate employees, and retirees. The best on-line prices and rooms are usually on the hotel's own website. Contacting the hotel directly might find you a lower rate.

3 Free Museum Days
Every museum in Balboa Park offers free admission on one Tuesday of every month to their permanent exhibits; special traveling exhibits or programs still charge admission. The Museum of Contemporary Art in La Jolla and in downtown San Diego is free on Thursdays 5–7pm.

4 Coupons
Stop by the tourist brochure racks at hotels, restaurants, and visitor centers to pick up discount coupons for museums, SeaWorld, the Zoo, car rentals, hotels, and restaurants. Promotional coupons can often be found in Sunday papers and the *San Diego Reader* (see p104).

5 Entertainment & Attractions For Free
Unwind in Balboa Park, daydream in the lobby of Hotel del Coronado, or hang out on the Mission Beach boardwalk. Hear a free Sunday concert at the Spreckels Organ Pavilion. Check out the local talent in cafés and bars. Walkabout International organizes free daily walking tours.

6 Parking
Many hotels operate shuttles to SeaWorld and other attractions. Parking at the Zoo, Balboa Park, and Old Town is free, as well as at many trolley stops. At Horton Plaza, buy anything and receive a few hours of validated parking. At the Tijuana border, park for free on the street in front of the outlet center.

7 Gasoline
San Diego has some of the highest gas prices in the US. If you fill up in La Jolla or along the freeways, you'll be broke. Look for stations away from the coast and tourist attractions; Arco stations tend to be the lowest priced.

8 Multiple Theme Park Passes
The "Best of Balboa Park Combo" includes the Zoo and park museums for a set number of days. Other packages include variations of the Zoo, Wild Animal Park, and SeaWorld. The "Go San Diego Card" includes the Zoo, Wild Animal Park, Legoland, and many other attractions.

9 Arts Tix
Tickets for music, dance, and theater performances throughout the San Diego area are available for half price at a kiosk in front of Horton Plaza. A small service fee is charged.

10 Transportation Passes
Stop by the Transit Store to pick up a transit pass good for buses of the Metropolitan Transit System, the North County Transit District, and the San Diego Trolley. Passes are available for 1–4 days, the last half of the month, or an entire month.

Directory

Airlines
• *Southwest Airlines: (800) 435-9792*
• *JetBlue: (800) 538-2583*

Walkabout International
• *(619) 231-7463*

Arts Tix
• *(619) 497-5000*

Transportation Passes
• *Transit Store: www.sdcommute.com*

Left **Disabled sign at hotel entrance** Right **Disabled-friendly trolley**

🔟 Special Needs Tips

1 Disabled Parking
Reserved parking spaces are marked by a blue curb, a blue-and-white wheelchair logo on the pavement, and by a posted sign. You may also park with no charge at any regular parking metered area. A special disabled placard must be displayed at all times.

2 Hotels & Restaurants
Hotels with over five rooms must provide accessible accommodation to disabled guests. Always call in advance to reserve one of these rooms, and specify if you need a roll-in shower. When making restaurant reservations, do clarify that you require access.

3 Transportation
All buses, the San Diego Trolley, and the Coaster are equipped with lifts. Amtrak trains have a limited number of accessible spaces and recommend advance reservations. Greyhound provides a lift-equipped bus with advance notice. The Cloud 9 Shuttle provides transportation from the airport, also with advance notice.

4 Accessible San Diego
The excellent booklet *Access In San Diego* gives specific access information on many hotels, restaurants, and shopping centers. Also included are tour bus companies, public and private transportation firms equipped with lifts, and car rental agencies that offer hand-controlled vehicles. You'll also find a directory of medical equipment suppliers and disability organizations.

5 Power Beach Chairs
Imperial Beach and Mission Beach have power and manual beach chairs, while Ocean Beach, La Jolla Shores, and Coronado offer manual chairs. Advance reservations and ID are required. You must be able to get into and out of the chair.

6 Ramped Curbs
Every intersection and sidewalk in San Diego has ramped curbs or at least a ramped driveway. Ramped access is standard in government buildings, universities, concert halls, museums, some theaters, and large hotels and restaurants.

7 Accessible Toilets
The universal wheelchair symbol indicates those restrooms that are private unisex or single occupancy with locking doors.

8 San Diego Zoo
The park map indicates walkways where you may need extra assistance if your mobility is limited or you're in a wheelchair. Have any employee call for shuttle assistance if you need it. Regular and motorized wheelchairs are available for rent near the zoo entrance.

9 Balboa Park
Older buildings are now in compliance for disabled access. Free park trams have been equipped with wheelchair lifts, and most restrooms are wheelchair accessible. For those with special needs and with advanced arrangement, the education office of most museums can supply a staff member to escort and narrate tours.

10 Tijuana
No federal law in Mexico requires businesses to provide disabled access. Many curbs in Tijuana are ramped, but the drawback is the poor, often hazardous condition of the sidewalks. Yet, many mobility-impaired people do successfully navigate the streets.

Directory

Cloud 9 Shuttle
• *(800) 974-8885*

Accessible San Diego
• *(858) 279-0704; www.accessandiego. org*

Beaches
• *Imperial (619) 685-7972*
• *Mission (619) 525-8247*

Left **Fire Engine** Center **Pharmacy sign** Right **Women's restroom sign**

🔟 Security & Health

1 Consulates
Some European consuls only deal with trade issues; they do not issue passports or visas. In an emergency, contact your embassy in Washington, DC or LA. Dial 411 for assistance.

2 If You Lose Everything
Before leaving home, it is advisable to photocopy all important papers. If you lose your wallet, make a police report, notify your credit card companies, and notify the credit-reporting companies to prevent identity theft. You can have money wired through Western Union.

3 911
During an emergency, dial this number free from any telephone. Be prepared to specify if medical and/or police assistance is needed and your location. Call the police department for all other matters.

4 Hospitals
San Diego has some of the country's best hospitals. If your situation is not life threatening, urgent care clinics are less expensive. Call your insurance company for a referral to a local doctor or clinic.

5 Pharmacies
CVS and Rite-Aid have 24-hour pharmacies.

6 Helplines
If you don't have health insurance, head to a community clinic. Expect to pay on the spot for services rendered. Look in the Yellow Pages under "clinics" to find a walk-in clinic.

7 If You're in a Car Accident
Call 911 if anyone is injured. Call the police if property damage appears to be over $500 and/or you need a police report. Drivers must exchange driver's license information and all vehicle insurance details. If you're in a rental car, report any accidents or vehicle damage to the agency immediately.

8 Seatbelts
It is California law for all passengers in the car to wear seatbelts. If not, you can be pulled over by the police and ticketed. Children under six and who weigh less than 60 lbs (27 kg) must be secured in a car safety seat. If renting a car, request the agency for a child seat in advance.

9 Public Restrooms
All major attractions have restrooms, as do gas stations and restaurants. Shopping centers, public buildings, libraries, and large hotels are other places to try. Beach restrooms are an option if you can't find a better alternative.

10 Food & Water Safety
All restaurants are required to post a letter grade, indicating the sanitation level, in their front window. An "A" means the restaurant has passed inspection; a "B" is passing, but sanitation issues exist; with a "C," a restaurant has 30 days to improve or risk closure. Water from the faucet is safe to drink but may not taste great.

Directory

Consulates
• Consulate General of Mexico: (619) 231-8414
• US Consulate, Tijuana: (664) 622-7400
• British Consulate, Tijuana: (664) 686-5320

Emergency Numbers
• San Diego Police Department: (619) 531-2000 • Medical or police assistance: 911

24-hour Emergency Rooms
• Scripps Hospital, La Jolla: (858) 457-4123
• Scripps Mercy Hospital: (619) 294-8111

Pharmacies
• CVS: 313 E. Washington • Rite-Aid: 535 Robinson Ave

Helplines
• Council of Community Clinics: (619) 542-4300
• 24–hour Rape & Battering Hotline: (858) 272-1767

Left **Bureau de Change** Center **ATM** Right **UPS post boxes**

🔟 Banking & Communications

1 Exchange
San Diego International Airport has international exchange kiosks in Terminal 1 and Terminal 2. Major banks handle most transactions; bring plenty of ID. Large hotels exchange currency as well, but offer low rates. Exchange windows in San Ysidro handle transactions in dollars and pesos.

2 ATMs
There are 24-hour Automatic Teller Machines all over the city. Look behind your ATM or credit card to see which banking network it's associated with. ATMs inside convenience stores or malls charge you for the convenience, as does your own bank if you go outside the network.

3 Banks
Most major banks are found throughout San Diego. Banking hours are usually 9 or 10am–6pm, Monday through Friday, with Saturday hours from 9am–1 or 2pm.

4 Traveler's Checks
Traveler's checks are good for backup in case your ATM card is swallowed. Most hotels, restaurants, and shops cash them with ID; sometimes banks charge a fee. Checks should always be in US dollars. Personal checks are difficult to cash.

5 Telephone
If using a telephone at a hotel, ask what the specific charges are first. Coin-operated pay phones can be found at hotels, some restaurants, and at gas stations, but not all of them accept incoming calls. If calling Mexico, dial 011–52 followed by the three-digit city code and seven-digit local number.

6 Phone Cards
Available all over the city, pre-paid phone cards eliminate the need for coins at public phones. Read the card before buying it; many of them charge a three-minute minimum even if you talk for less than that.

7 Internet
The San Diego Public Library offers Internet access, as do hostels. San Diego has more than 200 Internet cafés with Wi-Fi. Several Starbucks coffee shops offer coffee while surfing. Lestat's Coffee House (see p56) and the Gelato Vero Caffe offer free wireless access.

8 Post Offices
Regular post office hours are 8:30am–5pm Mon–Fri, with some branches open on Saturday mornings. Stamps are usually available from vending machines in the lobby, and signage indicates the cost of postage for mail sent to domestic and international addresses. Hotel concierges can post mail for you.

9 Shipping
Franchised United Parcel Service stores throughout the city will package and ship for you. Regular parcel post at the post office is the cheapest, and some branches sell boxes and tape. Packages shipped internationally can take over a month for delivery.

10 Courier Services
Federal Express, DHL, and UPS have guaranteed overnight delivery and reliable international service. Many offices sell packaging supplies. Much cheaper, the US Postal Service offers overnight service in the continental US and two–three day service internationally.

Directory

Exchange
• Travelex:
177 Horton Plaza

Internet
• Starbucks:
511 F St
• Gelato Vero Caffe:
3753 India St

Post Offices
• Downtown:
815 E. St

Courier Services
• DHL: (800) 225-5345
• FedEx: (800) 463-3339
• UPS: (800) 742-5877

> You'll need a laptop to use the free wireless access at Lestat's and Gelato Vero Caffe; they do not offer computer terminals.

Left **Pilar's Beachwear shop at Mission Bay Beach** Right **Drugstore in Tijuana**

TOP 10 Shopping Tips

1 Bargaining in Mexico

Bargaining is an ancient art and social exchange in Mexico. The rule of thumb is to offer half the asking price and work up from there. If the vendor senses you really want an item, he or she will stand firm. Remain polite and remember the vendor needs to earn a living. Department stores, upscale shops, and restaurants all have fixed prices.

2 Kobey's Swap Meet

Wear comfortable shoes, bring cash, and come early to walk the 21 aisles of this enormous outdoor flea market. Merchants sell clothing, plants, jewelry, luggage, electronics, sporting goods, and much more. Always ask sellers: "Is that your best price?"

3 Shopping Malls

The best shopping mall bargains can be found around public holidays. Department stores sometimes bring in outside merchandise to sell at "bargain" prices. Malls with concierge services sometimes have discount booklets.

4 Outlet Centers

San Diego has three outlet centers within an hour's driving distance: the Carlsbad Company Stores in North County,

the Shops at Las Americas at San Ysidro, and Viejas Outlet Center on the Viejas Indian Reservation east on I-8. You can usually find good deals at the designer spin-off shops.

5 Garage Sales

To meet San Diegans, drive around residential areas on any given Saturday and you'll find them selling items in their driveways. To locate garage sales, look for signs posted on telephone poles or find a copy of the *Pennysaver*, which lists addresses.

6 Senior Discounts

Senior discounts are offered at movie halls, restaurants, hotels, and shops. Some theater chains deem senior status at age 55, and many retail stores designate a certain day of the week for senior discounts. Use your AARP (American Association of Retired Persons) card when booking hotels.

7 Taxes

Current sales tax in San Diego is 7.75 percent. A non-refundable sales tax is added to all retail purchases and restaurant checks. Food items in grocery stores are not taxed unless they are for immediate consumption. If a store is shipping your purchase to an out-of-state address, you

shouldn't pay sales tax. Hotel tax is 10.5 percent.

8 Shopping Hours

Retail shops usually open at 10am and close from 5–6pm. Regular hours at shopping malls are 10am–9pm Mon–Sat and 11am–7pm Sun. Department stores sometimes open at 7am for super sales or extend their hours during the Christmas season. Malls close only during a few major holidays.

9 Open 24 Hours

You shouldn't have any trouble finding a 24-hour convenience store selling groceries. Many Ralph's and Albertson's supermarkets are open all night. A 24-hour CVS *(see p110)* has grocery items, and some office supplies can be found at FedEx Office.

10 Returns

Most stores accept returns, unless the item was bought on sale. Stores usually post their returns policy in a prominent place. Many accept returns for in-store credit only.

Directory

Kobey's Swap Meet
• *3500 Sports Arena Blvd*
• *7am–3pm Fri–Sun*

FedEx Office
• *8849 Villa La Jolla Dr, La Jolla*

Left **Farmers' Market** Right **Liquor bottles on sale in Tijuana**

🔟 Eating & Accommodation Tips

Farmers' Markets
Local farmers sell fresh vegetables, fruit, and specialties such as tamales, cheese and bread at special markets around the city. Seasonal produce is usually of much better quality and price than at the super-market. Take a supply of single dollar bills to make quick purchases.

Lunches & Early Bird Dinners
Entrées on the lunch menu are often half the price of those at dinner. Some restaurants offer early-bird dinners from 4–6pm, with a limit-ed number of entrées at a considerable discount.

Picnics
Make the most of San Diego's beautiful parks and beaches. Get items to go from restaurants, or stop by markets such as Trader Joe's (see p99) in Pacific Beach to pick up salads, sushi, and deli items.

Tipping
Most food servers expect a 15–20 percent tip; leave it in cash or add it to your credit card bill. If the service is truly awful, you're not obliged to tip. With large parties, 18 percent gratuity is automatically added to the check.

Alcohol Age Limit
The legal drinking age in California is 21.

If you look under 30, restaurant servers and merchants selling alcohol will ask to see your photo identification. In Tijuana, the legal drinking age is 18.

Fast Food
Fast food restaurants are the cheapest way to eat, are easily found, and many are open all night. San Diego is the birth-place to two fast food chains, Rubio's and Jack-in-the-Box.

Happy Hours
Many restaurants and bars offer happy hours on weekdays. For the price of a drink and a few dollars, snack on anything from a hot buffet to chips and dip. Some Mexican restau-rants sell cheap tacos on "Taco Tuesdays." Check out the advertisements in the San Diego Reader (see p104).

Motel Chains
Staying at a motel chain offers standardized accommodation. Most major chains can be found in Mission Valley's Hotel Circle. Parking is generally free, breakfast is often supplied, and you aren't charged countless petty fees.

Apartments & Extended Stay
If you plan to stay in San Diego for more than a few weeks, consider renting an apartment.

Summer rentals, especially along the beach, are more costly. Always ask what amenities are included.

Camping
The only comfortable place to camp legally near the city is in Chula Vista. The well-located campground offers a swimming pool, hot tub, and bicycle rentals. If desperate, try sleeping at the airport, or rent a cheap car and sleep in a motel parking lot. RV owners can try Campland on the Bay, who also accept tent campers.

Directory

Farmers' Markets
- 3960 Normal St, Hill-crest: 9am–1pm Sun
- 1st & B, Coronado: 2:30–6pm Tue • Ocean Beach: 4–8pm Wed
- Horton Square: 225 Broadway 11am–3pm Thu
- Mission Blvd (btw Reed & Pacific Beach Blvd): 8am–noon Sat

Apartment Rentals
- Penny Property Management: (858) 272-3900
- San Diego Vacation Rentals: (619) 296-1000

Camping
- San Diego Metro KOA: 111 N. 2nd Ave, Chula Vista, (619) 427-3601
- Campland On the Bay: 2211 Pacific Beach Dr, (858) 581-4200

Left **The Lodge at Torrey Pines** Right **Façade of W**

TOP 10 Luxury Hotels

1 The Lodge at Torrey Pines

Located on the cliffs of Torrey Pines, this lodge offers exquisite accommodation. Rooms look out onto a courtyard which reflects the surrounding coastal environment and the greens of the Torrey Pines Golf Course. Early California Impressionist art graces the walls and signature restaurant. ◉ Map D2 • 11480 N. Torrey Pines Rd, La Jolla • (858) 453-4420 • www.lodgetorreypines. com • $$$$$

2 Hilton San Diego Gaslamp Quarter

Beautifully appointed rooms with down comforters, loft apartments, and individual attention from the staff make this downtown's best choice. It's located right next to the Convention Center, the Gaslamp Quarter, and Petco Park. ◉ Map K6 • 401 K St • (619) 231-4040 • www.hilton.com • $$$$$

3 Westgate

No expense was spared in re-creating the anteroom of the Palace of Versailles in the front lobby. Baccarat crystal chandeliers, Persian carpets, and French tapestries are just backdrops to the gracious service. European furniture graces rooms equipped with marble baths. ◉ Map J4 • 1055 2nd Ave • (619) 238-1818 • www. westgatehotel.com • $$$$$

4 W

Everyone wants to be part of the W's hip weekend scene. It's all about sleek design and "anytime, anywhere" service. The rooms are fun and have window seats. ◉ Map H4 • 421 West B St • (619) 398-3100 • www.whotels.com • $$$$$

5 Hotel Parisi

The Mediterranean meets Feng Shui design in this boutique hotel. The rooms are tranquil and minimalist, yet hip. Try one of the 30 in-room spa treatments and then roll into Egyptian cotton sheets and a goose down duvet. ◉ Map N2 • 1111 Prospect St, La Jolla • (858) 454-1511 • www. hotelparisi.com • $$$$$

6 Marriott Coronado Island Resort

Lush grounds with a few flamingos, a relaxed ambience, and a dedicated staff make this resort a top choice. A California and French styling decorates large, comfy rooms, with the best ones looking out across the bay to San Diego. The hotel runs a water taxi service. ◉ Map C6 • 2000 2nd St, Coronado • (619) 435-3000 • www.marriott. com/sanci • $$$$

7 Pacific Terrace

Sunset views over the Pacific define high living at one of San Diego's finest beach hotels. Large guest rooms come with a balcony or patio. There's no full-service restaurant, but the friendly staff can suggest neighborhood choices. ◉ Map A3 • 610 Diamond St • (858) 581-3500 • www.pacificterrace. com • $$$$

8 Hotel Solamar

This hip boutique hotel in the Gaslamp Quarter offers a complimentary wine hour every evening in the fireplace lounge. California cuisine features at the JSix restaurant, and the fourth-floor pool deck with J6Bar and fire pits is popular with locals and visitors. ◉ Map J5 • 435 6th Ave • (619) 819-9500 • www. hotelsolamar.com • $$$$$

9 Manchester Grand Hyatt San Diego

Two high-rise towers hold 1,625 rooms, many with personal work areas and all with high-speed Internet. The lounge on the 40th floor is one of San Diego's best. ◉ Map H5 • 1 Market Place • (619) 232-1234 • www.manchester grand.hyatt.com • $$$$$

10 La Casa del Zorro

Accommodations range from large rooms to private *casitas*, and most have private pools and fireplaces. You can swim, hike, or play golf or tennis. ◉ Map F1 • 3845 Yaqui Pass Rd, Borrego Springs • (760) 767-5323 • www.lacasa delzorro.com • $$$$

Unless otherwise stated, all hotels accept credit cards, have private bathrooms, air conditioning, and provide dis. access.

La Valencia

🔟 Heritage & Vintage Hotels

1 Hotel del Coronado

This National Historic Landmark re-creates a bygone golden age. Suites in the original Victorian building have balconies that face a lovely white-sand beach. Restaurants, boutiques, and swimming pools add to the aristocratic character. ◎ Map C6 • 1500 Orange Ave, Coronado • (619) 435-6611 • www. hoteldel.com • $$$$$

2 La Valencia

Since 1926, the "Pink Lady of La Jolla" has enchanted with its splendid Mediterranean ambience, exquisite decor, and ideal location on the cliffs above La Jolla Cove. Rooms vary from quite small to large ocean villas. ◎ Map N2 • 1132 Prospect St, La Jolla • (858) 454-0771 • www. lavalencia.com • $$$$$

3 Horton Grand Hotel

Rebuilt from two Victorian-era hotels, this hotel reflects the character of the Gaslamp Quarter. Rooms are individually decorated in period style and each has a gas fireplace. ◎ Map J5 • 311 Island Ave • (619) 544-1886 • www. hortongrand.com • $$$

4 U.S. Grant

Ulysses S. Grant Jr. commissioned this stately 1910 Renaissance palace. A $56-million renovation has restored its past glory, with mahogany furniture and paneling, tile floors, and luxurious rooms. ◎ Map J4 • 326 Broadway • (866) 837-4270 • www.usgrant. net • $$$$$

5 Gaslamp Plaza Suites

Now on the National Register of Historic Places, much of the 1913 craftsmanship of this building remains, such as Australian gumwood, Corinthian marble, and an elevator door made of brass. Complimentary breakfast is served on the rooftop terrace. ◎ Map K4 • 520 E St • (619) 232-9500 • www. gaslampplaza.com • $$$

6 Glorietta Bay Inn

Many of the original fixtures of John D. Spreckels' (see p25) 1908 Edwardian mansion remain, including hand-made plaster moldings, chandeliers, and a marble staircase. Splurge on one of the antique-filled guest rooms inside the house. ◎ Map C6 • 1630 Glorietta Blvd, Coronado • (619) 435-3101 • www. gloriettabayinn.com • $$$$

7 The Grande Colonial

La Jolla's first hotel was designed by Richard Requa (see p44). The 1913 building houses luxury suites, while a 1926 building contains the main hotel. Elegantly appointed rooms are in keeping with the hotel's European ambience. ◎ Map N3 • 910 Prospect St, La Jolla • (858) 454-2181 • www.thegrande colonial.com • $$$$

8 Balboa Park Inn

This B&B is housed in Spanish-Colonial style buildings constructed in 1915. The Orient Express room features a Chinese rosewood bed, and the Beach House is decorated in shades of ocean blue. ◎ Map D5 • 3402 Park Blvd • (619) 298-0823 • No dis. access • www.balboapark inn.com • $$

9 Park Manor Suites

This 1926 inn was popular with Hollywood celebrities en route to holidays in Mexico in the 1920s and 30s. The original fixtures lend a delightful retro touch. ◎ Map C5 • 525 Spruce St • (619) 291-0999 • No air conditioning • No dis. access • www.parkmanor suites.com • $$

10 The Inn at Rancho Santa Fe

Refined elegance distinguishes this romantic country inn. Many of the red-roofed adobe casitas scattered about the lush grounds boast comfy queen-sized beds, fireplaces, and kitchens. ◎ Map E2 • 5951 Linea del Cielo, Rancho Santa Fe • (858) 756-1131 • www.theinnatrancho santafe.com • $$$$

Left **Façade of San Diego Marriott Hotel & Marina** Right **Fountain at Westin Hotel**

TOP10 Business Hotels

1 San Diego Marriott Hotel & Marina

Most rooms at this busy hotel are set up with worktables and high-speed Internet. The marina and waterfall swimming pool make great distractions. ☒ Map J6 • 333 W. Harbor Dr • (619) 234-1500 • www. marriotthotels.com • $$$$

2 Omni San Diego Hotel

A skyway links the hotel to Petco Park, and you can even see the ball field from some rooms. Comfy rooms sport great bathrooms, and if you must tend to business, the Convention Center is a few blocks away. ☒ Map K6 • 675 L St • (619) 231-6664 • www. omnihotels.com • $$$$

3 Wyndham San Diego at Emerald Plaza

You can't miss this hotel's green silhouette of hexagonal glass towers. Amenities include ergonomic work chairs and high-speed Internet access. The Convention Center is within walking distance. ☒ Map H4 • 400 W. Broadway • (619) 239-4500 • www.wyndham.com • $$$

4 Westin Gaslamp Quarter San Diego

Attached to Horton Plaza, this downtown hotel is close to restaurants and entertainment venues.

Business travelers appreciate the workout room and swimming pool. Gaslamp and the Convention Center are within walking distance. ☒ Map J4 • 910 Broadway Cir • (619) 239-2200 • www. westin.com • $$$$

5 Embassy Suites Hotel San Diego Bay

Guests enjoy spacious suites that have a living area and a separate bedroom. All rooms open onto a palm tree-filled atrium and a view of the bay or city. Ask for the complimentary airport transportation. ☒ Map H5 • 601 Pacific Hwy • (619) 239-2400 • www.embassy suites.com • $$$

6 Sheraton San Diego Hotel & Marina

Conveniently located near the aiport, this immense property has over 1,000 rooms, bike paths, a marina, a tennis court, and a swimming pool. ☒ Map C5 • 1380 Harbor Island Dr • (619) 291-2900 • www.sheraton. com • $$

7 Hilton La Jolla Torrey Pines

This low key but chic hotel is located next to the Torrey Pines Golf Course. A valet can look after your immediate needs, and a car service is available to drive you to La Jolla. All rooms have balconies

or terraces and many have ocean or harbor views. ☒ Map D2 • 10950 N. Torrey Pines Rd, La Jolla • (858) 558-1500 • www. hilton.com • $$$$$

8 San Diego Marriott Mission Valley

At this hotel, a business center and accommodating staff attract a regular business clientele. Take advantage of the swimming pool, fitness room, tennis courts, and jogging trail. ☒ Map D4 • 8757 Rio San Diego Dr • (619) 692-3800 • www.marriott hotels.com/sanmv • $$

9 Town & Country Resort & Convention Center

This sprawling 50-year-old resort has an on-site convention center and 1,000 rooms. Next door is a golf course, a trolley stop, and the Fashion Valley Mall. ☒ Map C4 • 500 Hotel Circle N • (619) 291-7131 • www. towncountry.com • $$

10 Hyatt Regency La Jolla

Post-Modern architect Michael Graves designed this Italian-style palace hotel. A large fitness spa and highly acclaimed restaurants are next door. Business travelers appreciate the business center. ☒ Map B1 • 3777 La Jolla Village Dr, La Jolla • (858) 552-1234 • www. lajollahyatt.com • $$$

Unless otherwise stated, all hotels accept credit cards, have private bathrooms, air conditioning, and provide dis. access.

Price Categories

For a standard double room per night (with breakfast if included), taxes and extra charges.

$	under $100
$$	$100–200
$$$	$200–250
$$$$	$250–300
$$$$$	over $300

Best Western Hacienda Suites

TOP 10 Moderately Priced Hotels

1 Humphrey's Half Moon Inn & Suites

Its summer concert series (see p51), tropical landscaping, private marina, and long list of activities make this hotel an entertaining choice. Pay a little more to get a room with a view of the bay. ◐ Map B5 • 2303 Shelter Island Dr • (619) 224-3411 • www. halfmooninn.com • $$

2 El Cordova

At this 1902 Spanish-style hotel, Mexican tiles line stairways and wrought-iron balconies overlook the street. A swimming pool is set amid lush landscaping. Good restaurants are next door. ◐ Map C6 • 1351 Orange Ave, Coronado • (619) 435-4131 • www. elcordovahotel.com • $$$

3 Best Western Hacienda Suites

On a hillside overlooking Old Town, the rooms at this charming hacienda-style hotel have private balconies or look onto a courtyard. There is complimentary airport transportation. ◐ Map P5 • 4041 Harney St • (619) 298-4707 • www.best western.com • $$

4 Crowne Plaza San Diego

In the 1960s, a wave of Polynesian-themed hotels sprang up and those that survived have almost a retro coolness factor to

them. The tropical decor still rules the public areas, but the rooms are contemporary and overlook the pool or neighboring golf course. ◐ Map Q4 • 2270 Hotel Circle N • (619) 297-1101 • www. cp-sandiego.com • $$

5 The Dana on Mission Bay

Families love this hotel. All the water activities of Mission Bay are close by, and the hotel operates free shuttles to SeaWorld. Tropical landscaping surrounds the grounds, and the swimming pool is a hit with kids. Free parking. ◐ Map B4 • 1710 W. Mission Bay Dr • (619) 222-6440 • www.thedana.com • $$

6 The Coronado Village Inn

This European-style B&B offers individually decorated rooms with antiques and lacy comforters. A full kitchen is available to guests, and a daily Continental breakfast. ◐ Map C6 • 1017 Park Place, Coronado • (619) 435-9318 • No air conditioning • www.coronadovillageinn. com • $$

7 Holiday Inn Express Old Town

Spanish-Colonial architecture befits the neighborhood's origins, and a sunny interior patio provides respite from the streets of Old Town. This above-average Holiday Inn offers a free break-

fast buffet and a swimming pool. ◐ Map P6 • 3900 Old Town Ave • (619) 299-7400 • www. hioldtownhotel.com • $$

8 Bay Club Hotel & Marina

Rattan furniture and tropical fabrics give a Polynesian cast to this hotel. The best rooms are at the back, and have views of the marina and Point Loma. Breakfast is included. ◐ Map B5 • 2131 Shelter Island Dr • (619) 224-8888 • www. bayclubhotel.com • $$

9 Inn Sunset Cliffs

A 180-degree ocean view distinguishes this inn. Many rooms have kitchens, and a whirlpool tub in the presidential suite overlooks the sea. A swimming pool is located between rooms. ◐ Map A5 • 1370 Sunset Cliffs Blvd • (619) 222-7901 • www.innatsunsetcliffs. com • $$$

10 Les Artistes

Rooms are named and decorated after famous artists, such as the tropical Gauguin room, the French-country Monet, and the rustic Mexican look inspired by muralist Diego Rivera. The Japanese-style Furo room has sliding Shoji screens and a soaking tub. ◐ Map D2 • 944 Camino del Mar, Del Mar • (858) 755-4646 • No air conditioning • www. lesartistesinn.com • $$

Hilton San Diego Resort

🔟 Waterfront Hotels

1 Crystal Pier Hotel
Reservations are essential for these 1927 Cape Cod-style cottages which sit directly on the pier. Many have kitchenettes, and patios with views of Pacific Beach. ⊛ *Map A3 • 4500 Ocean Blvd • (858) 483-6983 • No dis. access • www.crystalpier.com • $$$$*

2 Catamaran Resort Hotel
This Polynesian-themed hotel offers a long list of water activities. Within walking distance to many restaurants, Tiki torches light your way through lushly landscaped grounds. The upper floors of the towers have great views. ⊛ *Map A3 • 3999 Mission Blvd • (800) 422-8386 • www.catamaran resort.com • $$$$*

3 Hilton San Diego Resort
Mediterranean in style, this resort is perfectly located to watch the evening fireworks at SeaWorld. Kid's Klub can keep the kids entertained as you relax at the enormous swimming pool or spa. The best rooms are near the bay. ⊛ *Map B3 • 1775 E Mission Bay Dr • (619) 276-4010 • www.hilton.com • $$$$*

4 Harbor Vacations Club
At San Diego's most unique hotel, you have a choice to stay in eight different yachts, from a sailing catamaran to a 55-ft (17-m) coast cruiser. These floating dockside villas have a cooking galley and luxury cabins. ⊛ *Map B5 • Marina Cortez, 1880 Harbor Island Dr, G-Dock • (619) 297-9484 • No dis. access • www.shell vacationsclub.com • $$$*

5 Bahia Resort Hotel
This venerable Mission Bay Hotel is right next to the bay and Mission Beach. At night, you can enjoy live music on the Bahia Belle, a stern-wheeler that floats on the bay every evening. ⊛ *Map A4 • 998 W. Mission Bay Dr • (858) 488-0551 • No dis. access • www.bahiahotel.com • $$$*

6 The Beach Cottages
Detached cottages with full kitchens and laundry facilities are a good option for families who don't need luxury. Other accommodation choices include apartments and basic, inexpensive motel rooms. ⊛ *Map A3 • 4255 Ocean Blvd • (858) 483-7440 • No air conditioning • www.beachcottages.com • $$$$*

7 Ocean Park Inn
Restaurants are within walking distance of this contemporary inn, and the boardwalk action is just outside the door. Quiet rooms with the best views are on the third floor. All rooms feature a balcony or patio. ⊛ *Map A3 • 710 Grand Ave • (858) 483-5858 • www.oceanparkinn.com • $$$*

8 Best Western Blue Sea Lodge
Head to the pool or the Pacific Ocean for a morning swim and then down the boardwalk for breakfast. New rooms and suites have brightened this lodge, but the older rooms have the beach view. ⊛ *Map A3 • 707 Pacific Beach Dr • (858) 488-4700 • www.bestwestern-bluesea.com • $$$*

9 Carlsbad Inn Beach Resort
Families love this sprawling resort. Rooms and time-share condominiums are available nightly or weekly. Several activities and classes are held daily, and there's a good Mexican restaurant. ⊛ *Map D1 • 3075 Carlsbad Blvd, Carlsbad • (760) 434-7020 • www.carlsbadinn.com • $$$*

10 Oceanside Marina Suites
Surrounded by water on three sides, large, breezy rooms have lovely views. Suites are great value with a balcony, kitchen, and fireplace. During summer, a boat ferries guests to a miles-long beach. ⊛ *Map D1 • 2008 Harbor Dr. N, Oceanside • (760) 722-1561 • No air conditioning • www.omihotel.com • $$*

Unless otherwise stated, all hotels accept credit cards, have private bathrooms, air conditioning, and provide dis. access.

Price Categories

For a standard double room per night (with breakfast if included), taxes and extra charges.

$	under $100
$$	$100–200
$$$	$200–250
$$$$	$250–300
$$$$$	over $300

Paradise Point Resort & Spa

🔟 Spas

1 Four Seasons Resort Aviara

With impeccable service and a superb setting, this hotel is one of the most highly rated in Southern California. Choose between indoor and outdoor treatment rooms, or a couple's suite with a whirlpool. ⬥ Map D1 • 7100 Four Seasons Point, Carlsbad • (760) 603-6800 • www.fourseasons.com/aviara • $$$$$

2 Golden Door

Modeled after the ancient honjin inns, Japanese gardens, streams, and waterfalls make a glorious backdrop to a week of fitness and meditation. For most of the year, the spa is a women only domain. ⬥ Map E2 • 777 Deer Springs Rd, San Marcos • No dis. access • (760) 744-5777 • www.goldendoor.com • $$$$$

3 La Costa Resort & Spa

The Spanish-Colonial complex contains two PGA championship golf courses, a tennis center, a spa with assorted massage and body treatments, and a fitness room. ⬥ Map D1 • 2100 Costa del Mar Rd, Carlsbad • (760) 438-9111 • www.lacosta.com • $$$$$

4 Loews Coronado Bay Resort

The "Sea Spa" at this self-contained resort includes Watsu, which combines the buoyancy of water and the pressure techniques of Shiatsu massage. For an ultimate splurge, check into one of the bayside villas with views across San Diego Bay. ⬥ Map E2 • 4000 Coronado Bay Rd, Coronado • (619) 424-4000 • www.loewshotels.com • $$$$

5 Rancho Valencia Resort

Bougainvillea cascades over the Spanish casitas in this stunning resort. Many rooms feature cathedral ceilings, private terraces, and fireplaces. Rejuvenation treatments include reflexology, aromatherapy treatments and various massages. ⬥ Map E2 • 5921 Valencia Circle, Rancho Santa Fe • (858) 756-1123 • www.ranchovalencia.com • $$$$$

6 Cal-a-Vie

Exhilarating programs focus on fitness, nutrition, and personal care. The Mediterranean-style villas provide the most luxurious accommodation. ⬥ Map E1 • 29402 Spa Havens Rd, Vista • (760) 945-2055 • www.calavie.com • $$$$$

7 L'Auberge Del Mar Resort & Spa

Join the list of Hollywood notables who relax at this boutique hotel and spa near the Pacific. The rooms feature marble baths and many have private balconies and fireplaces. ⬥ Map D2 • 1540 Camino del Mar, Del Mar • (858) 259-1515 • www.laubergedelmar.com • $$$$$

8 Rancho Bernardo Inn

Two-story, red-tile-roof adobe buildings and bougainvillea-adorned patios evoke images of early California at this gracious resort. Life here revolves around the adjoining golf course, spa or tennis courts. ⬥ Map E2 • 17550 Bernardo Oaks Dr, Rancho Bernardo • (858) 675-8500 • www.ranchobernardoinn.com • $$$

9 Paradise Point Resort & Spa

At this Indonesian-style spa, jasmine-scented or hot stone massages can precede a soak in a rose petal bedecked tub. The brightly decorated cottage rooms have private lanais. ⬥ Map B4 • 1404 Vacation Rd • (858) 274-4630 • www.paradisepoint.com • $$$$$

10 Rancho La Puerta

Since 1940, guests have pursued body and mind fitness at this beautiful Mexican-Colonial style resort. Lodgings are in casitas decorated with folk art and bright fabrics. The dining room specializes in homegrown organic food. ⬥ Map F3 • 476 Tecate Rd, Tecate, Baja California, Mexico • (858) 764-5500 • www.rancholapuerta.com • $$$$$

The Golden Door is considered America's best spa. The Japanese honjin inns were places where travelers could come to rest.

Left **B&B Inn La Jolla** Right **View from B&B Inn**

🔟 Bed & Breakfasts

1 Heritage Park B&B

This 1889 Queen Anne mansion offers charming rooms reminiscent of its original era. Relax on a wrap-around veranda, or try a claw-footed bathtub for two. Breakfast is included. ◎ *Map P5 • 2470 Heritage Park Row • (619) 299-6832 • www. heritageparkinn.com • $$*

2 B&B Inn La Jolla

This delightful home with its individually decorated rooms was designed in 1913 by renowned architect Irving Gill, and Kate Sessions *(see p19)* planted its original gardens. ◎ *Map N3 • 7753 Draper Ave, La Jolla • (858) 456-2066 • www.innlajolla.com • $$$*

3 Keating House

The vintage 1888 Queen Anne home and adjoining 1905 cottage have been restored to Victorian perfection. Ask the hosts about the benevolent ghost that haunts the inn. ◎ *Map J2 • 2331 2nd Ave • (619) 239-8585 • No dis. access • www.keatinghouse.com • $$*

4 The Cottage

This city hideaway surrounded by a herb garden has two rooms with king-size beds and private entrances. The "Cottage" is furnished with unique Victorian antiques such as a wood burning stove; the "Garden Room" is in the owners' home. ◎ *Map C4 • 3829 Albatross St • (619) 299-1564 • No dis. access • No air conditioning • www.sandiegobandb. com/cottage.htm • $$*

5 Villa Serena

An Italian-style villa boasts three bright and cheerful rooms. Facilities include a microwave, refrigerator, laundry, and a swimming pool. Breakfast is provided. ◎ *Map B5 • 2164 Rosecrans St • (619) 224-1451 • No dis. access • www.inn-guide. com/villaserena • $$*

6 Crone's Cobblestone Cottage B&B

At this restored 1913 Craftsman-style bungalow, choose either the Elliot or the Eaton room, both furnished with period antiques. The walls are lined with thousands of volumes. ◎ *Map C4 • 1302 Washington Place • (619) 295-4765 • No credit cards • Shared bath • No air conditioning • www. cobblestonebandb.com • $$*

7 Cardiff-by-the-Sea Lodge

Rooms at this romantic seaside hideaway can be either contemporary in design or borderline Victorian. In the Sweetheart Room, find a heart-shaped tub and a etched-glass window with a sweeping ocean view. Many rooms feature four poster beds, ocean views, and fireplaces. ◎ *Map D2 • 142 Chesterfield Dr, Cardiff-by-the-Sea • (760) 944-6474 • www. cardifflodge.com • $$*

8 Loma Vista B&B

Ideally situated for touring the Temecula vineyards, rooms in this Mission-style inn have private balconies, Jacuzzis, and fireplaces. Rates include a continental breakfast with fresh pastries. ◎ *Map E1 • 33350 La Serena Way, Temecula • (951) 676-7047 • www.lomavistabb.com • $$*

9 Orchard Hill Country Inn

At this most luxurious of Julian's B&B inns, pick a Craftsman-style cottage with a whirlpool tub, fireplace, and private porch. Tasty breakfasts make a good start to the day. ◎ *Map F2 • 2502 Washington St, Julian • (760) 765-1700 • www. orchardhill.com • $$$*

10 Julian Gold Rush Hotel

Built in 1897 by a freed slave from Missouri, this quaint inn is the oldest continually operating hotel in Southern California. Its lacy curtains might remind you of your grandma's house. ◎ *Map F2 • 2032 Main St, Julian • (760) 765-0201 • No dis. access • No air conditioning • www.julianhotel.com • $$*

Unless otherwise stated, all hotels accept credit cards, have private bathrooms, air conditioning, and provide dis. access.

Price Categories

For a standard double room per-night (with breakfast if included), taxes and extra charges.

$	under $100
$$	$100–200
$$$	$200–250
$$$$	$250–300
$$$$$	over $300

USA Hostels Gaslamp

🔟 Budget Hotels & Hostels

1 La Pensione
In the heart of Little Italy, rooms contain a queen bed, TV, and refrigerator. A coin-operated laundry is on the premises, as well as free parking. Great Italian restaurants are just outside. ⊗ Map H3 • 606 W. Date St • (619) 236-8000 • No air conditioning • www.la pensionehotel.com • $$

2 Porto Vista Hotel
This Little Italy hotel offers a free shuttle to the airport, SeaWorld, and San Diego Zoo, and a swimming pool. It is convenient to both the Gaslamp Quarter and the Convention Center. ⊗ Map H3 • 1835 Columbia St • (619) 557-9303 • www.portovistasandiego.com • $$

3 Old Town Inn
Rooms are clean and comfy, and the hotel offers one of the better breakfasts around. An efficiency unit comes with a microwave, refrigerator, and range top. Parking is free. ⊗ Map B4 • 4444 Pacific Hwy • (619) 260-8024 • www.oldtown-inn.com • $

4 Vagabond Inn Point Loma
This motel is well situated for sportfishing activities and the Cabrillo National Monument. Along with the clean and cheery rooms, enjoy the free breakfast, airport shuttle, parking, and the swimming pool. ⊗ Map B5 • 1325 Scott St • (619) 224-3371 • www.vagabondinn.com • $$

5 Days Inn Harbor View
Clean and functional, every room comes with a mini-refrigerator and satellite TV. Amenities include a swimming pool, coin-operated laundry, and a free airport shuttle. The trolley runs to the Convention Center. ⊗ Map H3 • 1919 Pacific Hwy • (619) 232-1077 • www.daysinn.com • $

6 Motel 6 Hotel Circle Mission Valley
The parking is free, as are local phone calls. Kids under 17 stay free with parents; there's a pool, coin-operated laundry, and free HBO. Motel 6s in Chula Vista and San Ysidro are even cheaper. ⊗ Map Q4 • 2424 Hotel Circle N • (619) 296-1612 • No dis. access • www.motel6.com • $

7 Moonlight Beach Motel
This motel is located near shops, restaurants, and Moonlight Beach, one of the county's most highly rated beaches. All rooms have kitchenettes and the third-floor rooms offer great views. ⊗ Map D2 • 233 2nd St, Encinitas • (760) 753-0623 • No air conditioning • www.moonlightbeachmotel.com • $$

8 Ocean Beach International Backpackers Hostel
Passports and/or air tickets are required for check in. Teachers and out-of-county residents who hold hostel membership cards may also stay. They offer free breakfast and barbecue evenings, a kitchen, videos, and free lockers and airport transport. ⊗ Map A4 • 4961 Newport Ave • (619) 223-7873 • No dis. access • No air conditioning • No private bathrooms • http://members.aol.com/OBIhostel/hostel/ • $

9 USA Hostels Gaslamp
Centrally located, they offer dorm and some private rooms, Internet access, a laundry, kitchen, lounge area with videos, free lockers, and all-you-can-make pancake breakfasts. ⊗ Map K5 • 726 5th Ave • (619) 232-3100 • No dis. access • No air conditioning • No private bathrooms • www.usahostels.com • $

10 HI San Diego Downtown Hostel
This bright hostel offers dorm and some private rooms, free airport transport and breakfast, kitchen and lounge facilities, laundry and Internet access. ⊗ Map K5 • 521 Market St • (619) 525-1531 • No dis. access • No air conditioning • No private bathrooms • www.sandiegohostels.org • $

General Index

*Page numbers in **bold** type refer to main entries.*

Acknowledgements

The Author

Born in San Diego, Pamela Barrus is an unapologetic vagabond, having traveled solo through some 200 countries. She is the author of *Dream Sleeps: Castle and Palace Hotels of Europe* and has contributed to a number of national magazines. She still finds San Diego one of the best places in the world to come home to and enjoy the sunshine.

The author would like to thank Mary Barrus and Roger Devenyns for sharing their exceptional knowledge and insight of San Diego with her.

Photographer Chris Stowers

Additional Photography

Max Alexander, Geoff Dann, Frank Greenaway, Derek Hall, Neil Mersh, Rob Reichenfeld, Neil Setchfield, Scott Suchman

Factchecker Paul Franklin, Nancy Mikula, Paul Skinner

AT DK INDIA:

Managing Editor Aruna Ghose
Art Editor Benu Joshi
Project Editors Anees Saigal, Vandana Bhagra
Editorial Assistance Pamposh Raina
Project Designer Bonita Vaz
Senior Cartographer Uma Bhattacharya
Cartographer Suresh Kumar
Picture Researcher Taiyaba Khatoon
Indexer & Proofreader Bhavna Seth Ranjan
DTP Co-ordinator Shailesh Sharma
DTP Designer Vinod Harish

AT DK LONDON:

Publisher Douglas Amrine
Publishing Manager Lucinda Cooke
Senior Art Editor Marisa Renzullo
Senior Cartographic Editor Casper Morris
Senior DTP Designer Jason Little
DK Picture Library Richard Dabb, Romaine Werblow, Hayley Smith, Gemma Woodward
Production Rita Sinha
Revisions Design & Editorial
Sonal Bhatt, Nicola Erdpresser, Anna Freiberger, Claire Jones, Juliet Kenny, Meredith Smith, Hugo Wilkinson, Ros Walford

Picture Credits

t-top; tl-top left; tlc-top left center; tc-top center; tr-top right; cla-center left above; ca-center above; cra-center right above; cl-center left; c-center; cr-center right; clb-center left below; cb-center below; crb-center right below; bl-bottom left, b-bottom; bc-bottom center; bcl-bottom center left; br-bottom right; d-detail.

Every effort has been made to trace the copyright holders of images, and we apologize in advance for any unintentional omissions. We would be pleased to insert the appropriate acknowledgements in any subsequent edition of this publication.

The publishers would also like to thank the following for their assistance and kind permission to photograph at their establishments:

Balboa Park, San Diego; San Diego Aerospace Museum; San Diego Automotive Museum; Birch Aquarium; San Diego Chinese Historical Museum; Horton Plaza;

San Diego Maritime Museum; San Diego Museum of Art; Santa Fe Depot; Spanish Village Art Center; The Putnam Foundation, Timken Museum of Art, San Diego; Villa Montezuma; San Diego Union Historical Museum; Wells Fargo Museum; and all other churches, missions, museums, parks, hotels, restaurants, and sights too numerous to thank individually.

Works of art have been reproduced with the permission of the following copyright holders: The Putnam Foundation, Timken Museum of Art, San Diego: Frans Hals *Portrait of a Gentleman* (1634) 18bc; Alan Bowness, Hepworth Estate, *Figure for Landscape*, Bronze (1960) 18tl.

The publishers would like to thank the following individuals, companies and picture libraries for their kind permission to reproduce their photographs.

ALAMY: MARK Gibson 66tl; Popperfoto 51tr; Robert Harding World Imagery 20-21; Andrew Slayman 22-23c. BALBOA PARK: Brett Shoaf 66tr; BAZAAR DEL MUNDO: Ted Walton 82tr; BUBBLES BOUTIQUE: 74tl CORBIS: 14-15c, 38tr, 39tr; Art on File 48t; Bettman 35tl; Jan Butchofsky-Houser 36-37; Anthony Cooper,

Ecoscene 107tl; Richard Cummins 10-11c, 25cra, 38tl, 66c, 67tl, 67tr; Raymond Gehman 87bl; Mark E. Gibson 98tr; Philip Gould 52 tl; Kelly Harriger 63tr; Dave G. Houser 1c; The Mariners Museum 13br; Museum of History & Industry 38c; Fred Greaves/Reuters 12t, 12bl; Bill Ross 24-25c, 88-89; Bob Rowan 62t; G.E. Kidder Smith 38tc; Underwood & Underwood 39bl. HILTON SAN DIEGO RESORT: 118 LA JOLLA FIBER ARTS: 99tl; LA VALENCIA: 115tl; THE LODGE AT TORREY PINES: 114tl; LONELY PLANET IMAGES: Richard Cummins 26-27c, 68-69, Anthony Pidgeon 102-103 MASTERFILE: Dale Sanders 4-5 MURPHY O'BRIEN PUBLIC RELATIONS: 56tl SAN DIEGO HISTORICAL SOCIETY: Tom Ladwig 73bl; SAN DIEGO MUSEUM OF MAN: 75T; SAN DIEGO ZOO & WILD ANIMAL PARK: 2tr, 14tr, 15b, 16tr, 16tl, 16cra, 16bl, 17cr, 52cl, 62cra, 70cl, 94tr. SCRIPPS INSTITUTION OF OCEANOGRAPHY: 33cb. SEAWORLD: 7cr, 30-31c, 30tl, 30crb, 30bc, 31tl, 31cr, 31b, 94cr, 95tr. THORNTON WINERY: 96c

All other images are © Dorling Kindersley. For further information see www.dkimages.com

Special Editions of DK Travel Guides

DK Travel Guides can be purchased in bulk quantities at discounted prices for use in promotions or as premiums. We are also able to offer special editions and personalized jackets, corporate imprints, and excerpts from all of our books, tailored specifically to meet your own needs.

To find out more, please contact:

(in the US) **SpecialSales@dk.com**

(in the UK) **travelspecialsales@uk.dk.com**

(in Canada) DK Special Sales at **general@toumaline.ca**

(in Australia) **business.development @pearson.com.au**

Selected Street Index